The
Politics
of American
Democracy

Marian D. Irish

Charles O. Lerche, Jr. Professor,
School of International Service, The American University,
Washington, D. C.

James W. Prothro

Professor, Department of Political Science,
and Director, Institute for Research in Social Science,
University of North Carolina

Prentice-Hall, Inc., Englewood Cliffs, New Jersey

The
Politics
of American Fourth
Democracy Edition

© Copyright 1959, 1962, 1965, 1968 by Prentice-Hall, Inc.,
Englewood Cliffs, New Jersey.
All rights reserved. No part of this book may be reproduced in any form
without permission in writing from the publishers.
Library of Congress Catalog Number: 68-16374.
Printed in the United States of America.
Designed by Walter Behnke.

The Politics of American Democracy,
FOURTH EDITION   *Irish and Prothro.*

PRENTICE-HALL INTERNATIONAL, INC., *London*
PRENTICE-HALL OF AUSTRALIA, PTY., LTD., *Sydney*
PRENTICE-HALL OF CANADA, LTD., *Toronto*
PRENTICE-HALL OF INDIA PVT. LTD., *New Delhi*
PRENTICE-HALL OF JAPAN, INC., *Tokyo*

Current printing (last digit):
15 14 13 12 11 10 9 8 7 6 5 4 3 2 1

C

PREFACE

The original idea of writing this book came after a long faculty meeting devoted to considering possible texts for an introductory American government course at Florida State University. We and our colleagues were trying to find a basic text that was suitable for a one-semester course, that would apply the most advanced findings of the discipline to an explanation of American politics, and that would at the same time convey to undergraduates a sense of the excitement and importance of politics. The search was unsuccessful. Neither of us had ever expected to write a textbook—we were more interested in pursuing our own research than in attempting to synthesize the wide range of research on American politics. But we lingered behind after the meeting and, to our mutual surprise, found ourselves agreeing that we should write the kind of book we wanted our students to have.

That decision was made ten years ago, yet each revision of the book has been guided by the original commitment to give our students a book suitable for a one-semester course and, more importantly, a book that attempts to explain American politics on the assumption that students will understand and enjoy as much as political science has to offer on the subject. We have been gratified that students besides our own have found this effort worthwhile.

In this fourth edition, we have again attempted to apply the latest research findings and theoretical developments to an understanding of how American democracy works and why it works as it does. We have not been able to supply final answers to all questions. Indeed, the chief educational value for the authors in revising a text is the necessary confrontation with both the tentative and the cumulative nature of our knowledge of politics. The fifth edition of this text should be better than the fourth; if we have taken proper advantage of developments in the discipline, this edition is better than the third.

Insofar as we fail to explain realistically the way American government works, the failure can be attributed to the shortcomings of the authors or of the discipline of political science—not to any feeling that undergraduates are incapable of understanding the best that the discipline has to offer. We are convinced that the most advanced propositions on American politics can be made not merely comprehensible but also challenging and exciting to undergraduates. We have therefore kept both our colleagues and our students in mind throughout the preparation of this book. In the many areas where the authors themselves have engaged in no original research, we necessarily turn to our colleagues for data, explanations, and unanswered questions. We have thus attempted to write *from* a professional viewpoint. But we have attempted to write *for* undergraduate students—to give them a sense of the excitement, the basic processes, and the unanswered questions that characterize American politics.

We have avoided the idea that theory and practice can be separated. Instead, we have taken the view that "facts" have little meaning except as a route to explanatory generalizations, and that "theory" is of little value unless it explains actual practice. We emphasize analysis more than mere description, and current politics more than historical background. Thus fact and theory, past and present, are inextricably intertwined. Although an effort to explain the workings of the political system abjures the encyclopedic or journalistic approach, it necessarily introduces those descriptive details the student needs in order to understand the system. Facts are essential for understanding, but we have attempted to present them only for that purpose—i.e., not as isolated bits of information to be learned for their own sake, but as the basis for explanation or for doubt.

The book is organized around the concept of politics as a system of activities. Chapter 1 is devoted to spelling out the basic features of American politics as a system with identifiable boundaries and interrelated parts, and with linkages to the environment through both inputs and outputs. Here we also specify the basic functions of any political system for the larger society of which it is a part. Chapter 1 thus sets the theoretical framework for the book as a whole. Recognizing the tentative nature of all scientific findings, we conclude the chapter with a discussion of the limitations of the systems approach to politics.

To underscore the fact that any system of activities responds to its environment, Part I considers the cultural, ideological, constitutional, and federal context of American national government. Part II is concerned with inputs—the demands, supports, and apathy which are injected into the system through political opinions, political parties, pressure groups, public relations, and the electoral system. Part III focuses on the activities of authoritative decision-making which represent the core of the governmental process. In Part IV, we consider outputs—the rewards and deprivations that accompany every decision, formal or informal. In analyzing these substantive activities, we focus throughout on the functions they perform and the structures through which they are implemented. The bibliographical essay at the end of the book offers the student a guide to new materials and different approaches to the study of contemporary American politics.

In addition to new illustrative materials and new research findings that are incorporated throughout the book, the principal changes from the preceding edition are three. First, we devote a separate chapter to the problem of studying American politics in order to provide a clearer statement of the theoretical framework of the book. Second, we have introduced more comparative materials. The focus is still, of course, on American government, but we attempt to illuminate the American system by relating its key features to those of other systems. Third, we have completely reorganized the four chapters on official decision-making agencies—Congress, the presidency, the bureaucracy, the

PREFACE

courts. In preceding editions, the actors in each of these agencies were analyzed with concepts that appeared useful for understanding their individual performances. But we finally realized that this approach was hardly consistent with our view that each decision-making agency should be viewed not as a unique phenomenon but as one case out of a universe of decision-making agencies. Our concern is for generalities, for the regularities that characterize all decision-making agencies; even their unique or particular characteristics can be better understood as deviations from characteristics common to all decision-making agencies. Each of these four agencies is accordingly analyzed through the same concepts, based principally on "role theory." This strikes us as such an obvious improvement that we feel ashamed of not having made it earlier.

We have received valuable help from many people in the preparation of this book. A principal source of encouragement has been the students who have read earlier editions, not only our own students at American University and the University of North Carolina, but also those at institutions other than our own who have gone to the trouble of writing to us. If we have succeeded in stimulating new undergraduates in this book, much of the thanks must go to three astute editors: James J. Murray, III, Wilbur E. Mangas, and William S. Green of Prentice-Hall. Among our colleagues, particular assistance in this revision has been given by Edward C. Dreyer of San Diego State College, Heinz Eulau of Stanford University, Richard F. Fenno, Jr., of the University of Rochester, Robert McCloskey of Harvard University, Michael O'Leary of Syracuse University, William Riker of the University of Rochester, Francis E. Rourke of Johns Hopkins University, Martin Shapiro of the University of California, Irvine, and Raymond E. Wolfinger of Stanford University. We owe a special debt to Elke Frank of Hunter College for her counsel in the preparation of the manuscript and assistance in editing the proof. Finally, we express our appreciation for the unflagging interest and assistance of Mary Prothro, who has seen us through all four editions after swearing that each was her last.

As we have tried to suggest above, some of the inadequacies of this book may be attributed to the nature of political science as a growing discipline. Readers who discover factual errors or faulty interpretations, however, are invited to call them to the attention of those who are individually and jointly responsible — the authors.

MDI　　　　JWP

Washington, D. C.
Chapel Hill, North Carolina
January, 1968

CONTENTS

PART ONE   The Context of American Politics

Page 1

1

Some Basic Concepts. Political Activities as a Political System. Theory and Theories in Studying American Politics.   **The Study of American Politics,** 3

2

Politics as a Cultural Heritage. The Physical Environment as a Political Setting. The People at the Base of American Politics. Class Structure as a Political Force. Economic Influences on Politics.   **The Cultural Context,** 23

3

Democractic Political Theory. What Is Democratic Government? The American Creed and Its Detractors. Threats to Democracy. A Reaffirmation of the Democratic Faith.   **The Context of Ideas,** 61

4

First Steps Toward Nationhood. The Politics of Constitution Writing. New Intentions and New Framers.

"The First New Nation", *91*

5

Concepts of Federalism. The Constitutional Prescription. "Creative Federalism."

The Federal System, *137*

PART TWO **Inputs of The Political System: Demands, Supports, and Apathy**

Page 175

6

The Nature of Political Opinions. Political Socialization. The Continuing Socialization of Adults. The Expression of Political Opinions. Political Opinions in the Political System.

Political Opinions and Participation, *177*

7

The American Party System. Functions of Political Parties. The Structure of American Parties. The Doctrinal and Social Base of American Parties. Criticisms of Political Parties.

Political Parties, *219*

CONTENTS

8

The Importance of Pressure Groups in Politics. Bases of Pressure-Group Strength. Pressure Group Tactics and Public Responses. Professional Public Relations. From Unofficial to Official Input Activities.

Pressure Groups and Public Relations, *255*

9

The Electoral System as an Official Agency of Government. Formal Voting Requirements. Nominating the Candidates. Campaigns and Elections. Elections and the Political System.

The Electoral System, *289*

PART THREE   Decision-Making Agencies and Activities

Page 329

10

Legislators in Political Systems. The Recruitment of Legislators. The Role of Congressmen. Role Performance: The Structure of Congressional Activity. Congressional Relations with Other Decision-Making Agencies. The Functions of Congress.

The Legislators, *331*

11

The Executive in the Political System. Recruitment of the President. Constitutional Status and Roles of the President. The Structure of Presidential Activities. The Functions of the President.

The President, *381*

12

Bureaucracy in the Political System. Organization and Management in the National Government. Background and Recruitment of Bureaucrats. Roles of the Bureaucrats in the Policy Process. A Democratic and Responsible Bureaucracy. Congressional Controls over the Bureaucrats. Functions of the Bureaucracy.

The Bureaucrats, *439*

13

Judges in the Political System. The Rulers of Law: Their Background and Recruitment. Constitutional Status and Role Concepts of the Judiciary. Structure of Judicial Activities. The Judicial Functions.

The Judges, *487*

CONTENTS

PART FOUR Outputs of the Political System: Rewards and Deprivations

Page 543

14

The Constitutional Statements. Privileges and Immunities of Citizens. The Great Rights. Equal Protection of the Laws.

Civil Rights, 545

15

General Welfare in the Changing Environment. The General Welfare: Demands, Supports, and Apathy. Decision-Makers and Decisions: General Welfare and Common Defense.

General Welfare and Common Defense, 597

16

Foreign Policy and International Politics. The Domestic Environment of American Foreign Policy. The Inputs of Foreign Policy: Demands and Supports. Decision-Makers and Their Decisions in Foreign Policy.

Foreign Policy and National Security, 653

17

The American Political System in Perspective, 713

xiii

A Bibliographical Essay

Page 725

The Declaration of Independence

Page 749

The Constitution of the United States of America

Page 752

Index

Page 763

The Politics of American Democracy

PART ONE

The Context
of American Politics

THE STUDY OF

AMERICAN POLITICS

1

"On January 20, 1965, in Washington, D.C., a wildly enthusiastic crowd of Democrats and a goodly number of polite Republicans witnessed the inauguration of Lyndon B. Johnson as the thirty-sixth President of the United States."

This statement—the first sentence in the preceding, 1965 edition of this book—was written months before the 1964 presidential election. Our confidence in committing such a statement to print before the election took place testifies to the growing ability of political science to explain and account for political phenomena—sometimes even before they have occured. Yet the truth of this statement should not be exaggerated. Political science is still unable to predict or explain many things. If we had been required to predict who would receive the Republican nomination for President in 1964, for example, we would have been wrong. The reasons for both our assurance of Johnson's victory and for our inability to anticipate the Republicans' choice of Barry Goldwater as his opponent will become clear in later pages. It is enough to say here that political science as a discipline, even though it is far from having the answer to every question, has the capacity to clarify enough of what happens in politics to be taken seriously. Our aim in this book, then, is to impart the basic knowledge of the constants, variables, and recurrent patterns of American politics that permits a citizen to understand what is going on in politics, and why.

Future research will no doubt show that some of today's apparent answers are wrong. A couple of generations ago, physicists defined the atom as "the largest indivisible unit of matter." Since then, the usefulness of the definition and the phenomenon to which it refers have both been shattered with spectacular results. Since political science is a relatively "soft" science in comparison with physics, the student certainly needs to take certain of our hypothetical explanations as tentative rather than as final. Although our hypotheses are advanced responsibly—that is, on the basis of some evidence—political scientists are themselves divided on some of them. Our effort is to take the mystery out of politics. Knowing in advance that no one can succeed completely in this effort, we undertake it with the conviction that we can go far enough to make the effort worthwhile.

Some Basic Concepts

Politics, power, and *government* are terms that we all use in everyday conversation. We also talk, from time to time, about business, religion, sex and sports, and everyone recognizes when the subject is being changed from one of these topics to another. To be sure, they are not always distinguishable —golf is usually a sport for the great majority of those Americans who overrun the suburban courses of the nation on pleasant summer weekends, but it may be a business activity if an amateur uses it to sell insurance or when an Arnold Palmer or a Jack Nicklaus pursues it for a livelihood. Sex usually represents recreation or procreation, but it is sometimes "the world's oldest profession." Without expecting to draw a firm line between politics and other activities, we can identify those activities that are peculiarly political in nature, and we can specify the circumstances under which a normally nonpolitical act becomes political.

Power

The atmosphere surrounding a victorious candidate is heady with excitement. To some extent the excitement is the same as that infecting a college football team that has just defeated its traditional rival. Everybody likes to win, especially against a familiar foe. But the exhilaration of victorious politicians goes beyond satisfaction in winning for its own sake—they have also gained the right to exercise *power*. Although power is a central concern of politics, it cannot be handed to someone in a neatly wrapped bundle. The winning candidate gains a status or position in which he is expected—and legally authorized—to exercise power in various relations with others. These expectations about how a person in an official position should and will behave define his particular political *role*. The actual extent of his power will depend upon his *role performance,* that is, upon the manner in which he takes advantage of his official position.[1]

Political power is not something that can be grasped in the physical sense that a monkey can grasp a coconut; it is not a tangible *thing* like a coconut that can be thrown from a tree to the ground or from one person to another. Rather, it is a *relationship*. It can no more exist without someone to respond to the claims of the powerful than it could without someone to assert such claims.[2] A relation of power exists whenever one individual or group is subordinate to another with respect to some form of activity. A person thus enjoys power whenever he can influence the behavior of others according to his own intentions. Under this definition of power, it is not only possible but altogether common for Jones to have power over Smith with respect to one kind of activity and for Smith to have power over Jones with respect to a

---

[1] See Richard Neustadt, *Presidential Power* (New York: John Wiley & Sons, Inc., 1960). The concept of *role* is more fully developed in Chapters 9 and 10.

[2] See H. D. Lasswell, *Power and Personality* (New York: W. W. Norton & Company, Inc., 1948), p. 10; and H. H. Gerth and C. W. Mills (trs. and eds.), *From Max Weber: Essays in Sociology* (New York: Oxford University Press, 1946), p. 180.

4

different kind of activity. One of the authors of this book, for example, recently challenged one of his students to a tennis match. The disparity in abilities was so great (the student failed to mention that he had been captain of the tennis team at another university) that the "match" was transformed into a series of tutorial sessions. On the tennis court, the power relationships between student and professor were the reverse of what they were in the classroom. Each exercised power over the other—influenced the other's behavior in accord with his intentions—in one form of activity, and each responded to the other's power in another form of activity.

Politics

Although each of the individuals in a group might conceivably have equal power, this situation seldom occurs. Ordinarily, some have more authority than others. This is where *politics* comes in. In its broadest sense, *politics* may be defined as the "pursuit and exercise of power." The distinctive power relations we have in mind when we generally speak of "politics" are those in which some people fix policies or rules of behavior that others are obligated to follow. This means that politics is indistinguishable from government.[3] The late V. O. Key, Jr., one of our most distinguished political scientists, equated politics with the "workings of governments generally, their impact on the governed, their manner of operation, the means by which governors attain and retain authority."[4] This point of view is quite different from the assumption of occasional luncheon-club speakers that politics is something evil and somehow quite distinct from government. On examination, however, *politics* is frequently used on such occasions to refer to the acquisition or exercise of power for ends which the speaker disapproves of; "governance," "statesmanship" and other sonorous terms he reserves for the acquisition or exercise of power for ends he does approve. If we disregard his personal values, it is apparent that he is talking about the same kinds of activities in both cases. Political scientists go to an opposite extreme from that of the luncheon-club speaker; they use *politics* interchangeably with the broad term *political system*.[5] We shall accordingly refer to *American politics* or the *American political system* as synonymous with *American government*.

Government

In its broadest sense, *government* is the process by which rules of behavior are set up and enforced to realize group interests and protect individual rights. But for our purposes this definition

---

[3]Our reference to "government" here should not be taken to imply that the term has a *real* meaning that all right-thinking people can discover. Like all words, *government* is merely a term invented by human beings to help them communicate; we use it here to mean government as the term is generally defined. Unless we specifically stipulate a definition (as we shall, immediately below, for *government*), we shall attempt to use all words in their generally accepted (or lexical) meanings throughout this book.
[4]*Politics, Parties, and Pressure Groups* (New York: Thomas Y. Crowell Company, 1958), 4th ed., p. 4.
[5]Gabriel A. Almond and James S. Coleman (eds.), *The Politics of the Developing Areas* (Princeton, N.J.: Princeton University Press, 1960), pp. 5–9.

is obviously too broad, for it takes in such institutions as the family, business corporations, labor unions, churches, and college fraternities as well as the formal government. When fraternity members tell plebes how to behave, they are exercising governing power in the broad sense. But fraternity rules and regulations are certainly not what we have in mind when we speak of *"the* government." We are not directly concerned with the internal politics of such private groups; they will come into our analysis only insofar as they affect the broader political system of which all Americans are a part. So we shall have to narrow the definition down to the process by which rules or laws are made that apply to society as a whole.

Our definition of formal or *public* government, then, might read like this: *Government* consists of the structures and processes through which rules or policies are *authoritatively* determined for society as a whole.[6] These rules may be directed toward realizing such contradictory goals as continuing peace or military victory, widespread prosperity or class privilege, popular freedom or strict conformity. But whatever its substantive goals, public government differs from private governing agencies in that it can legitimately rely on physical compulsion, which means that its rules are *authoritatively* prescribed. Furthermore, only the policies of the government apply to *society as a whole*. If a man loses faith in the creed of his church, even its power to excommunicate him no longer operates as a punishment; but if he loses faith in the policies of his government, its power to put him in jail remains very much in force.

If you are in the habit of thinking about government as nothing more than official agencies and the legal decisions they make, you may need to reread the above definition. We are using the term in a more comprehensive sense, to include all the interactions that influence public policy or its enforcement. We stress that *politics* and *the political system* are synonymous with *government* because it is easier to think of these substitute terms as referring to more than formal institutions and legal codes. Our analysis will include not only official agencies like Congress, but also the political aspects of informal structures like political parties, the media of communication, and social classes. We shall be greatly concerned with laws as formal policies, but we shall also be concerned with unofficial norms that govern our behavior. If the norms of an area deny Negroes access to public facilities, these denials—and the threat of coercion that supports them—are actually part of our political system. The political system includes all the activities that shape public policy and that determine how it is enforced.

Political Activities as a Political System

We have focused thus far on the *political* aspect of the concept, "political system." What are the implications of viewing American politics as a *system*? To begin with, just what is a system? The notion of "system" is common to all

---

[6] See David Easton, *The Political System: An Inquiry into the State of Political Science* (New York: Alfred A. Knopf, Inc., 1953), especially Chapter 5, for a discussion that supplies much of the orientation of this section. See also Harold D. Lasswell and Abraham Kaplan, *Power and Society: A Framework for Political Inquiry* (New Haven: Yale University Press, 1950).

of us; we talk easily about such things as the electrical system of a house or the fraternity system in a college and have at least a vague notion of what a system entails. Social scientists sometimes use the term just as loosely, but the concept of a "political system" is sufficiently important to warrant as careful attention to the noun as to the adjective.

The Concept of a Political System

The eminent political theorist Carl J. Friedrich has offered this definition of a system: "When several parts that are distinct and different from each other compose a whole, bearing a defined functional relation to each other which establishes a mutual dependence of these parts upon each other so that the destruction of one entails the destruction of the whole, then such a constellation shall be called a system."[7] This definition is broad enough to apply to any sort of active system—a solar system, the human body, an economic system, or, of course, a political system.[8] Like any system of activity, the American political system has certain basic attributes simply by virtue of the fact that it *is* a system.

Let us examine the meaning of *system* more closely. First, a system has identifiable parts or elements—units of which it is composed. The elements of a political system are political actions, all those activities that bear on the formation and enforcement of authoritative policies. These activities tend to structure themselves in political roles and political groups. In the United States, the political structure is highly visible and differentiated—our elaborate system of courts, for example, settles disputes in the application of public policy to particular individuals. In more primitive cultures, these activities may not be so highly differentiated or visible, but they exist nonetheless. Political structure appears to be a universal attribute of human societies, despite considerable variations in the nature of the structures.[9]

Second, a system constitutes an identifiable whole, which means that it has recognizable boundaries and that the different activities of the system are to some degree integrated or coordinated. How a system works is in part determined by the environment in which it operates; the environment includes other systems of activity that affect the political system, but from which it must be distinguished if it is to be examined in full detail. We have already seen that politics can be abstracted from other activities by determining whether they directly affect public policy. Thus when a church endorses a given code of behavior, it is normally engaged in religious activity. But if the endorsement calls for legislation to prohibit the sale of contraceptives or of alcoholic beverages, it has directly entered the political system. In addition to

---

[7] *Man and His Government: An Empirical Theory of Politics* (New York: McGraw-Hill Book Company, 1963), p. 25.

[8] It would not include such usages as "a mountain system," since the definition we are using implies activity by the system rather than merely the combination of things or parts into a complex whole.

[9] See Gabriel A. Almond, "A Functional Approach to Comparative Politics," in Almond and Coleman (eds.), *The Politics of the Developing Areas*, pp. 10–11.

recognizable boundaries to the political system, the idea of an identifiable whole also implies some measure of cooperation among the different units of the system. Even though they may be performing different kinds of activities, one element of a system cannot operate in complete disregard of the activities of other elements without disrupting or destroying the system. The American system of law (a subset of activities and doctrines within the total political system) was seriously threatened, for example, when Governor George Wallace of Alabama "stood in the doorway" of the University of Alabama to prevent the entrance of two Negro students whose admission had been ordered by a federal court. Had he not capitulated, the American political system would have been threatened with destruction or drastic modification.

Third, the constituent units of a system are interdependent—each part affects and is affected by all the other parts. Although some differentiation or division of labor exists in all systems, the performance of each part is to some extent a function of the performance of the other parts. Yet Friedrich's stipulation that the destruction of one part of a system entails the destruction of the whole seems to go too far.[10] Systems tend to persist and to adapt to changes both in their environment and within themselves. If the planet Venus were destroyed, for example, every other part of the solar system would be affected, but the system itself would persist in a modified form. The American political system might similarly survive the loss of the Senate. The loss of both houses of Congress, however, would probably lead to the creation of an entirely different political system. The interdependence of all elements within a system does not mean, then, that all elements play equally vital roles. The relative functional importance of the component parts of the American political system will accordingly be a recurrent concern in this book.

The General Characteristics of a Political System

What are the other consequences of viewing American politics as a system of activity? Some of the more important are illustrated in Fig. 1-1, which diagrams the preliminary features of a political system.

To begin with, the area in white, which represents a political system, indicates that political life is separable, at least analytically, from other activities and systems. Second, in viewing politics as a system, we are forced to recognize that "the operation of no one part can be fully understood without reference to the way in which the whole itself operates."[11] The entire political system is therefore presented in Fig. 1-1 as linked together in a pattern of interrelated activities. Third, the operation of the entire political system (and therefore of its parts) can be understood only in terms of the environment in

---

[10] Professor Friedrich is aware of this: despite the unqualified nature of the statement of mutual dependence in his definition, in his book he immediately thereafter distinguishes between constitutive elements, which are necessary to survival of the system, and supplementary elements, which may play important roles but which could be lost without the entire system necessarily being destroyed.

[11] David Easton, "An Approach to the Analysis of Political Systems," *World Politics*, IX (April, 1957), 383. Although our diagram of a political system departs radically from Professor Easton's, this entire discussion has benefited greatly from his work. His concept of the political system is further elaborated in *A Framework for Political Analysis* (Englewood Cliffs, N.J.: Prentice-Hall, Inc., 1965) and *A Systems Analysis of Political Life* (New York: John Wiley & Sons, Inc., 1965).

THE STUDY OF AMERICAN POLITICS

which it operates. The shaded area around the political system suggests that it is a part of a broader culture by which it is influenced, and which it in turn influences. Fourth, the system's ungeometric shape and the breaks in its boundaries means that, although it is identifiable, the area of society occupied by the system varies with circumstances and with the activities of other systems. During World War II, for example, the economic system of the United States was almost totally absorbed by the political system, the government determining price levels and deciding which goods should be produced. America's political and economic systems overlap in peacetime too, but the economy is not completely dominated by the government then as when the nation is at war.

In addition to these general characteristics, the diagram is designed to suggest the substance of the basic processes of government. As a system of activities, American government—any government, for that matter—is made up of an interrelated set of activities, all bearing on the authoritative determination and implementation of policies. This broad function is what we mean by *governance,* or the act of governing. But to say that the function of the political system is to govern is almost a truism, and it is at best such a general statement that it offers few clues on how to analyze American politics. The diagram attempts to break up this all-encompassing function into different stages of political activity. (In the next section, we shall add more specific functions to the diagram.)

At the core of the governmental process are the interrelated *activities of authoritative decision-making,* which are performed by identifiable political agencies or structures. These are represented by the "charmed circle" at the center of the political system. In a tribe ruled largely by custom, with a few elders who interpret the meaning of the customs in rare cases of uncertainty, these official decision-making activities may not be highly structured or even easily discovered. African specialists report that early British requests to "take me to your leader" sometimes produced bizarre results in areas where the leadership structure was not only loosely defined but was also described in different terms. In the United States, on the other hand, the highest levels of political leadership are occupied by full-time politicians with distinctive titles, office buildings, seals of office, and all the other paraphernalia of authority. The President is a constant fo-

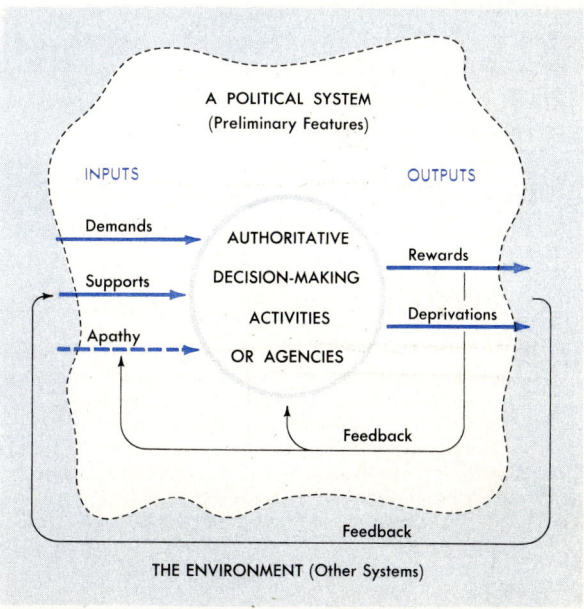

Figure 1-1

cus of public attention, whether he is lifting a dog by its ears or using dozens of pens to sign an Act of Congress. Both houses of Congress, the Supreme Court, and—to a lesser extent the vast bureaucracy under the President are also visibly engaged in the decision-making activities by which we are governed.

But keep in mind that the boundary lines between the environment and the political system and between the political system and its authoritative decision-making activities are designed to identify activities, not people. Despite the merciless attention of the mass media, even a President can hope that part of his life will remain purely private and therefore outside the area of the political system. Similarly, some of his political activity will represent not *authoritative* decision-making but efforts to influence other decision-makers, as when he delivers an appeal for public support of legislation he has proposed to Congress. Thus the official decision-makers act partly outside the political system, mostly within it (but still outside the core area of authoritative decision-making), and partly in the core area of authoritative decision-making itself.

The neat circle which represents these decision-making activities should not suggest an undifferentiated or perfectly harmonious set of activities. The diagram vastly oversimplifies complex realities in order to draw attention to the principal features of the system. The decision-making circle could be broken up into a number of subsets representing different departments and agencies, each connected to the others by crisscrossing arrows representing inputs and outputs. No matter what their internal relationships were, however, all these departments and agencies would be engaged in authoritative decision-making.

The term *inputs* refers to those activities which keep the system going. The most obvious forms of inputs are *demands* on the decision-makers—a "March on Washington" demanding congressional enactment of a civil rights act, a flood of letters to the President urging him to veto a statute, a lawsuit challenging the constitutionality of a local ordinance regulating picketing, an application from a college professor seeking National Science Foundation funds to support a research project. These and countless other demands —many of them only indirectly reflected at election time—of citizens on a democratic government are often generated outside the political system. A hurricane in Texas or an earthquake in Alaska will dramatically demonstrate how nonpolitical events create conditions that are translated into political demands. Political demands may also be generated *within* the political system, as when, for example, the President urges Congress to pass a particular bill. In recognition of this pattern of influence, the diagram includes feedback arrows to represent inputs on decision-makers from within the political system as well as from the nonpolitical environment.[12]

The input of *supports* in the political system includes attitudes and behavior

---

[12]Professor Easton uses the term "withinputs" to refer to this generation of inputs by the political system itself. Such an awkward term appears necessary because his diagram of a political system includes only what we have labeled "authoritative decision-making activities or agencies." Inputs therefore appear to be entirely outside the political system in his model. If the political system is more broadly conceived to include inputs, decision-making, and outputs as analytically separable parts of the same system, then one part of the system can easily be understood to affect other parts.

supporting the political system at every level: the political community, the structure of government, the current administration exercising the power of government, and particular government policies. American children learn to support "America the Beautiful" and the American constitutional system so early that support for the most basic levels of our system is largely taken for granted. But the fact that we take them for granted as we do sanitary drinking water, does not lessen their importance. The turmoil in some of the new African nations in which support for the very idea of a political community is weak, demonstrates the importance of support at this level for any political system. On the other hand, the stability of the French system has suffered, despite strong support for the idea of France as a political community, because of weaker support for the established structure of government at any given time. Major drop-offs in support in the United States apply only to the next level—the current administration controlling the government. And even there, Republicans *accept* and *pledge to support* (though not to prefer) a Democratic administration until the next election. Democrats, of course, return the compliment when the Republicans win. Support for new policies is not nearly so widespread, although most Americans at least accept official decisions as legitimate. But the input of supports for established policies goes beyond acceptance of their legitimacy; in the United States, it usually includes widespread belief in their effectiveness and desirability. Once established, an originally controversial program is not easily changed, as indicated by the mixture of amusement and shock that greeted Senator Barry Goldwater's suggestion that the federally operated Tennessee Valley Authority—once widely denounced as socialistic—should be sold to private corporations.

Many political scientists would probably protest the inclusion of the third input identified in our diagram—*apathy*. How can apathy influence the decision-making activities of government? It certainly operates in more indirect fashion than the demand and support inputs, and we recognize this by using a broken line to indicate its linkage to decision-making activities. Nevertheless, widespread apathy may be almost as important as active demands on government in shaping public policy. In a thorough study of the attitudes and behavior of the American voter, a research team at the University of Michigan found woeful ignorance on the most prominent issues in American politics. On sixteen "burning" issues of the day, the number of citizens who had an opinion, some notion of what the government was doing, and some feeling about the differences in party policy constituted a rousing 28 per cent![13] A majority of American citizens would thus have great difficulty in making intelligent demands or offering meaningful support in connection with most public policies. Ignorance does not necessarily mean apathy, of course, as is demonstrated by the fact that a majority of American adults—al-

---

[13]Angus Campbell *et al., The American Voter* (New York: John Wiley & Sons, Inc., 1960), p. 182. These findings are based on a most generous application of the criteria: if an individual thought he knew the position of the government on an issue, for example, he was counted as informed even if he misinterpreted that position.

most two-thirds—has voted in recent presidential elections. But a sizeable proportion of the citizenry—at least a fifth and probably a third—is both ignorant of and indifferent to politics. This apathy is not the same as support, although it implies at least acquiescence in basic governmental arrangements. With respect to particular policies it is entirely neutral, which means that the freedom of decision-makers to act without concern for public reactions increases with the proportion of apathetic citizens. In an indirect fashion, then, the degree of apathy in a political system has important consequences for the way it performs.

Because we view the political system as a set of activities related to authoritative decision-making, the *outputs* of the system are, by definition, decisions or public policies. The substance of these policy outputs may be identified, as in Fig. 1–1, as *rewards* and *deprivations*. These outputs represent the translation of demands, supports, and apathy by the decision-making agencies into rules or policies that maintain order and, therefore, promote the survival of the system by adapting it to changing circumstances. The consequences of inputs show up primarily in the way the political system operates, the consequences of outputs in the impact of its operation on the environment. National tax policies, for example, profoundly affect the economic system. The arrow representing the rewards and deprivations of public policy in our diagram, therefore, moves into the general environment, but it also circles back to the inputs of the political system itself. When the Supreme Court interprets an act of Congress—and most dramatically, on the rare occasions when it rules an act of Congress unconstitutional—the content of the decision has a direct effect on the Congress no less than on the nonpolitical environment. This aspect of the political system—in which the decision outputs directly affect decision-making agencies and the inputs to which they respond—is simply the other side of our earlier observation that *inputs* affecting decision-makers may be generated by the decision-making agencies themselves.[14]

Throughout this book, we shall conceive of government decisions as simultaneously bestowing rewards and imposing deprivations. When an irate citizen seeks an injunction to prevent his neighbor from practicing the trombone at 2:00 A.M., the court's decision will quite evidently please one of the parties and displease the other. If the judge grants the injunction, the trombone player will lose the freedom to exercise his talents when he chooses; if the plaintiff's petition is denied, he loses not only the case but undisturbed sleep. The rewards to the winner, whatever the decision, are equally obvious. But what if the judge refuses for some reason to render a decision? Even then, a decision has been reached, so far as the citizens are concerned, in favor of music and against sleep.

That the failure of government to act involves a decision (which is viewed as a deprivation by some and as a reward by others) is obvious when we are talking about a lawsuit. But many people are not so quick to see that the same reasoning applies to the refusal of *any* government agency to decide a question put to it. Under the rules of the United States Senate, for example, a

---

[14]This pattern of influence is not included in Easton's model, since his "political system" includes only what we call "authoritative decision-making activities or agencies." Adopting his terminology with regard to inputs, however, this output linkage would be called "withoutputs."

minority of members (33 per cent plus 1) may prevent a majority from bringing a proposal to a vote. One justification advanced for this practice is that important decisions should not be made by a bare majority of 50 per cent plus 1; if a larger majority is required, genuine support approaching consensus will be achieved. Whether the requirement of an extraordinary majority is wise or foolish, this particular argument ignores the fact that *a refusal to decide involves a decision itself*—a decision to continue the *status quo*, which is rewarding to some but not to others. If a minority can block action, it has at least a negative control over policy.

We have talked thus far about rewards *and* deprivations as the substance of policy decisions, as if every decision included both. Can a decision carry *only* rewards or *only* deprivations? Political scientists are divided on this question, some maintaining that no outputs of government are neutral, while others argue that in certain cases government may act to the benefit of all. Our position throughout this book will be that political decision-making is never neutral, and that the outputs of the political system always involve differential effects. Notice that we speak of "differential effects" rather than of rewards and punishments. This is to take account of the fact that some decisions of government involve no direct deprivations. Someone in the Post Office Department for example, must decide, what colors will be used on a particular stamp. Most of us are wholly indifferent to such routine decisions. Even so, philatelists may be quite interested, and some will be pleased and others disappointed by the choice. No one suffers a serious loss from this sort of decision, but within the general atmosphere of indifference those who *are* affected will react differently. The less consequential a decision is, the closer it may appear to approach neutrality. The greater its consequences for the citizenry, however, the more obvious are the rewards and deprivations that it entails.

The concept of *feedback* in our diagram of a political system simply gives explicit recognition to points we have already made—the interdependence of the political system with the other systems of society. Governmental decisions represent not only the adaptation of the system to its environment but also the efforts of the system to modify that environment.

Functions of the Political System

In adapting to and modifying the environment in order to survive, every political system performs certain basic functions. Up to this point, we have talked about the basic elements of politics without much concern for the functions which make a given set of activities recognizable as a political system. We have already mentioned that the underlying function of politics is the authoritative determination of policy for society as a whole and that activities can be identified as political insofar as they bear on this process. The general concept of functions has thus already been put to use. But we have talked about the basic elements of politics without concern for their specific functions. Nor have we explained what we mean by *function*. Like so many English words, this one is used with a variety of meanings. We refer to a college dance or a cocktail party, for example, as a "social function." But when we talk of the "functions of government," we certainly do not have public gatherings of this sort in mind.

Another usage, and one closer to our usage concerning governmental functions, identifies functions with *motives* or *purposes*. From this point of view, the *function* of an act of Congress could be determined by finding out what Congress intended to accomplish when it passed the act. But, from the point of view of political science, the *function* of a law—or of any activity or structure—is not necessarily the same as its *purpose*; the function of anything is understood more clearly in terms of its *effect*. In other words, we may undertake an activity with a firm purpose in mind, only to find that the ultimate effect or outcome of the activity is quite different from what we had expected. Thus our *purpose* in going to college may simply be to get a college degree or to kill time between leaving preparatory school and entering the family business. Contrariwise, the effect—that is, the *function*—of going to college may be the stimulation of a permanent intellectual curiosity or the development of new career plans. To determine the real function of college for an individual, we ask—"What would his life have been like without such an experience?" To clarify the primary functions of government we may ask the very same sort of question—"What would our lives be like without government?"

In the broadest sense, then, *functions* refers to the effects or consequences of an activity. Biological and social scientists have developed a more specific meaning, according to which *functions* refers to the consequences of activities that promote the survival of the acting system, and *dysfunctions* refers to consequences that tend to disrupt or destroy the system.[15] The basic output functions of the political system are fairly obvious: the system must furnish some general rules or policies to maintain order and to satisfy demands on the system. In addition to deciding on rules or policies, the system must carry them out, apply them in actual practice. Also, it must settle disputes among citizens, as in the case already mentioned of the nocturnal trombonist and his neighbor.

Figure 1–2, with these and other basic functions added, represents a more complete diagram of a political system than Fig. 1–1. The three functions we have mentioned—rule-making, application of rules, and settlement of disputes—are outputs or consequences of decision-making activity. They are easy concepts for Americans to grasp, because each tends to be centered in a highly visible political agency—the Congress, the President and the bureaucracy he heads, the Supreme Court and lower courts. When we look more closely at the decision-making agencies in later chapters, we will discover much more sharing of output functions by the agencies of American government than this neat trichotomy suggests. Whatever the form of government, however, these three output functions will somehow be performed. By adding these functions

[15]See Robert K. Merton, *Social Theory and Social Structure* (New York: The Free Press of Glencoe, Inc., 1949), p. 50. Merton also distinguishes *manifest* functions—consequences that accord with the declared purpose of an activity—from *latent* functions—the unintended consequences of an activity.

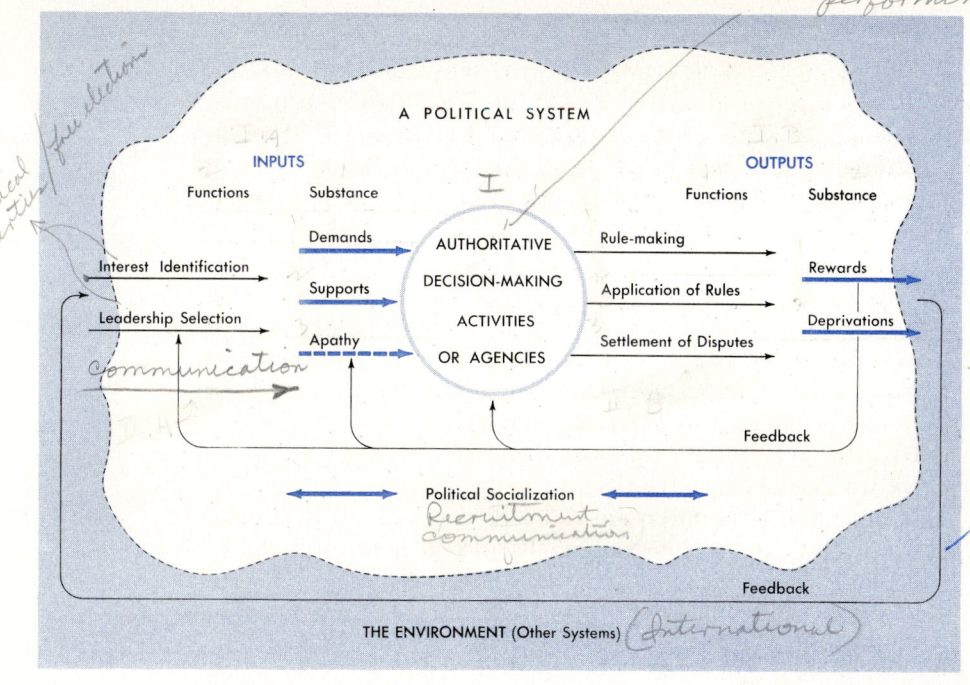

Figure 1-2

to our diagram of a political system, we are simply recognizing another dimension of the system's outputs. The decisions of a political system will thus be viewed as carrying the substance of rewards and deprivations, and as performing the functions of rule-making, application of rules, and settlement of disputes. Other dimensions of output might also be identified—for example, the kinds of goals toward which policy is aimed. The diagram should therefore be regarded as a representation of only some of the key features of a political system, not as a complete model.

The function of *political socialization* is presented as being at the base of the political system, between outputs and inputs. This is because political socialization supports the entire system, and also because the process is in some respects an output of the system and in other respects an input. (All aspects of the system are interrelated, but political socialization is so much a part of both inputs and outputs that it cannot be identified with one to the neglect of the other.)

Political socialization is "the process of induction into the political culture."[16] This definition should not be taken to imply that the individual who is "socialized" politically already exists as a social creature, and that he is brought into the political system by the addition of appropriate political attitudes to those he already has. The appropriate attitudes and behavior patterns *make* a human being. Children who have existed in a condition of

15

extreme isolation may be *homo sapiens* in a physical sense but they are not human beings in a social sense—that is, their only resemblance to human beings is physical. Such an isolated individual can be socialized through careful and expert guidance, but only if his isolation is ended at a fairly early age.[17] The process of socialization thus creates human beings; political socialization, as a part of this general process, creates citizens or subjects—human beings who share in some degree the political community's way of acting and thinking about politics.

From this point of view, political socialization is an output function of the political system. Political systems tend to perpetuate their own values and practices, and they do this by developing new members who share these values and follow those practices. In all political systems, children are somehow indoctrinated in the political processes and beliefs of their society. In Plato's *Republic,* political socialization can easily be recognized as an output function of government because children are to be brought up by an official agency of government rather than by their parents. In real political systems, the process is considerably more informal. Children learn largely from observation and imitation in informal contacts with others the normal way of doing things (including political things). The process begins in the family, is continued in contacts with playmates, and—in more highly developed countries—is furthered by formal schooling, television programs, and other contacts with the world far beyond the family. The acquisition of specifically political attitudes begins amazingly early[18] and it continues into adulthood, when individuals add new and perhaps contradictory attitudes through job contacts, marriage, and other experiences. Except for the public schools, these socializing agencies are not part of the official structure of government. But even the family is acting as a part of the political system when it imparts political knowledge and attitudes.

Although political socialization is thus an output of every political system, it can also be viewed, as we have said, as part of the input activities of the system. The kinds of demands and supports that enter the system, the general level of apathy, and the aspects of the system toward which citizens are indifferent—all these are heavily influenced by the processes of political socialization. Almost all American children grow up with the idea that American government is democratic and that democracy is the best system of government. Beyond this general set of facts and values, however, they may learn quite different things. A child whose parents never discuss politics will probably be a different sort of citizen from another whose parents insist that all politicians are crooked, and both will be different from a third child whose parents begin to pin campaign buttons on him during his infancy.

Two other broad functions are essential features of a political system: *Identification of interests* in the population and *selection of leaders* or official

[17]Kingsley Davis, "Final Note on a Case of Extreme Isolation," *American Journal of Sociology,* LII (March, 1947), 432–437. Professor Davis estimates that the maximum age to which a person could remain isolated and still retain the capacity for socialization is 10 to 15 years.

[18]Herbert Hyman, *Political Socialization* (New York: The Free Press of Glencoe, Inc., 1959). Socialization processes are more fully treated in Chapter 6.

decision-makers. These are more exclusively input functions than is political socialization.

Every political system must somehow identify the basic interests that unite and divide its citizens.[19] This function is performed in quite different ways and by quite different kinds of political structures from one country to another. In the United States, a congressman's difficulty in identifying the needs and desires of his constituents stems in part from the fact that they express their interests so freely. He gets a steady flow of mail from individual constituents; he hears from scores of pressure groups in and out of his district; he receives advice from local and national party organizations; and he reads about his duty in the newspapers. The massive census program carried out every ten years by the government may also be viewed as a way of identifying the interests to which government must respond. In a dictatorship, the flow of communication from individuals and groups to the decision-makers may not be so free as in a democracy. Nevertheless, every government, if it is to remain viable, must somehow identify the conditions in society on which it must act.

The second input function—selection of leaders—is equally universal. The process is exceedingly simple in some societies. For example, the eldest male of a particular family may be designated to hold the highest office. In such a system, leadership positions are ascribed rather than achieved through successful competition. In modern democracies, millions of people, not just one, are technically eligible for the highest office. The informal norms of the system usually reduce the active prospects for top positions to a mere handful, but those who reach this select position have usually survived a lengthy series of tests that many more have not. More people are elected to more offices in the United States than in any other democracy, and lower-level positions are frequently available to almost anybody who will take them. The political structures that perform the central tasks in American leadership selection are, of course, the political parties; but pressure groups, official agencies of government, the media of communication, and the voting public all play important parts, too.

[19]Our discussion of functions has benefited greatly from Gabriel A. Almond, "A Functional Approach to Comparative Politics," in Almond and Coleman (eds.), *The Politics of the Developing Areas*, pp. 3–64. It differs in four respects. He treats "political recruitment" as a specialized form of political socialization; we use instead the broader and separate concept of "leadership selection." He regards political socialization as an input function; we think it cannot be properly understood without also recognizing its importance as an output function. We omit one of his input functions, "political communication," because communication is inherent in both the substance and the functions of all political activities. Moreover, communication is as much a part of output activities as it is of input activities. Finally, he talks of "interest articulation" and "interest aggregation" as two separate functions. Since some combination of interests has occurred in virtually every expression of interests, and since aggregated interests are articulated, this does not seem to be a meaningful distinction. Hence we use the broader concept, "interest identification." Even interests that are not articulated may have important effects for policy. The Soviet Union, for example, goes to considerable expense and trouble to gain information on the unarticulated interests of citizens. See Alex Inkeles, *Public Opinion in Soviet Russia* (Cambridge: Harvard University Press, 1950).

Theory and Theories in Studying American Politics

We indicated at the beginning of this chapter that our objective is to *explain* the basic processes of American politics. Scholars occasionally distinguish explanation from "mere description"; but when you stop to think about it, *mere* description is impossible. If we started out to describe rather than explain American politics, what would we describe? You might say that an entirely descriptive work would simply present "facts" with no interpretation. But a "fact" is simply one particular characteristic of the concrete social world chosen by the observer from an infinite number of characteristics. The very act of deciding which facts to present therefore requires an interpretation of what's important and what's unimportant. And once you begin making decisions on what's important, you have entered into the task of explanation.

Explanation reaches the level of *theory* when it becomes precise and applicable to a number of different facts. Notice that we are not talking here about "theory" as the word is sometimes used in popular conversation. In the statement "that's the theory, but here's how the fraternity system really works," "theory" is used to mean an official or accepted but misleading explanation. This is not what physicists, economists, chemists, or political scientists have in mind as they work to develop explanatory theory. We would be horrified to think that college students might complete a course on American politics with the lament that their reading was "good in theory but inapplicable in practice." In the search for understanding of the world we live in, theories that fail to explain actual practices are simply bad theories.

The Paucity of General Theory

If a satisfactory general theory of politics existed—or if we had the wit and the wisdom to develop one—we would not hesitate to employ it in explaining American politics. Despite great strides by political scientists in explaining an ever-increasing range of political phenomena, the discipline has not yet arrived at a single, unifying theory that can account for the vast range of activities that comprise American politics.[20] But it has developed a "near-theory," an analytical framework that helps us decide which "facts" are important and which relationships among facts bear examination. Gabriel Almond, speaking as President of the American Political Science Association, put it like this: "The emerging analytical framework in contemporary political theory is the concept of system, whether it is employed at the level of subnational, regional, or structural units such as communities, legislative bodies or committees, at the level of national political units, or at the level of the international political system. The principal advantage of the system concept is that it analytically differentiates the object of study from its environment, directs attention to the interaction of the system with other

---

[20]For an analysis of developments in the study of American politics since World War II, see William R. Keech and James W. Prothro, "American Government and Politics, *Journal of Politics*, XXIX, May, 1968..

THE STUDY OF AMERICAN POLITICS

systems in its environment, to its own conversion characteristics, and to its maintenance and adaptive properties."[21]

The view that American politics comprises a system of activities governs the organization of this book. We have already employed the concept to specify which "facts" we need to examine—those that affect authoritative decision-making for American society. Because any system of activities responds to the environment in which it operates, we will consider next the context of American politics: the second part of the book is specifically concerned with the entry of demands, supports, and apathy into the system. Third, we shall focus on decision-making as the central activity of the system, the process by which inputs are converted into policy outputs. Finally, we shall consider the outputs of rewards and deprivations that accompany every decision. In analyzing these substantive activities, we shall focus in each case on the structures—both formal and informal—through which they are carried out and on their consequences for the maintenance, adaptation, or disruption of the political system.

The systems framework can thus prove helpful in organizing our thoughts about politics, in identifying relevant variables and studying their interrelationships, and in recognizing the consequences of political activities for society and its politics. It will also be helpful in the effort to avoid provincialism. Because this is a book on American politics, we constantly run two opposite intellectual risks—that of generalizing from American practices to all other peoples, and that of assuming that American practices are somehow unique. The systems approach facilitates our effort to shift from an examination of formal government institutions to an examination of the basic struc-

---

[21]"Political Theory and Political Science," *American Political Science Review*, LX (December, 1966), 876.

Drawing by Koren; © 1967 The New Yorker Magazine, Inc.

tures—formal or informal—through which the system responds to its environment. With this shift we can more easily compare American practices with those carried out by quite different institutions in other societies. Although our focus remains on the American political system, we will compare at least its most central features with those of other systems.

But the systems framework is a useful *approach* rather than a true *theory*. It does not offer a set of interrelated propositions that apply to all forms of political participation. Nor does it offer broad explanatory generalizations from which we can deduce specific propositions accounting for the great variety of political practices that make up the American political system. To argue otherwise would be pretentious. Systems "theory" is not even comprehensive enough to explain all that is important to know about so small a *sub*system as a congressional committee. Richard Fenno employed the system framework, for example, in a study of the House and Senate appropriations committees. But even for this smaller and more intensive explanatory task, he recognized that the available theory was fragmentary rather than comprehensive: "As befits their essential fragmentation, the bits of theory have not been used to formulate a series of interrelated and testable propositions. They have been used rather to help chart the terrain . . ., to point up relevant kinds of relationships, and to suggest directions for further research. Indeed, the appeal of the political system as a central idea lies in the fact that it sensitizes the researcher to the broadest range of relationships. And it may be precisely this kind of capacious sensitivity that is most needed at the present juncture. . . ."[22] For the systems approach to offer the advantages Fenno describes is enough to ask of it. If it cannot do more at the level of the congressional committee, we would be foolhardy to expect it to explain everything at the level of the national political system.

Dependence on "Theories of the Middle Range"

Some years ago, Robert Merton, an eminent sociologist, recommended that his colleagues could most fruitfully work with "theories of the middle range," by which he meant "logically interconnected conceptions which are limited and modest in scope."[23] Theories of the middle range have a broader scope than working hypotheses but are more restricted than general theories. Of the all-encompassing general theory, he said, "I assume that the search for a total system of sociological theory, in which all manner of observations promptly find their preordained place, has the same large challenge and the same small promise as those all-encompassing philosophical systems which have fallen into deserved disuse."[24] A prominent political scientist has more recently offered similar advice to his colleagues: "I am quite convinced that in the present state of the social sciences premature (and often pretentious) theoretical closure is the surest way to some sort of neoscholasticism. The social scientist, it seems to me, is at his best if he is sensitive to the open-endedness of all current theo-

[22]*The Power of the Purse: Appropriations Politics in Congress* (Boston: Little, Brown and Company, 1966), p. 680
[23]*Social Theory and Social Structure*, p. 5.
[24]*Ibid.*, pp. 5–6.

ries and maintains a healthy respect for those facts that do not fit his particular working theory of the moment."[25]

We think this call for middle range theories and for a recognition of the "open-endedness" of all current theories is sound. We will therefore not permit the systems approach to blind us to other useful ways of looking at politics. Instead, we adopt the stance for the national political system that Fenno adopted for the congressional committee subsystem: "The book which follows is eclectic in borrowing various kinds of theory which seem particularly helpful in describing varieties of committee [here, national] activity and in facilitating generalizations about that activity. No single all-embracing body of theory has been adopted and none is on trial."[26] We will find "role theory," for example, particularly useful in understanding how and why the official decision-making agencies operate the way they do. The structural factors emphasized by "stratification theory" will prove helpful in understanding political opinions and political participation. "Reference group theory" will add to our comprehension of political parties. And "group theory" and the "power-elite theory" will be tested for their applicability to the analysis of pressure groups in American politics.

None of these middle range theories is incompatible with the broad systems approach adopted for this book. And each has relevance for understanding some aspect, however modest in scope, of the political system. While the "capacious sensitivity" of our approach will be regarded as a weakness by theoretical purists, we are convinced that, in the current stage of political science, explanatory relevance should take precedence over theoretical purity. If eclecticism is unclean, we are prepared deliberately to sacrifice our purity in the interest of clear understanding.

[25]Heinz Eulau, review of Gerhard E. Lenski, *Power and Privilege* (New York: McGraw-Hill Book Company, 1966), in *American Political Science Review*, LXI (June, 1967), 482.
[26]*The Power of the Purse*, p. xviii.

THE CULTURAL

CONTEXT 2

The writer of "escape" literature characteristically focuses on the current action of his hero (James Bond, for example), and shows little concern for the forces that shape his personality or his behavior. But authors of more enduring literary works recognize that the true hero is, like Tennyson's Ulysses, "a part of all that he has met." Understanding a literary character requires some recognition of the forces that impinge upon him.

Political scientists may not resemble novelists in most respects, but they do have one thing in common: they both concentrate deliberately on one part of a mixed-up whole. Like the good novelist, the serious political scientist recognizes that his principal concern (in the latter's case, the political system) influences and is influenced by every other aspect of society. In focusing on politics, we must not forget that the political system is simply one aspect of a broader social system. The general culture and its physical, demographic, class, and economic aspects all affect the political system.

Politics as a Cultural Heritage

In a Miss America contest, we can safely forecast that American judges will not award first prize to the young lady with the most elaborate tattoos, the most elongated lips, or the most elegantly deformed feet. Although each of these attributes is essential to true "beauty" among some people, Americans choose to value different abnormalities, such as spectacularly large bosoms in combination with unusually small waists.

If beauty, which appears at first glance to be an inherent and universally recognizable quality, is subject to such extreme variations, surely political values must also be molded by culture. If we know that a person has been brought up as an American, we can predict how he will normally react to certain political situations. We can say, for example, that he will probably not support a man who claims an office to which he has not been elected. And if he is an elected official himself, he will relinquish his office whenever he is defeated in a popular election. True enough, you may say. But what do these obvious generalizations have to do with the details of American political behavior? They simply suggest that we ought to look at the relationship of culture to politics in a more systematic way than we usually do.

"Culture" and the Way We View the World

Our national peculiarities—which seem so "natural" and "right" to us—spring from our "culture." By *culture* we mean the habitual modes of thought and behavior characteristic of a given society—"a *way* of thinking, feeling, believing."[1] In other words, the culture of any society is its social heredity, the man-made part of the environment, the ideas and habits that are acquired by all normal people in the process of growing up—or of being "socialized"—in that society.[2] This means that culture includes political behavior no less than courtship practices and funeral customs. It means that politics is not isolated from other activities, even though we may study it separately. In a study focused exclusively on American government, this is an important point to bear in mind. It will help us to be more objective in our appraisal of political behavior, and will keep us from the pitfalls of provincialism.

John Dewey, the noted twentieth-century American philosopher, once suggested that the customs of the society in which an individual grows up may be compared with the total vocabulary of his native language, and that his own influence on that society may be compared with the number of special words that his immediate family picks up from his baby talk. On the basis of her long study of different cultural patterns, anthropologist Ruth Benedict concluded that this is no exaggeration. "The life history of the individual," she said, "is first and foremost an accommodation to the patterns and standards traditionally handed down in his community."[3] Thus our political expectations, aspirations, and activities arise in large measure from the simple fact that most of us have been reared as members of the American society.

Journalist Walter Lippmann painfully discovered the meaning of this truth for politics. After an early career in which he had vainly tried to convince Americans of the need for reforms, he concluded that we do not approach politics with an open mind: "For the most part we do not first see, and then define, we define first and then see. In the great blooming, buzzing confusion of the outer world we pick out what our culture has already defined for us, and we tend to perceive that which we have picked out in the form sterotyped for us by our culture."[4]

Opinions are not built in a neutral fashion, then, on the basis of systematic observation. Indeed, we have attitudes toward many things we may never observe, from British socialized medicine to French sex life. And we acquire attitudes toward countless other things, from college professors to communists, long before we actually observe the objects of our opinions. Having picked up the attitude unencumbered by experience, we tend later to notice particularly those events that support our preconception. If we expect college professors to be absent-minded, we perceive any absent-minded act by a professor as typically professorial, whereas we perceive similar acts by doctors or lawyers as personal idiosyncrasies. When we have strong feelings about a

---

[1] Clyde Kluckhohn, *Mirror for Man: The Relation of Anthropology to Modern Life* (New York: McGraw-Hill Book Company, 1949), p. 23.
[2] Robin M. Williams, Jr., *American Society: A Sociological Interpretation*, 2nd ed. (New York: Alfred A. Knopf, Inc., 1960), pp. 22–25; and Ralph Linton, *The Study of Man* (New York: Appleton-Century-Crofts, 1935), p. 288.
[3] Ruth Benedict, *Patterns of Culture* (New York: Mentor Books, 1934), p. 2.
[4] Walter Lippmann, *Public Opinion* (New York: The Macmillan Company, 1922), p. 81.

subject, like communism, for example, we find it hard to accept any facts that may be contrary to those feelings. Our culture not only shapes our *opinions* but it also helps determine which *facts* we will notice and how we will interpret them.

Students of politics have to be on guard against the danger of mistaking values for facts. They must also attempt the more difficult task of holding opinions, even those that were received ready-made from their culture, with enough flexibility to permit the recognition of contradictory evidence. The truly curious person is like the ideal scientist in that he welcomes facts that challenge his opinions. Unfortunately, most people rarely question the ideas with which they grow up.

Some Americans use such terms as "mick," "wop," "frog," or "nigger" in referring to the Irish, Italians, French or Negroes. In doing so, they are not simply using a neutral term for referring to an ethnic group, for these very terms carry with them certain "natural" attitudes toward these groups in particular and toward all "other" ethnic groups in general. For example, just from knowing that a person uses such terms, we would probably be safe in predicting that he would oppose such political measures as strong civil rights legislation. And he could also be identified as a potential follower of any demagogue who appealed to race prejudice. Our choice of terms often carries with it a built-in political meaning.

The "American Character" in Politics

The influence of culture on politics is especially obvious to the foreigner, for to him the politics of a new country appears fresh and alien rather than inevitable and natural. The American "national character" has been analyzed by an endless series of foreign commentators, and some of them—for example, Alexis de Tocqueville, an early nineteenth-century French visitor[5]—have given us precious insight into our national peculiarities. More recently, social scientists have tried to identify a systematic pattern of cultural traits so widely shared that they offer a general picture of how the "ideal" or "normal" American approaches politics. Hopefully, the contemporary student relies much more on a general theory of human behavior and less on sheer intuition than a journalist or a traveler like Tocqueville, but almost all students of American character have come to similar conclusions.[6]

Popular writers like Vance Packard occasionally wring best-selling books out of the allegation that American character has drastically changed; in

---

[5]See his classic, *Democracy in America* (New York: Vintage Books, 1954), I, II, first published in 1835.

[6]For a review of the literature on national character, see Alex Inkeles and Daniel J. Levinson, "National Character: The Study of Modal Personality and Sociocultural Systems," in Gardner Lindzey (ed.), *Handbook of Social Psychology* (Reading, Mass.: Addison-Wesley Publishing Co., Inc., 1954), II, pp. 977–1020. For a collection of contemporary foreign impressions, see Allen F. Westin, Julian H. Franklin, Howard R. Swearer, and Paul E. Sigmund (eds.), *Views of America* (New York: Harcourt, Brace & World, Inc., 1966).

The Small Society, drawing by Brickman; © 1967 Washington Star Syndicate, Inc.

Packard's view, because we have suddenly become "status seekers."[7] This sort of discovery generally represents not a change in American values but the recent perception (and exploitation) of long-standing values by the writer. Americans have been described as status seekers since the early nineteenth century. Tocqueville himself, in describing the destruction of aristocracy by American democracy, says, "They have swept away the privileges of some of their fellow creatures which stood in their way, but they have opened the door to universal competition."[8] In a penetrating work on American social character, the influential sociologist David Riesman submitted in 1953 that Americans have abandoned reliance on fixed, personal standards ("inner-direction") for a radar-like response to whatever standards appear in vogue with their associates ("other-direction").[9] But virtually the same language was used by Harriet Martineau, an English liberal visitor to the America of 1830: "[Americans] may travel over the world, and find no society but their own which will submit to the restraint of perpetual caution, and reference to the opinions of others."[10] The chief points made by these reassessments of American social character may be that Americans are self-critical and that they feel their criticisms will be more effective if they argue that we have abandoned the ways of our forefathers.

The image of radical change in social character is based on the assumption that material conditions determine social values. From this point of view, the shift of American society from a predominantly rural and individualistic way of life to a predominantly urban and bureaucratic pattern must necessarily entail a radical change in values. Much can be said for the Marxist view that material conditions determine values. But the values of a society also appear to influence the way it responds to materialistic changes. Thus Max Weber, a renowned German sociologist, argued that the "Protestant ethic," with its

[7] Vance Packard, *The Status Seekers* (New York: Pocket Books, Inc., 1961). (Originally published in 1959 by David McKay Company, Inc.)
[8] *Democracy in America*, II, p. 146.
[9] *The Lonely Crowd* (New York: Doubleday Anchor Books, 1953).
[10] Harriet Martineau, *Society in America* (New York: Sanders and Otlay, 1837), III, p. 14. Quoted in S. M. Lipset, "A Changing American Character?" in S. M. Lipset and L. Lowenthal (eds.), *Culture and Social Character* (New York: The Free Press of Glencoe, Inc., 1961), p. 143.

emphasis on individual responsibility and achievement, was a prerequisite for the development of a capitalistic economic system.[11] This is, of course, directly opposite to the Marxist view that values are mere "superstructure" shaped by material forces. Basic social values are highly stable; they help to shape the way we respond to technological change rather than being merely responsive to such change.

The basic value that appears to have shaped American social character from the outset is the *aggressive assertion of equality in social relations.* We began with the bold declaration that "all men are created equal" rather than with an aristocratic order inherited from the feudal caste system.[12] Despite the conspicuous exception of slavery (which Jefferson denounced in the original draft of the Declaration of Independence), this emphasis on equality is probably the unique feature of American society. Urbanization, industrialization, and political democracy are characteristics we share with others; the deeply ingrained and insistent stress on equality, however, has been peculiarly American. Thus *Baedeker's* handbook for the European visitor to the United States late in the nineteenth century warned that he "should, from the outset, reconcile himself to the absence of deference, or servility, on the part of those he considers his social inferiors."[13]

America's stress on equality leads to three other basic social characteristics that have also long been noted by foreign visitors: *competition* or *individual achievement, status uncertainty,* and *conformity*. At first glance, some of these attributes may appear incompatible, but on examination each may be seen to lead to the other. Democratic egalitarianism, as Tocqueville saw, leads to intense competition and stress on achievement. If one's "station in life" is not fixed by a rigid class system, he must establish it himself. And in America we tend to measure achievement primarily in terms of money. With hereditary rank eliminated, cash value becomes the most obvious measure of status. As one anthropologist puts it, "Money comes closer with us than with any other people to being the universal standard of value."[14] Ask an average American, "What is Tom Smith worth?" and you are likely to get an answer in terms of dollars rather than class position, religious standing, military rank, knowledge, or political or social contributions.

The fact that Americans must achieve whatever rank they claim for themselves—that they cannot assume it as their birthright—may explain what appears to be a sense of insecurity and uncertainty about their status. Because of its unique rate of immigration and its possibilities for social and geographical

---

[11]Max Weber, *The Protestant Ethic and the Spirit of Capitalism,* trans. Talcott Parsons (London: George Allen & Unwin, Ltd., 1930). First published in German, 1922–1923.

[12]For an interpretation of American political thought that emphasizes the continuity of this value and the importance of this beginning, see Louis Hartz, *The Liberal Tradition in America* (New York: Harcourt, Brace & World, Inc., 1955).

[13]Quoted in Lipset, "A Changing American Character?" in Lipset and Lowenthal (eds.), *Culture and Social Character,* p. 143.

[14]Kluckhohn, *Mirror for Man,* p. 241.

mobility, America is in some respects a nation of *parvenus*.¹⁵ Early foreign observers of American society insisted that our emphasis on equality and opportunity actually led to greater consciousness of status than was found among the aristocracies of Europe. After all, people are unsure about positions they have newly acquired.

Status uncertainty has expressed itself in such things as an addiction to titles, "exclusive" resorts, and fraternities and sororities. Commenting on these efforts to create badges of superiority, D. W. Brogan, a British political scientist, explains, "It is only an apparent contradiction in terms to assert that the fundamental democratic and egalitarian character of American life is demonstrated by the ingenuity and persistence shown in inventing marks of difference and symbols of superiority. In a truly class-conscious and caste-dominated society, the marks of difference are universally recognized even if resented. In America, they must be stressed, or they might easily be forgotten. . . ."¹⁶ The conspicuous display of wealth is, of course, the most simple and direct way of advertising one's status. Texas, as the new frontier of the new rich, is noted for the most vulgar current display of sudden riches—without his Neiman-Marcus wardrobe, the oil millionaire might be indistinguishable from the farmer he was yesterday.

Status uncertainty leads to conformity. Whereas Europeans have found security in following the standards of earlier generations, Americans tend to feel insecure unless they are "up-to-date" in clothing, slang, furniture, and child-rearing practices. Some anxiety inevitably attends such a form of conformity, for what is "up-to-date" changes from day to day. The person insensitive to cues or without enough money to replace his wardrobe with each shift in fashion is in constant danger of being left behind. As our earlier quotation from Harriet Martineau reveals, the American's extreme sensitivity to the opinions of others was discussed more than a hundred years before David Riesman coined the term "other-directed personality."

How do these traits of "American character" show up in political attitudes and behavior? In a sense, this whole book is an extended answer to this question, but the impact of each basic characteristic deserves at least one illustration here at the outset.

In attempting to link national character to specifically political attitudes, we need to recognize that, as Professor V. O. Key said in an early draft of *Public Opinion and American Democracy*, the hazardous task of delineating national character requires "heroic guesswork." Kindly man that he was, he changed the phrase in galley proofs to read "educated intuition."¹⁷ Whether they are based on heroic guesswork or educated intuition, our statements on American character do not represent firmly established propositions. We have firm data on recent political attitudes, however, thanks largely to the research of the University of Michigan Survey Research Center and to Professor Key's synthesizing book based on that research. If we find widely shared political ideas

---

¹⁵Gabriel A. Almond, *The American People and Foreign Policy* (New York: Frederick A. Praeger, Inc., 1960), p. 62.
¹⁶D. W. Brogan, *U.S.A.: An Outline of the Country, Its People and Institutions* (London: Oxford University Press, 1941), p. 116.
¹⁷V. O. Key, Jr., *Public Opinion and American Democracy* (New York: Alfred A. Knopf, Inc., 1961), p. 42.

that might be said to stem from the apparent traits of American character, then, we can be more confident that the traits have been correctly identified.[18]

First, a vast majority of Americans are suspicious of power, regardless of who exercises it. This is precisely the attitude that would be predicted from the proposition that Americans are peculiarly and aggressively committed to equality. American opinion surveys consistently find large majorities who feel that the bosses, labor unions, or business corporations have "too much power."[19] Moreover, the people who believe that "big business" should not have too much say in the way government is run have the same belief about labor unions. The suspicion is not just of a particular group; it applies to any accumulation of power that appears to threaten our basic equality. Moreover, if no threat to equality is clearly present, we can always invent one. Many a candidate for public office has directed his campaign against some invisible "power elite" that threatens the public.

Second, the American value of individual achievement appears to be reflected in a number of political attitudes. The problems that concern Americans are overwhelmingly personal, not political, and most people are optimistic about their personal prospects. Moreover, the American parent thinks his children have a good chance to be better off than he is. This tendency of Americans to rely on themselves rather than on government seems to be a facet of their general optimism rather than an indication of antigovernmental convictions. The typical attitudes are simply *non*governmental. When asked if they think the government ought to engage in a particular program, such as medical care for the aged, most Americans will answer affirmatively. But the issue is not at the center of their interests, which leaves officials considerable discretion and permits small groups who are actively interested to play a role that far outweighs their numbers.

The status uncertainty of Americans can be seen in the high degree of ethnocentrism that marks their political attitudes. This is so conspicuous that it is the first trait of American "political character" noted by Professor Key: "The American characteristically manifests an uncommonly high degree of loyalty and satisfaction with things American—an attitude that, on occasion, approaches smugness and, at times, extreme intolerance of matters regarded as un-American."[20] Proponents of any new measure must be able to demonstrate that it is not an alien practice before it can receive serious consideration. Thus policies that have become commonplace in most other democracies may be long delayed here precisely because they were developed elsewhere. A cataclysmic economic depression was required before we could join other democracies, for example, in providing Social Security for our citizens.

The social trait of conformity expresses itself most obviously in a disposition

---

[18]The discovery of political attitudes logically deducible from traits of national character does not, of course, demonstrate a causal connection. But it does lend additional credence to traits that have been identified on the basis of different evidence.

[19]Key, *Public Opinion and American Democracy*, p. 44. Unless otherwise noted, other references to political attitudes in this section come from the same source, pp. 41–50.

[20]*Ibid.*, p. 42.

to abide by the majority will. As Key says, acceptance by the minority of an unwanted majority decision may stem simply from "resignation to the fact that the majority has more spears and dissent is futile."[21] But the quality of acceptance of majority decisions in the United States seems to go beyond mere resignation. Indeed, immediately after an election, about 10 per cent more voters claim to have supported the winner than actually voted for him on election day! People like a winner, some so much that they cannot face the fact that they did not contribute to his victory. Once a new administration has had a chance to stabilize itself, bare-knuckled opposition reappears. But even opposing politicians tend to rally 'round the winner long enough to give him a brief "honeymoon" during which consensus seems to prevail.

The existence of a national "political character" can be demonstrated on the basis of attitudes shared by a large majority of the population. And the content of these attitudes is consistent with what would be expected from more speculative propositions about the national "social character." But the linkage of social character to political attitudes rests on logical inference, not demonstrable evidence. The linkage must accordingly be taken as highly tentative. In inferring that status insecurity is tied to ethnocentrism, for example, we cannot say that the former is a necessary and sufficient cause of the latter. Other causes of ethnocentrism no doubt exist. The French, Chinese, and English also appear to be highly ethnocentric without similar backgrounds of status uncertainty. Hence status insecurity is not absolutely necessary to ethnocentrism. Moreover, such insecurity might exist without leading to ethnocentrism. It could express itself in such nonpolitical forms as conspicuous economic display or alcoholism. Hence status insecurity is not a sufficient condition, by itself, to produce ethnocentrism. With these reservations in mind, we can only say that the American social character *seems* logically related to Americans' political attitudes.

The Physical Environment as a Political Setting

Concealed beneath what we have been calling the "American character" are all kinds of variations. The newly arrived foreigner thinks all Americans look and act alike, but the longer he observes us the more he comes to see our differences. If we are to appreciate the true impact of culture on politics, we must look closely at the geographic, demographic, class, economic, and historical roots of these differences.

From the very dawn of civilization, leaders of men have had to take into account the facts of geography—the distribution of natural resources, the effect of a territory's size and location on its armed strength, the pattern of natural trade routes. And yet nowadays many of us give little thought to the influence of geography, forgetting that the American political tradition is in large part a product of the physical setting in which it developed. Although federalism exists only as a possibility in a small land like Switzerland, in a vast country like the United States it is almost a necessity.

[21] *Ibid.*, p. 48.

The Natural Environment and the American Tradition

Three geographic factors have contributed mightily to shaping the American political tradition: The country's isolation from Europe, the vastness of its territory, and the richness of its natural resources.[22] As with American social character, these geographic factors are not necessary and sufficient to explain the American political tradition. Latin America, for example, has also experienced isolation from Europe, has a vast territory and abundant resources. But it did not develop in the same way as did the United States, perhaps basically because it was not consolidated into a single nation. As a result, the resources in one area were of little help in another area under a different government. Because political unification must be added to geographic attributes to explain the North American development, any notion of geographic determinism must be rejected. As one among many influences, however, geographic conditions helped to make the American political tradition possible.

Isolation from Europe meant, among other things, the absence of a feudal tradition and the accompanying concept of fixed status. Consequently, Americans took equality and freedom for granted almost from the outset, whereas in Europe the fight for equality consumed the political energies and dominated the ambitions of the "lower classes" for centuries. The vast land always stretching on beyond the frontier gave a new vitality to the principles of equality and freedom for individual achievement to every generation of Americans up to the twentieth century. The availability of cheap or free land served as a psychological "safety valve" and as a form of cheap economic relief for those who were denied equal opportunity in the settled regions of the East. Our natural resources, combined with political freedom, meant that Americans could turn to commerce and industry while European and Latin American contemporaries were struggling to win basic rights from oppressive governments.

One of our most eminent historians, the late Carl Becker, concluded that America's social equality and political freedom were casual and lavish gifts bestowed by nature rather than hard-won privileges earned through battle or careful reasoning.[23] Receiving so many advantages with such relative ease, Americans have tended to pursue a politics of self-congratulation. Even the Puritans came to assume that God was the special servant of the American people rather than vice versa. Today we easily forget how much we owe to the abundance of our natural resources and the lucky accident that we came to span the continent just when technological developments made it possible to weld the land into a political and economic unit. We tend to give ourselves all the credit; Reinhold Niebuhr, a contemporary theologian, ironically notes that on Thanksgiving Day we have come to "[congratulate] God on the virtues and ideals of the American people, which have so well merited the blessings of prosperity we enjoy."[24]

---

[22]See Carl L. Becker, *Freedom and Responsibility in the American Way of Life* (New York: Vintage Books, 1955), p. 12.
[23]*Ibid.*, p. 21.
[24]*The Irony of American History* (New York: Charles Scribner's Sons, 1952), pp. 52–53.

This spirit of complacency promotes our characteristic ethnocentrism, the feeling that all things American are superior. This feeling helps explain our failure to take advantage of successful experiments with new policies elsewhere. By definition, they are non-American; ethnocentrism translates non-American into un-American, meaning "treacherous." Our self-satisfaction also throws light on the prejudice and discrimination to which every generation of immigrants has been exposed. In international politics our pride sometimes leads to an emotional rather than a rational appraisal of events; assuming that America is omnipotent, we find it hard to adjust foreign policy to the unpleasant fact that some things are beyond our easy control. When the communists won power in China after World War II, for example, many Americans assumed that someone in the United States government must have been responsible. And we were shocked in 1961 when an ill-organized invasion failed to overthrow the Castro regime in Cuba. We disliked the Castro dictatorship, so we assumed that it could not last, just as we had assumed in 1917 that the communist regime in Russia could not survive.

The kindness of geography has been a mixed blessing in American politics. To be sure, it helped to give us great prosperity, but it also led us to accept our good fortune without thinking how to sustain it. It permitted a foreign policy of isolationism for over a century, and left us ill-prepared for both the responsibilities of world leadership and the realities of world politics.

The Natural Environment and Political Differences

Li'l Abner has more in common with a New Yorker than with a Samoan. And yet even within the United States there are important regional variations in the food people eat, the language they speak—and in the way they behave politically. For example, anti-Catholic attitudes seem to be more common among Southerners than among other Americans. President Kennedy was estimated to have suffered a 17 per cent loss of votes in the South in the 1960 presidential election simply because he was a Catholic (in the rest of the nation, he picked up a 1.5 per cent advantage because of his religion).[25] Opinions on many political problems vary in this way from one region to another. During the 1950s, when excitement about alleged communist control of American business, labor unions, government offices, military commands, and churches was at a peak, people were questioned on their willingness to grant certain rights to socialists, atheists, communists, and persons accused of communism. The largest proportion of relatively tolerant people was found in the West, and the smallest proportion in the South.[26] Even when the comparison is between Westerners and Southerners with the same amount of education, or living in the same kind of community (urban or rural), the regional differences are still significant.

These regional contrasts are remarkably endurable, but they should not mislead us into adopting the notion of geographic determinism. People who

---

[25]Philip E. Converse, et al., "Stability and Change in 1960: A Reinstating Election," *American Political Science Review*, LV (June, 1961), 269–280.
[26]Samuel A. Stouffer, *Communism, Conformity, and Civil Liberties* (Garden City, N.Y.: Doubleday & Company, Inc., 1955), pp. 129–130.

move from one section of the country to another tend to keep the political attitudes of the region where they grew up rather than picking up the viewpoint of their new environment. And when the newcomers are the dominant group in the locality, they can maintain their political distinctiveness for generations. A place like Edwards County in southeastern Illinois, which was settled in 1818 by relatively well-off, well-educated, antislavery colonists from England, remains more Republican to this day than the surrounding counties that were originally settled by proslavery southerners. Because Edwards County has the same geographic characteristics as the surrounding counties, its political distinctiveness suggests that political habits are an autonomous force rather than a simple reflection of the natural environment.[27]

The combination of regional contrasts and local variations within regions lends great variety to American politics. The candidate for Congress in Seattle, for example, will campaign quite differently from the candidate in a South Carolina farming community. The former will normally be less critical of nonconformists, less hesitant to adopt a position that might be denounced as "un-American," and more inclined to support proposals for the admission of more immigrants into the United States.

The People at the Base of American Politics

We can at least say two things about the American people in general: there are continually more and more of them, and they are all immigrants or the descendants of immigrants. Both characteristics have many important political implications.

More People with New Characteristics

In the first census of the United States in 1790 we numbered about 4 million. Just after the Civil War, we were 30 million Americans. A century later, in 1967, the population clock at the Bureau of the Census ticked past 200 million. And we are told that, given present population trends, we will be 300 million in the year 2000.

We are now 200 million Americans. According to the Census Bureau, in round numbers, about 102 million of us are females:

98 million	males
19 million	under 5 years of age
19 million	over 65 years of age
175 million	white
25 million	nonwhite
91 million	married

---

[27] V. O. Key, Jr., *American State Politics: An Introduction* (New York: Alfred A. Knopf, Inc., 1956), p. 225. Also see V. O. Key, Jr., and Frank Munger, "Social Determinism and Electoral Decisions: The Case of Indiana," in Eugene Burdick and Arthur J. Brodbeck (eds.), *American Voting Behavior* (New York: The Free Press of Glencoe, Inc., 1959), pp. 281–299.

11 million	widows or widowers
120 million	old enough to vote
6 million	in college
50 million	in other schools
33 million	white-collar workers
27 million	blue-collar workers
9 million	foreign-born
125 million	city-dwellers
33 million	home-owners
123 million	church members
85 million	born since July 1, 1945.*

The 1960 census was a record of dramatic change, and changes in the population always have political repercussions. Between 1900 and 1950, the population of the United States doubled; in the single decade between 1950 and 1960 it increased 18.5 per cent. This rapid growth has meant a greater drain on natural resources that were once exploited with abandon. Conservation programs have become more than just pious notions to be forgotten in the competitive drive for profit. With every leap in population, the efforts of lumber and cattle interests to exploit the public domain, the fate of the offshore oil lands, and programs of soil conservation and reforestation, clean streams and clean air, all become matters of increasingly urgent domestic

Source: U. S. Department of Commerce, Bureau of the Census. *200 Million Americans* (Washington, D.C.: U.S. Government Printing Office, 1967). Unless otherwise stated, census figures after 1960 are from this source.

Figure 2–1

Source: Bureau of the Census, United States Department of Commerce, 1960 Census of Population: Advance Reports, Final Population Counts, p. 6.

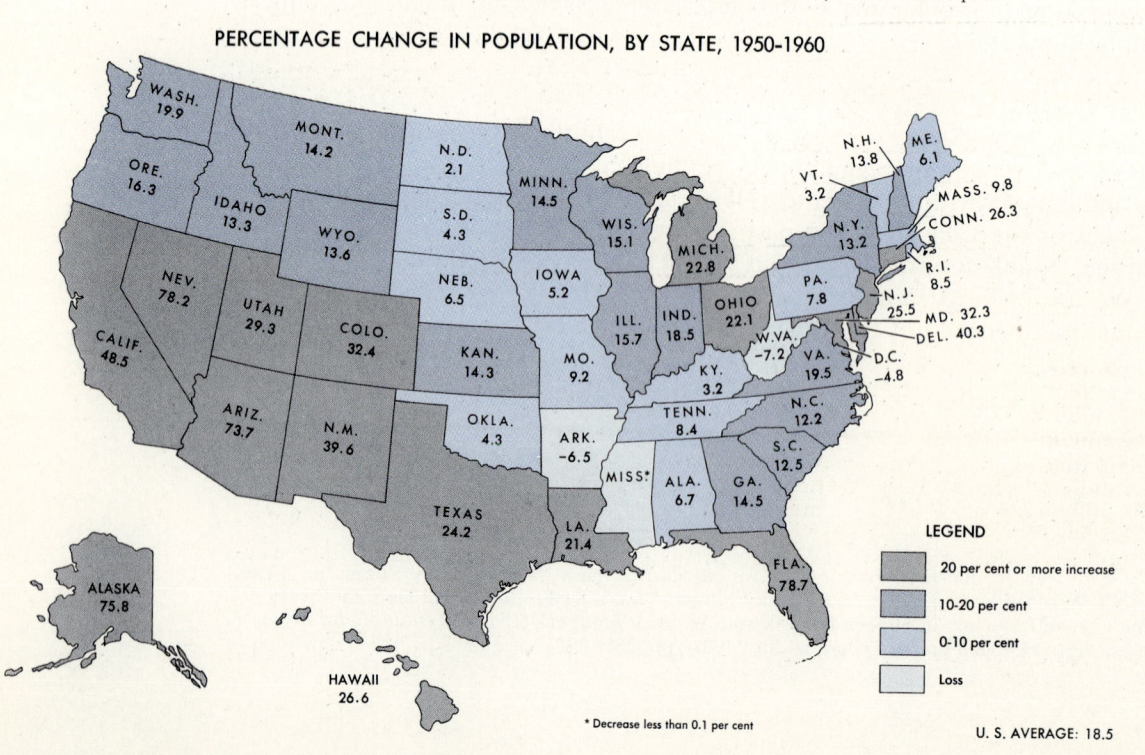

PERCENTAGE CHANGE IN POPULATION, BY STATE, 1950–1960

State	%	State	%	State	%
WASH.	19.9	MONT.	14.2	N.D.	2.1
ORE.	16.3	IDAHO	13.3	MINN.	14.5
CALIF.	48.5	WYO.	13.6	S.D.	4.3
NEV.	78.2	UTAH	29.3	NEB.	6.5
ARIZ.	73.7	COLO.	32.4	IOWA	5.2
N.M.	39.6	KAN.	14.3	MO.	9.2
OKLA.	4.3	ARK.	−6.5	TEXAS	24.2
LA.	21.4	MISS.*		ALA.	6.7
GA.	14.5	FLA.	78.7	TENN.	8.4
KY.	3.2	W.VA.	−7.2	VA.	19.5
N.C.	12.2	S.C.	12.5	WIS.	15.1
MICH.	22.8	ILL.	15.7	IND.	18.5
OHIO	22.1	PA.	7.8	N.Y.	13.2
VT.	3.2	N.H.	13.8	ME.	6.1
MASS.	9.8	CONN.	26.3	R.I.	8.5
N.J.	25.5	MD.	32.3	DEL.	40.3
D.C.	−4.8	ALASKA	75.8	HAWAII	26.6

LEGEND:
- 20 per cent or more increase
- 10–20 per cent
- 0–10 per cent
- Loss

* Decrease less than 0.1 per cent

U. S. AVERAGE: 18.5

THE CULTURAL CONTEXT

concern. (In Chapter 16, we shall be considering the problem of "population explosion" in the international environment and its impact upon American foreign policy.)

As they have grown in numbers, the American people have also shifted about the country. During the first half of the century, the population of the West grew at a rate of 499 per cent; the population of New England grew at a rate of only 67 per cent. The old westward movement has shifted to become a movement toward the relatively underdeveloped periphery of the country. The five states with the greatest rates of growth between 1950 and 1960 were Florida (78.7 per cent), Nevada (78.2), Alaska (75.8), Arizona (73.7), and California (48.5). In contrast to their phenomenal growth, only one New England state (Connecticut) had an increase greater than the national average (see the map of Fig. 2–1). Even if we ignore percentages and talk in terms of actual numbers of additional people, New York just beat out Texas for third place, while California and Florida were first and second. In political terms, these changes mean that in the future the old areas of the East can expect to exercise less influence over such crucial political contests as presidential elections. California and Texas are already supplying more national leaders to the major political parties.

This high rate of mobility makes some of the current arguments about "states' rights" seem rather anachronistic. An early Virginia congressman's boast, "My patriotism begins to wane as I leave the borders of Virginia," may have sounded meaningful in 1800, but it would make little sense to the mobile Americans of today. About 40 per cent of all native "white" Americans move from one state to another after growing up, and southern Negroes have been moving out of the South in a steady stream.[28] Between 1950 and 1960, the Census Bureau recorded the greatest migration for a single decade in American history—the movement of nearly 1.5 million Negroes from the South to other areas of the country. About one-half of American Negro citizens are now living in the central cities of metropolitan areas. The rate of moving has slowed down since the 1940s, when war industries attracted thousands of workers, especially Negroes, to industrial centers. Now the Census Bureau estimates that about 80 per cent of the population (mostly older people) continue to live in the same house and only about 20 per cent (mostly young people) move to a different house every year.

Americans who have lived in several states during their lifetime tend to keep the attitudes with which they grew up. Regardless of where they were reared, most Americans think of "the government" as the government in Washington, not the government of a county in which they may have resided for a few short months. And on election day they show where their primary political interest lies: The largest number of voters turn out for national elections, with state elections ranking second and local elections third in stimulating voter interest.

[28] Angus Campbell *et al., The American Voter* (New York: John Wiley & Sons, Inc., 1960), p. 442.

35

What about separate groups within this restless, shifting population? The percentage of the population 65 years old and over increased from 4 per cent in 1900 to 9.5 per cent in 1967. Despite the great increase in the number of old people, the median age of the population actually decreased in the last decade, for the first time in American history. (The median age of Americans in 1967 was a little less than 28 years old.) How can the median age drop when the aged portion of the population is increasing? The answer can be seen in crowded maternity wards and schoolrooms: the proportion of the population under 18 was increasing even faster than the very old group, and accounted for 36 per cent of the total population in 1960. A new trend may have set in, with a declining birthrate; in 1967 the birthrate reached a record all-time low. Various explanations are offered: "the pill" (although the decline in the birthrate, beginning about 1957, predates general use of the pill); the "new style" in family living, with working mothers, and parents planning to put their children through college; and possibly "fear of the bomb" (although previous wars have usually boosted the birthrate). Even so, the Census Bureau is predicting a baby boom in the 1970s, simply because there will be more women who can have babies.

Women began to outnumber men in the United States for the first time in 1950 (with 100 women to every 99 men) and their majority had increased by 1960 (to a 100–97 ratio). (See Fig. 2–2.) Americans are a marrying people. The trend is toward marrying at a young age, females marrying at an earlier age than males. There is a temporary "marriage squeeze"; for every 100 girls of ages 18 to 22 today, there are only 91 boys of ages 20–24. But the Census Bureau promises that "things should ease up for the girls" around the early

Figure 2-2

Source: *200 Million Americans*, p. 19.

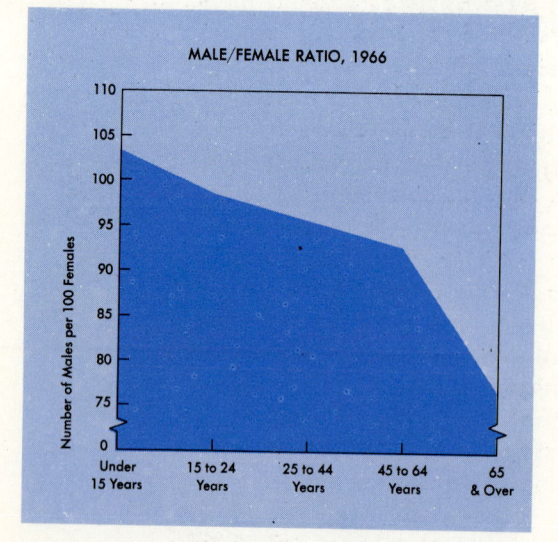

Figure 2-3

Source: *200 Million Americans*, p. 11.

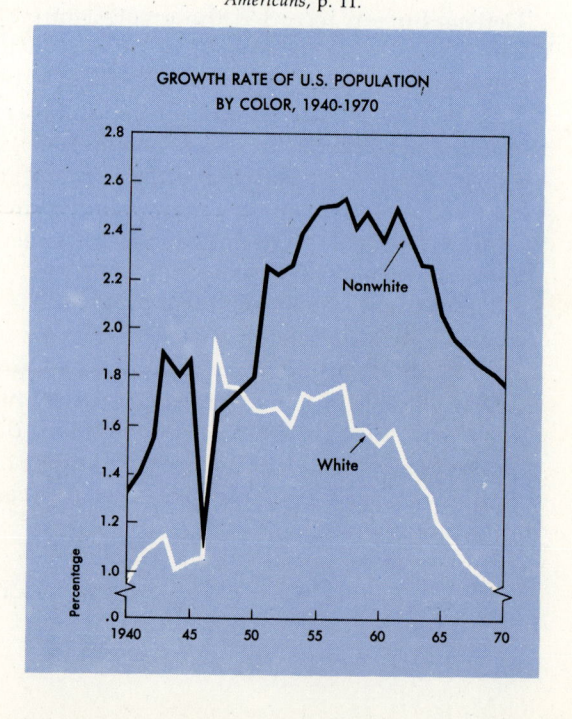

1980s! At present, however, 95 per cent of persons 45–54 years old are or have been married at some time in their lives.

Finally, the rate of growth of the nonwhite population has been going up slowly since 1950. (See Fig. 2–3.) The Census Bureau reports that the nonwhite population rose from 11.4 per cent to 12 per cent of the population in the years from 1960 to 1966. The percentage of increase for the white population during that period was 8.6, while the nonwhite population rose 14.2 per cent. The reason for the differences is attributed to the higher birthrate among nonwhites. (The deathrate is also higher among nonwhites, however.)

What effects do these changes have on government? The increasing number of very old and very young people means that a larger portion of the population is not engaged in productive work and must be supported by the smaller percentage that is actively employed. Only 4 out of 10 Americans are in "the productive years" (18 to 65). Some persons under 18 or over 65 are at work, of course, but in general, the youngsters and the oldsters do not make a major contribution to the economy. The elderly now require national programs of pensions and public assistance, and such programs have become a fixed part of the government's responsibilities. The high birthrate of the '40s and early '50s has already produced tremendous strains in our educational system. Because financing the public schools is beyond the capacity of local governments in many parts of the country, the federal government will have to play an increasingly important role.

The proportionate rise and greater number of women making up the total population will almost certainly accelerate their movement into industry and government.[29] In 1920, women made up 20 per cent of the labor force engaged in paid employment; by 1966 the figure had risen to 40 per cent. (See Fig. 2–4). The bulk of women workers are either women without children or mothers whose children have entered school, but the number of working mothers with children still at home has risen sharply. (See Fig. 2–5.) Contrary to popular impression, the urban environment continues to produce earlier marriages than were common in the old rural environment; this means that persistent demands will be heard for the construction of new homes, either in public housing projects or with government financing. And the increase in the nonwhite ethnic groups will bring increasing insistence on additional government guarantees of civil rights. Both political parties agree on the need for more federal activity to solve these and other problems, but they do not agree on how much aid and for what needs.

The most radical changes in American life have sprung from the shift of the population from farms to cities. In the first fifty years of this century, the ratio of urban to rural dwellers was almost exactly reversed, from 40–60 in 1900 to 64–36 in 1950.[30] The 1960 census reported an urban majority of 70 per cent,

---

[29]Report of the President's Commission on the Status of Women, *American Women* (Washington, D.C.: U.S. Government Printing Office, 1963).

[30]References, here and elsewhere, to the urban-rural division of the population rely on the findings of the Bureau of the Census, in which places are defined as "urban" if they contain over 2,500 persons and "rural" if they contain less than 2,500 persons.

Figure 2–4
Source: *200 Million Americans*, p. 69.

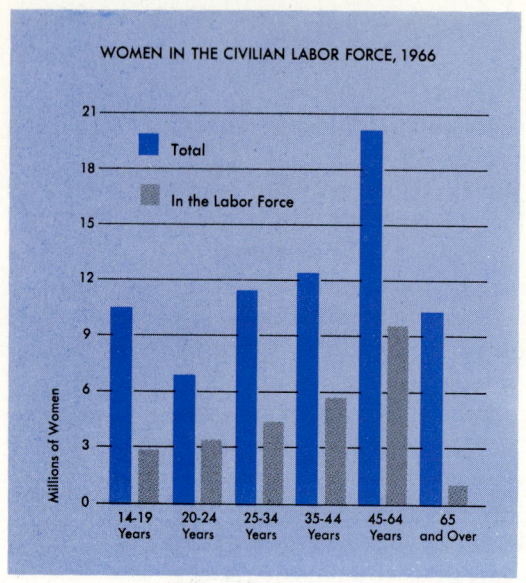

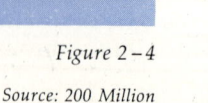

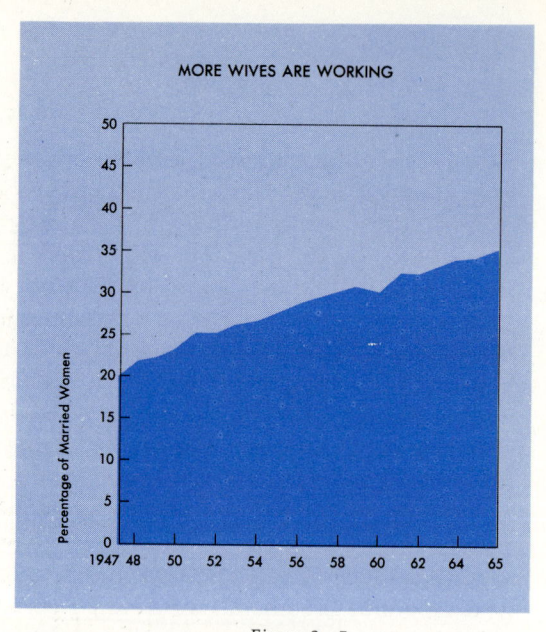

Figure 2–5
Source: *200 Million Americans*, p. 64.

but with a shift from central cities to their surrounding suburbs. The suburbs are now growing five times as fast as the central cities, twice as fast as the country at large. By 1966, more people were living in the suburbs (66 million) than in the central cities (59 million).

If cities were, as Jefferson said, "sores on the body politic," this concentration in urban and suburban areas would have imperiled the health of the democracy. Fortunately, however, the modern city-dweller is no less responsible a citizen than his country cousin. Indeed, he is generally both better-educated and better-informed on current political problems. The regional differences in toleration of unpopular political ideas that we mentioned above are matched by similar differences between urban and rural residents: in every section fewer rural people than city-dwellers are tolerant of nonconformists, even when the comparison is between groups with the same amount of schooling. We are not sure just what makes small-town and farm communities more intolerant of divergent opinions, in violation of the democratic tradition. But here is one suggestion: "In the anonymity of city life it is much easier for deviant behavior to flourish than in the goldfish bowl of a small community. In the large community there are sometimes so many goldfish that nobody bothers to look at them. In the small town a lone exotic specimen can be viewed with careful, critical, and occasionally devastating attention."[31]

Urban tolerance may, of course, be a greater blessing for the maverick than for the typical citizen. Although the city has been the breeding ground for most of the great achievements of mankind, it has also displayed many of the

[31]Stouffer, *Communism, Conformity, and Civil Liberties*, p. 130.

THE CULTURAL CONTEXT

worst aspects of human behavior. Rural and smalltown life may suggest tight-lipped disapproval of those who neglect church or PTA functions, or—in extreme cases—it may bring to mind the posse or the lynch mob. But many Americans have recently been shocked at the emergence of an opposite extreme in the cities: for several dozen citizens to witness a public act of murder without intervening or even calling the police goes beyond mere tolerance; it reaches the point of extreme indifference to the fate of one's fellows. Thus many people have felt that the excitement of life in the city is not worth the loss of freedom to stroll safely through the park at night. The movement of the American population to urban areas has accordingly shifted from central cities to the suburbs.

Urbanization has intensified old problems of local government and has added countless new ones. With so many people living together in close quarters, such familiar municipal functions as police and fire protection, sewage and garbage disposal, and providing water and street lighting have become much more important, difficult, and costly. People in a modern metropolis are more dependent on one another for the things they need to survive, but at the same time are more impersonal in their relationships. Unable to meet their own needs either on an individual basis or through the occasional help of friends and relatives, urban dwellers have grown more dependent on government. New programs are being added to satisfy their growing list of needs—planning, zoning, health, employment, recreation, slum clearance, water- and air-pollution control, noise abatement, traffic engineering, and—always—parking.

Municipal budgets are generally inadequate to cope with many of these problems. But city dwellers have painfully learned that, even if "only God can make a tree," only the government can make a park. If city and state governments cannot meet urban needs, then the national government must act. Hence the creation of national departments of Housing and Urban Development (1965) and of Transportation (1967). Even the control of rats takes on major proportions in today's urban slums. The rural majority of the past could

"Well, that's democracy for you. My vote nullifies your vote."

Drawing by Mirachi;
© 1967 *The Saturday Review*.

leave the control of rats to the family cat. And the rats that survived the cat had enough sources of food that they rarely attacked humans. But in the slums of major cities today, ratbites constitute one of the major sources of injury to children. Despite an initial defeat in the House of Representatives by congressmen little acquainted with rats as a serious threat to safety, public indignation and publicity led to the passage of a rat-control bill in 1967. The rural humor brought to bear in the original rejection of the proposal to eradicate rats would have seemed more appropriate in the early years of this century and in the small towns where most of today's congressmen grew up. (The problem of gaining majority representation for the urban majority in state legislatures and in Congress will accordingly be examined in considering "THE LEGISLATORS," Chapter 10.)

The American as Immigrant

President Franklin Roosevelt once alienated the Daughters of the American Revolution by greeting them as "My fellow immigrants. . . ." He was, of course, chiding those Americans who feel superior to more recent arrivals. The "melting-pot" character of the American population does seem to be a source of strength rather than weakness. John Gunther reported in *Inside U.S.A.* that both Arkansas and Mississippi proudly claim to have the highest percentage of native-born population in the country.[32] The 1960 census reveals, however, that both of these states are among the three that *lost* population in the previous decade. The alleged advantages of homogeneity seem to be ignored by Americans when they decide where to live.

However varied the languages, religions, and political ideas they brought to the United States, all Americans (except the Indians) are alike in one respect—they are immigrants or the descendants of immigrants. Today, fewer than 6 per cent of Americans are foreign-born. Nevertheless, the political habits of Americans have naturally been influenced by their common immigrant backgrounds.

[32]*Inside U.S.A.* (New York: Harper & Row, Publishers, Inc., 1947), pp. 658–659.

"I have nothing to offer but blood, toil, tears, sweat and . . . oh yes, rats . . ."

Drawing by Fischetti;
© 1967; reprinted by permission of Publishers-Hall Syndicate.

According to Margaret Mead, all Americans exhibit the "third-generation" trait of rejecting the father as a model of authority.[33] Whatever success the father may have had in becoming "Americanized," he is still marked by the "old country," or—if he is not in fact second-generation—he at least follows some of the old and therefore outmoded ways. The desire to "belong" is so powerful that each generation is encouraged by the fathers themselves to "go further," to achieve more, to be somehow different. For a son to follow in his father's footsteps generally produces as great a sense of failure in the father as in the son. In this tendency to reject the father as a model, Miss Mead finds a basic source of the American's disrespect for authority.

Although this interpretation is a prime example of the "educated intuition" about which Professor Key spoke, it may help to explain Americans' deep-seated distrust of power. For a fuller explanation, however, we must remember that America's political history has been marked by a similar rejection of authority. The American Revolution has been interpreted as a rejection of authority *per se*, rather than as a rebellion against English rule alone. And the weakness of the state governments that were set up in the new nation suggests that the newly independent American was almost as distrustful of his own government as he was of the British King's. The governors elected under the first state constitutions were so strait-jacketed that one might almost think they were still being appointed by the Crown.[34]

When an immigrant child is sent to the neighborhood school to be "Americanized" along with native-born children, he learns that the revolution against England was a praiseworthy act. He reads in his elementary-school texts that the English were black-hearted villains and the colonists shining heroes. In effect, then, the child is taught that the rejection of both family and political authority is sanctioned by adults. The very idea of authority becomes repugnant to him, and to reject it becomes a laudable—a peculiarly "American"—action. We must not go too far with this interpretation today, when many Americans seem to be looking on government and authority with less and less disfavor.[35] But it highlights an underlying aspect of political socialization that has by no means disappeared.

The American's desire to belong reflects an insecurity about his status as a "real American"—an insecurity that gives rise to the peculiar practice we have noted of condemning activities because they are un-American. Swedes, Lebanese, and Australians denounce practices that they think unwise, but the notion of an un-Swedish, un-Lebanese, or un-Australian activity is not common political currency. Yet Americans who are only shortly removed from

---

[33]*And Keep Your Powder Dry: An Anthropologist Looks at America* (New York: William Morrow & Company, Inc., 1942).

[34]See Geoffrey Gorer, *The American People: A Study in National Character* (New York: W. W. Norton and Company, Inc., 1948).

[35]Attitudes toward strong leadership and expanding government programs are not unfavorable, even though a generalized suspicion of authority may remain. See Campbell, *et al.*, *The American Voter*, especially Chapters 8 and 9; and H. McClosky, *et al.*, "Issue Conflict and Consensus among Party Leaders and Followers," *American Political Science Review*, LIV (June, 1960), 406–427.

immigrant status (whether in fact or in their fears) are insecure enough to feel that they must proclaim their Americanism more loudly than others. Ironically, they are joined by some of the "old" Americans who feel that their status is threatened by the rise to acceptance and influence of more recent arrivals.

In the competition to "prove" that one is a "true American," the easiest route may lie in demonstrating that one is *more* American than others. This impulse quickly leads to direct accusations that others are *un*-American, with all the attendant dangers of bigotry and the excitement of ferreting out heretics. Unfortunately, the insecure attain their greatest sense of Americanism through impugning the loyalty of those who appear beyond reproach: to be more American than one's next-door neighbor may be gratifying, but to be more American than a national leader is a glorious achievement. In the era after World War II, when Senator Joseph McCarthy (R.-Wis.) was leading the self-proclaimed superpatriots, the Secretary of State was a favorite target.

Recent immigrants are not the only Americans beset by feelings of status insecurity. The irony of "old" families joining superpatriotic movements may result from the fact that some of them see society changing from the simple forms under which they played dominant roles to a mass-based politics and a corporate economy in which old family names carry less weight. The rise of recent immigrants to prominence and the demands of the underprivileged in general for more recognition may lead those old families whose status was tied to the pre-urban economy to feel threatened. Up until the time of McCarthy in the 1950s, the superpatriotic movements in the United States were basically nativist movements, as is the current John Birch Society. One may thus feel uncertain about his place in society either because of recent immigrant status or because he feels threatened by the influx of immigrants and by associated changes in society.

We noted earlier that status insecurity is not a necessary and sufficient condition for ethnocentrism. Nor should it be taken as a complete explanation of the rise of superpatriotic movements. At least another necessary condition is the presence of a substantial number of politically disaffected people who join the movement and give it leadership for other reasons. In the case of McCarthyism, for example, the bulk of the support came from Republicans who strongly resented the fact that their party had been out of office for twenty years.[36] Thus the political system itself is important in molding the cultural factors that impinge upon it. Indeed, if the cultural factors provided a sufficient explanation for political phenomena, we would not need to examine the political system separately. The political system absorbs immigrants and turns most into supporting citizens, not insecure superpatriots. And, conversely, the political system may operate in such a way as to add support to superpatriotic organizations from people whose only disaffection is political.

[36]See Nelson W. Polsby, "Towards an Explanation of McCarthyism," *Political Studies*, VIII (October, 1960), 250–271.

THE CULTURAL CONTEXT

Class Structure as a Political Force

Although the American people share a common culture, they are by no means a homogeneous group. We have already found, for example, that political attitudes vary according to region and urban or rural residence. Do they also vary according to social class? Or can we say that Americans are free from class-consciousness—that their only differences are purely individual ones within a single predominant class? The American emphasis on social equality leads to some embarrassment even in admitting the possibility of class differences. But the emphasis on achievement and uncertainty about status suggest that class differences may actually be quite pronounced. Questions of this sort have preoccupied every serious student of politics. Aristotle was just as convinced that a large middle class was essential to stable government as Karl Marx was that class conflict would persist until communism produced a completely classless society.

America's first politicians disagreed about the role of class in politics, but in a fashion that would seem most peculiar today—the conservatives talked about class hostility while the liberals stressed class harmony. In the early years of the Republic—when the vote was limited by property and tax-paying qualifications—conservative leaders of the Federalist and Whig parties (men like Alexander Hamilton and Daniel Webster) stoutly emphasized the inherent antagonism between classes, while Jeffersonian and Jacksonian Democrats denied that class conflict was inevitable. Thus an arch-conservative Federalist, Chancellor Kent, argued in New York's Constitutional Convention of 1821 that "the tendency of universal suffrage is to jeopardize the rights of property," while an unknown liberal opponent replied, "Let us not, sir, disgrace ourselves in the eyes of the world, by expressing such degrading opinions of our fellow citizens."[37] When a majority of adult males won the vote in the 1820s and 1830s, conservative leaders began to use less insulting terms to describe them, while liberal leaders borrowed discarded conservative arguments about class differences.

Why the switch in arguments? If we recognize that politics is the pursuit of power, the change of positions is easy to understand. Before the Jacksonian Democrats had extended the right to vote, conservatives could hope to keep the suffrage restricted by alarming worthy citizens with the threat of lower-class hostility. In order to win the vote for their poorer supporters, on the other hand, the liberals had to argue that Americans were not separated by basic class differences. With suffrage extended, however, the desire of each group to win elections produced a different emphasis: conservatives wooed the new and poorer voters by maintaining that all Americans were really "one big

[37]From debates in the New York Constitutional Convention of 1821, as quoted in Alpheus Thomas Mason, *Free Government in the Making: Readings in American Political Thought* (New York: Oxford University Press, 1949), pp. 400–405.

happy (and classless) family"; liberals sought their votes by insisting that the interests of the "rich, well-born, and able" were opposed to those of the "common man."

Class Differences in Political Participation at the Popular Level

Americans like to think that class differences are less acute in the United States than in Europe; indeed, some even insist that the idea of "classes" is alien to our way of life. Nor has there been a lack of evidence to support this point of view. George Gallup has reported, for example, that 88 per cent of our population say they are middle class, whereas only 6 per cent identify themselves with the upper or lower classes. A *Fortune* magazine survey found that 79 per cent of the people identify themselves with the middle class. These findings suggest that "class-consciousness" is of no real importance to American politics, that disagreements arise from individual rather than class differences.

But more rigorous research on class awareness, and on the relationship of class to political behavior, tells quite a different story. The overwhelming middle-class identification reported in such surveys as those cited above appears to stem from a desire on the part of workers to avoid the term "lower class" when the choices were arbitrarily limited to upper, middle, or lower class. Whatever their actual positions in society, Americans seem hesitant to claim that they are "upper class," and loath to say that they are "lower class." A growing body of research in the last two decades has demonstrated that, when the more common term "working class" is added to the list of choices, a majority of Americans describe themselves as working class rather than middle class.[38] In 1964, for example (as Table 2-1 indicates), 56 per cent of the American electorate claimed working-class status, while 39 per cent said they

[38] So few people claim upper- or lower-class identification that some researchers have dropped these terms from their list of choices. See Richard Centers, *The Psychology of Social Classes* (Princeton: Princeton University Press, 1949); Joseph A. Kahl, *The American Class Structure* (New York: Rinehart and Company, Inc., 1957); and Campbell et al., *The American Voter*.

Table 2-1 Subjective Class Identification of Adult Americans (1964)

PERCENTAGE SAYING

Middle class		39%
Aware of social class*	23%	
Unaware of social class*	16	
Working class		56
Aware of social class*	37	
Unaware of social class*	19	
Upper class		1
Reject idea of class		2
Don't know; not ascertained		2
Total (N = 1,571)		100.0

*Respondents were asked if they ever thought of themselves as belonging to the middle class or to the working class. The 60 per cent who said "yes" are labeled as "aware of social class"; the 35 per cent who said "no," but subsequently chose a class when asked to do so, are labeled as "unaware of social class."

Source: The 1964 presidential election survey conducted by the University of Michigan's Survey Research Center. It is based on a cross-sectional sample chosen by strict probability methods from all adult citizens living in private households in the United States. The authors are grateful to Aage Clausen, Study Director, for the special tabulation used for this table.

were middle class. Rather than a homogenized middle-class America, then, the evidence reveals a population divided into a working-class majority and a middle-class minority.

How meaningful is this class identification in political behavior? First, it has a direct impact on the basic question of who takes part in politics and who doesn't. Political activity may take many forms: seeking information about public affairs through newspapers or TV; voting; attending campaign rallies; talking with others about elections and trying to influence their votes; giving money to a party or candidate; and becoming a candidate for public office are among the most common. Only a tiny minority ever seek public office, but we like to think that practically all citizens get involved in the mass forms of political participation. Political involvement is not scattered evenly throughout the population, however; *a greater proportion of middle-class than of working-class people are active in every form of political participation.* (For figures on participation in 1964, see Table 2–2.)

Table 2-2   Political Participation in 1964 According to Class Identification

FORM OF PARTICIPATION CLAIMED BY RESPONDENT	MIDDLE CLASS N = 549	WORKING CLASS N = 788
Voting*	86%	72%
Talking to others about voting for a party or candidate	40	24
Giving money, buying tickets, etc., to help the campaign of a party or candidate	16	4
Attending political meetings, rallies, etc.	14	5
Working for a party or candidate	8	3
Belonging to a political club or organization	5	3

*For an explanation of the larger proportions reporting voting than the proportion of people who actually voted (60.6 per cent), see Campbell et al., *The American Voter*, pp. 93–96.

Source: Data furnished by the University of Michigan's Survey Research Center. (See Table 1-1 for information on the sample.) Entries are proportions in each class who reported participation of the type indicated.

In Chapter 6, we shall try to explain why some people vote and why others don't. As for the class factor, we may briefly note here that working-class people, when compared with the middle class, have less control over their own time, are more absorbed in the task of meeting their immediate family needs, feel less effective and self-confident in public affairs, and have less information on how governmental policies affect them.[39] Our concern here is not, however, to account for class differences in participation; it is simply to demonstrate that class is a general factor in American politics, influencing every form of participation. Whether we assign Americans to classes according to their own choices or according to some objective criterion (like income or

---

[39] For a more complete list of factors decreasing participation by lower-status people, see Robert E. Lane, *Political Life: Why People Get Involved in Politics* (New York: The Free Press of Glencoe, Inc., 1959), Chapter 16.

education), the results remain basically the same: lower-status groups observe, discuss, and take part in politics less than do higher-status groups.

Class Differences in Chances for Political Leadership

Although class differences show up clearly in mass forms of political participation, perhaps a look at the impact of class in a second area will tell a different story. Does our population enjoy equal opportunities to assume political leadership? Is the log-cabin-to-White-House motif, so prominent in American folklore, an accurate reflection of the facts of political life? Or does class status tend to open the door for some and slam it on others? The fact that political participation is less common for lower-status groups does not necessarily mean that these groups contribute less than their share of top leaders; the smaller proportion of the working class who participate might be enough motivated to rise to the top.

The evidence indicates, however, that class differences are even more acute in chances for political leadership than in mass participation. Donald R. Matthews, in a systematic study, *The Social Background of Political Decision-Makers*,[40] demonstrates that class distinctions in American society apply to political leadership as well as to other areas of behavior. Certainly the United States has no caste-like elite with a monopoly over all high offices; but those of higher class origin do fill a disproportionately large number of political offices, whereas those from the lower strata fill relatively few.

Examining the occupations of the fathers of American officeholders (see Table 2–3), Matthews concludes: "American political decision-makers . . . are, with very few exceptions, sons of professional men, proprietors and officials, and farmers. A very small minority were the sons of wage earners, low-salaried workers, farm laborers or servants. When this fact is compared

[40](Garden City, N.Y.: Doubleday & Company, Inc., 1954).

Table 2-3   Occupational Class of Fathers of American Political Decision-Makers

OCCUPATIONAL CLASS OF FATHER	PRESIDENT, VICE-PRES., CABINET, 1789–1934	HIGH-LEVEL CIVIL SERVANT, 1940	U.S. SENATORS, 81ST CONGRESS, 1949–51	U.S. REP., 77TH CONGRESS, 1941–43	LABOR FORCE, 1890†
Professional	38%	28%	22%	31%	5%
Proprietors & officials	20	30	33	31	6
Farmers	38	29	40	29	26
Low-salaried workers	*	3	1	0	5
Wage-earners	4	10	3	9	36
Servants	0	0	0	0	7
Farm laborers	0	0	0	0	15
Unknown, unclassified	0	0	1	0	0
	100%	100%	100%	100%	100%
	(N = 311)	(N = 180)	(N = 109)	(N = 186)	

*Less than 1%.
†Subject to substantial error because of incomplete data.
Source: Matthews, *The Social Background of Political Decision-Makers*, p. 23.

with the occupational distribution of the labor force in 1890 (about the median time of birth of all these groups except the first), the narrow base from which political decision-makers appear to be recruited is clear."[41]

Judged in terms of fathers' occupations, the impact of class on chances of political leadership is clear: 22 per cent of the population get 0 per cent of the offices considered, whereas 5 per cent of the population at the other extreme get an average of 30 per cent of the offices. Similar analyses in terms of race, ethnic origins, religion, education, and occupation lend further support to this point. In each case the group with higher social status enjoys a disproportionately large share of offices (in comparison with its proportion of the total population), whereas groups with lower status tend to be virtually excluded from office. The advantage lies, for each of these classifications, with whites over Negroes, native-born over foreign-born, and immigrants from Northwestern and Central Europe and Canada over those from Eastern and Southern Europe and Asia,[42] Protestants (especially Congregational, Presbyterian, Episcopalian, and Unitarian) over Catholics and Jews, the highly educated over citizens at large, and lawyers over everyone else.[43]

The explanation of this upper- and upper-middle class domination of important political offices lies not in any "ruling-class" plot but in certain evident features of American society. First, only those at the upper level of the social scale are likely to enjoy the money, experience, and contacts required for active political life. Second, some occupations possess a greater degree of what social scientists call "role dispensability." Whereas the doctor or architect would find his professional competence impaired if he became preoccupied with politics, political activity is actually an advantage in the profession of the law; moreover, a lawyer's training and daily work prepares him in some measure for a political career, whereas a doctor's or architect's training and experience do not. Hence the lawyer's dominance in public office. Third, opportunities for rising to positions offering status, money, and leisure are highly unequal, with those who start nearer the top having a great advantage. Finally, as members of a stratified society with recognized symbols of success, even those citizens at the lower levels tend to prefer people of established "worth" as their representatives.[44]

In emphasizing unequal class opportunities, we must not forget that leaders of upper-class background sometimes become strong champions of the underprivileged. A group or class need not be *literally* represented in public

---

[41]*Ibid.*, pp. 23–24.

[42]In many areas it is a definite advantage to be a first- or second-generation American of a dominant ethnic group, but this generalization still holds for the country at large and especially for higher offices.

[43]See Matthews, *The Social Background of Political Decision-Makers*, pp. 24–32. John R. Schmidhauser has more recently reported similar findings on the social backgrounds of justices of the Supreme Court. See his *The Supreme Court* (New York: Holt, Rinehart & Winston, Inc., 1960), p. 32.

[44]Three of these four points may be found in Matthews, *The Social Background of Political Decision-Makers*, p. 32.

office in order to have access to and influence on the decision-making process. A given group may well find its most effective spokesman in an individual from a quite different class. But in terms of extent of personal participation, the class structure does serve to "freeze out" a sizeable portion of the total population.

Economic Influences on Politics

Discerning Americans have long realized that there is an intimate relationship between economics and politics. "'Tis . . . certain that *property* in fact generally *confers* power, tho' the possessor of it may not have much more wit than a mole or a musquash," wrote James Otis almost two centuries ago.[45] James Madison, the "father" of our Constitution, put it this way: "The most common and durable source of factions has been the various and unequal distribution of property. Those who hold and those who are without property have ever formed distinct interests in society. . . . *The regulation of these various and interfering interests forms the principal task of modern legislation.* . . ."[46]

The historian Charles A. Beard made this same point a century and a quarter later, in his controversial book, *An Economic Interpretation of the Constitution of the United States.*[47] Although Beard elaborated on Madison's thesis in explaining the ratification of the Constitution, he was condemned by the press for "insulting" the Founding Fathers! This ironic turn of events supports the assertion that "in popular American mythology there has been a tendency to assume that economics and property relationships are areas of human interest and activity quite distinct, and properly so, from the political and governmental spheres. The fact that the myth has had little if any relation to historic conditions even in the United States has not shaken the faith of many that such an artificial line may be drawn."[48]

The Idea of Economics as Independent of Politics

What had happened in the 125 years between the publication of Madison's argument in *The Federalist* and Beard's restatement of the same position in his *Economic Interpretation*? What had encouraged the popular delusion that the Professor sullied the memory of the Founding Father when he developed the same thesis—that economics conditions politics?

[45] James Otis, *The Rights of the British Colonies* (Columbia, Mo.: University of Missouri Studies, 1929), IV, p. 51.
[46] Alexander Hamilton, John Jay, and James Madison, *The Federalist* (New York: Random House, 1937), Modern Library Edition, p. 56. (Originally published as a series of letters in New York newspapers in 1787.) Emphasis added.
[47] *An Economic Interpretation of the Constitution of the United States* (New York: The Macmillan Company, 1913).
[48] Richard C. Snyder and H. Hubert Wilson, *Roots of Political Behavior: Introduction to Government and Politics* (New York: American Book Company, 1949), p. 315.

THE CULTURAL CONTEXT

In the first place, America had turned to an exaltation of material values that was to make its way of life known as "Our Business Civilization."[49] Preoccupied with the rugged job of civilizing a new continent, Americans had little time for intellectual or artistic pursuits. Because the most immediate problems were physical and tangible, the person who could accumulate *things* came to enjoy more respect than the person who could manipulate *ideas*. Clyde Kluckhohn underscores the American identification of worth with wealth in the comment, "'Success' is measured by two automobiles—not by two mistresses as in some cultures."[50] The point was more bluntly made in the official organ of the Chamber of Commerce: "A man is worth the wages he can earn."[51] This exaltation of the material received something close to official sanction in 1893 when a justice of the United States Supreme Court explained human motivations in this fashion:

> The man who writes books, paints pictures, moulds statues, builds houses, pleads causes, preaches sermons, or heals the sick, does it for the money there is in it; and if, in so doing, he acquires a reputation as an author, painter, sculptor, architect, jurist, or physician, it is only an incident to his success as a money-getter. The motive which prompted Angelo to plan the dome of St. Peter, or paint the frescoes of the Sistine Chapel was essentially the same as that which induces a common laborer to lay brick or dig sewers.[52]

The Justice, in his exclusive emphasis on economics, might appear to have outdone both Madison and Beard, even to have rivaled Karl Marx. But notice that he meant to bestow unstinted praise on economic motivation, rather than to complain about the influence of economics on politics.

The idea that economics can be separated from politics was encouraged, in the second place, by the American's traditional distrust of authority. The first struggle against arbitrary power was directed at the British government, not at some powerful economic or social class. Developed during the revolutionary struggle to throw off British rule, the belief that government is a threat to freedom continued to flourish in nineteenth-century America. Although Americans today generally do not single out government as a particular target of suspicion, their generalized fear of authority seems to have taken a particularly antigovernmental form at least up to the twentieth century.

"Government is a necessary evil" and "That government is best which governs least" are ideas which went virtually unchallenged by nineteenth-century Americans. To be sure, the people who recited such maxims were actually using the government to promote a variety of economic interests. The

---

[49]See, for example, James Truslow Adams, *Our Business Civilization* (New York: Boni, 1930).
[50]*Mirror for Man*, pp. 242–243.
[51]Eden Phillpotts, "A Reply to Socialism," *Nation's Business*, XVII (January, 1929), 26.
[52]Henry B. Brown, "The Distribution of Property," *Reports of American Bar Association* (Philadelphia: Dando Printing and Publishing Company, 1893), XVI, 226–227.

government was furnishing homesteads to settlers, subsidizing shipping interests, maintaining tariffs to protect American manufacturers from foreign competition, and building roads and canals to benefit western settlers. And yet the colonial distrust of government persisted—government was worthy of promoting economic interests but it could not be trusted to regulate them. Indeed, our natural resources were so great and opportunities so widespread that voters had little reason to consider the government as a force for controlling the economy.

Once the frontier had disappeared and "big business" had begun to dominate the economy, however, farmers and workers started to demand that the government regulate business interests. Government interference in the economy—in the form of subsidies, land grants, and tariff benefits—had long been accepted as "the American system," but regulation was something new. Business interests suddenly began to complain that it was un-American for the government to tamper with the economy! And the antigovernmental bias of most Americans was so deep that they were blind to the inconsistency. Government controls over the economy were achieved later in the United States than in any other democracy.

Several nineteenth-century assumptions about economic behavior and institutions furnished a third support for the belief that economics could be separated from politics. Like the American's materialism and his distrust of government, these assumptions led to the idea that economics was an independent domain with which government had no proper concern.

First was the assumption that most people owned *private property*, and that ownership carried with it control over and responsibility for the management of that property. Second, *wealth* was thought of primarily in terms of such tangibles as wheat, buildings, shops, land, and ships. Third, *private enterprise* suggested an individual or a small group of partners actively engaged in directing a business they owned. Fourth, *individual initiative* was believed to have wide latitude, with daring, ingenuity, and nonconformity reaping rich rewards. Fifth, the *profit motive* was conceived as the mainspring of progress, in view of man's innate desire for material acquisition. Sixth, *free competition* was thought to assure that the interests of consumers, laborers, and other businessmen could not be ignored without economic loss. And, finally, permeating all these six assumptions was the belief in a *natural economic order* in which the price mechanism guaranteed an equable distribution of economic rewards.[53]

The reluctance with which these assumptions have been sloughed off (and the nostalgic stubbornness with which they are still invoked by some) can be explained by the fact that they worked so well for so long. Particularly suited to a young and growing nation rich in resources and on the threshold of the industrial revolution, they helped promote tremendous technological advancement, the spanning of a continent, and the development of a material standard of living that is the envy of the world. These assumptions were never held with complete seriousness or consistency, of course, but they were

---

[53]This series of assumptions is drawn primarily from Adolph A. Berle and Gardiner C. Means, *The Modern Corporation and Private Property* (New York: The Macmillan Company, 1932).

widely enough accepted to give business a relatively free hand in extending the nation and building its economic facilities.

The Twentieth-Century American Economy

We have already seen that America's commitment to *laissez faire* had never been quite genuine. The Constitution itself was at least in part an economic document, providing general protection for property, insuring the rights of creditors, and preserving the binding force of contracts. In 1789, the first session of the first Congress of the United States violated free competition by establishing tariffs and providing subsidies for shipping interests. Later, the disposal of the free land of the West served as a vast public relief program. In fact, government promotion of economic interests has marked our entire political history. *Laissez faire* and free enterprise have been enthusiastically displayed whenever government regulation was mentioned, but they were hidden away when the question of government aid came up.

With the closing of the frontier and the development of a corporate economy, more serious defects showed themselves in the old assumptions. The severe depression of the 1930s convinced many thoughtful Americans that economics could not be separated from politics. Adolph A. Berle and Gardiner C. Means, in their study, *The Modern Corporation and Private Property*, pointed out in 1932 that the classical economic theory dating from Adam Smith's eighteenth-century writings was not applicable to the realities of the twentieth century.

Private property is no longer widely owned, and it plays a less influential role in our economy than it did a century ago. Small plants, privately owned and managed, still exist, but they produce only a small part of our industrial output. The important property now is not really private; it is found in the business corporation's great *instruments of production.* These are quite unlike the old blacksmith's hammer and anvil—they are huge machines and complicated plants too costly to be owned by a single person. Thousands of stockholders legally "own" these industrial plants, but most stockholders never see "their" plant and would have no idea of how to manage it. The property is actually controlled by a corps of nonowning managers, not by a private owner. Similarly, *wealth* has taken on new meanings. It refers more often to *intangible rights* to income from corporate stocks and bonds than to such tangible things as buildings, land, or ships.

The *private enterprise,* then, has been replaced by the *corporate enterprise* as America's dominant economic unit. And a modern corporation hardly resembles a private shop. In the typical small private enterprise, the same person is owner, worker, and manager; in the corporation, some people (stockholders) are owners, others are workers, and still others are managers. The corporation is a device, then, for combining the money, labor, and managerial skills of

51

many people under unified direction. Without the unified efforts of all these people, we could not enjoy such intricate, mass-produced products as airplanes and television sets. Such unified efforts, however, cannot be achieved without sacrificing *individual initiative* in the interest of *conformity;* careful coordination geared to the assembly line cannot tolerate wide personal deviation from the prescribed routine. The rugged individualist of frontier days has been replaced by the "organization man" who can follow orders and cooperate with fellow members of the "team."

The *profit motive* that classical economists thought of as underlying all economic activity has also been drastically modified. The profits of a modern corporation go to the stockholders, not to those who actually direct the work of the enterprise. Since the top directors do not receive the profits, they must be motivated by the desire for other rewards, such as large *salaries,* generous *bonuses,* extravagant *expense accounts,* and the *prestige* that comes from exercising *power* over other people. Formerly, it was assumed that the drive of many concerns competing for profit would produce *free competition,* which in turn would keep prices down to a "natural" level at which only the most efficient individuals could prosper. But today most sectors of the economy—such as automobiles, steel, and oil—are dominated by a few large concerns, which compete for sales through advertising wars rather than through price wars. These industrial giants *fix prices by administrative decision* rather than leaving them to be fixed by the uncertainties of consumer demand. And, as the Senate Subcommittee on Antitrust and Monopoly revealed in 1961, the giants sometimes get together and *fix prices by collusion.*

Finally, the underlying assumption of a *natural economic order* has come to sound increasingly anachronistic in the twentieth century. Anthropologists were demonstrating in the 1920s that what seems "natural" at one time or in one place may seem quite "unnatural" at another time or in another place. The anthropologists' term for describing these variations in values from one society to another—*cultural relativity*—is now an accepted part of the vocabulary of most literate Americans. And the concept of cultural relativity does not fit well with the idea that a single economic order is "natural" (and therefore "right") for all men at all times. In particular, how could *laissez faire*—leaving nature alone—be justified in view of the fact that most human progress has been made by *controlling the forces of nature*? "Unnatural" levees prevent annual floods, and careful interference with nature breeds grain and roses in lieu of weeds. In brief, the laws of men are sometimes preferred to the laws of nature.

Even under the old assumptions, the government, as we have noted, promoted business interests, regulated certain industries, and attempted to protect competitive markets. Mass unemployment in the early 1930s—with a fourth of the labor force out of work—helped undermine the old assumptions and produce more active government participation in the economy. Direct payment of relief funds to hungry citizens was the emergency response, but this was replaced by a number of "automatic stabilizers"—Old Age and Survivors Insurance, minimum wage and maximum hours legislation, and unemployment compensation.[54] Reforms to redress the imbalance posed by

[54]On both the traditional and the newer government activities, see Michael D. Reagan, *The Managed Economy* (New York: Oxford University Press, 1963), pp. 169–189.

"big business" led to (1) extensions of government regulatory activities, such as in the regulation of corporate offerings of stocks for public purchase; (2) the provision of price supports to protect farmers—whose sector of the economy was about the only important one that remained competitive according to the classical theory of the market—from the vicissitudes of unbridled competition; and (3) legislation guaranteeing labor the right to organize for purposes of collective bargaining. The final burial of the notion that government is not responsible for the nation's economic well-being came with the passage of the Employment Act of 1946. The Act assumed that indirect controls of the economy through fiscal policy (taxes and government expenditures) and monetary policy (decisions on the availability and cost of credit) would suffice to achieve the nation's economic goals. These indirect controls would work if the economy were truly competitive. In fact, however, the competitive determination of prices through the mechanism of the market has been largely replaced by administrative determination of prices through the planning activities of major corporations. The Employment Act of 1946 is important primarily, then, for its formal assertion of government responsibility for the nation's economic well-being. How this well-being can best be promoted is subject to continuing debate.

In practice, the presumed power of a free and competitive market to control prices—and, through prices, to control economic activity—exists today in only limited areas of the economy. The mixture of government and corporate economic activity greatly reduces the area within which the market mechanism works in the assumed fashion. A nation of small shopkeepers, farmers, and entrepreneurs not only could, but perhaps would, have to rely upon the market to determine their activities. But with the government—as spender, contractor, and regulator—vitally affecting the economy, and with "private" corporations bigger than most governments creating and controlling markets, the free market of competitive small producers is a thing of the past. John Kenneth Galbraith, a prominent Harvard economist, points out that three so-called private businesses (General Motors, Standard Oil of New Jersey, and Ford Motor Company) had a greater gross income in 1965 than did all the farmers in the nation.[55] Each of these corporations has an income far in excess of that of any state in the nation. The revenues of General Motors in 1963 were one-fifth those of the national government, eight times those of New York state, and fifty times those of Nevada. Such a corporation hardly acts in the manner of a cobbler running a small shop. The scale of its operation requires planning, and planning requires control of supply, demand, and capital to the end of minimizing risk.

Some sectors of the economy, however, are still left largely to the unplanned vagaries of the market. "The impersonal magic of the market," as Galbraith puts it, is still of primary importance for shopkeepers, plumbers, barbers, repairmen, independent craftsmen, and others operating service enterprises.[56]

[55] *The New Industrial State* (Boston: Houghton Mifflin Company, 1967), pp. 75–76.
[56] *Ibid.*, p. 355.

Even these entrepreneurs attempt to control the market, however; lacking economic resources comparable to those of giant corporations, they turn to the political system to control the effects of free competition. State licensing boards for barbers and cosmetologists, for example, serve to restrict entry into these occupations and hence to avoid excessive price competition. Other economic areas in which Galbraith deplores the results of reliance on the market rather than comprehensive planning are surface transportation, both within and between urban centers; urban and suburban housing; conservation of natural resources; outdoor recreation; and forestry in the Eastern section of the United States.[57]

America's mixed system of government and corporate planning interspersed with market allocations is highly productive, but many citizens fail to receive the outputs of the system. In 1963, Michael Harrington underscored this failure in a popular and influential book, *The Other America*—the America of "internal exiles," people living in a land of luxury but trapped themselves in a cycle of poverty.[58] Because the truly poor live off the beaten track—along rutted roads around Pennsylvania mining towns, in city tenements only glimpsed from the trains or the freeways that lead to suburbia—the other America is less visible than ever before. But such people as the poor farmers, the unskilled workers, and the minority groups who suffer from a combination of slum dwellings, poor schools, and restricted opportunities do not share in the general prosperity. Harrington's shocking conclusion was that America's poor include, at a minimum, some 32 million people and that the figure probably approaches 50 million. To say that these people are better off than the average citizen of Hong Kong or than the medieval upper class is not, Harrington submits, relevant to their needs. "The American poor are not poor in Hong Kong or in the sixteenth century; they are poor here and now, in the United States. They are dispossessed in terms of what the rest of the nation enjoys. . . . They live on the fringe, the margin. They watch the movies and read the magazines of affluent America, and these tell them that they are internal exiles."[59]

Many Americans, accustomed to hearing about our high standard of living, find it hard to believe that 20 to 25 per cent of their fellow citizens share none of the prosperity of which we boast. For one thing, the cheapest foods are fattening, so when we do see the poor they do not look emaciated. Then again, most of us are unaware that, partly because of our poverty and partly because of our lack of general medical assistance programs, our infant mortality rate is higher than that of ten other countries.[60] Unpleasant statistics of this sort very rarely receive much attention. And for those who are statistically minded, figures on family income look better every year, even for our poorer citizens.

---

[57]*Ibid.*, pp. 354–369.
[58]Michael Harrington, *The Other America* (Baltimore: Penguin Books, 1964). Originally published in 1963 by The Macmillan Company.
[59]*Ibid.*, p. 190.
[60]See Gabriel Kolko, *Wealth and Power in America* (New York: Frederick A. Praeger, Inc., 1964), p. ix. Except for the Preface, this is the same as the 1962 edition.

The dollar income of almost all Americans has been going up, partly as a result of general increases in prosperity and partly as a result of gradual inflation, which means that a dollar today buys much less than it did during earlier periods. The extent to which inequalities have been reduced can therefore be approached better by finding out what proportion of the nation's total personal income a group receives than by examining its dollar income.

If we divide America's families and unattached individuals into ten groups, from the poorest to the richest, and look at their shares of the national income, the persistence of extreme inequality is startling. Table 2–4 shows that the share of the poorest tenth in 1910 was only 3.4 per cent of the national personal income. By 1959, this low proportion had *dropped* to a depressing 1.1 per cent! Indeed, if we total the portion of the national income received by half the population in the five lowest groups, we find a decrease from 26.8 to 22.7 per cent of the nation's personal income. At the other extreme, the best rewarded tenth of the population enjoyed 33.9 per cent of the income in 1910 and 28.9 per cent 50 years later. The extreme inequalities show no signs of disappearing.[61]

[61] The U.S. Census Bureau reported in 1967: "Those in the lowest 20 per cent are still getting only 5 per cent of the aggregate income just as they were 20 years ago."

Table 2-4 Percentage of National Personal Income, Before Taxes, Received by Each Income-Tenth*

	HIGHEST TENTH	2ND	3RD	4TH	5TH	6TH	7TH	8TH	9TH	LOWEST TENTH
1910	33.9	12.3	10.2	8.8	8.0	7.0	6.0	5.5	4.9	3.4
1918	34.5	12.9	9.6	8.7	7.7	7.2	6.9	5.7	4.4	2.4
1921	38.2	12.8	10.5	8.9	7.4	6.5	5.9	4.6	3.2	2.0
1929	39.0	12.3	9.8	9.0	7.9	6.5	5.5	4.6	3.6	1.8
1934	33.6	13.1	11.0	9.4	8.2	7.3	6.2	5.3	3.8	2.1
1937	34.4	14.1	11.7	10.1	8.5	7.2	6.0	4.4	2.6	1.0
1941	34.0	16.0	12.0	10.0	9.0	7.0	5.0	4.0	2.0	1.0
1945	29.0	16.0	13.0	11.0	9.0	7.0	6.0	5.0	3.0	1.0
1946	32.0	15.0	12.0	10.0	9.0	7.0	6.0	5.0	3.0	1.0
1947	33.5	14.8	11.7	9.9	8.5	7.1	5.8	4.4	3.1	1.2
1948	30.9	14.7	11.9	10.1	8.8	7.5	6.3	5.0	3.3	1.4
1949	29.8	15.5	12.5	10.6	9.1	7.7	6.2	4.7	3.1	0.8
1950	28.7	15.4	12.7	10.8	9.3	7.8	6.3	4.9	3.2	0.9
1951	30.9	15.0	12.3	10.6	8.9	7.6	6.3	4.7	2.9	0.8
1952	29.5	15.3	12.4	10.6	9.1	7.7	6.4	4.9	3.1	1.0
1953	31.4	14.8	11.9	10.3	8.9	7.6	6.2	4.7	3.0	1.2
1954	29.3	15.3	12.4	10.7	9.1	7.7	6.4	4.8	3.1	1.2
1955	29.7	15.7	12.7	10.8	9.1	7.7	6.1	4.5	2.7	1.0
1956	30.6	15.3	12.3	10.5	9.0	7.6	6.1	4.5	2.8	1.3
1957	29.4	15.5	12.7	10.8	9.2	7.7	6.1	4.5	2.9	1.3
1958	27.1	16.3	13.2	11.0	9.4	7.8	6.2	4.6	3.1	1.3
1959	28.9	15.8	12.7	10.7	9.2	7.8	6.3	4.6	2.9	1.1

*In terms of "recipients" for 1910–1937 and "spending units" for 1941–1959.
Source: Kolko, *Wealth and Power in America*, p. 14.

The income tax is supposed to reduce these inequalities, but its effect is less than one would gather from the pained protests of those in the upper tax brackets. Those with the highest incomes enjoy advice from the best tax experts, and Congress has provided countless loopholes through which they can earn their fees. Before the 1964 revision of the income tax, for example, the theoretical maximum tax was 91 per cent. But the average tax of individuals earning over a million dollars a year was 42 per cent.[62] As a move to "combat poverty," the theoretical maximum tax was reduced to 70 per cent in 1964. Aside from tax loopholes, the most affluent Americans also enjoy benefits from corporate hunting lodges, yachts, safaris to Africa, "business" trips to Paris, and expense accounts, none of which counts as "income." Finally, 9 to 14 per cent of the nation's personal income is not reported on income-tax returns, and most of the oversight comes from those with the highest incomes. Because the salaried worker has all of his income tax withheld before he receives his pay check, the inequality in American incomes is not greatly decreased by our system of taxation.[63]

Although the share of the national income received by the poor has not increased, their purchasing power has. Moreover, they are the chief beneficiaries of expanded government services, such as public parks and housing, Medicare, hot school lunches, that—like the corporate fringe benefits enjoyed by the wealthy—are ignored in most studies of personal income. The poor may be as deprived as ever in comparison with their fellow citizens, but their absolute standard of living has improved. The United States Department of Health, Education, and Welfare (HEW) reported in 1964 that the number of families with incomes below $3,000 (measured in terms of the 1962 value of the dollar) had decreased from 32 per cent in 1947 to 20 per cent in 1962.[64]

Although perfect agreement concerning the dividing line between poverty (inability to satisfy basic and irreducible needs) and a minimum standard of subsistence is impossible, a conservative estimate of the number of impoverished Americans is between one-fifth and one-sixth of the population. HEW estimates 20 per cent, The Bureau of the Census 15 per cent; social scientists claim that 25 per cent is a more realistic estimate. No matter which figure is most accurate, it is clear that many millions of Americans do not enjoy what we like to think is the American standard of living; the unskilled, the uneducated, and the nonwhites lag behind. Of increasing political significance is the differential in incomes between white and nonwhite families. In 1966, the average nonwhite family income was only about 60 per cent of the average white family income. (See Fig. 2–6.) But that was an improvement over the 51 per cent of 20 years ago. Moreover, the improvement is likely to continue if nonwhites are able to take advantage of better educational opportunities.

[62]Kolko, *Wealth and Power in America*, p. viii.

[63]Indeed, because most state and local taxes are regressive (taking a greater percentage of income from the poor than the rich), the percentage of income paid in all taxes does not vary as much as expected from one income level to another. Those who receive less than $2,000 a year pay about 21 per cent of their income in taxes, compared with 22 per cent for those with $10,000–15,000 incomes and 34 per cent for those with over $15,000. The data in the footnote and in the preceding paragraph are from Kolko, *Wealth and Power in America*, p. 37 and *passim*.

[64]*Health, Education, and Welfare Indicators*, February, 1964, p. ix.

THE CULTURAL CONTEXT

(See Fig. 2–7.) Nonwhites with four or more years of college were doing about 82 per cent as well as whites with the same educational background.

Back in the depression years of the 1930s, President Franklin Roosevelt called for a New Deal because of the shameful fact that one-third of our nation was "ill-fed, ill-housed, and ill-clothed." After more than a generation of prosperity, we have reduced this proportion by a little more than ten percentage points, but the absolute number of people enduring poverty has hardly decreased at all. In 1964, President Lyndon Johnson's call for a War on Poverty shifted America's attention from the problems of achievement back to the needs of equality.[65] But the proposal was for a limited "war," calling for expenditures of $970 million, or only 1 per cent of the national budget. That the program sounded radical to many people, in and out of Congress, attests to the continued importance of our nineteenth-century economic assumptions, bias against government interference, and materialism. After all, we happily

[65] *The War on Poverty: The Economic Opportunity Act of 1964*, a compilation of materials relevant to S. 2642 prepared for the Select Subcommittee on Poverty of the Committee on Labor and Public Welfare, United States Senate, 88th Congress, 2nd Session (Washington, D.C.: U.S. Government Printing Office, 1964).

Figure 2-6

Source: *200 Million Americans*, p. 59.

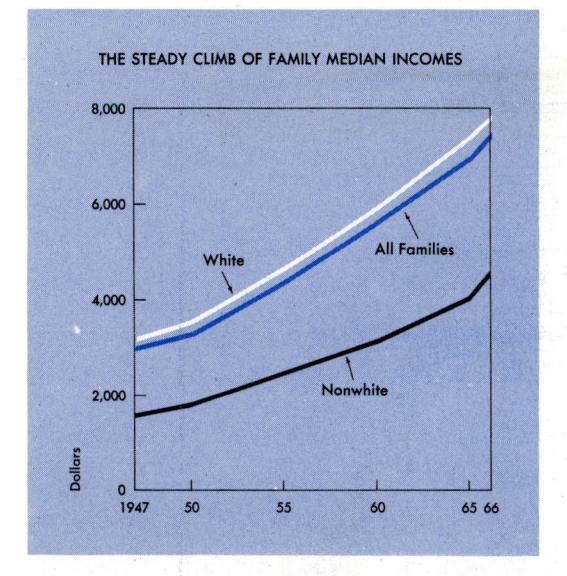

THE STEADY CLIMB OF FAMILY MEDIAN INCOMES

Figure 2-7

Source: *200 Million Americans*, p. 60.

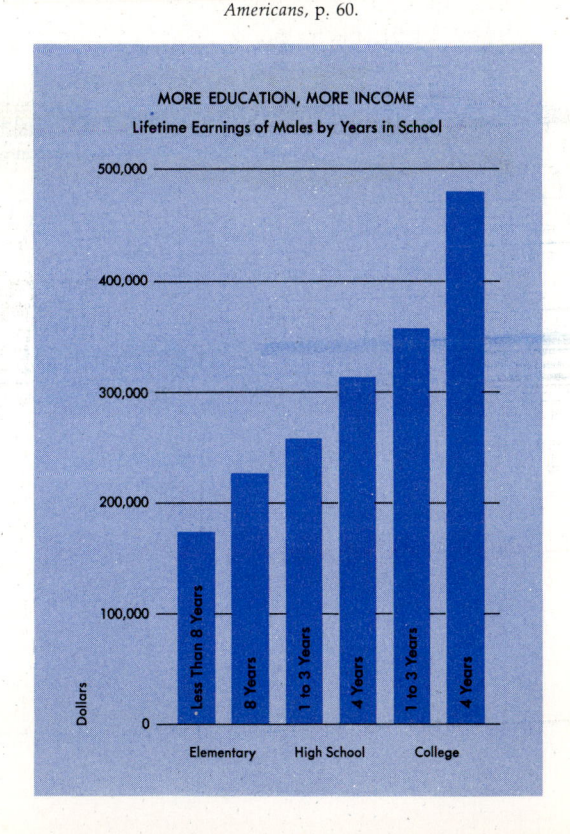

MORE EDUCATION, MORE INCOME
Lifetime Earnings of Males by Years in School

spend over $10 *billion* a year on advertising, spending the nation's resources to create new desires, often for bizarre products.

Although any corporation that did not enlarge its budget and its outstanding stock (that is, its debt) would be regarded as a poor risk, President Johnson had to juggle figures to make his new program appear *not* to enlarge the national budget. Rather than regarding an expanding budget and debt as a sign of strength, as we do for business corporations, we view such signs of activity by government with suspicion. So long as we view production for the satisfaction of private wants as the all-important goal of our economy and look on public services as a necessary evil, this contrast will continue. We will continue to regard the manufacture of school toilet seats as an increase in our wealth and education itself as a burden. We will manufacture more and bigger automobiles, and waste precious hours looking for a parking space.

Why do we emphasize private production for even the most dubious needs and neglect public services of the most pressing sort? The answer is, at least in part, that we continue to think of economics as a private sphere that operates best without government interference. "To suggest that we canvass our public wants to see where happiness can be improved by more and better [government] services has a sharply radical tone," Professor Galbraith submits. "By contrast the man who devises a nostrum for a nonexistent need and then successfully promotes both remains one of nature's noblemen."[66] Galbraith's underlying theme is that our real problem is not *how much* but *what* we should produce, and for *whose benefit*.[67] If the decision about what should be produced were made deliberately, he says it would almost inevitably involve increased control by the government over economics.

Despite our long-standing prejudice to the contrary, politics and economics have in fact grown ever more interdependent, and the process has been hastened by a relatively recent phenomenon that can be described as a "balance of bigness." The political response to "big business" has been the development of "big government," and both have stimulated the emergence of "big labor" as another powerful "countervailing" force. Indeed, in our "mixed" economy of today, government and economics have become virtually inseparable. We are not socialistic in any doctrinaire sense, as the existence of private control of key instruments of production like the railway and steel industries attests. But neither are we capitalistic or *laissez faire* in any doctrinaire sense, as our publicly owned and operated schools, highways, post offices, and power plants attest. Even such apparently private enterprises as railroads and power companies are subject to a variety of government regulations. In short, much of our industry—and our economy as a whole—stands between the extremes of *laissez faire* and socialism.

Although it is the way we conduct our politics that primarily distinguishes American democracy from other systems of government, our politics itself is a part of the more general pattern of human interactions that we call "the American Way of Life." Beginning with the American culture at the most

---

[66]*The Affluent Society* (Boston: Houghton Mifflin Company, 1958), p. 269.
[67]On the latter, see his article, "Let Us Begin: An Invitation to Action on Poverty," *Harper's* (March, 1964), 16–26.

general level, we have suggested how culture and the related factors of the natural environment, population, class structure, and economics affect government. With this broad cultural picture in mind, we shall turn now to the context of ideas that shapes our government.

THE CONTEXT

OF IDEAS   3

Democracy is more than a way of governing; it is also an idea. And ideas provide the key to understanding human behavior. The carpenter who builds a house, the clerk who sells shoes, the lawyer who defends the property rights of his client—all may be convinced that they are dealing more directly with "reality" than the student of ideas. But the way we produce, distribute, protect, and evaluate material objects stems from those elusive human attributes variously called opinions, myths, stereotypes, prejudices, convictions, or principles. American politics, like any other facet of our behavior, may be understood only within the context of the ideas that shape our lives.

In the United States, the general pattern of ideas that pervades politics—and against which we are urged to judge politicians—is found in democratic political theory. Public opinion surveys have shown that an overwhelming majority of Americans regard democracy as the only proper form of government. And apparently this conviction is just as strong among public officials, as anyone who has ever been exposed to Fourth of July oratory can testify.

Democratic Political Theory

Just what do we mean when we claim to be democratic? There is no simple, ready-made answer. The model state of communism or fascism is relatively easy to define, but the ideals of democracy are much more elusive.

Democracy is more ambiguous than ideologies with a fixed creed. Indeed, the whole notion of democracy revolves around the belief that each generation can fix its own goals. A contemporary political scientist, employing formal logic to produce a "rational justification" of the superiority of democracy to other forms of government, proposes the following injunction as the ultimate "must" of democracy: "Do not block the possibility of *change* with respect to social goals."[1]

Despite their emphasis on change as central to beliefs, however, political philosophers have identified several other ideals as implicit in any democratic society.

Identifying these ideals, like identifying traits of "national character," is

[1] Thomas L. Thorson, *The Logic of Democracy* (New York: Holt, Rinehart and Winston, Inc., 1962), p. 139. Emphasis added.

largely a matter of "educated intuition." Philosophers—more library-oriented than anthropologists—can perhaps claim an advantage over the latter in terms of formal education. Anthropologists—who, unlike philosophers, benefit from field trips—may claim the advantage of intuitive insights based on observations. For the most part, however, neither can claim that his propositions are supported by the same sort of systematic empirical observation as the chemist's or the physicist's. Nevertheless, political philosophers offer helpful commentaries on the ideals logically implied by a democratic way of life just as anthropologists furnish us with helpful clues on national character.

Any political philosophy is built on a few guiding beliefs or assumptions about the nature of man, the nature of society, and the nature of politics. Half a dozen beliefs of this sort characterize classical democratic theory. The democratic view of the nature of man is based on the principles of *equality* and *humanitarianism;* the democratic view of the nature of society is based on the principles of *individualism* and *progress;* the democratic view of the nature of politics is based on the principles of *majority rule* and *minority rights.* Democratic theory is built on these beliefs—equality, humanitarianism, individualism, progress, majority rule, minority rights—and from them gains its enduring appeal.

The Democratic View of Man

The most fundamental belief of democratic theory—that which distinguishes it from all other political creeds—is the concept of *equality*. Critics of democracy sneer at the concept that "all men are created equal," pointing out that men obviously come in a great variety of sizes, shapes, and colors, and with a great range of endowments. But this is an attack on a straw man. Even Thomas Jefferson, the patron saint of America's equalitarian tradition, recognized that people are unequal in talent and virtue no less than in appearance. What Jefferson and other equalitarians insist on is that differences in prestige and position should not be determined before birth, that they should reflect unequal talents rather than unequal opportunities, personal ability rather than artificial advantage.

People do not resemble each other like identical twins, but neither are they so different that they must be classified into different species. Since potential ability may turn up anywhere, in the slum as well as in the mansion, democratic theory disapproves of inherited privileges. Hereditary leadership in politics or business is as senseless as a hereditary professorship in political science. Simply by virtue of their common humanity, all men share equally an intrinsic moral worth. They ought, therefore, to have equal opportunity to develop their own personalities according to their inclinations and their abilities.

The democratic view of human nature adds the concept of *humanitarianism* to the belief in equality. Despite his capacity for evil, man is viewed as being somewhat closer to the angels than to unreasoning animals. Although some enthusiasts have expanded this idea to a belief in human perfectibility, realistic democratic theory makes the more modest claim that man's capacity for good outweighs his potential for evil. Conflict arises wherever men live together, but so does cooperation. And since cooperation is necessary even in waging conflict, it appears to be more basic to human nature. Controversy and competition lend zest to life, but it is man's cooperative efforts that make social life possible.

62

Both *laissez faire* and Marxian materialists picture man as the helpless pawn of economic forces—forces that he may understand but cannot direct. Democratic theory, however, emphasizes that man is capable of pursuing humane values. Trying to control his own destiny, but tinged even in the attempt with concern for the welfare of others, man has demonstrated an inextinguishable desire to grope for a broader good than pure self-interest. The willingness of the Soviet government to let millions of peasants starve while it established collectivized agriculture is incomprehensible to the democrat. Even if the objective itself were desirable, he feels that nothing justifies such a deliberate squandering of human life. Democracy will not sacrifice human beings for the "long-run" interest of any abstract system; its humanitarianism bent simply will not allow the sanctity of human life to be forgotten.

The Democratic Concept of Society

Extended from man to society, the democratic principles of equality and humanitarianism take the form of *individualism* and *progress*. The democrat evaluates the processes, institutions, and power structure of society according to the effects they have on the individual. Regarding society as nothing more than interrelationships among individuals, democratic thought rejects the idea of any "national interest" separate from the needs of the citizens. The democrat thinks it absurd to sacrifice the welfare of any citizen or group of citizens for that of the "fatherland"; for him the fatherland exists only to promote the welfare of its citizens and to secure their rights as individuals.

Similarly, democratic theory sets a higher value on the individual than on any segment of society. It recognizes that the military, the church, the academic, and the business communities all make important contributions to society, but it gives none of them pre-eminent status on that account. A former head of General Motors turned Secretary of Defense touched off an uproar early in the Eisenhower Administration when he was quoted as having innocently remarked that "What's good for General Motors is good for the country."[2] The resulting excitement stemmed, not from disrespect for General Motors, but from the conviction that the general welfare begins with the welfare of the *individuals* who constitute the society. Other values are important, of course, but they are secondary to individual freedom. Whether the argument is for "freedom of enterprise" or "freedom from economic royalists," "academic freedom" or "freedom from propaganda," democratic theory judges the argument by what it means for the individual as a free agent.

Democratic thought is dedicated to the irrepressible ideal of social progress. Indeed, the ideals we have already mentioned virtually assume that progress

---

[2]This remark was attributed to Charles Wilson during hearings before the Senate Armed Services Committee on his nomination to the office of Secretary of Defense. The record shows that, in response to a question about whether he could make a decision "extremely adverse to the company, in the interests of the United States Government," he actually said: "Yes, sir; I could. I cannot conceive of one because for years I thought what was good for our country was good for General Motors, and vice versa. The difference did not exist." See *Hearings* before the Committee on Armed Services, United States Senate, 83rd Cong., 1st Sess., January 15, 1953, p. 26.

is part of the democratic creed, for most governments throughout history have violated the democratic ideals of equality, humanitarianism, and individualism. A democrat living under an undemocratic regime must either believe in progress or else abandon his other political beliefs. Although we need no longer agree with Rousseau that "man is born free but everywhere in chains," anyone who is committed to the ideals of equality and humanitarianism can always find ways to improve the lot of the individual.

Social conditions undergo constant change, and it is the task of democracy to translate this change into progress for the individual. At the very heart of democracy is the continuing attempt to direct rather than to thwart change. New forms of privilege and new threats to the individual constantly crop up to replace the old, making it impossible for democracy to be permanently dependent on any one set of policies or governmental agencies. The progress exalted by democratic theory consequently takes two forms. First, there is the constant attempt to bring society closer and closer to the basic values of democracy. Second, there is the constant attempt to improve policies and institutions so that the gains that have already been won will not be lost in a changing world.

The Democratic Theory of Government

What happens when we apply this rather abstract democratic theory to government in operation? The central principles of government based on democratic theory are majority rule and minority rights. Although the simple phrase "majority rule and minority rights" can only hint at the complex attitudes and habits that support democracy, taken together, these principles constitute the briefest possible definition of democracy.

If one genuinely accepts the principles of equality and individualism in his appraisal of man and society, he must inevitably embrace the idea of *majoritarianism* in the conduct of government. If men are basically equal, and if each has an inherent moral worth by virtue of his humanity, no individual or group can have a monopoly on truth. Thus it follows that the only way we can approach truth is through the free flow of ideas, through the process of give-and-take by which a wide variety of special "truths" are compromised. This implies that each individual must enjoy the freedom to work out and contribute his own version of truth. And, since self-development requires self-government, the democratic theory in government is firmly based on the concept of popular consent or majority rule.

The ambiguity of democratic theory stems largely from an apparent conflict between *majority rule* and the equally basic principle of *minority rights*.[3] In its extreme form, majoritarianism holds that the majority view is always right; in less extreme form, that it must always be followed, right or wrong. But democracy, in its true, self-perpetuating form, holds certain freedoms to be "unalienable rights," rights that even the majority cannot abridge. Since absolute truth is revealed to no one, even the majority is quite capable of

---

[3]For a strong majoritarian statement, see Henry Steele Commager, *Majority Rule and Minority Rights* (Gloucester, Mass.: Peter Smith, 1943). For a strong defense of minority rights, see Walter Lippman, *Essays in the Public Philosophy* (Boston: Little, Brown and Company, 1955).

making mistakes. And the individual who finds himself temporarily in a minority need not automatically renounce his own beliefs and adopt the majority opinion: he need not submerge his individuality in the majority. Those who voted for Stevenson in 1956 did not suddenly decide that Eisenhower was after all the better candidate, nor did the Goldwater supporters in 1964 switch their preference to Johnson as soon as the election returns were in. And although they accepted the outcome as binding—that is, as if the majority had been "right" and they had been "wrong"—at the same time they reserved the right to insist that the majority had erred and to work actively against the policies of the new government.

The majority-minority relationship in a free election is, when you stop to think about it, one of its most valuable aspects. But the possibility of extreme conflict between majority rule and minority rights raises difficult questions. Minority acceptance of the majority's victory reflects the realization that it is outnumbered and that defiance would be rightfully suppressed. And for the winners, who exercise the power of government, respecting the rights of the losers requires self-restraint rather than simply a sense of being restrained. But what if the majority were to deny the minority the right to oppose the new government, or even the right to enjoy such other basic freedoms as the right to a fair trial? In this situation does democratic theory favor majority rule or minority rights?

Absolute majoritarianism says the majority decision must be followed. This means that if today's majority succeeded in making opposition unconstitutional, democracy would be extinguished. Such risks, this argument continues, are among the costs of democracy; putting its faith in majority rule, democracy must accept the possibility of mistaken judgments without cringing. At worst, the people may destroy democracy by endorsing a dictatorship that eventually eliminates not only minority rights but even majority rule. But majority preference cannot be denied, argues absolute majoritarianism; one can only hope that self-restraint and self-education will come to the majority through a realization that it has erred.

Much can be said for this argument, but democratic theory has generally avoided its obvious pitfalls by emphasizing that the principle of minority rights is an essential restraint if majority rule is to work at all. The Declaration of Independence may have placed somewhat more emphasis on majority rule and the Constitution may have been somewhat more concerned with minority rights, but both principles are clearly present in both documents. The general theory underlying this interpretation is that no individual or group can have absolute power. Not even the majority is competent to speak perfectly or permanently for all. If such a privilege were granted—which would have to be at the cost of minority rights—majority rule itself could not survive. For majority rule to exist as a *continuing* principle, today's minority must have a chance to become tomorrow's majority. Majoritarianism thus implies the corollary principle of minority rights.

What Is Democratic Government?

Democracy as One Way of Governing

If the "man in the street" were asked to define the different systems of government, he would probably find it very difficult to engage in such abstractions. A few who are well-read and articulate might reply that democracy is government by the many, that aristocracy or oligarchy is government by the few, and that monarchy or dictatorship is government by one. Actually, this collective definition is neither clear nor true. But it has been offered since Aristotle's day, and consequently enjoys so much prestige that even contemporary political scientists occasionally use it. As a matter of cold, hard fact, "the many" can never participate directly in the process of governing, simply because it is physically impossible to bring them all together. The Greek city-state would not qualify as a democracy on this count, since only a minority were citizens; and even the famous New England townmeeting of colonial times appears to have been controlled by interested minorities, such as Sam Adams' Caucus Club. The full-time task of governing is always allocated to a relatively few specialists.

At the other extreme, no one person can govern by himself, for it is physically impossible for him to make all the important necessary decisions. Hitler and Stalin may have enjoyed much more power than any other single individual, but neither was able to govern entirely by himself. Even in the most totalitarian nation, there is always a small core of the party faithful who share in the burdens of government.

Government, then, is always by the few. To identify different forms of government by the proportion of citizens who take part in governing is therefore not feasible. The effort is as pointless as trying to identify a bird as a pigeon, eagle, or robin by asking whether it has one, two, or four wings—all birds have two wings and all governments are conducted by a small minority of the citizens. We may accordingly discard the idea that democracy is government by the many and that dictatorship or monarchy is government by one.

If all governments are by the few, we clearly must find some grounds other than the number of rulers for distinguishing between different political systems. The most important feature that varies from government to government is the *relationship* between the governing few and the governed many. Where a responsible relationship exists, we may say that democracy exists, regardless of the structure of government, the content of policy, or the number or quality of the rulers. Where the relationship is irresponsible, the government is an oligarchy or—in more contemporary terms—a dictatorship.

Democracy is singularly lacking in dogma; it is without absolutes. There is no democratic theorist to whom we can turn, as can communists to Karl Marx, for the "correct" attitude on every problem. Indeed, to identify democracy with a single formula would be to reject its very essence. Notice that we have come right back to the two basic principles of the democratic theory of government. These principles refer to a *method* of governing—or, more precisely, to a method of deciding who shall govern—rather than to a complete, fixed creed. This means that we can identify democracy by two essential features: (1) major-

ity rule, which exists so long as the public at large is free to choose the men who make public policies; and (2) *minority rights,* which exist so long as those in the minority may openly attempt to win majority support for different leaders and policies without a loss of the individual rights enjoyed by the majority. Democratic theory thus puts only one restriction on majority rule: no one may be denied individual freedoms because he opposes the majority, either as an individual or as part of a concerted effort to persuade a majority to join the opposition.

Of course, no government meets these two standards in an absolute sense. No democracy insures the perfect and continuous response of rulers to majority opinion; and no democracy tolerates freedom of dissent to the extent of permitting dissenters to overthrow the government by force or violence. Conversely, even the most totalitarian regime covets the support of the majority and may even permit some freedom for dissenters. Neither democracy nor dictatorship, in other words, reaches the logical extremity of its principles in actual practice.

And yet these two features—majority rule and minority rights—are useful criteria for identifying some governments as democratic and others as dictatorial. If we were allowed only two questions to identify a government as democratic or dictatorial, we would first ask: Are its rulers chosen by the votes of a majority? A country in which elections are hard fought between opposing parties, neither of which is certain of victory, insures enough government responsibility to the voters to be meaningfully called a democracy. On the other hand, a country where the voters can only approve the official slate, with no chance to choose between candidates, provides nothing more than false majority rule; it must be called dictatorial. Second, we would ask: Do the losers —the minority—enjoy the same basic rights in relation to government as the majority, including the freedom to make demands on the government and to advocate the selection of new leaders in the next election? If minorities are free to agitate, organize, and propagandize for the peaceful overthrow of the ruling party without fear of punishment, they are "free" in the democratic sense. But if dissenting minorities are punished for demonstrating their opposition to the ruling party, they are "unfree" in the democratic sense.[4]

Basic Institutions of Democratic Government

When our discussion shifted from democratic theory to democratic government, you may have noticed that we began to mention some of the institutions (such as political parties and elections) through which the theory expresses itself in concrete situations. This is because democratic government depends on certain peculiar institutions, some official and some unofficial. For free communication of ideas, we rely on such agencies as the press, pressure groups, and the schools. The very first article in the American Bill of Rights guarantees freedom of speech, freedom of press, and freedom of association. As Justice William Douglas has pointed

[4]For a penetrating analysis of the meaning of freedom, see Felix E. Oppenheim, *Dimensions of Freedom: An Analysis* (New York: St. Martin's Press, Inc., 1961).

out, "Full and free discussion has indeed been the first article of our faith. We have founded our political system on it."[5] When the institutions by which public opinion is formed and expressed begin to lose their vigor, democracy itself is in danger. If majorities and minorities are to discover the areas in which they agree and the areas in which they conflict, and if they are to influence the course of government accordingly, they must be free to give and take in the "market place of ideas."

Political parties are the unofficial institutions, and a free election system is the official institution, that are most essential for majority rule on a continuing basis. Political parties enable interested citizens to join forces in their attempt to win control of government and to get what they want through political action. The party system is thus one of the principal structures through which a democratic polity performs the key input functions necessary to any political system—identification of basic interests in society and leadership selection. Equally crucial to the democratic performance of these functions is a system of popular elections. Elections permit the combination of interests that make up a political party to compete peaceably with any opposing party for control of the government's decision-making apparatus. Democracy counts ballots instead of bullets. The citizens of a democracy can express their support for or dissent from government policies and personnel through political parties and elections rather than through conspiracies and assassinations.

Because the precise forms taken by these institutions vary widely from time to time and from place to place, we cannot say that they must exist in some "ideal" form in order for a government to be regarded as democratic. After all, the perfect democracy is just as unattainable as the perfect dictatorship. Even imperfect and erratic responses to majority opinion indicate that democratic processes are at work, though perhaps at a crude, immature level. But to say that democratic institutions vary widely in form does not mean that we have no way of evaluating them. Specifically, we can evaluate any political institution in terms of how good a job it does in promoting *majority control* on a *continuing* basis—that is, with respect for the right of today's minority to become tomorrow's majority. Within this frame of reference, we can say, for example, that pure one-party politics is *un*democratic, because it fails to keep rulers accountable to changing public opinion. And even if party leaders are chosen by popular vote, we can say that a one-party system is *less* democratic than a two-party system; because competition in one-party politics is merely between personalities, group responsibility for the conduct of government is lacking.

Perhaps American educators are not completely free in the pursuit of truth, perhaps freedom of the press is diluted for newspaper readers by the decline in the number of competing newspapers, perhaps some pressure groups have a disproportionately loud voice in public affairs while others are scarcely heard. Still, in spite of their imperfections, our schools, press, and pressure groups enjoy enough freedom to place the United States in the democratic camp. The search for truth does go on, information about public affairs is widely disseminated, and every group can present its viewpoint. There is

[5]Dissenting opinion in *Dennis* v. *U. S.*, 341 U.S. 494 (1951).

room for improvement, of course, but these institutions operate far differently here from the way they operate under totalitarian governments. On rare occasions, Russian schools, newspapers, or special group spokesmen are permitted to deviate from the opinions of the dominant group, but it is always on sufferance, always about incidentals rather than fundamentals, and always at some risk to life and freedom.

The loose organization and lack of discipline in American political parties leave legislators free to vote against their party's platform without fear of being punished by party leaders. We might conclude that American parties are less democratic than the more united and disciplined British parties, because unified parties can better carry out their pledges to the national majority who put them in office. But even our loosely organized parties give us a measure of majority control that makes our system so different in degree as to be different in kind from that of Franco's Spain, with its one-party rule.

The important point is this: Just because we judge one form of an institution to be *more* democratic than another, the latter does not automatically become *un*democratic. Somewhere between universal suffrage and the complete absence of popular elections, for example, democracy is lost; but it does not make sense to suppose that there is an *exact point* at which democracy ceases to exist.

Remember that throughout most of American history only a minority has enjoyed the right to vote. And yet we think of the United States as having been democratic from the very start. Clearly, we do not regard voting qualifications based on age, sex, and literacy as necessarily out of keeping with democracy. But we *do* regard qualifications based on religion, race, or property ownership as undemocratic. In other words, it is the *function* of the restriction that determines whether or not the restriction itself is compatible with democratic principles.

When a large group of citizens is denied the right to vote only because their interests are in conflict with those of the ruling group, we have a denial of democracy. Excluding slaves from voting in this country, for example, was clearly undemocratic, for it denied the right of suffrage to an entire racial and economic group. If we grant that the United States was democratic before the Civil War, it can only be because the excluded group was relatively small in number. The denial of the vote to women, on the other hand, was less a denial of democracy as such, because women constituted a less homogeneous class or set of interests and their needs were not totally unrepresented in our government.

At one extreme in political theory is the model of the perfectly democratic government, in which rulers are clearly responsible to majority opinion and all citizens are completely free to express every viewpoint. At the other extreme is the model of the perfectly dictatorial government, in which rulers are utterly unresponsive to public opinion and citizens have no opportunity to dissent. All governments fall somewhere between these extremes.

Since rulers must suppress opposition if they wish either to ignore or to control majority opinion, the criteria of majority rule and minority rights are closely related—irresponsible rulers and suppression go together just as responsible rulers and freedom of dissent go together. But the close relationship is not perfect. Figure 3-1 suggests the degree to which a few major powers may be said to meet these two criteria. (The diagram should not be accepted as a precise location of nations in terms of democracy or dictatorship; it is presented simply to suggest *how* our criteria may be applied.) Although France

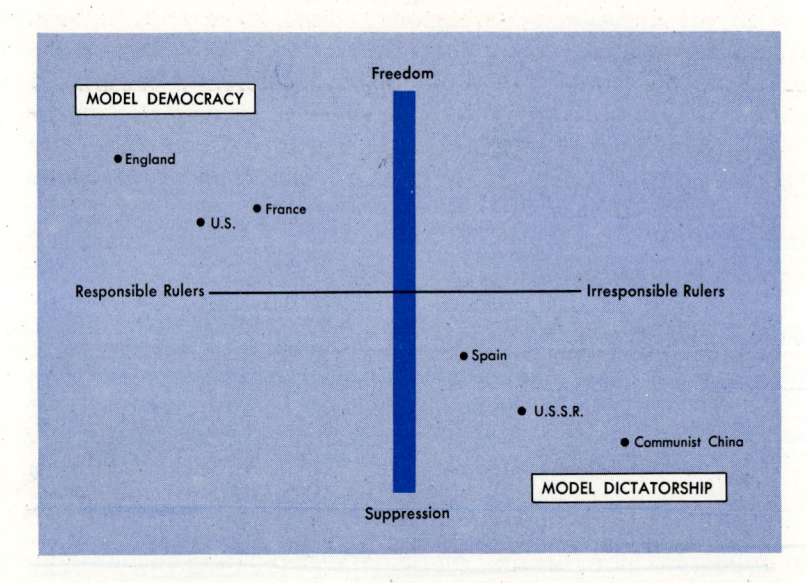

Figure 3-1 Location of selected major powers in terms of majority control and minority rights.

may be as tolerant of dissenting opinions as the United States, her chaotic multi-party politics is more likely to obscure responsibility, even under such a charismatic leader as de Gaulle. Notice that the government of the United States lies well within the gravitational field of *both* majoritarianism *and* freedom. As the diagram suggests, we are probably not so close to the democratic ideals as England (which has more highly developed party responsibility and ingrained toleration of even the most hated opinions), but we are probably closer than France, and we have an entirely different kind of government from Spain, Communist China, and Russia.

The American Creed and Its Detractors

So far this chapter has dealt with democracy in general rather than with American politics in particular. In talking about democracy, Americans naturally tend to have their own country in mind. We need to remember, however, that democracy is by no means exclusively American. Our general discussion of the concept applies to Australia or Sweden or India as well as to the United

THE CONTEXT OF IDEAS

States. In this perspective, how does American political thought fit into the general pattern of democratic beliefs?

On the surface, America gives an impression of extreme contrasts—religious, ethnic, class, and regional. Beneath this surface, however, where individuals and groups seem to be struggling for conflicting ends, the astute observer detects a remarkably homogeneous and stable political faith. The Swedish economist, Gunnar Myrdal, in his classic study of the Negro in America, concluded at one point that the American Creed is unique both in its clarity and in its acceptance by the people:

The Declaration of Independence: The Conscience of America

When the American Creed is once detected, the cacophony becomes a melody. The further observation then becomes apparent; that America, compared to every

Drawing by Hunt; © 1967 The New Yorker Magazine, Inc.

*"Every day they sit like that—
right-of-center, left-of-center, and middle-of-the-road."*

other country in Western civilization, large or small, has the *most explicitly expressed* system of general ideals in reference to human interrelations. This body of ideals is more widely understood and appreciated than similar ideals are anywhere else. The American Creed is not merely—as in some other countries—the implicit background of the nation's political and judicial order as it functions. To be sure, the political creed of America is not very satisfactorily effectuated in actual social life. But as principles which *ought* to rule, the Creed has been made conscious to everyone in American society.[6]

Almost every one of us has experienced what Myrdal is talking about here. Recently, a college student was arguing that the generally accepted norms cited by Myrdal do not really exist in America. In making his case, he referred to an injustice he had observed in a student Honor Court meeting—specifically, a denial of the concept of equality for all before the law. But in pointing out this injustice, he was in fact applying the American Creed itself as a norm, and he was perfectly confident that the people he was talking to would automatically accept it as a norm. Admittedly, we depart from our standards on occasion, in national politics no less than in campus politics, but the point is that we *do* have a recognized and semiofficial norm by which to identify our departures.

Myrdal says that "America is continuously struggling for its soul." That "soul" is embodied in the Declaration of Independence. Sometimes it seems that crass material forces dominate American life, but somehow the high ideals of the American Creed as developed by Thomas Jefferson and the other leaders of the Revolution have always reasserted themselves. "Call it a dream or call it vision," wrote John Dewey, "it has been interwoven in a tradition that has had an immense effect upon American life."[7]

The enduring appeal of the Declaration of Independence as the foundation of the American Creed springs from these propositions: (1) There is a *higher law*, found in the "laws of nature and of nature's God," that embodies certain self-evident truths against which institutions and practices may be judged. (2) Society must recognize that *"all men are created equal,"* with the right to make their own decisions, to have an equal opportunity to develop their talents, and to enjoy equality both under the law and in the chance to influence the law. (3) All men have *"certain unalienable Rights,"* including those of "Life, Liberty and the pursuit of Happiness," by virtue of their common humanity and equality under God. This list of rights was not made exhaustive, to insure that as situations changed new rights could be asserted. But the recognition of the moral worth of every life, and the freedom to use that life as one sees fit, was specifically included. (4) *Government is an instrument of the people*, to be used by them for the twofold purpose of protection and service, or, in the words of the Declaration, of "Safety and Happiness." As a tool "to secure these rights," government is not an object of veneration or an end in itself. (5) *"Consent of the governed"* is the only legitimate basis of power; this proposition implies the *right of revolution*—"That whenever any Form of Government becomes destructive of these ends, it is the Right of the People to alter or to

---

[6]*An American Dilemma: The Negro Problem and Modern Democracy* (New York: Harper & Row, Publishers, Inc., 1944), p. 3. The McGraw-Hill Book Company brought out a two-volume paperback edition in 1964.
[7]*Freedom and Culture* (New York: G. P. Putnam's Sons, 1939), p. 55.

abolish it, and to institute new Government. . . ."(6) *Democracy cannot be identified with any fixed principles or forms of government*; instead, democracy consists of a *method* of governing by popular consent. All people should be free to organize their government as they see fit, "laying its foundation on such principles and organizing its powers in such form, as to them shall seem most likely to effect their Safety and Happiness." (7) *Popular government is practical and stable*, despite its continuing dependence on popular consent. ". . .All experience hath shown, that mankind are more disposed to suffer, while evils are sufferable, than to right themselves by abolishing the forms to which they are accustomed." (8) When government becomes irresponsible, citizens have more than a right to rebel—"it is their *duty to throw off such Government.*" The prospects of popular government depend on the capacity of the people to accept burdensome duties.

These are the high standards with which the American nation began—standards which, as we shall see in the next chapter, were to influence the Constitution and inspire the Bill of Rights. True, we have repeatedly fallen short of realizing them, but the very existence of the creed has made us conscious of and dissatisfied with our shortcomings. Vernon L. Parrington, the great interpreter of American ideas, had this to say about the influence of the Declaration of Independence:

> The humanitarian idealism of the Declaration has always echoed as a battle-cry in the hearts of those who dream of an America dedicated to democratic ends. It cannot be long ignored or repudiated, for sooner or later it returns to plague the council of practical politics. It is constantly breaking out in fresh revolt. . . .Without its freshening influence our political history would have been much more sordid and materialistic.[8]

The eight central propositions that we have just set forth appear in the writings of John Locke as well as in our own Declaration of Independence—a reminder of our indebtedness to the heritage of the entire Western civilization of which America is only a part. Our ideals are the general ideals of democracy, and no nation has a monopoly on them. "The American Creed is older and wider than America itself."[9]

Agreement on the Idea of Democracy

The central ideas of the Declaration of Independence are more or less America's official creed. Does the ordinary citizen champion this creed so much as students of our heritage seem to think he does? In a democracy, there cannot be too great a gap between the official creed and the beliefs of the people at large, but the two are not necessarily identical.

---

[8] Vernon L. Parrington, *Main Currents in American Thought* (New York: Harcourt, Brace & World, Inc. 1930), III, p. 285.
[9] Myrdal, *An American Dilemma*, p. 25.

One of the most impressive facts about Americans is that they are almost unanimous in their commitment to the concept of democracy. And yet opinion surveys show that the public is startlingly ignorant about even the most important political issues of the day.

Several years after the United Nations was created, and after it had held several well-publicized meetings in the United States, one out of every four Americans admitted that they either had never heard of the U.N. or had no idea what its purpose was. In presidential elections, about half the people may be unable to name the vice-presidential nominees of either party. The University of Michigan's Survey Research Center reports that only about a fourth of the eligible voters can be said to have the minimum information necessary for their votes to be informed on important public issues. By "minimum information," we mean that this one-fourth meets three simple conditions: they have opinions on important issues; they think they know what the government is doing about the issues; and they think they know what the party differences on the issues are.[10] In April of 1961, 63 per cent of the people admitted they had never heard of the well-publicized John Birch Society; and of those who had heard of it, a number said that this extremist right-wing and anticommunist organization was "too radical" or was "dominated by communists."

On the basis of consistent findings of this sort, students of public opinion have come to the conclusion that at least 20 per cent of the American public is completely ignorant on almost any given subject (and the figure is usually closer to 40 per cent). But when we check the results of surveys designed to find out what Americans think about democracy, we find that an overwhelming majority of them endorse democracy as the most desirable form of government. Moreover, *four out of five Americans can give a meaningful definition of the concept "democracy."* The public at large is not at home with abstractions. And yet 80 per cent choose to define democracy in terms of its two essentials, popular rule and freedom—both of which are highly abstract concepts. Americans are unmistakably committed to democracy, at least in general terms.

As soon as we begin to probe beyond the concept of democracy, however, the picture becomes less reassuring. When asked to identify the Bill of Rights—the constitutional amendments that formally guarantee our basic freedoms—Americans do very poorly. In one survey, 31 per cent of the adult population said they had never heard of the Bill of Rights, an additional 36 per cent said they had heard of it but were unable to identify it, and another 12 per cent identified it incorrectly. Only 21 per cent could identify it correctly. Still, even this seeming ignorance is less alarming than it appears at first glance. What is important to democracy is not the "Bill of Rights" label but the ideas behind the label. If Americans are genuinely dedicated to popular freedoms, it matters very little whether or not they know that these freedoms are enumerated on a piece of paper. Democracy draws its vigor from living ideas, not from legal principles.

More disquieting are the inconsistent attitudes that Americans show toward the specific problems of democracy. Although nearly everyone endorses the

---

[10]Angus Campbell *et al.*, *The American Voter* (New York: John Wiley & Sons, Inc., 1960), pp. 171–183. The "informed" percentage would have been further reduced had incorrect perceptions of government activities or of party stands been taken in account.

principle of free speech, a majority would deny socialists and atheists the right to speak in their own communities. About 57 per cent of the general electorate agree with the statement, "Freedom does not give anyone the right to teach foreign ideas in our schools." Americans are nearly unanimous in endorsing the idea of a free press, but they divide evenly on this proposition: "A book that contains wrong political views cannot be a good book and does not deserve to be published."[11]

Even here, however, the situation may not be so alarming as it first appears. The problem is not that Americans consciously reject democracy, but rather that they fail to see the connection between *different values*. As one student of the "American mind" has perceived, most Americans tend to place equal stress on a whole battery of values, not recognizing that values must be arranged in some sort of hierarchy if the most fundamental ones are really to operate.[12] When an American is asked a question about atheists or socialists, he tends to give an antisocialist or antiatheist answer, not stopping to think that it may also be antidemocratic. When the inconsistency of his response is called to his attention, however, he usually modifies it in favor of the more basic values of democracy. Hostile as he may be to communists, he is reluctant to deny anyone his civil liberties.

Community leaders tend, moreover, to reply in a far more tolerant or democratic way to questions about unpopular groups. Accordingly, they may be expected to lead others in recognizing that an attack on the freedoms of an unpopular minority is an attack on democratic values. This higher level of tolerance is shown by the leaders of the most conservative groups as well as by the leaders of the most liberal groups in America.[13] The implication is clear: the American creed is so liberal in itself that even our conservatives work to preserve what is essentially a liberal heritage. Unlike the citizens of European democracies, almost all Americans are committed to the concept of liberal democracy. So strongly are they committed, in fact, that they label the infinitesimal minorities of "right" and "left" who openly reject democracy as the "lunatic fringe."

What Is the Public Ideology?

The fact that almost all Americans claim to believe in democracy, coupled with the nation's early and stirring expression of democratic sentiments in the Declaration of Independence and the Bill of Rights, has led many observers to conclude that consensus among virtually all citizens of the United States exists on both abstract and specific

---

[11] Herbert McClosky, "Consensus and Ideology in American Politics," *American Political Science Review*, LVIII (June, 1964), 367. Earlier references to public opinions are from the American Institute of Public Opinion (Gallup Poll) and Herbert H. Hyman and Paul B. Sheatsley, "The Current Status of American Public Opinion," in Daniel Katz *et al.* (eds.), *Public Opinion and Propaganda* (New York: The Dryden Press, 1954), pp. 33–48.

[12] Henry Steele Commager, *The American Mind* (New Haven: Yale University Press, 1950), p. 39.

[13] Samuel A. Stouffer, *Communism, Conformity, and Civil Liberties* (Garden City, N.Y.: Doubleday & Company, Inc., 1955), pp. 26–48. McClosky, "Consensus and Ideology in American Politics."

principles. But can we assume that liking democracy means accepting the specific principles it implies?

The average American's commitment to democracy is most impressive, to be sure, but his inconsistent attitudes suggest that the nature of the commitment requires further examination before we can talk about a democratic ideology is not surprising. Americans are distinctively nontheoretical in their approach to public problems. Continuing investigations of political attitudes in the most general terms. Consensus—agreement by majorities approaching 100 per cent—exists on the abstract idea of majority rule and minority rights but on little beyond that. Continuing majority rule logically requires, for example, the right of any group peaceably to increase its influence through the ballot. But recent research has found no consensus on even such a statement as the following: "A professional organization like the AMA (American Medical Association) has the right to try to increase the influence of doctors by getting them to vote as a bloc in elections." Researchers have failed to find consensus on a whole series of such statements, all similarly derived from the principles of majority rule and minority rights. [14] They have accordingly been forced to conclude not only that consensus disappears when democratic principles are put in concrete terms, but also that citizens are closer to complete discord (a 50–50 split) than to perfect consensus (a 100–0 split) on many such questions.

What, then, is the average voter's ideology? It includes a belief in democracy and the abstract principles by which it is defined. But, contrary to the assumption of some political theorists, that's about as far as any conscious consensus goes. The bulk of the citizenry fails to carry through the notion of democracy to a consistent democratic creed, principally because most citizens lack the inclination, the information, or the intellectual skills needed to entertain *any* coherent ideology. If we consider the real people behind the abstract "public," rather than the logical expectations of theorists, the lack of popular ideology is not surprising. Americans are distinctively nontheoretical in their approach to public problems. Continuing investigations of political attitudes by the Survey Research Center of the University of Michigan demonstrate that most citizens respond to (or ignore) each new issue on its merits, not in terms of any well-defined system of ideas—whether generally democratic, or specifically liberal or conservative. If by a political ideology we mean a close-woven structure of attitudes that expresses a person's basic values and determines his stand on particular issues, less than 3 per cent of the total population can be said to have a genuine ideology.[15]

If it is so vaguely accepted, how does the American Creed work as well as it does? Widespread acceptance of certain specific rights (such as the right of a professional organization to act as a political bloc) seems logically necessary if one accepts the abstract principles of majority rule and minority rights. And we will tend to assume that what people *should* (logically) believe is what they *do* (in fact) believe. But real human beings, certainly pragmatic Americans, somehow fail to follow the neat logical patterns of the political philosopher.

---

[14]James W. Prothro and Charles M. Grigg, "Fundamental Principles of Democracy: Bases of Agreement and Disagreement," *Journal of Politics*, XXII (May, 1960), 276–294.

[15]Philip E. Converse, "The Nature of Belief Systems in Mass Publics," in David E. Apter (ed.), *Ideology and Discontent* (New York: The Free Press of Glencoe, Inc., 1964), pp. 206–261.

Professor V. O. Key, Jr., systematically pursued the specter of consensus on fundamentals and discovered that it haunts the learned observer rather than members of the general public, most of whom couldn't care less about such a rarefied subject as ideology.[16] Examining the actual distribution of opinions on a wide variety of subjects, Key discovered consensus where conventional doctrine predicts disagreement and disagreement where doctrine prescribes consensus. First, near unanimous agreement, or consensus, prevails on some concrete questions of public policy, such as support for public education or for social welfare benefits to the aged. But this is not the kind of agreement called for by the doctrine of consensus on the fundamentals. Second, a little data and a lot of heroic guesswork indicate that consensus exists on some general attitudes of the sort we described as part of the "American character" in Chapter 2, but these attitudes are not directly political. Third, except for the highly general commitment to democracy mentioned above, no consensus can be found on the basic principles of democracy.

Professor Key's analysis suggests that the democratic system works, not by consensus, but *as if* consensus prevailed. One explanation for this seeming paradox is that consistently democratic values and habits are more prevalent among the politically active minority. However much they may disagree on issues, political activists seem to serve as the carriers of the democratic creed, learning through actual experience to recognize the problems of others, to compromise differences rather than insisting on total acceptance of their own particular principles, and to appreciate the relation of specific actions or issues to broader democratic principles. But leaders imbued with democratic values are not enough. A second reason why the system can work as if we had a conscious public ideology lies in the continuing interaction between leaders and the mass of the population: the expectations and opinions of the general public are, if not highly systematic, at least compatible with democratic procedures. A complete democratic ideology is not necessary throughout the population so long as the public accepts the ways in which political power is won and exercised—that is, so long as agreement exists on the general idea of democracy. The key word here is *acceptance*: "Apathy can play a constructive role if it leads those who reject the techniques called for by the democratic creed to inactivity or to acceptance of decisions they themselves would not have made."[17]

Discussions of democracy tend to overlook the functional nature of apathy for the system. No one is surprised that what people say they believe is not necessarily consistent with what they actually do. We usually assume that verbal positions represent a higher level—a more "democratic" stance—than nonverbal behavior. But something close to the opposite may also be true: Many people who express undemocratic principles in response to questioning

---

[16]V. O. Key, Jr., *Public Opinion and American Democracy* (New York: Alfred A. Knopf, Inc., 1961), Chapter 2.
[17]James W. Prothro and Charles M. Grigg, "Societal Coordination by the Educated Minority," *Political Research: Organization and Design* (now *American Behavioral Scientist*), III (January, 1960), 8.

are too apathetic to act on these principles in concrete situations. And in most cases, fortunately for the democratic system, those with the most undemocratic principles are also those who are least likely to act. For example, a sizeable number (42 per cent) of the voters in a southern city, in reply to a survey, said they thought that a Negro should not be allowed to run for mayor of their city. A few months before the survey was taken, a Negro had conducted an active campaign for that office without any obstruction.

In this case, the behavior was more democratic than the verbal expressions. If leaders—the carriers of the creed—had encouraged undemocratic action, it might have materialized (as it did in the murder of civil rights workers who attempted to encourage Negro voter registration in Mississippi). But, in fact, people with basically undemocratic opinions either abstained from acting or acted in a perfectly democratic fashion. "The successful working of the system is not deliberately aimed at by those who work it," John Plamenatz says, "but is the result of their behaving as they do."[18] The American Creed depends then, on leaders at all levels (from the local PTA to Congress) who are dedicated to a coherent democratic ideology. But it also depends on followers who are dedicated to the general idea of democracy and who either (1) recognize, when leaders point it out, the connection between a specific issue and the basic ideals of democracy, or (2) accept the creed in practice without thinking about the principles that imply such behavior, or (3) entertain notions inconsistent with the basic creed but are too few or too apathetic to carry out their undemocratic beliefs.

Threats to Democracy

Democracy may be threatened in two quite different ways: first, by the deliberate attempt of totalitarians to replace democracy with some other form of government, and second, by the provincial tendency to narrow the meaning of democracy to the institutional patterns of a particular time and place. We shall speak of the totalitarian threat in the next section. Here we shall focus on provincialism, which, because it is less obvious and sometimes unintended, is the more insidious.

Provincialism as a Threat to Democratic Values

Surveys reveal that 88 out of every 100 Americans consider the United States a democracy; only 60 per cent regard Great Britain as a democracy, and even fewer believe that France is democratic.[19] These findings demonstrate the tendency of Americans to identify democracy—which is a *method* of governing that may follow a variety of forms of principles—with one particular form and one particular set of principles. Chances are that a good many English and French citizens would say that the United States is not a democracy, just because it is neither England nor France. This does not, however, make the tendency *rationally defensible*. You may have

---

[18]"Cultural Prerequisites to a Successfully Functioning Democracy," *American Political Science Review*, L (March, 1956), 123.

[19]Hyman and Sheatsley, in Katz et al. (eds.), *Public Opinion and Propaganda*, p. 41.

once regarded your high school as the best in the land, but certainly you would never have insisted that it was the *only* real high school in the country and that all the others were reformatories!

Thomas Jefferson once argued that men are willing to put up for a long time with the worst possible arrangement simply because it is familiar to them. They are even more inclined to find all virtue in a situation that is satisfactory as well as familiar. This feeling might be laudable if it were not carried to extremes, and if it were not so suspiciously confined to the most uninformed citizens. In its extreme form, it constitutes a serious threat to democracy. It leads men to insist on conformity of ideas. If this insistence became widespread, only the ideas of the dominant majority would survive. In other words, it would kill democracy. Since democracy, unlike totalitarianism, does not make government synonymous with society, even the most loyal citizen needs the freedom to criticize government when he feels that criticism is necessary.

Only the misguided patriot insists that democracy is limited to a single set of institutions and principles. Because change is the one unchangeable feature of human life, again, such an insistence dooms democracy. The Constitution has been changed twenty-five times by formal amendment and countless times by interpretation and usage, and our economic and social life has undergone constant transformation over the years. How can anyone say that *now* at a given moment of a particular day, all change must cease?

Many of us assume, without reflection, that such prized American achievements as a written constitution, separation of powers, checks and balances, judicial review, federalism, and private enterprise are essential to the very existence of democracy. We shall look closely at these features of our government in later chapters, but here we shall just make two observations about their relation to democracy.

First, none of these institutions is functionally necessary to a political system with majority rule and minority rights—the two requisites of democracy. They all bear some relation to both these requisites, but none of them is perfectly identified with either—i.e., they are *supplementary* rather than *primary* institutions. More specifically, we cannot enjoy majority rule or minority rights unless we are free to organize political parties, select leaders in free elections, and have access to a free press (these are primary institutions, without which the functions of leadership selection and interest identification could not be performed in response to changing public opinion). But we can very well have both majority rule and minority rights without separation of powers or federalism (these are merely supplementary institutions, which may be functional or not for a democratic system, depending on circumstances of time and place).

In the second place, as any well-traveled or well-read person knows, democracies *do* exist without many of the characteristic features of American government. Although other democracies may seem less attractive to us than our own, we must recognize that they too can be responsible to their majorities without becoming "Americanized." Federalism and checks and balances may be more suitable to our country than a unitary government with integrated powers, but this gives us no reason to argue that *all* governments must have these particular features before they can be regarded as democracies.

An institution is essential to democracy *only if* its absence means the end of majority rule on a continuing basis. A member of the British Labour Party once claimed, in a debate with an American businessman, that private enterprise leaves vast amounts of power in the hands of men who do not have to account to the public for their use of that power; and because democracy requires that those vested with power be responsible to the people, he argued, private enterprise is undemocratic by definition. The point he missed was that Americans have simply not chosen to nationalize key industries, even though they are perfectly free to do so should they ever change their minds.

The American businessman, in turn, argued that the British had automatically relinquished democracy when they gave the socialists control of the government in the 1945 election. Because democracy means liberty and private enterprise is a form of liberty, he argued, any socialist government is undemocratic by definition. The American was blind to the same point that had escaped his opponent. The British, who had freely chosen to nationalize certain key industries, were equally free to return them to private control should they ever change their minds.

This debate could never be won, for neither spokesman could prove that either private enterprise or socialism is *directly related* to majority rule and individual liberty. The doctrinaire socialist might argue—as some do—that economic power in irresponsible hands leads inevitably to such complete domination of the newspaper, radio, television, and school systems that elections degenerate into a meaningless ritual in which the "big business"

Drawing by Reilly; © 1967 The New Yorker Magazine, Inc.

"Before we go voting for frills like an auditorium, some of us would like to know who's going to say what in it!"

candidate always wins. The facts disprove this argument, however, for in six out of eight national elections in the United States from 1936 through 1964, "big business" sided with the loser. Similarly, the doctrinaire advocate of private enterprise might argue—as some do—that the combination of economic and political authority under socialism grants government officers so much power that a dictatorship and the end of free elections is inevitable. Here, too, the facts contradict the argument, for after five years of socialist rule, the British voters returned the Conservative Party to power in an election that was as free as any ever held, and then went back to the Labour Party in 1964.

Naturally, in the United States we hear more extreme arguments in favor of private enterprise than in favor of socialism. During a recent municipal election campaign, one issue was whether the city should retain its municipally managed power plant or sell it to a private utility company. The company ran the following advertisement in the local press: "He who fights for private business fights for democracy and for freedom. If that war should be lost to us we cannot have the consolation that the struggle was a matter of little moment, for private business, political democracy and Christian religion all go down together." As it turned out, the citizens of the city voted in favor of municipal management, but no disruption of business activities, church services, or scheduled elections was ever reported. Although the utility company never recanted, democracy seems to survive despite the "inroads of socialism."

Totalitarian Attacks on Democratic Ideas

So far we have examined the corrosive effect of the false friends of democracy. Now we turn to the frontal attacks from democracy's avowed enemies. Here we meet the antidemocratic position in its baldest form. Throughout Western history the champions of oligarchy—whether in the guise of monarchy, theocracy, militarism, fascism, or communism—have consistently denied the democratic assumptions about man, society, and government. They have viewed human nature through the lenses of "elitism" or materialism rather than through the lenses of equality and humanitarianism. They have interpreted society in terms of the needs of the "fatherland," an elite class, or the single "true" party, rather than in terms of the needs of the individual. They replace progress with stability and order as the goals of society. In government, they supplant majority rule with the dominance of a superior and irresponsible minority; they substitute conformity for freedom.

The most powerful contemporary form of dictatorship is communism, and communist rejection of democracy illustrates the nature of totalitarian attacks on democratic ideas. Communist rulers in the Soviet Union, the People's Republic of China, and Eastern Europe have so reinterpreted Karl Marx's theories that he might scarcely recognize them; but these are the communists with whom we are concerned, because they are the ones with power. As the word "totalitarian" suggests, theirs is a form of dictatorship in which an irresponsible minority tries to absorb the total power of society and to command unquestioning obedience. Thus communism, in all its varying forms, flatly rejects the two essentials of democratic government.

The communists discard the notion of majority rule as a "bourgeois" sop to the masses, and look on man as a reed buffeted about by economic forces. So misguided that he votes against his own best interests, man is clearly not competent to govern himself. Despite the communists' use of such slogans as "Workers of the world unite—you have nothing to lose but your chains," communist practice is based on the idea of an elite. The superior few who can understand and take advantage of economic determinism become, of course, the leaders of the communist movement. Only through these leaders—who always constitute the "vanguard of the proletariat"—can the majority be led to perceive what is best for them.

What happens when communists succeed in gaining power? Considerable variation exists from one communist nation to another, as indicated by the differences among the Soviet Union, China, Yugoslavia, and Poland. Each nation tends to interpret communism in terms of its own political heritage. Nevertheless, communists have much in common in all countries. Convinced that they possess final and absolute truth, they leave little room for freedom to dissent—the freedom basic to democracy. Once a man has come face to face with perfect truth, why should he tolerate error?

Intellectuals in many underdeveloped countries have little patience for the emphasis on procedure shown in our criteria for classifying governments as democratic or dictatorial—they are concerned with *results*. They would accordingly reject our emphasis on the methods by which rulers are selected, and would argue that general progress takes priority over minority rights. Like the private utility company mentioned earlier, they associate Western democracy with capitalism. Unlike the utility company, however, they associate capitalism with the exploitation they have so long experienced. Moreover, in countries like Brazil, which has had competitive elections from time to time without producing any noticeable change, the current military dictatorship does not seem much different from earlier "democratic" regimes. But these intellectuals see real change in Cuba. For these people, the "dictatorship of the proletariat" is often taken seriously to mean a true people's democracy—a system that produces results without bourgeois concern for gentlemenly methods of winning or exercising power.

The communist practice of seizing power without waiting for a majority vote in a free election is enough, in itself, to damn communism to most people in Western democracies. But this characteristic has little effect on the attitudes of people who have never experienced self-government, and they make up a vast majority of the world's population. The present generation seems to be engaged in a "participation explosion" which is injecting mass opinions—often violently—into the decision-making processes of governments all over the world. People in established democracies are tempted to interpret this as meaning that other people clamor for democracy as we know it. But the form that mass participation will take is in real doubt. The central aspects of Western culture that are most easily exported are its industrial technology and rational bureaucracy. These have obvious payoffs that are desperately needed in underdeveloped areas. They are found in the Soviet Union, however, no less than in

82

the United States or Britain. Political modernization can clearly be achieved without the element we would most like to share—our democratic political culture. The abstract ideals of democracy have wide appeal, but the attitudes and practices that support those ideals are not easily transmitted to people who have not grown up with them. Two students of mass attitudes and political culture warn us, "What must be learned about democracy is a matter of attitude and feeling, and this is harder to learn."[20] In the rush for national independence and modernization, the "participant subject" mode of participation is, they warn, as likely a fate as that of "influential citizen."

Imagine a country, like so many in Asia, Africa, and Latin America, where no government has ever been chosen by the people. A new group, called the communists, organizes enough mass support, with help from Russians or Chinese, to seize control of the government. The lack of a majority vote in a free election would hardly be noticed if the country had never known a free election. This coup might appear different from all the previous ones only in its greater efficiency, its somewhat larger base of popular support, and in its claim to represent a true people's democracy. Such an excitingly new kind of dictatorship might look like genuine democracy to a habitually oppressed people. And the demonstrated scientific achievements of the U.S.S.R., or the increased military might and claims of progress by China, would certainly have glamorous appeal and stir the ambitions of people in the new "democracy."

The unpleasant fact then, is that communism does have great appeal for millions of people, especially among the relatively underdeveloped areas of Africa, Asia, and Latin America. Americans themselves occasionally feel that Russia is "doing the better job of winning people around the world to its point of view."[21] The response to communism is greatest in countries marked by mass illiteracy and poverty, where the oppressed peasants agree that they "have nothing to lose but their chains." Familiar with misery and squalor, but strangers to democracy, these people are ill-equipped to analyze communist slogans about a blissful "people's democracy" in which all needs are perfectly met. Whereas fascism represents a comparatively naked evil to adherents to democracy, communism is cloaked in a humanitarian disguise that makes it all the more dangerous. Quick to exploit any weakness that will serve their ends, communist leaders promise dignity, economic security, and national independence to people who are desperately in need of all three.

In most democracies, on the other hand, as Mr. Justice Douglas has pointed out, communists are "miserable merchants of unwanted ideas." Because the evils that Karl Marx perceived in early industrialism have been reduced by democratic means themselves, Marxist ideology appears to be a set of outmoded slogans, and communist practice a brutal assault on human dignity and freedom. Even in democracies, however, there are minorities—ranging from the

[20] Gabriel A. Almond and Sidney Verba, *The Civic Culture: Political Attitudes and Democracy in Five Nations* (Princeton: Princeton University Press, 1963), p. 5.
[21] American Institute of Public Opinion (Gallup Poll), *Public Opinion News Service*, February 3, 1961.

infinitesimal in the United States and Britain to the sizeable in Italy and France—who embrace communism. This support is most likely to exist, as in the "colonial" areas, where severe grievances stand unresolved.

Of the millions of people who vote for the Communist party in France and Italy, only a small minority are actually party members. These protest voters, compared with the electorate in general, come disproportionately from male workers in lower income and educational categories. These are not people who reject the ideals of the system so much as they reject the system because of its failure—in their experience—to realize professed ideals. The average communist voter is more often reformist than revolutionary; he recognizes shortcomings in the Communist party, but it still gives him a way of expressing his dissatisfaction with the shortcomings of the established system. Most communist voters are caught in a "politics of despair," voting against the system they see as responsible for their bleak lives without really wanting a communist regime. A large-scale study of communist voters in France and Italy ends with this quotation from a French tool-and-die-maker, who robustly expresses the alienation of most communist voters from *any* available ideology:

Hell, I have to work under any system. I got my family to think of. The kids need shoes and the wife needs a coat. Where the hell do you think I can get the money? What the workers want is a good standard of living and more opportunities for themselves and their kids.

I don't care if the workers get a good standard of living under capitalism or socialism. It doesn't make any difference to me. I don't want a revolution; I just want change. It's none of my business what workers do in other countries. They don't concern themselves about me; why the hell should I concern myself about them? Let them fight their own battles, and I'll fight mine.

But nothing I say is going to make any difference.

All I want is to enjoy myself in this life. For all I know it may be the only one I have. When you're dead, maybe you've had it. Hell, I don't know. All I want is to have a good life, that's all. Is that too much?[22]

But what motivates others, who do not suffer any apparent deprivations, to submerge themselves, even at great risk, in the Communist Party? For these the chief appeal of communism seems to lie in the very feature that makes it so repugnant to democrats—its guarantee of an authoritative answer to every problem. Apparently not everyone desires freedom and self-government, for freedom involves responsibilities as well as privileges. And the burdens of self-responsibility are more taxing than the perverted kind of freedom that comes with a surrender of independence. When a man gives up his freedom of choice, he at least gains freedom from the difficult responsibility of making his own independent decisions.

Erich Fromm has analyzed this tendency in his brilliant book *Escape from Freedom*.[23] In a complex, urban, industrial society the individual finds himself

[22]Quoted in Hadley Cantril, *The Politics of Despair* (New York: Basic Books, Inc., 1958), pp. 211–212.
[23]*Escape from Freedom* (New York: Farrar, Strauss & Giroux, Inc., 1941). Also see David Riesman, *The Lonely Crowd* (New Haven: Yale University Press, 1950); and T. W. Adorno et al., *The Authoritarian Personality* (New York: Harper & Row, Publishers, Inc., 1950). Gabriel Almond's *The Appeals of Communism* (Princeton: Princeton University Press, 1954) is a systematic analysis of why people join and quit the Communist Party.

surrounded by the "bigness" of impersonal forces that challenge his understanding and belittle his powers of control. Oppressed by feelings of insecurity, impotence, and loneliness, he may, if he is not made of sturdy stuff, join the search for subjugation rather than face the uncertainties of self-responsibility. The Communist Party holds out the promise of belonging to a worldwide movement in which one is told what to think and do, and in which the painful doubts of democracy are replaced by the absolutes of an authoritarian creed. In a democracy, the individual must live with ambiguity. But the authoritarian personality cannot bear the burdens of uncertainty.

A Reaffirmation of the Democratic Faith

Because democracy as an ideal is older than democracy as a practice, a number of unrealistic assumptions crept into the ideal along with the enduring truths. Early theorists of democracy, unacquainted with the everyday operation of popular government and eager to stir people into radical change, overstated their case. Today's theorists, who enjoy the advantage of living in a democracy, are in a position to isolate and discard these unrealistic assumptions.

Discarding Unnecessary Assumptions

The existence of democracy assumes that a sizeable proportion of voters are rational in their electoral choices—or, in Professor Key's straightforward terms, that "voters are not fools."[24] But some theorists assume that *rationality must be a characteristic of individuals uninfluenced by group affiliations*. This assumption is both unnecessary and unwarranted. If we define rational voting as a vote that reflects one's values, then Key's research nicely demonstrates that American voters are, by and large, rational. As we shall see when we consider political opinions and political parties (Chapters 6 and 7), voting preferences are closely related to such characteristics as socio-economic status, religion, region of residence, and parental party preference. That people's political values are largely shaped by their life experiences does not, of course, mean that their choices are "irrational." Americans are so sensitive to any apparent slur on the electorate, however, that some infer from these findings a denial of citizens' rationality. William Riker of the University of Rochester, for example, accepts the validity of the empirical findings but complains that "the implied conclusion is that factors such as these rather than rational calculations of advantage are what bring about choices in voting."[25] Why rational calculations of advantage cannot involve one's socio-economic status, religion, region of residence, and family upbringing is not spelled out by Professor Riker. His only evidence in support of his position is that, in 1960, several million Protestant Democrats voted for a Protestant Republican (Richard M. Nixon) and that several million Roman

[24]V. O. Key, Jr., *The Responsible Electorate* (Cambridge, Massachusetts: The Belknap Press of Harvard University Press, 1966), p. 7.
[25]*Democracy in the United States*, 2nd ed. (New York: The Macmillan Company, 1965), p. 48.

Catholic Republicans voted for a Catholic Democrat (John F. Kennedy). This he takes as proving that "a very large number of voters, when faced with a real conflict of values (i.e., party affiliation against religious affiliation), *thought deeply* about the conflict and made some sort of rational calculation of which affiliation was more important for them."[26] We agree with Riker that this example illustrates rational voting (in the sense of maximizing the values of the voter), but we disagree with his conclusion that such rationality is somehow incompatible with group influences on the vote. His own illustration reaffirms the impact of group affiliations on the voter's values.

We disagree also with the assumption that people whose votes were influenced by religious affiliation in 1960 necessarily "thought deeply" about conflicts between their party and religious affiliations. Associated with the false assumption that the rational man must be an isolated individual is the notion that ordinary people think deeply and are vitally concerned about politics, i.e., that *man is the "political animal."* First cousin to the "economic man" of classical economic theory, man as political animal was presumed to be heavily laden with virtues—an intense interest in politics, tireless activity in gathering accurate information on which to base political decisions, keen logicality in reaching conclusions, and an unwavering eagerness to register his views at the polls.[27] This glowing picture was useful in arguing for a more broadly based government, but it has proved a woefully inaccurate description of real citizens in real democracies. The average American is only mildly interested in politics. The little information he has he picks up from sources that agree with his preconceived convictions or prejudices. And when it comes to voting, only a little over half of the eligible voters appear at the polls.

The traditional image of political man is unnecessary to democratic theory. Democracy does not really require that all citizens be highly involved or keenly interested in politics. In the first place, nonvoters account for at least some of the most uninterested and uninformed citizens—those who are least qualified to vote. In a sense, these people are automatically disqualified from participation in politics. We set up no barriers of race, sex, religion, or wealth, but we do require that the adult citizen be sufficiently motivated to register and vote. From this point of view, get-out-the-vote campaigns are pernicious if they induce uninterested, uninformed citizens to vote. Only if they generate genuine interest in the important issues of the day do they produce properly qualified voters at the polls.

A second reason why democracy does not depend upon a nation of political men stems from the specialization and division of labor through which modern society operates: a high level of political power and knowledge are required in only a relatively few specialists. Just as we do not expect everyone to know how to make shoes, we need not expect every citizen to know how to make public policy. Some commentators are horrified at how few Americans show any interest in public policy or can even name such important officials as the

---

[26]*Ibid.*, p. 49 (emphasis added).

[27]In the following discussion we are indebted to Carl J. Friedrich, *The New Image of the Common Man* (Boston: Beacon Press, 1950); and Bernard R. Berelson, Paul F. Lazarsfeld, and William N. McPhee, *Voting: A Study of Opinion Formation in a Presidential Campaign* (Chicago: The University of Chicago Press, 1954), pp. 305–323. The latter volume sets up a straw man to attack by imputing ideas to contemporary political theorists that few of them actually hold.

Secretary of Defense. But would the ability to name the Secretary of Defense make a person more capable of deciding what our defense policy should be? And even if the average citizen were convinced that he knew what our policy should be, would he not be foolish to believe that he as an individual could get his idea adopted?[28] What actually happens is that various organized groups with expert representatives exert a real and informed influence on policy. Most Americans are members of such groups and, responding in a realistic way to the specialization that marks twentieth-century America, they usually leave it to their spokesmen to represent their interests. The minority who take the time to write letters to their congressmen supplement this organized representation. But only through organized representation can most people influence policy and at the same time take care of their routine daily commitments.

A third reason why democracy does not require that all citizens be highly politicized is that democracy depends on different kinds of political participation. Too many good citizens could actually be bad for the system. If we were all highly motivated in politics and stubbornly committed to well-conceived principles, for example, the flexibility of our system would be lost and our politics might reach permanent stalemate. True, democracy requires reasonable men who reasonably disagree; but it may also benefit from less reasonable men who are only occasionally interested. The less highly motivated citizens vote less regularly and change their party affiliation more often. But what would our politics be like without this kind of behavior? With all adults voting in every election and firmly dedicated to their principles, we would be divided into solid, permanently opposed voting blocs. Elections could be permanently cancelled except to record the preferences of those who had just reached voting age. Successful democracy needs *both* stability *and* change, and these are qualities that are not supported by the same individuals. The requirements of the system call for variety among the citizens who comprise it.

Three other assumptions that have needlessly encumbered democracy are more or less implicit in the image of political man. Perhaps most closely related is the assumption of *extreme individualism*—that any "common man" is competent to play any political role. As Andrew Jackson put it in his first message to Congress in 1829, "The duties of all public officers are, or at least admit of being made, so plain and simple that men of intelligence may readily qualify themselves for their performance. . . ." In practice, Americans abandoned this assumption long ago. For example, we have designed rigorous civil service examinations that only a small minority can hope to pass. But some defenders of democracy still feel obliged to talk as if the common man as an individual were capable of any political task. All that the democratic faith really requires, however, is a more modest assumption that *the people in a collective sense* are capable of giving general direction to public policy.

A second assumption that is related to the romanticized picture of the political man is that *"the voice of the people is the voice of God."* In countering the

[28]For an application of this line of reasoning to foreign policy, see Gabriel A. Almond, *The American People and Foreign Policy* (New York: Harcourt, Brace & World, Inc., 1950), pp. 226–241.

royal claim to rule by divine right, early crusaders for democracy made equally extravagant boasts for the citizenry at large. But experience has made it clear that voting returns have no mystical quality that renders the majority verdict unerringly wise. Nor does democracy need such a belief. It need only assume that over the long run the majority shows relatively greater wisdom than any minority. When we consider that the self-appointed "wise men" of history resemble Adolf Hitler more than Plato's "philosopher king," the fallible majority seems preferable to the fallible elite.

Finally, the assumption that the "common man" can make *correct decisions on technical matters* requiring expert judgment or rare taste is both unnecessary to a belief in democracy and indefensible as a logical proposition. American voters are not called upon to decide whether the TVA should have a new generator or how to build spacecraft. Although they would be incapable of solving such problems intelligently, they are able to judge broader questions related to specific problems. Arguments about public versus private power or the state of our space program do enter election campaigns. And all that democracy requires is that the judgment of the voters be applied to *general questions of public policy*.

Democracy as a Practical System

Agreeing that most men are little interested in politics and that those who are can be wrong, defenders of democracy sometimes go a step further and argue that instability and inefficiency are the price democracy pays for popular freedom. But history suggests that democracy is actually more stable and efficient than dictatorships that curb freedom in the name of stability and efficiency. The two oldest and most stable governments among the major powers are those of Britain and the United States. On the other hand, Hitler's Third Reich, which boasted that it would endure for a thousand years because it had escaped the uncertainties and confusions of democracy, lasted scarcely a dozen.

How is it that the system which exalts freedom over order actually enjoys greater order with its greater freedom? Apparently the political arrangement that endures is the one that makes room for conflicting aims and turns mistaken judgments to advantage. A dictatorship seems efficient only because it shoves its inconsistencies and errors beneath the surface. To wash one's dirty linen in public may be to admit that mud has been thrown, but it also indicates that the mud has been discovered and washed away. Studies conducted in Germany and Japan after World War II reveal that gross miscalculations were made simply because people were afraid to admit their own mistakes or criticize the mistakes of their superiors. Undetected or concealed from those in top positions, errors tended to breed further miscalculations. Everyone makes mistakes; democracy benefits from mistakes by discovering and correcting them.

If democracy has these advantages, why has it not become the universal form of government? Although democracy seems best adapted to the needs of free men, the people of many cultures do not even desire it. Certain conditions are necessary before even the desire for democracy arises: (1) a relatively high level of literacy, (2) some measure of widespread economic security, and (3) an acceptance of the dignity of human life. The first two conditions seem to be necessary for the last. An illiterate and poverty-stricken people can hardly develop the ideals, the power, and the organizational skills necessary for the achievement of responsible government.

Although literacy and economic security are *necessary*, they are not always *sufficient* to produce a recognition of human dignity. And without wide respect for man's worth, democracy does not develop. Employing advanced methods of propaganda and coercion, a modern dictatorship may continue to violate human dignity and to forestall democracy long after the population has achieved literacy and decent standards of living. In Russia, for example, the newly literate peasantry read only ideas approved by the Communist Party, and their economic security is tied to political conformity. Consequently, they may never develop the idea of democracy in the Western sense.

Another reason that may help to explain why democracy has not been embraced by all the people of the world is that it has no "set" creed to sell. An eminent historian puts it forthrightly: "We should not ask [other countries] to adopt our 'philosophy' because we have no philosophy which can be exported."[29]

Democracy is rooted in *patterns of behavior* rather than in *consensus on principles*. Suppose you were to ask a banker waiting for a haircut in an American barbershop if he and the lawyer, carpenter, mechanic, and college professor sitting with him were "equal." Chances are he would answer with a flat "no," or else ask you to clarify the question. But when the barber asks "Who's next?" each of the men would automatically look at the others in trying to decide who had arrived first, and would then wait his turn. In other words, even though they may have no well-defined or rational principle of equality, they all *behave* as if they consciously endorsed the principle.[30] This customary behavior rather than overt agreement on well-defined principles is what characterizes democracy. Habitual behavior of this sort is not easily destroyed—that is why democracy is much sturdier than its enemies realize. Unfortunately, however, habitual behavior is not easily or quickly created either—that is why it proved impossible to set up a series of democracies simply by writing democratic constitutions for European countries after World War I.

Ultimately, democracy rests on the simple idea that every person has an equal right to make his own choices, to say what he likes, to be heard. And if everyone has an equal right to be heard, the only practical way of deciding on public policy is by majority vote. There is only one alternative to majority control: if rulers are not held responsible to the majority, they will be responsible to a minority. But minorities are made up of imperfect human beings, too, and their imperfections are magnified by irresponsible power. As Thomas Jefferson put it, "Sometimes it is said that man cannot be trusted with the government of himself. Can he, then, be trusted with the government of others? Or have we found angels in the form of kings to govern him? Let history answer this question."

[29]Daniel J. Boorstin, *The Genius of American Politics* (Chicago: The University of Chicago Press, 1953), p. 1.
[30]See Friedrich, *The New Image of the Common Man*.

"THE FIRST NEW

NATION"

4

The primary fact of our national existence is that the United States was born in revolution against British colonialism. Today the United States is a great world power whose political stability, economic prosperity, technological proficiency, and military capability make it the foremost nation.

Since 1945 more than a billion people in Asia, Africa, and Latin America have resorted to revolution against colonialism. Eager to dissolve their traditional societies, most of them are determined to achieve the modern way of life. Approximately one-third of the members of the United Nations are new nations that obtained their political independence after World War II. Nearly all of them can be described as economically underdeveloped and politically unstable. No doubt the success of the American Revolution of 1776—measured by the powerful position of the United States today—has been one basis for the "revolution of rising expectations" among these newly independent countries. On the other hand, nearly a billion people under communist regimes are testing a very different mode of modernization through revolution. The Soviet Union is no mean rival: its rapid industrialization and fantastic economic growth within one generation after revolution, its vast military complex, its extraordinary advances in missiles and rocketry, its technical and scientific achievements all add up to an impressive demonstration of how to modernize a backward people in record time.

In this chapter, we treat the beginnings of the American government as a problem in "nation-building." How did the United States, breaking ties with the mother country, create and develop its own national system? To what extent does the early American experience offer guidelines to the newly developing nations today?

First Steps Toward Nationhood

The Prototype of Nation-Building: From Colonialism to Independence

Statesmen and politicians currently engaged in the making and breaking of nations have discovered that American history offers them many practical pointers: how to break away from colonial rule; how to stage and win a revolution; how to legitimize a new government and obtain consent of the governed; how to write a constitution and set up new political structures; how to make government an ongoing political process. Students of comparative politics, testing their theories of modern nation-building, find a variety of empirical data in the early American experience: colonists reacting to a different environment develop different values and perspectives; in the new nation they build new patterns of communication, and as the personal, commercial, and political transactions multiply among them they begin to identify themselves as a distinct community; detachment from the mother country becomes psychological as well as physical and old loyalties give way to new commitments; an integrated political community emerges as a new nation.

When does a new nation "emerge"? What is its birthdate? Most legalists date the inception of the United States from the Declaration of Independence, July 4, 1776: "When in the course of human events, it becomes necessary for one people to dissolve the political bands, which have connected them with another, and to assume among the powers of the earth, the separate and equal station to which the Laws of Nature and of Nature's God entitle them . . . ." From a legal standpoint, 1776 also marks the final disintegration of British authority within the boundaries of thirteen North American colonies, although Great Britain did not formally recognize this fact until the Treaty of Peace in 1783. Constitutionally, the thirteen independent states were not joined as the United States of America until the Articles of Confederation had been ratified by all the states, which did not occur until 1781. The "more perfect union" was not achieved until the new Constitution, written in 1787 by delegates from twelve of the states in Philadelphia, was ratified by nine state conventions in 1788. And the government under this Constitution technically did not go into operation until after George Washington was inaugurated as first President of the United States on April 20, 1789. If you were asked to determine the birthday of the United States, which date would you give?

Legal documents cannot tell us when British authority began to disintegrate, or even when and how the American community began to assume a separate political identity. But historians remind us that even before the Declaration of Independence a succession of formative events tended to transform British colonists into American nationalists. The French and Indian Wars, for example, represented common dangers and engendered various plans for common defense. Noteworthy is Benjamin Franklin's "Albany Plan" for intercolonial union in 1754, which proposed that a General Government representing all of the colonies and with power to handle Indian affairs dispose of the western lands and determine other matters of common concern. Neither the British nor the Americans were prepared to accept the Albany Plan, but the idea of political union was to grow steadily thereafter. The Stamp Act and the Sugar Act (taxation and regulation of trade without representation) and other acts of the British Parliament in the 1760s and '70s provoked common resentment throughout the colonies against economic imperialism; the Quartering Act (requiring the colonists to house British troops) and the Intolerable Acts (petty punitive acts against the American Patriots) prompted a spirited defense of the rights and liberties of free men.

Fighting and winning the Revolutionary War was of course the major event in the integration of the American people into a viable political community. The Revolutionary War was not a popular war; it was a true civil war which divided families and villages. Those who preferred to keep their ties with the British Empire considered themselves "Loyalists;" those who chose to fight for independence called themselves "Patriots." The distinguished American historian Samuel Eliot Morison has hazarded a "guess" that not more than 10 per cent of the white population of the United States was actively Loyalist, that about 40 per cent was actively Patriot, and that the other 50 per cent was either neutral or apathetic. To Morison, "the significant fact is that nowhere, except in Georgia and in occupied seaports, were the British able to organize a Loyalist civil government."[1]

As John Adams had predicted, the American Revolution was "a long, obstinate, and bloody war." No charismatic national leader emerged during the war years. As Commander-in-Chief of the Revolutionary armed forces, General George Washington was accorded the highest respect and trust by the Patriots, but he earned his reputation as a statesman only after the Revolution. Perhaps because the Americans had personified in George III the power of the British Crown in the colonies, they were disinclined to accept another chief of state, even one of their own choosing. Even in the throes of revolution, the Patriots consciously tried to create a "government of law," a constitutional government with specific and limited power. Almost immediately after its Declaration of Independence, the Second Continental Congress began to consider the Articles of Confederation.

Directing the war was such a time-consuming activity that debate on the details of the proposed constitutional union of the states was delayed more than a year. But in November, 1776, Congress formally adopted the Articles and forthwith submitted them to the state legislatures for ratification. All of the states except one promptly approved the Articles (Maryland ratified them in March, 1781). Thus almost up to the surrender of General Cornwallis at Yorktown—that is, virtually until the end of the war—Congress acted as a central government for the states in what might be regarded as a common law arrangement, conducting foreign affairs, managing interstate relations, and doing what it could to bring the Revolution to fruition. Although the Revolutionary government was poorly financed and inadequately supported, although sacrifices were unevenly and unfairly distributed and innumerable problems were simply put aside, fewer than 3 million Americans successfully defied the world's greatest colonial power and took "the first steps, however faltering, toward a more satisfactory union among themselves."[2]

Since World War II, dozens of revolutionary governments have gained their independence from colonial powers, but few have been able to establish a democratic political system capable of projecting the national interest and at the same time sustaining individual rights and liberties. To understand the remarkable achievement of the North Americans in the eighteenth century, we

---

[1] Samuel Eliot Morison, *The Oxford History of the American People* (New York: Oxford University Press, 1965), p. 236.
[2] Richard Hofstadter, William Miller, and Daniel Aaron, *The United States: The History of a Republic* (Englewood Cliffs, N.J.: Prentice-Hall, Inc., 1957), p. 116.

must look at more than events and legal documents; we need to examine the *process of nation-building* which had its beginnings among the colonists more than half a century before the outbreak of revolution.

Lucian Pye, analyzing the problems of nation-building in modern Asia, conceives of the process of political development before and after colonial rule as a series of crises: *identity, integration, penetration, participation,* and *distribution*.³ The American experience can be illuminated within this modern conceptual framework. Moreover, the comparative approach, although it spans centuries and continents, can clarify not only what happened in the United States before and after 1776 but also what is now occurring within most of the new nations of the world. Conditions of nation-building were not the same for Americans in the eighteenth century as they are for Asians and Africans in the twentieth—the disparities of input and output are obvious—but the basic similarities make the analogy meaningful.⁴

The first crisis in nation-building (following Pye's model) is the acquisition of a sense of common identity. For Americans this was a natural experience, since most of the colonists were of British descent. John Jay made this point in supporting the idea of a strong federal union in 1788: "Providence has been pleased to give this one connected country to one united people—a people descended from the same ancestors, speaking the same language, professing the same religion, attached to the same principles of government, very similar in their manners and customs."⁵

Although we cannot say exactly when the colonists came to identify themselves more as Americans than Englishmen, recent studies in American history, using some of the newer tools of social science, offer evidence that this first crisis in nation-building antedated the Declaration of Independence. Through a systematic examination of symbols of common identity in the colonial press, Richard L. Merritt is able to trace the growth of a distinctly American political community between 1735 and 1775, a growth which he depicts not as smooth and steady, but rather "a typical learning curve, cyclical and spiral." His research tentatively identifies some time during 1763 as the crucial date when the colonists crossed the threshold of common American identity.⁶ In other words, had it been possible to make annual surveys of pre-revolutionary American opinion, 1763 was probably the first year in which a majority of colonists would have identified themselves as "Americans" rather than as British subjects.

By this time coastal shipping was growing at a much more rapid rate than

---

³"Transitional Asia and the Dynamics of Nation Building," in Marian D. Irish (ed.), *World Pressures on American Foreign Policy* (Englewood Cliffs, N.J.: Prentice-Hall, Inc., 1964), pp. 154–172.

⁴Seymour Martin Lipset views the United States in historical and comparative perspective in *The First New Nation* (New York: Basic Books, Inc., 1963). The title of this chapter is taken from Lipset's seminal study. See also Richard L. Merritt's essay, "Nation Building in America: The Colonial Years," in Karl W. Deutsch and William J. Foltz (eds.), *Nation-Building* (New York: Atherton Press, 1963), pp. 56–81; and Richard L. Merritt, *Symbols of American Community, 1735–1775* (New Haven: Yale University Press, 1966).

⁵*The Federalist* (also known as *The Federalist Papers*), No. 2. Many editions of *The Federalist* are available, including: Max Beloff (ed.) (New York: The Macmillan Company, 1950); Henry Steele Commager (ed.) (New York: Appleton-Century-Crofts, 1949); Edward Mead Earle (ed.) (New York: Modern Library, 1937).

⁶Merritt, *Symbols of American Community, 1735–1775*, p. 126.

commerce with the mother country. Meanwhile, the building of post roads and marked improvement in transportation facilities had brought about a great expansion in intercolonial trade, which was accompanied by population expansion. Merritt also notes that by the 1700s a fairly continuous line of settlement ran from Penobscot Bay in Maine to Savannah, Georgia. The establishment of a postal system in North America as early as 1753 encouraged a great deal of intercolonial communication, including the circulation of newspapers and pamphlets. Religious groups—Baptists, Friends, Methodists, and others—organized intercolonial meetings; mass revivals like the Great Awakening cut across colonial boundaries.

Public education, which is today's approach to fostering nationalism, was virtually nonexistent in colonial America. Massachusetts and Connecticut laws required that all children be taught to read, but education was generally a private (usually church-related) enterprise and a matter of local concern. By 1766, however, eight colonial universities were attracting students, mostly from the middle and upper classes, but from all parts of the country. They were, in effect, developing an intercolonial, i.e., American, intellectual elite which would furnish most of the leadership, first in the revolutionary movement, then in the new government under the Articles, and subsequently under the Constitution of 1787.

It would be stretching the facts too far to claim that the colonists were developing what Walter Lippmann terms "a public philosophy."[7] Nevertheless, increasing intercolonial exchange—of ideas, things, and persons—did build up a sense of community that came to encompass the peoples of all thirteen colonies. And this longtime process of political socialization was a most significant input for what Pye describes as the second crisis of nation-building.

The crisis of *integration* involves the relationship of the political system to the social structure: "It is concerned with the manner and degree to which the various elements and communities are interrelated with each other and with the system of national government"[8] We have already noted that continuing clashes with the British government fostered the idea of an American union. In the decade before the final break with the mother country, intercolonial Committees of Correspondence, a kind of interlocking intellectual elite, functioned as unofficial agents of the colonists, consciously institutionalizing the political ties. The First Continental Congress, meeting in Philadelphia in 1774 to coordinate colonial opposition to the so-called Intolerable Acts, established a structure of political bodies which acted, albeit tentatively and inadequately, as a national government. The Second Continental Congress, which so boldly proclaimed "these United States are, and of right ought to be free and independent states," deliberately assumed the role of a constituent assembly and meantime with due modesty served as a national legislature.

In stressing the prerevolutionary antecedents of the American community, we do not want to leave the impression that the United States of America

---

[7]Walter Lippmann, *Essays in The Public Philosophy* (Boston: Little, Brown and Co., 1954).
[8]Pye, *op. cit.*, p. 163.

emerged to full nationhood in 1776. Americans had met the crisis of common identity and had approached the crisis of integration before the Declaration of Independence, but they still had a long way to go, well past the middle of the nineteenth century, and through another long and bloody civil war, before it was finally settled among them that the United States *is* rather than the United States *are*.[9]

Developing a sense of common identity and winning the fight for independence—these are but preliminaries to achieving nationhood. The most crucial crises lie beyond: the establishment of a decision-making structure that the people themselves will recognize as legitimate and authoritative (*integration*); the development of a political system that will reach out to the local communities and respond to their various demands and supports (*penetration*); growing recognition of a mutual commitment on the part of governors and the governed that transcends the pragmatic relationships of coercion and obedience, influence and compliance (*participation*); continuing controls over the outputs of the political process—the rewards and deprivations—that promote the national interest and general welfare and secure for the individual his rights and liberties (*distribution*). This, of course, is a model of nation-building; it pictures an ideal process which in reality is never quite achieved. Such a model is useful, however, for understanding the dynamics of political development.

Undoubtedly the seminal contribution of eighteenth-century Americans to the modern model of nation-building was writing a constitution to serve as a warrant of authority and legitimacy for their government. Most governments today—and especially those newly established—have written constitutions, but the Americans were the first to implement the idea in modern times. Written constitutions did not originate in the United States; the idea is older than Aristotle, whose political philosophy reputedly rests on a thorough investigation of 258 ancient constitutions, including the famous written constitution of Athens. At the time the American government was founded, however, no major power in the world was operating under a written constitution.

In every new nation born of revolution, the crisis of integration must face up to the problem of legitimacy: How can the people be made to recognize and accept the authority of the new government? One of the most remarkable aspects of the American revolution was the inclination, as well as the ability, of its leaders to engage in constructive political efforts in the midst of their war activities. Even before the Declaration of Independence, seven of the colonies had established independent governments, and by 1777 all the states had adopted new constitutions except Massachusetts, which adopted hers in 1780.

The First Constitutions: "Warrants of Legitimacy"

---

[9]Students who wish to pursue further the initial problems of nation-building in the modern context should examine the several "Studies in Political Development" sponsored by the Committee on Comparative Politics of the Social Science Research Council; among them are *Communications and Political Development* (1963), edited by Lucian W. Pye; and *Bureaucracy and Political Development* (1963), edited by Joseph LaPalombara; (Princeton: Princeton University Press). See also *The Integration of Political Communities*, edited by Philip E. Jacob and James V. Toscano (Philadelphia: J.B. Lippincott Co., 1964), especially "Communication Theory and Political Integration" by Karl W. Deutsch; *The Politics of the Developing Areas*, edited by Gabriel A. Almond and James S. Coleman (Princeton: Princeton University Press, 1960); and David E. Apter, *The Politics of Modernization* (Chicago: University of Chicago Press, 1965).

Benjamin Fletcher Wright, one of the keenest students of American constitutional history, reminds us that this "great feat of constitution-making was unprecedented and remains unparalleled in the history of modern constitutionalism."[10]

A constitution need not be written. A constitution is a fundamental set of political practices, not a historic piece of paper. A textbook on British government cannot conveniently include in its appendix a concise copy of the British constitution, for it has never been written out as a single document. But this does not mean that the British people do not live under a constitutional government. Indeed, many of the great landmarks in the development of British constitutional government, such as Magna Carta (1215), the Petition of Right (1628), and the Bill of Rights (1689), are part and parcel of the American constitutional background. Because the American colonies had long been governed by written charters, however, the American states quite naturally chose to launch their new governments with formal written documents. Most of the states framed entirely new constitutions, but some, such as Connecticut and Rhode Island, simply made minor changes in their old charters.

A constitution need not be ratified by the whole people. In fact, most of the early state constitutions were established through ordinary legislative procedures. But the Massachusetts Constitution of 1780 came to be regarded as a "model constitution" because it was written by a convention elected especially for that purpose and submitted to the people for final ratification. Thus it is a more concrete expression of the eighteenth century notion of a "social compact," an agreement setting up a government by the people themselves.

A constitution embodies the fundamental political philosophy of the people. It outlines the basic structure and the major functions of the government. And, in a general way, it describes the relations between individual citizens and their government. One would therefore expect to find much the same democratic philosophy in these early state constitutions and in the Declaration of Independence.

The framers of the first state constitutions, like the authors of the Declaration of Independence, borrowed most of their ideas from seventeenth- and eighteenth-century English and French political philosophers.[11] Americans were deeply impressed with the doctrine of "popular sovereignty," the idea that all political power is derived from the people and that every government must have the consent of the governed. The Declaration of Independence was signed "in the Name and by Authority of the good People of these Colonies." The Massachusetts Constitution explicitly stated that "the People in this commonwealth have the sole and exclusive right of governing themselves as a free, sovereign, and independent state."

All of the new state constitutions were republican: they recognized the principle of popular representation and provided for government by officials who were accountable to the public and who held office for a fixed term or

---

[10]Benjamin Fletcher Wright, *Consensus and Continuity, 1776–1787* (Boston: Boston University Press, 1958), p. 8.

[11]The debt to English thinkers, especially to John Locke, was very great. There is, however, scholarly controversy about the direct influence of French writers in the American colonies.

"during good behavior." Popular sovereignty, or "consent of the governed," did not, however, necessarily imply universal suffrage. One authority on state government says of this period, "Popular sovereignty was more nearly property sovereignty."[12] But property and tax-paying qualifications were really not so onerous as to restrict the vote to a wealthy elite. Recent research indicates that on the eve of revolution, in most of the colonies one-half to three-fourths of the male adults possessed the franchise; in Massachusetts probably 95 per cent were eligible to vote.[13]

The new constitutions made no clear break with the past. The idea of "natural rights" or "unalienable rights" expressed in the Declaration of Independence is rooted deep in our English heritage, as far back as the English Bill of Rights, the Petition of Right, and the Magna Carta. A bill of rights was attached to nearly all the state constitutions. The revolutionary leaders did not regard these bills of rights as conferring any new rights, but merely as protecting those rights already possessed by Englishmen and therefore by Americans from "time immemorial." The Virginia Bill of Rights states the general principle:

> All men are by nature equally free and independent, and have certain inherent rights of which, when they enter in a state of society, they cannot, by any compact, deprive or divest their posterity, namely the enjoyment of life and liberty, with the means of acquiring and possessing property, and pursuing and obtaining happiness and safety.

These bills of rights, for all their sweeping generalizations about "popular sovereignty" and "natural rights," were not mere abstractions. They included such fundamental rights as freedom of speech, freedom of press, freedom of religion, and freedom of assembly. Just as the Declaration of Independence spelled out the grievances of the colonists against the British king, so these early constitutions specified the civil rights of the people: speedy and public trial, trial by jury, protection against unreasonable search and seizure, protection against self-incrimination, and all the other guarantees of fair procedure that Americans still cherish as their heritage of constitutional rights.

It would be an exaggeration, however, to claim that our modern notions of civil rights were tailored in the eighteenth century. By today's standards these early American interpretations appear quite rudimentary. Until very recently our legal definitions of civil rights have been rather vague and ill-developed, which accounts in part for the many serious political misunderstandings that have arisen—and continue to arise—over the definition of "constitutional rights." (We shall be discussing this further in Chapter 14.)

Although the revolutionary leaders were more concerned with the principles of freedom than they were with the structure of government, they nevertheless realized that institutions were necessary to protect individual liberties. The writers of the first constitution were highly practical and most of their political propositions were rooted in their own experience. Some of them may have read and been impressed by the contemporary writings of "the celebrated Montesquieu" but more likely they got their idea of separation of powers from colonial practice rather than from the French political philosopher.

---

[12]Arthur W. Bromage, *State Government and Administration in the United States* (New York: Harper & Row, Publishers, Inc., 1936), p. 25.
[13]Robert A. Dahl, *Pluralist Democracy in the United States* (Chicago: Rand McNally & Co., 1967).

Paradoxically, the American revolutionaries were fairly conservative in that they were not eager to scrap existing machinery that seemed to work well enough. Hence six of the new state constitutions expressly proclaimed "separation of powers" as a principle of popular government. The Virginia Constitution of 1776, for example, declared, "The legislative, executive, and judicial departments should be separate and distinct so that neither exercises the powers properly belonging to the others." And yet, in practice, the new governments reflected legislative supremacy. The governor in some states and judges in most states were appointed by the legislatures.

All the new constitutions set up various combinations of checks and balances to restrain executive power. The American Revolution was ostensibly fought against the British King, but the King was a symbol thousands of miles away. Consequently, the Revolution turned against the royal governors and the King's judges within the colonies. This animus was reflected in the first state constitutions. Within a year after the Declaration of Independence, however, the New York Constitution provided for the popular election of the governor, a pattern followed by Massachusetts in 1780 and by all the states within a few years. Nevertheless, state governors have never quite overcome the handicap imposed by these first constitutions.

While the states were setting up their new constitutions, the second Continental Congress began to draft a constitution for the government of the states as a whole. In July, 1775, Benjamin Franklin presented to Congress a design for "Perpetual Union" and, immediately following the Declaration of Independence, Congress appointed a committee to consider Franklin's proposals. This committee quickly made its report to Congress in the form of *Articles of Confederation.* Congress debated the report for more than a year before finally agreeing on a new draft, which it submitted to the state legislatures with the stipulation that the Articles would not go into effect until every state had approved them. Legally the Articles did not go into effect until the last state, Maryland, had ratified them in 1781. Thus between 1776 and 1781 the United States as a single nation had no constitutional government; there existed only thirteen separate and independent state governments.

The Articles of Confederation proclaimed "a firm league of friendship" explicitly protecting each state's "sovereignty, freedom, and independence, and every power, jurisdiction, and right, which is not by this confederation expressly delegated to the United States, in Congress assembled." Throughout history, most federations and confederations have begun as fighting organizations, and this one was no exception. The states joined together "for their common defense" in a mutual security pact, "binding themselves to assist each other, against all force offered to, or attacks made upon them."[14] The

---

[14]For varying accounts of the United States under the Articles, see John Fiske, *The Critical Period of American History, 1783–1789* (Boston: Houghton Mifflin Company, 1916); Merril Jensen, *The New Nation: A History of the United States During the Confederation, 1781–1789* (New York: Alfred A. Knopf, Inc., 1950); A. C. McLaughlin, *The Confederation and the Constitution* (New York: Harper & Row, Publishers, Inc., 1905).

Articles accordingly represented a compact among states and not a government "of the people, by the people, for the people." The United States under the Articles was more comparable to an international organization than a national state.

Under the Articles, Congress was the center of governmental organization. But Congress merely represented the states; like the United Nations today, it could not make laws directly governing the people of the member states. Delegates to Congress were chosen by the legislatures of each state, and no state was represented by less than two or more than seven members; no matter how many delegates a state had, it enjoyed only one vote in Congress. Oddly enough, although the state constitutions made much of the principle of "separation of powers", the Articles totally disregarded it. They made no provision for an executive, although a "committee of the states," consisting of one member of Congress from each state, managed the general affairs of the government when the whole Congress was not assembled. This committee appointed one of its members to act as president; the term of office was one year, and no one could serve two terms in succession. The Articles established no national judiciary, but Congress acted as a sort of Supreme Court for disputes between states concerning "boundary, jurisdiction, or any other cause whatever."

Numerous important responsibilities assigned to Congress by the Articles actually represented little more than a transfer of British colonial functions to the government of the United States. Congress was given "the sole and exclusive right and power of determining on peace and war," of sending and receiving ambassadors, of entering into treaties and alliances, and in general of making the rules for the conduct of war, which was of immediate and common concern. Congress also had "the sole and exclusive right and power" to regulate the value of coins; to fix the standard of weights and measures throughout the United States, to regulate trade with the Indians and to manage Indian affairs, to establish and regulate post offices, to appoint all officers of the navy and to commission all other officers in the service of the United States, to make all rules for the regulation of land and naval forces and direct their operations.

Critics of the Articles of Confederation have emphasized that the loose organization of government under the Articles encouraged the states to take off in different directions rather than work closely together for the general good. The text of the Articles, however, suggests that its framers meant to establish a constitutional union and not merely to affirm the friendship of the member states. The people of each state were guaranteed the freedom to travel to and return from any other state, and the citizens of each state were entitled to the "privileges and immunities" of citizens in all the states, including all privileges of trade and commerce. The Articles provided that fugitives from justice could be extradited from one state to any other. And each state was required to give "full faith and credit" to the records, acts, and judicial proceedings of the courts and magistrates of every other state.

Moreover, the states, in ratifying the Articles, agreed to accept certain limitations on their sovereignty. Without the consent of Congress no state could enter into any "conference, agreement, alliance, or treaty with any king, prince or state," engage in diplomatic relations with foreign governments, or enter into any interstate compact or agreement. No state could levy any imposts or duties that might interfere with treaties made by the United States. Without the consent of Congress no state could engage in war unless it was actually invaded or threatened with imminent danger. No state could maintain a navy, but every state was expected to keep up a well-regulated militia and enough armament to defend itself.

But quite clearly if a state were to disregard or violate any of these restrictions, the Congress would be practically impotent to bring that state back into line. The Articles of Confederation, despite the embryonic unionism implied by some of their provisions, could scarcely be regarded as forming a new nation. Rather the emphasis remained on the sovereignty and equality of the separate states. Congress was not to legislate on any matter unless it had the consent of nine of the thirteen states; and no alteration could be made in the Articles unless it was unanimously accepted by Congress and then confirmed by the legislature of every state. But the possibility of achieving unanimity became less likely as the Revolution drew to a close and the states no longer faced a common foe.

The weakness of the government under the Articles was due to a more fundamental matter than political structure, however. Although the colonists had developed a sense of community in their fight against the British government, the end of the war brought the letdown a new nation usually experiences once they have achieved their independence. Joined together in a common grievance, they fought valiantly for a common cause. But when the shooting was over, they fell to quarreling as they had to discard one set of beliefs for another. It is one thing for revolutionary leaders to capitalize on dissent, encourage iconoclasm, and incite violence. It is quite another, much more arduous, matter to return to constructive efforts and work for consensus among dissident groups.

By emphasizing the sovereignty and equality of the separate states, the Articles tended to minimize *national identity*. Since the national government under the Articles did not directly govern the people, the average citizen was less impelled to offer his political loyalty to the new United States and more inclined to give his first allegiance to his own state. But for the United States to become one nation, the people in all of the states would have to develop enough political cohesion to think of themselves primarily as Americans rather than as Virginians or Pennsylvanians.

To cope with the crisis of *integration*, a new government must be able to exert its authority and the people prepared to accept that authority. But the spirit of revolution, once quickened among the citizenry, does not immediately abate when the war is won. The American Revolution of 1776 had been not only a war against Parliament and King in London, but also a series of local uprisings against unpopular tax-collectors and county judges. A decade after the Declaration of Independence, many Americans throughout all the states were still in arms against political authority; debtors were released from jails, records were destroyed, mob violence prevented courts from sitting. Many of the wealthy, upper-class Tories who normally would have served to temper revolutionary extremism had gone into exile. A transfer of power and an establishment of authority had to be effected not only on paper but in the minds of the people.

The crisis of *integration* is essentially a problem of communication—the task of bridging the gap between political leaders and divergent factions among the people. (Lacking mass media, the problem in the eighteenth century was perhaps more serious than in our time, when radio and television can keep the government in immediate touch with the whole citizenry.) Thus the American revolutionary leaders, alarmed by the persistent tendency of the people to resist any form of government, moved into the official positions which Tory leaders had vacated and tried to restore public order and protect private rights. We have already noted the revolutionary leaders' efforts to establish constitutional governments in the states. Effective integration at the national level was more complicated because the Articles made no provision for direct communication between the national government and individual citizens. The impact of national authority was scarcely felt in the local communities by the time it was transmitted through state agencies.

The United States almost foundered on what Pye calls the third crisis in nation-building—the crisis of *penetration*. Under the Articles, the central government could not take direct action in the states and local communities and hence was virtually impotent in economic affairs. True, Congress had exclusive power over coinage, but the states were free to issue great quantities of paper money in an attempt to appease the increasing number of debtors. The resultant monetary confusion aggravated the business depression that followed the Revolution. Congress was unable to regulate interstate commerce, which rapidly developed into an economic "cold war" among the states. Moreover, it had to depend on contributions from the states to cover all expenses for the common defense and the general welfare, the contributions being based on the relative value of the land, buildings, and improvements in each state. The central government could not levy taxes; only the legislatures of the states had that power. Actually, the flow of funds into the national treasury depended on the good will and good faith of the individual states; and as time passed, the states showed themselves less and less inclined to meet their obligations to the central government. Congress could borrow money on the credit of the United States but, since it had no means of its own to raise revenue, its credit became increasingly shaky. During the last years under the Articles of Confederation, the United States was unable even to meet the interest due on its foreign and domestic debt.

The crisis of *participation* is closely related to the crisis of identity, but it goes beyond psychological identification since it is concerned with drawing the general citizenry into the national political process. Under the Articles of Confederation the citizens in the several states did not vote directly for any representatives in the national government. The members of Congress, chosen by the state legislatures, were under no pressure to respond to popular mandate. Since Congress had no power to levy taxes on individual citizens, or to pass other laws affecting them directly, the people as a whole did not feel personally involved in the nation's affairs. If the national government were to succeed, it would have to establish a more direct and functional relationship with the many interest groups and various factions that comprised the dynamic community.

The final crisis in nation-building is that of *distribution,* the problem of deciding who gets what under the new system. Rising expectations are a part of every revolution, in any century, among all peoples. The criterion of success for the new government, from the viewpoint of those who helped create it, is the payoff. The American Revolution had strong ideological motivations: It was a fight to secure "certain unalienable rights." But it was also an economic war, a struggle to toss off the yoke of colonialism and to promote American commercial and business interests. In fact, the greatest dissatisfaction with the Articles seems to have come from the merchants, planters, and businessmen who thought that the national government should be more actively concerned with the economic development of the country.

The first moves to amend the Articles stemming from dissatisfaction with the existing pattern of distribution reflected the demands of economic groups who equated their rising expectations with a stronger national economy. Twice under the Articles amendments were proposed to permit Congress to levy duties on imports. In 1781, a proposal to levy a 5 per cent duty on enumerated imports was defeated by the single veto of Rhode Island. Two years later a similar amendment proposed duties on sugar, molasses, tea, coffee, pepper, and other commodities; all proceeds were to be used to pay the public debt. This one was defeated by the veto of New York. Moreover, although Congress could regulate foreign commerce, it had no power over commerce among the states. In an attempt to exclude the commerce of their neighbors, many states had set up tariff barriers and tonnage duties. Economic rivalry among the states reached such a high pitch of tension and frustration that the states themselves began to demand a stronger national government.

Then an unanticipated series of events led fortuitously to the resolution of these problems. In 1785, delegates from Virginia and Maryland met in Alexandria, Virginia, to work out an agreement on problems of navigation and commerce on the Potomac River and Chesapeake Bay. Because the conference was unsuccessful, the Virginia legislature called a general economic conference to meet in Annapolis, Maryland, in September, 1786. The Annapolis Conference was also a failure, for only twelve delegates appeared to represent five states whose interests were predominantly commercial: New York, New Jersey, Pennsylvania, Delaware, and Virginia. The report of these delegates, under the leadership of Alexander Hamilton of New York, observed that the situation of the United States under the Articles had become "delicate and critical," and recommended that all the states appoint commissioners to meet in Philadelphia on the second Monday of the following May (1787) "to devise such further provisions as shall appear to them necessary to render the Constitution of the Federal government adequate to the exigencies of the Union."

Immediately after the Annapolis Conference several of the states began to name delegates to the meeting in May. In February, 1787, Congress itself finally endorsed the movement for a convention, resolving that it was "expedient" for a convention to meet "for the sole and express purpose of revising the Articles of Confederation and reporting to Congress and the several legislatures such alterations and provisions therein as shall when agreed to in Congress and confirmed by the states render the federal constitution adequate to the exigencies of Government and the preservation of the Union." All the states except Rhode Island eventually responded by appointing delegates to the Constitutional Convention that was to meet in Philadelphia in May, 1787.

The Politics of Constitution Writing

The "Framers" in Philadelphia, 1787

The goal of a successful revolution is the founding of a new political order, but seldom do revolutionary leaders become constitution-makers. It takes one kind of talent to organize rejection of the existing political order and to engineer its overthrow by force and violence. It takes another kind of talent to work out a new basic agreement between the governors and the governed that will satisfactorily reflect the values, beliefs, and interests of the new community.[15] It is quite remarkable, then, that American revolutionary leaders in the midst of war framed the Articles of Confederation to bring all the states into a constitutional union and also provided written constitutions in each state. Nevertheless, by 1787 a considerable turnover had occurred in American political leadership, and the young men moving into positions of power and influence were notably more conservative, more concerned about the public order, and less fixed by libertarian ideas than their revolutionary predecessors.

Few of the popular leaders who had been the most active agitators during the Revolution appeared in Philadelphia. In general they feared that any central government would serve the aristocracy just as the English government had, and their suspicions were strengthened as they noted that those most critical of the Articles were also inclined to be most skeptical of democracy. They scorned imagined "aristocratic plots" and were confident that they could block any attempt to transfer power to the gentry simply by controlling a single state legislature. Understandably, they made little effort to seek nomination as delegates, or even to accept the opportunity when it fell their way. Only eight of those who had signed the Declaration of Independence were appointed as commissioners to the Convention of 1787. Four of them were from Pennsylvania—Benjamin Franklin, Robert Morris, George Clymer, and James Wilson; and all four signed the Constitution. Elbridge Gerry of Massachusetts, who had signed both the Declaration of Independence and the Articles of Confederation, took an active part in the Convention but would not give his approval to the outcome. Roger Sherman of Connecticut and Robert Morris of Pennsylvania were the only men who put their names to all three of the great documents of the period: the Declaration of Independence, the Articles of Confederation, and the Philadelphia Constitution. Colonel George Mason of Virginia, who in the fight against ratification was to denounce his

---

[15]Political order and political community are not synonymous. Carl Friedrich has written a most perceptive chapter, "Founding the Political Order," in his monumental book *Man and His Government: An Empirical Theory of Politics* (New York: McGraw-Hill Book Company, 1963).

colleagues in the Convention, wrote to his son that he was pleased to find in the Convention "many men of fine republican principles . . ., many gentlemen of the most respectable abilities . . ., of the purest intentions." James Madison wrote one of his friends that he was impressed with the good company: "In several instances the most respectable characters in the United States and in general . . . the best contribution of talents the states could make for the occasion." William Pierce of Georgia, on whose contemporary notes we depend for characterizations of individual members, said that he was gratified to sit in "the wisest council in the world."

Many of the Convention delegates were gentlemen of learning; about half of them were college graduates from such schools as Princeton, Yale, Harvard, Columbia, Pennsylvania, and William and Mary. In his "character sketches," William Pierce called special attention to their educational qualifications: Dr. Samuel Johnson of Connecticut, "one of the first classics in America"; Colonel Hamilton of New York—"reputed to be a finished scholar . . ., he enquires into every part of his subject with the searchings of phylosophy"; William Paterson of New Jersey, "possesses a good education and some reading"; James Wilson of Pennsylvania, "is well acquainted with Man, and understands all the passions that influence him. Government seems to have been his peculiar Study, all the political institutions of the World he knows in detail and can trace the causes and effects of every revolution from the earliest stages of the Greecian commonwealth down to the present time"; John Dickinson of Delaware, "a Scholar, and said to be a Man of very extensive information"; George Wythe of Virginia, "the famous professor of Law at the University of William and Mary. . . . From his close attention to the study of general learning he has acquired a compleat knowledge of the dead languages and all the sciences. . . No Man it is said understands the history of Government better than Mr. Wythe. . . ."; James Madison of Virginia "blends together the profound politician, with the Scholar"; Governor Randolph of Virginia, "a young Gentleman in whom unite all the accomplishments of the Scholar, and the Statesman"; Charles Coteworth Pinckney, "a Gentleman of Family and fortune" from South Carolina, "has received the advantage of a liberal education and possesses a very extensive degree of legal knowledge"; Abraham Baldwin of Georgia, "having laid the foundation of a compleat classical education at Harvard College, he pursues every study with ease." And so down the roster; of only a few could Pierce say, "but little education."

Most nationalist leaders in modern nation-building are relatively young men whose professional ambitions and personal fortunes are tied to the central government. For the most part, they belong to the elite class, the well-born and able, ideological innovators, social and economic promoters. Not too surprisingly, the Founding Fathers of "the first new nation" fit neatly into this pattern. Three-fourths of the men at the Philadelphia Convention were under fifty; the average age was forty. Many of those whose voices were strongest during the debates were in their thirties: Alexander Hamilton thirty-three, James Madison thirty-seven, Gouverneur Morris thirty-eight, Elbridge Gerry thirty-seven, Edmund Randolph thirty-two, Charles Pinckney twenty-four, William Paterson thirty-four. The term "Founding Fathers" conjures up images of old graybeards. In fact, however, the American Founding Fathers were like most nation builders—relatively young men—and more important, they were zealous young men fired with ideas and ideals. That the work of the Founding Fathers has survived the test of time may be attributed to their preoccupation with the fundamental principles of government as well as their very practical interest in workable solutions for immediate problems. The conscious joining together of scholarship and statesmanship in the Convention of 1787 resulted in a political design that did far more than merely meet the exigencies of the new republic. The delegates to the Constitutional Convention of 1787 deliberately developed a public philosophy based on certain concepts concerning the nature of man, the nature of society, and the nature of government. That this public philosophy happened to bolster the self-interest and personal predilections of the framers does not detract from the intrinsic merit of the Constitution which they made the "supreme law of the land." The gentlemen at Philadelphia were not only rich and well-born; they were also exceptionally able. Combining their own practical experience in government with the insights of the ancient and contemporary political philosophers, they developed basic rules

Drawing by Martin; © 1967 The New Yorker Magazine, Inc.

"Mr. President, Delegates, and fellow-Forefathers . . ."

that still apply amazingly well to vastly changed circumstances.

General Washington expressed the consensus of his colleagues when he wrote to General Lafayette, his old ally of Revolutionary years, that what the Convention hoped for was "a government of respectability under which life, liberty, and property will be secured to us." In the term often used by the Founding Fathers themselves, they were "gentlemen of principle and property." In the course of debate, the gentlemen passed many remarks that have frequently been cited as evidence that they were less concerned with securing the blessings of liberty than with protecting rights of private property and the sanctity of contacts. Gouverneur Morris of Pennsylvania, arguing that wealth as well as numbers should be represented in Congress, declared: "If property then is the main object of government, certainly it ought to be one measure of the influence due to those who are to be affected by the government." John Rutledge of South Carolina echoed these sentiments, saying, "Property is certainly the principal object of society." On the other hand, according to Madison's notes on the Convention, James Wilson, counsel for extremely wealthy interests in Pennsylvania, "could not agree that property was the sole or primary object of government and society. The cultivation and improvement of the human mind was the most noble object. With respect to this object, as well as to other personal rights, numbers were surely the natural and precise measure of representation."

Charles Beard, in *An Economic Interpretation of the Constitution*, analyzed the personnel of the Constitutional Convention in terms of their economic interests and professional pursuits. He found that a majority of the members were lawyers by profession; that not one represented the small farming or mechanic class; that the overwhelming majority held government bonds which they were eager to protect; that many were land speculators anxious for a strong government which would insure their interests; that many were wealthy merchants who hoped to advance their commercial interests; that many were slaveholders who wanted their property rights regarding slaves specifically guaranteed.

Beard's thesis was shocking and provocative when it was first published in 1913. He charged that the Constitution was based "upon the concept that the fundamental private rights of property are anterior to government and morally beyond the reach of popular majorities"; that it was "an economic document drawn with superb skill by men whose property interests were immediately at stake"; and that "as such it appealed directly and unerringly to identical interests in the country at large."[16] In time, these pioneering generalizations from Beard's carefully collected data have become part of the conventional wisdom in the literature of American government. No single modern study has been so influential in the interpretation of the Constitution of 1787.

Not all historians and political scientists, however, have been willing to accept all of Beard's economic interpretation. In *The Making of the Constitution*, Charles Warren, a long-time student of our constitutional background, makes a

---

[16]Charles Beard, *An Economic Interpretation of the Constitution of the United States* (New York: The Macmillan Company, 1913).

careful analysis of the daily debates at Philadelphia. On the basis of what was said and how the voting went at the Convention, Warren disagrees with Beard's view that property interests of the members shaped the main outlines of the Constitution.[17]

More recent critics of the economic interpretation, pursuing Beard's own methodology, have arrived at different conclusions. Forrest McDonald, after gathering much new data, especially from the state ratifying conventions, declares that "it is impossible to justify Beard's interpretation."[18] He finds that the delegates in the Convention "behaved as anything but a consolidated group." Furthermore, Beard's thesis that the contest over ratification was between large personal property interests on the one hand and small farming and debtor interests on the other "is entirely incompatible with the facts." Examining the voting records in each of the state conventions, McDonald finds no grounds for Beard's claim that the holding of public securities was a significant factor in ratification. Economic interests were certainly important, but they were not so simply and clearly aligned as Beard claims; the conflicts were too numerous and complicated to assign any single motivating economic force either for or against the Constitution. [19]

Political Strategy at Philadelphia

The critical point for constitutional government in a new nation usually occurs shortly after independence is won. Because first attempts at self-government rarely measure up to popular expectations, the threat of counterrevolution is great and the new government, usually unable to fulfill its promises, is vulnerable to overthrow by military coup or to subversion by one-party dictatorship. This is the now-familiar pattern in contemporary nation-building. The American nationalists, however, managed to dispose of their first constitution and to substitute a more viable system, not by violence or coercive techniques, but rather by masterful political expertise. A small group of dedicated nationalists, supported by a variety of private interests to whom a stronger government meant bread, butter, and more gravy, skillfully pushed for constitutional reform. Actually the politics of the Philadelphia Convention got under way before the delegates were selected in the states. Certainly it was not happenstance that more than half the delegates to the Convention had served or were then serving in Congress, where they developed a nationalist viewpoint.[20]

[17]Charles Warren, *The Making of the Constitution* (Boston: Little, Brown and Company, 1937).

[18]Forrest McDonald, *We the People* (Chicago: The University of Chicago Press, 1958), pp. 350, 357. For still another attack on the Beard thesis, see Robert E. Brown, *Charles Beard and the Constitution* (Princeton: Princeton University Press, 1956).

[19]To exercise your own judgment in this controversy, read what the various members had to say about the role of property in government, the basis of representation, qualifications for franchise, individual liberties, and property rights. Notice that some of the most articulate and colorful delegates in debate were frequently outvoted. Three of those most conspicuous in the proceedings (Randolph and Mason of Virginia and Gerry of Massachusetts) refused to sign. Be sure to take a hard look at the final text of the Constitution. However heated the debates, the cold decision is what counts. See Max Farrand, *The Records of the Federal Convention of 1787* (New Haven: Yale University Press, 1911), 3 vols. Unless otherwise noted, the many quotations in this chapter from the debates in Philadelphia are taken from these records.

[20]For a fresh look at the strategy of the Constitutional Convention of 1787 see John P. Roche, "The Founding Fathers: A Reform Caucus in Action," *American Political Science Review*, LV (December, 1961).

Seventy-four delegates were appointed to the Philadelphia Convention. Nineteen of them never appeared, and of the fifty-five who attended only thirty-nine signed the final document which became the Constitution. On May 14, 1787, the day fixed for the opening session, only Virginia and Pennsylvania were represented. Bad weather and impassable roads made travel exceedingly difficult, especially from New England. But gradually the delegates began to arrive, and a quorum of nine states was obtained on May 29. The Georgia delegates arrived two days later; the Maryland delegates, though close by, did not show up until June 2. The New Hampshire delegates, among the first appointed, were the last to arrive, some time in July. Rhode Island appointed no delegates and boycotted the whole proceeding. The New England representation was small, and only six men stayed on hand to sign the Constitution. The southern delegations were the largest in attendance and the most influential in debate; fourteen southern delegates gave their support to the very end.

The proceedings of the Constitutional Convention were intended to be kept secret. A secretary, Major Jackson, was appointed to keep a record of all the motions and votes cast on them. In order to encourage a spirit of accommodation, the record of voting was kept by states rather than by members; this permitted delegates to change their votes during the course of debate without filling the records with apparent inconsistencies. Convention rules forbade members to make copies of the resolution; after the Convention was over, however, it became apparent that several delegates had spent the evenings transcribing their notes on the daily debates. But during the Convention they saw to it that neither the general public nor even close friends and relatives were informed on the nature of the discussions under way in the State House.

This was probably the most practical way to proceed with the business; once men are forced to defend their positions in public, any compromise tends to appear as a retreat from principle. "Open covenants openly arrived at" makes a better slogan than it does a bylaw. If, in the early weeks of the Convention, the press had been allowed to report the debates, it seems most unlikely that the members would have been able to continue their deliberations until they reached final agreement. Even as it was, the early differences of opinion threatened the success of the Convention. The differences, however, were over structural more than ideological matters. In the main, the delegates, thanks to the politics involved in their appointment, were in fundamental agreement on the main purposes of their business at Philadelphia.

Governor Edmund Randolph, who headed the Virginia delegation, presented fifteen resolutions at the opening session on May 29. These "Virginia Resolutions" proposed substantial changes in the structure of the national government in order to bring it into a direct and functional relationship with the people in the states. The immediate introduction of the Virginia Resolutions was shrewd strategy on the part of the nationalists, for in this way the most important decision of the Convention was induced at the outset, and with little debate; that is, the decision to write an entirely new constitution rather than to tinker with the Articles was implicit in the agreement to use the Virginia Resolutions as the point of departure for discussion. Men like James Madison and James Wilson, nationalists who had done their homework, were obviously well-prepared to defend their positions in logical and learned discourse. The Virginia Resolutions, because they were deliberately extreme and because they were introduced at the very beginning, so shook most delegates' preconceptions that the subsequent and much more moderate federalist proposals seemed relatively feasible. Both the nationalists and their opponents at the Convention were politicians who understood that compromise is the road to consensus. And it was in this frame of mind that they tackled, throughout the summer of 1787, the basic problems of political science: (1) how to strengthen the national identity through a more effective central government and still recognize the diverse and vested interests of the people in the thirteen states; (2) how to establish a republican and democratic government which the people in all the states would accept as both authoritative and representative; (3) how to redesign the political structure so that it could function most vigorously, advancing the national interest, promoting the general welfare, and protecting individual liberties; (4) how to legitimize their own efforts, utilizing existing machinery to obtain consent of the governed to the radically different system of government proposed under the new constitution.

The Basic Problems at the Convention

A more vigorous national government. The Virginia Resolutions proposed a strong consolidated union which, Governor Randolph candidly admitted when he submitted them, was intended to be stronger than any federal government. His plan was to establish a national legislature with two branches: the first branch to be elected directly by all the people, the second to be chosen by the first from a list of persons nominated by the state legislatures. Representation of the states in both houses would be determined by their population or the amount of taxes they paid. This national legislature would retain all the functions that Congress performed under the Confederation and would also be empowered to "legislate in all cases in which the separate states are incompetent or in which the harmony of the United States may be interrupted by the exercise of individual legislation." In addition, the national legislature would have the authority to nullify any law passed by the states that it felt contravened the Constitution, and to call out the full force of the Union against any state that failed to meet its obligations under the Constitution.

The Randolph Plan proposed a modified parliamentary form of government. The national legislature was to choose the national executive for a fixed term. It would also choose the members of the national judiciary, who would hold office "during good behavior." The executive and the judiciary would comprise a "council of revision," with the power to veto all laws, national or state, that it judged to be contrary to the intent of the Constitution. Obviously the doctrine of separation of powers—that is, the independence of the executive, legislative, and judicial branches—had not as yet made much impression on the thinking of Governor Randolph, or of James Madison (who probably had more to do with shaping the plan than the young Governor who had the honor of presenting it).

110

For several weeks the delegates at Philadelphia debated the Randolph Plan. Naturally it was favored by the large states and attacked by the small. Under the Articles all states, whether large or small, enjoyed equal representation in Congress, whereas under the Randolph Plan the more populous states and the wealthier states would have proportionately greater representation in both houses.

On June 15, William Paterson of New Jersey brought in a combination of counterproposals that had been worked up by delegates from Connecticut, New York, New Jersey, and Delaware. Whereas the Randolph Plan had scrapped the Articles in order to set up a strong national government, the Paterson Plan proposed to preserve and strengthen the existing Confederation. The Paterson Plan would add to the powers of the present Congress the authority to regulate commerce among the states, to raise revenue by tariff, and to obtain financial contributions from the states in proportion to the number of citizens. It would also give Congress the power to choose an executive who would serve a single term. It would establish a judiciary, the judges to be appointed by the executive and to serve during good behavior. The "king-pin clause," later to appear in the Constitution, appeared first in the Paterson Plan. This clause made the acts of Congress passed under the Articles and all treaties ratified under the authority of the United States "the supreme law of the respective states and of their citizens anything in the respective laws of the individual states to the contrary notwithstanding."

The Randolph Plan and the Paterson Plan presented the Convention with two clear-cut alternatives: on the one hand to construct a new and strong consolidated union; on the other, to continue a fairly loose association of states—a confederation. Both plans were republican at the national level and at the state level. Under the Randolph Plan, Congress was composed of two houses and each state's representation was to be determined by its population or the amount of taxes it paid to the national government. Under the Paterson Plan, the Congress would remain unicameral, the state legislatures would choose the representatives, and the states would be represented equally. The Randolph Plan would give Congress plenary power to legislate in all matters of national concern affecting the general welfare. The Paterson Plan would give Congress only enumerated powers. Both plans were calculated to strengthen the national government; they differed only in terms of the degree to which it would be strengthened.

The Paterson Plan for a unicameral Congress with equal representation of the states sparked the great debate over whether the United States should become a national union or remain a confederation of states. According to Madison's notes, Colonel George Mason of Virginia declared that "notwithstanding his solicitude to establish a national government, he never would agree to abolish the state governments or render them absolutely insignificant." Luther Martin of Maryland agreed with Colonel Mason on the importance of the state governments: "He would support them at the expense of the general government which was instituted for the purpose of that support."

James Wilson of Pennsylvania advocated the Randolph Plan; he did not think "state governments and state sovereignties to be so much the idol of the People that they are averse to receive a national government." Alexander Hamilton was the most outspoken in denouncing the idea of a mere confederation. He felt that "great economy might be obtained by substituting a general government" for the state governments, though he admitted he would not shock public opinion by pressing for such a drastic measure. James Madison reviewed the history of ancient and modern confederations and found in all of them "the same tendency of the parts to encroach on the authority of the whole"; he begged the smaller states to drop their "pertinacious adherence" to the Paterson Plan.

The text of the Constitution bespeaks for the "great compromise" that was finally worked out between the large and small states. The "more perfect union" is neither a consolidated national government nor a confederation of sovereign states. In the Congress of the United States there are two houses: The House of Representatives represents the people of the states and representation is proportioned to their number; the Senate represents the states as equal political units, and has two senators from each state. And the Constitution provides that equal representation in the Senate cannot be abridged even by constitutional amendment.

A republican and democratic government. The critical issue in 1787 was how to accommodate the thirteen states in the greater context of one nation. Note, however, that the issue was *how to* and not *whether to*. The delegates were in fundamental agreement on the need to strengthen the national government and were nearly unanimous on the desirability of retaining the separate state identities in the federal union. The second issue, less critical at the time but more basic if the new government was to endure, was how to establish authority and to provide for popular participation. Again there was practical consensus that the national government should be established under a constitution, and that it should be republican in form and democratic in action. But several pressing problems were inherent in this second issue: How to count the slaves who then comprised nearly one fifth of the population; whether the frontier farmers should participate in the national government on equal terms with the eastern commercial interests; whether the national elections should be based on national suffrage requirements, and if so, whether the electorate should comprise all citizens or be limited to "freeholders" (property-owners).

For the purpose of establishing proportional representation in the House, it was agreed that "the people" would include the free inhabitants and three-fifths of the slaves in each state. (It was also part of the final compromise to include three-fifths of the slaves in the apportionment of "direct taxes.") There is no moral or logical defense for this compromise. It is simply a formula to which the free and the slave states were willing to agree. Northerners generally thought that the number of free inhabitants was the proper basis of representation, for the northern states had the preponderance of free inhabitants. Southerners generally thought that wealth, particularly wealth invested in slaves, should be counted in apportioning representation—the southern states had the preponderance of slaves. Elbridge Gerry of Massachusetts cynically remarked, "Why then should the blacks, who were property in the South, be in the rule of

112

representation more than the cattle and horses of the North?" Gouverneur Morris of Pennsylvania pointed out that if the Negroes were counted for purposes of representation, the people of Pennsylvania would revolt at the idea of being put on a footing with slaves. In reply, William Davie of North Carolina announced that if the eastern states meant to exclude slaves from representation, "the business was at an end."

A few of the Framers yearned to establish an aristocracy. In the debates on the bicameral legislature, Gouverneur Morris of Pennsylvania argued almost plaintively, "The second branch ought to be composed of men of great and established property—*an aristocracy* . . . . Such an aristocratic body will keep down the turbulence of democracy." As the debates went on, however, it became increasingly evident that Morris' claim for aristocracy was intended to give greater weight in the government to the eastern commercial interests. "He thought the rule of representation ought to be so fixed as to secure to the Atlantic States a prevalence in the National Councils." He was opposed to any rule of representation based on mere numbers, for this would give too much power to the western people: "They will ruin the Atlantic interests. The Back members are always more averse to the best measures." His opposition to counting slave property in apportioning representation can also be interpreted as a reluctance to give the southern states too much power.

The class-consciousness of Gouverneur Morris and his supporters must have seemed shallow and pretentious even to their contemporaries. As Louis Hartz points out in *The Liberal Tradition in America*, would-be aristocrats have always been frustrated in American politics because of "the absence of an aristocracy to fight, the absence of an aristocracy to ally with, and the absence of a mob to denounce."[21] Certainly, in 1787, the gentlemen who debated the Constitution could not look to any *ancien régime* outside the Convention to put up a fight for special privileges. And certainly no angry mobs ever besieged the State House in Philadelphia to force the Framers to form a democratic government.

The Convention attempted to meet the problems of popular participation and of penetration first by providing for direct representation in the House of Representatives and then by giving Congress the power to levy and collect taxes from all the people. The individual with a pocketbook interest in his government (whose leaders he helps to choose) is not so likely to be indifferent to how that government operates. When it came to determining the basis of representation and taxation, everyone agreed that at least all the free inhabitants should be counted. But disagreement arose over what the qualifications of the electorate should be. Only a few of the delegates were willing to trust all the people with the vote. John Dickinson of Delaware urged that the right of suffrage be limited to the freeholders of the country; he felt that such a limitation was a "necessary defense against the dangerous influence of those multitudes without property and without principle, with which our country like all others will in time abound." James Madison of Virginia was inclined

---

[21]Louis Hartz, *The Liberal Tradition in America* (New York: Harcourt, Brace & World, Inc., 1955), p. 96.

to agree with Dickinson, for he too feared the time when "the great majority of the people will not only be without landed, but any other sort, of property." Such people, he argued, were bound to become "the tools of opulence and ambition." The good Dr. Franklin objected, reminding the Convention that "our common people" had displayed much virtue and public spirit during the Revolution, and that he would not disfranchise them for their pains.

Many delegates to the Constitutional Convention showed little feeling for democracy in the modern sense. In protesting against the popular election of legislators, Elbridge Gerry of Massachusetts declared, "The evils we experience flow from the excess of democracy." No doubt Shays' Rebellion in Massachusetts on the eve of the Convention had pointed up the gentleman's fear of "the levilling spirit." On the other hand, James Wilson of Pennsylvania argued that the legislators in the lower house be chosen by popular election, because "he was for raising the federal pyramid to a considerable altitude, and for that reason wished to give it as broad a base as possible." When the work of the Convention was finally done, the delegates had indeed raised the federal pyramid to a considerable height above the general citizenry. "The people" were given a direct part only in the election of the House of Representatives. The Senate was to be chosen indirectly through the state legislatures. The President was to be selected by electoral colleges in the states. The judges were to be appointed by the President, with the confirmation of the Senate.

The delegates failed to reach a compromise on voting qualifications, however, and simply returned the problem to the states. To this day, the Constitution makes no guarantee of the right to national suffrage; whoever has the qualifications to vote for the most numerous house of his state legislature may also vote for United States senators, representatives, and presidential electors.

In assessing the democratic—or aristocratic—intentions of the Framers of the Constitution, keep in mind what they did rather than what they said. Certainly they were not zealots for democracy as we think of democracy today; on the other hand, they did provide for popular participation in the national government, and they did give initial power over the purse—the taxing power—to the House of Representatives. They did enlarge the powers of the national government while carefully limiting these powers by specifically enumerating them; furthermore, they circumscribed in considerable detail the authority of those who were to exercise these powers. As hard-headed politicians they recognized that power is the pivot for all political action. Hamilton put it bluntly: "Men love power. . . . Give all power to the many, they will oppress the few. Give all power to the few, they will oppress the many. Both therefore ought to have power, that each may defend itself [sic] against the other." And for that very reason they worked out their elaborate system of separation of powers and of checks and balances—to protect the country against both "the excesses of democracy" and "the mischief of aristocracy." The great majority of them claimed, whether they believed it or not, that this new country comprised "one great and equal body of citizens." Indeed, members who spoke out boldly for "kingly power" and "natural aristocracy" usually ended up by apologizing for any remarks they may have made that were susceptible to misinterpretation. The Framers were not democratic in the sense that they were ready to offer political power to the masses. Yet they were

114

firmly republican in their principles and determined to establish a strong representative government for the country as a whole.

The Philadelphia Convention was particularly concerned with the problem of legitimate leadership. A revolutionary government which has come to power by overthrowing traditional authority inevitably finds it difficult to secure an effective substitute for the rejected authority. Seymour Lipset, a prominent political sociologist, points out the extraordinary role played in this context by George Washington, who presided over the Constitutional Convention. Lipset suggests that the charismatic leadership of General Washington—"first in war, first in peace, first in the hearts of his countrymen"—successfully bridged the critical years between the revolution against the British king and the constitutional establishment of a strong President.[22] Happily, the Commander-in-Chief of the Revolutionary forces, who was also slated to be the first President of the new republic, was committed to the idea of constitutional government.

Almost all members of the Convention agreed that the new government had to be republican—that is, nonmonarchical—in form. Some may have felt privately that the British monarch was the best model, for this was, after all, the age of monarchy. Only a few years had passed since all the delegates had been pleased to describe themselves as "His Majesty's most faithful subjects." The grievances against the Britsh king spelled out in the Declaration of Independence, however, had made a deep impression on the popular mind. The people were bound to repudiate any plan for a hereditary ruler.

The Randolph Plan provided for a national executive to be chosen by the national legislature. Gouverneur Morris of Pennsylvania opposed this scheme because he thought it would tend to make the President a mere creature of the legislature; he preferred election-at-large by the freeholders of the country. But Mr. Pinckney of South Carolina objected to election by the people on the practical grounds that the most populous states could join in support of one candidate and manage to carry every election. Colonel Mason of Virginia felt it would be "as unnatural to refer the choice of a proper character for chief magistrate to the people, as it would, to refer a trial of colours to a blind man." Not until nearly the end of the Convention was a compromise effected: The President and Vice-President were to be selected by electoral colleges appointed by the states in whatever manner their legislatures might direct. James Wilson of Pennsylvania insisted that this device favored aristocracy, for it meant that the people would have no more than an indirect part in the election. Most of the other members were better pleased with it, though probably none of them was completely satisfied.

Randolph had initially proposed that the President's term of office run for seven years. Dr. McClurg of Virginia moved that the President be permitted to serve "during good behavior"; Morris seconded the motion, announcing that he was indifferent to how the executive was chosen so long as good

[22] *The First New Nation*, p. 18.

behavior determined tenure. Colonel Mason thought that to base tenure on good behavior was but a step away from hereditary monarchy. The final compromise set the President's term at four years, with no restrictions concerning successive terms.

The question of the judiciary provoked comparatively little discussion at the Convention. There was no disagreement on the need for a supreme national court; the establishment of inferior courts was left to the discretion of Congress. The Convention was not persuaded to accept the Randolph proposal for a "council of revision" in which the executive shared with the judges the power to declare national and state laws "unconstitutional." Elbridge Gerry of Massachusetts objected to the idea of "making statesmen of the judges; and setting them up as the guardians of the rights of the people; he relied for his part on the representatives of the people as the guardians of their rights and interests." James Madison argued that, since experience showed the powerful tendency of the legislature "to absorb all power into its vortex," it was necessary to give "every defensive authority to the other departments that was consistent with republican principles." Whether the Convention meant to give the courts the power of judicial review—the power to declare acts of the legislature or of the executive unconstitutional—is uncertain, for they did not write their intentions regarding this matter into the document itself.

Following Beard's model (discussed earlier), many writers have attempted to demonstrate that the Constitution was essentially an economic instrument for the protection of property and the promotion of commerce. To support this interpretation they have emphasized the several specific provisions dealing with the public debt, taxation, commerce, sound money, bankruptcy and obligations of contract, weights and measures, patents and copyrights, post offices and post roads. This emphasis is somewhat misleading, however, for the delegates to the Convention spent considerably more time debating problems of governmental structure—the relation of the states to the Union and to one another; the separation of powers (executive, legislative, and judicial); and the check and balance of these powers—than questions of governmental functions. The Constitution's treatment of the enumerated powers of Congress and the functions of the national government seems incomplete, oddly deficient, even deliberately ambiguous. Many special powers were suggested during the course of debate, such as the authority of Congress to create corporations, but apparently they were struck out in order to make the document politically palatable. If serious objection was raised to any one provision, it was usually omitted—and the argument postponed to future congresses—in the interest of promoting agreement on the general plan of the Constitution.

The most spirited debate on the functions of the national government focused on the power of Congress over foreign commerce. The southern states, whose economy depended on agricultural exports, feared that the northern states might succeed in levying taxes on exports to the disadvantage of the South. Colonel Mason of Virginia stated the problem clearly: "A majority when interested will oppress the minority." If the interest of the eight northern states was recognizably different from that of the five southern states, the southern states had good reason to be suspicious. Pierce Butler of South Carolina strenuously opposed giving the national government power to tax exports as "unjust and alarming to the stable states." The upshot was that an explicit limitation on Congress was put into the Constitution: "no tax or duty shall be laid on articles exported from any state." Northern business interests were pleased, however, by a provision that granted Congress the power to tax *imports*, for they felt that this would enable them to throw up a tariff wall behind which new manufacturers could prosper.

Perhaps what disturbed the southern delegates most was the possibility that, if the national government were granted power over foreign commerce, the northern states might try to prohibit the slave trade. Mr. Pinckney of South Carolina vehemently attacked every proposal for extending the power of Congress in this matter; his state was "expressly and watchfully" opposed to any "meddling with the importation of negroes." Colonel Mason of Virginia, attributing "this infernal traffic" to the "avarice of British merchants" and to the "lust of gain" of "some of our Eastern brethren," believed it "essential in every point of view that the general government should have the power to prevent the increase of slavery." Because Virginia already had more than enough slaves, its delegates could therefore afford to be moral concerning this issue while the delegates from South Carolina and Georgia, which still had a pressing need for cheap labor, could not. John Rutledge of South Carolina warned the Convention that the people of South Carolina and Georgia would never be such fools as to give up so important an interest. The final decision was an attempted compromise between morality and economics: Congress was not to prohibit the slave trade before 1808 but could levy a head tax of ten dollars on all slaves imported into the states until that time.

The most complete and detailed powers retained in the Constitution were those dealing with war, for the imminent danger of foreign aggression induced the delegates to give ample authority to the central government as a fighting organization. The Constitution grants the national government almost absolute authority in time of war. Even the writ of habeas corpus may be suspended when the country is threatened by insurrection or invasion. The only concession the Convention made to the widespread yearning for peace—in 1787 the people were tired of war and its chaotic aftermath—is the clause that forbids Congress to make any appropriation for the army for a term longer than two years.

The Fight for Ratification. The work of the Convention ended on September 17, 1787. Dr. Franklin rose to urge all "for our own sakes and for the sake of posterity" to act "heartily and unanimously" in recommending the Constitution. Three members who stayed to the end, though they confessed that they were "painfully embarrassed," declined to sign the document—Governor Randolph, Colonel Mason, and Mr. Gerry. Thirty-nine delegates, representing twelve states, did affix their names.

Three members of the Convention—James Madison of Virginia, Rufus King and Nathaniel Gorham of Massachusetts—were also members of Congress, and they immediately carried the document to New York City, where Congress was in session. On September 28, 1787, without making any recommendation of its own, Congress submitted the proposed Constitution to the states.

How to legitimize the result of the Philadelphia Convention was a rather delicate problem. In writing a new constitution, the delegates had clearly exceeded their authority—which was simply to propose amendments to the Articles of Confederation. Since the members of both Congress and of the state legislatures were sworn to the "perpetual union" under the Confederation, they could hardly vote to scrap the Articles. Even before the Convention had met, James Madison had written to Thomas Jefferson that he felt it expedient "to lay the foundation of the new system in such a ratification by the people themselves as will render it clearly paramount to their legislative authority."

In the Convention itself, some of the members demurred at departing from the amending procedure outlined in the Articles, which demanded the unanimous consent of the state legislatures. The complete absence of a Rhode Island delegation at the Convention, however, made unanimity out of the question. Moreover, as Madison pointed out, because the powers that the Constitution granted to the general government had been taken mainly from the state legislatures, the legislatures might decide to reject the document. To refer the document to state conventions elected for the express purpose of considering the new Constitution seemed a feasible solution. And so the Convention decided that the Constitution would be "ordained and established" when nine state conventions had ratified it. Certainly the legitimacy of the proposed new government could only be enhanced by popular participation in the ratification procedure.

Conventions called by the state legislatures in Delaware, Pennsylvania, New Jersey, and Georgia swiftly and unanimously adopted the new Constitution. The debate in other states was more prolonged and the voting, in some instances, was very close. It is hard for us now, looking back over the years, to analyze the climate of public opinion during the fight for ratification. Propaganda for and against the new Constitution took many forms: pamphlets, editorials, letters to newspapers, caricatures, handbills, and platform lectures. Probably the most important single contribution to the literature of American political theory, and also the most effective piece of propaganda in the program to explain and justify the proposed Constitution, was *The Federalist (The Federalist Papers)*, which first appeared as a series of letters in the press explaining and defending the Constitution to the people of New York. The three authors, Alexander Hamilton, John Jay, and James Madison (writing under the name of "*Publius*"), while careful not to reject the popular doctrines of natural rights, individual freedom, and popular participation, argued a skillfully wrought case for a strong national government, limitations on the powers of the states, and "stability in government." Madison wrote to his father that *The Federalist* was "the best commentary on the principles of government which was ever written."

The Federalist certainly had an influence on the New York convention. Later, when the letters were collected in book form, they were effectively used in the Virginia campaign as well. They made a particularly strong impression on John Marshall, who was fighting for ratification in the Virginia convention; not many years later, as Chief Justice of the Supreme Court, Marshall referred frequently to *The Federalist* in citing the intentions of the Framers of the Constitution. We must bear in mind, however, that *The Federalist* was not an impartial exposition of the original Constitution, for it was first published as a piece of electioneering. We must also remember that during the campaign for ratification a great deal was said and written in opposition to the proposed Constitution. But, because most of this material never found its way into book form, and because it championed the losing side, it has disappeared while *The Federalist* has lived on.

As counterpropaganda to *The Federalist*, for example, "Agrippa" (James Winthrop) wrote in the *Massachussets Gazette*, "The question before the people is whether they will have a limited government or an absolute one. . . . It is the opinion of the ablest writers on this subject that no extensive empire can be governed upon republican principles and that such a government will degenerate to a despotism unless it be made up of a confederacy of smaller states each having the full powers of internal regulation." And "Cato" (Governor Clinton) warned the people of New York to beware "the proferred constitution of Caesar" which denies the doctrine of separation of powers and gives authority to the President that is too vast and important for any one man without limited tenure. "Sidney" (Robert Yates) argued in the *New York Journal* that the new Constitution would "destroy the rights and liberties of the people."[23]

The opponents of the proposed Constitution hammered away at its most conspicuous weakness: the absence of a bill of rights. This omission was especially glaring in view of the fact that eight of the new state constitutions contained separate bills of rights, and three guaranteed fundamental liberties within the main text. And yet, until the very end of the Philadelphia Convention, no one had mentioned the idea of a bill of rights. Even after it had been suggested, none of the members showed much interest. Later, James Wilson explained to the Pennsylvania ratifying convention that a "Bill of Rights is neither essential nor a necessary instrument in framing a system since liberty may exist and be as well secured without it." Charles C. Pinckney told the South Carolina convention that the Framers had hesitated to enumerate specific rights lest it be construed that the government could take away any rights that were not enumerated; but he also candidly admitted that a bill of rights generally begins with a declaration that all men are born free and equal, and that the members of the Philadelphia Convention felt they could not honestly make such a statement in that "a large part of our property consists in men who are actually born slaves."

The arguments of the Framers, however logical, were not convincing. The Framers had thought that the principle of separation of powers combined with an ingenious system of checks and balances and the enumeration of the specific powers of the central government were sufficient safeguards against tyranny. But the majority of the citizens believed they were entitled to a bill of rights and that no just government "should refuse or rest on inference." The New York, Massachusetts, and Virginia conventions agreed to ratify the new Constitution only after receiving the solemn promise of its advocates that it

---

[23] The primary source for the fight over ratification is Jonathan Elliot, *The Debates in the Several State Conventions and the Adoption of the Federal Constitution* (Philadelphia: J. B. Lippincott Co., 1888).

would immediately be amended to include a bill of rights as part of the supreme law of the land.

The fight over ratification was in part a sectional one: The eastern seaboard and the tidewater south were generally in favor; westerners were inclined to be suspicious and doubtful. Economic lines were rather roughly drawn: Merchants and bankers, slaveholders and persons of property were more often in favor of ratification than were the small farmers, shopkeepers, mechanics, and debtors. But the contending groups were not solid blocs: There were both advocates and opponents of the proposed Constitution in every state, in every community, among all classes. Gentlemen of property and learning participated in the debate on both sides. Samuel Eliot Morison, concludes, "The only generalization that can stand the test of fact is that the cleavage was one of age against youth. . . . The warmest advocates were eager young men."[24]

At the level of practical politics, the nationalists, outside of Virginia, seemed to have a near monopoly on effective leadership. With the same political finesse that secured them their delegations to the Philadelphia Convention in the first place, the proponents of the Constitution skillfully succeeded in garnering support. On the other hand, except for pointing out the need for a bill of rights, the opponents had little to offer of constructive value; their objections were vague suspicions rather than specific dissents. But however it was achieved, the important fact is that a majority of the conventions in nine states were persuaded to approve the new Constitution.

On September 17, 1788, Congress resolved to put the new Constitution into effect. The first Wednesday in January, 1789, was fixed for choosing the presidential electors; the first Wednesday in March for the opening session of the first Congress under the Constitution and on April 20, 1789, George Washington was inaugurated as the first President of the United States.

"Intentions of the Framers"

Students of American government have extended and re-examined the "intentions" of the Framers.[25] While conducting such an examination we must remember, however, that not even the official records of the Convention are absolutely dependable. At the end of the Convention, the secretary was instructed to turn over his notes and the official journal to the presiding chairman. In 1796, President Washington deposited this material with the State Department, observing at the time that the notes had been imperfectly kept, some pages of the journal were loose, other papers were missing, and the whole was in disorder. In 1819, following the instructions of Congress, Secretary of State John Quincy Adams worked over the official notes and the journal of the Convention to prepare them for publication, at the same time writing letters to James Madison and Charles Pinckney asking them to check their records and recollections of what had happened. In the meantime, the autobiographies and memoirs of the Founding Fathers were beginning to appear in print, offering variations on "the Philadelphia story." Even as early as Washington's administration, men who had participated either

---

[24]*The Oxford History of the American People*, p. 313.
[25]See William Anderson, "The Intention of the Framers," *American Political Science Review*, XLIX (June, 1955), 340–352.

in the framing of the Constitution or in its ratification were voicing conflicting interpretations. The authors of *The Federalist*—Jay, Hamilton, and Madison—soon parted company in the political battles that arose during the early years of the Republic.

Compared with the Declaration of Independence, which only a decade before had boldly proclaimed to all mankind the doctrine of revolution, the Constitution of 1787 seems almost reactionary. But judgments of this kind—"revolutionary" or "reactionary," "liberal" or "conservative"—depend largely on the frame of reference. In the age of monarchy, the Framers established in the New World a republican, representative government on a scale hitherto unventured at any time, in any place. True, some were apprehensive of popular government, but their view of human nature made them distrustful of all men in office. Their major concern was to prevent despotism and to check tyranny, whether by one man, by a few people, or by the masses.

Separation of powers combined with checks and balances may seem to us a deliberate barricade against majority rule, but the "enlightened patrons of liberty" in the eighteenth century believed otherwise. All the state constitutions, including those written at the peak of the Revolutionary fervor, embodied this fundamental principle. The Massachusetts Constitution, adopted in 1780 by statewide referendum, spells it out most clearly because the Massachusetts voters had rejected an earlier draft that did not provide adequate checks and balances. Federalists and Antifederalists were agreed on the principle of separation of powers—both Adams and Jefferson vigorously defended it. All the delegates to the Convention of 1787 seem to have taken the principle for granted; only Franklin and Hamilton showed opposition, and these two were poles apart in their perspective on popular government. Madison, in *The Federalist*, refers to separation of powers as "this essential precaution in favor of liberty" and as "the sacred maxim of free goverment."

Whether we should consider the Constitutional Convention more conservative than the Second Continental Congress depends in part on which documents we have in mind. If we compare the Articles of Confederation with the Constitution, we note a considerable progress in notions of democratic government between 1776 and 1787.[26] Under the Articles, the people had no feeling of participation in the central government, largely because members of the unicameral Congress were chosen in the state legislatures. The Constitution of 1787 gave the people direct representation in Congress in proportion to their numbers in each state, a novel feature in the history of federalism. Although the executive was not to be popularly elected, Madison explains in *The Federalist* that "it was desirable that the sense of the people should operate in the choice of the person to whom so important a trust was to be confided." If we accept Madison's explanation, the electoral college was not undemocratic in conception; on the contrary, it was designed to give the people in the states a more active role in determining the leadership of the national government. As to

---

[26]For a discerning study of democratic ideology from 1776 to 1787, see Wright, *Consensus and Continuity*, "Was the Constitution Reactionary?", pp. 40–60.

the appointment of the federal judges, that was simply following prevailing practice in the states. The idea of electing judges as part of democracy is a nineteenth century innovation.

That the Framers considered the issue of individual liberties is evidenced by specific provisions in the original text protecting the individual against being held for a crime without cause (writ of habeas corpus), punished for an act that was not illegal when it was performed (ex post facto law), singled out for punishment by an act of Congress (that is, being punished by bill of attainder), or convicted of treason except for offenses and by procedures spelled out in the Constitution. True, the Constitution did not grant national suffrage, but neither did it impose suffrage restrictions, as some members had urged. And the Constitution, as approved, did prohibit religious tests for any office or public trust under the United States, though such tests were common in the state governments. It seems fair to conclude that the omission of a more complete bill of rights was a tactical error, not a sinister calculation. Significantly, James Madison, who had been most conspicuous in the Convention, took the lead in the First Congress to secure a bill of rights.

The articles were never submitted to the people; they went into effect as soon as all the state legislatures had approved them. In contrast, the Constitution was approved in state conventions popularly elected for the purpose of considering ratification. (The election of these state conventions constituted the only national referendum in our political experience until voters in 1933 elected conventions to consider ratification of the Twenty-first Amendment.) The Articles could only be amended by consent of all the state legislatures. Certainly the Constitution was much more liberal in its provisions for changes.

From the vantage point of the present day, the Constitution of 1787 seems undemocratic in many respects: Separation of powers, checks and balances, indirect elections of the President, indirect election of senators, appointment of judges for life tenure contingent on good behavior, the presidential veto, and judicial review. But in the context of the times, the very idea of writing a constitution, with the consent of the whole people, guaranteeing a republican form of government in every state, providing for the direct election of representatives in the national government, and limiting the powers both of the national government and of the states was indeed most remarkable. Whether strengthening the national government was more democratic or less democratic in tendency is an argument that still rages. But over the years, the greatest concern for civil liberties and human rights has been manifested in the national government rather than in the states or local communities in general.

Several incidents indicate that the Framers themselves could not agree on what "intentions" they had expressed in the Constitutional Convention. When, for example, President Washington approached the Supreme Court in 1793 for advice on questions of international law that had arisen as a result of the French Revolution, Chief Justice John Jay informed the erstwhile Chairman of the Convention that the Framers had not intended the judiciary to furnish advisory opinions to the executive. In 1796, Alexander Hamilton and James Madison took opposite sides in the constitutional debate over a treaty negotiated by their former collaborator in *The Federalist Papers,* John Jay. The House precipitated the issue by refusing President Washington's request for appropri-

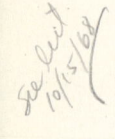

122

ations to implement the treaty. Hamilton and Chief Justice Ellsworth, both of whom had helped shape the decisions at Philadelphia, advised the President that the House was under a constitutional obligation to appropriate funds to carry out the treaty. James Madison, "Father of the Constitution," disagreed, arguing that the Constitution did not make the House a rubber-stamp for international commitments made by the executive. And so the arguments continued, the meaning of the Constitution following the party battles of the period.

James Madison, who had kept voluminous notes at the Convention, apparently went back over his papers from time to time, making additions and alterations. Without impugning his integrity, we may say that his memory over the years seems to have been somewhat influenced by the partisan politics in which he played so energetic a part. Madison's *Notes on the Convention* were not published until 1840, a few years after his death. Because they are the most detailed record we have of the proceedings, they have come to be regarded as also the most authentic. And yet we might do well to recall Madison's own warning following the publication of the official *Journal:*

> As a guide in expounding and applying the provisions of the Convention, the debates and incidental decisions of the Convention can have no authoritative character. However desirable it be that they should be preserved as a gratification to the laudable curiosity felt by every people to trace the origin and progress of their political institutions, and as a source perhaps on the science of government, the legitimate meaning of the Instrument must be derived from the text itself; or if a key is to be sought elsewhere, it must be not in the opinions or intentions of the Body which planned and proposed the Constitution, but in the sense attached to it by the people in their respective State Conventions when it received all the authority which it possesses.

Madison's advice holds good today; constitutional law begins with the living text of the Constitution, not with the proceedings of the Convention that were kept secret at the time and that remain ambiguous to this very day.

We cannot regard the Constitution merely as a monument to the memory of the Founding Fathers. A constitution, if it is to be the organic law of the people and not merely a holy relic, must grow and change with the country, for it reflects as much as it determines the political relations among the people. The American Constitution is the oldest written constitution in the world. The constitutional histories of France and America span nearly the same period of time; but while we have been able to keep our Constitution in relatively good working order, the French have tried and discarded fourteen different constitutions. That the work of the Framers has stood the test of time so well may in part be attributed to their own doubts and dissatisfactions. None of them wholly approved the Constitution they finally proposed. All hoped and anticipated that suitable changes would be made later on. That is why they made sure that the new Constitution would be far more flexible than the old Articles of Confederation.

New Intentions and New Framers

When the final draft of the Constitution was read to the Convention in 1787, Benjamin Franklin expressed the general sentiments of those who signed it:

The Constitutional Amendments

> I doubt whether any other Convention we can obtain may be able to make a better Constitution. For when you assemble a number of men to have the advantage of their joint wisdom, you inevitably assemble with those men, all their prejudices, their passions, their errors of opinion, their local interests, and their selfish views.

Franklin was willing to sign, not because he thought the Convention had designed a perfect instrument of government, but because he thought that the members had done the best they could under the circumstances. No one who signed was entirely satisfied. It was for this very reason that they had written a flexible constitution, one that could be changed fairly easily.

The Framers provided two methods for proposing amendments to the Constitution and two for ratifying them. An amendment may be proposed either by a two-thirds vote in both houses of Congress or by a national convention called by Congress at the request of the legislatures of two-thirds of the states. An amendment may be ratified by approval of either three-fourths of the state legislatures or by three-fourths of special state conventions. All the amendments except one (the Twenty-first) have been adopted by approval of the state legislatures.

Despite the belief of Jefferson and other early leaders that every generation should call a national convention for general constitutional revision, the method of proposing amendments through a national convention has never been used. In the mid-1960s, however, Everett Dirksen, long-time Republican leader in the U.S. Senate, was urging state legislatures to petition Congress to call a constitutional convention for the express purpose of nullifying recent Supreme Court decisions that had forced reapportionment in some state legislatures. The proposal appealed to proponents of "states rights" and especially to many state legislators who had a vested interest in resisting reapportionment. Within a surprisingly brief time the "Dirksen Amendment" was endorsed by thirty-two state legislatures, just two short of the Constitutional requirement of two-thirds of the state legislatures. The specific intent of Dirksen's proposal was to restore the right of each state to apportion one of its legislative houses on the basis of geography or of political criteria, regardless of population distribution. But once a national Constitutional convention comes into being there is no assurance that it will restrict its activities to a narrow cause or a single amendment. The Convention of 1787, for instance, totally disregarded its instructions merely to amend the Articles and decided to write a new constitution. As the prospects of a national constitutional convention became more real in 1967, warnings arose that such a convention might tamper with the Bill of Rights, modify the pattern of federalism, or alter the system of checks and balances. Thus popular enthusiasm waned as people were alerted to what might be involved in "returning to the faith of the Fathers" or in "updating to modern needs."

In *The Federalist*, Alexander Hamilton indicated that some zealots would have amended the Constitution even before it was established. In any event, twelve amendments were adopted in the first fifteen years of the Republic. The Framers themselves were willing, even eager, to make changes in the original document. Professor William Munro in his study of *The Makers of the Unwritten Constitution* remarks that "it would be difficult to find, at any stage in American history, a group of men more benevolently inclined toward amendments than were the Fathers themselves."[27] Indeed, subsequent generations have added only thirteen amendments to the twelve that were adopted before 1804. All told, although some 5,000 amendments have been introduced in Congress only thirty-one of these have been submitted to the states and only twenty-five have been ratified by the required three-fourths of the states.

Drawing by Herblock;
© 1967 The Washington Post.

Pandora Project

The Constitution puts only two restrictions on amendments. One of these, which relates to the slave trade, has long been obsolete. The second is still in force, for no state may be deprived of its equal suffrage in the Senate. Otherwise, there is no restriction on the content or substance of amendments. Congress specifies whether ratification of any one amendment shall be by state legislatures or by state conventions. A state is not free to substitute any other mode of ratification; when Ohio submitted the Eighteenth Amendment to the direct vote of the people, the United States Supreme Court held that the Ohio legislature had no authority to delegate its constitutional obligations.[28] Congress may also fix a time limit on ratification; if Congress does not choose to fix "a reasonable time," then the states are free to approve at any later date.

The most conspicuous weakness of the original Constitution was the deliberate omission of a bill of rights. The fight for ratification pivoted on this point

---

[27] W. B. Munro, *The Makers of the Unwritten Constitution* (New York: The Macmillan Company, 1930), p. 5.
[28] *Hawke* v. *Smith*, 253 U.S. 221 (1920).

in both the New York and the Virginia conventions, which were finally persuaded to approve the Constitution only with the understanding that it would be immediately amended to include the traditional guarantees of private rights and personal liberties. Consequently, the first session of Congress almost at once proposed twelve amendments in the form of a Bill of Rights. Three-fourths of the states forthwith ratified ten of these proposals, and they at once became an integral part of the Constitution.

The Bill of Rights guarantees the free exercise of religion, freedom of speech and of the press, rights of assembly and petition (Amendment I); the right of the people to keep and bear arms (II); protection against quartering of soldiers in private homes (III); protection against "unreasonable searches and seizures" of persons, houses, papers, and effects (IV); procedures protecting the rights of persons accused of a crime, and "due process of law" with respect to life, liberty, and property (V); further rights of the accused, including trial by jury and the right to counsel (VI); provisions for trial by jury in civil cases (VII); prohibition of excessive bail or fines or cruel and unusual punishments (VIII); the reserved rights of the people beyond those enumerated (IX); the reserved powers of the states (X).

The first eight amendments spell out individual rights and liberties, but the Ninth Amendment clearly states that this enumeration must not be regarded as complete and exclusive. One proposed amendment—which James Madison, its sponsor, declared to be "the most valuable of the whole list"—was rejected by the Senate. It read as follows: "The equal rights of conscience, the freedom of speech or of the press, and the right of trial by jury in criminal cases shall not be infringed by any state." The first nine amendments were regarded as restrictions on the national government—"Congress shall make no law. . . ." This one would have placed restrictions on the states. But the state legislatures were not yet willing to accept such specific restrictions on state power from the outside, although the state constitutions included similar provisions.[29]

The Framers of the Constitution of 1787 *created* a new government, "a more perfect union." Accordingly, their main concerns were, on the one hand, to establish the basic pattern of the central government and to give it specified powers and, on the other hand, to restrict the states in certain areas where supreme national authority seemed necessary and proper. The addition of the Bill of Rights was in essence Part II of the Constitution. Part I, the Constitution of 1787, establishes the new government; Part II, the Bill of Rights, applies restraints to the government, particularly in its relations with individual persons.

Ironically, in view of the furor over the Framers' omission of a bill of rights, American civil rights were hardly at issue until after the Civil War. As Ray Forrester, Dean of the Law School at Tulane University, points out, "before the Civil War not one great case is to be found in the Supreme Court under the First Amendment—the amendment which many regard as the keystone of our society as well as of our Constitution."[30] But constitutional conflicts may be settled by agencies of government other than the Supreme Court. For example,

---

[29]For an authoritative analysis and interpretation of the Constitution of 1787 and its amendments, see *The Constitution of the United States of America*, prepared by the Legislative Reference Service, Library of Congress, Norman J. Small (ed.) (Washington, D.C.: Government Printing Office, 1964).

[30]Ray Forrester, *Constitutional Law* (St. Paul, Minn.: West Publishing Co., 1959), p. 533.

a serious problem relating to the First Amendment was posed by the Sedition Act of 1798. This was the Act that called forth the Virginia and Kentucky Resolutions, in which Madison and Jefferson challenged the whole doctrine of national supremacy. In the election of 1800, the Jeffersonian Republicans attributed the consequent abridgment of individual rights to the deterioration of states' rights and won a great victory at the polls. In the short period that the Sedition Act was on the federal statute books, some 70 persons, mostly vociferous Republican editors, were jailed and fined. But before any of them had time to appeal to the Supreme Court, the Jefferson Administration moved to free all who had been jailed, returned all the fines collected under the Act, and suffered the Act itself to expire without mourning. Not until 1940, with the passage of the Smith Act, did the federal government again in peacetime attempt to legislate against "sedition."

In the period before the Civil War, the most important decision of the Supreme Court affecting basic federal relations in the area of civil rights was *Barron* v. *Baltimore* (1833). In this early case, Chief Justice John Marshall interpreted the Bill of Rights as referring only to the national government. Barron, a citizen of Baltimore, thought he had been deprived of his property without just compensation when the city had destroyed the usefulness of his wharf while grading the streets. Barron brought suit for damages in federal court. The Supreme Court held that the suit was improper in a federal court since the Fifth Amendment restrained only the national government and was not applicable to the states or their local governments.[31]

After the Civil War, however, the Thirteenth and Fourteenth Amendments extended national guarantees of civil rights into the states themselves. The Thirteenth Amendment forbids slavery or involuntary servitude any place in the United States. The Fourteenth, an extremely complicated amendment, has been the subject of seemingly endless litigation in the courts. It defines United States citizenship in accordance with the English principle of *jus soli*—place of birth: "All persons born or naturalized in the United States, and subject to the jurisdiction thereof, are citizens of the United States and of the state wherein they reside." The Framers of the Constitution had deliberately omitted any such definition of citizenship, no doubt because they had so recently been subjects of His British Majesty. The Fourteenth Amendment also forbids the states to abridge "the privileges or immunities of citizens of the United States," but the Amendment does not set forth in detail just what these privileges and immunities are. Finally the Amendment prohibits the states from depriving "any person of life, liberty, or property without due process of law," and from denying to "any person within its jurisdiction the equal protection of the laws."[32]

National Power and States' Rights

The debates between the proponents of strong nationalism and the advocates of states' rights were sometimes sharp at the Philadelphia Convention, but they became even sharper dur-

[31]*Barron* v. *Baltimore*, 7 Pet. 243 (1833).
[32]For further discussion of individual rights and judicial review see Chapter 14.

ing the fight for ratification. To allay any fear that the national government might use the new Constitution to absorb the states, the Tenth Amendment provides that, "The powers not delegated to the United States by the Constitution, nor prohibited by it to the states, are reserved to the states respectively, or to the people."

What did the Tenth Amendment actually add to the Constitution? Supporters of national power and advocates of states' rights have always answered this question differently. The answer in terms of government practice, however, has generally favored national power. And the evidence indicates that the framers of the Amendment themselves merely intended to reaffirm the principle of federalism implicit in the original text of the Constitution—that the national government has delegated powers and the states have reserved powers. When the Amendment was drafted in 1789, Congress voted down an attempt to insert the word "expressly" before the word "delegated." Apparently, then, the framers did not mean to limit national power only to those powers expressly delegated.

A new undeveloped nation, emerging from colonialism, is bound to pressure its government for economic assistance. The first new nation was no exception. As Lipset points out, Washington's administration, especially the Treasury Department under Alexander Hamilton, was greatly concerned with promoting industry and manufacturing through a national tariff in accordance with the commerce clauses of the Constitution. Although the Constitution gives Congress no express power over banking, the First Congress (the same Congress that sponsored the Tenth Amendment) established a national bank to carry on the financial business of the national government. True, the Federalists were in control of the Congress that established the first Bank of the United States and they were exponents of strong central power, but years later, when the anti-Federalists were in control of Congress, they in turn set up the second Bank of the United States, even though they were exponents of states' rights. Finally, Chief Justice John Marshall, in the famous case of *McCulloch v. Maryland* (1819), upheld the right of Congress to create a national bank as an "implied power."[33] Under this doctrine, Congress may employ whatever powers are "convenient and useful" in carrying out any powers delegated to the national government. What is "convenient and useful," of course, changes with the times.[34]

The Eleventh Amendment was adopted in 1798 as a special concession to the sensibilities of the anti-Federalists and states' rights partisans of the period. It protects states from being sued in federal courts by citizens of other states. In 1793, the Supreme Court had permitted a private citizen, named Chisholm, to sue the state of Georgia. Article III of the Constitution had extended the judicial power of the national government to controversies "between a state and citizens of another state. . . ." This was probably no more than a stylistic error; it is doubtful that the Convention contemplated such presumption and effrontery as appeared in the person of Chisholm! Indeed during the debates over ratification in 1787, when the anti-Federalists pointed out that under the judicial article an individual could hale a state into a federal court, the Federalists replied that of course no "sovereign state" would ever be sued without its

[33] *McCullock v. Maryland*, 4 Wheat. 316 (1819).
[34] For expansion of this section see especially Chapter 15, "General Welfare and Common Defense."

consent. When Chisholm dared to sue the "sovereign state" of Georgia, all the states were so indignant that Congress moved with "vehement speed" to prevent subsequent affronts to the dignity of states.[35] More than the dignity of a sovereign state was probably at issue, however. When the Eleventh Amendment was proposed, many states were in financial difficulties and had defaulted on their debts. The states could therefore use the new amendment not only in defense of theoretical sovereignty but also, in a more practical way, to forestall suits by individual creditors.

In conclusion, one can say that the Framers of the Tenth and Eleventh Amendments to the Constitution made no great alteration in the principles of federalism laid down in the original document. The national government has powers expressly granted and it also has any implied powers that are "necessary and proper" in carrying out its delegated powers. The states have reserved powers—all powers that are not granted explicitly or implicitly to the national government and that are not denied to the states. The states are also entitled to respect in the federal union and cannot be sued by individuals in the federal courts.

Democratizing the Constitution

The problem of popular participation has been a continuing crisis in American politics. Since 1787, eight Amendments to the Constitution have very considerably broadened the political basis of the national government.

The Twelfth Amendment (1804) provides that the electoral colleges must cast separate ballots for President and Vice-President. This change in itself is not very significant, but it shows how the Constitution must be kept abreast of changing conditions—in this case, the emergence of a national party system, something the original Framers had not anticipated. The Framers specified that in presidential elections the candidate with the highest number of votes (provided it were a majority) would become President; if there were a tie, or if no one received a majority, the decision would go to the House of Representatives. The candidate with the second highest number of votes would become Vice-President; if there were a tie, the decision would go to the Senate. In 1800, Thomas Jefferson was the Republican Party's candidate for President and Aaron Burr the party's candidate for Vice-President. When the members of the electoral college cast their votes, each Republican elector voted for both men. As a result, Jefferson and Burr tied for first place. The House, in which the Federalists still held a majority, almost prevented the popular choice from taking office; it took thirty-six ballots to give the presidency to Jefferson. In order to prevent this sort of thing from happening again, the Twelfth Amendment was adopted before the next election came around.

Although the Twelfth Amendment made only a slight change in procedure, its adoption was necessary because of a development of fundamental impor-

---

[35]*Chisholm* v. *Georgia*, 2 Dall. 419 (1793).

tance—the rise of political parties as agencies "democratizing" the choice of the President. National party conventions now nominate candidates for President and Vice-President. The people themselves now vote for the members of the electoral colleges, and in each state these electors are morally pledged if still not legally bound, to cast their votes for the candidates named by their respective party conventions. The electoral college has thus become an automatic voting machine in which the electors simply record, state by state, the peoples' choice of party candidates. Although the electoral college system is still far from accurate in recording popular preferences, political parties have succeeded in turning it into a basically democratic device for majority rule.

We must mention here, however, that the Twelfth Amendment has itself generated certain changes. For instance, as its opponents predicted, it tended to minimize the role of the Vice-President. The first two Vice-Presidents of the United States, who were elected before the Amendment was passed, were men of such stature that they later moved on to the presidency in their own right. Following the passage of the Amendment, only one Vice-President, Martin Van Buren, became President without succeeding to the office through the death of the elected President.

The Fifteenth (1870), Nineteenth (1920), Twenty-third (1960) and Twenty-fourth (1964) Amendments have promoted universal suffrage, the very thing that many of the Framers feared the most. The Fifteenth, adopted after the Civil War, forbids any restriction of suffrage on the basis of race, color, or previous condition of servitude. The Nineteenth, ratified after World War I, forbids any restriction of suffrage on the basis of sex. And yet, even with these amendments, the Constitution does not give Negroes and women the right to vote, for the federal Constitution grants no rights of suffrage at all. The states themselves still decide on qualifications for voting, and these vary considerably from one state to another. All that the Fifteenth and Nineteenth Amendments say is that no state may deprive any person of the right to vote because of race, color, or sex.

The Twenty-third Amendment allows citizens of the District of Columbia to vote in presidential elections. The District of Columbia is entitled to the number of presidential electors assigned the least populous state (three). The electors meet in the District and cast their ballots for President and Vice-President in the same manner as presidential electors in each of the states. As originally introduced, the Amendment also gave the District a nonvoting delegate in the House of Representatives, but to expedite ratification this provision was dropped before the Amendment went to the states. Some opposition came from race-conscious southerners—a majority of the population of the District is Negro. Some Republicans were also wary that this move might put three more votes into the Democratic column of presidential electors, since the Negro vote is overwhelmingly Democratic. But national sentiment in favor of a vote for all Americans produced ratification in the record time of 286 days (repeal of the Prohibition Amendment took 288 days).

The Twenty-fourth Amendment provides that "the right of citizens of the United States to vote in any primary or other election for President or Vice President, for electors for President or Vice President, or for Senator or Representative in Congress, shall not be denied or abridged by the United States or any state by reason of failure to pay any poll tax or other tax." This Amendment affected only five southern states in which a poll tax was still a prerequisite for voting. The tax had long since lost whatever effectiveness it may have had, when first adopted, as a means of disfranchising southern Negroes and poor whites,[36] so the Amendment may be regarded as a "cleaning-up" operation in affirming the national principle of universal suffrage. It was not expected to produce basic changes in the peculiar political order of the South. Indeed, any state which insists on placing a price tag on the vote is free under the Amendment to retain the poll tax as a requirement for voting in elections of local and state officials.

The Seventeenth Amendment (1913) provides for the popular election of senators. Originally the Constitution stipulated that senators be chosen by the state legislatures. Too often this resulted in state party machines or special interest groups dictating the choice of senators. Even when no corruption or malpractice was charged, people still complained that too many senators were wealthy men tied more closely to the business community than to their state as a whole. During the first decade of this century, progressives and "muckrakers," insisting that "the cure for the evils of democracy is more democracy," stirred widespread demand for direct election of senators by the people. The Seventeenth Amendment, although it was blocked for a long time in the Senate itself, was the result.

The Twentieth Amendment (1933) fixes the twentieth of January as the beginning of the terms of the President and Vice-President, and the third of January as the beginning of the terms of congressmen. This is known as the "Lame Duck Amendment." Prior to its passage, congressmen who were defeated in the November elections continued to sit (like "lame ducks") in the December session following their defeat, while the new congressmen could not, except for a special session, take their seats until the thirteen months after they had been elected. Before the adoption of the Twentieth Amendment, the President and Vice-President did not take office until March following their election.

The Twenty-second Amendment (1951) revises the judgment of the original Framers that the President should be permitted to run for office as many times as he wanted. President Washington set a precedent for his successors by retiring after two terms. The election of Franklin D. Roosevelt to four terms outraged many, although he received a majority of the popular vote in each election. Early in the Truman administration, the Twenty-second Amendment was proposed in Congress and was speeded through the required number of state legislatures without much debate or publicity. Under its provisions no person may be elected to the office of President more than twice; and no person who has acted as President for more than two years may run again more than once. The incumbent was specifically excluded, so that President Truman, after having served out the remainder of President Roosevelt's fourth

---

[36] V. O. Key, Jr., *Southern Politics* (New York: Alfred A. Knopf, Inc., 1949); Frederic A. Ogden, *The Poll Tax in the South* (University, Alabama: University of Alabama Press, 1958).

term, and after having been elected for one term on his own, could have chosen to run for another term. (He did not so choose.) This restriction on the number of terms a President can serve may actually decrease rather than enhance democratic control. In the first place, it denies future majorities the chance to continue a successful President in office, a freedom of choice that might be critically important in a time of crisis. For this reason, former President Eisenhower urged repeal of the restrictive Amendment. Another probable effect is a decline in presidential leadership during second terms. The degree to which Eisenhower's influence in national politics decreased during his second term is difficult to assess, for his concept of presidential leadership was one of restraint from the outset. In general, however, other office-holders are less likely to pay attention to an incumbent who has no chance of heading the next party ticket.

Economic and Social Changes

The Sixteenth and Eighteenth Amendments were the first to deal with matters of taxation. The history of both starts in 1894, when Congress levied a 2 per cent tax on incomes over $4,000. The next year the Supreme Court declared the law invalid on the ground that a tax on income from real estate was a "direct tax" and that the Constitution required direct taxes to be apportioned among the states according to their population.[37] The decision was finally overridden by the Sixteenth Amendment, despite vociferous opposition from the "rich and few" to what they regarded as "socialism."

The Sixteenth Amendment (1913) authorizes Congress "to lay and collect taxes on incomes, *from whatever source derived*, without apportionment among the several States, and without regard to any census or enumeration" (emphasis added). This Amendment has had a revolutionary impact on the American economy. Not only did it shift the burden of financing the government onto those who were most able to pay; it also brought about a gradual redistribution of national wealth. Most local and state taxes remain regressive—that is, they take larger proportions of incomes from the poor than from the rich. But the principle of progressive taxation developed under the Sixteenth Amendment redresses the balance in favor of those with lower incomes. Moreover, the great revenue brought in through the income tax has permitted a vast expansion of public services, on which poorer citizens are especially dependent. The Sixteenth Amendment is probably the most important change that has so far been made in the text of the original Constitution.

The Eighteenth Amendment (1919) was an extraordinary attempt to change the moral character of American society. Its passage through Congress as a "war measure" (corn and rye, bread and cereal for the boys in the trenches!) in 1917 and its subsequent ratification in three-fourths of the state legislatures make an outstanding case study in pressure politics. The Anti-Saloon League, organized in 1893 to wage war against "Demon Rum," pressed first for temperance legislation in the states. Early in the twentieth century, the League marshalled its forces for nationwide prohibition of alcoholic beverages; by 1917 it

---

[37] *"Polluck v. Farmers' Loan and Trust Co.,* 157 U.S. 429 (1895).

had become one of the most powerful pressure groups in the country, strong enough to persuade two-thirds of Congress and three-fourths of the state legislatures to vote the whole country "dry."

The Eighteenth Amendment prohibited the manufacture, sale, or transportation of intoxicating liquors within the United States, and their import into and export from the United States, for beverage purposes. This attempt to incorporate a moral principle of one part of the public into the organic law of the nation failed, for too many people simply would not recognize the code as binding. Bootlegging and gangsterism flourished throughout the country. Violation of prohibition under the Eighteenth Amendment was so general and widespread that a dangerous disrespect sprang up for the "supreme law of the land."

One of the earliest and most popular acts of President Franklin Roosevelt's New Deal was to end "the noble experiment" by promoting the passage of the Twenty-first Amendment (1933), which specifically repeals the Eighteenth Amendment. The Amendment gives some constitutional aid and comfort to those who are set on keeping their own states "dry," however, for it forbids the transportation or importation of intoxicating liquor into any state in violation of that state's laws.

The Twenty-fifth Amendment (1967) remedies an initial deficiency by clarifying who shall exercise presidential power and in what manner when the President is incapacitated or dies. This problem was emphasized by the serious illness and hospitalization of both Presidents Eisenhower and Johnson and dramatically posed by the assassination of President Kennedy, all of which occurred within the short span of less than ten years. The Amendment makes explicit the conditions for succession of the Vice-President to the presidency. If the President is unable to discharge the powers and duties of his office because of illness or any other reason, he must notify the Speaker of the House and the President *pro tempore* of the Senate so that the Vice-President can become Acting President. If the President is so stricken that he does not realize his infirmities, the Vice-President, with approval of the majority of the Cabinet, is charged with deciding whether he (the Vice-President) needs to take over as Acting President, a position which exists only until the President himself is able to inform Congress that "no disability exists." If the President and Acting President are in disagreement over the issue of presidential disability, Congress decides the issue; a two-thirds vote is required in both houses to uphold the Acting President. When the Vice-President succeeds to the presidency because of the death of the President (a situation that has occurred eight times), he is authorized to name his Vice-President, subject to approval by both houses of Congress.

The Continuing Constitution

When the Constitution was written, the Framers were moved to awe and apprehension over the magnitude of their task. A gigantic task it was: designing a federal union for thirteen distinct and independent states; setting up a republican government for nearly four million people; ruling a "vast territory" outlined by fifteen hundred miles of coastline and stretching all the way from the Atlantic Ocean to the Mississippi River. The Framers could not possibly have imagined that the instrument of government they fashioned would be operating, more than 175 years later, for more than 200 million people, in fifty states, from Florida to Alaska, from Maine to Hawaii.

In 1787, the size of the country alone overawed the Framers; a republican government had never before been tried on so grand a scale. Yet today it takes less time for Hawaii's congressmen to reach the national capital by plane than it did for the New York delegates to travel by stagecoach to the Philadelphia Convention. In 1787, Philadelphia, then the second largest city in the states, had a population under 30,000; New York, which had been the capital under the Articles of Confederation, had a population of about 40,000. Today the population of New York City alone is approximately three times the total population of the country as reported in the first census of 1790. More than 90 per cent of the population was living on farms and plantations when George Washington was inaugurated as the first President; today less than 15 per cent of the people are engaged in farming. "The butcher, the baker, the candlestick maker" typified the village business in late eighteenth-century America, a very different world from the nationwide economy of Armour, National Biscuit, and Westinghouse. When the delegates, after the Constitutional Convention had adjourned, returned to their homes by horseback, stagecoach, and sailboat, they could have had no idea of the mass communications and rapid transportation of the future—American Telephone and Telegraph, Columbia Broadcasting System, General Motors, General Dynamics. In 1787, there were only a few hundred corporations in the entire country, mainly banking and transportation enterprises. Individual proprietorship was the prevailing pattern of business in "commerce among the states." As the delegates stopped along the way at taverns and blacksmith shops, they could not have conceived of what has since become the American Way: United States Steel, Alcoa, Firestone, Metropolitan Life, Borden, Woolworth, the corporate form, absentee multiple ownership, mass production, professional management, collective bargaining.

The Framers of the original constitutional document were, as we pointed out earlier, scarcely democratic in the modern sense; they were not too concerned about pleasing the current majority. Their great task was to write a constitution that would serve as "the supreme law of the land," not only for themselves but their posterity. They had to decide what principles of government were so basic and fundamental to the whole people that they ought to be placed above and beyond ordinary political action. This is the real meaning of constitutionalism—the idea that even if a change is attuned primarily to popular opinion, it will not achieve the force of law if it is not in pursuance of the Constitution.

When, however, we try to ascertain "the plain meaning of the Constitution," we must go beyond the text of 1787. The Framers include not only the members of the Philadelphia Convention but the many thousands of congressmen, state legislators, and members of state conventions who have been involved since 1787 in the introduction and ratification of the Amendments which are now an integral part of the formal written Constitution.

In brief summary, the Framers (all of them over the years) intended: (1) a *federal* government in which powers are divided among and functions shared by the national government and the states; (2) a *national* government supreme in all external affairs and in certain enumerated domestic matters; (3) a *republican* government—national and state—in which the people choose their principal policy-makers, executive and legislative; (4) a *democratic* government in which the citizens enjoy universal suffrage in periodic elections and directly influence public policies; (5) a *limited* government in which specific prohibitions are placed on both the national and state government; a government in which fundamental *individual rights* are guaranteed even against *majority rule;* (6) a *representative* government with the people of each state directly represented in proportion to their numbers in the House of Representatives and approximately in the same proportion in the presidential electoral colleges; (7) a *presidential* government with independent tenure and a *separation of powers* (but also *checks and balances*) between the executive and legislative branches.

Constitutional lawyers often emphasize that the Constitution is designed to serve the *status quo.* In order to change an existing situation by law, the instigator must surmount a series of constitutional hurdles. He must obtain approval of his proposal by a majority in both houses of Congress. He must then win the approval of the President or run the risk of a veto which could not be overriden without the consent of a two-thirds majority in both houses. Even so, a proposal enacted into law may still be declared null and void by the courts. All these blocks in the normal legislative process seem to be opposed to one of the principles that we have described as essential to democracy—majority control. But the Constitution is a conservative instrument only in a procedural sense. It was never intended to be a rigid straitjacket embracing a single economic or social philosophy. The Constitution can be amended in any part, with no limitations or substantive modification. The Framers themselves recognized the ultimate need for freedom of dissent, leaving the way open for future generations to alter the Constitution as they might see fit.

In this chapter, we have deliberately focused on the constitutional text of 1787 and the twenty-five amendments that have been formally affixed to it. But it should be clearly understood that the contemporary Constitution is continuously changing. It has grown enormously and matured remarkably since 1787, not so much by formal amendments as by statutory enactments, presidential interpretations and executive orders, administrative rules and regulations, judicial decisions, popular attitudes and opinions, and customary behavior, official and unofficial. The Constitution is not merely an historical document; it is rooted in the experience of the nation; it retains its vitality and validity because it is both input and output in the ongoing political process. All policy-making is conditioned by constitutional prescription. In short, the Constitution sets the outer limits of permissability for all government activities; and in this broad sense of constitutional law, all the following chapters may be seen as amplification of what Americans regard to be "the supreme law of the land."

THE FEDERAL

SYSTEM 5

When the French political writer Alexis de Tocqueville visited America in the 1830s, he considered the Constitution of the United States to be "the most perfect federal constitution that ever existed." He felt, after an extended look at America and its institutions, that the United States combined the advantages of both large and small states—"happy and free as a small people, and glorious and strong as a great nation."[1] K. C. Wheare, a contemporary British political scientist, regards the American Constitution as the prototype of "what federal government is" today.[2] Students from abroad apparently perceive more clearly what we ourselves see but dimly. Certainly no principle of American government has been more controversial in these (or this) United States than federalism.

Concepts of Federalism

Federalism as a Functional Device for Nation-Building

Most Americans, even many politicians, have only the vaguest idea of what federalism really means. They tend to think of federalism as whatever it is that America has; and our political ethnocentrism is such that we think whatever we have must be the best. But many other countries, such as the Soviet Union, Canada, Australia, the Federal Republic of Germany, Mexico, and Brazil, also are federal political entities. Their common political structure nevertheless leaves room for significant differences among them. The Soviet Union is a dictatorship, for example, whereas Australia is a democracy; the United States has a two-party system of government, whereas Mexico has a one-party system. They can all claim to have a federal form of government, however, because in each the powers and functions of government are divided, on a constitutional basis, between a general or national government and regional units or states.

A definition of federalism in terms of structure is relatively simple, but when we try to describe how federalism actually operates—in terms of policies,

---

[1] Every student of American government should examine Tocqueville's *Democracy in America*. Originally published in 1835, it still is most discerning in its observations on American political character. It is now available in an inexpensive paperback edition edited by Phillips Bradley (New York: Vintage Books, 1954), 2 vols.

[2] K. C. Wheare, *Federal Government*. This classic, first issued under the auspices of the Royal Institute of International Affairs in 1946, is now available in its 4th edition as a paperback Galaxy Book (New York: Oxford University Press, 1964).

programs, and activities that affect the daily lives of the people—the problem becomes much more complex. A federal system of government is designed to accommodate diversity within a country but also to bolster the basic national unity that makes it a distinctive political system. Every society is more or less pluralistic, with variations in race, nationality, language, religion, economic groupings, and class. When significant differences develop along geographic lines, each territorial unit tends to demand a political arrangement that will respect its peculiar values and interests. No new nation is wholly unified; and the persuasive rationale of a federal union is that it functions to protect political, economic, social and cultural variations within territorial units and at the same time functions to develop a national political system (e.g., in the Pye model,[3] strengthening the sense of *national identity*, hastening the processes of *integration, penetration, participation*, and *distribution*.)

Although federalism is a basic principle in the American system of government, neither the word *federation* nor the word *federal* appears in the Constitution. The Preamble does no more than declare the intent of the people "to form a more perfect union." Perhaps we are lucky that the Framers did not precisely define "federalism." If they had, we would have been required to invent a different term for the system of government they helped create—for they used the term "federal" as the adjectival form of "confederation." They were simply striving to add to the structure operating under the Articles of Confederation some features of a more "consolidated" (i.e., integrated) national government. As James Madison put it, "the *federal* form . . . regards the Union as a *Confederacy* of sovereign states," whereas "a *national* government . . . regards the Union as a *consolidation* of states." In the thirty-ninth in a series of essays that was later to be called (ironically, it seems now) *The Federalist*, he carefully explained that the proposed Constitution was neither "federal" nor "national" in nature, but was a "mixture" of the two. This new combination, a league between sovereign states and the unitary government of consolidation, is what we call federalism.

If we follow Madison's analysis of "this mixed constitution," the American concept of federalism emerges as a synthesis. Beginning with a thesis (a league of states) and confronting it with an antithesis (a unitary national state), the Constitutional Convention of 1787 resolved the tension with a novel political structure. The American federal union was the first of its kind, and has subsequently served as a working model for many federal unions in the modern world. Whether the original idea of American federalism—or any of its subsequent phases of development—has any substantial relevance to the problems of nation-building today is not for us to decide. The problems perceived by the Philadelphia Convention in the late eighteenth century were different in both kind and degree from those that face contemporary constitution-makers. But even conceding that nation-building is unique in terms of time, place, and people concerned, one may still find in the American experience some of the reasons why many new nations are adopting some version of federalism.[4]

[3] See discussion of the Pye model in Chapter 4.

[4] For a germane discussion of federalism and nation-building today see *Federalism and the Nations of Africa*, David P. Currie (ed.) (Chicago: University of Chicago Press, 1964). Note especially "Foundations and Developments of American Federalism: the Experience of an Older Federation" by Paul A. Freund.

THE FEDERAL SYSTEM

First Intentions

Various factors tended at the outset to enhance state separatism. The thirteen colonies were founded at different times, by different kinds of settlers, and for different purposes, and the historical circumstances extending over more than a century and a half served to perpetuate different traditions and distinct loyalties. Moreover, the distribution of population was such that the small states had good reason to be apprehensive of what might happen to them in a "consolidated national government" such as that proposed in the Virginia Resolutions. Virginia was twice as populous as Massachusetts, a dozen times more populous than either Delaware or Rhode Island. Slavery was also a divisive issue; more than one-fifth the inhabitants of the United States in 1787 were slaves, most of them concentrated in the southern states. There were also serious economic cleavages: between the southern states, which were dependent on the export of raw products, and the New England states, which had major mercantile and manufacturing interests; between the inland and frontier communities and the commercial interests in the seaport towns. Conflicts of interest, jealousies and rivalries, discriminations and recriminations—these were the factors that conditioned interstate relations in the decade following independence and made it seem impossible, yet increasingly imperative, to join the thirteen states in a more effective union.

The Articles of Confederation provided a constitutional framework for at least an embryonic national government. But because the central government under the Articles could operate (outside of foreign affairs) only through state agencies, its influence was scarcely felt at the local level. Although the colonists had been reaching toward a national identity even before 1776, the process of Americanization was slowing up, even foundering, in the decade under the Articles. Most Americans still thought of themselves as Pennsylvanians, Virginians, or North Carolinians, and had no intention of relinquishing these distinctive identities. Although they had fought together in a common cause against the British Crown, when independence was achieved they were not fully prepared for the consequent shift in roles—from British subjects to American citizens. The removal of external threat pointed up the relative lack of internal cohesion. (A similar psychological lag occurs today in many new nations, where people have been learning the hard way that the break from colonialism does not in itself bring about a new polity.)

The Framers of 1787 were experienced politicians. They recognized that the intensity of state pride, the extent of state rivalries, and the multiplicity of state loyalties (by which they themselves were torn) ruled out any real prospect of a unitary national state. But they also perceived the advantages that would ensue from a stronger union. And they recognized that, despite the many frictions under the Articles, there was a common sense of nationality, a common pride in having established the first republic in the new world, and a common resolve to achieve "a more perfect union." Thus it was with conviction that John Jay, propagandizing for the stronger national government proposed by the new Constitution, could write:

139

To all general purposes we have uniformly been one people; each individual citizen everywhere enjoying the same national rights, privileges, and protection. As a nation we have made peace and war; as a nation we have vanquished our common enemies; as a nation we have formed alliances, and made treaties, and entered into various compacts and conventions with foreign states.[5]

The basic problem of the Philadelphia Convention was how to work out a practical design for government which could accommodate the *diverse interests* as well as the *uniform needs* of the American people. To this end the Convention made four crucial decisions: to create a strong national government, to preserve the states, to form a federal union that would embrace both the states and the national government in a *new* constitutional framework, and finally to bring the national government into a direct and functional relationship with the people.

Arguing for the adoption of the new Constitution, *The Federalist* stressed the *utility* of the federal union. Hamilton singled out the principal purposes of the union as "the common defense of the members; the preservation of the public peace, as well against internal convulsions as external attacks; the regulation of commerce with other nations and between the States; and superintendence of our intercourse, political and commercial, with foreign nations" (No. 23). Madison, after analyzing the kinds and quantity of power delegated to the national government, reached two complementary conclusions: (1) that no part of the power vested in the national government by the Constitution is unnecessary or improper for accomplishing the functions of the union and promoting the national interests; (2) that strengthening the national government will not weaken the portion of authority left to the states (No. 41).

The Framers intended to establish a viable federal union; creating an energetic national government was central to that intention. *The Federalist* tried to allay apprehensions that federalism was inimical to the states. Thus Madison points out that the principal branches of the national government —the President, the Senate, and the House of Representatives—owe their existence more or less to the favor of the state governments. On the other hand, the component parts of the state governments are in no way indebted to any agents of the national government. Governors, state legislators, and all other decision-makers in the state government are chosen by and responsible only to the constituents of their respective states. The powers delegated to the national government are few and defined; those which remain to the states are numerous and indefinite, extending to all the ordinary course of affairs. Finally, and this was the clincher to Madison's argument, "both the national government and the states are in fact but different agents and trustees of the people, constituted with different powers and designed for different purposes" (No. 45).

The Federalist views the federal union as one political system. Madison sharply rejects the idea that the national government and the states will become enemies or mutual rivals. The ultimate authority for both resides in the people alone, and it therefore will not depend "on the comparative ambition or address of the different governments, whether either, or which of them will be able to enlarge its sphere at the expense of the other." Madison be-

[5]*The Federalist*, No. 2.

lieved that "the first and most natural attachments of the people will be to the governments of their respective States," but he also boldly suggested that if the national government bettered its administration, "in that case, the people ought not surely to be precluded from giving most of their confidence where they may discover it to be most due" (No. 46).

New Framers and New Concepts

What the authors of *The Federalist* had to say about the intentions of the Framers is still of historical interest to us. But to treat the essays as if they were an authoritative exposition of contemporary federalism is to indulge in antiquarianism. Today's Constitution is substantially different from the text that was so painstakingly hammered out at the Philadelphia Convention. Even if we were to limit our discussion to the written document, quite clearly the addition of some twenty-five amendments has considerably altered and extended the original text. The Bill of Rights, for example, goes well beyond the initial intentions of the Framers. Hamilton declared in *The Federalist* (No. 84) that a bill of rights "would sound much better in a treatise of ethics than in a constitution of government." He argued that a bill of rights was "not only unnecessary in the proposed constitution, but would even be dangerous." After the first ten amendments became an integral part of the Constitution, Hamilton's previews became irrelevant. Likewise, the addition of the Civil Rights amendments following the Civil War carried the process of national penetration much further into the jurisdiction of the states than the original Framers could have contemplated. Whatever the original Framers' intentions, new Framers with new concepts have materially modified functional relationships, not only between the national government and its citizens but also between the national government and the states, with respect to individual rights.

Of all the amendments, the Sixteenth, which authorizes the national government to "lay and collect taxes on incomes from whatever source derived without apportionment among the several states" has most materially changed the original prescription. A graduated income tax is intended to apportion the support of government activities according to the taxpayer's ability to pay; those with higher incomes pay taxes at higher rates, those with lower incomes pay at lower rates. In effect, the national income-tax system provides a more equitable distribution of wealth throughout the country. Moreover, the vast revenue which the income tax brings to the national government is now shared in increasing percentages with states and local communities through grants-in-aid for a variety of public assistance and welfare programs. Later in this chapter we shall be discussing in more detail some implications of these shared finances as part of "cooperative" and "creative" federalism.

As the organic law of the nation, even more than as a written legal document, the Constitution as "supreme law of the land" has come to reflect the massive changes in American society and the impact of science and technology since 1787. Successive concepts of federalism and new patterns of intergovernmental relations have emerged without changing the original text. Probably the most marked change in functional relationships—between the national government and the states and between the national government and people in the states—have occurred under the congressional power to regulate commerce. The changing character of commerce—brought about by new transportation methods, from stage coach to supersonic jet; new media of communications from town crier to Telstar; new means of production and distribution from handicrafts to automation, from Main Street to Madison Avenue—has given entirely new and different meanings to the clause in Article I, Section 8: "The Congress shall have power . . . to regulate commerce among the several states." Without feeling the need for formal amendment, decision-makers have simply responded to new demands and different supports in a fast-changing environment. The power to regulate commerce, once regarded as somehow restricted, has now fully met "the crisis of penetration," reaching almost everywhere into the economy. Literally there has been no change in the commerce clause, but congressional statutes, administrative rules and regulations, and judicial decisions over the years have set forth continuously contemporary translations of "commerce among the states."

The orthodox idea of American federalism, which embraces the twin principles of national supremacy and state sovereignty, is called "dual federalism." Because there is potential conflict and competition between the two jurisdictions, a major concern of both the national and state governments is to prevent encroachment upon their respective functions. The national government, therefore, possesses only certain enumerated powers; all other powers not denied to them are reserved to the states (or to the people); and in accordance with this neat distribution of authority, the activities of each jurisdiction remain separate and distinct. But like so many of our orthodox ideas, dual federalism has more often been elevated to principle rather than reduced to practice.

Unquestionably, the concept of federalism became more and more diluted as the nation expanded beyond the first union of the thirteen states. The early settlers came to Connecticut, or to Virginia, or to Georgia; but millions of immigrants who came to the new world in the nineteenth century knew only of "America." The belief in "manifest destiny," the westward movement of settlement from the Atlantic seaboard to the Pacific, fostered a spirit of nationalism. Frontiersmen were not nearly so interested in the legal or theoretical aspects of federalism as they were in its utility. Federalism meant cooperation and joint enterprise between the national government and the states, partnership rather than rivalry in building a prosperous nation. The new states in the Union, with little of the traditional separatism of the original states, looked to the national capital for all kinds of federal aid.

Daniel Elazar's study of intergovernmental relations in the United States in the nineteenth century,[6] based on very careful sifting of data and documents in national and state archives, demonstrates that many governmental activities

---

[6] Daniel J. Elazar, *The American Partnership* (Chicago: The University of Chicago Press, 1962). See also his *American Federalism: A View from the States* (New York: Thomas Y. Crowell Company, 1966).

since the early days of the Republic have been cooperative endeavors shared by national and state agencies. Indeed, the beginning of cooperative federalism antedates the Constitution; the Northwest Ordinances of 1785 and 1787, pledging the national government to grant a section of land in each township of the Territory for the support of common schools, established the precedent of national-state collaboration in public education.

Probably the most crucial problems in building a new nation, especially a democratic one, is the improvement of communication and transportation facilities. The Philadelphia Convention had recognized this need by giving Congress power to establish post office and post roads. Congressional power to develop a nationwide system of communication was the subject of many heated debates in the early years. It was critically important for the new nation to maintain close ties—political, economic, and cultural—between the people in the original states and the ever-increasing number of settlers moving westward. Strict constructionists in the first half of the nineteenth century, who interpreted the powers of the national government under the Constitution in the narrowest sense, succeeded in blocking an American system of internal improvements planned and financed by the national government. Nevertheless, the exigencies of nation-building on a continental basis generated a variety of cooperative intergovernmental programs. Ironically, John C. Calhoun, best known for his passionate espousal of states' rights in the slavery issue, was one of the leading architects of cooperative federalism in the broad field of internal improvements.

For those brought up to believe that the national government has only recently carried its activities into the local communities, Elazar's account of national-state cooperation in *The American Partnership* provides an entirely different basis for understanding the federal system of government. Intergovernmental cooperation in the nineteenth century included a multitude of internal improvement projects (roads, canals, railroads, harbors, public buildings, river improvements, mineral extraction and refinement, agricultural development); a variety of land-grant programs (the development of common schools in the states carved out of the Northwest Territory, the establishment of colleges of agriculture and mechanical arts in every state and territory); and land grants, cash grants, material grants, and services for all kinds of purposes in the states (railroad construction, irrigation of desert lands, drainage of swamp lands, soldier homes, agricultural experiment stations, welfare institutions).

It was the New Deal, however, that dealt the deathblow to the concept of dual federalism. In dramatic political response to the Depression, the Roosevelt administration launched a battery of nationwide programs affecting agricultural production, industrial labor-management relations, rates and services in transportation and communications, stock market operations, public utilities, public works, and social security. At the outset the New Deal encountered difficulties in the Supreme Court, which took a dim view of the wholesale extension of national powers into the economy. But soon the Court itself was revolutionizing constitutional law and giving judicial sanction to national penetration into all spheres of the economy. The Court swept out many of its own landmark decisions that had long given aid and comfort to free enterprise on the state as well as the national level.[7]

But rather than push national power to its utmost limits, the Roosevelt administration created a new pattern of intergovernmental relations to effect new nationwide policies. Since the power to tax (and to appropriate) for the general welfare has virtually no constitutional restrictions, the New Dealers stepped up the national income taxes and then used the burgeoning revenue of the national government to offer grants-in-aid to states willing to implement, in accordance with national guidelines, various New Deal programs: distribution of surplus farm products to the needy, free school lunches, child welfare, old age assistance, aid to dependent children, aid to the needy blind, and many more. Before 1933 such grants-in-aid to the states (except, after 1916, for highways) involved no great sums and made little impression on the political system as a whole. The New Deal grants-in-aid, however, especially those for welfare programs, were massive and so had a definite skewing effect on state functions as well as state finances. The New Deal version of federalism, whether viewed as an expansion of national powers in Washington or as more cooperative relations with the states, made drastic and permanent changes in American government and politics.

An important aspect of New Deal federalism was the bypassing of state agencies to make grants-in-aid directly available to local communities for emergency relief programs. These early New Deal grants were precedents for a major trend after World War II, when the national government began to give direct grants on a large scale to local governments for airport aid, urban renewal, and education programs.[8] By the mid-'60s this trend was seemingly irreversible. As a recent study by the Senate Subcommittee on Intergovernmental Relations reports, "Whatever direction President Johnson's emergent 'creative federalism' may take, it is clear that the power distribution in American federalism, as it has emerged since the New Deal, bears little resemblance to earlier days."[9]

So far we have emphasized the functional nature of federalism in terms of its unifying aspects. Remember that an institution or activity can be called "functional" if its consequences promote the survival of the system without major disruption. Thus we can certainly say that some aspects of federalism are highly functional for the American polity. It would be highly unrealistic, however, to deny or ignore the dysfunctional aspects of American federalism, for it has had divisive and separatist tendencies as well as unifying effects. Reverberations of the great debates of the nineteenth century—between the promoters of national power and the supporters of states' rights over slavery

---

[7] For further discussion of the impact of the New Deal upon the national economy and general welfare, see Chapter 15.

[8] The last section of this chapter, "Creative Federalism" (a term popularized by the Johnson Administration), discusses further shifts in functional emphases and new concerns in intergovernmental relations.

[9] Harry N. Scheiber, *The Condition of American Federalism,* a study submitted by the Subcommittee on Intergovernmental Relations to the Committee on Government Operations, U.S. Senate, October 15, 1966 (Washington, D.C.: Government Printing Office, 1966). The author is an historian.

THE FEDERAL SYSTEM

and other issues—still rankle in the minds of many Americans. To some of us, the doctrines of dual federalism, of division of powers and separation of functions, of nullification and secession, may be little more than verbal images, but once they were potent enough to tear the country asunder and to provoke four years of civil war. The current battles over congressional legislation and judicial decisions in the area of civil rights dramatically attest to the persistence of disunity in the American Union. Despite past crises and current strains, however, the continuous pattern of formal and informal intergovernmental activities that constitutes American federalism has promoted unity no less than diversity.

The trend toward nationalism in most aspects of American life vitiates some of the old arguments for political decentralization. Urbanization, industrialization, and especially rapid and convenient means of transportation have made Americans the most mobile people in history. Each year since World War II one-fifth of the American people have changed their places of residence. He is a rare person today who lives his whole life in the community in which he was born and reared. The media of mass communication, radio and TV, play up national affairs to the extent that the average citizen is much more aware of what goes on in Washington or in distant communities than he is of the run-of-the-mill news in his home town. The national systems of social security and veterans' benefits encourage citizens in every state to look to Washington for extension of the general welfare. We talk about "national interests," "national purposes," "national goals" even in areas long regarded as local concerns, such as health, housing, education, farm prices, labor standards, and civil rights.

If a national constitutional convention were called today to reconsider the fundamental principles of American government, it would probably make substantial modifications in the distribution of powers between the national government and the states. Most probably, however, it would retain the federal system, which is still highly functional. For all the talk about uniformity and conformity in American life, the United States remains a panorama of many different regions with marked variations in diet, dialect, cultural patterns, degrees of urbanization and industrialization, and political backgrounds. The initial motivation for American federalism—thirteen unlike states—continues as a tradition among the present fifty states.

The states are convenient means by which to multiply the choices of the American people on issues where national uniformity is unnecessary or even undesirable. Alternatives are especially important when the majority of the people in a given region dissent from national views. In such cases, the states may delay or may brake action by the national government. On the other hand, as Lord Bryce observed many years ago, "Federalism enables a people to try experiments in legislation and administration which could not be safely tried in a large centralized country."[10] Thus the states may serve as laboratories

[10]James Bryce, *The American Commonwealth* (New York: The Macmillan Company, 1914), new ed., I, 353.

for new policies and progressive legislation which the country as a whole might not be ready to try or to accept.

The Constitutional Prescription

The constitutional prescription for American federalism is to be found in the original text; in some of the amendments; in orthodox and modified interpretations of these; in tradition and settled usage; and in new and developing patterns of behavior. Despite the seeming confusion of sources, the main outlines of the constitutional prescription are fairly clear; and decision-makers—whether in the nation's capital, the statehouses, the county courthouses, or the city halls—know that they must shape their policies and implement their programs in accord with the main points of the prescription: (1) the states, more than the national government, determine the political structure of the union; (2) all of the states—old and new—are on equal footing within the union; (3) the union is indestructible; (4) the states have certain obligations to one another; (5) the national government has certain obligations to the states; (6) the powers of government are distributed between the national government and the states; (7) when the chips are down—i.e., in terms of functions—the national government enjoys supreme power over the states.

The States in the Union The decision to retain the states in the union determined the basic character of federal or intergovernmental relations in the United States. In a sense, there is almost no national government in the United States. Congress, the President, federal judges, even the civil service reflect state interests. The Senate represents the states directly and equally, with two senators from each state standing guard over the state's rights. The House of Representatives represents the people within the states; the representative's constituency is not the nation as a whole but the people in his own district who have elected him to promote their particular interests. The boundaries of each congressional district are still determined by the respective state legislatures, subject to the judicial guiding principle that districts within the state must be substantially equal in size of population.[11]

The Constitution requires that senators and representatives be inhabitants of the states they represent. It is the custom, though it is not required by the Constitution, that congressmen also be legal residents of the district they represent. Residence requirements of this sort make it impossible for Americans to elect a national legislature such as the British Parliament. Members of the House of Commons are chosen by local constituencies, but British voters are far more willing than Americans to support a nonresident candidate so long as he represents their point of view on national issues. The British Parliament has traditionally been a council of the wise and great men of the realm. As Edmund Burke remarked in 1774: "Parliament is a deliberative assembly of one nation, with one interest, that of the whole; where, not local

---

[11] *Wesberry v. Sanders*, 376 U.S. 1 (1964).

purposes, not local prejudices, ought to guide, but the general good resulting from the general reason of the whole." Under the American system, however, we simply have to assume that every state and every congressional district can recruit favorite sons capable of serving as outstanding statesmen for the nation at large. Or, granting that our local representatives will not take a national view, we assume that the national interest will emerge when all the local interests are added together.

The years have borne out James Madison's prediction that "a local spirit" will usually prevail among the members of Congress. The first concern of every congressman seems to be how to get as much as he can out of the nation for his own state—appropriations for hydroelectric projects, flood control, disaster relief, military installations, post offices, airports, veterans' hospitals, improvement of rivers and harbors. It is customary, for example, for a congressman to seek appointment to those committees whose activities most vitally concern his constituency. Thus a congressman from a dominantly agricultural district may request assignment to the committee on agriculture. There he will not only occupy a key position with respect to legislative policies affecting agricultural interests but also, through the administrative oversight responsibilities of this committee, he (and his constituents through him) will have greater access to the bureaucracy dealing with agricultural matters. For like reasons, the congressman from a heavily industrialized constituency may be appointed to the committee on labor, and the congressman from a maritime district to the committee on public works (which in the House authorizes river and harbor expenditures). Moreover, whatever his committee assignments, every congressman makes his office an important point of contact between the national bureaucracy and the state and local interests which he represents. Some congressmen actually give more time to their "casework" than to their legislative tasks. The case may be arguing with authorities in the Pentagon about closing down an obsolete military installation in his state, or introducing a group of businessmen from back home to officials in the Agency for International Development for advice and assistance on how to get government insurance for investments abroad. This kind of interaction between congressmen and bureaucrats in the furthering of state and local interests may appear to be only remotely connected with the constitutional prescription. Nevertheless, it is a significant aspect of federalism in the political process.[12]

The President and Vice-President are the only national officers chosen in nationwide elections. Having a national constituency, the President is more likely to represent the national viewpoint than does the Congress, but the Constitution makes his office, too, a creature of the states. Technically, the President is elected not by the people of the United States, but by an electoral college in which each state has as many electors as it has representatives and senators in Congress. Each state legislature may decide how the state's presidential electors are to be chosen; today, all of them are chosen in statewide

[12]See Daniel Elazar, "The States, the Parties, and Congress," *American Federalism*, for more extensive coverage of this point.

elections, although other procedures have been followed in the past. And in the national conventions held by the major parties to nominate their candidates for President and Vice-President—which come months before the election itself—the state is again the basic unit.

The national legislature and the national executive are not alone in reflecting strong state and local interests and influence; the same can be said of the national judiciary. The Constitution requires that the President nominate and appoint justices of the Supreme Court, and all other officers of the federal courts, with the advice and consent of the Senate. "Senatorial courtesy" further requires that the President clear all nominations in advance with the senators (or party officials) of the state in which his nominees legally reside. The Senate Committee on the Judiciary, which has first look at all presidential nominations for federal judges, is most solicitous in checking with the senators from the states concerned. Nearly all appointments to the district courts actually originate with the President's party organization within the judicial district concerned. Moreover, the Supreme Court has tended to pass the buck back to the district courts for implementing its decisions in cases involving national issues, *e.g.*, desegregation of the public schools and reapportionment of the state legislatures or congressional districts. Stereotypes of the federal judiciary pitting its alien (i.e. national) views against the customs of the local community are somewhat exaggerated. Federal judges (and U.S. marshals too) are almost always local people who have reached their official status in the national government via state and local politics. How else could they have been appointed under the prevailing rule of party patronage?[13]

The states are also powerful political units in national administration. Again, according to the custom of senatorial courtesy, the President—before making patronage appointments in a state—is expected to consult with the senators and representatives of the state concerned. If the senator or representative is not of the President's party, the President is expected to clear appointments through party officials in the state. Senatorial courtesy also enters into the appointments of purely national officers, such as members of the Cabinet, ambassadors, heads of executive agencies, and foreign service officers. Finally, appointments to the civil service in Washington follow a quota system, roughly proportionate to the population of each state. This rule is not strictly followed in practice, but even its existence is a concession to the continuing influence of "the indestructible states."

The constitutional prescription of federalism not only determines the governmental structure but conditions the political process. The Constitution does not mention political parties. Nevertheless, parties have become the principal instruments through which American politics are organized and made explicit. But note that the two major parties,[14] the Democrats and Repub-

[13]On the other hand, election or appointment to a national office is likely to develop a more national outlook in the individual. The Senator from Texas who is elected President, the Governor of California who becomes Chief Justice of the Supreme Court, the state legislator from Florida who goes to the U.S. House of Representatives, the local lawyer from Jackson, Mississippi who becomes a Federal District Court judge—all of these apparently react to the role expectancy of the office they hold. But it also remains evident that no one ever leaves home completely.

[14]Much is written nowadays pointing up the centralization of power and politics in Washington. Daniel Elazar emphasizes the opposite view: "American political parties rarely centralize power at all. . . . [Rather they serve] as a canopy under which special and local interests are represented." *American Federalism*, p. 50.

148

licans, operate on a federal basis. The fifty state party organizations are loosely bound together into a national organization whose main goal is periodically to elect a President; but the real centers of power and influence remain in the state and local organizations. Most special interest groups are also organized along federal lines. Thus the American Bar Association functions most actively and most effectively as fifty state bar associations; likewise the American Medical Association is a federation of fifty state medical associations; and the American Federation of Labor comprises fifty state federations of labor. The Constitution was originally designed to accommodate both the uniform and diverse interests of the American people; the designers accomplished their purposes far better than they could have realized at the time. Because the governmental structure is federal in form, the whole political process becomes federal in action.

"An Indestructible Union"

When the Constitution was written, the Framers anticipated the new states would shortly be admitted to the Union, but they left the conditions of admission entirely to the discretion of Congress. It is now a firm doctrine of constitutional law that all states, new and old, enjoy equal rights and hold identical powers in the Union. In 1787, however, the Philadelphia Convention was not ready to accept such a doctrine; by a vote of nine to two, it actually voted down a proposal that would have guaranteed equality for new states. The delegates from eastern states had no intention of admitting the western territories on an equal footing, but Congress decided differently. Each of the first two states to be admitted—Vermont and Kentucky—came in "as a new and entire member of the United States of America." When Tennessee was admitted in 1796, it was "on an equal footing with the original states in all respects whatsoever." The precedent became so well established that in 1911 a unanimous Supreme Court declared, "The constitutional equality of the state is essential to the harmonious operation of the scheme upon which the Republic was organized."[15]

The Constitution does not specify the procedure to be followed for the admission of new states. It only prohibits Congress from creating a new state within the jurisdiction of an established state, or from joining two or more old states together to form a new state, without the consent of the state legislatures concerned. Ordinarily, when a substantial number of persons within a territory have desired statehood, they have petitioned Congress to pass an "enabling act." If Congress reacts favorably to the request, it will by legislation "enable" the people of the territory to elect a constitutional convention. The territorial convention then meets and frames a constitution, which it presents to Congress for approval. If Congress finds the proposed constitution acceptable,

---

[15]*Coyle* v. *Smith*, 221 U.S. 559 (1911). The congressional enabling act for the admission of Oklahoma had provided that the capital of the new state should be at Guthrie and that it should not be moved from there before 1913. In 1910, the Oklahoma legislature moved the capital to Oklahoma City. The Court held that Oklahoma was as free as any other state to locate its capital wherever the people wanted it. Congress may put restrictions into the enabling act but these cannot be enforced when the territory becomes a state if they are not generally found in all the states.

it passes a joint resolution recognizing the territory as a new member of the Union and seats the elected senators and representatives of the new state. Although the procedure seems simple enough, it is always complicated by political, social, economic, and even personal issues.

Before 1861, lively arguments were waged over whether a state has a constitutional right to secede from the Union. In 1861 it became the one constitutional debate that Americans have settled by civil war. Finally the Supreme Court declared in 1869, "The Constitution in all its provisions looks to an indestructible union, composed of indestructible states."[16] No state can break its constitutional bonds, for the Union is considered perpetual and indissoluble.

The right to interpose state sovereignty and nullify federal laws that go beyond constitutional limits has been claimed at one time or another by states in every section of the country. The most recent and vigorous claims have come from the southern states since the 1954 school desegregation decisions of the United States Supreme Court. But notice that in earlier cases the states were protesting against *acts of Congress*. The 1956 version of interposition claimed that the Supreme Court had no constitutional authority to settle disputes between the national government and a sovereign state.

Brown v. Board of Education (1954 and 1955)[17] — the desegregation decision of the Supreme Court — prompted a hundred congressmen from eleven southern states in March 1956 to present "A Declaration of Constitutional Principles." This manifesto excoriated the Court using such language as "naked judicial power," "the clear abuse of judicial power," and "the unwarranted decision" which is "in derogation of the authority of Congress" and which "encroaches upon the reserved rights of the states and the people." It commended "the motives of those states which have declared the intention to resist forced integration by any lawful means." With Alabama and Virginia in the lead, most of the southern legislatures proceeded to draft their own declarations of "interposition." None went so far as to declare the Supreme Court decision null and void, but all were intent on circumventing it.

In the fall of 1960, in response to a federal court order, the New Orleans School Board announced its plan to begin desegregation in the New Orleans public schools. Five Negro girls, of first-grade age, were to be admitted to formerly all-white schools. This plan so aroused the Louisiana Legislature that, in an extraordinary session, it passed twenty-seven measures, including an Interposition Act designed to prevent integration in the state's public schools. Nationwide TV audiences viewed angry mobs besieging the schoolhouses to which the Negro children were admitted under armed guard. Nevertheless, the Federal District Court stood firm: "The conclusion is clear that interposition is not a constitutional doctrine. If taken seriously, it is illegal defiance of

---

[16]*Texas* v. *White*, 7 Wall. 700 (1869).

[17]*Brown* v. *Board of Education*, 347 U.S. 483 (1954). The different basis of this decision from earlier ones is probably more apparent than real; the words of the Constitution are not self-interpreting. For years the Court has openly interpreted various provisions in the light of social and economic facts. Even the decision that first interpreted the "equal protection" clause to permit state-enforced segregation was based on sociological considerations about the difficulty of changing human nature by law. The difference appears to be that in the more recent case the sociological reasoning of the justices was buttressed by scholarly authorities rather than simply taken for granted. See. Mr. Justice Brown's opinion in *Plessy* v. *Ferguson*, 163 U.S. 537 (1896).

constitutional authority." The Court held unconstitutional the whole package of laws enacted by the Louisiana Legislature with respect to school integration. The U.S. Supreme Court, by refusing to rehear the case, upheld the ruling of the District Court. It found that Louisiana's claim of the right to interpose its authority in the field of education was "without substance."[18]

The arguments supporting states' rights and the doctrines of nullification and interposition usually cover up other issues. One must also admit that judicial resolution of these issues in accord with "the supreme law of the land" is sometimes rather superficial. On the racial issues, for example, the Supreme Court has firmly declared that enforced segregation is a violation of equal protection of the laws. But the implementation of this decision has been generally left up to the states and the local communities. In the past decade, three-fourths of the states have enacted civil rights legislation with even higher standards than the national legislation in this field. Segregation persists as the prevailing behavior, however, not only in a handful of recalcitrant states but also in many other communities throughout the country.

Ten years after the *Brown* decision, only 9 per cent of schoolchildren in the border states and less than 1 per cent in the Deep South were attending integrated schools. Federalism in action is a political process, and what the political authorities do in terms of the constitutional prescription depends on the dynamics of demands and supports in the political area. Thus when the Office of Education in the Department of Health, Education, and Welfare tried to speed up desegregation in schools receiving national grants-in-aid, senators and representatives from the southern states successfully persuaded the 90th Congress (1967) to cut back the enforcement duties of the Office of Education. Decision-making in the political arena, it appears, is much more complicated than settling cases in the courts.

Patterns of behavior deeply rooted in the social and economic institutions of the community are more effectively changed by persuasion than by coercion. In the federal system, the problem is rarely one of eye-to-eye confrontation—the power of the national government versus the power of the states. Federalism in action means that the national government is continuously responding to pressures from diverse interests in the states and local communities; that the states and local communities are continuously stimulated and conditioned by the pressure of national interests and out of these cross-pressures comes an ever-changing compromise.

"A More Perfect Union"

"The better to secure and perpetuate mutual friendship and intercourse among the people of the different states in this Union," the Articles of Confederation provided that: (1) *full faith and credit* be given in each of the states to the records, acts, and judicial proceedings of every other state; (2) the citizens of each of the states be given the *privileges and immunities* of citizens in all states; (3) *extradition* of fugitives

[18] *Bush v. Orleans Parish School Board*, 364 U.S. 500 (1960).

from justice be obtained on demand of one governor to another; (4) *interstate compacts* be made with the consent of Congress. The Constitution of 1787 incorporates all four provisions with virtually no change in wording.

Full Faith and Credit. The Constitution provides that "Full Faith and Credit shall be given in each state to the public Acts, Records and judicial Proceedings of every other state." As Americans move about the country more and more freely, this provision becomes more important. Those who go out of their state to get married; those who seek a divorce outside their own state; those who try to evade alimony or child support by moving out of the state whose court decreed the financial settlement; the beneficiaries of an estate who are not residents of the state in which the will was probated; the out-of-state owner of a car involved in a traffic accident—all these instances, and many more, come under the coverage of the Constitution.

The intent of the full faith and credit clause is clear; it is to protect the everyday legal rights of the citizen as he moves from one state to another. It is also intended to prevent a person from evading his legal obligations simply by crossing state lines. But in practice one of the most acute problems in interstate relations today is the failure of the states to meet their obligations under the full faith and credit clause. This is particularly true in cases of divorce and alimony. For example, a couple may be legally married in one state but their marriage may not be recognized in another state.[19]

Privileges and Immunities of Citizens. The Constitution reads: "The Citizens of each State shall be entitled to all Privileges and Immunities of Citizens in the several States." The meaning of this clause has never been entirely clear even to constitutional lawyers. It stems from the common citizenship which the colonists enjoyed when all were subjects of the British monarch. The original Framers included the "privileges and immunities" clause in order to continue this concept of common citizenship. In general, what it means is that no state may discriminate against citizens from another state in favor of its own.[20]

There is no dependable rule for determining the privileges and immunities of citizens in the several states. They seem to include rights to police protection, to sue in court, to acquire and hold property, to move in or out of a state, to reside in any state, and to earn a living without discriminatory restrictions. The citizen does not take with him all the privileges and immunities of his home state, however, when he enters another state; nor does the out-of-state citizen immediately acquire all the privileges and immunities of legal residents in a state. For example, a state may charge tuition to out-of-state students who enter its public schools; it may require a doctor or lawyer moving in from another state to meet its own standards for professional practice; it

---

[19]Since divorce is so common, it is at least entitled to a small footnote. The status of "out-of-domicile" divorces is sharply controverted under the full faith and credit clause. Because divorce proceedings are difficult and unpleasant in some states, the unhappily married in these states are tempted to seek divorce in other states where residence requirements are short and divorce laws are lenient. Such out-of-domicile divorces, however, are frequently questionable in the light of Supreme Court decisions. In *Williams* v. *North Carolina,* 317 U.S. 287 (1942) and 325 U.S. 226 (1945), the unfortunate Mr. Williams, a resident of North Carolina who went off to Nevada to get a divorce and remarry and who then returned to North Carolina with his second wife, was unable to obtain reversal of his conviction for "bigamous cohabitation" under North Carolina law.

[20]Further interpretation has excluded corporations from protection under the clause, although their full coverage as "persons" under "due process of law" has more than made up for this.

may require a period of residence in the state as a prerequisite for holding a state job; or it may restrict political privileges, such as voting, to citizens who have resided in the state for a certain time.

Extradition. The Constitution provides for the "interstate rendition" or "extradition" of fugitives from justice. The obligation and the procedure are clearly stated: "A Person charged in any State with Treason, Felony, or other Crime, who shall flee from Justice, and be found in another State, shall on Demand of the executive Authority of the State from which he fled, be delivered up, to be removed to the State having Jurisdiction of the Crime." But there is no way to enforce the obligation. The duty to surrender fugitives is a moral one; the Supreme Court concedes that it has no power to compel the governor of a state to fulfill his constitutional obligation. Ordinarily, of course, since no state wants to harbor the criminals of another state, in a sense the provision is self-enforcing. Because extradition is such a cumbersome and uncertain process, Congress has simplified the problem of dealing with criminals who flee across state lines by making it a federal offense for a person to move from one state to another in order to avoid prosecution or imprisonment.

Interstate Compacts. The Constitution provides that "No State shall, without the Consent of Congress . . ., enter into any Agreement or Compact with another State." In practice, this provision has been read to mean, "with the consent of Congress the several states may enter into compacts or agreements with each other." In our federal government we recognize that some problems are too big for a single state to tackle, yet too limited to warrant the attention of the national government. For such problems, which involve more than one state but do not concern the whole country, the interstate compact appears to be a reasonable approach.[21]

In years gone by, most interstate compacts were nothing more than agreements on boundary lines. More recently, however, the interstate compact has been used as a regulatory device to meet social and economic problems shared by several states. For example, several interstate agreements deal with the conservation of natural resources; here the efforts of one state would be fruitless without the cooperation of others. Thus interstate agreements are used to protect the salmon resources of the Columbia River and migratory fisheries of the Atlantic states. Similar agreements govern the amount of petroleum produced in different states and establish interstate flood control along the Connecticut River. New compacts in the welfare field provide for interstate cooperation in dealing with such problems as parole supervision, control of juvenile delinquency, and care of mentally ill patients.

Interstate compacts have often been used by adjoining states to improve navigation and transportation facilities. In 1921, New York and New Jersey,

---

[21]The Council of State Governments has dealt with the subject of interstate compacts in numerous publications. See also Vincent V. Thursby, *Interstate Co-operation: A Study of the Interstate Compact* (Washington, D.C.: Public Affairs Press, 1953); Richard H. Leach and Redding S. Sugg, Jr., *The Administration of Interstate Compacts* (Baton Rouge, La.: Louisiana State University Press, 1959); and Weldon V. Barton, *Interstate Compacts in the Political Process* (Chapel Hill, N.C.: University of North Carolina Press, 1967).

joined in compact to erect the Port of New York Authority, the planning and administrative agency for the entire port of New York City. A new development in compact activities is now appearing in the area of urban mass transportation. A recent amendment to the 1921 Port of New York compact authorizes the interstate Authority to take over and operate the electric rapid transit system between New Jersey and Manhattan terminals. Interstate agreements have also been worked out for such objectives as public utility regulation, civil defense, and highway safety.

"The consent of Congress," express or implied, has been readily obtained for more than a hundred interstate compacts. Only once has Congress reacted unfavorably toward a proposed interstate agreement. In 1947, the Conference of Southern Governors called on Congress to authorize a regional agreement for the improvement of professional and higher education in the southern states. Congressional debates on the southern compact centered on the segregation issue. Eventually the Senate killed the compact by referring it back to the Judiciary Committee. Having failed to receive the consent of Congress, the southern states decided that the consent of Congress is necessary only when a compact infringes on national power, and that since education is "reserved" to the states, congressional sanction for their compact was not required. Thus they went ahead with their compact and with their plans to develop graduate and professional schools on a regional basis. The Southern Regional Compact continues in force; it has served as a model and impetus for similar compacts in the New England region and among the western states.[22]

The Delaware River Basin Compact represents a new departure in intergovernmental relations. Its Commission, organized in 1961, comprises a representative from each of the member states (Delaware, New Jersey, New York, and Pennsylvania) appointed by the respective governors, and also a representative of the United States government appointed by the President. This is the first interstate compact to which the national government is a signatory and a party. Activities of the Commission include the planning and construction of flood prevention and water supply facilities and other water resource needs. As an experiment in national-regional administration, it bears watching.

More pervasive, and in many ways more visible, examples of "federalism without Washington" are the many interstate activities that emanate from the Council of State Governments. The Council is a governmental agency of the fifty states, created, supported, and jointly directed by all of them; it fosters interstate cooperation, provides a clearing house for research and information services, and acts as secretariat for numerous associations of state officials, including the Governors' Conference, the National Legislative Conference, and the National Association of Attorneys General. In recent years, the Governors' Conference has assumed an increasingly important role in national politics, affording the states a forum for political negotiations on national issues—even foreign policy—as well as serving as a staging area for consideration of interstate problems. The Council also maintains cooperative ar-

---

[22]See Redding S. Sugg, Jr., and George H. Jones, *The Southern Regional Education Board: Ten Years of Regional Cooperation in Higher Education* (Baton Rouge, La.: Louisiana State University Press, 1960) for an account and an appraisal of the Compact in operation.

rangements with the National Conference of Commissioners on Uniform State Laws. Working closely with the American Bar Association, the National Conference of Commissioners has successfully supported an interstate Commercial Code designed to simplify interstate transactions (and also to forestall national intervention in local business activity).[23]

At the local level, the United States Conference of Mayors, the National Association of County Officers, the National League of Cities, and other organizations of local officials and jurisdictions have joined to maximize the interests of local governments (and their own professional interests) in outputs of the federal system. Their political techniques are much the same as those of other special interests groups in the political process. Indeed, in the politics of federalism, it is sometimes as hard to differentiate the public from professional and private interests as it is to discern the lines of functional separation among the territorial jurisdictions.

Interstate Disputes. In 1787, at the time the Constitution was drafted, ten of the thirteen states were involved in serious disputes over boundaries, lands, and river rights. Under the Articles of Confederation, Congress had the authority to hear such interstate disputes. And while the Constitution gives the Supreme Court power to settle *all* cases involving two or more states, the Court itself has refused to hear what it considers "non-justiciable" disputes—that is, disputes that cannot be settled by some rule of law. In recent years, the states have brought an increasing number of suits to the Supreme Court—not only over boundary rights but also over such matters as water rights, disposal of sewage and garbage, and diversion of water resources.

The problem of enforcement is one reason why the Supreme Court is so choosy in the kind of interstate disputes it will hear. How can the Court compel a state to accept its judgment? The problem is illustrated in a long drawn-out conflict between Virginia and West Virginia. When West Virginia seceded from Virginia (when Virginia seceded from the Union), West Virginia agreed to assume its just proportion of the public debt. West Virginia later refused to meet this debt obligation, and Virginia finally commenced suit in the Supreme Court in 1906. The Supreme Court decided against West Virginia in 1915, but West Virginia ignored the decision. In 1917, Virginia again petitioned the Supreme Court for an order that would compel the West Virginia legislature to levy a tax to pay its debt to Virginia. While the Court was stalling on this proposition, West Virginia accepted the Court's earlier judgment and finally paid its debt to Virginia. But if West Virginia had not given in, how could nine justices of the Supreme Court have made the West Virginia legislators act against their will?

When states are in conflict with each other or with the national government,

---

[23]The American Bar Association appointed a special committee on uniform state laws in 1899; its first assignment was to investigate the possibilities of a uniform divorce law. Since then approximately one hundred uniform acts have been drafted, *e.g.*, in the administration of justice, inheritance of property, absentee voting, but so far the ABA has produced no satisfactory uniform divorce act.

it is essential to a stable system of federalism, that some agency of the national government have the last word. Judicial enforcement of the "supremacy clause" of the Constitution is the principal device through which the American system has met this necessity. The Constitution requires judges in every state to recognize the Constitution, the laws of the United States in pursuance of the Constitution, and treaties made under the authority of the United States as "the supreme law of the land . . . any Thing in the Constitution or Laws of any State to the Contrary notwithstanding." Although, as Justice Oliver Wendell Holmes observed, our system could endure without the Supreme Court's power to invalidate an act of Congress. (British courts, for example, do not have the power to annul acts of Parliament.) It is hard to conceive of a federal system without judicial authority to pass on the constitutionality of state laws as well as to settle disputes between states and between citizens of different states. Without this ultimate national authority, the system might be disrupted by fifty conflicting interpretations of constitutional law.

Obligations of the National Government to the States

The Constitution specifies that the states shall have certain rights and privileges in the Union. It is the obligation of the national government to insure these rights: (1) the United States shall guarantee to every state in the Union a republican form of government; (2) it shall provide equal representation for all the states in the Senate and representation proportional to population in the House; (3) it shall protect each of the states against invasion or domestic violence.

The guarantee of a republican form of government has never been put to a real test. When two opposing factions claimed to be the legitimate government of Rhode Island in the 1840s, the Supreme Court held that Congress has the power to decide which is the legitimate—the "republican"—government in a state.[24] When Congress admits the senators and representatives of a state, it thereby recognizes the authority of the government they represent.

For many years, the Supreme Court steadfastly refused to consider "political questions," but more recently the justices have appeared willing, even eager, to jump into what Mr. Justice Frankfurter aptly called "the political thicket." Long before Congress was ready to enact civil rights legislation to insure constitutional voting rights, the Supreme Court recognized the national interest in suffrage and elections in the several states. Declaring that "the United States is a constitutional democracy," the Court has consistently maintained the right of all qualified citizens to vote in state as well as in national elections, in party primaries as well as in general elections, without discrimination. The Court holds that citizens not only have the right to cast their ballots but also to have them counted and that the national government has the power to enforce these rights.[25]

More recently, the Supreme Court has taken on the much more complicated problem of legislative malapportionment in the states. Pointing out that

---

[24]*Luther* v. *Borden*, 7 How. 1 (1849).
[25]See Chapter 14 for an extended discussion of voting rights protected by federal authority. The quotation here is from Justice Reed's opinion, delivered for the Court, in *Smith* v. *Allwright*, 321 U.S. 649 (1944); this case in effect outlawed "white primaries" in the southern states.

"legislators represent people, not trees or acres," the Court held in 1964 that "as a basic constitutional standard, the Equal Protection Clause (of the Fourteenth Amendment) requires that the seats in both houses of a bicameral state legislature must be apportioned on a population basis."[26] The Court has rejected application of the "so-called Federal analogy" to state legislative apportionments. As the Court views it, equal representation of states in the Senate is the result of a compromise on the part of the original thirteen states, which surrendered some of their sovereignty and delegated some (but not all) of their powers to the national government when they entered the federal union. The political subdivisions of the states—counties, cities, or whatever—never were sovereign; they have, in fact, always been subordinate entities within the state.

In return for national protection against invasion or insurrection, every state in the union must give up the privilege of maintaining arms. No state, without the consent of Congress, may keep troops or ships of war in time of peace or engage in war unless it is actually invaded. The Constitution provides that the national government will protect any state against domestic violence whenever the legislature or the governor asks for it. On several occasions, however, the national government has intervened without such a request. Lincoln called out the national militia to put down insurrection in the southern states. In 1894, despite the protest of Governor Altgeld, President Cleveland sent federal troops into Illinois, ostensibly to protect the United States mails but actually to break up a railroad strike. A dramatic use of this power occurred in 1957, when President Eisenhower ordered federal troops to Little Rock, Arkansas to enforce a desegregation decree of the federal district court in Arkansas, despite vigorous opposition of the state's governor. In less dramatic fashion, President Kennedy sent U.S. Marshals into Alabama in 1961 to protect "Freedom Riders" who were interstate bus passengers; and in 1964, President Johnson ordered several hundred U.S. sailors to assist in the search for missing civil rights workers in Mississippi. Apparently, whether the state approves or not, the national government will send federal forces into any state whenever it seems necessary to avert national danger or serious industrial strife, to protect the constitutional rights of citizens, or simply to enforce federal laws.

Enumerated Powers and Implied Powers

We could work out a very neat pattern that shows how powers are distributed between the national government and the states: (1) Certain powers are assigned to the national government and belong to it exclusively—the conduct of foreign affairs, for example, or the control of currency. (2) Certain powers are assigned to the national government but are also held concurrently by the states—taxation or regula-

---

[26]The quotation is from Chief Justice Earl Warren's opinion in *Reynolds* v. *Sims*, 377 U.S. 533 (1964). For a more detailed discussion of developments on reapportionment and their implications for policy outputs, see Chapter 10, "The Legislators."

tion of commerce. (3) Certain powers are specifically denied to the national government—for example, Congress may not tax exports or give preference to the ports of one state over those of another. (4) Certain powers are specifically denied to the states—for example, no state may enter into any treaty, alliance, or confederation, or lay any imposts or duties on imports or exports. (5) All other powers belong to the states—that is, those powers that are neither delegated to the national government nor denied to the states or to the people.

This neat pattern of federalism looks fine on paper. But in actual practice, lawyers and politicians have almost as much difficulty in drawing a sharp line between national power and states' rights as churchmen and laymen do when they try to separate what belongs to God from what belongs to Caesar. Those who stress national power point to Article VI, Section 2, which they regard as the keystone in the arch of American federalism because it explicitly states that the Constitution and the laws and treaties of the United States shall be the supreme law of the land. Proponents of states' rights point to the Tenth Amendment, which provides that "The powers not delegated to the United States by the Constitution, nor prohibited by it to the States, are reserved to the States respectively, or to the people." What the Tenth Amendment added to the original intentions of the 1787 Framers, however, is not at all clear.[27] When the Amendment was drafted in 1789, Congress rejected a proposal to insert the word "expressly" before the word "delegated." Nevertheless, to this day, the advocates of states' rights continue to claim that the national government is limited to powers *expressly* delegated to it.

The Articles of Confederation plainly held that each state retained "every power, jurisdiction, and right" not *expressly* delegated to the United States. The Constitutional Convention was well aware of this wording; so was the First Congress, which rejected similar wording for the Tenth Amendment. In the case of *McCulloch* v. *Maryland*,[28] Chief Justice Marshall declared that the Framers, both of the Constitution of 1787 and of the Amendment in 1789, had experienced "such embarrassments" from this restrictive wording that they "probably omitted it to avoid those embarrassments." But for those not satisfied with Marshall's interpretation alone, the constructive actions of Congress may be more convincing.

When Congress in 1791 chartered the Bank of the United States, the action was bitterly criticized before and after the passage of the act. Indeed the establishment of the Bank was one of the major party issues during the first decades of the federal union. Alexander Hamilton, who proposed the Bank, felt it was a "necessary and proper" exercise of power delegated to the national government. As Secretary of the Treasury, he planned to make the Bank sole depository for government funds. Also, since the Treasury minted only gold and silver coins, he counted on the Bank to issue notes that could be used as currency in business transactions. Jefferson and his friends, who opposed the establishment of the Bank, maintained that Congress should not act beyond its

---

[27] For a brief and scholarly essay see Walter Bern's "The Meaning of the Tenth Amendment," in Robert A Goldwin (ed.), *A Nation of States* (Chicago: Rand McNally & Co., 1961). For an opposing viewpoint, see "The Case for 'States' Rights" by James Jackson Kilpatrick in the same collection of essays. Berns is a professor of political science at Cornell University; Kilpatrick is editor of the Richmond *News Leader*.

[28] Wheaton 316 (1819).

expressly assigned powers. Behind their opposition on legal grounds, however, was the fear that a Bank of the United States—in which the national government had a proprietary interest—would offer too formidable competition to the state banks. Moreover, they looked on a central banking system as a device to give the merchants and financiers more influence and greater stakes in the national government. Nevertheless, Congress voted to approve the charter and its constitutionality was never attacked in the courts.

A Second Bank of the United States was chartered by Congress for another twenty years in 1816, again amid sharp controversy between the advocates of states' rights and the supporters of national power. The Second Bank was initially sponsored by the Democrats to help the national government manage some of the financial problems that beset the country after the War of 1812. Later the Bank was attacked by the Jacksonian Democrats, ostensibly on constitutional grounds, actually for a variety of reasons: that the Bank was a political machine for the Federalists; that it represented the commercial interests of the eastern seaboard as against the western farmers; that its stock was held largely by British and other foreign investors; that its inefficient and corrupt management contributed to the failure of many local banks in the postwar depression. The Second Bank became such an object of popular mistrust that a number of states passed laws restricting its activities.

In *McCulloch* v. *Maryland*, the Supreme Court considered the question of whether a state could legally restrict the activities of a federal instrumentality. Before answering the question, the Court first determined that Congress had the power to incorporate the Bank even though the Constitution does not specifically mention banking as one of the national government's enumerated powers. The Court pointed out that the enumeration of powers in Article I, Section 8, ends with a blanket clause giving the Congress power "to make all laws which shall be necessary and proper for carrying into execution the foregoing powers, and all other powers vested by this Constitution in the government of the United States, or in any department or officer thereof." This clause is placed with the *powers* of Congress—not among the limitations on its powers—and it purports to grant additional power, not to restrict those already granted. As Chief Justice Marshall construed the meaning of "necessary and proper," Congress had the discretion to choose whatever means it deemed convenient, useful, or essential to perform its legislative functions. Since Congress chose to establish a Bank to facilitate the fiscal operations of the national government, the Bank must be regarded as a federal instrumentality.

The same constitutional interpretation that upheld the establishment of the Bank of the United States has also given judicial sanction to subsequent acts of Congress extending national controls over banking—the National Banking System inaugurated in 1863, the Federal Reserve System established in 1913, and the Federal Deposit Insurance Corporation in 1933. Indeed, the doctrine of implied powers which developed out of this early case has become the crucial doctrine justifying expansion of national instrumentalities and activities to meet the increasing and changing needs of the American people.

In answering the primary question of *McCulloch* v. *Maryland* the Court established a second doctrine important in setting the functional pattern of federalism—the immunity of national government activities from state controls. Maryland had attempted to restrict the Bank by placing a heavy tax on its activity within the state. The Court held that the tax was unconstitutional. The Chief Justice argued that the power to create implies a power to preserve. And since the national government had the power to create the Bank, it logically follows that the national government had also the power to preserve the Bank. Marshall then argued that the power to tax involves the power to destroy; again it follows logically that, if a state has the power to tax, it would also have the power to destroy a federal instrumentality. As Marshall saw it, the people of the United States created a national government and made its laws supreme. The states have no power, *by taxation or otherwise*,[29] to impede or in any manner control the operations of the national government that are undertaken either under the powers specifically enumerated or under those which can be reasonably implied. Thus the Maryland law was declared null and void by the Court.

The opinion of Chief Justice Marshall in *McCulloch* v. *Maryland* is generally conceded to be one of the great state papers in exposition of American federalism. Keep in mind, however, that it was the policy decision of Congress to create the First Bank and the Second Bank which in fact set the federal pattern of implied powers. The Court did no more than give judicial affirmation to congressional policy. The decision of the Supreme Court was not delivered until 1819, but Congress chartered the First Bank of the United States in 1791. Judicial interpretations over the years have justified a great many changes in the functioning of American federalism. Policy-making at any time, however, represents a continuous intermeshing of legislative, executive, and judicial decisions, in the national government and in the states.

"Creative Federalism"

A discussion of federalism entirely in terms of constitutional law would be both superficial and incomplete. The "indestructible states" within the "indestructible union," all on an "equal footing" with one another, each claiming "sovereign rights" and "reserved powers"—while these are important concepts, they also are part of the stereotyped vocabulary of endless and fruitless debates. A functional approach to federalism offers a more realistic account of intergovernmental relations as they have developed in actual practice within the constitutional framework. As we turn our attention to specific governmental policies (i.e., courses of political action) it will become obvious that changes in environment since the eighteenth century—physical, technological, economic, cultural, intellectual, and political—have had a tremendous impact on American federalism.

[29]In numerous cases, the Court has since upheld extension of the national taxing power over many kinds of state activities, and vice versa. In answer to Marshall's dictum, the "power to tax involves the power to destroy," Justice Holmes once retorted, "but not while this court sits."

Federalism in Action

The relationship between the national government and the states may be viewed from various perspectives. The most familiar one is to regard the federal structure as a three-level hierarchy—the local communities at the base, the state governments at the intermediary level, and the national government at the apex. Another model focuses on the national government as the central government, remote from the people who live in the states and local communities, some of which are at great physical (and cultural) distance from the national capital. If we accept either of these models of federal government, we are led to believe that state and local governments are "closer" to the people than the national government. If, however, without referring to either of these models (which are, after all, no more than arbitrary abstractions) you take a fresh look at American federalism in action, you will observe that many agencies of the national government are at work in your local community. As a matter of fact, most activities of the national government are administered locally, and about 90 per cent of the federal civilian employees live and work outside of the District of Columbia. Certainly the national government is "close" to the people, whether we think of "closeness" in terms of physical proximity, communications, or direct controls and primary services. Consult your telephone directory and see how many *local* phone numbers are listed under "United States Government": the Post Office, the Department of Justice, the Department of Agriculture, the Veterans' Administration, the Treasury Department, Health, Education, and Welfare, and others.

That the Founding Fathers well understood the operational as well as the structural side of federalism, even in 1787, is implicit in the numerous constitutional provisions for cooperative and concurrent action by the national government and the states.[30] Some years ago, Morton Grodzins of the University of Chicago, was asked to examine "The Federal System" for the President's Commission on National Goals. In his study, he found that American federalism has never been a system of separated governmental activities. Throughout our history, the national and state governments have shared activities, powers, and responsibilities. Grodzins maintained that this is a first principle and a continuing practice in American federalism.[31]

The Commission on Intergovernmental Relations, created by Congress at the request of President Eisenhower, points up the complexity of federalism in the mid-twentieth century. The Commission examined the major fields in which the national government and the states were both active: agriculture, civil aviation, civil defense, education, employment security, highways, housing and urban renewal, natural disaster relief, natural resources and conservation, public health, vocational rehabilitation, and welfare. Not one of

---

[30] Daniel Elazar tabulates seventeen constitutional provisions for "sharing." See *The American Partnership*, p. 309.

[31] The President's Commission on National Goals, *Goals for Americans* (an American Assembly book) (Englewood Cliffs, N.J.: Prentice-Hall, Inc., 1960).

these fields is even mentioned in the Constitution of 1787, although today all of them are of vital nationwide concern. The Commission pointed out that broad interpretations of the Constitution have given the national government almost unlimited power. Faced with the practical problem of allocating responsibilities, the Commission found that the crucial question is not which government—national or state—has the constitutional right to perform a given function, but rather which government can perform it most effectively in meeting the needs of the people.

Because the Commission did not evolve a national policy or prepare any blueprint for the improvement of intergovernmental relations, President Eisenhower next persuaded the Governors' Conference to establish a Federal-State Joint Action Committee. The hope was that this Committee would make some specific recommendations for unwinding the complicated pattern of modern federalism—that is, for returning to the states as many activities as they were willing and able to handle without federal interference or assistance.

The Federal-State Joint Action Committee labored diligently over its assignment to "decentralize" the federal government.[32] It finally came up with the following recommendations, among others: that the states assume full financial support for some of the older programs in vocational education, such as practical nurse training and the training program for the fisheries trade; that the states manage and finance their own solutions to problems of sewerage and water pollution. But even these modest recommendations came to grief in the political arena when the interest groups affected converged on Washington. State departments of education, educational interest groups, the nurses' associations, and the fishing industry all sent representatives to oppose any cuts in federal aid for vocational education. The United States Conference of Mayors, the American Municipal Association, and various sportsmen's associations also sent their spokesmen to ask for more, not less, federal aid for local waste disposal, which they testified was a grave national problem. And so Congress was persuaded not to cut back these particular programs in health, education, and welfare.

Thus concrete proposals to curtail specific activities of the national government are usually defeated by local demands on Washington for continuing and increasing federal aid. In fact, cooperative federalism correlates with the pattern of political power in America today. The alliance between conservative rural representatives and powerful economic interests in many states resists regulatory activities by the state government and also produces economy-oriented budgets which do not adequately meet public needs. Because state governments have failed to respond to the urgent demands of urban and industrialized communities, city-dwellers, a majority of the population in most states, have turned in their frustration to the national government for help. U.S. senators serve statewide constituencies, U.S. representatives come from congressional districts much more populous than state legislative districts, and

---

[32]The Federal-State Joint Action Committee was organized at the Governors' Conference at Williamsburg in 1957. Upon its first *Report to the President* in 1958, President Eisenhower immediately requested Congress to follow through with appropriate legislation, but Congress was persuaded not to take action. Later the Governors' Conference voted to continue the Committee but did not extend its approval to the Committee's specific proposals for the transfer of programs from the national government to state governments.

the President of course represents a nationwide electorate. Hence the national government has been more accessible to people in the cities, who because of underrepresentation could less easily influence their state legislatures. But now that state legislatures are elected on the principle of equal representation of people—in accord with recent mandates from the U.S. Supreme Court —changing patterns of power and influence may redress the balance between urban and rural interests in state politics.

Often the arguments for or against activities of the national government are really arguments for or against governmental activities in general. Indeed, it is difficult to single out programs of the national government in which state and local governments do not participate. Even in matters of national defense, the state and local governments play a considerable part. The national guard is composed of state militia units which remain under command of their respective governors until called into emergency service by the national government; training must meet the national standards and, in return, the national government pays most of the costs. The Selective Service is responsible for implementing the Universal Military Training and Service Act, but its administration is left largely to the state headquarters and local draft boards. And quite obviously, the location of military bases throughout the country reflects local community pressures as well as national strategic considerations; the payroll of a military base is a bonanza for any Main Street.

In the area of law enforcement, state and local police agencies have access to the fingerprint files, reporting service, and other facilities of the Federal Bureau of Investigation, including special courses in the FBI's famous National Academy for training in modern police methods. Immediately following the passage of the Civil Rights Act of 1964, the new Director of Community Relations personally conferred with state and local officials, especially in the southern states, to plan for the implementation of the controversial legislation through "voluntary compliance." This is the usual pattern of intergovernmental relations—personal conferences, joint planning, continuous consultation, interchange of facilities, awareness of common enterprise in the public interest. Whatever the field of intergovernmental activity, professional interests and professional standards at the program level are likely to be more important than legal verbalisms and political platitudes. The U.S. geologist works professionally with the state geologist on the problems of conserving water resources. Inspectors from the Food and Drug Administration meet their counterparts in the state departments of agriculture. Rangers in the U.S. Forest Service cooperate with state forest rangers to preserve our forests. Examples of official collaboration and cooperation can be cited until they cover the whole range of intergovernmental activities.

Shared Finances

The most friendly personal relations do not alone make a partnership. In a truly federal system, shared activities mean shared finances. Earlier in this chapter, we gave some account of the development of grants-in-aid from the national government to the states—land grants, service grants, and cash grants. Most important in modern federalism are the cash grants. The grant-in-aid has become an essential tool of modern federalism, a device employed not only to alleviate the wide disparities in financial resources among states and among local communities, but also to promote minimum national standards for the general welfare of the people in all the states. In this regard, the national government systematically supplements state finances with cash grants for some one hundred programs in areas of national concern.

Figures on governmental expenditures are always impressive, even awesome, in total amounts. But because the methods of reporting often vary from one governmental unit to another and even from one year to the next, tables and charts of public finances are never too reliable. Nevertheless, the distribution of fiscal resources is so crucial to cooperative federalism that to understand how cooperative federalism works we must scrutinize (and carefully interpret) the basic facts and figures. Gross figures can be quite misleading, and a quite different picture emerges when we take into account such variables as (1) increasing population; (2) changes in the economy (including the fluctuating value of the dollar) and basic patterns of living; (3) new and different political demands and supports.

All governmental expenditures—national, state, and local—have skyrocketed since the Great Depression year of 1932. In analyzing these ever-increasing expenditures, however, we must keep in mind that in the same period the population of the United States has also been rapidly growing. In 1932, there were about 124 million persons in the United States; in 1966 there were about 196 million. This "population explosion" has various implications for public finances. Growth in population increases the number of people who need public services, while it also increases the number whose taxes support government programs. Thus per capita figures may be more illuminating than gross figures. Table 5–1 shows that governmental expenditures have increased more than eighteen times between 1932 and 1966; Table 5–2 reveals that the per capita increase between 1932 and 1966 was about eleven times the 1932 figure.[33]

Government expenditures are reported annually in terms of the current value of the dollar; over the years, however, the value of the dollar has fluctuated considerably. Thus if we were to use the 1954 dollar as a standard ($1.00), then we would note that the 1932 dollar bought $1.97 in goods and services whereas the 1966 dollar was worth only 83¢.[34] A recent study of government spending in the twenty-five year period between 1936 and 1961 indicates that the 1961 expenditures of all American governments (national, state, and local) were almost nine times those of 1936. But when the investi-

---

[33]On the other hand, per capita figures may actually distort the picture in that still other factors alter the equations between demands and supports. For example, rising percentages of old people and of schoolchildren (the current trend) increase the demand for welfare and educational programs, whereas the corresponding decrease in the percentage of adult workers in the population means fewer taxpayers to foot the bill for these additional services.

[34]Tax Foundation, Inc., *Facts and Figures on Government Finance*, 14th Ed. (New York: Tax Foundation, Inc., 1967), "Purchasing Power of the Dollar, 1909–1966," as measured by consumer price index, p. 62.

gators took into consideration the decline in purchasing power of the dollar over this period, they found that the increase was only about three-and-one-half times. When they adjusted the figures further to cover population growth, they discovered that the 1961 expenditures—in constant (1961) dollars on a per capita basis—were but two-one-half times those of 1936.[35]

TABLE 5-1 Governmental Expenditures
(in millions of dollars)

YEAR	TOTAL: NATIONAL, STATE, AND LOCAL	NATIONAL	STATE	LOCAL
1932	$12,437	$4,266	$2,568	$5,609
1936	16,758	9,165	3,144	4,449
1940	20,417	10,061	4,545	5,811
1946	79,707	66,543	6,162	7,011
1952	99,847	71,568	13,330	14,948
1956	115,796	75,991	18,379	21,426
1962	176,240	113,428	29,210	33,601
1966	219,500	137,800	38,200	43,500

Source: Tax Foundation, Inc., *Facts and Figures on Government Finance*, 14th ed. (New York: Tax Foundation, Inc., 1967), p. 19.

TABLE 5-2 Governmental Expenditures—
dollars per capita distribution
(in dollars)

YEAR	TOTAL: NATIONAL, STATE, AND LOCAL	NATIONAL	STATE	LOCAL
1932	$100	$34	$21	$45
1936	131	72	25	35
1940	155	77	35	44
1946	581	485	45	51
1952	648	461	86	96
1956	695	456	110	129
1962	955	614	158	182
1966	1126	707	196	223

Source: *Facts and Figures*, p. 20.

Still another yardstick which helps one to gain a true perspective on public finance is the relationship of governmental expenditures to the gross national product (GNP). (GNP = total market value of all the nation's goods and services over a given time-period.) The GNP was $58 billion in 1932, $681 billion in 1965; in 1932, total governmental spending amounted to 18.3 per cent of the GNP, in 1965 27.3 per cent, an increase of 50 per cent in terms of the national economy (see Table 5–3). In other words, the costs of government keep going up, but just how high and at what rate depends on which yard-

---

[35] Frederick C. Mosher and Orville F. Poland, *The Costs of American Governments, Facts, Trends, Myths* (New York: Dodd, Mead & Co., 1964).

TABLE 5-3 Gross National Product
and Government Expenditures
(in billions of dollars)

			AS A PERCENTAGE OF GNP		
YEAR	GNP	TOTAL: NATIONAL STATE, AND LOCAL	TOTAL	NATIONAL	STATE & LOCAL
1932	$58.0	$10.6	18.3%	5.5%	12.8%
1936	82.5	16.0	19.4	10.4	9.0
1942	157.9	64.0	40.5	35.5	5.0
1946	208.5	45.5	21.8	17.0	4.7
1952	345.5	93.6	27.1	20.5	6.5
1956	419.2	104.1	24.8	17.2	7.7
1961	520.1	149.0	28.6	19.6	9.0
1965	681.2	185.9	27.3	18.1	9.2

Source: Facts and Figures, p. 32.

stick you use. Beware of the sweeping statistics and look for the meaningful interpretation.

Furthermore, analysis of governmental expenditures is entirely unrealistic unless it is related to who gets what. A political system functions and survives only so long as it continues to serve the needs and interests of the people. Sooner or later we must all face the fact that "The American Way of Life" is not what it used to be—in 1790, 1890, 1932, or even in 1967. Industrialization, urbanization, population explosion, and other contemporary phenomena have made basic changes in patterns of living, which in turn account for (in fact, demand) new and different notions of what constitutes essential governmental services. Government is expected to provide much of the overhead costs for our industrialized and urbanized society: interstate highways, education, health facilities, welfare programs, recreation programs, control of air and water pollution, etc. What was good enough for the fathers and mothers is not enough for the sons and daughters. We expect a cloverleaf at the crossroads; a nuclear reactor for the state university, as well as a stadium and modern dormitories; a golf course, a Little League baseball field, and a civic auditorium for the townspeople, as well as streetlights and paved roads; mass transit and parking facilities for the suburbanites; soil conservation experts for the farmer and home demonstration agents for the farmer's wife.

Returning to the distributive aspects of federal financing, we note that all of our tables show that the greatest increase in governmental expenditures over the past thirty or forty years has been at the national level. This fact is frequently used to prove the "nationalization" of the federal system. But the proportion of national outlays devoted to purely domestic programs over the same period has decreased: only about 26 per cent of the national budget in 1967, as compared with about 31 per cent in 1930, was allocated to domestic civilian activities (see Table 5–4).

By assuming leadership of the "free world" (i.e., of the noncommunist nations) since World War II, the United States has had to bear the brunt of two major wars—in Korea and in Viet Nam. Since Hiroshima and Nagasaki we have been determined to keep the lead in nuclear weapons; as other powers have joined the nuclear club, the costs of trying to maintain that leadership

TABLE 5-4   Federal Budget Expenditures by Selected Function*
(in millions of dollars)

YEAR	TOTAL EXPENDITURES	NATIONAL DEFENSE	INTERNATIONAL AFFAIRS & FINANCE	VETERANS' BENEFITS	INTEREST	ALL OTHER
1789	$ 4	$ 1	$ - - -	$ - - -	$ 2	$ 1
1900	521	191	- - -	141	40	149
1920	6357	3887	435	332	1024	569
1930	3320	734	14	821	697	1054
1945	98303	81216	3312	2095	3662	8018
1953	74120	50442	2216	4368	6583	10511
1961	81515	47494	3954	5414	9050	15603
1967	112847	50541	4177	5721	12854	29554

Source: *Facts and Figures*, p. 76.
*The years selected include maximum budgets for World War II (1945) and the Korean War (1953); 1967 reflects mounting costs in Viet Nam. Selection of 1930 as a year of "normalcy" is purely arbitrary; it is a year of isolation in foreign policy, with minimum international commitments. Note also that these figures are from current budget presentations and do not show constant dollar values.

have become staggering. Military budgets for nuclear and conventional warfare, multiple defense-related activities, space research and technology, veterans' benefits, and interest on debts incurred for such purposes are the main reasons for the tremendous increases in national expenditures. But not even the strongest proponents of states' rights suggest that the national government abdicate its responsibilities for programming and financing our military and foreign policies.

The "revolution" in federal financing—in terms of grants-in-aid from the national government to states and local communities—is older than federal union, if we take into account the school grants to the states under the Northwest Ordinance of 1787. But as we have noted above, not until the New Deal of the 1930s did national cash grants become numerous and sizeable enough to affect the overall fiscal pattern. In recent years, national grants have become a significant aspect of cooperative federalism. But, as the President's Advisory Commission on Intergovernmental Relations reported in 1964, although the amounts seem to have zoomed, the percentages of total federal expenditures in terms of GNP reduce the whole grant-in-aid system to chicken feed[36] (see Table 5–5).

When we examine the grant-in-aid system in greater detail (who gets what) a realistic picture of cooperative federalism begins to emerge. First, there is considerable variation in federal contributions to state and local revenues. In early grant programs, the states were usually expected to match the federal grants dollar for dollar. More recently, equalizing features have been introduced—allocation formulas calculated to grant federal aid on the basis of program need or financial need. "Equalization" of federal grants, however, may mean equal grants to all the states, equal grants per unit of need, or

[36] In his 1968 budget message, President Johnson noted that "grant outlays have risen steadily and substantially in recent years," and recommended another increase for 1968. Scrutiny of the Budget, however, reveals that the estimated $16.7 billion recommended for grants-in-aid (compared with $14.8 billion in 1967) was 1.2 per cent of the total budget in 1968 compared with 1.1 per cent in 1967, whereas the GNP had grown from 1966 to 1967 by nearly 5.4 per cent.

TABLE 5-5 Federal Aid to State and Local Governments
(in millions of dollars)

YEAR	TOTAL FEDERAL AID	FEDERAL AID AS A PERCENTAGE OF STATE & LOCAL REVENUE	FEDERAL AID AS A PERCENTAGE OF FEDERAL GENERAL EXPENDITURE TOTAL	CIVIL	FEDERAL AID AS PERCENTAGE OF GNP
1932	$232	3%	6%	12%	0.4%
1936	948	11	10	17	1.1
1940	945	10	10	14	0.9
1946	855	7	1	10	0.4
1952	2566	10	4	21	0.7
1956	3335	10	5	20	0.8
1962	7857	14	8	26	1.4

Source: Advisory Commission on Intergovernmental Relations, Report, "The Role of Equalization in Federal Grants," January, 1964.

grants designed to bring about more equal program levels in the different states. The problem is highly complicated by the fact that the states are unequal or unlike in various ways. Different states have not only unequal capacities to finance, but also quite different inclinations toward supporting public programs fostered by the federal government. And it is the very essence of federalism to tolerate differences from state to state—even in the face of a "strong national interest."

The national government now makes available to the states several hundred grant-in-aid programs. Despite this great proliferation, 85 per cent of the grants in 1967 fell into three categories, which were, in rank order: health, labor, and welfare; highways; and education and research. National grants-in-aid for highways were introduced in 1916; grants for health, labor, and welfare reflect the profound change in public philosophy brought about by the New Deal; grants-in-aid for education in the schools did not amount to much until the 1960s.

No doubt federal grants-in-aid stimulate the states to provide services they might not otherwise undertake. No doubt, also, a state legislature is sometimes stimulated by the promise of federal money to undertake programs that the taxpayers of the state cannot afford. Legally, the states are quite free to reject grants-in-aid, for strictly speaking there is no coercion to accept grants-in-aid. State legislators, however, find it extremely difficult to explain to their constituents why their state should be denied a slice of the national pie. Thus the same state legislature that berates the national government for encroaching upon states' rights in one field will do everything it can to qualify for federal grants-in-aid in a half-dozen other fields.

The national government provides grants-in-aid to the states only if the states are willing to meet conditions specified by Congress. National agencies that administer the funds require the states to submit their plans for advance approval. Many of the "conditions" attached to the grants are worked out through personal consultation and professional collaboration between the federal and state agencies concerned. For some programs, the conditions are but one-shot affairs; that is to say, when the program is established, the state may have to agree to do something in particular (set up a governmental agency, provide a merit system for personnel involved). Usually the only continuing condition is that the state or locality must appropriate matching funds. For some programs, however, federal agencies examine the state programs in operation, inspect the work that is done with federal aid, and audit the accounts of the cooperating state agencies. State officials are naturally inclined to resent excessive federal "meddling" in such "state" affairs. In this respect, the most controversial "guidelines" so far established by Congress appear in Title VI of the Civil Rights Act of 1964, which stipulates:

> No person in the United States shall, on the ground of race, color, or national origin, be excluded from participation in, be denied the benefits of, or be subjected to discrimination under any program or activity receiving Federal financial assistance.

Whenever federal agencies have attempted to implement the "clear intent" of Congress, charges and countercharges have assailed the unhappy bureaucrats—usually that they have exceeded (or fallen short of) their duties in establishing congressional policy with respect to facilities or services in local communities underwritten by the national government. In response to these and other expressions of dissatisfaction—mainly with the rigidity of conditions sometimes attached to grants-in-aid—President Johnson emphasized that "the basis of creative federalism is cooperation."[37] Recognizing that cooperative federalism is more than a matter of shared finances, the President specifically directed heads of the major federal departments and agencies concerned with grants-in-aid to consult directly with the chief officials of state, county, and local governments so that intergovernmental programs could be joint and cooperatively planned, organized, and managed.

"Metropolitan America: Challenge to Federalism"

In Chapter 2 we noted that the most radical changes in American life arose from and have been reflected in the shift of population from farms to cities. In the past twenty years, however, the old distinction between rural and urban areas has been largely obscured by the new population pattern that we call the metropolitan area.[38] A metropolitan area is an economic, social, and cultural community rather than a single political unit; it may embrace more than one county—even sprawl over several states—and include a maze of cities, boroughs, townships, and special administrative districts. According to the 1960 census nearly two-thirds of the nation's

---

[37]Memorandum of President Johnson, November 11, 1966, to heads of departments and agencies concerned with federal grants-in-aid. Quoted in Advisory Commission on Intergovernmental Relations, *Eighth Annual Report*, January 31, 1967, Washington D.C. The agencies to whom the memorandum was addressed included: the Departments of Defense; Justice; Interior; Agriculture; Commerce; Labor; Health, Education, and Welfare; Housing and Urban Development; the Office of Economic Opportunity; and the Office of Emergency Planning.

[38]The "standard metropolitan area" first used in the 1950 census refers to any county or group of counties which contains at least one city of 50,000 or more inhabitants. The 1960 census term "standard metropolitan statistical area" modifies the 1950 criterion in order to break down the largest metropolitan areas for purposes of statistical convenience.

population was living in metropolitan areas, half of these in metropolitan areas with more than a million inhabitants.

The bulk of American business activities is now carried on in the metropolitan areas; four-fifths of our taxable wealth is located in these areas; and more than 80 per cent of the national revenues from personal income taxes come from them. The metropolitan areas are the centers of economic power and affluence; but concentrated in these same areas is the major proportion of the nation's underprivileged, uneducated, undernourished, unemployed, and unemployable. Here are great cultural and educational opportunities. Here also are racial ghettos; slums; centers of crime, juvenile delinquency, and drug addiction; and a disproportionate number of broken homes, indigent elderly people, and illegitimate children. Here also is the weakest link in the American federal system, an amazing and appalling fragmentation of political power, a tangled web of multijurisdictional lines. In the 212 metropolitan areas counted in the 1960 census,[39] more than 18,000 units of government—counties,

---

[39]*Metropolitan America: Challenges to Federalism*, a study submitted to the Intergovernmental Relations Subcommittee of the Senate Committee on Government Operations by the Advisory Commission on Intergovernmental Relations, October, 1966 (Washington, D.C.: U.S. Government Printing Office, 1966), p. 7. Much of the material in this section is derived from studies and hearings of this Subcommittee. *Megalopolis* by Jean Gottmann (Cambridge, Mass.: M.I.T. Press, 1961) depicts in scholarly and dramatic fashion the problems of the urban northeastern seaboard, "more the size of a nation than a metropolis . . ., one of the largest industrial belts in existence and the greatest financial and political hubs on earth." This "partitioned land" crosses the boundaries of ten states and the District of Columbia, with 117 counties subdivided—in overlapping layers—into municipalities, townships, boroughs, and special districts.

Figure 5-1

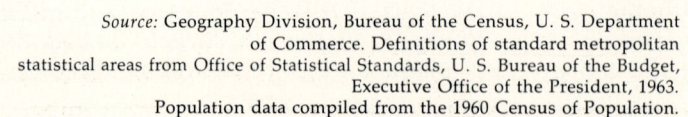

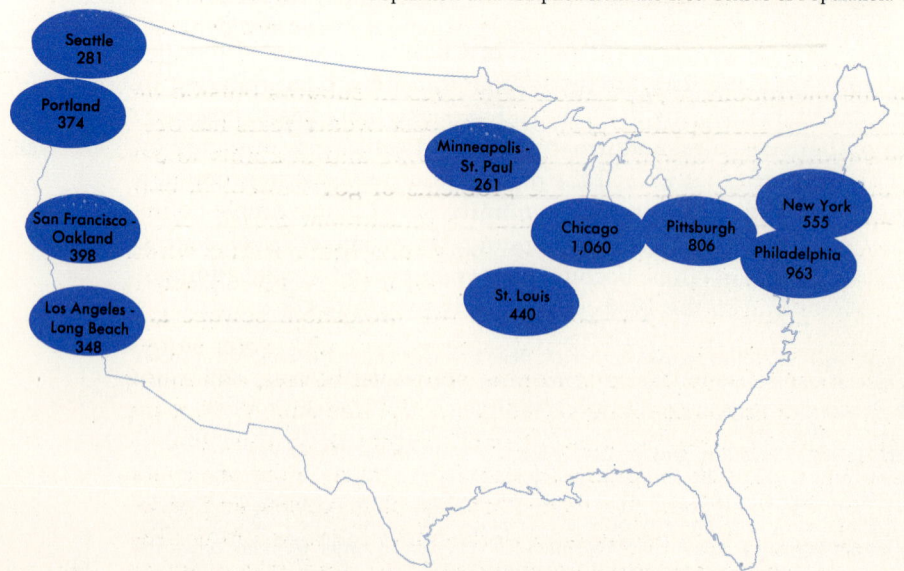

Source: Geography Division, Bureau of the Census, U. S. Department of Commerce. Definitions of standard metropolitan statistical areas from Office of Statistical Standards, U. S. Bureau of the Budget, Executive Office of the President, 1963. Population data compiled from the 1960 Census of Population.

Seattle 281
Portland 374
Minneapolis - St. Paul 261
San Francisco - Oakland 398
Chicago 1,060
Pittsburgh 806
New York 555
Philadelphia 963
Los Angeles - Long Beach 348
St. Louis 440

townships, municipalities, school districts, special districts—were variously responsible for public policies and public services. (The map on the facing page shows the number of local governments subsumed in the ten largest metropolitan areas in 1962.)

The democratic process usually moves slowly under any conditions, but in a federal system with multiple authorities and multiple constituencies, intergovernmental action sometimes resembles an old-fashioned game of parchesi: Take one step forward, lose a turn, go forward three steps, go back one step, lose two turns, and so on to the final goal. Figure 5–2 indicates the complexity of intergovernmental relations in federal aid programs by illustrating the necessary approval process for a hypothetical community's application for a national grant to improve its water system. Note how many different agencies are involved at the various points of (1) initiative, (2) review, (3) authority to disapprove, and (4) authority to approve. Note also how many different channels may be followed from one point to another, leaving open multiple possibilities for delay, for duplication of efforts, and ultimately for neglect of dangerous situations. Newark, New Jersey, for example, was one of the first cities in the country to apply for a wide range of national grants under the Demonstration Cities Act of 1966; by the summer of 1967, when terrible riots broke out in that city, the applications were still "in process"—not yet even approved, much less implemented.

Local governments somehow manage—though not always adequately—to operate the schools, pave the streets, collect the garbage, and provide police and fire protection. But when it comes to the broader issues of metropolitan concern—such as commuter transportation, water supply, air polution, slum clearance, open housing, city planning, and zoning for the area as a whole—then the institutional base, the legal authority, and—most important—the sense of community which must underpin governmental action are generally lacking or inadequate.

Nearly half the metropolitan population now lives in suburbs outside the central city; most of the metropolitan growth in the past twenty years has been in these same suburbs. The disparity in levels of living and in ability to pay for essential public services aggravates the problems of government in both the suburbs and the cities. On the one hand, the mushroom growth of the suburbs puts extraordinary pressure upon recently rural communities which hardly are prepared—psychologically or financially—for the required tremendous expansion in public services: police and fire protection; sewage and garbage disposal systems; paved streets and streetlights; and a water supply adequate for sprinkling lawns, air-conditioning split-level houses, and filling the swimming pools in the burgeoning subdivisions. Parents who move to the suburbs usually claim "it's for the kids," but the higher proportion of children in the suburban population puts an unexpected strain on the taxpayers' ability and willingness to support the needed schools, playgrounds, and parks.

On the other hand, the more poorly paid workers and depressed minorities who generally comprise the residential population of the central city are forced

APPROVAL PROCESS FOR WATER AND SEWER PROJECTS

PROJECT: Water System for a Hypothetical Community
- of less than 5,500 people
- in an economically depressed area of the Ozarks
- near a larger city
- in an area with a metropolitan planning agency

1 Possible Point of Initiative **2** Possible Review Point **3** Authority to Disapprove **4** Authority to Approve

LOANS AND GRANTS CAN BE REQUESTED FROM:
- DEPT. OF HOUSING AND URBAN DEVELOPMENT
- DEPT. OF AGRICULTURE — Farmer's Home Administration
- DEPT. OF COMMERCE — Economic Development Administration

Nonprofit Corporation	Special District	City Government	County Government	Metropolitan Planning Agency*	State Government	Interstate Regional Agency	Federal Regional Office	EXECUTIVE DEPT., WASHINGTON
1	1	1 2	1 2	2	1 2		3 2 HUD Regional Administrator, Ft. Worth, Tex.	3 4 HUD
1	1	1 2	1 2	2	1 2		3 2 FHA State Director, Columbia, Mo.	3 4 Agriculture
1	1	1 2	1 2	2	1 2	2	3 2 EDA Area Director, Detroit, Mich.	3 4 Commerce

→ 2 DEPT. OF INTERIOR (Water Pollution Aspects)

Applicant is notified of the appropriate agency to apply to after Washington review of Preapplication Form No. 101

*Review required by Section 204, Demonstration Cities and Metropolitan Development Act of 1966

APPROVAL PROCESS Could Follow Many Possible Intergovernmental Channels Depending on
- nature of applying agency
- nature of project
- law and administrative regulations *different for each agency*
- decisions by federal officials as to appropriate nonfederal reviewing agencies

Source: Bureau of the Budget, *Creative Federalism,* Hearings before Senate Subcommittee on Intergovernmental Relations, Part I, p. 292.

Figure 5-2. *Intergovernmental Relations in Federal Aid Programs.*

to live in the rundown quarters which the suburbanites left behind. City-dwellers therefore find it hard to pay taxes for even the minimum services which government must provide when people in large numbers live closely together. Just the costs of basic sanitation and police and fire protection run inordinately high in city slums. But even higher are the many overhead costs of modern industry and commerce which are written into city budgets—and these are paid through the taxes of city people, even though nonresidents may be benefiting most from these services, which include airports, bus terminals, parking facilities, and water works (not only to meet residential needs for sanitation and drinking water, but also to air-condition skyscraper offices and to provide steam for industrial plants, which in turn contribute most to the air pollution problem).

It is useless to argue how the 1787 Framers would have had us cope with the government of modern metropolitan areas. There is no mention of metropolitan areas, nor for that matter of cities, in the Constitution. In 1790, New York was the largest city in the country with a population of some 33,000; Philadelphia, the capital, was second in size with less than 29,000; the District of Columbia was an undeveloped project not yet named, but only referred to as "the Federal City." Today all three of these cities are located in metropolitan areas that embrace governments in multiple states and localities. Along with more than 200 other metropolitan areas, they face social, economic, technological, and political problems which the Founding Fathers could not even have imagined.

Perhaps the greatest challenge to contemporary federalism is how to devise intergovernmental machinery—national, state, and local—which will function cooperatively and creatively to make the American Way a reality for the great majority of American people who now live and work in these metropolitan areas. Because neither local nor state governments have been able to deal effectively with fast-deteriorating and increasingly critical conditions in the urban centers, the national government has been drawn more and more into the vortex of community relations. As the President's Advisory Commission on Intergovernmental Relations explains it," economic consideration alone, and the predominant position of the metropolitan areas in the national economy, make the development of these areas a vital concern of the federal government."[40] But more than economics is involved, as the riots of the past few summers in Watts, Chicago, Jacksonville, Harlem, Brooklyn, Newark, Detroit, and many more sore spots festering across the country have made obvious. Policies that have penned minority groups into city slums and denied them equal opportunities to enjoy "the American standard of living" have stirred previously apathetic citizens to a violent expression of their alienation.[41]

In Part IV we shall be discussing more fully some of the outputs of our federal system. Here it is sufficient to indicate that the most significant aspect of "creative federalism" has been the increasing responsibility of the national government for the care and development of "Metropolitan America." Perhaps the most dramatic political move was the creation of the Department of Housing and Urban Development in 1965 and the subsequent appointment of a distinguished Negro, Robert Weaver, to head it. Although the Department of Housing and Urban Affairs now directs the principal programs of the national government affecting the physical aspects of the metropolitan areas, many other federal agencies (the Department of Health, Education, and Welfare, the Office of Economic Opportunity, the Department of Labor, and the Department of Commerce, to name but a few) are also deeply involved in local community projects.

Although the "blight of the cities" is a nationwide problem, uniform national solutions are not possible—because of great diversity among the cities themselves, because of the multigovernmental authorities involved, and

---

[40]*Metropolitan America*, p. 119.

[41]A few days after the 1967 summer riots in Newark, Joseph Kraft, columnist in *The Washington Post*, called attention to Newark's own description of itself in its application for participation in a national grant-in-aid program: "Among major American cities, Newark and its citizens face the highest percentage of substandard housing, the most crime per hundred thousand of population, the heaviest per capita tax burden, the sharpest shifts in population and the highest rate of venereal disease, new cases of tuberculosis and maternal mortality." *Washington Post*, July 20, 1967.

because of the American tradition of "grass roots" democracy. Consequently the most hopeful approach appears to be "creative federalism," which is a concerted and planned use of intergovernmental resources with intergovernmental decision-making at every stage from planning to implementation and maintenance. At least this is the rationale of the Demonstration Cities and Metropolitan Act of 1966, which authorizes national grants-in-aid to furnish social services to entire neighborhoods, to help local communities plan and carry out comprehensive rehabilitory programs, and to advance the development of entire metropolitan areas. The primary role of the national government under the Act is to provide incentives for cities to plan their projects and tackle their problems themselves. "Demonstration cities" receive the whole range of national grants-in-aid, as well as supplemental grants to support innovation and experimentation in meeting special needs. Success of the Demonstration Cities Program is posited on more cooperative functioning of the intergovernmental machinery and more effective sharing of the financial costs than in the past. As one high federal official remarked after a congressional hearing on appropriations for grants-in-aid, it does little good to paste a Band-Aid on a cancer.

PART TWO

Inputs
of the Political System:
Demands, Supports,
and Apathy

POLITICAL OPINIONS

AND PARTICIPATION   6

What do people want from their government? How much public support do the practices, policies, and leaders of government enjoy? And to what extent are citizens simply indifferent to their government? These questions get to the substance of what we have called the "input" activities of the political system. And they suggest that public opinions—or, more specifically, ==political opinions—are the ultimate foundation on which all governments==, democratic or dictatorial, ultimately rest.

The importance of public opinion is more obvious in democracies, of course, for many of their institutions depend on public preference. But all political systems must somehow perform the basic function of identifying the interests of the public. Even the absolute dictator is aware that public opinion sets limits that he can violate only at his own peril. The elaborate pretensions for maintaining public support that Machiavelli recommended to heads of state in his treatise, *The Prince*, are almost as complicated as the processes of a genuine democracy. And by the time the rulers of the Soviet Union were forced to modify their campaign against religion, they had painfully discovered that Machiavelli's warning that the people cannot be entirely ignored still applies in the twentieth century. Although the antireligious laws did not lead to actual rebellion, they proved so difficult to enforce and so destructive of morale that they had to be relaxed. Today the Soviet government goes to great trouble and expense to keep its knowledge of public opinion up to date.[1] The shrewd dictator never forgets that inefficiency, chaos, and revolution represent the range of prices that may be paid for a complete disregard of public sentiment. The elected leader is of course even more directly dependent on the opinions of his public.

The Nature of Political Opinions

When a prince, dictator, prime minister, or president worries about public opinion, exactly what is he concerned with? Most of us understand what the President means when he pulls the report of an opinion survey out of his pocket and says that public opinion supports his latest proposal to Congress.

---

[1] See Alex Inkeles, *Public Opinion in Soviet Russia* (Cambridge: Harvard University Press, 1950).

To analyze the place of public opinion in American politics, we need to make that understanding more precise.

What Is Public Opinion?

We shall consider *public opinion* as the *expression of attitudes on a social issue*. Notice that this definition includes three parts. First, unless an attitude is *expressed*, it is neither public nor opinion, since attitudes are internal predispositions that cannot be directly observed and opinions are the expressions of those predispositions. Thus we say that a milquetoast employee has no opinions in the presence of his boss even though we assume that he does have attitudes of some kind. Attitudes must somehow be communicated to others—that is, they must be expressed—to become part of public opinion. Suppose that three-fifths of the people in a country harbor secret attitudes disapproving of their rulers, but that they fail for some reason to express their disapproval in talking with friends, in behavior at political meetings, in voting, in responses to interviewers, or in any other way. Such attitudes would not be part of public opinion, although they would constitute a highly important potential or latent public opinion. Unexpressed opinions have an influence in government, but only because public officials must make guesses as to what opinions a given course of action would bring into play.[2]

Second, public opinion requires an *issue* on which people take different positions. An opinion is always evaluative, pro or con. If a person has neither favorable nor unfavorable feelings about an issue—the Johnson administration's conduct of the war in Viet Nam, for example—we say he has no opinion on the subject.

Third, public opinion deals with *social* rather than purely private questions. A hypochondriac's operation, however enthusiastically he expresses opinions about it, is not a social issue. It becomes a social issue, and an object of public opinion, only if others are stimulated to form opinions on the subject. Public opinion refers, then, to the opinions of an aggregation of individuals rather than to those of a single person. Despite our tendency to assume that the only *real* social issues are those *we* know are important, public opinions exist on a tremendous range of questions—from whether Roger Maris really broke Babe Ruth's home run record to problems of world peace. Any question on which people have favorable or unfavorable attitudes can, in other words, become an object of public opinion.

We started with a deliberately broad definition of public opinion as a reminder that every question of public concern is not necessarily political.[3]

---

[2] M. Brewster Smith, Jerome S. Bruner, and Robert W. White refer to the individual as "holding" an opinion to describe the predisposition we call an "attitude"; they say he "expresses" an opinion in the same way that we do. See *Opinions and Personality* (New York: John Wiley & Sons, Inc., 1956), p. 40. Either usage seems satisfactory; we use different terms to make certain that the distinction between unobserved attitudes and announced opinions is clear.

[3] From our point of view, V. O. Key's definition of public opinion as "those opinions held by private persons which governments find it prudent to heed" is thus too narrowly political. It is also subject to the charge of employing one of the terms defined in the definition. V. O. Key, Jr., *Public Opinion and American Democracy* (New York: Alfred A. Knopf, Inc., 1961), p. 14. The narrow definition reflects Professor Key's specific concern for returning the study of public opinion to a governmental setting. Our chapter's concern is similarly with political opinion, but we do not want to imply that all public opinion is political.

Some sort of public opinion is undeniably created and expressed by every change in the weather. But these opinions become political only as they acquire relevance for government—if they deal with the need for more municipal snowplows, for example. If we use *public opinion* to mean the expression of attitudes on a social issue, then *political opinion* refers somewhat more narrowly to the expression of attitudes on a political issue. The issue may be presented by any politically relevant object of opinions, such as candidates, parties, or policies.

Not only must we guard against the temptation to claim that all public opinion must deal with our favorite kind of *issues*, but we must also be careful not to assume that the particular people we are interested in make up the entire *public*. Unqualified references to opinions of *the* public are frequently misleading. Statements about "the public" scarcely ever mean literally everyone in the country; the person making the statement is usually thinking of a more restricted group. Some people, for example, confuse the opinions of newspaper publishers with the opinions of the population as a whole, and others assume that only rational and well-informed people have opinions.[4] Most of us are guilty of assuming that our own contacts are *the* public, but election results occasionally bring us sharply back to reality. Once the voting lever has been pulled or the ballot marked, the opinion is registered—no matter what the profession, the rational prowess, or the social contacts of the person who has expressed it.

The Functions of Opinions for the Individual

Like other forms of behavior, expressions of political opinions reflect the current adjustment of personalities (created by past interaction of organism and environment) to their present situation and experiences. One way of viewing opinions, then, is by describing the way they express an individual's personality. Someone who is incapable of dealing in abstractions, for example, will have a limited range of opinions dealing with specific and unrelated subjects. We could describe his opinions simply as consistent with his innate capacities or as expressive of his personality. In functional terms, however, we would say that his limited range of opinions serves to reduce his environment to manageable size. This is to suggest that just as we analyze the political system in terms of its functions for society, so we may analyze political opinions in terms of their functions for individual personalities.

Opinions are functional for an individual insofar as they promote his response to—or survival in—the environment without serious disruptions or disturbances. This view of opinions as mediating between the inner demands of the individual and the outer demands of the environment does not imply that "functional opinions" are merely defensive adjustments to the environment. At the highest level of sophistication, such mediation involves probing and testing the environment through the rigorous methods of scientific

[4]See, for example, A. Lawrence Lowell, *Public Opinion and Popular Government* (New York: Longmans' Green and Company, 1926), pp. 16–27. First published in 1913.

inquiry. In such cases, the individual actively seeks evidence that might contradict his ideas and he readily modifies them in the light of changing evidence. Most people, however, arrive at their opinions more casually and modify them more reluctantly.

After a quasi-clinical study of the opinions of ten normal men, a team of Harvard psychologists identified three basic functions that opinions perform for the individual—object appraisal, social adjustment, and externalization of inner requirements.[5] These functions are served by opinions about every sort of object, from the writings of Plato to the performance of football teams, and all three may consequently be explained in terms of opinions about politics as well.

By *object appraisal*, we mean that an individual's opinions serve to orient him to the world in which he lives, enabling him to categorize and to "size up" the objects and events around him. Since an opinion expresses a favorable or unfavorable predisposition toward some set of objects, it enables the individual to react without much trouble to any new object that can be classified as falling in some set about which he already has an opinion. If a person has been reared a loyal Republican, for example, he has an immediate clue for evaluating candidates and proposals—his initial predisposition will be favorable if they are Republican or unfavorable if they are not. Without such convenient categories for evaluating the countless stimuli that confront us, the world would appear, as Walter Lippmann once said, as a great buzzing confusion. Each event simply cannot be approached with the genuine innocence and naïveté of an infant, or we would never manage to react to the countless stimuli that surround us. Accordingly, when voters must react without the convenience of differentiating party labels—as in party primaries and nonpartisan elections—preferences are much more unstable and more responsive to influence by such agencies as the mass media of communication.

Social adjustment refers to the consequences of opinions for improving, disrupting, or maintaining an individual's relations with others. In the family, the child discovers early that some opinions win approval, others disapproval. And anyone who has ever been an uncertain freshman in college knows that the consequences of opinions for social adjustment do not end with departure from the home environment. Family and college associates tend to constitute "reference groups"—groups with which we feel a sense of identity or kinship and from which we derive standards for judging ourselves. But a reference group may also be quite impersonal, involving no face-to-face contact, and it may be negative as well as positive. The lonely intellectual in a small town may willingly and even eagerly incur the disrespect of his neighbors in order to enjoy the feeling that he is acting in ways that would satisfy the editors of *The American Scholar*. In this case, his immediate neighbors constitute a negative reference group (his self-esteem is enhanced by their disapproval) and the editors of *The American Scholar* represent a positive reference group (his self-esteem is enhanced by the feeling that he conforms to their standards).

An individual thus tends to find his social identity and his self-esteem by relating his opinions to those of others. When a person asks himself, "What

[5] Smith, Bruner, and White, *Opinions and Personality*, pp. 39–46.

am I?" he tends to answer in terms such as "a human being," or "a carpenter." When he asks himself, "What am I in politics?" he tends to answer "a Democrat" or "a Republican." The most important clue to his political identity is his party preference, and it will color his responses to all other political stimuli. When a political party is a positive reference group, it furnishes the standards to which an individual adjusts his opinions. Should he answer "What am I in politics?" with "I don't know," he has no specific political group with which to identify. The chances are that he will be a nonvoter or an inconsistent (independent) voter who responds to transient factors.

By *externalizing inner requirements*, opinions may serve to reduce a sense of anxiety produced by some unresolved psychological problem of the individual. Herbert McClosky of the University of California at Berkeley has discovered, for example, that people who are personally insecure and afraid of the future tend to adopt a conservative political philosophy that extols the merits of stability, the wisdom of the past, and the dangers to society that social experimentation would bring.[6] And Robert E. Lane of Yale University found that people unable to tolerate ambiguity showed some tendency to vote for a candidate who offered simple solutions to difficult problems.[7] Such adoption of political opinions because of a feeling, often unconscious, of analogy between an issue and a personal psychological difficulty is not likely to represent a rational approach to political ends. But it is not a tendency that is associated with one party more than another. One difficulty in attempting to understand politics through psychological analysis is that, while it may permit the prediction of certain psychological tendencies, these tendencies may take opposite political forms. Intense sibling rivalry, for example, has been cited as the source of habitual hostility and aggressiveness, but for some this condition leads to fascist tendencies and for others to communist tendencies. For still others, it no doubt leads to mistrust of all politics. On rare occasions when such political opinions serve the function of externalization for great numbers of people, a Hitler or a McCarthy era emerges.

Political Socialization

Opinions thus help the individual relate to the world around him, to other people, and to himself. Where do his political opinions come from? They come partly from immediate political stimuli—a particular candidate or an exciting issue, for example. But the citizen does not react to each new stimulus as if it were his first political experience. His reaction is largely shaped by his learned predispositions—all the preferences, images of reality, and loyalties which he has acquired through previous experiences. (In helping him react to current

---

[6]Herbert McClosky, "Conservatism and Personality," *American Political Science Review*, LII (March, 1958), 27–45.
[7]Robert E. Lane, "Political Personality and Electoral Choice," *American Political Science Review*, XLIX (March, 1955), 181.

political figures and issues, these predispositions are, of course, performing the function of object appraisal.) The term *political socialization* refers to the process by which these guiding predispositions are inculcated. Political socialization, then, is the process of initiation into politics, the process through which the initiate's general conceptions, knowledge, and opinions about the political world are shaped.[8]

The Family Heritage

The first of many opinion-shaping agencies to affect the individual—first in influence as well as in time—is his family. The citizen inherits his political preferences just as he inherits his church preference, for both are part of a general attitudinal structure that dictates what he "naturally" thinks. Schoolchildren have been found to be uniformly warm and positive in their attitudes toward their political communities.[9] Although we could hardly have imagined that they would have rejected their own nation in favor of Castro's Cuba or some other alien (in the sense of "unknown") political environment, we might have expected them to be childishly indifferent about the matter. But American satisfaction—at its extreme, ethnocentricism—apparently comes early.

Many college students, who set a high value on rationality and independence of mind, resent the implication that their political opinions have been acquired in such a seemingly irrelevant, almost thoughtless, fashion. But the fact that the process begins with the individual's first awareness of the world around him, and is so nearly automatic, so little marked by critical scrutiny, is precisely what makes it so effective. Ideas that are as natural as breathing are built into the personality so intimately that they stand without being questioned. The biological function of the American family is to propagate the species in a physical sense, but its social function is to propagate *Americans* rather than just human beings—that is, to transmit the general norms of the American culture appropriately modified by a particular subculture. It is this function that also perpetuates sectional variations in opinion.

Moreover, when we look more closely, this automatic acquisition of ideas within the family is more logical than it might seem. Only an extreme deviant would reject the one nation he has known. In terms of more specific loyalties within the national community, the fledgling citizen is a member of the same ethnic group as his parents, and he tends to be identified with the same religion and social class. Consequently, the attitudes that are appropriate to his parents as members of these groups will be no less appropriate for him. Because the Democratic Party has, for the last generation, been regarded as the champion of ethnic "out-groups" such as the Negroes and the immigrants from Slavic countries, the children in these groups have the same reasons to vote Democratic as their parents had. Despite Republican appeals to such groups, the Democrats continue to win a higher percentage of support from minority groups than from the population as a whole. By the same token, if members of the professional and managerial class find Republican policies

---

[8] See Fred I. Greenstein, *Children and Politics* (New Haven: Yale University Press, 1965), Chapter 1.
[9] David Easton and Robert D. Hess, "The Child's Political World," *Midwest Journal of Political Science*, VI (August, 1962), 236–237.

more in keeping with their needs than Democratic policies, they and their children will have the same reasons for supporting the Republican Party.

Family influence on political opinions does not only operate indirectly, through the transmission of religious, ethnic, and class identifications. At a remarkably early age, children pick up direct political cues from their parents and express similar attitudes on a wide range of political issues. But the strongest and most persistent influence is on party identification. Issues may be too complicated for children to understand, but even the dullest child learns at an early age to tell the "good guys" from the "bad guys" on TV. In politics, when his parents agree (as most do) in their attitudes toward the parties, the child has an ordering device almost as simple as that of TV westerns: he can tell the good guys from the bad guys—not by whether they are clean-shaven or unkempt but by their party labels. As a result, when children are asked how they would vote in an election, a vast majority report the same preference as their parents.[10] And this inherited party preference continues to exert influence in adult life: Among those voters who remember that both parents supported the same party, around 80 per cent report that their first vote was also for that party; 69 per cent of all adults say they are still for their parents' party, as compared with 13 per cent who support the other party and 17 per cent who call themselves independents.[11]

Relying upon interviews with grade-school children rather than on the memory of adults, Fred Greenstein of Wesleyan University offers even more convincing proof that the family directly transmits political attitudes. He finds that children in interviews speak of party affiliation as a general family characteristic rather than as an individual choice. "All I know," said one pony-tailed 10-year-old when asked about her party preference, "is *we're* not Republicans."[12] Greenstein discovered that children not only mirror their families partisanship but also pick up an earlier awareness of those aspects of the political system that are more important for their parents. Thus children usually grasp the significance of the offices of the President, Governor, and Mayor earlier than institutions such as Congress, state legislature, and town council, and understand the national level before the state—just as adults are more aware of executives and of the national government.[13]

If children of active party members tend to support their parents' party, what political heritage is shown by children of people who shift parties or who fail to vote? They, too, reflect their upbringing—such children, as might be guessed, are much more likely to identify with no party at all. Among voters whose parents were for the same party, only 17 per cent are independ-

---

[10]Herbert Hyman, *Political Socialization* (New York: The Free Press of Glencoe, Inc., 1959); H. H. Remmers, "Early Socialization of Attitudes," in Eugene Burdick and A. J. Brodbeck (eds.), *American Voting Behavior* (New York: The Free Press of Glencoe, Inc., 1959), pp. 55–67.

[11]Less than 1 per cent of the offspring of parents who agree in their party choice have no identification. Key, *Public Opinion*, p. 301n, and Table 12.1, p. 296.

[12]Greenstein, *Children and Politics*, p. 73. This book contains, in addition to its own findings, an excellent discussion of the literature on political socialization.

[13]*Ibid.*, pp. 56, 63.

ents; among those who do not know how their parents voted, or whose parents did not vote, 32 per cent are independents; and among voters whose parents shifted parties, 39 per cent are independents.[14]

Similarly, people reflect in their adult life the degree of interest their parents had in politics in general. The greater the parents' interest, the greater the children's sense of involvement and efficacy in politics. Family influence can also be spotted in attitudes on policy questions, such as foreign affairs or labor-management disputes, but not so clearly as on questions of party choice or political involvement. Family cues on policy are less clear to begin with, and new issues leave the adult more nearly on his own. Like our parents, we tend to identify with a party more than with specific positions.

If the family influence is so strong, how do we account for the minority who depart from the politics of their parents? An obvious answer would be simply to say that some children hate their parents and take joy in voting against their parents' party at the first opportunity. Some psychologists have toyed with this notion, but they find that even among children who reject their parents the act of rejection generally takes a nonpolitical form. (Only in highly politicized families is politics important enough for the rebellious offspring to choose it as his vehicle for rebellion.[15]) So we must turn to less dramatic

[14] Ibid., p. 296.
[15] See Henry W. Riecker, "Primary Groups and Political Party Choice," in Burdick and Brodbeck (eds.), *American Voting Behavior*, pp. 162–183; and Eleanor E. Maccoby *et al.*, "Youth and Political Change," *Public Opinion Quarterly*, XVIII (Spring, 1954), 23–39.

Drawing by John A. Ruge; © 1966 *The Saturday Review*.

"Roger and I have stayed in the Republican Party because of the children."

influences to account for the erosion of family agreement. Most people seem somehow to select marriage partners with similar political views, but when they don't, one or the other is often ripe for political conversion. Since politics is culturally defined as more masculine than feminine in the United States, the agreement is most often reached by wifely acquiescence in the husband's view.[16] Consequently, agreement between husbands and wives is usually even greater than agreement between parents and children.

Other forces eroding family influence include exposure to a different class environment, residence in a community in which the dominant sentiment runs counter to the parental party choice, the experience of political events that work to the disadvantage of the parental party or to the advantage of a different party, and contact with friends and co-workers predominantly identified with a different party.[17] Although we discuss all these influences below, be sure to keep two points in mind: (1) most people live in the same kind of political environment as their parents, so that conflict between family and other influences is the exception; (2) even when conflict is created, as by membership in a class different from that of one's parents, the family influence on political opinions never disappears completely.[18]

Class Status Americans are not acutely class-conscious. In 1964, for example, a nationwide cross-section of the adult population was asked, "There's quite a bit of talk these days about different social classes. Most people say they belong either to the middle class or to the working class. Do you ever think of yourself as being in one of these classes?" Even with the encouraging assurance that most people say they belong to a class, only 60 per cent replied that they ever thought of themselves in class terms.[19] If over a third of the voters never picture themselves as belonging to a class, we might conclude that class identification is of little consequence for political opinions in America. But a closer look suggests that such a hasty conclusion is unwarranted.

In the first place, less than 2 per cent of American adults flatly reject the idea of classes. Of the people who say they do not think of themselves as belonging to a social class, almost all are willing and able to say what class they would call themselves if they had to make a choice. In the second place, however tenuous class-consciousness may seem in America, it "works" in the sense that it has significant effects on attitudes and behaviors. Indeed, we saw in the second chapter of this book that both political participation and chances for political

---

[16]Whereas in other areas, such as furnishing the home, our culture expects the husband to defer to the wife. See Robert E. Lane and David O. Sears, *Public Opinion* (Englewood Cliffs, New Jersey: Prentice-Hall, Inc., 1964), p. 30.

[17]Excellent sources on these influences are Herbert McClosky and Harold F. Dahlgren, "Primary Group Influence on Party Loyalty," *American Political Science Review*, LIII (September, 1959), 757–776; and Bernard R. Berelson, Paul F. Lazarsfeld, and William N. McPhee, *Voting: A Study of Opinion Formation in a Presidential Campaign* (Chicago: The University of Chicago Press, 1954).

[18]*Public Opinion*, p. 313.

[19]From data furnished by the University of Michigan's Survey Research Center.

leadership vary markedly along class lines. Americans are not so different from other people on the question of class, then, as we sometimes like to believe. A UNESCO survey in nine countries found a pattern of class identification among other peoples surprisingly similar to that of Americans. Moreover, when the people in each country were asked if they felt that they had "anything in common" with fellow countrymen who were not members of their own class, Americans were not at all unique in their feeling of common interests across class lines. The percentage in each nation who acknowledged something in common with different classes of their fellow citizens was: Australia, 78; United States, 77; Britain, 67; Norway, 64; Germany, 64; France, 63; Mexico, 56; Netherlands, 50; Italy, 50.[20]

How meaningful is this class-identification as an influence on political opinions? Granted that class is important in determining whether a person will participate in politics, does it also have an influence on the content of his opinions—that is, on the direction of his preferences? Let's look at this question in terms of opinions on two of the most important elements of politics—public issues and political parties.

Class identification has a direct impact on many political attitudes. Richard Centers, a social psychologist who carried out one of the first systematic studies of this problem a generation ago, found that people who thought of themselves as middle-class were significantly more conservative than those who identified with the working class. The political importance of working-class radicalism as opposed to middle-class conservatism may be seen from the highly charged political nature of the attitudes Centers used to measure "conservatism-radicalism." He found that working-class people were more likely than middle-class people to believe the following: America is not truly a land of opportunity; people in the United States do not get what they deserve; we would all be better off if working people had more power and influence in government; wages and salaries would be fairer, jobs steadier, and unemployment lower if the government took over and ran our mines, factories, and industries; the government should guarantee every person a decent and steady job and standard of living; workers rather than employers are usually right in strikes and industrial disputes; employers sometimes take advantage of working people. American attitudes on the most basic political questions, then, cannot be understood without taking class differences into account.

A huge variety of studies since Centers' seminal investigation in 1945 have rounded out his findings. And, whether class is determined subjectively by the choice of the individual or objectively by such criteria as occupation, income, or education, the results are much the same. Class is a sufficiently vague concept in the United States, however, that about a fourth of Centers' respondents were "misidentifiers"—blue-collar workers who thought of themselves as middle-class or white-collar people who thought of themselves as working-class. Do these misidentifiers react to public issues according to their "subjective" class or to their "objective" status? Generally they think and act like hybrids, neither as liberal as the blue-collar, working-class identifiers nor as conservative as the white-collar, middle-class identifiers. If these

[20]William Buchanan and Hadley Cantril, *How Nations See Each Other* (Urbana: University of Illinois Press, 1953), p. 18.

misidentifiers are divided according to degree of political involvement,[21] however, we discover that subjective class outweighs occupational status as an influence on the party choice of those voters who are politically involved to the point of interest in and concern about an election. Among the most apathetic third of the population, on the other hand, the misidentifiers are more likely to vote according to their occupational status than according to their subjective class. For these uninvolved, apathetic citizens, the choice of a class is relatively meaningless. For them, "the pressure stemming from class identification is weak relative to that stemming from the actual social group, and partisan choice . . . reflects occupation primarily."[22] But these are the exceptions: three-fourths of all adults identify with a class that objectively "fits" their occupations.

Perhaps the most significant modification in our understanding of the relation between class status and political opinions is the discovery that "conservatism" and "liberalism" have several dimensions, and that a person who is conservative along one dimension may be liberal along another. Academicians and journalists have tended to think of liberalism as a coherent set of beliefs that includes at least three dimensions: approval of government measures to help the underprivileged and promote equality; belief in social experimentation rather than automatic acceptance of the *status quo*; and tolerance toward the rights of others.

Centers' measure tapped only the first dimension of liberalism, since he dealt with issues of equality and social welfare. On questions of this kind, lower-status individuals are consistently and markedly more liberal than those of higher status. But it turns out that they are *less* liberal on both the other dimensions that were once assumed to go along with the first. On underlying attitudes toward social change, for example, Herbert McClosky has found that lower-status individuals are much more likely than upper-status people to

---

[21] Political involvement is measured by intensity of party preference, interest in the campaign, concern over the election outcome, sense of citizen duty, and sense of political efficacy. See Angus Campbell et al., *The American Voter* (New York: John Wiley & Sons, Inc., 1960), pp. 102, 106–107.
[22] Ibid., p. 373.

Table 6–1 Status (Educational) Differences in Conservatism-Liberalism as Measured by Attitude Toward Change

ATTITUDE	GRADE SCHOOL	EDUCATION HIGH SCHOOL	AT LEAST SOME COLLEGE
Liberal	6.2%	16.3%	30.5%
Moderately liberal	15.9	32.7	35.7
Moderately conservative	34.6	32.3	23.8
Extremely conservative	43.3	18.7	10.0
Total (N = 1,082)	100%	100%	100%

Source: Herbert McClosky, "Conservatism and Personality," *American Political Science Review*, LII (March, 1958), 35. The data are from a Minnesota survey.

accept the ways of the past and to resent innovation.[23] As Table 6–1 indicates, two-thirds of the people with college training are liberal in their attitudes toward change, while less than a fourth of those with only grade school training are liberal.

On our third measure of liberalism—tolerance toward the rights of others—lower-status individuals once again rank low. This dimension of liberalism was measured by willingness of respondents in a national sample to permit free speech and other civil liberties for unpopular groups like communists, alleged communists, critics of churches and religion, and champions of nationalized industry. Table 6–2 points up the extent to which tolerance toward nonconformists increases as we go up the occupational scale. Even when tolerance is measured in terms of support for the rights of ethnic minorities, such as Negroes, higher-status people are markedly more tolerant than are those of lower status.[24]

Table 6–2   Status (Occupational) Differences
in Conservatism-Liberalism
as Measured by Tolerance of Nonconformists

PERCENTAGE OF MEN SCORING "MORE TOLERANT"

Professional and semiprofessional	66%
Proprietors, managers, and officials	51
Clerical and sales	49
Manual workers	30
Farmers or farm workers	20

Source: Samuel A. Stouffer, *Communism, Conformity, and Civil Liberties* (New York: Doubleday & Co., 1955), p. 139; and Seymour M. Lipset, *Political Man* (Garden City, N.Y.: Doubleday & Company, Inc., 1960), p. 104.

What conclusions can we draw from the findings on all three dimensions of liberal and conservative opinions? The most compelling is that class, whether determined by personal feelings or by educational and occupational status, is an essential concept for understanding political differences. Perhaps even more significant, class-related opinions are not systematic enough to form the base of an ideology. On the contrary, political opinions more nearly approximate *ad hoc*, unrelated responses to each issue in terms of immediate and fairly obvious self-interest. On the bread-and-butter, social-welfare issues, the working class emerges as more liberal than the middle class. But when we move into more complex questions that involve long-run goals or the ability to relate abstract principles to specific problems, the middle class looks more liberal. This conclusion is not only called for by the findings above; it is also necessary if we are to account for additional attitudes that would otherwise be inexplicable. Take the question of whether taxes should be reduced even if it means the government must postpone things that need to be done. People with low income agree with this proposal more than people with high income!

[23]See citation in Table 6–1.
[24]See Herbert H. Hyman and Paul B. Sheatsley, "Attitudes Toward Desegregation: 1942–1963," *Scientific American*, CCXI (July, 1964), 16–23. In the South, however, a very high level of education is necessary before anti-Negro attitudes are basically modified. Donald R. Matthews and James W. Prothro, *Negroes and the New Southern Politics* (New York: Harcourt, Brace & World, Inc., 1966).

"Although this finding runs counter to political folklore," it is not so surprising when we discard "long-standing assumptions about ideological structure on these matters."[25] To the sophisticated observer, it may seem inconsistent for a low-income person to favor both expanding social welfare benefits and postponing needed government activities in order to cut taxes. But the apparent inconsistency stems from the sophisticate's assumption that other people are as ideologically oriented as he is. The simple desire to improve one's economic lot, without regard to ideological niceties, renders both views consistent to the average citizen—should he bother to think of one in connection with the other.

Even with the ideological trappings eliminated, a serious qualification must be noted to round out our picture of class and attitudes on public issues: Sharp class differences do not exist on all issues, nor are these differences equally strong or weak at all times. Although every problem we have discussed so far involves differences, not every issue produces real disharmony. We would not expect to find class differences in attitudes on the weather, of course. (That is, although farmers and lazy baseball players might prefer rain when carpenters and eager golfers would prefer sunshine, these are not systematic class differences.) But we might expect more difference than Table 6–3 shows on the proposal that "government ought to see to it that big business corporations don't have much say about how the government is run." The general endorsement of the statement seems to reflect a feeling among all occupational groups that, while business should have a say, it should not be allowed to dominate the government. Another reason for the lack of sharp differences, and one that is often overlooked, is that the lower-status groups are much less likely to have an opinion on such difficult questions. Once again, the lack of political information and involvement on the part of the working class becomes important. Almost half the unskilled workers reported no opinion on the role of big business in 1956, a time of prosperity. During a depression, these people would probably have an opinion: to repeat, class differences vary from time to time as well as from issue to issue.

[25]Campbell et al., The American Voter, p. 196.

Table 6–3 Status (Occupational) Differences on the Question of Restraining Big Business Influence

	PROFESSIONAL	BUSINESS	CLERICAL	SKILLED	UNSKILLED	FARMERS
Agree[a]	53%	48%	52%	56%	42%	54%
Depends	8	8	5	6	3	5
Disagree	23	24	20	13	10	14
No opinion	16	20	23	25	45	27
	100%	100%	100%	100%	100%	100%
N	163	243	169	487	235	180

[a]"The government ought to see to it that big business corporations don't have much say about how the government is run."
Source: Key, Public Opinion, p. 126. The data are from the 1956 presidential election survey of the Survey Research Center, University of Michigan.

Re chapt. 2

In the second chapter, we saw the importance of class for mass participation and chances for political leadership. We have just seen how it affects attitudes on public issues. An even more direct political consequence is the influence of class identification on voting behavior. Members of the working class typically vote Democratic, while middle-class voters tend to favor the Republicans. Tables 6-4, 6-5, and 6-6 present the voting differences in these classes for three presidential elections. In every case, whether the victor was a Democrat or a Republican, the Democrats fared relatively better among the working class and the Republicans among the middle class. Even in Franklin Roosevelt's decisive defeat of Thomas Dewey in 1944, middle-class people voted as heavily for Dewey as they did for Roosevelt; and Eisenhower's great triumph over Stevenson in 1952 still saw working-class voters preferring Stevenson.

Neither political party, faced with these facts, can afford to forget where its heaviest support comes from. Hence, while both parties urge people to "vote

Table 6-4 Voting Preferences of Middle-Class and Working-Class People in 1944

VOTING PREFERENCE	MIDDLE-CLASS RESPONDENTS N = 415	WORKING-CLASS RESPONDENTS N = 472
Democratic	49%	70%
Republican	49	29
Other, don't know, refused	2	1
Total	100%	100%

Source: Centers, *The Psychology of Social Classes*, p. 124. Class membership was by the respondent's choice of his own class affiliation. The sample included white males only; while this is unfortunate, subsequent studies indicate that the differences would not have been substantially reduced had Negroes and females been included.

Table 6-5 Voting Preferences of Middle-Class and Working-Class People in 1952

VOTING PREFERENCE	MIDDLE-CLASS RESPONDENTS N = 389	WORKING-CLASS RESPONDENTS N = 811
Democratic	30%	54%
Republican	69	43
Other, don't know, refused	1	3
Total	100%	100%

Source: Heinz Eulau, "Perceptions of Class and Party in Voting Behavior: 1952," *The American Political Science Review*, XLIX (June, 1955), 364. Class membership was determined on the basis of the respondent's occupation, income, and education.

Table 6-6 Voting Preferences of Middle-Class and Working-Class People in 1964

VOTING PREFERENCE	MIDDLE-CLASS VOTERS N = 470	WORKING-CLASS VOTERS N = 570
Democratic	56%	77%
Republican	43	21
Other, don't know, refused	1	2
Total	100%	100%

Source: The 1964 presidential election survey conducted by the University of Michigan's Survey Research Center. Class membership was by the respondent's choice of his own class affiliation.

as you please but please vote," the Republicans make a special effort in upper-income precincts and the Democrats go all out to mobilize the lower-income districts. The Democrats have to be particularly concerned about turnout, since more of their potential supporters fail to vote. On the other hand, American class division in voting is a far cry from incipient class warfare. Each party gets substantial support from both the broad classes. Moreover, the influence of class varies considerably from one election to the next. Class awareness seems to have been much less marked in 1960 and 1964 than in 1944 and 1948, for example. Philip Converse has demonstrated that the relation between class and attitudes dropped sharply from 1945 to 1956, as did the relation between class and voting.[26] Class awareness is not a constant factor, then, in American politics. It is reduced by the emergence of issues that cut across class lines, such as problems of war and foreign policy, by the appeal of a magnetic personality like Eisenhower, by the injection of an issue like religion into a campaign, or by the extreme positions of a candidate like Goldwater. It presumably reaches a peak of influence during depression periods, when resentment over the uneven distribution of wealth is keenest; and attachments formed at such times may carry over into periods of prosperity. Despite its varying influence, class identification ranks second only to party affiliation as a general clue to political attitudes and behavior.

Residence A generation ago, sectional conflicts would probably have received major attention in a discussion of forces shaping public opinion. Considering the regional distribution of opinion in the last decade, however, Professor Key concluded that *similarities from one region to another are more characteristic than differences*.[27] The Midwest has long been viewed as a center of isolationist sentiment, for example, but World War II and subsequent events have largely obliterated the regional differences in public attitudes on broad foreign-policy questions. Most Americans accept U.S. commitment to an active internationalist role, and the dissenting minority is not much greater in the Midwest than in the rest of the country. Similarly, we tend to think of the South as peculiarly conservative on economic issues—opposing such government activities as aid for medical care, the guarantee of a job for everybody who wants to work, and electric power and housing programs. On these and similar questions, however, Southerners turn out to have a range of opinions remarkably similar to other Americans. Only when these questions impinge on race relations does the South adopt a distinctive position.

Why, then, do we so often hear American politics described as if the people of different regions held sharply opposing views? First, the greatest sectional

---

[26]"The Shifting Role of Class in Political Attitudes and Behavior," in Eleanor E. Maccoby *et al.* (eds.), *Readings in Social Psychology*, 3rd ed., (New York: Henry Holt and Company, 1958), pp. 388–399.
[27]*Public Opinion*, Chapter 5.

difference that does exist centers on an issue of the gravest national and international import—racial injustice, which cuts to the core of the democratic creed. The extreme anti-Negro sentiments and measures in many parts of the South, the increasingly effective expression of Negroes' dissatisfaction with second-class citizenship in the South and widespread sympathy with their demands among white and Negro voters outside the South all tend to identify politics with sectional differences. Second, the press exaggerates any sectionalism that shows up in other areas of politics, because journalists thrive on conflict and because sectionalism is an easy and dramatic way to describe differences. Third, our system of representation, with a single legislator representing an entire district, magnifies regional differences. We tend to think of representatives or senators as reflecting the opinions of entire districts or states rather than the opinions of some constituents who may be bitterly opposed by others in the locality. Assuming that congressmen reflect the preferences of a majority of their constituents, 51 per cent in favor of a bill in one section and 51 per cent opposed in another section would be translated into solidly opposed sectional blocs in Congress. Small differences in the public can thus create marked differences in Congress. Fourth, sectional differences do exist on some questions other than the rights of Negroes.

We mentioned in Chapter 2 that people in different regions vary in the degree to which they are willing to tolerate nonconformists. Why is this true? Why, for example, are people in the West more likely than people in the South to respect the freedom of speech of socialists, atheists, communists, and persons accused of being communists? An easy explanation would be that the difference is not regional at all—that it disappears when we take into account such things as the lower educational level of the South. But the differences are still significant, even when the comparison is between Westerners and Southerners who are matched in terms of educational and other characteristics. So we must conclude that different regions develop political subcultures that are distinctive in some respects.[28] Perhaps this results from the original sources of settlement—consider the wider variety of backgrounds represented in the West. Perhaps it also results from important events particularly affecting a region—for instance, the development of slavery as the "peculiar institution" of the South. While American opinions on most of the broad issues of politics do not show marked regional influences, then, regional distinctiveness in attitudes has certainly not disappeared entirely.

Residential differences in political opinions today are actually more clear-cut when the comparison is in terms of size of place—metropolitan center, suburb, small city, or county—than when it is in terms of regions. On international issues, the rural residents are, as expected, more isolationist. Similarly, rural residence is associated with intolerance of nonconformity. But on social-welfare measures, rural people are not the most conservative, as many would expect. The most liberal attitudes on these bread-and-butter issues are in the metropolitan centers, and the most conservative attitudes are in small cities. Higher-status groups seem to dominate the politics in small cities (from 10,000 to 50,000 people) more easily than anywhere else. Competing centers of

[28] For data on the continuation of regional differences, see Norral D. Glenn and J. L. Simmons, "Are Regional Differences Diminishing?" *Public Opinion Quarterly*, XXXI (Summer, 1967), 176–193.

political influence, such as politically active labor unions, are rare in such cities, but they are large enough for the views of the Chamber of Commerce and the businessman's service clubs to find effective expression. Laborers are accordingly much less likely to vote Democratic if they live in a small city than if they live in a metropolitan center.[29]

Ethnic Groups The influence of religion on political opinions in America, though it is quite apparent in some cases, is sometimes overemphasized. Systematic differences on social-welfare issues are found in the major religious groups in the United States. Despite individual and sectional variations, in the country as a whole the Congregational, Presbyterian, and Episcopalian groups rank as most conservative, and the Jewish, Catholic, and Baptist groups rank as most liberal. With the exception of the Jewish group, however, these differences appear to be based more on class status than on religion. The ranking of every one of the other major denominational groups on politico-economic questions is identical with its class-status rank, whether class is measured in terms of education, income, or occupation. Differences of opinion also occur *within* each denominational group and the differences are again related to class status. Baptists as a group are more liberal on politico-economic questions than Episcopalians, but rich, college-trained executives are equally conservative whether they are Baptists or Episcopalians. In summary, class rather than religion seems to be the decisive factor.[30]

But religious affiliation does sometimes outweigh other influences. Upper-class Jews, for example, continued to be overwhelmingly Democratic in the Eisenhower era, in contrast to other people in the same educational, economic, and occupational positions, because of special circumstances that applied to them as a group. Aware of anti-Semitism as a widespread prejudice, even upper-class Jews may have felt deprived of prestige and therefore may have been influenced by psychological pressures not unlike those that beset lower-class groups. Moreover, the Jewish creed encourages a liberal political view, and the Jews were historically identified with the Democratic Party because of the party's earlier opposition to Nazism (which was responsible for acts of genocide against the European Jews).[31]

The situation of the Catholics is perhaps more ambiguous. Although their religion does not appear to influence their attitudes on general issues, Catho-

---

[29] See Nicholas A. Masters and Deil S. Wright, "Trends and Variations in the Two-Party Vote: The Case of Michigan," *American Political Science Review*, LII (December, 1958), 1078–1090; Leon J. Epstein, "Size of Place and the Two-Party Vote," *Western Political Quarterly*, IX (March, 1956), 138–150.

[30] The discussion in this paragraph is based on Wesley and Beverly Allinsmith, "Religious Affiliation and Politico-Economic Attitude: A Study of Eight Major U.S. Religious Groups," *Public Opinion Quarterly*, XII (Fall, 1948), 377–389.

[31] See Lawrence E. Fuchs, *The Political Behavior of American Jews* (New York: The Free Press of Glencoe, Inc., 1956).

lics do tend to vote Democratic more often than the population at large, even when we compare voters in similar socio-economic positions. This is one of the many regularities in political behavior that have not yet been explained. One reason may be that the immigration of the Irish, Polish, and Italians to the United States was heaviest at a time when the Democratic Party controlled most of the eastern cities where these immigrants settled. Predominantly Catholic, they developed into good Democrats at the same time they developed into good Americans. And they may have passed on their party identification to their children along with their new nationality. Party identification may itself shape behavior; it need not always depend on some other force. In this case, the descendants of these immigrants seem to be voting simply as Democrats, not as Catholics.[32]

When a religious issue is injected into politics, however, religious preference becomes highly relevant. Members of some Protestant denominations regard the consumption of alcoholic beverages as sinful, for example, and many Catholics regard the use of birth-control devices similarly. Given a chance to vote on such questions, members of the churches concerned will tend to vote according to their religious beliefs. The important question, then, is this: how salient is religious affiliation for politics? When a candidate is criticized because of his religion, his fellow religionists will suddenly find that their church membership is highly salient and directly relevant to politics. In 1960, Catholics who had voted for Eisenhower in 1956 returned in overwhelming numbers to the support of the Democratic candidate—a Catholic under fire because of his religion. Since Nixon's Protestantism was not under fire, religion played a much smaller role for many Protestants. Even so, Protestantism was not irrelevant to political preference; Protestant Democrats who attend church most regularly were much more likely than infrequent attenders to vote against Kennedy.[33]

Racial identification and national origins appear to influence political opinions in much the same way as do religion and other ethnic characteristics. When members of any ethnic group are deprived of political rewards—or even of prestige alone—because of their ethnic identification, they will tend to support policies or candidates that recognize their interests. Hence the hot conflicts between Italian and Irish groups in many New England cities as the more recently arrived Italians fought for a foothold in Irish-dominated city politics. The desire for recognition in the form of public office, appointive jobs, and improved municipal services heavily influences the votes of people who are hungry for acceptance but who have also been just plain hungry. In many industrial areas, both parties offer a "United-Nations" slate of candidates—a ticket carefully chosen to include every significant ethnic group.

The importance of ethnic minorities in politics, especially in the Northeast, is generally taken—even by scholars—as a mark of their assimilation into American society.[34] But Raymond Wolfinger of Stanford University argues that

[32] Angus Campbell and Homer C. Cooper, *Group Differences in Attitudes and Votes: A Study of the 1954 Congressional Elections* (Ann Arbor: Survey Research Center, Institute for Social Research, University of Michigan, 1956), p. 36.
[33] Philip E. Converse *et al.*, "Stability and Change in 1960: A Reinstating Election," *American Political Science Review*, LV (June, 1961), 269–280.
[34] See Robert A. Dahl, *Who Governs?* (New Haven: Yale University Press, 1961), pp. 33, 59.

this is a mistaken interpretation. Because parties compete for the support of ethnic minorities by offering them recognition—candidates in New York manfully and publicly eat their way through a grand assortment of blintzes, salami, manicotti, and similar ethnic concoctions—the campaign process "heightens separate identification and structures politics as ethnic conflict."[35] Wolfinger's implicit model of a "good" or "effective" structure of politics seems to be one organized more exclusively along class lines. Class politics, he feels, calls for expanded programs in education, welfare, and recreation; for progressive taxation; for laws favorable to labor; and for other liberal measures of benefit to lower classes in general. Ethnic politics calls for recognition of the ethnic group by awarding public offices to its members (usually its higher-status members) and by making much of celebrations on St. Patrick's Day, Columbus Day, and the like. Accordingly, ethnic politics becomes dysfunctional for most members of the ethnic groups themselves. "By structuring politics so that expectations are for recognition rather than substantive policies, ethnic struggles divert working-class energies away from substantive policy demands. If the vote of a worker who happens to be of Italian descent can be won by putting an Italian on the ticket, why should the party promise him better schools?"[36] This argument appears somewhat oversimplified; for when *both* party tickets include Italo-Americans, *additional* appeals are necessary. Moreover, the other sections of the country, which do not have a basically ethnic politics, manifest no more clear-cut class politics than the Northeast.[37] Whatever its effect in discouraging a pure class politics, ethnic politics has at minimum given otherwise underprivileged groups a leverage in politics that they have not achieved in the economic or social systems.

Ethnic groups want to achieve both welfare and status objectives, but specific public issues occasionally pose a painful conflict between the two kinds of goals. Should Negroes support a new public housing project in an all-Negro area? This would meet the welfare need for more housing, but at the expense of the status need to escape from the ghetto. Negro leaders in New York recently split on just this question, with the result that the Housing Authority took advantage of divided Negro opinions to win approval for the project.[38] In most elections, the lower-status group has a more clear-cut choice: the party or candidate most responsive to its material needs is generally also most attuned to its need for symbolic recognition. In many areas of the South, no candidate positively supports Negroes' interests; in that milieu, the only practical course is to vote for the candidate who is least *anti*-Negro. The civil rights issue is so acutely important to Negroes that they probably constitute,

---

[35]"Some Consequences of Ethnic Politics," in M. Kent Jennings and L. Harmon Zeigler (eds.), *The Electoral Process* (Englewood Cliffs, N.J.: Prentice-Hall, Inc., 1966), p. 51.
[36]*Ibid.*, p. 47.
[37]For a good general discussion of ethnic groups in America, see Nathan Glazer and Daniel Patrick Moynihan, *Beyond the Melting Pot* (Cambridge, Mass.: MIT Press and Harvard University Press, 1963).
[38]See James Q. Wilson's penetrating analysis of Negro politics outside the South, *Negro Politics: The Search for Leadership* (New York: The Free Press of Glencoe, Inc., 1960), p. 211.

as a result of this one overriding consideration, the most issue-oriented ethnic group in American politics. Ironically, many Americans who deplore the lack of attention to issues also deplore this strong issue commitment as "bloc voting." But two points should be kept in mind on bloc voting: (1) no group, including southern Negroes, votes as a perfectly solid bloc; (2) bloc voting in the sense of predominant support for a given candidate is characteristic of *all* groups when the group itself is a target of rewards or deprivations. So long as ethnic groups are made such a target, they can be expected to respond in terms of their group needs. The nearly unanimous support of President Johnson by Negro Americans in 1964 was a dramatic demonstration of this point.

The Continuing Socialization of Adults

The secondary socializing forces that we have been exploring—family, class, residential, and ethnic influences—give the individual an early political slant that conditions his response to more immediate and less constant factors for the rest of his life. The basic function of these forces for the political system, then, is to lend continuity to politics by perpetuating the basic distribution of political opinions.

Proximate forces, however, also play a significant role in influencing political opinions. Were this not so, dramatic shifts from one election to the next (as from 1928 to 1932, or from 1948 to 1952) would never occur. An individual's identification with family, culture, class, section, and ethnic group is far more stable than his political allegiances. Clearly, then, such secondary factors can only begin to explain the formation of political opinions. Political learning, viewed as the socialization of citizens in their role in the political system, continues throughout a lifetime. And even though most adult learning is limited to refining or reinforcing the orientations acquired earlier, enough change takes place nonetheless to merit examination.

The Mass Media of Communication

Eighty per cent of all Americans are exposed to a daily newspaper, and 88 per cent of American homes have television sets. The output of newspapers, television, radio, and magazines so inundates the United States every day that Americans seem to have little excuse for not being well-informed on politics. But a closer look suggests a different conclusion. Political news is submerged in an even greater outpouring of entertainment and trivial or sensational news items. Newspapers still reflect enough of their early tradition of deep political commitment to print news rather than advertisements or comics on the front page, in marked contrast to the secondary emphasis on news on radio and TV. Even in newspapers, however, reports on sporting events constitute the largest proportion of items.[39] Moreover, political events are typically reported as "spot" news —that is, as brief reports of isolated events with no interpretation indicating

---

[39] Charles E. Swanson, "What They Read in 130 Daily Newspapers," *Journalism Quarterly*, XXXII (Fall, 1965), 411-421.

which interests stand to be hurt and which to be helped by the development. Local television and radio, which operate in the tradition of the frontier medicine show and of vaudeville rather than of the crusading press, present capsule versions of the spot news appearing in newspapers.

Exceptions to the above comments are the national television networks' news and public affairs programs. Although they receive secondary emphasis, the journalistic level of the networks' news programs is infinitely higher than the artistic level of their entertainment programs. The news departments of the networks are operated by men who seem to have a different set of values from their counterparts in other departments. For example, they take pride in the monetary *losses* suffered by their department; the higher the losses, the greater the proof that the news departments are engaged in a responsible journalistic enterprise rather than in hucksterism.[40] In effect, then, the money-making programs subsidize the news departments. Moreover, the nationally-known commentators genuinely regard themselves as news analysts rather than performers. A commentator who simply reads copy written by others is accordingly frowned upon by his peers. As part of the effort to get away from the Hollywood "star" concept, the thirty-minute evening news programs on CBS and NBC increasingly rely on specialists in different policy areas and on reporters from the scene of action rather than on their "stars" (Cronkite, Huntley and Brinkley).

The major networks are sufficiently conscious of prestige that they are willing to underwrite the losses incurred in the effort to do the best job of news reporting. But the journalistic enterprise of the networks operates within ever-present, if ill-defined, commercial restraints. In 1966, Fred W. Friendly resigned as President of the CBS News Division because higher officials insisted on carrying a fifth rerun of "I Love Lucy" and an eighth rerun of "The Real McCoys" instead of permitting him to present live television coverage of Senate hearings on the Viet Nam war. Mr. Friendly's letter of resignation, which presents the role of the newsman in the mass media much better than we could, read in part:

> I am resigning because C.B.S. News did not carry the Senate Foreign Relations Committee hearings last Thursday, when former Ambassador George Kennan testified on Vietnam. It was the considered news judgment of every executive in C.N.D. [Columbia News Division] that we carry these Vietnam hearings. . . . I am convinced that the decision not to carry them was a business, not a news, judgment.
> . . . . What happens to [the] sense of fairness and balance . . . when one day's hearings, and perhaps the most comprehensive, are omitted? How can we return on Thursday and Friday of this week without denying [the] argument that "the housewife isn't interested?" Why were N.B.C.'s housewives interested? . . .

[40]This observation is based on personal conversations with officials, researchers, writers, and commentators in the news departments of CBS and NBC. Because these were conversations rather than interviews, and because the "respondents" were not selected by rigorous procedures, the observations should be taken as impressions, not "facts."

The concept of an autonomous news organization responsible only to the chairman and the president was not a creation of mine. It is a concept almost as old as C.B.S. News, and is a tradition . . . . The dramatic change in the concept is, to my mind and that of my colleagues, a form of emasculation.

******

My departure is a matter of conscience. At the end of the day it is the viewer and the listener who have the biggest stake in all this. Perhaps my action will be understood by them. I know it will be understood by my colleagues in news and I know Ed Murrow would have understood. A speech he delivered . . . in 1958 spelled it all out:

"One of the basic troubles with radio and television news is that both instruments have grown up as an incompatible combination of show business, advertising, and news. Each of the three is a rather bizarre and demanding profession. And when you get all three under one roof, the dust never settles. The top management of the networks, with a few notable exceptions, has been trained in advertising, research, sales, or show business. But, by the nature of the corporate structure, they also make the final and crucial decisions having to do with news and public affairs.

******

"There is no suggestion here that networks or individual stations should operate as philanthropies. I can find nothing in the Bill of Rights or the Communications Act which says that they must increase their net profits every year, lest the republic collapse."[41]

The commitment of the newsman to a professional role, his rejection of the profit-and-loss criterion, his desire for an autonomous operation governed by professional considerations, and the strains he undergoes in trying to follow these norms in today's mass media—all these points are clear in Mr. Friendly's analysis.

Should we condemn the mass media for offering meager and superficial coverage of public affairs? Before we do, we should realize that the comics get more attention than any other category of newspaper content. And, as their chief source of political information, more people rely on TV—the most superficial source—than on any other medium. Magazines, a few of which offer serious analyses of public affairs, come in last as a source of political information.[42] Spokesmen for the mass media are quick to point out that most people do not want the political information that is available; millions of viewers would no doubt be lost if "The Beverly Hillbillies" were replaced by a public affairs program. The critics often fail to recognize that the business of the mass media is to sell advertising rather than to inform the public. And the public seems to seek more diverting entertainment rather than more information on public affairs.

In addition to the pervasive criticism of superficial and inadequate news coverage, three complaints are frequently lodged against the mass media. First, local sources of news—and therefore different interpretations of local affairs—have decreased, largely due to the decline in daily newspapers. During the first half of this century, the population of the twenty-five largest cities

---

[41]*New York Times*, February 16, 1966. For further elaboration of this theme, see Newton Minow, *Equal Time: The Private Broadcasters and the Public Interest* (New York: Atheneum Publishers, 1964).
[42]Key, *Public Opinion*, Chapters 14 and 15.

increased by 133 per cent; over this same period, the number of daily newspapers in these same cities *decreased* by 44 per cent. In 1910, some 57.1 per cent of the nation's cities had competing dailies; by 1960, the figure had dropped to 4.2 per cent.[43] In 1967, the *Boston Traveler* and the New York *World Journal Tribune* (which only months before had been formed from the ailing *World Telegram,* the *Journal American,* and the *Herald Tribune*) were added to the list of defunct dailies. The Senate Antitrust and Monopoly Subcommittee opened hearings on the problems of the newspaper industry amid predictions by an industry spokesman that "if present trends continue, soon no city less than 650,000 in population will be able to support more than one newspaper."[44] The decline of newspapers is offset to some extent by the availability of competing sources of news through network radio and TV. For local news, however, few citizens have a wide range of choices. They have a single newspaper, and their local television stations, many owned by the newspaper firm, make little effort to offer depth reporting.

Second, the media are often charged with a conservative bias. This particular "complaint" is advanced, of course, by critics of the *status quo;* to a conservative, such a characteristic of the media would be very appealing. In any case, the same observation could probably be made about the mass media of any stable society. As socializing agents supported by the society, the mass media can hardly be expected to reject the fundamental features of the system of which they are part. The liberal complaint in the United States takes the following form: Dependent on a mass audience, the media must be careful to avoid offending any commercially significant group—and virtually everybody buys soap. If no distasteful views can be presented, and if communication is impossible without some opinions creeping in, then the media must take care to echo currently accepted opinions. In avoiding divisive issues, then, the mass media serve to support the *status quo.*[45] When the *status quo* is challenged in such a newsworthy way that the mass media must discuss the challenge, they are more likely to please the manufacturer of the soap than the fellow who needs it for dirty fingernails. This does not mean that advertisers "buy" the mass media; they don't need to. Because the media of communication are big businesses, too, the men who control them quite naturally share the convictions of other businessmen.

The third criticism leveled against the mass media is the opposite of the second: They are charged both with inflaming controversy and with a liberal bias. The first part of this charge is clearly true. Some moderate Negro civil rights leaders complain that only the most virulent condemnations of "whitey" from Negro militants receive press attention, and that protest leaders are thus driven to more and more extreme statements. The local and national atten-

---

[43]Raymond B. Nixon and Jean Ward, "Trends in Newspaper Ownership and Inter-Media Competition," *Journalism Quarterly,* XXXVIII (Winter, 1961), 5. Thirty-one per cent of the TV stations are affiliated with this declining number of newspapers.

[44]*Congressional Quarterly Weekly Report,* XXV (July 14, 1967), 1199.

[45]Joseph T. Klapper, *The Effects of Mass Communication* (New York: The Free Press of Glencoe, Inc., 1960), pp. 38–43.

tion focused on a minor racial incident can turn it into a major conflagration. The media may not challenge the overall structure of the political system, but they love a fight so much that they occasionally help to create one. The accusation of a liberal bias is harder to assess. Because the journalist's professional commitment is different from the commercial commitment of the newspaper publisher or of the TV networks' top executives, some tension continually exists between the journalist and his employer. For the past thirty years, most newspaper reporters covering presidential campaigns have been consistently pro-Democratic and their publishers consistently pro-Republican. Which bias emerges in print depends on the heavy-handedness of the publisher. Our impression is that in recent years television output has been generally pro-Democratic and newspaper output generally pro-Republican.

All these complaints frequently lead to an image of the mass media as irresistible manipulators of public opinion. Such an image, however, is wildly unrealistic. In the first place, no more than 10 per cent of all adults can be called careful followers of political events. If you don't see the propaganda, it can't manipulate you. Those who are attentive tend to notice items agreeable to their own preferences and to neglect items that make them uncomfortable—that is, items that do not fit their biases. What political activist has not turned off the TV set when he could no longer endure listening to a hated candidate? Subtle propaganda may not register, or the listener may reinterpret it to fit his frame of reference. And, when the message is unmistakable but distasteful, we begin to use it to decide how *not* to vote. A political leader dependent on lower-class votes in a one-newspaper town explained to one of the authors that he loved having the local paper against him—it insured his election!

Realistically, while the mass media cannot be said to have direct control over political opinions, they do have significant effects. Short-run effects can be great enough to make any candidate nervous about the way the press might treat last-minute charges which he will have no chance to refute. The candidate can expect his supporters to discount such charges, but he knows that undecided voters are more susceptible to propaganda because of their lack of clear preferences. Most people may lack standards by which to judge new issues or candidates, such as sudden developments in international affairs or unknown opponents in a party primary. Appraisal of such unfamiliar events and personalities may be markedly affected by the way the press describes them. In the long run, however, party, union, lodge, church, and other sources of political cues dull the impact of newspapers and TV. The residual effects of the mass media are extremely hard to judge. Because of their heavy emphasis on entertainment, perhaps their chief political function is to divert Americans from serious attention to politics. And, because inattention favors the *status quo*, the tone of the mass media may help to set the conservative limits within which American politics operates.

Primary Group Influences: Home, Friends, Co-Workers

Another proximate factor conditioning the adult's political attitudes is his personal environment. Just as the individual's earliest view of politics comes from the family he is born into, so his current opinions are molded by his own family, his friends, and his co-workers. Since opinions are formed and expressed through such primary groups, we cannot really understand even the effects of the mass media without considering primary group influences.

Communication does not flow in a single direct step, from media to an undifferentiated mass of individuals; as an influence on opinions, it can better be understood as a two-step flow, from media to informal opinion leaders, and from opinion leaders to small groups.[46] These opinion leaders—or "influentials"—are found in all sorts of groups, in all walks of life, and at every educational and social level. And different people may act as influentials in the same group depending on what topic is under consideration. In the family, for example, the influential on politics is normally the father; on interior decoration, it is the mother; and on choice of breakfast cereals, it is the children ("Get the box with the psychedelic rocket-launcher in it, Mommy!"). Political influentials follow public affairs more closely and in more media than their associates do; hence they are better able to interpret public events in the light of the group's informal norms. In the process of interpretation, they may, of course, modify or reinterpret the meaning that the mass media give to events. The fact that the trusted, face-to-face informant has more influence than an impersonal source also helps to explain the inability of the media to manipulate a mass audience. Instead of directly reaching an undifferentiated audience, the messages of the media filter through—perhaps in modified form—to myriads of small-group audiences.

The pressure to conform to group judgments is perhaps most dramatically demonstrated by the fact that people respond to group influence even in their perception of physical objects. Psychological experiments have shown that when other members of a group unanimously maintain that the longer of two objects is really the shorter, for example, people tend to reject the evidence of their own senses and to acquiesce in the group judgment.[47] The need for social adjustment appears, in this instance, to outweigh the need for accurate appraisal. If the individual thus manages to adjust his perception of purely physical objects to the norms of his group, consider how easily he can adjust his attitudes on the much more ambiguous subject of politics. Through group experiences, individuals not only develop their definition of themselves—their social identity—but also their picture of the external world.

Most of us associate with people from similar family, class, residential, and ethnic backgrounds. As a result, we tend to find ourselves in a basically homogeneous political environment. To the extent that we do not find such homogeneity, we create it. The highest level of political agreement is found in the immediate family; about 90 per cent of husbands and wives, for example, vote for the same candidates. In the rare cases where political agreement is not reached in the home, the offspring will tend to be politically apathetic or

---

[46] See Katz and Lazarsfeld, *Personal Influence*.
[47] See S. E. Asch, "Effects of Group Pressure upon the Modification and Distortion of Judgments," in Dorwin Cartwright and Alvin Zander (eds.), *Group Dynamics* (Evanston, Ill.: Peterson, 1953), pp. 151-162. This and other studies of group influence are cogently summarized in Lane and Sears, *Public Opinion*, pp. 34-39.

independent—and ripe for political conversion if they marry someone from a politically unified family. Even our friends tend to be politically like-minded. As Table 6–7 indicates, young people more often find themselves with at least one friend of a different political persuasion. But with advancing years, one's immediate friends tend to be increasingly unified in their political outlook. From middle age on, a vast majority can comfortably report that they and their three closest friends all vote for the same candidates. Moreover, the minority who cannot report such political agreement are most unstable in their own preferences.

Table 6–7   Age and Political Agreement of Friends

AGE	SAME VOTING INTENTIONS AS THREE BEST FRIENDS
21–25	53%
26–34	69
35–44	75
45+	77

Source: Berelson, Lazarsfeld, and McPhee, *Voting*, p. 97. Percentages include only respondents who knew the voting intentions of all three friends.

The degree of consensus among co-workers is not quite so great as among friends, since the individual cannot ordinarily choose the people with whom he works.[48] But the more homogeneous the political environment in which a person works, the firmer his attitudes will be. Labor-union members, whose normal Democratic predilections are intensified by their union contacts, are more likely to vote Democratic than are nonmembers, even when the comparison is between workers whose occupation, class, education, age, religion, and nonpolitical attitudes are identical.

Conversely, individuals in a personal environment that is politically divided are more vulnerable to the pressures of the dominant attitudes in the larger community. In a predominantly Republican community, the Republicans win more votes than the Democrats from people whose friends and co-workers are politically divided. In the 1952 election, for example, voters of the Jewish faith who had the fewest contacts with non-Jews—housewives in Jewish neighborhoods and students in Jewish colleges—voted more heavily Democratic than did Jews as a whole; Jewish voters in predominantly Republican suburbs, on the other hand, showed greater defections to the Republicans.[49]

Political Influences: Issues, Candidates, Parties

Three additional influences—issue orientation, candidate orientation, and party identification—modify the impact of all the other proximate factors we have discussed. After a whole generation of presidential victories, the Democrats lost votes in 1952 and 1956 from almost every social group. Unless we take into account the appeal of the issues, candidates, and parties, the Eisenhower victories remain inexplicable.

How sharply a citizen perceives the chief issues of the day, and how strongly

---
[48] Berelson, Lazarsfeld, and McPhee, *Voting*, p. 98.
[49] Fuchs, *The Political Behavior of American Jews*.

he feels about them, affect both his inclination to vote and his voting preference. If he has an overriding interest in a single current issue, the stand of the candidates or parties on that one question may determine his vote. Thus the position of southern Democrats on civil rights seems to have induced great numbers of Negro southerners to shift from a Democratic to a Republican vote in 1956. Similarly, Kennedy's telegram of sympathy to Martin Luther King, the highly respected Negro leader who was arrested on traffic charges in Georgia during the 1960 campaign, helped set a tone that brought Negro voters in the South back to the Democratic column. Senator Goldwater's vote against the Civil Rights Act of 1964 brought him votes from southern segregationists who were concerned with that issue alone. When an issue is not of critical importance to a voter, however, he tends to ignore his own party's disagreement with his opinion, or the opposing party's agreement with it, and proceeds to project his own opinion onto his favored candidate.[50]

Issues play a more important part in some elections than in others. In 1948, issues were the decisive factor: the popular preference for the Democratic Party's stand on domestic economic problems probably motivated the last-minute swing to Truman. In 1952 and 1956, issue orientation was outweighed for most voters by the personal appeal of "Ike" Eisenhower. And yet the very nature of the issues in any postwar period enhances the attractiveness of a great war hero. Suddenly, citizens lack the unifying exhilaration of the war effort, and are beset by the uncertainties and tensions that wars always create. So the issues of the time call for the hero of war to resolve the perplexities of peace—after World War II both Democrats and Republicans courted General Eisenhower as a presidential candidate. The central issue of 1960 was John Kennedy's Catholicism: defections among Protestant Democrats reduced his victory to a razor-thin margin. In 1964, Senator Barry Goldwater's "extremism" returned the advantage on issues to the Democrats.

Certainly candidate orientation played a predominant role between 1948 and 1952, when the nation's most popular general entered onto the political battlefield.[51] The resounding 1952 victory of the Republicans, achieved with the support of about 25 per cent of those who had voted Democratic in 1948, was based on the Republican candidate rather than on the party or its position on issues. The University of Michigan's Survey Research Center reports that the new Republican voters of 1952 showed little enthusiasm for the Republican Party or for its stand on issues, but their preference for the Republican candidate was great enough to outweigh issue orientation and party identification.[52] The appeal of the new President was almost universal: except for the Negroes and two groups (the college-educated and the professional-managerial class) which were already heavily Republican in 1948, every economic and

[50]Berelson, Lazarsfeld, and McPhee, *Voting*, p. 220.
[51]So great was his appeal that Eisenhower apparently could have won as handily in 1948 as he did in 1952. See Herbert Hyman and Paul B. Sheatsley, "The Political Appeal of President Eisenhower," *Public Opinion Quarterly*, XVII (Winter, 1953–54), 442.
[52]Angus Campbell, Gerald Gurin, and Warren E. Miller, *The Voter Decides* (Evanston, Illinois: Row, Peterson and Company, 1954).

social group shifted in some degree to the Republican candidate. In the 1956 election, Eisenhower won even greater support from virtually every group, despite his party's failure to win control of either house of Congress—a fate that had befallen no party with a winning presidential candidate since 1848.

While Republicans were voting for the man in 1956, the more faithful Democrats were voting on the basis of party preference, despite the fact that many of them too admired Eisenhower greatly. For many people the political variable of party identification is thus a crucial factor, influencing or overshadowing opinions about both issues and candidates. Over three-fourths of the voters support the same party from one election to the next, and most have decided how they will vote even before the post-convention campaigning begins.[53] Although voters are much less "regular" than party leaders in their opinions on issues, they do tend to change their opinions during the course of an election campaign to conform with their party's position. If they differ with their party on issues they regard as particularly vital, or if they find the other candidate particularly appealing, of course, they may break away to the other party. But for some voters the attachment to party, regardless of issues or candidates, appears virtually unassailable.

To talk about party attachment simply as another political force that intervenes between secondary influences and a specific electoral decision somehow fails to do justice to the importance of party identification. Unlike reactions to the transient issues or personalities of particular campaigns, party identification, like family and class background, may be viewed also as a socializing influence that helps to shape our view of the political world in an enduring way. Remember that the process of political socialization which begins in the family is to a large degree a process of inculcating attitudes toward political parties, and that children pick up parental party preferences remarkably early. Party attitudes not only influence our votes, then, but also our responses to the mass media and our evaluations of people and policies.

The staunch party adherent is sometimes chided for his allegedly blind loyalty—"You'd vote for an idiot or a crook if he ran on the Democratic (or Republican) ticket!" But the critics neglect the convenience of party as a valuable clue in evaluating men and issues. Using party labels as a guide, even relatively uninformed voters can make fairly reasoned choices without knowing very much about the candidates themselves. If a man wins the nomination of a party, its faithful followers will decide that he must have sterling qualities. Formed early and generally growing more intense with age, party identification is the most important single factor both in shaping general political outlooks and in determining voting preference.

Journalists frequently convey the impression that political opinions oscillate wildly in response to politicians' every subtle move. This tendency to exaggerate stems partly from eagerness to find something newsworthy for each day's deadline, partly from the notion that other journalists, cab drivers, and bartenders represent the general public, and partly from ignorance of the basic forces that form political opinions. The underlying distribution of party preference is, in fact, remarkably stable. Table 6–8 shows that in the period

[53]Berelson, Lazarsfeld, and McPhee, *Voting*, p. 18.

from 1952 to 1964, for example, virtually no change in party identification occurred, despite variations in the fates of the respective parties at the polls during the same period. The Democrats now enjoy an impressive advantage, claiming about 60 per cent of those who have some degree of party identification; and earlier surveys show that this advantage extends back to the 1930s.[54] But the Republicans' 1952 and 1956 victories, and their near-victories of 1948 and 1960, demonstrate that voting does not perfectly mirror party identification. Why not?

Table 6-8 Distribution of Party Identification in the United States, 1952 to 1964

	OCT. 1952	OCT. 1954	OCT. 1956	OCT. 1958	OCT. 1960	NOV. 1962	OCT. 1964
Strong Republican	13%	13%	15%	13%	14%	12%	11%
Weak Republican	14	14	14	16	13	16	13
Independent Republican	7	6	8	4	7	6	6
Independent	5	7	9	8	8	8	8
Independent Democrat	10	9	7	7	8	8	9
Weak Democrat	25	25	23	24	25	23	25
Strong Democrat	22	22	21	23	21	23	26
Apolitical, "Don't know"	4	4	3	5	4	4	2
Total	100%	100%	100%	100%	100%	100%	100%
	1,614	1,139	1,772	1,269	3,021	1,289	1,571

Source: Survey Research Center, University of Michigan.

The Democrats' dominance is reduced, in the first place, by the fact that a higher percentage of Democrats than Republicans have a low level of political involvement. Hence they are more likely not to vote or to cast a casual vote for the other party's candidate.[55] When these features of low involvement are taken into account, the Democratic edge is reduced from 60–40 to about 54–46 or 53–47.[56] With the Democrats' effective party identification reduced to 53 or 54 per cent, we can more easily see how short-term influences give the Republicans a good chance to win elections. Just *how* good a chance is a difficult question to answer. Donald E. Stokes, having made a careful analysis of variations in the presidential vote from 1892 through 1960, concludes that, with the present division of party loyalties, the minority party has about three chances out of ten to get into office as a result of short term influences.[57]

Every election has its own peculiarites—a new blend of events, issues, and

---

[54]The Republicans presumably enjoyed a similar advantage in the 1860–1932 era.
[55]We do not elaborate the point here; the relatively low level of involvement found in groups identifying with the Democrats is discussed in Chapter 7.
[56]Philip E. Converse, Angus Campbell, and Warren E. Miller, "Stability and Change in 1960—A Reinstating Election," *American Political Science Review*, LV (June, 1961), 274.
[57]"Party Loyalty and the Likelihood of Deviating Elections," in Angus Campbell et al., *Elections and the Political Order* (New York: John Wiley & Sons, Inc., 1966), pp. 125–135.

personalities—and the short-term influences are as likely to help one party as the other. Granted the importance and the stability of party loyalties, the minority party cannot win office unless the short-term influences run fairly strongly in its favor. The peculiarities of the 1960 election, for example, aided the Republicans, but not quite enough to put them in office. With a greater boost from short-term forces in 1964, the Democrats won by the largest margin in America's history of popular elections.

The Expression of Political Opinions

When we defined *public opinion* as *the expression of attitudes on a social issue*, we left open the question of just *how* opinions are expressed. Americans express their political opinions most conspicuously on election day, but voting is only one of many ways in which popular preferences are revealed.

Forms of Political Participation

Political participation is many things. A street-corner gang beefing about their lack of places to go and do things, housewives planning over morning coffee how to confront the superintendent of schools with a problem, a farm family attending a campaign barbecue, a union member contributing his dollar to a labor political committee—all are taking part in the daily round of democratic government. Political participation includes all these activities and many more besides; it can perhaps be best described as all behavior through which people directly express their political opinions.[58]

Various kinds of political participation are so closely correlated that they can be viewed as different dimensions of the same activity. When a successful candidate is formally sworn into office, and when a disgruntled voter informally swears to a friend that the new office-holder will never be re-elected, both are taking part in politics. But running for public office is a much more demanding and costly activity than merely talking with friends about the candidates. Hence different kinds of participation can be ranked in a hierarchy from the cheapest (least demanding of time, energy, and ability) to the most costly (those which demand an application of almost all one's resources). Professor Lester W. Milbrath of the State University of New York at Buffalo has prepared such a hierarchy of the most common political activities found in a democracy (see Fig. 6–1). The first thing to note concerning this hierarchy is that the activities are *cumulative*. That is, people who engage in the more demanding forms of activity, such as soliciting political funds, will almost certainly engage in all the less demanding forms. And a person who fails to express his opinions in the least costly ways, such as merely talking about politics, will rarely express them in any of the more demanding ways. A second point of interest about the hierarchy of participation is its relative stability. People who rank low or high in one election tend to maintain the same position in future elections. Some movement occurs, of course—candidates and active party workers must be recruited, and some old party work-

[58]This definition and many of the ideas in this section are from Matthews and Prothro, *Negroes and the New Southern Politics*, Chapter 2, "Levels of Participation."

206

horses grow weary and curb their activity—but the distribution remains remarkably stable over time.

How many adult Americans fall into each of the broad categories? About one-third are completely outside the hierarchy of activity; they are the apathetic people who are for the most part literally unaware of their political environment. About 60 per cent can be called mere spectators: "they watch, they cheer, they vote, but they do not battle."[59] The people who could be called gladiators according to Fig. 6-1 make up no more than 5 to 7 per cent of the adult population, even with "gladiator" generously defined to include those who engage in such minor campaign activities as mailing literature or passing out bumper stickers.

What leads to political participation? How do those who participate at least at the spectator level differ from their inactive fellows?[60] To a considerable extent we have already answered these questions in our discussion of the childhood and adult socializing process, which focused on direction of preference and tendency to participate. Disregarding direction of preference, we can recall that participation is encouraged by parents who are interested in politics and agree in their partisanship; by high levels of education, income, and occupation; by ethnic identification, especially when it becomes politically salient; by attention to the mass media; by reinforcement through primary group contacts; and by sensitivity to political parties, issues, and candidates. People for whom all of these forces are positive will be active participants; so far as these forces are mixed or negative, participation is less probable. But *why* do some characteristics lead to active participation, while others do not?

Drawing by Chon Day;
© 1966 *The New Yorker Magazine, Inc.*

"It isn't just the election. Should we put more money in the market or leave it in savings bonds? Is public or private school better for the children? Shall we take a winter vacation or wait till spring? Shall we have the house painted first or the inside redecorated? We're undecided about everything!"

---

[59] This distribution is from Lester Milbrath, *Political Participation* (Chicago: Rand McNally & Co., 1965), p. 21.

[60] We will be concerned with the attributes of the small number of true gladiators in the next chapter on political parties and in later chapters on Congress, the President, the bureaucrats, and the judges.

Structural Factors and Participation

At a primitive level of explanation, we can say that some people participate in politics more than others because they have greater interest. Digging a little deeper, we discover that people with more political sophistication are more interested in politics than others, that people with more education have more political sophistication, that people from higher-class backgrounds have a chance to get more and better education, and so on. While these observations help to round out the picture, they do not get us far beyond the primitive level at which we started if they lead us simply to conclude that people with given attributes are more likely than others to "decide" to participate. For this misses the essential point that some people have great opportunities to "decide" to participate, while other people have no such opportunities.

Each individual does not decide whether to attend party meetings, ring doorbells in a political campaign, vote, or run for office. The possibility of such activity is so completely foreign to the way many people live that the thought of active participation never occurs to them. And we can better explain the decisions of those for whom political activity is feasible by examining "the definitions of appropriate behavior for particular categories of persons in the society, i.e., the norms governing participation and involvement."[61] In a study of political involvement in four Wisconsin cities, Robert Alford and Harry Scoble conclude: "Political involvement may . . . be usefully conceived as a social role, with attached normative expectations for the self and others, varying with group and community membership. . . . Involvement is seen in this way as connected to the social and political structure through a process of role definition and learning."[62]

Gabriel Almond and Sidney Verba, in a five-nation study, have distinguished three roles citizens play that roughly correspond to the activity levels described above: parochial (apathetic), subject (spectator), and participant (gladiator).[63] The point here is that the socialization process *trains* people to see themselves as properly occupying one or the other of these roles. In Milbrath's inventory of propositions accounting for political participation, a clear syndrome emerges if one moves from social to personal to

Figure 6-1

Source: Adapted from Milbrath, *Political Participation*, p. 18.

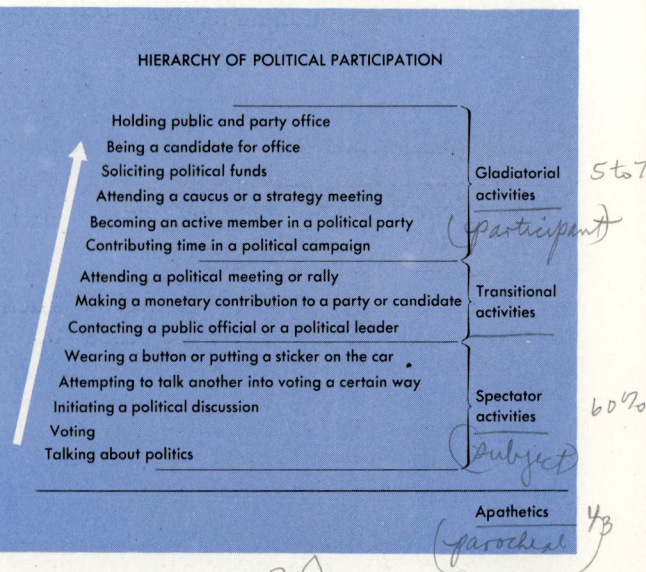

HIERARCHY OF POLITICAL PARTICIPATION

Holding public and party office
Being a candidate for office
Soliciting political funds
Attending a caucus or a strategy meeting
Becoming an active member in a political party
Contributing time in a political campaign
} Gladiatorial activities

Attending a political meeting or rally
Making a monetary contribution to a party or candidate
Contacting a public official or a political leader
} Transitional activities

Wearing a button or putting a sticker on the car
Attempting to talk another into voting a certain way
Initiating a political discussion
Voting
Talking about politics
} Spectator activities

Apathetics

---

[61] Robert R. Alford and Harry M. Scoble, "Sources of Local Political Involvement," unpublished manuscript, 1967. The same point of view will be found in their book, *Bureaucracy and Mobilization in Urban Politics* (Chicago: Rand McNally & Co., 1968).

[62] Alford and Scoble, "Sources of Local Political Involvement." We will develop the concept of "role" more formally in Chapters 9 and 10.

[63] See Almond and Verba, *The Civic Culture* (Princeton: Princeton University Press, 1963).

immediate factors. First, using findings from all the Western democracies, he reports that a social position toward the center of society rather than toward its periphery is conducive to a politically active role:

> Persons close to the center occupy an environmental position which naturally links them into the communications network involved in policy decisions for the society. They become identified with the body politic. They receive from and send more communications to other persons near the center. They have a higher rate of social interaction, and they are active in more groups than persons on the periphery. This central position increases the likelihood that they will develop personality traits, beliefs, and attitudes which facilitate participation in politics. There are many more political stimuli in their environment, and this increases the number of opportunities for them to participate.[64]

This concept of "centrality" is somewhat vague—like the notion of the "mainstream" in popular politics—and deliberately so, since it is designed to include more factors than social class. But clearly every advantage listed for "centrality" is more common among those in higher than in lower status positions. The next body of findings Milbrath cites supports the crucial point that participation is consistently more likely among higher-class than among lower-class persons. Shifting to personal factors, he reports that participation is a function of psychological involvement, feelings of political efficacy, sense of civic duty, political sophistication, lack of absorption with personal problems, self-confidence, and lack of cynicism toward politics. For *every one* of these attitudinal or personality traits, persons of higher socio-economic position (as measured by income, occupation, and—especially—education) are more likely to have the pro-participation trait. The immediate factors—political stimuli—follow the familiar pattern: a person is more likely to participate the more political stimuli he receives, people who are attracted to politics have higher media exposure, political information-seeking is cumulative, and so on, leading to the proposition: *"Persons who lack education and sophistication about politics tend to shut out political stimuli . . . as a way of protecting themselves from messages which they do not understand and cannot absorb."*[65]

This group of findings, all related to class position, suggests that lower-status children somehow learn that their role in society does not require active participation. Indeed, they might expect only discomfort from trying to understand, much less get involved in, the abstract, middle-class world of politics that their parents ignore. At the lowest level, the role is defined as parochial—the world of authority, even (or especially) the "cops" are "they," another world with its own peculiar norms and sanctions. Best to avoid it. The appropriate role for someone slightly higher on the scale—perhaps upper-lower to lower-middle class—is that of the subject, aware that the government affects him, and concerned enough perhaps to vote, but certainly not enough to participate actively or to get deeply concerned.

[64]*Political Participation*, p. 113.
[65]*Ibid.*, pp. 45–46 (emphasis in original).

Greenstein's study of fourth- to eighth-grade school children supports this interpretation of role definition. Despite the fact that the children picked for the study enjoyed the same amount of formal education, upper-status children even at these ages exceeded lower-status children in the capacity and motivation for political participation.[66] Greenstein concludes that "deeply imbedded psychological impediments to the participation in politics of lower-status groups . . . seem to result from lack of self-direction and self-confidence and from inability and unwillingness to express personal feelings and ideas."[67] Thus the role of the nonparticipant is learned early and well. And the marginal role depicted by these findings gives clearer meaning to the concept of "central" location in the social structure.

Political Participation Outside and Against the System

Among students in Latin America, particularly those from countries with dictatorial regimes, the chief criticism of North American political science is that it too heavily emphasizes stability and "system maintenance." Many of these students want neither stability nor maintenance for their authoritarian regimes. Nor, from all appearances, do they want a United States-style democracy. They would vociferously object to our hierarchy of forms of political participation in Fig. 6–1 on the ground that it omits revolution, assassination, and other essential and

[66]Greenstein, *Children and Politics*, p. 94.
[67]*Ibid.*, p. 106.

"When I joined the reform movement, I sure never thought I was joining an 'in-group'"

Drawing by Ed Fisher; © 1961 *The New Yorker Magazine, Inc.*

effective ways by which people express their opinions.[68] They would be correct in doing so.

We have been considering only those forms of participation that take place within the normal channels of the American political system. But how do those Americans, the one-third described as being outside the system except in their passive role as objects of the system's actions, express themselves? The usual answer is that they do not. That is why we describe them as outside the system. In recent summers, however, we have been unforgettably reminded that not all Americans are interested in "system maintenance." Some unknown number, but presumably reaching tens of thousands, are ready on proper provocation to kill, burn, and pillage as a way of expressing their disgust with their lives in the United States. Where do we fit them into our scheme? Are they parochials, subjects, or participants; apathetics, spectators, or gladiators?

In all candor, we are even less certain about these questions than about the others we try to answer in this book. All our answers must be taken as tentative and subject to correction. Any effort to answer these questions must be highly speculative for the very reason that our foreign critics cite: North American political science has not produced enough research to offer well-grounded conclusions on the role of violence in the United States. We can, however, apply the reasoning of the preceding section to this problem.

Robert Lane of Yale University tells us that the upper-lower-class worker regards the overall system as sound and, despite some hardships, usually blames his personal fate on his failure to go far enough in school.[69] This person is even realistic enough about his personal limitations to have a certain *fear* of equality: he knows he would be uneasy in social contact with upper-status people. But what about the person in the lower-lower class? He knows that he has been defined out of the system of rewards—social, economic, and political. He devotes his energies to the most basic problems of survival, and these leave little time for political philosophy or civic improvement activities within the system.[70] Indeed, the system is completely alien to him. Granted an opportunity to break out of his miserable existence he is available for "riot duty"—especially since he can see that most people live quite differently—against the system, or perhaps simply against the world. Concerning what he is for, other than a change in his lot, we are even more uncertain. We suspect that he, too, is most uncertain about his specific personal goals. But destructive violence at least performs the function of externalizing his desperately felt inner needs.

[68]These observations are based on the experience of teaching graduate students in Latin America. The reader should not generalize from these comments to all Latin American countries. Chile, for example, has had as stable a democracy as the United States for many years.
[69]*Political Ideology* (New York: The Free Press of Glencoe, Inc., 1962).
[70]See James C. Davies, *Human Nature in Politics: The Dynamics of Political Behavior* (New York: John Wiley & Sons, Inc., 1963).

Political Opinions in the Political System

Our consideration of political opinions underscores a point made in Chapter 3, where we considered the context of ideas of the American political system: An overwhelming majority of Americans have no ideology in the sense of a structured and functionally interdependent set of ideas. On the direction of preference in mass opinions, we have therefore concentrated on specific party, candidate, and issue preferences. And although we have talked about liberal versus conservative orientations, we had to break that discussion down into specific and poorly related components—positions on social welfare issues, attitudes toward change, relative tolerance of nonconformists, and views of "big business" influence. That the general public responds to political issues without any well-structured set of ideas thus complicates the task of explaining the contributions of public opinion to the political system.

The Policy Implications of Political Opinions

When General Eisenhower was elected President in 1952, his victory was interpreted by most commentators as a popular demand for a shift toward conservatism.[71] From the point of view of 2 or 3 per cent of the adult population, this was a highly meaningful interpretation; this small fraction, which includes the journalists who offered the interpretation, represents the proportion of adults who can be said to have any generally coherent ideology. In fact, however, the Eisenhower victory was attributable to voters with no notion of what abstract terms like "liberalism" and "conservatism" mean: "the stirrings in the mass electorate that had led to a change in administration and in 'ruling ideology' were primarily the handiwork of the very people for whom assumptions of any liberal-conservative dimensions of judgment were most far-fetched."[72] Very few of the extremely few people with an ideological orientation shifted at all.

This case is typical. The few people whose profession is to interpret political events tend to assume that the general public shares their own abstract and logically consistent view of politics. Professors are no less guilty than journalists in this respect. With great frequency they develop a hypothesis they regard as logical but are disappointed to find that their theory "works" only when applied to the 10 per cent of adults who have completed college. The problem is that they expect the general public to employ the sophisticated orientations which "educated people come to take for granted as initial ingredients of thought but that the most cursory studies will demonstrate are not widely shared."[73]

The concept of a liberal-conservative continuum on which candidates and parties can be located is not part of the intellectual equipment of most voters.

---

[71] For one of the most influential of these interpretations, see Samuel Lubell, *Revolt of the Moderates* (New York: Harper & Row Publishers, Inc., 1956).

[72] Philip E. Converse, "The Nature of Mass Belief Systems in Mass Publics," in David E. Apter (ed.), *Ideology and Discontent* (New York: The Free Press of Glencoe, Inc., 1964), p. 218. The other data in this paragraph are from the same source.

[73] *Ibid.*, p. 255.

Instead, they appraise political objects with more fragmented and less organized bits of information, the most general and useful of which is that one party is better than another—better because conditions are good when it is in power and bad when the other party is in power, better because it favors the groups one identifies with, better because of its foreign policies or style of operation, or just better because one has always known it was better.[74] If politicians make the mistake of imputing a refined ideological significance to voting shifts like the one from 1948 to 1952, however, the grand irony is that the policy results will be the same as if the general public *had* behaved in ideological terms! We did get more conservative policies under the Eisenhower administration. Such misperceptions are undoubtedly comfortable for the politician because they allow him to assume that everyone shares his way of thinking. But the misperceptions can be dysfunctional, too, because they lead to surprises that are inexplicable according to the view that public opinion is ideologically oriented. The so-called conservative shift of 1952 was thus followed by a "strange" and unbroken series of Democratic triumphs in every congressional election since that date, including the year (1956) when Eisenhower was overwhelmingly re-elected President. In ideological terms, this did not make sense. From the point of view of actual public opinion, it makes great sense—people both "liked Ike" and liked Democratic policies.

None of the above means that mass opinion plays a negligible role in government; it simply means that the role of public opinion is less simple and direct than old-fashioned oratory suggests. In assessing the policy influence of public opinion, we need to distinguish between two kinds of decision-making—day-to-day decisions on the specifics of policy, and relatively enduring decisions on the broad direction of policy. In the first sphere of decision-making, unorganized public opinion plays little direct role. The authors of *The American Voter* put it this way: "Of course, those involved in policy formation do exercise intensive 'public' pressures for and against particular policy alternatives. But these emanate almost entirely from limited, special publics, often speaking through organizations, and not from the electorate as a whole." Decision-makers try to anticipate possible reactions of the general public to their policies, but "the fact that the details of these policies will be very largely unknown to the general electorate"[75] gives the officials considerable latitude.

When we turn to the broad goals of public policy, however, we find that general public opinion is considerably more influential. Fortunately, this is the only policy area where a democracy, according to democratic theory, requires public opinion to play a controlling role (see Chapter 3). To begin with, the general bounds of public policy are set by latent public attitudes. Some matters, such as government control of the press or nationalization of industry, are ruled out as possible policies in the United States by underlying public

---

[74]See Donald R. Matthews and James W. Prothro, "The Concept of Party Image and Its Importance for the Southern Electorate," in Jennings and Zeigler (eds.), *The Electoral Process*, pp. 151–159.
[75]Campbell *et al., The American Voter*, p. 544.

attitudes. In addition to this negative influence, mass political opinions play a more positive role through the election system. The broad goals of public policy are set on election day. Although the typical election carries no clear mandate for a particular set of policies, it empowers the winners to act as if it did. To remind ourselves of the importance of the ballot box, we need only compare the public services received by Negroes in communities where they can vote with those in communities where they cannot. Once their candidate has won, the "payoffs" (favorable policies) that large numbers of voters expect may be exaggerated.[76] But in areas where *no* Negroes are allowed to vote, as in some Mississippi counties, their helplessness in relation to government drives home for us the importance of the franchise.

The Functions of Opinions for the Political System

In stable political systems, political opinions support the system and help it adapt to changing circumstances. From the point of view of the controlling regime, opinions are considered functional insofar as they support the personnel and policies of the regime. But what is "functional" at one level may be "dysfunctional" at another. Dissatisfactions with the scheme of American government under the Articles of Confederation were dysfunctional for that particular regime (they helped destroy it), but they seem to have been highly functional for the American political community (they strengthened it and helped it to survive changing circumstances). Only rarely do rulers recognize that opinions which support their regime may be highly dysfunctional for the political community as a whole. The cynical but penetrating remark of Louis XV, eighteenth-century King of France—"After me, the deluge!"—represents the exceptional case in which a ruler was able to recognize that the perpetuation of his regime was dysfunctional for the perpetuation of the political community.

Favorable or indifferent public opinions are not only necessary to the survival of a political system but also are necessary to its creation. Without some sense of community or of common identity among a people, they can hardly create a common political system. Active consensus on principles is too much to expect, but a common frame of reference—at least to the point where disagreements center on what is best for a recognized society—is essential. Karl Deutsch of Harvard observes, for example, that a necessary condition for the integration of small political units into a larger whole is "compatibility of the main values held by the politically relevant strata of all participating units."[77] Although extremist groups such as the John Birch Society and the Ku Klux Klan demonstrate that basic democratic values are not pursued by all Americans, even these groups drape their appeals in terms of the needs of the American political community. Even the American communists insist that they seek to improve American society, not to promote Russian interests.

Political opinions thus create the sense of community necessary to a political

---

[76]See William R. Keech, *The Impact of Negro Voting: The Role of the Vote and the Quest for Equality* (Chicago: Rand McNally & Co., 1968).
[77]Karl W. Deutsch et al., *Political Community and the North Atlantic Area* (Princeton: Princeton University Press, 1957), p. 48.

system and promote the survival of the system. So far as democratic politics is concerned, another necessary function of political opinions is to create a widespread sense of the relevance of government, of its importance for and accessibility to the mass of citizens. Only when government is regarded as a potential instrument of the people does a democratic polity become possible. If most people regard the government as an alien and inaccessible creature and cannot imagine it otherwise, they may constitute a political community but it is highly unlikely that they will ever develop a democratic political system.

The three underlying functions of political opinions that we have suggested all apply to the society as a whole and deal with conditions necessary for the emergence of political systems. What about the functions of opinions *within* the political system? These are much more difficult to assess. In the first place, research on political opinions so far has dealt primarily with mass attitudes or with elite activities. The difficult and complex task of tracing the connective thread between mass opinions and the attitudes and performance of government officials has scarcely begun.[78] Moreover, political opinions do not represent a separate institution or structure of government, even though they are vitally important for every institution and function of the political system. Mass opinions are particularly important for the input functions of interest identification and leadership selection, but their importance is expressed through such structures as political parties, pressure groups, and the electoral system. When we talk about the functions of these institutions in the next three chapters ("Political Parties," "Pressure Groups and Public Relations," and "The Electoral System"), we shall accordingly be considering the functions of political opinions also.

Despite the difficulties that confront any attempt to relate political opinions to specific government actions, three functions can be roughly sketched out. First, political opinions perform a *permissive function*. Public indifference or ignorance about most public questions is so widespread that official decision-makers enjoy a wide range of discretion. Even though the public may favor government action on an issue, it may be a long time before the government acts, often because mass sentiment may not be strongly expressed. On the admission of Hawaii to the Union and on the right of the residents of the District of Columbia to vote in presidential elections, for example, a vast majority of the public expressed approval ten to fifteen years before Congress took favorable action.[79] The people did not feel strongly on either subject, however, and the chances are that no member of Congress felt that his re-election was threatened by failure to support public opinion on these subjects. The consequence of such a situation is that government officials find

---

[78] In *Public Opinion and American Democracy*, Professor Key's primary objective was to analyze the "linkages" between public opinion and official actions, but the section on linkages is the weakest part of the book. Significant research in this area by Warren Miller and Donald Stokes of the University of Michigan will be considered in Chapter 9.

[79] Key, *Public Opinion*, pp. 32–33. The data on the two following functions of political opinions are also from Key, pp. 29–39.

Drawing by Ed Fisher;
© 1967 Saturday Review.

"Don't you see,
by protesting and making it
look like this is still
a free country,
we play the power
structure's game. . . ."

it easier to act as they see fit—or at least convenient—without fear of public reprisal.

Second, political opinions perform a *supportive function,* endowing existing policies and actions with a general sense of legitimacy and public approval. However intense the opposition to a measure, it tends to receive widespread support once it becomes the "law of the land." The Social Security Act of 1935, for example, was bitterly opposed by Republicans, but its provisions were approved by about 90 per cent of the voters as soon as it was enacted. This supportive function tends, of course, to stack the cards (or the votes) against those who try to change approved policy. As a candidate for President in 1964, Senator Barry Goldwater took pains to endorse an extension of the Social Security system in order to counteract the impression made by his earlier proposal that it be made voluntary. The importance of the supportive function is underscored when it is missing. Consider the difficulties that confronted officials who were charged with carrying out the provisions of the prohibition amendment.

Third, political opinions sometimes perform a *demand function*. At all times, of course, small segments of the public stridently support particular measures. And permissive support often enables a small but intense group to block legislation about which the vast majority of the general public is relatively unconcerned. (The American Medical Association's long success in opposing general government aid for medical care is perhaps the prime recent example.) But the opinions of the general public occasionally take such clear form that officials can ignore them only at their peril. Although opinion survey data do not go back to the early 1930s, the voters of that era seem to have been in a mood that demanded some government response to the country's economic depression. More recently, the intense dissatisfaction of American Negroes with the stigma of "second-class citizenship," coupled with the supportive or permissive attitudes of most other Americans, required (and achieved) some kind of positive response from the government.

The permissive and supportive functions of political opinions apply to all political systems. The demand function is constitutionally supported only in democracies. In the next three chapters, we shall consider the principal institutions—political parties, pressure groups and public relations, and the electoral system—through which these functions are carried out in the United States.

POLITICAL

PARTIES

Politics is the struggle for power among groups, not among isolated individuals. Early democratic theorists assumed that individuals could exist in a "state of nature" quite apart from groups. Today this notion seems untenable, for we know that even such essential human attributes as speech cannot be developed by children in isolation from other human beings. As David Truman, a student of interest groups, puts it, "We do not, in fact, find individuals otherwise than in groups; complete isolation in space and time is so rare as to be an almost hypothetical situation."[1] Both opinions and behavior are largely shaped by group affiliations. Having identified the political attitudes and behavior patterns that differentiate various groups within the population, we now turn to groups in the purer sense of the term—that is, as aggregations marked by some degree of *interaction* or *relationship* among the members.

Among the unofficial agencies through which public opinion performs the basic input functions of selecting leaders and of communicating public interests to official decision-makers, the most important are political parties, pressure groups, and professional public relations organizations. We shall concentrate first on the political party, which is both the broadest of these three kinds of groups and the one that is most central to a democratic system.

The American Party System

In all societies that we know about, human beings are born and grow up under some kind of government. Realistically, this means that the enduring problem of politics is not that of devising a form of government and selecting people to man it. The truly enduring problem is the management of transfers of power. Instead of devising a government, human beings are presented with the problem of maintaining or changing the governments under which they live. Responses to this problem vary from apathy to support for established rulers to demands for a change.

The questions of who shall succeed to power and through what processes have been answered by different kinds of political systems in different ways. Hereditary monarchies solve these questions through a biological lottery,

---

[1] David B. Truman, *The Governmental Process: Political Interest and Public Opinion* (New York: Alfred A. Knopf, 1951), p. 48.

219

although bloodshed following or leading to the death of rulers was at one time frequent enough to furnish gory material for Shakespeare and other writers.[2] Modern dictatorships have been equally troubled by the problem of succession when rulers have fallen into disfavor, become senile, or died. Perhaps the greatest achievement of democracy is the development of political parties as peaceable agencies for expressing public reactions to rulers and preferences for their successors. Political parties may be viewed as democratic equivalents of groups found in all governments—those supporting the established regime and those conspiring to overthrow it.

Given the importance of political parties for democracy, we might expect them to be among the most respected groups in America. That they are *not* is one of the mysteries of politics that we cannot fully explain. One explanation of this irony is that both the Framers and the original opponents of the United States Constitution mistakenly expected that popular elections would give citizens direct control over government without the need for intermediary organizations. Generations of political experience, however, have convinced observers that parties are essential to the functioning of any group of people. No large group of individuals can behave as a unit until they are organized by those who are actively seeking to speak for the group and to formulate its policies. "Affairs of a group—be it a nation, a church, a union, or a chamber of commerce—do not and cannot take care of themselves; small factions of men must advance proposals and put themselves forward as willing to assume responsibility for handling the affairs of the group."[3] In democratic societies, political parties seek to exercise this leadership in quite a different way from the strong-arm tactics adopted by the rulers of nondemocratic societies.

The Common Purpose of Political Parties

What is a political party? It can be distinguished from other political groups by its peculiar purpose and methods.[4] The *purpose* of a party is to win and exercise political power—specifically, to gain control of the government. It is this purpose that sets political parties apart from other institutions that struggle for political power. Pressure groups, for example, try to influence public policy, but they are concerned with *specific* policies rather than with control of the government *as a whole*. The Women's Christian Temperance Union would like to determine policy on matters relating to alcoholic beverages, but is uninterested in assuming responsibility for policies of taxation and foreign affairs. The Chamber of Commerce and the AFL-CIO have interests that are just as sober and much broader, but not even these groups press for continuous control of the entire government. If any one of these organizations were to move beyond the attempt to influence specific policies and seek to win general control of the

---

[2] The notion of a biological lottery and much of the substance of the above paragraph are from V. O. Key, Jr., *Politics, Parties, and Pressure Groups*, 5th ed., (New York: Thomas Y. Crowell Company, 1964), Chapter 1.

[3] *Ibid.*, 3rd ed., p. 217.

[4] For a brief discussion of the concept of party (similar to that employed here) and the formulation of the concept by noted authorities, see Alfred de Grazia, "Party," in J. Gould and W. L. Kolb (eds.), *A Dictionary of the Social Sciences* (New York: The Free Press of Glencoe, Inc., 1964), pp. 482–483.

government, then that group would, by definition, become a political party.

The effort to take over responsibility for the overall conduct of the government, then, distinguishes the political party from the pressure groups. And proximity to power distinguishes the true political party from the "minor" parties that operate on the fringes of politics. To be an authentic party, a political group must either enjoy power now or have a fair prospect of gaining power in the future. Consequently, such organizations as the Socialist, Prohibitionist, Greenback, and Vegetarian parties, which neither gain nor lose in American elections, are more properly educational movements or interest groups rather than political parties. Many state laws require this distinction, and require that an organization must have received a specified percentage of the vote in the preceding election (2 per cent in California, 5 per cent in Illinois, 10 per cent in Colorado)[5] before it can be classed a "political party" and appear on the official ballot.

If we try to define political parties in terms of more specific purposes, rather than simply in terms of the attempt to gain control of the government, the definition loses its generality. Perhaps the most famous concept of party is that advanced by Edmund Burke, a British statesman of the eighteenth century: "Party is a body of men united, for promoting by their joint endeavours the national interest, upon some particular principle in which they are all agreed." But what "particular principle" serves to "unite" such Democrats as Senators Robert Kennedy of New York and James Eastland of Mississippi, or such Republicans as Senators J. Strom Thurmond of South Carolina and Edmund Brooke of Massachusetts? Their disagreement on principles is exceeded only by their lack of unity in Senate voting. Clearly, principles vary from one member to another within the same party, but *all* the members are united in their desire to win control of the government. Although individual motives and objectives would have to be taken into account in a study of a given party, a definition general enough to apply to all parties must stop short with the statement that their broad objective is to acquire political power.

The Distinguishing Method of Political Parties

The method by which a political party tries to achieve its objective of winning power is based on attempts to mobilize votes. Indeed, David Truman insists that we should forget purpose altogether and define political parties exclusively in terms of this distinguishing method.[6] Nonparty organizations, like public relations and pressure groups, also try to mobilize votes, but they do not themselves offer candidates for office. The customary method of seeking power through ballots rather than through bullets is peculiar to democratic regimes. It may be that the party is

---

[5]See Joseph P. Harris and Leonard Rowe, *California Politics*, 2nd ed. (Stanford, California: Stanford University Press, 1959), p. 31; Austin Ranney, *Illinois Politics* (New York: New York University Press, 1960), p. 18; Curtis Martin, *Colorado Politics* (Denver: Big Mountain Press, 1960), p. 35.

[6]"Whatever else it may be or may not be, the political party in the United States most commonly is a device for mobilizing votes, preferably a majority of votes." Truman, *The Governmental Process*, pp. 270–271.

primarily an organ for the expression of combative instincts, but it serves to sublimate those instincts and to promote a peaceable settlement of differences.

The peaceable method of parties in a democracy distinguishes them from the "parties" of totalitarian regimes like the People's Republic of China. To "become a party" to something means to identify oneself with one group rather than with another—in other words, to make a *choice*. Since totalitarian regimes deny individuals this right to choose one party instead of another, they never permit multiple parties to function. For parties to operate in a meaningful way, they must be tolerated by the government. Conversely, they must "tolerate" the form of government once they have achieved power—that is, they must not transform the government simply into an arm of one party. Although totalitarian parties may win wide support in a competitive party system—as the communists do in France and Italy—their success at the national level would destroy the system itself, for all totalitarian parties aim to become the only "party."[7] The party apparatus in such regimes performs important functions for the political system, of course, but these functions are radically different from those of competitive political parties. As we shall see below, these functions are such that a one-party regime becomes a no-party regime.

Functions of Political Parties

Because freely competing political parties are unique to democracy, students of political parties have suggested that almost anything essential to the maintenance of democracy must be a consequence of party activities.[8] When we described the basic political functions of public opinion (Chapter 6) as the choice of leaders and the communication of public interests to official decision-makers, we also pointed out that political parties are indispensable to the democratic achievement of these results. In the broadest terms, then, the consequences of party activity for the political system as a whole are the public choice of leaders and the open and organized expression of public interests. Political parties can therefore be said to democratize the input functions that must be performed by all viable political systems.

In addition to their contribution to the input functions common to all political systems, political parties perform more specific functions for the individual as well as the political system. At the individual level, parties are

[7] Note that our reference here is to totalitarian parties, not to parties with any particular label. In Chile, for example, the Communist Party appears committed to democratic techniques whereas the Socialist Party recommends revolution by violence.

[8] Samuel J. Eldersveld, for example, has recently discerned seven "critical" functions of parties for democracies: "to recruit leadership, formulate policy, organize decision-making, communicate upward and downward between leaders and public, promote consensus, enforce responsibility, and thus move society toward the effective and expeditious resolution of its conflicts." *Political Parties: A Behavioral Analysis* (Chicago: Rand McNally & Co., 1964), p. 22. Frank J. Sorauf speaks of three manifest functions (electing, propagandizing, and governing) and of six latent functions of parties: "They reduce effectively the number of political options to manageable numbers, bring order and focus to the political struggle, simplify issues and frame alternatives, compromise conflicting interests, recruit political leadership, personalize and dramatize politics, stabilize political debate and allegiances, and enhance the political power of the 'insignificant' individual." *Political Parties in the American System* (Boston: Little, Brown and Company, 1964), pp. 165–166.

222

reference groups which help the citizen organize his opinions. They thus perform the function we called "object appraisal" in talking about public opinion. Once the citizen has decided which party he prefers, he has a reliable cue for reacting to new issues and personalities with a minimum of effort—he need only discover where his party stands or, if he likes real economy of effort, he can support his party on the assumption that it supports the correct position. Second, party activity tends to increase voting turnout, to strengthen party loyalty, and to create more favorable attitudes toward active partisan work among those who are exposed to it. Third, exposure to party activity results in greater interest in and information about public affairs. Even among citizens who frequently watch television, those exposed to local party activity are much better informed on national affairs than those not so exposed.[9] The competition of parties for votes thus leaves citizens more politically oriented, more active, more interested in politics, and better informed about public affairs.

At the level of the political system, political parties serve many functions in addition to their basic role in leadership selection and interest identification. If you can imagine what our political life would be like without political parties, you will be able to identify these additional functions. With no political parties, the struggle for power would certainly be less open, less predictable in its outcome, more susceptible to minority manipulation, and more likely to take the form of coups or even of revolution. Without parties, countless groups could be expected to pursue extremely different policies, and so many opposing alternatives would be available that choice would be difficult. Each election, assuming that elections continued to prove feasible, would present such an overwhelming array of individual candidates that voters could hardly know what policies or even general tendencies they were supporting. Finally, with no party program to help organize their work, official decision-makers would presumably rely much more heavily on those interest groups that were organized to promote special interests. If these speculations are valid, we have identified at least three additional functions that political parties perform for American politics.

First, parties structure the conflicts of society. Parties did not create the struggle for power; the struggle for power in the context of a democracy created parties. Thus parties function to control, direct, and stabilize conflict and thereby permit a peaceable expression of differences.[10] In structuring social conflict, parties develop legitimate opposition to those in control of government and become the functional equivalent of revolutionary movements.[11] Second, political parties serve to moderate the differences among opposing groups, to stabilize political allegiances, and, in Lord Bryce's phrase,

[9] Eldersveld, *Political Parties*, p. 542. The second and third findings are both from Eldersveld's research in the Detroit metropolitan area.

[10] Clinton Rossiter calls this the primary function of a democratic party from which all others are derived. *Parties and Politics in America* (Ithaca, New York: Cornell University Press, 1960), p. 39.

[11] As Professor V. O. Key put it, "The strivings of the outs for office become . . . a sublimation of revolutionary movements," *Politics, Parties, and Pressure Groups*, p. 204.

to "bring order out of the chaos of a multitude of voters." In order to win majority support, they must avoid taking extremist positions. Consequently, they must appeal to a wider group than just their own hard core of doctrinaire and dogmatic faithful.[12] Third, political parties organize the decision-making activities of government in such a way as to give ordinary citizens a much better chance of having their interests recognized. William Chambers, in a study of the origins of American political parties, finds this the "great role" of parties and party competition: "shaping and clarifying options for popular choice or decision, and . . . giving such choices some effect in the conduct of government."[13]

In all these functions, political parties have a strong majoritarian bias that we can better appreciate by again considering what our politics would be like without parties. This consideration need not be entirely speculative: in the early days of the Republic, before the emergence of the party system, future members of Jefferson's Republican Party complained about the advantages enjoyed by "the Weight of Talent, Wealth, and personal and family interest." Melancton Smith argued that the influence of

. . . the well-to-do and eminent will generally enable them to succeed in elections. [Those of] conspicuous military, popular, civil, or legal talents . . . easily form associations; the poor and middling classes form them with difficulty. . . . A substantial yeoman, of sense and discernment, will hardly ever be chosen. From these remarks, it appears that the government will fall into the hands of the few and the great. This will be a government of oppression.[14]

We still hear charges that the "poor and middling classes" are too little recognized in decision-making. But they now have a weight that they could not possibly have achieved without political parties.

The Two-Party System

The most important single feature of the political wars in the United States is that they are conducted within a two-party system. True, we have many so-called "minor parties"; but parties are power vehicles, and political power in the United States is effectively monopolized by the Republican and Democratic parties. In 1966, for example, the minor parties failed to win a single seat in Congress, the governorship of any state, or even one of the 7,734 seats in the state legislatures. Quite clearly, ours cannot be described as a multi-party system. Nor can it be called a one-party system. The Republicans almost always win the elections in about nine states, and the Democrats in about thirteen, but both parties *share*

---

[12]This is more true in two-party than in multi-party systems, but even in multi-party systems the most extreme of the "class parties," the communists, lay claim to representing the true interests of society as a whole. See Sigmund Neumann, *Modern Political Parties: Approaches to Comparative Politics* (Chicago: The University of Chicago Press, 1956), p. 397. Three of the functions listed here may be found, in somewhat different form, in this same source.
[13]*Political Parties in a New Nation* (New York: Oxford University Press, 1963), p. 13.
[14]Quoted in *ibid.*, p. 13.

political power in the national government and in a majority of the states.[15] Moreover, areas completely dominated by a single party are apparently disappearing everywhere outside the South, and even there one-party rule is weakening.[16]

How does the two-party system compare with the single-party and multiparty systems? The single-party system at the national level appears incompatible with democracy, but this is not necessarily the case at the subsystem level. In southern states, even though the Democratic candidate is assured of victory in the official election, the Democratic party primary gives voters a choice between competing personalities or factions. But competition between individuals—which inevitably means that there is no continuing group responsibility—seems a poor substitute for competition between parties. One-party politics can promote popular control of policy only through competition between factions that are so well organized that they resemble parties.[17]

Organized, continuing, and visible factions are the exception in a one-party system. And when a bifactional pattern of competition develops, the absence of recognizable party labels and programs renders the one-party system less stable than the two-party system. In Professor V. O. Key's classic analysis of the consequences of one-party factionalism for southern politics, he used Louisiana as a principal example of the bifactional state.[18] Less than two decades later, Louisiana was outranked only by Mississippi in the multiplicity

---

[15]On the basis of elections for President, United States senator, and governor between 1914 and 1953, Austin Ranney and Willmoore Kendall have developed a threefold classification of state party politics in the United States: (1) *two-party states,* "in which the second party had won over 25 per cent of the elections"; (2) *modified one-party states,* "in which the second party, while winning less than 25 per cent of all elections, has won over 30 per cent of the vote in over 70 per cent of all elections and has won over 40 per cent of the vote in over 30 per cent of all elections"; and (3) *one-party states,* "in which the second party has won less than 25 per cent of all elections, and has also won over 30 per cent of the vote in less than 70 per cent of all elections and won over 40 per cent of the vote in less than 30 per cent of elections."

The one-party states during this period were: *Republican*—Vermont; *Democratic*—Alabama, Arkansas, Florida, Georgia, Louisiana, Mississippi, South Carolina, Texas, and Virginia. The modified one-party states were: *Republican*—Iowa, Kansas, Maine, New Hampshire, North Dakota, Oregon, Pennsylvania, South Dakota; *Democratic*—Kentucky, North Carolina, Oklahoma, Tennessee. The remaining twenty-six states were two-party. "The American Party Systems," *American Political Science Review,* XLVIII (June, 1954), 477–485. Attempts to establish more refined systems of classification may be found in Robert T. Golembiewski, "A Taxonomic Approach to State Political Party Strength," *Western Political Quarterly,* XI (September, 1958), 494–513; Edward C. Cox, "The Measurement of Party Strength," *Western Political Quarterly,* XIII (December, 1960), 1022–1042; Joseph A. Schlesinger, "The Structure of Competition for Office in the American States," *Behavioral Science,* V (July, 1960), 197–210.

[16]On the "erosion of sectionalism," see V. O. Key, Jr., *American State Politics* (New York: Alfred A. Knopf, Inc., 1956), pp. 26–28. While competition diverges in some degree from the perfect two-party model in most states, the politics of even the pure one-party states can be understood only as an integral part of a national two-party system. See Angus Campbell *et al., The American Voter* (New York: John Wiley & Sons, Inc., 1960), p. 557.

[17]Lewis Bowman and G. R. Boynton, "Coalition as Party in a One-Party Southern Area: A Theoretical Case Analysis," *Midwest Journal of Political Science,* VIII (August, 1964), 277–297.

[18]See *Southern Politics* (New York: Alfred A. Knopf, Inc., 1949), Chapter 14.

of its factions!¹⁹ In the one-party system with multiple factions, the voter is confronted by a bewildering array of candidates. Florida, for example, typically has about ten candidates for governor alone in its first primary elections. Party label is meaningless because all candidates are in the same party. Hence a one-party politics—even with factions—is in fact, as we observed earlier, a no-party politics.

To identify the functions of political parties, we tried to imagine what our politics would be like without parties. Since the one-party systems in several southern states actually operate as no-party systems, they give us a chance to test our conclusions against actual cases: that is, some of the consequences of no-party politics must be the obverse of the consequences of two-party or multi-party politics. At the most general level, factional competition in one-party states results in public selection of leaders and the identification of public interests. But the kind of leaders selected tend to be different and the interests identified tend to be more restricted. Why? For an answer we look to Professor Key's analysis of the more specific functions of the one-party system, reorganizing his conclusions to make them comparable to our analysis of the functions of the party system.

At the individual level, a no-party system offers the citizen no stable reference groups or reliable clues for reacting to political stimuli. As Key puts it, "Discontinuity of faction both confuses the electorate and reflects a failure to organize the voters into groups of more or less like-minded citizens with somewhat similar attitudes toward public policy.... The voters' task is not simplified...."²⁰ Second, factional politics leads to relatively low levels of voter turnout. Indeed, the original purpose of southern one-party systems was to disfranchise the Negro. But the lack of clarity in factional competition also leads to lower rates of participation by poorer and less-educated whites. Third, no-party politics fails to stimulate citizen interest in and information about public affairs. "You can't tell the players without a program," shout the vendors at sporting events. In one-party politics, the citizen not only lacks a "program" to identify the "players," but his interest also suffers from the fact that, in the absence of opposing teams, everyone on the field wears the same uniform.

At the system level, the discontinuities of one-party politics prevent the structuring of political strife even to the point where the "outs" can attack the "ins": "the 'ins' do not exist as a group with any collective spirit or any continuity of existence."²¹ Each candidate for the legislature, for the governorship, and for various cabinet offices has campaigned and will campaign in the future without ties to other candidates, so that there is really no way to "throw the rascals out." Second, the every-man-for-himself context of one-party politics "places a high premium on demagogic qualities of personality that attract voter-attention."²² The lack of organization for screening out extreme types, the proliferation of candidates, and the lack of clues for appraising them

---

¹⁹See Donald R. Matthews and James W. Prothro, *Negroes and the New Southern Politics* (New York: Harcourt, Brace & World, Inc., 1966), pp. 159–160.
²⁰*Southern Politics*, p. 303.
²¹*Ibid.*, p. 303.
²²*Ibid.*, p. 304.

226

all combine to the advantage of the flamboyant personality. Third, the conduct of government under a one-party system eludes the control of ordinary citizens. "Factional fluidity and discontinuity probably make a government especially susceptible to individual pressures and especially disposed toward favoritism.... The erratic changes in personnel and policy associated with control by a succession of unrelated and irresponsible factional groups make the consideration, much less the execution, of long-term governmental programs difficult."[23]

At both the individual and system levels, then, one-party politics appears less functional for the general public than does competitive party politics. Leaders are selected and public interests are identified through both systems, of course, but with vastly different consequences for the citizens. We concluded our consideration of party functions by noting their strong majoritarian bias. Professor Key concluded his consideration of one-party functions with an opposite emphasis:

> The significant question is, who benefits from political disorganization?... Politics generally comes down, over the long run, to a conflict between those who have and those who have less. In state politics the crucial issues tend to turn around taxation and expenditure....
>
> It follows that the grand objective of the haves is obstruction, at least of the haves who take only a short-term view. Organization is not always necessary to obstruct; it is essential, however, for the promotion of a sustained program in behalf of the have-nots.... It follows, if these propositions are correct, that over the long run the have-nots lose in a disorganized politics. They have no mechanism through which to act and their wishes find expression in fitful rebellions led by transient demagogues who gain their confidence but often have neither the technical competence nor the necessary stable base of political power to effectuate a program.[24]

The antimajoritarian bias of one-party systems make them an anomaly in a democracy. And note carefully that the one-party systems we have been discussing are *subsystems* that are greatly influenced by the larger two-party system of which they are a part. Where one-party politics extends to an entire political system, its antimajoritarian bias typically expresses itself more strongly as dictatorship.

A multi-party system, on the other hand, can claim two advantages over a two-party system: it permits more shades of opinion to be represented in the legislature, and it vests party membership with greater meaning. And yet, to most American observers, the two-party system seems to be more satisfactory, for the following reasons:

First, it guarantees that both parties will have a wide appeal to the electorate. This sometimes makes the parties so similar that any choice between them means little or nothing; but the two-party system also produces certain advan-

[23]*Ibid.*, p. 307.
[24]*Ibid.*, pp. 305–306.

Drawing by Reilly;
© 1967 The New Yorker
Magazine, Inc.

"Come quick! The G.O.P.
is offering
a viable alternative!"

tages. Since both parties must seek majority support in order to acquire power, they both must please substantially the same people, at least in a diverse society such as ours. (If the people were divided into two sharply opposing groups, each party would be driven toward an extreme.[25]) The fact that the two parties resemble each other so closely, then, may simply mean that both are doing a good job of interpreting public opinion, and their similarity certainly strengthens the unifying and moderating function of parties. Because a majority coalition cannot be built on an extremist position, the age-old fear of a "tyranny of the majority" becomes unrealistic in a heterogeneous society like our own.

Second, the two-party system encourages compromise *within* each party

[25] Anthony Downs, *An Economic Theory of Democracy* (New York: Harper & Row, Publishers, Inc., 1957), Chapter 8; Robert A. Dahl, "Some Explanations," in Dahl (ed.), *Political Oppositions in Western Democracies* (New Haven: Yale University Press, 1966), p. 376. The nonideological orientation of most voters and the multidimensional nature of political stimuli render most unlikely the possibility of an alignment of voters into two extreme groups, in intragroup agreement and intergroup conflict on all issues.

228

before the election, rather than compromise among several parties after the election. This means that the ultimate coalition in control of the government is chosen by the voters rather than by legislative blocs. This method of reaching compromise enhances the role of the voters in choosing their government, and it also tends to *fix responsibility* on a continuing and recognizable group. (This advantage is often said to be reduced in the United States by the failure of the winning party to maintain a high degree of unity in Congress.)

Third, by making certain that *someone* will win a majority in every elected body, the two-party system increases the chances of coherence and stability in government. The classic argument is that, under a two-party system, control of the government is fixed by the voters for the entire period between elections, rather than being subject to overthrow with every shift in alliance among a multitude of parties. The second part of the argument clearly fits the American system: with only two parties, post-election maneuvers do not determine which party will control the government. But the first part of the argument refers too neatly to "the government" to fit the American system without modification. In a federal system like ours, with separation of powers in both state and national governments, "control of the government" is considerably more complicated than in a unitary and parliamentary system like that of Britain. An election in an American locality may mean victory for nonpartisan city officials, a Republican governor and state senate, a Democratic state house, a Republican President, and a Democratic Congress. In such a case, which party can be said to have control of "the government"—or, for that matter, of any level of government?

In fact, the two-party system is less certain to produce coherence and stability in the United States than its proponents claim. Even so, control of each elective body goes to one winning party rather than to an (unknown) post-election coalition. More important, the tendency is toward unified control at each level of government—the President and Congress usually represent the same party, as do most governors and state legislatures.[26] While we cannot accurately claim, then, that the voters in the American two-party system always put control of the government in the hands of one winning party, we can say that the system works in that direction. The confusion is in our separate election of many governing bodies, not in the two-party system. Just imagine how much *more* complicated our system would be with the various branches of our different levels of government each controlled by different combinations of minority parties.

A fourth advantage of the two-party system applies more clearly to the United States: it insures that the Chief Executive will represent a general body of opinion. Where only two parties are competing for power, the successful

---

[26]In 1965, for example, the same party controlled the governorship and both houses of the legislature in 29 states, as compared with 19 states that had a party division. (The two remaining states, Minnesota and Nebraska, have nonpartisan legislative elections.) In 1967, 23 states had a party division. At the national level, from 1900 to 1968, the President and both houses of Congress were of the same party for 54 years; at least one house of Congress was of a different party for only 14 years.

candidate for President or governor must inevitably represent the broad base of one of the two parties. With "energy in the executive" even more essential today than when Alexander Hamilton first argued for its necessity, this is a real advantage indeed.

Finally, recent research casts doubt on the old claim that the multi-party system necessarily heightens citizen interest. A comparison of French and American political attitudes reveals a lower level of awareness of political parties in France than in the United States. On the other hand, the citizens in another multi-party system, Norway, are much more aware of party differences than are Americans.[27] A determination of what accounts for these differences awaits further research, but at least it can no longer be confidently asserted that citizen interest is greater in multi-party systems. At least in France, the multiplicity of parties seems to confuse citizens and lessen their interest.

Why Two Parties? Clearly, democracy thrives when there is more than one party. But why do some countries stop at just *two* while most establish more?[28] Let us look at a few of the explanations. Some say that "the two-party system seems to correspond to the nature of things," because "political choice usually takes the form of a choice between two alternatives."[29] Thomas Jefferson pointed to the nature of man rather than to the nature of things: "The sickly, weakly, timid man fears the people and is a Tory by nature. The healthy, strong, and bold, cherishes them and is formed a Whig by nature. . . ."[30] Alexander Hamilton found the explanation in economic factors: "All communities divide themselves into the few and the many," he argued before the Constitutional Convention. "The first are the rich and the well born, the other the mass of the people."[31] Some observers cite the historical fact that the United States divided into two parties early in its history, although this is circular reasoning and throws no light on the reasons behind the division. Others emphasize the lack of irreconcilable religious, racial, or class cleavages among the American people. In explaining Britain's two-party system, one observer has even suggested that the division is rooted in "the sporting instincts of the British people, which lead them to view political campaigns as a match between rival teams"!

Now these explanations may or may not be relevant to the reasons behind the two-party system. But one general technical factor—the officially prescribed electoral system—is the key to the party system in *every* country. The

---

[27]Philip E. Converse and Georges Dupeux, "Politicization of the Electorate in France and the United States," and Angus Campbell and Henry Valen, "Party Identification in Norway and the United States," in Campbell *et al.*, *Elections and the Political Order* (New York: John Wiley & Sons, Inc., 1966), pp. 269–291, 245–268.

[28]Only eight out of thirty countries with recognized opposition parties in 1964 had two-party systems. See Dahl, *Political Oppositions*, p. 333.

[29]Maurice Duverger, *Political Parties: Their Organization and Activity in the Modern State*, trans. Barbara and Robert North (New York: John Wiley & Sons, Inc., 1955), p. 215.

[30]See Charles A. Beard, *Economic Origin of Jeffersonian Democracy* (New York: The Macmillan Company, 1936), pp. 420–421n, for letter to Lafayette (November 4, 1823).

[31]Max Farrand (ed.), *The Records of the Federal Convention of 1787* (New Haven: Yale University Press, 1911), p. 299.

single-member district system with plurality election correlates almost perfectly with the two-party system. The "single-member district system" is the system under which only one representative, rather than several, is elected to a given office from any one district. "Plurality election" means that the candidate with the largest vote is elected even if he fails to win a majority, so that there is never any need for a second balloting to produce a majority vote. Because parties always direct their efforts toward winning elections, the election procedures that are prescribed by law cannot help but mold the character of party politics. A country that has a two-party system almost always uses this electoral scheme; and if it uses this electoral scheme, it will almost certainly have a two-party system.[32]

The way in which the single-member district system freezes out minor parties is fairly obvious. Only one victor is possible in each race, whether for the presidency or for the legislature. And since the minor parties have no chance at all of capturing the presidency, and very, very little chance of ever enjoying any legislative power, they quickly die out.

The influence of plurality election, often overlooked, is also important. In countries where a majority vote is required for victory, a second balloting between the candidates who led on the first ballot is necessary. This system encourages minor parties to offer candidates in the first election in the hope of slipping into the runoff election. (The second ballot was one of the causes of the multi-party system in France's Third Republic.) But in countries where only a simple plurality is needed for victory, minor parties are encouraged to join forces with one of the major parties, in the hope that they may become identified with the winner. Understandably, the major parties tend to make concessions to the minor parties in order to broaden their base of support. Where there is only one election, then, coalitions must be formed before the election rather than in the interval between the first and second balloting.[33]

Although these technical features of the electoral system seem particularly well adapted to two-party politics, we still cannot say that the party system of a country is a direct result of its electoral system. From data on five European countries, John G. Grumm of the University of Kansas concludes that the party system shapes the electoral system rather than the other way around.[34] Some European systems like Denmark's once had the single-member district and the plurality system of elections, but maintained a multi-party system. The parties

---

[32] As Duverger explains, the exceptions to this rule are rare (Canada offers the only current exception) and result from special conditions. He accordingly finds the limits of this system's influence to be as follows: "It tends to the creation of a two-party system inside the individual constituency; but the parties opposed may be different in different areas of the country." Duverger, *Political Parties*, p. 223. For insight into this problem, the authors are particularly indebted to Duverger's discussion on pp. 216–228, and to E. E. Schattschneider, *Party Government* (New York: Farrar, Straus & Giroux, Inc., 1942), Chapter 5.

[33] These propositions find support in the conduct of Democratic primaries in the South; more factions appear in those states requiring a "run-off" primary than in those in which nomination is by a plurality in a single primary.

[34] "Theories of Electoral Systems," *Midwest Journal of Political Science*, II (November, 1958), 345–376.

then changed the electoral system to help themselves. Without attempting to unravel cause and effect, we can say that single-member districts and plurality elections are found together with two-party systems, just as proportional representation from multi-member districts and majority elections (calling for runoff elections) are associated with multi-party systems.

So many factors work to shape both the electoral and the party system of a country that the question of *why* such systems are followed probably cannot be answered exactly.[35] In general terms, the cultural context is important in making our election system seem "natural" to us. Early in our history, Americans divided sharply into groups supporting and opposing adoption of the Constitution. Once that fight was settled, each side adjusted remarkably well to the Constitution's basic procedures, even though they continued to represent opposed interests. America has never been marked by the social homogeneity and consensus of one-party systems or by the social fragmentation and unbridgeable cleavages of multi-party systems.[36] After a bitterly fought election, Thomas Jefferson observed in his first inaugural address, "We have called by different names brethren of the same principle. We are all Republicans, we are all Federalists." With the "American Creed" so widely accepted, the differences among Americans have not been basic enough to drive many voters into splinter parties.

Finally, any pattern of behavior, once established, tends to perpetuate itself. People with political ambitions gravitate to the existing parties (two in the United States). And party loyalty is fantastically enduring among the general public. Although this tells us little about the origins of our two-party system, it reminds us that American practices were influenced by the English background of most of our first politicians. Since their day, the *idea* of the two-party system has been a part of American political socialization. Generations of citizens have been taught the superiority of the two-party system, and it has been elevated from mere habit to the level of a celebrated tradition.

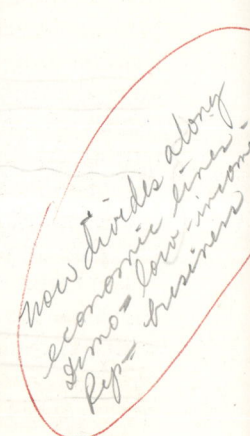

The Structure of American Parties

Like the overall party system, the internal organization of each party is also shaped by the country's official electoral practices. Because the purpose of each party is to gain control of the government by winning elections, party organization is built around the electoral system. Accordingly, the formal organization of our political parties has taken on a pyramidal structure. As we shall see when we begin to identify the points of power within this structure, however, its neatness is most deceptive.

Formal Party Organization

On paper, the *national committee* of each party represents the capstone of the pyramid. Actually, though, the national committee is the point of final authority only in a purely formal

---

[35] Aaron B. Wildavsky offers a sharp criticism of Duverger for neglecting the multiplicity of factors productive of two-party politics in "A Methodological Critique of Duverger's *Political Parties*," *Journal of Politics*, XXI (May, 1959), 303–318. For a general discussion of the electoral and party systems, see Avery Leiserson, *Parties and Politics* (New York: Alfred A. Knopf, Inc., 1958), pp. 108–113.
[36] Sorauf, *Political Parties in the American System*, pp. 30–31.

sense. In both the Republican and Democratic parties, the national committee is composed of one man and one woman from each state (plus members from the territories). The Republicans also give a bonus of an additional seat to any state committee chairman whose state voted Republican in the last presidential, gubernatorial, or congressional election. A territorial chairman is similarly a national committee member if his territory elected a Republican delegate to Congress. The national convention of both parties officially elects the two regular committee members from each state, but in reality it merely accepts the nominees submitted by the state's delegation to the convention. These nominations are made, in accordance with state law, by a primary election, a state convention, the national convention delegation, or a state committee. The duties of the national committee amount to little more than deciding when and where the next convention will meet and preparing a temporary roll of delegates—tasks that are only incidental to the chief concerns of the party.

The *national chairman* acts as the official spokesman for the party. Other party members, especially congressmen, who frequently and vociferously dissent from the chairman's pronouncements, demonstrate, however, that the party has no single voice. The national chairman is officially chosen by the national committee, but in practice he is named by the party's presidential nominee. His primary job is to manage the presidential campaign. In choosing party candidates for Congress, in executing the party program after victory, indeed even in choosing the presidential candidate, the national committee and its chairman normally play only minor roles, and certainly not leadership roles. Selected merely to oversee the presidential campaign, these party officials reflect rather than exercise the real power of the party. The great agitation among Republican leaders about removing Dean Burch as Republican national chairman in 1965 was not an effort to win a post of great power; rather, it was a move to demonstrate that the Goldwater wing was no longer in control of the party.

The national chairman and his committee lack real power over the party's policies and choice of candidates, but they can sometimes play a role of true importance. Because of its limited official authority, the committee tends to be as strong or as weak as its chairman.[37] In addition to his usual role as campaign manager, the national chairman serves his party as fiscal leader and as mediator for its hundreds of state and local units as well as its major factions. An occasional chairman has the qualities to build considerable influence on the basis of these functions, even attempting to coordinate party policy.

To discover the normal functions of the national committee, however, perhaps we should simply ask what a party would lose if its national headquarters disappeared. Hugh A. Bone, one of the few students of the national committees, supplies this answer: "If the headquarters were abolished the parties would lose an agency that has sought to coordinate the infinite variety of effort of numerous party affiliates, to raise money, and to obtain publicity

[37]See Abraham Holtzman, "Party Responsibility and Loyalty: New Rules in the Democratic Party," *Journal of Politics*, XXII (August, 1960), 491.

for the party as a whole."[38] Professor Bone notes, in massive understatement, that neither national committee has performed its purported role of coordination "in a spectacular way," and he points out three weaknesses of the committee which account for this failure. First, turnover in the chairmanship is so frequent that an effective national office can hardly be created. From 1940 to 1962, for example, the Republicans had thirteen chairmen and the Democrats eleven. Second, the national committee has no firm base in the party, with no official place in either the state or congressional party organizations. Nor do committee members normally have power as informal leaders; frequently they are relative unknowns who are selected because of financial contributions to the party. The occasional committee member who is a powerful figure in his state derives his influence from some source other than his position on the committee. Third, the national committees have no constitution or bylaws giving them definite authority and functions. The rules of the Democratic Party, for example, specifically note that the national committee is limited to powers granted by the national convention and that no convention has authorized "formulation of proposals which might be construed to be in the nature of platform declarations" by the committee.[39]

Alongside the national committee in the party structure are the national *congressional* and *senatorial campaign committees*, chosen by each party's representatives in the House and Senate. Their independence of the national committee further suggests the extent to which power in American parties is dispersed. Although the demands of modern campaigning have produced an increasing amount of personalized cooperation between the various party committees, this is primarily at the staff level, not at the decision-making level. "For all practical purposes both committees in both houses are autonomous," Professor Bone submits. "The four Capitol Hill committees remain jealous of their independence and are quick to resist 'encroachment' by the national committees. Especially in the realm of policy, there has been the frequent tendency of party leaders to suggest that the national committees concern themselves with raising money and let the congressional leaders determine the general policy line."[40]

Why do the Capitol Hill party committees each go their own way, rather than function as units subordinate to the national committee? Most of the explanations can be attributed to the separation of powers provided by the American constitutional framework. The national committee is concerned primarily with the presidential race, so the congressman feels that he would be a party orphan without his own organization; congressional staffs are impressed with split-ticket voting and the consequent possibility of furthering their own campaigns without dependence on the presidential candidate, if need be; local appeals, which may be at variance with the party's national interests, can be better exploited through the Capitol Hill committees; the national committee favors the President's supporters but the congressional and senatorial committees are essentially service agencies, helping any mem-

---

[38]*Party Commmittees and National Politics* (Seattle: University of Washington Press, 1958), p. 123.
[39]Clarence Cannon, *Democratic Manual for the Democratic National Convention* (Washington, D.C.: Democratic National Committee, 1956), p. 9.
[40]*Party Committees and National Politics*, pp. 128, 150.

ber with the party label regardless of his stand on national policies; and, finally, separate committees are a way to avoid inconvenience from the three-million-dollar limit on expenditures that the law imposes on each party agency. Under these circumstances, says Bone, "One national level party committee may exert influence on another at times, but this is not the result of systematic organizational relationships. Rather, it comes from the temporary transference of personal influence of particular leaders."[41]

At the next level are the *state committees*, which reveal great variety in functions, modes of selection, and even titles. All these committees are concerned with conducting state campaigns, but some of them also exercise control over state party activities in general. Unlike the "higher" levels of the party structure, which are controlled only by the rules of the party, the organization of these committees is generally governed by state law. Whether weak or powerful, however, none of them is subordinate to the national committee.

County and *city committees* are organized around such subdivisions as townships, precincts, and wards. The chairmen of these committees often possess real power in local politics and, because of their influence over elections to national offices, they frequently make their power felt in national politics as well.

The Pattern of Power

This brief sketch of formal party organization suggests that American parties are little more than loose coalitions of state and local factions, brought together to conduct presidential campaigns and, if their party wins, to distribute public offices to loyal supporters. Except when the party's presidential candidate is seeking re-election, the national committee supports no "organization slate"; nomination is controlled by unofficial and temporary alliances of state and local leaders, not by the national committee. Occasionally, some of these leaders refuse to support the party nominee, as did a number of southern Democrats in 1948 and a few in 1964. In 1964, Republican candidates in several states tried to disassociate themselves from the Goldwater candidacy, but most of them—like most southern Democrats—at least went through the formality of announcing general support for their party's ticket. Generally, the party achieves at least a surface unity during campaigns. But this unity is loose and voluntary rather than close and disciplined—the Democrats' decision in 1965 to deny seniority privileges to two representatives who had actively supported Barry Goldwater for President was the first such punitive action since 1925. Even in these cases, the representatives were not denied their status as Democrats.

Candidates for Congress are even more clearly the products of local rather than national machines. Under the Constitution, a member of the House of Representatives must be a resident of the state in which he is elected, but local machines have informally narrowed this requirement to residence in the

[41] *Ibid.*, p. 153.

electoral district itself. The national committee never boosts a promising party member by designating him as *the* party candidate for Congress, especially in a district where he does not reside. But if the Bell Telephone Company were to send a young executive from Des Moines to head its San Francisco office, no one would take offense; he would be judged—as the candidates of British political parties are—according to his competence in promoting the aims of the national organization. Local biases in America are often extreme in politics, and a candidate for public office is expected to be a long-time resident of the electoral district and a product of the local party organization. Hence the route to political office—national, state, or local—is controlled by local party leaders.

The great furor over recent exceptions to this rule appears merely to demonstrate its basic validity.[42] In 1964, two prominent figures in the late President Kennedy's administration sought election to the Senate from states where they had not lived for years—Pierre Salinger, former press secretary, from California and Robert Kennedy, the late President's brother and Attorney General, from New York. Although Salinger is a native Californian who had lived in the state most of his life, and although he was running as an incumbent (having been appointed in the summer of 1964 to the vacated seat under contest), he was defeated by a political newcomer, former movie actor George Murphy. The outcome was attributed to the charge that Salinger was a "carpetbagger." Robert Kennedy was subjected to the same charge (more accurately, since he had lived in New York only briefly as a child), but he won, defeating the widely respected Republican incumbent Kenneth Keating. Both these candidacies were exceptional—one could hardly imagine them occurring other than in the two largest and most heterogeneous states, and the Kennedy victory rather than the Salinger defeat appears truly exceptional. New York gave President Johnson such an unprecedented majority (68 per cent) that almost any Democratic candidate could have ridden in on his coattails. Californians gave Johnson 60 per cent of their votes, not quite enough to include Salinger in the victory. Kennedy trailed Johnson by 12 percentage points (over a million votes), whereas Salinger trailed by 11 percentage points (three-quarters of a million votes). That Salinger actually came a little closer than Kennedy to matching the Johnson vote suggests that the local route to office has not been replaced by the drawing power of a national personality and a beloved name.

To locate the real controlling power in a party, we must answer two questions: Who controls the nominations? and Who controls the government when the party is in power? As we have already discovered, it is the local machines, alone or in combination, that control party nominations. Even a presidential aspirant, who must ultimately win a national majority, depends initially on a coalition of state and local leaders for his nomination. No less a politician than Franklin D. Roosevelt needed the support of bosses like Mayor Frank ("I Am the Law") Hague of Jersey City and Mayor Edward J. Kelley of Chicago to win his nomination before he could appeal to the voters of the nation. The power of television, added to the decline of the old-style local boss, may modify this

---

[42]These exceptions could, of course, represent signs of an opposite trend. This is something to watch for in future elections.

dependence. As of 1964, however, Senator Goldwater's careful cultivation of local Republican leaders over the preceding four years was counted as a major factor in his landslide nomination for the presidency.

A party's success in winning control of the government probably means less in the United States than in any other democracy. Since election to the presidency requires national support, the President and the chairman of the national committee stand for the views of the party as a national organization. But party members in Congress enjoy a considerable measure of independence from the national party. Since they are chosen by local organizations and depend on these same organizations for re-election, they reflect the parochial bias that we would expect. Local machines are more concerned with patronage and limited local projects than with national policies. Consequently, senators and representatives are largely free of any party control, either national or local, on the matters that are of greatest national importance. A variety of interest groups concerned with national policies, however, are only too happy to fill this vacuum.

Party Personnel: "Members" and Leaders

The French student of political parties Maurice Duverger notes that the expression "party member" has different meanings in different parties and countries, and he adds in fascination, "For American parties, it even has no meaning at all...."[43] What he has in mind is the lack of party members in the sense that Boy Scout troops, for example, or Rotary Clubs, or college fraternities, or mass political parties in Europe may be said to have members. "Republicans" and "Democrats" undergo no official initiation (except, in some states, when they indicate their party affiliation in registering to vote), need meet no standard of fitness for membership, and pay no dues. Nor are they required to show any obligation to the party or to attend regular mass meetings. Duverger concludes, however, that there are three different degrees of participation in American parties, just as there are in parties with regular membership rolls: *electors* who vote for the party's candidates; *supporters* who go a step further by openly acknowledging their support, and who occasionally even contribute time or money to the party; and *militants* who direct the work of the party and organize its campaigns. ("Members," if we had them, would fit somewhere between supporters and militants.)

It has been estimated that only about 3 to 5 per cent of the adult population in the United States are militants, or "political gladiators."[44] Lumped together as "political spectators," electors and supporters make up 60 to 65 per cent of the eligible voters. About one-third of the adult population falls completely outside Duverger's system of classification; these are the "political apathetics," who pay no attention whatsoever to politics—neither participating in nor

[43]Duverger, *Political Parties*, p. 61.
[44]Lester W. Milbrath, "Predispositions toward Political Contention," *Western Political Quarterly*, XIII (March, 1960), 5–18.

observing the performance. For most Americans, clearly, politics is a spectator sport. If simply voting for a party made one a member of that party, then by the same reasoning thousands of faithful fans in New York play baseball for the New York Mets.

The passive attitude of most Americans toward party organizations is hardly surprising. Historically, the mass political parties of Europe, which actively try to organize the electorate, appeared only after extended suffrage had been achieved. Typical of these parties were the socialists, who sought both to educate the workers and to reform the existing order. In order to avoid becoming dependent on the "moneyed interests" that opposed reform, they were obliged to finance their campaigns by levying membership dues.

American workers, however, are not so class-conscious as their European counterparts, and America lacks an active socialist party. Could it be because we extended the suffrage *before* the full impact of industrialism was felt? Whatever the cause of our greater conservatism, Duverger convincingly concludes that "the archaic organization of American parties . . . seems the consequence of the essential conservatism of American politics, in the European sense of the term."[45]

The few militants who actually operate the local machines exercise the leadership of American political parties by default; indeed, for all practical purposes they *are* the political parties. What are these "political gladiators" like? What distinguishes them from the great mass of spectators who are interested enough to vote but who go no further in political participation, and from the apathetics who neither participate in politics nor observe the efforts of those who do?

As we saw in Chapter 6, gladiators tend to be recruited from the higher socio-economic strata. They come from positions in the structure of society that *define* and *train* them as potential leaders. The people who respond to this training tend to be more self-expressive, more optimistic, and more self-accepting than are their politically inactive peers.[46] Some continue to be trained for politics as adults. This is particularly the case for people in *brokerage* occupations—people like lawyers, realtors, salesmen, and independent merchants, whose jobs require skills in mediating, bargaining, and negotiating with others.[47] Not only do they find these skills applicable to politics but—unlike doctors, engineers, architects, or teachers—they also find political participation a professional asset rather than a liability.

Party activists also differ from rank-and-file party members in policy orientations. We already know from our consideration of political opinions that the leadership stratum has more ideologically consistent views than does the general population. In partisan terms, this means that Democratic and Republican leaders disagree more sharply on issues than do their followers. Herbert McClosky of the University of California at Berkeley has studied the attitudes of party activists and general party members on twenty-four political issues grouped under five headings: public ownership, government regula-

---

[45]Duverger, *Political Parties*, p. 23.
[46]Milbrath *op. cit., Western Political Quarterly*, XIII (March, 1960), 17–18.
[47]The applicability of this interpretation to people in county-level public offices is demonstrated by Herbert Jacob in "Initial Recruitment of Elected Officials in the U.S.—A Model," *Journal of Politics*, XXIV (November, 1962), 703–716.

tion of the economy, equalitarianism and human welfare, tax policy, and foreign policy. He found that Democratic and Republican leaders were far apart on 23 of the 24 issues, but that the rank-and-file Democrats and Republicans were significantly divided on only 7 of the 24 issues. Even on the minority of issues on which the rank-and-file differed, the differences were not as great as among the leaders.[48] Figure 7–1 shows the location of party leaders and followers on an average index of support in each of the broad policy areas; note that in every case the leaders are farther apart than the followers. The moderating function of a two-party system thus operates despite the fact that the leaders would *not* converge unless the system and the underlying distribution of public opinion forced convergence upon them.

The second striking feature of the distribution of opinions in Fig. 7–1 is that *the rank-and-file Republicans are generally closer to the Democratic leaders than they are to the Republican leaders*. The first three policy areas presented in Fig. 7–1 can be taken as rough measures of liberalism-conservatism on economic and social policy. On these issues the Republican leaders are conspicuously more conservative than anyone else, including their own party's rank and file. Nevertheless, under the constraints of the two-party system these very leaders (delegates to the Republican national convention of 1956) overwhelmingly renominated Eisenhower for President. They wanted to win. So did their predecessors in 1952 who, although presumably equally conservative, bowed to the necessity of winning in rejecting the great leader of Republican conservatism, Senator Robert Taft of Ohio, for the popular General. In 1964, the Republican convention delegates either ignored mass opinion or managed to confuse the vocal minority of extreme conservatives with the majority of the general public.[49] Departing from the center in nominating

AVERAGE SUPPORT RATIOS* IN FIVE POLICY AREAS AMONG PARTY LEADERS AND GENERAL PARTY MEMBERS

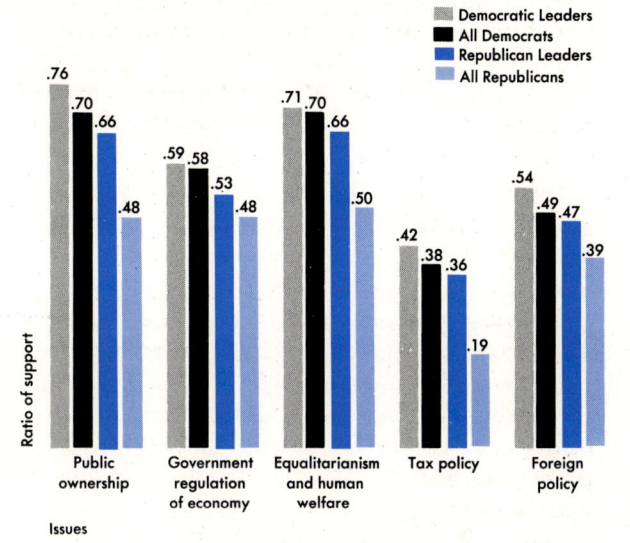

Legend: Democratic Leaders, All Democrats, Republican Leaders, All Republicans

Public ownership: .76, .70, .66, .48
Government regulation of economy: .59, .58, .53, .48
Equalitarianism and human welfare: .71, .70, .66, .50
Tax policy: .42, .38, .36, .19
Foreign policy: .54, .49, .47, .39

Source: McClosky, Hoffmann, and O'Hara, *op. cit.*, American Political Science Review, 410–415.

*"Support Ratio" is scored by assigning a weight of 1.0 to each response favoring an "increase" in support of policies in each issue area, 0 to each "decrease" response, and 0.5 to each "reamin as is" or "same" response.

Figure 7-1

---

[48]Herbert McClosky, Paul J. Hoffmann, and Rosemary O'Hara, "Issue Conflict and Consensus Among Party Leaders and Followers," *American Political Science Review*, LIV (June, 1960), 406–427. The authors selected as "leaders" the delegates to the Republican and Democratic national party conventions in 1956.

[49]For an analysis of the difference between the world of mass opinion and the world of opinion of the minority who write political letters, see Philip E. Converse, Aage R. Clausen, and Warren E. Miller, "Electoral Myth and Reality: The 1964 Election," *American Political Science Review*, LIX (June, 1965), 321–336.

Barry Goldwater, they suffered the most disastrous defeat in the history of the Grand Old Party.

Bosses and Machines

Many observers roundly condemn American political parties for being oligarchical. But so few persons take an active part in politics that roles of leadership are amazingly easy to come by, and frequently are even uncontested. The ambitious young man with talent but without connections accordingly finds more opportunities to "make a name for himself" in politics than in private business. In grass-roots politics, the "quality" of one's connections may be less important than their quantity. Consequently, newly assimilated immigrant groups have often found politics a more open route to prestige than business. Each new wave of immigration has tended to be followed by a wave of political activity as soon as the new group has reached economic and social levels high enough to produce effective leaders. Until recently, the term "political boss" automatically evoked the picture of a jovial Irishman—Jim Curley of Boston, Frank Hague of Jersey City, Edward J. Kelley and Pat Nash of Chicago. Samuel Lubell, a widely read political commentator, reports that of late, however, "the plight of the Irish Democratic bosses . . . is not unlike that of the wearied rulers of the British Empire, who are everywhere on the defensive before the rising 'nationality' elements they once ruled."[50]

The Italo-Americans in Rhode Island are a good example of the rise to power of new ethnic groups. In 1946, John Pastore became the first Italo-American to be elected governor of any state and, four years later, the first United States senator of Italian origin. Pastore's rise appears to have been linked to the increase in numbers and in socio-economic status of Rhode Island's Italo-Americans. In 1907, when he was born, Italians made up only one-thirteenth of the state's population. But in 1938, the Rhode Island legislature declared Columbus Day a legal holiday, perhaps less in tribute to Columbus' discovery of America than to the discovery that every fifth voter in the state was Italo-American. With a rising middle class to provide leadership, and with money to accompany their growing voting power, the Italo-Americans in Rhode Island had arrived politically.[51]

The old-style political machine has itself been undergoing drastic change. In both national and, to a lesser degree, local campaigns, the mass media of communication have helped popular personalities to force themselves on the machines. However much they would prefer "one of their own," the machine bosses know that victory at the polling place is still their prime goal. Rising standards of living, the assimilation of immigrant groups, and the development of social welfare services under the New Deal have all militated against the continued dominance of local machines. The political boss can no longer win elections simply by distributing baskets of food on Christmas, acting as an informal employment agency, helping with citizenship papers, and talking about common ties with the "old country." A character in *The Last Hurrah*, a

---

[50]Samuel Lubell, *The Future of American Politics* (New York: Harper & Row, Publishers, Inc., 1951), p. 66.
[51]*Ibid.*, pp. 67–75.

bestselling novel of 1956, pointed up these factors in explaining why an old party boss in Boston had finally been defeated:

> Well, of course, the old boss was strong simply because he held all the cards. If anybody wanted anything—job, favors, cash—he could only go to the boss, the local leader. What Roosevelt did was to take the handouts out of local hands. A few little things like Social Security, Unemployment Insurance, and the like —that's what shifted the gears, sport. No need now to depend on the boss for everything; the Federal Government was getting into the act. Otherwise known as a social revolution. So you can see what that would do in the long run. The old-timers would still string along with the boss, of course, because that's the way they always did things. But what about the kids coming along? . . .
>
> To begin with, they were one step farther away from the old country; he didn't have the old emotional appeal for them. You know, the racial-spokesman kind of thing. . . . And finally, most of them had never had the slightest contact with him because it wasn't necessary. When they got out of the army, for example, and needed a little spare cash to tide them over, what did they do? Did they go to the boss? Not on your life; they didn't have to. They joined the 52–20 Club and got twenty bucks a week for the next year, all supplied by good old remote, impersonal Washington. And when they went to work at last, and then got laid off for awhile, the same thing happened. No boss; Unemployment Insurance instead. It was a new era, sport. . . .[52]

If developments of this sort really serve to broaden and nationalize the political concerns of Americans, they are probably a wholesome influence. But if they mean simply that the organizational continuity and responsibility of the old party machines are to be replaced by the confusion of recurrent popularity contests, they may well create a new, less easily identifiable "machine" of professional public relations men and their employers. John Crosby, the television critic, has described this danger in the following comments on national party conventions:

> The smoke-filled room is gone, possibly forever, to be replaced by the electronic living room full of 120,000,000 people. Naturally, no more cigars, no more open-necked shirts, avoid the bold patterns in [neckties] and watch those mannerisms. Well, the smoke-filled room was a deplorable political institution, but at least it was filled with human beings who smoked and chewed and spoke their minds.
>
> There were some cussed individuals in them, but they were colorful. Now that the mass media experts have taken over, we can hardly expect horny-handed individuality. After they get the bold patterns out of the ties, the next step is to get the bold patterns out of the phrases and out of the ideas. The perfect candidate will look just like somebody out of a Chrysler ad—well-bred, well-shaved, and thoroughly antiseptic.[53]

---

[52] Edwin O'Connor, *The Last Hurrah* (Boston: Little, Brown and Company, 1956), pp. 374–375.
[53] Excerpts from John Crosby's column, August 13, 1956, © 1956, New York Herald Tribune, Inc.

The Doctrinal and Social Base of American Parties

The doctrines of a party reflect the needs of the groups and interests with which it tries to build electoral victories. Those who maintain that parties are groups of men in agreement on basic principles are doomed to disillusionment by what must appear as unpardonable shifts in basic party policy. But it is precisely as organizations trying to win elections by fostering the aims of a coalition of interests, and not as groups dedicated to fixed principles, that American parties "make sense." After all, doctrines are created simply to serve human interests.

Shifting Doctrines

Shifts in party doctrines are the direct result of a very simple set of related factors: (1) voters try to maximize their own interests; (2) parties try to win elections; (3) to do this, parties must enlist the support of a broad coalition of interests; (4) to enlist such support, they must promote the aims of these interests; and (5) the needs of different interests undergo continuous change.[54]

We cannot undertake a history of party principles here. By comparing the present positions of our two great parties with the positions of their predecessors, however, we can suggest the extent to which changing economic and social conditions have led parties to modify their doctrines. The original party lineup in the United State found the Jeffersonian Republicans (later to become known as the Democratic Party) on one side, and the Federalists (the grandfathers of the present Republican Party) on the other. The Jeffersonians stood for the needs of an agrarian society, which they sought to foster by emphasizing the concepts of "least government" as the best government, states' rights, decentralization, *laissez-faire*, legislative rather than executive power, and economy in government. The Federalists, on the other hand, held the vision of an industrial, urban society, which they sought to foster by emphasizing the ideas of energetic government, nationalism, centralization, government intervention in the economy, executive rather than legislative power, and a managed public debt.

Notice that the two present-day parties have neatly changed positions on every one of these issues. Does this mean that they have abandoned their principles, that the Democrats have rejected Jeffersonian values for Hamiltonian values, while the Republicans were executing the reverse maneuver? We need reach that conclusion only if we confuse technique with goal, instru-

---

[54] Anthony Downs develops an intriguing model of party government on the basis of three fundamental assumptions: that both voters and parties behave rationally at all times, that parties are guided only by the desire to win and keep office, and that every voter tries to promote his own self-interest with the ballot. See his *An Economic Theory of Democracy*. In analyzing the party system of the United States, we cannot assume perfect rationality, nor can we rely on other assumptions of his model, such as that the winning party after every election takes complete control of the entire government. Nevertheless, his analysis has been most helpful to us; the analytically minded student will find it fascinating. Also see Donald Stokes, "Spatial Models of Party Competition," in Angus Campbell *et al.*, *Elections and the Political Order*, pp. 161–179.

mental values with root values. Jefferson was imbued with faith in the masses, and, in a predominantly rural society in which the government was the only agency powerful enough to threaten popular freedoms, he was naturally suspicious of government power in almost any form. Hamilton was more impressed with the superiority of the "rich, well-born, and able," and was equally anxious to create a strong government that would reflect that superiority and would control the "unthinking majority." By now the Jeffersonian view has triumphed to such an extent that no politician would reject majority rule as such. But the Democratic Party is still more concerned with the needs of the "underprivileged," and the Republican Party, like the Federalists, is more attuned to the preservation of greater rewards for the "deserving." The development of an industrialized and urbanized society has simply changed the policies that seem most appropriate for gaining these respective ends.

The first great shift in party doctrines occurred in the 1820s and 30s, when Jacksonian Democracy established the President as the chief spokesman for popular majorities. The Whigs (unlike the Federalists who preceded them) rejected the idea of a strong executive and supported instead a strong legislature, in which minority interests would have more opportunity to block the majority; and the Democrats began to prefer strong executive power to strong congressional power. The rapid industrialization that took place after the Civil War concentrated private power in the hands of corporations strong enough to constitute a potential threat to majority interests. The Democratic Party tended to look on this concentration of private power as the chief danger to popular needs, and on the government as a means of coping with this danger rather than as a "necessary evil." Republicans, on the other hand, adopted the old Jeffersonian fear of government when, late in the nineteenth century, government began turning to such "socialistic" schemes as income taxes and business regulation.

The Great Depression that fell on the country in 1929 revealed these new orientations in a naked light. Increasing numbers of voters seemed to feel that the only way to achieve the goals of Jefferson was to adopt the techniques of Hamilton. "So the Democrats stole the Republicans' clothes, and this is always most embarrassing to the party which has gone bathing."[55] The extent of this switch in party doctrines is indicated by the roll-call votes recorded in Congress during Eisenhower's first term. Although Eisenhower himself favored such "New Deal" measures as expanded social security and higher minimum-wage levels, a majority of the Republicans in Congress voted to curb executive power, to restrict government intervention in the economy, and to prevent extensions of social welfare programs. Specifically, they favored restrictions on the President's authority to reduce tariffs and supported proposals to decrease executive power in foreign relations. Similarly, they opposed government development of power projects and federal action to combat unemployment in chronically depressed communities. And they also opposed extensions

[55]Roland N. Stromberg, *Republicanism Reappraised* (Washington, D.C.: Public Affairs Press, 1952), p. 13.

of government aid in such areas as housing, education, health, and social security.[56] A majority of Democrats voted for each of these measures while a majority of Republicans voted against them.

In 1964, when a Democratic rather than a Republican President was urging positive governmental measures, the contrast between the parties in Congress was even more clear-cut.[57] The basic differences in party doctrine still seemed to exist, then; to understand these differences, we must turn to the continuing social base of the parties.

Persisting Bases of Support

During the Eisenhower administration, when a majority of the Republicans in Congress opposed, and a majority of the Democrats supported, a move to replace a tax cut on income from stock dividends with a $100 increase in the personal tax exemption, each party was assuming its "natural" position.[58] Good arguments could be advanced on both sides: a tax cut for the small minority of the people who own corporate stock would make more money available for the investments that spur general progress; an increase in the personal tax exemption would primarily benefit those with low income, and would increase the mass purchasing power that is also essential to general prosperity. The former approach automatically made more sense to the Republicans, and the latter approach automatically made more sense to the Democrats. Why? Because the parties are identified with different social groups in the population.

The persistence with which the Democrats have looked first to the needs of those who have lower socio-economic status, and the Republicans to the needs of those who enjoy higher status, is illustrated by Wilfred Binkley's comment on the Democratic-Whig division in the nineteenth century:

> Jacksonian Democracy originated as the personal following of one who symbolized the idea of justice for the masses. He was represented as a champion of the under-dog and the Democratic Party has always relied for its voting strength primarily upon the counties with poorer soils and the crowded wards of the great cities largely populated with recent immigrant stock. . . .
>
> To the well-to-do, however, Jackson was a demagogue, a preacher of social discontent, and the prosperous became the backbone of the opposition to Jackson. The dominant elements of the Whig party consisted of the great financial, commercial, and emerging industrial interests of the East, the more prosperous agrarians of the North and the great slaveholding planters of the South.[59]

Save for the inclusion of great slaveholding planters, this statement aptly describes the bases of strength on which Democrats and Republicans respectively rely to this day. And the heavy vote for Goldwater in the old slavehold-

---

[56]These statements are based on an examination of roll-call votes in one or both houses of Congress.

[57]See *Congressional Quarterly Weekly Report*, XXII (October 30, 1964), 2593–2597.

[58]The vote in the House was 10 Republicans for and 201 against the substitute, and 193 Democrats for and 9 against. The Senate vote on a similar measure was 2 Republicans for and 45 against, 43 Democrats for and 4 against. See *Congressional Quarterly Weekly Report*, XIV (October 5, 1956), 1189.

[59]*President and Congress* (New York: Alfred A. Knopf, Inc., 1947), pp. 86–87.

ing counties of the South in 1964 suggests that even this element might be restored to its position in the opposing coalitions of the 1830s. While the programs which the contending political groups in America require have changed radically, each group is fairly consistent in the party it looks to for the realization of its needs.

The success with which each party has mobilized its own supporters and enticed those of the opposition into its camp has varied enough to produce three distinct eras of party dominance. The period from 1800 to 1860 was a time of Democratic supremacy. As the suffrage was gradually extended, the opposition was able to erase the stigma of its original distaste for democracy only twice, and then only by establishing a new party (the Whigs) and by nominating two war heroes for President—William Henry Harrison (1840) and Zachary Taylor (1848).

The Republicans enjoyed the longest period of supremacy, from 1860 to 1932. With sectional conflict over slavery disrupting the established competition between parties, the Republicans attained their first success by capturing the mass appeal the Democrats had long enjoyed. Despite its radical origins, the Republican Party emerged from the Civil War with a more "right-wing" character. "The Republican party that Grant brought out of the Civil War period was not the same Republican party that Lincoln had taken in," observes Ivan Hinderaker, a specialist on political parties.[60] "Lincoln's party had been a farmer-worker party with Declaration of Independence overtones. Grant's party from 1868 was farmer-capitalist in nature with a declaration of independence to give the capitalist a free hand in the exploitation of America's natural resources." While the Republicans were

[60]*Party Politics* (New York: Henry Holt and Company, 1956), p. 312.

Drawing by Stevenson;
© 1960 *The New Yorker Magazine, Inc.*

"*It's probably some kind of Democratic trick.*"

appealing to business, they also compaigned for the labor vote with the promise of a "full dinner pail." Even the "silver-tongued" promises of William Jennings Bryan, three-time presidential candidate of the Democratic Party, were unable to win the eastern labor vote. During this period of great industrial progress, the Democrats were able to defeat the Republicans only under the leadership of Grover Cleveland and Woodrow Wilson.

The third great period of dominance returned the Democrats to power in 1932. With the severe depression that began in 1929 suddenly making the business community unpopular, the Democrats took advantage of the opportunity to label the Republicans as the party of "big business." Long-run influences that had already been working in the Democrats' favor reinforced the "no-confidence" vote against the Republicans in 1932. The increased voting strength of immigrants and their children, the high birthrate of lower-income groups, the shift of people from farms to cities, the increasing political awareness of ethnic minorities—all of these gave more votes to Democrats than to Republicans. Al Smith, the Democratic presidential nominee in 1928—an effective Governor of New York but, more important, a Catholic who had an "East Side" New York City accent and occasional grammatical difficulties—created for many an image of the Democrats as the party of the underprivileged. The depression gave them a perfect opportunity to capitalize on this image just when it had the most appeal. Vestiges of their success can still be seen in the 1960s; many voters still view Republicans as sympathizing with "big business" and Democrats as favoring the "little man."

Eisenhower's victories in 1952 and 1956 represented a temporary "housecleaning" in the midst of a Democratic period rather than the inauguration of a new era of Republican control. It took a Civil War to shatter the original Democratic hold on the country, and a cataclysmic depression to terminate the Republican era. The lack of any such major upheaval in contemporary America, and the inability of the Republican Party to win control of Congress even when Eisenhower scored his second presidential victory, indicated that the Democratic tide was still running. As the representative of the majority party, John Kennedy managed to win the presidency in 1960 despite a formidable opponent and a massive resurgence of anti-Catholicism. In 1964, for the first time since 1936, short-run election forces favored the Democrats; President Johnson won with the greatest percentage of the popular vote in American history. Barring another upheaval like the Civil War or the depression of 1929, the present Democratic era can be expected to continue.

Party Support Today

The two major parties still depend on electoral bases that are remarkably similar to those of the early nineteenth century. You can demonstrate this for yourself by applying the discussion on political opinions in Chapter 6 to the Republican and Democratic parties, with the Republicans as the party of the "right" and the Democrats as the party of the "left." Both American parties are essentially conservative when compared with their European counterparts—our "left-wing" Democratic Party is more conservative than Britain's Conservative Party! Within the cultural context of American politics, however, the Democrats win more "leftist" support and the Republicans win more "rightist" support. In the extremely close presidential election in 1960, 55 per cent of those who

Table 7–1 Relative Strength of Parties in Major Population Groups[a]

POPULATION GROUPING	DEMOCRATIC	REPUBLICAN
Sex	Men	Women
Age	Younger voters	Older voters
Religion	Catholics, Jews	Protestants
Race	Negro	White
Type of Community	Metropolitan centers	Suburban and rural areas
Education	Noncollege	College
Occupation of Family Head	Unemployed, skilled and unskilled labor	Professional, business or managerial, sales
Labor Affiliation	Union	Nonunion
Income	Low	High

[a]These findings may be found in almost any voting-behavior study. For a good summary, see Angus Campbell and Homer C. Cooper, *Group Differences in Attitudes and Votes* (Ann Arbor: University of Michigan Institute for Social Research, 1956). For an analysis, see Campbell et al., *The American Voter*.

identified with the working class reported voting for Kennedy, in contrast to only 36 per cent of those identified with the middle class.[61] Each party tends to be relatively stronger in the major population groups indicated in Table 7–1.

Notice that the groups are sources of *relatively* greater strength for the parties. In any given election, the Republicans might gain majority support among younger voters, for example, but they will still tend to win *a larger proportion* of the older than of the younger votes. Notice, too, that none of the sources of strength represents *solid* voting blocs; with regional variations added to individual peculiarities, and with both parties using broad appeals, no social interest in the United States can be perfectly mobilized behind either party. Unusual issues or personalities may, as they did in both Eisenhower victories, deflect substantial numbers from their normal voting habits. Finally, these general characteristics should not be regarded as the basic *determinants* of the voter's allegiance. The fact that a larger proportion of women than of men vote Republican, for example, appears to be a function of class rather than of sex differences: the general tendency of women to vote less than men is more pronounced in lower than in higher socio-economic levels; within the same class, however, the sex difference in party preference disappears.

Current trends could modify the traditional bases of party support. The increasing population shift to the suburbs, along with the tendency of the suburban vote to go heavily Republican, was spotted as one such trend during the Eisenhower era.[62] But recent analyses indicate that Republican strength increased no more in the suburbs than it did in other areas,[63] and the general decrease in Republican support in 1964 characterized the suburbs no less than other areas. The Republican environment of the suburbs accordingly seems

[61]From a special tabulation furnished by the Survey Research Center of the University of Michigan.
[62]Louis Harris, *Is There a Republican Majority?* (New York: Harper & Row, Publishers, Inc., 1954), pp. 123–125.
[63]Bernard Lazerwitz, "Suburban Voting Trends: 1948 to 1956," *Social Forces*, XXXIX (October, 1960), 29–36; Jerome G. Manis and Leo C. Stine, "Surburban Residence and Political Behavior," *Public Opinion Quarterly*, XXII (Winter, 1958–59), 483–489.

not to affect newly arrived Democrats as much as it was once assumed to. Perhaps the children of these new residents, by virtue of their predominantly Republican environment outside the home, will be more susceptible to Republican appeals. By their nature, however, gradual changes are difficult to observe.

The region most deviant from national political norms is the South; and in view of its small proportion of the total population and resources of the country, its impact on our national political system has been extraordinary. If the states of the Confederacy that once tried to secede from the United States had succeeded, the country would much more closely resemble the other democracies of the Western world. In discussing the most significant changes that he would expect to occur in the American political system, Robert Dahl of Yale recently concluded that the two most fundamental and likely are

> . . . the removal of the ancient issue of Negro rights from its central (if not always public) place in politics by defeating the South on this question . . . and the development of a two-party system in the South. For one condition above all created the pattern of cleavage that has dominated American politics. . . . This was the power of the one-party South in elections and in Congress and its virtually unbreakable unity on the institution of white supremacy in the South. A party that would not do business with the South on its own terms, i.e., yield to white supremacy in the South, has for nearly a hundred years stood in perpetual danger of being defeated in elections or in Congress, or both, by a party that would. Both parties yielded to this imperative. As a result, the South was at once a permanent opposition (on all questions involving racial segregation) and a permanent partner in government.[64]

A slow partisan drift toward the Republicans in the South supports Dahl's expectation of change. The South appears destined to rejoin the Union. But the implication that a party realignment can be expected in the near future appears overly sanguine. The conclusion of a thorough study of the prospects for major realignment in the South is that, ignoring short-run fluctuations, "the underlying drift is one which was underway not too long after the turn of the century, and one which may well continue its evolution to the turn of the next, barring dramatic and unforeseen interventions."[65]

Criticisms of Political Parties

Popular Complaints

The popular image of politicians and political parties is far from flattering. For those who regard politics as inherently evil, political parties are veritable cesspools of iniquity. This notion has undemocratic origins that are seldom recognized by those who hold it. At their inception, popularly based political parties were naturally opposed by those who resisted democracy and distrusted the masses. Since parties promise to achieve popular control, Americans who still fear "majority tyranny" are logically antiparty. But this bias is a strange one to be entertained by the majority itself, for whom parties provide a voice in public affairs.

A familiar variation on this theme is that, although parties themselves are

---

[64]*Political Oppositions in Western Democracies*, pp. 68–69.
[65]Philip E. Converse, "On the Possibility of Major Political Realignment in the South," in Campbell *et al.*, *Elections and the Political Order*, p. 237.

not inherently evil, the "wrong kind of men" always seem to take over politics and turn parties into something unsavory. To test the validity of this complaint we need only refer to the studies by Milbrath and Jacob.[66] Actual investigation of the kind of people who are active in politics supports the view that they are superior in talent to the population at large. And when we compare their moral standards with those of business, labor unions, and some professions—where nepotism, lavish expense accounts, luxurious gifts from clients or customers, and vacation trips are all taken for granted—leaders of political parties come off very well indeed. True, we should apply high standards to political behavior, but we should also make realistic appraisals. After all, politicians are a product of the same society in which all the rest of us live.

A more substantial complaint is that political parties are undemocratic in their organization. Certainly the mass of Republican and Democratic voters do not maintain an active and continuing control over their parties' procedures, nominations, and policies. Democracy is rooted in the responsibility of the ruling few to the many, however, not in the actual conduct of party activities by the entire membership. Since party membership is such a vague allegiance in the United States, it is not easy to judge the extent of membership control. But the active members of political parties probably exercise as much control as union members, corporate stockholders, church members, or fraternity brothers do over their respective organizations.

We may also observe that internal democracy in political parties is not essential to popular control of the government. What *is* essential is competition *between* parties, which insures that elections cannot be won without popular candidates and policies. Even if the parties were internally autocratic, the desire to win elections would still force them to offer attractive candidates. We assume that our economic system will best serve the needs of the public if competition exists between different firms, regardless of whether the internal policies of the firms are democratic or autocratic. Surely the same assumption can be made in politics. Moreover, in politics we are more certain that competition actually exists, that the public plays a greater role in the choice of the "product" to be offered, that no one is allowed multiple votes, and that virtually all interested adults are guaranteed an equal vote. Sigmund Neumann, a student of party systems, reminds us that in a democracy "it is the competitive scheme, the choice between at least two oligarchies, which guarantees the quality of its leadership."[67]

The Basic Criticism: Irresponsibility

The most valid basis for evaluating the performance of any organization is in terms of how well it performs its primary function. At the beginning of this chapter, we suggested that the central functions of political parties for a democracy are the public choice of leaders and the open and organized expression of public interests. Since these functions mark the difference between democracies and dictatorships, they

---

[66] See footnotes 44, 46 and 47.
[67] *Modern Political Parties*, p. 397.

offer a basis for evaluating the performance of our parties—at least for those who agree that democracy is desirable.

The most basic and meaningful criticism of the political parties is that they fail to function as the essential mechanism of popular control—that they are irresponsible. To political scientists, "Party responsibility means the responsibility of both parties to the general public, as enforced in elections."[68] In light of this simple criterion, the Committee on Political Parties of the American Political Science Association has concluded that "an effective party system requires, first, that the parties are able to bring forth programs to which they commit themselves, and, second, that the parties possess sufficient internal cohesion to carry out these programs.[69]

The great weakness of American parties lies in their failure to meet this second requirement—that is, to achieve the requisite cohesion in Congress. Although there is more straight party voting in Congress than is often recognized, party disunity is still common enough for the majority party to be uncertain about carrying through its policies. Both parties usually attain an admirable measure of cohesion during campaigns, with the rejected aspirants manfully joining in to support the party nominees. When the parties succeed in winning a majority of seats in Congress and have only to vote together in order to carry out their platform pledges, however, this unity tends to evaporate. Since state and local organizations control nominations and elections, the party as a national organization is in a poor position to demand cooperation. Consequently, congressmen often respond to the local or special interest groups that influence their chances for re-election.

This failure of the parties to achieve the post-election unity they need to carry out their programs makes the general public more receptive to *any* criticism directed against political parties. But there is a contradiction here: many voters seem to respond to criticisms of "party hacks" and to praise of "independent statesmen." They condemn the congressman who is consistently loyal to his party and praise his colleague who responds to other pressures for his "independence." But is the real choice between statesmen and party ciphers? Or is it between control of Congress by coalitions of unidentifiable minority interests and control by political parties responsible to a broader public? If the party organization leaves a power vacuum, it will eagerly be filled by groups that have not been endorsed by popular election.

Some observers insist that more effective party government would decrease the freedom of the elected official to vote as he pleases—or as his conscience dictates. But even if we assume that a congressman could stand completely free of pressure from any source, this idea represents a peculiar view of the purpose of elections. Elections are held not to give a few people a chance to win popularity contests but to give the citizens a chance to influence government policy. Advocates of strong parties carry this argument a step further. If we accept the basic importance of the voter, they say our preference must be for internal party discipline. Even a nation of Einsteins could not manage to

---

[68]Report of the Committee on Political Parties of the American Political Science Association, *Toward a More Responsible Two-Party System* (New York: Holt, Rinehart & Company, Inc., 1950), p. 22; also see *American Political Science Review*, XLIV, Part 2 (September, 1950).
[69]*Ibid.*, pp. 17–18 (emphasis omitted).

hold 535 men responsible as individuals for the enactment of legislation, but ordinary citizens *could* enforce responsibility on unified parties.

Another variation on the antiparty theme is that the office-holder should respond to the views of his local constituency rather than to those of the party's national majority. Although this argument is appealing, it does not fit the facts of political life. In order for fragmented responsibility of this sort to operate, the average citizen would have to follow the performance of each individual office-holder from his district. The fact is, however, that local newspapers and radio and television stations all tend to present syndicated, nationally oriented news of party stands in Congress. It is not easy for the average voter to follow the detailed performance of his own representative and senators, even if he is interested enough to try. But he *could* get a good idea of the overall record of his party if it operated as a unit. Responsibility to the majority of voters cannot be effective when it is fragmented; fragmented responsibility, however, does offer advantages to pressure groups.

Ultimately, of course, one's position on this question depends on his personal values. The bias of the present party system is against rapid policy changes, whereas the bias of disciplined parties would be in favor of quicker response to public demands for new policies. Hence most political scientists who recommend more disciplined political parties do so as a way to get reformist policies. (Those who oppose the recommendation may be equally reformist, but they regard proposals for party discipline as an unrealistic or ineffective way to get reformist policy and as conflicting with other, more important values.) The 1950 report of the Committee on Political Parties, however, is a carefully developed argument directed toward the implicit goal of reformist, majoritarian policies. Researchers have found that a large majority of political scientists are liberal or reformist in their values.[70] The endorsement of strong party government by an official Committee of the American Political Science Association thus represents an attempt to promote the values of a majority of the Association. While the values being promoted cannot be validated or invalidated by the techniques of political science, the report of the Committee can be read as a series of *prescriptive* statements: "*If* you agree on value X, *then* you ought to pursue course A." In this case, X equals policies responsive to the (presumably liberal) wishes of the current majority, and A equals measures designed to promote strong party government.

The Improbability of Reform

Many political scientists do not agree with the Committee on Political Parties that more "responsible party government" is desirable. Some reject X as a goal, regarding policies closely geared to the changing wishes of the majority as undesirable. Roland Pennock,

---

[70] Paul F. Lazarsfeld and Wagner Thielens, Jr., *The Academic Mind* (New York: The Free Press of Glencoe, Inc., 1958); Seymour M. Lipset, *Political Man* (Garden City, New York: Doubleday & Company, Inc., 1960), Chapter 10; Henry A. Turner, "The Party Affiliations of American Political Scientists," a paper delivered at the annual meeting of the American Political Science Association, September 8, 1960.

a thoughtful political theorist, argues that "responsibility" in government has two meanings. In addition to answerability to the public, responsibility also means maturity of judgment and rational actions supported by careful investigation and deliberation.[71] More of the first kind of responsibility would, Pennock thinks, mean less of the second kind—and would substitute responsiveness to momentary whims for responsiveness to settled opinions. Ernest S. Griffith, a student of Congress, disapproves of the policies and techniques he associates with disciplined party government as practiced in Britain:

> A bureaucracy . . . increasing by leaps and bounds; the two parties outbidding each other with promises of governmental largesse, so as to attract marginal groups; a division of the nation along class lines; the sacrifice of independence of thought and action on the part of the individual member; the pressing home of such a drastic measure as the nationalization of steel, though a majority of the voters supported candidates opposed to it at the last election.[72]

Most dissenters from the Committee's report do not join Griffith in rejecting the goal of policies closely geared to public opinion or, for that matter, the implicit preference for more liberal policies. But they do charge the Committee with ignoring the nature of political realities in America and with overlooking the heavy price that would have to be paid for cohesive and disciplined parties. The probable price of centralized and disciplined parties, in the view of the defenders of the present system, would include (1) the breakdown of federalism; (2) the deterioration of compromise among opposed groups; and (3) the development of a multi-party system.[73] The dissenters support their position with as much force as does the Committee majority. First, they argue that unitary and centralized parties are ill-suited to a heterogeneous and complex country like the United States. The great variety of interests in such a sprawling country, this argument holds, could not be accommodated in parties more cohesive than we have today. And even if such an arrangement could fit the informal power structure, the federal system of government makes it politically unattainable. Pendleton Herring, supporting the second argument, points out that the very generality and ambiguity of party platforms is what makes for peaceable compromise in this country. "The accomplishment of party government lies in its demonstrated ability for reducing warring interests and conflicting classes to cooperative terms."[74] Third, Austin Ranney maintains that unity in American parties would destroy the two-party system:

> It has often been remarked that the congeries of bipartisan and intraparty "blocs" in Congress is, in effect, a multiple-party system masquerading under the labels and formalities of a two-party system. To the extent that this is an accurate description of our present national party system, it results, not from any

---

[71] J. Roland Pennock, "Responsiveness, Responsibility, and Majority Rule," *American Political Science Review*, XLVI (September, 1952), 790–807.

[72] *Congress: Its Contemporary Role* (New York: New York University Press, 1951), pp. 156–157.

[73] For a good summary of these arguments, see Austin Ranney and Willmoore Kendall, *Democracy and the American Party System* (New York: Harcourt, Brace & Company, 1956), pp. 527–533. Also see Ranney's *The Doctrine of Responsible Party Government* (Urbana: University of Illinois Press, 1954).

[74] *The Politics of Democracy: American Parties in Action* (New York: Holt, Rinehart & Company, Inc., 1940), p. 132.

mere organizational deficiency in our national party machinery, but rather from the diversity and multiplicity of our interest groups and the heterogeneity and complexity of the political conflict they express. So long as the basic nature of the American community remains the same, therefore, centralizing and disciplining our national parties would very likely result in a multiple-party rather than a two-party system.[75]

Despite these arguments, there are a number of ways in which party responsibility could be increased in the United States. The Committee on Political Parties recommends the following measures: the tightening of national party organization to reflect actual party support in the areas represented; the coordination of state and local party organizations by the national organization, including the "excommunication" of disloyal groups; the promulgation of authoritative interpretations of the platform by the national organization; the tightening of party organization in Congress by having the party caucus make binding decisions on party policy, and by selecting committee chairmen on the basis of party loyalty and service rather than on the basis of seniority. Rewards to cooperating members—in the form of campaign help and favorable committee assignments in Congress—would be stressed rather than punishment. But the Committee also advocated that discipline be applied where necessary: "It is possible to refuse to seat delegates to the National Convention; to drop from the National Committee members representing the dissident state organization; to deny legislative committee assignments to members of Congress sponsored by the disloyal organization; and to appeal directly to the party membership in the state or locality, perhaps even promoting a rival organization. The power to take strong measures is there."[76]

The power to take these strong measures may be there, but the will to do so is not. American politics is so localized that early prospects for responsible party government seem poor indeed; the very men whom many political scientists exhort to centralize our parties are themselves products of loose alliances of local groups. If either party began to act with real unity in Congress, the voters might be so impressed that they would force the opposition to follow suit. But the centers of power in both parties appear satisfied with the present decentralized structure. The expectation of voluntary reform of the party system by congressmen ignores a fundamental law of politics: those who enjoy power do not advocate reform of the system that gives them power.

Perhaps such factors as our federal system, the separate election of President and Congress, the great variety of problems and viewpoints in the United States, and the interests that promote political localism will always forestall the unity required for completely responsible party government. But these factors themselves are not necessarily immutable. If recent court decisions guaranteeing urban residents an equal voice in state legislatures and in the House of Representatives effect a basic change in the balance of the federal system, other parts of the system will be modified, too.

[75]*Democracy and the American Party System*, p. 531.
[76]Report of the Committee on Political Parties, *Toward a More Responsible Two-Party System*, p. 23.

PRESSURE GROUPS AND

PUBLIC RELATIONS 8

Because one of the goals of democracy is widely shared political power, and because complete equality is never achieved, social scientists have engaged in lively—often acrimonious—debate over the question, "Who governs?" Three theories—or, more properly, schools of thought—have developed in the attempt to answer this question. They can be roughly labeled as log-rolling, group or pluralistic, and power-elite explanations of the policy process. Each of these explanations offers a different view of the influence of pressure groups on public policy.

The log-rolling interpretation sees policy as the product of a decentralized bargaining process in which the relationship among pressure groups is one of "mutual noninterference."[1] The participants do not share common interests and the process is not one of compromise. "Given . . . interests whose objectives are intrinsically of mutual indifference, collaboration for support of the whole demands of each can be readily effected."[2] Some see this rolling together of different interests as adding up to an expression of majority needs, but it is more generally viewed as biased in favor of narrow special interests.

Group theory or the pluralistic model is probably the dominant point of view among political scientists today.[3] In group theory, mutual noninterference is replaced by conflict among groups with "shared attitudes." Majority coalitions must be created on each issue, and many individuals and groups fail to apply their potential resources in the coalition-building effort. As a result, the system contains considerable "slack." "Thus, power is highly decentralized, fluid, and situational. There is no single elite, but a 'multicentered' system in which the centers exist in a conflict-and-bargaining relation to each other."[4]

The power-elite explanation does not deny the importance of pressure

---

[1] See Theodore J. Lowi, "American Business, Public Policy, Case-Studies, and Political Theory," *World Politics,* XVI (July, 1964), 677–715. We have drawn upon this article both for the discussion of the three competing theories and for the discussion of their synthesis in the section on "policy systems" below.

[2] Grant McConnell, *Private Power and American Democracy* (New York: Alfred A. Knopf, Inc., 1966), p. 112. A classic development of the log-rolling interpretation is E. E. Schattschneider, *Politics, Pressures and the Tariff* (Englewood Cliffs, N.J.: Prentice-Hall, Inc., 1935), reprinted in 1963 by Archon Books, Hamden, Connecticut.

[3] The best known and most influential works in this *genre* are David B. Truman, *The Governmental Process* (New York: Alfred A. Knopf, Inc., 1951), and Robert A. Dahl, *Who Governs?* (New Haven: Yale University Press, 1961).

[4] Lowi, "American Business . . . ," loc. cit., 679.

groups, but it does deny that power is decentralized.[5] The distribution of power is viewed as inherently hierarchical and those at the top of the pyramid —particularly those in the highest industrial, military, and political positions —make all the "key" decisions. Their resources are overwhelmingly greater than those of lower-status people, and the theory assumes that power resources are applied without "slack." Occupants of these "command post" positions are recruited and socialized so as to reduce basic conflicts among them. Policy can thus be settled by informal gentlemanly accord without the formal trappings of debates and votes. Group conflict and coalition-building occur, but only on issues that are not fundamental and among people at the "middle levels of power."[6]

The Importance of Pressure Groups in Politics

Which of these interpretations of the importance of pressure groups in American politics is most valid? Let us postpone an answer until we have looked at the nature and function of pressure groups and at the nature of the group struggle in politics.

The Nature and Functions of Pressure Groups

Pressure groups have much in common with political parties and even with official decision-making agencies such as the United States Congress. All fall within the general meaning of "political interest group" if we accept David Truman's definition of that concept as "a shared-attitude group that makes certain claims upon other groups in the society" by acting "through or upon any of the institutions of government. . . ."[7] Decision-making agencies such as the House of Representatives or the Supreme Court are clearly distinguishable from political parties and pressure groups by their official status, despite the fact that they too make claims on other groups by acting through or on government institutions. Political parties and pressure groups are both unofficial agencies, but they differ on other grounds. The current practice of regarding "political interest group" simply as a more neutral way of saying "pressure group" is therefore highly misleading. The former concept includes the latter and a lot more too—such as political parties. For example, a political interest group involves "shared attitudes toward what is needed or wanted in a given situation." This is as true for the Democrats as it is for the A.M.A. (American Medical Association). The Democrats want to win elections, and the A.M.A. wants to block government health insurance. There are members within each

---

[5]The best known and most influential applications of this approach are Floyd Hunter, *Top Leadership, U.S.A.* (Chapel Hill: University of North Carolina Press, 1959), and C. Wright Mills, *The Power Elite* (New York: Oxford University Press, 1956). For a keen examination of all these approaches, see Nelson W. Polsby, *Community Power and Political Theory* (New Haven: Yale University Press, 1963).

[6]Mills, *The Power Elite*, p. 245.

[7]David B. Truman, *The Governmental Process*, p. 37. Although he offers this broadly inclusive concept of political interest groups, Truman then uses it in reference only to what we call pressure groups. See, for example, his chapter on "Interest Groups and Political Parties," which suggests that political parties are not political interest groups.

256

group who share attitudes on what is needed. Moreover, a political interest group "makes certain claims upon other groups in the society." Thus the Democrats demand the loyalty of voters, and the A.M.A. claims support from pharmacists, patients, and physicians.

We may regard both the political party and the pressure group as political interests groups, but we must also recognize that they differ enough to require distinct labels. The *purpose* of the pressure group is to influence specific policies, rather than to achieve control over the government as a whole. Another difference is in the *method* of acquiring power: the political party concentrates on winning elections, whereas the pressure group never offers its own candidates to the voters. The pressure group may be vitally concerned with every stage of the election process, but it does not campaign under its own banner; and it is just as interested in other means of influencing policy as it is in elections themselves.

We can define a pressure group, then, as an organized attempt to influence government policy decisions without officially entering election contests. Despite the unfavorable connotations that have come to be associated with the term "pressure group," we shall use it in referring to this unofficial kind of nonparty political interest group.[8]

Pressure groups are based firmly on the constitutionally guaranteed freedoms of assembly and petition. Consequently, they are no less characteristic of democracy than are political parties. Freedom of speech and freedom of the press would mean little if various interests could not translate them into organized attempts to gain recognition. And the basic function of pressure groups is just that: to give political expression to the values or interests of minority groups. Just as political parties strive to mobilize a majority of the voters, pressure groups serve to give special representation to minorities. For the political system as a whole, then, they play an indispensable part in identifying the various interests in society. Additional functions of pressure groups include stimulating interest and participation in politics and, through demands on candidates, clarifying issues during election campaigns.[9] Groups of this sort are an integral part of politics in every democracy.

Politics as a Struggle among Groups

We opened our discussion of political parties with a recurrent theme of this book: politics is a process of interaction among groups. This point deserves emphasis, because so many of us retain eighteenth-century illusions about the nature of political power. We focus on the individual and neglect his group identifications; we tend to praise the "independent" voter and the "independent" congressman as ideal

---

[8] In a brief and penetrating analysis of pressure groups in American politics, Harmon Zeigler bows to the popularity of the term "interest groups" in his title: *Interest Groups in American Society* (Englewood Cliffs, New Jersey: Prentice-Hall, Inc., 1964). Nevertheless, his definition of pressure groups (p. 30) is virtually identical to that above.

[9] *Ibid.*, p. 39.

types in the exercise of political power. But in doing so we ignore the hard fact that power—the motivating force in politics—springs from organization. "In a great part of our political life the average citizen is an innocent bystander and also a bewildered one. He feels that his vote is futile, but he seldom grasps the fact that the Congress, like the state legislatures, never has functioned as a truly representative body, but only as a means of registering organized pressures. It does, in that way, represent all the forms of *organized power* in the nation. . . ."[10]

This statement is a bit extreme, for unorganized and even latent public opinions set limits within which the power struggle tends to be confined. As we saw in Chapter 6, a basic function of political opinions is to support those policies that were so often described in the 1964 presidential campaign as the mainstream of American politics. The boundaries of the mainstream are not precise, however, and unorganized opinions seldom have a positive influence on the direction of policy. Even if the "independent" legislator or President felt that he really owed his office to the "independent" vote, he would hardly know how to serve it, "for it is truly both dumb and divided, while the organized forces that press upon him . . . are both unified and highly articulate."[11] Here is another way of putting the point: "Organization represents concentrated power, and concentrated power can exercise a dominating influence when it encounters power which is diffuse and not concentrated, and therefore weaker."[12]

In speaking of the sources of group affiliations and activities, James Madison observed in his classic *Federalist* essay No. 10 that they are ". . . sown in the nature of man." Beyond their individual peculiarities, men are conditioned by their group loyalties, contacts, and needs. No two members of any pressure group have identical native characteristics or life experiences, but their identification with a common group means that they share certain interests or attitudes. Precisely what attitudes they share may vary almost infinitely. As Madison put it,

> . . . the most common and durable source of factions has been the various and unequal distribution of property. Those who hold and those who are without property have ever formed distinct interests in society. Those who are creditors, and those who are debtors, fall under a like discrimination. A landed interest, a manufacturing interest, a mercantile interest, a moneyed interest, with many lesser interests, grow up of necessity in civilized nations, and divide them into different classes, actuated by different sentiments and views.

Although many noneconomic organizations, such as the American Civil Liberties Union and the League of Women Voters, play an active role in politics, economic differences are just as predominant in the activities of pressure groups now as they were in Madison's day. Indeed, the specialization that has been brought about by our industrial economy has created so

---

[10] Harvey Fergusson, *People and Power: A Study of Political Behavior in America* (New York: William Morrow & Co., Inc., 1947), pp. 109–110 (emphasis added).
[11] *Ibid.*, p. 114.
[12] Earl Latham, "The Group Basis of Politics: Notes for a Theory," *American Political Science Review*, XLVI (June, 1952), 387.

many pressure groups that we can only guess at their total number. Even according to the most conservative estimates, the number of groups active at the national level of government alone would have to be counted in at least four figures.[13] Primitive societies in which there is little division of labor have few pressure groups. But complex industrial societies tend to produce them in ever-increasing numbers.

The banker in California has more in common with another banker in New England than he has with a fruit-picker in his own county. Moreover, organizations like the American Bankers' Association keep him constantly aware of these common interests and provide a power structure through which they can be continuously represented before all the agencies of government. The fruit-picker, with no pattern of interaction with other farm laborers, seldom discovers that his interests are shared by other farm laborers scattered across the country; consequently, he has little political influence. Understandably, the legislator who is presumably representing both the banker and the fruit-picker is more aware of the interests of the organized group. Only if the fruit-picker's interests happen to become part of some political interest group (either a pressure group or a political party, or both) will they carry any real weight in the policy-forming process. The more nearly the fruit-picker resembles the "independent" citizen, the more completely will he find himself isolated from power.

Since Tocqueville's time, America has been described as a nation of joiners. But in focusing on the proliferation of pressure groups, we should not overstate the extent to which Americans are formally involved in such organizations. About a third of the adult population belong to no formal organizations of any kind, and another third belong to organizations that never take a stand on political questions. This leaves only one-third of the population as members of formal organizations that sometimes take a stand on housing, better government, school problems, or other public issues. Only about 2 per cent claim membership in specifically political organizations.[14] Millions of Americans are members of pressure groups, then, but equal numbers are members of no groups at all or of groups that they perceive as totally nonpolitical. As a political resource then, pressure group members constitute a minority of the population.

Pressure Groups in Different Policy Arenas

An old fable relates how three blind men encounter an elephant and then describe their sensations: one, feeling his way along the creature's side, says he has walked into a wall; the second, touching a leg, says he has walked into a tree; while the third, grasping the trunk, yells, "Run, run—there's a snake here!" The fable may be usefully applied to interpreters who describe the contribution of pressure

---

[13]Truman, *The Governmental Process*, p. 59.
[14]Robert E. Lane, *Political Life: How People Get Involved in Politics* (New York: The Free Press of Glencoe, Inc., 1959), p. 75.

groups to public policy with reference to log-rolling, to group conflict, or to a power-elite: the interpretation of each may be "true," but only with reference to one area of the object of inquiry. Instead of singling out one system as *the* instrument of policy-making, one student of Congress suggests that "it might be more helpful to conceive of a set of 'policy systems,' in which all parties involved in a particular category of issues share regularly in the making, alteration, and execution of policy."[15] Perhaps the influence of pressure groups varies systematically from one area of policy to another. Theodore Lowi of the University of Chicago has attempted just such a reappraisal of domestic policy systems (or *arenas*, his term) in the United States. Classifying policies according to their expected impacts on society, he identifies three functional arenas of public policy: *distribution*, *regulation*, and *redistribution*.[16]

The term *distributive* was first coined to describe nineteenth-century land policies in the United States, but Lowi uses it as synonymous with *patronage* in the broadest meaning of that term. All decisions on the dispensing of fairly specific favors are thus distributive, including "most contemporary public land and resource policies; rivers and harbors ('pork barrel') programs; defense procurement and R & D [Research and Development]; labor, business, and agricultural 'clientele' services; and the traditional tariff."[17] Decisions in the distributive policy arena tend to be highly individualized, each more or less isolated from the other. We said in explaining our scheme of a political system (in Chapter 1) that all policy decisions include both rewards and deprivations, but that in some decisions deprivation might be present only in the sense of differential rewards. Such is the case with distributive policies; the deprived and the rewarded may never confront each other in conflict. If the deprived are those who get a smaller piece of the pie, or those who are out of this particular policy arena and who support the distribution in their tax payments, they may not even have a sense of deprivation.

In the regulatory arena, deprivations are as clear as rewards. When Congress enacts a statute on labor-management relations, the deprived party is as aware of his loss as the rewarded party is aware of his gain. "Regulatory policies are distinguishable from distributive in that . . . the regulatory decision involves a direct choice as to who will be indulged and who deprived."[18] Here, too, decisions tend to have specific and individual impact; each decision, however, involves the application of a general standard which tends to carry over to others who are subject to the regulation. A regulatory policy is accordingly more nearly a general policy than the accumulation of an almost infinite number of individual decisions.

Redistributive policies are similar to regulation in their application to broad categories of people and in the interrelation of individual decisions. But redistribution applies to much broader segments of the population and carries still greater rewards and deprivations. "The categories of impact are much broader, approaching social classes. They are, crudely speaking, haves and

---

[15]Ralph K. Huitt, "Congress, the Durable Partner," in Elke Frank (ed.), *Lawmakers in a Changing World* (Englewood Cliffs, N.J.: Prentice-Hall, Inc., 1966), p. 19.
[16]"American Business . . . ," loc. cit.
[17]*Ibid.*, 690.
[18]*Ibid.*, 690–691.

have-nots, bigness and smallness, bourgeoisie and proletariat. The aim involved is not use of property but property itself, not equal treatment but equal possession...." Professor Lowi's only examples of redistributive policies in the United States are the income tax and various "welfare state" programs, and he concedes that these are only mildly redistributive. Nevertheless, "the aims and the stakes involved" render these policies redistributive.[19]

This classification of policy outputs may be viewed as a further specification of the general outputs of rewards and deprivations explained in the scheme of a political system around which this book is organized. Each of these types of rewards and deprivations describes a real arena of power that differs systematically from the others.[20] What are the differences? The most important difference is that each of these policy arenas seems to correspond to a different "theory" of the policy process. Like the three blind men exploring the elephant, the holders of each theory may have touched part of reality and confused it with the whole.

Distributive politics appears to be best explained by the log-rolling interpretation. The primary political unit affected by these decisions is an individual or a particular firm or corporation. The Public Works Committee of the House, for example, decides billion-dollar issues with reference to rivers and harbors, but these are broken down into a series of million-dollar and thousand-dollar decisions. This kind of policy-making multiplies the number of interests involved and creates a relationship of mutual noninterference within a coalition whose members have nothing in common except a desire for some share of the rewards. Rather than conflict, the goals of distributive policies lead to a structure of mutual accommodation among the key decision-makers and their supporters—"you scratch my back and I'll scratch yours." Power relations are involved here, of course, and the relative strengths of pressure groups vary. But when thousands of separate and obscure decisions are merely packaged together as a "policy" of rivers and harbors development, or of defense subcontracting, or of natural resources development, those who have access to the key decision-makers will tend to support them. The result is a stable power structure dominated by key decision-makers and their supporting groups. The primary locus or cite of decisions in these cases is generally specialized agencies such as congressional subcommittees and executive bureaus.

The policies that have been most widely studied by political scientists are regulatory. Perhaps this is why pluralistic or group theory is so widely ac-

---

[19]*Ibid.*, 691. Here he shifts from functional analysis—which deals with effects—to what might be called anticipatory functional analysis—which deals with possible effects.

[20]Each arena could no doubt be broken down into still smaller and more homogeneous "political systems." But we think Lowi is on the right track in striving for a more general level of explanation. The chief deficiency of the scheme is that it is not broad enough to incorporate foreign policy. As we shall see in Chapter 16, however, in foreign policy the United States is a subsystem acting within a larger international system. This is one reason for the inability to incorporate in the above scheme those aspects of foreign and military policy that have no direct domestic implications. See Lowi, "American Business . . . ," *loc. cit*, 689n.

cepted, for it best explains regulation. The principal units affected by regulations are the "shared attitude" groups we described above. Regulatory decisions deal with direct conflicts that go beyond individual rewards and deprivations and affect all people with similar interests. A decision that a given labor or management practice is "unfair" concerns more than a single firm or union. Conflict over this kind of decision leads to bargaining between coalitions made up of people with common interests. Dependent on the changing interests of the various groups in the coalition, the resultant power structure tends to be unstable. And the pluralistic nature of the power structure militates against the decision of policy in specialized agencies—policies tend, from time to time, to be fought out on the floor of Congress. This is the policy arena that political science best explains. Lowi goes so far as to conclude, "Within this narrower context of regulatory decisions, one can even go so far as to accept the most extreme pluralist statement that policy tends to be a residue of the interplay of group conflict."[21]

By now the perceptive reader has guessed which interpretation of the policy process best explains the redistributive arena. Since the log-rolling explanation has been applied to the distributive arena, and the pluralistic explanation to the regulatory arena, we have only one explanation left for redistribution—the power-elite theory. Professor Lowi reaches the expected conclusion. He sees distributive issues as dividing the participants into two cohesive peak associations that broadly represent "money-providing" and "service-demanding" groups. With one elite for each side, the only negotiation that is possible is on increasing or decreasing the impact of redistribution. Decisions here tend to be made by top leaders in the executive and in peak associations, not on the floor of Congress or in specialized agencies. Because of the stability of broad classes in the United States, and because of what he calls the "impasse (or equilibrium)" in the relations between classes, Lowi concludes that the power structure of redistribution is highly stable.[22]

We think this interpretation of the distributive arena is strained, developed in the interest of giving a sense of closure or completeness to Lowi's scheme of classification. (See Table 8–1 for a diagrammatic summary of the scheme.) Income tax policy, for example, is cited as redistributive, but it does not take the form of dividing participants into two homogeneous groups, nor is it politely settled in private negotiation. Tax issues can divide the "haves" as well as the "have-nots"—as does the 27½ per cent depletion allowance for oil producers, for example—into smaller groups that compete to maximize their varying rewards and to minimize their varying deprivations. This kind of conflict hardly fits the neat categories of explanation summarized in Table 8–1.

Although we agree with Lowi's imaginative analysis of the distributive and regulatory arenas, we cannot agree with his view that the power-elite theory explains the redistributive policy arena.[23] But we agree that the pluralistic model does not *disprove* the existence of some kind of elite control in this area. The redistributive policy arena may turn out, on the basis of future research, to differ from the distributive and regulatory not so much by the way *decisions*

---

[21]*Ibid.*, 695.
[22]*Ibid.*, 711.
[23]See Polsby, *op. cit.*, for the methodological and theoretical weaknesses of power-elite theory.

are made as by the way questions are *prevented from being presented* for a formal decision.

Table 8-1   Arenas and Political Relationships:
A Diagrammatic Summary

ARENA	PRIMARY POLITICAL UNIT	RELATION AMONG UNITS	POWER STRUCTURE	STABILITY OF STRUCTURE	PRIMARY DECISIONAL LOCUS
Distribution	Individual, firm, corporation	Log-rolling, mutual non-interference, uncommon interests	Nonconflictual elite with support groups	Stable	Congressional committee and/or agency**
Regulation*	Group	"The coalition," shared subject-matter interest, bargaining	Pluralistic, multicentered, "theory of balance"	Unstable	Congress, in classic role
Redistribution	Association	The "peak association," class, ideology	Conflictual elite, i.e., elite and counterelite	Stable	Executive and peak associations

*Given the multiplicity of organized interests in the regulatory arena, there are obviously many cases of successful log-rolling coalitions that resemble the coalitions prevailing in distributive politics. In this respect, the difference between the regulatory and the distributive arenas is thus one of degree. The *predominant* form of coalition in regulatory politics is deemed to be that of common or tangential interest. Although the difference is only one of degree, it is significant because this prevailing type of coalition makes the regulatory arena so much more unstable, unpredictable, and non-elitist ("balance of power"). When we turn to the redistributive arena, however, we find differences of principle in every sense of the word.

**Distributive politics tends to stabilize around an institutional unit. In most cases, it is the Congressional committee (or subcommittee). But in others, particularly in the Department of Agriculture, the focus is the agency or the agency *and* the committee. In the cities, this is the arena where machine domination continues, if machines were in control in the first place.

Source: Lowi, "American Business . . . ," *loc. cit.*, 713.

What, then, takes the place of the power-elite theory? The orthodox pluralist theory does not fill the gap. The pluralists have chosen to study issues on which conflict occurs, so naturally they have discovered conflict in decision-making. They have also chosen issues that are decided by office-holders in the formal political system, so naturally they have missed any potential issues that were barred from presentation. "Standing decisions" that certain practices are beyond debate may exist in the nation or in particular communities.[24] And pressure groups and other unofficial agencies may be more important than official decision-makers in shaping the standing decisions within which the official decision-makers are bound. As Professor Schattschneider puts it:

> All forms of political organization have a bias in favor of the exploitation of some kinds of conflict and the suppression of others because *organization is the mobilization of bias.* Some issues are organized into politics while others are organized out.[25]

[24]For the concept of the "standing decision," see Todd Gitlin, "Local Pluralism as Theory and Ideology," *Studies on the Left,* V (Summer, 1965), 21–45.

[25]E. E. Schattschneider, *The Semi-Sovereign People* (New York: Holt, Rinehart & Winston, Inc., 1960), p. 71.

The mobilization of bias may be indirectly and even subconsciously applied to define some issues out of politics. Picture the school administrator in a rural, conservative, and religiously fundamentalist school district who feels that sex education should be introduced in the local schools. A prudent person in this position would probably decide that the mobilization of bias in the community was such that he should not introduce the issue to the school board. Here a decision is made—a decision not to raise an issue—but it is made outside the formal system. For the formal political process, then, it is a *nondecision,* an issue never raised. At the national level, questions that challenge the private enterprise system, fundamental constitutional arrangements (and how many other policies?) may similarly be "defined out" of the political system. But the process of suppressing issues is not always indirect. "In those instances when a latent issue of the type which is usually submerged is successfully pushed forward and emerges as a public issue (for example, the recent emergence of Negro demands in the South), it is likely that the mobilization of bias will be directly and consciously employed against those who demand a redress of grievances by the decision-making organ. In such instances, the decision-making process preempts the field previously occupied by the nondecision-making process. And in so doing, it necessarily jeopardizes the previously-established mobilization of bias."[26]

Is American politics under the control of a small ruling elite? In the distributive and regulatory arenas, the answer appears to be negative. In the redistributive arena, the necessary research for a confident answer has yet to be carried out. When such research is undertaken, it will have to include a consideration of the process by which issues are suppressed as well as the process by which they are resolved once they are raised.[27] At this stage of our knowledge, we are confident that the mobilization of bias favors upper-status groups. Indeed, it would be truly amazing if the dominant values and rules of procedure in a stable society did not favor those in more powerful positions. But we are not at all confident that this bias can be equated with positive control by a narrow power elite. Some hybrid theory (biased pluralism or multicentered elitism) may be the answer.

Bases of Pressure-Group Strength

If we are correct in the argument that different policy arenas develop different power structures, is it still possible to talk about pressure groups in general terms? We think it is. Although the political units and relationships in different policy systems are not the same, some general bases of pressure-group strength can be identified.

The Political Environment as a Source of Strength

The strength of all pressure groups, whatever their makeup or their goals, is affected by the political environment in which they operate. In a democracy, for example, political

---

[26]Peter Bachrach and Morton S. Baratz, "Decisions and Nondecisions: An Analytical Framework," *American Political Science Review,* LVII (September, 1963), 642.

[27]For a statement of what such research should investigate, see Peter Bachrach and Morton S. Baratz, "Two Faces of Power," *American Political Science Review,* LVI (December, 1962), 947–952.

practices make it a simple matter for different interests to advance their claims before the government. "Liberty is to faction what air is to fire," Madison observed. The techniques employed and the degree of influence achieved by pressure groups vary greatly from society to society, but in every democracy these groups are at least given an opportunity to seek power.

The formal organization of the government is a second factor that affects the strength of pressure groups. In the United States, the existence of three levels of government—national, state, and local—and the separation of powers at each level among the legislative, executive, and judicial branches, produce many points at which government policy may be influenced. This system is disadvantageous for agencies that seek control of the entire government—that is, the political parties. But it is clearly advantageous for agencies that seek only to influence specific policies—that is, pressure groups.

When a pressure group is trying to *block* government action that it regards as detrimental, for instance, it finds that opportunity knocks not just once but over and over again. If a group cannot prevent an issue from being raised, its cause is not necessarily lost, for if it fails in one house of Congress, it can try the other. Indeed, as we shall see in Chapter 10, the manner in which Congress is organized provides pressure groups with a number of points of access in each house. Since power in Congress tends to be personalized and scattered rather than institutionalized and concentrated, to impress just one key congressman with the group's needs may be enough. If he is a member of a committee that is considering an objectionable measure, especially if he is the chairman of the committee, he may kill the measure before the membership of the house ever has a chance to vote on it.

If the pressure group fails to win the backing of any of the congressmen, it may still strive for a presidential veto. But the end of the trail does not come even there. Once a law has been passed, it is still subject to challenge in the courts, where, even if it is held constitutional, the group may succeed in having it interpreted to the group's advantage in specific cases. And when a law is put into operation, the group can continue to contact the administrators who interpret and administer the law day by day.

Our federal system offers another series of opportunities for interest groups at the state level. If a group cannot muster effective power at any point in national politics, it may still realize its ambitions in at least some of the states. The old saw, "If at first you don't succeed, try, try again," is taken very seriously by American pressure groups. If none of these efforts to influence the government is successful, the group may finally attempt to influence nominations and elections to state or federal office.

A third factor in the political environment that enhances the strength of pressure groups in the United States is the weakness of political parties. The diffusion of power in the official government structure strengthens the efforts of pressure groups to *block undesirable* policy decisions. And the weakness of political parties strengthens the efforts of these groups to *promote desirable* policy decisions. The failure of the majority party to organize Congress effectively and to act with cohesion on policy matters produces a power vacuum that tends to be filled by organized interest groups. "Because the legislator's tenure in office depends on no overarching party organization, he is accessible to whatever influences are outstanding in his local constituency almost regardless of more inclusive claims."[28] On questions that are of no direct concern to prominent interests in his locality, the weakness of party structure leaves the congressman susceptible to appeals from national pressure groups that have little or no identification with his constituency.

Group Characteristics as Sources of Strength

In a political environment, then, in which pressure groups are free to organize, in which government power is highly diffused, and in which weak parties leave the majority largely unorganized, pressure groups have golden opportunities to reach their goals. How successful they are in taking advantage of their opportunities depends largely on the same group characteristics that determine the success of political parties—namely, organization, leaders, social base, and doctrines. In the three policy arenas analyzed above, and in the foreign policy arena as well, each of these group characteristics has a bearing on the success of a pressure group in achieving its intermediate objective: gaining access to key points of decision-making in government.[29]

Status is, however, probably the most influential of all characteristics in determining the strength of a pressure group. If it occupies a position of high prestige, its leaders will enjoy an easy access to key points of decision that is denied to low-status groups. A junior legislator or administrator may actually be flattered to have a leader of a group like the American Bar Association or the American Legion come to him for help. But an organization of the far left, like the National Council for American-Soviet Friendship, or of the far right, like the John Birch Society, may find it difficult even to get a hearing. Until the 1930s, labor spokesmen generally had a hard time finding a sympathetic ear in government. This situation has changed over the decades, mainly because labor has achieved far more powerful organization and, with it, higher status. But in some sections of the country, notably in rural areas and in certain parts of the South, endorsement of a candidate by the AFL-CIO would still be the kiss of death. Consequently, labor in these areas has little access to legislators.

High-status pressure groups and their spokesmen also have the advantage of talking the same language as office-holders. Since they have similar class backgrounds, similar experiences, and similar contacts, they quickly discover similar interests. Moreover, a high-status group is able to develop common interests with other pressure groups and enlist their support in its efforts. Finally, since status is tied so closely to money in the United States, the group with greater status will almost automatically be able to command greater financial resources. And it costs money to engage in pressure politics, as our discussion of pressure-group tactics will make clear.

In addition to status, organization is another characteristic that helps determine the power of pressure groups. The closer and more frequent the interaction among members, the more cohesive—that is, the more effectively organ-

---
[28]Truman, *The Governmental Process*, p. 325.
[29]*Ibid.*, p. 264.

ized—the group will be. And organization means power. Although the official organization charts of pressure groups often give the impression that they are as decentralized as the political parties, they generally enjoy a much greater concentration of power at the national level than do the latter. Pressure group leaders try to avoid the localism that keeps the structure of political parties weak and makes it difficult for any one person to speak authoritatively for the organization as a whole. Ironically, the very groups that have the highest degree of concentrated nationwide control, such as the Chamber of Commerce and the National Association of Manufacturers, are frequently the loudest champions of states' rights for political parties and the government.

Tight organization allows a pressure group to keep in constant contact with the government. The good lobbyist works hard to gain the respect of sympathetic congressmen by offering material for speeches, data on impending legislation, detailed information on the needs of the lobbyist's clients, and other services. Conversely, the congressman can keep the lobbyist informed on new developments and on his own and his colleagues' inclinations. This kind of relationship demands time no less than skill. One lobbyist for a business group explained that he concentrated on a few strategic members of Congress because he could not maintain a sufficiently close relationship with a larger number. "To keep these friendships alive and genuine, I have to stop around to see them quite often just to say hello. For example, if I don't see _____ at least once a week, he'll say, 'Where the hell have you been? You only stop around when you want something from us.' Even a few contacts on the Hill demand a good deal of time and attention."[30] Only a group well enough organized to have a staff of spokesmen constantly on the job can hope to build this kind of mutually rewarding relationship. Another lobbyist has said, "We are just getting to the point where members of Congress and agency officials come to us and seek information. This office is only ten years old, and you know it takes time to establish a reputation."[31] Without a well-organized effort, it cannot attain this respect. It will have trouble securing enough information to protect its interests—to say nothing of advancing new interests.

The quality of *leadership* is a third characteristic that affects the strength of a pressure group. In order to advance its claims effectively, a group needs spokesmen with official contacts and with an intimate knowledge of the political process. Many administrators and legislative assistants become lobbyists for various groups after leaving government service—an indication of both the know-how and the contacts that lobbyists need. One study of Washington lobbyists disclosed that "over half of the lobbyists had worked for the federal government either in a staff position on the 'Hill' or in one of the agencies or as an appointive or elective officeholder."[32] Contrary to popular

---

[30]Quoted in Donald R. Matthews, *U.S. Senators and Their World* (Chapel Hill: The University of North Carolina Press, 1960), p. 181.
[31]Lester W. Milbrath, *The Washington Lobbyists* (Chicago: Rand McNally & Co., 1963), p. 289.
[32]Lester W. Milbrath, "The Political Party Activity of Washington Lobbyists," *Journal of Politics*, XX (May, 1958), 346.

assumption, only a few former congressmen are found among the lobbyists in Washington. The greater reliance on people with administrative and legislative staff experience indicates the increasing importance of lobbying before administrative agencies: a lobbyist needs access to administrators as well as legislators, and he must "know the ropes" well enough to take advantage of his access. To know whom to see and when to see him, what information will be most helpful, how best to advance one's case—these are invaluable assets.

Unless leaders maintain cohesion within their own organization, they will have little impact in Washington, even if they employ the best of lobbyists. And the greatest threat to cohesion for groups active in the regulatory and redistributive arenas stems from overlapping membership in various groups. Since few people are totally identified with a single group, members may be alienated or even lost from an organization if it presents too many conflicts with other loyalties. A member of the American Legion, for example, may also be a Baptist, a fisherman, a pipefitter, a father, a union member, and a Mets fan. The effective leader must somehow minimize the cross-pressures that arise from conflicting group loyalties and maximize the members' identification with his own group. To this end, skillful leaders use such devices as internal propaganda, services to members, and the maintenance of at least the appearance of membership control. Ultimately, however, the perceptive leader must sometimes recognize that other organized and potential interests among his followers impose restraints on his leadership that no skill can overcome. When John L. Lewis tried to lead the United Mine Workers into the Republican Party in 1940, the overwhelming Democratic vote that was rolled up in the mining districts was a sharp reminder of the reality of these conflicting interests.

In the distributive policy arena, on the other hand, overlapping memberships pose no problem because of the isolated nature of distributive decisions. Indeed, in the quest of some share of widely distributed benefits, overlapping membership may actually help promote group cohesion. Overlapping thus becomes a form of specialization through which members of group X can pursue in groups Y and Z those goals that might be disruptive if introduced into group X.[33] And if group X is concerned with distributive rewards—a tariff decrease on steel, or the deepening of a river channel—it can steer clear of broader issues on which its members might be in extreme disagreement. The availability of other groups and the overlapping of memberships thus promote the cohesion of groups trying to influence distributive policy decisions. Opponents of a log-rolling coalition, recognizing that its members differ greatly on other questions, often try to disrupt the coalition by injecting broader issues—labor relations, civil rights, communism—into the decision-making process.

The social base of a pressure group is a fourth characteristic that affects its strength. The number of members that a group can claim is important, of course. But size does not always bestow strength; in fact, the larger a group grows the more likely it is to become disunited. If the AFL-CIO could main-

---

[33]Lowi, "American Business . . . ," *loc. cit.*, 697. Also see Raymond A. Bauer, Ithiel de Sola Pool, and Lewis Anthony Dexter, *American Business and Public Policy* (New York: Atherton Press, 1963), pp. 332–333.

tain the cohesion in politics that it does in collective bargaining, its political power would be greatly magnified. Its millions of members are cross-pressured by so many other loyalties, however, that its power is not commensurate with its size. Thus it is readily seen that *cohesion* is a key determinant in *every* element of group strength.

The geographical distribution of the members is another important factor in the social base of a group. If members are widely scattered, the group will probably be less unified than it would be if they could frequently meet face-to-face. On the other hand, if almost all the members live in a *single* area, as importers tend to be concentrated in New York, their effectiveness before Congress may suffer. Since the importer is not an important force in most constituencies, when tariff increases are under consideration "his opposition is taken for granted, discounted in advance, and if he is heard it is with irritation."[34] If the members of a group are fairly well concentrated in urban areas, as the members of labor unions are, the group will enjoy greater influence in the office of the President (who depends on national majorities) than in Congress (where rural areas are more heavily represented). The strong influence of farm groups on Congress, conversely, springs in part from the wide geographical distribution of their members.

Finally, the *doctrines* or policy objectives of a pressure group have a direct influence on its strength. If the aims of a group fit the prevailing pattern of values in the country at large, the group will enjoy easy access to the government and cross-pressures among the members will be kept at a minimum. Eveyone is in favor of good health, for example, so the American Cancer Society has the advantage of almost no opposition. (On the other hand, it may not be able to count on very *strong* commitment; mild approval may lead to an absence of opposition, but not necessarily to active support.) If the doctrines of a group run counter to prevailing values, however, its chances of breaking through the mobilization of bias will be slight, and its status will suffer accordingly. Extreme examples are the communist groups in the United States today. And, despite widespread race prejudice in the South, the departure of the Ku Klux Klan from the accepted "rules of fair play" in attempting to preserve "white supremacy" has relegated it to the "lunatic fringe," in the view of most southerners.

In order to succeed, the pressure group, no less than the political party, must be willing to modify its doctrines with changing times. Until the 1930s, the American Federation of Labor championed *laissez-faire*. But when it discovered that the government could be used to promote as well as to block its needs, and when the depression demonstrated that its needs could not be met *without* government help, it was quick to shift its support to social welfare legislation. On the other hand, the ultraconservative Minutemen, after Barry Goldwater's defeat in the 1964 presidential election, asserted that "the hopes of millions of Americans that the communist tide could be stopped with

---

[34] E. E. Schattschneider, *Politics, Pressures, and the Tariff*, p. 162.

ballots instead of bullets have been turned into dust."[35] Thus the organization, it was announced, was henceforth to concentrate on the training of "combat teams" that would employ the tactics of infiltration, subversion, and psychological warfare developed by communists. This particular modification of doctrine—if it can be called that—was in effect *against* the changing times, and consequently made the Minutemen presumably even more unpopular than before.

The more goals a group tries to achieve, the weaker it becomes in the pursuit of any one of them. If it can concentrate on a single overriding aim, as the Anti-Saloon League did in battling for prohibition, its chances of maintaining cohesion and winning success are enhanced. The Americans for Democratic Action, on the other hand, is committed to a whole series of programs, and the diffusion of its efforts thus reduces its effectiveness in each.[36] Since the pressure group is unconcerned with winning general control of the government, however, it need not, like the political party, develop an overall political program for the country at large.

Pressure Group Tactics and Public Responses

The persistent efforts of pressure groups to advance their particular interests are felt at every stage of the political process. Day after day, they work to create a favorable public opinion, to influence nominations and elections to public office, and to sway governmental decisions.

When most people consider pressure groups at all, they tend to think of efforts to influence the behavior of public officials. Actually, though, pressure groups have become so aware of the importance of public opinion to their causes that they are now spending millions of dollars every year on mass propaganda. Not only groups with broad concerns, such as the National Association of Manufacturers, but even individual companies maintain elaborate bureaucracies to sell "correct" ideas on general political questions along with favorable attitudes toward the company. The idea behind these efforts is that if the public can be induced to define the "American Way" precisely as the pressure group or the company does, mass support will be forthcoming whenever a critical issue arises. And the mobilization of bias may be such that still more critical issues never arise.

The General Mills food company, for example, which most people think of as simply trying to sell Wheaties, "The Breakfast of Champions," at one time maintained a Director of Educational Services in its Department of Public Services. This organization has made available to secondary-school teachers, without charge, such aids as fully planned teaching units on economics, complete with comic books in color and examinations on economic questions accompanied by answers. Schoolchildren are consumers not only of cereals but of ideas. And if they absorb the proper beliefs along with the proper foods,

---

[35] *The New York Times*, November 12, 1964.
[36] Clifton Brock, *Americans for Democratic Action: Its Role in National Politics* (Washington, D.C.: Public Affairs Press, 1962).

they will one day grow into sturdy supporters of sound public policies.

There have been rumblings of discontent, chiefly from competing pressure groups, about these general educational campaigns. It is argued that the general public unwittingly pays for the costs of the programs. Since the costs are regarded as company operating expenses, they reduce the amount of taxes paid by the company to the government; in addition, the costs are presumably included in the price of the company's product. In 1952, Representative Robert L. Ramsay (D.-West Virginia) introduced a bill to make it unlawful for corporations to reduce their taxes by charging to "business expense" the cost of advertisements with "political purposes." In endorsing the bill, one labor publication editorialized:

> An increasing flood of this institutional advertising is pouring into newspapers, magazines, radio programs, and the mail. It can be recognized by the fact that it tries to sell—not a product—but the political and economic prejudices of a businessman or corporation. . . .
> The businessmen who publish these institutional advertisements have a right to their personal opinions, but do they have a right to spread them at Government expense, which means at the expense of other taxpayers?[37]

Because labor groups cannot subsidize their own propaganda efforts in this way, it is hardly surprising that they should object to the practice. But the effectiveness of such campaigns is hard to prove,[38] and it would be difficult for legislators to frame laws that would distinguish between "product" advertising and "political" advertising. Finally—and most important—opposing groups have not managed to stir up enough public disapproval of the practice to bring about restrictive legislation.

Another tactic used by pressure groups—*electioneering*—overlaps these general educational programs. If the citizen is properly oriented on politics in general, the pressure group assumes that he will vote "correctly" in any given election. Consequently, pressure groups try to influence elections by appearing before platform committees at party conventions, by making monetary contributions to cooperative candidates, by offering propaganda services to candidates endorsed by the group, and by making direct exhortations to their members and general pleas to the public. If the right man can be elected in the first place, the group's interests will be almost automatically insured once he has taken office. In some cases, a pressure group may succeed in capturing the local party almost completely—as the United Automobile Workers have captured the Democratic Party in the Detroit area. Then it may simply install its own members in office and forget about the whole problem of influencing official decisions. Generally, however, pressure groups follow the practice of rewarding their friends and punishing their enemies.

The tactic most generally associated with pressure politics is that of at-

---
[37]*Congressional Record,* February 28, 1952, Appendix A1278 ("Extension of Remarks of Hon. Robert L. Ramsay"). Daily Edition.
[38]See William H. Whyte, Jr., *Is Anybody Listening?* (New York: Simon and Schuster, 1952).

tempting to influence official decision-makers, or, more bluntly, *lobbying.* Many citizens have a lurid picture of lobbying efforts. One lobbyist reports that he once overheard a revealing conversation between two women in the Senate waiting room. One lady, apparently a resident of Washington, was pointing out the sights to her visiting friend. "That's Senator _____," she said in a stage whisper, "and that"—pointing to the man with whom the Senator was talking—"is _____, the lobbyist for what's-its-name." "O-o-oh!" responded the impressed tourist. "Is he bribing him now?"[39]

Despite the negative popular image of lobbying efforts, modern lobbyists rarely resort to the use of corrupt practices or unlawful pressure. Instead, they serve as conveyors of useful information, both technical and political. The legislator and administrator must depend on the professional services of the lobbyists to keep themselves informed about the needs and preferences of important segments of the population. So the relationship is reciprocal: the official contacts the lobbyists for advice, information, or help, perhaps as often as the lobbyist contacts the official. An exhaustive study of the communication between congressmen and businessmen on the politics of foreign trade found "innumerable cases in which interested members of Congress get businessmen to make statements which it is hoped will influence other members of Congress."[40]

Whenever the spokesman for a pressure group violates the American concept of "fair play," he endangers the cohesion of the group's members —who are perhaps more committed to the general concepts of fair play than to the group itself. Moreover, he exposes the group to attack from other interests, and himself to prosecution. In 1956, for example, independent producers of natural gas seemed to have an excellent chance of winning exemption from federal rate control, a measure President Eisenhower himself had indicated he supported. Then, in the midst of debate, Senator Francis Case (R.-South Dakota) announced that he had rejected a $2,500 campaign contribution from an individual who was interested in the passage of the bill, and that the offer had changed his position from probable support to opposition. "I object," the Senator submitted, to "doing something so valuable to those interested in natural gas that they advance huge sums of money as a down payment, so to speak, on the profits they expect to harvest." The Senate promptly undertook an investigation of the incident. Although little came of the investigation itself, and the bill was actually passed by Congress, it was subsequently vetoed by the President.

Here was dramatic evidence of the existence of an unorganized "majority interest" in the basic concepts of fair play. The cynic may argue that the natural-gas bill was opposed to the majority interest regardless of the tactics used to support it. He may also emphasize that the President would have signed the bill had public attention not been aroused. But the incontrovertible fact, regardless of one's views on the merits of the bill itself, is that the public interest in fair play had *set limits* that the pressure group seemed to have violated. And the President—who, more than Congress, is the spokesman for the general interest of which we are speaking—was sufficiently responsive to

[39] Matthews, *U.S. Senators and Their World,* p. 176.
[40] Bauer, Pool, and Dexter, *American Business and Public Policy,* p. 197.

veto the bill because of "highly questionable activities" which he deemed to be "so arrogant and so much in defiance of acceptable standards of propriety as to risk creating doubt among the American people concerning the integrity of governmental processes." This is a point that we should keep in mind whenever we evaluate the charge that pressure groups, by themselves, can determine public policy.

The proposal of the Kennedy Administration to extend the social security system to health care for the aged (the King-Anderson bill in 1961) illustrates how pressure politics enters into the legislative process. Dozens of different organizations took formal stands and published statements, for or against the idea. A few groups with direct but different economic or professional stakes in the measure were extremely active. The American Medical Association, the American Dental Association, the National Association of Manufacturers, the Chamber of Commerce, and the insurance companies threw their combined weight on the negative side. The Americans for Democratic Action, the National Council of Senior Citizens' Clubs, and organized labor—especially AFL-CIO affiliates—worked most energetically for the proposal.

The American Medical Association is a high-status pressure group, professing to speak for about three-fourths of the nation's doctors. It opposed the Kennedy proposal on ideological grounds: "socialized medicine for the aged" would end up in "socialized medicine for every man, woman, and child in the country." It fears that "socialized medicine" might mean bureaucratic interference with the medical profession, that extension of public health service might turn the medical profession into a class of civil servants, that government payments based on "reasonable cost" might reduce doctors' fees and income. The A.M.A. maintains an aggressive lobby in Washington, with registered lobbyists paid to keep the views of the organization continuously before Congress. The central office also makes a wide appeal to the public through advertisements, "press kits" for editorial writers, and the provision of lecturers for state and county medical associations and for civic groups in general.

The most effective use of tactics of the A.M.A. is at the local level. The *A.M.A. News* urges physicians to tell their patients "the truth about socialized medicine, the danger in tying medical care to social security, the pitfalls in compulsory government insurance." To carry out its adverse publicity campaign, the A.M.A. furnishes suitable posters and pamphlets for the doctors' waiting rooms and texts for local television and radio spot announcements. The A.M.A. also urges its individual members not only to write personal letters to congressmen but to persuade local civic groups to join in a letter-writing campaign against "socialism."

While the A.M.A. pitches its campaign on ideological and professional grounds, its allies in the health insurance industry are frank to admit their large economic interests. Mutual of Omaha, Continental Casualty, Metropolitan Life, Aetna Life, and Equitable Life Assurance are among the companies with multimillion dollar stakes in this issue. Under Medicare, these big companies feel certain they will lose much of the business they now get from people over 65; and if the plan were carried further to cover the health needs of people under 65, they fear that the private health insurance business would be ruined. As might be expected from their strong commitment to private enterprise, the National Association of Manufacturers and the Chamber of Commerce join in the fight against the extension of government enterprise.

Organized labor, unlike the A.M.A., has only an indirect interest in the medical aid issue. The labor unions, however, have generally supported redistributive measures. Labor lobbyists in Washington pressure congressmen, and local affiliates are urged to write letters to their respective representatives. Many "senior citizens" have an obvious interest in the legislation, and nearly 10 per cent of the population is 65 or older. During the 1960 campaign, Senior Citizens for Kennedy were organized in a number of states. In 1961, the National Council of Senior Citizens' Clubs emerged as a broad federation that has lobbied not only for medical care but for other government aids for the aged.

"O Beautiful For Spacious Roads That Spread From Slum To Slum"

Drawing by Herblock;
©1967 The Washington Post.

The failure of the Kennedy proposal for medical aid to the aged in 1961 can be attributed at least partly to the cross-currents of pressure politics. In numbers, in broad social base, the labor groups and the organized senior citizens were certainly more outwardly impressive; but their interests and their efforts were both probably too diffuse. On the other hand, the high status of the opposition groups, their direct economic interest in the issue, their concentrated attack, their lavish expenditures, and their grass-roots approach to Congress seem to have been more effective.

By 1965, however, the picture had changed. The same groups played out their familiar roles once again but with different results. During the presidential campaign of 1964, the president of the National Council of Senior Citizens denounced the Republican platform as a "cruel hoax." The A.M.A. hired the firm of Fuller, Smith, and Ross to handle a million-dollar advertising campaign against Medicare. The achievement of Medicare under the Johnson administration cannot be attributed to a change in the lobbying forces, but rather to a greater popular mandate for the President and an increase in the number of liberal Democrats in Congress.

So long as official decision-makers are rather closely divided on an issue, pressure group efforts may block action. But the pressure group that is out of step with a concerted majority will eventually lose, however great its resources. The A.M.A. and its allies blocked Medicare for at least seventeen years—no small accomplishment—but they could not overcome a Democratic President who was supported by overwhelming majorities in both houses of Congress in 1965.

When lobbyists themselves are asked to assess the importance of different factors influencing public policy, they rank the executive branch, the composition of Congress, and voters' preferences far ahead of lobbying efforts. And the congressmen agree. Lester Milbrath of the State University of New York at Buffalo reports, on the basis of interviews with 101 lobbyists and 38 congressional objects of lobbying, "It is rather striking that both the practitioners and the recipients of lobbying think that lobbying is of so little importance in making public policy." He quotes one lobbyist who had great difficulty in rating the forces that operate in policy-making:

> I don't know where in the world I would fit the lobbyists as a group. Some of them have been up here for years battling for lost causes. On the whole, and speaking of all lobbyists in general, I think they are a lot less effective than most people believe.[41]

Pressure groups make several important contributions to democratic politics. They play an indispensable function in identifying the interests in society to which the political system must respond. They also serve to increase participation and to clarify issues in connection with the other great input function of the political system—leadership selection. In our single-member district system of representation, each legislator is presumed to represent everyone within a given geographical area. But political differences occur between interests that transcend district lines more often than they do between distinct territorial units. Pressure groups thus offer an important supplement to the official system of representation. By permitting a more precise expression of special interests than can be expected through the broad political parties or through a district's representative, pressure groups prevent a sense of alienation from taking hold and enhance the stability of the system.[42]

For a number of reasons, however, pressure groups appear less satisfactory than political parties as agencies to express broad public interests: (1) all interests are not represented equally through pressure groups, especially the underprivileged and noneconomic interests; (2) the complexity of current domestic and international problems demands a coherent and stable overall policy, and this kind of policy cannot be achieved if every problem is tackled

---

[41]Milbrath, *The Washington Lobbyists*, p. 352.
[42]*Ibid.*, pp. 357–358.

by a different coalition of special interests; (3) since every person, no less than every district, has a variety of interests, the pressure group leader can speak no more accurately for all the members of his group than the elected representative can for all his constituents; and (4), most important of all, pressure groups cannot be held accountable by the general public for the manner in which they use their power, because they do not win it through popular election.

We said earlier that the mobilization of bias in the United States favors upper-status interests and prevents some controversial questions from ever being raised as political issues. A bias against issues that might disrupt the system is no doubt built into the social, economic, and political systems of all stable societies. And the American mobilization of bias contains some strong majoritarian features, such as political parties and a system of popular elections. Hence, in the absence of evidence to the contrary, we see no reason to infer the existence of a small and self-conscious ruling elite that decides which issues can be raised. As noted earlier, further research must be done before we can talk confidently about the weight of different groups in the *non*decision arena. But even for the issues that are *raised*, some people view policy as being shaped exclusively by pressure groups and in total disregard of the unorganized mass of people.[43] This, too, strikes us as an oversimplified and inaccurate view.

In our discussion of the strength of pressure groups, we have already referred to their *overlapping memberships*. These criss-crossing relationships constitute a kind of natural restraint on the power of pressure groups to dominate general policy. Overlapping membership means that all the members of a pressure group cannot be mobilized completely on any question of general importance, for the members of any group are also involved in other groups in varying degrees. Consequently, group leaders are obliged to modify their own demands in order to accommodate the competing demands of other groups. Moreover, loyalty of members to any group varies—as in a college club, where involvement ranges from complete indifference to zealous participation by a few eager souls.

The latent power of *unorganized interests* and *potential groups* constitutes a second natural check on pressure group power. Unorganized interest groups and potential interest groups may be aroused to counteraction if they are flagrantly neglected. Even in a dictatorship there are certain bounds beyond which the ruler cannot move with impunity. And in a democracy the amorphous majority interest—the underlying expectations about how the government should operate and what sort of policies are fair—is a much more realistic check on organized minorities (remember the fate of the natural-gas bill). In a sense, then, even the submerged, potential interests enjoy a kind of representation, simply because they may organize if they are too severely mistreated. In recent summers the riots in American cities represented particularly destructive examples of submerged interests finding means of self-expression. Overlapping memberships and potential, unorganized groups thus serve as natural checks on pressure group government.[44]

[43]Fergusson, *People and Power*, p. 109.
[44]Truman, *The Governmental Process*, p. 514.

Some observers of politics, either unimpressed by these natural checks or unaware of their existence, have suggested various reforms to neutralize or purify the power of pressure groups. Many of these reforms consist of impractical constitutional revisions, generally in the direction of parliamentary government. James Madison and his contemporaries were relatively free to embody in the Constitution their ideas on how to cope with factions; but we have lived with the document too long and have become too attached to it for wholesale revisions to be anything other than visionary. Reformers must cope not only with the public's traditional attachment to the Constitution but also with the vested interests that grow up around any established constitutional practice. The forces working for constitutional revision must be strong indeed to surmount these obstacles. A proposal to give the President the power to "dissolve" Congress if it fails to enact his major recommendations, for example, would certainly not get much support from congressmen. So how could Congress be expected to approve such a revision by the two-thirds vote necessary to propose amendments?

More modest efforts at regulating pressure groups culminated in the Federal Regulation of Lobbying Act of 1946.[45] This law imposes no real restriction on lobbying, however, for it simply insures that the money spent by pressure groups to influence legislation be made part of the public record. It requires that professional lobbyists before Congress register their names and file information about themselves and their employers, and submit quarterly reports of receipts and expenditures. The Supreme Court has greatly reduced the effect of these provisions by narrowly interpreting the act to apply only to direct lobbying before congressmen.[46] The Court thus excludes from regulation the more modern technique of indirect lobbying through propaganda beamed at the general public. The failure of the act to provide an enforcement agency and the failure of the press to publicize the information that is reported further reduce the potential effects of the law. Obviously, this act "regulates" lobbying in name only.

We return to the political party, then, as the unofficial agency that is most capable of checking the power of interested minorities by mobilizing the power of the majority. Overlapping memberships and potential interest groups represent vital passive checks, but the political party operates as a more positive and active restraint. Only the party has a real stake in organizing the underlying majority interest and in stimulating potential groups to action. Political parties thus offer the possibility of restraining organized power with greater organized power.

Although American parties already restrain pressure groups to some extent, our earlier discussion suggests that we may never see really cohesive parties here of the sort that the British, for example, have developed. It is difficult to

---

[45]Title III of the *Legislative Reorganization Act of 1946*, Public Law 601, 79th Cong., 2d Sess., 1946.
[46]*United States* v. *Harris*, 347 U.S. 612 (1954). For a discussion of "The Dilemma of Lobby Regulation," see Donald C. Blaisdell, *American Democracy Under Pressure* (New York: The Ronald Press Company, 1957), pp. 82–98.

imagine an American legislator whose constituency contained strong pressure groups opposed to the national platform of his party persisting in supporting his party's position. But a judicious distribution of rewards and punishments might at least lead him to support his party more consistently on positions that are not strongly opposed in his constituency. Even now, the willingness of many legislators to respond to party pressure is impressive.

A fourth check on pressure group power is found in the official decision-making agencies themselves—the electoral system, the Congress, the presidency, and the courts. Official decision-makers are far from being passive pawns; they are active participants in the political process.[47] Official agencies find pressure groups vitally important sources of information and services, but not all-powerful forces before which they cringe. A leading student of Congress concludes from a study of the Senate: "Lobbying is important. The Senate could not possibly operate in the mid-twentieth century without it. But the effects of lobbying are not what most observers have assumed them to be."[48] The lobbying relationship is a reciprocal one in which the official decision-maker commands resources that give him considerable maneuverability. When pressed to support a bill, for example, the legislator may refuse, he may agree to vote for it but offer no further aid, or he may agree to lend it his all-out support. If he is known to oppose the bill, the smart lobbyist favoring passage will not even approach him, lest he lose good will and the possibility of future access to the legislator. Moreover, such futile pressure may have a boomerang effect and lead the legislator not only to vote negatively but actively to oppose the bill.

The ideology that the decision-maker brings to his office and the commitments he makes during his campaign for election probably have more to do with his decisions than all the activities of pressure groups. This means that important pressure groups in his constituency may have a special claim on him—to the point where he doesn't regard their advice as "pressure"—but it also decreases the likelihood that pressure groups can do more than reinforce predispositions he already has. And remember that the decision-maker generally shares the widespread but unorganized attitudes about what constitutes fair play in American politics. In this light, pressure groups appear much less menacing than they are frequently pictured to be. Milbrath's study of the positive and negative features of pressure group activities led him to conclude, "If we had no lobby groups and lobbyists we would probably have to invent them to improve the functioning of the system."[49]

Professional Public Relations

A few years ago, a survey of the unofficial agencies of politics would have ended with the discussion of political parties and pressure groups. But today the public relations expert is so ubiquitous in American politics that he demands special consideration. In party politics, the dominance of the local

[47]Zeigler, *Interest Groups in American Society*, p. 25.
[48]Matthews, *U.S. Senators and Their World*, p. 196.
[49]Milbrath, *The Washington Lobbyists*, p. 358.

boss and his machine is on the wane; in pressure group politics, the technique of trying to influence officials directly has begun to be overshadowed by appeals to the general public. In both cases, professional public relations organizations have been the beneficiaries of the shift and, to some extent, the agents responsible for it.

As Stanley Kelley makes clear in his *Professional Public Relations and Political Power*,[50] the new politics in America is no longer characterized by the local bosses who once "delivered" the votes of their organized followers, but by public relations firms like Batten, Barton, Durstine and Osborn, and the Joseph Katz Company,[51] whose business is to manipulate the attitudes of great numbers of voters. The tactics of pressure groups are directed less toward convincing office-holders than toward shaping the opinions of individuals and groups within the general public. One realistic party official, recognizing the emerging role of public relations, concludes, "If present tendencies continue, our federal elections will increasingly become contests not between candidates but between great advertising firms."[52] Was John Steinbeck looking too far into the future when, in his novel, *The Short Reign of Pippin IV*, he described the French government as unable to employ Batten, Barton, Durstine and Osborn because the firm was engaged on two more important accounts — rewriting the U.S. Constitution and marketing a new golfmobile with pontoons?[53]

Madison Avenue and Modern Public Relations

Democratic politics has always dealt in relations with the public. But there is something distinctly modern in the professional public relations men who now peddle their skill in selling ideas, candidates, and causes on a mass scale for millions of dollars a year. It is this technical skill that supports the role of professional public relations in politics — a skill based on expert knowledge of the mass media of communication, the nature of public opinion, and techniques for manipulating attitudes.

"Madison Avenue" is a new symbol in American politics — on this famous street in New York the plush offices of the broadcasting chains, advertising agencies, and public relations firms are all clustered together. The role of Madison Avenue could not have emerged 150 years ago when there was no mass circulation press and no radio or television, when most Americans were illiterate, and when suffrage was restricted to a few. The mass media of communication, universal suffrage, and higher levels of literacy, then, are among the forces that have produced this new elite. But the more immediate explanation for the political rise of the public relations expert is, of course, his

---

[50]This section is largely based on Kelley's *Professional Public Relations and Political Power* (Baltimore: The Johns Hopkins Press, 1956). In the decade since Kelley's research, political scientists have done little to develop more systematic understanding of this subject.
[51]These two important firms were retained at one time by the Republican and Democratic Parties, respectively.
[52]Quoted in Kelley, *Professional Public Relations*, p. 2.
[53]*The Short Reign of Pippin IV* (New York: The Viking Press, 1957), p. 72.

superior skill, as compared with professional politicians, in using the channels of communication.

The basic function of the public relations man is to create attitudes that are favorable to his client. As a person, he himself may have a strong preference for Ultrabrite toothpaste over Crest, or for Republicans over Democrats, but his services as a publicity expert are for sale to the highest bidder. He finds it easy to transfer his technical skill in molding attitudes from one assignment to another. The public relations director of a food company or of a health foundation may shift with equal expertise to selling a government policy or a candidate for public office. Whatever the substantive problem—the molding of proper attitudes toward toothpaste, or Democrats, or cigarettes, or Republicans, or health, or national defense—the technical problems are much the same. Thus, when President Kennedy continued Eisenhower's practice of infrequent press conferences, the critical reaction was as much in terms of the poor public relations that might result as it was in terms of the public's need for information. President Johnson's unscheduled contacts with the press are similarly evaluated more in terms of showmanship than content.

The enterprising public relations expert is not content to function merely as a tactician. Nor does he consider himself simply a press agent. He has become a "practical social scientist" whose profession is "managing human relations." In business corporations, he is found more and more often as a member of the policy-making "team." And in politics, he expects to have a say in determining what issues his client will espouse as well as the manner in which the issues will be presented. Even when he does not formulate policy, he must be close to those who do in order to advise them on how to "package" their policies attractively for the public "market." In government, the public relations expert has thus transformed the eighteenth-century principle of "consent of the governed" into the twentieth-century practice of "engineering consent."[54]

After he has created a popular image of the candidate—investing him with a public personality that makes him a "salable product"—the conscientious professional manager, whether his office is in Hollywood or Washington, expects his "star" to perform according to public expectations. But the candidate sometimes fails to cooperate. Some critics of Adlai Stevenson, for example, argue that he would have received more votes in 1952 and 1956 if he had relied more on his public relations advisers. Stanley Kelley quotes the somewhat plaintive comments of the late Clem Whitaker, at the time one of the country's outstanding public relations men, on this problem:

> An automobile is an inanimate object; it can't object to your sales talk—and if you step on the starter it usually runs. A *candidate on the other hand can and does talk back—and can sometimes talk you out of an election, despite the best you can do in campaign headquarters.* . . . We have the problem of human relations . . . [and the candidate's] ability or inability to measure up to the character you give him by your carefully prepared build-up.[55]

[54]This term was coined by Edward L. Bernays, one of the leading public relations experts. For a fuller discussion of this topic, see his book, *The Engineering of Consent* (Norman: University of Oklahoma Press, 1955).

[55]Quoted in *Professional Public Relations*, p. 222. Emphasis in original.

Some candidates, however, have shown little inclination to "talk back." In 1951, a group of senators investigating alleged malpractices in the Maryland campaign of Senator John Marshall Butler and Jon Jonkel, his Chicago public relations counsel, remarked, "It was a matter of the campaign manager and the campaign headquarters directing candidate Butler rather than candidate Butler directing the campaign manager and the campaign headquarters."[56]

Although the services of a professional public relations firm are now a standard part of political campaigns, their efficacy may easily be exaggerated. Party identification, for example, is a stable political factor that cannot be changed by even the cleverest of gimmicks during a brief campaign. And the established records of candidates cannot be transformed to suit the adman's schemes, even if the candidate is willing to follow his every direction. Finally, the advertising expert's talents may not be as easily transferred from deodorants to hundred-millimeter cigarettes to politics as he would have his client believe.

In 1964, the Democrats relied on one of the most creative agencies, Doyle Dane Bernbach, which handles the advertising campaigns of such products as Volkswagen, Avis Rent-a-Car, and Clairol. But the light touch of the Volkswagen ads was somehow missing from the material they prepared for the Democrats. The highly dramatic, "tactile" techniques of the TV spot showing a beautiful little girl picking flowers in a meadow, with the scene suddenly obliterated by the mushroom shape of a nuclear blast, and of the film showing a pair of hands tearing up a social security card seemed in bad taste. They may be fine techniques for dealing with hair rinses or automobiles, but not with the nation's future. We all know the former choices are not very serious. Somehow, the propriety of such crude emotional appeals becomes less acceptable as the seriousness of the subject matter increases. Perhaps because we are inured to it, we are not horrified to be told that the wrong hair rinse for a mother will lose both the admiration of her children and the amorous attention of her husband. But such emotionalism seems out of place when "Brand X" is identified with the destruction of mankind. Moreover, the appeal represents a level of hucksterism to which the same agency does not stoop in its commercial accounts.

On the Republican side, the 1964 advertising campaign was entrusted to a leading firm, Erwin, Wasey, Ruthrauff & Ryan. Immediately after the election, an official of the firm explained that the voters' lack of familiarity with Senator Goldwater "was but one of several problems that had to be solved in 'merchandising' him."[57] The official conceded that President Johnson's lead at the start of the campaign was probably too great for his firm to overcome even "if the problems in advertising had not existed," although he implied that the margin of defeat could have been greatly reduced. The burden of his argument was that the campaign period was too short to achieve the two objectives

---

[56]Senate Committee on Rules and Administration, *Maryland Senatorial Election of 1950*, 82d Cong., 1st Sess., p. 9.
[57]*The New York Times*, November 5, 1964.

necessary to win the undecided vote. First, the agency had to introduce Senator Goldwater to the voters (much, presumably, as a Mr. Clean is unveiled—a full-blown personality with no past and therefore perfectly adjusted to today's market); second, it had to tell the voters what he stood for. Capsuling these objectives into a short period produced what the adman called a confusion of "product claims."

The confusion of "product claims" was brought into the open when Senator Goldwater repudiated a film prepared by some of his admen and refused to let it be shown because of its blatant racism. (The film attempted to link President Johnson with race riots, nudism, pornography, and other symbols of "moral decay.") Such incidents as this may explain the complaint of an unidentified adman to *The New York Times* that the agency was "unable to effectively choose and then capitalize on campaign issues."[58] This complaint suggests that the parties have not turned all the issues of the campaign over to their public relations firms. The same executive's additional complaint could be turned around. He says, "Further, members of a party's national committee generally do not understand or appreciate the purpose or nature of advertising." Could it be that the advertising moguls do not fully understand or appreciate the purpose or nature of politics?

Public Relations Tactics in Politics

Some of the finest exemplars of political campaigning as a business were found in the late 1950s in the California public relations firm of Clem Whitaker and his wife, Leone Baxter, who said that they operated "just as we would if we were merchandising *commodities* instead of selling *men* and *measures*."[59] Although it would be unwarranted to speak of even the most efficient firm as the "cause" of victory, Whitaker and Baxter's record of success in about 90 per cent of their efforts for a variety of candidates and causes was highly impressive. Kelley identifies the principles that guided this firm's campaign tactics, and the most significant feature he describes is the systematic fashion in which the tactics were applied, in conformity with a meticulously planned campaign blueprint and budget.

The first principle is to conduct an offensive campaign, for this enables the firm to choose the battleground and to define the issues. In conducting a three-and-one-half-year campaign for the American Medical Association against President Truman's proposed compulsory health insurance, for example, Whitaker and Baxter posed the issue as "Socialized Medicine" versus "The Voluntary Way."

Four devices are used to give a campaign its aggressive tone. First, complicated issues are reduced to simple themes or slogans—"Political Medicine is Bad Medicine!" "The Voluntary Way is the American Way!" Second, the firm uses showmanship, employing "the appeal that is beyond politics," the appeal that can compete with comics, variety shows, and murder mysteries for the voter's attention. "There are thousands of experts bidding for every man's attention—and every man has a limited amount of leisure," Whitaker warned. But, he added, "Most every American loves *contest*. . . . So you can interest

[58]*Ibid.*
[59]Quoted in Kelley, *Professional Public Relations*, p. 39.

him if you put on a fight! No matter what you fight for, *fight for something....* Then, too, most every American likes to be entertained.... So if you can't fight, PUT ON A SHOW!"[60] Third, a "gimmick," some unusual phrase or trick, is used to command attention and "fix" a name or preference in the lazy voter's mind. Jon Jonkel employed this device effectively in his Maryland campaign by broadcasting spot announcements that droned, in the fashion of the familiar Bromo-Seltzer advertisements, "Be for Butler, be for Butler, be for Butler, be for Butler, be for Butler, be for Butler, be for John Marshall Butler, Republican candidate for United States Senator." Fourth, proper "pacing" is used to insure that the campaign will build to a climax just before the election. About 75 per cent of the total funds are spent during the last three weeks of the campaign.

A second general principle is to adapt the themes of the campaign to market conditions of time, place, and audience. Aware that society is made up of many groups, the public relations firm recognizes that no one group affiliation will dominate the average voter's preferences. If he cannot be reached as a veteran, perhaps he can be reached as a father; if not as a Methodist, perhaps as a businessman. If the various group identifications of, say, a union member, can be stimulated more than his opposing loyalties, he may even be induced to support an "antiunion" position. Public opinion polls are an invaluable aid in planning just the right appeal for different groups and places. Indeed, more empirical research in political behavior is probably being conducted by commercial agencies than by the universities.

A third general principle is to distribute the correct ideas with the maximum effect on the consumer-voter. The well-organized firm has its own apparatus for distributing pamphlets, films, and similar materials. But it is keenly interested in communicating its message through the "normal" and presumably unbiased channels of communication as well. The extent and success of its efforts to do so are sug-

"*Grin and Bear It*" by George Lichty; reprinted by permission of Publishers-Hall Syndicate.

"These days, people haven't got time for long-winded, involved programs . . . Just write me a snappy political plank that fits a bumper sticker!"

[60]*Ibid.*, p. 50 (emphasis Whitaker's).

gested by the conclusion of *Fortune* magazine that almost half the contents of the better newspapers come from publicity releases.[61] Public relations experts may accomplish more by furnishing "news," by alerting editors to the importance of a problem, and by mobilizing natural allies than they can by direct propaganda.

H. Walton Cloke, coordinator of public relations for the Henry J. Kaiser Corporation, has explained how his company improved its public relations program in Washington by a comprehensive information campaign.[62] The firm discovered that the fifteen states and territories in which it had plants or other facilities were represented by sixty-eight senators, congressmen, and territorial delegates in Washington. So it decided to "tell the Kaiser Story to this Congressional group." It printed a colorful brochure to celebrate its fortieth anniversary and gave copies to the congressional group in addition to 100,000 employees, stockholders, and customers. It provided each congressman with manuals to inform him on such matters as what Kaiser plants were in his district, the number of employees, and the annual payroll; it also provided him with data on the overall corporate structure, such as a "who's who" in management, the number of stockholders, the net earnings, and the net sales. The company put the congressmen on its mailing list for all news releases about company activities, and invited them on plant tours so that they could see for themselves how much Kaiser plants meant to their constituents. Finally, it held a public relations conference in Washington, attended by the company's top managers, and invited the sixty-eight congressmen to join in discussions of government programs affecting Kaiser business. The conference was also used to bring in several cabinet officers to talk over the general relationship of government and business. "In addition, several government public relations men told the group how to work with government agencies and departments to the mutual public relations advantage of all concerned."

How extensively are such public relations tactics applied to politics? Beyond doubt, both pressure groups and political parties are increasingly relying on the public relations approach. Its influence even on the presidency is unmistakable. During President Eisenhower's first year in office, the gentleman who was chosen to merchandise his policies explained, "We all suddenly realized we were busy manufacturing a product down here, but nobody was selling it."[63] In this environment, it was not surprising that, in 1955, an unprecedented decision was made: a cabinet meeting, which never before had been opened to the public, would be televised. Given this decision, it is even less surprising that the firm of Batten, Barton, Durstine, and Osborn, with its experience in handling such hit programs as the Jack Benny show, was put in charge of the production. The day after the premiere performance, defenders of the company were insisting it was the best show they had produced, and *The New York Times* impartially reported the meeting both on its front page and in its television section. The television reviewer was the more critical, suggesting that this might be good politics, but it was poor theater.

---

[61]"Business Is Still in Trouble," *Fortune* (May, 1949), 69.
[62]Allen H. Center (ed.), *Public Relations Ideas in Action* (New York: McGraw-Hill Book Company, 1957), pp. 269–272.
[63]Kelley, *Professional Public Relations*, p. 2.

President Eisenhower introduced the practice of having press conferences televised "on tape" for later editing and public release. President Kennedy, fresh from his success in live TV debates with Nixon, went all the way and permitted live television coverage of press conferences. Cautious observers were fearful that an ill-advised impromptu remark might jeopardize the national interest, but the presumably greater audience interest in live coverage outweighed the risk of such dangers. President Johnson appears more at home in small, informal gatherings, but the need for maximum "exposure" has led him to continue live coverage of press conferences.

Shall Madison Avenue Inherit the Earth?

What does commercialized, public relations politics portend for American democracy? While it is too early to answer precisely, we can be sure that, like any new route to political power, it will work to the advantage of some groups and to the disadvantage of others. At first, the advantage appeared to lie with the Republican Party and with business groups. The old machine politics of urban areas probably worked to the advantage of the Democrats, because it was built on skills in meeting the needs of their "natural" base of support—the immigrant, the uneducated, the poor, and the underprivileged. The politics of public relations depends on quite different skills—the manipulation of attitudes among great masses of voters. The Republicans got a head start in using modern public relations techniques, partly because of their closer identification with the business community and the "businesslike" approach, and partly because they were the "outs," and more in need of a new approach, when the mass media came into their own. But the Democrats seem to have closed the gap. Their public relations counsel insisted that he conceived the idea of the first "saturation" television campaign through spot announcements before it was hit on by the firm hired by the Republicans. If the new politics does work to the long-run advantage of the Republicans, then, it will only be because the Republican Party is more successful in raising funds for this expensive type of campaigning. The ability of the Democrats to match Republican outlays in 1960 and 1964, however, indicates that the Republican advantage may have already disappeared.

Forgetting for a moment the effect on political parties, we may credit public relations in politics with three positive gains. First, it serves to increase popular participation in elections. Since the power of the political boss was rooted in his ability to deliver a regular vote from an organized following, he preferred a low turnout from the general public. He could always count on the "party faithful" to vote, and the larger their proportion of the total vote the more secure was the boss's position. The public relations expert, however, deals with unseen and unknown audiences to whom he has rendered no personal favors and with whom he has no personal contact. His interest is served by mass appeals that stimulate the greatest possible number to vote.

A second gain from public relations is that it tends to nationalize American politics. The political leaders of the old school, dependent on personal ties, had little interest in broad national questions. The national public relations firm, however, with its centralized and standardized approach, necessarily concentrates on broader concerns. It can hardly promise to deliver a bucket of coal, but it can promise to "deliver" a new foreign policy. Since the cost of a professional public relations approach renders it less feasible at the local level than at the national level, public relations should tend to decrease the localism that plagues American parties. If a candidate for Congress uses the advertising kit of his party's national headquarters during his campaign, he may find it embarrassing to depart from the national party line after he has been elected.

A third gain is that public relations tends to emphasize issues. The political boss was seldom interested in issues, especially not national issues. But the public relations expert is. As Stanley Kelley describes it:

> Jon Jonkel, in the Maryland senatorial campaign of 1950, had little in the way of a local organization on which to depend. In his strategy, he gave real importance to an issue and the power of that issue to determine an election's outcome. This much must be granted, whatever one may think about the way the issue was framed or the intellectual integrity of Jonkel's arguments. If there is one belief that the public relations man holds sincerely, it is his belief that words can shape men's actions and mold men's minds. He is serious about talk.[64]

Both pressure groups and political parties have become somewhat more issue-oriented as a result of the shift to public relations techniques. "This has been the chief motive back of the vast expansion of public relations programs by businesses, industries, and interest groups: to control government policy by standardizing and enforcing public opinion."[65]

Despite these apparent advantages, the threats represented by public relations politics are considerable. To begin with, access to public relations skills is highly unequal; if an individual or a group is unable to invest large sums of money in public relations, that individual or group is effectively excluded from the public "debate." Financial limitations are especially important in campaigns for nomination through primary elections; without competing party labels to help voters evaluate candidates, the citizen may be more easily influenced by propaganda through the mass media. There is no "right to counsel" in facing what Madison Avenue likes to call "the bar of public opinion."

Furthermore, public relations alters the nature of public debate. Discussion and examination of issues are replaced by slogans, capsule notions, and "gimmicks" designed to standardize opinions. The potential voter is viewed as a victim of prejudices and intellectual laziness, uninterested in politics or in serious ideas. "Fortunately," one public relations expert submits, "the sincere and gifted politician is able, by the instrument of propaganda, to mold and form the will of the people."[66]

When Americans are faced with a problem, they usually turn to education as the route to secular salvation. Certainly a citizenry that was educated to

---

[64]*Professional Public Relations*, pp. 217–218.
[65]*Ibid.*, p. 218.
[66]Edward L. Bernays, *Propaganda* (New York: Horace Liveright, 1928), p. 92.

examine ideas with critical discrimination could force the public relations expert to give political propaganda more rational content. The high sensitivity of this profession to market conditions suggests that it would quickly modify its appeals if the voters failed to respond to the current offerings. In more practical terms, however, the solution probably lies in achieving more equitable access to the agencies able to conduct large-scale public relations campaigns. Better organization of more groups, and some form of financing party and pressure-group campaigns from membership dues or contributions, appear to be the most feasible way of assimilating modern public relations into democratic politics.

From Unofficial to Official Input Activities

To this point, we have been talking about the input activities of the political system solely in terms of unofficial agencies—the small groups and large organizations (from the family to the mass media of communication), political parties, pressure groups, and public relations organizations through which political opinions are formed and expressed. All these unofficial agencies help to create the demands, supports, and apathy that constitute the inputs of the political system. And, in addition to their particular functions, each is involved in some degree in the broad functions of political socialization, interest identification, and leadership selection.

These are functions that, we have argued, are carried out in one way or another in every political system. But the functions of leadership selection and interest identification cannot be understood, in the American context, without also including the official electoral system in the analysis. The demands, supports, and apathy that make up the input activities of American politics are authoritatively represented through the electoral system, which we describe in the next chapter.

THE ELECTORAL

SYSTEM 9

The American system for choosing public officials is, by world standards, an unpopular one. Only about a quarter of the nations of the world hold elections in which the adult population freely chooses among competing candidates.[1] Heredity is the route to public office on the island monarchy of Tonga, the military coup is most common in Argentina, and choice by the Communist party followed by ratification (without opposition) at the polls is the practice in the Soviet Union. Although Americans regard competitive elections as the "natural" way to decide who will manage public affairs, the system is a relatively recent innovation which is not so widespread as people tend to suppose.[2]

The Electoral System as an Official Agency of Government

Elections are a conspicuous and important part of American politics. The Constitution emphasizes output functions so heavily, however, that we tend to overlook its official recognition of this input function common in one form or another to all political systems. Rules and policies cannot make and enforce themselves; every political system must somehow provide for the selection of those who will wield the official power of government. Although it is well-nigh inconceivable that the Constitution would have neglected procedures for selecting leaders, had this been the case, informal procedures would have been developed out of necessity. In fact, the Constitution only roughly sketches the outlines of the leadership selection process, and most of the crucial authoritative decisions have fallen to unofficial agencies. But in elections no less than in law-making, the formal decisions are made by official agencies of government. Accordingly, the Constitution stipulates who is eligible for public office and provides means for choosing among those eligible, the two essential features of any election system.

[1] See Robert A. Dahl (ed.), *Political Oppositions in Western Democracies* (New Haven: Yale University Press, 1966), p. xi.
[2] We talked about the underpinnings of this system in Chapters 2 and 3; here we are concerned with its operation.

Constitutional Provisions on Political Recruitment

The constitutional provisions on eligibility for national office are quite simple. Representatives must be at least twenty-five-years old, to have been U.S. citizens for at least seven years, and to be inhabitants of the states in which they are elected. For senators, the age and citizenship figures are raised to thirty and nine, with the same residence requirement. The President must be at least thirty-five and a natural-born citizen who has resided in the United States for at least fourteen years. No eligibility requirements are provided for judges and other national officials appointed by the President. Such minor restrictions on eligibility represent an opposite extreme from the restrictions of some systems. Where no one is eligible for an office except a single person—the eldest male in a particular family, for example—the office may be said to be officially *assigned;* where many people are eligible, as in the United States, official status is based on *achievement* rather than official assignment.[3]

If eligibility requirements are simple, the machinery for choosing national officials from the many who are eligible is extremely elaborate. The Constitution does not include detailed procedures: the system for choosing congressmen is left to the states, subject to alteration by Congress; election of the President must be by electors, again selected as the state legislatures may provide; judges and other officers of the United States are appointed by the President with the advice and consent of the Senate. The varying details of these procedures will be discussed later. Here we need only note that they insure a different constituency for every branch of the government. The Constitution also provides different terms of office for members of each branch—two years for representatives, six for senators, four for the President, and during "good behavior" for judges.

Nominating procedures are not mentioned in the Constitution, except for the provision that the President "shall *nominate,* and by and with the advice and consent of the Senate, shall appoint" Supreme Court justices and certain other national officials. Again, diversity is assured, since the President is not given the power to appoint either his own successor or congressmen. Although nominating procedures for these elected officials have developed outside the written Constitution, the procedures are clearly a part of our official constitutional system. The Supreme Court has recognized the official character of the nominating system as well as of the final system of elections: "A primary election which involves a necessary step in the choice of candidates for election as representatives in Congress, and which . . . controls that choice, is an election within the meaning of the constitutional provision and is subject to congressional regulation as to the manner of holding it."[4]

---

[3] As we shall see below, informal requirements add considerably to the restrictions on eligibility—women, for example, have been effectively if informally banned from the presidency.

[4] *United States* v. *Classic,* 313 U.S. 299 (1941).

Who Performs the Authoritative Decision-Making Roles?

The selection of public leaders is clearly a central function of all political systems. "Man's rise to political power is, after all, one description of the political system; the classical definitions of government, of monarchy, oligarchy, and democracy, hinge upon the manner in which the political leaders are chosen."[5] But who are the decision-makers concerning this vital question of who shall rule?

If we try to answer this question by looking for the people in public office who make legal decisions or pronouncements regarding who shall hold office, we come up with bizarre results. For members of Congress, we would conclude that the authoritative decisions are made by the minor election officials who supervise the counting of votes and report the results from each county, and by the state officials who receive their reports, total the votes, and issue certificates of election to the winners. For the President and Vice-President, our study would focus on the members of the electoral college in each state and the President of the United States Senate, to whom the electoral votes are delivered for official counting. These are about the only public officials who take part in the legalities of selecting national leaders.

To avoid the absurdity of such a focus, we need to locate election activity within the broad concept of the political system. First, remember that the "charmed circle" in our model of a political system represents authoritative decision-making *activities*, not people, offices, or titles. And the activity may or may not be performed by someone who holds a public office—the authoritative force of the activity, not the person who performs it, places it at the core of the political system. Second, we need to recall our earlier assertion that political activities tend to structure themselves in specialized political roles. In the division of labor that characterizes all political systems, some roles include routine chores and others carry great discretionary power.

By role we mean "the ways of behaving which are expected of any individual who occupies a certain position."[6] To say that certain behavior is "expected" of anyone who occupies a particular position is to say both that this behavior probably *will* occur and that it *ought* to occur.[7] When the behavior does not correspond to expectations, both our sense of understanding the political system and our sense of what is proper are affronted. Accordingly, every role is composed both of predictions and of norms, i.e., of beliefs about what will be done and of attitudes about what *ought* to be done by people in particular positions.

---

[5] Joseph A. Schlesinger, *Ambition and Politics: Political Careers in the United States* (Chicago: Rand McNally & Co., 1966), p. vii.

[6] Theodore M. Newcomb, *Social Psychology* (New York: The Dryden Press, 1950), p. 280. The seminal work on role theory is George Herbert Mead, *Mind, Self and Society* (Chicago: The University of Chicago Press, 1934). Richard Fenno, *The Power of the Purse: Appropriations Politics in Congress* (Boston: Little, Brown and Company, 1966) systematically applies the concept of role in analyzing the appropriation process in Congress and we are here following Professor Fenno's lead.

[7] The idea of role is thus normative in both the statistical and the ethical senses of the term. See John C. Wahlke *et al.*, *The Legislative System: Explanations in Legislative Behavior* (New York: John Wiley & Sons, Inc., 1962), n. 8, pp. 8–9.

The role expectations associated with the official position of election judge call for facilitating the act of voting by those who are eligible and for ratifying the results. In both these activities, the official is expected to perform more as a clerk than as a decision-maker; his activity is rigorously controlled both by state laws and by community sentiment so as to prevent any effort on his part to influence the election outcome. Hence he is almost totally (and wisely) ignored in the vast literature on electoral behavior. On the rare occasions when election officials are charged with deviating from this restricted role, a scandal ensues. Clearly, these official actors perform routine chores that permit the authoritative decisions of others to be realized.

Members of the electoral college are in a different legal position. Article II of the Constitution states that the President and Vice-President "shall . . .be elected as follows: Each State shall appoint, in such manner as the legislature thereof may direct, a number of Electors, equal to the whole number of Senators and Representatives to which the State may be entitled in the Congress . . . ." Amendment XII then specifies, "The Electors shall meet in their respective states and vote by ballot for President and Vice President . . . ." Nothing in the formal Constitution would prevent the electors from serving as the key decision-makers in the selection of the President. But the informal definition of the role of elector has reduced him, too, to a mere recording agent. So miniscule is his part in the electoral process that a recent volume on presidential elections contains not a single reference to the role of the individual elector.[8]

Where, then, do we find the activities governing who will hold national office? The crucial, if obvious, decisions concern: (1) Who will be the candidates for each party's nomination? (2) Who will be nominated? (3) Who will be elected? As we go from the first to the third decision, the number of actors involved in the decisions increases from hundreds to thousands to millions. However much it may sound like Fourth of July oratory, we must conclude that the authoritative decision-making on the choice of rulers in the United States involves all its many millions of voters.

The flexibility of the circle of authoritative decision-making activity is thus demonstrated most vividly in the electoral system. Each voter has, of course, only a minute fraction of the decision-making authority. But on election day, the normally small circle of authoritative decision-making is expanded fantastically to include every voter. In the prior decisions concerning who shall run, a smaller number of party leaders perform more specialized and individually weighty roles. In this chapter we shall accordingly focus first on the voters, second on nominations, third on the election process, and finally on the general place of elections in the political system.

Formal Voting Requirements

In our discussion of public opinion (Chapter 6), we implied that nonvoting is mostly voluntary—lack of interest accounts for some 75 per cent of all failures to vote. But we must remember that certain legal qualifications have to be met

---

[8] The book, by Nelson W. Polsby and Aaron B. Wildavsky, is *Presidential Elections: Strategies of American Electoral Politics* (New York: Charles Scribner's Sons, 1964).

THE ELECTORAL SYSTEM

before a citizen can enjoy the franchise, regardless of how interested he is in politics. Failure to meet residence requirements alone prevented 8 million citizens from voting in 1960.[9] The seemingly innocuous requirements that Americans must take the initiative in registering to vote, that they must often do this long before the election, and that elections are held on working days, help to account for the fact that less than half of all eligible citizens vote in congressional elections and less than two-thirds in presidential elections. In Italy and Germany, where registration is automatic and elections are held on Sunday, voter turnout has been much higher since World War II: over 92 per cent in Italy and from 78.5 per cent to 87.8 per cent in West Germany.[10] Clearly, we cannot understand voting behavior without taking into account official controls over elections.

[9]President's Commission on Registration and Voting Participation, *Report on Registration and Voting Participation*, November, 1963, p. 13.
[10]*Ibid.*, p. 8. In Italy the polls are open not only on Sunday but on Monday until noon.

"It's exactly the kind of life I've always wanted, Yvette; it's just that I feel I ought to be home in Canton, Ohio, voting."

Drawing by Ed Fisher;
© 1964 *The Saturday Review*.

The Extension of Voting Rights

In addition to leaving the manner of choosing presidential electors to the state legislatures, the United States Constitution provides that representatives and senators shall be chosen by those voters in each state who are qualified to vote for "the most numerous branch of the State legislature." Legal requirements for voting in all elections are thus established by the states, subject to certain limitations imposed by the Constitution. Since the Constitution adopts state suffrage requirements for national elections, voting qualifications have varied from state to state as well as from time to time. And yet the history of suffrage in the United States has been one of steady expansion, until in the twentieth century virtually universal adult suffrage has been achieved.

The first general restrictions on voting to be eliminated were religious qualifications. These qualifications prevailed in the original New England colonies, but had been generally replaced by economic restrictions before the Revolution. Somewhat slower to fall were property-holding and taxpaying barriers, but even they could not withstand the assaults of the Jacksonian Democrats; by the time of the Civil War practically all free men could vote. Today the only vestiges of the idea that men devoid of property are necessarily "devoid of principles," and that only citizens with a "stake in society" should have the right to vote, are found in provisions that restrict the vote in local bond elections to those who pay property taxes.

A third arbitrary limitation on suffrage—the denial of the vote on grounds of race or color—has resisted attacks more stubbornly. Although the Fifteenth Amendment, adopted shortly after the Civil War, forbade the states to deny the vote "on account of race, color, or previous condition of servitude," this prohibition was effectively nullified in the southern states by a variety of devices, legal and illegal, until well into the twentieth century.

The basic subterfuge for about the first forty years of this century was the device of the "white primary." By restricting membership in the Democratic Party and thereby participation in its primary elections to white voters, this device effectively excluded Negroes from influencing the choice of candidates in areas where the Democratic nominee always won the general election. The Fifteenth Amendment outlawed denial of the vote by *states*, but the Supreme Court viewed the Democratic Party as a private association to which state election regulations did not apply. Consequently, the white primary seemed a perfect weapon for the guardians of "white supremacy."

In the 1944 case of *Smith v. Allwright*, however, the Supreme Court took a closer look at the situation and decided that the white primary was an integral part of a continuous process for choosing public officials.[11] Since the primary was endorsed and enforced by the state—for example, the state certified party nominees for inclusion on the general election ballot—the Court ruled that the action of the Democratic Party constituted state action in violation of the Fifteenth Amendment. When South Carolina tried to evade this decision by repealing all laws dealing with primaries, U.S. District Judge J. Waites Waring

---

[11]*Smith* v. *Allwright*, 321 U.S. 649 (1944). In *U.S.* v. *Classic*, 313 U.S. 299 (1941), the Supreme Court had already determined that, "where the primary is by law made an integral part of the election machinery," Congress has constitutional power to regulate primary as well as general elections.

ruled that the plan was unconstitutional on the ground that the choice of public officals was still controlled through the primary. "It is time," said Judge Waring, himself a native of South Carolina, "for South Carolina to rejoin the Union."[12]

The effects of this Court decision provide us with an interesting commentary on the old saw, "You can't legislate prejudice out of existence." Official decisions actually do not try to regulate prejudice; they attempt to control overt acts. And illegal *behavior*, as distinguished from the attitudes that prompt such behavior, is susceptible to official modification. The estimated number of Negro voters in the South was 250,000 in 1940; the number had doubled within two years after the Supreme Court decision, in 1960 it had reached 1,414,052, and by 1964 it had climbed to 2,164,000.[13] Since 1945, Negroes have been elected to scores of offices in the South, from city commissioner to state legislator, and every southern state has had at least one Negro in elective office.[14] As the maps in Figure 9–1 indicate, the proportion of voting-age Negroes who were registered in 1964 exceeded one-third in every southern state except Mississippi, Alabama, and Louisiana. This represents impressive increases over the level of Negro registration in 1960, when the proportion exceeded one-third in only one state (Tennessee).

The lower map in Fig. 9–1 reflects the dramatic story of the impact of the southern Negro vote in the presidential election of 1964. The increased Negro vote, coupled with the near-unanimous support of Negroes for President Johnson, was clearly responsible for the President's margin of victory in four states (Arkansas, Tennessee, Virginia, and Florida). Indeed, Texas is the only southern state that the President could have carried comfortably without the votes of Negroes. These figures indicate that the last few years have witnessed truly giant strides toward the effectuation of the Fifteenth Amendment.

Much of this progress has been due to the Civil Rights Acts of 1957, 1960, 1964, and 1965, which all had as their major goal the elimination of racial discrimination in voter registration in the southern states. These laws demonstrate that, if legislation cannot eliminate prejudice, it can greatly reduce prejudicial behavior. The first Act empowered the Attorney General of the United States to seek court injunctions when an individual is illegally deprived of his right to vote, and the second provided for the appointment of federal "referees" to register potential voters when the courts find a "pattern or practice" of depriving Negroes of their rightful vote in a specified area. The 1964 Act was much stronger. It made the unequal administration of voting

[12]*Elmore* v. *Rice*, 72 F. Supp. 528 (1947).

[13]These estimates are only rough approximations because of the decentralized character of registration records. They are based on: Henry Lee Moon, "The Negro Vote in the South: 1952," *The Nation*, September 27, 1952, 245–248; Margaret Price, *The Negro and the Ballot in the South* (Atlanta: Southern Regional Council, 1959); *Report of the United States Commission on Civil Rights; 1959* (Washington, D.C.: U.S. Government Printing Office, 1959); and *1961 Commission on Civil Rights Report: Voting*, Book 1 (Washington, D.C.: U.S. Government Printing Office, 1961); and *The New York Times*, November 22, 1964.

[14]By "the South" we mean the eleven states of the Confederacy. Mississippi can be included in this statement only because one of its cities, Mound Bayou, has an exclusively Negro population.

THE GROWING IMPORTANCE OF THE NEGRO VOTE IN THE SOUTH

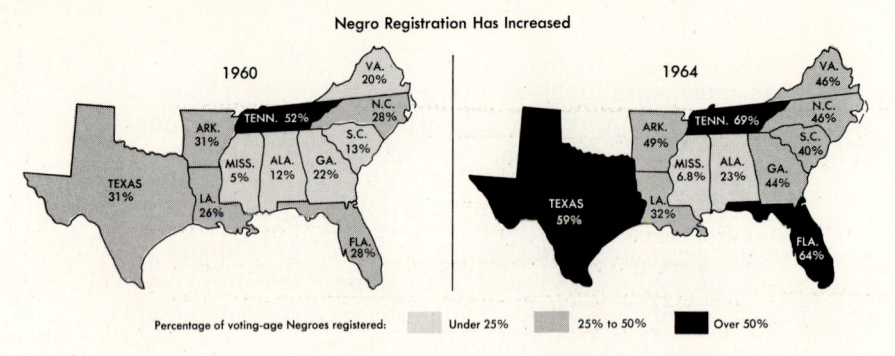

Negro Registration Has Increased

1960
- VA. 20%
- TENN. 52%
- N.C. 28%
- ARK. 31%
- S.C. 13%
- MISS. 5%
- ALA. 12%
- GA. 22%
- TEXAS 31%
- LA. 26%
- FLA. 28%

1964
- VA. 46%
- TENN. 69%
- N.C. 46%
- ARK. 49%
- S.C. 40%
- MISS. 6.8%
- ALA. 23%
- GA. 44%
- TEXAS 59%
- LA. 32%
- FLA. 64%

Percentage of voting-age Negroes registered: Under 25% | 25% to 50% | Over 50%

Negro Vote Was a Major Factor in Johnson Total

- ARK.: 67,600 / 65,400
- TENN.: 165,200 / 126,000
- VA.: 166,600 / 77,000
- N.C.: 168,400 / 173,900
- TEXAS: 521,000 / 247,000
- FLA.: 211,800 / 37,800

Carried by Johnson | Negro vote | Carried by Goldwater | Johnson plurality

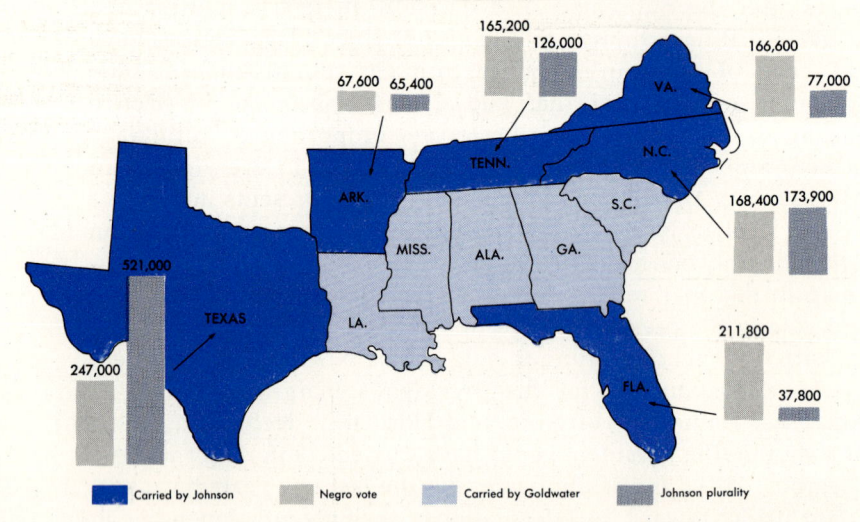

Maps reproduced from *The New York Times*, November 22, 1964.

Figure 9–1 The per cent of Negroes registered was lowest—under 45—in the five states carried by Goldwater. Johnson's name was not on the ballot in Alabama. In four of the six states won by Johnson the Negro vote, almost 100 per cent of which was cast for the President, exceeded his plurality. Figures are from the Southern Regional Council.

requirements a federal crime, prohibited the denial of the right to vote on the basis of minor errors in the voting application, required that all literacy tests be given in writing and that applicants be able to examine these tests after taking them, and stated that a sixth-grade education must be considered proof of literacy. But political leaders outside the South regarded these efforts as inadequate. In 1965, a new Voting Rights Act

(1) suspended literacy tests and similar devices in all states or counties in which less than 50 per cent of the voting-age registrants were registered to vote on November 1, 1964;

(2) provided for the appointment of federal examiners to register persons in these areas to vote;

(3) directed the Attorney General "forthwith" to institute court action against the enforcement of poll taxes as a prerequisite to voting in state and local elections.

By July of 1967, federal examiners had been sent into sixty counties. In the five states principally affected by the Act—Alabama, Georgia, Louisiana, Mississippi, and South Carolina—Negro voter registration had reached 1.25 million, an increase of 78 per cent in the first twenty-two months after passage of the Act. The proportion of adult Negroes registered to vote in these states had increased from 28 to 52 per cent.[15]

The fourth and last general barrier to voting—the denial of the vote to women—was not broken down completely until the Nineteenth Amendment was adopted in 1920. The struggle for female suffrage, antedating the Civil War and closely linked to the abolition movement, had been long and ably fought. Success had been achieved in fifteen states before the federal amendment was adopted. The extremist arguments on both sides now seem amusingly anachronistic, for women have neither been "unsexed" and degraded by political participation, nor have they purified our politics by their loftier morals. According to leaders of the women's suffrage movement, however, powerful interests opposed the extension of the franchise for more practical reasons. As one of the official historians of the crusade put it, two "supreme influences were implacably opposed to suffrage for women; the corporations because it would vastly increase the votes of the working classes, the liquor interests because they were fully aware of the hostility of women to their business and everything connected with it."[16] As things turned out, the first of these groups need not have worried: Women vote less frequently than men, and the lower their economic class the less inclination they show to vote.[17] As a result, women's suffrage has probably worked to the advantage of corporate interests in politics. The liquor interests, on the other hand, did have reason to worry, for in all countries where votes can be compared in terms of sex, women appear to favor more stringent regulation or curtailment of the liquor industry than do men.

Once these general barriers had been eliminated, the right to vote in the United States became for all practical purposes universal. True, three general requirements must still be met in all states before one can claim the right to vote, but none of these is an arbitrary denial of the franchise to a whole class of the adult population.

First, voters must be citizens of the United States. Aliens were at one time

---

[15]The two paragraphs above are from Donald R. Matthews and James W. Prothro, *Negroes and the New Southern Politics* (New York: Harcourt, Brace & World, Inc., 1966), pp. 18–20; and from a release from the Department of Justice, July 6, 1967.

[16]Ida Husted Harper, *The History of Woman Suffrage* (New York: National American Woman Suffrage Association, 1922), V, xviii. Quoted in V. O. Key, Jr., *Politics, Parties, and Pressure Groups* (New York: Thomas Y. Crowell Company, 1964), 5th ed., p. 614.

[17]Angus Campbell and Homer C. Cooper, *Group Differences in Attitudes and Votes* (Ann Arbor: Survey Research Center, Institute for Social Research, University of Michigan, 1956), p. 20.

permitted to vote in twenty-two states and territories; but in 1926, the last holdout, Arkansas, joined the other states to make citizenship a universal requirement.

Second, voters must be a certain age—twenty-one years in all but four states. Georgia and Kentucky have reduced the minimum to eighteen, Alaska to nineteen, and Hawaii to twenty. Although President Eisenhower recommended a constitutional amendment in 1954 to reduce the voting age to eighteen in all states, Congress did not respond to the recommendation. Again in 1963 President Kennedy's Commission on Registration and Voting Participation recommended that the states themselves consider reducing the required voting age to eighteen. Because those in their twenties are less interested in politics and are less likely to vote than their elders, these proposals are not supported by intense demands from young voters. But the President's Commission advanced the interesting hypothesis that the low participation of younger citizens stems from the fact that by the time they become twenty-one "many young people are so far removed from the stimulation of the educational process that their interest in public affairs has waned."[18] This theory assumes that people *younger* than twenty-one, more of whom are still in school, are (or would become) more interested in politics if this interest did not suffer from a lack of exercise in the late 'teens—a plausible hypothesis, but one whose validation depends on future research.

The third general voting requirement is that voters must have resided for a specified period in one state, one county, and one voting district. Although the periods required vary considerably, they are generally one year, ninety days (or even less), and thirty days (or less), respectively. The most liberal residence requirements appear in the nine states that require six months residence in the state and thirty days (or less) in the county and district.[19] At the other extreme, Mississippi sets the periods at two years in the state and one year in the district.[20] Since certain groups—fruitpickers, southern Negroes, and professors, for example—are more migratory than others—doctors, and lawyers, for example—residence requirements in some measure serve as property qualifications.

The Census Bureau reports that more than 20 million adults changed residence in 1961; 13 million of these moved within a single county, but 6 million moved across county lines, and 3 million across state lines. With this high rate of mobility, *any* residence requirement is certain to keep sizeable numbers from voting. Recognition of this problem has grown to the point where, since 1953, fifteen states have modified their residence requirements to permit new residents to vote in presidential elections, and four others permit absentee voting in presidential elections by former residents who are not yet qualified to vote in their new state.[21]

In addition to these general requirements, there are several bases of disqualification that vary from state to state. Such people as the insane, prison inmates, and those convicted of specified crimes are frequently disqualified.

---

[18] *Report on Registration and Voting Participation*, 1963, p. 43.
[19] The states are Idaho, Kansas, Maine, Michigan, Minnesota, Nevada, New Hampshire, Oregon, and Wisconsin.
[20] For a complete tabulation of voting qualifications by state, see *The Book of the States, 1966–67* (Chicago: The Council of State Governments, 1966), pp. 22–23.
[21] *The Book of the States, 1966–67*, pp. 15, 22.

Until recently five southern states required the payment of an annual poll tax of one or two dollars before a citizen could vote. This requirement, generally thought to be directed against Negroes, affected enough white voters to fall into disfavor even in the South. In 1964 the ratification of the Twenty-fourth Amendment made the poll tax unconstitutional as applied to national elections. In addition, as we saw above, the Voting Rights Act of 1965 directed the Attorney General to challenge the constitutionality of state poll taxes even in state and local elections. Thus when four indigent Negroes in Virginia, with the assistance of the American Civil Liberties Union, sought an injunction against enforcement of Virginia's $1.50 poll tax (each complainant owed $5.01 in back taxes and penalties), the U.S. Solicitor General joined in the case, seeking rejection of the poll tax as unconstitutional. In 1966, the Supreme Court favorably responded to these pleas on the ground that, "once the franchise is granted to the electorate, lines may not be drawn which are inconsistent with the Equal Protection Clause of the 14th Amendment."[22] Justice Douglas, speaking for the court, held that one of the lines that may not be drawn is one which makes the "affluence of the voter" an essential factor in his right to vote.

Literacy tests are required by fifteen states. These tests were initiated in Connecticut (1855) and Massachusetts (1857) as a substitute for the property qualification, with the specific aim of denying the vote to recent immigrants. Since the ability to read is related to the ability to achieve an informed judgment, properly administered literacy tests have been less harshly criticized than poll taxes. Abuses of the literacy tests by election officials in some southern states, however, led to the provisions concerning such tests, discussed earlier, in the Civil Rights Act of 1964.

In at least some areas of all states, citizens must demonstrate that they meet the voting requirements by registering some time before the election. In small rural communities, the election officials may know all the prospective voters and their qualifications on sight. But in the big cities some form of registration is necessary to insure that voters actually meet legal requirements.

There are two systems of registration: periodic and permanent. The periodic system seems more desirable at first glance, because it should produce a "clean" list of voters at regular intervals. In practice, however, these decentralized registrations, conducted by part-time employees chosen by party stalwarts at the precinct level, may be more conducive to fraudulent and padded lists. No system is foolproof, of course, but most states now use permanent registration.

The chief advantage of permanent registration is that a small, permanent staff, appropriately supervised, develops a professional spirit that reduces the chances of fraud. And the problem of revising the voting lists can be handled on a continuing basis. Such organizations as the National Municipal League and the League of Women Voters have endorsed permanent registration. But party organizations—loath to surrender the patronage accompanying the periodic employment of registration officials in each precinct—generally oppose it.

[22]*Harper v. Virginia State Board of Elections*, 383 U.S. 663–686 (1966).

Perhaps the worst arrangement of all is the combination of permanent registration and the use of part-time political appointees to maintain the system. The combination of professional, full-time personnel and permanent (but continuously revised) registration lists appears most conducive to the fair and efficient conduct of elections.

All members of the official electoral agency do not work in harmony. The federal system lends itself to departures from general legal standards whenever the dominant elements in a given geographical area are bent on imposing deviant norms. Even in the most rural, Deep South county, however, election officials are part of a national agency. The Civil Rights Act of 1964 included specific regulations to insure that all applicants for the franchise in a county will be expected to meet the same standards and that these standards shall be reasonable.[23]

Nominating the Candidates

Over 70 million American citizens were legally eligible for election as President in 1964.[24] But in the election, the voters had an effective choice between only two people. What happened to the other 70 million or more possibilities? They were eliminated by the nominating process. If nominations take care of 99.9 per cent of the political recruitment function, they are quite evidently a major part of the electoral system.

Caucuses and Conventions

The first stage in the official election process in the United States is the nomination of candidates to represent each of the parties (or independent groups) that are seeking public office.[25] In other democracies, nominations are made informally by party organizations or caucuses. But in the United States the nomination has taken on an official and elaborate form. The basic reason for this difference is probably that American political parties are less responsible as a group for the conduct of government than are the parties in other democratic regimes. Consequently, the person who seeks office under the party label takes on greater importance as an individual.

Another contributing factor is that the reformist movement in the United States after the industrial revolution moved more in the direction of "direct democracy" through institutional reform than, as in Europe, in the direction of socialism. Official regulation of nominations by the states was begun late in the nineteenth century at the urging of reformists who were bent on democratizing every aspect of American government. This development was particularly important in the one-party states, where nominations are tantamount to elections.

[23] See Chapter 14 for a discussion of the specific provisions of the Act.
[24] This figure is only an approximation. The 1960 census reported 76,698,688 people in the United States thirty-five years of age or older. We reduced this number to account for naturalized citizens, aliens, and natural-born citizens disqualified by the fourteen-year residence requirement.
[25] Although most states permit independent candidates to secure nomination, generally by a petition signed by a given percentage of the voters, party nominees dominate. We therefore confine ourselves to the processes of nomination by political parties.

The first nominating device used by American political parties, for both national and state office, was the legislative caucus. The caucus was composed of party members in Congress (or in the legislature for state elections). But the Jacksonian Democrats denounced the caucus as an undemocratic device, and advocated the party convention as a means of insuring at least indirect nomination by the party rank and file. Although the convention came into universal use during the nineteenth century as the means of choosing nominees to state offices, it came to be associated with boss rule and domination by special interests during the Progressive Era in the twentieth century. Like the caucus before it, the convention was discarded for a more popular method of nomination. Today, representatives, senators, and most state officers are nominated by direct primary elections, and party conventions persist only in nominations for the presidency.[26]

The Direct Primary Election

The direct primary really serves as a preliminary official election. It is usually conducted under state laws, just as the subsequent general election is, and it provides the members of each party with an opportunity to take part in choosing the party's nominees. Aspirants to the United States Senate or House of Representatives, and to various state offices, secure a place on the primary ballot either by simply announcing their candidacy and paying a fee, or by presenting a petition signed by a required number of voters. The candidate for nomination may enter only his own party's primary, and in most states he must be able to demonstrate that he is actually a member of the party—by attesting that he supported its nominees in the last general election, for example.

Direct primary elections are either "closed" or "open." In the closed primary, a voter must be able to demonstrate that he is a party member, and he may vote only in the primary of his own party. The tests of party allegiance are often quite simple, involving merely an assertion of past, present, or future identification with the party—that he voted for the party nominees in the last general election, that he is a member of the party, or that he plans to vote for the candidates nominated by the party. In about half the states, however, his party affiliation is recorded at registration, and he is not permitted to vote in the primary of any other party. In the open primary, on the other hand, any qualified citizen may vote in the primary of any party. Party regulars resent the idea that nonmembers can affect the choice of party nominees and vehemently denounce the open primary as corrosive of party responsibility.

But party leaders are probably overly suspicious in thinking that staunch Democrats or Republicans will be so Machiavellian as to neglect their own party's primary in order to promote the least attractive candidate of the opposition. Few voters actually engage in such devious and subtle reasoning. From 1913 to 1959, for example, California law permitted "cross-filing," an arrangement that enabled candidates to enter both party primaries at the same time.

---

[26]Connecticut, Delaware, Indiana, Maryland, Michigan, New York, and Utah still use conventions to nominate candidates for some or all statewide offices. See *The Book of the States, 1966–67*, p. 18.

For most of this time, a large majority of successful primary candidates won the nomination of both parties. Although Democrats have far outnumbered Republicans in California since the 1930s, the Republicans had better-known "local notables" as candidates and a better press, so the practice of cross-filing worked to their advantage. A few years before cross-filing was abolished, however, the Democrats marshaled enough strength to amend the law to require that the ballot show each candidate's party identification. This seemingly trivial change—which still permitted cross-filing—almost put an end to candidates' winning both primaries: Voters were not nearly so willing to vote for the other party's candidate once they knew what his party was. The result for California was that the Democrats captured control of the governorship and both houses of the legislature for the first time in 1958. In 1959, cross-filing was abolished.[27] For us, the important point is that many voters are so ill-informed about candidates that they will vote for a well-known figure without even knowing his party affiliation. Once they do know, however, they respond to the party cue.

To what extent has the direct primary succeeded in "democratizing" party nominations? Experience suggests that primaries may have decreased organizational control, but without bringing the promised increase in popular interest and participation. Let's look first at the effect of the primary on the party hierarchy's control over nominations. In some states, the party organization endorses a slate of candidates on the primary ballot, but these "regular" candidates meet with varying success. Even where the organization is uniformly victorious, the necessity of securing the party members' approval in the primary may have already influenced the organization's choice. Where there is no official organization slate, the primary may be fought out between fairly well-defined factions within the party, or simply between individual candidates with whatever personal organizations they can manage to put together. In any case, direct control over the choice of nominees by a few powerful leaders appears less likely than it was under the convention system.

Nomination by direct primaries has decreased the extent to which a statewide organization can control nominations. But it has not brought about the selection of candidates by a broad cross-section of party members. In the first place, participation in primaries has been disappointingly low. A study of gubernatorial elections in fifteen states between 1926 and 1952 demonstrates this vividly. In a majority of the primaries, less than 30 per cent of the potential electorate voted, whereas in a majority of the general elections, over 60 per cent voted.[28] In the second place, the small number who do vote in primaries do not accurately represent the entire party following. In Massachusetts, for example, the Boston area has supplied about half the Democratic Party's primary election votes but only a third of the party's general election votes. As a result, Boston—which supplied only one out of four Democratic nominees under the convention system—came to supply over 80 per cent of the Democratic nominees under the primary system.[29]

[27]Joseph P. Harris and Leonard Rowe, *California Politics*, 2nd ed. (Stanford: Stanford University Press, 1959).
[28]The states selected were all nonsouthern. Turnout in general elections in the South is much less than elsewhere, and turnout in primaries is also no greater. V. O. Key, Jr., *American State Politics* (New York: Alfred A. Knopf, Inc., 1956), p. 135.
[29]*Ibid.*, pp. 154–156.

The Direct Primary in One-Party Politics

Nominations in two-party areas reduce the voter's choice to two candidates, but in one-party areas they actually eliminate any real choice in the general election. And the one-party system—the domination of general elections by a single party—is much more widespread in the United States than is generally realized. In talking about political parties, we classified about half the states as two-party because "the second party had won over 25 per cent of the elections" for President, United States senator, and governor. This criterion leaves room, even in two-party states, for many elections to be effectively settled by the direct primary. In the fifty-year period from 1896 to 1946, in the United States as a whole, over half the elections to the House of Representatives were won by a plurality of at least 20 per cent, which means that the winner received 60 per cent or more of the votes while his opponent mustered no more than 40 per cent.[30] Even with the close presidential race in 1960, a majority of the House seats were still won by the same large plurality. In 1966, 280 of the 435 congressional victories were by margins of 60 per cent or more.

From a functional point of view, elections are the process by which the people choose public officials, and nominations are the process by which the support of similar or allied groups is concentrated behind a candidate. In these terms, in one-party areas the primary of the major party *is* the election. What, then, constitutes the nomination in these areas? The real nomination takes place through informal bargaining in which various leaders and factions agree to support a common candidate. In some one-party states, such as Louisiana, these intraparty factions have enough continuity to resemble political parties. In other one-party states, such as Florida, nominations usually emerge from a chaotic struggle between purely personal followings.

Primary elections generally give the nomination to the candidate who receives a plurality (the largest number) of the votes. But in most one-party states a "run-off" (or "second primary") is held between the two leading candidates if neither receives a majority in the first primary. Without the primary election to give expression to political differences, the one-party system could hardly endure. In two-party states, on the other hand, the primary is much less decisive. Because the meaningful choice in two-party states occurs in general elections, the primary in these states may even be dropped altogether. Thus the few states that retain nominating conventions for statewide offices all enjoy fairly even competition between the parties.

Functions of the National Convention

Although the party convention has been replaced by the direct primary in nominations for Congress and most state offices, it remains conspicuously alive in the nomination of presidential candidates. Indeed, the national nominating conventions of the political parties are as American as baseball and hotdogs. Spectators at national conventions

---

[30]This conclusion is based on the comprehensive analysis of Cortez A. M. Ewing, *Congressional Elections, 1896–1944* (Norman: University of Oklahoma Press, 1947), pp. 328–333. Also see Malcolm Moos, *Politics, Presidents and Coattails* (Baltimore: The Johns Hopkins Press, 1952), pp. 24–29.

are usually awed, shocked, or repulsed by the noise, numbers, and hard bargaining that characterize this quadrennial political pageant. Many observers regard the circus atmosphere as inappropriate to the choice of a candidate for one of the world's most powerful positions. Defenders of the convention, on the other hand, point out that the quality of American presidents has been generally competent and occasionally truly great. Like war veterans, businessmen, and other nonpolitical conventioneers, American politicians do make a holiday of the convention, but they also manage to accomplish serious and generally successful work.

The principal function of the national convention is to nominate candidates who will serve as the party's standard-bearers in the quest for America's most prized political plum—the presidency of the United States. A second function is to create enthusiasm, both inside and outside the convention, for the party and its presidential and vice-presidential candidates. Third, the convention serves, perhaps more by the candidates it selects than by the platform it adopts, to suggest the party's position on the key issues of the day.

The selection of candidates, the creation of support, and the adoption of positions on issues are the intended consequences or the purposes of the convention. They may accordingly be called its *manifest* functions.[31] But the convention system also has latent (unintended) functions that are frequently overlooked. While the manifest functions of the convention are important primarily for the parties themselves, the latent functions are also vitally important for the political system as a whole.

Looking first at latent functions of national conventions for the parties themselves, the most important is the creation or ratification of party consensus. Through the bargains and the compromises that seem so offensive to the uninitiated, the convention serves to unite fifty state parties into a single national party, at least for the duration of the campaign. The first conventions in the early nineteenth century functioned merely to *ratify* an established consensus on who should head the ticket, and they generally failed to create party unity in support of a vice-presidential candidate. The nomination of James K. Polk as the Democratic candidate in 1844 is cited as the first case in which a convention created "an original synthesis," nominating a candidate who received no votes at all on the first ballot and uniting the party behind him.[32] From that point on, the conventions have been able to *create* as well as merely to ratify party consensus.[33]

Occasionally, the convention fails to bring about this unity, and such failures serve to spotlight the importance of this latent function. In 1948, for ex-

---

[31] As we indicated in Chapter 1, the functions of any specified unit are understood in terms of its consequences, whether intended or unintended. This distinction between intended consequences (manifest functions) and unintended consequences (latent functions) should keep us aware that both exist. Professional political scientists sometimes become so fascinated with the discovery of latent functions that they forget the importance of manifest functions. For the distinction as we employ it, see Robert K. Merton, *Social Theory and Social Structure* (New York: The Free Press of Glencoe, Inc., 1949), p. 63.

[32] Key, *Politics, Parties, and Pressure Groups*, p. 398.

[33] Republican conventions have more often achieved unity by ratifying consensus and Democratic conventions by creating consensus. Since the Civil War two-thirds of the Republican candidates for President and one-half of the Democratic candidates have been named on the first ballot. See *ibid.*, p. 425.

304

ample, the Democratic Party organizations in four southern states, embittered by President Truman's stand for a positive civil rights program, broke from the national party and presented a different candidate (J. Strom Thurmond, the States' Rights or "Dixiecratic" nominee) as the Democratic nominee in their states. The fact that dissension of this sort rarely develops is a tribute to the success of the convention in unifying the party behind a single candidate. The Republican convention of 1964 could be called dysfunctional so far as party unity is concerned. Even so, none of the major Republican leaders bolted the party to support the Democrats, and most manfully went through at least the motions of supporting Senator Goldwater.

The convention's second latent function which is important primarily to the parties is that of a ceremony or ritual in which the democratic nature of parties is celebrated. For a few days every four years, hundreds of minor figures enjoy the official right to decide on the destiny of their party. Although most members are committed to take their cues from their state or national leaders, any delegate may rise to challenge the vote as reported by his delegation's chairman. The exercise of this right, and the subsequent poll of the delegation, reaffirms the dependence of the leaders on their followers.[34]

Third, the national convention, by virtually nullifying the intent of the electoral college procedures prescribed in the Constitution, has become one of the key devices through which political parties have democratized the choice of the President. Here we see a latent function of great importance for the political system as a whole rather than simply for the parties themselves. The expectation of the Constitutional Convention that members of the electoral college would exercise independent judgment in voting for a President and Vice-President was quickly dashed by the development of political parties. And the convention has succeeded better than the party caucus in turning the electoral college into a recording device for its choices as endorsed by the electorate. Conventions as noisy gatherings of the party faithful, representing members in all the states and territories, give the party rank and file an influence that would have horrified the more genteel among the Founding Fathers, who recoiled at the thought of such turbulent "mob action."

The basic nature of our national party system is a fourth indirect consequence of the national convention. V. O. Key went so far as to imply that our national system of party government itself is a direct function of the national convention: "When the national convention was contrived to designate presidential nominees, viable national party came into existence."[35] This is probably too strong a statement, as a subsequent comment by Key himself suggests. "Without [the national convention] or some equivalent institution party government for the nation as a whole could scarcely exist." The crucial phrase here is "or some

[34]In order to prevent TV-conscious delegates from delaying proceedings to get "on camera," both major parties have ruled that the poll of delegations may take place while the work of the convention proceeds. See Paul T. David, Ralph M. Goodman, and Richard C. Bain, *The Politics of National Party Conventions* (Washington, D.C.: The Brookings Institution, 1960), p. 388.
[35]Key, *Politics, Parties, and Pressure Groups*, p. 431.

equivalent institution"—other nations without national nominating conventions have national party systems. Without this particular nominating device, we would probably also have developed some equivalent. If this line of reasoning is correct, the national nominating convention is a sufficient but not a necessary condition of national parties.

Whether necessary to the system or not, our quadrennial conventions for nominating presidential candidates have done much to shape the nature of our party system. For one thing, the national convention includes a broader base of members—and therefore of potential candidates—than the congressional caucus. Members of the losing party in congressional races would go unrepresented in a congressional caucus, but their districts are represented in the national convention. During the period when the Democrats nominated Roosevelt, Truman, and Stevenson, Southerners held as many as 45 per cent of the Democratic seats in the Senate and 50 per cent of those in the House, but they got only 25 per cent of the seats at Democratic national conventions. Without a noncongressional channel for advancement, such as the national convention affords, the kinds of nominations we have experienced would certainly have been quite different. Roosevelt, Truman, and Stevenson, for example, would probably have failed to win the nomination under different circumstances, and Eisenhower could certainly not have won the Republican nomination from Senator Taft if the battle had been fought on different terrain.

The convention system has probably functioned to turn the President into the one national leader who must be responsive to the needs of national majorities. Notice the shift from a congressional to a broad popular orientation with Jackson, the first President to capture office outside the caucus system. Granted the particularistic or local orientation of Congress, the national orientation of the presidency has probably been functional for the American system.[36]

Choosing Convention Delegates

The management of these great conventions is completely in the hands of the political parties, except that some states regulate the selection of delegates by law. The methods of selecting delegates vary greatly, and differences in party rules as well as state laws create an extremely complicated national picture. Fifteen states and the District of Columbia conduct presidential preference primaries in which the voters may indicate their preference among the contenders for their party's nomination.[37] In a number of these states, however, including Illinois, Massachusetts, New Hampshire, New Jersey, and West Virginia, the outcome of the presidential preference vote is not binding on the delegates. In Nebraska, candidates for election as delegates must file affidavits pledging themselves to abide by the

[36] Of course, if Congress were more directly involved in the choice of Presidents, and if congressional service led more directly to the presidency, the orientation of Congress might be much less particularistic. If a national orientation is functional for the democratic polity, then, the national nominating conventions may be dysfunctional in their effects on Congress. While this reasoning is speculative, it is not entirely unsupportable by data. See, for example, the more national orientation of the British Parliament. At minimum, it reminds us that a given institution may be functional for the system as a whole and for some of its elements while, at the same time, it is dysfunctional for other elements.

[37] *Congressional Quarterly Weekly Report*, XXII (January 17, 1964), 92–100.

outcome of the presidential preference voting; but in practice this pledge has often been ignored, the presidential primary being interpreted as advisory only. In three states with presidential primaries—Indiana, Maryland, and Pennsylvania—some or all of the delegates are chosen by party conventions. Most of the states choose all their delegates through party conventions, but in a few they are chosen by party committees or by a combination of methods.

Most of these complications arose from attempts in the first two decades of this century to extend the direct primary to the nomination of presidential candidates. Reformers reasoned that, if the national convention could not be eliminated as most state conventions had been the direct election of delegates pledged to a specific candidate would at least transform the national convention from a decision-making body into a mere recording device. If the movement had succeeded, it would have left the national convention with no more discretion in nominating the President than the electoral college now has in electing him. By 1916, half the states were using the presidential primary in one form or another, but since that time the tide has turned back in favor of the convention. If the convention is to perform its latent function of unifying the party, as well as its manifest function of nominating candidates, the delegates must retain some freedom to maneuver, bargain, and compromise. As a result, the attempt to turn the function of the convention over to the primaries produces such complicated rules as those binding Oregon delegates, who must support the winner of the presidential preference primary until he wins less than 35 per cent of the convention votes, until he releases the delegates, or until two ballots have passed. Most of the states that bind delegates now bind them only for the first ballot.

The chief function of the presidential primaries is to gauge public opinion, and in this respect primaries are far from satisfactory. Since the presidential primaries are held on different dates, the results in one state inevitably affect the campaign in other areas; candidates wisely refuse to enter the contest in states where they may lose more than they can gain; local "favorite son" candidates are entered in order to postpone committing the state to any national contender; grueling campaign efforts are imposed on the candidates; and the expense is enormous. Moreover, public opinion surveys furnish nationwide reports on the popularity of the candidates that are probably more meaningful than the results of the scattered primaries. In view of these defects, it is disquieting to consider the number of potential candidates—Goldwater, Kennedy, Humphrey, Stevenson, Eisenhower, Stassen, and Willkie come quickly to mind—whose hopes have been dashed or exalted by presidential primaries.

Despite their limitations, however, presidential primaries do constitute an important factor in the battle for a party's nomination. Aside from the delegate votes they pick up, they can impress party leaders in other states with a candidate's vote-pulling power. Thus the "Minnesota miracle" in 1952, when over 100,000 voters went to the trouble of writing in Eisenhower's name in the Republican primary, gave great impetus to the Eisenhower campaign everywhere.

The crucial primary for Kennedy in 1960 was in West Virginia, where he demonstrated that his Catholicism was not an insurmountable barrier to success among predominantly Protestant voters. In 1964, the California primary virtually assured Goldwater of the Republican nomination. He had garnered only 23 per cent of the Republican votes in New Hampshire and only 18 per cent in Oregon. Coupled with survey findings which consistently showed minority support for him among Republicans throughout the nation, these primaries came close to eliminating him. Even with strong support among delegates chosen through conventions, another defeat in California would most probably have been ruinous. His razor-thin victory over Governor Rockefeller in California, however, erased the stigma of previous defeats.

Because primaries can assume such importance, they tend to limit the field to national figures who can, moreover, command considerable preconvention financial backing. When Hubert Humphrey, then a senator from Minnesota, attempted to compete against Kennedy in the 1960 primaries, he found himself handicapped by the limited organization that he could finance.

The allotment of delegates to each state and territory is controlled entirely by party regulations. Originally it was based on the electoral college vote: for many years, each state got two convention votes for each of its electoral college votes. Then, after 1912, in order to reduce the influence of traditionally Democratic states, the Republicans worked out an arrangement that gives greater influence in the convention to states and districts that can be expected to support the Republican nominees. States with relatively few Republican votes are thus penalized and those with heavy Republican turnout receive "bonus" delegates. In 1964, the Republican convention included 1,308 delegates, each with a single vote. The allocation of these delegates followed this formula: *at-large delegates*—4 per state, 2 additional for each U.S. representative-at-large, 6 additional for each state that voted for Nixon in 1960 or that elected a Republican U.S. senator or governor in 1960 or later; *district delegates*—1 for each congressional district that cast 2,000 or more votes for Nixon in 1960 or for the Republican House candidate in 1962, 1 additional for each district that cast 10,000 or more votes for Nixon in 1960 or for the Republican House candidate in 1962.[38] This formula makes dull reading, but it is arithmetic with a message. The Republican system of at-large bonus delegates rewards Republican states and the district system rewards areas in proportion to the Republican votes therein.

The Democrats traditionally allotted delegates to every state and district without regard to their voting records until 1964, when they came up with a reform that carries a significance overlooked by the press. The Democrats adopted a bonus system designed not only to reward states which supported the preceding Democratic presidential candidate but also to reward states with a heavy turnout of Democratic votes, regardless of who carried the state. Moreover, unlike the Republican formula, the Democrats' bonus system is *keyed to the presidential race alone.* The new Democratic formula for 1964 was: 3 convention votes for each electoral vote, 1 vote for every 100,000 popular votes (or major fraction thereof) cast for Kennedy in 1960, a bonus of 10 votes if

---

[38]*Congressional Quarterly Weekly Report,* XXII (January 17, 1964), 84.

the state cast its electoral votes for Kennedy in 1960, and 1 vote to be cast by each state's national committeeman and committeewoman.[39] In order to avoid the embarrassment of all-white delegations from states like Mississippi and Alabama in 1968, the Democrats further ruled that all state delegations must be "broadly representative of the Democrats of the state" and that any "nonrepresentative" delegation would be refused seats.[40]

Because the new Democratic bonuses are keyed to the presidential race only, they will not automatically accrue to southern states that, although they always elect Democrats to the Senate and governorship, occasionally vote Republican in presidential contests. Nor will they go to states that, like Mississippi in 1960, elect an unpledged slate of Democratic electors who cast the state's electoral vote for some Democrat (Senator Harry Byrd of Virginia in this case) other than the convention's nominee. Finally, by rewarding states that turn out heavily for the Democratic presidential candidate, the new system of bonuses will work to the relative disadvantage of states with low levels of participation—and these are primarily in the South. These reforms were adopted by the Democratic National Committee in a mood that suggested they constituted the first step in a trend. Even this first step modestly shifts the relative power in the convention toward the large industrial states and away from the parochial Democrats of the South.

The national conventions are held in the summer of the election year, at a time and place designated by the national committee of each party. The preliminary work is done by four standing committees. The committee on *credentials* judges the qualifications of delegates and recommends solutions of disputes to the convention as a whole. In the convention, the "temporary roll," compiled by the national committee, determines which of the contending delegates will be seated. Bitter disputes occasionally produce an early indication of which faction controls the convention. In the Republican convention of 1964, supporters of Governor William Scranton (Pa.) offered an early motion to bar the seating of any delegate who had been selected by rules or procedures "which had the purpose or effect" of racial discrimination. This motion was supported with the charge the "forces at work in this country" want to turn the Republican Party into a "lily-white party." This statement was loudly booed by the delegates and the motion was resoundingly defeated. From this point on, it was clear that Goldwater supporters, against whom the charge was implicitly made, controlled the convention.

The committe on *permanent organization* nominates a permanent chairman, standing committees, and other functionaries to replace the temporary officers who were appointed by the national committee. Both the temporary chairman, whose chief function is to deliver a keynote address customarily praising his own party and condemning the opposition, and the permanent chairman, who presides over the convention, are key officers, and their selection is another indication of which faction holds control. The President usually controls these

[39]*Congressional Quarterly Weekly Report*, XXII (January 17, 1964), 131.
[40]*Congressional Quarterly Weekly Report*, XXV (July 21, 1967), 1260.

choices for his party, but they may be hotly disputed in the opposition party.

The committee on *rules* recommends a set of rules to govern the convention. Generally, it recommends that the rules of the House of Representatives be adopted insofar as they are applicable.

The committee on *resolutions* draws up the party platform, a statement of the policies the party proposes to follow if its candidates are elected. Although party platforms are generally ignored by voters and condemned by scholars for their evasiveness and generality, they are closely watched by leaders of special-interest groups. The committee conducts hearings at which interested persons may appear, but the basic platform is settled in advance by the group in control of the convention. This group tries to bridge differences within the party by careful ambiguity. Despite these efforts, bitter floor fights—like the one on the civil rights plank in the 1948 Democratic platform—sometimes disrupt the convention.

The chief business of the convention—the nomination of a candidate for the presidency—begins with an alphabetical roll call of states. This is an occasion for florid nominating and for seconding speeches in behalf of those seeking the nomination. Then the voting begins, again by the states in alphabetical order, and is continued until one of the candidates receives a majority. The Democrats formerly employed a "unit rule," under which the entire vote of each state delegation was cast for the candidate favored by the majority of the delegation. But present practice is for the convention to recognize and enforce whatever instructions have been given to the delegates by their state party organizations. Under this rule, most delegations are no longer bound to vote as a unit in Democratic conventions. In Republican conventions also, state delegations are not required to vote as a unit.

If no candidate captures a majority on the first ballot, the negotiations among factions are intensified. At this point, minor or "favorite son" candidates often gain considerable influence—or perhaps even the vice-presidency—by shifting to the apparent winner at a propitious moment. By means of such bargaining, the convention performs its function of uniting the party behind a single candidate. The symbol of this achievement is the common practice of making the vote unanimous once the outcome has become clear.

The nomination of the vice-presidential candidate has traditionally been a much more perfunctory matter, despite the fact that eight of the thirty-five men who have served as President were elevated from Vice-President upon the death of their predecessors. The presidential nominee, of course, has a strong voice in the selection of his running-mate, and his nod frequently goes to an opponent whose supporters ultimately helped the winner gain his majority. This is especially true if the opponent can "balance the ticket" by representing a different section, policy position, or faction of the party. Ironically, then, the vice-presidential candidate has often been one of the party figures *least* likely to ensure continuity should the President die in office.

This custom has been on the decline ever since the importance of Vice-President Nixon during the Eisenhower administration. Kennedy's choice of Johnson as his running-mate in 1960 followed the theory of the balanced ticket, but it also gave him a Vice-President with great political experience. President Johnson's 1964 prospects looked so bright after the Republicans nominated Goldwater that he was under minimal pressure in his choice of a running-mate. In Senator Humphrey, he too, chose a Vice-President with impressive political experience.[41] Goldwater's choice of retiring Congressman William Miller (N.Y.) clearly departed from the "balancing" theory in every sense except the geographical; Miller represented the same brand of conservatism as Goldwater himself. As the challenger of an incumbent President, Goldwater's departure from the custom of the balanced ticket may have reduced his chance of pulling an upset. The ambiguities and apparent contradictions of the usual platform and ticket were completely missing in the Republican campaign of 1964. In the 1962 edition of this book, we said, "When the chips are down in an election, party leaders can ill afford to forget the convention's function of unifying the diverse elements that make up the party." Senator Goldwater forgot—or chose to ignore—this function at his own peril.

Campaigns and Elections

Campaign Strategy

Campaign strategy is designed to win elections by influencing public opinion. This strategy is directed at the processes by which the voters form their political opinions. In a pioneer study of election behavior made in 1940 in Erie County, Ohio, the principal effects of campaign strategy were identified as *reinforcement, activation,* and *conversion.*[42] For most voters (about 53 per cent in the 1940 study), the campaign serves simply to *reinforce* preferences and intentions already formed. Most voters prefer the same party from one election to another. These members of the party faithful need only to be reassured on the rectitude of their position. Even among voters who change their party preference, more appear to switch their preference before the campaign, as a result of events since the last election, than are changed by the campaign itself. The reinforcement function is consequently central to the success of the campaign.

The campaign also stimulates the undecided or indifferent by *activating* or crystallizing latent preferences for a particular candidate or party. Without the vote of those who are only weakly attached to the party, the election may easily be lost.

Finally, the campaign tries to *convert* voters who have already decided to vote for the opposition. Although the casual observer might assume that this is the primary function of the campaign, only a small percentage of voters are induced to change their preference. Even the 8 per cent who switched parties in 1940 are usually enough to decide an election, however, so they cannot be ignored.

[41] See Gerald Pomper, "The Nomination of Hubert Humphrey for Vice-President," *Journal of Politics,* XXVIII (August, 1966), 639-659.

[42] Paul F. Lazarsfeld, Bernard R. Berelson, and Hazel Gaudet, *The People's Choice,* 2nd ed. (New York: Columbia University Press, 1948), p. 103. In addition to the 53 per cent who were reinforced and the 8 per cent who were converted, the campaign had these effects: activation, 14 per cent; reconversion, 3 per cent; partial conversion, 6 per cent; no effect, 16 per cent.

Campaigns are planned, with varying degrees of precision, to perform these three functions. Rule-of-thumb, traditional tactics may still predominate, but they are being supplemented more and more by the advice of experts in the art and science of "engineering consent." A successful campaign strategy must achieve three objectives, whether by design or by luck: (1) get the party's propaganda before the voter; (2) produce attitudes favorable to the party's candidates; (3) stimulate people to *vote*—for the right candidate. These objectives are easiest to achieve where reinforcement is all that is necessary and most difficult or impossible to achieve where conversion is required.

Getting the Message Heard and Believed

Both the traditional party institutions and the newly important public relations organizations are drawn into service in the effort to get the message heard. All the media of communication, from give-away pamphlets to television, are mobilized in efforts to make the voters familiar with the party's candidates and policies. Movie stars, athletes, and scholars contribute their assorted talents. Every conceivable avenue for reaching every group of voters seems to be exploited, including the candidates' families. In 1964, Mrs. Johnson toured the southern states on a campaign train known as the "Lady Bird Special" in an effort to shore up support among wavering Southerners. With Mrs. Johnson's Southern charm becoming more Southern at every stop, and with pressure from the White House becoming less gentle, various Southern politicians who had remained

Drawing by John A. Ruge; © 1967 *The Saturday Review*.

"He's got to be dumb enough to believe that we think he has a chance of winning, but not so stupid that the voters'll think we're not serious about the two-party system—and it can't look like we're holding back our good guys until 1972."

312

aloof during the campaign found themselves climbing aboard the Lady Bird Special. Although Mrs. Goldwater was less active in her husband's behalf, the Goldwater children were highly active.

Since few people vote for an unknown candidate, a politician must be known to the voters if he is to win. One of Stevenson's biggest disadvantages in 1952 and 1956 was his relative lack of national prominence. In 1936, 1940, and 1944, Roosevelt's challengers suffered a similar disadvantage. Moreover, Roosevelt understood that it is worse for a candidate to be ignored than criticized; consequently, he avoided mentioning his opponents by name in order not to give them free publicity. Before the 1960 campaign, Nixon was a much more familiar figure than Kennedy, but Nixon's willingness to meet his opponent in the famous TV debates largely dissipated this advantage. President Johnson, wrapping himself in the duties and dignity of the presidency, refused to make the same mistake; indeed, he followed Roosevelt's lead, avoiding mention of Goldwater until very late in the campaign.

Although familiarity is an essential element in winning elections, simply becoming known is not enough for the political candidate, his party, or its policies; they must also be known in a favorable light. The manner in which a personality is projected to the voters has a great deal to do with how they evaluate him as a candidate. Because of their "double exposure," the Kennedy-Nixon TV debates in 1960 gave the candidates a unique opportunity to create favorable images in both political camps—to watch your favorite you were virtually forced to watch his opponent. Unfortunately for Nixon, his predebate image called for a superb competitive performance. A candidate may be preferred primarily for a warm and sincere *personality* (Eisenhower), for his *political role*, such as the policies he espouses (Truman), or for his *performance* in a technical sense. The last was Nixon's forte. A *New York Times* article early in 1960 said that both Democrats and Republicans in Washington regarded Nixon as the most masterful TV performer in politics.[43] Even people who suspected his sincerity and disliked his policies admitted his skill as a campaigner. In light of these attitudes, the wide-spread feeling that Kennedy performed better in the first debate tended to blur and damage the Nixon image. Opponents were fortified in their anti-Nixon feelings; those who had condemned him for his consummate skill as a political in-fighter could now condemn him for his shortcomings as a political in-fighter. The undecided were left with a less clear or a less favorable image. And his supporters had to de-emphasize, as his opponents had previously done, the importance of mere debating skills, stressing personality or political role instead.[44]

Kennedy, on the other hand, was little known nationally before the 1960 election. The manner in which he won the Democratic nomination gave the impression of a cool, competent, and vital young man. But his maturity was suspect, and so was his ability to "stand up to Khrushchev" as Nixon had done

[43] Sidney Hyman, "What Trendex for Lincoln?" *The New York Times*, January 17, 1960.
[44] See K. Lang and G. E. Lang, "Ordeal by Debate: Viewer Reactions," *Public Opinion Quarterly*, XXV (Summer, 1961.) 277–288.

in an impromptu debate in Moscow. Even Kennedy's supporters expected Nixon to look more impressive in face-to-face debate, and were all set to explain that forensic skills are of little importance. In the debates, Kennedy's command of facts and facility with words served to allay suspicions just where they were most acute. In addition to positive features of personality and of political role, his ability to perform under fire and to turn adversity to advantage became part of the Kennedy image.

Turning from candidates to issues, we must admit that most political argumentation takes place without the "debaters" ever getting together—either in a physical sense or in terms of the issues. Even when candidates meet face-to-face, they frequently talk past one another. In the normal campaign situation, the best way of stimulating voters to adopt the desired attitude toward campaign issues is to reiterate one's strong arguments and to ignore those of the opposition. If this appears a dubious debating practice, remember that most observers of political campaigns are partisan themselves. Voters for each party tend to ignore rather than rebut the strong points of the opposition and to concentrate on the reassuring points that support their own decision; they would be only distressed if "their" party reminded them of unpleasantries.

Timing is also important in selling a party's issues and candidates to the voters. Thus Eisenhower's last-minute campaign promise that he would "go to Korea" in 1952 was timed for maximum effect. In terms of general intensity of organizational effort, Kennedy's presidential campaign is said to have reached too early a "peak"; had a few thousand votes in the right places been cast the other way, pundits would have given part of the credit for Nixon's victory to superior timing. Both parties try to pace their efforts so as to build up to a climax in the last weeks before election. Saturation TV coverage in the last days of the campaign has now become standard practice.

Attitudes toward political parties are less amenable to good salesmanship than attitudes toward candidates and issues. Since the political parties themselves are continuing institutions, the task of changing public attitudes toward them is far more difficult. The party in power gets blamed when times are bad and takes the credit when times are good. So the best campaign strategists can do in this regard is de-emphasize the importance of the party when its reputation is poor (as the Democrats did after the Civil War and the Republicans after the depression), and emphasize the importance of the party when its popularity is high (as the Republicans did during the prosperous 1920's, and the Democrats have done since the depression).

Getting Out the Vote

After the campaign strategists have caught the citizen's attention and have created a favorable attitude, their third objective is to get him to the polls. At this stage, party organization at the precinct level becomes crucially important. Personal contact provided by good precinct captains is invaluable, especially with uninterested and undecided citizens. Mass media can create a favorable general frame of reference, but they scarcely touch the indifferent. And they cannot ring doorbells, provide babysitters on election day, or furnish transportation to the polls. All political figures piously urge everyone to "vote as you please, but please vote"; nevertheless, their special efforts are naturally devoted to getting out all the votes that may be cast in their favor. Republicans worry about indifference and smugness in the suburbs, and Democrats fret about apathy and alienation in the tenements.

In our attention to mass media appeals and to responses in terms of various social characteristics, we often forget the importance of old-fashioned organizational effort at the local level. Granted the relative indifference of many citizens to politics, the effort of neighborhood leaders must be a crucial factor. Research has demonstrated that an active precinct organization can make a difference of 10 per cent in the vote division for President.[45] Precinct work is even more effective when—as in referendums, contests for minor offices, and primaries—voters are less familiar with the alternatives and less interested in the outcome. Although social and economic considerations influence American elections, purely political forces play an independent and distinctive part.

At the national level, exhortations to vote—and to vote right—reach their peak in the large doubtful states, where a shift of a few votes can radically alter the verdict of the electoral college. In 1952, for example, the Republicans blanketed forty-nine crucial counties with a last-minute "saturation" campaign of spot television appeals. One journalist, alarmed by the emotionalism, the timing, and the sheer number of these appeals, discussed them with Democratic Party officials after the election. He was surprised to hear, not an indignant complaint, but a wistful admission that the Democrats had thought of the tactic first but had lacked the money to carry it out.[46] Goldwater was criticized for making only one visit to New York during his entire campaign, but this fitted logically with his strategy—to build victory with the support of Western and Southern states. He made frequent appearances in California, the largest of these states.

Another common device to stimulate voters is the special appeal to the "cross-pressured"—those inclined for some reasons to vote Democratic but for others to vote Republican. Through such organizations as "Democrats for Eisenhower" and "Republicans for Roosevelt," waverers in the opposition camp are encouraged to think that changing their vote is not incompatible with their traditional preference. Open support from well-known figures in the opposing party can even better serve this end. Thus the switch of Senator J. Strom Thurmond of South Carolina, formerly a Democrat (and, earlier, a States' Rights candidate for President) to the Republican Party in 1964 was a boon to Goldwater in the deep South. The Democrats effectively countered in the nation as a whole with such organizations as Republicans and Independents for Johnson, Inc., which spread the motto, "Split your ticket, not your country."

We must not forget the so-called "independent voter," that improbable hero of much of the literature on politics. Independent voters were long thought of as those who change preference or make up their minds late in a campaign, who

---

[45] Daniel Katz and Samuel J. Eldersveld, "The Impact of Local Party Activity Upon the Electorate," *Public Opinion Quarterly*, XXV (Spring, 1961), 1–24.
[46] William Lee Miller, "Can Government Be 'Merchandized'?" *The Reporter* (October 27, 1957), 11–16.

are so interested that they wait until all the evidence is in, until they have carefully studied the platforms, until they have dispassionately weighed the relative merits of the candidates. Empirical studies show, however, that independent voters are generally the most uninformed, uninterested, and confused group within the voting public.[47] The average independent voter delays making a decision not because he is analyzing the evidence, but because he is hardly aware that a campaign is in progress. He changes his voting preference, not because new facts force a reappraisal, but because he holds his preference so lightly that he is steered by the last person he sees on election day.

Some independent voters, perhaps including some of the professors who helped create the romanticized portrait, undoubtedly do behave according to the myth. But if we consider our friends who are most highly interested and best informed on politics, we usually discover that they are strongly partisan rather than independent voters. A cushion of independent voters is highly useful to the democratic *system,* because they prevent the perpetuation of one party in power, but this does not mean that such voters are the best of citizens as *individuals.* For the campaign manager, of course, they are the group that respond best to last-minute—and, if possible, face-to-face—contact.

Money in Elections

Since money is essential to all these campaign efforts, the small minority who donate large sums generally have greater access to and influence on key officials. This may be not so much a matter of "buying influence" as it is of contributing to those who are already known to hold the desired points of view. The suspicion that those who hold the purse strings control politics periodically inspires regulations on campaign finances that are as ineffectual as they are well intentioned. Federal laws, for example, impose four types of regulation. First, national "political committees" and candidates for the Senate and House are required to file *reports of receipts and expenditures.* These reports have not produced the glaring publicity that was anticipated, partly because journalists fail to analyze them systematically, and partly because they are realistically regarded as woefully incomplete. Political committees that operate in only one state and a great variety of "educational" committees are exempted from this requirement. The provision does not apply to primary elections or to expenditures made without the "knowledge or consent" of the candidate.

Second, the *amounts spent* are subject to varying limits of $10,000 to $25,000 for a Senate election campaign, and $2,500 to $5,000 for a House campaign, depending on the number of voters in the constituency. This limitation is qualified too, however, for it applies only to general elections, to expenditures made by the candidate or with his knowledge, and only to certain types of expenses. Consequently, this limitation is as unrealistic as the $3 million annual limit that is placed on receipts and expenditures by any one "political committee" in a presidential campaign, a provision that has simply brought about a proliferation of committees.

Third, the *size* of individual contributions is limited to $5,000, but a well-

[47]Lazarsfeld, Berelson, and Gaudet, *The People's Choice,* p. 69; Campbell et al., *The American Voter,* pp. 143–145.

wisher may make any number of such donations to different election committees and, through his family, contribute even more to a single candidate.

Fourth, certain *sources* of funds — corporations and labor unions, for example — are barred from contributing to campaigns for federal office. There is no limitation on lobbying outlays, however, nor on contributions by corporate officers or by organizations voluntarily affiliated with unions.

For years the political funds of labor unions have simply been transferred in lump sums to state committees which in turn transfer the money to individual candidates; as committees operating in only one state, such organizations do not have to report the names of recipients. Corporations evade — and are encouraged by the parties to evade — the law with equal ease. In 1964, for example, the Democrats secured an estimated $1.5 million from advertisements in their convention program at $15,000 a page, a device that permitted corporations not only to make political expenditures but to classify them as tax – deductible "advertising" outlays. Ads in the Republican's 1964 National Convention programs were a comparative bargain at $3,500 to $5,000 a page. But when they discovered the higher rate the Democrats were charging, they brought out an additional publication later in the year and reaped $247,000 from ads priced at $10,000 a page. Playing it safe, about 50 corporations bought full-page ads in both the Democratic and Republican Convention programs.[48]

How much do the national parties actually spend in presidential election years? Because of the loopholes in the law requiring reports of expenditures, this is not an easy question to answer. In 1964, the two national committees reported a combined outlay of $47.8 million, $14.9 million more than the previous record expenditure of 1960.[49] Disregarding spending by labor and other nonparty groups, the political parties themselves spent almost $42 million in the national campaign for President and Congress. Although this seems like a tremendous expenditure, it boils down to less than 30 cents spent by each party to reach each voter. Considering that expenditures on commercial advertising during the same year amounted to $14.2 *billion*,[50] suspicions about an excess of money in politics appear to be exaggerated.

To be sure, the figures we have been citing do not tell the full story. If we add in the costs of nominating campaigns, and of all state and local outlays for national, state, and local races, total campaign costs in presidential election years reach these figures: $140 million in 1952, $155 million in 1956, $175 million in 1960, and $200 million in 1964. The contrast in actual and reported outlays depicted in Fig. 9–2 underscores the inadequacy of current reporting pro-

---

[48]The data in this paragraph and in the paragraphs to follow come, unless otherwise indicated, from a special report, "1964 Political Campaign Contributions and Expenditures," *Congressional Quarterly Weekly Report*, XXIV (January 21, 1966) 57–240.

[49]This figure includes expenditures reported to the Clerk of the House of Representatives and the Secretary of the Senate and an additional $1.2 million estimated deficit of the Democratic National Committee. The Treasurer of the Committee refused to give exact figures to the press. See *ibid.*, 57.

[50] Bureau of the Census, *Statistical Abstract of the United States 1966* (Washington, D. C.: Government Printing Office, 1966), 837.

cedures. Alexander Heard, author of the most definitive study of election campaign spending, reminds us that "these sums result basically from the functional necessities of a democratic system of government."[51] Insofar as Americans fill well over half a million public offices by popular election, and insofar as elections call for communication between candidate and electorate, our system makes such outlays an inevitable cost of democracy.

Expenditures during the last two decades tend to dispel the idea that the Republicans, the party of the "fat cats," always enjoy an advantage over Democrats in campaign spending. The findings suggest some Republican advantage but also support the axiom that "everybody loves a winner." The right-hand pie charts in Figure 9–2—which indicate the percentages of reported national outlays by both major parties, by labor, and by other groups—show that Republicans outspent Democrats in every national election from 1952 through 1964. But the Republicans' greatest advantages were during the Eisenhower years when Stevenson's chances for victory were slight. The gap was narrowed in the close race of 1960. In 1964, with a popular Democratic incumbent challenged by a Republican regarded as extreme by many in his own party, Republican

[51] The 1952 and 1956 estimates are from Heard's book, *The Costs of Democracy* (Chapel Hill: The University of North Carolina Press, 1960), p. 8.

Figure 9-2

Source: From a special report, "1964 Political Campaign Contributions and Expenditures," *Congressional Quarterly Weekly Report*, XXIV (January 21, 1966), back cover.

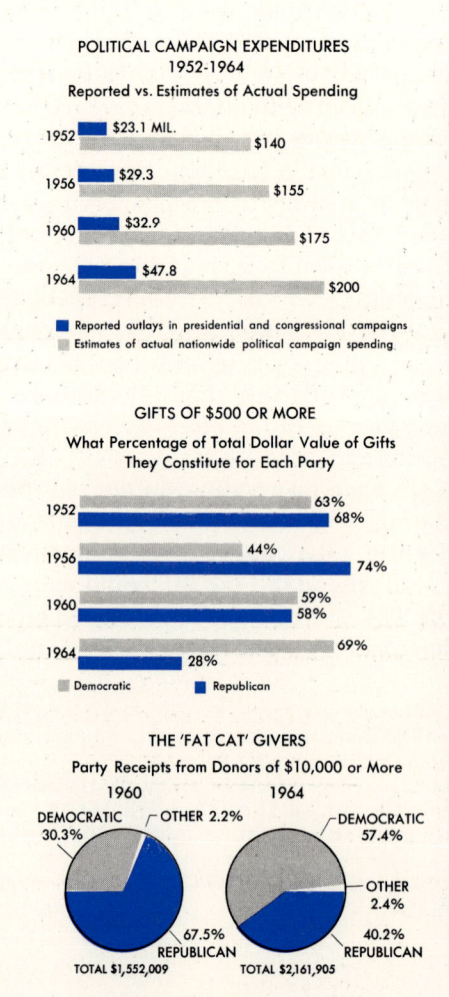

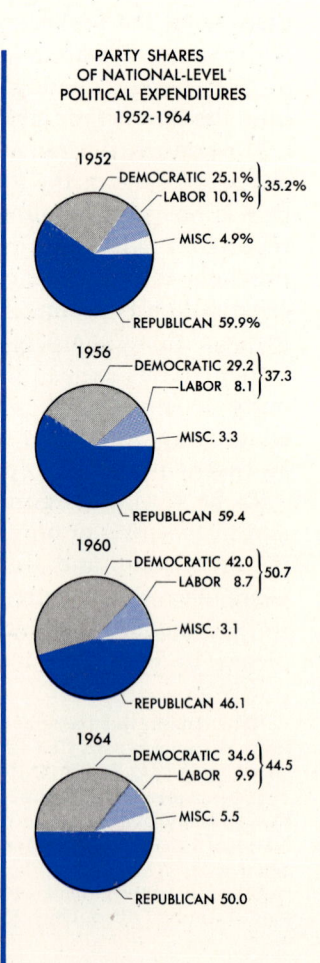

POLITICAL CAMPAIGN EXPENDITURES
1952-1964
Reported vs. Estimates of Actual Spending

Year	Reported	Estimate
1952	$23.1 MIL.	$140
1956	$29.3	$155
1960	$32.9	$175
1964	$47.8	$200

■ Reported outlays in presidential and congressional campaigns
▫ Estimates of actual nationwide political campaign spending

GIFTS OF $500 OR MORE
What Percentage of Total Dollar Value of Gifts They Constitute for Each Party

Year	Democratic	Republican
1952	63%	68%
1956	44%	74%
1960	59%	58%
1964	69%	28%

THE 'FAT CAT' GIVERS
Party Receipts from Donors of $10,000 or More

1960
DEMOCRATIC 30.3%
OTHER 2.2%
REPUBLICAN 67.5%
TOTAL $1,552,009

1964
DEMOCRATIC 57.4%
OTHER 2.4%
REPUBLICAN 40.2%
TOTAL $2,161,905

PARTY SHARES
OF NATIONAL-LEVEL
POLITICAL EXPENDITURES
1952-1964

1952
DEMOCRATIC 25.1%
LABOR 10.1% } 35.2%
MISC. 4.9%
REPUBLICAN 59.9%

1956
DEMOCRATIC 29.2
LABOR 8.1 } 37.3
MISC. 3.3
REPUBLICAN 59.4

1960
DEMOCRATIC 42.0
LABOR 8.7 } 50.7
MISC. 3.1
REPUBLICAN 46.1

1964
DEMOCRATIC 34.6
LABOR 9.9 } 44.5
MISC. 5.5
REPUBLICAN 50.0

expenditures were only half the total. To be sure, all the spending by labor and other groups would have to be added to the Democrats' 34.6 per cent of the spending for them to equal the Republicans. But most of the labor money did support the Democrats; were this added to unreported sums from the President's Club and from advertising, the Republican advantage would be reduced so much that it might disappear.

Big contributions seem to go to apparent winners and incumbents (see the middle left-hand bar charts of Figure 9–2). In elections from 1952 to 1964, the percentage of total donations represented by gifts of $500 or more to each party differed most sharply in 1956 and 1964. When Eisenhower ran for re-election against Stevenson (1956), the Republican percentage of large donations was the highest and the Democratic percentage the lowest of all these election years. Large donations may reflect a sense of obligation for advantageous policy outputs already received (hence the incumbent advantage) or of outputs expected (hence the advantage of the expected winner). Eisenhower enjoyed both advantages in 1956. So did Johnson in 1964, the year in which the largest percentage of Democratic contributions and the smallest percentage of Republican contributions came from donations of $500 or more.[52]

"Everybody loves a winner," and the "fat cats"—the extremely wealthy—are just like "everybody." The lower lefthand circles in Figure 9–2 represent the breakdown of donations over $10,000 in 1960 and 1964. In 1960, when the presidential election outcome appeared highly uncertain, 67.5 per cent of these large contributions went to the Republicans. Because Nixon enjoyed the advantage of "semi-incumbency" as the incumbent Vice-President and Kennedy the somewhat offsetting advantage of unusual personal wealth, perhaps the edge of the Republicans in "fat cat" contributions was about normal for this election. If so, the reversal in 1964 is truly startling: 57.4 per cent of these large contributions went to the Democrats, a gain of 27 per cent over 1960.

The shift of the Republicans to small contributions in 1964 was not simply a result of their poor chances for victory. It was also a result of the ideological nature of the Goldwater campaign. The small minority who were Goldwater supporters were sufficiently intense in their views to pour in vast numbers of small contributions. And there were enough large contributions to keep the Republicans the biggest campaign spenders; indeed, their 1964 expenditures set an all-time record for both parties.

Campaign contributions are an advanced form of political participation. Accordingly, they show the same biases as political opinions: Officials of labor unions give mostly to the Democrats and officials of major corporations give mostly to the Republicans.[53] But the patterns of American politics are extremely

---

[52]From the data available, we cannot disentangle the relative advantages of incumbency and apparent chances for victory. The latter are rarely certain, for one thing, and major donors probably think in terms of a series of elections including contests other than the presidency. Add other factors (family tradition, personal ideology) that enter in, and it is clear that any effort at interpretation faces serious difficulties.

[53]Senate Subcommittee on Privileges and Elections, *1956 General Election Campaigns,* 85th Cong., 1st Sess., 1957.

complicated. In the 1960 election, for example, the Teamsters Union launched DRIVE—Democratic Republican Independent Voter Education—to demonstrate that labor was not solid for the Democrats. And the chairman of the Republicans and Independents for Johnson, Inc. in 1964 was a former president of the Pepsi-Cola Company. Neither labor nor corporate interests like to be exclusively identified with any one party even though, over the long haul, the direction of their preference seems fairly obvious.

Since campaigns are expensive, money naturally plays a role in their outcome. If those who possess wealth usually want to avoid changes in the status quo, it is not surprising that conservative parties and conservative candidates find it easier to gain financial support than more liberal groups. But the apparent winner always finds his money-raising tasks simplified, especially in relation to "political businesses" such as defense contractors, builders, realtors, architects, liquor interests, and industries closely regulated by government. Personal motives, the power of mass organization, the influence of person-to-person contact, the impact of public events, the cohesion of social classes, and the force of effective leadership—all work to invalidate the notion that the more expensive campaign always ends in victory.

The Mechanics of the Ballot

Most Americans vote by marking secret ballots issued to them by local election officials. The ballots list a great number of offices sought by candidates whose names are usually grouped in columns according to party affiliation. Elections are conducted, according to state law, by precinct officers under the immediate, if rather casual, supervision of county or city election authorities.

While a majority of voters still mark paper ballots, over thirty states allow local governments to install voting machines which record and count the votes automatically, speed up elections, and reduce the opportunities for fraud.

Whether by paper ballot or by machine, voting is now secret throughout the United States. In the post-Civil War period, votes were still cast by voice, or by means of easily identifiable ballots printed by the parties. But labor and other reform-minded groups, convinced that intimidation and bribery were damaging their cause, agitated for secret voting, which was generally achieved by 1900 with the adoption of the Australian ballot in a majority of the states. The Australian ballot is an official ballot which is printed by the government and lists the names of all candidates for public office.

There are two basic ways of listing candidates on the ballot, whether paper or machine. The *party-column ballot*, used in twenty-nine states, groups the names of all candidates in columns according to party affiliation. On this type of ballot, it is usually possible to vote a "straight ticket" (for all the candidates of one party) by making a single mark or by pulling a single lever at the head of the column. The *office-block ballot* groups all candidates according to the office they seek rather than by their party. This design forces the voter to consider who should control each individual office rather than who should control the government as a whole. Because this approach encourages split-ticket voting, party officials generally deplore the office-block ballot.[54]

[54]In at least one state, Pennsylvania, the office-block ballot is combined with the opportunity for straight-ticket voting by a single mark or pull of the lever.

320

The mechanics of the ballot have little effect on the voting behavior of people with intense convictions. Anybody who feels so strongly that he would go through "hell or high water" to register his views will certainly not be influenced by the mere form of the ballot. But most citizens do not have strong political convictions, and the ballot form may influence their votes.

Voting a straight ticket is easy in states with *single-choice ballots*—a ballot form that permits a single mark or the pull of a single lever to register a vote for a single party's candidates for every office. Straight-ticket voting requires more effort in states with *multiple-choice ballots*—a ballot form that requires every office to be voted on separately. A comparison of the extent of straight-ticket voting under these two kinds of ballots give us a good chance to see the influence of ballot form on voting. In those states with single-choice ballots, straight-ticket voting is significantly higher than in states with multiple-choice ballots. None of the difference is supplied, however, by people with strong party identification. When an individual's vote is based on strong party identification, it is not influenced at all by the mechanics of voting. But it's a different story for those with weak party identification and, more particularly, for independents.

TABLE 9-1 Effect of Different Ballot Forms on People with Different Levels of Party Identification

LEVEL OF PARTY IDENTIFICATION	PERCENTAGE OF STRAIGHT-TICKET VOTES	
	SINGLE-CHOICE BALLOT	MULTIPLE-CHOICE BALLOT
Strong	77%	77%
Weak	70	55
None (independents)	48	30

Source: Survey data on 1952 and 1956 presidential elections reported in Angus Campbell and Warren E. Miller, "The Motivational Basis of Straight and Split Ticket Voting," *American Political Science Review*, LI (June 1957), 307.

Table 9–1 summarizes the effect of mere ballot form on straight-ticket voting for people at different levels of party identification. Reading across the table, we see that 77 per cent of those with strong party identification vote a straight ticket regardless of the form of the ballot. Looking at independents, we see a different story: 48 per cent of them vote a straight ticket when the ballot form permits them to do so by making a single choice, but only 30 per cent vote a straight ticket when they must make multiple choices. The 18 percentage-point drop represents a sizable minority of independents who have such weak political commitments that their vote, following the principle of least effort, is determined by the form of the ballot. If they can cast a straight ticket at minimum cost of energy, i.e., by making a single choice, they vote a straight ticket. If voting a straight ticket is harder, i.e., if they have to choose for each office in terms of some consistent principle like party identification, then they vote a split ticket—selecting one candidate because they have heard of him, another because they like the sound of his name, and another because his name comes first on the list. Such erratic behavior is not, of course, characteristic of most independents, but it is found in a significant minority. Again, the independent voter appears somewhat less the model citizen than political folklore might lead one to believe.

Elections and the Political System

Aside from their direct significance, elections are important for what they tell us about how choices are made and how power is distributed among individuals and groups, in and out of government. They may also be viewed in historical perspective, each election regarded as a single political event, as one unit in a continuing series of electoral decisions with consequences for the total political system.

Types of Elections

Elections may be classified according to two criteria. The first and most obvious is in terms of *which party wins*. If the incumbent party, the election results in *party continuity*; if the party out of office, a *party change* is the result. Since the question of who will control the government is the central concern of any election, this first criterion tends to dominate popular discussion. In 1928, then, the Republicans were jubilant because they retained control of the presidency by a handy margin.

A professional horse player differs from an amateur, however, in that his concerns go beyond the simple question of which horse won a particular race. He is also alert to the promise of strength in a loser and to signs of future weakness in the winner. And so it is with careful observers of elections. They are concerned with the second and less obvious criterion: whether the election reflects change or continuity in the party *preferences of significant groups* in the electorate. If deviations from the usual party preferences of major voting groups are not very great or enduring, the election may be called one of *electoral continuity*. If significant and enduring deviations occur, the election is one of *electoral change*. Viewing the 1928 election from this perspective, the Republicans seem to have won a battle while they were losing a war.

The Herbert Hoover-Al Smith presidential contest of 1928 has been called a critical election because, viewed as one in a series of electoral decisions, it accentuated and crystallized a realignment of significant groups within the electorate. Specifically, the candidacy of Al Smith intensified and solidified the movement of low-income, Catholic, urban voters of immigrant stock into the Democratic Party.[55] Because of the American penchant for viewing elections with the psychology of a novice at the races—"do they pay off on my bet?" —we forget that the long-run consequences of an election may be in terms of shifts in the electorate that do not show up in the win column. Franklin Roosevelt's victory in 1932 was not the only critical election, then, for Democratic dominance during the last generation. The identification of low-income and

[55] See V. O. Key, Jr., "A Theory of Critical Elections," *Journal of Politics*, XVII (February, 1955), 3–18.

minority groups with the Democrats was carried further in 1932, but—because almost all groups showed some shift to the Democrats in 1932—the contrast between low- and high-status groups may actually have been greater in 1928.

So far as the outcome of the elections was concerned, Eisenhower's victories in 1952 and 1956 seemed to reflect an impressive change in the electorate. But the capture of congressional power by the Democrats in 1954, 1956, and 1958 —and the capture of the presidency and Congress in 1960 and 1964—demonstrates that the Eisenhower victories were based on transient appeals rather than on an enduring change in the electorate. The varying impact of these presidential elections—1928, 1932, 1952, 1956, 1960, 1964—indicates that we must distinguish between the *electoral* and the *party* implications of each election. Table 9–2 sets up four types of elections in terms of these two dimensions.[56]

Table 9–2 Illustrations of Types of Elections in Terms of Consequences for the Political System

PARTY CONSEQUENCES	ELECTORAL CONSEQUENCES	
	CHANGE	CONTINUITY
Continuity	Type A: *1928* (1796)[a]	Type C: *1964* (1864, 1900)
Change	Type B: *1932* (1860, 1896)	Type D: *1952* (1884, 1912)

[a]We are reasonably confident that the italicized presidential elections are properly classified. For earlier years, before opinion survey techniques were developed, a greater amount of guesswork underlies the classification. We enclose these dates in parentheses to indicate that the classification is only suggestive.

In Chapters 6 and 7 we stressed the supporting function of political opinions and the moderating function of political parties. We also emphasized the impressive stability of party identification, which permitted us to divide the nation's political history into only three periods in terms of basic majority coalitions—the Democratic majority, 1800-1860; the Republican majority, 1860-1932; the Democratic majority, 1932 to the present.

If recent elections are viewed in the light of these stable factors, they can be understood as deviating more or less from a "standing decision" rather than as unique events. In 1952, Eisenhower won despite the standing decision in favor of the Democrats, because transient influences strongly favored the Republicans—his great personal appeal, the feeling that the Republican leaders would better insure peace, and charges of corruption in the Truman Administration. The first two of these forces, plus the great advantages of an incumbent, returned Eisenhower, in 1956. But the lack of any basic realignment was demonstrated by the election of Democratic Congresses during six of Eisenhower's eight years in office. Again, in 1960, the short-run influences

[56]Members of the Survey Research Center of the University of Michigan have also proposed a classification because it does not consistently recognize that party and electoral consequences of an election may be different. See Campbell *et al.*, *The American Voter*, pp. 531–538; and Philip E. Converse *et al.*, "Stability and Change in 1960: A Reinstating Election," *American Political Science Review*, LV (June, 1961), 269–280.

—chiefly Nixon's personal appeal and the religious issue—worked in the Republicans' favor.[57] Unlike Stevenson, however, Kennedy also had widespread public appeal and, while his religious identification cost him dearly in the South, it helped him enough in other sections to reduce his net loss from the religious issue to an estimated 2.2 per cent. The peculiarities of the electoral college and the lack of separate opinion surveys in all 50 states complicate estimates of the net effect of the religious issue, but it is nonetheless clear that the underlying preference for the Democratic Party barely gave Kennedy the base of support he needed to win.[58]

In 1964, for the first time since the Roosevelt era, the short-run influences favored the majority party. The result was the overwhelming victory depicted in Fig. 9–3, which gave President Johnson the largest vote in American history (42.1 million), the largest margin over an opponent (15.5 million), and the greatest percentage of the total vote (61.3).[59] The net effect of Goldwater's campaign was to reduce support for the Republicans, already a minority party, to a minimum level. In addition to the debacle of his own campaign, the 1964 election gave the Democrats a 38-seat gain in the House of Representatives, which added up to the biggest Democratic margin (295-140) since 1936. The Democrats added 2 seats to their comfortable Senate majority for a 68-32 margin. The sweep of the Republican defeat is seen most dramatically in the loss of over 500 seats in the state legislatures, with most of the losses occurring in states where Goldwater's candidacy hurt Republican chances at all other levels of office.[60]

In effect, the Goldwater campaign challenged the moderating function of political parties and the supporting function of public opinion. His refusal to make concessions to liberal elements in his own party and his denunciation, at one time or another, of America's basic foreign and domestic policies offered a supreme test of the myth of the "hidden conservative vote." Given "a choice, not an echo," the American public resoundingly chose the echo. Indeed, the most common view of voters, few of whom had read or heard of *The Conscience of a Conservative*,[61] was that Goldwater was a "radical." His broadscale attack on policies supported by past administrations, including those of President Eisenhower, paid off only in the Deep South. His vote against the Civil Rights Act of 1964 won him Georgia and the four states that had supported J. Strom Thurmond in 1948 (Louisiana, Mississippi, Alabama, and South Carolina). And his victory margin came from counties in this tier of black-belt states in which a majority of the population is Negro but where few Negroes vote. Had the Negroes in those counties voted, and had they supported Johnson as overwhelmingly as did Negroes elsewhere, Goldwater would have carried only his home state of Arizona.

[57]Donald Stokes says, "The really surprising aspect of the 1960 campaign, one that faces a struggle to survive in the popular histories, is how favorable an impression Mr. Nixon made on the public." See "1960 and the Problem of Deviating Elections," a paper delivered at the annual meeting of the American Political Science Association, September 6, 1961.
[58]Converse *et al.*, "Stability and Change in 1960: A Reinstating Election," pp. 269–280.
[59]In percentage of the two-party vote, Johnson fell slightly below Roosevelt's 1936 percentage (62.5); the above statement refers to total popular vote, which includes minor party vo...
[60]*Congressional Quarterly Weekly Report*, XXII (November 20, 1964), 2709.
[61]Barry M. Goldwater, *The Conscience of a Conservative* (Sheperdsville, Ky.: Victor Publishing Co., 1960).

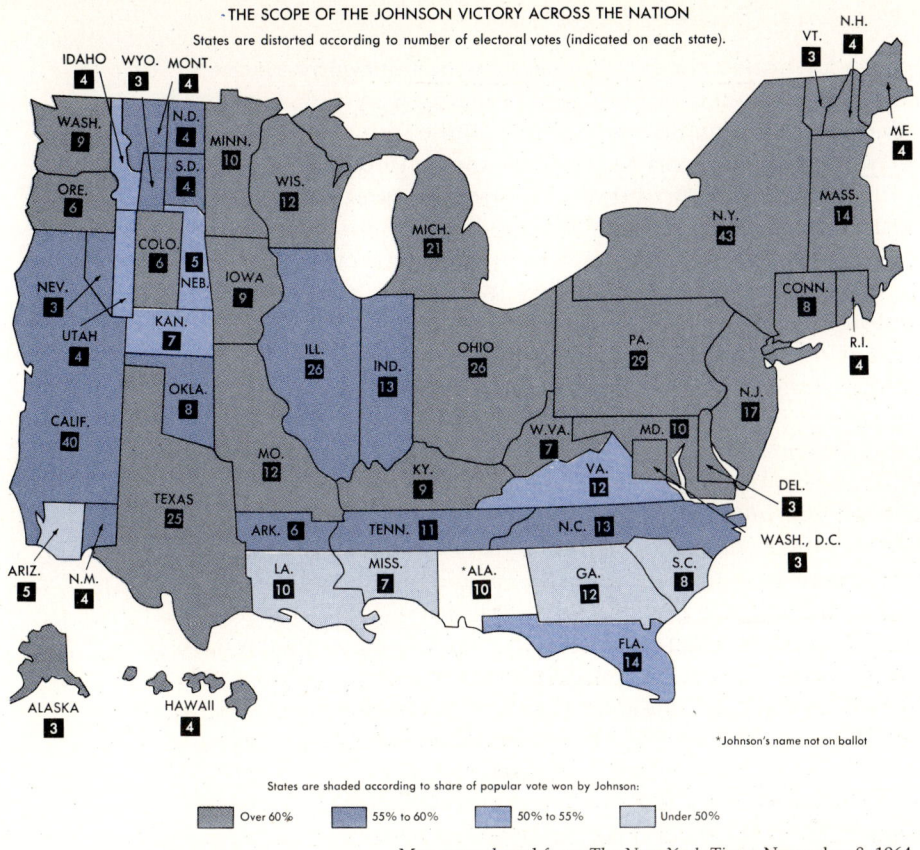

THE SCOPE OF THE JOHNSON VICTORY ACROSS THE NATION
States are distorted according to number of electoral votes (indicated on each state).

States are shaded according to share of popular vote won by Johnson:
Over 60% | 55% to 60% | 50% to 55% | Under 50%

*Johnson's name not on ballot

Map reproduced from *The New York Times*, November 8, 1964.

Figure 9-3

Every election has its own peculiarities, with a new blend of events, issues, and personalities, and the short-run influences are as likely to help one party as the other. But, in the absence of cataclysmic crisis, these short-run influences act against the backdrop of a standing decision that is buttressed by stable party loyalties and support for established policies. "Other things being equal," the Democrats in the present era should win with 53 to 54 per cent of the popular vote. The "other things" were highly unequal in 1964.

The Functions of the Electoral System

From the perspective of the political system as a whole, the electoral system functions, as intended, to select the official decision-makers. It contributes less clearly to the second major input function of the polity—the identification of citizen interests. During the 1950s, for example, when Americans elected a Republican President twice and Democratic congresses three times, what were they trying to achieve in policy outputs? Both the election results and the findings of public opinion surveys suggest that officials have great discretion in interpreting such election "mandates." Nevertheless, the effort of commentators and politicians to read some clear mandate into every election attests to the fact that elections are assumed to have—and therefore have—the function of identifying citizen interests. Perhaps they are poorly identified simply because they are not clearly conceived.[62]

In addition to these manifest functions, the electoral system has several consequences that might be unanticipated. First, the entire process of popular elections serves to celebrate and to reinforce the concept of self-rule. The result is to legitimize governmental power, to convince everyone of the right of the elected officials to make general policy. The losers of American elections are expected to show their good sportsmanship by rallying around the winner. Even the press observes a honeymoon period in which it minimizes direct criticism of the winning candidate, a practice which helps to build consensus in support of the victor.[63]

A second latent function of a system in which some people are allowed to vote is the extension of participation. At the outset, the right to vote may be enjoyed by selected elements of the population, such as property-owners and taxpayers early in American history. But the logic that won the franchise for some and, perhaps more important, the competition of opposing factions for votes tends to extend the franchise to new groups. A little democracy is thus a dangerous thing, exactly as antidemocrats have long argued.

Third, a popular electoral system changes the context within which public decisions are made. As we have seen, some elements in the population have a greater opportunity for leadership than others. But decisions on public policy in a system without popular elections are vastly different from similar decisions in a democracy. Even if elections cannot positively direct policy, decision-makers must always anticipate public reactions to their decisions. In V. O. Key's words, the suffrage means that "the wishes and probable actions of a vast number of people at the polls must be taken into consideration in the exercise of public power."[64]

To this point, we have talked about broad functions of popular elections for political systems in general. But just how do American elections serve to link public preferences (and indifference) to the policy outputs of government? Political opinions, political parties, pressure groups, and public relations all converge in the electoral process. Democratic theory assumes that, out of this convergence, the elected official will somehow represent the interests or views of his constituents.

At least three concepts of the relationship between constituents and decision-makers have been presented as describing either the actual or the desired model. The *instructed delegate* model holds that an official acts (or should act) as a spokesman for the preferences of his constituency, following its mandate in his decisions. The view traditionally opposed to that of the instructed delegate sees the representative performing as an *independent statesman*, acting in the interest of his constituents as he sees it, even though this may be contrary to their preferences. The *responsible party* model sees the representative as an agent of a national rather than a local constituency. The second and third concepts both view the official as free to act contrary to constituency preferences,

---

[62]See Philip E. Converse, "The Nature of Belief Systems in Mass Publics," in David E. Apter (ed.), *Ideology and Discontent* (New York: The Free Press of Glencoe, Inc., 1964), pp. 206–261.

[63]This statement is based on an unpublished content analysis of editorials on a series of presidents by William Blough in a graduate seminar at the University of North Carolina.

[64]*Politics, Parties, and Pressure Groups*, p. 622.

but they differ in that the independent statesman acts in terms of his own view of constituency or national interest rather than in response to his party's national constituency. Which relationship holds true in America?

Through an imaginative combination of data on the attitudes and voting records of congressmen with data on the attitudes of their constituents and their opponents for Congress, Warren Miller and Donald Stokes have brought systematic data to bear on these concepts for the first time.[65] Miller and Stokes specify two ways in which constituency control over a congressman's voting behavior is possible: (1) the constituency may elect a representative who shares the views of a majority in the area so that he will automatically vote their preferences in voting his own; (2) the representative may have a reasonably accurate idea of constituency preferences which he follows regardless of his personal views. The possibility of either form of constituency control over a congressman's behavior depends on three requirements.

First, the representative's votes must agree either with his own views or with his perception of constituency views. At first glance, this requirement might appear to be obviously met, but on reflection one recognizes that a congressman might instead follow the advice of the President, of party leaders in or out of office, or of pressure-group spokesmen. Examining the position of congressmen on roll call votes in three areas of legislation—social welfare, foreign policy, and civil rights—Miller and Stokes find this first condition to be realized in all three issue areas. Even so, a minority of congressmen were found to follow the lead of the administration regardless of their own preferences or their perception of constituency preferences.

A second requirement of constituency control is that either the representative's own attitudes or his perception of constituency attitudes must correspond with the actual opinions held in the district. This second requirement is not as well fulfilled as is the first. Congressmen most accurately perceive their constituents' preferences on the civil rights issue, but neither their own attitudes nor their beliefs about constituent attitudes are strongly related to actual constituency opinions on issues of foreign policy or social welfare. But these are severe tests. Popular opinions on questions of foreign policy are so unstable and so poorly supported by information that the congressman could hardly be expected to have a highly accurate impression of them. And on social welfare issues, if we compare the representative's perceptions and attitudes with the majority who supported him rather than with the entire constituency, a stronger relationship is found.

The third requirement of constituency control is that the constituency take account of the candidates' issue positions in deciding how to vote. This is the necessary condition for constituency control that is least satisfied. In contested congressional elections in 1958, only 24 per cent of the voters had heard or read something about both candidates, and only 54 per cent had read or heard

---

[65]This, the preceding, and the following paragraphs are based on their article, "Constituency Influence in Congress," *American Political Science Review,* LVII (March, 1963), 45–56. For a full report, see their *Representation in Congress* (Englewood Cliffs, New Jersey: Prentice-Hall, Inc., 1967).

something about either candidate.[66] Of those who could comment on the candidates, most offered general judgments—"he's a good man"; "he understands problems"—and only 3 per cent mentioned legislative issues of any kind. For that matter, a majority of the public could not say which party had controlled Congress during the preceding two years. If the vote was not in response to differences on issues, what was it based on? The overwhelming factor in congressional voting is *party identification*. Only one vote in twenty was cast by people with no sense of party identification and nine out of ten of those who did so identify supported their party's nominee.

Despite the public's use of congressional elections as a vehicle for expressing their party loyalties, four-fifths of the congressmen who were opposed for re-election felt that the outcome was strongly influenced by their voting records in Congress. Nor are they completely incorrect in this estimate. In the first place, with stable party voting among most of the electorate, the congressman in a competitive district needs only to win an extra increment of votes through his record to gain re-electon. Similarly, his record might reduce his stable party base enough to cost him his seat. Second, the two-step flow of communication we discussed in Chapter 6 may mean that votes apparently based purely on party identification are indirectly based on a congressman's record. Such mediating agencies as local party leaders, union or business associates, or informal opinion leaders in countless small groups react to the congressman's legislative record and pass their evaluations on to others. The ordinary member of such formal and informal groups may retain only the final evaluation—"he understands problems"—from contacts with opinion leaders, but the evaluation itself may relate back to the details of the Legislative record. Third, the congressman from a safe district may correctly view his record as important in that he needs to avoid angering constituents by taking a stand opposed by strong local interests. The influence of local opinions is still felt in this circumstance, most conspicuously in Southern voting on civil rights.

In varying degrees, then, the requirements of constituency influence through popular elections seem to be realized. The model of constituency-representative relationship that is actually adopted varies from one issue to another. The instructed delegate model appears predominant in the area of civil rights. On this issue, the congressmen's perceptions of district attitudes are twice as influential as their own attitudes in determining variations in their roll-call votes. The responsible party model more nearly explains the relationship on social welfare issues, where party differences have been clear enough to enable the voter to rely on party label as a way of communicating his preferences. Finally, the independent statesman model finds some support in congressional behavior on foreign policy questions, in that the congressman does not look to his district in making up his mind. But even here the congressman does not make an independent decision: ". . . the reliance he puts on the President and the Administration suggests that the calculation of where the public interest lies is often passed to the Executive on matters of foreign policy."[67]

---

[66]"Constituency Influence in Congress," 54. If nonvoters were included, the percentages would be much lower.
[67]*Ibid.*, 56.

PART THREE

Decision-Making

Agencies and Activities

THE

LEGISLATORS   10

The Constitution of the United States begins with this declaration: "All legislative powers herein granted shall be vested in a Congress of the United States which shall consist of a Senate and House of Representatives." This statement has an appealing simplicity; we prefer to picture government as being neat rather than as a confusing struggle among shifting and indistinct power groups. Generations of schoolchildren have been taught that government is the business of three coordinate branches: Congress enacts laws, the President executes them, and the courts settle disputes under the law. This breakdown tells part of the story and it correctly emphasizes a principle function of each branch of our government. But if taken too literally it can be misleading. Later on, the Constitution itself assigns powers to the different branches of the government that clearly call for a sharing of functions. When the Secretary of Defense issues an order putting certain areas "off limits" as potential residences for servicemen because its realtors refuse to rent to Negroes, he is engaged in rule-making. So is the President when he asks Congress to pass a foreign aid bill. And so is the Supreme Court when it declares that election districts must be drawn so as to give each vote a roughly equal weight in choosing legislators.

If "legislation" is defined as all enactments of Congress, then Congress is our only legislative agency by means of a circular definition. But if legislation is viewed as those activities that result in the establishment of general and authoritative rules for society, all the official decision-making agencies of government play some part in the process. And, although they cannot make officially binding decisions, unofficial agencies such as political parties, pressure groups, and professional public relations organizations are the structures for expressing most of the inputs that shape public policies. Despite the Constitution's reference to "*all* legislative powers," then, we can hope to understand Congress only as one part of a complex rule-making system.

Legislators in Political Systems

Suppose the readers of this book were dropped by parachute at random all over the world and each asked the first person he saw (in the appropriate language), "Who makes the rules that the people in this country have to follow?" The answers would probably vary fantastically. For some people the question would be meaningless, because their lives and their horizons do not extend beyond the clan or tribe and they do not think of themselves as being part of something broader called a "country" or "nation." For others, the question would be unanswerable, because they have never thought about the source of the rules by which they live. Although their lives are governed by enforceable norms, the norms for them are simply "givens"—required patterns of behavior that are unquestioningly observed. Still others accept the rules as "givens" but regard them as emanating from some identifiable source such as a hereditary ruler whose authority stems from the deity. In this case, however, they are likely to think of the rules as being *discovered* rather than *made*, so they too would find the question puzzling.

So long as a king's subjects think that he impartially discovers and declares what is lawful (whether stemming from God's will or from tradition), specialized structures for rule-making will hardly emerge. Indeed, they will deny the very concept of a rule-*making* function as essential to all political systems. But once this function is recognized, more specialized structures tend to develop. The idea that the enforceable rules of society are actually made by men is thus historically associated with the emergence of the representative assembly as a regular institution of government. Ralph Huitt, a long-time student of Congress, describes "the taming of the executive" as the "great historic achievement" of the representative assembly.[1]

In many countries with specialized legislative structures, our interviewers would receive quick, appropriate answers—"Parliament," "Congress," and the like. But even in these countries, the truly well-informed observer might find the question of who makes the rules very difficult to answer. Guides in Buenos Aires proudly show sightseers Argentina's imposing *Palacio del Congreso*, the huge edifice erected for the country's National Congress. But the guides explain that the building is not used for anything now because the Ongonía government has disbanded the Congress. Clearly, rule-making is taking place elsewhere. And, whenever the government decides to permit elections to the National Congress, discerning citizens will not necessarily conclude that the authoritative decisions are actually being made in the *Palacio del Congreso* just because the building is once again in use.

Legislators as Peripheral to Authoritative Decision-Making

The idea of representative government has great appeal. Article 30 of the Soviet Constitution, for example, specifies that the Supreme Soviet is "the highest organ of state power in the U.S.S.R.," and Article 32 adds that "the legislative power of the U.S.S.R. is exercised exclusively by the Supreme Soviet." This sounds like parliamentary supremacy. But a recent study of rule-making in the U.S.S.R.[2] dismisses the Supreme Soviet in a few pages and concentrates on the full-time party functionaries (*apparatchiki*). The reason for this is simple: the author takes a functional approach and tries to determine which decisions are crucial in authoritative rule-making. That they are not those of the Supreme Soviet is

---

[1] Ralph K. Huitt, "Congress, the Durable Partner," in Elke Frank (ed.), *Lawmakers in a Changing World* (Englewood Cliffs, N.J.: Prentice-Hall, Inc., 1966), p. 9.
[2] Jeremy R. Azrael, "The Legislative Process in the U.S.S.R.," in Frank (ed.), *op. cit.*, pp. 83–100.

evident: "It suffices merely to report that the Supreme Soviet is only in session for a few days a year, that these few days are almost entirely occupied by official speeches, and, finally and most indicatively, that the Supreme Soviet has never witnessed a negative vote or even so much as an abstention."[3]

Why should the Soviet Constitution make such exaggerated statements about its parliament? And, regardless of the Constitution, why does the regime bother with all the trouble of holding annual meetings of the Supreme Soviet if rule-making occurs elsewhere? However unimportant these perfunctory meetings may appear to Americans, students of Soviet politics find them useful for the regime in several ways: (1) they "provide the leadership with a ceremonial sounding board for important statements of policy and purpose"; (2) they provide a means of "giving status rewards to particularly diligent 'activists' . . . while simultaneously recruiting new 'activists' . . ."; (3) they create a sense both of political representation and of political participation.[4]

If the Supreme Soviet is peripheral to the rule-making function that we associate with legislatures, it may nevertheless be highly functional in communicating the goals of the regime and in mobilizing citizen support through the sense of representation and participation. This should warn us, in examining the United States Congress, to be alert to the possibility that authoritative rule-making may take place outside the agency officially granted "all legislative powers" and that the legislature itself may have other functions important to the system.

A look at the British Parliament, because it has stood as "the mother of parliaments" within the democratic tradition, may be even more helpful in giving us insight into the peculiarities of our own Congress. Parliamentary government reached its peak in mid-nineteenth-century England. In the period from 1846 to 1860, the House of Commons administered eight major defeats to various administrations. (On six of these occasions, the cabinet resigned; on the other two, the cabinet in power dissolved Parliament and called a general election.) This power of a parliament to control and overthrow an administration is the heart of what we mean by *parliamentary government*. In view of legislators' historic achievement in thus "taming" the executive, Professor Huitt points out, "it is ironic that the representative assembly . . . is now almost everywhere submissive once more to him and his establishment."[5] The irony is nowhere more striking than in Britain. The last time a defeat in the House of Commons forced a British government to resign was in 1923, and the party controlling the cabinet at the time had a minority of House members. The last parliamentary defeat for a cabinet whose party originally enjoyed a majority of all House seats was in 1885![6]

What happened to change a system of parliamentary government to one of

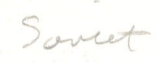

[3]*Ibid.*, p. 84.
[4]*Ibid.*, pp. 85–86.
[5]Huitt, "Congress, The Durable Partner," *loc. cit.*, p. 9.
[6]The material on the British Parliament in this section comes, unless otherwise noted, from Samuel H. Beer, "The British Legislature and the Problem of Mobilizing Consent," in Frank (ed.) *Lawmakers in a Changing World*, pp. 30–48.

cabinet government? Samuel Beer of Harvard University points primarily to the greater party discipline of Members of Parliament today. The rarity with which MPs vote against their own party permits even a government with a razor-thin majority in the House (such as the Labour Party, with a five-man majority from 1964 to 1966) to carry through its proposals. But executive power has also increased in other countries with or without a corresponding increase of party discipline among legislators. Hence Professor Beer is required to look for additional factors that have permitted party government to shift British power so strongly in the direction of the executive. He finds these in the requirements of war and of the welfare state.

We do not intend to equate the conduct of war and defense policies with government participation in management of the economy and in the provision of welfare benefits. Nevertheless, both these broad areas of decision-making require decisions of great technicality, complexity, and specificity. Because large parliamentary bodies appear best equipped to decide on general policies reflecting broad goals for society, and least equipped to settle highly specific, complex, and technical problems, the legislative importance of Parliament has declined. A larger area of decisions is left to administrative discretion and even the general grants of authority to the executive originate in the cabinet rather than among the general membership of the House of Commons. The central function of Parliament accordingly becomes less that of rule-making than of representing and identifying citizen interests. And this function is performed primarily by criticizing, and thereby to some degree controlling, the executive.[7]

The United States Congress: Is It an Exception?

What is the condition of the U.S. Congress? Does it, like the Supreme Soviet, function merely to create the illusion of citizen participation and representation? Has it, like the British Parliament, lost the function of rule-making but retained the function of representation and presentation of conflicting interests? Or has it escaped the general demise of parliamentary bodies to remain the center of authoritative rule-making?

Although no serious student of Congress thinks its activities are as peripheral as those of the Supreme Soviet, answers to the last two questions differ. "Congress is in a legislative dilemma because opinion conceives of it as a legislature," says Samuel Huntington, a student of Congress and of military policy. "Explicit acceptance of the idea that legislation was not its primary function would, in large part, simply be recognition of the direction which change has already been taking."[8] (Wouldn't those two statements confuse a high-school civics class!) Professor Huitt has a quite different emphasis. Speaking of the general decline of legislatures, he says, "The notable exception among national legislatures is the Congress of the United States . . . Congress

---

[7]Professor Beer recommends another function—that of mobilizing consent—but does not make clear the extent to which he feels this function is in fact being performed.

[8]Samuel P. Huntington, "Congressional Responses to the Twentieth Century," in David B. Truman (ed.), *The Congress and America's Future* (Englewood Cliffs, N.J.: Prentice-Hall, Inc., 1965), pp. 29, 30.

has maintained its place in the constitutional partnership . . ."[9] The contrast in the conclusions of these two recognized authorities suggests that political science as a discipline has some distance to go before precise and verifiable interpretations will take all the mystery out of politics. And the contrast should remind readers that the interpretations advanced in this book cannot be taken as some distilled "final word" on American politics—the final words have yet to be written and the tentative words are not always in agreement.

So which interpretation do *we* say is correct? A tempting answer is to say that both positions are sound and that they simply emphasize different facets of the same phenomena. But such an evasion would be unfair to the reader. We think Professor Huitt's emphasis on the continuing and unusual importance of Congress in the American political system—including the manifest function of authoritative rule-making—is more accurate.[10]

Both these interpreters recognize in the United States the same factors that have shifted the function of the British Parliament away from rule-making —namely, that the problems of a highly industrialized, urbanized society heavily involved in international affairs call for decisions that are increasingly technical, complex, and specific. Despite his view that Congress continues to perform its assigned functions, Professor Huitt notes: "Congress itself is ultimately utterly dependent on the bureaucracy for most of the information upon which it acts." And: "Legislatures learned more than a century ago that they cannot legislate in detail for very much of the varied life they seek to regulate."[11] Professor Huntington emphasizes that such conditions as these mean that "the President now determines the legislative agenda of Congress almost as thoroughly as the British Cabinet sets the legislative agenda of Parliament."[12]

Those who say Congress has lost the power to legislate virtually equate the *initiation* of legislation with *power* over legislation. Because Congress responds to executive initiatives, they conclude that it must play only a peripheral part in legislation (although they would concede that the power to obstruct, delay, and amend makes Congress more important than the Supreme Soviet in rule-making). Control of the agenda is important. But it does not shift the rule-making function entirely to the executive. This view overlooks, among other things, the "rule of anticipated reactions," which states that the bureaucrats are constrained by the necessity to anticipate the response they will receive in Congress.[13] It also forgets that a proposal originated by a congress-

---

[9]"Congress, the Durable Partner," *loc. cit.*, p. 9.
[10]In comparative terms, Huntington himself would accept our reference to the "unusual" (though perhaps not the "continuing") importance of Congress, for he concedes that "Congress has lost less power over legislation . . . than other parliaments." See Truman (ed.), *The Congress and America's Future*, p. 31.
[11]"Congress, the Durable Partner," *loc. cit.*, p. 15.
[12]"Congressional Responses to the Twentieth Century," *loc. cit.*, p. 23.
[13]On the rule of anticipated reactions, see Carl J. Friedrich, *Constitutional Government and Democracy* (Boston: Ginn & Co., 1946), pp. 589*ff.*

man may, because of the highly technical nature of most legislation, be drafted by a bureaucrat and thus be technically "initiated" by the executive. Wherever its origins, and they are usually so complex that an "ultimate first cause" or true origin can hardly be located,[14] legislation is painstakingly shaped in the committees and on the floor of Congress. These are rule-making activities.

The remainder of this chapter will attempt to explain both the increasing influence of the executive and the continuing importance of Congress in the rule-making function of the American political system.

Studying Legislators as One Class of Decision-Makers

Although we are primarily interested in Congress, we must view it as but one case in a universe of authoritative decision-making agencies. Hence the effort to broaden our perspective by comparing Congress, at least briefly, with other national legislatures. This view of all official agencies of political systems as different ways of structuring the same phenomena—authoritative decision-making activities—also applies to the study of a single political system. It suggests that, in focusing on American politics, we should apply the same categories of analysis to all of the official agencies. Political science is concerned not with descriptions of unique, nonrepetitive (and therefore inexplicable) events or activities but with explanations of the general, repetitive patterns through which men are governed. The peculiarities of Congress and of the other output agencies of government[15] will accordingly be important not as mere idiosyncracies to be appreciated but as deviations to be explained.

To understand the place of congressmen—or, for that matter, of Presidents, bureaucrats, and judges—in the American political system, we need answers to the following questions: (1) What kind of people does the system recruit for positions in the decision-making agency? (2) How is the role (of congressman, President, bureaucrat, or judge) defined—that is, what is the behavior other people expect of anyone who occupies the position, and what behavior does the occupant himself think the position calls for? (3) How are the roles structured by the actual performance of people in these positions? (4) What are the relationships among different structures or agencies of authoritative decision-making? (5) What functions does the agency perform for the broader political system? We shall accordingly organize our consideration of official decision-making activities around five topics: recruitment, role expectations, the structure of role performance, relations with other agencies, and functions. In our discussion of all these topics, we shall keep in mind the consequences of our findings for the policy outputs of the system.

[14]See the pioneer case study by Stephen K. Bailey, *Congress Makes a Law* (New York: Columbia University Press, 1950).

[15]The discerning reader may note that we shift from the assertion that *all official* agencies should be analyzed with the same categories to the statement that all *output* agencies will be so analyzed. The consideration of the electoral system in Chapter 9 was not organized in terms exactly paralleling those for the other official agencies. Logically, perhaps it should have been so organized, but the dominant part played by unofficial agencies in leadership selection seemed to call for a different organization. Even so, the key concept (role) and the key variable (relationships among interdependent elements of a common system) to be employed below, did govern the approach to the electoral system.

The Recruitment of Legislators

Membership in the Supreme Soviet of the U.S.S.R. is designed so as to reflect the ethnic, sex, and other demographic attributes of the Soviet population; the regime can boast that few parliaments include such a high proportion of women, workers, and members of minority groups. The United States Congress, on the other hand, has never been "representative" in the sense of mirroring the characteristics of the general population. This does not keep it from representing different citizen interests, of course, but the composition of Congress does affect the way in which it functions.

What Kind of People Become Legislators?

Perhaps the most noticeable characteristic of congressmen is that they are, by and large, older men. The average age of the members of the 90th Congress (1967–69) upon entering office was 52.1 years. The average senator was about fifty-eight, the average representative about fifty-one. Even the newcomers are not very young. The seven freshmen senators who took seats in 1967 had an average age of forty-six years, and the seventy-three new representatives had an average of forty-three years. Clearly, the official policies of the United States are not made by inexperienced young firebrands. Moreover, even at their relatively advanced age, most congressmen notice that there are few women in their midst. In the 90th Congress, for example, there were only eleven women representatives and one woman senator.

The fact that so many congressmen are middle-aged males does not mean, however, that the interests of youth and women are ignored in Congress. Groups need not be physically represented in order for their interests to be recognized. Leaders are different from average people almost by definition, and the characteristics of congressmen are a reflection of what Americans admire rather than of what Americans are. Most men come to Congress, as we would expect, from occupations of at least upper-middle-class standing. As Table 10–1 indicates, lawyers account for more than half the membership of Congress, and businessmen and bankers fill almost a third of the seats. Congressmen are similarly unrepresentative with respect to family background, race, ethnic origins, education, and religion. The groups of higher social status enjoy a disproportionately large share of offices in comparison with their proportion of the total population; groups of lower status tend to be virtually excluded from office.[16]

The constitutional qualifications for congressmen are quite simple: a representative must be at least twenty-five years of age, a citizen for seven years,

---

[16] See "Class Differences and Chances for Political Leadership," Chapter 2.

Table 10-1 Occupational Background of Congressmen

OCCUPATIONAL BACKGROUND	87TH CONGRESS SENATE	87TH CONGRESS HOUSE	90TH CONGRESS SENATE	90TH CONGRESS HOUSE
Agriculture	18%	11%	18%	9%
Business or banking	31	31	23	37
Journalism	10	8	10	8
Law	63	56	68	57
Medicine, engineering	3	2	3	2
Teaching	14	9	15	13

Sources: Congressional Quarterly Almanac, XVII (1961), 35; *Congressional Quarterly Weekly Report,* XXV (January 13, 1967), 65. Percentages total more than 100 because some members had engaged in more than one occupation.

and an inhabitant of the state from which he is elected; a senator must be thirty years old, a citizen for nine years, and an inhabitant of the state from which he is elected. Any citizen can meet these requirements simply by staying alive. But various informal requirements narrow the field sharply. If one plans to be a congressman, it will normally be to his advantage to arrange to be the following: a late-middle-aged male lawyer whose father was of the professional or managerial class; a native-born "white," or—if he cannot avoid being an immigrant—a product of Northwestern or Central Europe or Canada, rather than of Eastern or Southern Europe or Asia; a college graduate; and a Protestant, preferably a Methodist, Presbyterian, Episcopalian, or Baptist. On church membership, for example, the religious affiliations of congressmen in 1967–69 were: Protestant, 76 per cent; Catholic, 20; Jewish, 3.[17] He should also have some political experience before seeking election to Congress—as did 97 per cent of the senators and 86 per cent of the representatives in the 90th Congress. Finally, he will do well to serve at least briefly in the armed forces—65 per cent of the senators and 74 per cent of the representatives in the 90th Congress were veterans. If, however, after going to all this trouble, he seeks office in a constituency made up principally of Negroes, immigrants from Asia and Southeastern Europe, or pacifists, his efforts will have been in vain. The "typical" congressman is, after all, a product of the "typical" constituency.

Although we expect congressmen to be different from the rank and file, how do they compare with other top-level leaders? Comparing the one hundred members of the Senate with the presidents of America's one hundred largest industrial corporations in 1959, Andrew Hacker of Cornell University found important contrasts. First, despite the fact that the 1958 election produced an unusually heavy turnover,[18] the median tenure of the senators (seven years) was almost twice that of the corporation presidents (four years). Legislators, then, are men who have been at their jobs a relatively long while. This has not always been the case, as the figures in Table 10–2 demonstrate. In the Congresses of the late nineteenth century, almost half the members of the House

---

[17]Percentages do not total 100 because of rounding and because of two representatives who were Greek Orthodox and accounted for 0.4 per cent of the total. Six members whose religious affiliation was not given were excluded in figuring these percentages. The list of Protestant denominations in the preceding sentence is a ranking in order of number of members in Congress. See *Congressional Quarterly Weekly Report,* XXV (January 13, 1967), 62.

[18]Prior to the 1958 election, the Senate had 49 Democrats and 47 Republicans; after the election it had 65 Democrats and 35 Republicans. See Andrew Hacker, "The Elected and the Anointed: Two American Elites," *American Political Science Review,* LV (September, 1961), 539.

and over half the members of the Senate were serving in their first elective term. But the length of tenure has steadily increased to the point where around 80 per cent of all congressmen in the 1967–69 term had been elected more than once. Professor Huntington sees the top administrators under the President, no less than business leaders, as characterized much more by the "rotation-in-office" principle that is thought to bring in new blood and keep decision-makers attuned to changing public needs: "In this century the administration has acquired many of the characteristics of a representative body that Congress has tended to lose . . . . A continuous adjustment of power and authority takes place within each administration . . . . A thousand new officials descend on Washington, coming fresh from the people, representing the diverse forces behind the new President, and bringing with them new demands, new ideas, and new power. Here truly is representative government along classic lines and of a sort which Congress has not known for decades."[19] At the moment we are less concerned with Professor Huntington's argument that Congress is less "representative" than the administration than we are with making the point that congressmen enjoy longer tenures than other high-level leaders in government or in business. (The consequences of this and other characteristics of congressmen are the concerns of the remaining parts of this chapter.)

Table 10-2   The Percentage of Veteran Congressmen in Congresses from 1871 To 1967

CONGRESS	DATE	REPRESENTATIVES ELECTED TO HOUSE MORE THAN ONCE	SENATORS ELECTED TO SENATE MORE THAN ONCE
42nd	1871	53%	32%
50th	1887	63	45
64th	1915	74	47
74th	1935	77	54
87th	1961	87	66
90th	1967	86	80

Source: Figures for the period 1871–1961 are from Samuel P. Huntington, "Congressional Responses to the Twentieth Century," loc. cit., p. 9. The 1967 figures were calculated independently.

A second marked difference between congressmen and other national leaders is that congressmen are much less "national" in background and orientation. A far smaller proportion of congressmen, for example, come from the metropolitan centers that dominate American life (outside of Congress): 52 per cent of the corporation presidents but only 19 per cent of the senators grew up in areas with a population of over 100,000.[20] And the proportion of senators (32 per cent) whose fathers were farmers was more than twice as high as it was for administration leaders or corporation presidents. Congressmen not only

[19] "Congressional Responses to the Twentieth Century," loc. cit., p. 17.
[20] This paragraph is based on data from the Hacker and Huntington articles cited in the two preceding footnotes.

come from a more bucolic environment but, more importantly, they seem to prefer it. The average senator traveled a bit farther than the average corporation president from his home town to go to college, but the senators' early identification with the section of the country where they grew up is demonstrated by their greater tendency to return to the home environment after college. The median distance between the childhood home and the current residence of senators is 22 miles, for corporation presidents, 342 miles. Congressmen are thus peculiarly "home town" types, and their homes have a distinctively rural and small town quality in comparison either with other national leaders or with the total population.

These social characteristics do not determine the congressman's behavior in any complete sense, of course, but they do have an influence. Forget for the moment that we are talking about Congress and imagine that someone had just characterized for you the members of a wholly unknown political group. You discover that this group is almost entirely male, that its members are mostly middle-aged or older, that a large majority are "WASPS" (white-Anglo-Saxon-Protestants), that the members tend to remain in office for increasingly long periods, and that—despite their high education and high status—they tend to come from rural and small town backgrounds and continue to live near where they grew up. With no more information than this, you could safely predict that such an organization would have a highly conservative outlook.

The congressman is not a free agent. His actions are constrained by, among other things, his party affiliation and the characteristics of his constituency. But the individual congressman's own personal characteristics do have important consequences. A study of the voting records of congressmen on the reciprocal trade issue from 1948 to 1958 bears out the importance of the individual in a congressional seat regardless of party or constituency. The votes cast for districts which were represented by a single congressman during this entire ten-year period were compared with the votes cast for districts who elected more than one congressman of the same party. Considerably less variation was found in the votes when they were cast by a single person than when they were cast by different people, even when the different people were of the same party and from the same type of constituency.[21] And a major study of influences on foreign trade policy finds that the legislator has "nothing like a clear mandate from the people" and that his policy inclinations are more important in understanding his activity than interest group pressure on him.[22]

If we consider the kind of people who are congressmen and their relative discretion in decision-making, the remarkable thing is that the record of Congress is not more conservative. But the influence of constituency and party helps make the record more understandable and less remarkable.

The Constituencies of Congressmen

When the newly arrived congressman takes his seat in the Senate or House, he does not have to make a completely fresh start. As a mature and probably prominent person in his

---

[21]Lewis A. Froman, Jr., *Congressmen and Their Constituencies* (Chicago: Rand McNally & Co., 1963), Chapter 8.
[22]Raymond A. Bauer, Ithiel de Sola Pool, and Lewis Anthony Dexter, *American Business and Public Policy* (New York: Atherton Press, 1963), p. 453.

constituency, he has fairly well-established opinions on a variety of public problems. And he also has established contacts with different groups in his constituency who will offer cues whenever he is uncertain about his role. His role as a congressman may ultimately broaden his views, but he starts out as the representative of a particular constituency; and the problem of being re-elected by the folks back home keeps their picture bright in his mind. For that matter, his colleagues would regard him as a maverick if he forgot his constituents' special needs. Congressmen from agricultural constituencies champion price supports for farmers, those from predominantly immigrant areas favor liberal immigration quotas, those from the Deep South oppose civil rights bills. Since these stands can be taken for granted regardless of the congressman's party or personal characteristics, the constituency is an important element in policy-making.

Lewis A. Froman, Jr., of the University of California at Irvine has found systematic support for the long-standing assumption that the makeup of a constituency has a direct bearing on congressional voting.[23] Democrats vote on the liberal side of social welfare questions more than Republicans not just because of their party identification or ideology but also because they come from different kinds of districts than Republicans. Outside the South, Democratic districts are more urban, more racially mixed, have smaller proportions of owner-occupied dwellings, and have more people per square mile than Republican districts. Constituencies with these characteristics are generally expected to be on the liberal side of social welfare questions. The discovery that they tend to elect Democrats is therefore not surprising. But Froman goes on to demonstrate that, even when the comparison is between representatives in the same party, differences in these constituency characteristics still make a difference—Democrats from lower status districts vote even more for liberal measures than Democrats whose constituents are of higher status.

The larger a constituency is, the more likely it is to include diverse and heterogeneous interests. "Extend the sphere, and you take in a greater variety of parties and interests," James Madison advised in arguing for the adoption of the Constitution.[24] And the greater the variety of parties and interests in a constituency, the more liberal will be its representatives on broad questions of social and economic policy.[25] Hence presidential candidates, faced with the unit rule in the electoral college that gives all of a state's electoral votes to the candidate who wins a plurality in the state, are sensitive to the liberal demands of the most populous states. After all, a person can win the presidency if he gets a plurality in the eleven largest states and the District of Columbia and loses in all thirty-nine of the smaller states. The Senate, on the other hand, is oriented more to the small states. With two senators for every state regard-

---

[23] *Congressmen and Their Constituencies*, Chapter 7.
[24] This is from his famous Federalist essay No. 10. See Charles A. Beard (ed.), *The Enduring Federalist* (Garden City, N.Y.: Doubleday & Company, Inc., 1948), p. 74.
[25] See Grant McConnell, *Private Power and American Democracy* (New York: Alfred A. Knopf, Inc., 1966), pp. 103–118.

less of population, a majority of the Senate representing the twenty-six smallest states represents only 17 per cent of the population.[26] The Senate constituencies thus produce a less liberal outlook than the presidential constituency. By the same token, House constituencies, because they are yet smaller and more homogeneous, produce a still more conservative body.

We have been talking in the preceding paragraph about the Senate and the House as a whole. By the same logic employed there, a number of senators should be no less liberal than presidential candidates on social and economic policy. The senators from the eleven most populous states are elected from the very constituencies with diverse economic, ethnic, and religious groups to which presidents must appeal. Accordingly, both the Republican (Jacob Javits) and the Democratic (Robert Kennedy) senators from a state like New York must behave in a metropolitan rather than provincial fashion. And other senators or representatives with ambitions for higher office may respond to the needs of an anticipated constituency that is broader than their current constituency. The late Senator Kefauver from Tennessee is an excellent example of this source of deviation from our broad characterization of Congress. But the broad characterization remains, we think, valid. Stephen K. Bailey argues that "as each state and congressional district becomes more complex in its interest group structure, it becomes more and more a microcosm of the entire nation."[27] We agree with his argument, but disagree with his implication that a majority of the congressional districts have reached such a point of complexity.

The Party Membership of Congressmen

The reader should not conclude, just because constituency characteristics exert influence independent of a congressman's party affiliation, that representative government is simply a process through which constituency preferences are reflected by congressional agents. We have already seen that the congressman's personal background also has an independent influence. And the most important fact of all about congressmen is that they are all members of either the Republican or Democratic political party.

Despite the decentralization and loose discipline of American political parties, the basic differences in Congress are between Democrats and Republicans. If a person could ask for only one fact about a congressman in order to predict his voting behavior, the knowledgeable observer would ask for his party identification. Democrats and Republicans from the same constituencies in different Congresses differ drastically in their votes on issues important for those constituencies—for example, on a larger role for the national government in the social welfare area. A comparison of different party occupants of the same seats in 1957–60 and 1961–62 found that in every district the Democrat exceeded his Republican predecessor or follower in supporting a larger role for the national government; on the average the vote of the Democrats in favor of more national activity was 68 percentage points higher than that of Republi-

---

[26]Lewis A. Froman, Jr., *The Congressional Process: Strategies, Rules, and Procedures* (Boston: Little, Brown and Company, 1967), p. 4.
[27]*The New Congress* (New York: St. Martin's Press, 1966), p. 18.

cans from the same districts.²⁸ Although constituency characteristics have some influence independent of party affiliation, then, party affiliation has a far greater influence independent of constituency characteristics. Generally, of course, both forces work together: districts with "liberal" social and economic attributes elect Democrats and districts with "conservative" attributes elect Republicans. This normal congruence of constituency characteristics and party affiliation leads to great differences in party performance in Congress. Just as party identification emerged as the key explanatory variable in studying political opinions of the general public, so does it emerge as the principal factor for understanding Congress.

Party unity in the United States Congress does not approach that of either the Conservative or Labour parties in the British Parliament,²⁹ but it is much greater than most people realize. In 1966, for example, a majority of Democrats opposed a majority of Republicans on 198 roll-call votes. The average Democrat voted against his party on 18 per cent of these roll calls, the average Republican against his party on 15 per cent (see Table 10–3). If we recalculate the figures ignoring failures to vote, about 77 per cent of the Democratic votes and 82 per cent of the Republican votes are found to be in support of their party majorities.³⁰ This is far from perfect party unity, but it is even farther from perfect disunity.

Table 10-3 Congressional Votes on Roll Calls that Produced Party Division, 1966

	HOUSE DEMOCRATS	HOUSE REPUBLICANS	SENATE DEMOCRATS	SENATE REPUBLICANS	BOTH HOUSES DEMOCRATS	BOTH HOUSES REPUBLICANS
With Party	62%	68%	57%	63%	61%	67%
Against Party	17	15	21	18	18	15
Not Voting	21	17	22	19	21	18
	100%	100%	100%	100%	100%	100%

Source: Recomputation of data from the *Congressional Quarterly Weekly Report*, XXIV (December 9, 1966), 2990.

The greatest deviations from party unity in the United States come from southern Democrats. In 1966, the average southern Democrat in Congress voted against his party on about 36 per cent of the roll calls in which Democratic and Republican majorities were in opposition.³¹ (The average support

---

[28] Clarence N. Stone, "Inter-Party Differences and Congressional Voting Behavior: A Partial Dissent," *American Political Science Review*, LVII (September, 1963), 665–666.

[29] Richard Rose, *Politics in England* (Boston: Little, Brown and Company, 1964), pp. 208–209.

[30] One reason why the level of party support is underestimated is that some scholars misread the figures in the *Congressional Quarterly Weekly*, which does not report nonvoting. Thus Lewis A. Froman, Jr., reports that the average Democrat and Republican voted against their respective parties 31 and 29 per cent of the time in 1963–64. The actual votes *against* the parties were 16 and 17 per cent in 1963–64. See *The Congressional Process*, p. 6, and *Congressional Quarterly Weekly Report*, XXII (October 30, 1964), 2589.

[31] *Congressional Quarterly Weekly Report*, XXIV (December 9, 1966), 2990.

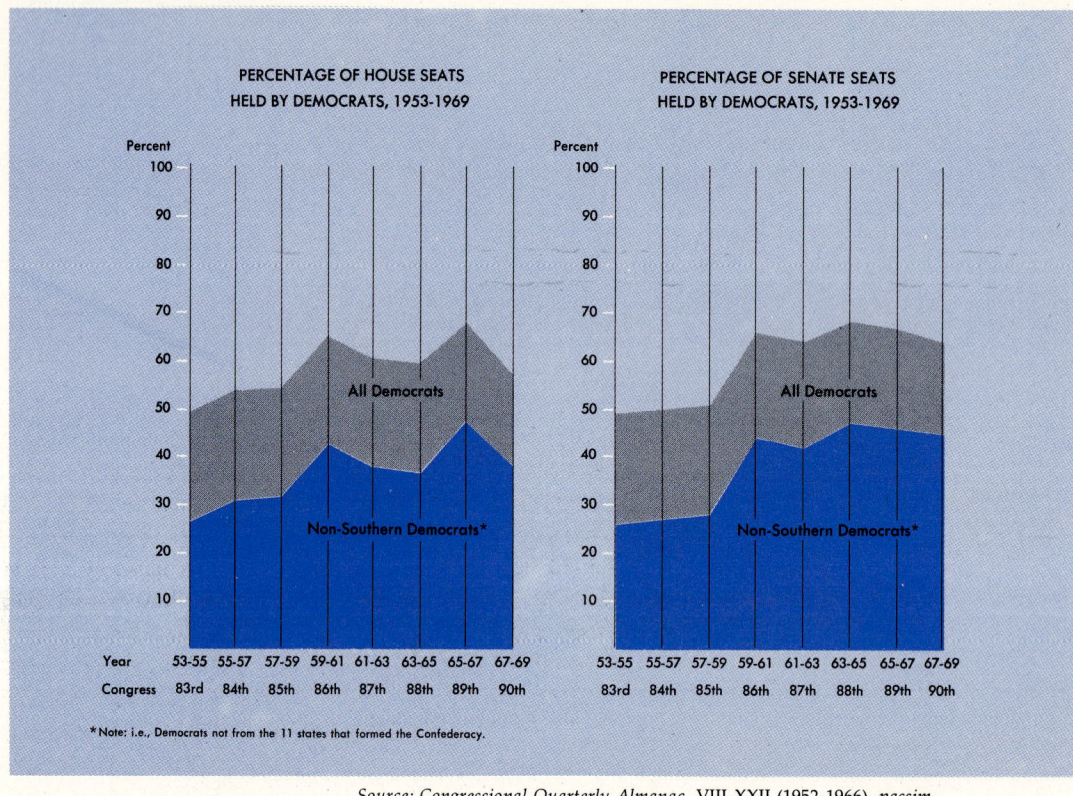

PERCENTAGE OF HOUSE SEATS HELD BY DEMOCRATS, 1953-1969

PERCENTAGE OF SENATE SEATS HELD BY DEMOCRATS, 1953-1969

*Note: i.e., Democrats not from the 11 states that formed the Confederacy.

Source: *Congressional Quarterly Almanac*, VIII-XXII (1952-1966), *passim*.

Figure 10-1

for the Democrats was about 41 per cent and abstentions were about 23 per cent.) Thus the Democrats usually need more than a bare majority to push through legislation. But when their majority reaches the point where the nonsouthern members of the party approach 50 per cent, as in 1965, one can confidently predict an upswing in legislation extending the social and economic welfare activities of the national government. (See Figure 10–1.) In discussing the generation-old controversy over Medicare in Chapter 8, we made the point that the legislation was finally passed in 1965 with no change in the alignment of pressure groups. The only difference was the election of 1964: the Democrats retained a large majority in the Senate and increased their majority in the House to 67.8 per cent, with the nonsouthern Democrats alone making up 47.1 per cent of the total membership. The election of 1964 and the changes it made in the party composition of Congress brought about the passage of Medicare.

The new student of political science may be surprised to hear that the explanation of the passage of Medicare recapitulated above was included in the third edition of this book, which was distributed by the publisher in April of 1965, three months *before* the Medicare bill was enacted into law. When the election of 1964 so greatly enlarged the Democratic majority in Congress, we were sufficiently certain that a Medicare bill would be enacted before September, 1965 (when students would begin to read the book), that we felt free to talk about its enactment to make several points. Perhaps this "inside story" will make the points more strongly: elections in the United States count; the party division in Congress counts; both count because they have *predictable* effects on the policy outputs of the political system.[32]

The Role of Congressmen

In considering the electoral system, we talked of roles as a combination of "will" and "ought" expectations (predictions and norms) about the behavior of people in particular positions. These expectations are supported by sanctions—both rewards and deprivations—of varying degrees of generosity or severity. How do they apply to congressmen?

External Expectations

Although the Constitution of 1787 does not stipulate the norms associated with the position of congressman, it clearly implies certain expectations. Underlying the formal phrases from the eighteenth century is the obvious expectation that congressmen would play a major role in the new government. Not only are they granted "all legislative Powers" but they are expected to enjoy large discretion in determining how to exercise those powers. Congress is expected to manage its own affairs—it is independently elected; "no Person holding any Office under the United States, shall be a Member of either house"; and each house determines its own rules of procedure, judges "the Qualifications of its own Members," selects its leaders (except that the Vice-President is designated as President of the Senate), and has the power to expel a member by a two-thirds vote. The assumption that congressmen should be free from harassment in carrying out their responsibilities is manifest in this protection: "They shall in all cases, except Treason, Felony and Breach of the Peace, be privileged from Arrest during their Attendance at the Session of the respective Houses, and in going to and returning from the same; and for any Speech or Debate in either House, they shall not be questioned in any other Place."

The greater power, autonomy, and protection granted to Congress is not given without restraints. And the restraints are equally revealing as to the official expectations about congressional behavior. The new congressman needs to read beyond the first sentence of Article I, with its grandiose reference to "all legislative Powers herein granted"; when he gets to Section 9, and later to the Bill of Rights, he discovers that some powers (primarily those that could be used for legislative punishment of individuals or denial of basic rights) not only are not "herein granted" but are specifically denied. He will also discover that the apparent congressional monopoly of those legislative

---

[32] Although political science may not have much more predictive capacity concerning future political events than meteorology has with regard to future rainfall, this story does suggest that political science is not totally devoid of predictive power.

powers which *are* granted is not complete—the President, for example, has the right to veto legislation and the duty to recommend legislation. In addition, the Constitution clearly envisages a Congress under public scrutiny: the provision for popular choice of its members (for senators, this dates from the adoption of Amendment XVII in 1913) is augmented by the requirements that each house keep and publish a "Journal of its Proceedings" and that "the Yeas and Nays of the Members of either House on any question shall, at the desire of one fifth of those Present, be entered on the Journal."

Officially, then, the position of congressman calls for the exercise of great—but not unlimited—rule-making power in a relationship of responsibility to other official agencies and to the public. Although about 60 per cent of adult Americans confess knowing nothing at all about their representative,[33] most are presumably aware that the position exists. Because Americans are virtually unanimous in endorsing the general idea of democracy, such vague ideas as they may have about the proper role of congressmen are no doubt within the limits of the official description.

But some people have more precise expectations about the role of congressmen. Among the general public, only about 15 per cent say they have ever written a letter to *any* public official.[34] Among the heads of business firms employing 100 or more employees, the contrast is striking: almost 80 per cent say they have communicated directly with Congress.[35] Frequently these constituent contacts with congressmen call for them to perform some service—furnish information or clarify a problem with an administrator, for example—that has nothing to do with their constitutionally defined role of law-maker. These requests carry the implication that the congressman is expected to represent his constituency not just as legislator but as intermediary and spokesman for constituent needs in relation to other agencies of government.

The local and national leaders of the congressman's party, all the people who invested time and money in his campaign for office, the President (especially when he and the congressman belong to the same party), organized interest groups in his constituency—all of these expect the congressman to give at least a sympathetic hearing to their demands. Some expect more than a sympathetic hearing; they expect a positive response. The more knowledgeable among them know that the congressman is the object of such a welter of expectations that no simple stimulus-response model will predict his behavior, whether the stimulus comes from constituents, party, pressure groups, or President.

Life in Congress: The Internal Demands of the Role

Congress has a group life of its own. Just as being a member of a Boy Scout troop, a neighborhood gang, or a college sorority influences a person's behavior and habits, so does being a member of Congress. And, like any other functioning group, Congress has certain norms to which the new member must adjust. To enjoy status within

---

[33] Donald E. Stokes and Warren E. Miller, "Party Government and the Saliency of Congress," in Angus Campbell *et al., Elections and the Political Order* (New York: John Wiley & Sons, Inc., 1966), p. 204.

[34] Philip E. Converse, Aage R. Clausen, and Warren E. Miller, "Electoral Myth and Reality: The 1964 Election," *American Political Science Review*, LIX (June, 1965), 333.

[35] Bauer, de Sola Pool, and Dexter, *op. cit.*, p. 201. The percentages for different sizes of firms are: 100 to 999 employees, 71 per cent; 1,000 to 9,999 employees, 79 per cent; 10,000 or more employees, 88 per cent.

this face-to-face group, the member must show respect for Congress as an institution, and he must adjust his behavior to the needs of the group. He will act, in other words, not merely as a particular kind of person with a given party identification and constituency background, but also as a member of Congress who is involved in its needs as an organization. The "club atmosphere" of the Senate demonstrates the deference members accord one another, even those who disagree on everything except the Senate's importance.

What norms do the Senate and House impose on new members? These norms are not formally spelled out, but the perceptive freshman quickly learns that they make up a well-defined role.[36] First, he is expected to be "seen and not heard," to serve—without complaining to the "upperclassmen"—a decent period of apprenticeship, during which he performs routine chores without glory. Second, he is expected to devote himself primarily to routine legislative tasks, rather than to seek publicity by proposing major policies or by trying to dominate public committee hearings or congressional debate. Third, he is expected to specialize in the area of legislation in which his committee or constituency has a particular stake; to try to take the lead in other legislative areas would be to challenge the leadership and the special prerogatives of his colleagues. Fourth, he is expected to cooperate with his colleagues, show himself willing to "give and take" rather than insist on his own principles without compromise. His ideology may be firmly fixed on his own mind, but he must subordinate it to the legislative necessity of compromise. Finally, and especially in the Senate, he is expected to show great respect for his colleagues as individuals and deep attachment to his branch of Congress as an institution.

Because of these norms, these unofficial rules of behavior, we hear very little from new members of the Senate or House during their first years in office. Even those who have made a name for themselves before going to Congress must—if they are prudent—be content to serve a period of apprenticeship. But this is a restrictive role, and rewards and punishments are necessary to encourage conformity. These sanctions are somewhat like the ones that lead fraternity pledges, and novitiates in primitive societies, to endure agonizing initiation ceremonies. Those who conform may live to be called "brother" or "true Senate men," to feel a warm slap on the back from their elders. The nonconformists, though not actually black-balled, are frowned upon for acting like "show horses" instead of "work horses" and are barred from the "inner ring" of the leaders. More tangible rewards are also offered: conforming members get the choice committee assignments, their bills receive more favorable consideration, and their states receive more favors.

[36]Material in this and the next paragraph comes largely from Donald R. Matthews, *U.S. Senators and Their World* (Chapel Hill: University of North Carolina Press, 1960). Richard F. Fenno, Jr., finds a strikingly similar set of norms to be functional for the integration of the House Appropriations Committee and their absence to be dysfunctional for the House Education and Labor Committee. See "The House Appropriations Committee as a Political System: The Problem of Integration," *American Political Science Review*, LVI (June, 1962), 310–324; and "The House of Representatives and Federal Aid to Education," in R. L. Peabody and N. W. Polsby (eds.), *New Perspectives on the House of Representatives* (Chicago: Rand McNally & Company, 1963), pp. 195–235.

The case of nonconformist Estes Kefauver (Tennessee) and conformist John Kennedy (Massachusetts) illustrates the way the system of sanctions works. In 1957, both these Democratic senators sought a berth on the important Senate Committee on Foreign Affairs. Under the normal functioning of the seniority system, the post would have gone to Kefauver because of his longer tenure. But Kefauver had conducted highly publicized investigations of crime and juvenile delinquency before two of the preceding presidential elections, and had spent considerable time campaigning, while Kennedy—although clearly ambitious—spent more time on the routine jobs of a senator. Kefauver had written a book, *A Twentieth Century Congress*,[37] in which he criticized various "outmoded" practices of Congress, including the system by which committee assignments are made on a seniority basis. Kennedy had also written a book, *Profiles in Courage*,[38] in which he eulogized the "greats" of Senate history. Kennedy got the coveted assignment. The seniority rule was relaxed—something that is rarely done—in order to keep the post from going to Kefauver, the critic of that rule, who wryly commented that he had not heard that the seniority rule was no longer in operation.

The force of congressional sanctions is enhanced by the longer tenure in office that congressmen enjoy today, a point we noted earlier. In contrast to their predecessors in the nineteenth century, congressmen have come to see service in Congress as a lifetime career, and have thus begun to pay more attention to the internal norms of Congress. These norms and the sanctions behind them were not so important when service in Congress was only one stage in a variegated career. But a career is more valued when it is a lifetime commitment; hence the internal norms of the legislature become more important.

Why do the norms take the particular form we have described? Donald Matthews, a student of legislative behavior, suggests that they are highly "functional"—that is, they are necessary if Congress is to survive without major change. His remarks about the Senate may be applied with almost equal force to the House:

> These folkways . . . are highly functional to the Senate social system since they provide motivation for the performance of vital duties and essential modes of behavior which, otherwise, would go unrewarded. They discourage frequent and lengthy speech-making in a chamber without any other effective limitation on debate, encourage the development of expertness and a division of labor in a group of overworked laymen facing unbelievably complex problems, soften the inevitable personal conflicts of a problem-solving body, and encourage bargaining and the cautious use of awesome formal powers. Without these folkways, the Senate could hardly operate with its present organization and rules.[39]

Other pressures on a congressman, such as ambition for the presidency, a fixed ideology, or the peculiar demands of his constituency, are sometimes strong enough to outweigh congressional norms in governing his behavior.

---

[37] In collaboration with Jack Levin, *A Twentieth Century Congress* (New York: Duell, Sloan and Pearce, 1947).
[38] *Profiles in Courage* (New York: Harper & Row, Publishers, Inc., 1958). Also published in a paperbound edition by Pocket Books, Inc.
[39] *U.S. Senators and Their World*, p. 116.

Behavior that is functional for Congress as a group may not be functional for an individual congressman's career—or, for that matter, for society at large. The nation needs an occasional nonconformist like the late Senator George W. Norris (R.-Nebraska), even if other senators grumble that he doesn't play the game. Thus a new congressman, responding to broader norms than those of the legislature itself, may embark on a wider range of activities than his colleagues think appropriate.[40] Nevertheless, the majority of freshmen seem to conform.

Role Performance: The Structure of Congressional Activity

Role performance does not always conform to role expectations: an occasional cleric absconds with the church treasury and organist. Some failures to conform violate internal rather than external expectations: an occasional doctor tells a patient that another medico's treatment was incompetent. Deviations from external expectations are likely to bring sanctions from the society as a whole (the erring minister would be incarcerated) and deviations from internal expectations are likely to bring sanctions from one's fellow group members (the erring doctor would receive few referrals of patients from colleagues).

The organization of Congress appears well adapted to role performance in keeping with internal expectations. Indeed, the norms of Congress are in large measure a product of the way it organizes its activities; the norms and the structure of activities are now so interrelated that each is both "cause" and "effect" in a mutually reinforcing relationship. Some critics argue, as we noted above, that Congress is *not* structured so as to fulfill the principal external expectation, authoritative rule-making. We will be in a better position to reassess this charge after considering the role performance of congressmen and their relations with other decision-making agencies.

Congress as a Separate System of Power

The chief peculiarity that distinguishes the United States Congress from most other national legislatures is its relative independence from the executive. In most western democracies both the chief executive and other cabinet officials are chosen from and retain membership in the legislature. Since the cabinet officers are leaders of both the executive and the legislature, the preparation of the legislative program is in their hands and little division of labor has developed in the legislature itself. The cabinet typically exercises strong control over the voting behavior of their fellow party members in the legislature. Indeed, if the legislative proposals of the executive are rejected by the legislature, the usual practice is for the government to fall, for the Parliament to be dissolved, and for new elec-

---

[40]See Ralph K. Huitt, "The Outsider in the Senate: An Alternative Role," *American Political Science Review*, LV (September, 1961), 566–575, and Professor Matthews' letter in the following issue of the *Review*.

tions to take place. In practice, as we saw for Britain, these drastic sanctions do not have to be applied. Parliament goes along.

The United States Congress is in a quite different position. Congressmen and the President are separately elected, they have different constituencies, and Congress chooses its own leaders. The constitutional prohibition against any member of Congress holding an office in the executive branch reinforces the status of Congress as a separate system of power. Despite the sharing of functions by President and Congress (the subject of our next section), "the institutions are clearly divided and so are the roles that go with each."[41]

With Congress thus separated from the executive, congressmen cannot, like members of a parliament, depend on those of its members who are in the cabinet for detailed information and consideration of legislative proposals. The cabinet is "they," an outside group with its own norms and procedures geared to the presidential constituency. The resultant necessity for Congress to have its own sources of information and its own agencies for consideration of legislation led to the committee system. If most parliamentary government is really government by cabinets, congressional government is, as Woodrow Wilson discerned, government by committees. And, as we shall see below, these committees are not only free from any direct control by the executive, but are also largely free from control by the internal leaders of Congress itself. Congressional government thus approaches maximum dispersal of power as closely as parliamentary government approaches maximum concentration of power.

A second peculiarity in the organization of Congress is that it is bicameral in fact as well as in name. Most other national legislatures also have two houses, but the lower house has generally acquired the exclusive power to legislate, with the upper house reduced to the point where it can delay but not block the enactments of the lower house. The necessity for positive action by both houses of the United States Congress further disperses power, multiplies constituencies, and adds more points at which legislation may be blocked.

The House of Representatives was originally conceived as the "popular" branch of Congress, with members elected directly by the people for two-

Drawing by Herblock;
© 1967 The Washington Post.

[41]Huitt, "Congress, the Durable Partner," *loc. cit.*, p. 11.

Fiddler 350

year terms. Each state was guaranteed at least one representative; beyond that provision, representation in the House was to be apportioned among the states according to population. Accordingly, the House was planned as the only popular agency of the national government—popular both in the manner in which the members were elected, and in the scheme of apportioning representation. The Senate, by contrast, was planned as the "nonpopular," or federal, branch of Congress. Its members were to be elected for six-year terms by the state legislatures, and each state was guaranteed two senators regardless of its population.

The hard facts of political power originally produced bicameralism, and chances are they will sustain it. All the talk about "states" having a "right" to an equal voice was and is a more attractive way of saying that people with extra power do not like to surrender it. The word "state" has no meaning except in terms of people. Political leaders from the less populous states enjoyed power at the national level disproportionate to their numbers before and during the drafting of the Constitution. And they refused to take part in the planning of the new government unless they were given a similar advantage in at least one branch of Congress. Delegates from the more populous states agreed to this hard bargain because they had more to lose under the Articles of Confederation (with no recognition of varying state populations) than under the new scheme.

The residents of Alaska or of Nevada would hardly argue that each Alaskan or Nevadan is worth over 100 New Yorkers. But if any proposal were made to abolish the Senate, their leaders would talk about the equal rights of states —not of people—and about federalism—not about majority rule. Moreover, with the amendment plan of the Founding Fathers still intact, the senators who represent only 3 per cent of the total population could block a proposal to amend the Constitution. Politics is the quest for power, and those who enjoy power do not voluntarily surrender it. Instead, they invent ideas to justify keeping it. Bicameralism is here to stay.

Some ironic twists have radically altered the intention of the Founding Fathers that the Senate be a conservative body checking the more liberal House members, all freshly elected by the people every two years and brimming with new ideas. Two things went wrong with these plans. First was the *democratization of the Senate* in the twentieth century as a result of the adoption of popular election of senators and the spread of two-party competition to a majority of the States.[42] As we noted in speaking of congressional constituencies, the greater heterogeneity of the senators' statewide electorates calls for a more liberal stance than is permitted by the more confined congressional districts often dominated by a single interest. By 1960, urban residents made up a majority of the population in thirty-nine states, so few senators can afford to champion the virtues of a simple and conservative rural way of life. And they face active competition to keep them attuned to the needs of their urban

---

[42]See H. Douglas Price, "The Electoral Arena," in Truman (ed.), *op. cit.*, p. 32. The data in this and the next paragraph are, unless otherwise indicated, from this source.

constituents. Of all senators elected in 1960 and 1962, for example, over half received less than 55 per cent of the votes.

The second twentieth-century change that has reversed the expectations of the Founding Fathers is the *professionalization of the House career.* "While the Senate has become more liberal and more subject to close competition, the House has become more conservative and less subject to competition in the great majority of congressional districts."[43] The smaller and more homogeneous House districts, instead of returning a fresh group of popular spokesmen every two years, return the same old representatives. In the period when over half of the senators were winning elections with margins of less than 55 per cent, only 23 per cent of the representatives won by such uncomfortably small margins. The relative homogeneity of House districts, the low level of public information about representatives, and the great advantage incumbents enjoy in being familiar to the public[44] combine to make at least three-fourths of all House seats relatively "safe" from party competition. As one experienced representative explained to a student of Congress, "You know I am sure you will find out a Congressman can do pretty much what he decides to do, and he doesn't have to bother too much about criticism."[45]

In the last decade, the apportionment of House seats has improved considerably. The number of seats each state gets has never been a serious problem because the Constitution requires that seats be allotted to the states "according to their respective numbers" after each decennial census. After taking the easy way out and permitting the membership of the House to increase steadily for over a hundred years, Congress finally called a halt at a total of 435 representatives. Since 1929, a virtually automatic arrangement has been followed. After each census, the Census Bureau calculates the number of representatives to which the population of each state entitles it, on the basis of a House membership fixed at 435. The President submits this reapportionment plan to Congress, and it automatically goes into effect unless Congress enacts a different plan within sixty days. This plan takes advantage of the difficulty of getting Congress to act—instead of requiring passage of a bill to *get* reapportionment, the procedure requires passage of a bill to *block* reapportionment.

But the apportionment of congressional districts *within* the states has been much more controversial. Since 1842, Congress has required states with more than one representative to choose their representatives from single-member districts.[46] But in 1929 it dropped the additional requirement that these districts be compact, contiguous, and as nearly equal in population as practicable. In other words, Congress left the state legislatures free to handle congressional districting without guidelines. As a result, the states adopted grossly unfair districting schemes with apparent impunity.

---

[43]*Ibid.*

[44]About 39 per cent of the citizens know something about their representative; about 20 per cent know something about his opponent. Donald E. Stokes and Warren E. Miller, "Party Government and the Saliency of Congress," *Public Opinion Quarterly,* XXVI (Winter, 1962), 540. Reprinted in Campbell *et al., Elections and the Political Order,* pp. 194–211.

[45]Lewis Anthony Dexter, "The Representative and his District," in Nelson W. Polsby *et al.* (eds.), *Politics and Social Life* (Boston: Houghton Mifflin Company, 1963), p. 498.

[46]When states fail to redistrict after a reapportionment and elect their new representatives from the state "at large," the House does not refuse to seat such representatives.

By mid-century, the rural minority of the population held about three-fifths of the House seats, and their overrepresentation in most state legislatures was even greater. The demands of urban residents for an equal voice in government were loud and clear, but they could hardly become effective inputs of legislative decision-making. Both the House of Representatives and the state legislatures (which are responsible for drawing congressional districts) were controlled by the very interests which stood to lose from reapportionment. But the political system functions as a whole and its elements are so interdependent that the activity (or inactivity) of one element affects all other elements of the system. A democratic political system must somehow respond to enduring majority interests if it is to survive; if one element of the system fails to respond, another element tends to meet the need.[47] Until the 1930s, for example, American workers' efforts to organize labor unions were severely handicapped by court enforcement of "yellow-dog contracts," which bound workers not to join a union and which the Supreme Court further interpreted as forbidding union officials from trying to organize such workers.[48] Long stymied in the courts, labor turned to Congress and won passage of the Norris-LaGuardia Act of 1932 outlawing yellow-dog contracts. Urban interests were similarly frustrated by malapportionment, but in this instance the legislature appeared unyielding; urbanites turned accordingly to the courts for relief.

In a series of decisions beginning in 1946,[49] the Supreme Court gradually worked its way to the position that the Constitution guarantees every citizen a vote roughly equal in weight in elections to both houses of the state legislatures and to the House of Representatives. The crucial decision for state legislatures came in 1962, when the Supreme Court ruled that a state's debasement and dilution of the effect of the votes of certain citizens violated the Fourteenth Amendment guarantee of equal protection of the laws.[50] Within two years this decision had led to some action on the apportionment of legislative seats in forty-two states.[51] The same criterion of "one man, one vote" was applied to the national House of Representatives in 1964.[52] Instead of the Fourteenth Amendment, the Court relied this time upon the constitutional provision that established the House as the popular branch of the national government: "We hold that, construed in its historical context, the command of Art. I, Sec. 2, that representatives be chosen 'by the people of the several States' means that as nearly as is practicable one man's vote in a

---

[47] Notice the qualifying word "tends" in the proposition above. We do not mean to imply any magical process by which some element of a system will *always* compensate for the dysfunctional performance of another element. The system may be destroyed or drastically altered, but the *tendency* is for systems to maintain themselves.
[48] *Hitchman Coal and Coke Co.* v. *Mitchell*, 245 U.S. 229 (1917).
[49] *Colgrove* v. *Green*, 328 U.S. 548 (1946). This was the first case in which a majority (4–3) of the justices participating held that congressional districting was a justiciable issue.
[50] *Baker* v. *Carr*, 369 U.S. 186 (1962).
[51] And in 1964 the Court applied the same reasoning to both houses of state legislatures. *Reynolds* v. *Sims*, 377 U.S. 533 (1964).
[52] *Wesberry* v. *Sanders*, 376 U.S. 1 (1964).

congressional election is to be worth as much as another's." Speaking for the Court, Justice Black emphasized the debates in the Constitutional Convention, the early practice of statewide election of all representatives (which automatically insured an equal weight for each vote), and Madison's emphasis in *The Federalist* on the popular character of the House. Within two years after this decision, 258 districts in twenty-seven states had been redistricted to meet its requirements.[53]

These bold pronouncements by the Supreme Court were roundly denounced by conservative interests, who correctly viewed them as threatening to change the particularistic biases that had developed within the federal system. The House of Representatives went so far as to adopt a proposal that would have denied the federal courts jurisdiction on matters dealing with state legislative apportionment. The House felt more threatened by the decisions on state reapportionment than those on national reapportionment because the shape of congressional districts is determined by the forces that control the state legislatures. Reaction to the decisions depended heavily on party affiliation: 78 per cent of the Republican representatives and 41 per cent of the Democrats supported the anticourt proposal. If southern Democrats are separated from others, the differences are even more dramatic: for the proposal were 84 per cent of the southern Democrats, 78 per cent of the Republicans, and 9 per cent of the nonsouthern Democrats.[54] When the same proposal came up in the Senate, it was resoundingly defeated (56–21), with only one nonsouthern Democrat and four Republicans taking the anticourt position. The difference between the two houses, between the two parties, and between the two wings of the Democratic party could hardly have been more clearly demonstrated.[55]

By the time of these 1964 decisions, the House of Representatives was not nearly as stacked in favor of rural voters as it had been at mid-century. Defining urban areas as those with populations of 50,000 or more, the *Congressional Quarterly* estimated that an "ideal" apportionment—the most feasible distribution of population among the districts of each state—would result in a net change of only about 16 out of the 435 House seats. The urban areas would gain 6 additional representatives, mostly in the South, and the suburban areas would gain 10.[56] Malapportionment of the House had thus developed in such a way that it was no longer so consistently biased in favor of rural residents as it was in favor of particular incumbents, parties, and interest groups.[57] These biases were most conspicuous at the state level. Despite the changes that had resulted from *Baker* v. *Carr*, a minority of the population in 1964 could still have elected a majority of the members of *both houses of every state legislative body*.[58]

In view of these deviations from the concept of an equal weight for every man's vote, radical changes can be expected in the state legislatures and lesser

---

[53] *Congressional Quarterly Weekly Report*, XXIV (April 15, 1966), 812.
[54] *Congressional Quarterly Weekly Report*, XXII (August 21, 1964), 1895.
[55] *Ibid.* (September 18, 1964), 2161.
[56] *Ibid.* (February 21, 1964), 352.
[57] See Malcolm E. Jewell, "Political Patterns of Apportionment," in Jewell (ed.), *The Politics of Reapportionment* (New York: Atherton Press, 1962), pp. 1–48.
[58] *Congressional Quarterly Weekly Report*, XXII (June 19, 1964), 1219.

changes in the House of Representatives. At the national level, these changes may not have great partisan consequences. After all, the suburban areas are those most underrepresented in the House, and the Republicans are traditionally strong in the suburbs. The vote of Republican representatives to deny federal courts the authority to rule on state legislative apportionment suggests, however, that state malapportionment has worked principally to the benefit of Republicans. (The South is, as usual, an exception: although southern malapportionment benefits local Democrats, southern representatives were so piqued at the Supreme Court for its civil rights rulings that they cast their votes to discredit the Court.)

Regardless of partisan implications, the consequences of a roughly equal weight for all votes will be to increase the national and urban orientation of *both* parties. When one reflects on all that could have been done about slum clearance, urban renewal, juvenile delinquency, mass transportation, and similar problems in the last twenty years if Congress had devoted the same attention to urban problems that it lavished on farm problems, the imagination is staggered. The feedback from these historic court decisions can be expected to become inputs of great importance for other decision-making agencies as well.

Rules of Congressional Procedure

Any aggregation of people must develop recognized leaders and rules of procedure if it is to function as a group. Just how elaborate its organization needs to be depends on the size of the group and the purpose it sets for itself. The House, for example, is more highly organized than the Senate. One reason is probably that the House is larger than the Senate. The executive branch, by the same token, is even more highly organized than the House. Administration calls for more unified and rapid action than does legislation, and the size of the executive establishment is too vast for any coherent action to be taken without a much more structured organization.

Table 10–4 juxtaposes the contrasting characteristics of the House and Senate, most of which stem from the larger size and smaller constituencies of the House. Taken together, these attributes lead to much greater specialization in the House than in the Senate. And differences in the degree of specialization are a key to understanding how each house contributes to policy-making. The committees where the specialized work is done are much more important in the House, and the individual is much more important in the Senate. With almost an equal number of committees (twenty in the House, sixteen in the Senate) and over four times as many representatives as senators, each senator will serve on three or four committees while each representative concentrates on one or two. Power is further dispersed in the Senate because a larger proportion of senators than of representatives have multiple positions of committee leadership. In one recent Congress, 12 per cent of the representatives and 51 per cent of the senators of the majority party were chairmen of at least two committees or subcommittees.[59] The senator is thus more important than the representative as an individual.

Table 10-4   Major Differences Between House and Senate

HOUSE	SENATE
Larger (435 members)	Smaller (100 members)
More formal	Less formal
More hierarchically organized	Less hierarchically organized
Acts more quickly	Acts more slowly
Rules more rigid	Rules more flexible
Power less evenly distributed	Power more evenly distributed
Longer apprentice period	Shorter apprentice period
More impersonal	More personal
Less "important" constituencies	More "important" constituencies
Less prestige	More prestige
More "conservative"	More "liberal"

Source: Froman, *The Congressional Process*, p. 7.

The rules of the House are necessarily much more elaborate and constraining than those of the Senate, just as administrative rules are more restrictive and detailed than those of the House. In view of the large number of representatives, the House must be more tightly organized if it is to act; the smaller number of senators permits a greater emphasis on full deliberation. It is a complicated job for 435 representatives to act on any matter, even one on which a majority is in strong agreement. During the early years of the House, when its membership was small, the only important function of the Rules Committee was to report a system of rules at the beginning of each Congress. As the House increased in size, however, the power of the Rules Committee grew to the point where it is the key coordinating committee of the entire body.[60] If the Rules Committee opposes a bill, it may simply refuse to recommend a rule under which it can be scheduled for consideration; when it does propose a rule for the consideration of a measure, the rule may drastically limit debate or it may limit the amendments that may be offered. The members of the House may reject the Rules Committee resolution (it is not subject to amendment), but to do so is to lose the chance to consider the measure at all and to incur the disfavor of a powerful committee. Affirmative action on the Committee's proposed rule is thus almost always assured. The representative who gets a chance to speak for five minutes on a bill is lucky.[61]

In 1965, the Democrats enjoyed their largest majority in the House of Representatives (295-140) since 1937. Moreover, their net gain of thirty-eight seats in the 1964 election had added liberal Democrats from outside the South; because seven of the nine Democratic seats lost to Republicans had been held by Democrats from Alabama, Mississippi, and Georgia who voted with the

[59]Froman, *The Congressional Process*, p. 11.
[60]Milton C. Cummings, Jr., and Robert L. Peabody, "The Decision to Enlarge the Commitee on Rules: An Analysis of the 1961 Vote," in Peabody and Polsby (eds.), *New Perspectives on the House of Representatives*, p. 169.
[61]The procedures for the conduct of business in both houses of Congress are well explained in Froman, *The Congressional Process*.

Republicans on key issues, the effective gain for the national Democratic Party was forty-five votes. This was enough to win a significant reduction in the power of the Rules Committee, which had long been the burying ground for liberal legislation. The House accordingly voted its Speaker power to speed bills from the Rules Committee. If the Committee failed to report a bill received from a policy committee for twenty-one days, the Speaker could recognize a member of that committee to move consideration of the bill. But the tables were turned in 1967 because the 1966 congressional election produced a net gain of forty-seven seats for the Republicans. Southern Democrats and Republicans joined forces to repeal the twenty-one-day rule; supporting repeal were 86 per cent of the Republicans, 79 per cent of the southern Democrats, and 5 per cent of the northern Democrats. Nevertheless, two Democratic vacancies on the Committee—seats formerly held by members of the southern Democrat-Republican coalition—were filled by administration supporters. And members of the Committee voted to meet on a regular schedule rather than merely on the call of the Chairman, William D. Colmer, a Mississippi Democrat. With

Drawing by Koren; © 1964 *The New Yorker Magazine, Inc.*

"Next I want to sing a song about the House Rules Committee and how the legislative functions of Congress are tyrannized over by its procedural calendar, dominated in turn by an all-powerful chairman hamstringing the processes of democracy."

regular meetings assured and with a majority of its members nationally oriented Democrats, the Rules Committee can no longer blatantly thwart the preferences of a House majority.

In contrast to the House, the Senate—"the greatest deliberative body in the world"—operates under a rule of unlimited debate. A "previous question" motion enables a House majority to bring a measure to a vote, but the Senate has no previous question rule. By permitting full debate, Senate rules also permit the "filibuster," a practice that enables a minority to prevent the passage of a law by talking it to death, never letting it come to a vote. Minorities also use the filibuster or the threat of a filibuster to extract concessions from the majority.

In 1959, the Senate adopted a "cloture" rule that requires a favorable vote by two-thirds of the senators *present and voting* to close off debate. For the Senate, this represented a small step toward majority control—from 1949 to 1959, the rule was that debate could be ended only by the approval of two-thirds of the *entire membership* of the Senate. Northern and western liberals argued that the change, which restored a 1917 rule, did not go far enough. Southern senators protested that its restoration was a move "to further curtail free speech in the Senate." The present cloture rule goes well beyond the attempts of the Founding Fathers to limit the majority; for the first twenty years of Senate history, debate could be ended by a simple majority vote![62]

Respect for the individual member is so great in the Senate that cloture is most difficult to apply. Only thirty-eight cloture votes have been taken since 1917, and only seven of these have been successful. If a truly decisive consensus builds up behind a measure, cloture is possible, as was demonstrated by the vote leading up to the passage of the Civil Rights Act of 1964. Seven cloture votes were taken in the 89th Congress (1965–67), and the only successful effort was in behalf of the Voting Rights Act of 1965. The first cloture vote in the 90th Congress (1967–69) continued the old story. This was a vote to end debate on a resolution that would have permitted a majority of three-fifths rather than two-thirds to apply cloture. Fifty-four per cent of the senators voted for cloture, twelve percentage points short of the necessary two-thirds. That the filibuster protects minorities is clear in the pattern of this vote: 100 per cent of the Democrats from the former Confederate states, 53 per cent of the Republicans, and 22 per cent of the non-Confederate Democrats opposed the cloture motion.[63]

The rules of the House show no such deference to individual members' right to debate. They do show special deference to the power of the standing committees. When a committee unfriendly to a measure refuses to report that measure to the floor for consideration, the only way the bill can be pried loose is by means of a "discharge petition" signed by a majority of the total House membership. Although this is not so extreme as the requirements for cloture in the Senate, respect for the committee system is so great—and absenteeism so regular—that the discharge petition is used infrequently. A majority cannot

---

[62] See George B. Galloway, *The Lesiglative Process in Congress* (New York: Thomas Y. Crowell Company, 1953), p. 560.
[63] *Congressional Quarterly Weekly Report*, XXV (January 27, 1967), 161.

be permanently frustrated in the House, but if it is to make its will prevail it may have to mobilize its strength completely and show real determination.

Elected Party Leaders

As these key rules and norms suggest, Congress is not dominated by strong leaders. If there is any overall leadership, it comes from the outside, from the President. Within the Congress itself, the bicameral system, combined with the lack of solidarity in our political parties, makes unified leadership out of the question. The Constitution permits each house to determine the power of its own leaders. As we would expect from the tighter organization of the House, the leaders there have more influence on their colleagues than do leaders of the Senate.

Before Congress convenes, the Republican and Democratic members of each house meet in party conferences or caucuses to select slates of candidates for the offices of their respective houses. Electing these officers is merely a formality, however, for in backing these candidates the party members achieve a solidarity that they rarely muster on policy questions. Voting as a bloc, the members of the majority party in each chamber always elect their slate.

In the House the principal officer is the Speaker. He is the leading member of the majority party in the House and is frequently described as "the second most powerful man in Washington." Before the powers of the Speaker were curtailed early in this century, his influence was even greater than it is today. At one time he exercised life-and-death control over legislation. Even today he is the strongest figure in Congress. The Speaker plays several roles: he is the presiding officer and a highly respected member of the House; he acts as contact man with the President when they are of the same party; and he serves as the leader of his party in the House. As presiding officer, the Speaker announces the order of business, puts questions to a vote and reports the vote, recognizes members who want the floor, interprets the rules, squelches dilatory tactics, refers bills to committees, and appoints the members of select and conference committees. While a decision of the Speaker may occasionally be overruled by the House itself, as in referring a controversial bill to a committee, his normal control over these functions gives him so much influence that even the House Rules Committee can ill afford to "buck" the Speaker. Indeed, he influences the selection of the majority members of the Rules Committee at the outset.

As a member of Congress, the Speaker is entitled to participate in debate and to vote. On the rare occasions when the Speaker descends from the rostrum to take a direct part in the debate, all the other members recognize that the issue must be an important one, and his fellow party members realize that a "wrong" vote may put them and their future projects in danger of the Speaker's disapproval. His close contact with the President lends further weight to his views. The elevation of a representative to the Speakership, though it may not require him to be so responsive to national sentiment as the

President is, does induce him to behave more as a national and less as a strictly parochial figure.

The Speaker is assisted by the Majority Leader (or "floor leader") and the Majority Whip.[64] These three represent a kind of triumvirate of general leaders who, together with relevant committee and subcommittee chairmen and perhaps other senior committee members, manage specific pieces of legislation. These three party leaders "are undeniably leaders in virtually all that goes on legislatively in the House."[65] The last eight Speakers all served previously as floor leaders; this career line underscores the importance of the floor leader's position and also suggests that he needs the same personal qualifications as an effective Speaker. These are pre-eminently the skills of a *negotiator*, a person who can bargain with fellow House members on a personal basis of trust and who is more devoted to the House than to any ideological cause. If these sound like strange qualifications for a party leader, remember that the parties in Congress are a reflection of the kinds of parties we have outside Congress. "Inside the House as well as outside," Richard Fenno reminds us, "the parties remain loose coalitions of social interests and local party organizations." Even though the Speaker and Majority Leader must negotiate rather than command, Fenno adds, "such centralization as the majority party is able to bring to House decision-making springs from them."[66]

The Majority Leader's task—so demanding that he traditionally abstains from serving on House committees—is to lead his party's efforts on the floor and to arrange the day-to-day House schedule. The Majority Whip, with the help of Assistant Majority Whips (eighteen for the Democrats; three Regional Whips and thirteen Assistant Whips for the Republicans) helps the majority cause in four ways: (1) he seeks to insure that a maximum number of his party's members are present when critical votes are taken; (2) he gives information to party members on pending measures; (3) he tries to find out how members of his party will vote on legislation important to the current administration's program; (4) he helps in the effort to induce wavering members of the majority to vote with their party.[67]

The success of these efforts by the party leadership is difficult to assess. One indication that they have some effect is that the majority party's attendance for voting on seventeen bills on which the whip organization was active in 1962 and 1963 was 94 per cent, more than 10 percentage points greater than for other roll-call votes.[68] Despite the relative weakness of political parties in the

---

[64] The minority party strives for a coherent opposition under a Minority Leader and a Minority Whip. The title "Whip" is derived from a British fox-hunting term, the "whipper-in," applied to the man responsible for keeping hounds from leaving the pack. The term came to be used in the British Parliament in the late eighteenth century. See Robert Luce, *Legislative Procedure* (Boston: Houghton Mifflin Company, 1922), pp. 501–502.

[65] Lewis A. Froman, Jr., and Randall B. Ripley, "Conditions for Party Leadership: The Case of the House Democrats," *American Political Science Review*, LIX (March, 1965), 53. The floor leaders for both parties and the Republican Whip are elected through the same process as the Speaker. The Democratic Whip is appointed by the floor leader (in consultation with the Speaker when the Democrats have a majority).

[66] Richard F. Fenno, Jr., "The Internal Distribution of Influence: The House," in Truman (ed.), *op. cit.*, pp. 62, 63.

[67] Randall B. Ripley, "The Party Whip Organizations in the United States House of Representatives," *American Political Science Review*, LVIII (September, 1964), 561–576.

[68] *Ibid.*, 571.

United States, then, party leaders in the House can be successful when they are willing to apply their bargaining resources (members are aware that a state is more likely to receive favorable consideration of a pet project if its delegation cooperates) and their control over events and information (for instance, arranging to have the departure of an Air Force plane for a subcommittee's foreign trip delayed and informing cooperating members of the subcommittee that they have time to remain on the floor for a crucial vote). Nevertheless, the chances of success in these efforts decrease as the issue becomes more visible and more important to particular constituencies.[69]

Senate leadership reflects the United States' separation of powers and decentralized political parties in even more extreme form than does the House leadership. These features of the general political system tend to disperse power, and the dispersal goes even farther in the Senate than in the House. Because each member of the smaller body is relatively more powerful, the possibility for centralized leadership is reduced. Leadership exists in the Senate, of course, but it is "highly personal and complex."[70] The Vice-President is the presiding officer but not a leader. As Vice-President Humphrey put it, he "stands as a servant of the Senate, rather than as an advocate in it."[71] The majority and minority floor leaders are the key leaders of the Senate, but their positions are even more personal and less institutional than those of their counterparts in the House.

Students of Congress generally agree that Lyndon B. Johnson was the most skillful and successful Senate floor leader in recent history. Johnson himself described the position in terms of persuasion, observing that "the only real power available to the leader is the power of persuasion. There is no patronage; no power to discipline; no authority to fire Senators like a President can fire his members of Cabinet."[72] One can argue that *all* power is ultimately based on persuasion,[73] but the Senate floor leader enjoys few of the resources that assist in persuasion. As the center of the legislative party's network of communication he can help keep a cooperating senator informed on crucial questions of timing, and he can help a member to secure an assignment to a special committee or even to get his pet legislation before the Senate for a vote. But the potential of the position is much more dependent on the personality of the occupant than is, say, the potential of the presidency. Writing both as a former Johnson aide and as a political scientist, Ralph Huitt reports that "persuasion was, in Johnson's case, overwhelmingly a matter of personal influence. By all accounts, Johnson was the most personal among recent leaders in his approach. For years it was said that he talked to every Demo-

---

[69] Froman and Ripley, *op. cit.*, 63.

[70] Ralph K. Huitt, "Democratic Party Leadership in the Senate," *American Political Science Review*, LV (June, 1961), 334.

[71] *Congressional Quarterly Weekly Report*, XXV (January 20, 1967), 87.

[72] Quoted in Huitt, "Democratic Party Leadership in the Senate," *American Political Science Review*, LV (June, 1961), 337.

[73] Richard Neustadt effectively argues this case for the President. *Presidential Power* (New York: John Wiley & Sons, Inc., 1960).

cratic senator every day. Persuasion ranged from the awesome pyrotechnics known as 'Treatment A' to the apparently casual but always purposeful exchange as he roamed the floor and the cloakroom."[74] This is personal and transitory power, not institutionalized and continuing power. When Senator Mike Mansfield (D.-Montana) succeeded to the position, his easy-going personal qualities produced radically different role expectations and role performance. General party leadership was reduced to the point where other senators complained that they were not being sufficiently led![75]

Party conferences (Democrats in the House call them "caucuses") do more than choose the official leaders in their respective houses. They are the governing bodies of the political parties in Congress. The conference is to the party in each house what the national convention is to the party in the nation; and it is almost equally ineffective as a real governing body. In addition to selecting the party leaders in each house, the conference sets up committees to make assignments to standing committees[76] and additional committees to try to create party consensus on policy and procedure. Both parties in the Senate and the Republicans in the House have "policy committees" for the consensus-building function. Although they have failed to build consensus, they do serve as agencies of communication and, to a lesser extent, of coordination. The Policy Committee of the Republicans in the House has been particularly active both as a focal point in internal battles for power in the House Republican Party and as an agency by which Republicans can try to alter their minority status.[77] The Democrats in the House have never created a Policy Committee, continuing to rely instead on a Steering Committee that seldom meets and never steers. In truth, the policy committees are about as far from policy-making as the Steering Committee is from steering.

Seniority Leaders and the Committee System

The basic organizational units through which Congress works are the *standing committees*. Every bill that reaches the floor of Congress has first been considered by a committee. And, in contrast to the practice in most state legislatures, no bill is reported out for the consideration of all the members until it has first won a majority vote in the committee.[78] The House has twenty, the Senate sixteen, of these virtually independent centers of power, each dealing with a different policy area—such as agriculture, appropriations, banking and currency, and foreign affairs —roughly corresponding to the major policy areas of the national government. Although they do not correspond exactly to the administrative structure, the committees provide regular channels of communication between the executive and legislative branches in all areas of policy formation. They also provide, as

---

[74]Huitt, "Democratic Party Leadership . . .," loc. cit., 338.
[75]See Huntington, "Congressional Responses to the Twentieth Century," loc. cit., p. 22.
[76]For the Republicans in both houses, this is a Committee on Committees; for the Democrats in the House, it is the Ways and Means Committee; for the Democrats in the Senate, it is the Steering Committee.
[77]Charles O. Jones, *Party and Policy-Making: The House Republican Policy Committee* (New Brunswick, N.J.: Rutgers University Press, 1964).
[78]As noted above, a measure may be discharged from a committee by vote of the House or Senate, but this is a rare and difficult procedure.

Roland Young points out, a practical instrumentality through which Congress can exercise control over the administration of policy by the governmental bureaucracy.[79] In policy-making, Congress and the administration function as integral parts of a single system, sharing rather than dividing powers. Hence each committee sets up its subcommittees to work closely with counterparts in the bureaucracy.

How is the membership of standing committees determined? The majority party in each house fixes the ratio of seats between the parties, always giving itself a majority in the committees roughly corresponding to its majority in the house as a whole. But the committee on committees in each party, which actually draws up the slates for the party conference, employs no fixed criteria in deciding which party member gets what committee assignment. Seniority is the most important qualification, although the committee on committees also takes other factors into account—reputation as a "responsible" legislator (one who is moderate in approach, politically pliant but not without conviction), for example, and the desire of congressmen to be on committees handling legislation of particular interest to their constituents.[80]

The party leaders are thus not so impotent as they are generally thought to be. Committee appointments constitute party leaders' chief weapon in affecting the output of the standing committees. The Democratic House leadership somewhat reformed the Rules Committee, for example, by adding two liberals in 1961 and filling two vacancies with administration supporters in 1967. Also, they put five liberals on the Appropriations Committee in 1963, and changed the ratio on the Education and Labor Committee, stacking it with liberals, in 1959. Here are cases in which the leaders molded the membership of committees with a view toward producing policies they favored.

Congressmen naturally go after seats on committees that deal with problems of special importance in their own locality. A committee that specializes in legislation affecting a particular economic interest tends, then, to be made up of the very congressmen who are most biased in favor of that interest. Thus the House Committee on Agriculture is controlled by representatives from predominantly rural areas; the Senate Committee on Interior and Insular Affairs, which considers laws on mining and public lands, by senators from western mining states; the House Committee on Merchant Marine and Fisheries by representatives from coastal regions. Although a choice committee assignment may be a reward for party service, disservice to the party—even sabotage of the national platform—is hardly ever punished by removal from a committee. Once appointed to a committee, a member stays. In the 1961 fight on the House Rules Committee, for example, some Democrats argued that

---

[79]*The American Congress*, Chapter 3, "The Internal System of Authority." The student will find the bibliographical essay at the end of this book extremely useful in pursuing further investigations into the legislative process.

Lists of the current committees of Congress and their members may be found in the *Congressional Directory*. Some committees publish an annual survey of their activities.

[80]Nicholas A. Masters, "Committee Assignments in the House of Representatives," *American Political Science Review*, LV (June, 1961), 345–357.

Representative William Colmer (D.-Mississippi), who had opposed Kennedy for President, should be removed from the Committee in favor of a Kennedy supporter. Recognizing the traditional independence of congressmen, however, party leaders decided that the most they could win was an enlargement of the Committee. In 1967, Colmer became Chairman of the Committee.

Just as Congress functions through its standing committees, so each committee functions through its chairman. But while the general power of Congress is scattered, committee power is concentrated in the hands of the chairman. Because he possesses the authority to call committee meetings, determine the agenda, appoint subcommittees, and refer bills to subcommittees, the chairman wields virtually autocratic power in every standing committee. As Woodrow Wilson observed, the United States government may be described as "government by the chairmen of the Standing Committees of Congress."[81] Chairman Howard Smith petulantly demonstrated his displeasure over enlargement of the Rules Committee in 1961 by not providing chairs for the new members!

How does a congressman reach this pinnacle of power? This is one question about Congress that can be answered very simply: by staying alive and getting re-elected. Complicated questions of service to party, commitment to party platform, and competence in the subject matter of the committee have little to do with seniority; therefore they do not enter into the choice of a chairman. Once a representative or senator takes his place on a committee, he need only keep his seat and some day he will find himself at the head of the class. A rare exception to this rule (the first since 1925) occurred in 1965. Democrats in the House deprived two representatives (from Mississippi and South Carolina) of their committee seniority because they had openly supported Senator Goldwater for President. Even though these representatives were not denied their claim to committee assignments as Democrats, this punitive action may represent a modest tendency toward the nationalization of American politics.

Despite the many critics of the seniority system—and there are more outside than inside Congress—it dominates the organization of both houses. If new members object to it, they find themselves left with the most minor committee assignments and cut off from the essential support of the old hands in carrying out their plans. Ernest Griffith, a long-time student of Congress, concludes that "Seniority is not only a rule governing committee chairmanships, it is also a spirit pervading the total behavior."[82] So long as he does not blatantly challenge the seniority system, a newcomer with ability and dedication can begin to exercise great influence after he has served in Congress for as few as two terms. By then he will begin to say that seniority at least assures that the top positions are held by men who know the ways of Congress, who have acquired specialized knowledge in the policy area of their committee, and who have "practical political wisdom on such matters as how to retain the support of a Committee, when to compromise on the contents of a bill, when to take a bill to the floor, how to maneuver in debate, and how to bargain with the Senate [or House] in conference—all in a special subject-matter area."[83]

---

[81]*Congressional Government* (Boston: Houghton Mifflin Co., 1885), p. 102.
[82]*Congress: Its Contemporary Role* (New York: New York University Press, 1956), p. 18. Also see the 3rd ed. (1961).
[83]Fenno, "The Internal Distribution of Influence: The House," *loc. cit.*, p. 58.

The seniority system helps explain why, during the Eisenhower and Kennedy eras, the "modern" and the "new" aspects of modern Republicanism and of the New Frontier were displayed by the executive rather than by Congress. The seniority system makes it almost inevitable that committee chairmen will be out of step with the majority elements of their party. As George Galloway says, "They represent districts made 'safe' by the poll tax and other restrictions on voting, or by the monopolistic position of one party, or by the ascendancy of a major interest group, or by city or rural machines."[84] Congressmen from districts where the competition between parties is livelier, where victory shifts with national elections, simply cannot outlast their colleagues from safe districts. The Roosevelt victory in 1932 initiated an era of Democratic control in Washington, but the seniority system excluded from

The Small Society by Brickman; © 1967 Washington Star Syndicate, Inc.

power the Democrats who came from the very areas that were responsible for the shift, and ensconced a number of anti-New Deal southerners in key positions. When the Dewey-Eisenhower Republicans won in 1952, the new committee chairmen turned out to be men from "Old Guard" Republican areas who opposed Eisenhower's attempts at "modernization." No matter which party is in control of Congress, a disproportionate number of strategic committee chairmen are bound to come from one-party areas.

Redistricting of congressional districts and increasing party competition in the South promise to change the pattern of southern dominance of the Democrats' seniority posts. In the last generation the number of "safe" Democratic districts in the South has decreased and the number outside the South has increased. In 1946, 79 per cent of the safe Democratic seats (those won by a margin of at least 65 per cent of the vote) in the House were held by southerners; by 1962, the percentage had dropped to 54 per cent and by 1964 to 36 per cent.[85] As nonsouthern Democrats replace southerners in seniority leadership positions, changes of great consequence may ensue. A careful study of

[84]*The Legislative Process*, p. 271.
[85]Raymond W. Wolfinger and Joan Heifetz, "Safe Seats, Seniority, and Power in Congress," *American Political Science Review*, LIX (June, 1965), 347.

changes in the seniority system concludes with this assessment: "Dissension in the Democratic party is due largely to Southerners. As the relative strength of the South decreases, the cohesive potential of the party as a whole will increase. . . . The decline of the Southerners will be accompanied by a Democratic president's greater ability to get his way with Congress. It appears, then, that present trends are in the direction of greater cohesion and 'responsibility' in the Democratic party."[86]

The Process of Policy-Making

The procedure by which Congress passes a bill requires completion of eight not-so-easy steps. As we trace these steps, we will see that getting an important measure through Congress is no routine matter. Policy-making always involves the tense drama of power in conflict and compromise.

First, the bill must be introduced. This is the easiest part of all. A representative simply hands his bill to the Clerk of the House or tosses it into the "hopper," a box on the Clerk's desk. A senator must be recognized by the presiding officer in order to announce the introduction of his bill; then he gives it to the Secretary of the Senate. Of the 10,000 or so bills introduced in every Congress, each has little better than one chance in ten of becoming a law. Most of these bills are relatively trivial, and many, despite efforts to reduce their number, are "private" bills dealing with such things as individual claims against the government. Although bills are actually introduced by congressmen, most of them are probably "thought up" by other actors in the policy-making performance. Major legislation usually represents the joint efforts of many people who have been called upon by a congressman for advice or support. Just who first conceived the idea for a given bill is perhaps as unanswerable as it is irrelevant to the merits of the bill.

The second step begins when the parliamentarian of the House (under the Speaker's direction) or the President of the Senate refers the bill to an appropriate committee for consideration. This is as far as most bills get. The committee, which enjoys virtual life-and-death power over all the proposals that come its way, may "pigeon-hole" a bill, disapprove it, rewrite it completely, amend it, or approve it as presented. But only if a bill wins the approval of a majority of the committee does it normally reach the floor of either house.[87] An unfriendly chairman may bury a bill by arranging the agenda so that it never comes up, or—if it is too important to ignore completely—by appointing an unfriendly subcommittee to consider it.

Measures that are found worthy of consideration are generally given open hearings at which interested government officials, lobbyists, and other experts are permitted to testify. Next the committee members assess the technical and political implications of the bill on the bases of the hearings, their own knowledge or convictions on the subject, the results of staff research, and their individual contacts with fellow legislators, party leaders, lobbyists, and constituents. Because Congress usually goes along with what the committees

---
[86] *Ibid.*, 348.
[87] Except in the rare event of a bill being reported out unfavorably or of a successful move to discharge the committee from consideration of a bill.

366

recommend, the work they perform is the real heart of legislation. Aware of this fact, the sponsor of a bill tries to stimulate publicity and support from influential groups outside as well as inside Congress. The chances of passing the bill are maximized, of course, if the sponsor is a senior member or, even better, the chairman of the committee.

In the Senate, the committee phase comes to an end when a majority of the committee votes to report the bill for consideration on the Senate floor. But in the House there is a second committee hurdle for all measures except money bills.[88] Before a nonmoney bill reaches the floor of the House, the Committee on Rules must rule whether, when, and under what conditions the bill may come up for floor debate. The Rules Committee may block a measure, report it to the floor with suggested amendments, recommend a substitute bill, or set up special rules to speed its passage. As we have seen above, the Rules Committee has been under increasing attack in recent years. Its position as "traffic cop" for legislation remains basically the same, but every time the size of the southern-Democrat–conservative-Republican coalition is decreased, the power or the membership of the Rules Committee is altered in the interest of expediting liberal legislation. Whenever an election enlarges the size of the conservative coalition, some power is restored to the Rules Committee. Should the Committee come under the control of northern Democrats for a lengthy period, both sides would no doubt revaluate their positions. In the last generation, however, the attitudes of the protagonists demonstrate that the Rules Committee normally favors conservative policies and obstructs liberal policies.

When one of the standing committees reports a bill back to the chamber in which it was introduced, it is placed on a calendar—a list of pending bills —where it awaits the third big step, floor debate. If the bill is important enough, however, its sponsor may not have to wait for it to take its turn on the calendar. In the Senate, the Policy Committee of the majority party serves as chief traffic manager. It establishes the order in which the bills are to be brought up, often—thanks to the cooperation of the Minority Leader—by unanimous consent of the Senate. In the absence of unanimity, the scheduling of bills is by majority vote. Debate in the Senate is unlimited unless it is limited by unanimous consent or cut short by a vote of cloture.

In the House, departures from the calendar are made at the direction of the Rules Committee, which also provides for limitations on debate. The Rules Committee may even provide a "closed rule," which permits only members of the reporting committee to offer amendments. If a representative objects to these rules, they are referred to the entire House for a vote, but in practice such appeals are hardly ever successful. When the House sits as the "Committee of the Whole," as it does in considering appropriation bills, for exam-

---

[88]In addition to bills from the committees on Appropriations and Ways and Means, certain bills from three other committees—Public Works, Veterans' Affairs, and Interior and Insular Affairs —may be brought to the floor at any time. Only the Appropriations Committee takes routine advantage of this privilege. Other committees prefer to go through the Rules Committee because this leads to consideration of their bills under favorable rules. See Daniel M. Berman, *In Congress Assembled* (New York: The Macmillan Company, 1964), p. 204.

ple, it transforms itself into one big committee so that it can operate more informally. No record is kept of the votes, the time for debate is divided equally between opponents and proponents, and debate on each amendment is limited to five minutes.

By the time a bill is ready for the fourth step—voting—its sponsor has a fairly good idea of what its chances for passage are. In the House, a vote may already have been taken on the rules governing debate (especially if a "closed rule" was involved), and in both chambers the votes on various amendments will have shown the alignment of the forces for and against. Indeed, the votes on amendments crippling the bill and on the motion to recommit the bill to committee are usually more revealing of sentiment than the final vote on passage. If opponents of the bill have failed in their efforts to weaken it or to send it back to committee, they know that they cannot block final passage. Accordingly, if the bill has strong popular appeal but is opposed by a strong pressure group, some of the members who have tried to defeat it at first may swing over to its support once its final passage is assured. The politics-wise pressure group will appreciate the fact that these representatives opposed the bill as long as they had any chance of defeating it. By pointing to their "yea" votes on final passage, however, they can also claim credit from the voters for supporting the bill.

Even after a bill has passed one house, it is still less than halfway through the process of becoming a law. We may lump together all the steps described so far as a fifth giant step—namely, the successful completion of the same steps in the other chamber. If the bill is rejected or ignored in this chamber, of course, it is dead. But if it manages to clear all the hurdles a second time, it need only be signed by the President to become a law. If it passes in slightly altered form, the house of origin must agree to the revisions before it goes to the President.

When a bill is substantially changed by the second house, it usually enters a sixth stage, in which it is sent to a conference committee made up of both senators and representatives who try to iron out the differences. The members of the conference committee are appointed by the presiding officer in each house from among the senior members of the committee that originally considered the bill. Again the cards are stacked in favor of the older members from the "safe" districts. As the safe districts become more equally distributed among regions and between rural and urban constituencies, however, the policy implications of the safe-district bias become less predictable. As of today, however, the implications are still predominantly conservative. Although technically the conference committee has no power to write a new bill, in practice its privilege of making final decisions on the contents of a bill means that the committee members exercise extraordinary power to alter it. If a majority of the members of the conference from each house agree on a compromise version, the bill is reported back to both houses in its new and final form.

If the compromise version is now approved by both houses, the bill is ready for its seventh step, presidential action. The President may allow the bill to become law (which is automatic after ten working days) without his signature, he may indicate his approval by signing it, or, if he disapproves of the bill, he may refuse to sign it and return it to Congress with a message explaining the reasons for his veto.

In this last event, the bill is probably doomed to failure, although it can still become law if both houses take it through the eighth step—namely, passing it by a two-thirds vote over the President's veto. But the chances that this will happen are not good. Disapproval by the President focuses public attention on the bill, and the vote to override his veto must be a roll-call vote. Since the President is more closely attuned to national sentiments than most congressmen are, his vetoes are generally in keeping with the desires and interests of the majority. And his power as a party leader cannot be ignored, especially by congressmen who want government contracts placed in their districts, or deserving constituents appointed to federal jobs, or presidential support in their next campaign. Congressmen who are perfectly willing to support a bill the first time around, when public opinion may not be aroused and the vote may not be recorded, are often not so eager to vote to override a presidential veto.

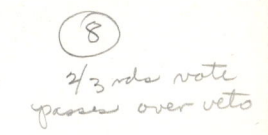

Congressional Relations with Other Decision-Making Agencies

Although Congress is the most visible site of authoritative rule-making, we have viewed it as only the center of a legislative system that includes local constituencies, pressure groups, and political parties. The other official agencies of government are also a part of the system. In Chapter 8 we said that the overall decision-making system can best be understood as made up of a set of policy "systems" or "arenas" in which all of the groups concerned with particular policies share regularly in making, modifying, and carrying out decisions. Specialization is thus recognized as characteristic not just of Congress but of other participants in the legislative system as well. "A particular policy is made by the people in the agencies, public and private, who are interested in and know about that policy area. There is an almost continuous interchange among committee members, their staffs, the executive (that is, agency personnel, White House staff, and private persons appointed to 'task forces,' and the like) and representatives of private associations at almost every stage of the process, from the first glimmer of an idea to compromise in conference and to administration of the act."[89]

Judges and Policy-Making

Although they are never seen on the floor of Congress or scurrying about the corridors, judges also participate in policy-making. Despite the myth that judges are neutral mediators in political wars, they help to make policy in several ways. First, every time they interpret an act of Congress they are making a declaration of policy. Legisla-

[89] Huitt, "Congress, the Durable Partner," in Frank (ed.), *Lawmakers in a Changing World*, p. 19.

tors usually write statutes in general terms that leave room for detailed policy-making by the courts. It is hard enough to pass a new law even in a fairly general form, and if the sponsors of a bill tried to spell out every detail of application they would make their task almost impossible. So instead of alienating elements that are at least willing to go along with a general policy, they postpone the fight over specific questions until they turn up in the courts.

A second, though more negative, means by which judges influence policy stems from the power of the courts to declare state or congressional enactments unconstitutional. When a court blocks a statute, it forces Congress to follow other lines of policy, and thus has at least a negative effect on policy formation. The Supreme Court has exercised considerable restraint in negating national laws, but the variety of state laws and practices has led to a much more active role for the Court in invalidating state actions. As has been so clearly demonstrated in the area of civil rights, the Court's review of state actions may almost single-handedly create new national policy.

Third, the possibility that the court may declare an act unconstitutional leads congressmen themselves to think in legalistic terms. Since the courts have the power of judicial review, congressmen must worry about the constitutionality as well as the political wisdom of every statute, and this alone makes the judges a constant factor in policy-making. Senator Barry Goldwater thus justified his highly publicized vote against the Civil Rights Act of 1964 on the ground that it was unconstitutional, leaving in abeyance the question of its wisdom as policy. Although he did not argue that the courts would agree with his legal analysis, his explanation for his vote demonstrates the pervasive nature of constitutional requirements.

The President and Policy-Making

The President's contribution to congressional activity is much more direct than is that of the judges. Both the formal Constitution and the informal pattern of American politics make the President our chief legislator no less than our chief executive. The Constitution underwrites the President's policy-making role in several ways. First, it stipulates that he shall initiate policy in his annual "state of the union" address and in other speeches and messages to Congress. Preparation of the congressional agenda is thus the work of the executive, not of Congress itself. Second, the Constitution gives the President the power to veto any legislation of which he disapproves. Although a stubborn Congress can override a veto by a two-thirds vote in both houses, the veto and the threat of a veto are powerful weapons. The clear intent of the Founding Fathers that the President should serve as a legislative leader is seen in a third Constitutional provision: the President has the authority to convene either or both houses of Congress in special session. Regular sessions of Congress are now so extended that the convening power hardly needs to be used, but it was important in originally establishing the President as the leader of Congress. Fourth, the Constitution specifies that the President "take care that the laws be faithfully executed." We have seen that laws are simply broad declarations of policy when they come from Congress, and that the courts continue the policy-making function as they interpret laws. But the executive branch plays an even greater role than the courts in filling in details and interpreting laws. Laws are not self-enforcing; the President decides how vigorously particular policies, such as civil rights guarantees and antitrust legislation, will be pursued.

The division of Congress into two houses and the decentralization of power in each house mean that the presidency is the only source of general leadership. Even congressmen who regularly disagree with a President depend on him to furnish a general program that they can attack. And his followers look to him for a coherent set of objectives that they can support. We have seen that party leaders in Congress are the principal source of coordination and that party affiliation is the principal influence on a congressman's vote. The President's status as head of his party therefore powerfully augments his legislative leadership. His party's leaders in Congress normally follow his lead and manage to rally most of the party faithful behind them. Some members of the President's party may feel that they owe their victories to his success in drawing votes to the party. If they won their seats by narrow margins and trailed behind the President in popular votes, they may find it helpful to be identified with the President and perhaps win his assistance in their efforts to get re-elected.

Unfortunately for the President, however, the key committee chairmanships generally go to representatives and senators from districts in which re-election is almost assured. Thus some of the most powerful figures in Congress are likely to be the very congressmen who are least dependent on the President's power as party leader. Democratic leaders in Congress, many of them permanent fixtures from the South, have frequently failed to support President Johnson. In Eisenhower's first administration, the Republican majority leader in the Senate, William Knowland of California, publicly opposed many of the President's policies, especially in the field of foreign affairs.

Despite these limitations on his power as party leader, all the President's roles nonetheless overlap to fortify him in the position of chief legislator. If he is a forceful leader, like Woodrow Wilson or either Roosevelt, he may appeal directly to the people for support in order to win still more influence over the members of Congress.

Bureaucrats and Policy-Making

Career bureaucrats furnish the detailed information and the expert knowledge that are necessary for congressional action. These career officials are vitally important parts of the different policy systems through which public policies are decided. Although they cannot openly oppose presidential recommendations, they may develop ties with private interests and with congressmen through which they covertly support policies contrary to the President's program.

The Army Corps of Engineers furnishes a striking example of bureaucratic independence in influencing decisions in the distributive policy arena. The

Corps, which is always eager to deepen channels, improve harbors, or strengthen levees, is closely tied to local officials and contractors, and to the congressmen from the lower Mississippi region. As part of what has been called "the lobby that can't be licked,"[90] the Corps of Engineers has repeatedly and successfully ignored orders from its Commander-in-Chief. In 1949, the Hoover Commission[91] recommended (to no avail) that the dam-building functions of the Corps be placed under the Bureau of Reclamation. The Corps, then, continues, unscathed, to battle the Bureau for appropriations—with or without presidential approval, and always with the cooperation of interested congressmen.

Every executive agency and operating division develops interests of its own, and every subordinate official is eager to preserve or extend his agency's role even while he is advising the President or interpreting his orders. Government agencies recommend legislation to Congress directly and through allied interests inside and outside the government. Although the executive departments are all legally subordinate to the President, their influence on policy is not that of a monolithic structure. Bertram M. Gross, from the vantage point of wide experience both in senatorial committees and in the Executive Office of the President, offers this conclusion:

> A bogeyman has been created of a vast Executive bureaucracy with such power and influence that the President can use it to dominate Congress and obtain whatever legislation he wants. One reason that this is not so is that no President has ever been able to avoid or overcome serious conflicts between the heads of the various agencies. . . .
>
> . . . Many agencies themselves are established only in response to the pressure of private organizations and their representatives in Congress and can continue in existence only by working with and serving such groups. . . . As a result of these diverse and often conflicting allegiances, there are more checks and balances within the executive branch itself than the Founding Fathers ever dreamed of when they wrote the Constitution.[92]

The sharing of functions by Congress and other agencies works both ways. A principal means by which Congress overlaps with executive agencies is through the device of committee investigations. The first congressional inquiry was conducted in 1792, when irate congressmen decided to find out why United States troops had been defeated in a battle with the Indians. Since then, there have been over a thousand investigations, and recent Congresses have been conducting them more frequently than ever. The most exciting inquiries during recent years have dealt with "reds" of a different kind—communists and alleged communists.

---

[90]Robert deRoos and Arthur A. Maas, "The Lobby That Can't Be Licked," *Harper's Magazine* (August, 1949).

[91]Officially known as the Commission on Organization of the Executive Branch of the Government.

[92]Bertram M. Gross, *The Legislative Struggle: A Study in Social Combat* (New York: McGraw-Hill Book Company, 1953), pp. 104–105. Roland Young treats Congress and the President as inseparable parts of the legislative process. He notes especially the manner in which the bureaucracy advocates and defends its interests in Congress even though it is not directly represented there. See Roland Young, *The American Congress* (New York: Harper & Row, Publishers, Inc., 1958).

The congressional power of investigation has never been seriously challenged, for it is evident that, as the Supreme Court put it, "the power of inquiry . . . is an essential and appropriate auxiliary to the legislative function."[93] Legislation deals with social and economic maladjustments about which congressmen are no more automatically informed than are college students and professors. In order to legislate wisely, lawmakers must be able to acquire the information they need, even if it means subpoenaing witnesses and compelling them to testify on pain of punishment for contempt of Congress. Many vital legislative reforms would never have been made if congressmen had been unable to investigate problems in this manner. The Securities and Exchange Commission, for example, which offers what is now regarded as minimum protection to investors, could hardly have been created without the technical information and political impact produced by the Senate Banking and Currency Committee's probe into Wall Street practices in the early 1930s.

This power of inquiry also gives life and meaning to congressional supervision of the administration. Under the separation of powers spelled out by the Constitution, Congress would be hopelessly overshadowed by the executive if it had no power to call administrators to account. A law acquires meaning only as it is administered, and congressmen would be rendered almost impotent if they were denied the right to inquire into whether administrative practices and rulings are in keeping with the broad policy directives of Congress. "Instead of the function of governing, for which it is radically unfit," John Stuart Mill submitted, "the proper office of a representative assembly is to watch and control the government . . . and, if the men who compose the government abuse their trust, or fulfill it in a manner which conflicts with the deliberate sense of the nation, to expel them from office. . . ."[94] Although Congress can expel executive officers only through the laborious process of impeachment, its power of investigation, coupled with its control over appropriations, assures it the power to supervise the work of even the most powerful executive officers. Finding the system of investigation "the main guarantee against dishonesty or inefficient administration," Harold Laski, a more recent British observer, concluded, "After all, a system which drove three cabinet members to resign in 1924 and resulted in imprisonment and two suicides may reasonably claim to have a measurable public value."[95]

The Functions of Congress

Evaluations of Congress depend on how much the evaluators like or dislike its policy output. The response to practices like the filibuster, for example, seem to depend on the critic's attitude toward the measures being talked to

---

[93] *McGrain* v. *Daugherty*, 273 U.S. 135 (1927).
[94] R. B. McCallum (ed.), *On Liberty and Considerations on Representative Government* (Oxford: Basil Blackwell, 1948), p. 172.
[95] Harold Laski, *The American Democracy: A Commentary and An Interpretation* (New York: The Viking Press, 1943), p. 89.

death rather than on his general beliefs about "majority rule" or "minority rights." Thus an attack by Vice-President Charles Dawes on filibustering in 1925, when labor was opposing measures supported by a majority of senators, brought from the American Federation of Labor's national convention a counterattack on Dawes for representing "the predatory interests." The AFL praised the filibuster for making the Senate "the only forum in the world where cloture does not exist and where members can prevent the passage of reactionary legislation."[96] By the 1940s, the political tides had changed; labor and other liberal groups were frequently in favor of measures supported by a majority of senators. The AFL accordingly reversed its position on filibusters and joined in a campaign with other liberal groups to establish "majority rule" in the Senate. The stand of the AFL is typical: the way most of us evaluate congressional procedures depends on our attitudes toward the laws being passed, not on any fixed principles about the "right" way of organizing Congress.

The Protection of Organized Minorities

We cannot easily lay aside our policy preferences in talking about the functions of Congress for the American political system. But we can try. By asking what the system would be like without Congress, we can hope to get some reasonably objective insight into the consequences of congressional activity for American politics.

Imagine we had no Congress. If we consider the policies advocated by Presidents, bureaucrats, and judges in the last generation, the United States would undoubtedly have had a more liberal set of social and economic policies than it now has. During the 1920s, the policies would have been more conservative than those adopted. (Remember that the ALF regarded the filibuster a pillar of "good" — that is, "democratic" — government, for Presidents were then so conservative that the filibuster was an asset to liberals.) In general terms, then, a basic policy consequence of congressional activity is to protect organized minorities in various policy systems from total eclipse by organized majorities. This is not necessarily a permanent function of Congress; but until a majority of congressional districts become microcosms of the national constituency, it is likely to remain.

Authoritative Rule-Making

The principal manifest function of Congress is legislation, the enactment of the laws that govern our lives. To conclude that Congress legislates may appear almost a redundancy. But, as we pointed out earlier, legislation is not the function of the Supreme Soviet in the U.S.S.R. or even of the British Parliament. And critics of the U.S. Congress charge that it, too, has lost the capacity to legislate. Has it? We conclude that it has not.

As we noted earlier, we need to distinguish between the initiation of legislation and the power to shape legislation. Although most bills are drafted

---

[96] As quoted in Gross, *The Legislative Struggle*, p. 418.

in the executive branch of our government, Congress does not simply give them a "rubber stamp" of approval. As the graph in Figure 10–2 indicates, the President's success in winning adoption of his proposals in recent years has varied from Kennedy's low of 27 per cent in 1963 to Johnson's high of 68 per cent in 1965. Presidential success is far from complete, and many of the proposals that are adopted are significantly changed in the process. Nor does Congress always simply react to presidential initiatives. In 1966, after his great success in winning congressional support for a massive domestic program in 1965, President Johnson decided to hold the line on spending. But Congress, with a large Democratic majority including seventy liberal freshmen, seized the initiative. "The committees in both houses, legislative and appropriations alike, . . . set about expanding the programs of the year before and inventing new ones. This bit of legislative history may require a simple explanation: that elections do count and representation does work."[97]

On balance, then, Congress does appear to perform its prescribed constitutional function of authoritative rule-making. Professor Froman is not exaggerating when he concludes that "the United States Congress is probably more powerful as a legislative body *vis-à-vis* the executive than is any other legislative body in the world today."[98]

Representation of Popular Interests

In rule-making, congressmen act in the name of their constituents—they stand for, or represent, the people. As we saw earlier in this chapter, constituency interests tend to coincide with party interests often enough to make party affiliation the key factor for understanding congressional performance. And many constituencies are sufficiently varied so that a Democrat's view of the needs of a given district will be quite different from a Republican's view of the same district. Indeed, in considering the linkage between the electoral system and congressional performance, we found in Chapter 9 that the congressman does not have a very accurate perception of actual constituency views on social welfare issues. When his perception is compared with the attitudes of his supporters, however, it is considerably more accurate. Where constituency opinions are clear, as on civil rights, the congressman's relationship to his constituents tends to be that of the instructed delegate.[99] Where party differences are clear and voters tend to react to party label, as on social welfare questions, the relationship is closer to the responsible party model. Where constituency preferences are least clear, as on foreign policy questions, the congressman must look elsewhere for cues; for members of the majority party, this means largely to the President and his administration. The congressman thus reflects constituent attitudes in an un-

[97] Huitt, "Congress, The Durable Partner," *loc. cit.*, p. 18.
[98] Froman, *The Congressional Process*, p. 3.
[99] Charles F. Cnudde and Donald J. McCrone, "The Linkage Between Constituency Attitudes and Congressional Voting Behavior," *American Political Science Review*, LX (March, 1966), 66–72.

even manner, with the accuracy of the reflection on each issue depending on the extent of public information and interest.

Most studies of Congress take the roll-call vote of congressmen as the one measure of their behavior. As we have indicated, however, most of the important decisions of Congress are made in committees and subcommittees. The principal energies of congressmen are expended in their committee work. Here is where most bills are killed and where the ones that pass are shaped. Since the members of Congress generally accept committee recommendations, this is where most of the positive as well as the negative decisions of Congress are actually made. And this is where the norms of Congress—especially respect for seniority and specialization and the willingness to compromise —exert their strongest influence. Two thoughtful students of Congress independently concluded, on the basis of separate studies of major House committees, that the importance of party is greatest for the final roll-call vote on the floor, and smallest for decisions at the "working level"—that is, in the subcommittees.[100] We should not exaggerate the importance of party affiliation, then, despite its great importance in roll-call voting, the most public of all congressional acts. Neither should we conclude that party is of no importance "behind the scenes." The congressman will act at different stages in response to different sets of pressures. Even at the subcommittee stage, he will take his cue from his party on measures of little direct effect on his constituency. In such a case, however, he will expend less energy on the measure than if important constituency interests were directly involved.[101]

Most congressmen want to vote with their party and feel more comfortable when they can. Party and constituency pressures are such that a congressman can usually represent both interests. Even at the roll-call stage, however, a vote may be so highly publicized that constituency pressures require the con-

[100]Richard A. Fenno, Jr., "The House Appropriations Committee as a Political System: The Problem of Integration," and Charles O. Jones, "The Agriculture Committee and the Problem of Representation," in Peabody and Polsby (eds.), *New Perspectives on the House of Representatives,* pp. 79–108, 109–127.
[101]Jones, *ibid.*

Figure 10-2

Source: Congressional Quarterly Weekly Report, XXIV (December 2, 1966), 2911.

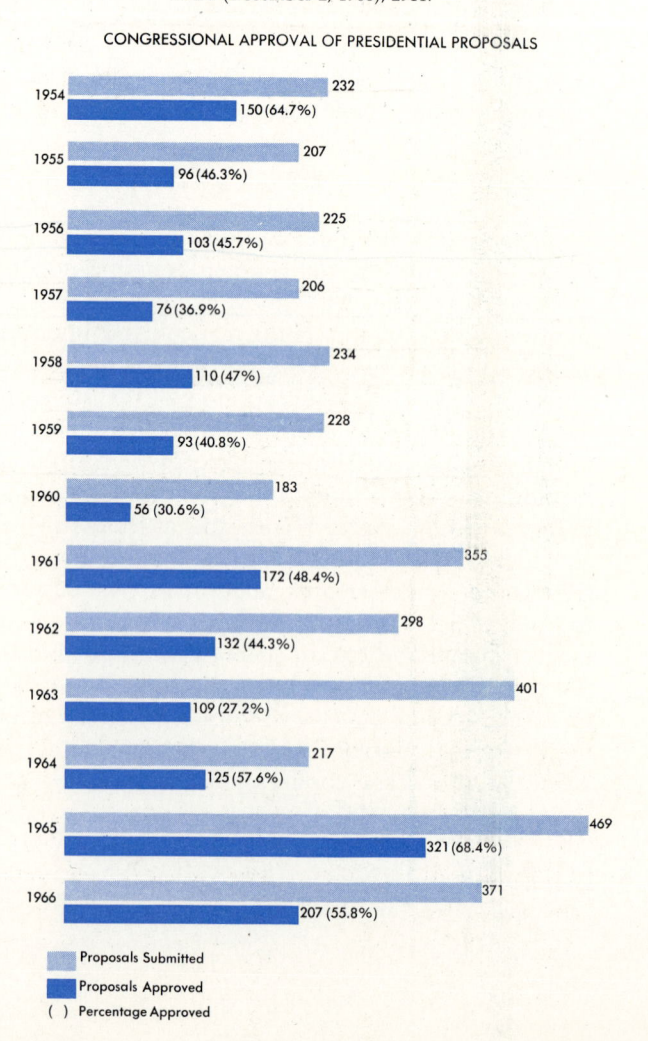

CONGRESSIONAL APPROVAL OF PRESIDENTIAL PROPOSALS

Year	Proposals Submitted	Proposals Approved	Percentage Approved
1954	232	150	(64.7%)
1955	207	96	(46.3%)
1956	225	103	(45.7%)
1957	206	76	(36.9%)
1958	234	110	(47%)
1959	228	93	(40.8%)
1960	183	56	(30.6%)
1961	355	172	(48.4%)
1962	298	132	(44.3%)
1963	401	109	(27.2%)
1964	217	125	(57.6%)
1965	469	321	(68.4%)
1966	371	207	(55.8%)

gressman to vote against his party's majority. Whether voting with or against his party's leaders, however, he feels that he is performing the function of representing popular interests.

The protection of minority interests, authoritative rule-making, and the representation of popular interests, appear to be so clearly anticipated in the organization and procedures of Congress that they can be called its *manifest functions*. Congressmen have always appeared to share the intent of the original Framers of the Constitution that Congress should perform these functions. What additional and less clearly intended functions does Congress perform? A complete list of all the consequences of congressional activity would be as exhausting to compile as it would be exhaustive. But we can identify several additional functions that appear particularly important to the maintenance of the political system. These can be roughly labeled special representation, communication, and legitimization.

We say "special" representation to distinguish this function from the expected kind of representation that occurs as part of rule-making. What we

Latent Functions

The Small Society by Brickman; © 1967 Washington Star Syndicate, Inc.

have in mind here is the importance of Congress in overseeing and controlling the vast bureaucracy. Some students of Congress believe that control of administration is replacing legislation as the primary function of the modern Congress.[102] In fact, critics of Congress probably overstate its effectiveness in general control of administration as much as they understate its effectiveness in legislation.[103] But the representation of the particular interests of individual citizens in relation to the bureaucracy is an undeniably important function of Congress. In the special representation of particular interests, the congressman

[102]Galloway, *The Legislative Process*, pp. 56–57.
[103]Huitt, "Congress, The Durable Partner," loc. cit., pp. 19–20.

is not so much concerned with general problems of administration as he is with helping the local businessman, farmer, social security applicant, and draftee as individuals in their dealings with the bureaucracy. "The actual work of congressmen, in practice if not in theory, is directed toward mediation between constituents and government agencies."[104]

Bureaucrats occupy a position that requires them to operate in a framework of abstract and general policies. Congressmen also want to act in terms of a broad national interest, but their roles make them particularly sensitive to individual problems in their constituencies. Indeed, the differences in the roles of congressmen and bureaucrats seem to dictate the different personality types which end up in the two positions; the former is a type who is "oriented to particular relations with persons" and the latter a type who "abstracts from persons to principles."[105] In any event, "the concern of the House with what may be the particular consequences of policies to minor local individuals and industries is one of its great functions and values."[106]

Like all official decision-making agencies in the American political system, Congress performs an important function in _communication_ of political information to the public. Woodrow Wilson felt that investigations of the administration were themselves primarily important for their effect on public opinion. "The informing function of Congress should be preferred even to its legislative function," he observed. "The argument is not only that discussed and interrogated administration is the only pure and efficient administration, but, more than that, that the only really self-governing people is that people which discusses and interrogates its administration."[107] In recent years, the informing function has been extended far beyond administrative matters, as Congress has pushed its investigations into such areas as civil liberties, concentration of economic power, labor and business practices, lobbying, campaign expenditures, and subversive activities. The recent hearings of Senator Fulbright's Foreign Relations Committee on the war in Vietnam have clearly been primarily designed as an educational enterprise.

In the process of realizing its other functions, Congress lends the mark of _legitimacy_ to the policies of the national government. Richard Fenno, one of the ablest students of Congress, submits that "the resolution of conflict and the building of consensus are among the major functions which Congress performs for American society."[108] Conflict is never resolved in any complete sense, of course, but the decision-making activities of Congress bring conflict into the open, permit it to find peaceable expression, and reduce its intensity by responding to citizen demands. Similarly, actual consensus can hardly be achieved for most legislation, but the fact that a public policy emerges from the congressional process of compromise, in which the minority is insured as much time in debate as the majority, serves at least to create a consensus on the legitimacy of that policy. After a law has been enforced for some time, acceptance often shifts into what we termed, in our discussion of political

[104]Huntington, "Congressional Responses to the Twentieth Century," loc. cit., p. 25.
[105]Bauer, Pool, and Dexter, *American Business and Public Policy*, p. 446.
[106]*Ibid.*, p. 445.
[107]Wilson, *Congressional Government*, p. 303.
[108]"The House of Representatives and Federal Aid to Education," in Peabody and Polsby (eds.), *New Perspectives on the House of Representatives*, p. 195.

opinions, "supportive consensus." Congress thus serves to unify the public behind the government by giving expression to differences of opinion as well as by turning the dominant opinions into legislation that is generally accepted as legitimate.

THE

PRESIDENT   11

"The executive Power shall be vested in a President of the United States of America . . . he shall take Care that the Laws be faithfully executed." This is the broad constitutional prescription of Article II, unchanged since it was written in 1787.

When the authors of *The Federalist* tried to explain to their contemporaries the meaning of "executive power," they declared that "the dim light of historical research" and the experience of other nations offered little instruction. As they viewed it, the office of "Chief Magistrate" in the new federal republic had no counterpart in any other country. They were especially anxious to reject the argument of anti-Federalists that the President would occupy a position similar to that of the British King. In their day executive power was thought of in terms of monarchs. A good part of the argument in defense of Article II was therefore designed to show that a vigorous executive is not inconsistent with republican government.

The Executive in the Political System

Browsing through *The Statesman's Yearbook*, we can discover all kinds of information about the world's chiefs of state: who holds what office, how each incumbent is formally selected, tenures in office, and constitutional duties and responsibilities. The wide variations in detail might suggest that each chief of state occupies a unique position; but when we consider that every nation-state is represented by a chief of state, we realize that the position is an institutional feature in every political system.

Suppose that the Big Five among the world's chiefs of state should accept an invitation from Pope Paul VI or the Secretary General of the United Nations U Thant to meet in a super-summit conference to rearrange the affairs of the world on a rational basis. Those attending would presumably include the American President, the British Prime Minister, the French President, the Russian Chairman of the Council of Ministers, and the Chinese Premier. All would have similar roles to play, each protecting and promoting the national interests of his country. Each would be empowered to act as *chief of state,* although they occupy quite different positions within their various political systems.

The chief of state may be the head of state, the head of government, or a person assigned both roles. In diplomatic protocol, the head of state takes precedent over all other persons from that state, even though his position is often only titular. In modern government, the head of state still performs distinct functions: he is a "symbol of unity, a magnet of loyalty, and a centre of ceremony."[1] In international law, the head of state is the sole agent of the state; the state is bound by his acts, and he is legally responsible for all the acts of his state. The *head of government* is the person who actually possesses the highest authority within the political system. In the policy process, the head of government is expected to formulate and recommend policies, and as chief executive to give general direction to all of the government's activities.

The American Constitution of 1787 was written at a time of transition. In Great Britain, the separation between the head of state and head of government had not yet been completely effected. The development of the British cabinet system and the emergence of the Prime Minister as head of government were still in the offing. Therefore, the American conception of a single magistrate combining the symbolic and ceremonial powers of head of state with the actual governing authority and administrative responsibility of head of government was really an early republican offspring of monarchy.

The American President would thus attend the super-summit meeting as both head of state and head of government. He is the principal spokesman of the United States in foreign policy, although he shares his powers and responsibilities in the policy process, foreign as well as domestic, with Congress. In contrast to parliamentary government, the American presidential system is based on separation of powers; the President is the recognized leader of his party, but his election and tenure in office are independent of the status of his party in the Congress. In 1954, when the American electorate returned a majority of Democratic legislators to both houses of Congress, Republican President Eisenhower was neither expected nor impelled to resign; when two years later the electorate chose him again to be their chief of state and chief executive and at the same time returned Democratic majorities to Congress, the situation was unusual but not inexplicable. As we pointed out in the previous chapter, the people "liked Ike" as a person and preferred the Democratic Party's policies.

In Great Britain, the monarch is still titular head of the state; the Prime Minister is Head of Her Majesty's Government. Constitutionally the British Prime Minister owes his appointment to the Crown, though actually his tenure in office is dependent on his leadership of the party which controls the majority of votes in Parliament. Within the British Commonwealth of Nations, all of the member states owe formal allegiance to the same head of state, Her Majesty Queen Elizabeth; but each member nation of the Commonwealth has its own government and its own head of government quite independent of Westminister (the British Houses of Parliament) or of No. 10 Downing Street (the London residence of the British Prime Minister). In the super-summit meeting, the British Prime Minister would speak only for the United Kingdom; he cannot bind the other members of the Commonwealth.

The President of the Fifth French Republic, like the American President, is

---

[1]Ernest Barker, *Essays on Government* (Oxford: Clarendon Press, 1945), p. 6.

head of state and, together with his Prime Minister, functions as head of government. His position, however, is quite different; he is head of a unitary state in which there is no sharing of powers and functions between the national government and the territorial departments, as in the American federal union between the national government and the states. Moreover, because the French President, together with his Prime Minister, acts as head of government in a parliamentary system, there is no separation of executive and legislative powers, as in the American presidential system. Because the French were not willing to give up their parliamentary system in favor of separation of powers, the Constitution of the Fifth Republic retains the post of a Prime Minister responsible to the Assembly; in fact, however, the Prime Minister owes his political authority and loyalty to the President who appoints him.

The Russian chief of state is Chairman of the Council of Ministers, the highest executive and administrative organ in the U.S.S.R. Constitutionally, the U.S.S.R. has a parliamentary system within a federal republic. Members of the Council of Ministers, including the Chairman, are responsible to the Supreme Soviet, the legislative body. The titular head of state is the Chairman of the Presidium of the Supreme Soviet, who presides over a collegial executive also responsible to the Supreme Soviet. Actually the number one power position is held neither by the Chairman of the Council of Ministers nor by the Chairman of the Presidium, but by the First Secretary of the Communist Party. This is because the U.S.S.R. is a totalitarian, one-party state in which the governmental structure is completely interlocked with the Communist Party. Similarly, in the totalitarian People's Republic of China, although the titular chief of state is the Premier, the Chairman of the Central Committee of the Communist Party actually acts as chief ideologist, chief strategist, and chief decision-maker.[2]

The interactions of chiefs of state reflect different roles within the varying political systems which they represent. The role which the American President plays is conditioned by his status within the American political system; conversely, his performance in the international system affects his position in domestic politics. Within his own political system, the President has top billing as Chief Executive. On the international stage, however, he must share the limelight with an all-star cast, for every chief of state has the lead role within his own system. In order to understand why the President is sometimes unable to fulfill the expectations of his American constituents, it may be helpful to note briefly some of the factors which determine the relative power and influence of chiefs of state in world politics. Summit performances offer us the most dramatic illustrations, although the same conditions enter into the

[2] Because the United States Government does not recognize the government of the People's Republic of China, and the country is off-limits to American political scientists, it is perhaps presumptuous to discuss the power structure of that country, the more so because party factions in the government seem to be in guerrilla warfare with each other. It would, however, be unrealistic to exclude the People's Republic of China from the super-summit, especially since it has joined the "nuclear club."

routinized day-to-day communications between chiefs of state acting as spokesmen for their own nationals.

The size and importance of a country usually determine the stature of its chief of state in international relations. At the Paris Peace Conference in 1919, for example, thirty-two nations were represented, but the Big Four who made the key decisions were the American President, Woodrow Wilson; the British Prime Minister, David Lloyd George; the French Premier, Georges Clemenceau; and the Italian Premier, Vittorio Orlando. Similarly, in World War II, twenty-six nations were at war with the Axis powers, but the Big Three determined the Grand Strategy: the American President, Franklin D. Roosevelt; the British Prime Minister, Winston Churchill; and Marshall Joseph Stalin of the Soviet Union.

Official status with authority to represent his government is the *sine qua non* of the nation's spokesman in international diplomacy. This was demonstrated at Potsdam, where the Big Three met in the summer of 1945 to settle the fate of the defeated enemies. Names and faces were quite different than at Yalta, where the Big Three had met only five months earlier. Harry S Truman, who had succeeded to the American presidency following the death of Roosevelt, now represented the United States; he had already used his power as chief executive to bring along with him his own appointee as Secretary of State, James F. Byrnes, replacing Edward R. Stettinius, Jr., who had accompanied Roosevelt to Yalta. Winston Churchill and his Foreign Secretary, Anthony Eden, represented Great Britain at the opening of the conference; Clement Attlee and Ernest Bevin, leaders of His Majesty's Loyal Opposition, were also in attendance just in case the scheduled parliamentary elections at home should result in victory for the Labour Party. That incredible event did occur; in the midst of the Potsdam meeting, ex-Prime Minister Churchill and ex-Foreign Secretary Eden packed up their attaché cases and went home, while Prime Minister Attlee and Foreign Secretary Bevin moved into the seats of power. Only the Russian team remained stable: Marshall Joseph Stalin and his veteran Foreign Affairs Minister Vyacheslav Molotov.

Obviously the politics of decision-making among chiefs of state demand that the participants have a realistic understanding of their respective domestic political situations. A classic example of what can happen when the actors on the international scene do not grasp changing situational factors on the home front is the story of President Woodrow Wilson's mission at the Paris Peace Conference after World War I. Wilson wrested from the Conference what he claimed the United States most wanted as the fruit of victory: the incorporation of the Covenant of the League of Nations as an integral part of the peace settlement. Apparently the American President did not realize the growing discrepancy between the role which he envisioned for himself on the world stage and his political status at home, where public opinion was sharply veering toward isolationism. A shift in party fortunes in the 1918 American congressional elections, which altered the balance of power between the Democratic President in the White House and the Republicans in Congress, literally made all the difference in the world in 1919. Influential as he was in international politics, the American President had lost control over the policy machine in his own country. And so, ironically, he failed to obtain the requisite consent of two-thirds of the Senate for the Peace Treaty, principally because it contained the Covenant!

Checks and balances in the American presidential system which the Founding Fathers designed so carefully to prevent corruption of men in office have sometimes weakened the bargaining power of the President in international politics. In 1967, President Johnson, about to meet with the Latin American presidents at Punta del Este, Uruguay, to discuss Latin American development plans, asked Congress for an advance commitment to support his pledges for increasing American aid to the Alliance for Progress. After acrimonious discussion, the Senate Committee on Foreign Relations only recommended that the Senate promise to "give due consideration to cooperation." The much publicized disagreement between the White House and Capitol Hill over appropriations for foreign aid (including funds for the Alliance for Progress) highlights the difficulties of any one administration in making pledges or commitments through diplomatic channels, even at the level of summitry among chiefs of state.

The turn of events and new situational factors have a way of changing power relations, even within a totalitarian system, and when these changes occur, a corresponding shift in power relations may take place in the international arena. As a result of Chairman Khrushchev's visit to the United States and his conversations with President Eisenhower at Camp David, a summit meeting was planned for Paris in May, 1960, to discuss the Berlin question. On the eve of that conference, however, an American U-2 reconnaissance plane was shot down inside the Soviet Union. When President Eisenhower assumed official responsibility for the act of espionage, an infuriated Khrushchev scuttled the summit meeting. Khrushchev, as chairman of the Council of Ministers and First Secretary of the Communist Party, was then at the peak of his power in the Soviet Union. President Eisenhower, as an outgoing President, was already moving out of the center of American politics; "the summit that never was" became a lively campaign issue that helped elect a vigorous young President to the office in November, 1960.

Interpersonal relations are probably less significant in international politics than in domestic politics. When chiefs of state meet at the summit, the degree of deference or respect which they pay one another is usually a direct consequence of national power positions rather than personal attributes. In his memoirs, Eisenhower observed about the "spirit of Camp David" that "the Khrushchev of the tea table was scarcely recognizable to one who knew him at the conference table."[3] When Lyndon Johnson and Alexei Kosygin met at Glassboro, New Jersey, in 1967, the informal small-town setting, the family-style entertainment, and the genial public appearances of the participants gave an initial impression of a *détente* between the United States and the Soviet Union through personal diplomacy. Thus the hard line which the Chairman took at a formal press conference at the United Nations after two days of

---

[3]Dwight D. Eisenhower, *Waging Peace* (Garden City, New York: Doubleday & Co., 1960), p. 558.

pleasant conversation with the American President came as a shock to the American public. But the fact is that neither the Russian Chairman nor the American President was really empowered within his own political system to initiate any significant policy changes.

As we look over the major countries of the world, whether totalitarian or democratic, we note that in none is the chief of state the sole embodiment of national power. The personal dictator survives only in small, backward, or underdeveloped countries. The very nature of modern big government implies a complex system of behavior in which all of the components continuously interact. No system of human behavior is impersonal, however, for the "components" are always persons.

All chiefs of state have one characteristic in common: they are politicians whose aptitude for leadership has differentiated them and lifted them above the rank and file of citizens or subjects. Some more than others seem to possess qualities of leadership which go well beyond executive ability, administrative skill, political manipulation, and articulation of prevailing political opinions. The charismatic leader is one who has force of will and inner conviction to carry his visions into execution and who identifies his own ego with national destiny and persuades his followers to reach for greatness through him. Charles de Gaulle adds this dimension of charismatic leadership to his role of chief of state when he claims, "I am France." In size or economic resources, France today is not a major power in the world; and yet under de Gaulle's leadership the Fifth French Republic has attained a position of primacy in Europe and great influence in international politics. The reluctance of President Roosevelt to deal directly with de Gaulle as leader of the Free French forces during World War II and the decision of the American State Department to deal officially with Premier Pétain in the Vichy government turned out to be diplomatic goofs with long-lasting effects. Failure to recognize the inspirational nature of de Gaulle's leadership, to assess the General's ambitions, capabilities, and will power, and to realize how these were tied to the aspirations of the French people are still factors in today's cleavage between the United States and France.

The American people have known some strong Presidents but few charismatic leaders. We might name Abraham Lincoln, Woodrow Wilson, and Franklin D. Roosevelt, but these in their own times were rejected by many; the myths of history serve now to exalt their memory. Certainly John Fitzgerald Kennedy had a charismatic appeal, especially for young people. The intelligence, the energy, the faith, the dedication which he brought to the presidency, his commitment to human rights at home and around the world, his inaugural promise to "light our country and all who serve it," these are the special qualities of leadership that we call charismatic. Yet, on the record, his administration proposed more than it accomplished. What he might have achieved, given time, is not known; he too has become a myth in American history.

Comparisons need not be invidious; they can in fact be very useful in perceiving patterns of behavior in any group. We have heard it said so often that we have come to believe that the President of the United States is the most powerful chief of state in the world. But would he really be *primus inter pares* at the super-summit meeting? To understand the relative power of the American President among chiefs of state, we have sketched above a number of power sources: the size and importance of the country or countries involved; the national interests and goals of the people; the official status of the principals within their own political system; the force and events and situational factors which may condition particular positions; new demands and pressures at home and in the world; and, finally, how each performer views and acts out his own role.

Robert Dahl has designed a neat little paradigm for comparison of power: "_____ is more influential than _____ with respect to _____ as measured by _____ and _____."[4] Try it out if you want to compare President _____ with President _____; or President _____ with Premier _____. Note that you cannot fill in the blanks without specific data.

The easiest way to explain the position of the President in the American political system is to take the institutional approach. The *United States Government Organization Manual* offers a neat symmetrical chart of the national government (see Fig. 11–1). At the very top of the chart is a box for the *Constitution*, from which all authority in the government is derived. The three branches of the government—*legislative* (Congress), *executive* (the President), and *judicial* (the courts)—are shown in three boxes on the same horizontal line, separate, equal, and coordinate. The President's box is set in the middle and lines of authority extend from it to the twelve boxes below, which represent the executive departments with Cabinet rank, and then to a giant box that includes thirty-odd independent offices and establishments.

The Chief Executive

The original concept of the President focused on his personal power in the office. "*He* shall hold his Office, . . . *he* may require . . . , *he* shall have Power, . . . *he* shall, . . . *he* may, . . . *he* shall take Care that the Laws be faithfully executed." The Constitution does not mention a *chief* executive; it simply vests executive power in the President. Nevertheless, in recent years, the Executive Office of the President has to a large extent bureaucratized and institutionalized the presidency. Although the President acts as Chief Executive, the White House comprises many offices (see Fig. 11–2).

Organization charts show official relationships and the authorized chain of command, but they do not give us any real notion of what government is like in action. Kremlinologists would not get far in studying the Soviet Union if they relied on this kind of information. An organizational chart of the Soviet Union places the Constitution in the top box just like the chart in the American *Government Manual*. Because the Soviet Union has a parliamentary form of government, the highest organ of state power under the Constitution is the Supreme Soviet; the Presidium and the Council of Ministers appear as func-

[4] Robert A. Dahl, *Modern Political Analysis* (Englewood Cliffs, N.J.: Prentice-Hall, Inc., 1963), p. 47.

THE GOVERNMENT OF THE UNITED STATES

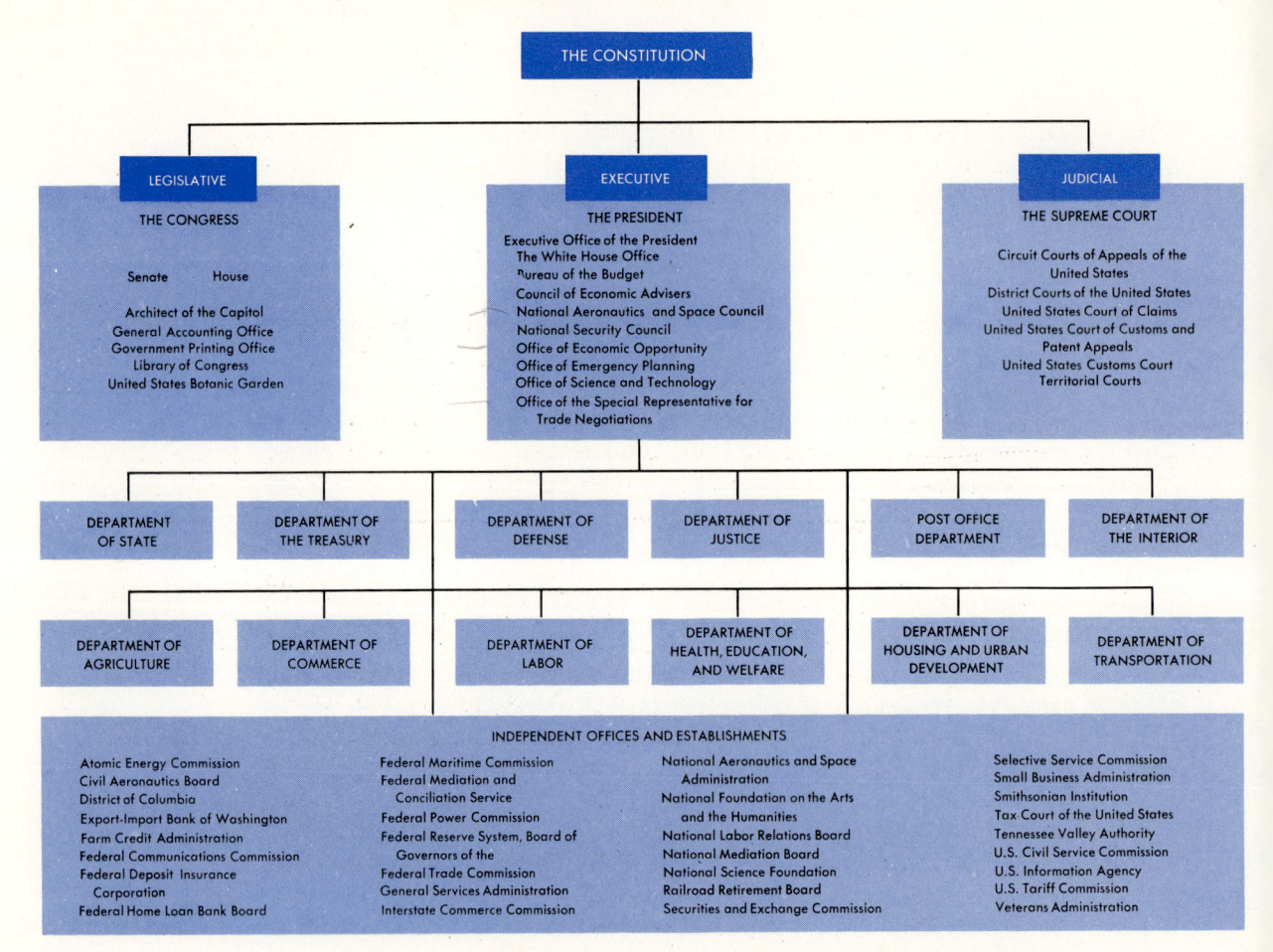

THE CONSTITUTION

LEGISLATIVE
THE CONGRESS

Senate House

Architect of the Capitol
General Accounting Office
Government Printing Office
Library of Congress
United States Botanic Garden

EXECUTIVE
THE PRESIDENT
Executive Office of the President
The White House Office
Bureau of the Budget
Council of Economic Advisers
National Aeronautics and Space Council
National Security Council
Office of Economic Opportunity
Office of Emergency Planning
Office of Science and Technology
Office of the Special Representative for Trade Negotiations

JUDICIAL
THE SUPREME COURT

Circuit Courts of Appeals of the United States
District Courts of the United States
United States Court of Claims
United States Court of Customs and Patent Appeals
United States Customs Court
Territorial Courts

DEPARTMENT OF STATE	DEPARTMENT OF THE TREASURY	DEPARTMENT OF DEFENSE	DEPARTMENT OF JUSTICE	POST OFFICE DEPARTMENT	DEPARTMENT OF THE INTERIOR
DEPARTMENT OF AGRICULTURE	DEPARTMENT OF COMMERCE	DEPARTMENT OF LABOR	DEPARTMENT OF HEALTH, EDUCATION, AND WELFARE	DEPARTMENT OF HOUSING AND URBAN DEVELOPMENT	DEPARTMENT OF TRANSPORTATION

INDEPENDENT OFFICES AND ESTABLISHMENTS

Atomic Energy Commission
Civil Aeronautics Board
District of Columbia
Export-Import Bank of Washington
Farm Credit Administration
Federal Communications Commission
Federal Deposit Insurance Corporation
Federal Home Loan Bank Board

Federal Maritime Commission
Federal Mediation and Conciliation Service
Federal Power Commission
Federal Reserve System, Board of Governors of the
Federal Trade Commission
General Services Administration
Interstate Commerce Commission

National Aeronautics and Space Administration
National Foundation on the Arts and the Humanities
National Labor Relations Board
National Mediation Board
National Science Foundation
Railroad Retirement Board
Securities and Exchange Commission

Selective Service Commission
Small Business Administration
Smithsonian Institution
Tax Court of the United States
Tennessee Valley Authority
U.S. Civil Service Commission
U.S. Information Agency
U.S. Tariff Commission
Veterans Administration

Source: *United States Government Organization Manual, 1967–68*
(Washington, D. C.: U. S. Government Printing Office, 1967), p. 618.

Figure 11-1

tional agents in boxes below the Supreme Soviet with lines of responsibility to the Supreme Soviet. We have indicated in the previous chapter, however, that the Supreme Soviet actually meets only for a few days each year, to rubber-stamp decisions that have been made elsewhere in the Soviet system, notably in the decision-making apparatus of the Communist party.

The tripartite model of decision-making—rule-making, rule-application, and settlement of disputes—is useful for structural as well as functional analysis in the American government, but it is not as serviceable in comparative politics. Most governments in the world, parliamentary in form, do not institutionally differentiate executive from legislative functions in the policy process. Hence political scientists who want to look at American politics within a universe of decision-making have tried to schematize the process itself without reference to the standing of the participants in the structural hierarchy.[5]

[5] A seminal model of decision-making is Harold D. Lasswell, *The Decision Process: Seven Categories of Functional Analysis* (College Park, Md: Bureau of Governmental Research, University of Maryland, n.d.).

388

In an abstract scheme the process of decision-making appears to follow a logical sequence:

(1) *Intelligence:* obtaining information and interpreting data which have a bearing on the problem.

(2) *Formulation:* identifying the values, interests, and goals, and determining priorities where there are conflicts.

(3) *Assessment of alternatives:* examining the array of alternatives, and appraising them through the intelligence and goal task, previously performed.

(4) *Recommendation:* recommending the preferred alternative in line with the previous assessment of costs, risks, and feasibility.

(5) *Authorization:* prescribing a general rule of behavior to achieve the recommendation.

(6) *Implementation:* planning the programs and setting up the operations to carry out the authorization.

(7) *Application:* applying the rules and settling disputes in specific cases in terms of the general authorization.

(8) *Reappraisal:* re-examining the programs and operations to determine whether the general rule and its specific applications have met the problem, in terms of the values, interests, and goals considered in the formulation of policy.

Like organization charts, the decision-making schema bears little resemblance to government in action. Critics point out that the actual policy process is never so logical or rational, that policy-makers may make decisions without waiting for full intelligence reports or even in the face of contradictory reports. Because interests, values, and goals are highly subjective, decision-makers may act from personal bias, class predilections, or from parochial prejudices.

EXECUTIVE OFFICE OF THE PRESIDENT

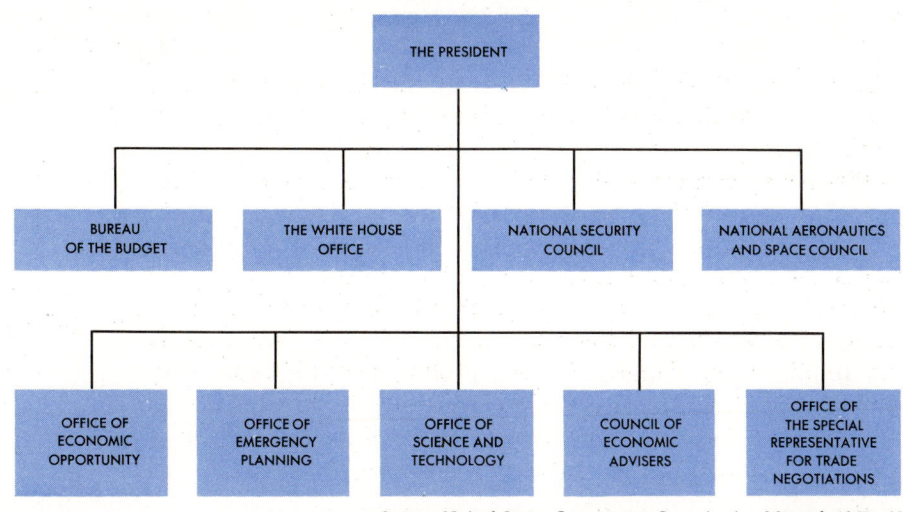

```
                        THE PRESIDENT
                             |
   ┌─────────────┬───────────┼───────────────┬──────────────────┐
 BUREAU       THE WHITE     NATIONAL        NATIONAL AERONAUTICS
 OF THE       HOUSE         SECURITY        AND SPACE COUNCIL
 BUDGET       OFFICE        COUNCIL
                             |
   ┌──────────┬──────────┬───┴──────┬──────────────┐
 OFFICE OF  OFFICE OF  OFFICE OF  COUNCIL OF   OFFICE OF
 ECONOMIC   EMERGENCY  SCIENCE    ECONOMIC     THE SPECIAL
 OPPORTUNITY PLANNING  AND        ADVISERS     REPRESENTATIVE
                       TECHNOLOGY              FOR TRADE
                                               NEGOTIATIONS
```

Source: *United States Government Organization Manual, 1967–68* (Washington, D. C.: U. S. Government Printing Ofice, 1967), p. 619.

Figure 11-2

They may promulgate a course of action without giving any consideration to other alternatives. A policy deliberately formulated and strongly recommended on the basis of maximum intelligence may fail to win approval in the agency that is empowered to authorize it, or a policy may be duly authorized but indifferently or inadequately supported. The general rule may be ignored in some cases and capriciously applied in others. A program once put into operation may be indefinitely continued without any reappraisal of its utility, or it may be arbitrarily discontinued by a new administration eager to try out new and different policies. Nevertheless, however well-grounded these criticisms may be, the schema of decision-making suggests the norms of the policy process.

Since we are concerned with the roles that the American President plays in the policy process as well as with his position in the official hierarchy, we shall from time to time refer to the schema of decision-making. As Chief Executive, the President is *primarily* responsible for activities in every stage of the process except authorization, which usually falls within the legislative prerogatives of Congress. In the preceding chapter on Congress, we have already pointed out the considerable interaction of Congress and the President, not only at the point of authorization, but throughout the policy process. In this chapter, we shall also observe how bureaucrats and judges enter into the process and how their various activities affect the exercise of the President's power.

Whatever the forms of government, presidential or parliamentary, democratic or totalitarian, the schema of decision-making can be used. One must keep in mind, however, that policy-making takes place in a specific environment, specific in time and place, that conditions the process. At the intelligence stage, for example, the vantage point for interpretation of data is within the cultural context of the community. That the American President and the Soviet Chairman could talk for two days in 1967 without arriving at any agreement on major issues is to be expected; they view the problems in the Middle East, or Southeast Asia, or Berlin from totally different perspectives. The national interests and goals of their respective countries are very different. By the same token, the British Prime Minister may recommend a very different policy toward trading with Cuba or China from that of the American President; although both are exponents of the "free world," their national interests in foreign trade are very different. Within the American system, decision-making is similarly conditioned by different interests and different values. A Republican President backed by the business community may recommend a quite different labor policy than would a Democratic President with strong support from organized labor. And within the same administration, the American Chief Executive has to decide what intelligence and whose assessments to take when he establishes budget priorities for our three major wars—against communist aggression in Asia, against hunger and population explosion in the less developed countries, and against poverty at home.

In an entertaining and discerning study of the American President, Sydney Hyman says, "He is, or can be, the essence of the nation's personality."[6]

---

[6]*The American President* (New York: Harper & Row, Publishers, Inc., 1954), p. 13.

Harold Laski, a noted British political scientist, made much the same observation in an earlier and more penetrating analysis: "The essence of the presidency is the fact that it is an *American* institution, that it functions in an American environment, that it has been shaped by the forces of American history, that it must be judged by American criteria of its response to American needs."[7]

Recruitment of the President

Thirty-six men have served as President of the United States. The constitutional requirements for the nation's highest office are very modest—a President must be a native-born citizen, he must have resided in the United States for 14 years, and he must be at least 35 years old. Actually, many additional political considerations of a practical nature govern the selection of presidential candidates. But here we run into the difficulties of generalizing over a long period in American history. All our presidents, of course, have met the constitutional specifications; the practical rules that determined their ultimate "availability" as candidates have changed considerably, however, since 1789.

Background and Qualifications

Despite American folklore that Presidents proceed "from log cabin to White House," less than a half-dozen Presidents have risen from the ranks of the very poor. Most Presidents have grown up in the upper-middle class; a few, like George Washington, Franklin D. Roosevelt, and John Fitzgerald Kennedy, have been very wealthy. In the 1964 election, both presidential candidates were multimillionaires. Neither Lyndon Johnson nor Barry Goldwater had to worry much about personal campaign expenses or how to support a family on a government paycheck. A modern national election, however, costs more than even a multimillionaire can finance on his own. Before a candidate has a chance to wage his campaign on a national scale, he must secure heavy outside financial backing.

Other factors, more or less personal, also condition the people's choice. The need to secure a majority vote in a very large and mixed electorate has prevented the candidacy of any overt representatives of special interests such as business or labor. Many of our presidents have been military leaders, ten have been army generals. President Eisenhower made his great reputation as a General of the Army, had little liking for politics, and never developed a strong sense of partisanship. Most presidents have been college or university graduates and a majority of them have been lawyers. President Kennedy majored in political science at Harvard College and his honors thesis became a best-selling book.[8] President Johnson graduated from Southwest Texas State Teachers College and taught debating and public speaking before he made politics his career.

[7] *The American Presidency* (New York: Harper & Row, Publishers, Inc., 1940), p. 7.
[8] *Why England Slept* (New York: Funk & Wagnalls Co., Inc., 1961, first published in 1940).

Religion and sex also enter into presidential politics. The American people are religious in sentiment if not always in behavior. Up to 1960, the Protestant tradition was strong enough to reject a Roman Catholic as President. In 1928, when New York's Governor Alfred E. Smith unsuccessfully ran for the office, his defeat was widely attributed to his Roman Catholic faith, although other issues in the campaign becloud this conclusion. But Kennedy's 1960 victory, however close, dispelled the myth that a Roman Catholic cannot be elected to the country's highest post. In 1964, the political pundits worried whether or not it would be strategically astute for President Johnson (Christian Church) to name a Roman Catholic for second place on the Democratic ticket; he chose Hubert Humphrey, a Congregationalist. Barry Goldwater (Episcopalian) selected a Roman Catholic, William E. Miller, to be his running mate.

Custom has long excluded women from most policy positions in American government, and it will probably continue to exclude them from the office of Chief Executive for some time to come. Senator Margaret Chase Smith's decision to try for the Republican nomination in 1964 was a gallant one, but the Republican convention at San Francisco gave her short shrift. Hitherto, a Negro candidacy has been inconceivable because of racial pride and prejudice on the part of the overwhelming majority of Caucasians who make up the electorate. But surely the time is coming when a candidate will not be barred because of sex, race, or color, just as the time finally came when a candidate was not barred because of his religion.

If the President is to represent "the essence of the nation's personality," he—and his family—must appear as one of us. Though well over half the American people now live in cities, the notion persists that city men are "slickers" and "wicked," whereas rural folks are "decent and respectable." Only two of our presidents, William Howard Taft and John Fitzgerald Kennedy, were born and raised in large cities. Harry Truman from Independence, Missouri; Dwight Eisenhower from Abilene, Kansas; Lyndon Johnson from Stonewall, Texas (population about 650)—all three typify American small-town talent, the Horatio Alger tradition of "luck and pluck," "work and win." Harry Truman's whistle-stop speeches in 1948 inevitably ended, "Howja like to meet my family?" and then he would introduce Mrs. Truman as "the boss" and his daughter Margaret as "my baby." Pictures of Ike and Mamie Eisenhower in the White House were obviously made to fit into the "American album of Presidents we like"; especially appealing were those of "Grandpa Ike" and little David. The Johnsons are similarly projected. Effective public relations keeps us informed of the daily doings of the First Family and vicariously we enjoy first-name familiarity with "Lyndon," "Lynda Bird," "Luci," "Pat," and "little Lyn."

The Kennedys brought a new kind of sophistication to the White House. They simply could not be pictured as "an average American family from Main Street." John Fitzgerald Kennedy belonged to the "melting pot aristocracy," Boston Irish, but also of Hyannis Port, New York, and Palm Beach. He had style, flair, an engaging personality, and lots of money. Youth was the hallmark of the Kennedy administration, but not inexperienced or naïve youth. The academic influence was perhaps more conspicuous in the Kennedy administration because it had been slighted in the Truman and Eisenhower administrations. But the New Frontiersmen were idea men rather than idealists or ideologists; most of them were also organization men, specialists in public and business administration. President Kennedy himself was a practical politician who came to the White House after fourteen years of toughening experience on Capitol Hill.

Each administration, however, inevitably bears the unique stamp of the President's personality and particular experience. Harry S Truman, Dwight D. Eisenhower, and John Fitzgerald Kennedy each had his own way of conducting the presidential business, for each was a very different kind of person. Although Lyndon B. Johnson was determined to carry on the program outlined by his predecessor, within a remarkably short time he headed a distinctively Johnson administration which was quite different in tone and techniques from the administration of President Kennedy.

President Johnson is the only powerful congressional leader since James Madison to reach the White House. He succeeded where Henry Clay and Robert A. Taft failed; and his legislative experience and associations have paid off well in the presidency. Sensitive to critical comparisons with his predecessor, Johnson is reported to have established his own norm for the role: "They say Jack Kennedy had style, but I'm the one who's got the bills passed."[9]

Lord Bryce, who served as British ambassador to the United States at the turn of the twentieth century, outraged the American public by devoting an entire chapter of his *American Commonwealth* to the question of "Why Great Men Are Not Chosen President."[10] He suggested several answers. First, a smaller proportion of first-rate ability is drawn into politics than into private business. Second, the methods and habits of Congress, with its emphasis on the committee system and loose party organization, offer few opportunities for personal distinction. Third, since eminent men are more likely to make enemies than are mediocre men, political parties tend to choose safe rather than outstanding candidates.

Some years later, however, another distinguished British observer of American politics, Harold Laski, took issue with Bryce's conclusions: "On any showing, eleven American presidents have been extraordinary men whatever may be our view of the handling of their office. That is a proportion not less high than the proportion of remarkable men who have become prime minister in the same period."[11] Laski charged that it was unfair of Bryce to compare American Presidents with the political leaders of England or of any other foreign government, because basically they are not comparable. A President is neither a king nor a prime minister. His single office combines the perquisites of head of the state and the powers of head of the government.

---

[9]Rowland Evans and Robert Novak, quoted in *Lyndon B. Johnson: The Exercise of Power* (New York: The New American Library, 1966), p. 2. Evans and Novak are a pair of knowledgeable Washington correspondents. Their book is a piece of journalistic reporting, based on some 200 personal interviews.

[10]James Bryce, *The American Commonwealth*, 3rd ed. (New York: The Macmillan Company, 1903), 2 vols.

[11]Laski, *The American Presidency*, p. 8.

observed that the only part of the Constitution to escape severe censure during the fight for ratification was the provision for an electoral college to choose the chief magistrate. According to the original plan, each state was to choose as many electors as it had senators and representatives in Congress. The Founding Fathers anticipated that the electors would be free agents who would act deliberately and recruit the most eminent candidate. A majority vote was required to elect the President; the runner-up to the successful candidate would become Vice-President. If the electors failed to cast a majority of votes for any one candidate, then the House of Representatives would designate the person most qualified for the office among the top five candidates considered by the electoral college. Hamilton was confident that this unique process of selection would virtually guarantee that the presidential office would be filled by "characters preeminent for ability and virtue."[12]

Ironically, this much admired electoral system was changed within the first decade of the new republic. The early development of political parties made it necessary to revise the procedure to guard against the possibility of electing the President from one party and the Vice-President from the rival party. Thus the Twelfth Amendment now requires separate balloting for President and Vice-President. As the system now works, the voters in each state do not vote directly for President and Vice-President, but rather choose between slates of presidential electors designated by the respective state party organizations. The slate of electors that wins the popular vote in the state gets to cast all the electoral votes of that state for their party's candidates for President and Vice-President. In reality, the electoral college never meets as an electoral unit; it has no recruiting function at all; it simply acts as a sort of automatic voting machine to record votes cast at the polls.

Recently there has been a rather strong movement to abolish the electoral college and to provide for the election of the President and Vice-President by direct, nationwide popular vote. A report from the Commission on Electoral College Reform of the American Bar Association (normally a conservative pressure group) pulls no punches: "The electoral college method of electing a President of the United States is archaic, undemocratic, complex, ambiguous,[13]

---

[12]*The Federalist*, No. 68.
[13]*Electing the President.* A report of the Commission on Electoral College Reform, to the American Bar Association, January 1967, p. 3.

The electoral system is no exception to our proposition that government procedures are never neutral in their consequences. Nelson Polsby and Aaron Wildavsky have analyzed the presidential election process in a markedly different fashion from that of the ABA. They point out that "the present method of electing the President tends to give greater power to the large, urban states, not the small, rural states, because the large states can deliver to the winner large blocks of votes he needs to win. Consequently Presidential nominees tend to come from big states, and tend to run on platforms likely to appeal to big-city interest groups." As political scientists, Polsby and Wildavsky are concerned with who gets hurt and who gets helped under different procedures. They submit that the net effect of abolishing the electoral college outright and weighing votes everywhere equally would undermine slightly the current strategic advantage now enjoyed by the party-urbanized states. An alternative proposal, to retain the apportionment of the electoral college (which gives numerical advantage to small rural states) and to abolish the unit rule for electoral votes (which operates strongly in favor of populous states), would confer an additional political bonus upon states already overrepresented in positions of congressional power. (Nelson Polsby and Aaron Wildavsky, *Presidential Elections* [New York: Charles Scribner's Sons, 1964], pp. 28–29, 166–67).

indirect, and dangerous." The report points out that under the present system a person may become President with fewer popular votes than his major opponent. No matter how close the voting may be in a state, the winner takes all electoral votes, thus canceling all minority votes cast in the state. The system also gives each state at least three electoral votes; fails to consider population changes in a state between censuses; and makes it possible for presidential electors to vote against the national candidates of their party.

Under the electoral college system, which has governed forty-five presidential elections, fourteen presidents have been chosen without obtaining a majority of popular votes. Of these fourteen, three received fewer popular votes than their major opponent. The House of Representatives has twice been assigned the responsibility of choosing the President after the electoral college failed to cast a majority vote for any one candidate: Thomas Jefferson was so chosen over Aaron Burr in 1800 (the fracas over this election provoked the passage of the Twelfth Amendment); John Quincy Adams was so chosen over Andrew Jackson in 1824. In 1876, the Democratic candidate, Samuel J. Tilden, won a clear majority of the popular vote but in a dispute about which electors should be certified from four of the former Confederate states, a bipartisan Electoral Commission was established by Congress to resolve the issue. On a strict party vote, eight Republicans versus seven Democrats, the Commission certified the Republican electors in each state, so that Rutherford B. Hayes became President. To avoid such anomalies in future elections, Congress is now considering a number of proposals to amend the Twelfth Amendment.

Because the electors do not serve a recruiting function, how does a candidate for the presidential office emerge? With the possible exception of George Washington, the man must first of all nominate himself: no President has ever been drafted for the office; every presidential candidate has sought the office and made his availability known to influential people in the party of his choice. Second, his party must choose him above all others who aspire to the position, presumably because he possesses personal and political attributes most likely to attract not only the popular vote but also the requisite majority of votes in the electoral college. Third, the people must elect him at the polls, preferring him to the alternative candidate who has also been selected by a major political party because of his attractive personal and political qualities.

Nearly all of our Presidents have been professional politicians. They have served as Cabinet officers, members of Congress, and governors of their respective states. In recent years, the U.S. Senate has furnished the candidates for both parties: Richard Nixon, John Kennedy, Lyndon Johnson, and Barry Goldwater. Normally, a candidate has a better chance if he comes from a pivotal state that has a large bloc of votes and where the parties have nearly equal strength in national elections. Of the thirty-six presidential candidates put forward by the major parties from 1868 through 1964, twenty-one were from three states—New York, Ohio, and Illinois. The Republican nomination of Barry Goldwater from Arizona simply flaunted the rule, for Arizona could add but five votes to the final tally.

After the Civil War, candidates from southern states were ruled out of practical consideration by both parties. Neither the Democrats nor the Republicans could figure much advantage in promoting a candidate from a region that was bound to vote Democratic in any event. But ever since the Dixiecrats walked out of the Democratic Convention in 1948, protesting Harry S. Truman's stand on civil rights, the Democratic Solid South has been crumbling. Many old-line southern Democrats became presidential Republicans in 1952, and remained such in 1956, when Dwight D. Eisenhower's record as a war hero enhanced the doctrinal appeal of Republicanism. In 1960, many southerners voted for Richard M. Nixon, partly to express their anti-Catholic opposition to the Democratic candidate, but also because the Republican Party appealed more to their politically conservative predilections.

Drawing by Herblock;
© 1967 The Washington Post.

"I'm feeling
a touch of disability myself"

By 1960, both parties recognized that the South had become a pivotal area in presidential politics. Unquestionably, Kennedy's choice of Lyndon B. Johnson as his running mate was intended to reassure southern moderates and to bring the defectors of 1952 and 1956 back into the Democratic camp. As Majority Leader of the Senate, Johnson was an outstanding figure in national politics, and fortuitously, he came from a southern pivotal state with 24 electoral votes. In 1964, President Johnson was in a position to nominate himself as the Democratic candidate.[14] The fact that Barry Goldwater carried five states of the old Confederacy meant that both parties would be looking over possible candidates from the doubtful southern states before the 1968 conventions.[15]

Louis Koenig, professor of government at New York University, writes: "To win the Presidency, the aspirant must travel a long, hard, treacherous road abounding in bumps and quicksand and divisible into three distinct seg-

---

[14]"When the President is sitting in the White House, the National Convention has never gone against his recommendations in the choice of a candidate or in the formation of a platform on which that Convention is to operate." Harry S Truman with reference to his own nomination by the Democratic Convention in 1948. *Memoirs* (Garden City, N.Y.: Doubleday & Co., Inc., 1956).

[15]For further discussion see Avery Leiserson (ed.), *The American South in the 1960's* (New York: Frederick A. Praeger, 1964), especially Donald R. Matthews and James Prothro, "Southern Images of Political Parties: An Analysis of White and Negro Attitudes," and O. Douglas Weeks, "The South in National Politics." Also see Paul T. David (ed.), *The Presidential Election and Transition 1960–61* (Washington, D.C.: The Brookings Institution, 1961), especially V. O. Key, Jr., "Interpreting the Election Results," and Paul T. David, "The Political Changes of 1960–1961."

ments: the pre-convention build-up, the national nominating convention, and the post-convention electoral campaign."[16] Since we have earlier (in Chapters 7 and 9) discussed those "three distinct segments" in the process of selecting a president, we move into a fourth segment, the period between election and inauguration when the President-elect is recruiting the principals for his new administration.

Presidential Transition

The inauguration of the President is an occasion for national celebration. But in the midst of celebration, the new administration is expected to carry on the business of government without crisis, without interruption. Actually, preparations for the shift in political power symbolized by the inaugural ceremony will have begun on election day and even before.[17]

The first presidential transition involving party turnover in the twentieth century was from William Howard Taft to Woodrow Wilson in 1913. Laurin Henry offers a memorable picture of Woodrow Wilson's inauguration: the leisurely pace and old-fashioned manners, the intimate scale of government activity (including the cow on the White House lawn), President Taft and President-elect Wilson riding together in a horse-drawn carriage to the Capitol. Taft's arrangements for delivering up the office and Wilson's for taking over the administration were personal, informal, and inadequate. It is almost incredible that into the middle of the twentieth century the American national government, ever beset by problems of increasing magnitude and complexity, at home and abroad, simply met the crises of executive succession on an *ad hoc*, unplanned basis. This is the crux of presidential transition as Henry puts it: "a party system that makes it both a minor miracle and a painful experience for the outparty to win a presidential election and then gives the President-elect little assistance in forming a government."[18]

President Truman made a determined effort to exit as a statesman. From his own experience, he knew how hard it was to go into the President's office without preparation. Shortly after the 1952 election, he invited the President-elect to the White House. Meantime he directed that General Eisenhower be furnished with important security information, including Central Intelligence Agency reports and policy papers of the National Security Council. The most crucial current problem was the Korean armistice negotiations. Evidently the President hoped that, in the interest of national unity, the President-elect would actually concur in foreign policy decisions. Eisenhower at once made plain, however, that he would not participate in any government decisions before taking office. As early as November, he appointed Joseph M. Dodge to

[16]Louis Koenig, *The Chief Executive* (New York: Harcourt, Brace & World, Inc., 1964), p. 35.
[17]Laurin Henry, *Presidential Transitions* (Washington, D.C.: The Brookings Institution, 1960).
[18]*Ibid.*, p. 737. In order to facilitate an orderly transition, Congress passed legislation early in 1963 which authorized the outgoing administration to provide some facilities—office space, secretarial assistance and the like—so that the President-elect and his incoming administration can set up shop in Washington between election and inauguration.

be his representative to the Bureau of the Budget and Senator Henry Cabot Lodge to be his liaison with the State and Defense Departments. Their function was simply to obtain information; they had no authority to participate in fiscal or foreign policy decisions. No doubt President Truman felt rebuffed. Nevertheless, he ordered each agency to prepare "briefs" on its organization and operations so that the incoming administration could be "informed to the point of action" on inauguration day. Thus, despite some personal animosity between the two principals, and considerable partisan bitterness between the outgoing and incoming administrations, the process of transition was systematized and institutionalized. The Eisenhower-Kennedy transition, patterned after this precedent, was smoother and more effective, partly because the personal relationships were less strained and partly because the party victory was so marginal in 1960.

In the few months between election and inauguration, the President-elect must choose the key officers of his administration, his personal advisers on the White House staff, top officers in the Executive Office, the heads of departments and principal agencies, the most important ambassadors abroad. Selection of personnel, however, is only the beginning of transition. The strategy of responsible leadership means coming to grips with important issues in a specific and practical way so that programs can be produced. As Henry points out, when a presidential candidate becomes the President-elect, he can no longer lead the opposition; in his new role he must learn to identify himself with an ongoing administration and a continuing bureaucracy. "The myths of opposition must be adjusted to the hard facts of limited alternatives."

Presidential transition with a party turnover is particularly difficult. The President-elect shares responsibility with the outgoing President for an orderly shift in political power and a continuity in administration. At the same time, as leader of a victorious party, he cannot risk tarring his new administration with the policies of the old administration. Franklin Roosevelt deemed it good politics to let the Hoover administration sweat it out even though the bankrupt state of the nation's economy called for immediate concerted effort. As a result, the Democratic administration would not be blamed for the depression and it could take all the credit for the New Deal. General Eisenhower scrupulously refrained from assuming any responsibilities for foreign policy until he was actually sworn into office. Thus the Truman administration could be indicted for taking us into the Korean War, while the Eisenhower administration would be remembered for bringing peace to the nation. But such partisan restraint, to keep the two administrations distinct in the minds of the electorate, can work to the disadvantage as well as to the advantage of the incoming President and his administration. Certainly, President Kennedy's administration was ill-starred in foreign policy at the outset—witness the Cuban fiasco—because the incumbent President and the President-elect could not assume joint responsibility for policy-making between election and inauguration.

In one sense, the presidential inauguration in January, 1965, marked the final transition from the Kennedy administration to the Johnson administration. President Johnson felt committed to fulfillment of the Kennedy program for the duration of what would have been Kennedy's first term. Throughout the 1964 campaign, however, Johnson made it clear that he intended to move forward with his own policies if the voters gave him a "mandate to begin." Thus the 1966 Budget, already in preparation before the election in November, 1964, and presented to the Congress after the inauguration in January, 1965, was designed to accommodate President Johnson's concept of "the Great Society" as well as his vision of America's role in world affairs. Moreover, in the period between election and inauguration, there were daily news reports of resignations and appointments in top policy positions. Kennedy people were moving out; Johnson people were moving in—with new loyalties, new viewpoints, new policy plans.

No incoming administration—whatever the nature of succession—can ever begin with a clean slate, however. A transfer of power in the White House will ultimately affect Congress, the bureaucrats, and even the judges. A new administration, given time, is bound to change the policy processes and alter the policy outputs. Because the President is only a part of the whole system, the actions of his administration will in large measure be constrained by the constitutional pattern, institutional practices, environmental conditions, and the course of events.

The input of policy is a continuum of economic, social, political, and personal factors that do not automatically stop and start with the election and inauguration of a new President. When President Eisenhower came into office in January, 1953, he had to accept his legacies from twenty years of Democratic control: New Deal, Fair Deal, Korean War, World War II, Truman Doctrine, Marshall Plan, Point Four, the North Atlantic Treaty, and Communist Containment. When the chips were down and the Republicans were actually responsible for policy-making, they were not even free to repudiate the war-time agreements which they had so viciously attacked in the heat of campaigning in 1952. By the same token, when the New Frontiersmen took over in 1961, they, too, found themselves bound, inextricably committed to policies at home and abroad that were not to their liking and certainly not of their own making.

Constitutional Status and Roles of the President

Article II of the Constitution briefly outlines the President's duties and responsibilities:

He is the Commander-in-Chief of the armed forces.

He may require the opinion in writing from his principal officers in the executive departments.

He may grant reprieves and pardons for offenses against the United States.

He may make treaties with the advice and consent of two-thirds of the Senate.

He appoints ambassadors, judges, and other officers of the national government with the advice and consent of a majority of the senators.

Aritcle II: "The Executive Power shall be vested..."

He informs the Congress from time to time on the State of the Union and recommends to them measures which he considers necessary and expedient.

He may on extraordinary occasions convene either or both houses of Congress, and if they are disagreed on the time of adjournment, he may adjourn them.

He receives representatives of foreign governments.

He commissions all officers of the United States Armed Forces.

He takes care that the laws be faithfully executed.

These are the general constitutional prescriptions according to which each President has developed his own style, or pattern of behavior, in office. Here is what Theodore Sorensen describes as "the limits of permissibility."[19] On entering office, every President must solemnly swear to "preserve, protect, and defend the Constitution of the United States." It is an oath which none has taken lightly. But each President has read Article II according to his own lights, and so all have played out their roles in office somewhat differently.

The authors of *The Federalist*, explaining Article II, let their own predilections be known, when they talked about "a vigorous executive," "an energetic executive," and "a man of tolerable firmness." Theodore Roosevelt, who was President at the turn of this century, wrote to the British historian, George Otto Trevelyan:

> While President I have *been* President, emphatically; I have used every ounce of power there was in the office and I have not cared a rap for the criticisms of those who spoke of my "usurpation of power"; for I knew that the talk was all nonsense and there was no usurpation. I believe that the efficiency of this government depends upon its possessing a strong executive.[20]

Speaking of his exploits as President, Roosevelt could say "I took Panama," which, in fact, he did, so that the United States could build its canal between the Atlantic and the Pacific. And he was the "bully" President who wanted to send the American fleet around the world to "show the flag" of the United States. When Congress balked at providing the necessary appropriations, he sent the ships halfway around the world and then asked Congress if it cared to bring the boys home, which, of course, it did.

Roosevelt's successor in office, William Howard Taft—who later became Chief Justice of the Supreme Court—took a strictly legalistic view of his powers in the presidential office:

> . . . the President can exercise no power which cannot be fairly traced to some specific grant of power or justly implied and included within such express grant as proper and necessary to its exercise. Such specific grant must be either in the Federal Constitution or in an Act of Congress passed in pursuance thereof. There is no undefined residuum of power which he can exercise because it seems to him to be in the public interest.[21]

---

[19] Theodore C. Sorensen, *Decision-Makin in the White House* (New York: Columbia University Press, 1963), p. 24.

[20] Letter by President Theodore Roosevelt to George Otto Trevelyan, June 19, 1908, quoted in John P. Roche and Leonard Wikery (eds.), *The Presidency* (New York: Harcourt, Brace & World, Inc., 1964), p. 22.

[21] William Howard Taft, *Our Chief Magistrate and His Powers* (New York: Columbia University Press, 1916), quoted in Roche, *The Presidency*, p. 23.

When President Harry Truman wrote his memoirs, he expressed the views of an old pro in politics:

> There are some people, and some time members of Congress and the press, who get mixed up in their thinking about the powers of the President. The important fact to remember is that the President is the only person in the executive branch who has final authority and if he does not exercise it, we may be in trouble. If he exercises his authority wisely, that is good for the country. If he does not exercise it wisely, that is too bad, but it is better than not exercising it at all.[22]

President Eisenhower, recruited from a distinguished military career to become the Chief Executive, confessed after three years in the office that he had "no great liking" for politics.

> Now, on the other hand, any man who finds himself in a position of authority where he has a very great influence in the efforts of people to work toward a peaceful world, toward international relationships that will eliminate or minimize the chances of war, all that sort of thing, of course it is a fascinating business. It is a kind of thing that would engage the interest, intense interest of any man alive.
>
> There are in this office thousands of unique opportunities to meet especially interesting people, because the Government up here in Washington has become the center of so many things that, again, you have a very fascinating experience in meeting scientists, leaders in culture, in health, in governmental action, from all over the world.[23]

Later, when Eisenhower wrote his memoirs—in part a dialogue with his predecessor—he was more inclined to stress the organizational and managerial aspects of his administration:

> Organization cannot of course make a successful leader out of a dunce, any more than it should make a decision for its chief. But it is effective in minimizing the chances of failure and in insuring that the right hand does, indeed, know what the left hand is doing.[24]

When Senator John Fitzgerald Kennedy announced his candidacy for the presidency in January, 1960, he offered his concept of the office:

> The times . . . and the people demand . . . a vigorous proponent of the national interest . . ., the head of a responsible party . . ., a man who will formulate and fight for legislative policies. . . . He must above all be the Chief Executive in every sense of the word. He must be prepared to exercise the fullest powers of his office—all that are specified and some that are not. . . . He must originate action as well as study groups. He must reopen the channels of communication between the world of thought and the seat of power.[25]

---

[22]*Memoirs,* Vol. I *(Year of Decisions)* (Garden City, New York: Doubleday & Co., Inc., 1955), p. 545.
[23]News conference, May 31, 1955.
[24]*Waging Peace,* p. 630.
[25]*The Congressional Record,* January 18, 1960, pp. A-353-354.

But after President Kennedy had been in the office two years he was much more restrained in his notions of what the Chief Executive could do:

> In the first place, the problems are more difficult than I had imagined they were. Secondly, there is a limitation upon the ability of the United States to solve these problems.
>
> . . .
>
> The responsibilities placed on the United States are greater than I imagined them to be, and there are greater limitations upon our ability to bring about a favorable result than I had imagined them to be . . . because there is such a difference between those who advise or speak or legislate and between the man who must select from the various alternatives proposed and say that this shall be the policy of the United States.[26]

The change in role perception notable in the views of Candidate Kennedy and President Kennedy remind us that even Presidents are but actors-in-an-environment. The President is chief of state and Chief Executive, but he cannot say, "I am the United States," or "I run this government." He is an integral part of the political system and his administration is a period in American history. Whatever the President's personal inclinations, he cannot ignore the Constitution or flout his statutory assignments; he cannot escape most of the guidelines, precedents, and commitments established by his predecessors; and he cannot move far in advance of or contrary to the well-understood notions of the American people who have made him their spokesman.

During his 1960 campaign for the presidency, Kennedy read with relish Richard Neustadt's *Presidential Power*.[27] As a political scientist, with staff experience in the White House, Neustadt chose to treat the subject of presidential power in terms of the man rather than the institution. Observing how Roosevelt, Truman, and Eisenhower performed in office, he notes that the President sits in a unique seat and works within a unique frame of reference. The power of a President is largely his personal influence upon the behavior of those who hold policy positions in the government. Whether history rates him "strong" or "weak," "leader" or "clerk," depends most of all on the President's own character and capabilities. "The more determinedly a President seeks power, the more he will be likely to bring vigor to his clerkship."

In Neustadt's thesis, presidential power is first of all the power to persuade: the authority and status inherent in the President's office give him great advantage in bargaining, which is but another facet of persuading. The bargaining power of the President is enhanced by his professional reputation and his popular prestige. These involve more than the image created by public relations experts. They stem from the opinions other men hold regarding his skill and will and also their appraisal of how his public views him. The presidency is no place for an amateur in politics; use of presidential power

---

[26]Radio-television interview, December 16, 1962. Reprinted in Donald Bruce Johnson and Jack L. Walker, *The Dynamics of the American Presidency* (New York: John Wiley & Sons, Inc., 1964), p. 142.

[27]Richard E. Neustadt, *Presidential Power* (New York: John Wiley & Sons, Inc., 1960). Professor Neustadt is now Director of the Institute of Politics in the John F. Kennedy School of Government at Harvard University.

calls for extraordinary expertise. The way a President sees his vantage points and uses his influence to get what he wants done—"his sense of power and of purpose and his own sense of self-confidence"—these are "politics of leadership."

President-elect Kennedy invited Professor Neustadt to participate in the pre-inaugural planning for the new administration and throughout the rest of his time in office Kennedy counted on Neustadt to help keep open "the channels of communication between the world of thought and the seat of power." Even so, it is doubtful that President Kennedy acted on the Neustadt prescription. According to Theodore Sorensen, who was one of the President's closest advisors, Kennedy's philosophy of government was keyed to power, but "not as a matter of personal ambition."

> Power was not a goal to be sought for its own sake. It was there, in the White House, to be used, without any sense of guilt or greed, as a means of getting things done. He felt neither uplifted nor weighted down by power. He enjoyed the Presidency, thinking not of its power but its opportunities, and he was sobered by the Presidency, thinking not of its power but its obligations. He was a strong President primarily because he was a strong person.[28]

No doubt the positive and forceful character of Franklin D. Roosevelt—coupled with times of crisis—enormously enhanced his role as Chief Executive in American government; but his successors picked up where he left off, each in turn adding a few more lines to the role. Paradoxically, the more popular an executive is, the graver becomes the danger of personal dictatorship. Democracy assumes, however, that the people know on whom they should bestow popularity.

As an extra safeguard against personalized power, the Constitution relies on checks and balances. A President who abuses his power may be removed from office by the process of impeachment. The President's treaty-making power is limited by the requirement that two-thirds of the Senate must concur. He may make no commitments involving expenditures without obtaining the necessary appropriations from both houses of Congress. His role as Commander-in-Chief of the armed forces is curtailed by congressional control over the purse-strings. Congressional hearings on the executive budget are extensive and intensive, exacting and exhausting. Congressional investigations of the President's administration can be thoroughly embarrassing and utterly discrediting.

Even when Congress is inclined to delegate its legislative powers to the President, the Supreme Court can be counted upon to invoke from time to time the constitutional doctrine of separation of powers. Thus the Court has denied the President power to ignore or override the legislative will (Truman and the *Steel Seizure Case*) and has held null and void congressional delegation of legislative responsibility (Congress and the New Deal). As a further barrier

---

[28]Theodore Sorensen, *Kennedy* (New York: Harper & Row, Publishers, Inc., 1965), p. 389.

to personal power, the Twenty-second Amendment provides that no person shall be elected President more than twice. But probably the most potent check on the tendency of any President to build up dictatorial powers is the American tradition itself; every incumbent has tried to live up to the honor and prestige inherent in the office.

Head of State

The President plays many roles, and in each role he exercises many kinds of power. He is head of state, director of foreign policy, Commander-in-Chief, Chief Executive, legislative director, head of the nation's economic program, party leader, and personal spokesman for all Americans.

As head of state, the President entertains visiting royalty and heads of other governments, he receives the credentials of foreign ambassadors and ministers, he addresses Congress on the state of the Union, and he speaks to the people on crises in world affairs. As the official personification of the national character, the President must play many parts, ranging from the most solemn to the downright silly. "Mr. President" is not a private person, and his time is not his own. His every waking moment is taken up with public acts; wherever he goes, he is under guard; whatever he does officially or informally is fully reported in press, radio, and TV. A steady stream of "callers" at the White House symbolizes the direct accessibility of a democratic leader to the people.

A typical presidential calendar, in any week, will include scheduled and sometimes special meetings with the Cabinet, the National Security Council, and the congressional leadership. The President will also have individual appointments with congressmen, administrative assistants, and various heads of departments. He may meet with the press in formal conference in the auditorium of the State Department, or informally as he walks about the White House grounds. He will brief American ambassadors before their departure and be briefed by them on their return from posts abroad. He will receive foreign ministers and ambassadors on their arrival, and as they leave the country. He will greet and entertain a never-ending procession of heads of states and heads of governments who want to do business with the United States. He will meet governors, mayors, bankers, defense contractors, labor leaders, military leaders, scientists, astronauts, Negro leaders, religious leaders, educational leaders—in short, all manner of spokesmen from the special interest groups that make up pluralistic America. He will usually take time out to have his picture taken with each visitor, for this is part of the presidential image—the people's chief lobbyist keeps in personal touch with all his many constituencies. And, finally, he will be on hand for a series of social events, including perhaps breakfast with legislative leaders, a luncheon or dinner at the White House for a foreign dignitary, and, of course, the luncheon or dinner given in return by the distinguished visitor for the President.

In his role as head of state, the President has endless tasks to perform. He has monuments to unveil, medals to bestow, public works to dedicate. He has speeches to make—to the Sons of St. Patrick and the Daughters of the American Revolution, to the Veterans of Foreign Wars, and the United Cookie Cutters of America, to the members of Congress assembled in solemn session and the families of America assembled in front of their television sets. He serves as Honorary President of the American Red Cross; he chips in the first dime to the March of Dimes; he tosses out the first ball of the baseball season; he memorializes Washington, Lincoln, Jackson, and Jefferson on their birthdays; he joins the children hunting Easter eggs on the White House lawn; he chats with Indian chiefs, movie actresses, and America's Mother of the Year; he proclaims the Fourth of July, Labor Day, and Thanksgiving; he buys the first Christmas seals. And he struggles with a mountain of paper work, much of it before a battery of cameras. There are treaties to sign, bills to approve, bills to veto, commissions to grant, appointments to make, diplomatic reports to study, gifts to acknowledge, letters to write, budgets to revise, economic reports to digest, military reports to review, more speeches to prepare. All these are routine matters in the President's daily round of activities. As President Truman wrote in his *Memoirs*:

> One of the hardest things for the President to do is to find time to take stock. I have always believed that the President's office ought to be open to as many citizens as he can find time to talk to; that is part of the job, to be available to the people, to listen to their troubles, to let them share the rich tradition of the White House. But it raises havoc with one's day, and even though I always got up early, usually was at work ahead of the staff, and would take papers home with me at night to read, there always seemed to be more than I could do.[29]

Director of Foreign Policy

Some years ago, Justice Sutherland of the United States Supreme Court referred to the President as "the sole organ of the federal government in the field of international relations."[30] Certainly the President has been the principal director of the nation's foreign affairs ever since the first administration of President Washington. Most of the historic foreign policies of the United States were announced originally in presidential messages and proclamations: Washington's proclamation of neutrality, the Monroe Doctrine, Wilson's Fourteen Points "to make the world safe for democracy," Franklin D. Roosevelt's Good Neighbor policy and the "Four Freedoms," the Truman Doctrine and "Point Four," and the Eisenhower Doctrine for the Middle East.

This practice of putting full power over foreign affairs into the hands of the President generally makes good sense. All the information that is gathered daily by our diplomatic, consular, and confidential agents abroad is made available to the President. Since national security frequently requires that information of this sort be kept secret, or that it be released only with extreme caution to appropriate authorities, the President can truly claim the most comprehensive knowledge of the conditions that prevail in every foreign country. As Justice Sutherland pointed out, "In this vast external realm, with

---

[29]*Memoirs*, Vol. II, p. 361.
[30]*United States v. Curtiss-Wright Export Corp.*, 299 U.S. 304 (1936).

its important, complicated, delicate and manifold problems, the President alone has the power to speak or listen as a representative of the Nation."

The Constitution, however, does not give the President an exclusive role in foreign affairs. Article II of the Constitution specifically grants to the President: (1) the power to make treaties, by and with the consent of the Senate; (2) the power to receive foreign ambassadors and ministers; (3) the power to nominate and appoint ambassadors, ministers, and consuls, with the advice and consent of the Senate; (4) the duty to report to Congress on the state of the Union and to recommend whatever measures he deems expedient; (5) and full authority as Commander-in-Chief over the military forces of the nation. Clearly, the Constitution provides for separation of powers and for checks and balances in foreign affairs just as it does in domestic matters; but of necessity the conduct of foreign affairs has become the primary responsibility of the President.

The President has the sole power to initiate and negotiate treaties. All the Senate can do is to approve or disapprove what the President has in effect already promised in the name of the United States. Actually, the Senate has rejected only about 1 per cent of the treaties sent to it by the President, has amended or made specific reservations in about 15 per cent, and has approved all the rest without change. The most notable rejection was the Senate's action on the Paris Treaty that Woodrow Wilson had negotiated after World War I. Aware of Wilson's experience, Franklin D. Roosevelt was careful to include strategic members of the Senate Foreign Relations Committee in negotiations on the various treaties arising from World War II, including the United Nations Charter. His action, however, was prompted by political wisdom rather than by any legal obligation.

The Constitution says nothing about the House of Representatives in defining the President's treaty-making powers. But Washington's second administration was nearly wrecked on this very point. Because Washington failed to inform the House on the negotiations that led to the unpopular Jay Treaty (1795), the representatives decided not to appropriate the funds he had requested to put it into operation. Washington insisted on the importance of preserving secrecy in diplomatic matters, and refused to send the House any enlightening papers or documents on the treaty. Thereupon the House threatened to impeach him. Although the House finally passed the appropriations, Presidents ever since Washington's time have profited by his unhappy experience. Because the House initiates the appropriations necessary to implement a treaty, the President finds it advisable to consult with House leaders as well as with Senate leaders in his conduct of foreign affairs.

Executive agreements, however, are used more often than treaties in the conduct of foreign affairs. Although the Constitution does not even mention executive agreements, the Supreme Court has declared that the President may enter into agreements with foreign governments as "a modest implied power" under his treaty-making authority.[31] Thus treaties, which must have the concurrence of the Senate, and executive agreements, which are made solely under the authority of the President, both have the force of law in the courts.

[31] *United States* v. *Pink,* 315 U.S. 203 (1942).

In 1953, Senator John W. Bricker (R.-Ohio) proposed a constitutional amendment specifying that no treaty or executive agreement could become law until it had been validated by Congress. Such a restriction would have put severe handicaps on the President's direction of foreign policy. President Eisenhower strongly opposed the amendment, but in 1954 it came within one vote of obtaining a two-thirds majority in the Senate. The Senate apparently still remembered and resented such executive agreements as the Roosevelt-Litvinoff Agreement of 1933, by which the United States officially recognized the U.S.S.R.; the "swap" of fifty American destroyers for the use of English naval bases on the eve of World War II; and the Yalta agreements, which set down the conditions under which Russia entered the war against Japan. All these agreements had been concluded by Roosevelt without consulting Congress.

In assigning to the President the authority to receive foreign ministers and ambassadors, the Constitution implies that he also has the authority to recognize foreign governments and new states. This issue was raised in the very first administration, when Washington *received* "Citizen Genêt" and thereby *recognized* the French revolutionary government. Subsequently, Citizen Genêt abused the President's hospitality by appealing directly to the American people for intervention by the United States in the war between France and England. Exercising another presidential prerogative, Washington responded by requesting the French government to recall its overzealous representative.

During most of our history, the President has followed the customary international practice of basing the recognition of a new foreign government not on its constitutional legitimacy but on its *de facto* capacity to fulfill its international obligations. Under President Woodrow Wilson, however, the American policy of recognition took a new turn when he refused in 1913 to recognize the *de facto* government of President Victoriano Huerta in Mexico on the grounds that Huerta had risen to power by force and did not rule by "consent of the governed." No doubt this withholding of American recognition contributed to the downfall of the Huerta regime. Wilson followed the same policy with respect to the communist government that was established in Russia in November, 1917, but this time the United States' lack of recognition did not break the new regime.

Since Wilson's time, every American President has frankly used recognition as an instrument of American foreign policy. Warren G. Harding, Calvin Coolidge, and Herbert Hoover each refused to recognize the U.S.S.R., even though the communist government continued very much in fact after 1917. Franklin D. Roosevelt's decision to recognize the U.S.S.R. was based on economic rather than legal considerations, and in extending recognition he did not seek congressional approval. Hoover, and subsequently Roosevelt, withheld recognition of Manchukuo on the grounds that Japan had violated China's territorial integrity in setting up the new government. And yet President Truman recognized the establishment of Israel immediately, despite protests by the Arabs that their territory had been violated. In the context of the Cold War, American presidents in the 1950s and 1960s have been quick to recognize new nations in Asia and Africa without questioning too sharply whether the peoples of these countries were ready for self-government—or whether the new governments were prepared to assume their responsibilities in the international community. On the other hand, although the communists without question are in actual control of the Chinese mainland, a fact recognized by most of the other nations in the world, Truman, Eisenhower, Kennedy, and Johnson each in turn have withheld recognition of the People's Republic of China for purely political reasons. Thus the decision to recognize or not to recognize a foreign government is a political decision that belongs to the President alone. Neither Congress nor the courts can legally force or forestall the President's decision.

The Constitution gives the President power to appoint ministers and ambassadors, but only with the consent of the Senate. He also appoints the Secretary of State, the Under Secretary, the assistant secretaries, and the key figures in other departments concerned with foreign affairs, such as Defense and Treasury. All these officials constitute the "President's team" in the making of foreign policy. Just how the President uses his team members, or whether he uses them at all, depends mostly on his personal inclinations—and his capacity for statesmanship. Franklin Roosevelt became so deeply involved in foreign policy and in his role as a world leader that he made his own decisions. In fact, Secretary of State Cordell Hull complained privately that the President scarcely kept him informed, much less sought his advice. Roosevelt personally met with other heads of state, and he usually sent his own representatives rather than the regularly appointed ambassadors to less important conferences. Apparently he trusted the on-the-spot opinions of his friend Harry Hopkins far more than the systematic studies made by the State Department.

President Kennedy was never his own Secretary of State, as was sometimes charged, but he did take a direct and strong personal interest in foreign policy. He used the institutional machinery—the Cabinet, the National Security Council, the Joint Chiefs of Staff, and the Central Intelligence Agency—but less regularly and less formally than his predecessor. He exerted his personal power in foreign affairs, hand-picked most of the assistant secretaries in the State Department, and brought his own specialists into the White House Office to create what Washington observers called "the little State Department" under McGeorge Bundy. He frequently crossed departmental lines to develop a "community of policy makers," with his Secretary of State, Secretary of Defense, Attorney General, and other high officials at the core of this group.

Whatever the President's relations with his Secretary of State or his personal advisers, every President has had to face up to the hard fact that final responsibility for every major decision in foreign affairs rests on him and him alone. No one can really speak for the President or make up his mind for him. President Truman described the President's plight with poignancy in his *Memoirs:* "The presidency of the United States carries with it a responsibility so personal as to be without parallel. . . . To be President of the United States is to be very lonely, very lonely at times of great decisions."

The Commander-in-Chief

The Constitution designates the President as Commander-in-Chief of the armed services of the United States and also of the state militia when it is called into the service of the United States. But the Constitution does not give the President sole or plenary powers over the military. Rather, it specifies that Congress shall have power to tax for the common defense; declare war; grant letters of marque and reprisal and make rules concerning captures on land and water; raise and support armies; provide and maintain a navy; make rules governing the armed forces; call out the state militia and provide for its training and discipline.

Although the Constitution specifically gives Congress the power to declare war, Congress has never done so except at the urgent request of the President. Indeed, as Commander-in-Chief, the President may dispose the armed forces in such a way that Congress has no alternative but to issue a declaration of war. The naval policies of Woodrow Wilson in 1915–17, and of Franklin D. Roosevelt in 1939–41, for example, were bound to involve this country in war. Moreover, the President may recognize a state of war, as Lincoln did in 1861, without ever asking for a formal declaration from Congress. The President may also order American troops into action to protect American citizens or American property abroad, to support our vital interests or national honor any place in the world, and to carry out our commitments in the international community. Although the United States is now engaged in a major war in Viet Nam, Congress has not declared war and the President has not asked it to do so.

The Federalist is quite frank in explaining the President's military power: "Of all the cares or concerns of government, the direction of war most peculiarly demands those qualities which distinguish the exercise of power by a single hand." Alexander Hamilton would have approved President Truman's action in removing General Douglas MacArthur from all commands in 1952 for presuming to differ publicly with his Commander-in-Chief. The Founding Fathers, who elected General George Washington as the first President, expected the President to assume direct command in time of war. In fact, President Washington personally headed the U.S. troops for a short period during the Whisky Rebellion of 1792. Abraham Lincoln frequently intervened in the operation of the Army of the Potomac until General Ulysses S. Grant finally insisted on sole command. President Wilson was more interested in "organizing for peace" than in supervising the military strategy of World War I, but President Roosevelt, along with Prime Minister Churchill, participated in all the top-level military decisions of World War II. President Truman made the most momentous decision of any Commander-in-Chief in history when he gave the order to drop the first atomic bomb on Hiroshima in August, 1945. President Johnson personally reviews and approves the strategic bombing in North Viet Nam.

Lincoln was the first to use his military position "to take care that the laws be faithfully executed." As Commander-in-Chief, he called out the militia to put down "the rebellion," paid the militia men out of the Treasury without getting any appropriation from Congress, proclaimed a blockade of southern ports, directed the seizure of rail and telegraph lines leading into Washington, suspended the writ of habeas corpus, and issued the Emancipation Proclamation. And he did all this without any authorization from Congress. In the *Prize Cases,* which upheld the blockade, the Supreme Court explained that the "Executive Chief of the Government" is not only authorized but *bound* to resist force by force, and to do so without waiting for any special legislative authority. Moreover, said the Court, the President must determine what degree of force the crisis demands.[32] Only when the war was over did the Supreme Court admonish the President that "no doctrine, involving more pernicious consequences, was ever invented by the wit of man than that any of its [the Constitution's] provisions can be suspended during any of the great exigencies of government."[33]

In World War I, President Wilson carried Lincoln's concept of the Commander-in-Chief still further, to embrace even more far-reaching "war powers." As Professor Edward S. Corwin points out in his classic study, *The President: Office and Powers,* the main difference between the Lincoln and Wilson patterns of administration was one of method.[34] Lincoln assumed that as Commander-in-Chief he had all the powers necessary to win the war, an assumption that was supported by subsequent congressional approval of his actions. In World War I, Congress moved at the outset to give the President extraordinary powers over the nation's economy; to conscript an army; to license trading with the enemy and his allies; to censor all communications with foreign countries; to control enemy aliens inside the country; to take over and operate the nation's water and rail transportation, its telephone and telegraph systems. Thus the American President, "fighting to make the world safe for democracy," had almost all the powers that a totalitarian dictator possesses—and he used most of them.

Even before American entrance into World War II, President Roosevelt began to assume "war powers." The Lend Lease Act, passed by Congress nine months before we entered the "shooting war," authorized the President to sell, transfer title, exchange, lease, lend, or otherwise dispose of all kinds of "defense articles," from buttons to battleships, to any foreign government whose defense the President deemed vital to the national defense of the United States. Also, before we were actually at war, Congress authorized the President to procure ships and war materials; to requisition and operate any private factory for defense purposes; to modify or cancel any existing contracts that interfered with the government's defense program; to give top priority to all government defense contracts. During World War II, President Roosevelt exercised tremendous power over the national economy—price control, food rationing, rent controls, plant seizures, materials allocations.[35] All these were

---

[32]*Prize Cases,* 2 Black 635 (1863).

[33]The noble words of Justice David Davis in *Ex parte Milligan* holding unconstitutional the suspension of the writ of habeas corpus outside an actual theater of war. 4 Wall. 2 (1866).

[34]Edward Corwin, *The President: Office and Powers,* 4th ed. (New York: New York University Press, 1957), pp. 237ff.

[35]The best monograph on this aspect of presidential power is Clinton Rossiter, *The Supreme Court and the Commander in Chief* (Ithaca, N.Y.: Cornell University Press, 1951).

powers either delegated to him by Congress or implied from his position as Commander-in-Chief.

During the Korean War, in 1952, when the country was faced with a nation-wide steel shutdown because management refused to accept a decision of government mediators, President Truman seized the steel mills. In this case, however, the Supreme Court by a vote of 6 to 3 refused to uphold the President's action.[36] Truman insisted that as Chief Executive and Commander-in-Chief he had acted to avoid national catastrophe. The six justices who ruled against the seizure all offered different reasons for their decision, but they all agreed that "separation of powers" means that Congress, not the President, is entrusted with the lawmaking power of the nation. Justice Hugo L. Black, who delivered the opinion for the majority, explained it quite simply:

> The President's power, if any, to issue the order must stem either from an act of Congress or from the Constitution itself. . . . The order cannot be properly sustained as an exercise of the President's military power as Commander in Chief of the Armed Forces. . . . Even though "theatre of war" be an expanding concept, we cannot with faithfulness to our constitutional system hold that the Commander in Chief of the Armed Forces has the ultimate power as such to take possession of private property in order to keep labor disputes from stopping production. This is a job for the Nation's lawmakers, not for its military authorities.

Those who fear "the man on horseback" and the military *coup d'état* may find comfort not only in Black's opinion in the *Steel Seizure Case* but also in Truman's immediate acceptance of the Court's decision.

It appears, then, that the President may assume whatever powers he deems necessary to carry on a war, for neither Congress nor the Court will seriously challenge his actions so long as the nation is fighting for survival. Under such conditions, a strong President will make use of whatever powers seem to him reasonable and realistic, whether they are plainly delegated to him by the Constitution, or only vaguely inherent, implied, or incidental to his office. Thus in 1967, when the Chairman of the Senate Committee on Foreign Relations officially challenged the power of President Johnson to escalate the war in Viet Nam, the issue was moot. Senator Fulbright himself conceded: "The only real sanction that Congress has is impeachment and that is politically impractical."

Chief Executive

Although the Constitution itself does not give even the sketchiest outline of how the executive branch should be organized, it does empower the President to "require the opinion, in writing, of the principal officer in each of the executive departments, upon any subject relating to the duties of their [sic] respective offices." Apparently the Founding Fathers anticipated the establishment of executive departments

---
[36] *Youngstown Sheet & Tube Co.* v. *Sawyer*, 343 U.S. 579 (1952). For an analysis of power politics in the steel seizure case, see Richard E. Neustadt, *Presidential Power*.

to assist the President, but they could not have imagined the tremendous superstructure of administrative organization which today almost dwarfs the legislative and judicial branches.

The Constitution charges the President to "take care that the laws be faithfully executed." Obviously he cannot carry out this task without help. He must have assistants and, to insure their responsibility to him, he must have the power to appoint and remove them. With the advice and consent of the Senate, the President appoints "ambassadors, other public ministers and consuls, judges of the Supreme Court and all other officers of the United States" not otherwise provided for by law. But Congress may empower the President alone, or the heads of executive departments, to appoint "inferior officers" without obtaining senatorial consent. The Constitution leaves it up to Congress to draw the line between "superior" and "inferior" officers.

"Superior officers" seem to include diplomatic officers, justices of the Supreme Court, members of the Cabinet, commissioners of the independent regulatory agencies, and top decision-makers in various civilian executive agencies. Whenever the President names someone to fill one of these posts, the nominee must be confirmed by the Senate. The Senate usually goes along without much debate on the President's choice of representatives overseas, members of his own Cabinet, and justices of the Supreme Court. Despite the fact that President Eisenhower had to deal most of the time with a Senate controlled by the opposition party, only one of his major nominations failed to obtain confirmation, that of Lewis Strauss as Secretary of Commerce, in 1959. In other appointments, the President is expected to consult with the senators of the state in which a position is to be filled. If these senators are of the opposition party, the President consults with the state leaders of his own party before making a nomination. Whenever a President fails to observe this rule of party politics, he is likely to encounter "senatorial courtesy"—a polite way of saying that, in courtesy to their slighted colleagues, the senators will refuse to confirm the President's nominee, no matter how qualified the nominee may be for the post.

Although the President's power of patronage is now curtailed by civil service regulations, thousands of presidential appointments are still made on the basis of party politics. Key offices in the administration are filled by the leaders of the party faithful, with preference going to those who backed the President most strongly during his campaign. In Chapter 9, when we discussed how a President is elected, we noted that a few persons donate large sums of money to the President's campaign. Custom reserves for these generous supporters certain positions of power and prestige, such as the ambassadorships to Great Britain, France, and Italy. Most presidential backers, however, prefer to take their rewards in the form of personal access to the White House or influence on administrative policies after the election has been won. Since the national parties are made up of local blocs, the President is in a unique position to pull local strings through his power to appoint thousands of tax collectors, postmasters, marshals, district attorneys, and federal judges throughout the country. And yet these same local strings are also pulling on the President. Sometimes the Man in the White House must feel that he himself is just a party puppet.

Not only party politics but special-interest groups condition the President's appointive power. Since the President's "national constituency" is formed by a winning combination of special-interest groups, we are not surprised to find that pressure politics operates on the presidency just as it does on Congress. The top spokesmen of business, labor, farmers, educators, racial minorities, religious groups, professional associations, patriotic societies—all the groups that helped put the President into office—are likely to be privileged callers at the White House. Because they have access to the President, they may influence his decisions.

The President's Cabinet is a carefully calculated consolidation of the various groups in his national constituency; and so is the membership of the regulatory commissions and the other important administrative agencies. The influence of pressure politics extends even to the hundreds of noncareer political officers such as undersecretaries and assistant secretaries in the national administration, and to all the "inferior officers" who have any part in policy formulation or decision-making. Not even judicial appointments are immune from political considerations. Indeed, when a vacancy occurs on the Supreme Court, the representatives of special interest groups jostle and crowd one another in their race to the White House to get their favorite nominee appointed.

To help him supervise and control the national administration the President relies on many high-level political executives. These fall into several distinct categories: (1) The President tries to place in strategic positions within the departmental hierarchies individuals whose personal loyalties will center on the Chief Executive. President Kennedy deliberately disrupted the orderly routine of bureaucracy in a number of agencies when he kept a direct line of communication between the White House and his personal appointees, notably with his "whiz kids" in the State and Defense departments. (2) The President must make certain patronage appointments which identify the party organization with the presidential administration. Many such appointments will have been arranged during the campaign, some of them part of the dickering and dealing before the convention. Turnover among these appointees is usually high. Many a "political executive" attracted by a high-sounding official title and a chance to advance "the New Frontier" or to help build "the Great Society" finds that the day-to-day tasks of public administration are not really glamorous and that the pay is comparably less than he could make in business or private practice. (3) The President (and his staff) are constantly engaged in a talent search to discover program executives with the special knowledge and technological background that are needed in the modern business of government. Again, turnover is high in this group, many of whom find it professionally frustrating and insufficiently rewarding to work in a political environment. (4) The continuous coming and going of political executives is partially offset by the career administrators who come up through the ranks of the civil service or foreign service. As a presidential administration settles down, presidential appointments to second and third echelons come to include an increasing number of persons recruited from the permanent bureaucracy.

Although the Constitution is fairly specific on the President's power of appointment, it is silent on the power of removal. A debate in the First Congress over whether the Senate should concur in the President's dismissal of superior officers for disciplinary reasons was resolved in favor of the executive. From that date on, the general principle has been that the President must have the power to dismiss subordinates, since he is responsible for the work of the executive departments. But the principle has not always been followed. During the serious quarrels that broke out between President Andrew Johnson and Congress in the period of Reconstruction, Congress passed the Tenure of Office Act, which provided that heads of departments should serve for the duration of the term of the President who had appointed them and one month thereafter, and that they could be removed earlier *only* with the consent of the Senate. President Johnson vetoed the act on the ground that it was an unconstitutional restriction on the President's power of removal, a power that had been exercised by presidents ever since Washington's time. His veto was overridden, however, and the Supreme Court managed to sidestep the issue until 1926.

In *Myers* v. *United States* (1926), the Supreme Court held that Congress could not restrict the President's power to remove executive officers whom he has appointed with the consent of the Senate. In a lengthy opinion, Chief Justice Taft, who had himself been plagued by the problem during his own term as President, held invalid the Tenure of Office Act of 1867 and subsequent legislation restricting the President's removal powers. Taft took the same position that the First Congress had adopted. Since the President alone is responsible for the actions of his executive subordinates, he must have the sole power to dismiss them.

[The President] must place in each member of his official family, and his chief subordinates, implicit faith. The moment that he loses confidence in the intelligence, ability, judgment, or loyalty of any one of them, he must have the power to remove him without delay.[37]

Not quite ten years after its firm decision in the *Myers Case*, the Supreme Court reconsidered the "constitutional principle" that the Chief Executive must have the sole power to dismiss his subordinates. This time the dispute had developed between President Roosevelt and a member of the Federal Trade Commission, Colonel William Humphrey. The President had invited Colonel Humphrey to resign from the Commission because his views differed sharply from those of the administration. When Colonel Humphrey insisted on serving out his statutory term, the President summarily dismissed him. The Supreme Court refused to uphold the dismissal, on the ground that Congress did not intend quasi-legislative or quasi-judicial agencies to be subject to the political control of the Chief Executive. After rereading the congressional debates of 1789, the Supreme Court decided that the President's "illimitable power of removal" extended only to "purely executive officers."[38]

[37]*Myers* v. *United States*, 272 U.S. 52 (1926).
[38]*Humphrey's Executor* v. *United States*, 295 U.S. 602 (1935).

As Chief Executive, the President acts in the role of general manager of his administration. To play this role most effectively and efficiently, he needs authority to control the entire national administration: the vast and complex organization of executive departments, regulatory commissions, government corporations, and miscellaneous agencies that carry on the business of the national government. Since 1939, Congress has periodically authorized the President to submit his plans for reorganization, always reserving to itself, however, the right to veto any proposed plan. An incoming administration usually has in mind some organizational changes which symbolize the transfer of power. Note, however, that the President actually has very little power on his own to make changes in the established pattern of administration. Congress determines the duties and structure of each agency in detail. Congress passes on the appointments to all key positions in the administrative hierarchy and keeps a tight rein on operations within the administrative agencies. It prescribes detailed procedures, sets the basic pattern of personnel practices, including position classification and compensation schedules, and through its various committees continuously investigates any and every aspect of agency activities.

The assumption that the Chief Executive is a "general manager" may be misleading. With the exception of Herbert Hoover, none of our presidents has ever shown much interest in, or capacity for, administrative management. It is rather unrealistic to suppose that a President will be more able to manage the national administration if the main lines of authority and direction reach directly and conveniently to his office. Nor does increasing the number of special and professional assistants at the White House insure the unified and energetic executive envisaged in *The Federalist*. The essential responsibility of the President is to see that the laws are faithfully executed, and this is a problem that calls for political leadership far more than skill in administrative management. This point is best illustrated perhaps in the President's role as chief legislator.

The Chief Legislator

The Constitution itself sketches in certain working relations between the President and Congress. The President is required from time to time to "give to the Congress information of the State of the Union and recommend to their consideration such measures as he shall judge necessary and expedient." President Washington, who thought of the President's role as somewhat like that of a monarch, delivered his messages to Congress in person, quite in the manner of the British "Address from the Throne." Thomas Jefferson, who was essentially a party President, made no such formal presentations, but he did manage to get his way in Congress by using the party organization. For example, the "floor leaders," who first appeared in Congress during Jefferson's administration, were recognized as "presidential agents." Jefferson constantly met with congressional leaders, in caucus and in conference, to promote his legislative program without seeming to impose executive direction over Congress. He also devised the practice of "executive bill drafting" to make sure that Congress would know exactly what kind of legislation he had in mind. Woodrow Wilson, who was always something of a schoolmaster, often attempted to teach Congress what he thought was best for the country and, at least on domestic matters, he was very successful.[39] In Corwin's estimation, "Franklin D. Roosevelt's accomplishment as legislator first and last surpassed all previous records."[40] Roosevelt himself felt that the presidency was not merely an administrative office but primarily a post of moral leadership.

The President, then, has the constitutional right to assume legislative leadership. But Congress is under no obligation to accept what the President judges to be "necessary and expedient." Time and political circumstances, as well as the character of the President himself, determine how much influence the Chief Executive actually exerts as legislative leader. Franklin Roosevelt's leadership, for example, ebbed and flowed with events. His first administration was marked by extraordinary enterprise and energy on the part of the executive, and by remarkable docility on the part of Congress. But in the second administration, which was launched on a high tide of popular support for the New Deal, relations between the executive and the legislature dropped to a new low when Roosevelt made his ill-timed demand for administrative reorganization and announced his ill-fated Supreme Court packing plan. Presidential leadership rose to new heights in his third and fourth terms, as the Commander-in-Chief asked for and got what he thought was required to win the war.

Party fortunes also have a lot to do with the check and balance between President and Congress. A President can always be "strong" if he has the backing of his own party organization in both houses. He is usually "weak" when both houses of Congress are controlled by the opposing party. This was the plight of President Eisenhower for six out of the eight years of his administration. Although Eisenhower won overwhelming popular endorsement in the 1952 and the 1956 elections, his following was obviously personal and detached from regular party politics. Indeed, his leadership toward "modern Republicanism" was as hotly contested by the so-called old-guard members of his own party as it was by the Democrats.

Constitutional separation of powers could result in a complete deadlock between the executive and the legislature. But assiduous liaison on a bipartisan basis between the administration and Congress gave President Eisenhower a creditable score in legislative effectiveness. Through prior consultation with the congressional leadership of both parties, the Eisenhower administration ascertained the outside limits of what it could expect from Congress and then realistically charted its program within those limits. If President Eisenhower had been able to count not only upon a Republican majority in the 83rd Congress, but also upon a majority of "Modern Republicans," he might have attempted a more ambitious legislative program. On the other hand, if, after the 1954 elections, he had been continuously confronted

---

[39]He had written his Ph.D. dissertation in political science at The Johns Hopkins University on *Congressional Government: A Study in American Politics* (Boston: Houghton Mifflin Co., 1885).

[40]Corwin, *The President: Office and Powers,* 4th ed. (New York: New York University Press, 1957), p. 272.

with a majority bloc of liberal Democrats, he might have gotten something less than his final record. The fact that he succeeded as well as he did with a Congress controlled by "the other party" must be attributed to a coalition of modern Republicans and conservative (especially Southern) Democrats who went with him down the middle of the road.

The lack of party responsibility for party programing, the lack of effective discipline within each party, the crossing of party lines without pains or penalties—these make congressional government possible when the electorate chooses its President from one party and the majority of Congress from the opposition party. Because we had more congressional government than presidential government under Eisenhower, the focus of political power shifted from the White House to Capitol Hill.

President Kennedy, who had very positive ideas about the legislative role of the President, was fairly successful in pushing his New Frontier on domestic issues: a new minimum wage law, urban renewal, public housing, aid to depressed areas, interstate highways, airport construction, to name but a few of his proposals that became law. Among his more conspicuous legislative defeats were: the creation of an Urban Affairs Department, aid to the public schools, income tax reforms, Medicare, and civil rights legislation. In a televised review of his first two years in office, the President attributed his legislative difficulties, not to the substance of his program, but to the way in which Congress was organized for business. He was incensed because the conservative coalition of Northern Republicans and Southern Democrats, although a minority group, was able to dominate the Rules Committee in the House and to hold the principal committee chairmanships in both houses. As he put it to his national constituency, it's not easy to move a presidential program "particularly when the seniority system may place particular individuals in key positions who may be wholly unsympathetic to your program, and may be, even though they are members of your own party, in political opposition to the President. . . ."[41]

Perhaps the most distinctive feature of the American presidential system is the independent tenure of the executive, whose term of office is in no way dependent on the will of Congress. Obversely, Congress assembles at least once a year and may stay in session as long as it pleases. The President has no power to dissolve it no matter how obstreperous or disagreeable it may be with respect to the "administrative program." The Constitution permits the President to convene Congress in extraordinary session; in case of disagreement between the two houses on whether or not they should adjourn, he may adjourn them to such time as he thinks proper. So far, however, no President has ever adjourned Congress.

The fact that Congress cannot force the resignation of an unpopular Presi-

---

[41]The complete text of the interview broadcast of December 17, 1962, appears in *U.S. News and World Report* (December 31, 1962), 54–63. For an academic analysis of the problems discussed by President Kennedy see James MacGregor Burns, *The Deadlock of Democracy* (Englewood Cliffs, N.J.: Prentice-Hall, Inc., 1963).

dent, nor the President dissolve a recalcitrant Congress, offers both advantages and disadvantages. It may mean that a stalemate in the legislative program will be prolonged throughout the two sessions between elections; or it may promote a more practical give-and-take between the President and Congress.

At this point, we need to recall that the veto power gives the President significant influence over legislation. President Truman considered his veto power one of the must instruments of his authority in dealing with Congress. His memoirs record that he vetoed more major bills than any other President, with the possible exception of Grover Cleveland.[42] Among the vetoes which involved him in bitter disputes with Congress were those applied to the Taft-Hartley bill (which restricted the activities of labor unions), the Kerr bill (which excused independent gas producers from the price-fixing authority of the Federal Power Commission), the Internal Security bill (which set up the Subversive Activities Control Board), the Walters-McCarran Act (which retained the national origins immigration policy), and the Tidelands resolution (which returned the oil rich tidelands to the states following a Supreme Court decision which had held that the United States government had the "dominant rights" to off-shore oil and minerals). The mere threat that a President might veto a measure serves to moderate Congress in drawing up the bill in the first place. Once the President has exercised his veto power, Congress ordinarily does not attempt to override him by passing the bill over his objections. Indeed, Congress sometimes passes a bill in the comforting anticipation that the President will veto it. This practice allows a congressman to fulfill his local commitments without jeopardizing national interests. Later on, when he is talking to his constituents back home, he can say, "I voted for the bill. The *President* vetoed it."[43]

The Constitution, as it was written, clearly intended that *all* legislative powers of the national government be vested in Congress. But the men who framed it had never been confronted with the mass vote in elections, nor with a multitude of active special interest groups. Instead, the restricted suffrage of that day, together with the convenient device of the single-member constituency, were guarantees that middle-class farmers and merchants would be vastly overrepresented in Congress. Consequently, it seemed perfectly safe to make the legislature all-powerful. Once the suffrage had become universal, the legislator, though still elected by a single constituency, was beset by the competing and conflicting claims of different groups within that constituency. He could no longer represent a single class; nor could he please or appease all the groups. The simplest solution was to pass the buck, to delegate "quasi-legislative" powers to the executive, especially in such controversial areas as social and economic policy.

James Bryce, in his study, *Modern Democracies*, written shortly after World

---

[42]*Memoirs*, Vol. II, p. 477.

[43]In many states today, the governor enjoys what is known as an "item veto," which means that he can veto part of a bill without rejecting the bill as a whole. President Eisenhower—and many of his predecessors—have sought the same power for the President, particularly on appropriations bills. Since the President cannot easily veto a general appropriations bill (although President Truman once did), Congress frequently attaches "riders" to them. "Riders" usually carry some policy that is repugnant to the President, a policy that he would probably veto if it were presented to him separately.

War I, observed everywhere in the world a decline of the legislature and a pathology of representative government. The great depression of the 1930s accelerated the decline, exaggerated the pathology. Overwhelmed by the complex problems of modern industrial society, the "representatives of the people" seemed more than willing to turn over the vastly expanding business of government to "the elite and the expert." And the delegation of extraordinary legislative power to the executive became a sign of the times: "executive dictatorship" in Italy, Germany, and the Soviet Union, and "executive leadership" in France, Great Britain, and the United States.

In 1933, Congress passed the National Industrial Recovery Act, which in effect empowered the major industries of the country to draw up "codes of fair competition," including minimum wages and maximum hours, provisions for collective bargaining, and the prohibition of child labor. If any industry failed to draw up such a code, the President was authorized to prescribe one for it. Judicial review, however, temporarily checked this abdication from legislative responsibility. The Supreme Court, though recognizing that a grave economic crisis had impelled Congress to delegate this policy-making authority, nevertheless stood firm: "Extraordinary conditions do not create or enlarge constitutional power." The Court felt that for Congress to permit either trade associations or the President to formulate and establish as law "codes of fair competition" was such a sweeping delegation of legislative power that it violated the constitutional doctrine of separation of powers. Hence, in 1935, it declared the NIRA null and void.[44]

Although the judges continue to hold that separation of powers forbids the delegation of legislative power, Congress nevertheless frequently passes laws that contain only general statements of policy, leaving the executive to fill in the details. In such cases, the judges have insisted that Congress set forth clearly the general policy and fix "an intelligible standard" for administering it. Not since the early New Deal, however, has the Supreme Court been inclined to question the legislative standards too closely. Moreover, Congress continues to add to its already impressive delegations of quasi-legislative power through "contingent legislation" which permits the Chief Executive to determine when or where a situation exists that calls for putting legislative policy into operation. The judges have upheld "flexible tariffs" which give the President power to key individual items to fluctuating costs of production at home and abroad.[45] They also sustained the neutrality laws of the 1930s which authorized President Roosevelt to prohibit the sale of American arms and munitions if he felt that such action would contribute to peace between the belligerents.[46] More recently, congressional resolutions have empowered

---

[44]See *Panama Refining Co.* v. *Ryan*, 293 U.S. 388 (1935); *Schechter Poultry Corp.* v. *United States*, 295 U.S. 495 (1935); both discuss at some length the constitutional doctrine of separation of powers. It should be noted, however, that the National Industrial Recovery Act was not invalidated on this ground alone; the Court held the act unconstitutional insofar as Congress had exceeded its commerce power and had thus invaded states' rights.
[45]*Hampton & Co.* v. *United States*, 276 U.S. 394 (1928).
[46]*United States* v. *Curtiss-Wright Export Corp.*, 299 U.S. 304 (1936).

President Eisenhower in the Far East and Middle East, President Kennedy in Berlin and Cuba, and President Johnson in Viet Nam to take whatever measures seemed necessary to curb aggression against the "free world."

Head of the Nation's Economic Program

A realistic approach to understanding the President's working relations with Congress is to analyze his authority as head of the nation's economic program. In his budget message to Congress at the beginning of each session, the President specifies the major items on which he requests Congress to take legislative action. Since the President releases his legislative recommendations through nationwide networks and news services, Congress is put on the political defensive. If the congressmen cut the budget, they must explain why they dare to minimize expenditures for the general welfare or national security. If they add to the budget, they must meet the charge of "pork-barrel legislation." Thus the President, through his initiative in fiscal legislation, can almost straitjacket Congress when it comes to making economic policies and decisions on expenditures.

The Constitution does not expressly grant any economic powers to the President. The Founding Fathers believed that the authority to raise revenue by taxation, to borrow money on the credit of the United States, and to appropriate money for government functions belonged to the people's representatives in the legislature. For more than a hundred years, Congress carried out its fiscal assignment unaided. But as the functions of the federal government expanded rapidly from year to year, there was increasing waste and extravagance, confusion and incompetence. Long after the need for more unified direction and more professional management was apparent, the President still had little influence and no supervision over the requests for appropriations or the spending practices of the various agencies of which he was "Chief Executive." Not until 1921 did Congress finally concede that it was unable to control the chaotic finances of the sprawling and disorganized federal government. In that year of "fiscal revolution," Congress passed a Budget and Accounting Act which provided that the President prepare and transmit an annual budget of the United States to guide Congress in making decisions on taxation and appropriations. The Bureau of the Budget established in 1921 was first located in the Treasury Department, but was transferred in 1939 to the Executive Office of the President. Its location in the Executive Office gives the President both the broadest and the most specific controls, not only over public finances but indirectly over the entire national economy.

Preparing the federal budget involves not merely estimating expenditures for the year to come, but also justifying the programs that are planned. It is a tremendous responsibility, and one that is not always politically palatable. In January of 1957, President Eisenhower, just beginning his second term of office, presented to Congress the highest peacetime budget that had ever been known in American history—hardly a budget calculated to please John Q. Taxpayer. On the same day, the Secretary of the Treasury told a press conference "there are a lot of places in this budget that can be cut . . . if Congress can find ways to cut and still do a proper job." It was certainly unusual strategy for a Cabinet officer to assail the President's budget on the very day it went to Congress. Even more amazing was the President's own press conference three days later when he declared he was in complete agreement with the Secretary's statements. The President said he thought Congress through its committees ought to find ways to save more dollars.[47]

Since the President's Bureau of the Budget had spent months examining the estimates and justifications from all the agencies and had failed to come up with any feasible cuts, Congress was understandably reluctant to accept such a vain assignment. So the House politely passed a resolution asking the President to advise Congress where *he* thought the Budget could be reduced. The President in turn bounced the problem back to the lawmakers, again urging *them* to revise downward—if they could—such programs as defense and security, veterans' and farmers' benefits. Thereupon, the House proceeded to chop off a substantial percentage of the funds that had been requested to run the White House and Executive Office. This amusing interplay of "You first, my dear Alphonse. . . . But no, you first, my dear Gaston" is a good illustration of party politics in action; the people had set the stage in November of 1956 by electing a Republican President and a Democratic Congress. The attempted exchange of roles, however, was disturbing from the point of view of public administration, for it marked a retreat from executive responsibility for overall planning.

President Kennedy, almost as soon as he entered office, revised the Eisenhower estimates upward to meet a much greater spending program. In fact, President Kennedy persuaded Congress to vote even higher appropriations in 1961 than he had initially proposed. (International crises prompted this extraordinary cooperation from Congress.) But when President Johnson took over the responsibilities as Chief Executive, almost his first important decision was to pare back the Kennedy Budget of 1965, then almost completed. His memorable directive to cut down on the use of unnecessary electric lights at the White House was a piece of effective public relations which served immediately to project a new presidential image. It was not, however, a piece of fakery, as everyone in the government employ soon discovered. President Johnson intended to make frugality the hallmark of his administration, and he succeeded in trimming the Kennedy Budget of 1965 and in holding his own Budget of 1966 to a figure even the experts in the Budget Bureau had first thought would be impossible. Unfortunately, however, by 1967 mounting costs of the war in Viet Nam and pressing needs in metropolitan areas forced the Johnson administration to change its fiscal image. The 1968 Budget far exceeded the financial demands of any previous administration, including Franklin D. Roosevelt's during World War II and Harry S Truman's in the Korean War. And so, despite upcoming presidential elections in 1968, President Johnson had to plead with the 90th Congress for tax increases.

[47]For a sharp analysis of this episode, see Neustadt's account in *Presidential Power*.

The Structure of Presidential Activities

So far we have been talking primarily about the President as a person, what *he* is empowered to do, *his* views of the office, what *he* wants to do. But even when the President is the principal actor we note that the drama of policy-making is likely to involve a rather large cast of other actors. Just as in the preceding chapter on Congress we found it necessary to consider at some length the part played by the President in the legislative process, so in this chapter we have already made frequent references to the part played by Congress in shaping presidential decisions. We turn now to look at other members of the supporting cast whose various parts affect the President's performance.

The Executive Office of the President

To appraise the presidential personality is relatively easy, since the way a President uses his constitutional *powers* and his political *influence* is closely followed by the press. To analyze the *operations* and *processes* of the *Executive Office of the President* is much more difficult, for its "staff services" are covered with the cloak of bureaucratic anonymity. Not so long ago, a President was expected to handle the business of his office with the help of just a personal secretary and several clerks. Today, the institutionalized presidency includes more than a thousand permanent employees and many more thousands of part-time employees. This somewhat amorphous organization—most of it designed and developed since 1939—presumably provides the Chief Executive with the "skills and tools of management" he needs at the highest level of our national administration.

In terms of prestige and protocol, the *White House Office* takes precedence in the Executive Office. The office of Secretary to the President goes back to the first administration, when Washington, at his own expense, employed his nephew to help him with clerical chores. Not until the Buchanan administration did Congress appropriate a salary for the President's secretary. President Hoover was the first President to appoint three secretaries, and the practice was followed by President Roosevelt. Then, in 1937, the President's Committee on Administrative Management, pointing out that the President needed more than just secretarial help, urged the addition of six administrative assistants, who were to be marked by a "passion for anonymity." The Reorganization Act of 1939 authorized these administrative assistants, and subsequent acts provided for additional special assistants.

The *White House Staff* has four main jobs: (1) to keep the President's finger on the pulse of public opinion through professional public relations advisers; (2) to brief the President on the current activities and problems of the executive departments and agencies, so that he can act as an efficient general manager of the national administration; (3) to act as liaison between the executive branch and the legislative branch so that the President can be more effective in maneuvering the administration's programs through Congress; (4) to advise the President on military matters and national security.

422

Truman was the first President to use the staff system in the White House. He met with the staff daily and listened to what each and all had to say, but then he retired to his office to make his own decisions. President Eisenhower, however, turned over the responsibility of chief of staff to Sherman Adams. Adams' position in the White House had no precedent. Many presidents have put unusual trust in personal advisers; Wilson had his Colonel House and Franklin Roosevelt had Harry Hopkins. But Sherman Adams as the Assistant to the President was more than a close confidant, more than an efficient chief of staff; in official circles he was the President's *alter ego*. From the outset, Adams presided over the White House Staff meetings and reported to the President the consensus of the group rather than the conflicting viewpoints of the members. He also sat with the President in Cabinet meetings, in the National Security Council, and in most of the President's conferences with party and congressional leaders. Significantly, during each serious illness of President Eisenhower, the Assistant to the President rather than the Vice-President made the important executive decisions.[48]

Today's President needs expert advice on all kinds of technical matters that bear on public policy: advice of economists on tax measures; advice of scientists on missions to the moon; advice of military men on guerilla warfare. But experts, however qualified they may be in their own fields, may be lacking in political sagacity or disinterested in policy implications. A President normally counts on his Cabinet officers to advise him on particular policies: the Secretary of Agriculture on farm problems; the Secretary of Health, Education, and Welfare on Social Security and Medicare; the Secretaries of State and Defense on foreign aid or defense commitments. But each Cabinet member has his own bailiwick to support, and he loses face within his own hierarchy if he fails to advance the departmental interests. Thus diversity of viewpoints in Cabinet meetings or in the National Security Council may represent bureaucratic parochialism or agency rivalry, and consensus from group dynamics may reflect compromise rather than rational resolution.

Theodore D. Sorensen, special counsel to President Kennedy, points up the role of the White House Staff in presidential decision-making: to review the advice of the experts and the bureaucrats within the framework of the President's perspective.[49] Responsibilities of the White House Staff are as broad as the President's: to look at the government as a whole and to view all special claims critically and skeptically. The primary assignment of the White House Staff is to serve the President's needs and to talk the President's language. Even so, the President must use his own judgment in determining whose

---

[48]For two somewhat varying accounts of the role of the White House Staff by members of the Eisenhower administration, see Sherman Adams, *First Hand Account* (New York: Harper & Row, Publishers, Inc., 1961); and Emmet John Hughes, *The Ordeal of Power* (New York: Atheneum Publishers, 1963). For further discussion of the White House Staff system in the Eisenhower administration, see Marian D. Irish, "The Cipher in the White House," *New Statesman* (December 7, 1957), 761–764; also Marian D. Irish, "The Organization Man in the Presidency," *Journal of Politics*, XX (May, 1958), 259–277.

[49]Sorensen, *Decision-Making in the White House*, especially Chapter 5.

advice to trust most in any given situation. The White House Office offers him personal loyalty but, in their zeal to serve him, staff members may sometimes be too officious. Moreover, their confidential relationship to the President may imbue them with a confidence that exceeds their competence. As Sorensen points out, a White House adviser may see a problem in a wider context than a Cabinet officer, but he may also be less knowledgeable about actual operations, about Congress, and about special interest groups.

The men who surround the President in the White House—the special counsels, the secretaries, the administrative assistants, the special assistants—are in a position to exert tremendous influence on their chief. Yet they are almost completely unknown to the public and cannot easily be held accountable for the "staff service" that they render continuously on the most important issues of the day. In the days of Franklin D. Roosevelt, political scientists were gravely concerned about the "personalized power" of the presidency; today, they are more disturbed by the fear that personal leadership cannot be reasserted in view of the institutionalization of the Executive Office.

The *Bureau of the Budget* is by far the largest and most important unit in the Executive Office of the President. Its Director is one of the few top officials the President has the power to appoint without asking the consent of the Senate. Though the Budget Director is a political appointee, solely responsible to the President, the Bureau itself comprises a permanent professional staff of seasoned and able employees. In its impact on the government, the Budget Bureau is more powerful than any other single agency. The main business of the Bureau is to prepare the Budget of the United States for the President to submit to Congress. The President's Budget, however, is more than an accounting of estimated receipts and expenditures; it specifies the personnel and materials needed for the work to be performed by every agency in the executive branch.[50]

No agency can request congressional appropriations without clearance by the Budget Bureau. The Bureau requires every agency in the executive branch to justify its proposed expenditures with detailed "work plans," and if the plans do not conform to the President's overall recommendations, the Bureau returns them to the agency for revision. The Bureau also acts as a clearing house for any other requests an agency might make to Congress. Thus it can alert the President to the legislative needs of his administration and advise the Congress whether the agency proposals have the President's approval. In addition, the Bureau continuously scrutinizes the organization and operations of all the agencies in order to recommend changes designed to promote efficiency and economy. Because the asking budgets of the operating agencies always exceed any budget that the President can prudently recommend, the Bureau is the hatchet-man for the administration.

The Bureau has been the target of many criticisms. The operating agencies are inclined to resent the extension of this managerial arm of the President into their "line activities" or special interests. On the other hand, Congress

---

[50]Aaron Wildavsky offers an exciting account of *The Politics Of the Budgetary Process* (Boston: Little, Brown and Company, 1964). See also James W. Davis and Randal B. Ripley, "The Bureau of the Budget and the Executive Branch Agencies," *Journal of Politics*, XXIX (November, 1967).

has sometimes felt that the Bureau has been too lenient with the agencies, more concerned with keeping books than with evaluating programs.

A congressional committee, reporting in 1961, noted that the budgetary process, if employed with sophistication, could be the most discriminating and effective tool of the Chief Executive.[51] "It reaches deep into the activities of the great departments; it is the one presidential management device common to all of them; it works on that most sensitive pressure point—the pocketbook nerve." But the Committee complained that the budgetary process has not kept pace with the requirements of modern government. Today's budget retains the essential format of the first budget President Harding submitted to Congress in 1921. It is an exhaustive document—it takes two years to prepare—filled with obscure, archaic, fiscal jargon.

Nevertheless, the President's budget represents the most crucial policy decisions in the national government. The most important budget decision of the President is on the overall fiscal policy for the year—whether to balance the budget, accumulate a surplus, or recommend "deficit spending" (current expenditures exceeding current income). This overall policy determines whether the government agencies will be able to expand their activities, hold the line, or have to retrench. Its details reflect various demands, supports, and apathy in the political system. Its effect is to imprint presidential values on national policies. Once the President has in a general way determined the size of the budget and the general pattern of allocation, all of the government agencies prepare their estimates for the Bureau of the Budget.

The President's budget has been described as "a vast network of bargains." The President uses his power over the budget to bargain with his executive officers who have different clienteles to please. Pressure groups outside vie with each other to press their claims for their share—or more than their share—of the fiscal pie. As head of a political party who must always keep in mind the next election—elections are always coming up—the President no doubt weighs very carefully the competing and conflicting claims. He has his expert advisers in the Bureau of the Budget; he also gets a great deal of solicited and gratuitous advice from business leaders, labor leaders, spokesmen for minority groups, governors, city mayors, party officials, TV commentators, university professors, and others. He makes the final decisions and seals his part of the bargains when he delivers his budget message to Congress in January every year. There the process of bargaining begins again in the congressional policy committees that authorize government programs, in the appropriations subcommittees which hold intensive hearings on agency requests, and in the floor debates in the House and in the Senate. Nelson Polsby sums it up: "The budgetary process comes close to being the ideal illustration of the maxim that power in the American political system is

---

[51]Subcommittee on National Policy Machinery, Senator Henry M. Jackson, Chairman for the Committee on Government Operations, U.S. Senate, *Organizing for National Security* (Washington, D.C.: U.S. Government Printing Office, 1961), Staff Reports and Recommendations, Vol. III, 89–100.

dispersed and shared among a large number of participants, with widely varying obligations, constituencies, and policy preferences"[52] (see Fig. 11-3).

As a whole, then, the budgetary process appears to be worked out according to the pluralistic theory that we found particularly applicable to regulatory policy in Chapter 8. If we broke it down into its component parts, however, we would probably discover that many specific decisions were made according to the log-rolling theory. And, of course, the "mobilization of bias" keeps some questions from being raised for decisions.

The *Council of Economic Advisers* has a small but high-quality professional staff, mostly economists and statisticians, whose collective job is to analyze the nation's economy, appraise the economic programs and policies of the national government, and assist the President in his annual Economic Report to Congress. The Council consists of three members appointed by the President with the consent of the Senate. Since its own staff is small, it relies heavily on the operating agencies to collect necessary data. Unlike the Bureau of the Budget, its recommendations tend to be general, so that it enjoys fairly cordial relations with the operating agencies. It has sometimes been accused of being too receptive to the interests of special groups (in sharp contrast with the Budget Bureau, which appears remarkably insulated from outside contacts); it has also been charged with tempering its economics with political expediency and its recommendations with too much "welfare." Nevertheless, the Council offers the President substantial assistance in program-planning for service and security. Congress itself has organized a Joint Committee to receive and act on the Economic Report that emanates from the Council.

The *National Security Council* is the primary policy-developing agency in

---

[52]Nelson W. Polsby, *Congress and the Presidency* (Englewood Cliffs, N.J.: Prentice-Hall, Inc., 1964), p. 97.

Figure 11-3
Source: *The Budget in Brief, 1968,* p. 55 (with modification to show pressure groups).

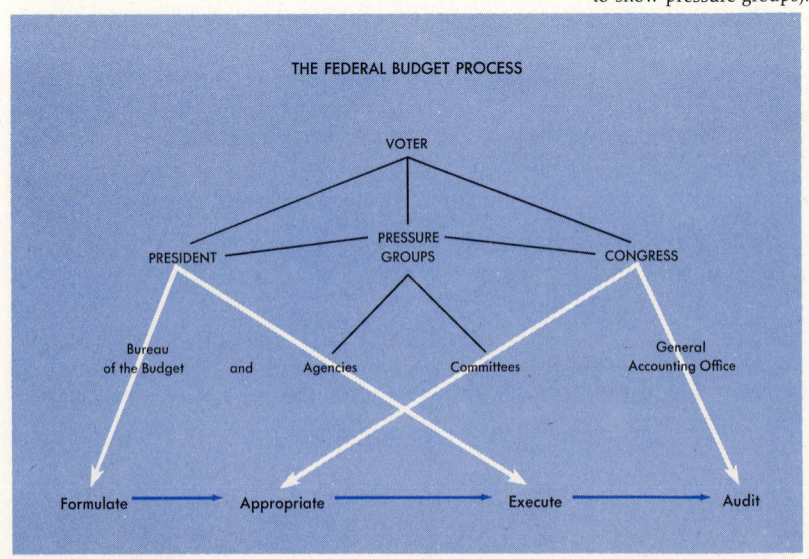

THE FEDERAL BUDGET PROCESS

426

preparing this nation for any possible war. Its function is to advise the President on the best way to integrate the domestic, foreign, and military policies that relate to national security. Its statutory members are the President, Vice-President, Secretary of State, Secretary of Defense, and Director of the Office of Emergency Planning. The President may, and frequently does, invite other strategic "decision-makers" to attend the Council meetings—the Budget Director, Chairman of the Joint Chiefs of Staff, Secretary of the Treasury, U.S. Representative to the United Nations, and others whose responsibilities are tied to national security. The Central Intelligence Agency, which coordinates all the intelligence activities of the departments concerned with security matters, reports to the Council through its director.

Each President is free to use the National Security Council in the manner he finds most suitable and helpful. He is solely responsible for determining what policy matters will be brought before the Council and how they will be handled. President Kennedy chose not to meet with the Council in full session as often or regularly as did President Eisenhower. He did, however, use it for discussion of basic national policy toward a number of countries. And he sought its advice on particularly pressing decisions as well as on long-term policies. When President Johnson took office, he was inclined to call Council meetings more frequently,[53] although, in part, this must be attributed to mounting crises in Africa and Asia.

The Office of Emergency Planning has gone through various statutory and administrative reorganizations. Under the Eisenhower administration, its activities covered all aspects of civil defense and defense mobilization. Its director advised the President on how to coordinate all plans for military, industrial, and civilian mobilization. In the face of mounting international tensions, President Kennedy directed that responsibility for civil defense—in such matters as health, food, manpower, and transportation—be transferred to the Department of Defense. The Director of the Office of Emergency Planning develops overall plans and guidelines for the national nonmilitary defense effort. He prepares for stabilization after an enemy attack. Part of his preparedness operations includes determination of what kinds and quantities of strategic and critical materials must be acquired and stocked against war emergency. President Johnson has used the Office of Emergency Planning mainly to cement federal relations; among other activities the Director administers the Federal Natural Disaster Program.

Prompted by the launching of the first Sputnik, President Eisenhower established the post of Special Assistant to the President for Science and Technology. President Kennedy upgraded the post by creating the *Office of Science and Technology*. The Director is charged with evaluating and coordi-

---

[53]Senator Jackson's Subcommittee on *Organizing for National Security* focused much of its investigation on the role of the National Security Council. Its published study (see footnote 51), including testimony from a variety of high officials from the Truman, Eisenhower, and Kennedy administrations, as well as staff papers from the Committee, is a goldmine of information, observations, and critical insights. For further discussion of the policy process and policy output relating to national security, see Chapter 16 in this text.

nating the major policies, plans, and programs of science and technology throughout the national government and with giving them appropriate emphasis in American foreign policy and national security efforts. The Office provides liaison between the governmental and nongovernmental communities in science and engineering, but most important it makes scientific counsel available at all times to the President. The range of scientific and technical activities in modern government is immense, "It goes from space to sonar, from microbiology to meteorology, from symbolic logic to systems engineering." No one person in the government can begin to comprehend the whole spectrum of specialized knowledge, and yet the President as Chief Executive must view the national policies in the round.

The role of the Vice-President vis-à-vis the President has always been a rather embarrassing anomaly in American politics. To put it crudely, the Vice-President's principal responsibility in the past has been to wait on the sidelines, pretending no eagerness, waiting for the moment when the President might be too disabled to function in office, of preparing to become President in the event of the President's removal from office by death, resignation, or impeachment. Because the Vice-President may become the President, he must meet the consitutional qualifications for the presidential office: he must be a native-born citizen, at least thirty-five-years old, and a resident of the United State for fourteen years. Both are formally chosen by the electoral college in separate balloting, or — if none of the vice-presidential candidates receives a majority of the electoral vote — the Senate shall choose one from the two top candidates.

The Vice-President

In the process of nominating candidates, each national convention concentrates on the presidential candidate. The vice-presidential candidate is usually chosen to "balance" the presidential ticket. In effect, this means that whatever the political qualifications of the presidential candidate, the Vice-President's are usually the opposite. If the President comes from the liberal, urban East, it is good politics to choose his running mate from the conservative, rural South — Kennedy vis-à-vis Johnson. If the President moves ahead of his party, his Vice-President should be a solid party man — Roosevelt vis-à-vis Truman. If the President is a senior statesman, his Vice-President should be a rising young politician — Eisenhower vis-à-vis Nixon. Although the balanced ticket is demanded by campaign strategy, it can have serious and even tragic consequences if the Vice-President is called on to fill out the President's term (as when Johnson succeeded Lincoln).

The tragedy of Dallas, Texas, on November 22, 1963, reminds us how important it is for the nation to choose its Vice-Presidents with the same seriousness that it considers the presidential candidates. A Vice-President has succeeded to the presidency eight times in American history; the eight presidents who died in office served less than eight of the thirty-two years for which they had been elected. Fortunately, Lyndon B. Johnson, who had been a contender in his own right for the presidential nomination in 1960, was eminently qualified to take over the presidential office and was wholly committed to the fulfillment of the Kennedy program. But, for the very reason that he knew from first-hand experience the enormous difficulties that face a Vice-President suddenly called to fill the top post, President Johnson was not beguiled by the usual political advice to choose an "opposite" that would balance the Democratic ticket in 1964. He personally selected Hubert Humphrey, who had also campaigned for the presidency in 1960. In an unprecedented move in American politics, the President appeared in person before the Democratic Convention in Atlantic City to announce that Humphrey was his choice for Vice-President. Declaring that Humphrey's experience as a legislator and administrator was marked with excellence and achievement, the President said "I will feel strengthened knowing that he is at my side at all times in the great work of your country and your government. . . . This is not a sectional choice, a way to balance the ticket. This is simply the best man in America for the job."

In earlier years, the position of the Vice-President has been mostly titular.[54] The Constitution provides that he shall preside over the Senate, but allows him to vote only to break a tie. As moderator in the Senate, he merely keeps parliamentary order and may not exercise his political influence overtly. The *United States Government Organization Manual,* which describes the important officers and agencies of the federal government, has no separate write-up for the Vice-President.

Vice-President Humphrey, in addition to his constitutional office of President of the Senate, holds a number of fairly important positions in the Johnson administration: he is a statutory member of the National Security Council, statutory chairman of the National Aeronautics and Space Council, and Chairman of the National Advisory Council of the Peace Corps.

President Truman, who served as Vice-President for less than three months of Roosevelt's fourth term, points out in his *Memoirs* one of the practical reasons for the anomalous position of the Vice-President. As President of the Senate, he is in between the legislative branch and the executive branch, responsible to neither, and trusted by neither. Senators rarely consult him on legislative matters; they may be outwardly friendly to him, but they do not admit him to the senatorial club. On the other hand, the President may not feel free to discuss confidential executive matters with him lest they be leaked prematurely to the congressmen with whom the Vice-President is in daily contact. Moreover, the very qualifications that made the Vice-President a good "running-mate" precluded close personal relations; Roosevelt could be cordial to Truman but not friendly.

Not since Martin Van Buren has any Vice-President won an election to the presidency in his own right without having become an incumbent through the death of his predecessor. In recent years, however, the Vice-President has begun to acquire political status in the administration. President Eisenhower deliberately built up the stature of his Vice-President. More conscious of the

---

[54]Irving G. Williams, *The Rise of the Vice-Presidency* (Washington, D.C.: Public Affairs Press, 1956) traces the history of the Vice-President, with a running account of the personalities that have filled the office and an analysis of their political activities in that office.

possibility of succession than his predecessors have been, probably because of his advancing age and severe illnesses, he took every opportunity to point to Nixon as "the most valuable man on my team." Vice-President Johnson profited by the more active role that Nixon enjoyed in the Eisenhower administration. Johnson also attended Cabinet and National Security Council meetings and was a bona fide member of the presidential community of policy advisers. He, too, served as a sort of roving ambassador on a number of trips abroad and undertook a number of special assignments on the domestic frontier, none more significant than his appointment to head the President's Committee on Equal Employment Opportunities. In the work of this Committee, he came to meet personally a cross-section of businessmen, bureaucrats, and civil rights leaders, an experience that paid off politically in the campaign of 1964.

Today, the Vice-President seems to be aquiring a new institutional status, predominantly in the executive branch, though, of course, he retains his constitutional post in the Senate. He holds the "second man" position in the administration, acting in the roles of deputy chief of state, deputy party leader, emissary for the President in foreign affairs, and *ad hoc* trouble-shooter for the President in various legislative and administrative assignments.[55] And under the Twenty-fifth Amendment, he will be Acting President if the President is disabled, and President if the incumbent is removed from office for any reason.

Interactions among Decision-Makers

If we return to the schema of decision-making introduced earlier in this chapter, we observe that although the President plays the primary role, the effectiveness of his performance depends in large measure on his supporting cast. The Central Intelligence Agency (CIA) and the Bureau of the Census, for example, are organized and operate for the specific purpose of furnishing the government's policy-makers with an extensive groundwork of systematic intelligence. Further, the President can call on a vast corps of professional experts in the executive agencies—historians, lawyers, economists, engineers, scientists, foreign service officers—to give him whatever specialized information he needs in the formulation of specific policies relating to national security, social security, labor-management relations, urban problems, and so on. Congress counts on receiving much of this intelligence as backstop for its legislative decisions. The President himself submits basic intelligence in his formal messages on the State of the Union, the Budget, and the Condition of the Economy. His principal officers spend a great deal of time on Capitol Hill providing additional intelligence to congressional committees considering specific administrative measures.

In the formulation of policy and in the assessment of alternatives, the President consults with many individuals and groups; he has his weekly luncheon engagements with the Secretary of State, the Secretary of Defense, his White House Adviser on National Security Affairs, and his Press Secretary; he meets

[55] For a recent discussion see Paul David, "The Vice President: the Institutional Evolution and Contemporary Status, *Journal of Politics*, XXIX (November, 1967).

more formally with the National Security Council and with his Cabinet officers collectively and individually. (For such meetings, specialists in the departments represented work up position papers and provide pertinent intelligence.) He confers with his Council of Economic Advisors, with the Director of the Office of Emergency Planning, and the Director of the Office of Science and Technology. He meets regularly with the leadership of his own party, with the leaders of his own party in Congress, with the bipartisan congressional leadership, and with various chairmen of congressional committees dealing with his current proposals. And his White House schedule of appointments indicates a continuous stream of callers from many interest groups in the organized and articulate public.

When Congress is at work on legislative policy, there is constant interaction between the policy committees on Capitol Hill and the White House assistants on congressional relations. The President himself may drop a note to his majority leader, or the chairman of a committee, or put in some strategic phone calls to personal friends. Every agency sends its congressional relations staff to help pilot its particular bills through each stage of the legislative process. And spokesmen from the interest groups will be on hand to furnish their various versions of intelligence and policy assessments to congressional committees and to individual congressmen.

At the implementation stage, after Congress has authorized and appropriated funds for specific policies, the executive agencies put their programs into operation. This implementation is subject to considerable presidential oversight, especially through the Bureau of the Budget, and to considerable congressional oversight, especially from members of the policy committees who are usually zealous in their concern that congressional prescriptions be followed. If additional personnel are required, the Civil Service Commission will have its say and the General Services Adminstration will lay down the rules for such activities as construction of buildings, procurement of supplies, and traffic and communications management.

In the application of policies in specific cases, the Chief Executive acts principally through the Department of Justice. Whether policies will be vigorously enforced is decided by the President or his executive agencies; but sometimes a congressional committee may undertake an investigation of what happened to a particular policy. At one point in the policy process the separation of powers is more than a matter of parchment barriers. Neither the President nor the Congress can control—or try to control—the judges. It would be highly improper for the President to schedule regular meetings with the Chief Justice to discuss pending cases, for example, even though the outcome of judicial decisions may be very important to the administration. A President may, in time, come to have indirect influence on the character of judicial decision-making through his appointing powers, as is attested by the "Roosevelt Court" of the early 1940s. (We shall discuss the implications of this in Chapter 13.) Certainly, judges, even though they are protected against political pressures, are nevertheless influenced by the same changing demands and supports which condition the behavior of all participants in the political process.

The reappraisal of policies is a continuous, interlocking process. In the normal course of legislative-executive relations, when disagreement occurs (as it inevitably does), both the President and the Congress are likely to make special appeals to the public to provide new supports, one against the other. And in the resolution of the conflict, new policies will be formulated. Occasionally, though not frequently, the judges may hold invalid a congressional statute, a presidential act, or an administrative order, which they consider out of constitutional bounds. This too will call for reappraisal and probably bring about consideration of new policy alternatives. The American government has no official counterpart to His Majesty's Loyal Opposition in the British government, but the congressional minority leaders serve a similar function. Moreover, the party conventions use their platforms to point out with pride or view with alarm the administration's policies; and the electorate is urged to vote for continuation or termination of the administration. Changes in the external environment or new situational factors in the domestic environment may force the administration to reconsider existing programs and to propose new policies. And so it goes, a continuous process of decision-making, many different patterns of interaction, and new policies always in the offing.

The Functions of the President

As chief of state and Chief Executive, the President functions as the nation's spokesman and principal policy-maker. His overall responsibility is to interpret, protect, promote, and implement the interests of the American people in international politics and in domestic politics. In the performance of these functions, the President must play many roles. But in the final analysis, how well he functions depends on the nature of his political leadership and the exercise of his presidential powers.

Political Leadership

The candidate for presidential office is the very personification of partisanship. To many voters the party labels have no significance except when they are used in presidential races. With the possible exception of General Washington, every President of the United States has entered office as a party man. The presidential campaign is actually an important factor in setting the stage for the successful candidate to perform his functions as President. In his campaign, the candidate meets a cross-section of the American electorate, and discovers from his own experience the plurality of American politics. This is the first testing ground for his skill as a decision-maker, identifying the values, interests, and goals of the American people, and determining priorities where there are competing and conflicting groups, so as to insure his own election by a majority of the people, or at least by a majority of votes in the electoral college.

Once elected, the President represents not only his party but the whole people. As the head of state, he is personal spokesman of "the people," even of those who voted against him and who still oppose him. Former President Truman, in a celebrated TV-radio interview with newscaster Edward R. Murrow in 1958, graphically described the President as "lobbyist for all the people." President Eisenhower, who was never comfortable in the role of party leader, often embarrassed his political mentors while he was in office by his somewhat derogatory views on party politics. On the other hand, the fact that he refused to indulge in sharp partisanship became an asset when he came to recommend policies to a Congress that was controlled by the opposition party.

The President is in a unique position to exercise political leadership for the nation at large. He is the only elected representative in the American government (except for the Vice-President) who can claim a national constituency. Even so, he cannot always count on the support of Congress, which represents many diverse constituencies across the country. Each national convention drafts a party platform at the same time it chooses its presidential candidate, but candidates for Congress are neither required nor even expected to stand on the party platform. Thus a President who tries to follow the party standard, even when his party controls both houses of Congress, may find himself out of step with the legislative decision-makers. The President may conscientiously act as spokesman for the nation, but the ears of election-wise congressmen may be more attuned to the voices of their more parochial constituents.

Although the President is the titular "head of the party," his political leadership may be largely personal. If he is able to sell his program to Congress, it is usually because he has first been able to persuade the public that his product is what they want. This is what Woodrow Wilson tried to do—and failed—when the Senate refused to buy his League of Nations. This is what Franklin D. Roosevelt tried to do—and succeeded—when he sold the New Deal to "My Friends." The development of mass communication has favored presidential leadership. Whereas Wilson had to make a killing lecture tour across the country, Roosevelt could sit in the White House and broadcast his "fireside chats" to a nationwide radio audience. President Eisenhower was able to telecast his personal appeals under the guidance of public relations experts whose profession it is to "engineer consent." Yet Calvin Coolidge's remark is still appropriate: "A President cannot, with success, constantly appeal to the country. After a while he will get no response."

We began this chapter with a sentence from the Constitution on the President's manifest function: "he shall take Care that the Laws be faithfully executed." Although the vigor with which various laws are carried out varies from administration to administration, the American presidency has realized the function of policy-implementation for which it was created. From the time when President Washington used troops to enforce a tax on whiskey in Pennsylvania to the use of the army to require compliance with school desegregation decisions in the twentieth century, presidents have suppressed open flouting of national policy decisions.

The President doesn't simply carry out policies; he also makes them. In executive orders under congressional grants of authority, he makes policies in his own right. The President is also the chief legislator. Not only does he have greater power over particular bills (e.g., through his veto power) than any congressman, but he also has the advantage of setting the agenda through which legislation is initiated. This initiation of legislation is also a presidential function intended by the Constitution.

As the center of attention and respect, the President is in a better position than any congressman—and probably than Congress as a whole—to communicate to the American people and the world the objectives of the American political system. And when the President signs a statute passed by Congress, it is unmistakably legitimized as the authoritative law of the land. Leaders of the particular "policy system" that passed the law—group leaders, agency members, congressmen—eagerly accept the fountain pens the President uses to legitimize it. As active participants in the policy system, they carry off a physical symbol of the fact that their efforts have been legitimized as a nationally binding decision.

In imagining what our national policies would have been like for the last generation without Congress, we concluded that they would have been much more liberal in the social welfare field. Because the constituency and policy biases built into the presidency are so nearly a "mirror image" of those built into Congress, we can easily conclude that, without the influence of recent Presidents, American policy would have been much more conservative. More than anyone else, the President speaks for and promotes the interests of the broad majority. The original Framers of the Constitution expected the President to serve as a conservative check on an impetuous Congress. Instead, recent presidents—Democratic and Republican alike—have consistently recommended more liberal legislation than most congressional leaders have liked.

As Chief Executive, the President provides policy leadership and implementation. But presidential leadership goes beyond the initiation and execution of policy. The position of chief of state implies something more—spokesman for the nation in relations with other political systems and mobilizer of national interests. The President stands as a symbol of national values.

The Exercise of Power

The President is powerful in international politics because he officially represents the most powerful democratic nation in the world. The President is powerful in domestic politics because the Constitution makes him the Chief Executive and authorizes him to act in every stage of the policy process. The President is powerful because history and tradition have endowed his office with extraordinary legitimacy, respect, and deference.[56] Louis Koenig speaks of "the imagined presidency" which, grounded partly in reality and partly in fancy, enhances the prestige of every incumbent, whatever his personal concepts of the office.[57] The imagined presidency "equates past presidential success, the nation's might, and expectations of how the world should go, with available presidential power."

From the moment he enters the office, the President of the United States

---

[56]Dahl, *Pluralist Democracy in the United States*, p. 380.
[57]Koenig, *The Chief Executive*, p. 5.

THE PRESIDENT

can never escape being a public figure. Whatever he does, wherever he goes, he is treated with pomp and circumstance: "Hail to the Chief." Even to his closest friends in Congress, with whom he had "wheeled and dealed" and been on a first-name basis for almost thirty years, Lyndon Baines Johnson became "Mr. President" from the moment that he took the oath of office.

In discussing the many roles of the President, we have observed that the sources of his real power extend beyond the constitutional authorization, if not as far as his personal inclinations. The President *is* the people's choice, he does have a national mandate, at least at the time of his election. His appointive powers give him many opportunities to move his own men into positions of influence and power not only in the executive offices but also in the judiciary. His access to intelligence, to expert counsel, and to all the top secrets of the government gives him enormous advantage in his assessment of alternatives and recommendation of specific measures. His central position in the whole policy machinery of the national government assures him whatever time or space he requests in the media of mass communications to function as the nation's principal spokesman on every facet of American political life.

Having said all this, it is anticlimactic to point out why the President is

"You don't seem to understand!"
"I am the strongest man on earth!"
thundered Uncle Gulliver.

Drawing by Haynie;
© 1967 Los Angeles Times Syndicate;
reprinted by permission.

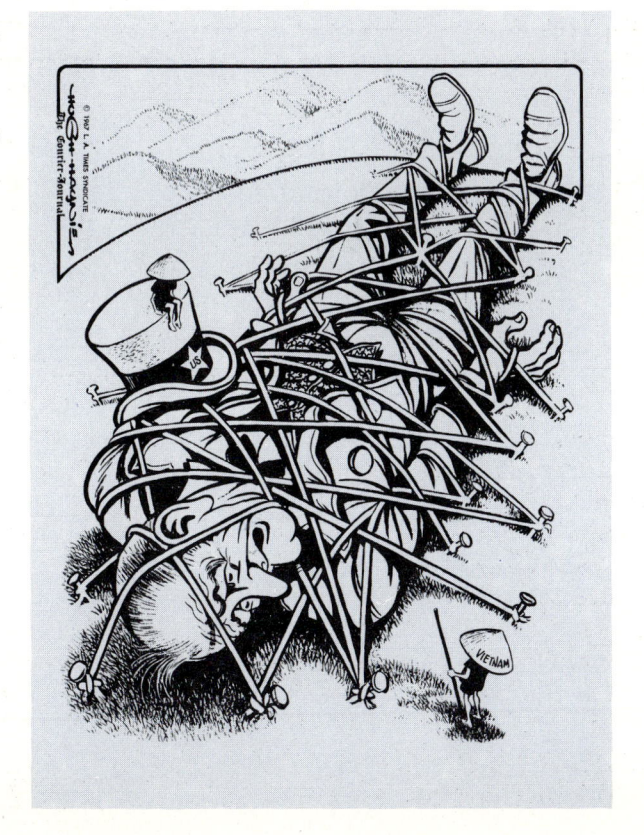

neither as powerful as he may want to be, nor as powerful as the nation expects him to be. Nevertheless, for a full understanding of how the President functions, we must realize that limitations on the exercise of presidential power are both real and substantial.

As chief of state and director of American foreign policy, the President has to recognize that his powers to command go no further than the boundaries of the United States. However well conceived his foreign policy may be in terms of American national interests, and the goals of the American people, if the policy runs counter to the interests, goals, and capabilities of another nation, the President may have difficulty in bringing his foreign policy to fruition. As Commander-in-Chief of American military forces, the President has at his instant disposal the most powerful and sophisticated weapons of modern warfare, but if the enemy refuses to capitulate or to bargain at the peace table, the President may not be able to terminate, much less win, the war. Indeed, the very fact that the President does possess "the most terrifying power in history" makes him less free than his prenuclear predecessors to use massive force as an ultimate weapon. President Johnson's "limited war" in Viet Nam is based on calculated risks in the atomic era.

With all his access to intelligence, the President may not be free to recommend what he personally thinks is the best course of action. He is bound by the guidelines of American history, by precedents set in past administrations, and by the network of commitments made by his predecessors in office. He has to take into consideration the ideological context of American politics, and he must stay close to the mainstream of public opinion. As a party leader, he can not promote unpopular causes which might jeopardize the success of his party at the next presidential election. He has to keep an eye on the opinion surveys to see whether a majority of those polled are approving or disapproving of the way he is handling his job as President; the upswing, or the downswing, may mean victory or defeat for his party in upcoming elections.

In this age of technology and specialization, the President is increasingly dependent on expert counsel. But sometimes the experts exceed the limits of their competence in offering political advice. Theodore Sorensen, in his analysis of decision-making in the White House, points out that "too many experts lack a sense of proportion, an ability to adapt, and a willingness to accept evidence inconsistent with their own."[58] Nevertheless, a President may hesitate to use his own common sense, or to substitute his own priorities, in the face of contrary advice from the Joint Chiefs of Staff or the Director of the Office of Science and Technology. If he does make an independent judgment and things go wrong, as it did for Kennedy at the Bay of Pigs, then he is damned for not having followed through on the best intelligence available.

Sorensen identified conflict as "the one quality which characterizes most issues likely to be brought to the President, . . . conflict between departments, between the views of various advisers, between the administration and Congress, between the United States and another nation, or between groups within the country: labor versus management, or race versus race, or state versus nation."[59] The President, at the center of the policy machine, may

---

[58] Sorensen, *Decision-Making in the White House* p. 65.
[59] *Ibid.*, p. 14. Sorensen's chapter on "The Outer Limits of Decision" is especially illuminating.

listen to all the points of view from official and nonofficial advisers, study all the intelligence he can get his hands on. But major conflicts which are really basic within our society cannot always be resolved by the political arts of persuasion and accommodation. At the presidential level, as President Eisenhower forewarned his successor, all the issues are "big ones." Decision-making for the "big ones," favoring one point of view over another, recommending this course of action rather than the alternative, rewarding some people and depriving others as a result of the decisions—this is the prime function of the President in the American political system. This above all is what makes his office so powerful, his job so exciting, and his position so hazardous.

THE

BUREAUCRATS 12

A long-time student of comparative government, Carl Friedrich, reminds us, in a discerning observation, that public administration is the core of modern democratic government: "All realistic study of government has to start with an understanding of bureaucracy (or whatever else one prefers to call it) because no government can function without it."[1] The elected representatives set forth the ground rules for public policy, but professional administrators in day-to-day decisions determine the courses of public action. Governmental bureaucracy is organized to administer the public business, but it is more than administrative machinery. Despite the abstract ring to such terms as "the executive establishment" and "the national administration," they refer to thousands of people, all public employees, engaged in all different kinds of jobs that comprise the government at work—the personnel administrator, the legal adviser, the mail carrier, the food inspector, the nuclear scientist, the budget analyst, the foreign service officer, and so on.

Bureaucracy in the Political System

Bureaucratic Models in the Comparative Context

Bureaucracy is the unavoidable consequence of bigness in our modern society. Any big organization, whether it is a big business, a big church, a big labor union, or a big government, is bureaucratic. Modern government, responsive to welfare and security needs in domestic and foreign affairs, calls for extensive public administration. A great many employees, brought together in large organizations designed to turn policies into programs, automatically constitute a bureaucracy.

Max Weber, a German economist in the early twentieth century, constructed an ideal model of governmental bureaucracy.[2] Since Weber's model serves as the basis for many studies in public administration, it may be helpful for our subsequent analysis of the American bureaucracy to indicate here the classic outlines of his bureaucratic model.

(1) *Hierarchy*. The offices of government are arranged in reference to each

---

[1] Carl J. Friedrich, *Constitutional Government and Democracy* (Boston: Ginn and Company, 1950), rev. ed., p. 57.
[2] Max Weber, *From Max Weber: Essays in Sociology*, trans. and ed. by H. H. Gerth and C. W. Mills (New York: Oxford University Press, 1946).

other, with lines of authority clearly drawn from apex to base, each lower office being under the constant supervision of a higher office.

(2) *Position Classification.* The organization is based on a division of labor; every office and each position is assigned the appropriate authority to perform their special tasks.

(3) *Professional Management.* An administrative class is developed, with special competencies and technical skills, to meet the qualifications required for the various positions. Bureaucracy becomes a career; entrance is by competitive examination and promotion is by merit.

(4) *Formal Framework.* Rules and regulations are formulated; records are written and filed; to obtain machine-like efficiency, the organization is made as neutral and depersonalized as possible.

The Weberian model is a mental construct which Weber himself admitted could not be found in reality. It was conditioned by his own knowledge and experience with European systems of public administration, which had developed out of army and church organizations. Probably it came closest to describing the Prussian bureaucracy of the nineteenth century, but even so it was an idealized version.

If we look at bureaucracies in different countries today we find not only basic similarities but also some quite significant differences. We can generally define bureaucrats in government as those people charged with taking measures to carry out the public policies. Bureaucratic structure usually includes the four salient features of the Weberian model: (1) *hierarchical organization*; (2) *differentiation* or *specialization* in the tasks assigned; (3) *qualifications* and *competence* as the basis for recruitment and promotion; (4) *institutionalization* of procedures. In Western democratic governments, the function of bureaucracy is instrumental: bureaucrats are expected to be politically neutral; divorced from party politics, they are more or less permanent agents of the government regardless of which party happens to be in power.

In the "civic culture" of the United States or of Great Britain, where elected public officials comprise a fairly stable government and provide continuous direction for and oversight of governmental activities, bureaucrats are regarded as public servants, "the civil service." In France or in Germany, which have experienced frequent and violent changes in constitutional authority and drastic shifts in policy leadership, bureaucrats have acquired higher status. In Germany, for example, the bureaucrats managed, by following their institutionalized routine, to carry on the day-to-day activities of government despite the revolutionary changeover from Imperial Germany to the Weimar Republic, the transformation of the Weimar Republic into the Third Reich, the upheaval of World War II, and the establishment of the Federal Republic. Between 1919 and 1954, thousands of German bureaucrats were responsible for maintaining government operations much as usual and at the same time taking what measures were required to effect the very considerable change of policies implicit and explicit in a transition from monarchy to a parliamentary republic, from democracy to a totalitarian system, and from National Socialism to a federal republic.[3] The bureaucrats performed similar services in the

[3] Elke Frank, "The Role of Bureaucracy in Transition", *Journal of Politics*, XXVIII (November, 1966), 725–753.

French government all through the political vicissitudes from the Third French Republic to the Fifth French Republic, and including the Vichy Government. It is therefore understandable why bureaucrats in these countries are regarded more as public officials than as public servants: in times of crisis they are often the only evidence of legitimate authority and continuity in government.

Bureaucrats in the Soviet Union and in other communist countries are expected to serve the policy goals of the party system as well as to carry on the government activities. Since the Communist party apparatus is interlocked with the governmental structure, obviously the bureaucrats cannot maintain a neutral stance; the problem for them of course is simplified by the fact that there is but one party, so they do not really have to serve two masters: the "party" and the government are one and the same. Moreover, on the basis of what we know about the bureaucracy in the Soviet Union, governmental activities are apparently carried on just as efficiently and effectively when the civil service is recruited from the single dominant party as when it is recruited on a nonpartisan basis in the western democracies. Once we have noted the difference in political background, we find that bureaucrats in the Soviet Union, just like bureaucrats in Great Britain or the United States, work in a hierarchical organization; they have specialized tasks, the same tasks that are required in any modern government; to perform these tasks they are recruited on the basis of professional qualifications and competencies; and the procedures they follow are generally routinized.

The relationship between ideology and policy is probably made most apparent by the magnitude of the public administration in socialist or communist countries. The traditional American respect for private enterprise and the belief (honored more in the breach than in the observance) that "that government is best which governs least" puts less demand upon the public sector in the United States than in Great Britain, or Germany, or France, or the Soviet Union. But even in the United States, in a civilian labor force of approximately 75 million in 1965, more than 10 million persons were working for national, state, and local governments. Moreover, demands for public services and public regulation in this country continue to increase, which of course means that still more bureaucrats must be recruited to take care of the additional activities.

The role of bureaucrats in the developing countries is perhaps more uncertain and more taxing than in the developed countries. The overriding goals in nation-building are political and economic development, and policies to meet these goals call for dynamic rather than stable government, innovation rather than continuity. In the early crises of nation-building, before the government has been able to institutionalize the political system and to integrate it with the social structure, the tenure of bureaucrats may be as brief as that of the current leadership. In most new nations, where authority is established by military dictatorship or promoted by charismatic leadership, bureaucrats are likely to be drawn from the dominant elite, who regard their functions as more political than administrative, more goal-oriented rather than task-minded. The high priority given to socio-economic progress requires a great deal of government planning and programing. The more grandiose the schemes to modernize the nation the more impossible it becomes for the elite to furnish enough experienced administrators with managerial capacity and development skills. Hence, on several accounts, it may appear that the bureaucracy is the weakest component in developing political systems.

The behavioral pattern of bureaucrats in the western democratic model is more or less prescribed by professional discipline. Friedrich suggests that "there are several behavioral traits that any government is apt to cultivate in a bureaucrat. Among these the most important are objectivity, discretion, precision, and consistency."[4] We have, however, already pointed out that "objectivity" is not one of the traits which a communist government is likely to cultivate in its bureaucrats. Certainly the National Socialists demanded a passionate commitment to the Third Reich. In the American ethic, it is considered reprehensible for the public administrator to enhance his private interests while taking measures for the government; we pass laws to prohibit such "conflict of interest." But in a developing country the interaction of public and private interests may have a highly respectable, pragmatic basis. In Chapter 4, "The First New Nation," we pointed out that the American Founding Fathers had some private vested interests in strengthening the national government. We might also observe that the salient features of the Weberian model were not nearly so well developed either in Great Britain or in the United States in the days when they were becoming modern states.

Friedrich notes that the professional discipline and the concept of rationality which circumscribe the behavior of public officials are culture-bound. What appears unethical or irrational in one system may seem quite correct and practical in another. This is a point to remember when one looks critically at "deviations" from the norms of bureaucratic behavior in other cultures, especially in the new nations.[5] In the United States, for example, we are inclined to forget that in the period of our own most rapid development American civil servants did not always make honesty and efficiency the *sine qua non* of bureaucratic behavior.

Ferrel Heady offers a "comparative perspective" from his background as a theorist and a practitioner of public administration in this country and abroad. After examining the role of bureaucrats in widely diverse settings, he finds that every modern government has a public service which meets the minimum structural requirement for bureaucracy, but he perceives "no standard pattern of relationships between public bureaucracy and the political system as a whole."[6] That is, bureaucrats function in every country, more or less effectively, regardless of whether the people generally participate in the political process, whether one or more parties exist, whether civil liberties are respected, whether public policy is responsible to demands and supports, whether there is a high degree of pluralism in the society or an all-pervasive ideol-

[4] Carl J. Friedrich, *Man and His Government* (New York: McGraw-Hill Book Co., 1963), p. 471.
[5] See Joseph LaPalombara (ed.), *Bureaucracy and Political Development* (Princeton, N.J.: Princeton University Press, 1963), especially the introductory essays by LaPalombara.
[6] Ferrel Heady, *Public Administration: A Comparative Perspective* (Englewood Cliffs, N.J.: Prentice-Hall, Inc., 1966), p. 110.

ogy. The effectiveness of the bureaucratic performance, however, must be measured within the framework of its own political system, and bureaucratic behavior must be judged within its own cultural context.

The Nature of the American Bureaucracy

From the very outset, American government has expanded at a steadily accelerating rate, until today its activities and services pervade the daily life of every citizen.

Although the powers delegated by the Constitution to the national government seem modest enough and there have been few additions to the original list, to set down what are regarded as the "necessary and proper" functions of our national government today would be a herculean job. Under its power to regulate "commerce among the states," the national government has assumed almost countless tasks—fixing rates in interstate transportation; regulating the stock markets; preventing unfair trade practices; protecting labor unions; prohibiting child labor; supporting farm prices; fixing agricultural marketing quotas; licensing radio and television stations; enforcing antitrust laws; requiring safety devices on trains, trucks, buses, and airplanes; and forbidding the transportation across state lines of women for immoral purposes.

National security, military defense, diplomatic activities, foreign aid, stockpiling strategic materials, social security, public assistance for the needy, old-age and survivors' insurance, veterans' benefits, atomic research, public health measures, medical research, regulation of banking, control of credit, hydroelectric development, flood control, postal service, park services, crime prevention, administration of justice, and aids for highway construction, housing, slum clearance, disaster relief, and hospital construction: these are only a few of the activities and services now undertaken by our national government—in extension of its enumerated powers.

The national administration is organized to do many different kinds of jobs for the American people. The governmental organization varies in pattern and grows in size in response to changing and enlarging public needs. Some Americans say, as former President Hoover once did, that the national bureaucracy is "immensely too big." But the reasons for big government today are plain enough. The extension of our national boundaries from Maine to Hawaii and from Alaska to Florida, and the growth of population from under 4 million to over 200 million; these two factors, without any other complications, would alone account for a tremendous expansion in the scope of American government. There are, however, many complications in the democratic government of a modern pluralistic society.

The Industrial Revolution and phenomenal developments in technology since 1787 have caused massive changes in the social and economic life of the nation. In this new environment—urban, industrial, vastly impersonal—the individual has often been described as alone and helpless in the crowd. But individuals join in groups, and in groups they bring pressures upon the government to promote their various interests and to regulate areas of conflict.

In Chapter 8 we noted some of the techniques of the many special interest groups active in American politics. The mushrooming bureaucracy of the modern state is in large measure the direct result of government's attempts to accommodate such private group pressures. The Departments of Agriculture, Commerce, and Labor are impressive examples of governmental agencies established at the behest of large organized groups within the general public. The causal link between technological development and governmental expansion is obvious in the creation of such regulatory agencies as the Federal Power Commission, the Federal Communications Commission, and the National Aeronautics and Space Administration.

If, as we have indicated, the expansion of governmental activities is in direct response to new needs and increasing demands in American society, if the bureaucracy is organized to serve the people, to administer the public business efficiently and impartially, why does the specter of bureaucracy haunt American politics? Why do so many Americans use the word "bureaucratic" as a sort of political cuss word?

One may plausibly reply that the closer American bureaucrats conform to the Weberian model or Friedrich's pattern of proper behavior, the more likely they are to irritate us. The bigger an organization gets and the greater the personnel force required to perform its many and complicated tasks, the more necessary it is for bureaucracy to become hierarchical, with increasing "red tape" and institutionalized procedures. Something in us all, however, rebels against being considered as Social Security No. 266–64–4732; Standard Oil National Credit Card 113–208–604–4; GTO license number 938951; Parking Permit No. 739; zip code 22101. We don't want to be treated equally; we want of the bureaucrat and the rigid rules by which he operates are needed to insure that the decisions of those in power are made on relevant grounds to be treated specially. We want the income tax collector, the customs inspector, the highway patrolman, and the school administrator to recognize that our case is different and to treat it accordingly. We understand, of course, that the standardized procedures of bureaucracy are a way of trying to attain fair treatment for others in large scale organizations, whether in big schools, big business, or big government. We realize that the objectivity and impersonality which are reasonably predictable and impartial. Still, we take cold comfort in knowing that if bureaucrats are not free to discriminate against us, neither are they free to do us favors.

The public administration in the United States is big, too big for us to deal with in all its aspects. Figure 12–1 indicates the size of the American bureaucracy and its distribution of workers in our federal system. In this chapter, as we go on to talk about bureaucrats we do not have in mind *all* the employees in the American governments (about 10 million of these), but only the executive and administrative class in the national government. In this selected group we include the presidential appointments to executive offices (about 1600) and the career executives in the top grades of the civil service (about 20,000).

Approximately 2.8 million persons are on the national government's civilian payroll, but this figure can be quite misleading as to the overall dimensions of the national bureaucracy. Despite a considerable increase in government activities, the statistics seem to show about the same number of employees in the national government since the cutback in personnel following World War II. Actually, the national government now contracts for the services of many people outside the official establishment to perform what are essentially governmental activities. Accurate figures in this area are hard to come by. According to one estimate, some 6 million persons are at work indirectly for the national government, which pays them through contracts, grants, and other arrangements.[7] One must also add some 3 million more men and women in the armed services, many of whom are assigned duties which might normally be performed by civil servants.

Approximately 2.4 million persons are employed in the competitive U.S. civil service; this comprises 90 per cent of all those employed in the country and 87 per cent of all those employed overseas. The composition of the national government's work force is extremely complex and is constantly changing in line with new policies that require new tasks. Currently, about 41 per cent of

THE SIZE OF THE FEDERAL CIVILIAN WORK FORCE — SOME COMPARISONS

U.S. Armed Forces
3,090,000 members

U.S. Government Civilian
2,760,000 employees

State Government
2,160,000 employees

Local Government
6,160,000 employees

Source: U.S. Civil Service Commission, 1967.

Figure 12-1

the civilian workers are employed by the Department of Defense, another 24 per cent work for the Post Office, and 6 per cent are in the Veterans' Administration; that leaves 29 per cent to cover all of the other agencies, including such big and diverse departments as Treasury; Health, Education and Welfare; Agriculture; and Interior.

Civilian workers in the national government are engaged in nearly every kind of job found in private employment, as well as many which are found only in the public administration. White-collar workers account for 52 per cent of all full-time employees; blue-collar 26 per cent; and the postal employees 22 per cent. Figure 12–2 gives a more detailed breakdown of the occupational distribution of the federal white-collar workers. About half of the white-collar

[7]Franklin P. Kilpatrick, Milton C. Cummings, Jr., M. Kent Jennings, *The Image of the Federal Service* (Washington, D.C.: The Brookings Institution, 1964), p. 40.

OCCUPATIONAL DISTRIBUTION OF FEDERAL WHITE-COLLAR WORKERS

Science, Medicine, Engineering — 14.0%
All Other Professional — 6.6%
Technical, Science Support — 8.7%
Administrative — 8.7%
All Other Administrative Technical — 4.5%
Government Occupations, (taxes, customs etc.) — 8.3%

Professional, Technical, and Kindred — 50.8%
Clerical and Kindred — 36.8%
All Other — 12.4%

Aid-Assistant — 4.1%
Specialized clerical — 8.5%
General Clerical — 24.3%
Police, Fire, Miscellaneous — 12.4%

Source: U.S. Civil Service Commission, 1967.

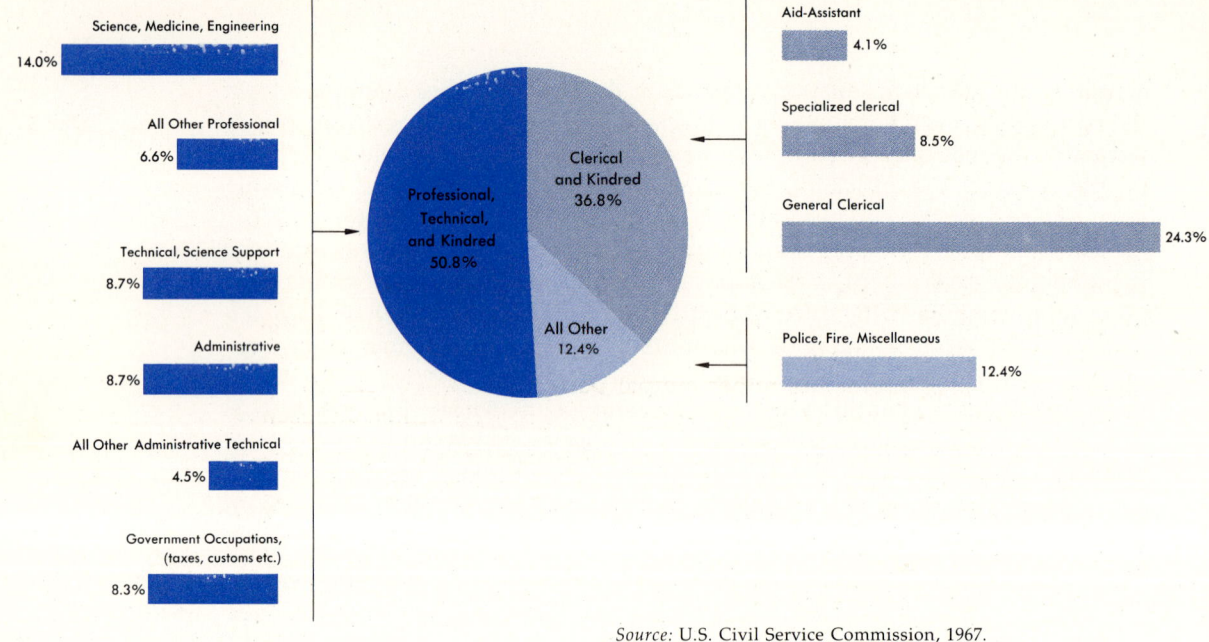

Figure 12-2

workers are in the professional and technical classification. Note that 8.7 per cent are classified as administrative. Only a small fraction of the national civil service is located in Washington; roughly 83 per cent are dispersed through the country, in every state; 5 per cent are stationed in foreign countries, and 1 per cent in the territories of the United States.

The United States Government *Organization Manual* presents some 40 organizational charts of the major executive agencies; each one seems to follow the Weberian model as to hierarchy in organization and differentiation of activities. But when we look at these same agencies, as they actually operate, we discover that neat and orderly charts can be quite deceiving. The American government has expanded so fast, especially since the 1930s, that like Topsy, its agencies "just growed." Despite recurrent reorganization, the lines of authority blur and activities seem to overlap, and even compete, from one office to another. As we shall see later, many of the agencies were created largely in response to pressure groups seeking favors from the government. Some agencies more than others appear to be clientele-oriented. When President Johnson proposed a merging of the Departments of Commerce and Labor in 1967, he was assailed by the highly vociferous clienteles of both departments as well as by the bureaucrats who had over the years developed their strong vested interests in separate organizations. The President beat a hasty retreat from that proposal.

Public administration in the United States has always been touched by personal and partisan considerations. The model of an objective and politically neutral body of administrators is alien to the American culture. The admini-

446

strative class on which Weber counted for professional management and special competence was slow to develop in the American civil service. Careers in public service have never been as prestigious in the United States as in the western European democracies. When de Tocqueville visited America in the 1830s he was struck by the fact that "public officers in the United States are not separate from the mass of citizens. . . . No public officer in the United States has an official costume but every one of them receives a salary." Tocqueville thought it important in a democracy that everyone be paid for public services "so that everyone has not merely a right but also the means of performing them."[8] From this rather simple point of view, we can say that the character of the American civil service was shaped by the democratic society in which it developed. And it is still true that American officials wear no uniforms, form no separate class, enjoy no special privileges or immunities, and move freely into and out of public employment.

Organization and Management in the National Government

The Constitution does not spell out how government activities should be organized and managed. It simply says that the President "may require the opinion in writing of the principal officer in each of the executive departments upon any subject relating to the duties of their respective offices." Today, however, many important federal activities are carried on outside the executive departments—in regulatory commissions, corporations, and other independent agencies.

The President's Cabinet

The government now has twelve executive departments: State (1789), Treasury (1789), Defense (1947), Justice (1870), Post Office (1872), Interior (1849), Agriculture (1862), Commerce (1913), Labor (1913), Health, Education, and Welfare (1953), Housing and Urban Development (1965), and Transportation (1966). Each executive department is headed by a Secretary appointed by the President with the consent of the Senate. The twelve secretaries are recognized as the top political figures in the national administration; they are in the so-called line of succession to the presidency; they sit in the President's Cabinet; each heads a large and important operating agency; and next to the President and Vice-President, they earn the highest salaries in the administrative hierarchy.

The President's Cabinet dates back to the first administration of George Washington. Washington had been snubbed when he tried to use the Senate as an advisory council, and had been rebuffed when he went to the Supreme Court for an advisory opinion. So he turned for collective advice to his principal administrative officers (the Secretary of State, the Secretary of Treasury, the

---

[8] Phillips Bradley (ed.), *Democracy in America* (New York: Random House, Inc. (Vintage Books), 1954), I, pp. 214–216.

Secretary of War, and the Attorney General). This was the informal beginning of the President's Cabinet. Soon it was institutionalized and given regular status, but not until the second administration of Theodore Roosevelt was it mentioned in federal law (1907). The Senate customarily confirms the President's nominations to his Cabinet with little hesitation, although Senators occasionally question a nominee's qualifications, as when they examined the business interests of Charles E. Wilson, Eisenhower's nominee for the Secretary of Defense in 1953.

Because Cabinet positions are regarded as top prizes in national politics, party loyalty figures high in the appointments. Sometimes for strategic reasons, however, a President will make at least a pretense of bipartisanship, as when Franklin D. Roosevelt appointed two distinguished Republicans, Henry L. Stimson and Frank Knox, to serve in his wartime Cabinet as Secretaries of War and Navy.[9] President Eisenhower thought it good politics to recognize the "Democrats for Eisenhower" by naming a Texas Democrat, Mrs. Oveta Culp Hobby, as his first Secretary of Health, Education and Welfare.

As a presidential candidate, John F. Kennedy promised that "all appointments, both high and low, will be made on the basis of ability." No doubt, however, the narrow margin of his party victory in 1960 induced President Kennedy to name two Republicans to key posts in the New Frontier: the Secretary of the Treasury, C. Douglas Dillon, and the Secretary of Defense, Robert McNamara. It is understood to be part of the President's prerogative to choose as his closest advisers persons whose judgment he can trust and whose personal loyalty he need never question. President Kennedy's appointment of his brother Robert as Attorney-General and of his brother-in-law Sargent Shriver as Director of the Peace Corps were obviously personal appointments.[10]

Upon the assassination of President Kennedy, Lyndon Johnson declared that he wanted no immediate innovations in the Kennedy administration. "President Kennedy left a program well outlined in its content; I will carry out all of the late President's commitments." To achieve this end, he felt that continuity of personnel was essential. Hence he urged all of the principal officers, including members of the Cabinet, to stay at their posts. He made the appeal partly on personal grounds, but also in terms of the nation's needs. When President Johnson was elected in his own right in 1964, many people expected immediate changes in the Cabinet posts. To the contrary, however, there was remarkably little turnover in the top positions. Indeed, Secretary of State Dean Rusk and Secretary of Defense McNamara set a record for tenure through two presidential administrations.

Although a President has a fairly free hand in the selection of his Cabinet,

---

[9] Announcement of these "patriotic" appointments was made on the eve of the Republican National Convention in 1940. Angry Republicans cried "double cross" and demanded that Stimson and Knox be "read out of the party." On the other hand, Democratic party regulars like Jim Farley denounced the "party betrayal."

[10] One remembers that President Eisenhower used his brother Milton on various confidential assignments and that he brought a number of his former military aides into the White House circle. See Marian D. Irish, "The Kennedy Administration: Appraisal at the Halfway Mark," in Jack W. Peltason (ed.), *1963–64 American Government Annual*, (New York: Holt, Rinehart & Winston, Inc., 1963), pp. 33–60.

certain demands are bound to limit his choice. The idea of a "balanced Cabinet" is based on recognition of party, geographic, and socio-economic factors as well as on special capabilities. Richard Fenno, who provides us with a first-rate analysis of the Cabinet in the period from Wilson to Eisenhower, points out that the process of Cabinet selection "finds its underlying consistency in the fundamental pluralism of American politics."[11] It is politic, for example, to name both a Jew and a Catholic to the Cabinet; it is also politic to include a representative of organized labor and other major interest groups. President Johnson's appointment of Robert Weaver as Secretary of Housing and Urban Development, the first Negro to attain a Cabinet position, was an appointment based on the qualifications and competence of the appointee; it was also shrewd political strategy.

Just how effectively the President and his Cabinet work together depends largely on their personalities. Franklin D. Roosevelt met regularly with his Cabinet, and played on rivalries among members to draw forth their conflicting views. But he never really used his Cabinet for collective policy-making. On such important matters as the "court-packing plan" and the development of the atomic bomb, he neither consulted with nor informed them in advance. President Truman introduced the device of a prepared agenda for Cabinet meetings, discussed all general policies with his Cabinet, and made a point of summarizing their collective judgment. Nevertheless, he made it clear that the Cabinet must follow the direction of the President. He simply would not brook public opposition from any Cabinet member. As he expressed it,

> When a cabinet member speaks publicly, he usually speaks on authorization of the President, in which case he speaks for the President. If he takes it upon himself to announce a policy that is contrary to the policy the President wants carried out, he can cause a great deal of trouble.[12]

President Eisenhower attempted to turn his Cabinet into a "political team." He established a Cabinet secretariat to deal with interdepartmental affairs, circulated a prepared agenda before meetings, called for "briefs" on different points of view, tried to achieve collective decisions, and authorized the release of "major policy statements" after Cabinet meetings. It does not appear, however, that this approach resulted in any greater sense of collective responsibility, for the Eisenhower Cabinet from the outset was marked by public bickering, which the President usually tolerated with rare good humor. President Kennedy, in an early TV talk to the public on how he expected to run his administration, explained that he preferred to meet with individual Cabinet members on particular problems and to keep in daily contact with the separate departments. He felt that large, formal, and regular meetings were "unnecessary and involve a waste of time."[13] When President Johnson sud-

---

[11] Richard Fenno, *The President's Cabinet* (New York: Random House, Inc. (Vintage Books), 1959), p. 87.
[12] Harry S Truman, *Memoirs* (Garden City, N.Y.: Doubleday & Company, Inc., 1955), I, p. 329.
[13] *The New York Times*, April 12, 1961.

denly was called to take charge, he relied much more on the Cabinet as an institution. Whereas Kennedy preferred dealing with Cabinet members individually, Johnson (at first) found greater support in collective meetings. But more recently President Johnson has been meeting less regularly with the Cabinet and more frequently with key members of his administration. The President's "Tuesday Lunch" with his Secretary of State, Secretary of Defense, and the White House Adviser on National Security Affairs suggests that he too finds it more helpful to deliberate on policy matters informally off the record rather than to engage in formal discussion at Cabinet meetings.

Professor Fenno concludes that "the Cabinet as a collectivity has only a symbolic value, a value which readily disappears when the need for action supersedes the need for a show window."[14] Indeed, the prestige enjoyed by the American Cabinet seems to spring more from political tradition and protocol than from actual power in the government. Individual Secretaries may be very important to the President, as Acheson was to Truman, Dulles to Eisenhower, and Robert Kennedy to his brother. But they have no responsibility as a group for furnishing broad political leadership. Moreover, the independent regulatory commissions and such important agencies as the Veterans' Administration and the Tennessee Valley Authority are excluded from the Cabinet. President Eisenhower frequently invited to Cabinet meetings such officials as the Chairman of the Civil Service Commission, the U.S. Ambassador to the United Nations, the Director of the Budget, and the Assistant to the President, but this never became a regular practice. The Cabinet seldom gets any further than discussing interdepartmental matters; its decisions are not binding even on its own members; and neither the President nor Congress is bound to heed its "major policy statements."

Many political scientists have proposed ways of strengthening the Cabinet's role in government. Some have suggested that Cabinet members be invited to sit in Congress and participate in debates that concern their particular departments. Senator Estes Kefauver long urged that Congress follow the British practice of a "question hour" in which congressmen could call on Cabinet members to answer questions about the executive policies of the day. Still another suggestion is that the Cabinet membership be expanded to include key congressmen, who could then participate in policy discussions. The Constitution, however, forbids congressmen to hold posts in the administration.

Some political scientists have urged fundamental constitutional reforms in the relations between the executive and legislative departments to provide for real Cabinet government, in which the heads of executive departments would be collectively responsible for policy decisions. W. Y. Elliott, Professor of International Relations at American University, has long advocated that the Constitution be amended to give the President the right to designate ten to twenty of his principal department or agency heads to sit and vote in both the Senate and the House. Elliott argues that this reform would strengthen the President's prestige in Congress and "bridge the appalling gap that exists between the two ends of Pennsylvania Avenue—the White House and the Capitol."[15]

---

[14] *The President's Cabinet*, p. 247.
[15] William Y. Elliott, Chairman, *United States Foreign Policy*, Report of a Study Group for the Woodrow Wilson Foundation (New York: Columbia University Press, 1952), p. 259.

Since separation of powers has created separate vested interests in the executive and legislative branches, however, constitutional reform of the Cabinet seems unlikely. We are thus inclined to agree with Professor Fenno that the Cabinet is both "useful and immovable." It will probably never serve as the central agent of government-wide coordination, as cabinets are expected to do in parliamentary governments, but it does serve as a consultative group to the President and in its very diversity represents the basic pluralism of the American political system.

The Executive Departments

The typical pattern of departmental organization (as indicated in the pyramidal charts in the *Organization Manual*) is hierarchical, with levels of authority clearly established from the Secretary as the chief executive of the department to the lowest level of boxes in the bureaucracy. Each department carries on activities that are more or less related to a single major function, such as conduct of foreign affairs, administration of justice, finance, or national security.

It is not entirely accurate to claim that each department carries on activities that are generally grouped around a single function. Obviously the Department of Health, Education and Welfare performs three disparate functions. Four of the departments—Agriculture, Commerce, Labor, and Housing and Urban Development—serve particular clienteles rather than more general functions. And the description of the departmental organization as hierarchical blurs the fact that a good many of the bureaus in the departments tend to be independent, e.g., the Federal Bureau of Investigation in the Justice Department, the Corps of Engineers in the Defense Department, and the Agency for International Development in the State Department. Autonomy of operating units within a department usually point to political demands outside the department which support this semidetached relationship.

The Hoover Commission in 1949 made an imposing report with many recommendations for improving the general management of the executive branch. The Commission was a bipartisan, six-man group under the chairmanship of former President Hoover, assisted by special research committees called task forces. The Hoover Commission was officially named "The Commission on Organization of the Executive Branch of the Government." It was said at the time that Congress avoided the term "reorganization" because it recognized that the executive branch had *never* been "organized." It was not organized in Washington's day, nor in Jackson's. Presidents Taft, Wilson, Hoover, Roosevelt, and Truman tackled the job, but none were really successful.

The Hoover Commission reported that the executive branch in 1949 was "a chaos of bureaus and subdivisions." The commissioners were appalled by the number of separate agencies, the proliferation of programs, and the lack of uniformity in structure, methods, and procedures. Great confusion existed within the departments and agencies as well as in their relations to the President and to one another. The commissioners searched in vain for clear lines of authority and responsibility. They could find no common conception of the organization, functions, or mission of an executive department. They were disturbed by the various degrees of congressional control over departmental organization and management. Approximately one-third of the bureau chiefs were appointed by the President with the consent of the Senate. In some instances the lack of coordination within departments was the direct result of congressional specifications on organization. Of all the departments and agencies that were operating field services, only in the Veterans' Administration had field workers developed a clear line of communications with the national offices, "and there was some question whether this was working effectively." Most of the departments were weak in "top management"; department heads were in desperate need of more assistance in policy-planning, programing, and public relations.[16]

[16]The Hoover Commission Reports are available in nineteen separate pamphlets printed by the Government Printing Office since 1949. The nineteenth summarizes and indexes the earlier pamphlets. It is entitled *Concluding Report: A Report to the Congress by the Commission on Organization of the Executive Branch of the Government* (Washington, D.C.: U.S. Government Printing Office, 1949). The reports of the research committees have also been printed by the Government Printing Office, designated as "Task Force Reports." Although the findings of the Commission and its numerous research committees appear to be entirely factual, we must be careful to interpret them within the Commission's particular frame of reference, which assumed that efficiency and economy are the paramount goals of government. The Commission endorsed centralization of responsibility, unitary organization, uniform procedures, integration of field services, and top management programing. Not all students of public administration, however, are so convinced that these principles comprise the *sine qua non* for good government.

"Testing — one billion . . .
two billion . . .
three billion . . ."

Drawing by Mort Temes;
© 1964 The Saturday Review.

Following the Report of the Hoover Commission, Congress passed the Reorganization Act of 1949 authorizing the President to reorganize the executive branch, subject to congressional veto of his proposals. Since then every President has struggled with the problem of how to reorganize the administration on a more rational basis. President Truman submitted 41 reorganization plans, Congress rejected 11 of them; President Eisenhower proposed 17 plans, Congress turned down 3; President Kennedy recommended 10 new plans, Congress vetoed 4. It is still too early to tally President Johnson's score; he is still at bat. The 1964 Reorganization Act authorizes him, however, to submit to Congress his plans to reorganize agencies through transfer, abolition, or consolidation of agency functions, with the proviso that the President may not create a new executive department by reorganization plan. Each presidential plan takes effect automatically within 60 days unless disapproved by a majority vote of either chamber.

The United States Government *Organization Manual* now takes about 50 pages of fine print to list the many reorganizations in the executive branch since 1933. But still it must be said that most of the departmental organizations are a long way from approaching the Weberian model.

The State Department is a good example of departmental organization. It is the oldest department in the national administration, having been created by the Continental Congress in 1781 and reconstituted without interruption of functions by an Act of Congress signed by President Washington in 1789. At the head is the Secretary of State, who sits in the President's Cabinet and usually acts as the President's right-hand man on all matters relating to foreign affairs. Sixty-three men have served as Secretary of State, from Thomas Jefferson in 1790 to Dean Rusk. Six of these later became President of the United States (Thomas Jefferson, James Madison, James Monroe, John Quincy Adams, Martin Van Buren, and James Buchanan); two were later appointed Chief Justice of the Supreme Court (John Marshall and Charles Evans Hughes). General George Marshall was the only noncivilian to hold the office.

The Secretary of State is responsible for all the activities of the Department (see Fig. 12–3). His alter ego is the Under Secretary, who is Acting Secretary in the Secretary's absence, a frequent occurrence in this era of summit diplomacy. In consultation with the assistant secretaries, the Under Secretary acts as principal coordinator of activities for the geographic and functional bureaus of the Department. Assistant secretaries head the geographic bureaus—Inter-American Affairs, European Affairs, East Asian and Pacific Affairs, Near Eastern and South Asian Affairs, African Affairs, and the Bureau of International Organization Affairs. Additional line or functional bureaus carry on a variety of activities, including liaison with Congress, intelligence and research, educational and cultural affairs, and public affairs. The bureaus are subdivided into offices with further differentiation of tasks calling for special competencies. An Under Secretary for Economic Affairs provides guidance and overall direction on matters of economic foreign policy and acts as the Department's policy representative for AID. A Deputy Under Secretary

DEPARTMENT OF STATE

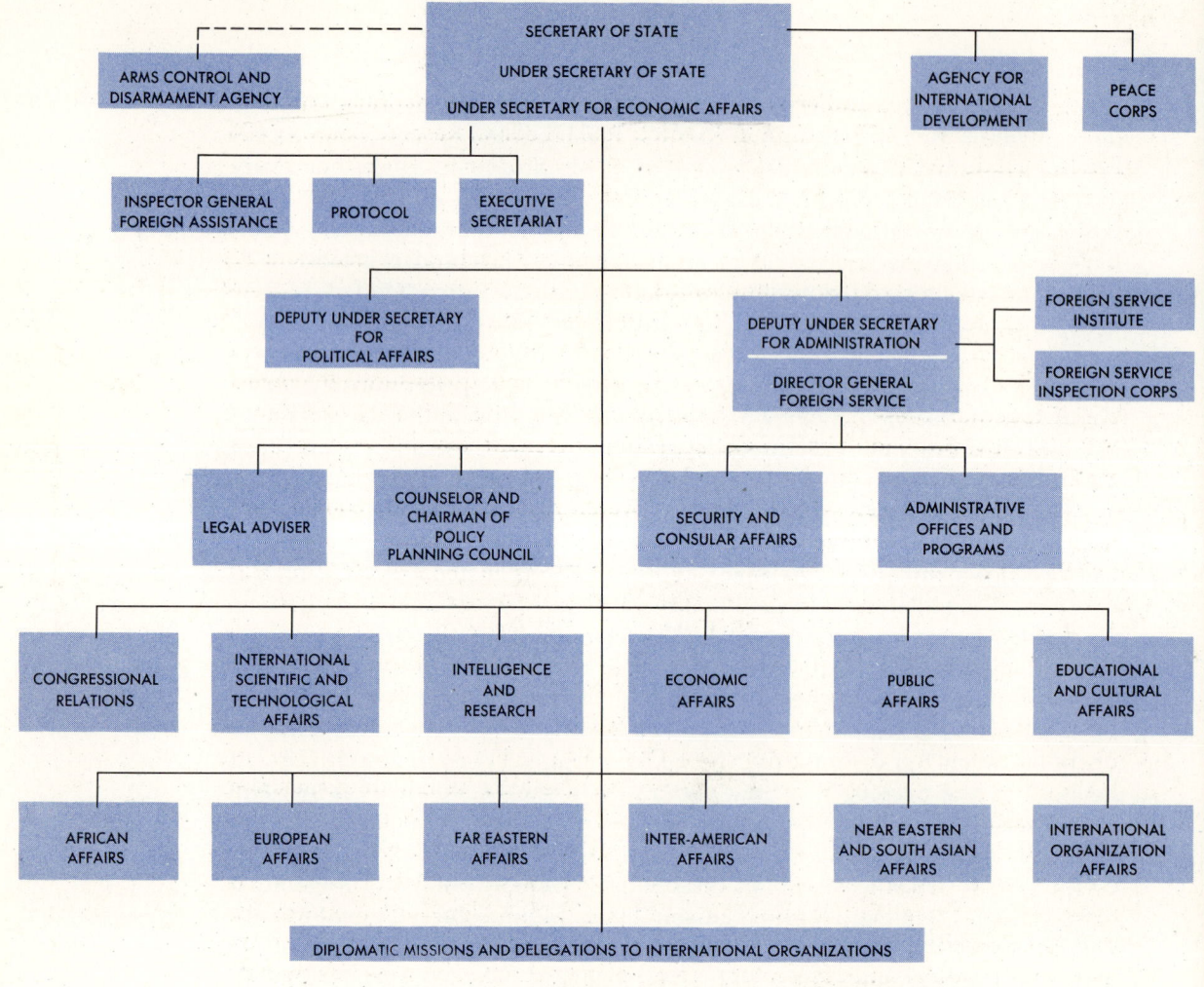

```
SECRETARY OF STATE
UNDER SECRETARY OF STATE
UNDER SECRETARY FOR ECONOMIC AFFAIRS
```

- ARMS CONTROL AND DISARMAMENT AGENCY
- AGENCY FOR INTERNATIONAL DEVELOPMENT
- PEACE CORPS

- INSPECTOR GENERAL FOREIGN ASSISTANCE
- PROTOCOL
- EXECUTIVE SECRETARIAT

- DEPUTY UNDER SECRETARY FOR POLITICAL AFFAIRS
- DEPUTY UNDER SECRETARY FOR ADMINISTRATION
  - DIRECTOR GENERAL FOREIGN SERVICE
- FOREIGN SERVICE INSTITUTE
- FOREIGN SERVICE INSPECTION CORPS

- LEGAL ADVISER
- COUNSELOR AND CHAIRMAN OF POLICY PLANNING COUNCIL
- SECURITY AND CONSULAR AFFAIRS
- ADMINISTRATIVE OFFICES AND PROGRAMS

- CONGRESSIONAL RELATIONS
- INTERNATIONAL SCIENTIFIC AND TECHNOLOGICAL AFFAIRS
- INTELLIGENCE AND RESEARCH
- ECONOMIC AFFAIRS
- PUBLIC AFFAIRS
- EDUCATIONAL AND CULTURAL AFFAIRS

- AFRICAN AFFAIRS
- EUROPEAN AFFAIRS
- FAR EASTERN AFFAIRS
- INTER-AMERICAN AFFAIRS
- NEAR EASTERN AND SOUTH ASIAN AFFAIRS
- INTERNATIONAL ORGANIZATION AFFAIRS

DIPLOMATIC MISSIONS AND DELEGATIONS TO INTERNATIONAL ORGANIZATIONS

Source: United States Government Organization Manual, 1967-68 (Washington, D. C.: U.S. Government Printing Office, 1967), p. 622.

Figure 12-3

for Administration manages the housekeeping activities of the Department, including security and consular affairs, personnel and fiscal matters. In the official hierarchy, the chain of command runs from Secretary to Under Secretary to Deputy Under Secretary to Assistant Secretary to Office Directors. When we come to discuss the role of bureaucrats in the policy process, however, we shall see that this is a model of administration and not the situation in reality.

Other Executive Agencies

The *United States Government Organization Manual* lists more than 40 independent agencies that function outside the departmental organization. Some are small and obscure; others are large and powerful. In the latter category are the *regulatory boards and commis-*

454

sions, whose services and activities affect vital areas in our national economy: Interstate Commerce Commission (created 1887), Federal Reserve Board (1913), Federal Trade Commission (1915), Federal Power Commission (1920), Federal Communications Commission (1934), Securities and Exchange Commission (1934), National Labor Relations Board (1935), Civil Aeronautics Board (1938), Atomic Energy Commission (1946). All have certain features in common. All are headed by boards or commissions with multiple membership. All are outside the executive departments and are free from direct responsibility to the President. All engage in policy-making and regulatory activities, mostly in the economic sphere. All have quasi-legislative and quasi-judicial powers. Taken together, these commissions exercise tremendous authority over transportation by railroad, bus, truck, pipeline, merchant marine, and airlines; communication by telephone, telegraphy, radio, and television; hydroelectric development, interstate electric power, water resources, flood control, and interstate transportation of natural gas; unfair trade practices in industry and commerce; unfair labor practices in labor-management relations; banking practices, credit policies, issuance of securities, and trading in the national stock markets.

Many reasons are suggested for setting up the independent regulatory commissions outside the departmental structure. Since the commissions have quasi-judicial duties, such duties can best be performed by independent and impartial persons. Also, since regulatory tasks often involve rule-making authority—quasi-legislative power which has the force of law upon business and industry—it is argued that such rule-making functions should be handled by a plural body in which several points of view may find expression. A more philosophical justification stems from the concept of separation of powers; because the regulatory commission exercises judicial, legislative, and executive functions, it ought not to be put wholly under the chief executive. In the more experimental and exploratory stages of regulation, Congress has thought it wiser to create new and independent agencies in order to insure maximum leeway in the development of new procedures and standards of administration. In some fields of policy-making, where regional representation seems desirable, the plural commission rather than the departmental unit more easily secures geographical distribution of decision-makers. Many of the tasks of regulation are complicated and technical, and experienced experts are more readily recruited if they are offered freedom from political pressures and partisan control. The Interstate Commerce Commission, first of the independent commissions, was considered generally successful; this encouraged Congress to continue the pattern and to promise the regulatory commissions their "independence from politics."[17]

[17] Robert E. Cushman sums up the more important reasons that led Congress to establish the commissions outside the departmental structure. See his Special Study, *The Problem of the Independent Regulatory Commissions,* in Report with Special Studies, President's Committee on Administrative Management (Washington, D.C.: U.S. Government Printing Office, 1937). A brief adaptation of the study is found in Dwight Waldo (ed.), *Ideas and Issues in Public Administration* (New York: McGraw-Hill Book Company, 1953), pp. 138–155.

The *government corporation* is another device for carrying on public business with a minimum of presidential direction or congressional control. The government corporation is organized much like its counterpart in private business, and its function is much the same—to conduct an economic enterprise. Since most government corporations have been creatures of war and depression, they have been rather short-lived experiments. Actually, however, the corporation is one of the oldest forms of federal administration. It dates back to the Bank of North America, chartered by the Continental Congress in 1781, and to the United States Bank, chartered by Congress in 1791.

In 1936, the President's Committee on Administrative Management listed 93 government corporations, presumably the peak number. The Committee spoke favorably of the "freedom of operation, flexibility, business efficiency, and opportunity for experimentation" that were possible in these autonomous, business-like organizations. Typically, the government corporation of that time was created by Congress with an act of incorporation that defined its functions and placed it under an independent board of directors. The corporation was generally given capital to carry on its activities, authority to borrow money, freedom to buy and sell commodities, the right to sue and be sued, and exemption from many overhead controls in budgeting, accounting, and personnel management. Powerful business groups, however, objected to the competition of these public corporations. Moreover, the bureaucrats in top management pressed for the adoption of the same procedures and practices required of other agencies, "coordination" with the rest of the executive branch.

The Corporation Control Act of 1945 subjected government corporations to most of the fiscal controls applied to other departments. Thus the General Accounting Office and the Bureau of the Budget have some control over the corporations, which must submit to a "customary commercial corporation audit" by the GAO, and must channel their budgets to Congress through the Budget Bureau and the President. The corporations must have specific congressional authorization for capital expenditures; and no corporation may be created except by Congress, thus ending the earlier practice of establishing them by executive order. In addition to these restrictions imposed in 1945, other laws have further reduced the autonomy of government corporations. Most have been placed under the Civil Service Commission, for example, thus depriving them of their discretionary power in hiring and firing.

As a result of these changes, it is hard to distinguish most government corporations from agencies in the regular departments. Indeed, many corporations are now pocketed away in the executive departments. The Farm Credit Administration in the Department of Agriculture is a holding company for all the government agencies that lend money to farmers. Federal Prison Industries, Incorporated, is located in the Department of Justice. Only a few corporations retain their independent status—the Export-Import Bank of Washington, the Federal Deposit Insurance Corporation, the Panama Canal Company, the Public Housing Administration, the St. Lawrence Seaway Development Corporation, the Tennessee Valley Authority. The TVA has proved especially hardy, having survived suits in constitutional law, investigations by Congress, internal dissension, and criticism from privately owned public utilities.

Background and Recruitment of Bureaucrats

"The Spoils System"

When President Washington made his several hundred appointments to the federal service, he declared that he had chosen from among the best qualified persons for each job. As his administration became increasingly pro-Federalist, however, it turned out that the "best qualified" were usually Federalists and, when Thomas Jefferson became President in 1800, he found that nearly all the jobs in the federal service were held by Federalists. As leader of the Democratic-Republican Party, Jefferson felt obliged to dispense what patronage he could to friends in his own party who had personally worked for "the great victory." Invoking a rule of "due participation" by both political parties, he immediately removed a great many Federalists to make room for Democratic-Republicans. But he explained that as soon as his party appointees equaled the number of Federalists already in office, he would "return with joy to that state of things when the only questions concerning a candidate shall be, Is he honest? Is he capable? Is he faithful to the Constitution?"

When Andrew Jackson became President in 1829, he at once threw out of office about 10 per cent of the 10,000 employees in the civil service. His enemies charged him with introducing a "spoils system," although Jackson chose to call it "rotation in office." Jackson feared the bureaucracy, convinced that no man could long hold public office without being corrupted. He opposed the development of an office-holding class, and urged Congress to limit all appointments throughout the federal service to four-year terms. In his first annual message in 1829, Jackson made his position clear:

> The duties of all public officers are, or at least admit of being made, so plain and simple that men of intelligence may readily qualify themselves for their performance; and I cannot but believe that more is lost by the long continuance of men in office than is generally to be gained by their experience.

There is still something to be said for "due participation" of the parties and "rotation in office." It is a democratic approach to self-government based on faith in the ability of the common man. It is also a practical way of strengthening the party in power and of achieving more direct political responsibility to the people. James Farley, Postmaster General and Democratic National Chairman during Franklin D. Roosevelt's first term, justified the spoils system as "fair, reasonable, and intelligent." He thought that merit and politics could well be wrapped in the same package. In passing out 150,000 federal jobs to deserving Democrats in the first year of the New Deal, he followed two simple rules: First, is the applicant qualified? Second, is he loyal to the party and sympathetic toward the program of Franklin D. Roosevelt? This was Farley's point of view:

Patronage is a reward to those who have worked for party victory. It is also an assistance in building party machinery for the next election. It is also—and this the public usually forgets—the test by which a party shows its fitness to govern.[18]

But as the federal government grew bigger and bigger over the years, and as its functions became more and more specialized, due participation of the parties and rotation in office were no longer enough to insure an effective public service. The mob scenes that occurred in Washington with every change of party fortunes in the presidency reached a tragic climax in 1881 when President Garfield was shot by a disappointed office-seeker. To cure these evils, a movement for civil service reform had been spearheaded by the National Civil Service Reform League, aided by such persuasive periodicals as *Harper's Weekly* and the *Nation*. At first, the politicians scorned the "snivel service reform" advocated by civic groups but they finally yielded to pressure politics. At last, in 1883, the Pendleton Act established a classified civil service under a Civil Service Commission.

The Competitive System

The Pendleton Act, sometimes called the "Magna Charta" of the civil service, originally affected some 14,000 positions, about 10 per cent of the federal service in 1883. The classified service has since been extended "upward, outward, and downward," until today 80 per cent of federal employees fall under the rules and regulations of the United States Civil Service Commission. Most of the few agencies that do not come under the Commission have established their own merit systems, as in the Tennessee Valley Authority, the Atomic Energy Commission, the Federal Bureau of Investigation, and the Foreign Service. The Classification Act of 1949 groups and grades positions in the civil service according to duties, difficulty, responsibility, and qualifications required. There are 18 grades in the General Schedule, with "equal pay for equal work" within each grade.

The U.S. civil service is open to all, without regard to sex, marital status, race, creed, color, or political affiliation. At least, that is what the law says. In actual practice, certain preferences and some discrimination do exist. Approximately two-thirds of the sub-professional, white-collar workers are women, whereas only a handful of women hold top jobs. Figures are not available on racial and religious backgrounds of civil servants, but in recent years strong political pressure has been exerted to give minority groups more visible representation in administrative and professional positions. In the Kennedy administration, departmental agencies vigorously competed with one another to attract qualified Negroes, especially for front offices. In the Johnson administration, when word went out that "the Chief" wanted more women in top jobs, suddenly an impressive number of qualified women were found deserving of promotion.

A team of researchers at The Brookings Institution, a major research foundation in Washington, recently surveyed national samples of the general

---

[18]James Farley, "Passing Out the Patronage," *American Magazine* (August, 1933), 21.

employed public, academic groups, groups in business, general federal employees, and special groups in the federal service, to ascertain what images come to people's minds at the mention of "federal civil servants." The single trait most frequently cited by the general public was "good personal character." Business groups, who rendered the least favorable overall reactions, frequently mentioned such qualities as "inordinate concern with security" or "lack of ambition and initiative." In answering why people enter the federal service, an overwhelming majority of the general public replied, "security and fringe benefits." Academic groups, particularly college teachers and high-school and college students, stressed the possibilities of service to others as well as security. Answers by the government workers may or may not reveal their own motives; at any rate they echoed the general public in emphasizing security and fringe benefits. But high-level federal employees offered a wide range of motives besides the security explanation, such as specific job opportunities, desire to be of service, and opportunities for self-advancement.

The Brookings staff was impressed by what the respondents did *not* say as well as by what they did say. Apparently, most Americans do not think that a person enters the federal service because it offers a prestige career. On the other hand, they do not believe that federal officials are attracted primarily by love of power. And there were virtually no attributions of low or bad personal character, from which we may infer that there is no widespread concern about corruption in the federal service.[19]

The Brookings study identifies a number of basic changes in the federal civil service since 1789. Among these are:

(1) *Increase in numbers*. In 1801, it is estimated that one American in 2,000 worked for the national government; by 1957, one American in every 80 was a federal employee. Of every 30 members of the civilian labor force, one was employed by the national government. The number of federal civil service employees has remained constant in recent years, but the federal government now farms out many of its activities through contracts, grants, and other arrangements, thereby reducing the official payroll.

(2) *Changing social composition.* In the early years, the federal service was principally attractive to members of the upper socio-economic class. Democratization of our political system, however, has promoted the recruitment of government workers from the total spectrum of American society.

(3) *Increased need for specialists and technicians*. Public administration in the eighteenth century, before the age of industrialization and urbanization, was a relatively simple matter. Today, because of the magnitude and complexity of governmental activities, the federal civil service has a high proportion of managerial, professional, technical, and scientific personnel. In 1960, one in every fifty employees in nongovernment service was engaged in scientific and engineering tasks; in the federal work force the ratio was one in fourteen.

[19]Kilpatrick, Cummings, and Jennings, *The Image of the Federal Service*. See also the companion volume, *Source Book of a Study of Occupational Values and the Image of the Federal Service* (Washington, D.C.: The Brookings Institution, 1964), which presents the detailed data for the entire study.

(4) *Changed ratio of military to civilian services.* Traditionally, the American people have been averse to a large-size, peacetime military force. Only during wartime did many Americans wear uniforms. Ever since the end of the Korean War in 1953, however, the number of persons in the military services has exceeded the number of persons in the civil service.

(5) *Increased fringe benefits.* With the creation of a federal retirement program in 1920, the federal service has developed a comprehensive system of fringe benefits that now include provisions for retirement, vacation and sick-leave pay, group life insurance, health insurance, career development programs, in-service training, and compensation schedules that, except at the very top, compare favorably with those in private enterprise.

The United States Civil Service Commission, set up in 1883, is bipartisan and composed of three members, only two of whom can be from the same political party. For many years, the Commission had two major assignments: (1) devising tenure regulations to insure continuity in administration and to protect civil servants from political pressures; (2) establishing a system of merit examinations to recruit qualified persons into a classified civil service. Over the years, the agency has developed an elaborate system of personnel management that covers the whole range of problems involved in a modern big bureaucracy: recruiting and examining, career development and training, incentive awards, pay and position classification, development of tests and standards, inspection and appraisal of personnel programs, investigations and security appraisals, appeals, retirement, and judicial review of administrative actions.

The Civil Service Commission acts as the central recruiting agency for the entire executive branch. Compared with the spirited brochures used in military recruitment, the announcements of civil-service openings seem very dull indeed. They are usually posted in such public buildings as post offices, although form letters are sometimes sent to organizations and institutions that might be able to contact prospective applicants. Recently, however, the Civil Service Commission has made a special effort to attract college-trained persons into the federal service, recruiting them on the basis of a "government career" rather than for any particular position. Since 1955, it has offered the Federal Service Entrance Examination several times a year. In the words of the Civil Service Commission's major recruitment brochure:

> The objective is not merely to fill current needs, but to bring into the Federal service a number of highly qualified, career-minded people who have the potential to grow and develop within the service and become the career managers, skilled technicians, and professional leaders of tomorrow.[20]

Examinations for the classified service are generally of a practical sort to test the applicant's ability to fill a particular position. Different tests measure aptitude, achievement, and specific skills; the nature of the examination depends on the specific duties and responsibilities of the position. Oral tests may be given to check on personal characteristics that do not show up on written work: appearance, manners, mannerisms, facility in speaking, ability

[20]See U.S. Civil Service Commission, *Federal Careers* (Washington, D.C.: U.S. Government Printing Office, 1956), p. 3.

to react in a given situation—whatever the examiners feel is pertinent. Veterans and their families are given preferential treatment. Since 1953, however, all veterans must make the passing grade before they become eligible for the additional points that used to be a standard bonus. Veterans with service-connected disabilities go to the top on many "registers" or lists of eligible job applicants. After World War II, Congress ordered that many examinations be open only to veterans, but since 1952 most of these have been reopened to nonveterans. Preference is also given to veterans when there is a "reduction in force"; the order of "separation" from the service is determined by length of tenure, efficiency ratings, and veteran or nonveteran status.

Before World War II, the Commission itself did most of the testing and made up the registers from those who passed. During the war years, when activities were still highly centralized under the Commission, so many bottlenecks built up that the Commission had no choice but to delegate more and more authority to the personnel offices of the individual agencies. Now the agencies, subject to standards fixed by the Commission, do almost all their own hiring, firing, promoting, demoting, and classifying.

Before a civil service appointment becomes official, the applicant must swear that he will support and defend the Constitution, that he is not a communist or fascist or a member of any other organization that advocates the overthrow of the government by force or violence, and that he will not strike against the government or belong to any organization of federal employees claiming the right to strike against the government. The Commission itself conducts a routine investigation of every applicant, checking references and making pointed inquiries to local law enforcement agencies, former employers and supervisors, school authorities, and even neighbors. If the position involves "national security," the investigation is more extensive, probably including a full field investigation by the FBI. The Commission acts as a central clearing house for all loyalty and security information on persons in the civil service, maintains central reference files and records, reviews derogatory information resulting from inquiries, and checks with other investigatory agencies such as the Department of Justice and military intelligence.

Special Ground Rules for the Civil Service

The original purpose of the merit system was to take politics out of the public employment. Appointments and promotions were to be based on relative fitness for positions without regard to political affiliations. Demotions and dismissals were to be made only on the grounds of incompetence, inefficiency, or moral turpitude. Over the years, civil service rules and congressional legislation have increasingly restricted the political activities of public employees. The Hatch Act of 1939 forbids any officer or employee in the classified federal service to take an active part in party politics or political campaigns. In 1940, a second Hatch Act extended this prohibition to state employees whose salaries are paid wholly or in part by federal loans or grants.

The Commission has worked out specific rules concerning what employees may or may not do in politics. The civil servant may vote, express his personal opinions, make voluntary political contributions, put stickers on his private car, and wear political badges or campaign buttons when off duty. He may also hold such local offices as justice of the peace, member of a school board, and member of a library board, or serve on any other civic but nonpartisan boards. He may write his congressman or sign a nonpartisan petition to Congress, and attend political rallies and join political clubs if he does not hold office in them. The civil servant may not run for any national or state office, solicit others to become candidates for such offices, campaign for or against any political party, distribute campaign material, march in any political parade (except when playing an instrument in the band!), solicit or receive political assessments, make or receive any political contributions in a federal building. If he violates any of these rules, he is subject to penalties ranging from 90 days' suspension to actual removal.

The purpose of these restrictions is to protect federal employees from political coercion and to protect the public from the spoils system. In 1947, the Supreme Court upheld the Hatch Act as a proper regulation designed to promote efficiency in the public service.[21] In a dissenting opinion, however, Justice Hugo L. Black pointed out that the act deprives public employees of basic civil rights:

> It relegates millions of federal, state, and municipal employees to the role of mere spectators of events upon which hinge the safety and welfare of all the people, including public employees. It removes a sizeable proportion of our electorate from full participation in affairs destined to mould the fortunes of the nation. It makes honest participation in essential political activities an offense punishable by proscription from public employment.

In his zeal for "the preferred freedom," the Justice may have overstated the case—and yet there is a case. It is ironical that the very people who are most familiar with the operation of our government should be prohibited from participating freely in the political activities that give it shape and substance.

The public expects its public service to be reliable, trustworthy, of good conduct and character, and loyal to the United States. After World War II, the mounting fear and suspicion of the international communist conspiracy, the disclosure that spy rings and espionage agents had operated in the top grades of our government and in strategic areas of our national defense, the rise of "McCarthyism" and the turn of public opinion to conservatism—all these developments led to the establishment of loyalty and security programs in the federal service.

In 1947, by executive order, President Truman launched the first full-scale, peacetime loyalty investigation in American history. The "loyalty" of every person in the federal service was checked and verified. Activities that could be considered as evidence of disloyalty included sabotage, espionage, treason, sedition, advocacy of revolution or violence, intentional and unauthorized disclosure of confidential documents to foreign agents, and serving the interests of another government. Other criteria included membership in,

[21] *United Public Workers* v. *Mitchell*, 330 U.S. 75 (1947).

affiliation with, or sympathetic association with any organization designated by the Attorney General as totalitarian, fascist, communist, or subversive. The machinery for settling individual loyalty cases consisted of a hierarchy of loyalty boards in the various agencies, and a Loyalty Review Board in the Civil Service Commission to which appeals could be taken from adverse findings in the agencies.

The "witch-hunting" sometimes went to incredible lengths. Loyalty boards actually reviewed such "derogatory information" as the books bought by a suspect, the magazines to which he subscribed, the pictures he hung in his living room (Picasso?), the records he played on his hi-fi (Prokofiev?), the friends he made in college, and the textbooks he was required to study in his undergraduate courses. And yet, in 1951, after all the public servants whose loyalty was open to reasonable doubt had been dismissed, it was found that they amounted to about one one-hundredth of 1 per cent of all who had been screened.[22]

Normally a civil service employee has permanent tenure. Under the rules of the Civil Service Commission he may be discharged only "for such cause as will promote the efficiency of the service"; and he may appeal his discharge from any agency to the Civil Service Commission for review. In 1950, however, Congress authorized the heads of certain agencies to dismiss summarily any person whose employment they deemed not "in the interests of the national security of the United States." Congress placed under this authorization all "sensitive" agencies whose activities are directly related to the country's security, such as the Departments of State and Defense and the Atomic Energy Commission. Under the loyalty program set up by Truman's executive order, employees charged with disloyalty could appeal from agency action to a central loyalty review board. But under the 1950 statute, employees who were dismissed from the "sensitive" agencies as security risks had no such right of appeal.

The Republicans who came into office in 1953 decided that the Truman loyalty program was far from adequate. Almost immediately after his inauguration, President Eisenhower replaced it with a much broader "security" program. To the existing loyalty tests were added such new grounds for dismissal as "any behavior, activities, or associations which tend to show that the individual is not reliable or trustworthy," and "any facts which furnish reason to believe that the individual may be subjected to coercion, influence, or pressure which may cause him to act contrary to the best interests of national security." As Leonard D. White, a former member of the Civil Service Commission, observed, "The new tests of reliability were extraordinarily vague and pervasive."[23]

---

[22]Federal Personnel Counsel, U.S. Civil Service Commission, *Facts About Government Work and Workers*, Revision No. 1 (Washington, D.C.: U.S. Government Printing Office, April, 1952).

[23]White, *Introduction to the Study of Public Administration* (New York: The Macmillan Company, 1955), 4th ed., p. 446. The reader will do well to consult White's entire chapter on "Loyalty and Security." White wrote from long-time, firsthand experience.

The Republican administration in its first two years of power in the executive branch did a pretty thorough job of ridding the civil service of alleged subversives and other security risks. Statistics on dismissals and sudden resignations turned into a "numbers game" in the 1954 congressional elections. In one of his campaign speeches Vice-President Richard Nixon jubilantly reported, "We're kicking the Communists and fellow travelers and security risks out of the government, not by hundreds but by thousands." Since, however, the American people returned a majority of Democrats to both houses of Congress in 1954, we may surmise that they were not overly impressed with the GOP's Great Crusade.

In effect, the Eisenhower security program extended the congressional legislation of 1950 to all government employees. In 1956, however, the Supreme Court held that Congress had not authorized such a sweeping presidential extension of its national security requirements. In *Cole* v. *Young* (1956), the Court considered the case of a food and drug inspector who had been dismissed as a security risk from the Department of Health, Education and Welfare. A majority of the Court found that the act of 1950 applied only to security risks in sensitive positions and that the President had acted beyond his powers in extending the criteria of "security" to all employees in all agencies. Three members of the Court vigorously dissented: "We believe the Court's order has stricken down the most effective weapon against subversive activity available to the government."[24]

Die-hard conservatives in Congress were unsuccessful in their numerous attempts to overrule the judges with legislation specifically authorizing summary dismissals for security reasons in all executive agencies. No doubt the judicial decisions did act as a brake on the arbitrary removal of persons whose loyalty was at issue. We must not, however, misinterpret the Court's position. In previous cases, the Court had upheld the right of the President to remove disloyal persons from the government services through proper procedures.[25] *Cole* v. *Young* holds that the President may not authorize dismissals without review except from those sensitive positions specified by Congress. Moreover, we cannot attribute loyal-security programs simply to party politics. The return of the Democrats to executive power in 1961 made no changes in basic policies. The Civil Service Commission still professes, and can uphold by proper procedures, the principle that the public's business must be conducted properly and by people of unquestioned loyalty and integrity.

Political Executives and Career Administrators

The merit system is extended by the shift of positions from a patronage basis into the classified service. When this is done, the incumbents acquire permanent status, despite their original patronage appointment. During the period from 1933 to 1953, when the Democratic Party was in power, some 193,000 employees acquired permanent status noncompetitively. Most of them, however, were required to meet

---

[24]*Cole* v. *Young*, 351 U.S. 536 (1956).
[25]*Bailey* v. *Richardson*, 341 U.S. 918 (1951). See also Justice Frankfurter's concurring and dissenting opinion in *Garner* v. *Board of Public Works*, 341 U.S. 716 (1951), involving a California loyalty test. "The Constitution does not guarantee public employment."

some noncompetitive standard of fitness in order to achieve permanent status.

When the civil service was first established, certain positions were included in the classified service—that is, they carried tenure—but were not subject to competitive testing. Since 1902 these "excepted positions" have been listed in "Schedule A." For many years Schedule A was restricted mostly to attorneys, employees in foreign countries, certain confidential and private secretaries, and some patronage jobs in customs, internal revenue, and the post office. Following an executive order of President Roosevelt in 1938, a number of "policy-determining" positions were added to Schedule A. Then, in 1940, the competitive service was extended under the *Ramspeck Act*, and most of the agencies responded by shifting many high-ranking positions into Schedule A. Under the Truman administration, either by executive direction or legislative action, many of these top-grade jobs were removed again from Schedule A and put back into the competitive service.

When the Republicans entered office in 1953, they claimed to be appalled at the number of "Democrats who had been covered into the civil service improperly," particularly in the higher grades. Almost no patronage had been left to the victorious party. President Eisenhower promptly requested the Civil Service Commission and the heads of all agencies to determine whether additional positions should be added to Schedule A.

In March, 1953, President Eisenhower by executive order created a new Schedule C for those positions in the policy-forming and confidential categories that had formerly been in Schedule A. All the agencies were directed to

Drawing by D. Fradon;
© 1967 The New Yorker Magazine, Inc.

submit to the Civil Service Commission requests for additional positions that they would like to have in Schedule C. The Commission was flooded by requests to add chiefs and assistant chiefs of bureaus, departmental directors of information, general counsels, heads and assistant heads of planning and legal staffs, and special aides or assistants to the political executives. Although the Commission manned the dikes with heroic resistance, a great many holes appeared in the merit system in the next two years. By the end of 1954, approximately 1100 positions had been placed in Schedule C and 350 more positions had been added to Schedule A. In percentages, these "exceptions" from the competitive service seem very small indeed. "But numbers alone do not tell the whole story," observed a Hoover Commission task force in 1955. "In importance of positions affected, Schedule C and the recent enlargement of Schedule A represent the most significant cut-back of the competitive service in its history."[26]

The Democrats returning to power in 1961 were similarly confronted with patronage problems. The Senate Post Office Committee published a 141-page book listing likely job openings in the new administration. But the pickings seemed small, just as they had appeared to the Republicans eight years earlier. The excepted service (not covered by competitive examinations) included three "schedules," about 13 per cent of the jobs in the national service; but relatively few of these were true patronage jobs. More than half the excepted service was in effect a special classification for lawyers, chaplains, narcotics agents for undercover work, and professional experts for temporary consultation purposes. Schedule B, also noncompetitive, was limited to a small number of specific and technical assignments such as communications intelligence activities.

Schedule C was the only really attractive recruiting base for the incoming administration. It included key positions which are "policy determining or which involve close personal relationship between incumbents and the head of agency or his key officials." Here are the political executives who make up the President's team: heads of departments, under secretaries, assistant secretaries, members of the regulatory boards and commissions, officers in the Executive Office of the President, and so on. In 1960, Schedule C listed about 1200 positions; this number has now gone up to about 1600, but even so they comprise less than one per cent of the positions in the national government.

Schedule C is a compromise between the traditional spoils system of American politics and the Weberian model of a permanent and professional bureaucracy. In the British or French governments, for example, political turnover will occur only at the very top of the ministries. The incoming ministers may head departments: their secretaries, under secretaries, deputy under secretaries, and assistant secretaries are all part of the higher civil service who stay at their posts, presumably providing competence and continuity in government operations throughout periods of executive succession and policy changes. By contrast, in the American system, each incoming administration feels obliged to fill all the positions in Schedule C with its own new appointees.

[26]Commission on Organization of the Executive Branch of the Government, *Task Force Report on Personnel and Civil Service* (Washington, D.C.: U.S. Government Printing Office, February, 1955), p. 192.

President-elect Kennedy indicated at the outset that he wanted "a ministry of talent," but the talent-hunt proved to be an arduous and large-scale project. His own staff undertook to screen tens of hundreds of applications for high and low positions and for this purpose scoured the business and academic communities especially. Theodore Sorensen, Kennedy's right-hand man in the 1960 election, and his Special Counsel in the White House, sums up the tremendous task of recruiting for an incoming administration:

> There were seventy-two days to inauguration. . . . Seventy-two days in which to form an administration, staff the White House, fill some seventy-five key Cabinet and policy posts, name six hundred other major nominees, decide which incumbents to carry over, distribute patronage to the faithful and fix personnel policies for the future. . . .[27]

Hundreds of new officials, many of them without any experience in the public service, joined the Kennedy administration to advance the New Frontier. The talent hunt, however, had also induced a number of key men from previous administrations to work with the new administration. It is not too difficult to attract first-rate executives to the Cabinet posts or other major policy positions in the national government. These are the glamorous positions that offer challenge, excitement, and prestige. It is not so easy, however, to recruit the assistant secretaries or others in the lower echelons who also have important jobs to do but who must play their roles for the most part out of the limelight. If they come to Washington, it is usually at a financial sacrifice; note that these presidential appointments do not include the "security blanket" or fringe benefits enjoyed in the civil service. A university professor may be paid more than an assistant secretary of education and a bank vice-president at Four Corners may draw a higher salary than an assistant secretary for international monetary affairs. Moreover, if the new appointee is not accustomed to the ground rules of bureaucracy in big government, he may soon get discouraged and go back to teaching political science at Podunk U. or to lending money at the bank in Four Corners. The turnover of political executives is very high in Washington.

Recognizing these problems in recruiting for second and third echelons in the bureaucracy, the Civil Service Commission has recently established the Executive Assignment System. This system is based on a career executive inventory, a comprehensive listing of civil service employees in grades GS–15 through GS–18, the top grades in the career service. The inventory provides a listing of some 20,000 persons of competence and experience in the public service who are available for new assignments outside the agencies in which they are employed. Thus the next incoming administration will have ready access to executive talent of known quality and experience. How the plan will operate, given the long tradition of partisan patronage in the American system, remains to be seen.

---

[27]Theodore C. Sorensen, *Kennedy* (New York: Harper & Row, Publishers, Inc., 1965), p. 227.

Roles of the Bureaucrats in the Policy Process

Different Assignments and Different Expectations

To portray the roles of bureaucrats in the policy process is somewhat more complicated than to discuss the roles of congressmen or of the President. The bureaucrat in the Executive Office of the President, the department head, the assistant secretary, the member of an independent bipartisan commission, the office director: all of these have different assignments in the policy machine. The roles that they play in the administration are determined not only by the nature of their assignments but by personal as well as political considerations.

The bureaucrat in the Executive Office of the President, on the White House staff, for example, is "the President's Man," and an official representative of the administration. He is appointed by the President, serves at the pleasure of the President, and his whole loyalty is to the administration of which he is an integral part; on the other hand, he is not a civil servant. "He is expected to jab and prod and push all the different bureaucracies."[28] He must project the President's point of view and see to it that bureaucrats throughout the executive branch produce whatever intelligence and recommendations the President needs in making policy decisions. He must keep in contact with the subbureaucracies and make sure that they are following through on whatever course the President has determined.

A department head may play several roles simultaneously: "His formal responsibilities extend both upward toward the President and downward toward his own department."[29] He is expected to implement the broad policy views of the President within his own department and also, within the functional area of his assignment, to Congress. He is expected to provide a direct line of communication from the White House to all the various offices in his department, and to see to it that the views of the people in those offices reach the President. This he may do, as we pointed out earlier, through his position in either the Cabinet or the National Security Council (if he is a member of the latter, interdepartmental group) or in other collective or individual, formal or informal, contacts with the President.

As chief executive of his department, he heads an immense organization whose activities he must direct and coordinate. Most department heads come to identify themselves with their respective organizations and feel an obligation to support the points of view and special interests of their own bureaucrats. But, in any case, the department head is responsible for seeing to it that the expertise of his bureaucrats reaches the right places in the policy machine and at the right time to count in decision-making. This involves knowledgeable oversight of the departmental activities and a great many consultative arrangements and policy meetings within the department.

Some department heads play still another role when they represent their clientele's interests in the policy process. We have already discussed the representative function of the Cabinet in the national administration. But

---

[28] Roger Hilsman, *To Move a Nation* (Garden City, N.Y.: Doubleday & Company, 1967), p. 569.
[29] Fenno, *The President's Cabinet*, p. 218.

some departments more than others have strong ties with constituencies outside the official hierarchy. Roger Hilsman points out that Presidents often choose certain men "precisely because they represent an outside, public constituency.... Having chosen men because of their affiliations with particular constituencies, a President can hardly be surprised if they speak for that constituency in the internal policy debate."[30] This factor may become a source of tension between a President and his own appointees. The more a President tries to balance his administration, the more likely are the chances that he will have to face conflict within his community of policy-makers.

Each department head acts primarily as "the President's principal adviser" within the functional area of his own department. The *Organization Manual* describes the Secretary of State as "head of the Department of State and the principal adviser to the President in the formulation and execution of the foreign policy of the United States," and the Secretary of Defense as "the principal assistant to the President in all matters relating to the Department of Defense." But the Secretary is expected to represent the expertise of his bureaucrats and also to represent the demands and support of his agencies' special clientele. Hence it becomes the responsibility of the President to make his own decision as to alternatives when, as sometimes happens, his principal advisers represent competing interests, or recommend conflicting policies.

The independent regulatory commissions are so set up that no one President gets to control the membership. Requirement of bipartisan appointments, along with lengthy and staggered terms, means that members of the regulatory commissions may act independently of the President or of the party in power. Nevertheless, the independence of the regulatory commissions has occasionally been overrated. Presidential appointments are usually based on personal and partisan considerations, and the Senate has always felt free to criticize presidential nominations to the regulatory commissions. When senators hold committee hearings on appointments, they never limit themselves to discussing the technical qualifications of the nominee or his professional fitness for the job. Senators are frankly interested in the nominee's political views, his economic and social philosophy, the degree of his sympathy with the objectives of the law he is to administer, his attitude toward those whom he is to regulate. Congressional lobbyists for pressure groups do everything they can to make sure that new appointments are "favorable." A glaring example of what this sort of pressure can lead to was the Senate's refusal to confirm President Truman's reappointment of Leland Olds to the Federal Power Commission in 1949. During his ten years on the Commission, Olds had bucked the public utility industry by pressing for price-fixing and federal regulation of natural gas. So the gas and oil lobby went to work on the senators to make sure that he would not serve a third term, with the result that the Senate rejected the Commissioner's reappointment.[31]

---

[30]Hilsman, *To Move a Nation*, p. 571.
[31]See Joseph P. Harris, "The Senatorial Rejection of Leland Olds: A Case Study," *American Political Science Review*, XLV (September, 1951), 674.

Every one of the commissions was created to reward some interests at the expense of others and has grown up in an environment of conflicting pressure groups. "The spirit and enthusiasm of a commission depends to a large extent on the general political setting."[32] When a commission is first set up, the public always shows a lively interest in its activities. This is the period when the commission can apply public policy most vigorously because public support is at its peak. As the public interest wanes, however, the political leaders tend to relax, leaving the agency to take care of specific problems as they arise. The commissioners in turn lose their initial zeal and settle into rules of procedure that are neither too arduous nor too disagreeable to either the regulators or the regulated. "Perhaps the most marked development in a mature commission is the growth of a passivity that borders on apathy."[33] The mature commission rarely goes out looking for new business. Since initiative and enterprise only stir up controversy, the commissioners are inclined to wait for private parties to bring in new cases.

At the outset, a new commission is operating in an area where public policy is inevitably rather experimental and exploratory. The commission's "experts"—most of them lawyers, engineers, and accountants—gradually work out the rules of conduct. As Marver Bernstein points out, however, "Expertness plays into the hands of the regulated interests."[34] The preponderance of lawyers is likely to give a strong legalistic flavor to commission activities. They tend, for example, to regard the special interests who are supposed to be regulated as clients who need to be protected from governmental attack. This was the issue between President Franklin D. Roosevelt and Chairman William E. Humphrey of the Federal Trade Commission: Although the Commission was supposed to promote and enforce codes of fair competition, Humphrey was reluctant to crack down on long-time friends who failed to meet the New Deal standards. Also, the commissioners are usually so busy with the immediate problems of regulations that they have no time for any long-range planning. Coordination between the commissions and the related departments is "loose and casual and sometimes nonexistent." For example, the National Labor Relations Board has no close relationship to the Department of Labor, and the Federal Commission has little to do with the Department of Commerce. Despite complaints regarding this lack of coordination, the Hoover Commission concluded that "the independent regulatory commissions have a proper place in the machinery of our Government."[35]

Before President Kennedy assumed office, he requested James M. Landis —who had been Dean of the Harvard Law School, Chairman of the Securities

---

[32]For a realistic study of the "life cycle of regulatory commissions," see Marver H. Bernstein, *Regulating Business by Independent Commission* (Princeton, N.J.: Princeton University Press, 1955), p. 83. Cornelius P. Cotter, *Government and Private Enterprise* (New York: Holt, Rinehart & Winston, 1960), treats government regulation of business in terms of policy-making and administrative processes. The emphasis is empirical, with background materials on the principal regulatory agencies.

[33]Bernstein, *Regulating Business*, p. 88.

[34]*Ibid.*, p. 118.

[35]The most useful exposition of independent regulatory commissions from an organizational standpoint is the *Task Force Report on Independent Regulatory Commissions*, prepared for the Commission of Organization of the Executive Branch of the Government (Washington, D.C.: U.S. Government Printing Office, March, 1949), p. 3.

and Exchange Commission, and chairman of the Civil Aeronautics Board—to study the independent agencies and to make appropriate recommendations for streamlining. The Landis Report which criticized the agencies more in terms of performance than of administrative structure, prompted President Kennedy early in his administration to urge Congress to provide for greater coordination among the agencies, and for a more hierarchical pattern in the executive branch. He recommended that the chairman of each agency serve at the pleasure of the President; that each chairman be granted greater authority over his agency's budget and staff; and that the commissioners be given the power to delegate more of their work to the technical staff. He singled out the Federal Communications Commission for specific reform. But the Kennedy administration came up against the same facts of political life that had defeated earlier efforts to bring the independent agencies into executive hierarchy. The interest groups that are most directly affected fought to maintain the "independence" of the agencies that regulate them.

Career Administrators in the Policy Process

The principal political appointments of any President constitute the "policy-makers" of his administration. As top men on the President's team, they share his political responsibility for the national administration. They have a representative role, and in that role they are expected to equate the public policy with the most recent expression of the public interest. Below them is the permanent bureaucracy in the classified civil service. Incoming political executives, eager to make policy changes, are likely to view the massive and seemingly immovable bureaucracy with dismay. Like the military conquerers of ancient China, who were ultimately absorbed by the culturally impenetrable mass of Chinese, so the new principal officers, especially in old-line departments like Agriculture and Interior, inevitably discover that they can get little done unless they work through the usual channels and adapt their ways to the departmental mores.

A political executive soon discovers that he is an organization man. He cannot make policies on his own, but must enter into the institutional process of decision-making. Administrative activity is group activity, and administrative decision-making is largely collective behavior. The head of a department may direct its activities, but he in turn is influenced by its activities. This is especially true in those governmental agencies where technical skill and expert intelligence are requisite to rational decisions—for example, in the Defense Department. Paradoxically, the development of technology and the emphasis on specialization in our modern society have decentralized and diffused decision-making.

In the administrative hierarchy, the crucial point of contact between the political executive and his operational staff is with the career administrators, who are not only experienced in programing for the department, but have also acquired know-how in governmental relationships with Congress and with other agencies. Political executives, new to their jobs, must lean heavily on the career administrators in their organization. When party changes bring hundreds of new political executives to Washington, the career administrators are important in furnishing continuity to governmental operations.

Since all public administration is laced with politics, it is almost impossible to draw a sharp line between political executives who help make policy and career administrators who carry out policy. The Hoover Commission regarded the two types as complementary. The political executives help make the policies of the Chief Executive and with him assume responsibility for the government. They come and go with the party in power. The career administrators, on the other hand, provide a reservoir of knowledge and managerial competence based on long-time experience. Politically neutral, they serve anonymously in the public service. Their main concern is with organization, methods, procedures, techniques; they are the professional experts who know *how* to do *what* the political executive decides should be done.

In the policy process, political executives and professional bureaucrats work closely together. Moreover, as one administration draws to a close, and vacancies occur at the top of the departmental hierarchies, the outgoing President is likely to fill the vacancies with professional bureaucrats who forego their permanent status while holding a political appointment. An incoming President takes his time in designating his second and third "teams," so that the career officers are generally responsible for carrying on governmental activities during presidential transitions. For example, distinguished foreign service officers usually command most of the top posts in the State Department during the period of presidential transition, because continuity in foreign policy is crucial for our international relations. As the new administration learns to make its own way in foreign policy, foreign service officers yield to political appointees and again take their tours of duty abroad.

A former Secretary of State, from his own experience at the head of the hierarchy, reminds us that "the work of the Department is performed by many thousands of trained, intelligent, and devoted men and women in all parts of the world and in Washington." Commenting on the notion that "policy originates at the top and is passed down," Dean Acheson, while agreeing that "great decisions are, for the most part, made at the top," insists that, in the sum total of departmental decisions, "the springs of policy bubble up, they do not trickle down."[36]

In Chapter 16, which deals with the policy process in foreign affairs, we shall find that the "community of decision-makers" is at considerable variance with the traditional models of administrative hierarchies. When President-elect Kennedy made a point of naming an Assistant Secretary of State, an Under Secretary of State, and the Ambassador to the United Nations *before* he designated the Secretary of State, he was in effect announcing his intention of directly injecting presidential power at operating levels of the Department. Each nomination was prefaced with a statement that the "post" was "second to none in importance." As President, Kennedy remained personally accessi-

---

[36]*The New York Times*, October 11, 1959. Recurrent crises in foreign affairs in the Eisenhower administration provoked much debate in professional and political cricles—how best to reorganize the State Department. The American Assembly discussed the problem from various points of view in its national meeting, October, 1960: Don K. Price (ed.), *The Secretary of State* (Englewood Cliffs, N.J.: Prentice-Hall, Inc., 1960), an American Assembly Book.

ble to many persons whose offices were far from the top of the administrative hierarchy; the emphasis was on personal relations rather than on bureaucratic channels. In a television interview at the end of his second year in office, the question was asked, "Is it true that during your first year, sir, you would get on the phone personally to the State Department and try to get a response to some inquiry that had been made?" The President replied, "Yes, I still do that when I can, because I think there is a great tendency in government to have papers stay on desks too long. . . . After all, the President can't administer a department, but he can at least be a stimulant."[37] President Johnson has also established a strong personal role for himself. He is more inclined, however, to stimulate the policy process at the points of formulation rather than implementation. Thus the Johnson style of administration calls for a great many phone calls to old colleagues in Congress rather than to the lesser bureaucrats.

Professional bureaucrats play a significant and sometimes crucial role at every stage in the policy process. They furnish most of the intelligence that constitutes the ground work for policy planning. When the agency's policy-makers are formulating new policies and assessing alternatives, they count on the objective judgments and experienced counsel of the career service. Bureaucrats are the permanent representative of conventional and pragmatic wisdom in the agency. They are the experts on how to do it and what it will cost to get it done. Moreover, bureaucrats are bound to develop some ideas of their own on how to cope more effectively with the problems that confront them daily; and so, as Dean Acheson reminds us, "the springs of policy bubble up" from the lowest echelons of the bureaucracy.

When the principal officers of a government agency go before congressional committees to obtain legislative authorizations and appropriations, they are inevitably accompanied by a full complement of their career officers to backstop their presentation, to interpret the supporting documents, and to answer the difficult and technical questions. When a new policy is authorized, bureaucrats prepare the blueprints for the structural organization, the personnel and fiscal requirements, and the operating procedures. Bureaucrats not only work out the rules and regulations for the implementation of policy; they also interpret and apply the rules in specific cases. Bureaucrats are expected to do all of this with professional competence, and always unobtrusively.

One can, of course, exaggerate the role of bureaucrats simply because their activities are so pervasive in the policy process. Roger Hilsman, one of Kennedy's talented appointees in the State Department, reflecting on possibilities for improving the policy machine, points out that "expertise should be given a full hearing, but experts themselves should be watched, at least for the narrowness of their interests."[38] This is probably the nub of the matter. Bureaucrats have an important role, but they must not move to the center of the stage; they belong to the supporting cast.

[37]From his radio-TV discussion of the presidency, December 16, 1962.
[38]Hilsman, *To Move a Nation*, p. 574.

A Democratic and Responsible Bureaucracy

We have observed that in some countries, where party government is unstable and there are frequent changes in political leadership, the civil service has a tendency to become permanently entrenched in power and to run the country unmindful of changes at the top that presumably reflect changing public opinion. We have also noted in one-party totalitarian systems that the bureaucracy is expected to act mainly as an instrument for advancing party policies within the government. In the United States, however, administrative officials serve under, and are responsible to, our elected leaders.

The President as General Manager

We recognize the President's role as general manager of the government when we speak of the Eisenhower administration, the Kennedy administration, or the Johnson administration. Because the President appoints most of the important officials in the executive branch—many of them his close friends, all of them presumably his political supporters—he puts a personal stamp on his administration at the very outset. This personal relationship is institutionalized in the meetings of the Cabinet and the National Security Council over which the President presides; in fact, the members of these groups are commonly called "the President's official family." About sixty key officials still report personally to the President, despite recommendations by the Hoover Commission to cut this number to a more manageable number. In practice, many of these officials deal more frequently with the White House Office than with the President himself, but the administrative responsibility is still the President's. Since nearly all presidential appointees serve at his pleasure, he is able to influence their attitudes and regulate their conduct, and even to dismiss them when their views differ too sharply with his.

Through the Executive Office, the President supervises all the activities of the executive branch. Every request for appropriations and every proposal for legislation coming from any administrative agency must be cleared through the White House before it is submitted to Congress. Congress has given the President authority to initiate administrative reorganization. Through the Bureau of the Budget, he reviews the budget estimates and apportions the congressional appropriations for each agency; and he scrutinizes the organization and operation of all the agencies in order to discover what changes are needed for economy and efficiency. All these phrases so familiar in bureaucratic circles sound bloodless and impersonal to the layman. Without using the technical language of officialese, we may simply say that the President acts as a general manager for the national government.

When a President comes into office, one of his first responsibilities is to chart the main policies of his administration. He must give his supporting officers a clear conception of what his administration proposes to achieve. And he must direct the various departments and agencies of the executive branch to prepare their work programs, with estimates of expenditures, in accordance with the overall aims of the administration. When President

Kennedy immediately revised President Eisenhower's budget estimates for 1961 and 1962, he was, in effect, recommending new courses of action for the national government. The most important budget increases occurred in the programs for agriculture, labor, and welfare, and for national security. And even before the first year was half over, crises in foreign affairs made it necessary for the Kennedy administration to request (and receive) still more money for the military establishment and for foreign aid.

As Chief Executive, one of the most complicated duties of the President is to coordinate the activities of the entire bureaucracy. The preceding chapter on the presidency called attention to the several managerial agencies in the Executive Office of the President. These included the White House Office, Bureau of the Budget, Council of Economic Advisers, National Security Council, National Aeronautics and Space Council, the Office of Emergency Planning, the Office of Science and Technology, and the Office of the Special Representative for Trade Negotiations. President Eisenhower made frequent use of the National Security Council for policy coordination in foreign affairs and military defense. For top coordination, he was inclined to rely on his White House staff.

President Kennedy, at the outset of his administration, hoped to cut through the red tape of countless interdepartmental committees. He was frankly not interested in "organization-chart thinking." He thought that staff operations should be minimized and that the President should personally assume more direct responsibility for decisions. One of his early reorganization moves was to abolish the Operations Coordinating Board that President Eisenhower had created to insure coordinated implementation of National Security Council recommendations. He abolished several dozen other interdepartmental committees which specialized in group thinking and group decisions. Wherever he could he attacked the idea of an institutionalized presidency and emphasized the importance of individual responsibility. In short, he played havoc with administrative orthodoxy.[39]

President Johnson's administration is neither as institutionalized as was Eisenhower's nor as personalized as was Kennedy's. President Johnson maintains a close working relationship with individual members of his White House staff, but no one approaches the role of Assistant to the President that Sherman Adams played for President Eisenhower. The heads of departments are probably more important politically in the Johnson administration, but lesser bureaucrats are not likely to get personal phone calls from the President. Communications to and from the President are normally routed through the White House staff. By its very nature, the role of general manager is instutionalized through the Executive Office of the President.

[39] For an exhaustive study of national policy machinery in the Truman and Eisenhower administrations, see the reports, hearings, and studies of the Subcommittee on National Policy Machinery, Committee on Government Operations, U.S. Senate, published in three volumes under the title *Organizing for National Security* (Washington, D.C.: U.S. Government Printing Office, 1961). For the Kennedy administration, the most discerning single volume is probably Theodore Sorensen's *Kennedy*.

Congressional Controls over the Bureaucrats

Congress has never been willing to give the President complete control over the administration of its policies. Congress determines the functions of the government and, accordingly, Congress also determines the tasks of the bureaucracy. It may spell out the details of administration, or it may merely supply a reasonable standard or guide for the administrator and leave the details to him. In any case, Congress possesses whatever power is necessary to keep the administrators in line with legislative policy. A large part of the *U.S. Code* (the official summary of federal laws in force) is devoted to congressional prescriptions of work methods and administrative procedures to be followed by the various executive agencies.[40]

In creating agencies for the administration of its laws, Congress over the years has followed no master plan. Consequently, the administrative structure today resembles a small house to which countless rooms, even whole new wings, have been added to accommodate a growing family. All the commissions that have studied the organization of the executive branch have disapproved of the rambling, ramshackle structure and have strongly recommended more functional "architecture." Presidents Roosevelt, Truman, Eisenhower, and Kennedy all proposed and obtained some "modern improvements." But Congress has always retained the right to look over the plans for proposed alterations.

Congress can create or abolish any administrative unit and decide whether a new unit will be established as a department, independent agency, regulatory commission, board, or corporation. Both Roosevelt and Truman tried without success to induce Congress to establish a new Department of Public Welfare in the President's Cabinet. Then Congress accepted Eisenhower's Reorganization Plan of 1953 and created the Department of Health, Education and Welfare as an executive department responsible to the President for the administration of health, education, and social security programs. President Kennedy, in the first year of his administration, asked for but failed to get a Department of Housing and Urban Affairs. President Franklin D. Roosevelt urged that independent regulatory commissions (such as the Interstate Commerce Commission or the Federal Trade Commission) be abolished and that their functions be transferred to the major executive departments directly under presidential management. But Congress rejected the proposal and subsequently set up still more independent commissions.

How frequently an administrative organization may be restructured is illustrated in our foreign aid program. In 1948, Congress established the Economic Cooperation Administration to administer the European recovery program. The Administrator was given rank equal to that of the Secretary of State, with whom he was directed to work "cooperatively." In 1951, Congress abolished the Economic Cooperation Administration and shifted its functions, considerably expanded, to a new agency, the Mutual Security Agency. The

---

[40]Joseph P. Harris, *Congressional Control of Administration* (Washington, D.C.: The Brookings Institution, 1964).

Director of the MSA held a position on the National Security Council equal to that of the Secretaries of State, Defense, and Treasury. Then, in 1953, the President's Reorganization Plan abolished the Mutual Security Agency and transferred its functions to the Foreign Operations Administration. The Director of FOA was charged with carrying on all our foreign aid programs but under policies established by the Secretaries of Defense, Treasury, and State, and with a network of interdepartmental committees to reconcile any conflicts of interest. In 1955, the Foreign Operations Administration was abolished by executive order and its principal functions were transferred to the International Cooperation Administration in the Department of State. The Director of ICA was made responsible to the Secretary of State, but an executive order again created a network of interdepartmental committees to work under, through, and above the ICA.

Each incoming administration attempts to present a new image by abolishing old organizations and replacing them with new ones. When President Kennedy came into office, he recommended that the International Cooperation Administration be abolished and that all of the foreign aid programs be consolidated in a single new agency, the Agency for International Development (AID). Congress obligingly authorized the President to carry out the functions of the Foreign Assistance Act of 1961 through any agency he deemed appropriate. And so AID was established by executive order, in the State Department, with the Director of AID reporting directly both to the Secretary of State and to the President.

In proposing AID, President Kennedy insisted that he was not merely reshuffling and relabeling old agencies, but that he intended to make a fresh start. But President Kennedy, like his predecessor, and also like his successor (who retained AID), was to discover that during all these reorganizations by statute and executive order, a fairly permanent corps of bureaucrats managed to transfer from one agency to the next, thus providing continuity and expertise for each new program, and also building up a core of resistance to any great changes in routine. Congressmen who try to tackle the basic problems of foreign aid, through authorizations and appropriations, sometimes emerge with the feeling that they are pushing against a wall of molasses. And so they end up by doing what comes naturally, cutting appropriations for projects but dimly perceived.

Congress placed the Budget Bureau directly under the President, but kept the General Accounting Office as a congressional "watchdog" over the Treasury. The Comptroller General, who heads the GAO, is principally responsible to Congress. Whereas the President alone can hire and fire the Budget Director, the Comptroller General is appointed with the consent of the Senate and can be removed only with the consent of both houses of Congress. The GAO has broad authority over government expenditures. Every government warrant must be countersigned by the Comptroller General. No money can be paid out of the Treasury unless the Comptroller General by his countersignature certifies the legality of the expenditure. A great deal of political and academic controversy has centered around whether the GAO should play such a decisive role in administration and yet be independent of the Executive Office. The fact remains, however, that Congress holds the purse strings, and the bureaucrats are as conscious of congressional control through the General Accounting Office as they are of presidential management through the Bureau of the Budget.

The committee system gives Congress another way of controlling the administration. Department heads may not appear on the floor of Congress to defend or promote pending legislation, but they are regularly called into the committee rooms of Congress to explain and justify their administrative programs. When, for example, the Senate Committee on Foreign Relations chooses to consider some current problem in foreign policy, it may summon the Secretary of State, the Secretary of Defense, the Chairman of the Joint Chiefs of Staff, and sometimes a whole crew of special assistants, assistant secretaries, office directors, bureau directors, and division chiefs to explain or defend their policies.

The most effective point of congressional control over the bureaucracy is in the appropriations process. The President's budget, as he submits it to Congress, is a single document. It is not only a complete financial report but also a planned program of activities for the entire executive branch. Congress, however, never debates the budget as such. In practice, each house accepts the recommendations of its appropriations committee, paying very little attention to general policy. Moreover, each appropriations committee normally accepts the bills proposed by its respective subcommittees. In effect, this piecemeal consideration of the budget vests the power of the purse in a score of small, relatively independent subcommittees.

The subcommittees on appropriations hold formal hearings at which administrative officials must appear to justify their budgets and programs. House subcommittee meetings are usually closed and Senate subcommittees open; both, however, publish transcripts so that the public can be informed. Interrogation may not be systematic, but it can be penetrating, for continuity of subcommittee membership is bound to build up familiarity with the work of the department concerned. Members may be as concerned with programs and policies as with allocation of funds. The recommendation of the subcommittee to grant the full request for one program, to deny or cut it back for another program is, in fact, a policy decision. Members of the subcommittee frequently have special interests to protect or promote. For example, congressmen from agricultural constituencies aim for an assignment to the subcommittee that deals with appropriations for the Department of Agriculture. Members on the subcommittee for the Interior Department are likely to come from such states as Arizona, New Mexico, Wyoming, California, or Nevada. Chairmen of the subcommittees usually come from safe districts, serve for long periods, and come to have a proprietary attitude (not always kindly) toward the agencies within their jurisdiction. Representative Otto Passman (D.-La.), as Chairman of the Subcommittee that considers funds for foreign aid programs, is notorious for his long-time resistance to administrative requests.

Congress also makes frequent use of its power to investigate administrative agencies. There is some doubt, however, about how far Congress can go in compelling officials to give testimony or produce documents. The courts have generally upheld the congressional power of investigation as essential to the legislative function. They have never recognized any inherent right of federal officials to withhold information from Congress (or the courts). Officials in certain departments, notably State, Defense, and Justice, have successfully claimed the "privilege" of refusing to give information on the ground that disclosure might jeopardize national security. Usually, however, officials cannot afford to appear unfriendly to Congress, for the consequences might be drastic. Although Congress has no effective authority to remove officials from office or to single them out for discipline, it does have the power to abolish any agency, to eliminate specific programs, and to "reduce force." Understandably, then, most administrators are eager and cooperative when they appear at committee hearings. In fact, some departments, such as State and Defense, employ special staffs to maintain constant liaison with Congress.

Summing up the relationship of the bureaucracy to the constitutional authorities is not easy. The President, as the overall manager, may be highly influential in top-level decisions; but for the great bulk of governmental business, which is handled administratively, presidential direction is nominal. And the same is generally true of the congressional controls over the day-by-day administration; they are nominal, or, more likely, nonexistent. Policy-making, in fact, is a complex process of group interaction within the bureaucracy. Pinning responsibility for a particular decision is almost impossible. When President Eisenhower assumed sole responsibility for the U-2 affair in 1960 and when President Kennedy did likewise for the Cuban invasion in 1961, few people really blamed the Chief Executive personally for what was obviously lack of coordination in the administration.

"Government under Law"

If we wanted to find the bulk of federal law that governs the country today, we would go not to the *Statutes at Large* passed by Congress, but rather to the *Federal Register,* which contains the executive orders, directives, rules, and regulations adopted by the national administration. Congress enacts general policies, but more and more it leaves the details of regulation to the administrative agencies. Beginning with the Interstate Commerce Commission in 1887, Congress has established nine independent regulatory commissions, each with rule-making authority over an important segment of the American economy, and each with what are called "quasi-legislative" and "quasi-judicial" powers. The Interstate Commerce Commission, for example, has power to fix maximum rates in interstate transportation. The Securities and Exchange Commission has power to grant or refuse approval for the offering of new securities on the stock markets. Each commission fixes standards of conduct and determines what individuals may or may not do within a specialized economic area. Clearly, this constitutes quasi-legislative administration. And each commission makes rules and hands down specific orders after conducting investigations and hearings, which constitutes quasi-judicial administration.

Many of the service agencies in the national government also perform quasi-legislative and quasi-judicial functions. For example, the Secretary of Agriculture regulates the marketing of basic agricultural products; the Wage and Hour Division in the Department of Labor prescribes fair labor standards for industries engaged in interstate commerce; the Fish and Wild Life Service in the Department of the Interior sets forth and polices the federal hunting regulations; the Food and Drug Administration in the Department of Health, Education and Welfare regulates the processing, packaging, and labeling of foods, drugs, and cosmetics that cross state lines. Today a hundred or more federal agencies are making rules that have the full force of law. Although Congress neither approves nor disapproves of all this administrative law, it does require each agency to give notice of proposed rule-making so that interested parties will have an opportunity to be heard before the rule is published. It also requires the publication of statements of general policy and procedures as well as of the rules, regulations, and orders themselves. These are published day by day in the *Federal Register* and are collected and systematized in the *Code of Federal Regulations.*

Government control of the modern economic system calls for highly technical knowledge and professional experience. Consequently, the administrators, who are appointed to furnish general policy leadership, must rely heavily on specialized staffs in making rules and quasi-judicial decisions. For example, a corps of lawyers, accountants, engineers, and other specialists is required to work out a railroad schedule that will meet the Supreme Court's requirement of a "fair rate of return on the fair value of the property." Another corps of technicians and specialists is required to allocate radio frequencies, to decide which sector of the broadcast band will be allotted to television, to assign specific frequencies to individual applicants, to check whether this station or that network is complying with the rule that calls for a balanced presentation of controversial public issues. In the American political system, the public official is not immune from ordinary law, as he is in some European governments. Any citizen who believes that an administrative order or rule is unjust, discriminatory, or a denial of his legal or constitutional rights may take his case into the ordinary courts. The Administrative Procedures Act of 1946 provides for judicial review of administrative decisions. A complainant, of course, is expected to seek redress in the administrative agency before resorting to court action. The courts, to protect themselves against a flood of litigation, may refuse to review questions of fact that do not also involve questions of law or questions of statutory or constitutional authority.

In practice, the administrative agencies enjoy a large measure of independence from judicial review. Because the administrator knows that his actions may be subject to judicial review, however, he consults continuously with the attorneys in his agency to be sure that he is acting in a legal manner. This very fact often discourages the private citizen from seeking legal redress. The great number of lawyers in the public service means that the individual has little hope of bucking the bureaucracy without high-priced legal counsel. Washington is full of lawyers who make a lucrative living by guiding clients through the procedural maze and legalistic ways of administrative agencies. But most people cannot afford the large fees of lawyers and the high costs of litigation, and the average citizen may lose rather than profit by a "rule of law" that is beyond his means.

Moreover, judicial restraint tends to favor the administration. The same reason that impelled the legislature to delegate rule-making authority makes the courts reluctant to review administrative decisions: the subject matter is often so technical that it is beyond the competence of the lay judges. Even when the courts do attempt review, they must listen to expert versus expert and then decide. Yet there is comfort in the democratic theory that no official is above the law, that all must operate within the law, and that any private citizen has the right to go to court and seek redress against arbitrary or excessive bureaucracy.

Public Service and "Special Interests"

The Hoover Commission reported to Congress in 1955 on "services, activities, and functions not necessary to the efficient conduct of government" and "nonessential services, functions, and activities which are competitive with private enterprise." To illustrate this basic theme, the Commission compiled a great amount of data on the industrial and commercial enterprises operated by the Defense Department and by the federal civilian agencies:

> The Federal Government today operates over a hundred business-type activities. It is, among other things, the largest electric power producer in the country, the largest insurer, the largest lender and the largest borrower, the largest landlord and the largest tenant, the largest holder of grazing land, the largest holder of timberland, the largest owner of grain, the largest warehouse operator, the largest shipowner, and the largest truck-fleet operator.[41]

Assuming that the private enterprise system is best for the national economy, the Commission was inclined to regard government in business as "creeping socialism." So we can understand how the Commission came to the conclusion that the federal government should get out and stay out of business as much as possible. It took its political cue from President Eisenhower, who stated:

> To bring Government closer to the people we will set up these principles and adhere to them: that no Federal project, large or small, will be undertaken which the people can effectively do or be helped to do for themselves; that no Federal project will be undertaken which private enterprise can effectively undertake.[42]

---

[41]Director of the Bureau of the Budget, A Speech to the Conference of the National Association of Bank Auditors and Comptrollers, New York City, December 7, 1954, cited by the *Commission on Organization of the Executive Branch of the Government, Subcommittee Report on Business Enterprises of the Department of Defense* (Washington, D.C.: U.S. Government Printing Office, 1955), p. 1.

[42]President Dwight D. Eisenhower, in 1952, *ibid.*, p. 1.

The Hoover Commission insisted that the government ought not to operate any public business in competition with private business. But some activities can be carried on only as public services—those that are necessarily monopolistic or those that are highly desirable for the general welfare, yet too expensive or too unprofitable for private business to undertake. Moreover, when private enterprise fails to satisfy the public needs, either in terms of performance or costs, the people are likely to use their political power to get what they want out of the government.

Often, however, minority pressures rather than public opinion create the demand for government services. The federal bureaucracy is generally organized on the "functional principle"—subordinate agencies carrying on similar activities and having common objectives are grouped in a single department. But the very fact that the government is organized on a functional basis makes the bureaucrats susceptible to the influence of private groups with corresponding interests. Thus the Department of Agriculture works closely with the Farm Bureau, the Department of Commerce with the Chamber of Commerce, and the Department of Labor with the AFL-CIO. Indeed, the working relationship is frequently so close that a line cannot be drawn between the objectives of the public agency and those of the private organization. This identification of the general welfare with special interests is even more complete where there is considerable mutual membership or overlapping personnel in the public agency and the private organization. For example, members of the National Education Association are constantly in and out of the Office of Education; and members of the American Legion hold key positions in the Veterans' Administration.

These personal contacts—the result of a natural affinity of interests—between the administrative agency and its private counterpart are calculated to produce agreeable working relations. Consultants, "dollar-a-year men," and semiofficial advisory committees attached to many of the public agencies represent the special interests of organized groups in labor, business, and agriculture. Such pressure politics is the more difficult to check, because it is covert rather than obvious. Lobbyists who try to influence the legislative process at least receive a certain amount of publicity; but public attention is rarely focused on special interests that work to influence the administrative process.

The bureaucrat has a natural tendency to believe that his own vested interests coincide with the public interest. Any agency that develops a sense of mission and *esprit de corps* will expand its own small bailiwick into a sizable empire if given the time and opportunity. In the chapters on outputs of the political system, we shall take a closer look at how administrative agencies sometimes act as pressure groups in the legislative process.

Whether or not a particular government agency serves the public interest depends on what it regards as its "public." The public is rarely if ever an organized majority with a single common interest; rather it is a changing coalition of many groups with various special interests. The administrator may think he is doing the best he can to serve the public if he simply satisfies his own clients. If, for example, the Farm Bureau is happy with the services and activities of the Department of Agriculture, the bureaucrats may assume that they have won the "consent of the governed." And yet there is a larger, inarticulate, unorganized public—the consumers—who must also be considered. The functional agencies, left entirely to themselves, tend to focus all their energies on the objective that constitute their *raison d'être*. But the private citizen has a right to expect top management to subordinate the special interests of pressure groups and the vested interests of bureaucratic agencies to broader public interests.

Functions of the Bureaucracy

The primary function of the bureaucracy is to administer the policies of the government, "to apply the rules" that have been worked out in the political process by the President and Congress. To perform this function the national administration comprises an immense organization based on rational division of labor; definite assignment of tasks graded according to degrees of difficulty, complexity, specialization, and responsibility; personnel generally recruited on the basis of merit to perform these tasks; and institutionalized procedures to guard against arbitrary, discriminatory, or capricious application of the rules.

When we try to ascertain how well the bureaucracy in the national government performs these functions, we run up against all kinds of problems. We begin by questioning the primary function, for we have observed that bureaucrats do not simply "apply the rules" that have been "made" by the President and Congress. Bureaucrats are also significantly engaged at every stage in the rule-making function, along with the President and Congress. Their specialized knowledge, their recognized expertise, and their experienced judgments make them invaluable partners in the decision-making process. Whether this is "good" or "bad" depends, of course, on one's vantage point. An incoming political executive may be much relieved to have on tap a supporting cast of qualified advisers who can carry on the show while he is learning his new lines. On the other hand, if he hopes to put a new show on the road, he may be discouraged to discover that even though he is cast as the principal actor he is expected to play in an old setting and cannot even choose his own company. The permanence of bureaucracy is both an advantage and a disadvantage; it offers continuity in the periods of transition between one set of principal actors and the next, but it also establishes a routine which tends to resist innovation and different roles.

When a new administration takes over, the obvious first step is to reorganize, as a signal that "top management" is planning policy changes. When the Kennedy administration tried to establish "new frontiers," especially in national security and foreign policy, its first move was to scrap much of the policy machinery of the previous administration and to set up different patterns of administration. But Kennedy's top aide ruefully tells us that "reorganization of the foreign AID program was hampered not only by the ineffective direction but by the refusal of Congress, the No. 1 critic of AID overstaffing and inefficiency, to authorize the elimination of deadwood' personnel, many of them placed there through Congressional influence."[43]

If the President is to act like a Chief Executive and to see to it that the laws be faithfully executed, then he must master the bureaucracy at the outset. In the phrasing of Richard Neustadt, the classic problem of the man on top in any political system is how to be on top in fact as well as in name. The lines of authority from the President's office must be clear and positive; all the books in public administration tell him so. Hence Presidents from Franklin D. Roosevelt to Lyndon B. Johnson have struggled to reorganize the national administration so that the President is unquestionably at the apex of the organization. But perennial study commissions are each in turn appalled to discover that our national administration is actually a chaotic structure of departments, bureaus, divisions, boards, commissions, corporations, and other independent establishments in which the lines of authority and responsibility appear hopelessly scrambled. Moreover, in some instances the lack of coordination within departments may be the direct result of congressional specifications on organization, reflecting the push and pull of various pressure groups. In effect, the principle of "efficiency" in organization is not uncommonly canceled out by practical considerations of pluralism in politics.

When a new President comes into office he is expected to recruit his own team to help him "clean up the mess in Washington," especially if his predecessor was of the other party. But immediately he and his chief administrators are inundated with policy problems. He must at once get his revised budget to Congress, which has already begun to hold hearings on the budget submitted by his predecessor. Getting a budget revised is such a technical business that he and his principal officers will have to depend a great deal on the counsel of bureaucrats who know the ropes. A pattern of relationships that will be difficult to break begins to develop.[44] Plans for reorganization may be delayed, then modified, and finally forgotten. Existing patterns of administration may begin to seem surprisingly rational.

Scrapping policy machinery is one thing, removing dedicated public servants is something else. Bureaucrats may be "highly qualified personnel," but who or what determines qualifications? Students of public administration generally agree that bureaucratic organization is "for the explicit purpose of achieving specific objectives and the organizational principle is administrative efficiency. . . ."[45] But, from the point of view of a new head of government, a smoothly running organization manned by highly competent personnel may pose greater problems for his administration than one which is obviously run-down. The obvious example, of course, is the State Department's impeccable Foreign Service.

The very fact that the Foreign Service is an elite career service makes it a formidable opponent to interference by amateurs, whatever their political

[43]Sorensen, *Kennedy*, p. 288.

[44]Sidney Mailick (ed.), *Concepts and Issues in Administrative Behavior* (Englewood Cliffs, N.J.: Prentice-Hall, Inc., 1962). See especially Norton Long, "The Administrative Organization as a Political System," p. 118: "The separation of policy formation from policy execution in any hard-and-fast way is probably as untenable as the old politics-administration dichotomy itself."

[45]Peter M. Blau, *The Dynamics of Bureaucracy* (Chicago: The University of Chicago Press, 1955), p. 264.

intentions. And the very skills of diplomacy sometimes appear as excessive caution and indecision to political executives in a hurry to make new policies. In 1953, when the Republicans came to office after twenty years out of power, their first target was the Foreign Service. In 1961, when the Democrats returned to office, President Kennedy forthwith declared his intention to make more effective the structure and the personnel of the State Department. But the Foreign Service is not easily dismissed or restructured; over the years it has come to dominate the State Department, both line and staff. In his first year in the presidency, Kennedy made several significant moves to "match men and jobs," but found that, given a qualified and permanent bureaucracy, such moves are necessarily limited and cannot penetrate very far into an agency.

Institutionalized procedures are both the rationale and the bane of bureaucracy. The bigger the organization the less practical it is to conduct business on a face-to-face basis. The bureaucracy of any modern government requires an enormous amount of paperwork for instructions, transaction forms, budget forms, personnel forms, purchasing forms, reports, record-making, and record-keeping techniques. A large part of the work time of government employees, or for that matter employees in any big organization—business or educational—is spent in the processes of paperwork.

In 1966, a congressional committee reported: "It takes 360,000 different forms prepared in 15 billion copies to keep the wheels of government turning. . . . In fiscal year 1966, the Federal Government is believed to have spent over $53 million to print its forms. . . . It was estimated in 1963, that directives cost the Federal Government $400 million for one million pages a year. . . . Records holdings now total more than 25 million cubic feet. Throwing away a page a second of these records, it would take 2,000 years to discard them all."[46] And so the Committee recommends additional professional staff, "fully trained and experienced in paper work" as well as more systematic automation through use of computers and related equipment. It is probably unfair to point out that just as the substitution of the typewriter for the quill pen did not cut down on clerical work, so introduction of automatic data processing is not likely to relieve by much the inherent problems of communication. In the final analysis, the performance of bureaucracy depends neither on organization nor on systematic procedures as much as it does on the quality of the human element in the system. In our judgment, the bureaucrats do a pretty fair job of carrying on the public business—a gigantic business—in a democratic organization and in a responsible fashion.

[46]Committee on Post Office and Civil Service, House of Representatives, 89th Congress, 2nd Session, October 1966, *How to Cut Paperwork* (Washington, D.C.: U.S. Government Printing Office, 1966), pp. 1–2.

THE

JUDGES   13

On June 23, 1967, President Lyndon B. Johnson nominated Thurgood Marshall to fill the Supreme Court vacancy left by the retirement of Associate Justice Tom Clark. After protracted hearings, the Senate Judiciary Committee recommended confirmation by a vote of 11–5. On August 29, 1967, after a six-hour debate that focused more on the nature of judicial power than on the qualifications of the nominee, the Senate approved the nomination in a 69–11 vote. After the roll-call, Senate Democratic Leader Mike Mansfield told his colleagues: "the confirmation of the nomination of Thurgood Marshall as an Associate Justice of the Supreme Court is also a confirmation of the vitality of the democratic system, . . . a shining hour for Mr. Marshall, for President Johnson, for the Senate, and for the United States of America."

The son of a Pullman car steward and the great-grandson of a slave, Justice Marshall served twenty-three years as counsel for the NAACP Legal Defense Fund. During those years, he carried thirty-two cases to the Supreme Court and won twenty-nine of them, including the celebrated case of *Brown* v. *Board of Education* (which resulted in the ruling that "segregation is a denial of the equal protection of the laws"). Many of these cases are now regarded as landmarks in American constitutional law. In 1962, President Kennedy appointed Marshall to the U. S. Court of Appeals for the Second Judicial Circuit. In 1965, on appointment from President Johnson, he left the bench to become Solicitor General of the United States. On October 2, 1967, Marshall was sworn in as a Justice of the Supreme Court, the first Negro to attain that position.

We shall return later in this chapter to the Senate debates on Justice Marshall's nomination. At this point, we merely note that only in the United States could the appointment of a judge occasion so much political excitement; for in the American political system, "the judicial Power of the United States," set forth in Article III of the Constitution, is coequal with "all legislative Powers" enumerated in Article I and "the executive Power" prescribed in Article II.

Judges in the Political System

The Nature of Judicial Power

In Chapter 1, we specified three basic functions common to every political system: rule-making, application of rules, and settlement of disputes. In the American political system, each of these functions is centered in a single agency: rule-making in Congress, application of the rules in the President and bureaucrats, settlement of disputes in the Supreme Court and lower courts. When we examined the activities of Congress, we discovered, however, that Congress performs all of these functions to some degree. Similarly, we observed that the President and the bureaucrats are more or less involved in every stage of decision-making. And, as we develop our discussion of the judges, we shall find that the judges do not confine their activities solely to the settlement of disputes.

Foreign observers of the American judicial system usually remark on its complexity. Tocqueville, who visited the United States in the 1830s, wrote, "The judicial organization of the United States is the institution which a stranger has the greatest difficulty understanding."[1] Tocqueville was especially struck by the "immense political influence" of the American judges, and he also thought it most remarkable that any American citizen could sue a public official in the ordinary courts. James Bryce, British Ambassador to the United States in the 1880s, was impressed by the "intricate judicial machinery" in the American federal union: "Every yard of ground in the Union is covered by two jurisdictions, with two sets of judges and two sets of officers."[2] He was gratified to find that in most respects America had followed the principles and practices of England. It surprised him, however, that in the United States any lawyer could take any kind of case and handle any aspect of it. The most characteristic peculiarity in the English legal profession had disappeared in America—the distinction between barristers, who take cases to court, and solicitors, who only do the paper work.

The American judicial system may differ in many details from the judiciaries of other countries, but basically the judicial function is much the same in every government. Judges are designated to hear and decide disputes within society: disputes between private persons, disputes between society and individuals, disputes between governmental agencies, disputes between public officials and private persons. The dispute may be a controversy as to facts, a difference of opinion as to the applicability of a particular rule, or an argument about whether an official is acting within or beyond his authority. In civilized society, the norms of judicial behavior are based on concepts of justice; a judge is expected to settle a dispute objectively, impartially. Courts are organized to provide an appropriate institutional setting for the performance of judicial functions. In most governments, the courts are established in a hierarchy: at the base, the trial courts; then a tier of courts of appeal; and at the top, a supreme court which exercises final judgment.

The dual system of courts in the United States—fifty sets of state judicial hierarchies and a separate federal judicial hierarchy—makes the American judicial process unusually complicated. The Constitution provides only that the national government include a Supreme Court and leaves it up to Congress to establish whatever "inferior courts" it deems necessary. The first Congress decided to set up a complete system of national courts—trial courts and appeals courts in addition to the Supreme Court. Most Americans take it

---

[1] Alexis de Tocqueville, *Democracy in America 1830*, edited by Phillips Bradley (New York: Vintage Books [Random House, Inc.], Vol. I, p. 102.
[2] James Bryce, *The American Commonwealth* (London: Macmillan & Co., 1891), Vol. I, p. 234.

for granted that this is the normal requirement of a federal government. Most federal governments, however—Australia, Canada, Germany, India, Switzerland, and U.S.S.R., for example—maintain a single unified judicial system. Only a few federal governments—such as Brazil and Mexico—have followed the American model.

Judges are recruited in several ways: In the United States, the President nominates all federal judges, and their appointment is subject to confirmation by majority vote of the Senate. Appointments of British judges are made by the Crown, which in practice means by the Prime Minister in consultation with the Lord Chancellor. In both countries, appointments are made both on the basis of party patronage and in recognition of professional qualifications. In France, prospective judges must complete a four-year curriculum at the National Center for Judicial Studies and then pass competitive civil service examinations. Russian judges in the appellate courts are appointed by the corresponding legislative bodies; thus the Supreme Soviet of the U.S.S.R. names the judges of the Supreme Court of the U.S.S.R. and each Union Republic Soviet names the judges of its Union Republic Court. Judges of the Federal Tribunal in Switzerland are chosen by the Federal Assembly. In a few countries—such as Bolivia, Honduras, and Finland—new judges are selected by the current members of the judiciary.

Judges in state courts are popularly elected in about three-fourths of the American states. In the Soviet Union, at the lowest rung in the judicial system informal meetings of citizens in factories or apartment houses may organize as "comradely courts" and choose judges from their own membership to settle local disputes. Judges of the Peoples Courts are also popularly elected; these courts, organized on a territorial basis throughout the U.S.S.R., have original jurisdiction in both civil and criminal cases, ranging widely from alimony to murder.

In the Anglo-American tradition, due process of law is built on judicial precedents, and judges are expected to be "learned in the law" and trained in jurisprudence. Although the Constitution does not require it, all federal judges are appointed from the legal profession, usually from among practicing lawyers, although sometimes a distinguished law professor may be chosen, especially in the appellate courts. British judges are elevated to the bench from the bar; also, there is a sharp social as well as professional distinction between barristers and solicitors, though both are lawyers. Much emphasis is placed on "the majesty of the law," symbolized by wigs and gowns still worn by the judges and barristers in court to set them apart from ordinary citizens. Members of the judiciary are generally recruited from upper-class groups who have enjoyed public-school (private) education, have attended one of the great universities, and who reside in one of the ancient Inns of Court.

On the continent, where entrance to the judiciary is by way of civil service examinations, a lawyer who elects to enter private practice cannot later switch to a judicial career. In France, the prospective judge, on passing his civil service examinations, receives an appointment as a judge, a public prosecutor, or a bureaucrat in the Ministry of Justice. Over the years he can expect to be promoted to more important posts, partly through merit, partly through political pull; the higher posts are never filled from outside as they are in the United States. French lawyers comprise three distinct groups: the *avocat*, who resembles the British barrister, argues the cases in court; the *avoué*, like the British solicitor, does the paper work preliminary to litigation; and the *notair* handles legal work that does not require court action.

German law students must also make an initial decision—whether to go into the regular civil service, into private practice, or into the judiciary. For judgeships, they must take rigorous examinations followed by lengthy probation; they begin their careers at the bottom of the judicial ladder and may gradually reach the upper rungs. As in France, appointments to the highest positions, even to the Federal High Court, are by promotion only. The German judge does not have either the social or professional status of his British counterpart. "He is, at all but the highest levels, very much like a civil servant, dependent upon the Justice Ministry for promotion within the hierarchy and imbued with a spirit and tradition very much akin to that of the regular civil servant."[3]

British courts were originally the King's Court; gradually, however, they have become autonomous organizations dominated by the legal profession. Today, although the judges owe their appointments to the Crown, they perform their functions quite independently of either Parliament or the Cabinet. The Lord Chancellor, who is Speaker of the House of Lords and a member of the Cabinet, has some administrative responsibility in the judicial system, but he has never assumed the role of a Minister of Justice. When the House of Lords holds a judicial sitting (an infrequent occurrence), the Lord Chancellor and Law Lords comprise the highest court of appeal in civil and criminal cases; the position of the Lord Chancellor is, then, somewhat like that of the Chief Justice of the Supreme Court. The French court system is administered by the Minister of Justice; justice is thus dispensed in a bureaucratic fashion, much as the postal service or any other public service; court officials are simply civil servants.

The Attorney General, who heads the U.S. Department of Justice, is neither a Minister of Justice in the continental sense nor a judge of the High Court like the Lord Chancellor. The Attorney General acts as legal advisor to the President and the executive departments and represents the national government in cases of exceptional importance before the Supreme Court. The Deputy Attorney General "handles" patronage appointments to the federal judiciary and presidential appointments in the Department of Justice; and the Solicitor General is responsible for all court cases in which the United States has an interest. But the Justice Department has no administrative or supervisory powers over the judicial system.

The Supreme Court of the U.S.S.R. shares with the Procurator General of the U.S.S.R. the responsibility for supervising the entire judicial system. The Procurator General, unlike the U.S. Attorney General, is not an agent of executive power, for he is appointed, not by the Council of Ministers, but by the Supreme Soviet of the U.S.S.R. The Procurator General appoints a procu-

---

[3] Arnold J. Heidenheimer, *The Government of Germany* (New York: Thomas Y. Crowell Co., 1966), p. 158.

rator as his personal agent at every level of the Soviet structure, from district to Union Republic. The procuracy embraces supervision of the courts, the administration of justice, and maintenance of due process of law. But, as is always the case in discussing totalitarian governments, we must keep in mind that constitutionalism is a façade for party dictatorship. In the U.S.S.R. the judges normally perform the same functions that judges do in every political system; that is, they settle disputes. But there is a marked difference between ordinary justice and political justice. Russian courts, like all other decision-making agencies in the Soviet system, are instruments of the Communist party. Russian judges are expected to educate the citizens of the U.S.S.R. in the norms of the socialist state, to promote respect for "soviet legality," to encourage a careful attitude toward socialist property, and to inculcate in the private citizen a proper sense of state and public duties. In the 1930s, Russian courts were used as showcases of orthodox Stalinism and served as efficient instruments for purging the government and the general citizenry of unorthodox communists.

It is probably fair to observe that American judges are also expected to serve an educational purpose; thus opinions of Supreme Court justices usually illuminate the democratic way of life and rationalize the capitalist economic system. If some of the justices appear to be "soft on communism" or refuse to legitimate attacks on "un-American activities," they can expect much criticism in the public forum.

French and German judges who settle disputes between private citizens have no authority to decide controversies which involve a public official. A case in which a public official is a party must be taken to an administrative court and be settled according to a special body of rules called *administrative law*. Students of French and German government point out that administrative courts are easily accessible to private citizens and relatively inexpensive for them. Moreover, the intent of administrative law is not so much to give the public official special consideration as to afford the citizen more effective protection against overzealous or arbitrary bureaucrats. According to the Anglo-American rule of law, all persons are subject to the law and none is exempt; hence public officials in the U.S. and Great Britain must be sued or prosecuted in the ordinary courts. We do not have administrative courts in the United States comparable to those generally found on the continent. Perhaps this is due to the fact that our civil service is relatively young compared to the European bureaucracies.

The Anglo-American courts follow an adversary procedure which was originally derived from *common law*—"what a reasonable man would think just"—but most of which is now specified in various statutes. In American federal courts, prosecution on criminal charges begins with indictment by a grand jury resulting from a preliminary presentation of evidence. In the trial proper, the judge acts as umpire between the lawyers for the defendant and for the government; the burden of proof is on the accusor (i.e., the government), and the rules of evidence are carefully devised to give the accused reasonable protection. In the French system, the proceedings are usually described as inquisitorial: a professional judge rather than a jury of private citizens makes the preliminary investigation and official accusation. The rules of evidence in the trial itself appear much less strict and formal than in the American or British Courts. Much of the courtroom activity seems to be in the nature of consultations and negotiations between the judges and lawyers.

British and American judges are governed, or profess to be governed, by rule of precedent, or *stare decisis*—what judges have ruled in previous cases on similar situations. It is part of the common law tradition even today that the judge "has obligations in every controversy to preserve the accumulated experience of the past."[4] Since judicial precedents have been piling up since the middle ages, the judge may have considerable discretion in choosing the applicable rule. It is also part of the same tradition for the judge to "anticipate the consequences to future generations, even as he seeks to dispense justice in the particular case before him,"[5] hence the claim that the judge in common law countries both "finds the law" and "makes the law."

Judges in the continental system have a less creative role; they apply to the case at hand the pertinent statute or rule from the code; they are not expected to build on precedents or to make new case law. It is easy, however, to exaggerate the difference between the two systems; no code is so rigid that it can be applied automatically. Whenever a judge has discretion in what rule he selects or in how he applies it, he becomes an active agent of justice. In general, then, there is perhaps a little more solicitude for the rights of the accused in the Anglo-American courts; and perhaps a little more concern for the public interest in continental courts.

Procedures in the Russian courts more nearly resemble the French than the British or American. As we have noted, the judges of the Peoples Courts (and the assessors who assist them) are elected by universal suffrage. Since there is no requirement that either the judges or assessors be lawyers, and since disputes do not have to be settled on the basis of judicial precedents, procedures and decisions vary considerably from one court to another in the Soviet Union. The Soviet Constitution declares that "judges are independent and subject only to the law"; but as a Soviet jurist explains it, "The independence of the judges . . . does not and cannot signify their independence of politics. The demand that the work of the judge be subject to the law and the demand that it be subject to the Communist Party cannot be in contradiction in our country."[6] Similarly, constitutional requirements that all cases be heard in public and that the accused have the right to be defended by counsel "unless otherwise provided by law" means that if policy demands it, trials may be conducted in secret and the accused may be denied access to counsel. The Great Purge of the 1930s under Stalin's dictatorship testifies to the grim implications of "unless otherwise provided by law."

[4]Glenn R. Winters and Robert E. Allard, "Judicial Selection and Tenure in the United States," in Harry W. Jones (ed.), *The Courts, the Public, and the Law Explosion* (Englewood Cliffs, N.J.: Prentice-Hall, Inc., an American Assembly Book, 1965), p. 147. The authors are respectively Executive Director and Assistant Executive Director of the American Judicature Society.
[5]*Ibid.*, pp. 146–177.
[6]N. N. Polyansky. Quoted in Merle Fainsod, *How Russia is Ruled* (Cambridge, Mass.: Harvard University Press, 1963), p. 375.

Both Tocqueville and Bryce marveled at the political influence of American judges, which both attributed to the power of judicial review possessed by all judges in the American constitutional system. It is the duty and right of the judges to settle disputes involving constitutional law according to their own views of what the Constitution means in specific instances. In pursuance of this duty and right, the judges may hold that a statute of Congress, or an act of the President—or the act of some bureaucrat, or some provision in a state constitution, or some state executive or legislative act—is unconstitutional. Although all judges in the American system are bound by this concept of constitutional law, the fact that the Supreme Court of the United States is the final court of appeal puts it at the apex of judicial power in the United States.

British judges, who enjoy a great deal of political independence, may interpret the laws as they think most reasonable, but they may not declare an act of Parliament unconstitutional. Judges in the ordinary French courts have no power of judicial review; the Constitution of the Fifth Republic sets up a Constitutional Council which may offer pronouncements on the constitutionality of executive and legislative actions. The Council has no power to enforce its decisions, however, and if the President or the Prime Minister or Parliament fails to consult with it, there is no way that the Council can make its views known. The Council is not accessible to the private citizen or open to appeals from the regular courts. Hence its position is far from comparable to that of the Supreme Court of the United States.

Special constitutional courts have been established in the postwar governments of Germany, Italy, and Austria in reaction to previous totalitarian regimes. German judges in ordinary courts do not have the power of judicial review, but the Constitutional Court is assigned special functions similar to those given to the Supreme Court of the United States. Judges of the Constitutional Court are elected for limited terms alternately by the Bundestag (lower house) and the Bundesrat (upper house) from panels of federal judges eligible for elevation to the Court and from other persons nominated for federal judgeships by the federal government, political parties, and Land (state) governments. The Constitutional Court has both "concrete" and "abstract" review jurisdiction. It may rule on constitutional questions in an actual ("concrete") controversy being heard in one of the lower courts; and it may give its opinion in an "abstract" controversy involving government agencies in dispute over constitutional meanings. In addition, it may declare its judgment when an ordinary citizen complains that his rights are infringed by specific legislation. The Court is empowered to settle disputes between the federal and Land governments and to decide on petitions charging infringements of basic individual rights. Further, the Court may deprive groups and individuals of normal constitutional rights if they engage in enumerated kinds of antidemocratic or unconstitutional behavior. (Under this latter provision, the Court has outlawed both the Socialist Reich Party, which was closely identified with the former Nazi regime, and the Communist party.) Thus it appears that the German Constitutional Court, like the U.S. Supreme

Court, is by the very nature of its judicial assignments frequently drawn into partisan conflict involving issues of paramount political importance. Because the Court is a recent innovation and the principle of judicial review is rather novel, however, the judges have not yet reached the peak of power which we attribute to the U.S. Supreme Court.

Among judicial institutions of the world, American judges, especially justices of the Supreme Court, enjoy a unique status as policy-makers. Many Latin American courts have been formally organized under constitutional and statutory prescriptions modeled after the federal system of the United States. In some Latin American countries, judges are the most prestigious officials in the government, but they are generally discreet in their exercise of judicial power. They may legitimate but they are not likely to invalidate the acts of executive or legislative agencies. Most of the developing new nations of Africa and Asia have replaced their tribal and traditional institutions with westernized judicial systems. Many of the judges in these countries have obtained their legal training in American or European universities. But as in Latin America, even when the constitution gives the judges the right to rule on the constitutionality of political acts, the power is not exercised. Judicial activism, judicial independence, and the exercise of judicial power in the political system—these are most characteristic of American judges.

The Nature of Law

To most laymen, the law is something to avoid. It's the highway patrolman lurking behind the billboard. It's the fine print in the insurance policy. It's the long delay in settling a small estate. It's the dog catcher when you've let your dog slip his leash. It's the game warden when you've shot one duck too many. It's the process-server with the jury summons for the week you planned to spend at the beach. It is prohibition and prosecution. It is words and phrases that only a lawyer can read and write. It is lawyer's fees and court costs. The power of the law is a policeman in uniform. The majesty of the law is a judge in black robes.

The law has been described in many ways. In Gilbert and Sullivan's *Iolanthe*, the Lord Chancellor sings:

> The law is the true embodiment
> Of everything that's excellent.
> It has no kind of fault or flaw,
> And I, my Lords, embody the Law.

Dr. Samuel Johnson said, "Law is the last result of human wisdom acting from human experience for the benefit of the public." But Mr. Bumble in *Oliver Twist* described it more graphically, "The law is a ass, a idiot."

Professional students of the law have viewed it in quite different ways. The nineteenth-century British scholar John Austin held that every law is a command from a political superior that is binding on inferiors—"superior" in this context signifying the power to force compliance. *Austinians* concede that custom may serve as a rule of conduct in society, but argue that it becomes positive law only when it is adopted as such by the courts of justice and only when the judicial decisions based on it are enforced by the power of the state.[7]

Other political scientists, from Aristotle to the present, have noted, "The law has no power to command obedience except that of habit, which can only be given by time." In this same vein, followers of the *sociological school* reject the concept that law is a command, for they believe that law springs from the customs of society. To them, government does not *make* law, but *guarantees* it. In *The Web of Government,* Robert MacIver describes "the firmament of law" as vastly greater and more intricate than could ever be devised by government. The "firmament of law" is derived from custom, cultural tradition, settled modes of procedure, and religious precepts, as well as from political rules. People observe the laws by "doing what comes naturally" rather than by complying with commands. Thus the real origins of the law, argues this school, are to be found with the help of anthropology, history, and even psychology, rather than through contemporary political science.

Justice Benjamin Cardozo, in deciding a case before the Supreme Court, once referred to "some principles of justice so rooted in the traditions and conscience of our people as to be ranked as fundamental."[8] Justice Felix Frankfurter held that law is "deeply rooted in reason," and that it cannot be arbitrary, capricious, or whimsical. What "shocks the conscience" or runs counter to the "decencies of civilized conduct" cannot be upheld as due process of law.[9] To Justice Frankfurter, due process of law was "compounded of history, reason, the past course of decisions, and stout confidence in the strength of the democratic faith which we profess."[10] Arthur Sutherland of the Harvard Law School notes, "Reasonableness is one of the commonest tools in the American lawyer's kit,"[11] To some, *stare decisis* is the "unrolling of reason in history;" since human nature is rarely original, almost any case that comes to court is bound to have a legal precedent. Thus law is the logical outcome of past experience.

Legal realists are less concerned with the origins and precedents of law than with its current impact. They regard law as a social science, and their real interest is in fact-finding, in arriving at conclusions supported by current evidence. Skeptical of legal magic, scornful of the "ancient word," they would make law serve its social purpose in the everyday world. Their approach to law is not only to study the statute books, the court reports, and the legal textbooks; they also dig into the data of economics, sociology, psychology, and political science. It is not enough, for example, to know the rules of bankruptcy; it is much more significant to understand the personal and the institutional causes of bankruptcy, and the social, economic, and psychological

---

[7]See "The Definition of Law," in *Lectures on Jurisprudence* (1832) quoted in Margaret Spahr, *Readings in Recent Political Philosophy* (New York: The Macmillan Company, 1935), pp. 105–131.
[8]*Snyder* v. *Massachusetts,* 291 U.S. 97 (1934).
[9]Frankfurter in *Rochin* v. *California,* 342 U.S. 165 (1952).
[10]*Joint Anti-Fascist Refugee Committee* v. *Magrath,* 341 U.S. 123 (1951).
[11]See Arthur E. Sutherland, *The Law and One Man Among Many* (Madison: University of Wisconsin Press, 1956), for a brief, original, and provocative discussion, "Perception of Justice."

causes of bankruptcy within a given period. Laws are not discovered, but rather must be made for a particular time in a specific place.

Legal realists reject the old saw, "More important that a case be settled than that it be settled right." Although *stare decisis* offers the advantage of certainty and stability, "outworn concepts which no longer fit the facts must be vacated. The judge should fit his decision to the facts; if he cannot find the precedents he must create new precedents."[12]

Jerome Frank, a legal realist and a distinguished federal judge, wrote a great deal about the "Law"—"that vague and troublesome word"—but eventually he tired of the "silly word-battle." For I think that one may say of 'Law' what Croce said of the word 'sublime'; it is 'everything that it is or will be called by those who have employed or will employ that name.'" Frank preferred to discuss what he called courthouse government, the pattern of social control that is imposed on us by lawyers and judges.[13] Justice Oliver Wendell Holmes once commented, "The prophecies of what the courts will do in fact, and nothing more pretentious, are what I mean by the law."

The study of public law (international law, administrative law, constitutional law) was once the core of the political science curriculum. It still is in many European universities. Until quite recently, students of American government were generally required to take one or more courses in constitutional law. What was taught as constitutional law usually included the text of the Constitution of 1787, its formal amendments, and judicial interpretations of these excerpted from the formal opinions of Supreme Court justices.[14] Most of the great issues that confront the nation have been recurrently argued before the Supreme Court: federal-state relationships, business-government conflicts, labor-management relations, police power versus private rights, majority versus minority interests, national security and individual liberties. The trenchant opinions of the justices, whether majority or dissenting views, provide a high level of discourse and usually a lively dialogue on the development of American constitutional government. Thus constitutional law has been widely regarded as "what the judges say it is"—from Marbury v. Madison (1803) to the most recent case decided in this October term.

The traditional approach to the study of constitutional law, in the law schools and in the political science classes, focuses on the substantive issues of case law. Landmark cases are examined and evaluated in light of legal reasoning, political philosophy, and constitutional history. Law students are usually more concerned with the court holdings, that part of the judicial opinion which is binding upon the parties in the case. Political science students are more likely to explore the *dicta* of the justices, opinions which may not be necessary to the decision in the case but which illuminate the personal or social values of the judge.

But just as legal realists claim that "it's not what judges say in their written

---

[12]William O. Douglas, "Stare Decisis," *Columbia Law Review,* XLIX (1949), 735.

[13]See *Law and the Modern Mind* (New York: Coward-McCann, Inc., 1930); *If Men Were Angels* (New York: Harper & Row, Publishers, Inc., 1942); *Courts on Trial* (Princeton: Princeton University Press, 1950).

[14]C. Herman Pritchett, "Public Law and Judicial Behavior: 1948–1968," *Journal of Politics,* XXX (February, 1968). This essay offers an excellent summary and critique of various approaches to the study of constitutional law and judicial behavior in American political science.

opinions but who wins that counts," so some political scientists are less interested in doctrinal analysis of case law and more concerned with the behavior of the judges in a political context. Thus Glendon Schubert, a leading exponent of the behavioral approach, tells us that "the major objective of studying constitutional law should not be to learn and to memorize what the Court has said but rather should be to understand the ecological process by which decisions of the Court are made."[15]

In this chapter we are committed to examine the role of the judges in the American national government in the same fashion that we looked at the legislators and bureaucrats, all as actors in a political setting, engaged in various aspects of the decision-making process.[16] We shall regard the Supreme Court as a political instrument and we shall treat its decisions as expressions of the behavior of the justices as political actors. We would, however, be most remiss if we concentrated our attention only upon the Supreme Court and its celebrated decisions in constitutional law. This chapter is about *all* the federal judges in *all* the federal courts who are expected to settle all kinds of disputes on the basis of law.

When we highlighted differences among judicial systems in the world, we referred to the common law tradition of the Anglo-American courts. Here we need to spell out a little more clearly what we mean by *common law* and *statutory law*.

Having read this far, you are ready to reject the notion that legislators make the law and that judges merely apply it to specific disputes. As a matter of fact, the great body of law in this country, in all states except Louisiana, has its roots in *common law*.[17] This is the law that has governed Englishmen everywhere "from time immemorial." "From time immemorial" dates from about the twelfth century, when Henry I attempted to regularize the administration of justice in England. The king's justices, who rode on circuit from one community to another, were instructed to apply the king's justice uniformly in all the king's courts. This meant that they were to render similar judgments in similar cases throughout the realm. In making a decision, each judge would refer to other cases he had decided elsewhere on the circuit, or to the precedents set by judges on other circuits. Contrary to popular misconception, common law is not unwritten law; it is very much written, for it has been recorded for hundreds of years in court reports. The origin of common law is to be found in customary law (the customs of the community), canon law (the

---

[15]Glendon A. Schubert, *Constitutional Politics* (New York: Holt, Rinehart and Winston, Inc., 1960), p. 6.

[16]Students interested in pursuing approaches to public law will find a variety of views in Glendon Schubert, "Ideologies and Attitudes, Academic and Judicial," *The Journal of Politics*, XXIX (February, 1967) 3–140; Wallace Mendelson, "The Untroubled World of Jurimetrics," *The Journal of Politics*, XXVI (November, 1964) 914–922; Martin Shapiro, *Law and Politics in the Supreme Court* (New York: The Free Press of Glencoe, Inc., 1964), Chapter 1, "The Supreme Court as Political Agency"; Theodore L. Becker, *Political Behavioralism and Modern Jurisprudence* (Chicago: Rand McNally & Co., 1964).

[17]Louisiana, originally a French colony, still maintains a separate system of law based on the Napoleonic Code.

laws of the Church), the Roman codes (for the Romans occupied Britain for a longer period than white men have lived in the Western Hemisphere), and merchant law (the laws developed in commercial transactions).

Since human beings tend to fall into the same kinds of trouble in every age, many of the cases heard in American courts today are not too different from the disputes decided long ago by the king's judges in England. Here are some familiar cases in court, any place, any time: the neighbors who argue over boundary disputes (*his* oaktree puts *my* rosebed in too much shade; the eaves of *his* house trespass upon *my* property; *his* well is drawing *my* water; *his* chickens wake *me* at the crow of dawn)—the husband and wife who find marriage disagreeable (*he* won't support me and the children; *she* doesn't understand me; *he* deserted me; *she* wouldn't leave her mother; *he* ran after another woman; *she* "entertained" while I was at work). Judges have been settling such disputes for centuries; there is no end to the legal precedents. But if an entirely new kind of case does happen to arise, one that cannot be settled by turning to precedent, under common law the judge may use right reason and decide "what a reasonable man would think just." Thus without benefit of any legislative law at all, judges may "make" everyday law for the community. Moreover, since common law exists and grows within the cultural context, most people abide by it habitually and conscientiously, without ever realizing that they are obeying the law.

Human nature may be much the same in the twentieth century as it was in the twelfth, but social and economic conditions are vastly different. In an era of atomic energy, the wheels of civilization turn infinitely faster than in the days when the king's justices rode on horseback from village to hamlet. To wait for the slow accretion of common law, case by case, seems too inefficient and cumbersome for modern society. And so legislators now enact a great deal of *statutory law*, which has largely replaced the old common law.

The legal system in the United States today is overwhelmingly a system of statutory law, adminstrative regulations, and recent judicial decisions interpreting these statutes and regulation. It is not a system of common law in the sense that we have described above. If you commit murder, divorce your wife, drive an automobile, pay your income tax, run a restaurant, sell insurance, build a swimming pool in your backyard, apply for a passport or a patent, teach school, or practice osteopathy, your actions are bound to be governed by statute and/or administrative regulation. Laws passed by the legislature, or rules made by regulatory agencies, presumably embody the public policy and represent the dominant will of the community. Since statutory law deals with general problems, however, rather than with specific disputes, a judge must still "find" the appropriate general rule, and then interpret it, in a particular case. Thus the style of judicial process is still colored by the common law tradition which is taught in the law schools as part of the requisite professional background.

All federal law is statutory law, made up of the laws passed by Congress and the rules and regulations that administrators make in carrying out those laws. When the federal courts hear cases that involve citizens of different states, however, they must apply the common law of the state where the controversy arose, unless that state has a specific statute to govern the case. For more than a century, federal judges were free to use their own judgment in the absence of state statutes, and had built up a body of federal common law. In 1938, however, in a decision that reversed precedent and practice dating almost from the beginning of our history, the United States Supreme Court ruled: "Except in matters governed by the Federal Constitution or by acts of Congress, the law to be applied in any case is the law of the state. . . . There is no federal general common law." But this "reform" has created a problem, for now the same federal court may have to apply different laws in deciding cases with identical facts because the cases arose in states with different laws on the subject.[18]

Federal courts handle both *criminal* and *civil* cases. Many kinds of crime make the front page of the newspapers: assault and battery, mayhem, rape, prostitution, bigamy, kidnapping, arson, burglary, larceny, embezzlement, robbery, forgery, counterfeiting, bribery. All these and many more are serious offenses against the public. In most states, criminal law is now generally covered by statutes that define the offense and prescribe the penalties. But any offense against the public morals, safety, or peace is "against the law" even if not in the statutes; the judge can always go back to the common law.

Our federal system vests primary responsibility for the maintenance of law and order in our state and local authorities. Since we have no national common law, offenses against the national government are limited to violations of federal statutes and administrative orders. Every year, Congress passes hundreds of statutes and the administrative agencies prescribe thousands of rules which have the force of law. Hence federal criminal law touches on everyday activities in every community. The Department of Justice, which is charged with enforcing federal criminal law, prosecutes individuals for violations of civil rights acts, internal security statutes, and antitrust laws; for evasion of federal taxes; for fraud in elections; for adulteration of food, drugs, and cosmetics; for violations of the narcotics, liquor, and gambling laws; for fraud against the government; and for fraud by mail. The Department of Justice enforces more than 600 federal criminal statutes covering treason, espionage, sedition, labor racketeering, bank robbery, bankruptcies, extortion, kidnaping, counterfeiting, transporting stolen motor vehicles across state lines, and many other offenses.

Cases in *civil law* do not usually make the front page of the newspapers. Most citizens, however, seem to get involved in civil litigation at some time or other, even when they stay home and mind their own business. If you fail to keep up the payments on your house or car, if your dog nips the newsboy or chases your neighbor's chickens, if your car even so much as dents the fender of another, you may find yourself the defendant in a civil suit. Or you may find it necessary to appear as plaintiff in a suit for libel, violation of contract, or abatement of nuisance.

The United States courts hear a great many civil suits involving federal laws

---

[18]The Supreme Court discusses the problem in *New York Central Railroad Company v. White*, 243 U.S. 188 (1917).

on such matters as copyrights, patents, trademarks, fair labor standards, labor-management relations, and civil rights. Then, too, even though no federal law is at issue, citizens of different states may bring their controversies into federal courts. For example, a citizen of Georgia may sue a citizen of Vermont, or a corporation organized in Delaware may bring suit against a corporation organized in Illinois. Many such suits go to federal courts under "diversity of citizenship," and in these cases the federal judges apply state rather than federal law. The increasing number of civil cases in both state and federal courts suggests that Americans are a very litigious people.

The Rulers of Law: Their Background and Recruitment

Lawyers

Americans are fond of saying that we have "a government of laws and not of men." But the fact is that all laws are made by men to rule other men. Although the United States has less than a quarter of a million lawyers, their influence in all branches of the government is great, and they have practically taken over the judiciary completely. In Anglo-Saxon countries especially, where respect for law is a tradition, lawyers enjoy a special status in society, because only they know how to read and write the language of the law. Whereas the law is unintelligible to laymen, hereinafter called the party of the first part; and whereas only lawyers, hereinafter referred to as the party of the second part, know what the law says or how to obtain standing under the law in the courts of justice; and whereas ignorance of the law is no excuse to the party of the first part; be it understood therefore by all those present that the party of the first part has the right, privilege, and every necessity to seek the advice and counsel of the party of the second part in due process of law and administration of justice.

When Tocqueville visited the United States, he was impressed by the conspicuous leadership of lawyers in American society. Everywhere he went, he found that the legal profession constituted a sort of privileged body, a political aristocracy that could be counted on to brake the excesses of democracy. "Men who have made a special study of the laws derive from occupation certain habits of order, a taste for formalities, and a kind of instinctive regard for the regular connection of ideas, which naturally render them very hostile to the revolutionary spirit and the unreflecting passions of the multitude." Tocqueville thought that the emphasis which Anglo-Saxon law puts upon precedents had a distinct effect on the character of its lawyers:

> In the mind of an English or American lawyer a taste and a reverence for what is old is almost always united with a love of regular and lawful proceedings. . . . A French observer is surprised to hear how often an English or an American lawyer quotes the opinions of others and how little he alludes to his own, while the reverse occurs in France. . . . This abnegation of his own opinion and this implicit deference to the opinion of his forefathers, which are common to the English and American lawyer, this servitude of thought which he is obliged to profess, necessarily gives him more timid habits and more conservative inclinations in England and America than in France.[19]

[19]Tocqueville, *Democracy in America*, 1830, op. cit., Vol. I, pp. 283, 286–287.

A more recent study of lawyers in politics by Heinz Eulau and John D. Sprague refers to lawyers as the "high priests of politics."[20] Eulau and Sprague point out that no occupational group stands in more regular and intimate relation to American politics than the legal profession. Lawyers have virtually a monopoly of public offices connected with the administration of justice, both in law enforcement and in the judiciary. They are also most prominent in the executive and legislative offices. Twenty-three of the thirty-six American Presidents have been lawyers. And we have already noted the large proportion of them in both houses of Congress.

Eulau and Sprague made an empirical study of lawyer-legislators and nonlawyer-legislators in four states: New Jersey, Ohio, Tennessee, and California. They found no significant difference in the ideological stance of lawyer-legislators and nonlawyer-legislators. They reject outright the argument that lawyers are likely to be politically conservative because the methods of the legal process are conservative. They point out that law seeks regularity and predictability of human affairs, but that it is also an instrument for social change. On the basis of a short attitudinal scale, in all four state legislatures a greater proportion of the lawyers than the nonlawyers scored "liberal."

Eulau and Sprague discount Tocqueville's notion that lawyers in America constitute a privileged social class. It just doesn't make sense to lump in one economic or social class the many small-town lawyers with private practices earning a few thousand dollars a year and the highly specialized corporation lawyers in New York or Washington who make a few hundreds of thousands of dollars a year. Moreover, lawyers differ widely in educational background and in the quality of their education; about half the lawyers in America are not college graduates. Eulau and Sprague observe that the status of a particular lawyer may be affected more by his ethnic or group affiliations than by his occupation. Addressing their inquiries to what they call the "professional convergence of lawyers and politicians," they found that there was a vocational affinity and a compulsion to pursue both the law and politics, but that the urge to enter politics usually preceded the decision to study law.

In this chapter, we are concerned not with the legal profession *in toto*, but particularly with lawyers who enter the federal judiciary. Lawyer-judges comprise a very small percentage of the lawyers in America, and what may characterize lawyers generally or even lawyer-legislators in four states may not hold true for federal lawyer-judges. A recent statistical breakdown of the legal profession shows that only 9 per cent of all lawyers are in any government service and only 3 per cent in the judiciary (and this includes national, state, and local judgeships). The overwhelming proportion of lawyers are in private practice.[21]

---

[20]Heinz Eulau and John D. Sprague, *Lawyers in Politics* (Indianapolis: The Bobbs-Merrill Company, Inc., 1964), p. 42.

[21]Eulau and Sprague, *Lawyers in Politics*, p. 135. According to the Martin-Hubbell census of 1958, there were 262,320 lawyers in the United States; 73 per cent were listed in private practice, 7 per cent salaried in private industry, 9 per cent in government service, 3 per cent in the judiciary, 4 per cent in law school, and 7.6 per cent in other employment.

Selection of Federal Judges

John R. Schmidhauser, of the University of Iowa, has done a pioneering job of data-gathering on the social and political backgrounds of the justices of the Supreme Court from 1789 to 1959. "The picture that emerges in the pattern of recruitment of Supreme Court justices is one which emphasizes the intimacy of judicial and political affairs."[22] Schmidhauser assumes that the social and economic backgrounds of the justices, especially family attitudes, "may be accounted subtle factors influencing the tone and temper of judicial decision-making." Only a handful of the justices were of essentially humble origin. Most of them came from politically active families in comfortable economic circumstances, from the gentry and professional classes. Only six of the justices were born abroad, five of these in the British Isles, Felix Frankfurter in Austria. In ethnic origin, nearly all the justices have been of British descent; only five of them of Central, Eastern, or Southern European descent; no person of Asian descent has ever been nominated. The largest percentage of justices have been Protestant, mainly Episcopalian, Presbyterian, Congregational, and Unitarian. Only 10 per cent have been Roman Catholic, Jewish, or Quaker. All the justices have had legal training of some kind, all practiced law at some stage in their careers, nearly all of them made law their major occupation. Up to 1861, most of the justices had pursued primarily political careers before appointment. Between 1862 and 1933, the percentage of judicial careerists increased considerably. In the whole history of the Court, over 50 per cent of the justices had prior judicial experience, although only slightly more than 25 per cent had really extensive judicial careers.

Because the Supreme Court justices are few in number and their business is of paramount national importance, they are most often singled out for political attack and academic study. In fact, however, most law-making by judges occurs in lower courts. The Supreme Court may consider about fifteen hundred cases in one term, giving its full opinions in perhaps a hundred of these. In the same term, the federal District Courts will handle more than a hundred thousand cases, of which only about 3 per cent will ever reach the appellate courts. To scrutinize the social, economic, and political background of all the judges whose decisions have made policy at different times in different sections of the country would be a highly rewarding but herculean task. The most we can attempt here is to note how district judges and judges of Circuit Courts of Appeals have recently gained their positions as decision-makers in the federal political system.

The Constitution provides that the President shall appoint judges of the Supreme Court with the advice and consent of the Senate, but it does not spell out how judges of the inferior courts are to be selected. Legally, the President appoints *all* federal judges with the advice and consent of the Senate; actually, the roles of the President and Senate vary considerably according to the level of appointments under consideration. In George Washington's time, perhaps the President could be expected to know personally who was qualified and

---

[22]John R. Schmidhauser, *The Supreme Court: Its Politics, Personalities and Procedures* (New York: Holt, Rinehart and Winston, Inc., 1960), p. 57. See also by the same author, "The Justices of the Supreme Court—A Collective Portrait," *Midwest Journal of Political Science*, III (1959), 1–57. The article contains extensive charts detailing the social and economic variations in judicial selection.

available for judicial appointments. But the modern President is much too preoccupied with policy matters to spend his time seeking out and screening candidates for lower level appointments. Thus it is now customary for the President to rely on the Department of Justice, and particularly the Deputy Attorney General, to organize the selection process.

Many different pressures enter into the selection of federal district judges. Although the Constitution does not specify any residence requirements, it is understood that judgeships in any given state will be filled by local candidates. Aspirants to judicial office normally seek the endorsement of their local and state party leaders and bar associations. A senator usually feels obliged to collect information on several contenders for judicial positions within his state. Operating on the old saw that "in making an appointment you make fifty enemies and one ingrate," most senators are inclined to suggest a number of "acceptable" candidates and then leave it up to the Department of Justice to take its pick for presidential consideration. The custom of senatorial courtesy gives the individual senators considerable influence in the selection of district judges within their respective states. But when it comes to appointments in the Courts of Appeals, the balance of power shifts to the presidential side. No one senator, or pair of senators, can claim a vital interest in a judicial appointment within a circuit that covers several states. Senatorial courtesy may be invoked by a senator of the state from which the nominee comes, but this is a rare occurrence. Ordinarily clearance on all nominations—including ratings by the American Bar Association, FBI checks, and party endorsements—is usually settled before the President takes any public action.

A *Congressional Quarterly* review of postwar judicial appointments—from the beginning of the Truman administration to the end of the Kennedy administration—covers all appointments to the Supreme Court, 92 appointments to the Circuit Courts of Appeals, and 329 appointments to District Courts.[23] All of the Supreme Court appointments were controversial, received considerable attention in the Senate, and got nationwide play in the press. Hardly a handful of the rest of the appointments evoked either debate in the Senate or national press coverage; only four nominations, all by Truman in the period of McCarthyism, were rejected.

Although the Constitution fixes no qualifications for federal judges, the method by which they are selected—presidential nomination and senatorial confirmation—makes their political views a paramount consideration. Most Presidents declare it their intention to make judicial appointments on a nonpartisan basis. Nevertheless, throughout the nation's history, judicial appointments have been used as patronage levers for the exercise of political power. Defeated in the presidential election of 1800, the Federalist administration of John Adams did all that it could to entrench good Federalists in judicial posts before the Republicans could come into office. Between 1933 and 1963, Presidents Roosevelt, Truman, Eisenhower, and Kennedy made a total of

[23]*Congress and the Nation, 1945–1964* (Washington, D.C.: Congressional Quarterly, Inc. 1965) pp. 1441–1454.

799 appointments to federal judgeships at all levels; of these 61, or less than 8 per cent, were to nominees of "the other party."[24]

During the 1960 campaign, the President of the American Bar Association asked both major candidates to pledge themselves in advance to the principle of bipartisanship. Candidate Kennedy replied that, "I would hope that the paramount consideration in the appointment of a judge would not be his political party, but his qualifications for the office."[25]

In President Kennedy's first year, Congress created 73 new federal judgeships, 10 in the Circuit Courts of Appeals, and 63 in the District Courts. President Eisenhower had urged the preceeding Congress to authorize additional judgeships in order to alleviate overloaded federal dockets. The Democratic Congress determined to hold off, however, until a Democratic President could dispense the luscious patronage plums. The Kennedy administration — campaign statements notwithstanding — made no bones about its policy of rewarding the party faithful, especially those who had worked for the nomination as well as the election of the President. During his time in office, President Kennedy got to appoint 128 federal judges; all but 11 were Democrats.

Since 1945, the American Bar Association, acting through a Standing Committee on the Federal Judiciary, has undertaken to pass on the qualifications of nominees. It offers an informal report to the Department of Justice on any person being seriously considered for nomination. After carefully investigating the potential nominee, the Committee rates him either "Exceptionally Well Qualified," "Well Qualified," "Qualified," or "Not Qualified." The ABA Committee considers a number of factors in their rating of judicial candidates. For instance, because judges have lifetime appointments — "during good behavior" — and the average age of incumbent judges is high, the ABA is on guard against stacking the courts with additional old men. They therefore do not recommend lawyers of sixty years or over. In addition, the ABA insists that a well-rated candidate have a reasonable amount of trial experience, fifteen years or so of legal practice, before he is elevated to the bench. The ABA committee also investigates the social and professional status of the candidate in his own community, a process which does not lend itself to scientific evaluation. (Meantime, the Department of Justice runs an FBI investigation of the candidate: federal judges, like Caesar's wife, are supposed to be above suspicion.)

A President need not be bound by ABA ratings. President Kennedy made a number of appointments in the face of a committee rating of "unqualified." Understandably, there is room for honest disagreement concerning the qualifications of a "good" judge. The ABA committee has shown a distinct bias toward corporate trial lawyers; but a negligence lawyer or a labor lawyer or a lawyer-politician may have more understanding of the problems that people take into courts. Morever, as in all political appointments, such factors as personal friendship with powers-that-be (a senator, someone in the Justice

---

[24]Data from *Congress and the Nation*. p. 1444. See also Sheldon Goldman, "Characteristics of Eisenhower and Kennedy Appointees to the Lower Federal Courts," *Western Political Quarterly*, XVIII (1965). 755–762.

[25]*The New York Times*, August 31, 1960.

Department, or the President himself), ethnic or religious considerations, group affiliations, as well as service to the party, may enter into the nomination.

Over the years, the ABA has been notably conservative in its political opinions. It has supported, for example, the Tidelands Oil Bill, which returned offshore oil rights to the states; the proposed Reed-Dirksen Amendment, which would have placed a 25 per cent limit on income tax; the proposed Bricker Amendment, which would have limited the treaty-making power of the President; and various congressional proposals to override Supreme Court decisions involving basic procedural rights. In the midst of the McCarthy era, the ABA commended the House Un-American Activities Committee and the Senate Internal Security Subcommittee on the manner in which they conducted their hearings and investigations. More recently, the ABA endorsed a constitutional amendment to override the decision of the Supreme Court with respect to reapportionment of state legislatures on the basis of one-man, one-vote. And in the current civil rights controversy, the ABA has been more concerned with the maintenance of law and order than with the issues of racial discrimination and denial of equal protection of the laws. Thus, although the political orientation of the ABA is certainly not the controlling factor in committee evaluations of particular candidates, no doubt some of the political bias of the ABA is reflected in the ratings of individuals under consideration by the Committee. Hence a Democratic President with the liberal views of a Kennedy or Johnson may find it quite preferable to disregard an ABA report on a particular nominee.[26]

Selection of Supreme Court Justices

Politics has always governed appointments to the Supreme Court. Because President John Adams had appointed John Marshall as Chief Justice of the Supreme Court, the Federalist Party remained entrenched in the national government for many years after the Federalists had ceased winning national elections. Indeed, every administration has tried to extend its political power through its appointment to the federal judiciary. Roger B. Taney, who succeeded John Marshall as Chief Justice in 1836, had been a member of Andrew Jackson's cabinet, and he carried his political views along with him when he went to the Court. Constitutional law was consequently revised considerably, for the Taney Court emphasized states' rights and "dual federalism" instead of the strong national government that the Marshall Court had supported.

Even more dramatic was the revolution in constitutional law that was staged in the 1930s. President Roosevelt's New Deal was blocked at the outset by the "nine old men" of the Court, the political appointees of previous administrations. Roosevelt eventually succeeded in replacing eight of the nine with his

[26]See Joel Grossman, *Lawyers and Judges* (New York: John Wiley & Sons, Inc., 1965) for a study of the influence of the ABA. The material in this chapter is also drawn from a monumental study (still in manuscript), by Harold Chase at the Brookings Institution, of federal judicial appointments.

own appointees, who were imbued with "the new constitutionalism," and the "Roosevelt Court" soon discovered dimensions in the federal system that made it possible to constitutionalize the national welfare state without any formal amendment.

Franklin D. Roosevelt's initial and unusual difficulty with the judiciary was in part simply a matter of bad luck; he had to wait four years to make his first appointment to the Supreme Court. As Robert A. Dahl notes in his revealing study of the frequency of presidential appointments to the Supreme Court, "Over the whole history of the Court, on the average one new justice has been appointed every twenty-two months. Thus a president can expect to appoint about two new justices during one term in office." Given even average luck, Roosevelt would have made two appointments in his first term and might have been able to avoid the head-on collision with the Court that occurred over the New Deal. A President does not normally appoint justices whose views on public policy are hostile to his own. Nor are the senators likely to confirm the nomination of a man whose stance on key questions is flagrantly at odds with the majority of the Senate. In other words, most justices are selected not so much for their "judicial" qualifications as for their "political" views. Hence Dahl draws the logical conclusion: "The policy views dominant on the Court are never for long out of line with the policy views dominant among the lawmaking majorities of the United States."[27]

"The good that Presidents do is often interred with their Administration. It is their choice of Supreme Court justices that lives after them."[28] President Eisenhower in his first administration had an opportunity to reshape constitutional law through his appointments to the Supreme Court. The Eisenhower appointments followed the custom of rating such factors as party affiliation, geographic background, religion, and political and social beliefs above legal training and judicial experience. His first appointment was Earl Warren as Chief Justice. This obviously fulfilled a party, and possibly a personal, commitment. Warren—three times Governor of California, and a vice-presidential candidate in 1948—was a national figure in Republican politics. Moreover he had contributed substantially to the Eisenhower victory in the West in 1952. Eisenhower's second appointment to the Court, John Marshall Harlan of New York, was also political: Harlan, who had served less than a year on the federal bench, was a personal friend of Governor Thomas E. Dewey, to whom Eisenhower was indebted for the eastern campaign in 1952.

Almost immediately, the Warren Court had to decide a number of cases on extremely controversial issues, involving such questions as segregation, sedition, and control of natural gas. Those who disliked the decisions criticized the justices for being "unjudicial." Some members of the American Bar Association were especially vocal in complaint. They managed to get introduced into Congress various proposals that would require more judicial training as a qualification for nominees to the Supreme Court. Individual

---

[27]Robert A. Dahl, "Decision-Making in a Democracy: The Role of the Supreme Court as a National Policy-Maker," *Journal of Public Law* (Emory University Law School), VI (1957), 279–295. This same volume contains a symposium, "Policy-Making in a Democracy: The Role of the United States Supreme Court," with contributions by well-known political scientists and lawyers.

[28]Editorial, *The Nation* (January 14, 1939), 52, on the occasion of Justice Frankfurter's appointment to the Supreme Court.

congressmen joined in the complaints against judicial forays into policy-making, but Congress took no action to change the composition of the Court.

President Eisenhower, however, did respond to public opinion. Instead of replacing Justice Sherman Minton, who had resigned, with another midwestern Republican, he appointed William Joseph Brennan, Jr., a member of the New Jersey Supreme Court with ten years of experience on the bench. Since this appointment was made on the eve of the 1956 elections, some cynical commentators noted that Brennan was a Catholic and a Democrat, and hinted that the appointment might have been calculated to bring some of Brennan's faith and party into the Republican fold. Eisenhower's fourth appointment did go to a Midwesterner, a lawyers' judge, Charles E. Whittaker. For twenty-five years, Justice Whittaker had been a successful trial lawyer; he had served as president of the Missouri State Bar Association; and he had sat for over three years as a federal judge. The retirement of Justice Harold Burton in the fall of 1958 gave President Eisenhower the opportunity of naming a fifth justice to the Court. He chose Potter Stewart, a judge of the U.S. Court of Appeals since 1954. Known as a "liberal" and a "humanitarian," Judge Stewart also admitted to "being a Republican" from Ohio.

In his less than three years in office, President Kennedy made two appointments to the Supreme Court, both in 1962. The first appointment went to Byron R. White, following the retirement of Justice Whittaker. The new justice was known to many Americans as "Whizzer" White, an All-American football star in the 1930's; but he was also a Rhodes scholar, a graduate of the Yale Law School, a law clerk of Chief Justice Fred Vinson, and a successful corporation lawyer. Probably more pertinent to the appointment, he had campaigned for Kennedy in 1960; and in 1961, as Deputy Attorney General, he had successfully handled the problem of attacks on "Freedom Riders" in Alabama. The chance to make a second appointment came with the resignation of Justice Frankfurter, who had suffered a number of heart attacks in the spring and summer of 1962. The President named Arthur Goldberg, then Secretary of Labor, who had achieved his reputation as a labor union lawyer.

No doubt the selection of White and Goldberg was calculated to tip the balance of power toward the "liberals" on the Court and to assure the President that he would have at least two justices on the Supreme Court who were in accord with the policies of the New Frontier. Some commentators on the Goldberg nomination, however, recalled the circumstances under which his predecessor had arrived on the Court. In 1939, Professor Frankfurter's appointment was generally regarded as part of President Roosevelt's strategy to pack the Court with "left-wing radicals"; but in 1962, when the Justice ended his long and distinguished career on the Court, conservatives felt they had lost their most effective spokesman.[29]

---

[29] James E. Clayton, on the Staff of *The Washington Post*, has given a nontechnical account of the October Term of 1962 in *The Making of Justice—The Supreme Court in Action* (New York: E. P. Dutton & Co., Inc., 1964). The account is particularly discerning because of its vignettes of the people who participate in the judicial process.

An appointment to the Supreme Court has usually been regarded as the culmination of a political career, although some justices have used their position on the Court as stepping stones to other political posts. When Justice Arthur Goldberg resigned in 1965 to become U.S. Representative to the United Nations, the career switch occasioned much puzzled comment. He was not, however, creating a new precedent. Justice Charles Evans Hughes resigned in 1916 to become the Republican candidate for the presidency; and twenty years later he returned to the Court as its Chief Justice, after an active career in politics that included the position of Secretary of State for President Harding. Justice James Byrnes resigned after little more than a year's service on the Court to become President Roosevelt's wartime Assistant to the President. Other Justices who are said to have nourished presidential aspirations while on the bench include Salmon P. Chase, Stephen J. Field, William O. Douglas, and Earl Warren. On the other hand, William Howard Taft always claimed that he reached the pinnacle of his ambitions not in the presidency but later as Chief Justice.

The fact that justices of the Supreme Court are selected on a political basis does not mean that they become stooges for the administration that appoints them. The members of the "Roosevelt Court" followed no White House party line, or any other one political line. In fact, they frequently disagreed with one another—Frankfurter versus Douglas, Jackson versus Black. The "Truman Court" turned on the administration in the *Steel Seizure Case*, when two out of four of Truman's personal appointees voted against his action. So when we speak of the "political" character of the Court, we do not mean that the justices make decisions in the manner of party hacks, or that their opinions simply reflect their personal prejudices. Most judges observe the ethics of their profession, and will not consciously use their position on the bench to advance their private views or even to support popular policies.[30]

The Constitution provides that "the Judges, both of the Supreme and Inferior courts, shall hold their offices during good behavior," but neither the Framers of the Constitution nor Congress have deemed it fitting to establish the kind of career service which characterizes judicial systems in the continental countries. As we have just seen, local political influence plays a large part in the selection of the District Court judges. A considerable number of judges on the Courts of Appeals have been recruited from the trial courts, but the American judicial hierarchy has no tradition of promotion from one level to the next. Relatively few justices in the history of the Supreme Court have had judicial experience before their appointment to the top tribunal. If judicial experience had been a requisite for Supreme Court appointments, the Court's roster would never have included such distinguished names as John Marshall, Roger B. Taney, Morrison R. Waite, Melville Fuller, John Harlan, Edward S. White, Louis Brandeis, Charles E. Hughes, George Sutherland, Harlan F. Stone, Robert H. Jackson, Fred Vinson, and Felix Frankfurter.

---

[30]Daniel Danelski has made an intensive study of the appointment of one Supreme Court justice—Justice Pierce Butler, who was appointed to the Court by President Warren G. Harding. He gathers all the data available on factors influencing the appointment and develops a theory of transactions to explain the process. *A Supreme Court Justice is Appointed* (New York: Random House, Inc., 1964).

Justice William O. Douglas refutes the myth that prior service on other courts or a long-time practice in law provides the "judicial" attitude and legal experience necessary for the work of the Supreme Court. He points out that most law firms, large or small, do not attempt to cover the wide range of problems with which the Supreme Court must deal. Most lawyers tend to become specialists, and many law offices never take a case in civil rights. The bulk of litigation in the lower courts is not concerned with paramount public issues but rather with the settlement of specific and technical legal questions. Justice Douglas, from his own experience, avers that it takes a decade or more for a justice on the Supreme Court to "run the length of the course and become familiar with its various features."[31] Certainly, the breadth of knowledge and wide experience in the law are desirable qualities in any judge. But because the courts play a positive and creative role in policy-making, it is also important for judges to have a broad understanding of public policy and a realistic concept of the impact of law on the structure of society.

Constitutional Status and Role Concepts of the Judiciary

Constitutional Prescription

The Constitution does not prescribe judicial behavior. It simply specifies that the judicial power of the United States shall be vested in one Supreme Court and in such lower courts as Congress chooses to establish. To help insure judicial independence, Article III provides that the compensation of judges shall not be diminished, but it does not forbid increases in compensation. Once appointed, a judge holds office during good behavior. If his behavior becomes questionable, he may be impeached, like any other national officer, in the House of Representatives, tried in the Senate, convicted by two-thirds vote. If convicted of "treason, bribery, or other high crimes and misdemeanors," he is removed from office and disqualified to hold any other office in the national government.

Under the Constitution, the "judicial power" of the United States extends broadly to two kinds of cases:

(1) According to the *nature of the controversy*
  (a) Cases arising under the Constitution, laws, and treaties of the United States.
  (b) Cases under admiralty and maritime law.
(2) According to the *nature of the parties*
  (a) Cases affecting ambassadors and other foreign diplomats.
  (b) Controversies to which the United States is a party.
  (c) Controversies between two or more states.
  (d) Controversies between citizens of different states.

The Constitution defines the *original jurisdiction* of the Supreme Court: "All cases affecting Ambassadors, other public ministers and Consuls, and those in

---

[31]Justice William O. Douglas, "The Supreme Court and Its Case Load," speech to the Cornell Law School, Ithaca, New York, April 8, 1960.

which a State shall be a Party." Otherwise, the Constitution leaves it up to Congress to determine the jurisdiction of the federal courts.

Article III provides that the trial of all crimes shall be by jury and take place in the state where said crimes shall have been committed. Further constitutional restraints on judicial procedures appear in the Bill of Rights, discussed in some detail in Chapter 14, "Civil Rights." Meantime, read for yourself the basic specifications for the protection of individuals in the administration of justice as they are laid down in Amendments IV, V, VI, VII, and VIII. Recently, the Supreme Court justices have been updating the meaning of these amendments to protect the rights of defendants against overzealous law enforcement. Moreover, through new interpretations of those clauses in the Fourteenth Amendment which require equal protection of the laws and due process of the law in the states, the justices have been actively remolding judicial procedures in the state courts to fit what the Supreme Court, or a current majority of Supreme Court justices, considers a national norm for justice in America.

The Framers of the Constitution had no intention of making the federal courts responsible to the people. On the contrary, in the original design of the Constitution, judges were three steps removed from direct election. They were appointed by the President (who was indirectly chosen by the electoral colleges), and were confirmed by the Senate (which was appointed by the state legislatures). As we have seen before, the Founding Fathers took a dim view of direct democracy. Hamilton, in *The Federalist*, counted on the judges "to do their duty as faithful guardians of the Constitution, where legislative invasions of it had been instigated by the major voice of the community." Hamilton anticipated that the legislature, as representatives of the people, might respond to the majority will of the moment and be persuaded into "dangerous innovations in the government." Therefore he put his trust in the "independency of the judiciary"—independence, that is, from popular control.[32]

No public officials of course are ever completely independent. All of them are conditioned by the social and economic environment in which they live and work, and their decisions are bound to represent some of those attributes which we call character in a man. Judges, however, are perhaps less free than legislators or bureaucrats to inject their personal opinions into the decision-making process. The high priests of the law are traditionally impersonal and rational in their professional stance; any deviation from strict neutrality or departure from *stare decisis* calls for extraordinary justification. Nevertheless, judicial behavior remains human behavior. Thus, to understand how the Court has reached a particular decision, or to predict how it may decide a pending case, the student needs to know how the judges themselves perceive their roles in the judicial system.

The Roles of Judges

When Robert Jackson was Solicitor General of the United States, arguing many of the New Deal cases before the Supreme Court, he charged that the Court is "almost never a really contemporary institution." He observed that the life tenure of judges in conjunction with the short elective terms for congressmen kept the average

---

[32] Alexander Hamilton, *The Federalist*, No. 78.

viewpoints of the judiciary and of Congress a generation apart. He felt that the conservative legal philosophy of the judges acted as a check upon a dynamic people "and nearly always the check of a rejected regime on the one in being."[33] Years later, as Justice Jackson, his views of the Supreme Court as a political institution had considerably mellowed. In his last lecture, written but not delivered the day before he died, he wrote,

> If an organized society wants the kind of justice that an independent, professional judicial establishment is qualified to administer, our judiciary is certainly a most effective instrument for applying law and justice to individual cases and for cultivating public attitudes which rely upon law and seek justice.[34]

Querying which comes first, an independent and enlightened judiciary or a free and tolerant society, Justice Jackson thought that an aggressive, activist judiciary could support but not guarantee a free government. "It is my belief that the attitude of a society and its organized political forces, rather than its legal machinery is the controlling force in the character of free institutions."

Justice Felix Frankfurter, an advocate of many liberal causes in the 1920s, a distinguished professor for many years at the Harvard Law School, was appointed to the Supreme Court by President Roosevelt at the height of the controversy between the New Dealers and the judges. Probably no Justice has given more deliberate thought to the role of the judge, nor expressed himself on the subject more eloquently. To the question "Does a man cease to be himself when he becomes a Justice? Does he change his character by putting on a gown?" he answered:

> No, he does not change his character. He brings his whole experience, his training, his outlook, his social, intellectual, and moral environment with him when he takes a seat on the supreme bench. . . . To assume that a lawyer who becomes a judge takes on the bench merely his views on social or economic questions leaves out of account his rooted notions regarding the scope and limits of a judge's authority. The outlook of a lawyer fit to be a Justice regarding the role of a judge cuts across all his personal preferences for this or that social arrangement.[35]

Justice Frankfurter was ever mindful of the constitutional division of labor in the American political system. He felt strongly that judges ought not to enter "the political thicket," but rather should leave what he considered "political questions" (such as reapportionment of the legislature) to the executive and legislative agencies, and to the vigilance of the people in exercising their political rights. In his nearly thirty years on the Court, he was frequently impelled to profess his notions of judicial restraint. Most poignant

---

[33] Robert H. Jackson, *The Struggle for Judicial Supremacy* (New York: Vintage Books [Random House, Inc., 1941), p. 315.

[34] Robert H. Jackson, *The Supreme Court in the American System of Government* (Cambridge, Mass.: Harvard University Press, 1955), p. 80.

[35] "The Judicial Process and the Supreme Court," a paper read at the Annual Meeting of the American Philosophical Society, Philadelphia, 1954. Reprinted in Philip Elman (ed.), *Of Law and Men* (New York: Harcourt, Brace & World, Inc., 1956).

is his dissenting opinion in the *Barnette Case* (1943), in which a majority of his colleagues held unconstitutional a West Virginia statute that required students in the public schools to salute the flag as part of the daily exercises:

> One who belongs to the most vilified and persecuted minority in history is not likely to be insensible to the freedom guaranteed by our Constitution. Were my purely personal attitude relevant I should wholeheartedly associate myself with the general libertarian views in the Court's opinion, representing as they do the thought and action of a lifetime. As a member of this Court I am not justified in writing my private notions of policy into the Constitution, no matter how deeply I may cherish them or how mischievous I may deem their disregard.

More recently, a Senate debate on the role of Supreme Court justices was touched off by President Johnson's nomination of Thurgood Marshall for the Supreme Court. Senator Sam Ervin (D.-N.C.), Chairman of the Senate Constitutional Rights Subcommittee, lectured the Senate for nearly two hours on the dangers of judicial activism. Identifying four activists already on the Court —Chief Justice Warren and Justices Douglas, Brennan, and Fortas—he warned his colleagues that if they approved the appointment of a fifth activist, "the American people will be ruled throughout the foreseeable future by the personal notions of the five rather than by the precepts of the Constitution."[36] Other southern senators also opposed Marshall as "a constitutional iconoclast" and an "ultra-liberal activist," as one bound to join the other activitists on the Court, who "substitute their own view of what the law ought to be for what the Constitution requires it to be."

Senator James Eastland (D.-Miss.), Chairman of the Senate Judiciary Committee, placed in the *Congressional Record* Marshall's previously expressed views on the nature of law and the judicial process: that law is not a set of abstract and socially unrelated commands of the sovereign but an effective instrument of social policy; that the Supreme Court is an example *par excellence* of judicial involvement in the process of social change.[37] Obviously Senator Eastland feared that Marshall would use his position on the Court not merely to effect social change, but to implement his "personal notions of contemporary communal values," which were diametrically opposite to the Senator's own notions of contemporary communal values.

Senator Jacob K. Javits (R.-N.Y.) suggested that if the senators really had to face up to a proposal to overturn Supreme Court decisions by legislative action, they would all have second thoughts on the matter: "We do not fear its decisions as much as many of us pretend we do." He reminded his colleagues that to conjure up how Judge Marshall might vote after he went on the Court, or how he might later affect the balance of the Court in decision-making, would be running in the face of experience with "that host of judges who have gone just the opposite way from what any one might reasonably have expected," such as Louis Brandeis, Felix Frankfurter, and Byron White. When the debate wound up, Justice Marshall's appointment was approved, 69–11; the 11 who voted against him were all from the states of the old Confederacy.

---

[36]*Congressional Record*, August 30, 1967, CXIII, No. 140, 1248. The whole debate is worth reading to gain insights into congressional images of the Supreme Court.

[37]The reference is to a speech that Justice Marshall made when he was Solicitor General of the United States at a Law Day Luncheon, University of Miami, April 27, 1966. Printed *in toto* in the *Congressional Record*, August 30, 1967, 12536.

The activism of the Warren Court in the '50s and '60s has stirred as much controversy as the activism of the Taft-Hughes courts in the '20s and '30s, but the ideological antagonists have switched views on what constitutes a proper judicial function. In the Taft-Hughes era, conservatives welcomed judicial activism as an appropriate legal defense of free enterprise against regulatory social and economic legislation. Today, these same conservatives attack judicial activism as an unwarranted usurpation of legislative authority. In the earlier period, liberals argued that judges should not substitute their social and economic views for those enacted into law by the elected representatives of the people. Today, these same liberals are gratified that judges are willing to stand up for the rights of minorities and individuals even against the majority of dominant interests that control legislatures. Since the justices appear to be playing the same role in both periods, it is fair to assume that it is not the Court's activism but its substantive policies that were and are in controversy.

Today, with libertarian justices in a majority, the Warren Court seems to be grasping for, rather than shying away from, opportunities to settle major controversies on the basis of constitutional law: race relations, legislative apportionment, First Amendment rights of political extremists (right and left), religion in the schools, law enforcement procedures, and the rights of defendants in court. As Herman Pritchett puts it, "The Court seems to be behaving more and more like the political scientist's model of a policy forming institution and less and less like the legal model of an enunciator of doctrine."[38]

Lawyers and political scientists have always been aware of and concerned about the policy role of judges. The older texts on constitutional history and biographical studies of individual justices inevitably develop their subject within a political context.[39] But more recently political scientists of the behavioral persuasion have been experimenting with methodologically more sophisticated tools for probing into judicial behavior. Pritchett's succession of books on the Roosevelt Court, the Vinson Court, and the Warren Court have employed bloc analyses to discover and verify the ideological bases for judicial affiliation. Other devices have been developed to measure the attitudes and value-beliefs of individual justices with respect to specific issues. Some political scientists have tried to discover through analyses of social backgrounds what attitudes and value-beliefs judges carry with them to the bench; and others have pushed further to relate background characteristics to specific patterns of decision-making.[40] Political scientists may argue among themselves

---

[38]Herman Pritchett, "Public Law and Judicial Behavior," *Journal of Politics*, XXX (May, 1968).

[39]Charles Warren's *The Supreme Court in United States History* is an example, par excellence, of a political treatment.

[40]The bibliographical essay at the end of this book lists many relevant titles. For a single reference, see the "Symposium on Social Science Approaches to the Judicial Process," *Harvard Law Review*, LXXIX (June, 1966), 1551–1628, which includes the following short articles: Joel Grossman, "Social Backgrounds and Judicial Decision-Making"; Walter F. Murphy, "Courts as Small Groups"; Samuel Krislov, "Theoretical Attempts at Predicting Judicial Behavior"; Joseph Tanenhaus, "The Cumulative Sealing of Judicial Decisions"; and Fred Kort, "Quantitative Analysis of Fact Patterns in Cases and Their Impact on Judicial Decisions."

as to which is the most effective methodology for examining the political functions of the judiciary, but there is little disagreement on the general proposition that all judges in all cases make policy to some degree, and that the Supreme Court, especially in the exercise of judicial review, functions as one of the primary policy-making agents of the nation.

Most scholarly pieces on the judicial process, and this includes articles in the political science journals as well as in the law reviews, are given to doctrinal analyses of substantive issues or charts and models on the batting averages and ideological positions of appellate judges. But 90 per cent of adjudication never gets beyond the trial courts. Obviously, then, we need to keep an eye on how trial judges perform their roles in the judicial process.

Through three editions of this textbook we introduced this chapter with an account of decision day, May 17, 1954:

> At 12:52 P.M., the Chief Justice began to read the unanimous opinion of the Court in the *Brown Case*. The accoustics were poor in the marble-columned, high-ceilinged room. The Associate Justices leaned forward in rapt attention. Everyone in the courtroom strained to hear the reading: "We conclude that in the field of public education the doctrine of separate but equal has no place. . . . Segragation is a denial of the equal protection of the laws." The reporters rushed out of the courtroom and the news was flashed around the world.

We thought this was a rather dramatic illustration of judges making policy in a political setting. But a lawyer well up the ladder in the national bureaucracy tells us: "Your fourth edition on "The Judges" should not start with the *Brown* case, but with some stinky little undramatic case (perhaps an income tax case) involving construction of an ambiguous statute, or a question whether a statute was implicitly repealed by a subsequent statute, or at worst a pre-emption case—one in which the existence of ambiguity could be made apparent to every student. Use this as a vehicle for developing the 'legislative' function of the judiciary and spend a good deal of time on that before ever reaching the Constitution."

His point, which we accept, is that most of the work of the federal judges is not a matter of expounding the Constitution but of interpreting statutes and applying their interpretations as rules of law to settle all kinds of disputes. He feels, and we agree, that political scientists tend to underplay the importance of nonconstitutional judicial decision-making relative to other kinds of decision-making in our society. Although the courts have a relatively small role with respect to most of our money-spending activities (like OEO or NASA), they have a very large role with respect to most of our regulatory activities. And while judicial interpretations of statutes can be overruled by Congress, they in fact rarely are—which means that great numbers of legislative decisions are left standing as judges in lower courts make them.

Harry W. Jones, Cardozo Professor of Jurisprudence at Columbia University, makes a similar point, especially with regard to the administration of justice in criminal cases.[41] He attacks "the upper court myth"—the notion that all is well in the house of justice as long as appellate justices are men of wisdom, expe-

---

[41]Jones (ed.), *The Courts, the Public, and the Law Explosion*, Chapter 5, "The Trial Judge—Role Analysis and Profile."

rience, and professional competence. He is much more concerned with how trial judges perform in the courtroom under different demands and strains. Appellate judges have a great deal of paper work, and their courtroom activities are largely confined to questioning contending lawyers on points of law. Trial judges must have unusual skill in dealing with people and understanding the problems of people who get into trouble with the law; trial judges must be able to communicate with litigants, witnesses, and jurymen who have no knowledge of the law, as well as with the lawyers. Thus Professor Jones, in setting up his criteria for "well qualified trial judges," puts first the qualities of personality and character. A trial judge must of course be a good lawyer, but, even more than professional competence, ideal specifications for his job in the courtroom include unusual emotional stability, exceptional firmness, and—not infrequently—psychic endurance. Moreover, the trial judge must be a man well thought of in his own community, whose judgment is generally respected, for in many cases he has to give full protection of the law to defendants in his court who are held in lowest esteem by the community. As Justice William O. Douglas observed in a contempt of court case, "judges are supposed to be men of fortitude, able to thrive in a hardy climate."[42]

Structure of Judicial Activities

The Trial Judges and Courts

The only federal court the Constitution mentions by name is the Supreme Court. The Constitution did, however, give Congress power to create any other courts that may be needed. Under this provision Congress has established a complete hierarchy of courts (see Fig. 13–1): (1) District Courts of the United States, (2) United States Courts of Appeals (sometimes also called Circuit Courts), and (3) the Supreme Court of the United States. Congress has also established other courts, such as the courts of the District of Columbia and various special courts.[43]

[42]*Craig* v. *Harney*, 331 U.S. 367 (1947).
[43]Congress has created a number of special courts: *The United States Court of Claims* handles claims cases in which the United States is being sued; the *Court of Customs and Patent Appeals* reviews decisions of administrative agencies in certain types of questions arising under the customs laws, patents, and trademarks; the *Customs Court* reviews appraisals of imported merchandise and decisions of collectors of customs; the *Court of Military Appeals* is the final appellate tribunal in court-martial convictions. Since all these "congressional courts" are outside the regular judicial hierarchy, constitutional provisions with respect to the appointment and tenure of federal judges need not apply.

The *Administrative Office of the United States Courts* was created by act of Congress in 1939. Its Director, appointed by the Supreme Court of the United States, is the administrative officer for all the federal courts. He works under the direction and supervision of the *Judicial Conference of the United States.*

The Judicial Conference is an annual meeting to which the Chief Justice of the Supreme Court summons the chief judges of the judicial circuits. The Conference keeps an eye on the volume of business in the federal courts, assigns judges to District and Circuit Courts according to how much judicial business is anticipated, and suggests to the various courts how they might expedite their business. The Chief Justice may invite the Attorney General to report to the Conference on court cases in which the United States is a party.

The *District Courts of the United States* are trial courts for both criminal and civil cases. These are courts of original jurisdiction; that is, all federal cases, except those few special cases which the Constitution reserves for the Supreme Court, begin in these courts. There are one or more District Courts in each state, with one to twenty-four federal judges assigned to each court, depending on how congested the docket is.

More than half the cases in the federal District Courts are in civil law. The government may bring suit in land condemnation or civil rights cases, or it may appear as plaintiff under such federal laws as the Fair Labor Standards Act, the Taft-Hartley Act, or the Food and Drug Act. The government may appear in a District Court as a defendent in tax suits, personal injury claims cases, or suits to enjoin federal agencies. Other civil suits arise from disputes over "federal questions," such as antitrust laws, labor laws, patent, copyright, and trade mark laws. Actually, diversity of citizenship cases—that is, controversies between citizens of different states—account for the greatest amount of court activity. Nearly four-fifths of all jury trials in civil cases in the federal courts do not concern the federal government and do not even involve a federal question.

The federal courts are open to private litigants and federal judges are empowered to settle disputes between individuals. About three-fifths of the civil cases in federal courts involve private litigants. If one party to a dispute

Fig. 13-1

JUDICIAL SYSTEM OF THE UNITED STATES

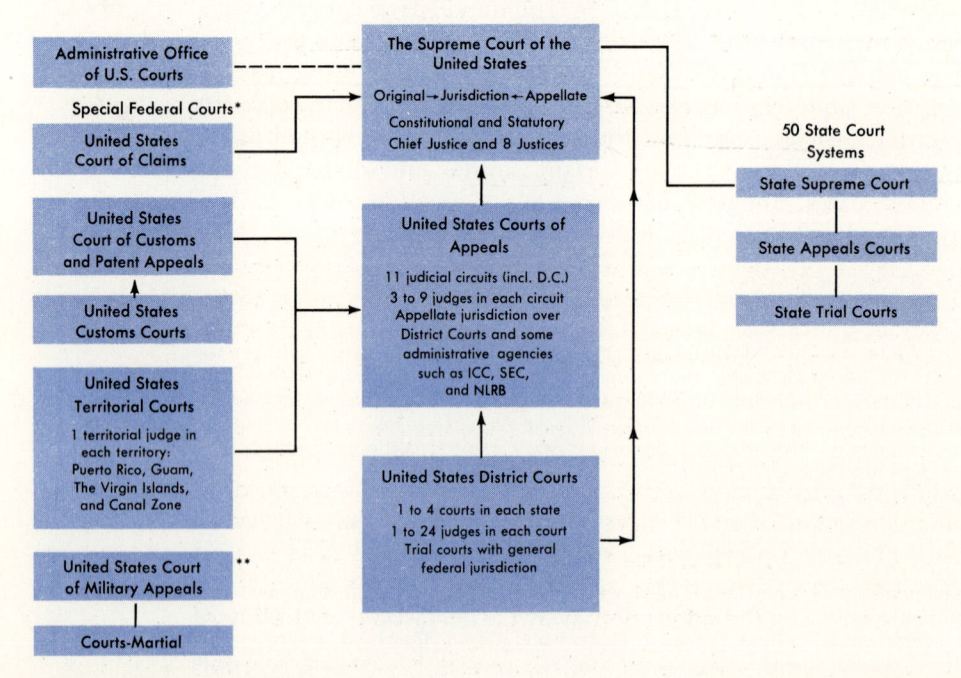

- Administrative Office of U.S. Courts
- Special Federal Courts*
  - United States Court of Claims
  - United States Court of Customs and Patent Appeals
  - United States Customs Courts
  - United States Territorial Courts (1 territorial judge in each territory: Puerto Rico, Guam, The Virgin Islands, and Canal Zone)
  - United States Court of Military Appeals**
    - Courts-Martial

- The Supreme Court of the United States
  - Original → Jurisdiction ← Appellate
  - Constitutional and Statutory
  - Chief Justice and 8 Justices

- United States Courts of Appeals
  - 11 judicial circuits (incl. D.C.)
  - 3 to 9 judges in each circuit
  - Appellate jurisdiction over District Courts and some administrative agencies such as ICC, SEC, and NLRB

- United States District Courts
  - 1 to 4 courts in each state
  - 1 to 24 judges in each court
  - Trial courts with general federal jurisdiction

- 50 State Court Systems
  - State Supreme Court
  - State Appeals Courts
  - State Trial Courts

* Created by Congress to perform special judicial functions
** Independent of the judicial system but highest tribunal for Courts-martial

goes into court and asks the judge to resolve the dispute, then the other party must submit to court procedure even though he may not want a judicial decision. An individual disputant who seeks a judicial settlement does not have to get permission from any government official to take a case to court. But if neither party wants a judicial settlement, the judge has no authority to require them to bring their case to court.

In federal civil cases, the litigants must furnish their own lawyers. The Constitution provides for jury trial in suits for damages, and Congress has extended the right to other kinds of cases. Jurors are chosen from a cross-section of the community. Following questioning by judges and lawyers to eliminate those who may be biased or otherwise unqualified to serve, twelve persons are selected to try the case before them "fairly and impartially." The individual who brings the case or makes the complaint is the plaintiff; the second party is the defendant.

When the case is tried in court, the lawyers for plaintiff and defendant each explain to the judge and jury what the dispute is all about. The plaintiff's lawyer submits evidence to support his client's contentions and calls witnesses to testify what they know about the facts pertaining to the issues. The defendant's lawyer may cross-examine each witness and challenge the evidence, and the judge decides whether the evidence is admissable. The defendant's lawyer follows the same course and the plaintiff's lawyer in turn has the right to cross-examine the defendant's witnesses and to challenge his evidence. Finally, the lawyers summarize the case to the judge and jurors, each showing why his client should win. The judge instructs the jury on the facts which have been brought out by the lawyers in court and on the rules of law which are applicable. The jury then retires to resolve the issues of fact and to apply the law which, according to the judge's instructions, is relevant. It returns to the courtroom with a verdict in favor of either the plaintiff or the defendant. The judge hands down his decision in accordance with the jury's verdict.

This model of civil procedure is, of course, much more simple than the actual procedure. The dual system of courts presents complicated questions of jurisdiction at the outset. Congress has provided concurrent jurisdiction in the federal courts and state courts for cases involving diversity of citizenship, but by statute limits federal jurisdiction to cases involving more than $10,000. A plaintiff may choose to sue in either a state or federal court but, if the defendant is sued in the court of a state of which he is not a citizen, he is permitted to have the case removed to a federal court. The increasing intricacy of questions in modern society frequently raises serious problems of jury competence, so that the disputants may prefer not to have their case tried by jury.[44] In cases where the United States is a party, government lawyers are notably successful in getting their cases settled before they reach the stage of trial by jury. The rules of procedure governing the admission of evidence and the credibility of

---

[44]See Charles W. Joiner, *Civil Justice and the Jury* (Englewood Cliffs, N.J.: Prentice-Hall, Inc., 1966) for a discussion of advantages and disadvantages of jury trials in civil cases. The author strongly defends the jury system.

witnesses are very complex and often evoke much argument in court among the lawyers themselves. When the judge instructs the jury as to the relevant rule of law, he usually has considerable discretion both as to selection and interpretation, and it is at this point that he exercises a legislative function.

District Courts are trial courts in both criminal and civil law and the same judges try both types of cases. All crimes against the United States are specified in statutes passed by Congress and all such crimes are prosecuted exclusively in federal courts. In federal criminal proceedings, the largest number of prosecutions are for auto theft involving interstate transportation, violation of liquor laws, forgery, counterfeiting, and tax frauds. Other federal offenses frequently tried in the District Courts include violation of the Selective Service Act, illegal use of a service uniform, white slave traffic, and narcotics cases. As in civil law cases, the courts are open for the government to prosecute public offenders but the judges do not and cannot solicit any business.

Judicial proceedings in criminal law are interlaced with the activities of the Justice Department and other law enforcement agencies. Agencies for detection and investigation of offenses against the U.S. government exist in the immigration service, the postal service, the internal revenue service, the customs offices, and other offices, but the principal agency charged with the investigation of federal crimes is the Federal Bureau of Investigation in the Department of Justice. The job of the Department of Justice is enforcing federal laws (see Fig. 13–2), and the *Attorney General of the United States* is ultimately responsible for the prosecution of all crimes against the United States; as a matter of practice, this responsibility is left almost entirely up to the local federal prosecutor, who is the United States Attorney in each judicial district.

The Attorney General is chief legal counsel for the President and the executive departments. This is an important political position, and it often leads to a career on the bench. Several Attorneys General in this century, for example, have been appointed to the Supreme Court: Wilson appointed his Attorney General, James McReynolds; Coolidge appointed his Amherst classmate, Harlan F. Stone, first Attorney General, then to the Supreme Court; Roosevelt appointed Robert H. Jackson; Truman appointed Tom Clark. The *Deputy Attorney General* supervises all the major units in the Department of Justice, including the Executive Office for United States attorneys. This office provides administrative assistance and supervision to the United States Attorneys in each federal judicial district. We noted earlier that the Deputy Attorney General plays a key role in the selection of federal judges. The *Solicitor General* represents the federal government in Supreme Court cases and, when requested by the Attorney General, he may conduct and argue cases in any federal court. He directs the activities of federal law officers throughout the country. When the United States District Attorney loses a case in the District Court, he may not appeal to a higher court except with the permission of the Solicitor General. The Solicitor General's Office is also regarded as a stepping stone to the Supreme Court. Robert Jackson's handling of New Deal cases as Solicitor General led first to his appointment as Attorney General and then to his Supreme Court judgeship. When Thurgood Marshall was being groomed for a Supreme Court appointment, it was regarded as politic to take him off the Court of Appeals and give him a workout as Solicitor General.

The *United States Attorney* in each district represents the United States in all

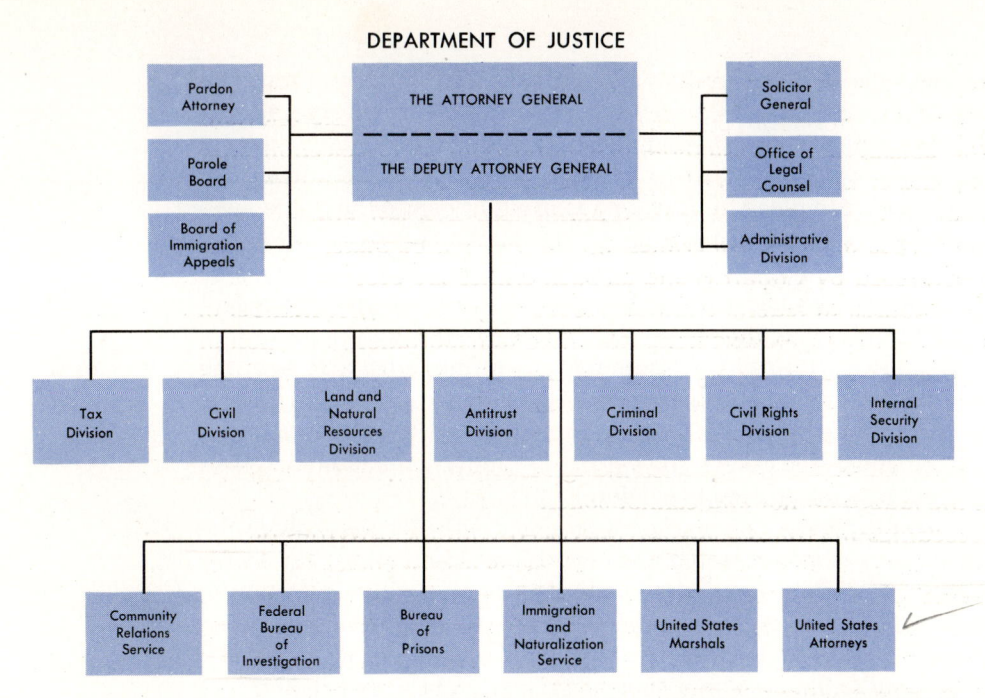

DEPARTMENT OF JUSTICE

```
                    THE ATTORNEY GENERAL
  Pardon Attorney   ─────────────────────   Solicitor General
  Parole Board      THE DEPUTY ATTORNEY     Office of Legal Counsel
                    GENERAL
  Board of Immigration Appeals              Administrative Division
```

Divisions: Tax Division | Civil Division | Land and Natural Resources Division | Antitrust Division | Criminal Division | Civil Rights Division | Internal Security Division

Sub-agencies: Community Relations Service | Federal Bureau of Investigation | Bureau of Prisons | Immigration and Naturalization Service | United States Marshals | United States Attorneys

Source: *United States Government Organization Manual, 1967–68* (Washington, D.C.: U.S. Government Printing Office, 1967).

Figure 13-2

cases initiated in District Court; he files suits on behalf of the United States in civil cases, and he conducts the prosecution in criminal proceedings. The *United States Marshal* in each district performs duties similar to those of the sheriff in state courts. He arrests and holds in custody persons accused of federal offense, summons jurors, serves subpoenas to witnesses, and executes the judgments of the courts. The *United States Commissioner* in each federal judicial district resembles a police magistrate or a justice of the peace. He issues warrants, holds preliminary hearings, fixes bail or holds suspects in jail pending trial in federal court. A *Clerk of the Court* keeps the records in each district. All these officers of the courts are political appointees. Their positions are covered neither by constitutional provisions for independence of the judiciary, nor by civil service regulations. The President fills them with members of the party faithful.

In the assembly line of justice, the trial judge occupies a key position, but not necessarily the crucial one. The administration of justice in criminal cases begins with detection and investigation, and many crimes are never reported, never detected, and never investigated. The judge has no part in proceedings until after an arrest is made; he may then be asked to issue a writ of habeas corpus, or to fix bail for the temporary release of the accused. Either before or after a preliminary hearing the District Attorney may decide to drop charges; if he does, that is the end of the case. If the District Attorney decides to prosecute, the Constitution requires that he carry his charges and preliminary evidence to a federal grand jury. The grand jury may refuse to indict; if it does, *that* is the end of the case. If the grand jury does bring in a bill of indictment,

519

and if the accused pleads "not guilty," then the District Attorney must be prepared to prosecute the case in court. At this point, however, bargaining is likely to take place between the District Attorney and the defendant's lawyer to obtain a plea of "guilty" and so to avoid a court trial. If the defendant chooses or is persuaded to plead "guilty," he is brought before the judge, who immediately imposes sentence according to the statutory provision. If the defendant pleads "not guilty," he is entitled to trial by judge and jury. The trial proceeds in much the same manner that we outlined for civil cases except that the District Attorney has the role which the plaintiff's lawyer plays in a civil case. At the close of the lawyers' summations to the judge and jury, the judge instructs the jury both as to the admissable evidence and the applicable law. The jury returns a verdict of "guilty" or "not guilty"; if the verdict is "not guilty," that is the end of the case; if the verdict is "guilty," the judge imposes sentence according to the statutory provision.

The constitutional rights of defendants in federal criminal cases include the guarantee against unreasonable search and seizure; the right to indictment by grand jury; the writ of habeas corpus; protection against double jeopardy; security against self-incrimination; the right to a speedy and public trial by an impartial jury; the right to be informed of the nature and cause of the accusation; the right to have witnesses subpoenaed; assistance of counsel at all stages from preliminary hearing to release or conviction, at public expense if the defendant is an indigent; and protection against excessive bail, excessive fines, and cruel and unusual punishments.[45] And yet, with all these rights and guarantees, less than 25 per cent of those who are charged with federal offenses choose to be tried in court.

Many explanations are offered as to why court trials are the exception and guilty pleas the normal procedure in criminal cases. A district attorney confronted with many more cases than he can prosecute in a court term picks the cases he wants to try—perhaps for their publicity value, if he has political ambitions. Naturally he chooses his best cases, those he is most likely to win; those that he thinks he will probably lose, he may *nolle pros*—simply drop from his list; in others he may try to negotiate with the defendants for pleas of guilty. The prosecutor's interest in maintaining a public image of effective law enforcement and successful prosecution; the defendant's interest in receiving as low a penalty, as much leniency, and the least repugnant charges (disorderly conduct, for example, instead of child molesting) as possible—these interests converge in a steady flow of guilty pleas and convictions. The judge from his elevated position on the bench may be uncomfortably aware of what goes on in the bargain basement of justice, but his job is only to adjudicate the cases that reach his court. If the defendant elects to stand trial, the judge is expected to see to it that all the rules of procedure are correctly followed. But with federal dockets already heavily congested, and the resultant delays of justice causing public annoyance, the trial judge is not likely to question guilty pleas too sharply, especially since all such pleas come into court with the consent of the defendant's lawyers.[46]

---

[45]David Fellman, *The Defendant's Rights* (New York: Rinehart & Co., Inc., 1958).
[46]President's Commission on Law Enforcement and Administration of Justice. *Task Force Report: The Courts* (Washington, D.C.: U.S. Government Printing Office, 1967), Appendix A, "Perspectives on Plea Bargaining," by Arnold Enker.

The Appellate Judges and Courts

Nine out of ten cases never go beyond the trial courts, but Congress has set up federal Courts of Appeals to consider cases which have for one reason or another not been satisfactorily resolved in the courts of original jurisdiction.

The United States is divided into eleven judicial circuits. In each circuit, there is a *United States Court of Appeals*. The District of Columbia constitutes one circuit; the states and the territories are grouped in the ten remaining circuits. From three to nine circuit judges are assigned to each Court of Appeals, depending on how much work has to be done. The chief judge of each circuit summons all the circuit and district judges to an annual conference to discuss and plan the year's business in the circuit. The chief judge also represents the circuit in the Judicial Conference of the United States (see Footnote 43).

The Courts of Appeals have appellate jurisdiction—that is, they hear cases on appeal from the District Courts. A Court of Appeals may review either the facts in controversy, or the lower court's interpretation of the law. They also hear cases on appeal from various administrative agencies, such as the U.S. Tax Court and the National Labor Relations Board. The Courts of Appeals are the last resort for diversity of citizenship cases if no federal law or constitutional rights are involved. No case can be appealed from the state courts to the federal Courts of Appeals.

The *Supreme Court of the United States* is the highest tribunal in the land. Congress fixes the number of Supreme Court justices. Since 1869, there have been nine justices on the Court at any given time, but the number has changed half a dozen times in the Court's history, ranging from as few as five to as many as ten. Under the Constitution, the Supreme Court has both original and appellate jurisdiction. Its original jurisdiction extends to (1) all cases affecting ambassadors, other public ministers, and consuls; (2) all cases in which a state is a party. In *Marbury v. Madison* (1803), Justice Marshall held that Congress does not have the power to extend this original jurisdiction. And the decision still stands. The Court hears perhaps one or two cases in original jurisdiction during each term (which runs from October to June).

Congress fixes the appellate jurisdiction of the Supreme Court. Under present law, the Supreme Court may review cases both from state courts and from lower federal courts. The Court must hear appeals from any lower court decision that invalidates an act of Congress. It must also hear appeals from final judgments of the highest courts in the states if (1) the question involves the validity of a federal law or treaty and the decision has been against its validity; (2) the state court has upheld the validity of a state statute alleged to be in violation of federal law or contrary to the Constitution. The Supreme Court of the United States will not review any cases from state courts, however, unless federal law or constitutional rights are involved.

The greatest number of Supreme Court cases reach the Court by means of the writ of certiorari, a court order calling a case up for review. Under certiorari, the Supreme Court may call up any federal case that at least four of the justices feel is of sufficient national importance to warrant the Court's attention. The writ is entirely discretionary, which means that the Court is free to deny most petitions for review. In a single Court term, some 2,000 appeals and petitions for certiorari may appear on the Court's docket. But the Court will give full review to less than 10 per cent of these cases.

The bulk of Supreme Court business is not likely to excite public attention. The 1965 Term of the Court is fairly typical. The Court disposed 9 cases on its *Original Docket;* 1182 cases on its *Appellate Docket* (cases from lower federal courts and state courts of highest appeal); and 1502 cases on its *Miscellaneous Docket* (nearly all cases from indigent persons, often prison inmates, appealing *in forma pauperis* for help from the Supreme Court). The Court gave only 107 full opinions in writing; all the rest of its decisions were in the form of "petition for certiorari denied," "judgment affirmed," "appeal dismissed," or "petition for rehearing denied." In the 1965 Term, the Court granted 124 writs of certiorari, and denied or dismissed 900 certiorari petitions. It dismissed 60 appeals; summarily affirmed, reversed, or vacated 49 appeals; and set 40 appeals for argument. Obviously the Court exercises considerable discretion in the appeals it considers as well as the petitions for certiorari which it grants. The statistics are sterile in themselves, but they do suggest that the Supreme Court generally serves as an instrument of support for lower court judges. When the Supreme Court decides not to review a case, whether on appeal or certiorari, in effect it is deciding to uphold the judgment—in many cases it is legitimizing the legislative function—of lower court judges.

A further examination of the 107 cases disposed of by written opinions gives us a better idea of the substantive value judgments which the Supreme Court superimposes upon its workflow. We may also perceive patterns of intercourt conflict and communications. Of the 107 cases, 41 dealt with questions of constitutional law and 66 with other issues. In original jurisdiction, the Court gave its written opinion in one case—brought by South Carolina against the U.S. Attorney General challenging the constitutionality of the Civil Rights Act of 1965.[47] The Court considered 59 civil, and 16 criminal, cases from the lower federal courts; constitutional issues were raised in 8 of the civil cases and in 6 of the criminal cases. The Court reviewed 31 cases from state courts and discussed constitutional questions in 7 out of the 9 civil cases and in 19 out of the 22 criminal cases. (See Table 13–1.)

In Chapter 14, we shall consider some of the 1965–66 cases in constitutional law, which included reversal of breach-of-peace convictions of Negro civil right demonstrators in Louisiana; invalidation of Virginia's poll tax as a prerequisite to voting; invalidation of the provision of the Subversive Activities Control Act of 1950, which required registration of individual members to Communist-action organizations; and procedural limitations on police interrogation of criminal suspects.[48] Here we call attention to the fact that the majority of Supreme Court opinions do not decide constitutional issues. Over 60 per cent of the decisions in 1965–66 ruled on statutory questions, such as government regulation of advertising, activities of regulatory commissions,

---

[47]*South Carolina* v. *Katzenbach,* 383 U.S. 301 (1966).
[48]*Brown* v. *Louisiana,* 383 U.S. 131 (1966); *Harper* v. *Virginia State Board of Elections,* 383 U.S. 663 (1966); *Albertson* v. *Subversive Activities Control Board,* 382 U.S. 70 (1965); *Miranda* v. *Arizona,* 384 U.S. 436 (1966).

Table 13-1   The Supreme Court at Work (Total, 1965–66 Term)

	PRINCIPAL ISSUE		OPINION	
	CONSTITUTIONAL	OTHER	FOR GOVT.	AGAINST GOVT.
Original jurisdiction	1	0	1	0
Civil cases from lower federal courts	8	51	23	16
Criminal cases from lower federal courts	6	10	8	8
Civil cases from state courts	7	2	4	3
Criminal cases from state courts	19	3	6	16
Total	41	66	42	43

Source: Archibald Cox, "The Supreme Court, 1965 Term," 80 *Harvard Law Review* 1 (November, 1966).

labor laws, patent laws, and tax laws. All of these issues are important, but they seldom rate headlines. When we consider the output of the Supreme Court, however, these decisions in nonconstitutional law cases are found to dominate its activity.

Table 13–1 also softens the stereotype which pictures the Supreme Court in sharp conflict with other decision-makers in the political system. In the 107 cases, the decision was for the government in 42 cases and against the government in 43 cases;[49] 22 cases in private litigation did not involve the government at all. In the 59 cases which the Court took from the lower federal courts, 31 decisions upheld the government action. The pattern is notably different, however, in the cases from the state courts; in these 31 cases, 19 decisions went against the state governments, 16 of these in the procedural area of criminal law. Quite obviously the Supreme Court is acting as a policy-maker in this area and communicating to the states its views on what it considers a national norm for the administration of justice.

Judicial Review

Now that we have made our point that the bulk of the business of the Supreme Court (or for that matter, of any court) is not the settlement of constitutional issues, we are prepared to examine the function of judicial review within the broad context of judicial power.

All laws passed by Congress must be "in pursuance of the Constitution." The President of the United States, sworn to uphold the Constitution, may veto any act he considers beyond the constitutional powers of Congress. All administrative rules and regulations are governed by constitutional limitations. In short, every public act—national, state, or local—must conform to constitutional requirements. Because the Constitution is "the supreme law of

---

[49]"The government" refers to national, state, or local government or to any individual participating in the suit in an official capacity; "for" means the government won, "against" that the government lost, as the Court settled the issue.

the land," it is binding on all parts of the American political system and must be enforced in all the courts of the country, "anything in the Constitution or laws of any State to the contrary not withstanding." The legal character of the Constitution has given rise to the practice of *judicial review*. Judicial review is the doctrine that gives courts the power to declare "null and void" any act of the national government or of the states which they deem contrary to the Constitution. Any court, national or state, may exercise judicial review, but because the Supreme Court of the United States is at the top of the judicial hierarchy, its judgment in constitutional law is final in any given case. What the judges think is unconstitutional may not at all affect actual practice unless someone takes the trouble to challenge the constitutionality of a particular act in the courts.

In the American system, judges rather than legislators have the final word in deciding what is constitutional law. The constitutionality of any statute may be challenged in the courts, and if the judges find it repugnant to constitutional law, they will invalidate it. An act that has been passed by both houses of Congress and approved by the President may still be declared null and void by the judges. And an act passed by a state legislature under the state's own constitution may be invalidated by the United States Supreme Court if a majority of the justices agree that the act conflicts with national law or contravenes the national Constitution. Although the President—and the fifty governors—are in fact interpreting the Constitution when they issue executive orders, their orders may be invalidated if the Supreme Court makes a different interpretation.

Thus in law the Constitution becomes "what the judges say it is"—for the time being. The Court may later reverse its own decisions; or the legislators may discover a way to do the same thing by slightly different means that the judges will find constitutional; or "we the People" may overrule the Court's judgment by constitutional amendment. The Eleventh and the Sixteenth Amendments attest to this ultimate power retained by the people.

The great precedent for judicial review is the case of *Marbury v. Madison* (1803), in which the United State Supreme Court declared invalid a part of the Federal Judiciary Act of 1789.[50] Before President Adams left office in 1801, he had appointed some sixty Federalists to newly created judicial positions. Among them was William Marbury, who had been appointed as a justice of the peace for the District of Columbia. Marbury's appointment had been approved by the Senate and his commission to office had been signed and sealed. But Madison, Secretary of State for President Jefferson, refused to deliver this commission and others, for he recognized them as a last-minute "court-packing" effort on the part of the Federalist Party. Marbury went directly to the Supreme Court for a writ of mandamus (an order from the court) to compel Madison to deliver his commission. Chief Justice Marshall —himself a leading Federalist politician—declared that Marbury had a lawful right to his commission, and that it was quite proper for Marbury to bring his suit directly into the Supreme Court. The Federal Judiciary Act of 1789 had authorized the Supreme Court to issue writs of mandamus in cases of original

[50] *Marbury v. Madison*, 1 Cranch 137 (1803).

jurisdiction (original jurisdiction refers to cases brought to the court in the first instance). After so scolding the administration, however, Marshall's opinion took a surprise twist and announced that the Judiciary Act was itself unconstitutional. Since the original jurisdiction of the Supreme Court is clearly defined in the Constitution, Congress has no power to enlarge this jurisdiction to include mandamus cases. The Court held that the act was repugnant to the Constitution and dismissed Marbury's petition for want of jurisdiction.

And yet we must not assume that in *Marbury* v. *Madison* Chief Justice Marshall simply seized for the federal judiciary supreme power over interpreting the Constitution. His argument for judicial review is entirely reasonable. If the Constitution is the supreme law of the land, and if it is the function of the Court to settle all controversies in law, it is the Court's duty to decide in favor of the Constitution when any conflict arises between the Constitution and ordinary law. Marshall's thesis was that this principle is essential to all written constitutions —namely, that any law contrary to the Constitution is void.

This thesis was not original with Marshall; Marshall's opinion shows striking similarity to Hamilton's words in *The Federalist* (Nos. 78 and 80). Although the Founding Fathers did not spell out the power of judicial review in the Constitution, they probably intended the judiciary to have such power. Back in the colonial period, the British Privy Council had established the precedent of judicial review over acts passed by the colonial legislatures. More influential perhaps was the fact that the courts in ten states prior to 1803 had already exercised the same power. Lower federal courts had also "reviewed" both state and national laws. But *Marbury* v. *Madison* was the first case in which a federal court actually decided that an act of Congress was unconstitutional.

The power of judicial review has been used sparingly and with restraint. After *Marbury* v. *Madison*, Chief Jus-

Drawing by Sidney Harris;
© 1967 *The Saturday Review*.

"It's nothing personal, Prescott. It's just that a higher court gets a kick out of overruling a lower court."

tice Marshall never declared an act of Congress unconstitutional again. No other act of Congress was ruled invalid until the eve of the Civil War when Chief Justice Taney, in the *Dred Scott Case,* held the Missouri Compromise unconstitutional after it had been in operation more than thirty years.[51] The Supreme Court has more frequently declared state laws unconstitutional. When we remember that the states enact thousands and thousands of laws every year, however, it becomes clear that the judges rarely overrule the legislators.

Justice Roberts once explained that when the United States Supreme Court considers a constitutional question, it "has only one duty, to lay the article of the Constitution which is involved beside the statute which is challenged and to decide whether the latter squares with the former."[52] But this explanation is much too simple. Every case that goes to the Supreme Court involves a controversy of paramount national importance. Probably every case in constitutional law that has been decided by the United States Supreme Court could reasonably have been decided otherwise. How else can we explain that the state legislatures or Congress—whose members are all sworn to observe and uphold the Constitution—have already passed the laws which the courts are asked to review? How else can we account for the frequent disagreements among the justices themselves and the Court's not infrequent departure from its own previous decisions? The idea that the Constitution clearly dictates the Court's decision in each case is a myth.

Quite obviously, when the Court engages in judicial review it is determining public policy and, in effect, making political decisions.

The Supreme Court and the Politics of Adjudication

The courts provide the institutional framework within which the judges establish the rule of law. Organizational charts, jurisdictional lines, and statistics on case loads do not tell us much, however, about the nature of the judicial process or the politics of adjudication. In the next part of this book, when we examine the policy outputs of the political system, we shall see that judicial decisions have been very important, not only in settling specific controversies, but also in shaping the main lines of public policy. Federal judges have played a dominant role in maintaining individual rights and liberties; and to a considerable extent they have also determined the constitutional limits of economic and social policies in the states as well as in the national government.

In our diagram of the basic features of a political system in Chapter 1, we represented all of the official decision-making activities by a neat circle. We noted then that the simplicity of the diagram should not be taken to imply perfect homogeneity among decision-makers. In fact, they are not only often in conflict, but the outputs of one decision-making unit may also be the inputs of another. Despite the ideal of an independent judiciary, the Supreme Court does not operate in a vacuum. The justices live and work within the contemporary social, economic, and political environment; their decision-making is influenced by that environment and their decisions affect that environment.[53]

[51] *Dred Scott* v. *Sandford,* 19 How. 393 (1857).
[52] *United States* v. *Butler,* 297 U.S. 1 (1936).
[53] For a more sophisticated discussion of material in this section see Walter T. Murphy, *Elements of Judicial Strategy* (Chicago: The University of Chicago Press, 1964), especially Chapter 1.

Inputs for judicial decision-making include demands, supports, and apathy. Constitutional arrangements insure the Court a position of relative independence from direct inputs of the electoral system or of unofficial agencies like parties and pressure groups. The demands to which the Supreme Court responds come from, or are filtered through, other official agencies. Appeals and petitions for certiorari from litigants in the lower courts constitute the bulk of direct demands upon the Court, though occasionally states or foreign diplomats demand the Court's attention in original jurisdiction. The controversies which these litigants bring to the Court frequently involve public issues of national magnitude. Hence the Court's docket, in any term, is likely to include demands for judicial arbitration from a variety of organized interest groups with conflicting claims—for example, in the field of race relations, in labor management disputes, or in church-state problems. When the government appears as party to a case—whether as plaintiff, prosecutor, defendant, or *amicus curiae* (friend of the court)—in effect it, too, is making demands for judicial support of its activities.

Mr. Justice Douglas reminds us that "each age brings the Court its own special worries, anxieties, and concerns." The main outlines of the life of the nation are mirrored in the controversies which the Court is called upon to decide. It is expected to hand down final answers to "questions in which important blocs of opinion in the nation have fixed and set opinions that no amount of argument would change.... The Court sits in a maelstrom which has increased in intensity with the growth of blocs and pressure groups."[54] The economic, social, and religious groups that press their claims to the highest court represent increasingly well-organized interests. They come before the Court not only as individual contestants, but also on behalf of those in similar situations. The frequent appearance of *amici curiae* before the Supreme Court indicates that many judicial opinions concern more than the parties named in a suit. In cases involving racial restrictions in housing, for example, labor organizations, neighborhood protective associations, real estate interests, and civil liberties organizations, no less than racial and religious groups, may enter briefs as *amici curiae*.

"The law is not made by judge alone, but by judge and company."[55] Here is a partial listing of *amici curiae* for a recent term of the Supreme Court: Religious Freedom Committee, American Civil Liberties Union, Railway Labor Executives Association, American Federation of Government Employees, National Association of Life Underwriters, Prudential Insurance Company of America, Chamber of Commerce of Metropolitan St. Louis, National Association of Retail Grocers of the United States, American Patent Law Association, Royal Netherlands Shipowners Association, American Committee for Protection of Foreign Born, American Federation of Labor and Congress of Industrial Organizations, Bureau of Information of Eastern Railways, the Southern

---

[54] Speech to the Cornell Law School, *op. cit.*
[55] A remark by Jeremy Bentham amplified by Paul Freund in his essay, "Judge and Company in Constitutional Law," *On Understanding the Supreme Court* (Boston: Little, Brown and Co., 1949).

California Gas Company, and the Chase Manhattan Bank. Many agencies of the federal and state governments also appeared as *amici curiae*, representing official special interests. This collection of "friends of the court" suggests the variety of company which may counsel the Supreme Court in a single term.

Arthur F. Bentley, whose book, *The Process of Government*, pioneered in interest group theory, asserts that the judges, as a functioning part of the government, are responsive to group pressures, representative of all sorts of pressures, and that they use their representative judgment to bring these pressures to balance.[56] Clement C. Vose, in *Caucasians Only*, has made a systematic study of how the NAACP operated as a pressure group over many years, claiming the attention of the judges as litigant and *amicus curiae*.[57] Samuel Krislov, who has examined *amicus curiae* briefs in a broader context, points out that by the mid-'20s the major types of interest groups had all availed themselves of the *amicus* brief as a device whereby to gain access to the judicial process. And he finds that the *amicus* has moved "from neutrality to partisanship, from friendship to advocacy."[58]

The supports for the Supreme Court as a decision-maker are both institutional and unofficial. The jurisdiction of the Court has been firmly established by the Constitution and by congressional statutes. But the judicial power is more than a matter of legal prescription. From the days of Chief Justice John Marshall, the Court has generally been supported by popular esteem. The high prestige of the Court can be attributed in part to a well-earned reputation for legal skill and professional integrity; but it is also a matter of tradition and habit for people to respect the judgments of the Court.

Because the Court considers only real controversies, it is bound to please one side and to displease the other when it makes a decision. Between 1900 and 1935, when the Court consistently resorted to *laissez faire* arguments to invalidate social and economic legislation, it won considerable support from the business community. On the other hand, in the 1960s, while the Court is actively trying to maintain equal protection of the laws for minority groups, its greatest support comes from "liberals" and various groups in the civil rights movement.

Apathy is a significant input of judicial decision-making. Most people, if they are not directly involved in litigation before the Court, tend to accept the Court's opinion because of ingrained respect for the law. Hence most litigants who lose their cases before the highest tribunal are not likely to win much sympathy or political backing from the general public. Paradoxically, seeming apathy on the part of public officials toward judicial decisions may represent a positive attitude. For example, congressmen, or the President, sometimes find it advantageous to let the Court serve as a scapegoat for decisions which they may want to accept but which they dare not, for political reasons, directly espouse. Thus, for nearly a hundred years after the Civil War, largely because of the apparent apathy of the "political branches," the Court was left to make most of the policy decisions on civil rights. Similarly, within the local commu-

---

[56] (Bloomington, Ind.: The Principia Press, 1935), p. 393.
[57] (Berkeley, Cal.: University of California Press, 1959).
[58] *Essays on the American Constitution*, Gottfried Dietze (ed.) (Englewood Cliffs, N.J.: Prentice-Hall, Inc. 1964), "Amicus Curiae Brief," pp. 77–98.

nity, school officials who would not have had the nerve to initiate integration readily comply with court orders; local merchants who hesitated to affront local mores may be quite willing to accept a court decision that enables them to serve all customers without discrimination.

We do not have much information on how the justices act in their conference sessions; such meetings take place behind closed doors and there are no reports to the press. We know that the Chief Justice presides, that he summarizes each case and indicates how he thinks it should be decided. Each of the judges, usually in order of seniority, expresses his separate view. During this presentation, however, some consensus is likely to emerge. When the members are ready to vote—the order is now reversed, with the junior justice voting first and the Chief Justice last—a majority of judges decide who wins (enjoys rewards) and who loses (suffers deprivations).

If the Chief Justice has voted with the majority in a case, he assigns the writing of the opinion to one of the judges in the majority—or chooses to write it himself. If the Chief Justice has voted with the minority, the senior justice in the majority takes the assignment. The writing of judicial opinions is not intended, however, to be a prima donna performance. Opinions are circulated and recirculated in the hope that all or most of the justices will be persuaded to join in "the opinion of the court." The ability of a justice to write an opinion which is reasonably attractive to all his colleagues on the bench is regarded as a mark of judicial craftsmanship.

To watch the Supreme Court in action is an impressive and dramatic experience, despite the fact that the oral proceedings are now mostly questions and answers between the justices and attorneys on points of law, with no opportunity for the impassioned pleas and bursts of oratory of a Daniel Webster or a Charles Pinckney that marked Court proceedings in days gone by. Before coming into court, counsel on both sides file voluminous briefs with supporting data which the justices presumably study before they grant a hearing. The proceedings are public but, because the courtroom is small and the rules of order strict, the audience is hushed and duly decorous. While the page boys prime the justices with glasses of water, and the lawyers privileged to practice before the Supreme Court Bar present their cases, the sightseers and friends of the participants may gaze on the panels of art around the room—"Powers of Evil" and "Defense of Virtue"—or lift their eyes upward to the murals of the historic law-givers—Menes, Mohammed, and Marshall. We are reminded of John Winthrop's words in 1644, "Judges are gods upon earth."

A decision requires a majority vote of the justices. If the justices disagree, and they frequently do, those who differ from the majority may prepare a dissenting opinion. Sometimes the justices reach even a majority decision by different lines of reasoning, and then they prepare separate concurring opinions. In the *Steel Seizure Case* in 1952, for example, six of the justices decided that the President had acted beyond his authority. Justice Black read the opinion of the Court. Justices Frankfurter, Jackson, Douglas, Burton, and Clark

Drawing by Ed Fisher;
© 1967 *The Saturday Review.*

"Some of us are getting mighty sick of these masterful dissents of yours, Bodgsly!"

each gave separate concurring opinions. And Justice Vinson, joined by Justices Reed and Minton, submitted a dissenting opinion.

The frequency with which the justices of the highest Court disagree has caused complaint and uncertainty (See Table 13-2 for dissents in recent terms.) Many people feel that the Court should develop a greater corporate spirit and should function "institutionally." Such is the opinion of Carl Swisher, professor of constitutional law at The Johns Hopkins University:

> We have a Court of nine justices not for the purpose of getting nine opinions in each case, or six or four opinions, or even two, but for the purpose of pooling into a unified decision and a unified statement of law the best that nine justices can offer. The people do not give the justices positions for life with guaranteed salaries merely to provide them with a forum for display of their individuality. The purpose is to build an institution.[59]

On the other hand, the late Justice Robert H. Jackson defended the practice of presenting dissenting opinions. Pointing to dissents of such great names in the Court's history as Oliver Wendell Holmes, Louis Brandeis, Benjamin

[59] *American Constitutional Development,* 2nd ed. (Boston: Houghton Mifflin Co., 1954), p. 1085.

Table 13-2 Supreme Court Opinions and Dissenting Opinions*
(October Terms, 1964, 1965, 1966)

JUSTICES	OPINIONS OF THE COURT '64	'65	'66	CONCURRING OPINIONS '64	'65	'66	DISSENTING OPINIONS '64	'65	'66	SEPARATE OPINIONS '64	'65	'66
Warren (Chief Justice)	10	9	11	1	0	1	5	6	3	0	1	0
Black	10	11	11	4	0	2	30	26	8	2	3	3
Douglas	10	12	12	7	6	5	27	25	15	2	0	1
Clark	12	11	12	2	2	1	11	9	4	1	0	1
Harlan	10	8	9	12	10	6	30	38	18	3	9	2
Brennan	10	13	11	2	4	2	2	5	2	1	1	1
Stewart	9	12	11	6	3	5	22	23	10	1	0	1
White	10	11	12	4	4	4	10	15	5	1	1	3
Goldberg	10	0	0	7	0	0	15	0	0	3	0	0
Fortas	0	10	11	0	3	4	0	15	9	0	0	2
Totals	91	97	100	45	32	30	152	162	74	14	15	14

*Does not include memorandum opinions of individual justices, dissents to *per curiams*, denial of certiorari petitions, etc.
Source: Statistics of the Clerk of the Supreme Court, as cited in G. Kenneth Reiblich, "Summary of October 1965 Term," 86 *Supreme Court Reporter* 248 (St. Paul, Minn: West Publishing Co., 1966) (for 1964 and 1965); and "Supreme Court Statistics" (Law Notes 3), *Congressional Quarterly Weekly Review*, Vol. XXV (June 23, 1967) (for 1966). p. 1073.

Cardozo, and Harlan F. Stone, Justice Jackson observed: "The right of dissent is a valuable one. Wisely used on well-chosen occasions, it has been of great service to the profession and to the law." He continued more critically, "But there is nothing good, for either the Court or the dissenter, in dissenting *per se*. Each dissenting opinion is a confession of failure to convince the writer's colleagues, and the true test of a judge is his influence in leading, not in opposing, his court."[60]

The volume of the Court's business has long since made impossible the early healthy practice whereby the justices gave expression to individual opinions. But the old tradition still has relevance when an important shift in constitutional doctrine is announced after a reconstruction in the membership of the Court.[61]

Most cases do not begin in the Supreme Court; by the same token, most of them do not end there. Many decisions go back to the lower courts for further judicial proceedings. In the school desegregation cases of 1954–1955, the Supreme Court did not make a final disposition of the issue. Quite the contrary, after stating the "fundamental principle that racial discrimination in public education is unconstitutional," the Supreme Court remanded the cases to the federal district courts "because of their proximity to local conditions."[62] When the Supreme Court declared that the New York State prayer program in the public schools violated the establishment clause of the First Amendment, and therefore the Fourteenth Amendment, it remanded the case to the New York court in which the case originated.[63] In 1962, when the Supreme Court held that a state's failure to reapportion its legislature may constitute denial of

[60] Robert H. Jackson, *The Supreme Court in the American System of Government*, p. 19.
[61] *Graves v. New York ex rel O'Keefe*, 306 U.S. 466 (1939).
[62] *Brown v. Board of Education*, 349 U.S. 294 (1955).
[63] *Engel v. Vitale*, 370 U.S. 421 (1962).

equal protection of the laws, it did not require all state legislatures immediately to reapportion. It simply found that the issue of reapportionment was justiciable and that, in this case, the complainants from Tennessee—which had failed to reapportion its legislature since 1901—were entitled to a trial and decision in the federal District Court in Tennessee.[64] In all these cases, although the Supreme Court stirred the whole country to action—and reaction—it simply stated the constitutional principle and then left the problems of policy implementation to the local authorities.

The Judicial Functions

To Settle Disputes

Settling disputes is the primary function of judges and their courts. Carl J. Friedrich claims that "dispute settling is perhaps the most basic kind of political process without which political order is inconceivable."[65] In the American federal system the responsibility for settling disputes is shared by federal and state judges. Article III specifies the kinds of cases and the kinds of disputants that come within the jurisdiction of the federal judges and courts. Except for the occasional cases that go to the Supreme Court within its constitutionally limited original jurisdiction, the judicial power of the United States is initially vested in the federal judges of the District Courts. In a single year, over a hundred thousand cases in civil and criminal proceedings will be heard—and 90 per cent of them will be settled—in these trial courts.

One point we have tried to make clear throughout this chapter: although settling disputes is a very important function in the political process, the judges never get to play a leading role. Even when grievous wrongs exist between individuals, the courts can do nothing about them unless the aggrieved parties present their cases to the courts for settlement. Lawlessness may exist in the community, but unless the officers of the law bring the offenders into court, no judge can pronounce sentence. Judges may decide cases, but they themselves have no power to enforce their decisions. Judicial review is the most important and delicate duty of the American courts, yet the judges may not take the initiative in passing upon the constitutionality of any statute. They may not render advisory opinions even at the request of the President or of Congress, nor may they hear any case that is not a real contest between parties. The judges may consider only controversies in which the constitutional or legal rights of the litigants are actually at stake.

As Chief Executive, the President is constitutionally required to take care that the laws be faithfully executed. "The laws" include decisions of the federal judges. How far the President may go in fulfilling his obligation to the courts was most dramatically illustrated during the Eisenhower administration, when the President ordered U.S. troops to Little Rock, Arkansas, to enforce an order of a federal judge in Arkansas even against interference by the Governor of the State. The federal judge in this instance was from Fargo, North Dakota, assigned by his superiors in the federal court system to sit

[64] *Baker v. Carr.*
[65] Carl J. Friedrich, *Man and His Government*, p. 423.

THE JUDGES

temporarily in the Arkansas district. The order was to prevent anyone from interfering with the opening of the newly integrated high school in Little Rock in September, 1957. When Governor Orval Faubus ordered the Arkansas National Guard to stop Negro children from entering the high school, the President of the United States proclaimed that he would "use the full power of the United States including whatever force may be necessary to prevent any obstruction of the law and to carry out the orders of the Federal Court." On the other hand, when the Supreme Court had earlier made its historic decision that segregation in public schools was unconstitutional, the President refused to say whether he approved or disapproved. After he had left the presidency, Eisenhower explained that although he "definitely agreed" with the Court's unanimous decision in the *Brown Case*, he felt it "could tend to lower the dignity of government" for the President to indulge in a practice of approving or criticizing Court decisions.[66]

Judicial decisions settle specific disputes concerning the rights of the parties who bring their cases into court. They do not become "the supreme law of the land," even when they are unanimous decisions of the Supreme Court. The decision in the *Brown Case* has certainly not settled the controversy over segregation in the public schools. A 1967 report from the Civil Rights Commission informs us that of the generation of Negro children that has passed through southern schools since the *Brown Case* the vast majority never attended class with a single white child. The Commission finds that the slow pace of desegregation, coupled with an expanding Negro population, means that more Negroes are attending segregated schools in the seventeen southern and border states than attended such schools at the time of the 1954 Supreme Court decision. What has been settled by the *Brown* decision is the unconstitutionality of compulsory segregation in public schools; no state or local government now requires racial segregation in the schools; but many state and local governments still provide segregated facilities.

To Administer Justice

Merely to settle a dispute is not enough; in the common law tradition, the judge is expected to settle a dispute "as a reasonable man would think just." Of all public officials, judges probably enjoy the highest esteem in the community, because they are professionally responsible for "the administration of justice." It is, of course, a circular definition, but one that pays tribute to the judicial function that justice is often defined as what the judges decide. The trial judge carries most of the burden for the administration of justice in the community. As Harry Jones observes, "the trial judge is the parish priest of our legal order."[67] Most citizens never see an appellate court in action but many of us experience the quality of justice at some time or other, whether as litigant, witness, or juryman, in a trial court.

---

[66] Dwight D. Eisenhower, *Waging Peace* (Garden City, N.Y.: Doubleday & Co., Inc., 1965), p. 150.
[67] Jones (ed.), *The Courts, The Public, and The Law Explosion, op. cit.*, p. 125.

The judge is a symbolic figure in civilized society; he personifies both the law and the conscience of the community. The "Cult of the Robe" can, of course, be overstressed. Jerome Frank (who wore the robe of a federal judge for many years) assures us that no major transformation takes place in a man when he puts on the judicial robe. Nevertheless, judges are supposed to act "like judges," to make impartial and reasonable decisions so that the decisions in themselves will have the sanction of legitimacy. Courts are supposed to serve as supports for the basic values, beliefs, and interests of a community. And to the extent that judges and courts measure up to these expectations, they perform a special function in the political process—they administer justice.

It is not enough, however, for judges to do justice; it is even more important that people know and see that justice is done. In the common law tradition, judges are inclined to lean heavily upon precedent, although the rationale of *stare decisis* is simply that persons in similar situations should be treated similarly. In *Courts on Trial* Jerome Frank was pretty rough on fellow judges who are occasionally persuaded to sacrifice justice so that the law may appear "certain"; he was equally scornful of judges who resort to legal trickery, who use oblique opinions to disguise departures from precedent. Judge Frank thought an important function of judges is to speak plainly, so that the people may have confidence in the judicial process, confidence based on understanding rather than belief in legal magic.

The Supreme Court has long considered promulgation of rules of procedure for federal courts an important aspect of its function as the nation's high court of justice. The procedural guarantees of the Bill of Rights apply, of course, *in toto* to all federal courts; but the Supreme Court has thought it desirable to spell these out more specifically in the light of modern law enforcement procedures. Recently, in a succession of headline cases, the Supreme Court has been reinterpreting the due process clause of the Fourteenth Amendment, so that the standards it has set for administration of justice in the federal courts have become applicable not only to procedures in state courts but also to local law enforcement activities. A majority of justices now seem to have reached the opinion that the dual system of courts need not result in a double standard of justice.

Law enforcement activities in the local communities often reflect parochial prejudices and predilections, and even the personal likes and dislikes of judges and company. The recent efforts of the Supreme Court to develop and impose a national norm of justice have met with some resistance, as evidenced by the citizen who affixes twin stickers on his car bumper "IMPEACH EARL WARREN," and "SUPPORT YOUR LOCAL POLICE." The concern of the justices for maintaining the constitutional rights of all defendants is sometimes regarded as "coddling criminals," or as being "soft on communists" (for example, by Daddy Warbucks in the comic strip "Orphan Annie"). Nevertheless, state and local judges and law enforcement officers have made notable efforts to follow the lead of the Supreme Court. Witness the action of the Florida legislature, establishing the office of public defender, following the *Gideon Case* decision that all defendants, including indigents, have a right to counsel in court.[68]

[68]*Gideon v. Wainright*, 372 U.S. 335 (1963). For further and more specific discussion, see Chapter 14 "Civil Rights," p. 545.

THE JUDGES

Uncertainty about the meaning of law, heavy congestion in court dockets, cumbersome trial procedures that were devised in the days of duels and ordeals by combat, brutality in law enforcement procedures, high fees for lawyers and heavy costs in courts, lawyers and judges touched with the bias and prejudice of class, the whole administration of justice seasoned with politics, from deputy marshal to Chief Justice of the Supreme Court—all these charges have been made against our "courthouse government." On the other hand, American judges and company do accept "equal justice for all" as their norm of professional and political behavior. As with all norms, there are bound to be deviations. But we do not have concentration camps; the writ of habeas corpus is a constitutional guarantee available to all. We have no gestapo; when law enforcement officers act too brashly or brutally, their cases fail in court. Due process of law is written into the supreme law of the land. We have no secret trials, no mass trials. Every man accused is entitled to a speedy, public, and impartial trial. He is entitled to counsel at every stage in the proceedings against him; he is entitled to know the charges against him, to be confronted with the witnesses and the evidence against him; and the government will subpoena witnesses for him. The federal system still holds to the grand jury, indictment by a representative body of the community, and trial by one's own peers. And over every court presides "His Honor, the Judge."

Communication The written opinions of the judges explaining the rational bases of their decisions provide us with learned discourse on the major political, economic, and social issues in every era of our nation's history. Judges take very seriously what they regard as the judicial function of communication. Unfortunately, the technical forms in which cases are presented in court and the professional style with which judges feel impelled to respond sometimes obscure the political message. Because judges are recruited more for their political interests than their legal qualifications, however, it seems safe to assume that the opinions which they prepare so painstakingly and deliver with such evident relish are intended to serve a political purpose that frequently goes well beyond informing the litigants of their legal rights. At the Supreme Court level, only controversies of paramount national importance are considered; the litigants themselves may be quite unimportant persons whose sole role in the proceedings is to offer the justices a vehicle of communication.

The only question which William Marbury took to the Supreme Court in 1801 was whether or not he was entitled to his commission as justice of the peace in the District of Columbia. The facts in controversy seemed to involve no more than "a trivial squabble over a few petty political plums."[69] But to Chief Justice John Marshall, the case of *Marbury* v. *Madison* presented a capital opportunity to expound the new Constitution, to deliver a stunning opinion on judicial review, and to effect a remarkable political coup for judicial power.

---

[69] John A. Gerraty (ed.), *Quarrels That Have Shaped the Constitution* (New York: Harper & Row, Publishers, Inc., 1962), "The Case of the Missing Commissions."

The opinion of Chief Justice Marshall in the case still stands as the single most important communication the Supreme Court has ever made to the President, to the Congress, and to the people. To poor Marbury it simply meant that he had to look for another job.

Judicial opinions are as enmeshed in the political process as are congressional debates or executive proclamations. The tendency of the Supreme Court toward increasing multiplicity and diversity of written opinions gives us some inkling of the clash in value judgments and political views among the justices. Opinions of the majority have become communications of public policy with sweeping effects on the nation's economy, on political practices, on civil rights, on nation-state relationships. But the dissenting opinions serve to push the controversy back into the public forum, and may constitute substantial inputs for different policies.

Of all the decision-making agencies in the American political sysem, the courts are least equipped to perform the function of communication. Unlike the President, Congress, or the big executive departments, the Supreme Court has no public information officers to bridge the gap between official action and public understanding. The nine justices have a tremendous responsibility. They must decide cases involving some of the most complicated and difficult social and economic issues of the day; but they have no staff services, no field services, no special consultants. They are expected to do their own work. Moreover, they are constrained by judicial protocol not to speak unofficially about what they have done officially. No matter how much abuse is heaped on the Court—billboards and bumper stickers urge the public to "HELP SAVE AMERICA, IMPEACH EARL WARREN"—the Chief Justice may not go on TV with a fireside chat explaining his own position or the actions of his Court.

Judicial decisions are supposed to speak for themselves. But a great deal of the animus aroused against the Supreme Court is based on public misconceptions of the role of the justices in decision-making. Inaccurate and inadequate reporting by the press is possibly the greatest barrier to public understanding of judicial functions. Most newspapers give cursory consideration to judicial decisions; the texts of judicial opinions are usually treated like routine government releases. *The New York Times* performs a public service when it prints in full the major decisions of the Supreme Court (Note how much coverage your local newspaper gives to the *content* of Supreme Court opinions.) NAACP WINS AGAIN or COMMUNISTS FREED BY SUPREME COURT are typical headlines which excite more than they inform. The complicated reasons why the Court has reached its decisions are usually left out of the news report or the accompanying editorials.

The justices also have their problems of communication with Congress. Again, unlike the executive agencies, the Court has no bureau of congressional relations to explain differences in viewpoints or policy positions. Because the power of judicial review can nullify congressional legislation, a certain amount of antagonism is inevitably inherent in the relationship between Congress and the Court. Congress is inclined to be wary of the power even when the Court professes to exercise judicial restraint. Frequently, in cases involving statutory construction, the Court is charged with trying to supersede the law-making branches when it attempts to decide in a specific case what the legislature or

Congress meant in a general law. Sometimes there is outright hostility, as when the Senator from Mississippi is Chairman of the Senate Committee on the Judiciary at a time when the Court is holding that the patterns of segregation in public schools and public accommodations are unconstitutional. The public, however, sometimes mistakes the voices of a few unhappy congressmen for congressional reaction in general. Despite pressures to limit the jurisdiction of the Supreme Court in certain kinds of controversies, or to reverse judicial decisions by statutory refutation or even by constitutional amendment, the majority of Congress has seemed satisfied to let the Supreme Court have its say and its way.

Policy-Making and Judicial Review

Justice Frankfurter once observed that the Court is the undemocratic organ in American government. The justices are not truly political agents within the democratic framework in that they are not accountable or responsible to any general body of constituents. The President and Congress are elected to office for limited terms; if their record as policy-makers does not meet with popular approval, they can expect to be defeated in the next election. Judges, on the other hand, may be appointed on political grounds, but once they sit on the bench they are there to stay during good behavior. They do not have to court public opinion or concern themselves with majority preferences. By constitutional design, they are insulated from most political pressures. They do not have to fight for appropriations to carry on their activities, and their compensation will not be cut if they invalidate laws passed by Congress and approved by the President. And *amici curiae* behave much more respectfully than the lobbies which clamor for congressional attention or the interest groups that continuously besiege the executive offices.

Critics of the Court sometimes deliberately misinterpret judicial decisions and then make political capital of the misinterpretations. In 1962, for example, the Court held that it was unconstitutional for the New York State Board of Regents to prepare an official prayer to be said aloud in unison by students in New York public schools at the beginning of each school day.[70] Justice Black, who delivered the opinion, declared that the official establishment of religious services in public schools was a violation of the establishment clause of the First Amendment. If one reads what Justice Black actually said, one knows that his opinion was in no way hostile toward religion or prayer. On the contrary, he made it perfectly clear that he was in accord with the Framers of the First Amendment, "Those men knew that the First Amendment which tried to put an end to governmental control of religion and of prayer was not written to destroy either." Nevertheless, the decision evoked demagogic misinterpretation. One southern congressman claimed, "They put the Negroes in the

[70] *Engel v. Vitale,*, 370 U.S. 421 (1962). For further discussion of the Court's views on religion in the public schools, see Chapter 14. For public reaction to the New York Regents' prayer case, see James E. Clayton, *The Making of Justice* (New York: E. P. Dutton & Co., Inc., 1964), pp. 17–23.

schools and now they've driven God out of them." Another declaimed, "The Court has now officially stated its disbelief in God Almighty." Others charged that the justices were trying to "abolish God." Depicting the decision as "the most tragic one in the history of the United States," a congressman from New York State introduced a constitutional amendment to sanction religious exercises in the public schools. Although these charges were absurd and had no basis in fact, many people, who never read any part of Justice Black's painfully conscientious opinion, were convinced that the Court was hell-bent on striking all vestiges of religion from public life.

Throughout this chapter, we have viewed the judges as active agents in the political process. We have noted that trial judges as well as appellate judges are engaged in fashioning the law, and in making policy, and that this occurs as much in statutory interpretation as in judicial review. Although the business of the courts appears as a succession of ordinary lawsuits, when the judges are asked to decide disputes on such issues as taxation, utility regulation, agricultural control, labor relations, housing, banking and finance, subversive activities, and public assistance for parochial schools, even though no constitutional issue is raised, the application of the relevant statute nevertheless inevitably involves a legislative function.

Policy-making through judicial review at the Supreme Court level is the ultimate function of the judiciary in the American political system. Even if the first Congress had exercised its initial option not to establish inferior courts, this ultimate power would still have been vested in the Supreme Court.

Charles Black, University professor of law at Yale, offers a thought-provoking analysis of judicial review within the context of legal realism: "Once it is recognized that judicial decisions are not the mechanical exercises they were once thought to be, it is clear that all judges, in all cases, make policy to some degree, and that the Court, so long as it performs the task of judicial review, must function to some extent and in some ways as one of the policy making organs of the nation."[71] As Black sees it, the Court participates in public policy whether it invalidates ("checks") or validates ("legitimizes") the political actions of our government. Professor Black finds no antithesis between the legal (or judicial) and the political functions of the Court. He is inclined to emphasize the affirmative or legitimizing work of the Court, which he regards as a "people's institution." The people rely on the Court not only to nullify what is unconstitutional, but also to uphold what is constitutional. When the Court upholds governmental actions, we can all "breathe the sweet air of legitimacy."

Professor Black stresses the concept of the Constitution as law, but he does not divorce law from policy. He talks about "vigorous judicial review," "a living body of constitutional law," and law which has "no demonstrable existence outside the facts of life." Judicial decision-making calls for technical competence and for expert knowledge of statutes, precedents, and procedures. "Law is and forever will be technicality. But law is also insight and wisdom and justice."[72] More than a technical lawyer is therefore needed to decide whether Congress has the constitutional right to appropriate public money for parochial schools or to regulate wages and hours in a western

[71]Charles L. Black, *The People and the Court* (New York: The Macmillan Company, 1960), p. 167.
[72]*Ibid.*, p. 182.

lumber camp, or whether the states can provide separate but equal education for Negro and white children, or remove smutty literature from drugstore magazine stands. In most cases that come before the courts, the controversy turns not upon the rule of law, but upon its application to the facts.

Fact-finding and fact-selecting as judicial function are not new ideas. In the *Brown Case*, when the Supreme Court drew on sociological data and psychological findings, it was widely criticized for introducing nonlegal techniques. But the justices did not, in fact, single out the school segregation issue for unusual treatment in this respect. The Brandeis Brief, filed in 1908 in a case involving the regulation of working hours for women in industry, included a great many background facts on the economic and social conditions of women workers.[73] The Brandeis Brief has become the prototype of numerous briefs and judicial opinions; lawyers and justices alike recognize the relevance of business facts, economic data, information concerning political practices and social customs, as well as legal precedents, in settling controversies of public importance.

Robert McCloskey, professor of government at Harvard University, places the exercise of judicial review close to the mainstream of American politics. The court is continuously forced to decide specific controversies within the broad context of the great issues that confront the nation: federal-state relationships, business-government conflicts, police power and private rights, national security and individual liberties. McCloskey repudiates the "myth of a perfect judiciary perfectly administering a perfect Constitution." At the same time, he discounts the view of those who treat the Court "as if it were not a court at all, as if its 'courthood' were a pure façade for political functions indistinguishable from those performed by the legislature."[74]

Drawing by Bill Mauldin;
© 1967 Chicago Sun-Times.

"Man, that's the fanciest place I ever got throwed out of!"

---

[73]This brief was prepared by Louis Brandeis, then counsel before the Court, later one of the justices. (*Muller* v. *Oregon,* 208 U.S. 412.) See Marion E. Doro, "The Brandeis Brief," *Vanderbilt Law Review,* XI (June, 1958), 783–799.
[74]Robert McCloskey, *The American Supreme Court* (Chicago: The University of Chicago Press, 1960), p. 19.

Drawing by Herblock;
© 1963 *The Washington Post.*

*"You know what?
Those guys act like they really
believe that."*

To begin with, the Constitution has never been perfect, and no amount of judicial review by mortal judges will make it so. Conceived in ambiguities, the Constitution has never lent itself to a single, consistent interpretation. In Chapter 2, "The Cultural Context," we pointed up some of the many ambivalences of the American character. The Convention of 1787 exemplifies our national inclination, even determination, not to choose but to compromise. The Framers were gentlemen of principle *and* property. They created a more perfect union *and* they conserved the states. They granted great powers to the national government *and* put various vague limitations upon it. They specified the powers of Congress *and* authorized additional necessary and proper powers to carry into execution "all other powers" vested in the government of the United States. They established a bicameral Congress—the House to represent the people in proportion to their numbers *and* the Senate to give the states equal representation. The familiar words and phrases throughout the document bespeak the many compromises that made the Constitution acceptable to factions that disagreed on basic principles and practices. The Framers gave Congress the power to regulate commerce *among* the states; the preposition made a nice distinction, something more than *between* the states, something less than *in* the states. They referred to "privileges and immunities of citizens in the several states" but nowhere did they define citizenship, either in the United States or in the several states, and nowhere did they attempt to spell out the meaning of privileges and immunities.

The article on the judiciary represents extreme forbearance on the part of the Framers. "Judicial power of the United States," surely a momentous power, is not defined. "Inferior courts" are neither prescribed nor described. What, then, could be more fuzzy and uncertain than the "appellate jurisdiction" of the Supreme Court? Assuming that Marshall's logic was good and his interpretation of the Framers' intentions reasonably accurate in *Marbury* v. *Madison*, how are the courts expected to exercise judicial review? What did the Convention really mean when it wrote so impressively, "This Constitution . . . shall be the supreme law of the land"?

Professor McCloskey calls our attention to the continuing and countervailing approaches to American constitutionalism: the rule of law *and* the will of the people. Although the Framers honored both doctrines, they accepted them side by side, not in synthesis. And this posed from the outset a dual development of constitutional interpretations. Americans believe that certain principles of government must be upheld as fundamental to a free society even when sometimes they are contrary to current popular opinions. But we also believe in the practice of majority rule and trust that the popular ideas will not really deviate too far from the constitutional tradition. Thus we expect the President and Congress to act in a political capacity to turn public opinion into public policy, "in pursuance of the Constitution." And we expect the Court to act in a judicial capacity, sustaining the supreme law of the land, observing the imperatives of public opinion.

The Constitution is what the judges say it is, but the judges must be careful what they say. When the judges expound the Constitution, they are not only exercising judicial review, but are also engaged in policy-making at the highest levels of statesmanship. The Court must draw a discreet line between what lawyers call judicial activism and judicial restraint. It must not be too modest. "America needs the Court's advice and control to help mitigate its own extravagances."[75] We are an impulsive nation; sometimes we act too much and too soon, and think too little and too late. We count on the Court to remind us of what is fundamental in our public philosophy. The Court must not be too aggressive. As McCloskey points out: "No useful purpose is served when the judges seek all the hottest political caldrons of the moment and dive into the middle of them." We count on the Court to blend its orthodox judicial opinions with a mixture of reasonably popular ideas. The function of the

[75]*Ibid.*, p. 20.

Court is to interpret the Constitution so as to maintain the stability and continuity of our fundamental principles and at the same time to permit necessary flexibility for changing times and new ideas.

PART FOUR

Outputs

of the Political System:

Rewards and Deprivations

CIVIL

RIGHTS

14

In the American political system, civil rights—for individuals, for minority groups, for all the people—are a matter of public policy. If you have followed the theoretical framework of this text, you will recognize that public policy is the output of the whole political process. We entrust our official decision-makers—the legislators, the Chief Executive, the bureaucrats, and the judges—with authority and power to determine public policy, but decision-making always occurs within an environment which conditions the official actors.

The political environment within which governmental decisions are made is an integral part of the whole society which constitutes the American Way of Life. The purposes, goals and objectives toward which governmental activities are directed—and it is essential that public policies have such rational direction—are deeply rooted in the cultural values, the political traditions, and the legal norms of the American people. Official actors make the authoritative decisions, but in a democratic system they are not likely to act without prompting from their various constituents. Public policies are never permanent; they must continuously reflect changes in the social environment and also react to changing demands and supports for governmental action within the community.

Since World War II, American public policy on civil rights has assumed great significance in international politics as well as in the domestic arena. Developing new nations, even those which have rejected democracy as we understand it, nevertheless are impelled to endorse liberal individual rights and values, whether as aspirations or as immediate new conditions. David Apter in *The Politics of Modernization* observes that "libertarian statements of intention embodied in constitutions are very important"; and he goes so far as to claim that "in the evolution of democracy, constitutionalism is dependent on the assertion of individuality in the modern world."[1] Because American civil rights are grounded in constitutionalism, the rising expectations of people in the new nations have inevitably focused attention on the output of the first new nation. How has the American government fulfilled the original intentions of the Constitutional Convention of 1787 "to secure the blessings of liberty to ourselves and our posterity"?

---

[1] David E. Apter, *The Politics of Modernization* (Chicago: The University of Chicago Press, 1967), p. 453.

The Constitutional Statements

"Unalienable Rights" in the Moral Context

The American Declaration of Independence holds that *all men* are "endowed by their Creator with certain unalienable rights, that among these are Life, Liberty and the pursuit of Happiness." The Constitution declares that *no person* shall be deprived of life, liberty or property "without due process of law" and further provides that no state shall deprive *any person* within its jurisdiction of "the equal protection of the laws." This is the American tradition and the supreme law of the land—that every individual possesses basic rights and liberties simply because he is a human being entitled to decent respect from his fellows.

The American government was instituted "to secure these rights," but the rights (with which men are endowed by the Creator) are *unalienable*; they may not be abridged by official decisions and they are deliberately placed beyond the reach of the current majority. These beliefs, which the authors of the Declaration of Independence proclaimed as self-evident "truths," still stand as the dominant rationale for our national policies in the area of civil rights.

The ideas of John Locke, Puritan philosopher in seventeenth-century England, permeate both the Declaration of Independence of 1776 and the Constitution of 1787. To Locke, man was amenable to reason and susceptible to the claims of conscience. Endowed by his Creator with these potentialities, man can shape his role in society and determine the kind of government to which he will give his consent. Locke believed that the good society is a free society in which men live by "right reason." The best kind of government is the one that governs least in matters of mind and spirit. When God gave Adam reason, he gave him freedom to choose, for reason is but choosing—so the great Puritan poet, John Milton, brought reason and freedom together in *Areopagitica* when he spoke for liberty of the press before the English Parliament: "Man is born free and rational." This basic tenet of seventeenth-century Puritanism became a basic tenet of eighteenth-century American political theory. The approach to civil rights was both intellectual and moral: government must guard the institutions of freedom.

The delegates to the Philadelphia Convention were more concerned with economic security than with political democracy. This concern was also part of the Lockean ideology. Locke himself was quite frank: "The reason why men enter into society is the preservation of their property." To Locke, however, the general term "property" encompassed the "lives, liberties, and estates" of every man. This explains, at least superficially, why Locke appealed both to the "radicals" of the American Revolution, who were primarily concerned with safeguarding personal liberties, and to the "conservatives" at the Philadelphia Convention, who were more concerned with protecting private property.

The doctrines of limited government and unalienable rights were not meant to imply license or absolute liberty, with every man free to say and do what pleases him personally. Civil rights are conceived in a moral context; the individual not only has a legal right but also a moral responsibility to seek the truth and to act according to "right reason." Moreover, every individual is constrained by the society in which he lives; he has a moral commitment as well as a legal obligation to respect the rights and liberties of his neighbor. Thus all rights and liberties, even those we regard as fundamental, are relative in practice. "No man is an Island, intire in itselfe"—no one of us can live alone. Clearly no individual has an absolute claim to a right if it is in conflict with a neighbor's claim; every personal liberty is restricted to certain ends and limits fixed by society. Though the individual may claim freedom of speech, he has no right to slander his neighbor, to incite his fellow citizens to rise up against the state, or to urge extremism that provokes mob action, even in defense of rights or liberties. As Justice Oliver Wendell Holmes once observed, "The most stringent protection of free speech would not protect a man in falsely shouting fire in a theatre and causing a panic." Liberty of conscience and freedom of worship are fundamental in a democratic society, but not even in the name of religion may American citizens engage in disorderly conduct, perpetrate fraud, or indulge in polygamy. Freedom of press is a primary right in our democracy, but it gives no license to publish what is seditious, obscene, malicious, or libelous.

Within the moral context of the American tradition, our individual rights and personal liberties carry with them corresponding responsibilities and obligations. Thus the claim to liberty of conscience assumes that each citizen has an obligation to make ethical decisions. The right to full and free discussion is tempered by the moral maxim that reasonable men may reasonably disagree—but they must stay within the bounds of reason. The right to publish books, newspapers, and magazines without censorship carries an obligation to inform, not inflame, public opinion. The right of the individual to read whatever he chooses implies some obligation to choose wisely—to read for information and counsel as well as for relaxation and diversion. If "the market place of ideas" is open to all, then we must count on the conscience and common sense of our citizens to reject the shoddy and false, to hold out for the good and true. Thus, the democratic creed in practice depends on both the intelligence and the moral character of citizens.

Civil Rights in Constitutional Law

The appeal to morality as a basis of individual rights and responsibilities is seemingly not so persuasive today as it was to our forebears. Supposedly unalienable rights have been alienated in so many parts of the world that we are less certain about the self-evident nature of our truths. Nevertheless, partly because the Founders implanted their notion of unalienable rights in our constitutional law, *civil rights* has an exalted position in our political and legal system today.

After the American colonists had broken away from the British Crown, the Continental Congress advised them to organize "conventions of the people" that would provide permanent constitutional government in each of the new states. Virginia was the first state to draft a constitution, a constitution prefaced by a Declaration of Rights that became the model for lawmakers in the other states.[2] The delegates to the Constitutional Convention in Philadelphia felt that these new state constitutions adequately protected the fundamental rights of the individual; they decided it would be superfluous to attach a detailed bill of rights to the federal Constitution.

They did, however, put some restrictions on both the national and the state governments with respect to personal liberties. Thus Congress was forbidden to suspend the writ of habeas corpus except in case of rebellion or invasion. Both Congress and the state legislatures were forbidden to enact bills of attainder, to pass ex post facto laws, or to impair the obligation of contracts. Treason was carefully defined, and punishment was limited to the life and person of the traitor. And religious tests were banned as a qualification for any office or public trust under the United States. The inclusion of these few restrictions, and the exclusion of other and more important ones, served to strengthen the popular demand for a comprehensive bill of rights as an integral part of the national Constitution. If promises had not been made in the state conventions assuring that such a bill of rights would immediately be added to the original text, the Constitution would certainly not have been ratified.

During the fight for ratification, more than a hundred civil rights amendments were proposed to the various states. In the first Congress, James Madison introduced a series of amendments to reassure the people that the new government had no intention of denying or disregarding "those rights of persons and property which by the Declaration of Independence were affirmed to be unalienable." The House actually passed seventeen of these amendments, although two of them were rejected by the Senate. The remaining fifteen were consolidated into twelve and then submitted to the state legislatures. Ten were ratified. These first ten amendments constitute the "American Bill of Rights," though only the first eight actually detail the rights of individuals.

The Bill of Rights, then, is an integral part of the Constitution. These amendments reveal what the eighteenth-century champions of popular freedom regarded as the most precious rights and liberties of the individual—the rights that must be most carefully guarded. In brief, these are: the free exercise of religion, freedom of speech and press, rights of assembly and petition (Amendment I); the right of the people to keep and bear arms (II); protection against quartering of soldiers in private homes (III); protection against unreasonable searches and seizures of persons, houses, papers, and effects (IV); the procedural rights of persons accused of crime and guarantees of due process of law with respect to life, liberty, and property (V); further rights of the accused, including trial by jury and the right to assistance of counsel (VI); provisions for trial by jury in civil cases (VII); and the

---

[2]See Allen Rutland, *The Birth of the Bill of Rights, 1776–1791* (Chapel Hill: The University of North Carolina Press, 1955), for an objective and accurate historical account of the background of the Bill of Rights. Authorship of the Virginia Declaration of Rights is attributed principally to George Mason and Patrick Henry—the same Colonel Mason who refused to sign the Philadelphia Constitution because it did not include a similar Bill of Rights for the whole people—the same Patrick Henry who refused to attend the Convention of 1787 because he "smelt a rat."

prohibition of excessive bails or fines and of cruel or unusual punishment (VII).[3]

Among the amendments that Madison originally proposed as part of the national bill of rights, one provided: "No State shall infringe the right of trial by Jury in criminal cases nor the rights of conscience, nor the freedom of speech, or of the press." Although this proposal was rejected by the Senate, Madison evidently wanted to place restrictions upon the states as well as upon the central government. At the time, four of the states had no bill of rights, and some of those that were adopted by the other states he judged "not only defective, but absolutely improper." Madison's proposal was probably defeated by senators from states whose established churches would presumably have been outlawed by this amendment, since these churches could have been held to infringe on rights of conscience. In any case, the rejection indicated that Congress intended the first eight amendments to restrict only the central government. Thus, the First Amendment begins, "Congress shall pass no law . . .," an implication that the Bill of Rights was designed to restrict only the national government. This interpretation was made constitutional law when Chief Justice Marshall in the case of *Barron v. Baltimore* (1833) firmly rejected the proposition that the Bill of Rights applied to the states as well. If Congress had so intended, "they would have declared this purpose in plain and intelligible language."[4] This interpretation was to be repeated in many cases over the next quarter century.

The addition of the Civil Rights Amendments—the Thirteenth, Fourteenth, and Fifteenth—after the Civil War considerably complicated the pattern of federalism in the area of civil rights. In their historical context, these amendments were specifically concerned with the rights of Negroes who had recently been freed in the southern states. The Thirteenth Amendment, prohibiting slavery, was intended to affirm the Negro's constitutional status as a freedman. The Fourteenth was intended to define his citizenship and to guarantee his privileges and immunities as a United States citizen: no state may deny him equal protection of the laws or deprive him of life, liberty, or property without due process of law. The Fifteenth was intended to guarantee that his right to suffrage would not be abridged because of race, color, or previous condition of servitude.

Congressional debates on the introduction of the Fourteenth Amendment show the intent, at least on the part of those who spoke out, to make the entire Bill of Rights applicable to the states. Immediately following the adoption of the Thirteenth Amendment, Congress had enacted the Civil Rights Act of 1866, which conferred citizenship on the newly freed Negroes and provided that Negroes should have "full and equal benefit of all laws and proceedings for the security of person and property as is enjoyed by white citizens."

---

[3] The incorporation of the Bill of Rights into the Constitution has already been discussed in Chapter 4.
[4] The Chief Justice was not usually such a stickler for strict construction; see *Marbury v. Madison* (1 Cranch 137), *McCulloch v. Maryland* (4 Wheat. 316), and *Gibbons v. Ogden* (9 Wheat. 1).

President Andrew Johnson vetoed the bill on the ground that it was beyond the constitutional power of Congress to "repeal all state laws discriminating between whites and blacks. . ." Congress passed the Civil Rights Act over the President's veto but meantime, to make legitimate national legislation in the broad area of civil rights, Congress introduced the Fourteenth Amendment. Unquestionably, the framers of the Fourteenth Amendment hoped to overrule the decision of *Barron* v. *Baltimore* and to bring the states under the same limitations as the national government with respect to individual rights and liberties. On the other hand, those who opposed the Amendment were just as certainly antagonistic to any transfer of responsibility for civil rights from the states to the national government.

In the American political system, no single set of decision-makers has the last word on public policy. No sooner was the Fourteenth Amendment ratified than the Supreme Court began to interpret its meaning without reference to the pertinent congressional debates. Within a decade the expressed intentions of the Congress were interred in a series of judicial decisions which in effect denied to Congress the power to pass general legislation on civil rights. The Court invalidated the Civil Rights Act of 1875 which had prohibited discrimination in public accommodations.[5]

Universal suffrage is generally regarded as one of the basic tests of democracy. We have already mentioned that the Constitutional Convention of 1787 could not come to agreement on this crucial test. Their decision was to leave it to the states to decide who should have the right to vote in the new Republic. Thus the members of the House of Representatives, according to the Constitution, are chosen by the same electorate in each state which votes for "the most numerous branch of the state legislature." Even to this day, we have no national policy with respect to congressional or presidential elections, except in a negative sense: the states still determine voting qualifications, subject to the restrictions of the Fifteenth, Nineteenth, and Twenty-Fourth Amendments. No state may deprive any person of the right to vote because of race, color, sex, or failure to pay a poll tax. In all the states, citizenship is the prime prerequisite for voting. Today, this is perhaps the most important right which a citizen can exercise and which an alien cannot. This, however, is a consequence of state policy rather than constitutional law or national policy.

We have already discussed, in Chapter 9, landmark decisions of the Supreme Court interpreting the constitutional statements on suffrage in state as well as national elections. The judges have invalidated so-called "grandfather clauses" in state laws or constitutions, Democratic "white primaries," and state poll taxes, on the grounds that such practices constitute either a denial of equal protection of the laws under the Fourteenth Amendment or violate the extension of suffrage under the Fifteenth Amendment.[6] On the other hand, they have upheld the 1965 Voting Rights Act, which provides for suspension of state voting rules and the use of federal examiners where less than half the

---

[5]See the *Slaughter House Cases* (1873), which virtually negated the privileges and immunities clause of the new Amendment (16 Wall. 36); and the *Civil Rights Cases* (1883), which declared void the Civil Rights Act of 1875 (109 U.S. 3).

[6]*Quinn* v. *United States*, 238 U.S. 347 (1915); *Smith* v. *Allwright*, 321 U.S. 649 (1944); *Harper* v. *Virginia State Board of Elections*, 383 U.S. 663 (1966).

citizens of voting age are registered, presumably because of discriminatory literacy tests or other regulatory devices. In the words of Chief Justice Earl Warren, "as against the reserved powers of the States, Congress may use any rational means to effectuate the constitutional prohibition of racial discrimination in voting"; his Court was in unanimous agreement that the congressional act of 1965 was "rational both in practice and theory."[7] Here we but note in passing the importance of voting rights in securing all other rights. People who can and do vote are in a much more strategic position to get what they want from government.

Privileges and Immunities of Citizens

Citizens of the United States

The Articles of Confederation mention "the free inhabitants of these States," "free citizens in the several states," and "the people of each State." The Constitution of 1787 speaks of "citizens of each State" and "citizens in the several States," but it adds a new phrase and a new concept: "citizens of the United States." Not until the adoption of the Fourteenth Amendment in 1868, however, do we find a constitutional definition of United States citizenship: "*All persons born or naturalized in the United States, and subject to the jurisdiction thereof, are citizens of the United States and of the state wherein they reside.*"

According to international law, each nation-state decides for itself who shall be counted as citizens. Until the Fourteenth Amendment, the prevailing view was that United States citizenship was derived from state citizenship. Thus, after the Declaration of Independence, all persons born in a colony or naturalized there became citizens in the new state. And, under the Constitution of 1787, the citizens in each state also became citizens of the United States. In the famous *Dred Scott Case* (1857), Chief Justice Taney argued that "citizens of each state" meant citizens of the United States as understood at the time the Constitution was adopted and that Negroes then were not considered capable of citizenship.[8] The Dred Scott decision was one that only the Civil War could reverse. When the war was over, Congress faced the problem of defining the status of the freed Negro. Through the Fourteenth Amendment, it deliberately overturned Taney's judgment in the Dred Scott case.

The United States Supreme Court has ruled that the Fourteenth Amendment means just what it says: *All* persons born in the United States are citizens of the United States. In the case of *U.S.* v. *Wong Kim Ark* (1898),[9] the Court held unconstitutional an attempt by Congress to exclude the children of aliens who themselves were ineligible to become citizens. Regardless of the race or na-

---

[7]*South Carolina* v. *Katzenbach*, 383 U.S. 301 (1966).
[8]*Scott* v. *Sandford*, 19 How. 393 (1857). Justice Curtis disagreed with Taney, asserting that as a matter of fact there were free Negro citizens in 1789 and that it was then understood that a state was free to extend citizenship to new classes of persons within its borders.
[9]*United States* v. *Wong Kim Ark*, 169 U.S. 649 (1898).

tionality of their parents, then, all persons born in the United States are citizens of this country. On the other hand, because corporations are created by law and are not natural-born persons, they cannot have the status of citizens. This particular interpretation has been important in excluding corporations from the constitutional privileges and immunities of United States citizenship. "Subject to the jurisdiction thereof . . ." has undergone both political and legal refinement. In brief, persons born in any of the states, in the District of Columbia, Puerto Rico, Guam, the Virgin Islands, American territorial waters, American missions abroad, and American public vessels —all are "subject to the jurisdiction of the United States."

A nation-state may establish its people's citizenship under two general principles of international law: (1) *jus soli* (law of the land) and (2) *jus sanguinis* (law of blood). Under *jus soli* the place, the country in which a person is born, determines citizenship; under *jus sanguinis*, the citizenship of the parent is transmitted to the child. The Fourteenth Amendment adopts the policy of *jus soli*.

Although the Fourteenth Amendment makes *jus soli* the basis for United States citizenship, Congress has by statute also adopted the policy of *jus sanguinis*. Thus a person born abroad of American parents may be an American citizen. Under present law, a person born abroad of American parents is an American citizen (1) if either of his parents is a citizen who has resided in the United States for at least ten years, five of them after the age of 16, and (2) if he himself resides in the United States for at least five years between the ages of 13 and 21.

Since other countries also define citizenship on the basis of *jus soli* or *jus sanguinis*, or both, many persons actually have dual citizenship. This dual citizenship may involve an individual in problems of conflicting jurisdiction in matters of military service, tax obligations, political activities, and protection in foreign countries. So far, however, the nations of the world have not been willing to accept any single, uniform basis for citizenship.

The Fourteenth Amendment prohibits the states from abridging the privileges and immunities of citizens of the United States. But nowhere in the Constitution is there any complete listing of these "privileges and immunities." From time to time, however, the Supreme Court has tried to enumerate some of them. In *Crandall* v. *Nevada* (1868), a case decided while the Fourteenth Amendment was before the states for ratification, the Court identified various "citizen rights": to have access to the government, to transact business with it, to seek its protection, to share its offices, to engage in administering its functions, to have entrance into its courts of justice and free access to the seaports.[10]

The first Supreme Court ruling on the meaning of the "privileges and immunities" mentioned in the Fourteenth Amendment was handed down in the *Slaughter House Cases* (1873).[11] These cases, which involved the validity of a

---

[10]Nevada had levied a head tax on every person leaving the state by public transportation. The Court held that because it is the right of the citizen to move freely from one state to another, a state tax restricting such movement was unconstitutional. 6 Wall. 35 (1868).

[11]*Slaughter House Cases*, 16 Wall. 36 (1873). Some constitutional authorities accord the *Slaughter House Cases* as much importance as *McCulloch* v. *Maryland*. Whereas Marshall's great decision enhanced the power of the national government, the decision in the *Slaughter House Cases* preserved the prestige of the states in the Union.

Louisiana statute, offer an excellent example of how vague and confused Supreme Court decisions can sometimes be. Under the state's power to protect public health, the Louisiana legislature authorized a slaughter-house monopoly in New Orleans. The independent butchers of New Orleans, in turn, protested that the monopoly deprived them of their privileges and immunities as United States citizens. The Court's decision was close—five to four. Justice Samuel F. Miller, speaking for the majority, held that when Congress framed the Fourteenth Amendment it had no intention of making any radical change in the relations between the state governments and the federal government, or in the relations of either of these governments to the people. The Justice "ventured to suggest" that Congress had considered the privileges and immunities of United States citizenship mainly as those that owe their existence to the federal government or that arise out of the nature and essential character of the national government. Quite understandably, the Court did not feel that butchering fell into this restricted category.

The decision in the *Slaughter House Cases* was hailed by the proponents of states' rights, especially in the South. According to the Court's interpretation, the Fourteenth Amendment gave the national government no additional positive power over civil rights. This interpretation also meant that the privileges and immunities of citizens of the United States which no state may abridge are the same as and no more than those which belonged to United States citizens before the amendment was adopted. The Court's list of such rights in *Crandall* v. *Nevada* was certainly scanty and unimpressive. But a citizen of the United States is also a citizen of the state in which he lives. The decision in the *Slaughter House Cases* reinforced this concept of dual citizenship: the Supreme Court's ruling left it up to the states to protect the privileges and immunities of citizens within the local cultural context.

Some students of constitutional law feel that the Court's decision in the *Slaughter House Cases* virtually nullified the privileges and immunities clause of the Fourteenth Amendment. True, the decision severely limited the privileges and immunities of *national* citizenship, but by the same token it gave greater emphasis to the privileges and immunities of *state* citizenship. The American citizen today looks to his state—not to the national government—to give him free schooling, to protect his home and other property, to grant his marriage license, his automobile license, his occupational license, his hunting and fishing licenses, and eventually to issue his burial permit!

Many people would still prefer to have the privileges and immunities of citizenship the same in every state and so guaranteed by the national government. Some argue that this is what Congress actually intended when it wrote the Fourteenth Amendment. Justice Stephen J. Field, who dissented in the *Slaughter House Cases*, thought that the Fourteenth Amendment meant that, "The fundamental rights, privileges, and immunities which belong to him as a free man and a free citizen, now belong to him as a citizen of the United States, and are not dependent upon his citizenship of any state. . . ." This interpretation has not prevailed, however. Just as rights of *persons* vary from state to state, so also do the rights and privileges of *citizens* in the several states.

The right to pass freely from state to state is a right of national citizenship; the nature of the federal union, however, requires that the right be extended to all persons in the United States. In the depression years, some states tried to bar the entrance of indigent migrants. In *Edwards* v. *California* (1941)[12] the Supreme Court considered a California statute which was aimed against the entrance of "Okies," poverty-stricken refugees from the Dust Bowl. The Court unanimously found the California statute unconstitutional: five of the justices said the prohibition imposed an unconstitutional burden upon interstate commerce; four thought the prohibition violated *the privileges and immunities of citizenship.* Justice Douglas was especially keen on this latter point: "The right of persons to move freely from state to state occupies a more protected position in our constitutional system than does the movement of cattle, fruit, steel, and coal across state lines. . . . The right to move freely from State to State is an incident of *national* citizenship, protected by the privileges and immunities clause of the Fourteenth Amendment against state interference." Whether one argues from the position of the majority or of the concurring four in the *Edwards Case,* it seems clear that constitutional law protects personal freedom of movement from state to state both under the commerce clause and under rights of national citizenship.

Early in the 1960s, mixed companies of Negroes and whites, all of them citizens of the United States, traveled as "Freedom Riders" across southern state lines, making frequent "rest stops" in railroad stations, bus terminals, and airports. They demonstrated quite dramatically that administrative rulings and judicial statements of constitutional law do not always reflect patterns of behavior.[13] Their freedom of movement was frequently curtailed by local "Jim Crow" regulations, and in some communities they were actually arrested for disturbing the public peace when they demanded equal protection of the laws. Since then, however, partly in response to their activities, racial discriminations have almost entirely disappeared from facilities and accommodations for interstate travel in the United States.

When an American travels abroad, his right to full protection of the United States government comes from national, not state, citizenship. The passport of the individual American citizen abroad is an impressive document: "I, the undersigned Secretary of State of the United States of America, hereby request all whom it may concern to permit safely and freely to pass and in case of need to give all lawful aid and protection to the above named citizen of the United States." But, as a by-product of the Cold War, the American government has put various controls on the travel of its citizens outside the country.

The Supreme Court has repeatedly declared that freedom of movement at home and abroad is an important aspect of the citizen's liberty, "deeply engrained in our history." In 1964, the judges invalidated a section of the Subversive Activities Control Act, which prohibited issuance of passports to Communists.[14] In the following year, however, the Court (with strong dis-

---

[12]314 U.S. 160 (1941).

[13]In 1955, the Interstate Commerce Commission had issued an order banning segregation on interstate trains and buses and also in railroad (but not in bus) stations.

[14]*Aptheker* v. *Secretary of State*, 378 U.S. 500 (1964).

sents) upheld the discretionary refusal of the State Department to validate a passport for travel to communist Cuba.[15] And similar restrictions on travel to communist China have been given judicial sanction.

Immigrants America is a land of immigrants. Not until the latter part of the nineteenth century did this country begin to close its gates against certain classes of foreigners. Some of the states, under pressure from vested social and economic groups, had earlier attempted to control the admission of "undesirable" aliens, but the Supreme Court declared all such state laws unconstitutional.

Congress passed its first major immigration act in 1882, barring the entrance of idiots, lunatics, convicts, and paupers. In the same year it enacted the first Chinese Exclusion Law, a controversial statute that was not repealed until World War II, when China was one of our allies. In 1885, largely at the behest of organized labor, Congress prohibited the importation of contract labor. Up to World War I, Congress continued to place qualitative restrictions that excluded such undesired persons as the feeble-minded, professional beggars, anarchists, and polygamists. (This specific exclusion suggests that these groups had been freely admitted previously.)

A phenomenal increase in immigration in the opening decades of the twentieth century—more than a million immigrants in a single year—caused great concern in many quarters. Organized labor thought that the flood of cheap labor aggravated unemployment and lowered wages. Increasing immigration from Southern and Eastern Europe posed new problems in social and political assimilation. Earlier immigrants, and their descendants, from Northern and Western Europe were determined to protect "the American heritage"—that is, their own background. A Presidential Study Commission, appointed in 1907, produced a forty-two-volume report in 1911. Congress took no action until 1917, however, when it established a simple literacy test for all immigrants and excluded virtually all immigration from most of Asia and the Pacific Islands.

Not until after World War I, when immigration from Europe was reaching the proportions of an invasion, did Congress impose quantitative limits. In 1924, Congress limited the total annual immigration to approximately 150,000, a mere fraction of the hundreds of thousands of pioneers and settlers who once came to our shores every year. This total was broken down into quotas based on "national origins": the number of immigrants admitted from any foreign country in any given year was reduced to one-sixth of 1 per cent of the number of persons in the United States in 1920 whose "national origin" could be attributed to that country. The "national origins" policy was designed to admit the largest number of immigrants from Northern and Western Europe, the smallest number from Southern and Eastern Europe. (The combined quotas for the British Isles and Germany accounted for nearly three-fourths of

---
[15]*Zemel* v. *Rusk*, 381 U.S. 1 (1965).

the legal total.) There are many arguments for this policy of "national origins," but most of them sound like pages out of Hitler's *Mein Kampf.*

The tides of immigration in this country have turned in large measure upon economic and political conditions in this country and abroad. Our country has traditionally been "the land of the free" for the politically oppressed or pursued, "the land of opportunity" for the economically depressed and ambitious. Even under the quota system, this pattern has prevailed. In the 1930s, the largest proportion of our immigrants came as refugees from Nazi Germany. But the 1930s left immigration generally at a low ebb, because the Great Depression in this country made us economically less attractive to settlers than at any other time in our history. World War II virtually stopped all immigration, although a token gesture to our Chinese allies provided for an annual quota of 105 Chinese immigrants. After the war, Congress was persuaded to make allowance for the influx of "war brides," and, as part of the Cold War strategy, to provide for the special admission of war-displaced persons and others who had fled, escaped, or been expelled from behind the Iron Curtain.

In 1952, the McCarran-Walters Act, which purported to overhaul American immigration policies, eliminated all racial barriers as such but retained both numerical restrictions and the national-origins quotas. (Immigration from the Western Hemisphere was not placed under the quota system.) President Truman vetoed the Immigration Act of 1952, declaring that its provisions were "insulting to large numbers of our finest citizens, irritating to our allies abroad, and foreign to our purposes and ideals." Nevertheless Congress passed the bill over his veto. Although Presidents Eisenhower, Kennedy, and Johnson each in turn requested Congress to modify our immigration policies, these remained unchanged until the end of 1965.

The Immigration and Nationality Act of 1965 finally made substantial changes in American immigration policy, not only in response to urgent requests from Presidents but also because of organized and articulate support from pressure groups. In congressional committee hearings preceding the floor debates, representatives from many different racial, nationality, religious, and patriotic groups spoke for and against continuation of the national origins policy. A representative from the American Coalition of Patriotic Societies expressed readiness to jettison the national origins policy (though he thought it "eminently fair and useful") in order to bargain for a more effective system of worldwide control, particularly greater restrictions on immigration from within the Western Hemisphere. A labor spokesman opposed the national quota system (which "conveys abroad an impression of ethnic meanness and racial bigotry"), but at the same time insisted that the number and classes of immigrants be carefully controlled to protect American workers.[16]

The 1965 Immigration Act fixes an overall annual limit of 170,000 immigrants, with a maximum of 20,000 allowed to any one country. Preference is given to: (a) children, spouses, and other relatives of citizens in the United States; (b) professional persons who because of exceptional ability in sciences and arts are most likely to benefit the national economy, cultural interests, or

---

[16]For an illuminating case study of official and unofficial demands and supports bearing on legislative action, see *Immigration,* Hearings before Subcommittee No. 1, Committee on the Judiciary, House of Representatives, March 3–June 1, 1965.

welfare of the United States; (c) skilled or unskilled labor, not of a temporary or seasonal nature, for which there is a shortage of willing and employable persons in the United States; (d) political refugees, especially from communist countries, up to 6 per cent of the total number in any one year. Immigrants from within the Western Hemisphere, classified as "special immigrants," may enter without numerical restriction until July 1, 1968, at which time a limitation of 120,000 per year is established (exclusive of immediate relatives), unless meantime a Select Commission on Western Immigration, charged with studying "demographic, technological, and economic trends," has brought about changes in the 1965 Act.[17]

Aliens and Naturalized Citizens

Although the Constitution does not mention immigration, it does specify that Congress shall have power to establish uniform rules of naturalization. In his first annual message, President Washington urged Congress to determine by law "the terms on which foreigners may be admitted to the rights of citizens." Congress passed the first Naturalization Act in 1790, making naturalization an activity of the national and state courts; and until early in the twentieth century, Congress left the procedures of naturalization largely to the discretion of these courts.

With little central control, standards were not uniform and procedures were often extremely lax. During those decades, when millions of immigrants were pouring into this country, political machines in many cities helped produce new citizens — and new voters — on a mass-production basis. On election eve, party workers rounded up aliens and rushed them into local courts where, after perfunctory hearings, they would be granted "final papers" just in time to vote for the machine's candidates at the polls. To correct such abuses — undignified and sometimes fraudulent — Congress in 1906 provided for special examiners to assist the courts with naturalization and placed the Bureau of Immigration and Naturalization in the Department of Commerce and Labor.

When the Department of Labor was created in 1913, a Bureau of Immigration and a Bureau of Naturalization were reorganized within the new Department. We were still welcoming immigrants in great numbers and looked upon them as a continuing source of labor power for the nation. In 1940, the Immigration and Naturalization Service was removed from the Department of Labor and transferred to the Department of Justice. By then, we were more distrustful of the strangers who came to our shores, more inclined to regard them with suspicion as potential subversives.

Under present law, naturalization of individuals is still a judicial process,

[17]The 1965 Act creates a bipartisan Select Commission on Western Hemisphere Immigration, composed of fifteen members, five appointed by the Speaker of the House, five by the President of the Senate, five (including the Chairman) by the President. See *Immigration and Nationalization Act* (with amendments and notes on related laws and summaries of pertinent judicial decisions), Committee on the Judiciary, House of Representatives (Washington, D.C.: U.S. Government Printing Office, 1966).

usually in a national court.[18] An examiner from the Immigration and Naturalization Service makes the preliminary investigation to determine whether the applicant meets the various legal requirements for admission to citizenship. Most judges do not question applicants in court, but accept the recommendations of the Immigration and Naturalization Service. Nevertheless, the court procedure is generally impressive and the ceremony of induction to citizenship is a solemn and memorable occasion for most of our naturalized citizens.

There are two stages in the formal process of naturalization: (1) the applicant files a petition with the court for an examination; (2) after a public hearing before a naturalization examiner, the court grants him "final papers." Any alien who has been lawfully admitted to the United States and who has resided here for five years may petition for American citizenship. He files an application with the nearest office of the Immigration and Naturalization Service, giving such personal information as marital status, employment record, and organization affiliations. Subsequently, he appears before an examiner with two United States citizens who can testify to his good character and loyalty. He must swear that he is not a polygamist, an anarchist, a communist, or a supporter of any totalitarian government and that he intends to reside permanently in this country. The final hearing is held in open court not less than 30 days after the preliminary examination.

An alien applying for naturalization must be "attached to the principles of the Constitution of the United States and well disposed to the good order and happiness of the United States." When the court grants his petition for naturalization, the applicant renounces allegiance to the foreign state of which he has been a citizen and promises to bear allegiance to the United States of America. Here is the legal crux of differentiation between the citizen and the alien—*allegiance*. The citizen is required to defend his country and to support its constitutional principles; he must be "loyal." Between World War I and World War II, in a series of naturalization cases, the Court persistently held that a person who refused for any reason to take an oath to bear arms in defense of the United States could not become an American citizen. Then, in 1946, the Supreme Court reversed itself and sustained the application of James Girouard, a Canadian conscientious objector, who refused to fight but was willing to accept noncombatant assignments.[19] Finally, in 1950 and 1952, Congress cleared up the judicial confusion by exempting conscientious objectors from the requirement that a new citizen must prove his loyalty by willingness to bear arms in defense of the United States. The "conscientious objector" who believes in a Supreme Being may now meet the naturalization requirement by promising to perform noncombatant service in lieu of military duty.

In 1952, all racial barriers to naturalization were removed. The law now requires that the candidate be able to speak, read, and write simple English, and that he have some knowledge of the history, principles, and form of our government. In most countries, a married woman takes the citizenship of her

---

[18]Congress has extended collective naturalization by treaty to the people of the Louisiana Territory (1803), Florida (1819), and Alaska (1867); and by the Statutes to the Indians (1924) and to the people of Hawaii (1900), Puerto Rico (1917), the Virgin Islands (1927), and Guam (1950).

[19]*United States* v. *Schwimmer,* 279 U.S. 644 (1929); *United States* v. *Bland,* 283 U.S. 636 (1931); *United States* v. *MacIntosh,* 283 U.S. 605 (1931); *Girouard* v. *United States,* 328 U.S. 61 (1946).

husband. Under American law, however, an American woman who marries an alien does not (since 1922) lose her American citizenship even though under the laws of her husband's country she acquires his citizenship. Similarly, an alien who marries an American citizen does not acquire American citizenship, though the process of naturalization is shortened and simplified for the alien spouse. This practice of separate citizenship for husband and wife often creates problems of dual citizenship. Since many of our troops abroad are now marrying foreign women who immediately lose their original citizenship without gaining United States citizenship, many of these brides cannot claim citizenship anywhere.

Naturalized citizens enjoy the same constitutional privileges and immunities as native-born citizens. There is only one exception: a naturalized citizen is not eligible to be elected President or Vice-President of the United States. A naturalized citizen of the United States automatically becomes a citizen of the state in which he resides. No state may deprive either a native-born or a naturalized citizen of his United States citizenship. It is nothing more than a popular misconception that a person who is convicted of felony thereby loses his citizenship. It is true, however, that a felon may by law be deprived of such privileges of citizenship as office-holding and suffrage. Whatever civil rights are implied as part of national citizenship—such as the right to participate in elections or to move without restrictions from state to state—belong equally to those who acquired citizenship at birth and to those who acquired it by choice through naturalization.

Expatriates and Denaturalized Citizens

The Constitution says nothing about expatriation or deprivation of citizenship. In 1868, Congress declared that the right of expatriation was "a natural and inherent right of all people." This was a fitting policy for a nation of immigrants who could acquire American citizenship only by severing ties with their native lands. The same policy was also extended to any person who wanted to renounce American citizenship. In 1907, Congress defined the grounds for loss of citizenship: (1) naturalization in a foreign state; (2) taking an oath of allegiance to a foreign state; (3) marriage by an American woman to an alien (a provision repealed in 1922). In addition, residence by a naturalized citizen in a foreign state for five years, or in his native country for two years, produced a presumption that his American citizenship had ceased. This, in brief, was our policy until the Nationality Act of 1940 expanded the grounds for expatriation to include: foreign military service, voting in a foreign country's political election, formal renunciation, conviction for desertion from U.S. military forces, or treason.

The power of Congress to expatriate a native-born citizen who has voted in a political election in a foreign state was upheld by the Supreme Court, in a 5–4 decision, in 1958.[20] Justice Frankfurter, speaking for the majority of the

---

[20]*Perez* v. *Brownell*, 356 U.S. 44 (1958).

justices, explained that such an act was "potentially embarrassing to the American government and pregnant with the possibility of embroiling this country in disputes with other nations." In 1967, again in a 5–4 decision, the Supreme Court reversed its earlier ruling.[21] The case involved a naturalized citizen, born in Poland, who participated in an Israeli election. Mr. Justice Black, who had sided with the minority in 1958, now declared for the majority that a citizen has a constitutional right to remain a citizen in a free country unless he voluntarily relinquishes that citizenship. (Justice Black for the majority and Justice Harlan for the minority both resorted to the intentions of the Framers, and especially to the legislative history of the Fourteenth Amendment, to support their divergent opinions!)

The Supreme Court has chipped away other provisions of the 1940 Nationality Act, generally on the ground that Congress has no constitutional power to "rob a citizen of his citizenship." In 1958, a majority of the Court invalidated the statutory provision for expatriation upon conviction for desertion during time of war.[22] In 1963, the Court struck out the section of the statute which automatically deprived a person of his citizenship if he left the United States or remained outside the country during wartime or in a national emergency in order to evade military service.[23] In 1964, the Court held that a naturalized citizen could not be divested of his citizenship because he chose to reside more than two years in the country of his birth. The Court held, "This statute proceeds on the impermissible assumption that naturalized citizens as a class are less reliable and bear less allegiance to this country than the native born."[24]

The general policy of the United States is not to force naturalization on any alien lawfully admitted to this country. Immigrants in this country may retain their alien status indefinitely. True, since 1940 the Smith Act has required that all aliens be registered and fingerprinted. And, as part of its internal security program, in 1952 Congress provided that the Justice Department should maintain a central file with information on all aliens in the United States. Aliens must notify the Department of any change of address and must file certain information with the Attorney General each year. Otherwise, however, except in time of war aliens are under no great disability in this country. Although they do not enjoy special privileges and immunities, as persons they are entitled to the same fundamental civil rights as citizens.

The basic civil rights guaranteed by the American Constitution belong to all *persons*, not just to *citizens*. This policy is expressed in the Fifth and Fourteenth Amendments. In everyday affairs, then, the status of the alien is not very different from that of the citizen. He must obey the laws, pay his taxes, and send his children to school. He has access to the courts and, if he is prosecuted or sued, he is entitled to the same fair procedures and due process to which a citizen is entitled. And yet the courts have upheld many special restrictions on aliens, especially in the economic field. For example, most states have laws that bar aliens from various licensed occupations and professions. Some states

---

[21] *Afroyim* v. *Rusk*, 385 U.S. 917 (1967).
[22] *Trop* v. *Dulles*, 356 U.S. 86 (1958).
[23] *Kennedy* v. *Mendoza*, 372 U.S. 144 (1963).
[24] *Schneider* v. *Rusk*, 377 U.S. 163 (1964).

have prohibited land from being owned by aliens who are ineligible for naturalization. The statutes were particularly aimed at preventing Asians from owning land. With the racial barriers now removed from naturalization, however, the point of such restrictions is lost. Some states deny aliens a share in welfare benefits, such as old-age assistance and workmen's compensation. All states now prohibit aliens from voting and generally bar them from public office, and, aliens are ineligible for most positions in the national civil service.

In one respect, the status of the alien in this country is totally different from that of the citizen. The alien has no *right* to stay in the United States. The Internal Security Act of 1950 codified the various grounds for deportation of aliens. Subject to deportation are those aliens who: (1) have entered the country unlawfully; (2) were admitted for a specific time or purpose and who subsequently violated the conditions of their admission; (3) have been lawfully admitted, but who have proved themselves to be undesirable residents through criminal, immoral, or subversive acts.

Deportation proceedings are handled by the Immigration and Naturalization Service, subject to review in individual cases by a Board of Immigration Appeals. In cases of subversion, the Attorney General has almost unlimited discretion. Most deportation cases are routine—catching up with stowaways or those who have slipped across borders. The most flagrant class of violators are Mexican nationals who steal across our southern border every year by the thousands.

The most difficult deportation cases are those involving aliens who "at the time of entering the United States" or "at any time thereafter" have been members of the Communist party. These cases, though few in number, are likely to be dramatized with pathos and political overtones. Even though the alien has no right to stay in this country, he does have the right to notice and a hearing before he is deported. The proceedings, however, are administrative. Although judicial review is possible, the Supreme Court has not been inclined to question the constitutionality of deportation, and it has generally upheld the administrative fact-finding.

The Great Rights

Citizens of the United States enjoy special privileges and immunities, but, as we mentioned earlier, in the American political system the "Great Rights" belong to all persons. The Fifth Amendment proclaims that "no person" shall be deprived of due process of law; and nowhere is there any mention of exclusive rights for citizens. In the early years of the Republic, it was understood that the Bill of Rights restricted only the national government; the addition of the Civil War Amendments buttressed the belief that the great rights were constitutionally protected against encroachment by state governments.

Before World War I it was generally believed that the First Amendment did not restrain the states. But during the "red scare" after the war and in the early 1920s, when a number of legislatures tried to curb political expression, the Court began to reinterpret the First Amendment precisely as if it read "Neither Congress nor any state shall make any law restricting freedom of religion, speech, press, peaceable assembly and petition of the people for redress of grievances." In 1925, in a case involving freedom of speech and the press in New York, Justice Sanford simply *assumed* that the fundamental freedoms of the First Amendment were incorporated in the personal rights and liberties protected by the due process clause of the Fourteenth Amendment from impairment by the states.[25]

Freedom to Differ

Most eighteenth-century Americans believed that the good society was a society in which every man was free to think for himself and to express his thoughts to others. They could put their trust in the consent of the governed so long as every man was free to follow the dictates of his own conscience and to form his opinions in full and free discussion with his fellows. This is the simple philosophy that underlies the First Amendment, "Congress shall make no law . . . abridging the freedom of speech, or of the press; or the right of the people peaceably to assemble, and to petition the Government for a redress of grievances."

In his great essay, *On Liberty*, John Stuart Mill said, "If all mankind minus one were of one opinion, and only one person were of the contrary opinion, mankind would be no more justified in silencing that one person, than he, if he had the power, would be justified in silencing mankind." Justice Holmes expressed this same sentiment: "If there is any principle of the Constitution that more imperatively calls for attachment than any other it is the principle of free thought, not free thought for those who agree with us but freedom for the thought we hate."[26]

Recurrent periods of social anxiety and economic stress, especially in the wake of wars, have, however, set in motion waves of collective hysteria and political repression. Thus public behavior has frequently been at odds with the public philosophy; and in these times the great rights have suffered.

The principle of free discussion was put to a severe test in the first decade of the Republic when the Federalists attempted to squelch the rising opposition of the Jeffersonian Republicans through the Alien and Sedition Acts of 1798. The victory of the Jeffersonian Republicans and the election of Thomas Jefferson in 1800 put a quick end to these acts. Not until World War I would Congress again try to control freedom of political expression. In 1917, Congress

---

[25]*Gitlow* v. *New York*, 268 U.S. 652 (1925). The Court declared that the fundamental freedoms contained in the First Amendment must be construed as part of the "liberty" that the Fourteenth Amendment guaranteed against restrictive state legislation. Under this interpretation, the Court held the states to the general principle that they may not pass any law that curbs freedom of speech or freedom of the press.

[26]The case, *U.S.* v. *Schwimmer*, 279 U.S. 644 (1929), involved a 49-year-old Hungarian woman, a professional pacifist, who was seeking U.S. citizenship. The majority of the Court refused to grant citizenship to a person who refused to bear arms in defense of the U.S. Though Holmes himself was no pacifist, he strongly dissented from the majority views.

passed an espionage act that was intended to restrict political dissent while the nation was at war.

In 1940, Congress passed the Smith Act, the first peace-time sedition act to be put on the books since the Alien and Sedition Acts of 1798. This Act forbids both the advocacy of the violent overthrow of the government and conspiracies designed to cause this overthrow. After World War II, as the international conflict of ideologies grew sharper, Congress turned its attention to the problems of "psychological warfare." To avert the dangers of subversion, and especially to guard against communism, Congress began to take steps toward the control of political thinking that was directly inimical to "Americanism." As early as 1947, Congress included in the Taft-Hartley Act a provision that required officers of labor unions to swear they were not members of the Communist party or any organization that believes in or teaches the overthrow of the government by force or by other illegal methods.

Also in 1947, President Truman by executive order prescribed "Procedures for the Administration of an Employees' Loyalty Program in the Executive Branch of the Government." A network of Loyalty Boards was established to investigate every employee in the federal service. Membership in organizations listed by the Attorney General as totalitarian, fascist, communist, or subversive was an important factor in determining "disloyalty." Following a hearing, many governmental employees were suspended, discharged, or they resigned under fire, because their political views made them "security risks."

The first half of the 1950s is known as the era of "McCarthyism," taking its name from the congressional campaign against communism spearheaded by Joseph McCarthy, the junior Republican Senator from Wisconsin. Many congressmen besides McCarthy, however, were involved in the witch-hunting. At one point at least a half-dozen congressional committees were simultaneously investigating un-American activities and subversives in all sectors of American society—university professors and public-school teachers; Hollywood actors, writers, and directors; news reporters and editors; clergymen; and especially ex-New-Dealers. A motley parade of informers and witnesses, many of them ex-communists, appeared before congressional committees to give testimony about communists, communist sympathizers, fellow-travelers, and "liberals." Individuals who refused to cooperate with the committees were liable to be held in contempt of Congress, and those who failed to tell the whole truth about their past or present political associations could be tried for perjury. The most celebrated case of the early 1950s was that of Alger Hiss, who had held a high post in the State Department; he went to prison not because he was found guilty of espionage, but because he perjured himself before the House Committee on Un-American Activities.

In 1950, Congress passed the comprehensive Internal Security Act. This Act set up a Subversive Activities Control Board charged with determining, at the request of the Attorney General, whether a particular organization is communist "action," communist "front," or communist "infiltrated." It required every communist organization to register annually with the Attorney General;

report the names of its officers and members; identify the sources of all its funds; and label as "communist propaganda" all its publications sent through the mails or across state lines. Also according to this Act, members of communist organizations could not obtain passports, hold elective federal positions, serve as officers or employees of a labor union, or work in a defense plant.

The outlawing of the Communist party as a political organization was maneuvered in 1954 by a group of liberal Democrats led by Senator Hubert H. Humphrey of Minnesota. Viewed as political strategy in an election year, this was a neat riposte to Senator McCarthy's charges that the Democratic Party had for twenty years stood for "communism, betrayal, and treason." Few congressmen at that time, in either party, could risk opposing the Communist Control bill, which quickly passed 79–0 in the Senate and 265–2 in the House. What Congress intended to accomplish in a substantive way is not clear. The Act declared that the Communist party was not a party but rather an agency of a hostile foreign power presenting a clear, present, and continuing danger to national security. Although it was generally agreed in the floor debates that individual membership in the Communist party should be treated as a felony, teeth to this provision were extracted before the final bill was passed; penalties for belonging to the party were relegated to enforcement of the Smith Act and the Internal Security Act.[27]

How effective was all this legislation aimed against communism in America? The Communist party has not put forward a presidential candidate since 1940 and its overt activities have reached a vanishing point. The requirements that Communists be registered was intended to make it easy for the government to prosecute party leaders and the most active members. But the Communists have never registered and only a handful have ever been convicted. The total number of party members is not known, but agents from the Federal Bureau of Investigation have so thoroughly infiltrated the movement that there may be more FBI men than Marxists in the apparatus!

Over the years, the Supreme Court has pursued a somewhat erratic course in its review of the Communist cases, reflecting changes in the composition of the Court as well as changes in the political environment. In 1950, organized labor argued before the Supreme Court that the non-Communist affidavit provision of the Taft-Hartley Act was a violation of the First Amendment guarantee of free speech. Chief Justice Vinson upheld the Taft-Hartley provision as a necessary and proper method for removing political obstructions (communist-inspired strikes) to the free flow of commerce. Although he paid tribute to "the high place in which the right to speak, think, and assemble . . . was held by the Framers of the Bill of Rights," he did not think that the First Amendment restrained Congress from making a legitimate attempt to protect the public from noxious ideologies. Only Justice Black could not agree with the assumption that individual freedom can be abridged whenever a majority of the Court is satisfied with the nature or purpose of the abridgment.[28]

[27]See Donald G. Morgan, *Congress and the Constitution* (Cambridge, Mass.: The Belknap Press of Harvard University Press, 1966), Chapter 12. Professor Morgan uses the Communist Control Act of 1954 as a case study of "individual rights and national insecurity."

[28]*American Communications Association, C.I.O. v. Douds*, 339 U.S. 382 (1950).

The Supreme Court upheld the Smith Act in the highly dramatic *Dennis Case* (1951), which sprang from the conviction of the eleven top communists in the United States for violating the act. The majority of the Court viewed the role of the Communist party in the United States as "a well organized, nationwide conspiracy." The Court held that it was not necessary for the government to wait until a *putsch* was about to be executed, with the plans laid and the signal awaited. It accepted the formula that Judge Learned Hand had applied in the Court of Appeals: "In each case [courts] must ask whether the gravity of the 'evil,' discounted by its improbability, justifies such invasion of free speech as is necessary to avoid the danger." In effect, this decision bestowed on Congress the power to determine when it is reasonable to restrict freedom of speech to safeguard public security.[29]

Justices Black and Douglas dissented vigorously in the *Dennis Case*. Black pointed out that the communist leaders had been charged neither with any attempt to overthrow the government, nor with any overt acts designed to overthrow it. Rather, they had been charged with something three steps removed from such an attempt—they had been charged with conspiring to advocate the overthrow of the government. Douglas could see no "clear and present danger" in the Communist party: "Some nations less resilient than the United States, where illiteracy is high and where democratic traditions are only budding, might have to take drastic steps and jail these men for merely speaking this creed. But in America they are miserable merchants of unwanted ideas; their wares remain unsold." The majority of the Court were unconvinced, unimpressed. The Smith Act was allowed to stand.

In 1957, the *Dennis Case* was somewhat modified by the decision of the Supreme Court in the *Yates Case*.[30] A group of California communists had been tried and convicted in the lower federal court on the charge of advocating the forcible overthrow of the United States government. Speaking for the majority, Justice John Marshall Harlan pointed out that "the Smith Act does not denounce advocacy in the sense of preaching abstractly the forcible overthrow of the government." Thus, in order to convict the communists under the Smith Act, the government would have to show that the defendants had advocated *overt action* toward the forcible overthrow of the government. Advocacy, said the Court, is criminal only if it urges persons to *do* something rather than merely to *believe* something. The Court therefore ordered a retrial of the California communists in line with this interpretation.

In 1961, the Court considered the membership clause of the Smith Act. In a lengthy and complicated opinion, Justice Harlan upheld the conviction of an *active* member of the Communist party, who had *knowledge* of the party's illegal purpose and specific intent to overthrow the government of the United States. Justices Black, Douglas, and Brennan and Chief Justice Warren dissented on various grounds. Justice Douglas charged the majority with making "a sharp break with traditional concepts of First Amendment rights." Justice

[29]*Dennis v. United States*, 341 U.S. 494 (1951).
[30]*Yates v. U.S.*, 354 U.S. 298 (1957).

Brennan argued that the Internal Security Act of 1950, requiring communists to register, was intended to give them immunity from prosecution under the Smith Act.[31]

In the same term, the Court also upheld the registration requirements of the Internal Security Act of 1950.[32] Justice Frankfurter, speaking for a majority of five, found that the Act neither violated the First Amendment freedoms nor constituted a bill of attainder. His opinion took cognizance of the world communist movement. He pointed out that the special requirements of registration, disclosure of membership, filing of financial statements, and identification of publications did not apply to all political groups but only to foreign-dominated organizations. Mr. Justice Black in dissent pressed the argument that "freedoms of speech, petition, and assembly guaranteed by the First Amendment must be accorded to the ideas we hate or sooner or later they will be denied to the ideas we cherish."

In the 1960s, the judges have been less and less inclined to help Congress combat communism. In 1965, the Supreme Court invalidated a 1959 statute which made it a crime for a member of the Communist party to serve as an officer or employee of a labor union.[33] Chief Justice Warren declared that the statute was in effect a bill of attainder inflicting punishment without trial. Four Justices took a different view, that Congress was merely trying to prevent political strikes by disqualifying Communists from leadership positions in the labor movement.

In 1964, the Supreme Court struck down the section of the Internal Security Act which prohibited the issuance of U.S. passports to American Communists: "[The section] sweeps too widely and too indiscriminately across the liberty guaranteed by the Fifth Amendment."[34] Two years later, the Court found that the registration of individual members was a violation of the constitutional guarantee against self-incrimination.[35] This decision seems to foreclose compulsory registration of *individual* Communists so long as the Smith Act (or other legislation) retains criminal penalties for membership in the Communist party. Finally, in 1967, when the Circuit Court of the District of Columbia held that the registration requirement for Communist *organizations* was also a violation of the Fifth Amendment, the Justice Department, worn out by fifteen years of litigation, gave up on efforts to enforce the registration requirement.

These legislative acts and judicial opinions reflect basic controversies in our current politics. Many people believe that the whole problem of national security, even national survival, is tied to the world communist movement. They say the American Way of Life can continue only if communism is stopped in America and contained in the world. Many persons are alarmed by what they regard as widespread un-American activities and disloyalty. Some have a tendency to equate opinions or practices of which they disapprove with "un-Americanism." Others, perhaps not so many, are seriously

---

[31]*Scales* v. *U.S.*, 367 U.S. 203 (1961).
[32]*Communist Party of U.S.* v. *Subversive Activities Board*, 367 U.S. 1 (1961).
[33]*United States* v. *Brown*, 381 U.S. 437 (1965).
[34]*Aptheker* v. *Secretary of State*, 378 U.S. 500 (1964).
[35]*Albertson* v. *Subversive Activities Control Board*, 382 U.S. 70 (1965). The Subversive Activities Control Board has been inactive since this decision but Congress has not acted to terminate its official existence.

disturbed by what they regard as ever-increasing abridgment of their constitutional rights and liberties.

Numerous citizens' groups have recently appeared in the public forum eager to battle against communism in a much wider arena than is now covered by official policies. The best known of these groups is the John Birch Society, though there are others with ideas even farther to the right. In general, these groups contend that the greatest danger to national security is from subversion and infiltration at home. They are prone to attack military expenditures and foreign aid programs as wasteful and as "phony defense." They are inclined to equate communism with socialism and socialism with liberalism. Their program of massive inoculation against communism has both an economic slant and a patriotic appeal. They view Americanism mainly in terms of the free-enterprise competitive economy. They are likely to attack, in the name of Americanism, an odd assortment of persons and programs: hippies and textbooks; pacifists and scientists; the Supreme Court and the Peace Corps; public libraries and the registration of firearms; preachers and professors.

How has the general public reacted to the charges of communism in America? Apparently few votes have been influenced by such accusations. Although the extreme Right went all out to support the Republican presidential candidate in 1964, President Johnson was overwhelmingly re-elected. Indeed, a Louis Harris survey reported that 45 per cent of the eligible voters regarded Goldwater as a radical, while only 1 to 3 per cent considered themselves or Johnson to be radical. (Johnson was predominately viewed as "middle of the road" or as "liberal," whereas Goldwater was predominately described as at the extremes—"radical" or "conservative.") For the ideologically pure, "radical" may suggest socialist or even communist economic policies, but it's just another term for "extremist" to many voters.

How do people react to governmental action to meet the "communist threat"? On the basis of a nationwide survey, conducted during the height of McCarthyism, Samuel Stouffer, a public opinion analyst, found very few Americans either worried about the internal communist threat or deeply concerned over any loss of civil liberties. Community leaders, particularly the better educated, were found to be relatively more tolerant than the general population was of such unpopular groups as suspected communists, socialists, and atheists.[36] A more recent study by a group of political scientists indicates that most Americans believe that no matter what a person's political views, he is entitled to the same legal rights and protections as anyone else. On the other hand, though he strongly supports the idea of liberty in the abstract, the average citizen is less likely than the political activist to support specific applications of civil rights.[37]

[36] See Samuel A. Stouffer, *Communism, Conformity and Civil Liberties* (Garden City, N.Y.: Doubleday & Company, Inc., 1955), p. 230.

[37] Herbert McClosky, "Consensus and Ideology in American Politics," *American Political Science Review*, LVIII (June, 1964), 361–382. See also James W. Prothro and Charles M. Grigg, "Fundamental Principles of Democracy: Bases of Agreement and Disagreement," *Journal of Politics*, XXII (May, 1960), 276–294.

Freedom of Speech and Press— and the Mass Media

Some members of the Constitutional Convention were frankly skeptical of democracy—and with good reason, for in their time a majority of the people were illiterate. For them to base the future of the Republic on the consent of the governed was for their time a remarkable expression of faith in the common sense of the people. In the generations since, free public schools and mass media of communication have virtually eliminated the technical reasons for mass ignorance. In our time, people throughout the country have every opportunity to become well-informed. Never before has so large a part of the population been able to read and never before have they had so much to read.

The Framing Fathers believed that consent of the governed should rest on full and free discussion. To this end they wrote into the Bill of Rights the guarantee of a free press. On the whole, to this day, the press as well as newer media of communication are free from governmental censorship, and the public is relatively free to make its choice in the "market place of ideas."

It has always been a point of common law—and the First Amendment incorporates this point—that neither speech nor press may offend public morals or public decency. It is within the police power of government to forbid the publication of whatever is "obscene," "lewd," or "lascivious." But we have seen how difficult it is to apply the formula of "clear and present danger" to political thinking, and it is even more difficult to test "evil thoughts" in the field of public morals.

Many people feel that the sharp upswing in sex crimes and juvenile delinquency can be attributed to the current popularity of lurid literature—particularly to what the poet e. e. cummings once called "uncomic non books." But we really do not have any hard data on the correlation between reading habits and criminal behavior. Nor has any one yet been able to tell us how to cope with the problems without violating civil liberties. The Supreme Court of the United States is frequently asked to act as a supercensor—to uphold or strike out community standards for preventing dissemination of material deemed harmful to children. But, as Justice Brennan recently observed, the judges really cannot condone the total suppression of such material lest the effect be to "reduce the adult population . . . to reading only what is fit for children."[38]

In 1948, the United States Supreme Court held invalid on the ground of "vagueness" a New York statute that prohibited publications "having a tendency to encourage or incite commission of any crime." With apparent regret, the Court declared that it did not know how the public could protect itself from sanguinary and salacious reading matter. Explained Justice Stanley Reed, "Though we can see nothing of any possible value to society in these magazines, they are as much entitled to the protection of free speech as the best of literature."[39] Ten years later in the *Roth* and *Albert* cases, the Court was still trying to deal with the question of whether obscenity in print falls within the area of protected speech and press.[40] In a confusing proliferation of opinions, the judges upheld convictions for obscenity under both federal law and

[38]*Jacobellis* v. *Ohio*, 378 U.S. 184 (1964).
[39]*Winters* v. *New York*, 333 U.S. 507 (1948).
[40]354 U.S. 476 (1957).

California law. Justice Brennan held, for the Court, that obscenity which is "utterly without redeeming social importance" is not within the First Amendment guarantee of free speech or press. The test of obscenity was "whether to the average person applying contemporary community standards, the dominant theme of the material taken as a whole appeals to purient interest."

Seven years later the justices were still struggling with the problem, still arguing among themselves. In the case of *Jacobellis*, involving a motion picture exhibitor convicted in an Ohio court for showing an obscene film, the Court found for the defendant.[41] The film in question had already been shown in approximately 100 of the larger cities in the United States and had been favorably reviewed in national publications. Justice Brennan, again speaking for the majority, explained that the Court's (his) previous reference to "the contemporary community" was not intended to carry a local connotation. The extent of social and cultural diversity among the local communities would result in too many different local standards. "The constitutional status of an alleged obscene work must be determined on the basis of a national standard." What Justice Brennan (or his fellow judges) did not—and probably could not—explain was how decision-makers at the national level are supposed to ascertain and establish the "national standard." Just how does one go about determining what constitutes "purient interest" in the mind of the "average person" in the United States?

The Supreme Court has always stood firm against "prior censorship" of the writer, publisher, and bookseller.[42] But licensing and prior censorship of movies and plays have long been practiced, especially at the local level. New York law, for example, until it was cut down by judicial review, provided that no film should be licensed for showing if it was "obscene, indecent, immoral, inhuman, sacrilegious or . . . of such character that its exhibition would tend to corrupt morals or incite to crime." Under this statute, the New York Board of Regents decided in 1950 that the Italian film *The Miracle* was "sacrilegious" and directed that its license be rescinded. The United States Supreme Court reversed the order, however, on the ground that "it is not the business of government in our nation to suppress real or imagined attacks upon a particular religious doctrine, whether they appear in publications, speeches, or motion pictures."[43] Shortly thereafter, the Supreme Court again reversed the New York Board of Regents for having refused a license for the French film *La Ronde* on the grounds that it was "immoral and tended to corrupt morals."[44]

Although moving pictures are included under the category of the press, whose freedom is guaranteed by the First Amendment,[45] the Court has been

---

[41]*Jacobellis v. Ohio*, 378 U.S. 184 (1964).
[42]See *Near v. Minnesota*, 283 U.S. 697 (1931).
[43]*Burstyn v. Wilson*, 343 U.S. 495 (1952). *The Miracle* had treated the Annunciation and Nativity in such a way as to offend many Christians.
[44]*Commercial Pictures Corp. v. Regents of New York*, 346 U.S. 587 (1954).
[45]*United States v. Paramount Pictures*, 334 U.S. 131 (1948). The real controversy in this case involved charges of monopoly in distribution. The statement cited is dictum only, the Court's opinion but not the basis for its decision in the particular case.

inclined to admit prior censorship of films. In a 1961 case,[46] the Court upheld a Chicago ordinance that required the submission of films to city officials, who had to grant a permit before they could be exhibited. This was a 5–4 decision in which the minority spoke out strongly against the "vice of censorship through licensing" and the "evil of previous restraint." Chief Justice Warren, who prepared the dissenting opinion, offered an astonishing list of films banned in various communities on different grounds: Chicago censors banned a scene depicting the birth of a buffalo; Memphis banned a film because it contained scenes of white and Negro children in school together; a Pennsylvania censor disapproved the duration of a kiss.

The First Amendment covers all kinds of freedom of expression. Early in the 1960s, the civil rights movement capitalized on the First Amendment to advance the cause of economic and social rights for the Negro people. Because desgregation of the schools following successful litigation was proceeding so gradually, civil rights workers, tired of tokenism, especially in southern communities, determined to try more direct action to obtain equal access to public accommodations. The first spontaneous "sit-in" demonstration occurred in 1960, in Greensboro, North Carolina, where some Negro college students demanded service at a dime-store lunch counter reserved for white people only. The Student Non-Violent Coordinating Committee (SNCC), impressed with the publicity given to the incident in Greensboro, forthwith organized further "sit-ins," "wade-ins," "stand-ins," "lie-ins," "kneel-ins," all to dramatize existing racial discrimination in public places. In a typical sit-in, Negroes would take seats at a lunch counter designated for whites, and, on being refused service, would "sit-in" until they were arrested or ousted by force. It is estimated that in a little over a year nearly 75,000 demonstrators had participated in these organized protests. More than 3500 were arrested.[47]

The legal issue of equal accommodations in public enterprises became moot after the passage of the Civil Rights Act of 1964. Nevertheless, the Supreme Court had to dispose of many cases involving the demonstrators. Since civil rights demonstrations (like labor picketing) usually take place in a hostile environment, the policeman on the beat has to make a snap judgment as to whether to permit freedom of expression, stop trespass, or prevent breach of the peace. Though the judges can make their decisions in insulated chambers, they too must balance competing constitutional rights. It is not surprising, therefore, that the constitutional line on rights of demonstrators sometimes seems rather wobbly. For example: the Supreme Court reversed trespass and breach-of-the-peace convictions of Negro students who had staged a sit-in at the lunch counter of a department store in Columbia, South Carolina, and had

---

[46]*Times Film Corporation* v. *City of Chicago*, 365 U.S. 43 (1961). In a more recent case, the Supreme Court has warned local communities that if they want to preview films before public showing, they must work out procedures that will not involve expensive or protracted adjudication. (*Freedman* v. *Maryland*, 380 U.S. 51 [1965]).

[47]The statistics are from *The Freedom Ride*, published by the Southern Regional Council, in a special report, May, 1961. For a succinct discussion of new tactics in the civil rights movement, written from the viewpoint of constitutional law, see Henry J. Abraham, *Freedom and the Court*, (New York: Oxford University Press, 1967), especially Chapter VII. For an account of the beginnings of the Negro protest movement, and especially the part played by southern students, see Donald R. Matthews and James W. Prothro, *Negroes and the New Southern Politics* (New York: Harcourt, Brace & World, Inc., 1966), especially Chapter 14.

been arrested by the local police for refusing to leave when so ordered.[48] The Court reversed the convictions of Negro students in Baton Rouge, Louisiana, who had picketed "near" the county courthouse in protest against the "illegal arrests" of other college students who had earlier participated in lunch-counter demonstrations.[49] On the other hand, the Court sustained the trespass convictions of Negro students in Tallahassee, Florida, who had demonstrated "in" the county jail yard against the detention of fellow students who had been arrested for picketing a segregated movie house.[50] (Demonstrating consisted of standing, sitting, singing, clapping, and dancing on the jail driveway and on an adjacent grassy area on the jail premises close to the jail entrance used for bringing prisoners to and from the courts several blocks away.) And the Court also sustained the convictions of a number of Negro leaders (including Nobel Peace Prize winner Dr. Martin Luther King) who participated in a "mass march" on Easter Sunday, 1963, in Birmingham, Alabama, in violation of a court injunction as well as local ordinances.[51] The above cases, and many more, were adjudicated on technical legal bases; the justices argued with each other and presented many different judicial views. But to civil rights defendants what really matters is whether or not they can be convicted and put in jail for having demonstrated their grievances to the public in a peaceable manner.

Academic Freedom

Thomas Jefferson once made this claim for the University of Virginia, which he had founded: "This institution will be based on the illimitable freedom of the human mind. For here we are not afraid to follow truth wherever it may lead, nor to tolerate an error so long as reason is free to combat it." If there is any place that should be free from propaganda and indoctrination, it is the university. Both professors and students must have the utmost freedom to find out all they can, to examine every doctrine and idea, to test out all opinions. This is the only way in which men can pursue the truth that makes them free.

We have heard much about the infiltration of communism into our colleges and universities. But, as Justice Douglas has pointed out, the communists have been for the most part "miserable merchants of unwanted ideas." Other groups have been far more successful in peddling their wares in our educational system. Business has a point of view that it wants taught—the doctrines of *laissez faire* and private enterprise. Labor wants recognition of its rights to collective bargaining, maximum hours, minimum wages. Patriotic societies want to promote their ideas of 100 per cent Americanism. Church groups are eager to strengthen "moral and spiritual values" on every campus. And so it goes—parents, alumni, taxpayers, special interest groups—all have something

---

[48]*Barr* v. *Columbia,* 378 U.S. 146 (1964).
[49]*Cox* v. *Louisiana,* 379 U.S. 559 (1965).
[50]*Adderly* v. *Florida* 385 U.S. 39 (1966).
[51]*Walker* v. *Birmingham,* 388 U.S. 307 (1967).

to say about what professors should and should not teach, about what students should and should not learn.

Tax-supported colleges and universities especially have been subjected to "loyalty programs" and popular agitation against "radicalism." During the 1950s, loyalty oaths were rather generally required as evidence of fitness to teach both in the public schools and in the state institutions of higher learning.[52] For example, the New York State Legislature, bent on weeding out "subversives" in the statewide educational system, passed the Feinberg Law which made membership in a subversive organization *prima facie* evidence of disqualification as a teacher. Under this act, the New York Board of Regents was authorized to make a listing, "after full notice and hearing," of subversive organizations. The Feinberg Law was upheld with unusual alacrity by a majority of the United States Supreme Court called upon to make a "declaratory judgment" even before the law actually became operative. Justice Sherman Minton, for the Court, pointed out that a state has a vital concern in the manner in which schools shape the minds of young people. He was not at all disturbed by the implication of "guilt by association." On the contrary, "One's associates, past and present, as well as one's conduct, may properly be considered in determining fitness and loyalty. From time immemorial, one's reputation has been determined in part by the company he keeps."[53]

McCarthyism took a sharp downturn after a 1954 Senate resolution censured the junior Senator from Wisconsin for his abuse of legislative power and demagogic tactics. The public began gradually to make more vigorous protests against the violation of civil rights on many fronts, including the academic. Legislative hearings showed more regard to due process of law and the judges were inclined to revise some of their previous opinions. Loyalty oaths were scrutinized more carefully, and many were struck down for "the vice of vagueness." Not until 1967, however, when the Cold War had largely abated, did the Supreme Court reverse its support of the Feinberg Law, and then only with bitter dissent in a 5–4 decision. In holding the New York law unconstitutional, Justice Brennan declared that academic freedom is "a special concern of the First Amendment, which does not tolerate laws that cast a pall of orthodoxy over the classroom." He pointed out that "our Nation is deeply committed to safeguarding academic freedom, which is of transcendent value to all of us and not merely to the teachers concerned." He continued, "The Nation's future depends upon leaders trained through wide exposure to . . . robust exchange of ideas."[54]

Communism as an issue in public education has turned out to be mostly a bugaboo. More insidious and pervasive is the problem of sterilized instruction. John Milton wrote in *Areopagitica*, "Where there is much desire to learn, there of necessity will be much arguing, much writing, many opinions; for

---

[52]Loyalty-security programs proliferated to all levels of government, national, state, and local. Loyalty tests were prescribed for government contract workers, lawyers, and street cleaners. One reliable estimate is that at least one person in five was required to pass some kind of loyalty test as part of his job qualification. See Arval A. Morris, "Academic Freedom and Loyalty Oaths," 28 *Law and Contemporary Problems* 487 (1963).

[53]*Adler* v. *Board of Education*, 342 U.S. 485 (1952). Note, however, that Justices Black and Douglas entered strong dissents.

[54]*Keyishian* v. *Board of Regents of New York*, 385 U.S. 589 (1967).

CIVIL RIGHTS

opinion in good men is but knowledge in the making." Nevertheless there is great pressure, especially in tax-supported schools, to keep controversial issues out of the classroom and extremist speakers, right or left, off the campus. For the administrator this is safe public relations; for the teacher it is realistic self-defense; for the student it is not good instruction. By the same token, when students heckle outside campus speakers, even attack them physically, to prevent freedom of expression for "the thought we hate," they too are denying themselves an education.

Religious Freedom and Liberty of Conscience

The First Amendment, which has been called "the First Article of our Faith," says, "Congress shall make no law respecting an establishment of religion, or prohibiting the free exercise thereof." The primary purpose of this amendment was to prohibit the establishment of a national church with a preferred status, such as the Anglican

Drawing by Robt. Day; © 1967 *The New Yorker Magazine, Inc.*

"*As president of a great university, sir, what would you say is the most significant change you have observed in the last twenty years?*"

Church in England. Since tax-supported religious institutions did exist in several states, however, it was generally understood that the First Amendment left to the state full power and free policy in religious matters. The Anglican Church had been disestablished in Maryland, the Carolinas, Georgia, and Virginia when the colonies' political ties with England were severed. But all the New England states except Rhode Island continued to give preferred status to the Congregational Church. Not until 1833 did Massachusetts amend its constitution to place all religious denominations on an equal footing. For many years, New Hampshire, New Jersey, Massachusetts, and North Carolina required that office holders be Protestants. Delaware, and even Pennsylvania, which had a Bill of Rights affirming the unalienable right of all men to worship God according to the dictates of their own conscience, disqualified Jews and other non-Christians for public office.[55]

The Founding Fathers for the most part were religious men. As Justice Story observed in his commentaries on the Constitution (1840)[56]:

> Probably, at the time of the adoption of the Constitution, and of the [First] amendment . . ., the general, if not the universal, sentiment in America was, that Christianity ought to receive encouragement from the State, so far as such encouragement was not incompatible with the private rights of conscience, and the freedom of religious worship.

As a matter of fact, through the years, the American government has officially encouraged religious practices and has offered special concessions to churches. By act of Congress, the pledge of allegiance to the United States is made to "one nation under God." The currency of the country carries the national motto, "In God We Trust." The Supreme Court of the United States opens each session with the intonement, "God save the United States and this Honorable Court." Each house of Congress appoints a chaplain who invokes divine blessings and prays for God's guidance in the daily proceedings. Chaplains are attached to all the armed forces of the United States; Sunday attendance at chapel exercises is compulsory at West Point, the Air Force Academy, and Annapolis. Church property and income are generally exempt from national and state taxes. Sunday is legally recognized as a day of rest in every state. Thanksgiving, Christmas, and Easter are observed in every community in the country. The Bible is commonly used in taking court oaths, usually ending in "so help me God." In some states, custody and adoption laws are tailored to religious beliefs.[57]

The Supreme Court has assumed that "liberty" under the Fourteenth Amendment includes all the basic freedoms specified in the First Amendment. Thus the fundamental relationship between church and state, which is defined for the national government in the First Amendment, is also implicit for the state governments in the Fourteenth. In other words, neither Congress nor the

---

[55]The most complete study in this topic is Anson Phelps Stokes, *Church and State in the United States* (New York: Harper & Row, Publishers, Inc., 1950), 3 vols.

[56]Joseph Story, *A Familiar Exposition of the Constitution of the United States: Containing a Brief Commentary* (New York: American Book Company, 1840), p. 261.

[57]When President Johnson, pressed hard for an immediate public policy in response to the riots in the cities in 1967, declared that July 30, 1967 should be a day for "national prayer," this, too, was in the American tradition.

states may establish a church or prohibit the free exercise of religion. This does not mean, however, that government cannot regulate religious practices that may offend public morals, jeopardize public health, or in other ways endanger the public welfare. For example, the practice of polygamy, the sacrifice of virgins, or wrestling with rattlesnakes may be forbidden without violating constitutional rights. State university students may be required to take ROTC training; first-graders may not be admitted to public schools without vaccination against smallpox; a couple may have to take blood tests before obtaining a marriage license. These and similar provisions come under the police power of the state, which is paramount to the dictates of individual conscience.

Thomas Jefferson was frequently criticized by clergymen for talking about a "wall of separation" between "Church and State." Especially in the sensitive area of public education, the controversy has sometimes been acute. For example, the Roman Catholic Church maintains parochial schools so that Catholic children may receive regular religious instruction along with the usual secular education. These parochial schools have given rise to many constitutional issues. Some years ago, Oregon passed a law requiring that all children attend the Oregon public schools; in effect, this law would have eliminated all private and parochial schools. Without referring directly to any religious rights involved, the United States Supreme Court held the law invalid under the Fourteenth Amendment on the grounds that it was a seizure of private property without due process of law. In Louisiana, where there are many Roman Catholics, the state provides free textbooks for parochial and public schools alike; this policy has been upheld as an aid to schoolchildren rather than a public assistance to church schools. The Supreme Court has also, on the grounds of public safety, sustained a New Jersey statute permitting free bus transportation for school children traveling to either parochial or private schools. And, after much argument among the justices, following knock-down-drag-out discussions in the public forum, the Court has upheld released time from the school schedules for religious instruction provided that parents give permission, that no public funds are spent, and that the instruction is not offered in the classrooms.[58]

The number of church-state questions that go into court attest to the many and deeply divisive opinions that Americans hold on the meaning of religious freedom. In 1962, the Supreme Court declared that it was unconstitutional for the New York State Board of Regents to prescribe a "prayer" as part of the daily exercise in the New York public schools.[59] Even though the Board of

[58]*Pierce* v. *Society of the Sisters of Holy Names of Jesus and Mary,* 268 U.S. 510; *Cochran* v. *Louisiana State Board of Education,* 281 U.S. 370 (1930); *Everson* v. *Board of Education,* 330 U.S. 1 (1947); *Illinois ex. rel. McCollum* v. *Board of Education,* 333 U.S. 203 (1948); *Zorach* v. *Clauson,* 343 U.S. 306 (1952).

[59]The prayer in question read, "Almighty God, we acknowledge our dependence upon Thee, and we beg Thy blessings upon us, on our parents, our teachers and our country." *Engel* v. *Vitale,* 370 U.S. 42 (1962). Mr. Justice Stewart who was the lone dissenter in the case said, "I cannot see how an 'official religion' is established by letting those who want to say a prayer say it. On the contrary, I think that to deny the wish of these school children to join in reciting this prayer is to deny them the opportunity to share in the spiritual heritage of the nation."

Regents claimed that the prayer was "non-denominational" and even though students who did not wish to participate in the exercise were permitted to remain silent or be excused from the schoolroom, the Court held that such an officially established prayer program violated the Establishment Clause and also the Free Exercise Clause of the First Amendment.

In 1963, the Court struck down a Pennsylvania statute which called for "at least ten verses from the Holy Bible to be read without comment, at the opening of each public school on each school day." (Any child was excused from the exercise upon written request of his parent or guardian.) The Court also held unconstitutional a similar requirement in the public schools of Baltimore—"reading without comment, of a chapter in the Holy Bible and/or the use of the Lord's prayer." In both cases the Court held firmly that the Establishment and Free Exercise Clauses of the First Amendment require the government to be strictly neutral in matters of religion, "protecting all, preferring none, disparaging none."[60]

The Court's decisions in the prayer cases—"taking God out of the schools"—outraged many people and stirred heated controversy in press and pulpit, in Congress and in state legislatures. Some groups have advocated passing a constitutional amendment to prohibit the Court from interfering with state educational policies, so that school children will not be deprived of their religious heritage or deprived of moral instruction.[61] On the other hand, spokesmen of the major denominational groups have generally supported the Court's doctrine of governmental neutrality with respect to religious activities. The separation of church and state, they point out, does not prevent people from praying at any time, nor from going to the church of their own choice. But because we are a religious people, a people of many different faiths, public policy—whether it is policy from the bench, the legislative chamber, or the office of the state superintendent of instruction—is not likely to settle the ancient issues of church, state, and school relations.

In the first edition of this book (1959), in discussing qualifications for the presidency, we pointed out that the Protestant majority had always insisted that the President, as a symbol of the national character, be at least nominally a Protestant. But the election of John F. Kennedy in 1960 dispelled the myth that a Roman Catholic could not hope to reach the White House. Ironically, the Kennedy administration almost immediately ran into a very bitter religious controversy when it proposed federal aid to public elementary and secondary schools, for classroom construction and for teachers' salaries. Even before the hearings on the bill began in Congress, bishops of the Roman Catholic Church insisted that federal aid to education should also be extended to private (that is, parochial) schools. President Kennedy told Congress that he thought federal aid to church-sponsored schools would violate the constitutional separation of church and state. Meanwhile, Catholic Church officials publicized numerous instances of federal funds used for church aid. Under the GI Bill of Rights, veterans had used federal grants to attend Catholic colleges.

[60]*School District of Abington Township* v. *Schempp,* 374 U.S. 203 (1963).
[61]Senate Minority Leader Everett Dirksen (R.-Ill.) in 1966 proposed a constitutional amendment to authorize local authorities to permit voluntary prayers in public school buildings. The proposal failed to obtain the requisite two-thirds majority vote in the Senate.

Under the National Defense Act, passed in 1958, students in Catholic colleges could obtain federal loans and scholarships. Catholic parochial schools were included in the national free lunch and milk programs for schools.

The great debate over federal aid to education in 1961 was not entirely fought on religious grounds. The Catholic hierarchy was joined by some southern leaders who hoped that if federal funds could be used by parochial schools, they might also be used for private schools set up to avoid integration. Many persons, like Senator Barry Goldwater, opposed the idea as another money-spending plank in the welfare program. Others fought the extension of federal power over an area traditionally reserved to the states. President Kennedy was in a peculiar spot: as the first Catholic President, he could not risk the charge of pushing the Roman Catholic position; on the other hand, he did not want to jeopardize the whole program of federal aid to education by refusing any aid to the parochial schools. As the battle moved to a climax in Congress, the White House remained aloof from discussion. No one following the congressional debates on federal aid to education, or the resultant editorial opinions in the newspapers, could remain under any illusion that church and state are separate in American politics or that religious prejudices do not enter into public policy.

President Kennedy's educational bill failed to pass, partly because he was in a poor position to give vigorous leadership in this issue. President Johnson was able to secure passage of the Education Act of 1965 by underplaying the religious issue. The grants-in-aid to school districts under that act went to educationally deprived children in public and nonpublic schools.

Liberty of conscience supported by religious convictions is protected under the First Amendment. The famous Flag Salute case, decided when the nation was at war in 1943, indicates the high priority which we officially accord to an individual's religious beliefs even when these run counter to prevailing patriotic sentiments. When children brought up in the faith of Jehovah's Witnesses refused to salute the flag as part of the daily exercises in Americanism prescribed for the public schools in West Virginia, the Supreme Court upheld the right of the children to follow the dictates of their religion.[62] In a still memorable opinion, Justice Jackson spoke for the majority of the Court:

> If there is any fixed star in our constitutional constellation, it is that no official, high or petty, can prescribe what shall be orthodox in politics, nationalism, religion or other matters of opinion or force citizens to confess by word or act their faith therein. If there are any circumstances which permit an exception they do not now occur to us.

Every American draft law since 1917 has exempted conscientious objectors from military service. Nevertheless, local draft boards are frequently unimpressed by claims for exemption on religious grounds. For example, when Muhammad Ali (formerly Cassius Clay), the heavyweight boxing champion of

---

[62]*West Virginia State Board of Education* v. *Barnette*, 319 U.S. 624 (1943).

the world, contended that he was entitled to deferment as a minister in the Nation of Islam ("Black Muslims"), he was inducted; when he resisted induction, he was jailed; and when he appealed to the Supreme Court, the judges refused to hear his case. The conscientious objector must be able to show the local draft board that he belongs to a recognized religious group with established pacifist principles. He must believe in a Supreme Being and cannot base his objections merely on political, sociological, or philosophical views.

The war in Viet Nam has highlighted the problem of the conscientious objector who feels that a particular war is not justifiable. Public officials have sometimes been rather impatient with outspoken critics of the war, but generally the objectors have been free to organize their demonstrations, parade their views, and be assured of police protection en route. When the Georgia House of Representatives refused to seat one of the first Negroes elected to the state legislature since Reconstruction, on the grounds that his antiwar posture and criticisms of the Selective Service laws were unbecoming a legislator, the Supreme Court declared that the First Amendment prohibited such a penalty for free speech.[63] On the other hand, when the objectors began to "symbolize" their protests by publicly burning draft cards and the American flag, Congress made such actions a federal crime. The judges have also been impelled to distinguish between speech and action. When William Miller, a twenty-two year old social worker in New York City, was convicted for burning his draft card in protest against American policy in Viet Nam, the Supreme Court refused to review his case.[64]

The civil rights of persons in the military establishment is now a major problem. The Constitution gives to Congress power "to make rules for the government and regulation of the land and naval forces." During the administration of President Washington, the problem was insignificant; Congress authorized an army of 840 men but less than 700 were actually in uniform. The situation today is vastly different. Some 2.5 million persons are now serving in the armed services of the United States, and every male resident is a potential member. The average male citizen may spend 4 per cent of his adult life in active military service and his reserve obligations may extend over 10 per cent of his lifetime.

Quite clearly military personnel cannot expect to enjoy the personal freedom that goes with civilian status. Freedom of expression is necessarily curtailed as a matter of discipline. This holds for the officer, the enlisted man, and the newest draftee. When General Douglas MacArthur persisted in publicly criticizing the political decisions which he felt were handicapping his military strategy in the Korean War, President Truman summarily removed the General from his high command. In 1967, when young Captain Howard Levy, an army doctor, refused to instruct Special Forces ("Green Berets") medical aidesmen how to treat skin diseases in Viet Nam, and also privately expressed to servicemen his disapproval of U.S. policy in Viet Nam, he was court-martialed and sentenced to military prison. The contention of his lawyers that he was acting on the "Nuremberg principle," disobeying orders that he felt constituted crimes against humanity, failed to impress his military judges.

[63]*Bond* v. *Floyd*, 385 U.S. 116 (1966).
[64]*Miller* v. *United States* 386 U.S. 911 (1967).

The Defendant's Rights

Mr. Justice Frankfurter once said that "the history of liberty has largely been the history of observance of procedural guarantees." The constitutional requirements of due process of law in the Bill of Rights are quite specific. They represent the usages and the modes of procedure under English common law that the eighteenth century considered basic to a "government of laws and not of men."

These requirements are: "The right of the people to be secure in their persons, houses, papers, and effects against unreasonable searches and seizures, . . . issue of a warrant only upon probable cause, supported by oath or affirmation, and particularly describing the place to be searched and the persons or things to be seized" (Amendment IV); "indictment by grand jury for capital or otherwise infamous crime, . . . the restriction upon double jeopardy, . . . immunity against self-incrimination" (Amendment V); "the right to a speedy and public trial, by an impartial jury in the state and the district wherein the crime was committed, . . . the right to be informed of the nature and cause of the accusation, . . . the right of the accused to be confronted with the witnesses against him . . . and the right to have compulsory process for obtaining witnesses in his favor, . . . the right to counsel" (Amendment VI); "protection against excessive bail, excessive fines . . . and cruel or unusual punishments" (Amendment VIII).

The judges have assumed that the rights of the First Amendment are incorporated in the guarantees of liberty in the Fourteenth Amendment. They have never been willing to concede, however, that all the procedural rights specified in the Bill of Rights are included in the guarantees of due process of law made applicable to the states by the Fourteenth Amendment.

In 1937, in the case of *Palko* v. *Connecticut,* Justice Cardozo attempted to rationalize the dichotomy of procedural rights in the American federal system.[65] A rather unsavory character, Frank Palko, who had been tried for first degree murder in a Connecticut court, was convicted of murder in the second degree, and sentenced to life imprisonment. Under Connecticut law, the state was able to appeal the case and secure a new trial. Palko objected to a new trial on the ground that it would constitute double jeopardy within the meaning of the Fifth Amendment. Nevertheless, he was retried and on the second go-around was sentenced to death. Palko's lawyer appealed to the Supreme Court that "whatever is forbidden by the Fifth Amendment is forbidden by the Fourteenth also." The Supreme Court affirmed the verdict in the second trial. Justice Cardozo perceived a "wavering and broken line" between the guarantees in the Bill of Rights binding on the states and those which were not so binding. As he explained it, those guarantees which were of "the very essence of a scheme of ordered liberty" were absorbed by the due process clause of the Fourteenth Amendment; but those less fundamental in the Anglo-Saxon traditions of justice were not carried by the Amendment to the states. To Justice Cardozo, the fact that Connecticut placed one of its citizens in double

---

[65] 302 U.S. 319 (1937).

jeopardy "is not cruelty at all, nor even vexation in any immoderate degree." To Frank Palko, however, double jeopardy meant the difference between life and death; he was executed.

Even before 1937, the judges had held that due process of law in the states need not include grand jury indictment, jury trial in either criminal or civil cases, or protection against self-incrimination, although these are constitutional rights respected in the national courts. Following the *Palko Case*, states continued to follow their own practices in the administration of justice provided that these did not "shock the conscience of the community" or violate the canons of "civilized decency." For almost a quarter of a century, Justice Cardozo's opinion swayed Supreme Court decisions, although some of the justices stoutly maintained that the double standard of justice (demanding for the national government, more lax for the states) was unconstitutional. In many dissenting opinions they argued that the Fourteenth Amendment was intended to nationalize all of the privileges, protections, and safegurds granted by the Bill of Rights.[66]

Beginning with the 1960s, a new spirit of judicial activism substantially altered the double standard. Case by case, the Supreme Court began to nationalize the procedural rights in the Bill of Rights. In 1961, the Court held that the Fourth Amendment's protection against unreasonable searches and seizures extended to the states and therefore evidence unlawfully seized could not be used as evidence in state courts.[67] Justice Clark, who had considerable experience with the practical side of administering justice when he was Attorney General of the United States, observed that the exclusion in court of evidence illegally seized "makes very good sense. . . . There is no war between the Constitution and common sense."

In 1962, the Supreme Court in effect nationalized the Eighth Amendment's guarantees against infliction of cruel and unusual punishment. At issue was a California statute which made drug addiction a crime punishable by a mandatory jail sentence. Justice Stewart, who delivered the opinion for the Court majority, felt that jailing a drug addict was akin to jailing a person mentally ill, or a leper, or some one afflicted with venereal disease — "a cruel and unusual punishment."[68]

In the celebrated case of Clarence Gideon,[69] decided in 1963, the Court, unanimously reversing a decision rendered twenty-one years earlier, ruled that a state must furnish counsel to indigent persons accused of noncapital offenses.[70] Gideon had been sentenced to serve a five-year term in a Florida

---

[66]Foremost champion of full coverage under the Fourteenth Amendment was Justice Hugh Black. See, for example, his dissenting opinion in *Adamson* v. *California*, 322 U.S. 46 (1947).

[67]*Mapp* v. *Ohio*, 367 U.S. 643 (1961).

[68]*Robinson* v. *California*, 370 U.S. 660 (1962).

[69]The best-seller *Gideon's Trumpet*, written by Anthony Lewis, former Supreme Court reporter for the N.Y. Times (New York: Random House, Inc., 1964), helped to celebrate the case.

[70]*Gideon* v. *Wainright*, 372 U.S. 335 (1963) reversed *Betts* v. *Brady*, 316 U.S. 455 (1942). Gideon had made his petition to the Supreme Court in a handwritten note on prison stationery. *In forma pauperis* is a proceeding whereby any citizen has a right to proceed in any federal court without payment of fees upon execution of a pauper's oath. The Supreme Court annually receives over a thousand *in forma pauperis* petitions, and grants about 3 per cent. Gideon's case was argued before the Supreme Court by Abe Fortas, one of Washington's most distinguished attorneys, appointed by the Court. Mr. Fortas subsequently became a Justice of the Court.

prison after he had unsuccessfully tried to conduct his own defense in a jury trial on the charge of breaking and entering a poolroom with intent to commit a misdemeanor. Without funds of his own, he had been unable to hire a lawyer, and under Florida law only a person charged with a capital offense was entitled to a public defender. The Supreme Court of the United States which received Gideon's petition (*in forma pauperis*) recognized that "in our adversary system of criminal justice, any person haled into court, who is too poor to hire a lawyer, cannot be assured a fair trial unless counsel is provided for him." Gideon's case was remanded to the Florida court for retrial with counsel, and subsequently Gideon was found not guilty. In the wake of Gideon's case, however, came a flood of similar petitions; the good citizens of Florida were shocked to learn that several thousand inmates currently serving time in the state penitentiary, who had been tried and convicted without counsel, were anticipating their freedom as a result of Gideon's case.

In 1964, the Supreme Court made still further inroads into the double standard. Overruling long-standing precedents, the Court held that safeguards against self-incrimination were also incorporated in the Fourteenth Amendment. In a Connecticut case, a prisoner convicted of gambling was ordered to testify further in a court-ordered inquiry of gambling and other criminal activities. When the prisoner claimed constitutional rights against self-incrimination, Connecticut judges informed him that the Fourteenth Amendment "extended no privilege to him." But a majority of five justices on the U.S. Supreme Court took a different view.[71] In the words of Justice Brennan, who spoke for the Court:

> The Fourteenth Amendment secures against state invasion the same privilege that the Fifth Amendment guarantees against federal infringement—the right of a person to remain silent unless he chooses to speak in the unfettered exercise of his own free will, and to suffer no penalty . . . for such silence.

The Supreme Court unanimously decided in 1965 that "the Sixth Amendment's right of an accused to confront witnesses against him is likewise a fundamental right and is made obligatory on the states by the Fourteenth Amendment."[72] The decision overruled a conviction in a Texas court (affirmed all the way up the Texas judicial hierarchy), which had in part been based on evidence in a transcript by a witness who had moved out of the state and who therefore did not appear at the trial.

In 1966, in *Miranda* v. *Arizona*, the Supreme Court reviewed the whole issue of police court procedures relating to constitutional rights.[73] The Chief Justice, speaking for a majority of his Court, ruled that an individual held for interrogation has a right to a lawyer and to have his lawyer present at the initial interrogation. Moreover, if the individual cannot afford a lawyer, then the

---
[71] *Malloy* v. *Hogan*, 378 U.S. 1 (1964).
[72] *Pointer* v. *Texas*, 380 U.S. 400 (1965).
[73] 384 U.S. 436 (1966).

court must appoint one for him. "The need for counsel . . . exists for the indigent as well as the affluent." The individual must be informed of these rights. Confessions obtained freely and voluntarily, after the accused has been allowed counsel, may be admissable as evidence. The Chief Justice noted that over the years the FBI has observed these procedures and still compiled an exemplary record of effective law enforcement. "The practice of the FBI can readily be emulated by state and local enforcement agencies."

To understand due process of law, of course, we must look to more than constitutional declarations, legal codes, and judicial opinions. The administration of justice, as a matter of public policy, involves a great many actors—policemen, lawyers, judges, lesser court officials, jail guards, prison wardens, and others—who play specific roles. All of these figures are actors-in-an-environment and the environment includes the unofficial norms, the conscience and culture (or lack thereof) of the community. Most persons haled into our criminal courts are "unrespectable" defendants—murderers, rapists, thieves, arsonists, dope peddlers, gangsters, racketeers, and just bums. Because they generally are such unsavory characters, the community is not likely to protest if some of those accused get short shrift, something less than due process of law, between arrest and imprisonment or execution.

Defendants associated with unpopular causes may find justice hard to get at any price. Obviously, defendants need lawyers to guide them through the intricacies of courtroom procedures. But atheists, communists, civil rights demonstrators, and political assassins may be denied due process of law because they cannot secure adequate counsel. Local lawyers in southern communities have sometimes been reluctant to take cases involving racial issues, especially if the accused were Negroes or northern integrationists. Similarly, persons accused of being security risks or subversives (especially from the Left) have found it difficult to obtain counsel. Lawyers know that if they take such cases they may be accused of being sympathetic with the client's cause which could seriously injure their professional status and practice in the community.

The Supreme Court has been under heavy fire for its extension of national standards of justice into local communities despite the fact that most state constitutions and most state laws equal or excel the national standard. Some people are opposed simply on the basis of states' rights, which they apparently rate higher than individual rights. Law enforcement officers complain that the standards set by the Supreme Court will seriously impair the efficiency of their operations and make it possible for more criminals to go scot free. They are particularly bitter about impediments in their way of obtaining confessions. They are also indignant about restrictions on their methods of getting evidence by wire tapping and other electronic devices. Some lawyers are apprehensive that their lucrative practices may be cut by mounting professional obligations to accept indigent clients under court order. (The determination of indigency is complex, but probably 30 to 60 per cent of all those charged with crime cannot afford to hire counsel.)[74] And finally, many

---

[74]The U.S. Department of Justice is well aware of the problems caused by the recent Supreme Court decisions requiring legal Counsel at all stages for the defendant. The Attorney General has instructed lawyers in the Justice Department that they may take on indigent clients.

good citizens, alarmed by the zooming statistics of crime in America, feel that if the Supreme Court is encouraging the coddling of criminals, then it is time to restrain the justices and "support the local police." To put the problem in perspective, which of the Great Rights would you like to give up "in the public interest"? And which of the rights that you claim for yourself are you unwilling to accord to others?

The constitutional rights of citizens overseas presents a special problem. Early in the nation's history, the Supreme Court held generally that the Constitution was inoperative beyond the nation's boundaries. Americans abroad—tourists, traders, students, merchants, and missionaries—accepted the fact that when they entered a foreign country they were subject to the law of that country and could not claim privilege and immunities of United States citizenship.

Drawing by Chon Day;
© 1966
The New Yorker Magazine, Inc.

"Well, what are you stalling for? Inform me of my rights!"

The tremendous expansion of American military bases around the world after World War II substantially changed this simple picture. Members of the armed forces, wherever stationed, are, of course, governed by military rules and regulations and subject to court-martial jurisdiction under the Uniform Code of Military Justice enacted by Congress. Generally, the judicial power of the civil courts does not extend to the treatment of military personnel under this code. The Supreme Court has made it plain, however, that court-martial proceedings can be challenged through habeas corpus proceedings in the regular courts if a defendant has been denied his fundamental rights. As Chief Justice Warren puts it, "Our citizens in uniform may not be stripped of basic rights simply because they have doffed their civilian clothes."[75]

The original intent of Congress when it passed the Uniform Code of Military Justice in 1950 was to establish military jurisdiction over all civilian employees and civilian dependents of the armed forces when stationed in foreign nations. The Act was implemented in 1953–1954 through the Status of Force agreements with those countries where the United States maintained military communities. These agreements permitted the United States to exercise extraterritorial jurisdiction over all persons covered by the Uniform Code of Military Justice, including the civilian employees and civilian dependents.

[75]"The Bill of Rights and the Military," 37 *New York University Law Review* (1962), 181.

Shortly thereafter, numerous appeals reached the United States Supreme Court challenging the right of military tribunals to try civilian persons. One of the first of these cases involved a civilian in the United States, Robert Toth, who had been discharged from the Air Force five months when American military authorities in Korea discovered evidence implicating him in the murder of a Korean national. Toth was arrested while at work in Pittsburgh and flown to Korea to stand trial by court-martial. The Supreme Court, in a 6–3 decision, ordered his release on writ of habeas corpus. Justice Black spoke firmly: civilians like Toth cannot be subjected to trial by court-martial. He declared invalid that part of the Uniform Code which extended court-martial to civilians charged with offenses committed during military service.[76]

Within months of the highly publicized *Toth Case* (1955), other civilians who had been court-martialed for offenses overseas were claiming a constitutional right to trial by jury and other procedural rights. The cases presented a variety of problems: capital cases involving civilian dependents; noncapital cases with civilian dependents; capital cases with civilian employees; noncapital cases with civilian employees. The issues were numerous, complex, and technical. Suffice it to say that in January, 1960, the Court declared invalid that section of the Uniform Military Code which provided for courts-martial of civilians in the overseas military establishments. Four cases were settled simultaneously, and in each case the civilians were freed.[77]

Equal Protection of the Laws

So far in this chapter, we have been concerned with our "American heritage," the blessings of liberty that are specifically guaranteed in the Constitution. You may have noticed that most guarantees of these individual rights are negative in character: "government *shall not do* this or that to any person." In recent years, however, a more positive concept of human rights has developed: "government *must do* this and that for all of us." For example, a whole new area of social security has been added to the conventional liberties and rights of the individual. President Franklin D. Roosevelt included in the Four Freedoms: (1) freedom of speech and expression, (2) freedom to worship God, (3) freedom from want, (4) freedom from fear. President Truman's Committee on Civil Rights declared that four basic rights were most important in the American Way: (1) the right to safety and security of the person, (2) the right to citizenship and its privileges, (3) the right to freedom of conscience and expression, (4) the right to equality of opportunity.

[76]*Toth* v. *Quarles*, 350 U.S. 11 (1955). The Justice also pointed up a very practical consideration. Over 3 million persons had become veterans since the Act was passed, and the number would increase. "These figures point up what would be the enormous scope of a holding that Congress could subject every ex-service man and woman in the land to trial by court-martial for any alleged offense committed while he or she had been a member of the armed forces."

[77]*Kinsella* v. *U.S. ex rel Singleton*, 361 U.S. 234 (1960); *McElroy* v. *U.S. ex rel Guagliardo*, 361 U.S. 281 (1960); *Grisham* v. *Hagan*, 361 U.S. 278 (1960); *Wilson* v. *Bohlender*, 361 U.S. 234 (1960).

Equal Protection Via "Judge-made" Law

The concept of "equal protection of the laws," stated in the Fourteenth Amendment, has undergone major surgery over the years. The Fourteenth Amendment was designed to extend the same civil rights to all persons without regard to race and color.[78] Specifically, Congress intended to remove any doubts about the constitutional validity of the civil rights legislation that had been passed during Reconstruction to protect Negroes. Ironically, the Supreme Court subsequently denied this specific intent in the *Civil Rights Cases* (1883).[79]

In these cases, the Court held unconstitutional the Civil Rights Act of 1875, which affirmed the right of all persons within the jurisdiction of the United States to the full and equal enjoyment of accommodations and advantages in hotels, public conveyances, theaters, and other places of amusement. In its decision, the Court made two important points. First, the Fourteenth Amendment gives Congress no positive powers over civil rights; Congress simply has the power to enact corrective legislation that is necessary to counteract state laws which violate privileges and immunities, due process, or equal protection. Second, the Fourteenth Amendment guarantees protection only against aggression by the states; it does not protect rights against encroachment by individuals unless such individuals are acting for the state. The Court's decision in these cases—a decision that in effect marked the end of Reconstruction—was widely applauded. The southern states were especially grateful for the institution of judicial review, since it allowed the "sound judgment" of the Court to reverse the "radical views" of Congress.

In denying Congress the power to establish a national policy with respect to civil rights, however, the Court in effect assumed for itself final authority over civil rights in the states. In matters of race relations, the Court was inclined to follow the path of least resistance, leaving this peculiar problem to local custom. For many years, the southern states counted on the courts to hold that laws requiring separate but equal facilities for "white" and "colored" met the constitutional standard of "equal protection of the laws." The leading case was *Plessy* v. *Ferguson* (1896), which involved a Louisiana statue that required separate railway carriages for white and colored passengers. Plessy, a citizen of the United States, described as of "seven-eighths Caucasian and one-eighth African blood," attacked the constitutionality of the act. Plessy had been arrested for refusing to leave a coach designated for whites and to take a seat in another coach assigned to Negroes. He claimed that such a legal requirement violated his constitutional rights under the Fourteenth Amendment. The

---

[78] Although the Fourteenth Amendment was undoubtedly intended to protect human persons only, very shortly the Supreme Court extended its coverage to "artificial persons." In 1886, Chief Justice Waite refused to hear argument on whether equal protection of the laws should be given to corporations; he simply announced, "We are all of the opinion that it does." See *Santa Clara County* v. *Southern P. R. Co.*, 118 U.S. 394 (1886). Roscoe Conkling, who had been a member of the Joint Committee on Reconstruction, had as counsel before the Court very plausibly argued this point of view a year or so earlier. Conkling's argument gave rise to the so-called "conspiracy theory" of the Fourteenth Amendment, that a joker had been deliberately slipped into the Constitution without the people's knowledge to give extraordinary protection to corporations.

[79] *Civil Rights Cases*, 109 U.S. 3 (1883).

Court upheld the Louisiana law, declaring that *"in the nature of things* [the Fourteenth Amendment] could not have been intended to abolish distinctions based upon color, or to enforce social, as distinguished from political, equality, or a commingling of the two races upon terms unsatisfactory to either."[80]

The justices of the Court made no effort in *Plessy* v. *Ferguson* to document their own sense of "the nature of things" with the findings of sociology, psychology, or philosophy. Instead, they upheld the practice of segregation on the basis of their own rule-of-thumb proposition that social prejudices cannot be overcome by legislation. Justice John Marshall Harlan, as the lone dissenter, was "of opinion that the statute of Louisiana is inconsistent with the personal liberty of citizens, white and black, in the United States."[81] The doctrine of separate but equal, established in *Plessy* v. *Ferguson,* long gave constitutional sanction, however, to the Jim Crow laws of southern states which required racial segregation (with "equal accommodations") in public transportation, public schools, and public meeting places.

Beginning in the 1930s, under the impetus of the New Deal, Negro interest groups began to press their claims for equal protection of the laws through systematic litigation. The first major breakthrough came in the field of public education. In the *Gaines Case* (1938), the Court held that a state must offer equal educational facilities to Negroes and whites and do so within the state. This obligation could not be fulfilled by providing tuition scholarships for Negroes to go out of state to obtain professional training available to whites within the state. The Court ruled that a state must accord all citizens within its jurisdiction equality of privileges regardless of race.[82] The effect of this decision was to improve educational facilities for Negroes in the southern states, though the facilities were still kept separate.

In 1950, the Supreme Court virtually abandoned the doctrine of "separate but equal" in higher education. It upheld the contention of a Negro graduate student at the University of Oklahoma that he had been denied equal protection. Although the Negro had been allowed to attend the university, he had been required to sit apart from the white students in the classrooms, the library, and the cafeteria. Conceding that these restrictions were "in form merely nominal," the Court nevertheless felt that the student had been substantially handicapped in the pursuit of his graduate work, since so much of education consists of discussion and association with fellow students.[83] In the same year, the Court held that the establishment of a separate law school for Negroes in Texas did not provide "equal protection," since the University of Texas Law School for whites and the new law school for Negroes were not substantially equal. In judging the Negro school inferior, the Court employed such criteria as the prestige of the faculty and the position and influence of alumni.[84] Under criteria of this sort—the intangible factors considered by any

---

[80]*Plessy* v. *Ferguson,* 163 U.S. 537 (1896). Emphasis added.

[81]Little more than half a century later, Justice Harlan's grandson, also named John Marshall Harlan, was to join in a unanimous opinion of the Supreme Court in 1955 which turned the "brooding spirit" of his grandfather into the "intelligence of today." 349 U.S. 294 (1955). This was the implementation opinion for *Brown* v. *Board of Education.*

[82]*Missouri ex rel. Gaines* v. *Canada,* 305 U.S. 337 (1938).

[83]*McLaurin* v. *Oklahoma State Regents,* 339 U.S. 637 (1950).

[84]*Sweatt* v. *Painter,* 339 U.S. 637 (1950).

prospective student—*no* racially segregated school could possibly meet the equal protection standard. Racial separation had not been rejected as such, but it had been subjected to a test that it could never pass in a specific case.

The Supreme Court heard five cases in 1952 that involved segregation in public schools below college level. In the earlier cases on higher education, the Court had avoided passing directly on the "separate but equal" doctrine. In these new cases, however, the Negroes did not contend that facilities were unequal, but that they were separate. The Court's decision, stated by Chief Justice Earl Warren in 1954, was unanimous: "We conclude that in the field of public education the doctrine of 'separate but equal' has no place. Separate educational facilities are inherently unequal." The opinion reads much like an academic term paper replete with footnotes from the "learned journals" in sociology and psychology. The Court firmly rejected *Plessy* v. *Ferguson*, but strategically left to the following term its "decree on implementation."[85] The states were thus given time to argue before the Court how they thought the judicial decision could be translated into specific and detailed court orders for desegregation.

Finally, in May, 1955, the Court handed down its implementation decrees in the antisegregation cases. It ordered a "prompt and reasonable start toward full compliance" but left it to the federal district courts to supervise this process in the local communities. No deadline was fixed and the Supreme Court's dictum that desegregation must proceed "with all deliberate speed" evoked more deliberation than speed. Ten years after the Supreme Court had declared that segregation in the public schools was unconstitutional, only 2.25 per cent of the Negro children in the eleven states of the Confederacy and 10.9 per cent in the entire region encompassing the southern and border states were attending school with white children. Approximately half the school districts were still fully segregated and many still had no plans for desegregation.[86]

The *Brown Case* focused on segregation in public schools. On week after that decision, however, the Court projected the principle of desegregation to other public facilities such as parks, theaters, and playgrounds. Earlier it had held state segregation laws an unconstitutional burden on interstate transportation. Obviously, the Court was giving general application to a policy decision—that segregation under color of law, wherever applied, is a denial of equal protection of the laws. Enforcement of this policy was to have nationwide repercussions, but its immediate massive impact was on the southern states.

At first, white political leaders in the South uniformly opposed desegregation. The issue thus did not lend itself to political compromise. The token responses to the new law of the land that did occur could be explained more

---

[85]*Brown* v. *Board of Education*, 347 U.S. 483 (1954).
[86]U.S. Commission on Civil Rights, *Survey of School Desegregation in the Southern and Border States, 1965–66*. Report, February 1966. See Table 14–1 for December 1966 desegregation statistics *after* passage of the 1964 Civil Rights Act.

in terms of the social and economic characteristics of southern counties than in terms of the political characteristics.[87]

Table 14-1 Public School Desegregation (Negro Pupils Attending School with White Pupils as of December 9, 1966)

	NEGRO PUPILS ATTENDING SCHOOLS LESS THAN 95% NEGRO		NEGRO PUPILS ATTENDING SCHOOLS 95 to 99.9% NEGRO		NEGRO PUPILS ATTENDING SCHOOLS 100% NEGRO	
	PERCENTAGE	NUMBER	PERCENTAGE	NUMBER	PERCENTAGE	NUMBER
TOTAL 17 States	17.3%	589,620	7.1%	239,770	75.6%	2,571,540
Southern States	12.5	363,290	4.4	126,160	83.1	2,410,000
Alabama	2.4	6,570	2.3	6,300	95.3	260,900
Arkansas	14.5	17,140	2.1	2,480	83.4	98,650
Florida	14.7	41,120	6.1	17,060	79.2	221,550
Georgia	6.6	22,610	3.3	11,300	90.1	308,450
Louisiana	2.6	6,850	.9	2,370	96.5	254,050
Mississippi	2.6	6,840	.6	1,580	96.8	254,700
North Carolina	12.8	44,850	2.8	9,810	84.4	295,650
South Carolina	4.9	12,120	1.1	2,720	94.0	232,550
Tennessee	21.9	40,600	9.8	18,170	68.3	126,550
Texas	34.6	117,050	12.7	42,960	52.7	178,250
Virginia	20.0	47,540	4.8	11,410	75.2	178,700
Border States	45.1	226,330	22.7	113,610	32.2	161,540
Delaware	84.8	20,440	15.2	3,660	0	0
Kentucky	88.5	38,230	0	0	11.5	4,980
Maryland	40.5	88,980	23.5	51,630	36.0	79,150
Missouri	26.7	34,710	37.5	48,750	35.8	46,540
Oklahoma	40.5	24,950	15.2	9,360	44.3	27,290
West Virginia	83.4	19,020	.9	210	15.7	3,580

Source: *Congressional Quarterly Almanac*, 89th Congress, 2nd Session, 1966, XXII, 478.

White Citizens Councils and other groups were organized to enlist public opinion against official compliance. Hundreds of new laws and ordinances were passed throughout the Deep South to prevent, restrict, or control school desegregation. A variety of tactics were used to circumvent integration in other public facilities. Public golf courses were converted to private clubs; public swimming pools were closed for extended repairs; picnic facilities were removed from public parks.

Racial tensions grew more critical within the region, although there was relatively little violence. Unfortunate incidents occurred — in Little Rock, Arkansas, where Governor Orval Faubus defied a federal court order by calling out the National Guard and instructing the guardsmen to prevent Negro students from entering the white high school; in New Orleans, Louisiana, where irate housewives resisted the entrance of Negro first-graders into the white elementary schools; in Athens, Georgia, where Klansmen and others joined in a

[87]See Donald R. Matthews and James W. Prothro, "Stateways Versus Folkways: Critical Factors in Southern Reactions to *Brown* v. *Board of Education*," in Gottfried Dietze (ed.), *Essays on the American Constitution* (Englewood Cliffs, New Jersey: Prentice-Hall, Inc., 1964), pp. 139–156; and a companion study, Donald R. Matthews and James W. Prothro, "Social and Economic Factors and Negro Voter Registration in the South," *American Political Science Review*, LVII (March, 1963), 24–44, and "Political Factors and Negro Voter Registration in the South," *American Political Science Review* LVII (June, 1963), 355–367.

violent student demonstration against the enrollment of two Negro undergraduates; in Oxford, Mississippi, where some "Ole Miss" students and assorted hoodlums followed Governor Ross Barnett's policy of defiance to engage in a pitched battle with United States marshals over the admission of James Meredith, a Negro, to the University of Mississippi. These isolated instances, played up by the mass media, disturbed many people in America and around the world. In general, however, both parties to this interracial cold war in the 1950s followed a strategy of nonviolent resistance. As white southerners counted on legislation, so Negro southerners countered with litigation, bringing hundreds of suits in federal and state courts on segregation, desegregation, and related issues.

By the 1960s, however, it was clear that litigation as a means of obtaining equal rights was not going to fulfill Negro expectations. The courtroom victories were dramatic, but somehow they seemed to have little affected patterns of behavior in most communities. Biracial conferences, committees, and councils made even less impression on community relations. "The time was ripe for rebellion—rebellion against white domination and segregation, against legalism, against gradual reform through governmental action, against established Negro organizations and leaders."[88]

We have already mentioned the student protest movement which took the form of "sit-in" and other "in" demonstrations to obtain equal access to public accommodations. Negro college students in large numbers engaged in a courageous educational enterprise to teach the rank and file of Negroes as well as white people the meaning of civil rights for all Americans. New leaders also appeared in the adult Negro power structure, advocating the tactics of direct action and civil disobedience, massive street demonstrations and community-wide boycotts. Most eloquent and probably most influential was Dr. Martin Luther King, who heads the Southern Christian Leadership Conference (SCLC), a loose confederation of ministers who have carried the Negro cause northward and into such areas of interracial contact as open housing and equal employment opportunities. Other militant groups that emerged, overshadowing the older and more conservative National Association for the Advancement of Colored People (NAACP) and the National Urban League, included the Congress of Racial Equality (CORE), which is interracial in membership and has been very active in demonstrations; the Student Non-Violent Coordinating Committee (SNCC), also interracial in membership and also active in the protest movement; and the Nation of Islam ("Black Muslims"), which is strictly for Negroes, advocates total segregation, and takes no interest in civil rights legislation. Not only Negro groups, however, but dozens of church groups, labor organizations, and others, such as the American Civil Liberties Union and the American Friends Service Committee, have been actively enlisting the support of public opinion for the civil rights movement.

[88]Matthews and Prothro, *Negroes and the New Southern Politics*, p. 411.

It is estimated that demonstrations for civil rights legislation were staged in more than 800 cities and towns across the country in 1963. In terms of propaganda value, none was more successful than the ill-fated demonstrations in Birmingham, Alabama, when thousands of Negro men, women, and children led by Dr. King and Reverend L. Shuttlesworth began a march for "human rights" and were met by police dogs and fire hoses, a sight seen on television around the world. High point of the protest movement was the March on Washington for Jobs and Freedom, August 28, 1963, when more than 200,000 persons participated in a nonviolent interracial demonstration, with groups descending on Washington from all parts of the country. In the light of increasing demands and obviously mounting support (and also in fear of incipient violence), decision-makers in Washington were forced to produce a more positive nationwide policy in the form of civil rights legislation.

Equal Protection Via National Legislation

How did the President and the Congress react to desegregation by litigation and judicial decree? In the Little Rock crisis of 1957, President Eisenhower ordered the use of federal troops to enforce federal court orders. Disclaiming any personal opinions as to integration, desegregation, or segregation, the President explained that drastic action was necessary because normal processes had failed. His action created a great furor; a nationwide debate raged over whether the President had exceeded his constitutional powers as Chief Executive. Federal troops arrived in Little Rock, however, and there they stayed, to afford military protection throughout the year to the handful of Negro children permitted to attend Central High School by court orders.

In September, 1962, President Kennedy took similar action when the Governor of Mississippi personally barred the entry of a Negro student at the University of Mississippi despite a federal court order requiring his admission. President Kennedy televised a message to the nation: "Americans are free to disagree with the law but not to disobey it. For in a government of laws and not of men, no man, however prominent or powerful, and no mob, however unruly or boisterous, is entitled to defy a court of law." Under presidential orders, U.S. marshals, and for a time regular U.S. troops, enforced the court order which admitted the first Negro student to the University of Mississippi. Little Rock, Arkansas, and Oxford, Mississippi, dramatically illustrate the exercise of presidential power to secure obedience to federal court decrees. They were, however, isolated incidents. Certainly neither President Eisenhower nor President Kennedy used full presidential powers to bring about desegregation of the public schools in line with Supreme Court decisions.

As for Congress, it simply sat tight, taking no action, though individual members expressed strong opinions pro and con in continuous debates. Less than a fifth of Congress joined in the celebrated Southern Manifesto which represented the official southern viewpoint. When Senator Jenner (R.-Ind.) tried to capitalize on widespread dissatisfaction with various judicial decisions relating to communists, subversives, and labor organizers, as well as racial minorities, Congress rejected his bill to curb judicial power and restrict jurisdiction of the Supreme Court. Indeed, Congress not only took no direct stand on the issue of desegregation and integration, but also continued to authorize and appropriate grants-in-aid to the states and local communities for health, education, and welfare projects which would operate on a segregated basis.

Congress did pass in 1957 and 1960 two modest Civil Rights Acts which pertained mainly to rights of suffrage and discrimination in voting practices. But not until 1964, a decade after the initial decision in the *Brown Case,* did Congress attempt to back up court decrees, executive orders, and administrative rules with a comprehensive Civil Rights Act that would make equal protection of the laws a positive national policy.

The year 1960 was crucial in the congressional decision to take affirmative action on civil rights. It was the year that sixteen African nations entered the United Nations and drastically altered the balance of power in the Cold War. The emergence of color as an issue in world politics inevitably had a considerable impact on American foreign policy, and those entrusted with our policies abroad were extremely concerned about how racial relations at home would affect our status and bargaining power in the international community. Also, 1960 was an election year, in which both major political parties stood on strong civil rights planks. The Democrats were returned to power in the White House and in Congress. The Negro electorate, which was especially strong in the big cities in the pivotal states, supported the Democratic candidate. President John F. Kennedy and his brother, Attorney General Robert Kennedy, were both personally committed to the principle of equal protection of the laws. Hence it was to be expected that the Kennedy administration would make every effort to push for a national policy on civil rights to be proclaimed as the law of the land. Moreover, Congress itself was subject to increasing demands from its grassroots constituencies.

The "Kennedy style," however, worked more successfully through executive orders and administrative rulings than by legislative action. The President's Committee on Equal Employment Opportunity was established to combat racial discrimination in government employment and in private businesses holding government contracts. The Attorney General petitioned the Interstate Commerce Commission to extend its ban on racial discrimination to interstate bus terminals and airport facilities. The Justice Department inaugurated more vigorous enforcement of voting rights under the 1957 and 1960 Civil Rights Acts. But not until June 1963 did the Kennedy administration give top priority to civil rights legislation. Then the President submitted to Congress the most sweeping civil rights bill since Reconstruction, including provisions to guarantee equal access to public accommodations, to cut off federal assistance in any area practicing discimination, to strengthen fair employment policies under government contracts, and to establish a Community Relations Service to help local communities resolve racial frictions. The bill bogged down in the summer months, however, in a congressional committee system dominated by southern Democrats. The House bill was formally reported out on November

20, but time had run out for the Kennedy administration. In his first address to Congress, following the assassination of President Kennedy on November 22, President Johnson pleaded for immediate passage of the civil rights bill: "No memorial oration or eulogy could more eloquently honor President Kennedy's memory than the earliest possible passage of the civil rights bill for which he fought so long."

The Kennedy bill failed to pass in 1963, but the Johnson administration continued the fight in 1964. It was not easy to get a civil rights bill through Congress, given the customary mutual distrust of Democrats and Republicans in an election year, as well as a marathon southern filibuster in the Senate. The Johnson administration and a bipartisan congressional leadership, however, worked with parliamentary skill and consummate political strategy to enact the bill with a minimum of personal bitterness betweeen proponents and opponents.

The Civil Rights Act of 1964 committed the national government to:

(1) enforce the constitutional right to vote for public officials;
(2) secure full and equal enjoyment of goods, services, and facilities in all places of public accommodation (hotel, motel, lunch counter, cafeteria, motion picture house, theater, sports arena, etc.);
(3) give the U.S. Attorney General power to initiate legal proceedings on behalf of persons denied equal utilization of any public facility, including the public schools;
(4) authorize the U.S. Commissioner of Education to assist local communities in the various problems that arise from desegregation of public schools;
(5) expand the activity of the Commission on Civil Rights as a national clearing house for information on denials of equal protection of the laws in the fields of voting, education, housing, employment, use of public facilities, transporation, and the administration of justice;
(6) forbid discrimination, on the ground of race, color, or national origin, in all federally assisted programs;
(7) make it an unlawful employment practice for an employer or a labor organization to hire or fire employees, or in any way to segregate employees, because of an individual's race, color, religion, sex, or national origin;
(8) create the Equal Employment Opportunity Commission to help police discriminatory employment practices;
(9) authorize the Secretary of Commerce (in connection with the decennial census) to compile registration and voting statistics;
(10) establish as part of the Department of Commerce a Community Relations Service to help local communities resolve disputes, disagreements, and difficulties relating to discrimination based on race, color, or national origin.

The most controversial provisions of the Act are those relating to fair employment practices and equal accommodations. Prior to passage of the Civil Rights Act, the Supreme Court had held that a privately operated restaurant within a public facility (a bus and parking terminal) could not discriminate among would-be customers. It also determined that a privately owned restaurant could not choose to serve only white customers, even though public policy in the local community, express or implicit, required or permitted segregation. The courts, however, had not made a final decision on what constitutes trespass in a private establishment when no official action is involved. But, in December 1964, the Supreme Court unanimously upheld the public accommodations section of the Civil Rights Act of 1964. The Court's action cleared the way for full-scale enforcement of the Act. Lawyers in the Justice Department and conciliators in the Community Relations Service of the Commerce Department had eagerly been awaiting the decision. Generally, however, there was immediate and widespread compliance with the act without coercion.

With the passage of the 1964 Civil Rights Act, the American people appeared to have reached a new consensus—that racial discrimination should be outlawed in our constitutional democracy. But within a month after passage, outbreaks of violence and mob looting in Harlem, Bedford-Stuyvesant, and upstate Rochester, New York revealed the many frustrations of the Negro even in a state with a strongly affirmative policy on individual and minority rights. A survey conducted in the New York area immediately after the 1964 street riots indicated that most Negroes regard civil rights as a minor public problem compared to economic complaints: low-grade, low-paid jobs; unemployment; bad housing, high rents, and overcrowded conditions.[89] Most of the Negroes polled said that they want their children to go to integrated schools with white children. They want to live in an integrated neighborhood with white families. On the other hand, most of them said they did not really like whites. Here is probably the crux of racial relations, the difficulty in attaining mutual respect between the two races, for bigotry exists on both sides of the color line.

. . .

This chapter was written in the "long hot summer" of 1967. To some it appears that the whole civil rights movement has collapsed in riots and rebellion. A new wall, under the name of Black Power, has arisen between the races. The headline news is of Negro riots to the point of guerilla warfare in major cities across the nation. Black Power is a militant and violent movement; it has no time for "sittin' in," "prayin' in," "kneelin' in," or any other kind of "-in." Interracial handclasping, with all singing "we shall overcome," is replaced by its slogan "burn, baby, burn." H. Rap Brown, new leader of the Student Non-Violent Coordinating Committee, told an audience in the nation's capital that "violence is as American as cherry pie."

In the wake of one of the worst riots in American history a national conference on Black Power met in Newark, New Jersey. There was no suggestion of moderation in the antiwhite resolutions that touched nearly every phase of life. The resolutions repeatedly called for the creation of a new black world, a new kind of black value system, a separate black world with everything black-operated. It was reported that the resolution receiving the most applause called for dividing the United States into separate states for Negroes and for whites.

[89]*The New York Times*, July 27, 1964.

Drawing by Isadore Parker; reproduced by permission of the artist.

"Under precedent established by King George III we are hereby granted the right to forcible search and seizure . . . ."

Following repeated requests from Michigan's Governor Romney, President Johnson sent federal troops to Detroit to assist the local police and national guardsmen restore order to that riot-torn city in summer, 1967. And he appointed a bipartisan National Advisory Commission on Civil Disorder to give him the answer to "three basic questions about the riots: What happened? Why did it happen? and What can be done to prevent it from happening again and again?" He gave the Commission a full year to conduct its investigation. The 90th Congress met the crisis of the cities in 1967 in much the same manner as did the Chief Executive. Following open hearings in which police officials from the riot cities told their stories of burning, looting, and killing, Congress passed the 1967 Anti-rioting Act. The Senate authorized its Permanent Investigations Subcommittee, headed by Senator John McClellan (D.-Ark.) to make a tough, searching, and detailed investigation of strife in the cities across the country.

It is too early to discern the contours of the emerging new relationships between the races in the United States. What appeared to be consensus on civil rights in 1964 more nearly approaches confrontation of the races in 1968. A political scientist can, however, draw some immediate conclusions as to why the civil rights movement in 1967 turned into riots and civil disorder.

Negroes have patiently pursued their rights in the courts through three decades. Judges have handed down many decisions in their favor, but judicial policy-making power is limited. Congress has passed civil rights acts, but these have not been sufficiently far-reaching to change basic social patterns. Congress rejected the 1966 civil rights bill proposed by the President which would have made open housing a national policy. The Negro ghettos in the metropolitan areas remain tightly sealed while white people continue their exodus to the suburbs. Though Negroes furnish the highest percentage of draftees and the highest percentage of casualties in Viet Nam, few Selective Service Boards in the nation include Negro members. The Negro leadership has voiced bitter criticism of national policy priorities evidenced in the Budget Message of 1967: No. 1, the Viet Nam War; No. 2, the space program; and No. 3, domestic programs. As Martin Luther King put it, "There is a striking absurdity in committing billions to reach the moon where no people can live and from which none can presently benefit, while densely populated slums are allowed miniscule appropriations."

The legislative record of the Johnson administration speaks for itself: the Civil Rights Act, the Model Cities Act, the Rent Supplement Act, Medicare and Medicaid, the Education Acts, Project Headstart, the Job Corps, the Neighborhood Youth Corps, the Teachers Corps, the Manpower Development Act, and many more. Even so, by 1967 it was clear that the Administration's high priorities for the war in Viet Nam and the space race had perceptibly slowed down the initial momentum of the War on Poverty. Moreover, the presidential election coming in 1968 was beginning to condition the policy-makers, both executive and legislative. Better to postpone decisions and meantime just "investigate" problems. The President's State of the Union Message for 1967 gave only a passing reference, less than 50 words, to civil rights *per se*. And obviously the 90th Congress had no intention of considering, much less passing, new civil rights legislation.

A Louis Harris survey in June, 1967, showed clearly the Negro impatience and disenchantment with the civil rights movement. Of those interviewed, 85 per cent felt that the movement should be stepped up immediately to accomplish the objectives of racial equality; 78 per cent wanted a federal open housing law *now*; and 76 per cent indicated that jobs were getting harder to find.

In a democratic system, the majority rules; but courts must function to protect the legal rights of individuals, and political channels must remain open to all so that the urgent demands of minority groups may be heard and heeded. If the system fails to operate in this manner, if the output of the policy process consistently denies any rewards to minority groups and offers them only deprivations, then the minority groups may take to the streets and attack the system itself.

GENERAL WELFARE AND

COMMON DEFENSE   15

What do we mean by public policy? As a rational concept it is relatively easy to define. It refers to the course of action taken by the government to achieve an objective or purpose. Note, however, that policy implies more than a *set* of governmental activities; it is an entire series of related goal-oriented activities. Note also that the policy base for governmental action, in any area, on any issue, involves significant decisions as to both means and ends. The decision-makers in American government—Congress, the President, the bureaucrats, and judges—determine the courses of action within an institutional framework. But the institutions of government are conditioned by the whole social environment, which embraces values, beliefs, ideas, and interests as well as the sensate, or material, culture of the people.

No policy is perfectly fixed or permanent, because politics—the attempt to influence policy—never ends. It never ends because laws are never neutral. The conflicting needs and views that various groups try to express in policy are constantly changing. Since every election, every law, every administrative ruling, and every court decision reflect some combination of conflicting claims, they are bound to please some political interest groups and to displease others. And in a democracy the losers are free to do what they can to modify or change the decision. Although this practice may distress those who seek permanence, or at least neutrality, in government, it is the essence of politics.

General Welfare in the Changing Environment

The Constitution of the United States was ordained and established to achieve certain great objectives, among these to "promote the general welfare." As a means to this end, the national government was given a variety of powers and Congress was specifically empowered to lay and collect taxes to provide for the general welfare of the United States. Nowhere in the Constitution, however, is general welfare defined or limited.

General welfare is in fact a social idea rather than a legal term, and because the American society is highly pluralistic, our ideas of general welfare vary considerably. In an open society, many different groups pursue political power for their own ends. The public interest—or the general welfare—appears as an accommodation of many different, competing, and conflicting interests. The policy base for governmental activities at any given time generally represents the goal orientation of the dominant or prevailing interests. All groups do not have equal power over every decision of government; policies therefore affect various interests differently. Because few groups in a democracy are willing to accept a subordinate role—or a "raw deal"—forever, policy becomes a nucleus around which politics continuously revolves. As the balance of power shifts within the political system, as it must in any dynamic society, governmental activities, insofar as they are goal-oriented, reflect continuously changing policies. As we said, politics knows no end.

In this chapter we propose to examine the policies of the national government within the expansive range of general welfare (and, less fully, of the common defense). To do this realistically, we must keep in mind the changing social environment which conditions the entire policy process. We shall look for guidelines in the constitutional background, for an ideological orientation, as well as for institutional prescriptions. We shall take a hard look at the input of policy-making, at the many and diverse unofficial agencies in our political system which are so influential in stimulating or blocking government action. Finally, we shall focus on the official decision-makers, and the various techniques they choose to employ for implementation of their decisions.

Constitutional Background: Ideological Orientation and Practical Accommodation

If we look at the bare text of the Constitution, we see that the Philadelphia Convention was practically concerned with the relations between the political order and the economy. In Article I, Section 8, about half of the powers enumerated to Congress pertain to economic matters: "to lay and collect taxes . . . ; to borrow money on the credit of the United States; to regulate commerce with the foreign nations, and among the several states . . . ; to establish . . . uniform laws on the subject of bankruptcies throughout the United States; to coin money, regulate the value thereof, and of foreign coin, and fix the standard of weights and measures; to provide for the punishment of counterfeiting the securities and current coin of the United States; to establish post offices and post roads; to promote the progress of science and useful arts . . . ; and to make all laws which shall be necessary and proper for carrying into execution the foregoing powers. . . ." If we analyze this listing of national powers, we see that the original document (a) authorized the national government to engage directly in business enterprise (postal services); (b) provided that the government furnish certain basic instrumentalities for business (currency, weights and measures, patents, trademarks and copyrights, and also communication and transportation facilities); (c) empowered the government to police the market (control bankruptcies, impose tariffs) and to regulate foreign and interstate commerce.

We may also infer from the Constitution certain principles that have a direct bearing on the relation of government to business: (1) the sanctity of private property; (2) the concept of limited government; (3) the federal pattern. Article I, Section 9, places specific limitations on the national government: no tax or duty shall be laid on articles exported from any state and no preference shall be given to one state over another in any national legislation on commerce or revenue. Section 10 puts other restrictions on the states: they may not coin money, issue bills of credit, or make anything but gold and silver legal tender; they may not pass laws impairing the obligation of contracts; and they may not levy taxes on imports or exports from out of state or out of the country. The Fifth Amendment prohibits the national government from depriving any person of property without due process of law and just compensation; the Fourteenth Amendment imposes a similar prohibition on the states. These provisions, within the federal system, limit both the national and state governments. On the other hand, the Sixteenth Amendment, which authorizes Congress to lay and collect income taxes, gives to the national government almost unlimited power to redistribute the wealth of the country. Attach the Sixteenth Amendment to the original power of Congress to lay and collect taxes for the general welfare and the national policy with respect to the economy becomes as pervasive as the prevailing concept of general welfare.

We do not find in the text of the Constitution any of the verbalisms which the business community likes to associate with the American Way: private enterprise, free enterprise, freedom of contract, freedom of competition, or the separation of government and business. Neither do we find any specifications about labor relations: the right to organize and to bargain collectively, the right to work, fair labor standards, or fair employment practices. There is no mention in the Constitution of profits, prices, income (except that it may be taxed from whatever source derived), interest rates, full employment, or wage controls. Observations of this sort led Mr. Justice Holmes to remark that the Constitution embodies no particular economic theory.[1]

By coincidence, Adam Smith, a Scottish professor of moral philosophy, published his book *The Wealth of Nations* in the same year that the United States proclaimed its independence from British colonialism and mercantilism. The doctrine of Adam Smith became a kind of economic theology for the American business community. Basically, Smith said that every man works best in his own interest, and therefore *laissez faire* ("hands off") government is the best kind of government. In terms of economics, Smith preached the message of the free market. The free market implies a self-regulating, self-adjusting economic system that operates under the "iron law" of supply and demand without need of governmental intervention. The doctrine was particularly appealing to American businessmen in the early years of the Republic. Adam Smith's natural law of economics was cut out of the same cloth as Thomas Jefferson's natural laws of politics. The free market offered "adventure, romance, and risk"; as one modern businessman explains it, "the market system fits the temper and character of the American people."[2]

From the beginning, however, the American people were able to keep both

---

[1] *Lochner* v. *New York,* 198 U.S. 45 (1905); a dissenting opinion.
[2] John R. Bunting, *The Hidden Face of Free Enterprise* (New York: McGraw-Hill Book Company, 1964), p. 21. Mr. Bunting is vice-president of the Federal Reserve Bank of Philadelphia. His book is a candid discussion of the businessman's views toward government and its role in the economy.

their political and economic ideologies comfortably apart from everyday activities. They might proclaim and even fight for the unalienable rights of all persons and still maintain the institution of slavery. They might talk about the free market and the strict separation of economics and politics and still use government to provide subsidies and other benefits to business. And, if they were troubled by logical inconsistency, apparently they were soothed by the felicitous thought which Grover Cleveland expressed so neatly, ". . . it is a condition that confronts us, not a theory."

The American economy *is* a condition, not a theory. It is not today—and it never was—the output of policy-planning either by business or by government. In *The Politics of Industry*, Walton Hamilton, an outstanding political economist, wrote about "the great transformation" in the socio-economic environment: "The machine process, the assembly line, the huge factory, the chain of stores, the speedy movement of commodities down the channels of merchandise, and the rise of corporations blessed with assets in excess of those of most of the states of the Union"—Hamilton attributed these modern economic phenomena to the scientists, the technicians, and the business executives who inadvertently fashioned a new order "with little thought of the impact of their innovations upon the established ways of society."[3]

A basic function of government is to deal with the conflicts and controversies that arise in society and to respond with policies that tend to promote order by distributing rewards and deprivations among the contending interests. As the character of society changes, as economic forces take new shape, new problems spring up for government to tackle. Thus what we regard as necessary and proper political regulation today is likely to be very different from what the Founding Fathers felt was appropriate for the circumstances that conditioned their thinking. It is pointless for us to argue whether the Constitution of 1787 was intended to regulate marketing quotas in agricultural products, to promote old age and survivors' insurance, to guarantee collective bargaining in industrial relations, and to develop public power projects. What is important to us is whether Congress and the courts can or should interpret the Constitution broadly enough to authorize such policies today.

The Constitution of the United States has survived because Americans have always been able to interpret it to meet current needs. To have held constitutional law to the literal "words and phrases" of the Founding Fathers would have rendered their work obsolete almost as soon as their signatures were dry. For instance, the Framers of the Constitution gave Congress the power to regulate commerce. The only instrumentalities of commerce they knew were sailing ships, stage coaches, and pedestrian traffic. But this does not mean that Congress is without power to regulate more modern instrumentalities of commerce like steam vessels, railroads, telegraph and telephone, air lines, trucks and buses, radio and television. Similarly, we cannot look in the dictionaries of 1790 to determine whether "due process of law" applied to wire-tapping and lie-detectors; whether "stomach pumps" come under the prohibition of "unreasonable search and seizure" or fingerprinting and alcoholic meter tests under "self-incrimination"; whether death in the electric

---

[3] Walton Hamilton, *The Politics of Industry* (New York: Alfred A. Knopf, Inc., 1957), p. 33.

chair or in the lethal gas chamber constitutes "cruel and unusual punishment." We must interpret the ancient words and phrases within the modern context.

We have seen that the Constitution itself reflects a continuous struggle over policy. The Founding Fathers simply began the debate over the meaning of the Constitution—they did not complete it. Ever since, the dominant groups in each generation of American politics have interpreted the document to correspond to their views. Minimum-wage laws were regarded as unconstitutional in the 1920s, not so much because of the "intention of the Framers" or the objective meaning of the Constitution, as because of the way in which the coalition then controlling American politics viewed the public interest—and their own. Minimum-wage laws finally became constitutional in the 1930s, not because of any change in the intentions of the Framers or in the words of the Constitution, but because of the Supreme Court's response to the new conditions and the new power relations that had developed during the current generation.

The Right to Private Property

If any one economic principle is imbedded in our political philosophy and our constitutional law, it is the right to private property. Blackstone, the great English law commentator, speaks of "the rights of persons and the rights of things." There is a tendency today to sharpen this dichotomy, to draw a line between *personal* rights and *property* rights. In the Lockean ideology, however, the rights of man include "life, liberty, and property" in indissoluble union. As John Taylor, principal theorist of Jeffersonian Republicanism, explained in considering the "principles of our revolution": "The rights to life, liberty and property, are so intimately blended together, that neither can be lost in a state of society without all; or at least, neither can be impaired without wounding the others."[4] John Adams, exponent of Federalist philosophy, wrote: "Property is surely a right of mankind as real as liberty . . . . The moment the idea is admitted into society, that property is not as sacred as the laws of God, and that there is not a force of law and public justice to protect it, anarchy and tyranny commence."[5]

But if we look carefully at the wording of the Constitution, we find that the protection of private property, as envisaged in the Fifth and Fourteenth Amendments, is conditional, not absolute. *A person* may not be deprived of property without due process of law, but a reasonable implication is that he *may be deprived of property with due process of law. Private property* may not be taken for public use without just compensation but it *may be taken for public use with just compensation.* No person has a claim of absolute right to private property against a counter-claim of his government that the property is needed for public use. Eminent domain—that is, taking private property for

---

[4]John Taylor, *From Construction Construed and Constitutions Vindicated* (1820), quoted in Francis Coker, *Democracy, Liberty and Property* (New York: The Macmillan Company, 1942), p. 496.
[5]In *Works*, VI, 8–9, quoted in Coker, p. 464.

public use—is an inherent and essential power of government. Although not specifically delegated to the national government, the power of eminent domain is implied as an attribute of government.

Just what constitutes public use at any given time depends largely on the prevailing concept of what governmental activities are proper and necessary. Thus, today, private property may be taken over to make way for *public roads* (including superhighways, bridges, tunnels, and roadside picnic areas); *public buildings* (including firehouses, police stations, courthouses, hospitals, libraries, and slaughterhouses); *public schools* (including cafeterias, bookstores, auditoriums, and stadiums); *public recreation facilities* (including ballparks, botanical gardens, zoos, swimming pools, skating rinks, and golf courses); *public works* (including water reservoirs, sewage-disposal plants, power plants, and gas works); and *conservation projects* (irrigation and drainage ditches, fish hatcheries, bird refuges, and forest preserves). There is almost no limit to the list.

In recent years, the national government has taken over a great deal of private property for military establishments and for huge hydroelectric and atomic energy installations. Several states and municipalities have taken private property in order to operate port facilities, piers, and warehouses. The Port of New York Authority, for example, exercised eminent domain on a gigantic scale to build the Holland and Lincoln tunnels, the George Washington Bridge, a huge railroad freight station, a large motor truck terminal, a central bus terminal, and the great airports at LaGuardia Field, Queens, Teterboro, and Newark. Many other cities have condemned private property to build airports, to clear slum areas, to construct civic centers. Although the courts still maintain that the question of public use may be settled by litigation, in practice judges tend to accept whatever the local political authorities decide. In effect, the courts have conceded that "public use" is a matter of social philosophy rather than a legal concept.

A decision of the United State Supreme Court illustrates how broad the current construction makes the power of eminent domain. In 1954, Justice Douglas upheld a slum-clearance and redevelopment project that had been enacted by Congress for the District of Columbia. A department store in the area protested the condemnation proceedings, arguing that the redevelopment project would simply shift its property to different private management. The Court, however, went no further than to affirm the initial public purpose: "a beautiful, healthy, spacious, clean, well-balanced, carefully patrolled" community. The Court regarded as immaterial the fact that Congress chose private enterprise, rather than public ownership or even government operation, as the means of accomplishing this purpose. Since the Court found the requisite public purpose in the housing project, it could then conclude: "The rights of these property owners are satisfied when they receive that just compensation which the Fifth Amendment exacts as the price of the taking."[6]

The tremendous expansion of government activities in recent years has vastly enlarged the judicial concept of public use. Because any property may

[6]*Berman* v. *Parker*, 348 U.S. 26 (1954).

be taken for public use, just compensation remains the sole legal bulwark of private property rights against eminent domain. Politically, of course, property owners are in a good position to demand protection of their interests by their elected representatives. The guarantee of just compensation is explicit in the Fifth Amendment with respect to the taking of private property by the federal government, and it is implicit in the due process clause of the Fourteenth Amendment with respect to the taking of private property by state or local governments. In general, the courts have held that just compensation represents "the fair value" of the property at the time it is taken, and fair value is usually regarded as the market value. If the owner of the property is not satisfied with the initial price offered by the government, due process provides that he be given a fair opportunity to present his case at some point during the condemnation proceedings. Public officials whose tenure depends on good will in politics are more inclined to be generous than otherwise with the taxpayers' dollars in these condemnation cases. In other words, the government price will more likely overvalue than undervalue the private property in most cases of eminent domain.

The government is not always obliged to compensate the owner when it takes private property. For example, in exercising police power to protect public health, safety, or morals, the government is not required to compensate private owners for the seizure and destruction of such property as illegal slot machines, bootleg liquor, lottery tickets, adulterated food or drugs, diseased or pest-infested plants, and substandard fertilizer. When national prohibition went into effect after World War I, the federal government offered no compensation to the distillers and brewers whose billion-dollar business had been closed out by the law.[7] Early in World War II, the military situation in the Philippines seemed so hopeless that the United States Army demolished a considerable amount of private property in Manila to prevent it from falling into enemy hands. The Caltex Company, whose terminal facilities and petroleum stock were destroyed, later demanded compensation, but the Supreme Court held that there was no constitutional right to compensation for property taken over by the military in wartime.[8]

The Constitution draws no line between personal and property rights—no persons may be deprived of liberty *or* property without due process of law. But what happens when claims to personal rights collide with claims to property rights?

The right to private property and free enterprise may be cardinal principles in American economic theory, but no one is free to use his property or carry on his business contrary to public policy. And in the final analysis it is the government that has authority to determine and enforce the public policy. If the law says (and it does) that an employer may not oppose labor union activities or refuse to bargain collectively with representatives chosen by his

[7] See *Hamilton* v. *Kentucky Distilleries and Wine Co.*, 251 U.S. 146 (1919).
[8] *United States* v. *Caltex, Inc.*, 344 U.S. 149 (1952).

employees, then an employer is not free to obstruct unionism in his business even though privately he thinks labor unions are un-American. If the law says (and it does) that an employer may not discriminate in hiring or firing employees, or segregate them in any way because of race, color, sex, religion, or national origin, then the employer is not free to engage in discriminatory practices even though he may be anti-Semitic or segregationist in his private views.

In the 1960s, the civil rights movement precipitated countless clashes between claims of private property rights versus personal liberties. The private motel on the interstate highway refused accommodations to Negroes. The gas station on the edge of town opened its "comfort room" to white customers only. The proprietor of the small lunch counter on Main Street maintained service for "exclusive clientele—whites only." The manager of the local movie house reserved the right to seat whites only, or to seat Negroes in a segregated section of the theater. When the Negroes staged sit-in demonstrations, picketed, or marched en masse to the tune of "We Shall Overcome," in many communities they were arrested for trespassing on private property or for disturbing the public peace.

Now the Civil Rights Act of 1964 makes it unlawful—as a matter of national policy—for any private business that offers public accommodations (hotel, motel, lunch counter, cafeteria, motion picture house, theater, sports arena) to deny goods, services, or facilities to anyone on grounds of race, color, religion, sex, or national origin. The Act was passed principally under the power of Congress to regulate commerce among the states. Public policy, however, is always open to challenge and changing interpretations. No one institution in American government ever has the last word on public policy. Test cases to determine the constitutionality of the 1964 Civil Rights Act were brought into court almost before the President had finished signing the Act. Segregationists who had been criticizing the courts for usurping the legislative power now counted on judicial review to invalidate congressional action!

The first two cases involving the 1964 Civil Rights Act to reach the Supreme Court came from a barbecue drive-in in Birmingham, Alabama, and a motel in Atlanta, Georgia. A federal District Court in Alabama held that the public accommodations section of the Civil Rights Act was unconstitutional when applied to a local and private business. Meantime, a federal District Court in Georgia had upheld the public accommodations provision when applied to the Atlanta motel, most of whose guests were admittedly travelers in interstate commerce. When the attorney for the motel argued his case before the United States Supreme Court, he indicated that the fundamental question was whether the Congress has the right to deny the owner of a private business freedom to run his firm as he wishes and to choose his customers. "The fact that Negroes are involved in this case is purely incidental," he said. "If Congress has the power to take away the personal liberty of the individual business man there is no limit to the power of Congress." Justice Clark, who delivered the opinion of the Supreme Court, in both the Birmingham and Atlanta case, observed that racial discriminations in local business had mounted to "a national commercial problem of the first magnitude." The Court upheld the 1964 Civil Rights Act as a "plainly appropriate technique to control the problem. Congress could have pursued other methods to eliminate the obstructions it found in interstate commerce caused by racial discrimination. But this is a matter of policy that rests with Congress, not with the courts."[9]

Developing a Natural Policy Base

In *The New American Political Economy*, Marshall Dimock attempted a "synthesis of politics and economics." He complains at the outset that "what America lacks is a policy base from which to reach sound decisions that are consistently right in the long run."[10] But a society which is (1) pluralistic, (2) dynamic, and (3) democratic does not expect its government to operate from any one policy base "in the long run." Government acts at any time in response to the combination of elements that make the most powerful demands on the decision-makers. Because the social and economic environment constantly changes, government policies must also undergo never-ending change. For one thing, new conditions may lead the powerful interests themselves to change their means or their goals, or both. But meantime, economic and social changes may give rise to new interests with different demands, and new coalitions may become sufficiently influential and powerful to redirect policy to their own ends.

In the early days of the American republic, the Hamiltonians wanted a strong national government that would provide a national market, a national currency, a national transportation system, and protection for the sanctity of contracts and the right to private property. The Jeffersonians, who came to power after the elections of 1800, represented rival economic interests and different social values. The policy base of Hamiltonianism was intended to promote the interests of manufacturing, commerce, and urbanism; the policy base of Jeffersonianism was intended to protect the interests of the rural communities and farmers who believed that "that government is best which governs least."

But the application of technology to industry transformed the socio-political environment and reversed the position of the classical antagonists. Big business no longer needed the help of government and so it embraced the Jeffersonian doctrine of *laissez faire*. On the other hand, the farmers, workers, and the less privileged elements of the general public tried to combat the new plutocracy by challenging big business with big government. Spokesmen for these groups, who had championed "strict construction" of the Constitution while government powers were being used to promote commercial interests, turned to "liberal construction" when they needed government to match the power of private economic interests. Whereupon the business community, which had once advocated a strong national government, began to espouse the "principle" of states' rights.

---

[9]*Katzenbach* v. *McClung*, 379 U.S. 294 (1964); *Heart of Atlanta Motel, Inc.* v. *U.S.*, 85 S. Ct. 1 (1964); 85 S. Ct. 348 (1964).

[10]Marshall Dimock, *The New American Political Economy* (New York: Harper and Row, Publishers, Inc., 1962), p. 17.

Power divided among the states could hardly cope with or control economic operations which were nationwide, or even international in scope. Once American resources and technology had developed powerful economic interests that wanted merely to continue established aids to business, and once American politics had extended the franchise to masses of people who felt a need for the government to curb those economic interests, the about-face in opinions on the role of government in economics swiftly followed.

After the mid-nineteenth century, in response to the rapid spread of the Industrial Revolution, European governments generally went into the business of providing the basic public utilities, especially in communications and transportation. In this country, however, there was almost no advocacy of socialism. Given the character of the American people, given their belief in individualism and their idea of progress through free competition, few in the United States wanted to substitute governmental enterprise for private business. On the other hand, a firm belief in equality, along with a deep-rooted humanitarianism, was also a part of the American democratic tradition. Gross abuses of economic power by individual entrepreneurs and oversized combinations in restraint of trade, monopolistic tendencies that belied the free market, disciminatory practices that denied fair play, distressing working conditions, and extremes of poverty and riches prompted many people to press for governmental regulations of the economy.

Meanwhile, the democratization of the suffrage, increasing pluralism in the electorate, and the extension of public education were changing the nature of the political arena. As in Europe, an awakening social conscience and rising expectations were parts of the output of the Industrial Revolution. Mass production and urbanization tended to shift the political emphasis from individual civil rights to social and economic reforms. In this country, the "revolt of the masses" took the form of populism and progressivism. Organized and articulate groups representing various sectors of the economy demanded that the police power of the state be used to promote the public health, safety, and morals and, indeed, to meet all public needs. The business community, outnumbered in the electorate, hence less influential in the legislative constituencies, counted more and more on the courts to protect the rights of private property and to brake the new "liberalism."

Although corporate business had revolutionized the American economy by the end of the nineteenth century, the courts continued to apply the principles of private property that had once protected the single proprietor, the individual entrepreneur. The courts still held that the due process clauses of the Fifth and Fourteenth Amendments restrained both the federal and state governments from regulating "private business." The first noteworthy break in this interpretation occurred in the 1870s, when organized pressure from midwestern farmers who were dedicated to "raising less corn and more hell" forced state legislatures to regulate the railroads.

In *Munn* v. *Illinois* (1876), Chief Justice Morrison R. Waite declared that "when private property is devoted to a public use, it is subject to public regulation." He found that, since grain elevators were devoted to a public use, their rates and services could be regulated by state legislatures. Justice Stephen

J. Field, however, took sharp issue with the Chief Justice. In Field's opinion, the due process guarantee extended to the use of property and to the fruits of that use: "The same liberal construction which is required for the protection of life and liberty . . . should be applied to the protection of private property." Field did not want property, any more than life or liberty, to be subjected to the will of the legislature, even when the legislature acted "under pretense of providing for the common good."[11]

For a half-century following the *Munn Case*, Field's views rather than Waite's tended to prevail in the courts. For example, the early attempts of the states to regulate hours of labor were frustrated by narrow judicial interpretation of due process of law. In *Lochner v. New York* (1905), the Supreme Court invalidated a New York statute which, under the guise of protecting public health, limited the work of bakers to sixty hours a week. Justice Holmes dissented in vain. Distressed by his colleagues' tendency to look to the *laissez faire* ideas of the popular English writer, Herbert Spencer, rather than to the Constitution, Holmes sharply reminded them, "The Fourteenth Amendment does not enact Mr. Herbert Spencer's Social Statics." Insisting that the public interest was "not in the slightest degree affected by this purely labor law," the majority of the Court gave the highest priority to "liberty of contract."[12] They believed that the liberty of workers and employers to contract with each other could not be regulated by the government. The high-water mark for this judicial concept of liberty of contract was approached in *Adkins v. Children's Hospital* (1923) when in a 5–4 decision the Court declared that a congressional act establishing minimum wages for women in the District of Columbia was a violation of the due process clause of the Fifth Amendment. The Court took a purely formal view, regarding the charwoman (Adkins) and the corporation (the Children's Hospital) as "persons" under the law, able to bargain as equals, both entitled to liberty of contract.[13]

Not until the 1930s, when the Great Depression forced the Court to face the facts of economic life, was there a turning of the tide in judicial interpretation of "business affected with a public interest." In the case of *Nebbia v. New York* (1934), the Supreme Court upheld a New York State statute regulating milk prices. Although the Court recognized that the milk business was in no sense a public utility, it nevertheless affirmed the right of the state to control any business for the public good. It found nothing "peculiarly sacrosanct" about the price a man may charge for what he makes or sells. It saw no reason why a state should not be free to adopt whatever economic policy it deemed necessary to promote the public welfare—including price-fixing—if the legislature thought such a regulation appropriate. Four justices dissented, subscribing to

---

[11] *Munn v. Illinois*, 94 U.S. 113 (1877).

[12] Subsequently the Court did retreat from this extreme position with respect to hours legislation. It later upheld an Oregon statute regulating hours of labor for women, and then a general hours law for men and women. *Muller v. Oregon*, 208 U.S. 412 (1908); *Bunting v. Oregon*, 243 U.S. 426 (1917).

[13] *Adkins v. Children's Hospital*, 261 U.S. 525 (1923).

the dire warning of Justice James C. McReynolds that to adopt the majority view was "but to declare the rights guaranteed by the Constitution exist only so long as supposed public interest does not require their extinction."[14]

As constitutional law now stands, the protection of liberty and property under the due process clause of the Fifth and Fourteenth Amendments does not forbid reasonable regulation of the economic system. In *West Coast Hotel Co.* v. *Parrish* (1937), Chief Justice Hughes specifically overruled the *Adkins Case* and sustained a minimum-wage law passed by Washington. In *Olsen* v. *Nebraska* (1941), Justice Douglas reversed another earlier decision by upholding the regulation of rates charged by employment agencies.[15]

This shift in judicial interpretation does not mean that business no longer has any constitutional protection against unreasonable, capricious, or confiscatory action on the part of government. Rather, it means that business can no longer claim complete immunity against the government's exercise of police power in the public interest, and that the judges are more inclined to examine the empirical evidence rather than deciding a case on economic myths.

"Commerce among the States"

In 1787, the Constitutional Convention had to make some momentous decisions. Given the contemporary social and economic context—a vast territory sparsely populated, an economy predominantly agricultural, and a people with as yet very little sense of national identity—the Philadelphia Convention could hardly justify a strong unitary national state. On the other hand, an aggressive business community, bent on developing a national economy, was frustrated by legislative policies in the states—steep taxes to pay off revolutionary debts, paper currency and inflation, statutory relief for debtors even to the point of liquidating debts, and tariff barriers at state boundary lines. The farmers were active in state and local politics, but the national leadership came almost wholly from the business community. Hence the Convention, appraising the alternatives, chose the ambiguous pattern of federalism which would permit the development of a strong national government and at the same time recognize the continued existence of the states as political entities.

The identification of the business interest with the national interest and vice versa—was most evident in the early days of the Republic. President Washington's selection of Alexander Hamilton as Secretary of the Treasury set the tone of the first administration and established policy bases which persist to this day. Hamilton proposed that the new national government assume all the public debts, national and state, at face value. By this refunding of all public debts, he established the credit of the United States and at the same time gained the support of its creditors. All those who hold government securities—and there are proportionately many more today than in the 1790s—have a vested interest in the national government. Hamilton proposed the establishment of a national bank as well as a national mint so that the national government could control the currency and regulate the fiscal policies of the country. Despite mounting opposition from the anti-Federalists, the Hamil-

[14]*Nebbia* v. *New York*, 291 U.S. 502 (1934).
[15]*Olsen* v. *Nebraska*, 313 U.S. 236 (1941); *West Coast Hotel Co.* v. *Parrish*, 300 U.S. 379 (1937).

tonian system became national policy, enacted by the Congress and implemented by the Washington administration.

The Jeffersonian Republicans, who opposed the Hamiltonian system, represented a variety of interests—small farmers, frontiersmen, some town laborers, and mechanics—the rank and file of citizens. Since most of them distrusted a government designed to build a national economy, in which they saw no direct benefits for themselves, they attached the principle of states' rights to a policy of minimum government. The victory of the Jeffersonian Republicans in the election of 1800 was a popular revolution, but the checks and balances in the constitutional system enabled the Federalists to retain a defensive position within the judiciary.

When an American political party loses control of Congress or of the presidency, it often looks to the courts to fight a rear guard action against major policy innovations by the incoming party. Since judges are appointed for life, the longer a party has been in power the more entrenched are its appointees in the judiciary. Thus, despite the overwhelming victory of the Jeffersonian Republicans over the Federalists in 1800, the federal judges who had won their appointments before the Republicans took over were able for many years to legitimate the doctrines of the defeated Federalists. Not until 1812 did the Jeffersonians obtain a dependable majority on the Supreme Court.

Chief Justice John Marshall's greatest decisions illustrate how a Federalist on the Court was able to advance his party's ideas—to strengthen the national government and to protect the interests of private property.[16] In *Marbury* v. *Madison* (1803), he claimed for the judiciary the power to declare an act of Congress unconstitutional. In *Fletcher* v. *Peck* (1810), he gave a narrow and literal translation of the constitutional provision that prohibits any state law from "impairing the obligation of contracts." His Court refused to sanction an act passed by the Georgia legislature rescinding past grants of public land that had been obtained by private companies through corrupt practices. The Chief Justice, who had the highest esteem for private rights, declared that once such rights were vested they could not be violated, even by legislative action. In *McCulloch* v. *Maryland* (1819), Marshall developed the doctrine of implied powers under which the activities of the national government can be indefinitely expanded so long as congressional policies appear "convenient and useful" in carrying out the constitutional powers. And in *Gibbons* v. *Ogden* (1823), he gave a broad and expansive interpretation to the commerce clause; the case concerned conflicting national and state rights to regulate steamboat navigation on the Hudson River. In upholding the congressional regulations, Marshall rejected the proposition that national power over commerce must stop at state lines.

Marshall's successor, Roger Taney, born of southern landed aristocracy, did what he could to emphasize states' rights; because he was on the Court nearly thirty years (1836–64), he was fairly successful in his efforts. Taney countered

[16]*Marbury* v. *Madison*, 1 Cranch 137 (1803); *Fletcher* v. *Peck*, 6 Cranch 87 (1810); *McCulloch* v. *Maryland*, 4 Wheat. 316 (1819); *Gibbons* v. *Ogden*, 9 Wheat. 1 (1824).

Marshall's earlier opinions on national power by building up a positive concept of police power in the states. (Police power is construed as the inherent power of the state to protect the general welfare of its citizens.) Without denying the supremacy of the national government in the use of its delegated powers, Taney stressed the Tenth Amendment as a guarantee of states' rights. In contrast to Marshall, who assumed that Congress had exclusive power over commerce among the states, Taney believed that a state had the right to protect the health, safety, and convenience of its own citizens, even if this meant regulating interstate commerce. He would not declare a state statute unconstitutional unless it seriously conflicted with an act of Congress. But his most famous decision, the *Dred Scott Case* (1857), invalidated the Missouri Compromise on the grounds that Congress had no power to prohibit slavery in a territory because such a prohibition amounted to taking "property" without due process of law.[17]

Congress in fact made little use of its power to regulate commerce among the states until near the end of the nineteenth century. For the most part, litigation under the commerce power was initiated by businessmen who appealed to the principle of national power over commerce in order to resist state regulations. So long as Congress remained silent and did not try to use its power affirmatively, free enterprise could flourish. Eventually the strategy backfired, however. Midwestern farmers, outraged by railroad extortions ("all the traffic would bear"), organized politically as the National Grange to secure state regulation of railroad rates and services. Such legislation, as we have already mentioned, was upheld in *Munn* v. *Illinois* (1877) as a reasonable regulation of a business affected with a public interest.

In 1886, the Supreme Court struck down an Illinois statute forbidding unjust rate discriminations by railroads. It held that legislation which restricted interstate commerce went beyond the state's authority; only the Congress of the United Staes could regulate interstate commerce.[18] An aroused public demanded that Congress act immediately. At that time, Congress had a choice of several courses of action. Like the European countries, it could have embarked on a policy of governmental ownership and management, but, as we know, the American people have always opposed the idea of socialism. It could have continued private ownership and management with government intervention to insure free competition, but this recourse would not have been economical. Students of the problem argued that the country really needed a unified transportation system that could offer adequate service even to sparsely settled and widely scattered communities. But the practical solution as Congress viewed it then—and now—was to leave the railroads under private ownership and management and to place them under national regulations which would protect the public against unreasonable rates. Thus the Act of 1887 created a national regulatory commission, the Interstate Commerce Commission, and established as national policy that railroad rates must be reasonable and just, and discrimination between places, persons, or commodities prohibited. In 1966, Congress finally established a cabinet-rank Department of Transportation to coordinate national transportation policies, func-

---

[17]*Dred Scott* v. *Sandford*, 19 How. 393 (1857).
[18]*Wabash, St. Louis and Pacific Ry.* v. *Illinois*, 118 U.S. 557 (1886).

tions and operations; but the new department does not replace the independent regulatory commissions, either the Interstate Commerce Commission or the Civil Aeronautics Board, and the Maritime Commission is left in the Commerce Department.

Congress has always shown special concern for the development of national transportation. The very first Congress in 1789 provided various benefits for shipping concerns, and the American merchant marine is still heavily subsidized by the national government. The improvement of rivers and harbors and the construction of roads have been major activities of the national government. Both the national government and the states provided substantial subsidies for the construction of railroads in the nineteenth century and for the development of commercial aviation in the twentieth century. Partly because of its importance for national military strength, transportation has received more direct federal aid than any other industry. Nevertheless, the industry has taken countless cases to the courts, claiming the rights of "free enterprise." Over the years the judges have gradually sanctioned the national power to regulate the rates and services of railroads, bus lines, and airlines, not only in interstate commerce but also in related intrastate commerce.

A second landmark in the extension of positive national power over commerce among the states was the passing of the Sherman Anti-Trust Act in 1890. By the end of the nineteenth century, giant industrial corporations and great financial holding companies threatened to dominate the entire economy. Huge combinations in restraint of trade were driving small businesses to bankruptcy in every community. In the 1880s, the same political forces that had secured the Granger legislation against the railroads—farmers, workers, and consumers—also sought legislation against the corporate monopolies. Obviously, however, a single state, or several states acting independently, could not begin to control the multimillion-dollar combinations that were turning into industrial and financial empires. Thus Congress was forced to take action on a national basis.

The Sherman Act declared unlawful "every contract, combination in the form of trust or otherwise, or conspiracy in restraint of trade or commerce among the several states, or with foreign nations." Congress could only declare the public policy, however; to put the policy into operation required supporting action from the other branches of the government. Judicial interpretations almost immediately nullified the original intent of Congress. As early as 1895, in the *E. C. Knight Case*, the Supreme Court held that the Sherman Act was not meant to regulate monopoly in manufacturing since manufacturing is not part of interstate commerce.[19] Pursuing this construction, the Court decided that a corporate combination with a monopoly on the manufacture of 90 per cent of the sugar refined in the United States could not be prosecuted under the Sherman Act.

Whatever Congress had expected to accomplish by the Sherman Act, the

[19] *U.S. v. E. C. Knight Co.*, 156 U.S. 1 (1895).

executive and judicial branches offered little support. Although the Supreme Court ruled almost immediately that the Act could not apply to manufacturing, it was quite willing to entertain suits brought by the Justice Department against labor organizations attempting to boycott manufacturing companies. Not until 1914, and then only after considerable pressure from organized labor, did Congress specifically exempt labor unions (and also agricultural and horticultural organizations) from the provisions of the antitrust legislation.[20]

Acting on the traditional assumption that the maintenance of free and fair competitive enterprise is "the keystone of the American economic system," Congress in 1914 established the Federal Trade Commission. It charged this independent regulatory agency with promotion of free and fair competition in interstate commerce and with prevention of price-fixing agreements, boycotts, and combinations in restraint of trade. Subsequent legislation has given the agency major responsibility for safeguarding the public against too free enterprise by regulating the dissemination of false or deceptive advertisements of food, drugs, cosmetics, and therapeutic devices. The agency relies principally upon the voluntary and cooperative compliance of business; it has no power of its own to punish those who violate its rules or orders but must rely on the courts for implementation of its policies. Over the years it has grown accustomed to frequent judicial reversals of its decisions.

The corporation, with multiple ownership, is the most characteristic organization for doing business in the United States today. There are more than a half-million corporations in the country, but the most important fact to note is the relatively small number of huge corporations which actually dominate the nation's economy. In 1965, the five hundred largest industrial corporations in the United States listed their total assets at better than $252 billion, their net profits as more than $20 billion, and the number of their employees as more than 11 million. Sixty industrial firms had sales of over a billion dollars.[21] (See Table 15–1.) John Galbraith points out that the gross income of the three largest industrial corporations in 1965—General Motors, Standard Oil of New Jersey, and Ford (see Table 15–2.)—together approximated the aggregate income of 90 per cent of all American farmers; it exceeded the income of any single state in the union (fifty times that of Nevada, eight times that of New York); and was about one-fifth of the total income of the American national government.[22]

The ownership of shares by millions of persons in these great corpora-

---

[20]"Judge-made" law continued to alter congressional output with respect to restraint of trade. The Court held that Congress did not intend to make *every* combination in restraint of trade unlawful (as the law plainly stated) but only *unreasonable* combinations. In the long-drawn-out case of *U.S.* v. *United States Steel Corporation* (251 U.S. 417 [1920]), the Court decided that mere size was not a criterion of unreasonable restraint. It found that the U.S. Steel Corporation was not an unreasonable restraint, that the U.S. Steel Corporation was not an unreasonable combination, even though it had the largest capitalization of any single corporation in the country, over a billion dollars, and was the leading producer (though not the only one) in its field.

[21]The *Fortune* magazine *Directories, 1954–65*, are reprinted by the Subcommittee on Anti-trust and Monopoly of the U.S. Senate Committee on the Judiciary, Part 5A, Concentration and Divisional Reporting, (Washington, D.C.: U. S. Government Printing Office, 1967). They provide detailed data on the assets, sales, income, and number of persons employed for the largest corporations in the American economy.

[22]John Kenneth Galbraith, *The New Industrial State* (Boston: Houghton Mifflin Company, 1967), p. 75.

Table 15-1   Corporate Finances, 1965

	TOTAL ASSETS	NET PROFITS	NO. OF EMPLOYEES
500 largest industrial firms	$252 billion	$20 billion	11,279,085
50 largest commercial banks	152 billion	10 billion	226,851
		(premiums and annuities income)	
50 largest insurance companies	136 billion	18 billion	350,735
50 largest transportation companies	36 billion	1 billion	856,044
50 largest utilities	84 billion	4 billion	1,180,214

Source: Fortune Directory for 1965.

Table 15-2   Corporate Finances, 1965

	ASSETS (IN THOUSANDS OF DOLLARS)	NUMBER OF EMPLOYEES
Ten largest industrial corporations		
1. General Motors	$12,586,170	734,594
2. Ford Motor	7,596,834	364,487
3. Standard Oil of New Jersey	13,073,437	148,000
4. General Electric	4,300,440	300,000
5. Chrysler Corporation	2,934,488	166,773
6. Socony Mobil Oil	5,212,380	80,660
7. U. S. Steel	5,451,740	208,838
8. Texaco	5,342,903	56,960
9. International Business Machines	3,744,918	172,445
10. Gulf Oil	5,210,833	55,200
Five largest commercial banks		
1. Bank of America (San Francisco)	16,358,951	27,051
2. Chase Manhattan Bank (New York)	15,117,859	15,646
3. First National City Bank (New York)	13,976,787	22,100
4. Manufacturers Hanover Trust Company (New York)	7,665,183	9,833
5. Chemical Bank, New York Trust Company (New York)	6,968,710	8,420
Five largest life insurance companies		
1. Metropolitan	22,485,524	55,909
2. Prudential	22,380,781	56,100
3. Equitable Life Assurance Society	12,223,632	18,955
4. New York Life	8,856,212	16,261
5. John Hancock Mutual	8,037,102	19,300
Five largest merchandising firms		
1. Sears Roebuck	4,909,325	280,000
2. Great A & P	835,795	132,000
3. Safeway Stores	576,703	69,248
4. Kroger	510,816	39,997
5. J. C. Penney	719,111	93,500
Five largest utilities		
1. American Telephone & Telegraph	32,819,689	195,294
2. Consolidated Edison	3,387,007	23,863
3. Pacific Gas & Electric	3,277,887	21,004
4. Southern California Edison	2,025,984	10,121
5. Commonwealth Edison	1,997,350	12,251

Source: Fortune Directory for 1965.

tions—the New York Stock Exchange calls it "people's capitalism"—is something quite different from the private enterprise of the individual entrepreneurs in the time of Tocqueville. Modern business is carried on by a complex organization of promoters, investment brokers, lawyers, bondholders, stockholders, advertisers, public relations men, management, and labor. It has become public business in which the owners assume no personal responsibility for the quality of the products, the fairness of the price, the conditions, of labor, or the soundness of securities. In the modern corporation, individual identity is subsumed in the organization man. The flamboyant tycoons and millionaire magnates in the early decades of this century were well-known public figures: Jay Gould, John D. Rockefeller, Henry Ford, Harvey Firestone, Andrew Carnegie, Andrew Mellon, and John Pierpont Morgan. You probably know by name your local tradesmen on Main Street or at the shopping center: the shoemaker, the watch repairman, the pizza vendor, and the dry cleaner. But who is the Chairman of the Board, or the President, or the First Vice-President of the national corporation from which you and your family buy insurance, a car, a television set, electric light bulbs, swimsuits, or bacon?

In 1950, Congress attempted to update its antitrust policy by bringing all types of corporate mergers under the prohibition of combinations in restraint of trade. Under the 1950 act, the Justice Department won its famous suit in court against DuPont de Nemours, which held 23 per cent of General Motors stock. As the judges finally viewed the facts in the long-drawn-out litigation, acquisition of the stock constituted a vertical merger of DuPont and General Motors in restraint of free competition, for DuPont was furnishing automotive finishes and fabrics for General Motors.[23] In a 1962 case, the Supreme Court held that the merger of the Brown Shoe Company (third largest shoe manufacturer) with G. R. Kinney & Co. (the country's largest independent shoe chain) was also a violation of the antimerger policy.[24] In 1964, in a case involving Continental Can, the judges observed that "where a merger is of such a size as to be inherently suspect, elaborate proof of market structure, market behavior, and probably anti-competitive effects may be dispensed with in view of [the congressional intent] to prevent undue concentration."[25]

In the 1960s, more vigorous prosecution of antitrust cases, along with an apparent change in judicial attitudes toward big business, brought about a sporadic trend of trust-busting.[26] Confronted with more output from its policy than anticipated, Congress was persuaded to take another look at the nature of economic concentration in modern America. In 1964, the Senate Subcommittee on Anti-trust and Monopoly launched a long-range inquiry into the corporate business of the country in order to determine whether traditional policies were still in line with current facts. In an election year, there were obvious partisan overtones, but the probe became more objective as it continued into the following years. The nation's top economists presented massive evidence and various expert opinions. Quite clearly, any ideological predilections,

[23]*U.S. v. E.I. DuPont de Nemours & Co.*, 353 U.S. 586 (1957).
[24]*Brown Shoe Co. v. U.S.*, 370 U.S. 294 (1962).
[25]*U.S. v. Continental Can Co.*, 12 L. Ed. 2d 1953 (1964). (The second largest metal container company had acquired the third largest glass container company.)
[26]For a brief discussion of recent governmental regulation of competition and trade practices, see Lloyd D. Musolf, *Government and the Economy* (Chicago: Scott, Foresman, 1965).

legislative acts, or judicial decisions to the contrary, the hearings demonstrated that the big corporations of the United States are getting bigger every year, that mergers are a principal factor in their gigantic growth, and that the corporate giants are building up their diverse interests into fantastic "conglomerations."[27]

Perhaps one illustration will suffice to indicate the new corporate type that plays such a prominent role in the political economy. (It is sometimes difficult to disassociate economic and political activities, hence "political economy.") The General Dynamics Corporation, incorporated in 1952, has had a meteoric rise through mergers to become the world's biggest manufacturer of weaponry. It has been the prototype builder of most of the U.S. nuclear submarines, a leading factor in space vehicles, and in commercial and military aircraft, and top recipient of the Defense Department's research and development contracts. By merger in 1957, it became the largest producer of carbon dioxide in the United States; it ranks fourth in the sale of industrial and medical gasses; and it produces flavoring extracts for carbonated beverages. By merger it acquired a major interest in building materials and ready-mixed and prestressed concrete; by merger it added brick and tile operations; and by merger it acquired a shipyard in Quincy, Massachusetts, to supplement its shipbuilding activities.[28] In the *Fortune Directory* for 1965 it ranked thirty-third among the five hundred largest industrial corporations in America. Its total assets were listed as $670 million; its sales totaled more than a billion dollars; and it was employing approximately 85,000 employees. General Dynamics is only one of several hundred conglomerate industries that represent the new technocracy in the American economy. But as yet, Congress has not decided whether—or how—to tackle the control of what Galbraith calls the New Industrial State.

Labor's Share in National Economic Policy

So far, we have said little about the role of labor in determining the national economic policy. In fact, the labor movement in the United States was at first much less aggressive than its counterparts in other industrial countries. The Knights of Labor in the 1880s represented an attempt by American workingmen to organize in one large national union, something comparable to the farmers' organization of the National Grange. But the Knights soon became embroiled in a succession of violent strikes, culminating in the disastrous Haymarket Riot in Chicago. In

---

[27]The U.S. Department of Commerce offers a "simplified explanation of input and output factors promoting American economic growth" in *U.S. Economic Growth* (Washington, D.C.: U.S. Government Printing Office, 1966). But for hard-core data and many different expert interpretations, see *Economic Concentration*, Hearings before the Subcommittee on Anti-trust and Monopoly of the Senate Committee on the Judiciary (Washington, D.C.: U.S. Government Printing Office (1964), I; (1965), II; (1965), III; (1965), IV; (1967), V.

[28]The bits of information offered here are from a much more comprehensive account offered by Harrison Houghton from the Federal Trade Commission in his testimony before the Subcommittee, September 9, 1965. (Hearings, *op. cit.*, Part I, p. 155). For further illuminating data on the five leading conglomerate corporations and how they grew by mergers, read Houghton's testimony.

1886, the Knights had planned a May Day demonstration to promote the cause of the eight-hour working day. In the course of demonstrating, the Knights tangled with a group of foreign-born anarchists and, when the Chicago police tried to break up the melee, a number of people, including several policemen, lost their lives and many were wounded. Organized labor was blamed for the bloody incident and the discredited Knights lost most of their membership almost overnight.

The American Federation of Labor (AFL), much less radical than the Knights, appeared next on the scene. Appealing to trade unions whose members were mostly skilled workers, the AFL worked for such general goals as the eight-hour working day, the six-day work week, decent wages, sickness and unemployment benefits, and restrictions on child labor. Not the least interested in forming a separate political party, the AFL supported candidates and platforms of any party that promised to promote labor interests. Though not inclined to violence, the AFL was prepared for direct action, to strike or boycott to gain its objectives. Under the leadership of Samuel Gompers, AFL membership increased from about 150,000 in 1886 to nearly 2 million at the outbreak of World War I.

Organized labor even in the 1930s was mainly concerned with better working conditions and higher wages for workers, especially skilled craftsmen. In the mid-1930s, John L. Lewis, head of the United Mine Workers, formed a Committee for Industrial Organizations, which undertook to unionize mass-production industries on a vertical basis, thus bringing into the labor movement hitherto unorganized, unskilled workers. The AFL fought the CIO for a number of years, but the CIO succeeded in building powerful unions in the steel, automobile, rubber, maritime, coal, electrical, and other industries. In 1938, the CIO became a permanent organization, the Congress of Industrial Organizations. In the 1940s, the CIO, through its Political Action Committee, became active in politics, getting out the mass vote and promoting candidates and policies favorable to labor. In 1948, the AFL also set up a political committee, the Educational and Political League (EPL); both the AFL and the CIO campaigned vigorously for President Truman's re-election. By the 1950s, the American labor movement was ready to accommodate both the horizontal crafts organization (AFL) and the vertical industry organization (CIO); the merger was officially accomplished as the AFL-CIO in 1956.

On the whole, American labor has had no quarrel with capitalism, nothing approaching the Marxist notions of the class struggle that motivated many labor movements in Europe. Even so, the reactions of American business were extremely hostile to labor union activities. As the labor unions learned to play the game of politics more effectively, they began to get what they wanted out of government. To offset the growing influence of labor among elected officials, businessmen counted on the judges, especially those appointed for life, to resist the pressure of "socialism" and "anarchism."

In 1914, under pressure from labor interest groups, Congress restricted judicial injunctions in labor disputes (Clayton Act) but not until 1932 (Norris-LaGuardia Act) did "the public policy of the United States" recognize the workers' need to organize and to bargain through their own representatives on the terms and conditions of their employment.

Although the national government had no positive labor policies until the mid-1930s, in many instances federal judges were able to govern labor relations by use of injunctions. If labor called a strike, the employer could seek an injunction ordering the strikers to cease and desist their interference with private business or their trespass on private property. To get the case into a federal court, it was not necessary to prove that the business in question was part of commerce among the states; if the parties to the suit came from different states, the federal judge could take jurisdiction under diversity of citizenship.

Before World War I, the opponents of labor unionism used all kinds of tactics, legal, extralegal, and illegal, to resist the organization of workers. A favorite device was the "yellow dog contract," which required a job applicant to abandon his labor union membership as a condition of hiring and made return to labor union membership a basis for firing. Prompted by labor lobbyists, especially by the brotherhoods of railroad workers, Congress (1898) made it a criminal offense against the United States for a railroad carrier in interstate commerce to discharge an employee simply because of his membership in a labor organization. A decade later, the Court held the provision to be an unconstitutional invasion of personal liberty as well as of the right of property guaranteed by the Fifth Amendment. Mr. Justice Harlan, who delivered the opinion of the Court (1908), professed that the employer has a legal right to discharge an employee, and an employee has an equal right to quit his job, "and any legislation that disturbs that equality is an arbitrary interference with the liberty of contract which no government can legally justify in a free land." As to whether Congress could prohibit yellow dog contracts under the commerce power, Justice Harlan asked, "but what possible legal or logical connection is there between an employee's membership in a labor organization and the carrying on of interstate commerce?"[29]

For more than three decades following the turn of the twentieth century, the Supreme Court construed the commerce power narrowly to keep national regulations at a minimum. Despite Justice Holmes' protest that the Constitution does not embody a particular economic theory, the Court managed to inject Adam Smith's concept of the free market into the supreme law of the land. Thus, in 1918, the Court held that, since manufacturing is not part of interstate commerce, Congress may not forbid interstate commerce in goods manufactured by child labor. And, in 1923, the Court invalidated a minimum wage act for women in the District of Columbia after finding that such legislation interfered with freedom of contract implied by the due process clause of the Fifth Amendment.[30] Meantime, the Court went even further in limiting the powers of the states over the business community. Citing the due process clause of the Fourteenth Amendment, in case after case, the Court prevented the states from restricting working hours, setting minimum wages for women, forbidding mining operations that endangered dwelling places, regulating

[29] *U.S.* v. *Adair,* 208 U.S. 172 (1908).
[30] *Hammer* v. *Dagenhart,* 247 U.S. 251 (1918); *Adkins* v. *Children's Hospital,* 261 U.S. 525 (1923).

fees charged by private employment agents, and fixing the prices of gasoline to prevent cut-throat competition.

The crash of the New York stock market in 1929, which signaled the beginning of the Great Depression of the 1930s, brought about a revolution in the relations between government and business in the United States. Between 1929 and 1932, the national income was cut approximately in half; the big factories cut down production and slashed their payrolls; mines were closed or worked only part-time; stores closed for lack of customers with cash; thousands of banks failed or suspended operations; millions of savings accounts were wiped out; nearly a hundred thousand business firms folded within three years; over 15 million persons became unemployed; millions of home and farm mortgages were foreclosed because people out of work could not keep up payments; people to whom normalcy meant prosperity stood in breadlines and many who couldn't stand the change in material circumstances committed suicide. Economists are still arguing among themselves just what happened to the American economic system and why. But at the time, most Americans were more concerned with their immediate condition, and seemed to think that the government ought to do something to meet the distressing situation.

When Franklin D. Roosevelt was inaugurated as President of the United States on March 4, 1933, the people were ready for a New Deal. The incoming President told the nation that he would ask the Congress for "broad executive power to wage a war against the emergency, as great as the power that would be given to use if we were in fact invaded by a foreign foe." His first action was to proclaim a bank holiday, call a special session of Congress—"The Congress of the Hundred Days"—and place the banks under national control. In a relatively short time, the New Deal constituted a kind of grand design for national recovery. It was not, however, so much a systematic national policy as it was a sequence of ad hoc reactions to pressing circumstances.

Although President Roosevelt had bipartisan support in both houses of Congress and overwhelming popular endorsement, the major policies of his first administration came to grief in the courts. Between 1934 and 1936, the Supreme Court invalidated the major acts of the New Deal. In 1935, the Court struck down the National Recovery Act, which was a package deal to establish codes of fair competition for every major industry in the country. For those industries which could not work out their own codes, the President was empowered to impose a "blanket" code prohibiting child labor, establishing maximum hours and minimum wage scales, and guaranteeing labor's right to organize and bargain collectively. By unanimous vote the Court held that such legislation exceeded the power of Congress to regulate commerce among the states and also violated the constitutional separation of powers by delegating legislative powers to the President.[31] In 1936, the Court nullified the Agricultural Adjustment Act, which proposed to regulate agricultural production as a way of raising farm prices and thus increasing farm incomes. Referring to "the accepted doctrine that the United States is a government of delegated powers," the Court decided (6–3) that the right to regulate agriculture was re-

[31] *Schechter Poultry Corp.* v. *U.S.*, 295 U.S. 495 (1935).

served to the states.[32] And a few months later, the Court (again 6-3) invalidated the Bituminous Coal Act; commerce among the states could no more apply to mining operations than it did to manufacturing.[33]

But the Constitution is more than what the judges say it is. It too reflects the social context and in the long run it stands for what the people think is necessary and proper for the general welfare. Two months after the Supreme Court nullified the NRA, Congress passed the National Labor Relations Act. The Act created a national regulatory agency, the National Labor Relations Board (NLRB), prohibited certain unfair labor practices, and reaffirmed labor's right to collective bargaining. Although the U.S. Chamber of Commerce, the National Association of Manufacturers, and similar interest groups were strongly opposed, organized labor, by then a potent force in national politics, more than counteracted the pressures from the business community.

Judges may be somewhat lagging in their responses to new demands and supports, but in the long run they too are sensitive to shifts in public opinion. All policy-making, including judicial decisions, is conditioned by the dominant interests in the community. In 1937, the Supreme Court upheld the National Labor Relations Act. As Chief Justice Hughes, speaking for the majority of the Court, explained it, the judiciary had finally opened its eyes to "the plainest facts of our national life."[34] In 1937, in the face of stormy controversy, especially from the South, Congress enacted the Fair Labor Standards Act, which fixed minimum wages and maximum hours for persons engaged in interstate commerce, including manufacturing. The Court also upheld this legislation in 1941, and in doing so flatly overruled its previous decisions.[35]

The interplay of pressure groups and official decision-makers within the contemporary context is reflected in the ups and downs of the labor movement. The NLRB was set up in 1935 as a result of organized labor's strategic position in the New Deal. For at least ten years, the Board showed a bias toward labor, just as the framers of the Act intended. Then, in 1947, a Republican Congress was elected with quite different views of the proper position of labor unions in the economy. During the war, labor had patriotically pursued a nostrike policy, but when the war was over a rash of major strikes outraged the public. Moreover, there was some suspicion that communists among the labor leaders might have deliberately stirred labor unrest as part of the tactics of the Cold War. Thus Congress passed the Taft-Hartley Act to purge the labor movement of communists[36] and to "reform" the mission of the NLRB.

---

[32]*U.S. v. Butler*, 297 U.S. 1 (1936). In this case, Justice Roberts refused to ascertain the scope of the phrase "general welfare" or to determine whether an appropriation in aid of agriculture falls within it. It is difficult for the layman to perceive how the Justice, simply by laying the AAA alongside the Constitution, could be so sure that aid to agriculture was not in keeping with the national power to tax for the general welfare but rather a violation of the Tenth Amendment.

[33]*Carter v. Carter Coal Co.*, 298 U.S. 238 (1936).

[34]*National Labor Relations Board v. Jones and Laughlin Steel Corporation*, 301 U.S. 1 (1937).

[35]*U.S. v. Darby Lumber Co.*, 312 U.S. 100 (1941). By 1941, a "Roosevelt Court" was in operation; seven of the nine justices had been appointed since 1937.

[36]The judges have since held this action unconstitutional. (*U.S. v. Brown*, 381 U.S. 437 [1965]). See Chapter 14, p. 566.

The 1937 Wagner Act had forbidden management to engage in unfair labor practices; the 1947 Taft-Hartley Act put a similar prohibition on the unions. Labor fought most bitterly against the inclusion of Section 14(b), which permitted states to outlaw union shops. Since twenty states have now banned union shops under the guise of "right to work" laws, labor claimed that the intent of 14(b) was to denationalize labor-management policies. Labor's charges were in part borne out when a politically reconstructed NLRB began, after 1947, to narrow its definition of interstate disputes and to return many labor-management disputes to the states for action.

Then, in 1959, Congress further curtailed union activities, ostensibly to protect the rank and file from abuses amounting to racketeering in some instances by labor leaders. The Labor-Management Reporting and Disclosure Act followed the highly publicized (televised) investigations of the Senate Select Committee headed by Senator John L. McClellan (D.-Ark.—his principal staff man was Robert Kennedy). The 1959 statute establishes a Bill of Rights of Members of Labor Organizations, which guarantees union members freedom to nominate their representatives, to vote in elections, to express their views in public, to petition their legislators, and to voice their individual opinions on dues, fees, and assessments.

Organized labor reached the peak of its power in national politics during the New Deal; since World War II, its influence has been perceptibly on the downgrade. This is reflected in a declining membership. The Taft-Hartley Act may be partially responsible, as labor claims; despite continuous pressure from the unions, backed by presidential requests from Truman to Johnson, Congress has made no move to change its policy. But, like the trade unions in western Europe, American labor unions have for the most part achieved their major political goals. They have gotten government support for social security, unemployment compensation, minimum wage guarantees, and virtually full employment. Most of labor's problems today—and there are many—are inherent in the organization and technology of our modern industrial system. These include outdated skills, automation, new products, new processes, and an increasing demand for white-collar rather than blue-collar workers. Congress, however, has only begun to raise questions regarding these problems; so far it has not formulated any policies that might alter the present system.

In the 1964 presidential election, the Democratic candidate supported most of labor's demands, including repeal of 14(b) of the Taft-Hartley Act. Labor in turn, endorsed Johnson and Humphrey. In 1965, President Johnson urged Congress to repeal 14(b); with top-heavy Democratic majorities in both houses he appeared to have a real chance to fulfill his campaign promises. But the conservative coalition defeated his proposals in both 1965 and 1966. The AFL-CIO leadership threatened to "take a new look at this entire question of our relationship with the political parties."[37] But President Johnson, expert in weighing political influence in national politics, made no specific promises to labor in his State of the Union Message in 1967.

---

[37]Political Memo from *COPE*, November 29, 1965. For an interesting treatment of labor's strategies over the years to get what it wants in national politics, see Robert Dahl, *Pluralist Democracy in the United States*, (Chicago: Rand McNally & Co., 1967), "Democracy and the Proletariat."

The General Welfare: Demands, Supports, and Apathy

In the preceding section, we scrutinized the changing social environment for clues to power shifts within the American political system. From an historical perspective, we observed how various economic interests have appealed to American ideology and constitutional principles to support quite different goals. We have also seen how the framework of federalism has been used over the years to accommodate quite different views of national power and states' rights with respect to interstate commerce. As we narrow our focus to policy-making in its contemporary context, we shall examine the inputs affecting specific issues to discover who wants what. For this purpose we have singled out national tax policies and national spending policies to see how public demands and supports are brought to bear on official decisions.

The National Tax Policy

The most revolutionary change in our national economy has proceeded from a broad construction of the fiscal powers granted by the Constitution to the federal government—"To lay and collect Taxes . . . to pay the Debts and provide for the common Defense and general Welfare [and] To Borrow Money on the Credit of the United States." From the first days of the Republic, Congress has used the taxing power not only to support the costs of government but also to carry out social and economic policies for the whole country. When Hamilton proposed a protective tariff in Washington's first administration, he was interested not only in raising revenue, but also in promoting and encouraging infant industries in the new nation.

Since Hamilton's day, Congress has used its taxing power to promote many other policies. Tax laws with policy objectives beyond the mere raising of revenue have included taxes on state bank notes, on colored oleomargarine, on dealers in such firearms as sawed-off shotguns and machine guns, on narcotics, on the "occupation" of gambling, and so on. Congress thus uses its tax power to carry out various policies that are not specifically included among its delegated powers. In doing so, it expands the meaning of the Constitution.

How far can Congress go in using taxes to enlarge its other powers? We have seen that the Constitution describes the taxing power in the most sweeping terms, authorizing Congress to tax "for the common defense and general welfare." But the Supreme Court in the 1920s and early 1930s imposed a "judge-made" limitation on the taxing power, holding that Congress could not use taxes to achieve purposes not included in its enumerated powers. It invalidated a tax on mines and mills that used child labor, a tax on coal operators who refused to accept the price-fixing and fair labor provisions of a New Deal code, and a tax on processors of agricultural products from which the proceeds were to be used for grants-in-aid to farmers cooperating in the agricultural program of the New Deal. In recent years, however, the Court seems to have returned to the Hamiltonian view that Congress has the broad power to tax for the "general welfare."

As a matter of fact, all taxes, even those exclusively intended to raise revenue, have other effects as well. Excise taxes on liquor, gasoline, tobacco, cosmetics, and other products, which bring in nearly 10 per cent of the federal revenue, raise the prices of these commodities. This effect on prices amounts to penalizing the consumers of these products, a penalty that is justified from various policy positions—that these products are nonessential, that they are injurious or perhaps even sinful, that excise taxes are "hidden" from citizens in the prices of products they purchase, and that, as an alternative to the income tax, excises decrease the burden on people with large incomes. No provision in the Constitution gives Congress direct power to penalize such things as fondness for "nonessentials," self-indulgence, or sin, but such penalties are very much a part of our constitutional practice.

The most regulatory tax of all—the one with the greatest policy implications and the greatest effect on the people—is, of course, the federal income tax. The Sixteenth Amendment authorizes federal taxes on "income from whatever source derived." The estimated revenues from income taxes make up about 80 per cent of the total federal receipts. The very fact that the income tax produces so much revenue makes it an effective governmental tool for redistributing the national wealth and for directing the nation's economic policy.

Changing tax laws bring into sharp focus the connection between policy and socio-economic divisions among the voters. Citizens have always had an intense interest in, not to say aversion for, taxes. In Biblical days, suppressed populations loathed the tax collector and his arbitrary ways; American colonists protested against "taxation without representation"; the small farmers of western Pennsylvania reacted to Hamilton's excise tax on whisky with the "Whisky Rebellion" of 1794; nor does the country ring with shouts of joy when Americans file their annual income tax returns today. No tax could ever be devised that all citizens would accept as fair and neutral; hence the government tends to follow the tax principle of "plucking the goose that squawks the least."

Until the twentieth century, the political power structure of the United States was such that the principal tax burden fell on those with low incomes. Duties on imports (tariffs) and domestic taxes on special commodities (excises) were the principal sources of revenue for the national government. Taxes of this sort have the same regressive effect as a sales tax: by raising the price paid by consumers for the items affected, they extract a greater percentage of income from the poor than from the rich. Ten dollars out of the weekly income of wealthy consumers may mean little or nothing; but it may be a big slice out of the income of others not so wealthy. This is the principle Jesus applied when he pointed out that the contribution of "two mites" by a poor widow was "more" than larger contributions from the wealthy.

When property qualifications for voting were removed, when public education was extended, and when workers and farmers began to organize, the tax base was shifted. In 1890, as a concession to the Populists—the most radical political force of the time—a 2 per cent tax was levied on incomes over $4,000 a year. But the sentiment of the people had not yet become the sentiment of the

Supreme Court. In an 1895 decision almost openly based on their attitude toward conflicting political forces, the justices corrected what they called "a century of error" in court interpretations of Congress' tax power and declared the income tax unconstitutional.[38] But the Court could not permanently substitute its own class biases for those of a newly restive majority of the voters. What had seemed a sudden outburst of class conflict to the Court had merely been the organization of new forces to give more effective expression to the views of people with lower socio-economic status. In 1913, the Sixteenth Amendment permitted the income tax to become the law of the land, and since then the geese with the most feathers have been regularly plucked.

When the Sixteenth Amendment was proposed, it was bitterly attacked in Congress and in the state legislatures as socialistic. Today, however, the idea of a progressive tax on personal and corporation income seems firmly written into the public policy. The rate of taxation goes up as income goes up; those with the highest incomes protest against "confiscatory" taxation; those with low incomes claim that the exemption base is unreasonably low. Notice that most arguments today focus on how to reform the tax structure rather than on the merits or demerits of the income tax *per se*.

One of the major goals of the Kennedy administration was to secure an equitable revision of the income tax law. Within a few months after his inauguration, President Kennedy directed the Treasury Department to prepare recommendations for a comphrehensive tax reform bill. The Treasury Department took twenty-one months to work out technical changes in the income tax system that would (1) broaden the tax base, (2) remove certain inequities and loopholes, and (3) permit tax reductions on both individual and corporate income. President Kennedy incorporated the Treasury recommendations in his tax message of January, 1963. The House Committee on Ways and Means and the Senate Committee on Finance held hearings and listened to hundreds of important witnesses, representing many different and influential groups in the economy.[39]

Obviously, all of the opinions expressed could not carry equal weight with Congress. The Chamber of Commerce of the United States, representing some 3400 local and state chambers of commerce and trade associations, argued that tax cuts were imperative but that reduction of federal expenditures was equally imperative. According to its spokesman, the Chamber opposed "the political arithmetic of rate making" and the popular philosophy of "tax and tax and spend and spend and elect and elect." Arguing that the present tax structure was one to encourage consumption and to discourage investment, the Chamber urged that immediate tax cuts be made in the top-income brackets to encourage "job making investments." On the other hand, the AFL-CIO, presenting its demands on behalf of 13 million industrial and trade

---

[38]*Pollock* v. *Farmers' Loan and Trust Co.*, 157 U.S. 429 (1895).

[39]The excerpts of testimony that follow on the Internal Revenue Act of 1963 are from the *Hearings* before the Senate Committee on Finance. 88th Congress, 1st Sess. (Washington, D.C.: U.S. Government Printing Office, 1962).

workers, favored immediate tax cuts for the low-income brackets but claimed that it would be disastrous to make such tax cuts conditional on reduction of federal expenditures. In fact, the AFL-CIO advocated greater government spending, especially for public works, as a means of relieving the unemployment situation. The AFL-CIO argued that low-income people would be sure to spend their tax savings, thus stimulating production and creating new jobs. It also insisted that the $600 basic deduction for dependents was unrealistically low, and suggested that, if the base were raised to $1000, the tax loss from this move could well be offset by closing the present loopholes with respect to mineral depletion allowances, dividend credits, and capital gains on transfer at death. Here, then, are two viewpoints, diametrically opposed, one from an organization of businessmen, the other from an organization of industrial workers. How to reconcile their divergent views in the public policy?

Those who appeared before the congressional committees represented a variety of interests: the Independent Petroleum Association of America (6000 independent oil and gas producers), pleaded with Congress to take no action regarding the special depletion allowance for oil and gas producers. The Association claimed that the oil and gas business was in such a state of decline, as to prices, employment, and business generally, that the atmosphere for capital investments in oil and gas production was already most unfavorable. Lest the industry appear too selfish, the Association spokesman pointed out how vital petroleum production is to the economic life of more than half the states and thousands of communities and also how important oil is in the national defense. The American Automobile Association testified on behalf of the millions of American motorists; its pitch was to include state gasoline taxes, car registration fees, and licenses as deductible items in the national income tax levy. The Association was indignant at the very idea that use of an automobile should be put in the same taxable category as consumption of alcoholic beverages; and it argued plausibly that, if the national income tax permitted deductions for furs, jewelry, and other items of luxury, then surely it could do no less for such a needed item as gasoline. A more modest request came from the National Federation of the Blind—an additional tax exemption for a taxpayer supporting a blind dependent.

The Farm Bureau Federation, representing 1.6 million farmers, told the Senate Finance Committee that any tax reductions not tied to reduced expenditures would be fiscally irresponsible. It stated unequivocally that it was opposed to any general tax reduction until the federal government was prepared to cut its expenditures. It was also opposed to raising the minimum standard deduction since this was bound to reduce the number of people who pay taxes and at the same time increase the number of voters who would feel free to demand and support additional programs to be paid for by others. On the other hand, the National Farmers Union, also representing farmers, offered complete support to President Kennedy's tax proposals. Believing that the basic cause of unemployment is underconsumption, it counted on tax cuts for the wage earners to increase their ability to purchase the goods and materials they produce. It was not in favor of allowing wealthy individuals to use farm losses to escape payments on off-farm income and it was opposed to the various loopholes which allowed great foundations to evade taxes.

The President of the National Association of Manufacturers pointed out that excessive income tax rates constitute a roadblock to the development of our entire national economy. He felt strongly that steeply graduated rates of income taxes contradict the principle of incentive which is vital in the free enterprise system of compensation. His Association urged tax cuts, especially in the middle- and upper-income brackets. It opposed high rates on corporate income as stifling capital formation and it specifically opposed repeal of the 4 per cent dividend credit, which exempts a portion of income from corporate dividends.

The Americans for Democratic Action decried the excessively heavy tax burdens borne by persons in the lowest income brackets, which lend a strong regressive bias to the national tax system as a whole. It also deplored the loopholes through which billions of dollars in income, mostly in the high-income brackets, evade taxation. It clearly expressed itself as opposed to any attempt to offset the loss of revenues from tax reduction by curtailing government expenditures. In support of this viewpoint, it called attention to the enormous unmet needs of the nation for increased public outlays for schools, public welfare, housing, urban redevelopment, water supply, mass transit, highways, and health and recreational facilities.

The American Bar Association, with a membership of 114 000 lawyers, many of them tax specialists, favored broadening the tax base, reducing income rates, simplifying technical provisions, simplifying administration, and easing the burden of compliance. Since it would take time to achieve these ends, the lawyers said it would be better not to tinker with piecemeal reforms. On the other hand, the Business Committee for Tax Reduction in 1963, whose membership included upwards to 2000 of the big names in big business, board members and officers of such firms as Ford Motors, Pennsylvania Railroad, American Telephone and Telegraph, the Chase Manhattan Bank, American Can Company, Commonwealth Edison, Westinghouse Electric, and others of similar magnitude, demanded across-the-board reductions on individual and corporate incomes. The Committee insisted that immediate tax cuts would not only stimulate consumer spending but also encourage business investment. Though it was opposed to deficit financing, it left it up to Congress to decide where and how federal expenditures could be cut; it was not willing to take a position on any particular items. If you were on one of these congressional committees, whose advice would you heed: the lawyers who counsel a wait-and-study period, or the businessmen who insist on immediate action?

In the next section of this chapter, we shall be looking at official decision-makers and their policy outputs. Who makes policy is always open to argument. In this text, we have taken the point of view that the unofficial agencies furnish important inputs in terms of demands and support, but policies are made by the official agencies. One bit of testimony before the Senate Committee on Finance relating to the 1963 Revenue Act suggests, however, the close interaction between the official and unofficial agencies. Following the presentation of the Business Committee for Tax Reduction in 1963, the senators' interrogation revealed that the idea for such a committee actually originated in the Treasury Department, which was sponsoring the proposed legislation. Five or six key businessmen had been invited to meet with Treasury officials to talk over the strategy of getting an omnibus tax bill through Congress in 1963. Subsequently, this small group divorced itself from the Treasury Department, organized on its own as a lobby to work on Congress, extended its membership, and sought and obtained financial contributions from hundreds of companies—insurance, utilities, distillers, automobile manufacturers, banks, department stores, iron and steel, coal and coke, oil, bus lines, air lines, shipbuilding—in short, a cross section of the nation's business. Was the Treasury Department indirectly engaged in lobbying?

The national political parties gather together a full range of issues and present them as platforms to the electorate. But because each party writes so many different planks into its platform, official policy-makers cannot always tell which issues are most influential in deciding the outcome of the national elections. Moreover, because congressional candidates frequently do not stand on the presidential platform of their party, and also because many citizens split their ballots, policy-makers are likely to be more responsive to the specific pleas of organized interest groups than to the confused and mulitple party lines.

The activities of lobbyists frequently go well beyond their special interests. As we have seen on the tax hearings, labor had much to say about business, and vice versa; farmers talked about business conditions and labor problems; consumer groups and veterans covered the whole range of legislation. The views of the large number of apathetic or uninformed citizens constitute effective inputs only as potential demands or supports that might be created by the feedback of policy outputs. Weighing all of these expressed and potential interests, Congress must discern the common interest and promote the general welfare.

National Expenditures

The constitutional power to tax—to pay the debts and provide for the common defense and general welfare—implies the power to spend the public monies for these ends. How official policy-makers decide to spend the public monies reaches to the very heart of politics—who gets what. In a democracy, all official policies are supposed to reflect the needs and goals as well as the opinions and votes of the citizens. But citizens have many conflicting viewpoints. Moreover, different political opinions and behavior are not randomly distributed through the population. These matters are still far from perfectly understood, but such variables as socio-economic status seem to have a weighty and persistent influence on the political preferences of voters. The perspective of a business executive gazing at the world through the tinted windshield of his chauffeur-driven limousine is likely to be quite different from that of an employee riding home on a bus or subway.

President Franklin D. Roosevelt's New Deal in the 1930s began as a great national effort to meet the exigencies of depression. Local charity and state activities had not been able to cope with the nationwide emergency. Most

Americans did not want outright relief; government handouts belied the American tradition of individual self-reliance. Work relief seemed a more respectable alternative to the dole. Hence the Roosevelt administration tried out various public works programs to put millions of unemployed people into useful jobs. No doubt there was some "boondoggling" or useless work in the hastily designed public works programs. But Arthur Schlesinger Jr., historian of the period, reminds us that the Public Works Administration put up the Triborough Bridge in New York, built a new sewage system for Chicago, a municipal auditorium for Kansas City, a water supply system for Denver; it rebuilt the Los Angeles schools after the earthquake of 1933 and constructed the bridges and highway between Key West and the Florida Mainland; it helped build the dams of the Tennessee Valley Authority, the Grand Coolee and Booneville Dams on the Columbia, Fort Peck Dam on the Upper Missouri, and Boulder Dam on the Colorado. Between 1933 and 1939 it spent about $6 billion dollars and in those few years it helped construct 70 per cent of the nation's new educational buildings, 65 per cent of the courthouses and city halls and sewage disposal plants, and 35 per cent of all the roads, bridges, and subways. As Schlesinger observes, all this must be counted a "prodigious accomplishment."[40]

Whether the PWA, and all the other alphabetical spending agencies of the New Deal, took us out of depression and up the road to recovery is still open to argument. To understand the New Deal, however, one must realize the full impact of nationwide social and economic distress; unprecedented conditions called for unprecedented government action. But in 1939, World War II totally changed the national as well as the international environment.

When the Republican Party returned to power after World War II, the Eisenhower administration carried forward its activities in a social and economic context vastly different from the early years of the New Deal. America was once more prosperous. American business had developed its technology and stretched its industrial capacity to win World War II and in doing so it entered into an entirely different relationship with the national government. The war effort had called for gigantic spending programs for military purposes as the government contracted with private enterprise to provide the weapons and materials for total war.

The Cold War and the Korean War which followed shortly after the end of World War II kept the government spending for national security at levels hitherto unimaginable in the American economy. Moreover, the three top industries of the country—modern weaponry, atomic energy, and space exploration—owed their very existence as well as spectacular development to government policies. The great spending programs of the government in the 1950s and 1960s were largely directed into these three industries. Government was in business in a big way but business was also in government in a big way. Again the magic nexus between government and business was in the

[40]Arthur M. Schlesinger, Jr., *The Coming of the New Deal* (Boston: Houghton Mifflin Company, 1959), p. 288.

form of profitable government contracts for private enterprise. As business prospered, the gross national product zoomed and American consumption patterns for family living were keyed to the economy of abundance. Science and technology in the service of government and business had made us the most "affluent society" in the modern world.

It came then as a sort of shock when the Johnson administration launched its "war on poverty" as a national policy. Some people, and not just Republicans, thought that the poverty issue was cooked up for the 1964 elections. It was hard to believe that poverty was, in fact, a widespread condition of living in the richest country in the world. But the millions of Americans who live in poverty are generally invisible to us who live fairly comfortably. Poverty exists off the beaten track, in the city slums where we seldom venture, in the mining towns off the main highways, in the backwoods country. Many of the very poor are old people, many are children, most of them are unemployable. As Michael Harrington points out in *The Other America*, these people at the bottom of our society rarely speak out for themselves—"The people of the other America do not, by far and large, belong to unions, to fraternal organizations, or to political parties. They are without lobbies of their own; they put forward no legislative program. As a group, they are atomized. They have no face; they have no program."[41]

Specific reactions to President Lyndon Johnson's plans for helping what Harrington calls "the other America" illuminate the nature of inputs affecting national spending policies. The specific demands and supports through which social interests are identified come from the decision-makers themselves no less than from groups outside the government structure. President Johnson first declared all-out war on poverty in his State of the Union message in 1964. In March 1964, the House Committee on Education and Labor began hearings on the Economic Opportunity Act, "a bill to mobilize the human and financial resources of the nation to combat poverty in the United States."[42] The administration plan, incorporated in the Act, was to test out a variety of programs in Appalachia, between the eastern Seaboard and the midwest Farm belt: basic education programs, community action programs, and special programs to combat poverty in rural areas. Adam Clayton Powell (D.-N.Y.), as Chairman of the Committee, introduced the Act as a first step toward helping "one fifth of our nation's population who have been left out of the flowing stream of prosperity." The Republican member from New Jersey countered, "We Republicans are unanimously of the opinion that it is unwise and a mistake to use an omnibus approach to this so-called war on poverty." Throughout the hearings, party lines were more evident than usual, because 1964 was an election year and both parties were alert to campaign issues.

The administration's initial presentation was by Sargent Shriver, Director of the Peace Corps and later head of the Poverty Corps when that agency was authorized. He told the Committee that in planning the proposed programs he

---

[41] Michael Harrington, *The Other America* (Baltimore: Penguin Books, 1963), p. 13. For further data on the extent of poverty, see Chapter 1.

[42] The excerpts of testimony that follow on the Economic Opportunity Act of 1964 are from the Hearings of the ad hoc subcommittee of the House Committee on Labor and Education, 88th Congress, 2nd Sess. (Washington, D.C.: U.S. Government Printing Office, 1964).

had consulted with many diffferent persons—college presidents and professors, prominent businessmen, representatives of foundations, labor leaders, state and local officials, and also with a task force from concerned agencies in the national government. Subsequently, every member of the President's Cabinet, except the Postmaster General and the Secretary of State, appeared before the Committee to explain how the proposed programs tied in with their particular areas of concern. Then began the parade of witnesses speaking for the pluralistic interests of America.

Labor leaders strongly supported the idea of a government war on poverty. The President of AFL-CIO took the opportunity to plug for extension of fair labor standards, claiming that more than a million Americans still earn less than fifty cents an hour. He also urged extension of national aid to primary and secondary education, national aid for area redevelopment, national aid for urban mass transit facilities, and national standards for unemployment compensation. The President of the United Auto Workers made the same pitch. Since Congress was then considering Medicare under Social Security, he added that item to labor's demands—"we are doing less to meet the medical care needs of our older citizens than any industrialized nation in the world on either side of the Iron Curtain."

Spokesmen for farm groups expressed different opinions. The National Grange favored the program, "the first time we have taken a broad look at the whole problem of American poverty." The National Farmers Union likewise gave all-out support. But the more conservative Farm Bureau was adamantly opposed to any additional national spending until the national budget could be balanced.

Strongest opposition to the antipoverty program came from the National Association of Manufacturers and the Chamber of Commerce of the United States. The Director of the Economic Research Department for the Chamber of Commerce questioned the statistical basis of the government's assessment of poverty in the country. "It goes without saying that our nation's level of living is the highest in the world." He pointed out that the federal government was already supporting more than forty programs related to the problems of poverty and the results were not impressive. He suggested that the President's concern with poverty was an election gimmick and that Congress should delay legislation until it could engage in "operational thinking." On specific questioning by Edith Green, the Democratic Representative from Oregon, the Chamber of Commerce spokesman expressed opposition not only to the Economic Opportunity Act but also to national spending for urban renewal, public housing, area redevelopment, mass transit, accelerated public works, hospital care for the aged under Social Security, public education, the Youth Employment Act, the Domestic Peace Corps, public power projects, TVA, the National Defense Education Act, and school construction. The Chamber favored tax cuts, fast tax writeoffs, subsidies to air lines, and the trade expansion act.

Republican members of the Committee frequently raised the issue of states' rights. And a number of witnesses objected to the national government bypassing the states to work directly with the local communities. Democratic members of the Committee argued that the problem of poverty had become too large for states and localities to solve without financial support from the national government. Governors from New Jersey, Kentucky, North Carolina, Indiana, and California appeared before the Committee to plead for the Act. Speaking for one of the largest and richest states, the Governor of California assured the Committee that his state not only needed help but was prepared to implement the national programs at once in its own battle against poverty. When a Republican member of the Committee intimated that the Act would allow "no role for the state government to play at all," the Governor replied that in his experience national agencies could be depended on to work cooperatively with state agencies. A succession of mayors —from New York City, Chicago, Detroit, St. Louis, and Syracuse—offered similar testimony, that their cities needed and wanted the kind of national assistance promised in the Economic Opportunity Act.

Drawing by Herblock;
© 1967 *Herblock in the Washington Post.*

"Can't you dig up a treaty or something to show that kind of commitment to us?"

How then do policy-makers arrive at reasonable decisions in the public interest when the input of political opinions is so strikingly divergent? That government must rest on consent of the governed is a fundamental principle of democracy, but how can our official representatives ascertain what all the people, or most of the people, really need or want?

Decision-Makers and Decisions: General Welfare and Common Defense

Thus far in this chapter we have focused on the cultural, social, and economic factors that condition the political environment within which our policy-makers determine what governmental actions are necessary and proper to promote the general welfare. We have observed especially the impact of science and technology on the economy and the consequent development of new inputs for the political system. We have looked at the changing demands and supports from the unofficial agencies in the policy process—political parties, pressure groups, opinion leaders—trying to influence the government to pursue this, or that, or still another kind of activity. Now we reach the authoritative decisions and the techniques of decision-makeup—the policy process itself. Here we attempt to identify the principal actors in the current policy process, not only the decision-makers within the constitutional and institutional setting but also the various "communities" of policy specialists. Finally, we take stock of the major policies which seem to be goal-oriented toward the general welfare, keeping in mind that such policies emerge as outputs from the entire political system.

All authoritative decision-making in American government takes place—or is supposed to—within the constitutional framework. In a democracy, it is assumed that every governmental activity may be rationalized, if not always justified, as directed toward the general welfare. Within this broad interpretation, every congressional statute, every executive order, every judicial decision relates to some aspect of the general welfare.

The Techniques of Decision-Making

Modern government uses a variety of techniques to control society and regulate the economy for the public welfare: by *subsidy*, by *regulation*, by *manipulation*. We have already touched on aspects of these in earlier chapters. In our discussion of cooperative and creative federalism, we noted the increasing use of grants-in-aid to raise levels of living in all the states and in the diverse local communities to something approaching a national standard. National price supports for basic agricultural commodities have been used by Congress since the 1920s to stabilize the purchasing power of farmers. Tax credits to the states willing to set up unemployment insurance programs were a similar subsidy technique which Congress found effective during the Depression to promote a new national policy.

The regulatory techniques of the national government cover a wide range of activities. We have in this chapter outlined the efforts, first in the states and then in the national government, to regulate rates and services of railroads and other public utilities. We have also observed the determination of Congress to preserve the myth of free enterprise through antitrust legislation, and to prevent unfair trade practices and unfair labor practices by establishing the Federal Trade Commission and the National Labor Relations Board. When the justices of the Supreme Court order the dissolution of a combination in restraint of trade, when the FTC issues a cease-and-desist order against price discrimination, when the NLRB orders an employer to reinstate an employee fired for union activities—all of these are regulatory techniques. When Congress levies excise taxes on playing cards and alcoholic beverages higher than it puts on checker boards or carbonated beverages, it is really trying more to regulate social behavior than to raise revenue.

When the government manipulates rewards and deprivations to favor one group at the expense of another, this too is a control technique. Our national tax policies are prime examples of governmental manipulation: inheritance and income taxes generally favor lower income groups at the expense of higher income groups, but loopholes in the tax fabric favor some special interests more than others—Texas oilmen, for example. The Federal Reserve Board and the Securities and Exchange Commission manipulate the financial structure of the country with many discretionary rules and regulations to safeguard the public. Congress manipulates social behavior even in the local communities when it prohibits racial discrimination in public accommodations. Social Security legislation and the whole gamut of measures to bring about the "Great Society" are obviously manipulatory techniques with far-reaching social consequences.

The kind of techniques which the government chooses to use in specific cases depends on many variables: external and internal pressures, quantitative and qualitative assessment of demands, supports, or apathy; whether many people are involved, a prestigeful or a despised minority group, or some nonconformist individual; whether the policy can be readily effected through voluntary compliance or will require coercion even to the point of sending in troops; whether the policy has bipartisan support or is likely to stir interparty rivalry or intraparty factionalism; whether the policy applies equally in all parts of the country or is aimed against a particular section (as was desegregation); whether programs to implement the policy call for one-shot or continuing appropriations, whether they will necessitate increased taxes.

The great diversity of public policies and the wide range of regulatory techniques generally discourage the political scientist from studying the politics of the policy process except through case studies. As Randall Ripley, who has recently edited a lively collection of case studies, observes, the techniques of government regulation can be studied by "looking at the related political process at any one (or combination) of a number of points . . . through the filter of congressional politics, electoral politics, group politics, bureaucratic politics, and the politics of federalism."[43]

The conventional approach of the textbook in American government to discussing governmental policies is to set up a number of "areas" and then to summarize the laws that fall into each—business, agriculture, labor, social welfare, finance, and foreign relations, for example. For this approach, the current *United States Government Organization Manual* is a convenient source. It indicates the constitutional and statutory authority of each agency, sketches the organization, outlines the official responsibilities and duties of each operating unit, and lists the principal officers. Its appendix includes a set of "organization charts" which point up the bureaucratic hierarchy in each major agency.

If we put policy-making in the context of politics, however, the summary descriptions and neat charts in the organization manual will not tell us who really made specific decisions or why one program got a green light and another got a stop signal, or why one technique rather than another was employed. Moreover, in the actual policy process, the official hierarchy may

---

[43]Randall B. Ripley, (ed.), *Public Policies and their Politics* (New York: W. W. Norton & Co., Inc., 1966). This chapter borrows from the editor's introduction, which offers "a brief catalog of techniques."

not be so important as an ad hoc "community of policy-makers." Membership in the community of policy-makers varies considerably according to the content of the policies under consideration. The community of policy-makers is a flexible concept, which in effect may disregard the constitutional designs for federalism or separation of powers or the institutional setting prescribed by statutes. Personal considerations may become more significant than positions and bureaucratic channels.

Social Security

Instead of cataloging all policy areas, we have singled out only two national policies to discuss within their institutional setting: Social Security legislation and the War on Poverty. How Social Security was established as a national policy is a long story that dates back to the beginning of the New Deal. The Democratic Platform of 1932 had declared, "We advocate unemployment and old age insurance under state laws." The official decision, however, provided for a much more complicated national system. The Social Security Act of 1935 was a three-in-one package, and a prime example of that "cooperative federalism" we discussed in Chapter 4. (1) It provided for a national system of social insurance against old age financed through national taxes and administered directly by the national government. (2) It provided for a nationwide plan of public assistance financed in part by matching grants-in-aid to the states, administered in state agencies under certain conditions specified by the national government. (3) It provided for a nationwide scheme of unemployment insurance, financed through national taxes with tax credits to the states, but administered under state plans approved by the national government. Congress has since made many changes in the original act that extend the coverage and liberalize the conditions under which benefits may be claimed. National administration of Social Security legislation has been reorganized in successive presidential administrations, but the whole Social Security system still operates in a pattern of working cooperation between the national government and the states.

Who made the initial decisions? The formulation of public policy always involves a variety of official actors. In this case, the principal actor was President Roosevelt, who was personally committed to the idea of public insurance.[44] We do not, however, attribute the specific programs to the President; a number of different bills had been proposed in Congress in 1933 and 1934 dealing with unemployment compensation, old age pensions, and assistance to the needy aged. The President asked Congress (June, 1934) to delay action on piecemeal legislation until his administration could work out (1) a truly federal program that would involve both the national government and the states; (2) a comprehensive measure that would be actuarially sound, financed by contributions rather than by any increase in general taxation. Meantime,

[44]The account of the New Deal period is borrowed largely from Schlesinger's *The Coming of the New Deal*.

the President appointed a Committee on Economic Security, headed by the Secretary of Labor, Miss Frances Perkins, to formulate an overall program.

The Committee on Economic Security comprised a group of "experts," drawn from the public (national and state) and private (labor and management) sectors of the economy, who represented a variety of views on how to set up, finance, and administer a social security system. Some advocated an exclusively national system; others preferred separate state systems; some urged financing by governmental contributions raised through general taxes; others thought that employers only should contribute since they could and presumably would shift payroll taxes to the consumer; others argued that employees ought to contribute so that they could more surely claim their benefits as earned rights. The President leaned toward the last view, not so much on the basis of economics, as on political grounds. Some time after the decision was made to finance old age insurance by joint contributions of workers and employers, the President explained privately, "We put those payroll contributions there so as to give the contributors a legal, moral, and political right to collect their pensions and their unemployment benefits. With those taxes in there, no damn politician can ever scrap my social security program."

Recently Governor of New York State, Franklin Roosevelt was inclined to favor a state system of administration; but as President of the United States, confronted with a nationwide depression, he recognized the need for national planning and national action. On January 17, 1935, he sent his message to Congress requesting national Social Security legislation. Senator Robert Wagner (D.-N.Y.) and Representatives David J. Lewis (D.-Md.) and Robert L. Doughton (D.-N.C.) introduced draft bills for the administration in the Senate and House respectively. Hearings began at once in the House Ways and Means Committee. A battery of witnesses from the administration, including members of the Committee on Economic Security and Henry Morgenthau, Secretary of the Treasury, discussed alternative programs and problems of financing and defended the compromise position of the administration. Interest groups, for and against, made their views known through committee hearings and with individual members of Congress. The business community generally viewed with alarm the ultimate outcome of such a socialist venture —"the result would be moral decay, financial bankruptcy, and the collapse of the republic." Many Republicans, first in committee sessions, then in floor debate, reflected the views of the business groups. Representative John Taber (R.-N.Y.) declaimed, "Never in the history of the world has any measure been brought in here so insidiously designed as to prevent business recovery, to enslave workers, and to prevent any possibility of the employers providing work for the people." But when the chips were down, and the people's representatives had assessed the weight of political opinions in their own constituencies, the House passed the bill 371–33 and the Senate, 76–6. Thus the principle of public insurance became a national policy as a result of many interactions, public and private, and with many persons officially and unofficially in the act.

Enactment of the Social Security Act and the establishment of the national agency was only the beginning. The initial decision—not to set up a unitary national system but rather to work through a federalized pattern—meant that actual implementation of the Social Security program was more or less left up to decision-makers in each state. It took some doing to get all the states into the system. When Congress passed the Social Security Act in 1935, only Wisconsin had an unemployment compensation plan. Most states did not support statewide welfare organizations, and less than half the states offered any kind of pensions or old age assistance and these plans applied only to the indigent. Although every state was persuaded to participate, the decision to participate had to be made within the constitutional and political framework of each state. To this day, our federalized Social Security system resembles a crazy quilt of varying state standards as to procedures, coverage, and benefits. And if we attempt to identify the principal actors in the policy process as well as in the institutional setting, we find a sort of interlocking directorate among the official decision-makers—national and state, executive and legislative, political and bureaucratic.

Even the judges got into the act through judicial review, and in so doing sanctioned the basic policy decisions. The constitutionality of cooperative federalism was thoroughly discussed by Justice Benjamin Cardozo in the case of *Steward Machine Co.* v. *Davis* (1937), involving the validity of the federal unemployment tax as applied to employers in Alabama.[45] The Court held that the tax did not involve national coercion of the states and did not invade powers reserved to the states under the Tenth Amendment nor violate any other restrictions implicit in American federalism. The Court agreed with the supporters of the Social Security Act "that its operation is not constraint, but the creation of a larger freedom, the states and the nation joining in a cooperative endeavor to avert a common evil." Congress passed the Social Security Act in a time of urgent national economic distress, and Justice Cardozo handed down his decision while the country was still emerging from a great economic depression. But the country has shown little inclination since then to repeal the congressional policy or to reverse the Court's opinion.

Old age, survivors, and disability insurance is financed through special taxes levied by Congress under its power to tax for the general welfare. All persons covered by the Act—nearly all workers, including self-employed persons, except doctors of medicine and federal government employees—pay their Social Security taxes to the Director of Internal Revenue. The Treasury Department maintains separate trust funds from which the benefits and administrative costs of the program are paid. The Social Security Administration in the Department of Health, Education and Welfare administers the program through some six-hundred district offices. For most Americans, this compulsory federal insurance constitutes the first line of defense against dependency in old age. The process of maintaining records of the lifetime earnings in more than 100 million active accounts is almost completely automated. Yet the main function of this vast and impersonal mechanism is to insure the economic independence of each individual to the end of his days.

[45]*Steward Machine Co.* v. *Davis*, 301 U.S. 548 (1937).

Social Security in the form of a basic retirement income is now an accepted national policy. Although many Republicans regarded the policy as socialistic in the early days of the New Deal, the return of the Republican Party to power in 1953 did not spell the end of social security. To the contrary, President Eisenhower's administration created the Department of Health, Education, and Welfare to administer the program, considerably extended coverage, and increased benefits under Social Security. By 1960, nearly 10 per cent of the population were over 65—thanks to improved sanitation and medical advances. Most of these old people depend on social security income to meet day-to-day living expenses; about 90 per cent of the population over 65 now claim social security benefits. (Figure 15-1 shows how benefit payments and number of beneficiaries have increased from 1950 to 1965.)

Public assistance was once the most urgent operation in the social security system. In the 1930s millions of Americans, most of them through no fault of their own, lacked the barest essentials of existence—food, clothing, and shelter. Local charity and state welfare programs could not begin to cope with all the hardship cases occasioned by the nationwide depression, but the Social

Figure 15-1

Source: *Annual Report 1966*, U.S. Department of Health, Education, and Welfare.

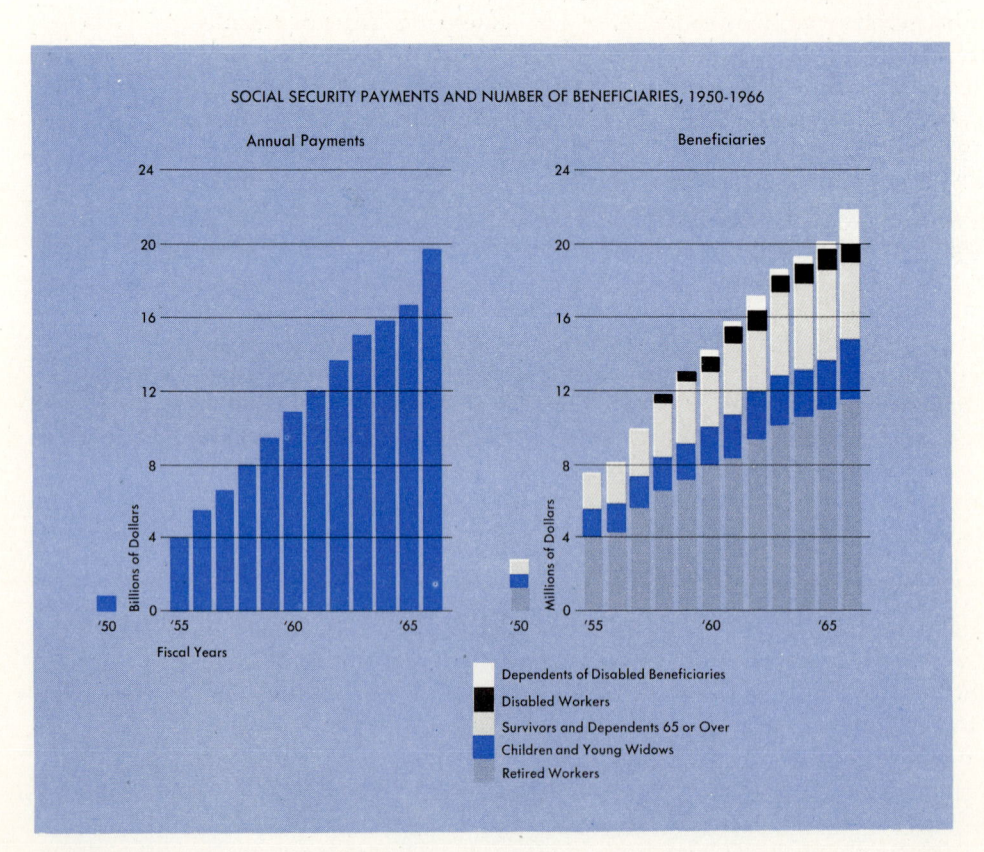

SOCIAL SECURITY PAYMENTS AND NUMBER OF BENEFICIARIES, 1950-1966

- Dependents of Disabled Beneficiaries
- Disabled Workers
- Survivors and Dependents 65 or Over
- Children and Young Widows
- Retired Workers

636

Drawing by O. Soglow;
© 1967 The New Yorker Magazine, Inc.

Security Act offered the advantages of cooperative federalism. Making full use of its power to tax the general welfare, Congress extended federal grants-in-aid for state programs of public assistance. The Act, many times amended since 1935, now provides for grants-in-aid to the states for five major categories of public assistance: aid for the needy aged, medical assistance for the needy aged, aid to the blind, aid to the totally and permanently disabled, and aid to needy families with dependent children. Minimum standards for such assistance programs are specified by the national government, although state programs reflect considerable difference in historical background, social custom, and degree of community concern. The Welfare Administration in the Department of Health, Education and Welfare is responsible for seeing to it that the state plans meet and maintain the basic federal prescription.

National expenditures for grants-in-aid to state public assistance programs are mounting every year. This fact is exploited by those who attribute the rising costs of government to socialism in Washington. Keep in mind, however, other statistical trends that help explain why expenditures for public assistance programs continue to increase even in these times of prosperity: the overall increase in population, the higher proportion of people over 65 in the population, the increased cost of living, higher costs of medical care, and higher charges for hospitalization. Actually, less than 5 per cent of the population receives any kind of public assistance. Since the depression years, emphasis in the social security system has shifted from giving relief to the dependent to building up earned rights to independence. Figure 15–2 (p. 638) graphically demonstrates the neglect of social welfare in the United States. Among the fourteen western democracies included in the figure, the United States ranks last in the amount of its Gross National Product devoted to social welfare measures.

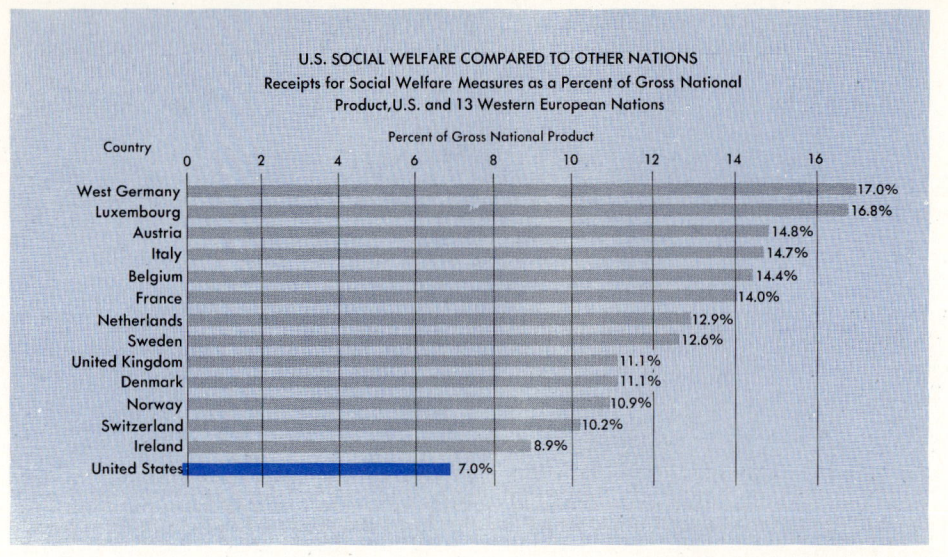

U.S. SOCIAL WELFARE COMPARED TO OTHER NATIONS
Receipts for Social Welfare Measures as a Percent of Gross National Product, U.S. and 13 Western European Nations

Country	Percent of Gross National Product
West Germany	17.0%
Luxembourg	16.8%
Austria	14.8%
Italy	14.7%
Belgium	14.4%
France	14.0%
Netherlands	12.9%
Sweden	12.6%
United Kingdom	11.1%
Denmark	11.1%
Norway	10.9%
Switzerland	10.2%
Ireland	8.9%
United States	7.0%

Source: *The Cost of Social Security 1958–60.* International Labor Organization (Geneva, Switzerland, 1964).

Figure 15-2

The Great Society and Its War on Poverty

The Great Society vision of the Johnson administration was disclosed to the American people in the President's now-famous speech at Ann Arbor, Michigan, in the spring of 1964:

The Great Society rests on abundance and liberty for all. It demands an end to poverty and racial injustice, to which we are totally committed in our time. But that is just the beginning.

The Great Society is a place where every child can find knowledge to enrich his mind and enlarge his talents. It is a place where leisure is a welcome chance to build and reflect, not a feared cause of boredom and restlessness.

It is a place where the city of man serves not only the needs of the body and the demands of commerce, but the desire for beauty and the hunger for community.

It is a place where man can renew contact with nature. It is a place which honors creation for its own sake and for what it adds to the understanding of the race. It is a place where men are more concerned with the quality of their goals than the quantity of their goods. But most of all, the Great Society is not a safe harbor, a resting place, a final objective, a finished work. It is a challenge constantly renewed, beckoning us toward a destiny where the meaning of our lives matches the marvelous products of our labor.

Although the speech was offered in a presidential election year, it was not just a campaign gimmick. Newly elected to the presidency in his own right, Lyndon B. Johnson officially provided the 89th Congress with his blueprint for legislative action to achieve "The Great Society." He promised that he would submit a number of special messages with detailed proposals for national action in specific areas. First in the promised series was the President's "Health Message," which called for medical aid for the aged as part of the national Social Security system.

Medicare had long been an issue in American politics, but not until the 1960s did it become a politically feasible policy. Senator John F. Kennedy led a floor fight for Medicare in the summer of 1960, and, on being defeated in the Senate, took the issue to the polls as the Democratic presidential candidate that year. Although Kennedy made Medicare an urgent policy recommendation of his administration, as President he was no more successful in persuading Congress to take action than he had been as Senator from Massachusetts. President Johnson made a heroic effort to get the Medicare program through the second session of the 88th Congress and almost succeeded. But at the very end of the session, the Medicare amendment to the Social Security program bogged down in a conference committee. Meantime an impatient Congress, eager to begin campaigning, left the issue wide open for the 1964 elections.

Medicare was not the most crucial issue in the presidential election but certainly it was one that swayed many votes—and the voters had a clear choice. Senator Goldwater (R.-Ariz.) had made a special flight from Phoenix to Washington in order to register a vigorous "No" when the Senate voted on Medicare. As Republican presidential candidate he continued his campaign against "socialism." (Toward the end of his campaign he was trying to explain rather frantically that he really was in favor of Social Security, if not Medicare.) He gained favor among those groups that had been pressuring Congress not to pass Medicare—the American Medical Association, the American Dental Association, and various business people who were opposed to any increases in governmental expenditures for welfare purposes. On the other hand, the groups that had been lobbying with Congress to support the Johnson administration on Medicare—the AFL-CIO, Americans for Democratic Action, the National Council of Senior Citizens, and others—urged the electorate to vote for the Democratic candidate who spoke firmly for increased Social Security benefits, including Medicare. The Democrats won, and, in July, 1965, President Johnson flew to Independence, Missouri, to affix his signature to a new Medicare Act in the presence of its original sponsor, former President Truman.

The extension of Social Security insurance to include Medicare for persons over 65 called for an intensive informational program. Practically all the media of mass communication were used to explain to the 19 million potentially eligible recipients how the program would operate. At the same time, administrative preparations to handle the program almost overwhelmed the bureaucrats in charge. Although the program was to be nationally implemented through the Department of Health, Education and Welfare, a great deal of "creative federalism" was involved. Arrangements had to be made with state health agencies to determine whether hospitals and nursing homes met quality standards for participation in Medicare, including the requirement of compliance with the 1964 Civil Rights Act. Finally, procedures had to be worked out for payment of doctors and nurses and for supplemental insurance with private companies such as Blue Cross.

In his 1967 State of the Union Message, President Johnson reported that three-and-one-half-million Americans had already received treatment under

Medicare. He next proposed extension of Medicare to disabled Americans of all ages. But Medicare for the elderly had already overtaxed the nation's medical facilities and, despite presidential requests, the 90th Congress was not persuaded to support a major drive for construction and modernization of modern hospitals throughout the nation.

The fight for Medicare for the aged was finally won, but the opposition forces to extension of Medicare were still in battle formation in 1967. The new President of the American Medical Association advised his fellow physicians that the many problems they face today "boil down to one issue, the single obligation to protect the American way of life [and] that way of life can be described in one word: capitalism." He warned the members of the AMA that they would have to face up to such challenges to their profession as "the concept of health care as a right rather than as a privilege."[46]

Following the official declaration of the War on Poverty, the national government launched some sixty "landmark" programs to achieve the Great Society: basic education legislation, new health programs, new conservation measures, demonstration and development programs for the cities, more assistance for consumers, the aged, and the needy. But despite all the speeches, all the new laws, and billions of dollars already spent to advance the programs, the American people were hardly stirred from apathy. A November, 1966 Gallup poll reported that only 32 per cent held a favorable opinion of the Great Society.

In March, 1967, President Johnson sent to Congress a special message on "America's Unfinished Business." Once again he mapped out a national strategy to combat rural as well as urban poverty. But criticism from the Right, deploring the rising costs of "socialist schemes" out of Washington, carping from the Left because the programs contained too many promises and too little action, a counterproposal from the Republicans which stressed more private initiative and less government intervention in an "opportunity crusade," racial overtones because a large proportion of antipoverty money has been going to Negroes, and the grim priorities of the war in Viet Nam—all of these factors, and probably others, made it unlikely that the 90th Congress would tackle the administration's "Unfinished Business." Not only was Congress reluctant to authorize new programs, but it also appeared determined to slash appropriations on programs which the previous Congress had authorized.

Chief target of congressional attack was the Office of Economic Opportunity (OEO), for which the President had requested over $2 billion, to be used principally for community action, training, and "Head Start" programs. In the midst of the big city riots in the summer of 1967, the House Committee on Education and Labor held hearings on the OEO request. Nearly all of the witnesses were asked the leading question, Should there be an OEO? Business leaders, labor leaders, health experts, social workers, conservationists, veterans, religious leaders, Negro leaders, city officials—representing the whole spectrum of organized interests in American society—almost unanimously answered in the affirmative, although many made specific suggestions for

[46]*Congressional Quarterly Weekly Report,* XXV (July 14, 1967), 1205. The AMA at its 1967 Convention also passed a resolution expressing opposition to the "race quota system" of HEW, referring to the efforts of the agency to force admission policies nondiscriminatory toward Negroes.

improvement of its administration. Representatives of the Urban League and the NAACP urged that Congress appropriate more, not less, for community action. Spokesmen for the bar associations testified that funds for the Legal Services Program should be tripled. The educators said, "Double Upward Bound."

The OEO was still fighting for its life late into the fall of 1967. Some Republicans were determined to scatter the administration's antipoverty functions among a half-dozen old-line agencies. Many congressmen were obviously in the mood to tighten controls over OEO programs. Representative Edith Green (D.-Oreg.) sponsored an amendment to give state and local government officials more authority over community action programs. OEO officials claimed that the "city hall controls" envisaged in the Green Amendment challenged the core concept of the poverty program—that the poor help themselves. Senator Jacob K. Javits (R.-N.Y.) charged that the Green Amendment would turn "a gifted idea" into "a new barrel of pork for patronage." The battle royal over authorization and appropriation of funds was prolonged way past the beginning of fiscal year 1967–68. Even the foreign assistance acts were finally passed ahead of the domestic antipoverty measures. But when the chips were down, few congressmen wanted to go on record as opposed to the War on Poverty; having vented their sharp criticisms against the conduct of the war, they wound up the altercation by adopting the Green Amendment and authorizing just under $2 billion for 1967–68 and just over $2 billion for 1968–69. Neither Democrats nor Republicans wanted to reopen the issue in the year of presidential elections; hence the OEO emerged with a two-year authorization and substantially the amounts originally requested for continuance of its programs. Appropriations for 1968, however, were substantially less than the authorized figure, $287 million less than the President had requested.

What did the Founding Fathers have in mind when they established a new republic with the avowed national purpose "to promote the general welfare?" Remember what the country was like in 1790: of its 4 million inhabitants, only 3 per cent of the population lived in towns of 8000 or more; 750,000 were Negro slaves. It is safe to say that the Founding Fathers did not worry about such problems as slum clearance, area redevelopment, mass transit, or public housing projects. Certainly, they were not then concerned with national public health programs or anything resembling Medicare. Public sanitation, as well as personal hygiene, were primitive, symbolized by the privy in the backyard. Medical science still endorsed such practices as cupping, bleeding, purging, and dosing with calomel, ipecac, opium, and mercury. Neither anaesthesia nor antisepsis existed. Obviously, President Washington had no thought of including a Secretary of Health, Education and Welfare—or for that matter a Secretary of Agriculture, or Commerce, or Labor, or Transportation—among the principal officers of his administration. In those days, paupers—the very young, the very old, the morons, the lunatics, and the totally disabled—were dumped in local jails or almshouses. But the most remarkable attribute of the American Constitution is its flexibility; it does not bind us to live as our forefathers had to live; succeeding generations of Americans have been—and will be—free to interpret "the general welfare" within the contemporary environment.

The New Industrial State and the Common Defense

No analysis of policies or policy-making in the national government is complete without some consideration of the overriding factors of "common defense." In the next chapter, we will turn our attention to foreign policy, and in doing so, we will examine the changing bases of our national security policies. But we cannot conclude this chapter without observing, at least briefly, the impact of war, space exploration, and defense policies on the political economy; and probably even more significant, the influence of industry in the formulation of these same policies. Figure 15–3, which depicts the magnitude of 1968 expenditures by function, demonstrates clearly the preponderance of national defense among the government's goals.

Figure 15-3

Source: *The Budget in Brief, Fiscal Year 1968* (Washington, D.C.: U. S. Government Printing Office, 1967), p. 19. The shaded areas in the chart marked "Trust Funds" refer to sources of funds other than appropriations, such as Social Security payroll taxes; the "−31" under "Education" is money owed the government—for example, from college housing loans. For a fuller explanation, see *The Budget in Brief*.

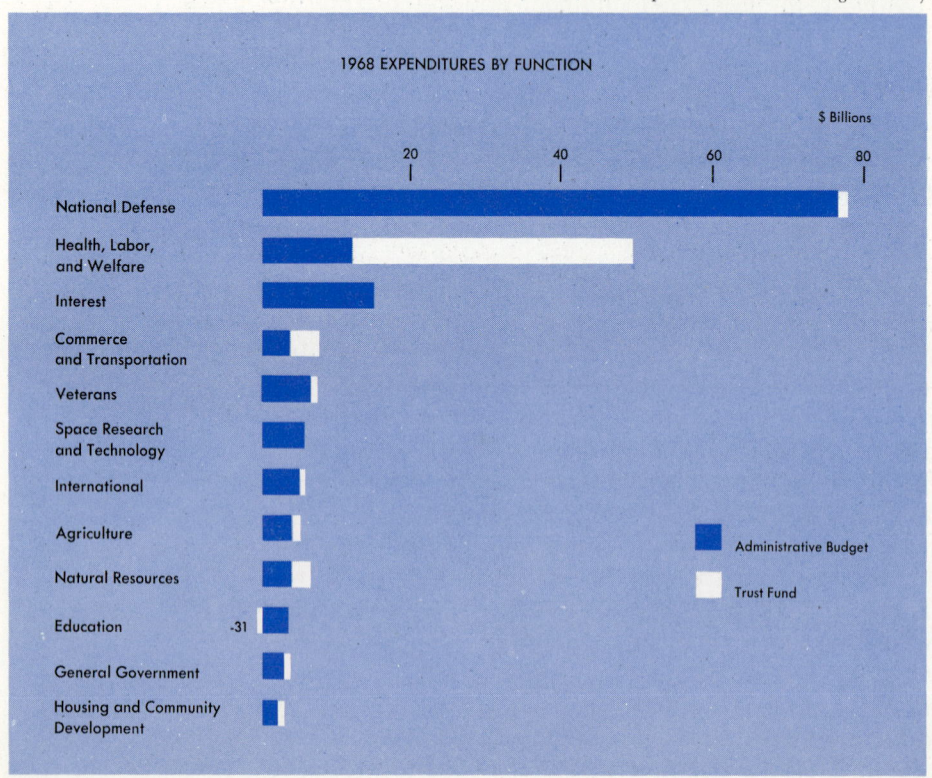

1968 EXPENDITURES BY FUNCTION

$ Billions

Function	
National Defense	
Health, Labor, and Welfare	
Interest	
Commerce and Transportation	
Veterans	
Space Research and Technology	
International	
Agriculture	
Natural Resources	
Education	−31
General Government	
Housing and Community Development	

■ Administrative Budget
□ Trust Fund

The United States was conceived as a "fighting organization," and nearly half of the powers of Congress enumerated in Article I, Section 8, relate directly to problems of common defense and the conduct of war. The Founding Fathers could have had no foreboding of modern warfare, with its techniques of mass extermination and total destruction. But they did give the national government all the powers necessary and proper to raise and support armies, to provide and maintain a navy, to call out the militia, to train the militia according to the discipline prescribed by Congress, to make rules for the regulation of land and naval forces, to declare war and make peace, to levy taxes for the common defense.

Congress has declared war five times—in 1812, 1848, 1898, 1917, and 1941; the President has twice recognized a "state of war"—in 1861 and 1950; and there have been numerous minor expeditions of American troops abroad. With muskets and rifles replaced by thermonuclear weapons and guided missiles, the concept of war has become increasingly total in scope.

The demands of war have inevitably led to the broadest interpretation of the Constitution. The Constitution, of course, gives no direction on how the government shall meet a civil war. When the southern states seceded from the Union in 1861, President Lincoln established a blockade against the southern ports; and the Court held in 1863 that as Commander-in-Chief the President had the power to determine what measures were necessary to suppress an insurrection.[47] Later on, as a "war measure," without any authorization from Congress, President Lincoln issued the Emancipation Proclamation freeing all slaves in the rebellious states. The Constitution gives Congress the power to coin "money," but in order to support the Union armies in the field Congress authorized the printing of "greenbacks," and made them legal tender in the payment of debts. In 1870, after the War was over, the Supreme Court declared that the greenback issue was unconstitutional; one year later, after President Grant had filled two vacancies on the Court, it reversed its decision and declared that the issue was constitutional.[48] Today we simply accept the practice of printing money as an implied power of Congress.

During World War I, the national government assumed unprecedented powers over the economy of the country. Congress authorized the President to regulate the importation, manufacture, storage, mining, or distribution of essential materials; to requisition foods, feeds, and fuels; to take over and operate factories, packinghouses, pipelines, mines, or other plants; to fix a minimum price for wheat; limit, regulate, or prohibit the use of food materials in the production of alcoholic beverages; to fix the price of coal and coke and to regulate their production, sale, and distribution. Other statutes gave him power to take over and operate the rail and water transportation system and the telephone and telegraph systems of the country. You will not find in the Constitution any such sweeping powers granted to Congress or to the Presi-

---

[47] *The Prize Cases*, 2 Black 635 (1863).
[48] *Hepburn v. Griswold*, 8 Wall. 603 (1870); *The Legal Tender Cases*, 12 Wall. 457 (1871).

dent. The explanation is simple, as Chief Justice Hughes put it: "The power to wage war is the power to wage war successfully."

Some of the acts passed by Congress during World War I were still on the books at the outbreak of World War II, and Congress enacted new ones to facilitate the defense effort. It set up rationing for consumers, control of industrial materials and production, and even empowered the President to seize plants where production was endangered by strikes. It also authorized price and rent controls. None of these provisions was ruled unconstitutional. Whatever economic theory the Court has used to interpret the Constitution in time of peace, in time of war it has generally upheld the plenary power of the Congress and President to mobilize and to command the total resources of the nation—not only to draft men for the armed forces but also to regulate the entire economy.

During World War II, Congress delegated such broad authority to President Roosevelt, not only over military matters but over the whole economy, that his powers under the Constitution approached those of *Il Duce* and *Der Führer* under dictatorship. On the other hand, during the Korean crisis in 1952, when President Truman ordered the Secretary of Commerce to take possession of the steel mills in order to avert a shutdown of the mills, the Court returned to the doctrine of "separation of powers." It held that, although the "theater of war" is an expanding concept, the Commander-in-Chief cannot, even in a military crisis, take possession of private property in order to keep labor-management disputes from stopping production.[49] Apparently, then, the Constitution can be interpreted not only to give tremendous war powers to the national government but also to put a limit on such war powers.

Since World War II, the United States has been determined to maintain a position of primacy among the military powers of the world. To the Eisenhower administration this meant the development of nuclear weapons with such delivery power that we could guarantee massive retaliation against any would-be aggressor threatening the United States or any of its allies. In the Kennedy administration, American national security policy shifted from a single strategy base to flexible response and called for a buildup of strike power along the whole military spectrum, from conventional weapons to the most sophisticated nuclear missiles. In his 1968 Budget Message, President Johnson declared it was necessary and prudent for the United States to maintain the "most modern, versatile and potent forces in the world."

The U.S. defense budgets of the 1960s give us awesome dollars and cents data on what it costs to promise the American people technological superiority in warfare. The President's budget may be regarded as an authoritative allocation of our national values, interests, and goals—subject of course to whatever alterations Congress chooses to make. In the past ten years (covering three presidential administrations), expenditures for national defense have risen from $43 billion in 1957 (actual) to over $70 billion (estimated) in 1967. In interpreting these figures, note that in this same decade the gross national product of the United States increased in almost the same ratio, from $431 billion in 1957 to $762 billion in 1967. Also note that national defense expend-

---

[49] *Youngstown Sheet and Tube Co.* v. *Sawyer*, 343 U.S. 579 (1952).

itures as a proportion of the administrative budget dropped from about 62 per cent in 1957 to about 55 per cent in 1967. But however one sets up the statistics, American taxpayers pay a high premium for the common defense (and for the defense of those countries to whom we have made "commitments").

President Eisenhower, in his televised farewell address to the American people, soberly warned of "the acquisition of unwarranted influences whether sought or unsought by the military-industrial complex." As he saw it, from his own experience, "the total influence—economic, political, even spiritual—is felt in every city, every statehouse, every office of the Federal Government." To put it more concretely, the Defense Department spends billions of dollars annually for services and the procurement of guns, missiles, airplanes, electronic devices, vehicles, tanks, ammunition, clothing, and other military goods. What to buy and how much to buy (aircraft carriers or strategic bombers, nuclear submarines or spaceships to the moon) involve military decisions; where to procure items and from whom to buy involve business arrangements, contracts with industrial corporations. The Defense Department has billions more to invest in real estate developments, for training camps, air bases, naval bases, arsenals, proving grounds. Where to locate them is a military decision that also concerns congressmen and their constituents, who are more likely to be interested in the local economic benefits resulting from a military establishment.

Providing for the common defense has become the nation's biggest business. Multimillion-dollar defense industries are almost wholly dependent on government contracts—and this in time of peace. Small business as well as big business vies for its share of military procurement. The Pentagon contracts with private firms for more than two million items a year, "from shoelaces to submarines." Adhering to the ideology of "free enterprise," the government calls on private contractors to design, develop, and produce the weapons systems that defend the free world—on a cost plus basis. But once a private firm enters what President Eisenhower called the "military-industrial complex," it is no longer engaged in much free enterprise. In order to insure uniform security practices within industrial plants, educational institutes, or other organizations working with classified materials, the Pentagon issues a bulky manual of detailed instructions and admonitions similar to those it issues to military installations. And these security regulations cover several million defense workers who are employed in private business under government military contracts.[50]

When the first "big bomb" was dropped on Hiroshima on August 5, 1945, President Truman reported that "what has been done[51] is the greatest achieve-

---

[50]Jack Raymond, reporter on defense affairs for the New York Times, discusses many important implications of the defense policies in *Power at the Pentagon* (New York: Harper and Row, Publishers, Inc., 1964). See especially chapters on "Research and the Federal Government," "Free Enterprise and National Defense," "The Military Lobbies," and "Questions of Probity."

[51]Harry S Truman, *Memoirs: Year of Decisions* (Garden City, N.Y.: Doubleday & Company, Inc., 1955), I, p. 420.

ment of organized science in history." In his farewell address, President Eisenhower more apprehensively called attention to the link between our "industrial-military posture" and modern science and technology. The crucial fact is that if national capability is to be measured by its modern weaponry, then national security policy requires large-scale programs of basic and applied research and development. The weapons of tomorrow have to be planned, designed, and tested now so that the hardware can be manufactured for delivery in 1984. And all of this implies a planned economy in an advanced industrial state.

The "new industrial state" has grown at a phenomenal rate since Sputnik alerted the American people to the necessity of gearing national security to the latest developments in science and technology. As Galbraith points out, the weapons competition, especially the nuclear race, has been enormously advantageous to the big industrial corporations in the United States. Government-sponsored space explorations have performed a similar function without the same destructive implications.

Running for the presidency in 1960, Senator John F. Kennedy made the "missile gap" and Sputnik major issues in his campaign. Immediately following his election, President Kennedy appointed a transition task force to enact a new course for American leadership in space exploration. And in his special State of the Union Message in May of 1961, the President asked for—and got—a national commitment to land a man on the moon and return him safely to earth "before this decade is out." He told Congress, "no single space project in this period will be more impressive to mankind . . . or so difficult or expensive to accomplish." Whatever prestige the United States has gained from its spectacular space programs, the price has run high. In the first year after Sputnik, the total expenditure for space research and technology was $145 million; in the first year of the Kennedy administration the figure was up to $744 million; and by 1968 the Johnson administration was budgeting $5.3 *billion.* (Table 15–3 shows how the figures soared within one decade.)

Business firms with government contracts to plan, develop, and produce nuclear weapons, antiballistic installations, spaceships, or moon rockets really enjoy free enterprise, although not in the classic sense of that term. They can make large-scale, long-term investments free from the hazards of the market,

Table 15-3 Federal Expenditures for Space Research and Technology (in millions of dollars)

Fiscal Year

	'59	'60	'61	'62	'63	'64	'65	'66	'67	'68
Manned space flight	11	113	279	565	1516	2768	3538	4210	3825	3575
Space science and applications	26	133	249	420	576	754	751	778	770	740
Space technology	21	52	87	159	303	432	484	435	450	440
Supporting activities	1	30	79	82	122	178	262	433	460	435
Aircraft technology	87	722	551	31	36	40	58	75	95	110
TOTAL	145	401	744	1257	2552	4171	5093	5933	5600	5300

Source: Table 19, *The Budget of the United States Government, 1968* (Washington, D.C.: U.S. Government Printing Office, 1964), p. 457.

price fluctuations, or changing demands. Moreover, although they operate in a planned economy, they have a major share in the planning. The unique functional relationship between Big Business, Big Government, and Big Science has been a mutually profitable arrangement.

Sputnik was a turning point in the defense policies of the United States. The immediate reaction of the Eisenhower administration was to create in the Executive Office of the President a new post, Special Assistant to the President for Science and Technology. Within a few years, this single post became a powerful bureaucracy charged with developing policies and evaluating and coordinating programs to assure that science and technology are used most effectively in the interests of national security and general welfare. Even more impressive is the upswing of government expenditures for research and development, especially in support of defense policies. In 1957, the Defense Department alone was spending $2.5 billion for research, development, testing, and evaluation; ten years later, the Defense Department's allocation for the same functions had soared to $7.2 billion.

Drawing by Herblock;
© 1967 Herblock in the Washington Post.

"There's money enough to support both of you—Now, doesn't that make you feel better?"

The distribution of government funds for research and development ("R & D," in Table 15–4, p. 648) is quite revealing. In 1966, the national government obligated up to $15.9 billion for research and development; 12 per cent for basic research, 22 per cent for applied research, and 66 per cent for development. Twenty per cent of the research was carried on in federal laboratories, 12 per cent was contracted out to educational institutions, and 63 per cent to private industry. Three agencies picked up 87 per cent of all national expenditures for research and development: the Department of Defense, the National Aeronautical and Space Agency, and the Atomic Energy Commission. In a preliminary analysis of the R & D estimates for 1968, the Budget Bureau made the not surprising announcement that the three top agencies to receive R & D funds would again be the Department of Defense, the National Aeronautical and Space Agency, and the Atomic Energy Commission, in that order. Total R & D obligations were estimated at $16.6 billion.

What do all these figures show? First of all, they give us some idea of what it costs the American people to link the credibility of their foreign policy to

Table 15-4   National Research Support—1966
             (Total Obligation = $15.9 Billion)

	PERCENTAGE
Summary by type of research	
Developmental research	66%
Applied research	22
Basic research	12
Summary by performer	
Industrial firms	63%
Intra-mural	20
Educational institutions	12
Other non-profit	4
Other	1
Summary by agency	
Department of Defense	47%
National Aeronautics and Space Agency	32
Atomic Energy Commission	8
Department of Health, Education and Welfare	7
Other	6
Summary by field of research	
Physical sciences	67%
Life sciences	25
Social sciences	3
Psychological	3
Other	2

Source: *Federal Funds for Research, Development, and Other, Fiscal Years 1965, 1966, and 1967,* National Science Foundation Survey of Science Series (Washington, D.C.: U.S. Government Printing Office, 1966), XV.

military capability. Secondly, they indicate that the bulk of nationally sponsored research and development is conceived in terms of potential payoffs in national security. Third, they point up the multibillion dollar stakes of private industry in continuation and development of big defense and space programs. Finally, they suggest that the science policy of the American government is mission-supporting: to meet conflict in international relations with the most sophisticated and powerful weapons of force and violence.[52]

When the Kennedy administration first came to office, it was dismayed by the number of private corporations handling top confidential assignments in national security. David Bell, then Director of the Bureau of the Budget, reported that "there have been instances—particularly in the Department of Defense—where we have come dangerously close to permitting contract employees to exercise functions which belong to our Government officials"[53] No doubt these contract arrangements between the government and private organizations are somewhat synthetic. Their purpose, in part, is to circumvent the civil service regulations with respect to salary limitations in order to secure the best brains in the nation to work on the toughest problems that confront us in the age of atomic energy and space science. As far as business is concerned, the arrangement offers extraordinary opportunities; the government takes the risk and the industry gets the profit. On the other hand, a business

[52]The discussion in this section is taken largely from Marian D. Irish, "Science, Technology, and Foreign Policy," in Abdul Said (ed.), *Theories of Foreign Policy* (Englewood Cliffs, N.J.: Prentice-Hall, Inc.) to be published in 1968.
[53]See Jack Raymond's commentary on the Bell Report in *Power at the Pentagon*, pp. 149–151.

that becomes wholly or significantly dependent on contracts may find itself in difficulties if for any reason the government shifts its research and development interests or changes its production plans.

Military leaders, defense contractors in big corporations, scientists and engineers in organized research have become influential in shaping, as well as in implementing, the policies of national security.[54] Obviously, this integration of public and private business, outside the constitutional framework, raises many questions about conflict of interest and personal loyalties. Don Price, Dean of the John Fitzgerald Kennedy School of Government at Harvard, suggests some of the far-reaching consequences of this breakdown in the old boundaries between public and private affairs:

> If anyone doubts that the boundaries are different today, let him reflect on the facts that Mr. Francis Powers, who flew the ill-fated U-2 over Russia, did so (or so the NASA announced) on the payroll of a private aircraft company; that technical assistance and international educational exchanges, which have become important arms of foreign policy, are largely conducted by universities and private institutions under contract for the government; and that some of the most important strategic studies are being made for the military not by staff officers in uniform but by a series of private institutions which began work under the somewhat narrower concept of operations research.[55]

Our enormous commitments in international relations, the total involvement of our economy in the national defense, and the unprecedented role of

---

[54]For informed analyses of this development in policy-making, see *Public Policy,* published annually by the Graduate School of Public Administration, Harvard University, edited by John D. Montgomery and Arthur Smithies (Cambridge, Mass.: Harvard University Press, 1964), Vol. XIII. See especially Wesley W. Posvar, "The Impact of Strategy Expertise on the National Security Policy of the U.S."; and Bruce L. R. Smith, "Strategic Expertise and National Security Policy: A Case Study." See also Don K. Price, *The Scientific Estate* (Cambridge, Mass.: The Belknap Press of Harvard University Press, 1965).

[55]The American Assembly, *The Secretary of State* (Englewood Cliffs. N.J.: Prentice-Hall, Inc., 1960), p. 169.

Drawing by Herblock;
©1967 *Herblock in the Washington Post.*

*"Some supersonic warplanes,
some money to pay for them—and,
oh yes,
some food for the peasants"*

science in both military and industrial technology—these require a great deal of skill in policy-making, top-level planning, and technical coordination in public administration. Again, the trend in modern government is to go outside the official agencies for consultants and advisers. Henry A. Kissinger, one of the most astute observers in the area of foreign policy, discusses this problem in *The Necessity for Choice:* "Crucial policy advice is increasingly requested from ad hoc committees of outside experts, as for example, the Gaither Committee on national defense or the Draper Committee on economic assistance or the Coolidge Committee on arms control."[56]

The ad hoc committee approach to public administration and what Kissinger aptly calls "the conversational approach to policy" pose new problems in American government. Our constitutional system is based on the proposition that those who exercise power can be held responsible, both legally and politically, for their public acts. But when power is achieved through the back door, as it were, by the private consultant, the technical adviser, or, on a broader scale, by the "community of strategic expertise," the constitutional guarantees are difficult to maintain.

Concerned as they were with "forms" of government, the Framers of 1787 would be surprised, perhaps aghast, to learn that some of the most important activities of the national government are carried on without regard to the careful contrivance of checks and balances in the Constitution. Nowhere is this more dramatically evident than in the policy process for national security. The Constitution gives to Congress, and only to Congress, the power to declare war; but the strategy of war in the nuclear age outmodes lengthy political deliberations. National security in the era of ICBM's and H-bombs calls for split-second decisions based on top-level military planning and highly confidential intelligence. How far decision-making can go without engaging the attention or authorization of Congress is illustrated by the "invasion" of Castro's Cuba in 1961. Apparently Congress had no knowledge of the role of the State Department, the Pentagon, or the CIA in this expedition until after the fiasco. More recently, President Johnson has escalated our military assistance in Viet Nam to the point of engaging the United States in a major war, without requesting a declaration of war from Congress—despite mounting criticism in Congress, especially in the Senate, and particularly from Senator Fulbright, Chairman of the Senate Committee on Foreign Relations. On the other hand, Congress has each year approved the administration's requests for defense appropriations, including those which support the war in Viet Nam and that maintain the string of bases that support American influence and the interests of our allies throughout the free world.

But, as Dean Price maintains, "as a matter of practical politics, we have fortunately recognized that the basic framework can be preserved best if we do not worship all the incidental apparatus and procedures that the Founding Fathers had in mind." He reminds us that technical advances in the twentieth century have broken down most of the old boundaries between peace and war, domestic and foreign problems, public and private affairs, which were

---

[56]Henry A. Kissinger, *The Necessity for Choice* (New York: Harper and Row, Publishers, Inc., 1960), p. 346.

implicit in the written constitution of the eighteenth century. Hence it has been "quite necessary, in order to maintain the general spirit of the Constitution, to work out an unwritten Constitution on new lines."[57]

[57] The American Assembly, *The Secretary of State*, p. 171.

FOREIGN POLICY AND

NATIONAL SECURITY 16

Foreign policy is perhaps the most complex area of decision-making in any government—certainly in ours. A month or so after taking office, Secretary of State Dean Rusk gave an informal talk to the policy-makers in the Department of State on how to think about foreign policy problems. "The problem . . . begins to take shape in a galaxy of utterly complicated factors—political, military, economic, financial, legal, legislative, procedural, administrative—to be sorted out and handled within a political system which moves by consent in relation to an external environment which cannot be under control."[1]

Foreign Policy and International Politics

Approaches to Foreign Policy

There are many approaches to the study of decision-making in American foreign policy. A traditional approach is to trace the development of our diplomatic relations with other nations, selecting and observing events in chronological sequence.[2] The approach is a valid one. The foreign policy of every nation is rooted in history, in established patterns of behavior, in principles, precedents, and commitments. It is difficult for a nation to deny its heritage or to forswear its history. American decision-makers are expected to take their current bearings from the great guidelines that have served in the past to advance our national interests in the world. Many of the opinions, beliefs, and attitudes which Americans hold most firmly today stem from courses of action taken in the past which have since been rationalized as basic principles.

Some of the problems that beset American foreign policy today go back to its foundations: to policies of isolationism and neutrality promoted in the early years of the republic, when we were distant and detached from the quarrels of the Old World and preoccupied with building "one nation under

---

[1]Selected papers, prepared by the Subcommittee on National Security Staffing and Operations, 87th Cong., 2d Sess., *Administration of National Security* (Washington, D.C.: U.S. Government Printing Office, 1962), Committee print, p. 23. Informal remarks made to the policy-making officers of the Department of State, February 20, 1961, by the Honorable Dean Rusk.

[2]There are many diplomatic histories of the United States. Samuel Flagg Bemis, *A Diplomatic History of the United States*, 5th ed. (New York: Holt, Rinehart & Winston, Inc., 1965) is a standard work. John W. Spanier, *American Foreign Policy Since World War II*, 2nd ed. (New York: Frederick A. Praeger, Inc. 1965) focuses on the period since 1945.

God" from the Atlantic to the Pacific. By the same token, opinions, beliefs, and attitudes which other nations hold about us are largely based on the record of our past performances in the international system.[3] To appreciate some of the difficulties that confront our policy-makers today trying to make a go of the Alliance for Progress in Latin America, we have to keep in mind the varying interpretations which we have given to the Monroe Doctrine and our Good Neighbor policies over the years, and to note the manner in which we have employed them to establish our hegemony in the Western Hemisphere.

Another traditional and useful approach to studying a nation's foreign policy is to examine the political and legal structure which prescribes the allocation of authority and defines the outer limits of permissibility.[4] For example, the constitutional prescription of checks and balances in American executive-legislative relations affects both the content and conduct of American foreign policy. When the President of the United States acts as "director of American foreign policy," his freedom of choice is considerably curtailed by constitutional provisions, congressional statutes and resolutions, judicial decisions, states rights, and individual rights. And as Theodore Sorensen points out in *Decision-Making in the White House,* the President's role in foreign policy is circumscribed by international law, "which cannot be dismissed as quickly as some claim."[5] Policy-makers (and therefore students of foreign policy) need to know which international charters, treaties, and agreements, decisions of international courts, and aspects of customary behavior in international relations are germane to specific decisions. Note that among President Johnson's justifications for our presence in Viet Nam the international legal commitments loom large. Because American foreign policy must be implemented outside the jurisdiction of the United States, studies of the legal and governmental variables which affect the choices of policy-makers, country to country, constitute basic intelligence not only in the making of our foreign policy but in evaluating it.

Foreign policy is, by definition, goal-oriented: the foreign policy of every country is intended to protect and promote its national independence, national honor, national security, and national well-being. Every nation has its own sense of national purpose and national mission; some appear to be more activated by ideology, or to be more messianic, than others. When the United States entered the community of nations in 1776, the Founding Fathers professed "a decent respect for the opinions of mankind." And ever since, American policy-makers have felt impelled to explain their courses of action on the world stage in a moral context.[6] In the words of Woodrow Wilson, we fought

[3]Alan F. Westin (ed.), *Views of America* (New York: Harcourt, Brace & World, Inc., 1966) provides a collection of foreign commentary, from the Communist bloc, the developing nations, and Europe, demonstrating that the rest of the world does not see us as we see ourselves.

[4]The best example of this approach is Elmer Plischke, *Conduct of American Diplomacy,* 3rd ed. (Princeton, N.J.: D. Van Nostrand Co., Inc. 1967). Burton Sapin, *The Making of United States Foreign Policy* (New York: Frederick A. Praeger Inc., 1966) also examines the organizational apparatus which carries out American foreign policy activities, but it is less institutional and more behavioral in approach than Plischke's work.

[5]Theodore Sorensen, *Decision-Making in the White House* (New York: Columbia University Press, 1963), p. 64.

[6]See Norman Graebner (ed.), *Ideas and Diplomacy* (New York: Oxford University Press, 1964) for a conceptualization of the intellectual milieu in which foreign policy is shaped. This is a collection of readings which records what decision-makers said, rather than what they did, in American diplomatic history.

World War I as "one of the champions of the rights of mankind" so that the world could be made "safe for democracy."[7] On the eve of the Second World War, President Franklin D. Roosevelt declared that "America hates war," and accordingly deemed it America's obligation to search actively for peace and to work "for the triumph of law and moral principles . . . in the world."[8] Since the breakdown of our wartime alliance with the Soviet Union, we have featured ourselves as the leader of the Free World, engaged in a great global struggle to counteract the communist ideology and to contain communist aggression and subversion.[9]

Another approach, the normative approach, has always appealed to some political scientists. In the 1920s and '30s, many students of foreign policy were influenced by the Wilsonian model; much of the teaching and academic writing of the period was concerned with problems of international organization and international law, with emphasis on the issues of war and peace. War was regarded as an aberration; peace could be achieved if nations would renounce war as an instrument of national policy and plan for collective security through international organization. World order through international law was the ultimate goal.[10]

After World War II, however, there was a notable decline in "idealism," among both decision-makers and students of decision-making. "Realists" decried the legalism and moralism of the earlier period. The Wilsonian model was largely replaced by the Lasswellian model—"who gets what, when, and how." National interest, defined as power, became the key to international politics; war was viewed simply as a fact of political life. The seminal contribution to the new school of realism is Hans J. Morgenthau's *Politics Among Nations*, significantly subtitled *The Struggle for Power and Peace*.[11] Political power, according to Morgenthau, is "man's control over the minds and actions of other men." Although Morgenthau rejects the "ideological pretenses" which blur the actual objectives of American foreign policy, he too takes a normative approach, for he believes that nations *should* use foreign policy to fulfill their "national purpose." In *The Purpose of American Politics*, Morgenthau tells us how Americans ought to act in the world: "We must make clear to

[7] Woodrow Wilson's War Message, April 2, 1917.
[8] Franklin D. Roosevelt's Quarantine Speech, Chicago, October 5, 1937.
[9] The official declaration of the Cold War may be read in President Harry Truman's speech to Congress, March 12, 1947, asking for aid to Greece and Turkey. As President Truman viewed it, the world in 1947 was faced with two alternative ways of life—freedom through democracy or terror and oppression under communism. The American strategy of containment, based on this view, would thereafter dominate American foreign policy in every administration to this day.
[10] A great outpouring of optimistic and idealistic literature marks this period. Two standard texts illustrate the approach: Pitman B. Potter, *International Organization* (New York: Appleton-Century-Crofts, 1922); and Clyde Eagleton, *International Government* (New York: The Ronald Press Company, 1932). Both of these texts were widely adopted and went through multiple editions into the immediate post-World War II period. Both authors were specialists in international law, actively involved in the great crusade for international peace and security, first through associations with the League of Nations and later with the United Nations.
[11] The first edition of this popular and influential textbook was published in 1948 (New York: Alfred A. Knopf, Inc.). Revised several times to take cognizance of the rapidly changing dynamics of "politics among the nations," the author still retains his key concept, that power politics is the core of foreign policy.

ourselves and to the world—by deeds rather than by proclamations—that equality in freedom still has a home in America and is still worthy of emulation."[12]

Escalation of the Cold War with the Soviet Union and the postwar nuclear arms race between the two great protagonists have revolutionized the substance and the theories of American foreign policy. Geared to power politics in international relations, American foreign policy is now almost completely dominated by military considerations involving vast and complicated systems of nuclear weaponry. More than half the national budget is allocated to national security programs of a military nature. And, as we noted in the preceding chapter, most of the federal money for research is "mission-supporting." Thus academic theorists as well as policy-makers now give unprecedented attention to the defense components and strategic side of foreign policy: how to deter atomic war, how to outmatch other atomic powers, how to bargain, how to calculate the risks, how to threaten, how to respond to threats, how to engage in brinkmanship, how to cope with reprisals, when to fight conventional wars, where to engage in guerilla warfare, how to stamp out wars of liberation, how to foment counterinsurgency, when to trust, when to cheat, when to attack, and when to come to the conference table.[13]

It is estimated that more than a hundred thousand studies on the strategic issues of war and peace have been published since 1945.[14] Much of this literature is "policy-oriented," exploring the problems of national security[15] (at the other end of the spectrum from the literature of the 1930s, when policy-oriented political scientists were exploring the problems of international security). Research institutes in foreign policy and defense study programs, have been established in many universities, reflecting a growing interest in theory, empirical analysis, and sophisticated methodology—and in federal research funds generously available for studies of foreign policy related to national security organization, defense strategies, and conflict resolution.

The analytical approach to foreign policy, based on empirical research, appeals to an increasing number of political scientists. On the one hand, foreign policy analysis is tied to comparative politics and cross-national studies, which examine internal influences upon external behavior; investigation begins with national goals, national capabilities, national inputs, national decision-making. Basic research depends on the collection of comparative political data, country by country. On the other hand, foreign policy analysis

[12]Hans J. Morgenthau, *The Purpose of American Politics* (New York: Alfred A. Knopf, Inc., 1960), p. 299.

[13]For examples, see Davis B. Bobrow (ed.), *Components of Defense Policy* (New York: Rand McNally & Co., 1965), with contributions from The Rand Corporation, Warner R. Schilling, Herman Kahn, Thomas C. Schelling, Roger Hilsman, and others.

[14]Harry Howe Ransom, "International Relations," *Journal of Politics*, XXX (May, 1968).

[15]It is difficult to single out typical studies. Probably the most influential was Henry Kissinger's *Nuclear Weapons and Foreign Policy* (New York: Harper & Row, Publishers, Inc., 1957). Disturbed by the predominance of fiscal considerations in the national security policies of the Eisenhower administration, Kissinger urged a more flexible defense doctrine that would enable the United States to exercise a variety of options short of massive retaliation. In *Necessity for Choice* (New York: Harper & Row, Publishers, Inc., 1960) Kissinger continues the argument for "a substantial strengthening of the conventional forces of the free world" and "a greater reliance on conventional strategy." The shift in American foreign policy in the Kennedy administration follows the Kissinger line.

is also tied to analysis of the international system, of the role of nation-states in the international community, and of external influences upon internal behavior.[16]

So far, neither the policy-makers nor the academic theorists have reached agreement on the relative influence or potency of variables in foreign policy. Some political scientists stress the environmental and nonhuman factors which condition the policy position of a nation, regardless of its societal values. Others place more emphasis on national goals and societal characteristics which determine capabilities, such as degree of national unity or extent of industrialization. Still others focus on the political factors which limit or enhance the roles of policy-makers within the national system. Of these, some are primarily concerned with the process of decision-making and the roles of decision-makers in the process.[17]

In this chapter we shall keep within the framework of analysis that we have used throughout the book. We are confronted at the outset, however, with the same dilemma that faces our decision-makers: foreign policy as a course of action determined within the national political system becomes a complicated pattern of interactions in the international system. Foreign policy is formulated in the context of national values, interests, goals, and capabilities; it is implemented in an external environment which is beyond the reach and control of the United States.

The United States maintains diplomatic relations with some 135 different countries in the world. Specific foreign policies are usually designed on a country-to-country basis, *we* and *they:* U.S. and U.S.S.R., U.S. and France, U.S. and Venezuela, U.S. and India. Basic intelligence for effective relationships calls for knowledge and understanding of *their* values, interests, goals, and capabilities, as well as *ours*. Country-to-country relationships, however, are affected by the dynamics of international politics and by cross-national transactions.

No country, including the United States, stands on its own in the international system; external conditions affect internal behavior; internal conditions affect external behavior. To understand American-Soviet relations, for example, one must recognize that the U.S. and the U.S.S.R. are each tied by numerous agreements and various commitments, bilateral and multilateral, to many

---

[16] James N. Rosenau (ed.), *International Politics and Foreign Policy* (New York: The Free Press of Glencoe, Inc., 1961) offers a wide variety of readings discussing the linkages between foreign policy and international politics. See also, R. Barry Farrell (ed.), *Approaches to Comparative and International Politics* (Evanston, Ill.: Northwestern University Press, 1966) for behavioral and traditional analyses of foreign policy in developed (Western) and developing countries, and in open and closed societies.

[17] For different theoretical approaches, see Harold and Margaret Sprout, *Man-Milieu Relationships in the Context of International Politics*, (Princeton, N.J.: Center of International Studies, 1956); Gabriel A. Almond, *The American People and Foreign Policy* (New York: Frederick A. Praeger, Inc., 1960); James A. Robinson, *Congress and Foreign Policy Making*, rev. ed. (Homewood, Ill.: Dorsey Press, 1967); James N. Rosenau, (ed.), *Domestic Sources of Foreign Policy* (New York: The Free Press of Glencoe, Inc., 1967); Richard Snyder, H. W. Bruck, and Burton Sapin, *Foreign Policy Decision Making* (New York: The Free Press of Glencoe, Inc., 1962).

different countries. Thus concerning the Berlin situation—which has reached a crisis more than once since 1945—what the United States does depends in large measure on what its partners in the Atlantic Alliance can do, will do, or want done. Likewise, what the Soviet Union does depends in large measure on what its partners in the Warsaw Pact can do, will do, or want done. And what happens in Europe is conditioned by what goes on in Latin America, the Middle East, and Southeast Asia. It takes an enormous bureaucracy in intelligence, research, and foreign policy analysis just to sort out and handle all "the utterly complicated factors" that enter into American foreign policy toward the U.S.S.R., on any issue, at any time.

Obviously we cannot turn this chapter into a position paper on American foreign policies. Taking advantage of academic license, we shall examine in a general way the international environment which conditions American activities in the world, and then turn our attention to the domestic side of American foreign policy.

National Power and International Politics

In any analysis of national power in international politics, it is fairly easy to identify the significant factors: population and manpower, geography and natural resources, productive capacity and technological development, national morale and political socialization, and, of course, military strength. But power is a useful concept only when it is applied to specific situations. Robert Dahl's paradigm is as helpful in understanding power relations among nations in the international system as it is in measuring the relative influence of actors in the national political system: "_____ more powerful than _____ with respect to _____ as measured by _____ and _____."

Most of the world lies outside our own borders and is not a world of our own making. This is the prime fact which confounds all our foreign policy. More than 3 billion people live on this planet; only 200 million are Americans. Statistics on world trends in population growth are increasingly alarming. If the present trend continues, the world will have to make room for another billion persons in the next fifteen years: moreover, four-fifths of this population increase will occur in the already underfed, developing countries in Asia, Africa, and Latin America. Already American policy-makers are beginning to prepare for the race against famine that is bound to overshadow the political problems that we now consider so crucial in Viet Nam, Cuba, the Congo, or Berlin. Statistics on population growth and food production sound the awesome warning that mass famine will overtake many countries in the world within the next decade if present trends are not curbed: population grows at the rate of 2 to 3 per cent annually in countries where increases in food production are annually less than 1 per cent or even at a standstill. Obviously the figures on population explosion have, or should have, a bearing on the shape of American aid programs and related policies toward population programs in the developing countries. (See Fig. 16–1 for projections of population growth in Latin America, Asia, and Africa, 1960–1980.)

Most of the people of the world are non-Western, non-Christian, and nonwhite. Of the ten most populous countries, five are in Asia, one is in

Africa, two are in Europe, one is in Latin America, and one (the U.S.) is in North America (see Table 16–1, p. 660). If we examine the rates of increases for these ten countries from 1958 to 1964, we perceive that the U.S. and U.S.S.R. are growing at about the same rate; that West Germany and Japan are also growing, but less rapidly; and that India, Indonesia, Pakistan, Brazil, and Nigeria are all growing at a much faster rate. Then, if we look at the 1966 projections of 1980 populations, we find that rate of growth of nonwhite population is much more pronounced. Data on the population growth of Communist China are not available, but note that the Chinese Communist population today is nearly four times that of the United States and about three times that of the Soviet Union.

The most important natural resource any nation can possess is its people. We assess the power position of any state on the basis of quantitative and qualitative population data. But mere numbers are not so significant today as when they represented potential military and industrial manpower. In the era of atomic fission and increasing automation, the real measure of a nation's military and industrial power is the number of its scientists, engineers, and technicians rather than the gross number of its soldiers and workers. The U.S. and the U.S.S.R. are well matched in natural resources. The U.S.S.R. has the larger population and its government is putting tremendous stress on science and technology to insure the specialized skills which are basic to modern, diversified military and industrial power. But because the Industrial Revolution reached the United States years before its influence was felt in Russia, the United States still seems to have the edge in the competition.

The geography and topography of a nation are still important, although not so critical as they once were, in conditioning foreign policy. Because our continental security seemed so impregnable before World War I, the United States could assume a stance of "neutrality" and even "isolation" from time to time in international relations. The English Channel long served as a strategic defense for England against the land armies of European powers. Nations once fought for rivers as natural boundaries—the Rhine, the Rio Grande, and the Yalu. But the development of air power and nuclear weaponry has drastically reduced the significance of natural defenses. On the other hand, conflicts in international relations can be resolved only once by all-out nuclear war. Meantime, the location of a country, its size, its accessibility by land and sea,

Figure 16-1

Source: United Nations
Demographic Yearbook, 1963.

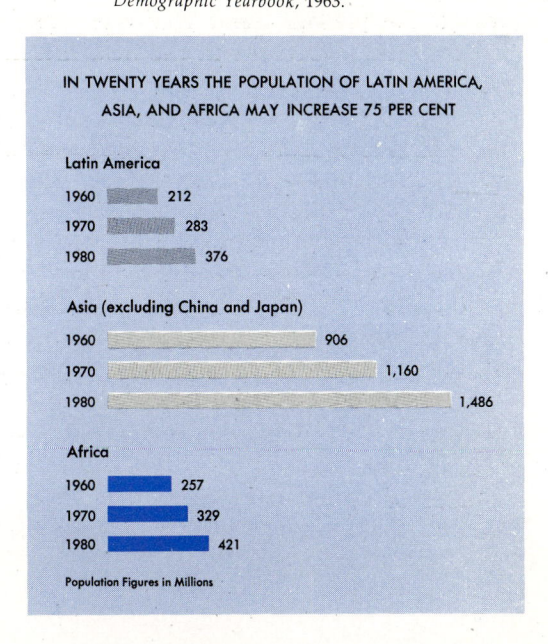

IN TWENTY YEARS THE POPULATION OF LATIN AMERICA, ASIA, AND AFRICA MAY INCREASE 75 PER CENT

Latin America
1960 212
1970 283
1980 376

Asia (excluding China and Japan)
1960 906
1970 1,160
1980 1,486

Africa
1960 257
1970 329
1980 421

Population Figures in Millions

Table 16-1 The Ten Most Populous Countries

	1964, IN MILLIONS	RATE OF INCREASE 1958–1964	PROJECTIONS IN MILLIONS, 1980
Communist China	690	—*	—*
India	472	2.3	682
U.S.S.R.	228	1.6	268
U.S.A.	192	1.6	241
Indonesia	102	2.2	152
Pakistan	101	3.2	183
Japan	97	1.0	111
Brazil	79	3.1	124
Nigeria	56	2.0	191
W. Germany	56	1.3	59

Source: U.S. Department of Commerce, *Pocket Data Book, USA, 1967* and *World Population Data Sheet*, 1966, Population Reference Bureau.
*No exact data.

and other geographic factors are still strategic in conventional warfare and guerilla fighting, as evidenced in the Congo and Viet Nam.

Natural resources are basic for military and industrial power. A nation need not possess all the essential resources within its boundaries (no nation does), but it must have access to them in order to develop a modern economy and to maintain national security. Even the United States, which was richly endowed and has made full use of its natural resources, is not self-sufficient; it must go into the world market for many such strategic and critical materials as chromite, tin, industrial diamonds, manganese, platinum, and uranium. To secure these vital imports has been a prime concern of American foreign policy.

The riches of this earth have not been equitably distributed over all parts of the world. It is oversimplifying the issue to divide nations into the "haves" and "have-nots"; but on the basis of such a rough classification, the "have" nations generally try to maintain the *status quo* and the "have-nots" attempt to break it up. Being rich in certain natural resources is no assurance, however, that a "have" country will remain one. New developments in technology may lessen the demand for certain natural resources or even render them useless. For example, in the jet age navigable rivers are not the crucial assets they once were in a nation's trade and commerce; and in the atomic age, access to uranium is perhaps more critical than natural water power.

Productive capacity depends, of course, on the availability of natural resources. But no matter how well endowed a nation may be, if it does not know how to utilize its resources it is going to remain a weak and underdeveloped country in the modern world. Many of the new African and Asian states have a wealth of natural resources, but so did the American Indians who had neither the inclination nor the know-how to use them. When we take a global look at industrial production, we find the United States and Canada in the lead, together being responsible for 34.3 per cent of the world's production; then come the Soviet Union and Eastern Europe, with 31.7 per cent; Western Europe produces 24.2 per cent; Asia 6.1 per cent; and Latin America 3.7 per cent (see Fig. 16–2).

A standard measure of economic power is the gross national product (GNP). In 1967, Secretary of State Dean Rusk told the Senate Foreign Relations Committee that the GNP of the United States equaled that of all the rest of NATO and Japan combined; it was twice that of the Soviet Union, ten times that of mainland China, and ten times that of all Latin America.[18] In presenting the Johnson administration's proposals to offer American assistance to the less developed countries of the world, Rusk pointed out that 29 per cent of the world's population has 83 per cent of the world's GNP and an average per capita annual income of just under $1800; and that 71 per cent of the world's population has 17 per cent of the world's GNP and a per capita annual income of roughly $154. Moreover, the gap between the more advanced countries and the less developed countries is widening.

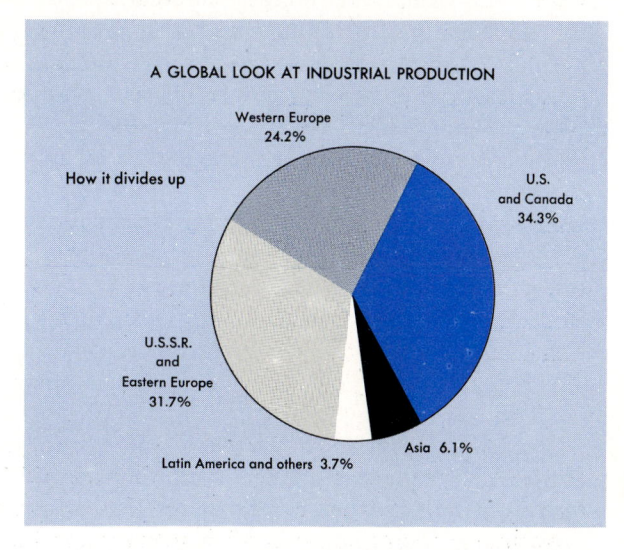

A GLOBAL LOOK AT INDUSTRIAL PRODUCTION

How it divides up
- Western Europe 24.2%
- U.S. and Canada 34.3%
- U.S.S.R. and Eastern Europe 31.7%
- Latin America and others 3.7%
- Asia 6.1%

Source: Fortune (September 15, 1967), 36.

Figure 16-2

Determining the most significant indices of standards of living, however, is another matter.[19] Bruce Russet, in his analysis of "trends in world equality," suggests that the GNP is a better measure of production than of welfare.[20] That is, Country A, although it may have twice (or ten times) the GNP as Country B., does not necessarily have twice (or ten times) as high a standard of living. For example, Russet finds that although the United States had the highest GNP in the world in 1950, it ranked fifth in provision for hospitalization; given present trends, the United States will still be the richest country in 1975 but will rank twelfth in this category. Russet also notes that greater access to means of communication in poorer countries provides the potential for the "revolution of rising expectations." Literacy, which is an index in this respect insofar as it implies basic access to information, provides a way of comparing one's status with that of others in the world. In 1950, all of the developed nations were at the level of virtually complete literacy—Canada 99 per cent, United States 97 per cent, etc.—while many countries in Asia, Latin America, and Africa were below 50 per cent levels; but given present trends, most of these countries are likely to be well over the 50 per cent levels in 1970.

---

[18] *Foreign Assistance Act of 1967*. Hearings before the Committee on Foreign Relations, U.S. Senate, 90th Cong., 1st Sess., on S. 1872, July 14, 1967, p. 125.

[19] *Fortune* used three indices for comparative standards of living in 1967: (1) cars, (2) TV sets, and (3) college enrollment. Fortuitously, the U.S. ranked at the top on all three indices; Sweden ranked second in cars per thousand population and in TV sets per thousand population; Japan ranked second in college enrollment per thousand; France ranked third in cars and in college enrollment; the United Kingdom was third in TV sets; Latin America was at the bottom on all three indices. Lawrence A. Mayer, "The World Economy," *Fortune* (September 15, 1967).

[20] Bruce M. Russet, *Trends in World Politics* (New York: The Macmillan Company, 1965).

In terms of national policy, one may query: Should a nation use its productive capacity first of all to strengthen its military establishment (some of the poorest countries in Latin America give higher priority to supersonic jet bombers than to electric power plants)? Should it gear its economy to what Daniel Boorstin calls the "consumption community" (the United States is a prime example of a people "who have a feeling of shared well-being . . . that comes from consuming the same kinds of objects.")?[21] Or should a nation, at least a rich nation, pursue Barbara Ward's idea of "tithing,"[22] contributing as a matter of course one per cent of its national GNP to the impoverished areas of the world? (The one percent standard was set by the Organization for Economic Cooperation and Development (OECD); the Japanese and the Canadians have adopted it as the government goal for sharing, and the French and the Belgians have gone beyond it.)[23] The answers to such questions depend on a nation's value judgments.

The new countries in Asia and Africa and some of the older countries in Latin America, as yet relatively untouched by the scientific revolution of the mid-twentieth century, stand in acute need of developing technologies.[24] To narrow the gap between the rich and poor countries is a prerequisite to an orderly and peaceful world. An important aspect of American foreign policy—and of the foreign policies of other advanced industrial nations in the West—is to help the new nations acquire the knowledge and technology essential for modern levels of living. In the preamble to its 1967 Foreign Assistance Act, the U.S. Congress recognized that "ignorance, want, and despair breed the extremism and violence which lead to aggression and subversion." Congress, however, was not carried away by its own rhetoric; its appropriation represented less than 0.6 per cent of the American GNP.

The new nations, although they have for the most part tried to maintain neutrality and nonalignment in the ideological battles of the Cold War, have nevertheless been pressured to choose one of two competing routes to modernization: democratic capitalism or Marxist communism. The American aid programs have been aimed to help the most promising countries "win the war against hunger," through technical assistance programs principally in the fields of agriculture, education, health, and population control. But, as we shall see later when we examine specific inputs for American policy, our foreign assistance programs are also designed to help American businessmen invest "capital, technical knowledge, and managerial ingenuity" in the developing countries and to provide government guarantees which will stimulate such private investments.[25]

Decision-makers in the realm of foreign policy must always be alert to

---

[21]Daniel J. Boorstin, "Welcome to the Consumption Community," *Fortune* (September 1, 1967).
[22]Barbara Ward, *The Rich Nations and the Poor Nations* (New York: W. W. Norton & Co., Inc., 1962).
[23]From the testimony of William S. Gaud, Administrator for AID. *Hearings* on the Foreign Assistance Act of 1967, before the Senate Commmittee on Foreign Relations, July 14, 1967, p. 222.
[24]Caryl Haskins, President of the Carnegie Institution of Washington, discusses the implications of science and technology in world politics, especially with reference to the new nations, in *The Scientific Revolution and World Politics* (New York: Harper & Row, Publishers, Inc., 1964).
[25]See, for example, AID pamphlets "The War on Hunger: A Challenge to Business," "Aids to Business (Overseas Investment)," "Commercial Exports Under AID Programs."

changing power relations in world politics; and they must not confuse past power with present power, nor present power with future power. In the case of the developing nations, the problem is how to gauge future power from what is known about potential power, in terms of resources, motivations, skills, and goals.

The great enigma in the external environment of U.S. foreign policy today is the People's Republic of China. Since the Communist regime of Mao Tse-tung came to power in 1949, we have almost no firsthand accounts by Westerners of Chinese scientific and technological progress. American policymakers have refused to extend diplomatic recognition to Mao's government and so far have successfully opposed the admission of Communist China to the United Nations. Without arguing the merits of the policy, we simply observe that faulty intelligence about China and the isolationism of China in world politics are in part outputs of the American foreign policy toward that country.

Mao's regime in China has called for total revolution and complete modernization in the fields of economics, politics, art, philosophy, culture, and warfare. Early in the 1950s, the U.S.S.R. was China's chief mentor in Marxist ideology and in Western science and technology. But by 1960, the Sino-Soviet bloc had begun to disintegrate. The Soviet Union discontinued its aid and trade programs with China and summarily recalled the many Russian scientists and technicians who had been directing and assisting China's industrial and nuclear programs. How much of a setback China suffered from its break with Russia is a matter of conjecture. But one fearful fact is as plain as a mushroom cloud in the heavens. China has produced her own atomic bombs and is now, it is assumed, capable of waging nuclear warfare. Moreover, the launching of the Great Proletarian Cultural Revolution in 1966—marked by Red Guards on the rampage, stamping out all vestiges of the "Olds" in thought, culture, customs, and habits—indicates that China has not only escalated her revolutionary movement, but that at the same time is fanatically resisting any notion of peaceful coexistence with the Western (especially American) "imperialists."

The China question is perhaps the toughest one on the American foreign policy agenda today. As late as 1957, Secretary of State John Foster Dulles believed that the Chinese Communist regime was a passing phase, and that we owed it to ourselves, our allies, and the Chinese people to do all that we could to contribute to that passing. Under his direction, American foreign policy moved on a collision course toward Communist China. But in a major policy address in 1963, Roger Hilsman, then Assistant Secretary of State for the Far East, bluntly reported to the American people that there was no reason to believe that the Communist regime would be overthrown. Presumably reflecting the views of the Kennedy administration, Hilsman urged the United States to adopt a new policy toward China—the "Open Door"—open to the possibilities of change: changes in China's domestic situation, changes in

China's role in international politics.[26] But ever since the days of McCarthyism, the China question has been such an emotion-packed issue, so interlaced with domestic politics and ideological controversy, that it has been virtually impossible to discuss Sino-American relations in a rational context, much less bring about a more flexible policy that would permit mutual accommodation.

The political development of a country is possibly more important that its economy in determining the conduct of its diplomacy. American foreign policy, for example, must be carried on within the constitutional framework and political institutions of the American system. By the same token, the American diplomat abroad must be aware of the constitutional and political pattern of the foreign government which he seeks to influence in favor of American interests. Because personal and institutional sources of power vary from one country to another, a considerable part of the continuing intelligence and research that underlies American foreign policy seeks to determine who are the decision-makers in foreign governments, and what supports, demands (or apathy) can be expected vis-à-vis policies that concern the United States.

In some ways, it is easier to do business with a totalitarian government, in which power is obviously located, than in a democracy, where public opinions may reflect a confusion of popular views. It is, for example, sometimes difficult for foreign diplomats to discover who speaks authoritatively on American foreign policy — is it the President, the Secretary of State, the Secretary of Defense, or the chairman of the Senate Committee on Foreign Relations? Or perhaps the Governor of Michigan or California? On the other hand, there is some diffusion of power even in a dictatorship, and the identity of all the members of its power elite may not be known by outsiders. Moreover, outsiders cannot easily assess the amount or type of rapport which exists between government and governed. We tend to underestimate the support which citizens in totalitarian systems give to their government because we think morale in such an environment must be low. Our fact-finders and diplomats must therefore guard against projecting their own values into a foreign situation.

In the absence of an international government, each nation must fend for itself. As a last resort (it is rarely the only resort), military strength may be crucial, depending on what a nation wants in the world and who has it. Military strength refers to many factors—military manpower, trained and in reserve; armaments up-to-date and ready for use; an industrial establishment geared for war; a civilian population prepared for defense against attack; a nation with the will to fight, an ideology to defend or extend. In the nuclear age, the ultimate weapon, given the capabilities, is the will to escalate the use of force even to all-out nuclear war. No matter how massive the deterrent, it

---

[26] Roger Hilsman, *To Move a Nation* (Garden City, N.Y.: Doubleday & Co., Inc., 1967). Hilsman criticizes John Foster Dulles' speech on America's China policy at San Francisco in 1957. Later, as Assistant Secretary of State for the Far East, Hilsman rejected the "tired and routine themes the State Department had been following since Dulles' speech of six years before." The Hilsman speech, given at the Commonwealth Club of San Francisco in December, 1963 (a few weeks after President Kennedy's assassination), outlined "a policy of firmness, flexibility, and dispassion." Shortly thereafter, Hilsman resigned from the State Department. There has been no perceptible change in the basic policy formulated by Dulles; it has perhaps been even more intensely applied since the escalation of the war in Viet Nam.

will not deter unless it conveys credibility that it will be used if necessary to carry out a policy.[27] No doubt the installation of Soviet missiles in Cuba was based on the assumption that the United States would not risk direct confrontation and nuclear war. By the same token, the withdrawal of the missiles was dictated by the reverse belief, when Chairman Khrushchev realized that President Kennedy was not bluffing.

Quite clearly the two major nuclear powers, the Soviet Union and the United States, prefer to avoid testing the consequences of nuclear strategy. The whole history of the Cold War has been a continuous interaction of confrontation and *détente*—over Berlin, Korea, Laos, Cuba, Viet Nam. Both sides negotiate, or refuse to negotiate, on the strength of their respective nuclear capabilities, but they are also joined in a common quest to control the nuclear arms race. Negotiations over five years culminated in the Moscow Test Ban Treaty of 1963.[28] Continuing negotiations produced a draft treaty in 1967, the purpose of which was to prevent proliferation of nuclear weapons. But granted the possibility of agreement between the U.S. and the U.S.S.R., by 1967 there were five, not two, nuclear powers, and within the next few years there will probably be several more members in the nuclear club.

The United States claims that its nuclear arsenal is necessary for national security; the threat of massive retaliation is intended to deter aggression. The Soviet Union makes the same sort of claim—that it maintains a stockpile of missiles and rockets as a defensive measure. In 1967, the strategy of nuclear defense was stepped up, first by the Russians, then by the Americans, with the introduction of antiballistic missiles (ABMs). The United States decision to establish a "thin line" of ABMs came only after diplomatic negotiations failed to secure an agreement not to do so with the Soviet Union. Russian reluctance to stop escalating its nuclear defenses may be a reflection of its mounting disapproval of American policies in Viet Nam and in the Middle East. But even if the Russians were ready to trust American overtures, they would still feel the urgency of a need for nuclear defenses against their neighbors, the hostile Chinese, who are not bound, nor are likely to be bound, by international agreements.

In large measure, the conduct of foreign policy revolves around the pursuit and use of power by each nation for the purpose of getting what it needs and wants in the world. But no nation is wholly self-sufficient, and no nation acts in isolation. As Robert Dahl observes, "The way a political system behaves is influenced by the existence of other political systems. . . . National govern-

---

[27] See W. W. Rostow, former Chairman of the State Department's Planning Council, more recently Special Advisor to the President on the White House Staff, who candidly discusses "American Strategy on the World Scene" in *View from the Seventh Floor* (New York: Harper & Row, Publishers, Inc., 1964). Amos O. Jordan, Jr. (ed.), in *Issues of National Security in the 1970's* (New York: Frederick A. Praeger, Inc., 1967), offers a collection of essays dealing with many facets of the military side of foreign policy, written mostly from the military viewpoint.

[28] Harold Karan Jacobson and Eric Stein, *Diplomats, Scientists, and Politicians* (Ann Arbor: University of Michigan Press, 1966) uses the Test Ban Treaty of 1963 as a case study to show the impact of science and technology on the negotiating process.

ments must adapt their actions to the hard fact that other national governments, alliances, coalitions, and international organizations also exist."[29]

Pluralism in One World

Extraordinary advances in communications and transporation since the mid-nineteenth century have made the concept of "one world" technically feasible. When the United States entered the community of nations, peoples could not speak to peoples. The largest audience reached by the human voice could be counted only in the thousands, and would have to be gathered in one place. Today radio and television carry the voice and image of nations' spokesmen to hundreds of millions of people in all parts of the globe, simultaneously listening and watching. Sailing ships were the principal links between nations when George Washington was President of the United States. But the maps that sailors used in the eighteenth century bear little resemblance to the navigation charts of today's air and space pilots. The arctic regions which were not navigable in the age of seapower are the shortest commercial and strategic routes today between many nations in the Northern Hemisphere. On old Mercator maps, the United States is separated from Europe and Asia by vast oceans and seas; but if we place the North Pole at the center of our maps, then our "detached and distant situation" is shown to be an optical illusion. President George Washington's farewell advice to his countrymen, to take advantage of their geographical isolation and stay clear of the quarrels of the Old World, has become outdated. In this generation, time and space have so diminished that the whole earth is now but a small sphere that an astronaut can encompass in a ninety-minute orbital flight.

Notwithstanding modern technology in communications and transportation, the dream of peoples speaking to peoples in a peaceful world has yet to materialize. While we were still engaged in World War II, fifty nations met in San Francisco, at "history's nearest approach to a global constitutional convention."[30] The Charter of the United Nations was signed with enthusiastic celebration in June, 1945. The United States had taken a leading role in planning for the San Francisco Conference and in shaping the great Charter. The United States Senate quickly gave its consent to our membership in the new organization, a momentous commitment on the part of the American people to the cause of international peace through collective security. In 1946, delegates to the First General Assembly from fifty-one nations met in London, eager to launch the experiment in international government. In 1967, the United Nations came of age, "in a world bristling with armaments and beset by war, charged with failure in the performance of its principal mission, the keeping of the peace."[31] The United States was engaged in a major war in Viet Nam; its

---

[29] Robert Dahl, *Modern Political Analysis* (Englewood Cliffs, N.J.: Prentice-Hall, Inc., 1963), p. 22.

[30] Inis L. Claude, Jr. *Swords into Ploughshares*, 3rd ed. (New York: Random House, Inc., 1964), p. 53. See also Claude's *Power and International Relations* (New York: Random House, Inc., 1962) for an analytical critique of the original notions of collective security expressed at the San Francisco Conference.

[31] *The United Nations at Twenty-One*, Report to the Committee on Foreign Relations, U.S. Senate, by Senator Frank Church, February 15, 1967 (Washington, D.C.: U.S. Government Printing Office, 1967), p. 16.

own casualties had passed the 100,000 mark; and the enemy casualties and civilian casualties were running to untold higher figures. What had happened to the high expectations for the United Nations, and to the commitment of the United States to work through the United Nations in order to maintain international peace and security?

To begin with, the United Nations was founded on the belief that the victorious nations in World War II would remain allies in the peace-keeping mission. The major powers, Great Britain, France, China, Russia, and the United States were made permanent members of the Security Council. But twenty-one years later, the power relationships in the world were very different than those written into the Charter. The British and French empires had disintegrated; forty-six new nations over which French or British flags flew in 1946 had now been admitted in their own right to membership in the United Nations. The defeated powers—Germany, Italy, and Japan—had once more risen to positions of power in world politics; but Germany was still excluded from the United Nations, and Italy and Japan were not accorded permanent seats on the Security Council. Nationalist China still held a permanent seat on the Security Council though it was actually an exile government in Taiwan. The United States remained implacably opposed to recognizing the People's Republic of China, which controlled the mainland; and year after year succeeded in blocking Communist China's membership in the United Nations (not to speak of a seat on the Security Council). The wartime alliance of the United States and the Soviet Union had collapsed within the first year of their participation in the United Nations; both powers used the organization as an international forum to advance their respective positions in the Cold War.

The charge that the United Nations has failed in its principal mission to keep peace in the world is not wholly correct. The United Nations played a major role in stopping the North Korean and Communist Chinese aggression against South Korea. That it was able to take action in this instance can be attributed in part to a parliamentary fluke: the Russians, who had absented themselves from the Security Council while the United States was pressing for international action, were not able to veto the UN decision. But, of course, the fact that the United States was anxious to use the UN machinery as an instrument of American foreign policy was the most influential consideration. On the other hand, in the Viet Nam war, the United States was not inclined to go through the UN to enforce what it considered a national commitment to South Viet Nam; neither North nor South Viet Nam were members of the UN, so they could not demand UN action; and, even if the United States had initially chosen to work through the UN, Russian commitments to North Viet Nam would have probably provoked the U.S.S.R. to block any UN action in the Security Council.

Although the United Nations has not been able to settle disputes in which the major powers—notably the U.S. and the U.S.S.R.—have been involved, it has kept open channels of communication and has made it possible for all members to publicize their views in times of crisis. This in itself has been an important function and has no doubt conditioned the foreign policy of the members; even great powers are sensitive to world opinion.

The Charter of the United Nations proclaims, "This organization is based on the principle of the sovereign equality of all its members." "Sovereignty" in its original context denoted absolute power, authority without accountability. The concept was developed toward the end of the Middle Ages to make legitimate the ruling claims of various temporal authorities and to justify their break from the Holy Roman Empire. First conceived as a personal attribute of the monarch, the doctrine of sovereignty was soon employed to rationalize the independence of nation-states in international affairs. Thus the government of a sovereign state—whether democratic or totalitarian, republican or monarchical, federal or unitary—has complete dominion over the land and people within its boundaries. No outside authority has a right to intervene in the domestic affairs of a sovereign state. Since sovereignty implies the idea of absolute power, all sovereign states enjoy equality under international law.[32]

Medieval as the idea of sovereignty may appear in the interdependent modern world, it nevertheless remains a significant factor in international politics. Obviously all nations are not equal—either in population, natural resources, economic development, political stability, cultural achievements, or national aspirations—but in the international system the fiction of equality is preserved as a principle of international law. Hence in the General Assembly of the United Nations, every member, the Maldive Islands, the United States, the Soviet Union, ministates to macropowers—each has one vote. And ironically, the proliferation of membership in the United Nations—from 51 in 1946 to 122 in 1967—has enhanced the emphasis on the sovereign equality of the members. Understandably the newest and the smallest states are most sensitive to the formal attributes of independence, but the principle of sovereign equality in practice has become a pattern of logrolling, obstructive strategy, and inaction in the United Nations.

The principle of equality in the United Nations does not apply to the financial support of the organization and its activities. Since 1946 the United States has contributed approximately $3 billion for UN activities, about half the total outlay of the UN during this period. Under a scheme of assessment based on ability to pay, the United States in 1967 paid for approximately 32 per cent of the cost of UN activities, including the operations of eleven specialized UN agencies. (The U.S.S.R. contributed 15 per cent, Great Britain 7 per cent, France 6 per cent, Japan 3 per cent and each of the fifty-five poorest nations 0.04 per cent of the UN budget.) In recent years, the largest percentage of American contributions to the UN has gone to development programs which provide preinvestment surveys and technical assistance to developing nations. The second largest percentage goes to the UN's regular operation budget, covering staff activities at headquarters in New York and in Geneva. Peace-keeping activities, as in the Congo or Cyprus, have accounted for only 9 per cent of U.S. contributions (admittedly a very small drop in the bucket compared to the huge annual expenditures of the United States for national defense). Major U.S. contributions have also been allocated to such UN opera-

---

[32] J. L. Brierly, *The Law of Nations* (London: Oxford University Press, 1955). "The Character of the Modern State System" provides an excellent discussion from the legal standpoint.

tions as assistance to Palestine refugees, the World Health Organization, the World Food Program, the Food and Agriculture Organization, and the Children's Fund.

The United States has not been able to dominate the United Nations either on the Security Council or in the General Assembly, where the many new governments now outnumber the original membership. Although the United States is most active in many UN operations and contributes twice as much as any other nation to the financial support of the organization, it has built up its own system of alliances and a massive power base for American foreign policy outside the framework of the United Nations.

The Cold War

For nearly the whole of its history the United States had abjured the balance of power system, following the advice of Washington and Jefferson against any "permanent" or "entangling" alliances. A revolution in American foreign policy occurred during World War II, when the United States, under President Franklin D. Roosevelt, became deeply involved in the power politics that would shape the postwar era.[33] At Casablanca, Cairo, Teheran, and Yalta, President Roosevelt entered into pivotal Allied decisions on postwar settlements: unconditional surrender of the Axis powers and a succession of territorial arrangements in the Far East and in Eastern Europe. And at Potsdam, President Truman helped to draw up the final and fateful arrangements for a totally defeated Germany and Japan.

The wartime and immediate postwar agreements engaged the United States in world affairs to an extent hitherto unimaginable to the American people. As late as 1951, Senator Robert Taft could still stage a "great debate" in the American Senate on whether the President of the United States could or should send troops to Europe in peacetime. But the die had been cast. American frontiers had already moved to the Elbe, the Black Sea, the Himalayas, the Mekong, and the China Sea. During the postwar period, the United States would enter into a network of defensive alliances with more than forty countries in Europe, the Middle East, Latin America, and the Far East, some multilateral, some bilateral. It would back up its vast new commitments with almost astronomical expenditures for military establishments and foreign aid programs. The American people would come to accept military conscription, overseas service, continued mobilization of the domestic economy, and even rockets to the moon as normal peacetime requirements for the national security.

The revolution in foreign policy was rationalized by most Americans as a necessary defensive measure against "the enemy." Just as they had subscribed to the "devil theory" when they fought the war against fascism and national

---

[33]William G. Carleton, *The Revolution in American Foreign Policy,* 2nd ed. (New York: Random House, Inc., 1967) narrates and interprets the course of American foreign policy since 1945 and views the contemporary situation from the perspective of history.

socialism, so Americans were now psychologically prepared to battle communism. A distinguished Secretary of State in the 1950s persuaded himself—and officially acted according to this persuasion—that WE were the free world and THEY were the communist menace and that all who did not join with us must be against us. As one well-known historian explains it, the notion of an international communist conspiracy fits neatly into the traditional American shibboleth of Old World wickedness and New World virtue.[34] One can do business with economic, political, or military rivals, but it is difficult for a moral-minded nation to come to terms with an ideological rival.

So long as we could view the Cold War in a bipolar context, as a moral crusade against monolithic, immoral communism, American foreign policy was strongly motivated, and impressively supported, at least at home. By the 1960s, however, it was clearly oversimplification and indeed a denial of plain reality to regard the world as divided into two power blocs or two ideological camps.

The war-torn countries of Western Europe to which we had extended aid under the Marshall Plan and a succession of European recovery and mutual security programs had miraculously recovered. Meantime, they had also established new and integrated economic systems. Six of them—France, West Germany, Italy, Belgium, Holland, and Luxemburg—traditional rivals in business, had formed a Common Market. Another seven had united in a European Free Trade Association: Britain, Denmark, Norway, Sweden, Portugal, Switzerland, and Austria. Moreover, as the peoples of Western Europe prospered, as business boomed and unemployment all but disappeared, American influence, which had been so all-pervasive immediately after the war, began to wane. The United States, which had once made the political unity of Europe a major goal in foreign policy, now found itself on the outside of what was largely its own creation. By 1967, at the behest of American agricultural, labor, and business groups, Congress was seriously reconsidering American trade policies, moving toward neo-isolationism with proposals for import quotas and higher tariffs. And European governments were threatening economic reprisal.

The Atlantic Alliance endures as the core of American foreign policy. Fifteen nations of Europe and North America comprise "a community with a common fund of history, traditions, loyalties, interests, and hopes that give life and make possible common efforts toward common goals."[35] The North Atlantic Treaty Organization, (NATO), however, is in disrepair. When the U.S. Senate approved the North Atlantic Treaty in 1949, circumstances were quite different than they appear today. In 1949, given the menacing military posture of Stalin's Soviet Union, our decision-makers were fully convinced that American vital interests in Europe were in immediate peril. NATO was conceived as a mutual defense alliance with coordinated military forces under a unified command. All of the member nations were expected to contribute conventional

[34]Henry Steele Commager, Professor at Amherst College, "Changing American Attitudes Toward Foreign Policy," Hearing before the Committee on Foreign Relations, U.S. Senate, February 20, 1967. (Washington, D.C.: U.S. Government Printing Office, 1967), p. 15.

[35]*The Atlantic Alliance: Unfinished Business*, a study submitted by the Subcommittee on National Security and International Operations to the Committee on Government Operations, U.S. Senate (Washington, D.C.: U.S. Government Printing Office, 1967), p. 1.

forces, but a central feature would be the continuing presence of American troops in Western Europe and, most important, a nuclear umbrella provided by the United States for the whole Atlantic community.

In 1949, it was not too difficult to persuade our allies that the Soviet Union posed a threat to the free world. The Soviet Union had opposed NATO with its own military alliance, the Warsaw Pact, comprising the communist countries of Eastern Europe; and the Soviet Union offered a similar nuclear umbrella. Such was the "balance of terror" that kept the peace in the 1950s. Today, however, the Soviet Union flies the banners of peaceful coexistence, and the United States is trying to build more bridges between the East and West. The Communist bloc actually began to break up as early as 1948, when Marshall Tito led Yugoslavia into defecting from the Soviet system of satellites. Since then, despite the fact that they are all ideologically oriented toward Marxism, Poland, Czechoslovakia, Rumania, Hungary, and Albania differentiate quite considerably in their practice of communism.

As a result of the thaw in East-West relations, members of NATO, no longer fearful of imminent military attack, began to bicker among themselves concerning military force requirements and strategic plans. France, especially irked by the predominance of American military power and consequent influence of the U.S. in the domestic affairs of Europe, pulled French forces out of NATO and, in effect, evicted NATO and U.S. military personnel and facilities from France in 1967. The shake-up in NATO has certainly discombobulated American foreign policy toward Europe; Congress has seriously debated a cutback of American troops in Europe.[36] We are, however, still determined to protect and promote our vital stakes in the Atlantic Alliance. The problem for our decision-makers now is how to develop a flexible response to the changing situation. As the Senate Subcommittee on National Security and International Operations summed it up, "the problem is complex, involving questions of national prestige, interallied confidence, strategy, and East-West relations."[37]

When we look at the world today in terms of rival ideologies, we no longer find two competing camps sharply distinguished one from the other. We see about 135 different independent countries, each with its own national traditions, its own kind of government, its own economic system. The United States remains the leading exponent of "free enterprise," but many of its allies are well advanced toward socialism. Indeed, socialism made its most spectacular gains in Europe following World War II, when victors and vanquished alike required a great deal of government planning, government aid, and government controls to recover from wartime destruction. On the other hand, as the European communist countries prosper under planned industrialization, the pressures of liberalism and individualism have made headway. In

---

[36]See, for example, *United States Troops in Europe*, Hearings before the combined subcommittees of Foreign Relations and Armed Services Committees, U.S. Senate, April 26 and May 3, 1967 (Washington, D.C.; U.S. Government Printing Office, 1967).

[37]*The Atlantic Alliance: Basic Issues*, a study submitted by the Subcommittee on National Security and International Operations to the Committee on Government Operations, U.S. Senate (Washington, D.C.: U.S. Government Printing Office, 1966), p. 11.

1967, the Russians celebrated fifty years of communism; it was a genuine celebration, for the Soviet Union of today is very different from the grim regime of Stalin in the 1930s and '40s. All of which is to say that we tend to oversimplify conditions in the external world—when actually we have to deal with an exceedingly complex and fast-changing situation.

In the 1950s, the official version as well as the popular American stereotype of the communist world saw it as an international revolutionary conspiracy with headquarters in the Kremlin, backed by the powerful might of the Soviet Union. Today, American decision-makers are trying to defuse the Cold War and to re-educate the American people to the new realities of the external environment. In the words of a high State Department official speaking to a local civic group in 1967: "Today we can no longer talk of a Sino-Soviet bloc. Indeed, we cannot properly refer to a Soviet bloc. The communist world has ceased to be a monolithic entity. . . . Doctrinal communism has proved no match for the powerful forces of national aspirations in our century."[38]

Since 1961, American policy-makers, in their attempt to reshape the strategy of the Cold War, have treated different communist countries differently, while still recommending resistance to communist aggression, by force if necessary, as in Viet Nam. The Johnson administration has been inclined to open the channels of communication, develop cultural contacts, and promote trade with communist countries in Eastern Europe. Because the issues of the Cold War had initially been presented in a moral context, the official decision-makers have had a tough time trying to get across to the American public that it is now "good business, good policy, and good sense" to develop friendly ties behind the Iron Curtain.

If we look at the external environment quite objectively, we perceive that, in varying degrees, among all peoples, in all countries, under totalitarian and democratic governments, under whatever economic system, the revolution of rising expectations is changing the relationships between the public and private sectors of society.[39] Everywhere, people (including most Americans) look to their governments to get what they need or want at home and abroad—and everywhere governments are getting bigger, more bureaucratic, more impersonal. This then is the external environment in which American foreign policy must be conducted. It is a complex world that cannot be comprehended by recourse to clichés and abstractions, influenced or conquered by slogans, or effectively projected by "images." There is no simple model for making or implementing foreign policy in the modern world. Decision-making in foreign policy—if it is to succeed in terms of goals and objectives, general or specific, long-range or immediate, strategic, political, economic, or cultural—calls for all kinds of highly specialized intelligence and the most sophisticated judgments.

[38]Foy D. Kohler, Deputy Under Secretary for Political Affairs, "Constructive Initiatives in East-West Relations," address to the Cincinnati Council on World Affairs, Feb. 17, 1967. Reprinted in State Department release, "Building Bridges to Eastern Europe."

[39]*World Pressures on American Foreign Policy*, edited by Marian D. Irish (Englewood Cliffs, N.J.: Prentice-Hall, Inc., 1964), examines the impact of changing international politics and external forces on American foreign policy. See especially Henry B. Mayo, "Theory, Ideology, and Foreign Policy"; Merle Fainsod, "The Future of the Communist Bloc and American Foreign Policy"; and Frederick M. Watkins, "Colonialism, Dictatorship, and the American Political Tradition."

The Domestic Environment of American Foreign Policy

Policy-making in a reasoned framework means choosing among alternative courses of action after carefully calculating the probable rewards and deprivations. Because the United States (or for that matter any country) must pursue its foreign policy beyond its own jurisdiction, the outside world in all its complexities conditions the policy choices of our decision-makers. The range of alternatives available is further limited by the domestic environment, by the ideological orientation of the people and their sense of national purpose, by constitutional and traditional prescriptions, and by the input of domestic politics and the pattern of interests within the political system. Most of this book has been given over to a general analysis of these factors. Here it should suffice to point out some of the factors which are particularly pertinent in the formulation and implementation of American foreign policy.

Ideological Orientation

The ideological orientation of the American people is rooted, as in any country, in historical experience. We are a revolutionary people, and because of this we are inclined to be sympathetic toward the revolutionary nations in today's world. We were once an exploited colony, and because of this we profess to dislike colonialism and imperialism even when practiced by our friends and allies. We entered the international community as an underdeveloped country, and because of this we feel obliged to give our aid and technical know-how to the less developed countries of today. As a constitutional democracy we identify ourselves with the Free World and expressly oppose totalitarianism, especially communism. Because we are a peace-loving nation, we are committed to the principles of international law and support the peace-keeping operations of the United Nations.

Every nation attempts to justify its foreign policy in sweeping ideological terms. This is effective strategy in modern psychological warfare, but it is not a new tactic. The American Declaration of Independence was consciously written with "a decent respect to the opinions of mankind." It is important, in domestic politics as well as in international relations, that a government appear to be acting in accord with the basic beliefs and moral convictions of its people. Political ideas which appeal to the minds of men and capture their imagination also move them to action. That an idea does not perform as promised does not necessarily detract from its function. For example, a great many Americans went into World War I "to make the world safe for democracy," and a great many more since 1947 have been stationed in military posts all over the world to "contain communism."

Historian Henry Steele Commager reminds us that it is in foreign policy especially that Americans are wont to exhibit a double standard of national

Drawing by Herblock; from *Straight Herblock* (New York: Simon & Schuster, 1964).

"Absolutely! We should stay out of foreign affairs and we should make other countries do as we say."

morality; what is right for "us" is wrong for "them."[40] For example, we profess to be deeply disturbed about Chinese policies of expansion and aggression in Asia, but tend to gloss over the facts of our own history: the United States in its first half-century of existence expanded from the Mississippi to the Pacific, trebling our territory at the expense of France, Spain, Mexico, and Britain, pursuing an ideology of republicanism that must then have appeared just as pernicious to the monarchies of Europe as communism does now to capitalist countries. We claim a vital interest in Southeast Asia and engage in war to support our "moral commitment" to South Viet Nam; but we would not tolerate a similar claim to vital interest or moral commitment on the part of the Soviet Union to Cuba. A foreign policy in support of ideology or in pursuit of moral purpose is usually viewed skeptically by the outside world.

Diplomats and scholars both agree that competing ideologies have a part in contemporary international relations, but we find widespread disagreement concerning the actual influence of ideology in the making or implementing of policy. Hans Morgenthau, best known for his debunking of "moralism" and "sentimentalism" in American foreign policy, nevertheless insists that "in

[40] "Changing American Attitudes Toward Foreign Policy," p. 7.

order to be worthy of our lasting sympathy, a nation must pursue its interest for the sake of a transcendent purpose that gives meaning to the day-by-day operations of its foreign policy."[41] Henry Mayo, in a perceptive analysis of "theory, ideology, and foreign policy," suggests that abstract theory may be relevant, but that as a political force it is never enough to control policy.[42] But whether or not ideology is a controlling factor in policy-making, public opinion at home and expectations abroad require every nation, and certainly a world power, to stand for something more than "national interest" or "national security and economic well-being." Thus the United States, as the oldest constitutional democracy, claims leadership of the Free World; the Soviet Union, as the most successful exponent of Marxism, claims to head the communist cause. It is, however, as we have already observed in our survey of the external environment, unrealistic to view world politics as a grand confrontation of two opposing ideologies. As Professor Mayo points out, the decision-makers in the Kremlin have "on the record adjusted Marxist ideology to their practice rather than the other way around." Over the years, Soviet foreign policy has been primarily directed toward strengthening the Soviet Union and only secondarily toward promoting world revolution. On the other hand, the "Free World" has not subscribed wholly to the American Creed, and has no agreed definable doctrine except perhaps a basic belief in the right of every nation to go its own way and for all to exist in diversity.

Toward the end of the 1950s, some high-ranking policy-makers became alarmed that the American people had lost their sense of national purpose. President Eisenhower actually commissioned a dozen distinguished citizens, representing a cross-section of leadership in American society, to establish a series of "Goals for Americans" both on the home front and in foreign affairs. Members of the Commission reached consensus on such generalities as "The basic foreign policy of the United States should be the preservation of its own independence and free institutions" and "Our principles and ideals impel us to aid the new nations." When the recommendations got down to brass tacks, however, individual members began to disagree with each other. The Commission agreed that "The healthiest world economy is attained when trade is at its freest," but not all members would go along with the specific recommendation that the United States should gradually reduce its tariffs and quota restrictions. The Commission agreed that the United States should stand firm and strong against communist aggression and subversion. The majority thought we should be prepared to negotiate specific issues with communist nations on a reasonable basis and to try continuously for mutual tolerance. The representative of organized labor, however, took exception to a specific suggestion that we enlarge personal and cultural contacts with the peoples behind the Iron Curtain, because he feared that, given an opportunity, Soviet trade unionists would attempt to subvert American labor organization.[43]

[41] *The Purpose of American Politics*, p. 8.
[42] In *World Pressure on American Foreign Policy*, p. 26.
[43] The President's Commission on National Goals, *Goals for Americans* (Englewood Cliffs, N.J.: Prentice-Hall, Inc., a Spectrum Book, 1960).

About the same time that President Eisenhower appointed his Commission, the Senate Committee on Foreign Relations requested the Council on Foreign Relations (a general interest group) to make a study of the "basic aims of American foreign policy." An *ad hoc* group of Council members, after examining the historic aims of American foreign policy, concluded that foreign policy in practice rarely corresponds fully to broad statements of aim and principle; that decisions are made and actions taken on the basis of "calculations of national interest in the specific circumstances." The Council's report to the Senate Committee covered diverse official policies: building an international order, strengthening the Atlantic Community, economic and technical assistance for the less developed areas, military needs to meet the communist challenge, limitation and control of armaments. The Report also underscored the massive unofficial contacts which Americans make today with peoples all over the world (trade relations, tourism on a grand scale, exchange of professors and students, exchange of scientific findings, and the movement of ideas across national frontiers via press, radio, and motion pictures). And it made the important point that the "national purpose," as judged abroad, is determined by the actual conduct of the American society. Moreover, the Report concluded, "as a free and pluralist society America speaks not with one voice but with many."[44]

A political ideology intended for export is not likely to be persuasive unless it is geared to the experiences of the people whom it endeavors to reach. This is the basic dilemma in American foreign policy: how can we convey the American appreciation of due process of law and the blessings of liberty to people who most of all seek equality, and especially equality in the economic sphere? How can we explain the advantages of democratic capitalism over totalitarian communism to a people who are not prepared for self-government and whose economy is far from modernized? On the other hand, the communist line comes closer to the aspirations of the new nations, challenging the inequities of the *status quo* and promising to raise the standards of living for the underprivileged masses. The Soviet Union, which has developed into a modern industrial state and acquired great power and prestige on the world stage within a single generation, becomes the very prototype of communism. Constitutional democracy, with its respect for individual rights and human dignity, may be more impressive in the long run, but meantime the new countries are most eager to improve their material conditions and to modernize their society in this generation. Hence American foreign policy toward the underdeveloped countries is a sophisticated mix of economic assistance and technological aid, along with information and propaganda to publicize the American ideology.

Constitutional Prescription and the Pattern of Federalism

Looking at the Constitution of 1787, we are struck by the Framers' preoccupation with foreign affairs. More than half of the powers enumerated to the Congress in Article I, Section 8, are related to problems of national security or international relations. Congress

---

[44]Council on Foreign Relations, *Basic Aims of United States Foreign Policy*, No. 7 in *United States Foreign Policy, Compilation of Studies*, prepared under the direction of the Committee on Foreign Relations, U.S. Senate (Washington, D.C.: U.S. Government Printing Office, 1961.)

has power to provide for the common defense; regulate commerce with foreign nations; regulate the value of foreign coin in the United States; establish uniform rules of naturalization; define and punish piracies and felonies committed on the high seas and offenses against the law of nations; declare war; make rules concerning captures on land and water; raise and support armies and a navy and make rules for governance of the armed services; provide for the organization, arming, and training of a militia. Add to this enumeration of specifics all the powers necessary and proper (or convenient and useful) to carry out the foregoing, and you see that Congress carries a considerable weight in foreign policy, even though Article II of the Constitution gives to the President the initiative and primary authority in foreign policy. (The President's various roles as head of state, Commander-in-Chief, and director general of foreign policy are discussed in Chapter 11.)

The overall concept of constitutionalism sets the outer limits of decision-making for the governors as well as the governed; it restrains Congress, the President, and the bureaucrats. The Constitution is intended to govern at all times, in war and in peace, in times of depression or inflation, as well as in times of "normalcy." It cannot be suspended to meet emergencies, however great. It is not merely a philosophical statement of aims, high purposes, and ultimate goals. It is a legal prescription for political behavior within United States jurisdiction, any law or practice in the several states notwithstanding.

The American pattern of federalism poses many problems in the foreign policy process. The Constitution makes it quite clear that, when it comes to international relations, the national government has complete power. Because this power was not granted to the national government by the states, they cannot recover it at any time. International law reinforces the Constitution on this point: under international law, every independent and sovereign nation has the inherent power to engage in foreign affairs. As Justice Sutherland pointed out, sovereignty in world affairs passed directly from the British Crown to the government of the United States in 1776.[45] None of the states (except Texas and Hawaii) has ever exercised independent power in the international community. Furthermore, the Constitution specifically forbids the states to enter into any agreements with foreign nations. In short, then, although the states may retain power over certain domestic matters, they can claim no power over foreign affairs.

The treaty power of the national government, for example, is *plenary*, or absolute, and it is an *exclusive* power that is not shared with the states in any way. As early as 1796, and again in 1816, the Supreme Court declared that a treaty was valid even if it conflicted with laws passed by the states. In the 1816 decision, when the Supreme Court overruled the highest court of Virginia, it touched off a storm of protest from advocates of states' rights. The Virginia court angrily responded that the Supreme Court did not have the authority to reverse a state court, for the sovereign states had created the Constitution and

[45] *United States v. Curtiss-Wright Export Corporation*, 299 U.S. 304 (1936).

they had reserved to themselves the right to settle their own problems. Justice Story, speaking for the Supreme Court, rejected the idea that the Constitution is a compact among sovereign states and declared it to be a supreme law created by the people themselves. He gave short shrift to the argument that the Supreme Court did not have the right to review actions of state courts.[46] Without such review, the nation would have no supreme law. A treaty is superior to any state law, then, and the Supreme Court has the authority to enforce it as part of the "supreme law of the land."

Unlike the laws of Congress, which must be made "in pursuance" of the Constitution, treaties are made "under the authority of the United States." The states have claimed time and time again that the treaty power ought not to be used to abridge their powers reserved under the Tenth Amendment, but this may only be the wishful thinking of states' rights advocates. For example, in the case of *Missouri* v. *Holland* (1920), the Supreme Court upheld a treaty between the United States and Great Britain calling for the protection of migratory birds in Canada and the United States.[47] Earlier, the Court had rejected a law passed by Congress to protect migratory birds, claiming that it was an invasion of the police power of the states to protect game within their respective jurisdictions; the Court could find no delegated or implied power under which Congress could enact such a law. Once the treaty had been concluded by the national government, the Court accepted substantially the same legislation, on the grounds that Congress had power to implement the treaty. In a more recent opinion—involving an executive agreement concerning the legal status of American soldiers in Great Britain—Mr. Justice Black declared that it would be "manifestly contrary to the objectives of those who created the Constitution" for the United States government to make agreements without observing constitutional prohibitions. He judged it "completely anomalous" to say that a treaty need not comply with the Constitution.[48]

The Constitution requires the consent of two-thirds of the Senate before the President can ratify a treaty. This provision assures the states some control over the manner in which the national government uses its treaty power. But they have no such control over "executive agreements" as a means of conducting foreign policy. The President may conclude an executive agreement with a foreign government without obtaining the consent of the Senate, and such an agreement is just as binding on the states as a treaty. In 1933, for example, President Roosevelt concluded an executive agreement with the Soviet government to settle claims and counterclaims arising out of the Communist Revolution of 1917. Under the terms of this agreement, the United States government was assigned a considerable amount of property rights in this country claimed by the Soviet government under its nationalization decrees. New York State, however, refused to recognize the extraterritorial effect of the Soviet decrees on the grounds that confiscation of private property was contrary to the public policy of New York. Hence, when the United States government sued to recover the assets of the New York branch of a Russian insurance company that had been "nationalized," the New York courts

---

[46]*Martin* v. *Hunter's Lessee*, 1 Wheat. 304 (1816).
[47]252 U.S. 416 (1920).
[48]*Reid* v. *Covert*, 354 U.S. 1 (1957).

refused to turn the property over to the national government. But the Supreme Court of the United States ruled against New York:

> No state can rewrite our foreign policy to conform to its own domestic policies. . . . The policies of the States become wholly irrelevant to judicial inquiry when the United States, acting within its constitutional sphere, seeks enforcement of its foreign policy in the courts.[49]

National supremacy in the foreign affairs of the United States is incontestable. In this respect, these Supreme Court decisions make several points clear: (1) the United States has plenary and exclusive power over foreign affairs; (2) this power is not shared with the states and need not be exercised so that it conforms to state policies; (3) Congress may exercise powers in carrying out a treaty that are neither delegated nor implied in the Constitution itself; (4) the President is our principal agent in foreign affairs and may make far-reaching agreements without even consulting Congress or obtaining its consent; (5) neither the President nor Congress may use the treaty power in violation of constitutional principles.

In terms of constitutional law, the national supremacy in foreign affairs is uncontestable. But, as we have pointed out in Chapter 5, the politics of federalism, as reflected in the decision-making process and in the policy output, is another matter. When we recall that congressmen are oriented toward constituencies in their own states (and this is especially true of senators, whose constituencies are the states), we can assume that state interests are specifically represented in the formulation of the national interest. Empirical evidence for this assumption appears, for example, in foreign trade and foreign aid bills, in various provisions calculated to protect or promote state industries, e.g., Indiana steel, North Carolina textiles, Texas cattle, Massachusetts fisheries, Nebraska wheat, and Minnesota minerals. The economic interests of the several states constitute a pervasive and persistent influence in American foreign policy.

The somewhat erratic course of American policy concerning the UN-sponsored Declaration of Human Rights shows how the proponents of states' rights may influence the national posture in international politics. The United States took a leading part in drafting the Declaration. The draft, which Mrs. Franklin D. Roosevelt, as Chairman of the Human Rights Commission, presented to the United Nations General Assembly, is a rousing piece of prose in which we join the peoples of the world in expressing our faith in fundamental human rights. But when it came to drafting the Covenant of Human Rights, which would have committed the nations to implement these "human rights," the American delegation was forced into an obstructionist role. For although the United States advocated personal liberties and private property rights, it was reluctant to include some of the social and economic rights now widely accepted by nations that are moving toward socialism. Furthermore, the

[49]U.S. v. Pink, 315 U.S. 203 (1942).

United States insisted on adding a federal-state article to the Covenant. Such an article would permit a federal government like ours to leave enforcement of the Covenant up to its states or provinces. Even this concession was not enough to satisfy the states' rights champions in the United States, who feared that the national government might use the Covenant to claim greater control over civil rights. And so we finally explained to our associates in the United Nations that the policy of the United States is to support the principles of the Declaration but to abstain from support of the Covenant which might have obligated us to take action.

Constitutionally, under the treaty power, the United States could have pledged its support to the Covenant of Human Rights; and Congress could then have passed civil rights legislation to implement the Covenant. To make sure that the pattern of federalism would not be disrupted in this way, Senator John W. Bricker (R.-Ohio), joined by fifty-eight of his fellow senators, proposed an amendment to the Constitution in 1952. As approved by the Senate Judiciary Committee, the Bricker amendment would have (1) nullified any treaty that conflicted with any provision of the Constitution; (2) permitted a treaty to become internal law only through legislation that would have been valid if there had never been such a treaty; (3) given Congress the same power over executive agreements with any foreign power or international organization that it has over treaties.

This attempt to restrain the President's hand in foreign affairs, particularly in making executive agreements, met with top-level opposition. President Truman and his Secretary of State (Dean Acheson), and President Eisenhower and his Secretary (John Foster Dulles), were equally firm in insisting that primary responsibility for making foreign policy decisions must rest with the President. And yet the discussion went on for several years, provoking a nationwide campaign against "un-American internationalism." Debates in Congress reached a sharp peak early in 1954, when both houses several times appeared on the verge of mustering the two-thirds vote needed to pass the amendment; the consent of three-fourths of the state legislatures was virtually assured. Then, in the showdown vote in the Senate, the requisite two-thirds vote was missed by only one vote.

As pointed out earlier, the constitutional pattern of executive-legislative relations—the whole complicated system of checks and balances—affects both the conduct and the content of American foreign policy. Although the Constitution requires that the President share his powers with Congress, continuing crises in international politics since World War II have tended to favor executive authority rather than legislative deliberation in the making of foreign policy.

There are, of course, good reasons for the enhancement of the presidential role in foreign affairs. It is argued that the advance of technology in modern warfare renders obsolete the notion of Congress debating a declaration of war; the Commander-in-Chief may have to make a split-second decision on how to repel an imminent nuclear attack. Another argument is that the President alone has immediate access to all kinds of secret and classified information that cannot be disseminated even to Congress, much less to the general public; hence only the President may know all the facts in a given situation. A third argument follows from the second;—that the President has a built-in relationship with experts and specialists in the bureaucracy, whereas the average congressman can hardly be expected to comprehend all the economic, military, scientific, and diplomatic factors which make foreign policy so intricate and so complex.[50]

Some congressmen, however, and especially senators who have had long legislative experience with foreign policy, are increasingly inclined to resist executive supremacy beyond what they consider the constitutional limits. Thus Senator Sam Ervin, Jr. (D.-N.C.), Chairman of the Senate Subcommittee on Separation of Powers (created in 1967), called on Congress to "recapture its paramount influence" and to reassert its constitutional powers in the determination of American foreign policy, "particularly the power to determine when the armed forces shall be used in offensive warfare."[51] The Senate Committee on Foreign Relations, under the chairmanship of Senator J. William Fulbright (D.-Ark.), has held highly publicized hearings on the conduct as well as the content of the foreign policy of the Johnson administration.

Congressmen—in committees, in floor debates, and as individuals—have raised many constitutional questions relating to the war in Viet Nam: whether the President as Commander-in-Chief has authority to conduct a major war without a declaration of war by Congress; whether Congress can delegate such authority to the President through a joint resolution endorsing whatever action he may deem necessary; whether the President can make—and carry out—commitments to other nations without seeking the advice and consent of the Senate; whether the Senate must deliberate and offer its advice, even, or especially, when it is not solicited by the President; whether the Congress should grant or withhold its consent on major administration policies according to its separate judgment or support the President in a show of national unity on foreign policy.

In 1964, following two days of North Vietnamese PT-boat attacks upon several U.S. destroyers in the Gulf of Tonkin, President Johnson asked Congress for a resolution supporting whatever action the President as Commander-in-Chief regarded as necessary to repel attacks on U.S. armed forces or to prevent communist aggression in Southeast Asia. (Congress had passed similar resolutions to support presidential authority in the past—for President Eisenhower to meet the threat to Formosa in 1955, and again in 1957 during the Middle East crisis; and for President Kennedy in the Cuban crisis of 1962.) After a brief and perfunctory debate, the Senate voted for the resolution, 88–2, on August 7, and the House voted for it on the same day, 416–0. Congress at the time regarded the resolution as an appropriate reaction to a rather minor incident; subsequently, however, the Administration chose to interpret the

---

[50]See statement of Ruhl J. Bartlett, Fletcher School of Law and Diplomacy, "U.S. Commitments to Foreign Powers," Hearings before the Committee on Foreign Relations, U.S. Senate, August 16, 1967 (Washington, D. C.: U.S. Government Printing Office, 1967), p. 9.
[51]Press release from the the office of the Senate Subcommittee on Separation of Powers, August 23, 1967.

Gulf of Tonkin Resolution as congressional authorization for a large-scale war in Viet Nam. When some congressmen began to have sobering second thoughts about the blank check they had given to the Administration's Asian policy, they were hardly reassured by a statement of Secretary of State Dean Rusk that "no would-be aggressor should suppose that the absence of a defense treaty, Congressional declaration, or U.S. military presence grants immunity to aggression."[52] This seemed to convey a significant message: that regardless of congressional action or inaction, approval or disapproval, the executive would pursue its own course against what it considered aggression in international politics.

The Chairman of the Senate Foreign Relations Committee, who had acted as floor manager for the Gulf of Tonkin Resolution, was one of those who bitterly rued the precipitant response of Congress in 1964. Somewhat belatedly, Senator Fulbright deemed it a proper function of the Senate Foreign Relations Committee to make itself available as a forum for recognized experts and scholars to present a variety of views on Viet Nam and on U.S. commitments to foreign powers. Some people feel that such hearings, with full coverage by the mass media, have given aid and comfort to the enemy by creating an image of disunity in the country. But Senator Fulbright believes that "dissent is not disloyalty, that a true consensus is shaped by airing differences rather than suppressing them." Hence he regards the public hearings of the Committee on Foreign Relations as "an experiment in public education" and "a beginning toward restoring the Senate to its proper role as adviser to the President on the great issues of foreign policy."[53]

The Inputs of Foreign Policy: Demands and Supports

The play of domestic politics and the pattern of interests (active or apathetic, public or private) within the political system inevitably affect the course of foreign policy. Foreign policy issues have always engendered sharp dissension in public opinions. One can trace the continuity of disunity from the Washington administration to the Johnson administration and the recurrence of party battles over our foreign relations in every election from 1800 to 1964.

Political Parties and Bipartisanship[54]

In modern times, we recall the fierce partisan quarrels immediately following World War I when Woodrow Wilson as the outgoing Democratic President tried and failed to persuade a Republican-controlled Congress to consent to United States membership in the League of Nations. Certain influential senators were personally piqued because they felt the President had slighted their constitutional prerogatives to

---

[52]Secretary Rusk's statement to the Senate Preparedness Subcommittee on August 25, 1966 is quoted in Senator J. W. Fulbright's statement before the Subcommittee on Separation of Powers of the Judiciary Committee, U.S. Senate, July 19, 1967. Press release.

[53]*The Arrogance of Power* (New York: Random House, Inc., Vintage Books, 1966), p. 56.

[54]Cecil V. Crabb, Jr., *American Foreign Policy in the Nuclear Age*, 2nd. ed. (Evanston, Ill.: Row, Peterson and Company, 1965) includes an excellent chapter, "Executive-Legislative Relations and Bipartisanship." See also Crabb's *Bipartisan Foreign Policy: Myth or Reality* (Evanston, Ill.: Row, Peterson and Company, 1957).

advise and consent. The President had not fully discussed with the Republican leadership problems likely to arise in the Paris peace settlements. He had not been sufficiently politic in his personal relations with the Senate to include Henry Cabot Lodge, the Republican Senator from Massachusetts and Chairman of the Senate Committee on Foreign Relations, in the official entourage that went to Versailles. Subsequently, the Republicans capitalized on the League issue and the war-weariness of the American people to win the presidential election of 1920. Warren G. Harding, the Republican Senator from Ohio who had participated in the partisan attack on the Covenant, succeeded Woodrow Wilson as President. And the American refusal to join the League was to have fateful consequences, not only for the American people but for the entire world.

The controversy over the League points out several significant aspects of policy-making. First, the constitutional prescripton of separation of powers enhances the possibilities of institutional discord between the official decision-makers, President and Congress. Second, partisan interests may be more influential than the so-called national interest when issues in foreign policy can be used to stir the electorate, turn out the party in power, and win the presidency for the opposing party. Third, interpersonal relations among the policy-makers may be crucial, even in decisions of paramount public importance. Fourth, foreign policy cannot be too far ahead of public opinion. Fifth, and perhaps most important, the policy process is no more rational than the men who sit as policy-makers.

The League of Nations fiasco taught the Roosevelt and Truman administrations some very practical lessons in how to conduct foreign policy more effectively during and after World War II. The idea that the leadership of both major parties should rise above partisan politics in the area of national security was consciously institutionalized. The American delegation to the Bretton Woods Conference in 1944, which laid the foundations for the International Bank and the International Monetary Fund, included bipartisan representation from both houses of Congress. Before President Roosevelt went to the summit conference at Yalta, he held a special bipartisan meeting with key members of the Senate to discuss with them what kind of world organization should be sought and how we might go about settling some of the postwar problems of Eastern Europe, including our relations with the Soviet Union.

The United States' part in the organization and operation of the United Nations is a good example of bipartisan foreign policy. The American delegation to the San Francisco Conference that drafted the Charter included Democrats and Republicans from Congress. Before the delegation went to San Francisco, the State Department offered bipartisan briefings, and during discussions and decision-making at the Conference the American delegates participated fully on a bipartisan basis. When the Charter was brought back to Washington, the Senate approved it by the overwhelming bipartisan vote of 89–2. Since San Francisco, American participation in all aspects of the United Nations organization and activities has been deliberately bipartisan. Thus two members of Congress—one Democrat and one Republican—are appointed in alternate years from the House and Senate to sit in the United States delegation to the General Assembly. President Truman, who strongly stressed bipartisanship in foreign affairs, appointed Warren Austin, former Republican Senator from Vermont, to head the first U.S. Mission to the United Nations and to represent us in the Security Council. President Eisenhower was more partisan in designating Henry Cabot Lodge (grandson of the Senator who fought against the League) to succeed Austin, and President Kennedy was just as partisan when he named Adlai Stevenson to the post.

In all important foreign policy decisions since World War II, the community of decision-makers has been bipartisan. Specific practices that set the pattern of bipartisan collaboration include: prior consultation between the Chief Executive and the congressional leadership on all measures that will call for legislative action or an outward show of internal unity; official briefings and continuous liaison between the Secretary of State, the Secretary of Defense, and other executive agencies with such congressional committees as the Senate Committee on Foreign Relations, the House Committee on Foreign Affairs, and both the House and Senate committees on the Armed Services; close working relations between the congressional subcommittees and the geographical and functional divisions of the Department of State and operating agencies in foreign affairs, particularly aid and information. Since the congressional leadership and the congressional committees are bipartisan in composition, these practices of executive-legislative liaison insure overall bipartisan collaboration. Another significant practice is the appointment of negotiators, consultants, and advisors from both major parties to insure bipartisan participation in important international conferences and to promote bipartisan support for the ensuing agreements.

Arthur Vandenberg, the Republican Senator from Michigan, was one of the principal architects of postwar bipartisanship. President Truman counted on the influential Senator to swing his fellow Republicans into line in support of the Marshall Plan, the Truman Doctrine, the China Aid Bill of 1948, the North Atlantic Treaty, the Mutual Defense Assistance Program, and the various economic and technical assistance programs under Point Four. Over and over Senator Vandenberg told the American public—and thus the world—that most Republicans were proud to join the Democrats in a show of national unity on major problems in foreign policy. The ideal, he said, is "an unpartisan American foreign policy—not Republican, not Democratic, but American—which substantially unites our people at the water's edge in behalf of peace."

American foreign policy—under Presidents Roosevelt, Truman, Eisenhower, Kennedy, and Johnson—has been largely bipartisan in planning, negotiating, deciding, and programing.[55] Nevertheless, every national election since World War II has focused on foreign policy as a major partisan issue. How then do we reconcile the continuous practice of bipartisanship with recurrent, fierce to vicious, partisan attacks on formerly agreed policies? First, in all honesty we

[55]See *Review of Bipartisan Foreign Policy Consultations Since World War II* by John Sparkman, 82d Cong., 1st Sess., Sen. Document, No. 87 (Washington, D.C.: U.S. Government Printing Office, 1952).

must point out that not all Republicans were glad to join with Senator Vandenberg in support of President Truman's foreign policy. Senator Robert Taft ("Mr. Republican") from Ohio launched an all-out attack in 1951 on the entire range of Truman's foreign policy, hitting especially hard the "troops-to-Europe" decision which the administration found necessary to implement the NATO agreement. President Truman's dismissal of General MacArthur for failure to support the official and political policies of his own government (and of the UN) touched off a highly partisan investigation and full-scale foreign policy debate that furnished much of the grist for the GOP campaign in 1952.

Second, personal relations as well as partisan considerations enter into the political situation. President Truman bitterly resented General Eisenhower's use of the Korean War as a campaign issue in 1952. President Truman had made General Eisenhower Chief of Staff of the U.S. Army and subsequently Commander of the Allied troops in Europe. In fact, Eisenhower had appeared as a witness for the administration in the congressional hearings on the troops-to-Europe issue. At the outset of the campaign, the President had offered the General complete and confidential briefings on matters of national security, thereby hoping to maintain the posture of national unity in foreign affairs through the election period. The General for his part became increasingly sensitive as President Truman's salty comments rubbed him the wrong way. Because the principals in the situation were hardly on speaking terms after the election, the 1953 transition from Democratic to Republican power in the White House had rough going, with repercussions in foreign policy.

John Foster Dulles, who had been an influential member of President Truman's community of foreign policy advisers and who had negotiated the Japanese Peace Treaty for the administration, was chief strategist for the Republican Party on foreign policy issues in 1952. The Republicans charged the Democrats with plunging us into the Korean War, abandoning the friendly nations of Eastern Europe to communist rule, and permitting the communists to take over China, and in general blamed the Roosevelt and Truman administrations for all the troubles in Latin America, the Middle East, the Far East, and Africa. After the Republicans clinched their victory at the polls, Dulles appeared before the Senate Committee on Foreign Relations as the President-elect's choice for Secretary of State. Responding to questions from committee members about how the election returns would affect the course of foreign policy, Dulles explained that a political campaign is like a legal contest. The parties play the role of lawyers rather than judges; they represent their clients in court and use what tactics are necessary to win their case. When the case is settled, the opposing lawyers can shake hands in professional fellowship. Thus, when a national election is won, campaign charges can be dropped. Said the incoming Secretary, "I believe we should try to work together on a bipartisan basis."[56]

[56]Hearing before the Committee on Foreign Relations, U.S. Senate, 83rd Cong., 1st Sess., on nomination of John Foster Dulles, Sec. of State designate, Jan. 15, 1953 (Washington, D.C.: U.S. Government Printing Office, 1953).

In January, 1960, when Senator John F. Kennedy from Massachusetts announced his candidacy for the Democratic presidential nomination, he attacked the Republican administration for the whole sorry state of the world. The attack, however, was on the *style* rather than the substance of administrative policy. This was the Kennedy image sustained throughout the campaign (and for the less than three years he was in office): a young man born in this century, dedicated to the public service, experienced in the political process, ready to make the most of presidential powers, alert to the crucial issues of our times, prepared to open and keep open the channels of communication between the world of thought and the world of action.

The incoming Kennedy administration stressed the "leadership of change," and in the revolutionary world of the 1960s change was certainly the order of the day. But the Kennedy administration had to learn (as every administration must) that the central themes of American foreign policy are more or less constant, regardless of the party in power. National traditions, historical precedents, legal principles, strategic interest, and policy commitments continue to shape the national policies without regard for individual administrations. Party changes in the American political system may affect the external environment, but only incidentally. The pattern of cross-purposes in the international community is determined by the ideas, interests, and institutions that condition policy-makers in more than a hundred independent nation-states.

In all policy planning, events have a way of altering the input even before the planners have had time to assess their data. The death of Premier Joseph Stalin in March 1953 was probably the most significant event in the first year of President Eisenhower's administration. Policy-makers in Washington had nothing to do with reorganizing the party and state apparatus in the U.S.S.R., but the new regime in Moscow immediately affected the plans of the Eisenhower administration to carry psychological warfare behind the iron curtain. Early in the Kennedy administration, Fidel Castro joined Cuba to the communist bloc; the rift widened between the Soviet Union and the People's Republic of China; the East German government built a concrete wall that sealed off East from West Berlin; Secretary General of the UN, Dag Hammarskjold, killed in a plane crash in the Congo, was replaced by U Thant, Burmese Ambassador to the UN, thus symbolizing the new Afro-Asian balance of power in international diplomacy; Russian troops, then Russian missiles, appeared in Cuba. To these events—and to many more in the world outside—the Kennedy administration had to react and the sum of the reactions became a large part of American foreign policy.

"New frontiers" were established in the Kennedy administration, such as the Alliance for Progress and the Peace Corps, but the grand design of foreign policy was not radically changed. As in every administration since World War II, national security was—and continues to be—the main objective. President Kennedy had no difficulty in obtaining bipartisan support for increased expenditures for military purposes, including a build-up in conventional weapons to implement a policy of "limited war" as an alternative to nuclear confrontation. When President Johnson, in his first budget, attempted to cut expenditures at points where he thought our defenses were already powerful, congressmen from both parties and in all parts of the country protested on behalf of constituents who had economic interests in defense installations and defense contracts.

As in the Truman and Eisenhower administrations, the second line of defense was—and continues to be—foreign aid, with emphasis shifting in the Kennedy and Johnson administrations from military to economic assistance, especially for the underdeveloped countries. Each year debates on foreign aid get rougher, however, as Congress becomes increasingly reluctant to appropriate the taxpayers' money for overseas projects. Nevertheless, on the record, both Democrats and Republicans voted for—and against—foreign aid programs in the Truman, Eisenhower, Kennedy, and Johnson administrations.

foreign aid

An incoming administration cannot start with a clean slate. It must begin with the policies and commitments of its predecessor. In the 1952 election, the Republicans claimed that if they were returned to power they would "repudiate all commitments contained in secret understandings such as those of Yalta." But, in fact, President Eisenhower found himself constrained to observe all agreements made in good faith by his predecessors in office. *Pacta sunt servanda*—agreements are observed. Even if the American President had wanted to undo the political and military decisions taken at Yalta and Potsdam, he could not have turned back the sequence of past events in countries outside the United States. Likewise, when President Kennedy took office he inherited policies and programs from the Eisenhower administration. Secretary Dulles had tied the United States into a network of mutual defense arrangements with forty-three different nations. Secretary Rusk accepted these treaties with all their implications as part of continuing American foreign policy. An incoming administration may recommend reversal of its predecessor's domestic policies, but in foreign affairs it cannot repudiate international agreements—i.e., the *continuum of policies* involving international agreements or commitments. Notice, however, that continuum of policies is not a static concept. The new party in power will have an opportunity to make its own choices of action as new events and new actors change both the external environment and the domestic situation.

Pressure Groups in Foreign Policy

The continuity of bipartisanship in American foreign policy suggests the existence of considerable consensus in relevant American public opinion. This is because American political parties, as well as the electorate, generally view foreign policy as a grand design to insure *national* security and *national* well-being. But if we look at foreign policy not so much in terms of high-level diplomatic relations but rather in the context of day-to-day operations from country to country, then we perceive that specific programs represent a wide range of special interests, rival interests, and conflicts of interest. We have already discussed in Chapter 8, how the activities of interest groups enter into the policy process. It would be remiss, however, not to point out some of the diverse demands and supports that press specifically upon decision-makers in *foreign* policy. The accommodation of various special interests within the framework of "national interest" explains what might otherwise seem to be an incoherent approach to national policies.

We began this chapter by stressing the "externalness" of American foreign policy. At this point, again we stress the obvious. Just as the United States maintains diplomatic missions in more than a hundred different countries for the purpose of advancing *our* national interests (and the interests of American nationals), so do these same hundred and more countries maintain *their* diplomatic missions in the United States to advance *their* national interests (and the interests of *their* nationals). In Washington, there is continuous traffic between the foreign embassies and the various administrative agencies in Washington that deal in foreign affairs—the State Department, AID, the Export-Import Bank, and so on.

The diplomat's job is a politically delicate one. He is expected to provide his own government with maximum intelligence about the country to which he is accredited. This means he must seek authoritative information. He is expected also to negotiate for whatever policies (programs) that might benefit his own government. He must therefore have access to those in authority and in positions to carry out commitments. Because diplomats are formally accredited to heads of states, it is generally understood that they will pursue their missions with the executive branch of the government, not with the legislative branch.

International law accords the diplomat many privileges and immunities which facilitate his mission, but it also places him under various restrictions. Thus it is not proper for a foreign diplomat in the United States to seek an engagement with a congressional committee, even though the committee may be considering a program very important to his country. By the same convention, a congressional committee may not invite foreign diplomats to testify, even though such testimony might be the shortest cut to first-hand information which the Committee needs to suggest intelligent legislation. On the other hand, congressmen and foreign diplomats may meet "for lunch" and talk on any topic. The constant round of social life in Washington affords congressmen, foreign diplomats, and other key actors a nonofficial setting where they can get together on matters of common interest. Who influences whom and how much depends on many factors.

That diplomatic missions try to influence American decision-makers is so obvious that it is often overlooked in analysis of inputs in the foreign policy process. Another set of influentials, usually not so obvious in their activities, are the many (about five-hundred) nondiplomatic individuals and organizations who act within the United States as private agents of foreign governments and interests.[57] Since 1938, these foreign agents have been required by law (1) to register with the Attorney General; (2) to identify the foreign governments or foreign interests which they serve; (3) to account for the activities they undertake on behalf of their foreign principals; and (4) to indicate any

[57]See *Activities of Non-Diplomatic Representatives of Foreign Principals in the United States,* Hearings before the Committee on Foreign Relations, U.S. Senate, 88th Cong., 1st Sess. (Washington, D.C.: U.S. Government Printing Office, 1963).

foreign propaganda which they circulate in the United States. Since these foreign agents are not diplomats, they do not have the latter's special privileges and immunities; but neither are they subject to the restrictions of international law. Provided that they declare their activities, they are legally free to influence legislative or executive decision-makers.

The number of foreign agents in the United States has increased in recent years, partly because the number of countries in the world has increased and also because many of the new nations do not have sufficient native talent for export. They frequently find it more effective to supplement their rather small diplomatic corps with American citizens paid to perform specific services. The Attorney General's list indicates that the largest number of such foreign agents in the United States are engaged in public relations, publicity, and information activities. The second largest group provides legal services; some of the most distinguished law firms in the United States are on the payrolls of foreign governments or foreign interest groups. The third largest category includes economic consultants, financial advisers, and trade promoters, the kind of experts most needed by the developing countries. These foreign agents work to influence governmental activities on behalf of their clients; they also may provide liaison between interest groups in this country and groups with similar interests in the country which they represent.

Gabriel Almond in his study of *American People and Foreign Policy* identifies and classifies American interest groups that influence foreign policy: (1) labor groups (e.g., AFL-CIO); (2) business organizations (U.S. Chamber of Commerce, National Association of Manufacturers); (3) agricultural groups (American Farm Bureau Federation, National Grange); (4) veterans' groups (American Legion, Veterans of Foreign Wars); (5) women's groups (League of Women Voters, American Association of University Women); (6) religious groups (National Council of Churches of Christ, specific church groups such as Methodists, Presbyterians, Roman Catholics, etc.); (7) ethnic groups (Jews,

"Grin and Bear It" by George Lichty; reprinted by permission of Publishers-Hall Syndicate.

"As a small, proud nation we refuse to be the captive of Yankee economic and military aid . . . but don't pay any attention to us!"

Germans, Poles, etc.). Here we add (8) government groups (vested and special interests *within* the government agencies).[58]

Government agencies, especially bureaucrats with specialized interests, do what they can to influence the political process in order to further particular programs to which they are professionally committed. The Pentagon, for example, effectively lobbies on military issues; AID on foreign aid; and USIA on information programs. Most administrative agencies now maintain a professional staff whose task it is to sell administrative programs. The Department of State has an Assistant Secretary of State whose job it is to handle "congressional relations," not only for the Secretary of State but also for all the various bureaus and offices in the Department. The Department of Defense also has an Assistant Secretary whose office manages legislative affairs for the many components within the Pentagon. The White House Staff coordinates the legislative liaison activities of the several agencies. When congressional committees are asked to authorize and to appropriate funds for specific programs and particular operations, it is the bureaucrats most concerned who really put mind and heart into "justifications."

Outside the government, the lineup of pressure groups varies considerably according to issues. A dramatic illustration of pressure groups in action during the course of decision-making occurred in the late summer of 1963, when the Treaty of Moscow was before the Senate.[59] The treaty, which culminated long-time negotiations between the United States and the Soviet Union, forbade participants to conduct nuclear weapons tests or nuclear explosions in the atmosphere, in space, in territorial waters, or on the high seas. The Senate committees on the Armed Services and Foreign Relations held joint hearings over several weeks, so that many interested individuals and organizations, official and nonofficial, could present their dissident views. Two groups with professional stakes in the issue, the militarists and the atomic scientists, were divided among themselves, with spokesmen supporting and opposing the treaty. Among those pressuring for ratification were the United World Federalists, the American Friends Service Committee, SANE, Methodist church organizations, and other religious groups. The American Legion endorsed the treaty subject to certain reservations, whereas the Veterans of Foreign Wars opposed it. A Citizens Committee for Nuclear Test Ban, including thirteen Nobel Prize winners, coordinated the activities of approximately twenty-five interest groups in a nationwide campaign to influence public opinion in turn to influence congressmen. Congressional offices reported an unusually heavy barrage of letters, telegrams, and personal visits from constituents. Thanks to the efforts of the Citizens Committee, support for the treaty became consolidated, whereas the opposition, though also intense, was not organized. The Treaty of Moscow was ratified by a bipartisan vote, 80–19. Among the nineteen senatorial votes against it was that of Barry Goldwater, a vote which Johnson and Humphrey exploited in the 1964 campaign as an indication that the Republican candidate was out of "the mainstream" of both parties.

[58] Gabriel Almond *The American People and Foreign Policy,* Chapter VIII.
[59] Mary K. Lepper, *The Nuclear Test Ban Treaty: Demands and Support* (Indianapolis: The Bobbs-Merrill Co., Inc., 1968) discusses the interaction of decision-makers and interest groups in mobilizing public opinion for new policies.

Foreign aid legislation offers a continuing example of interest groups at work shaping the content of American foreign policy. "Our programs of economic assistance are designed to serve a basic goal of U.S. foreign policy: to enlarge the security and well-being of the United States in a world of free nations increasingly able to provide a better life for their peoples."[60] This is the official rationalization of American foreign aid programs. But if we examine the record of hearings before the congressional hearings that authorize and appropriate funds for our foreign assistance policies year after year, we find that a variety of pressure groups manage to wedge their special interests into the sphere of national interest. Bureaucrats from AID, the State Department, and the Defense Department all appear in order to support the President's proposals; but, as we have recognized above, such "official inputs" may also represent vested interests within the administrative agencies; one would not expect AID officials to recommend sweeping cuts in economic assistance, or Pentagon witnesses to urge an end to military assistance; in this sense these officials consitute official pressure groups.

An important feature of the democratic policy process is the interaction of official decision-makers with "opinion-makers" in the unofficial sector of the political system. Congressional hearings serve as a convenient meeting place: they offer representatives of special interest groups legitimate access to a crucial point in decision-making; they give decision-makers an opportunity to survey the spectrum of organized demands and supports on a specific policy; and they provide a forum wherein the unofficial opinion-makers, as well as government officials, may seek to arouse public interest and mobilize support. Thus, every year, associational and institutional representatives appear to plead their special interests regarding pending foreign assistance legislation.

The National Association of State Universities and Land Grant Colleges expresses a special interest in continuing and expanding AID grants to foster educational programs and technical assistance programs in developing countries. The National Farmers Union voices an economic as well as a humanitarian interest in AID programs to speed agricultural growth in underdeveloped countries: the NFU wants AID to encourage cooperative developments and to promote people-to-people exchanges which will bring young farmers to the United States to observe how American agricultural cooperatives fit into the life of the farmers and the business community. The National Association of Home Builders specifies its interest in international housing programs and wants AID programs to include investment guarantees for private demonstration housing projects undertaken by American businessmen in Latin America. The American Federation of Labor and Congress of Industrial Organizations generally supports the nation's foreign aid program, subscribes to the target of 1 per cent of the GNP proposed by the UN as an appropriate national con-

[60]*Foreign Assistance Act of 1966*, Hearings before the Committee on Foreign Affairs, House of Representatives, statement of David E. Bell, Administrator, AID, March 16, 1966 (Washington, D.C.: U.S. Government Printing Office, 1966). Material for this section is taken largely from these hearings. The student may update the material by examining current hearings.

tribution of the industrial nations to the poorer countries, and specifically seeks technical assistance funds allocated to help labor unions to organize in the developing countries. The Chamber of Commerce of the United States wants increased emphasis on private resources in furthering foreign assistance objectives and reduction of government programs after these programs have served their catalytic purposes; the Chamber further urges a coordinating mechanism at the policy-making level whereby the business community will obtain adequate and specific opportunities to register its views on what should go into the foreign assistance legislation. And so it goes. . .

To what degree pressure groups are influential in the formulation or execution of foreign policy is difficult to ascertain. One can, of course, point to the policy output—who gets what. AID contracts with *American* colleges and universities, engineering and construction companies, private business firms, cooperatives, and farm and labor organizations to provide special kinds of assistance to governments and institutions in less developed countries. AID also sends *American* industrial and commercial products, not dollars, overseas—iron and steel, industrial machinery, chemicals, motor vehicles, fertilizers, copper, oil, etc.; approximately 90 per cent of these products are bought from *American* firms. Today foreign assistance appropriations cover approximately $3 billion guaranteeing *American* business investments in less developed countries against losses from inconvertibility of currency, expropriation, war, revolution, and insurrection.

We must be wary, however, of drawing any firm conclusions about the extent of pressure group influence in foreign policy. A group of distinguished scholars at the MIT Center for International Studies recently completed an in-depth study of the influence of pressure groups in U.S. trade policies.[61] They suggest that the traditional image of pressure group effectiveness is built up largely by the propaganda that the pressure groups have put out about themselves and their opposition. Dozens of pressure groups may be concerned with foreign policy, and vast sums of money may be spent in trying to bring about specific policies, but the overall pressure from unofficial groups is bound to be greatly diluted as it is variously divided among multiple differing interests.

Public Opinion in Foreign Policy

Consent of the governed is a tradition of American government as old as the Republic. But applied to foreign policy, the function of the tradition is at least open to question. In the fall of 1958, Secretary of State Dulles was engaged in "brinkmanship" over Quemoy and Matsu, two small islands offshore from the China mainland claimed by Chiang Kai-shek. From time to time, the Chinese Communists had pressed counterclaims by bombarding the islands. In September 1958, following such a bombardment, Secretary Dulles announced that the United States intended to use force if necessary to defend the offshore islands for Chiang. To underscore the Secretary's announcement, the United States forthwith began to concentrate its powerful air-naval fighting force in the Pacific. Letters

---

[61] Raymond A. Bauer, Ithiel de Sola Pool, and Lewis Anthony Dexter, *American Business and Public Policy: The Politics of Foreign Trade* (New York: Atherton Press, 1964), Chapter 28, "The Pressure Groups—A Summary."

692

to newspaper editors, to the White House, to the Secretary of State, and to congressmen immediately reflected an increasingly adverse public reaction to the Secretary's statement. Editorials throughout the country, TV and radio commentators, paid ads by interest groups, and a number of public opinion polls expressed a trend definitely opposed to the Secretary's announced policy. In a press conference, Dulles was asked whether he thought the reaction of the public, on one side or another, was important to the implementation of the policy. He replied that a policy involving grave decisions for the country should have the support of the American people "so far as practical," but he insisted that final decisions in foreign policy must rest with the President and his advisers, regardless of public approval or disapproval.

At the crest of public reaction to the Quemoy-Matsu affair of 1958, a subordinate in the State Department "leaked" to the *New York Times* a report that 80 per cent of the letters received in the Department were critical of the administrative position. This report touched off another phase in the debate when Vice-President Nixon said he was "shocked" at such a disclosure by a government employee. Secretary Dulles stood his ground, stating that "public opinion is always important because obviously you cannot carry out effectively a public policy without the support of public opinion. The question is always present as to whether the public opinion is sound or not. Certainly you cannot allow your foreign policy to be dictated by public opinion."[62]

Fortuitously, the crisis over Quemoy-Matsu blew itself out and the public almost forgot about the offshore islands until they were featured once again in the Kennedy-Nixon debates of 1960. Many questions raised in the 1958 incident remain unanswered, however. We do not know, for instance, whether all the sound and fury in the public forum, especially in the press, in any way altered — or would have altered — the conduct of official policy. We do not know whether the barrage of letter writing reflected opinions held by the general citizenry, by special groups, or by an assortment of aroused individuals. And we cannot say whether the administration would have been better advised if it had responded more sensitively to the opinions expressed in the press and mass media. Dorothy Fosdick, one-time member of the State Department's Policy Planning Staff, reminds us that "the wisdom of a policy bears no direct relation to the number of people favoring it."[63]

The making of foreign policy is a tortuous process involving many factors, not only within the domestic arena but also in the external environment, factors which the man on the street cannot know, much less appraise. The public, comprising many different groups with many different interests, cannot decide foreign policy by plebiscite or polls. Foreign policy may seem to be a paramount issue in a presidential election or in congressional elections, but the many studies on how America votes (including Chapter 6 of this book)

---

[62] For a brief case study, see Marian D. Irish, "Public Opinion and the Quemoy Crisis," *Political Quarterly*, XXXI (1960), 151–161.
[63] Dorothy Fosdick, *Common Sense and World Affairs* (New York: Harcourt, Brace & World, Inc., 1955), p. 188.

indicate that such factors as family background, class, residential and ethnic identifications, and party regularity are more likely to determine voting behavior than reasoned reactions to policies. In the final analysis, citizens must leave policy decisions up to their public officials. On the other hand, public officials in a democracy are constrained to consider the value judgments of the whole people from whom they receive their legitimate power. Alexander Hamilton wrote in *The Federalist* (No. 70), even as he was defining the concept of a vigorous and strong executive, "The circumstances which constitute safety in the republican sense are, first a due dependence on the people, secondly a due responsibility."

The increasing unpopularity of the Viet Nam war has subjected the Johnson administration to a great deal of public criticism. In a press conference, President Johnson, asked to appraise the public attitude, replied: "The important thing for every man who occupies this place is to search as best he can to get the right answer; to try to find out what is right; and then to do it without regard to polls and without regard to criticism." Asked whether he considered criticism of his policy in Viet Nam as "unpatriotic," the President drew a distinction between "conscientious responsible dissent . . . which we protect—and storm-trooper bullying, throwing yourself down in the road, smashing windows, rowdyism, and every time a person attempts to speak to try to drown him out." The President stated plainly that he considered "these storm-trooper tactics" to be "extremely dangerous to our national interest."[64]

The problem of communications between the governors and the governed is especially difficult in the area of foreign policy. "Open covenants openly arrived at" is more convincing as a slogan than as a diplomatic practice. By definition, foreign policy involves more than one government, more than one people. The American government is not free to disclose to the American people the full story of its relations with another country unless the government of that country is equally ready and willing to tell all. Moreover, an important part of decision-making is the gathering and analysis of strategic intelligence. Understandably it is not always feasible to offer up for public debate the top-secret plans of the State Department, Pentagon, or CIA. Sometimes officials think it necessary, as a part of strategy, to withhold information from the public or to manipulate news. Consider this a possible explanation, albeit not our justification, for what sometimes appears to be a "credibility gap" between public statements and subsequent courses of action in the Johnson administration, particularly on issues relating to Viet Nam.

American public officials, traditionally sensitive to public opinion regarding foreign as well as domestic policy, generally try to provide the public with adequate information regarding governmental activites in foreign affairs. The Bureau of Public Affairs in the Department of State maintains day-to-day relationships with the news media of the world: press, radio, and TV networks; motion pictures; and photographers. It also conducts a variety of programs that reach opinion-makers and groups especially interested in international affairs; arranges policy information conferences and briefing sessions in Washington and throughout the country; sends out knowledgeable

[64]*Washington Post*, November 18, 1967.

speakers for all kinds of public forums, from civic luncheons to academic commencements and veterans' conventions; and handles a great deal of personal correspondence on international affairs both for the Department and for the White House. A similar Bureau in the Department of Defense performs informational and public relations services for defense policies, plans, and programs.

The Bureau of Public Affairs in the State Department is charged with interpreting to the Department and to the Foreign Service what appear to be the demands and supports within the American public for American foreign policy. The Bureau of Public Affairs in the Defense Department carries out a similar responsibility with respect to defense policies and plans. Communications as an aspect of policy-making is a two-way activity: (1) the government provides the public—or opinion-makers and interest groups—with information on public policies and programs; (2) the public—or interested individuals and groups—responds in various ways to the government policies. Probably the weakest side of the communications system between the public and its officials is the feedback process—the way in which the government agencies attempt to ascertain public opinions and the way in which they respond to what they apprehend as public opinion.

James Rosenau, who has attempted to develop a "pre-theory" of public opinion and foreign policy, concedes that we have little knowledge about the role of public opinion in shaping foreign policy.[65] He perceives three distinctly different processes: (1) *governmental decision-making*, which presumably integrates the public opinions as they are perceived by the responsible officials; (2) the *opinion-submitting process,* in which individuals or groups convey their views to the decision-makers; and (3) the *opinion-making process*, in which ideas about foreign policy are articulated and circulated among the general citizenry. Rosenau observes that opinion-making in foreign policy takes place mainly at the national level, for that is where decision-making in foreign policy must take place.

Access to decision-makers is, of course, prerequisite to any effective role in the public opinion-foreign policy relationship. Rosenau categorizes opinion-makers as (1) *governmental* (e.g., a U.S. Senator); (2) *associational* (Commander of the American Legion); (3) *institutional* (Chairman of the Board of General Motors Corporation); or (4) *key individuals* (syndicated columnists). All of these, of course, have access to the national policy machinery and can be expected to articulate their various viewpoints. But here the curtain rings down. There is no visible connection between decision-making on the one hand or opinion-submitting and opinion-making on the other hand, although all these processes are interrelated. Thus, after holding public hearings a congressional committee goes into executive session to hammer out its own legislation, taking into account as it will—or will not—opinions circulating among the general citizenry or submitted by pressure groups to the committee.

[65]James Rosenau, *Public Opinion and Foreign Policy* (New York: Random House, Inc., 1961), p. 4.

Congress has generally frowned on any systematic polling of public opinion by official agencies and sometimes itself appears pretty casual and haphazard in the way it samples public opinion. Our interviews with a number of congressmen on this point indicate that the most widely used guides to public opinion in Congress are letters from constituents, chats with callers who happen into the office, and occasional visits with the folks at home.

Ernest May, a professor of history at Harvard who has done some recent research on the role of public opinion in foreign policy making, finds that not only the congressmen but the President and high-ranking officials in administrative circles, looking for clues to public reactions, are inclined first of all to look in the daily mail bag and then at the editorials and comments of their favorite columnists.[66] Bernard Cohen of the University of Wisconsin, who has also recently made a study of *The Press and Foreign Policy*, declares that most officials in the State Department use newspapers as their "daily measure" of how the American people are reacting to the course of foreign policy.[67] For students of political science who like to observe political behavior in a reasoned framework, it is somewhat dismaying to notice how our top decision-makers calculate public opinion—and make judgements accordingly—in the age of computer science!

Decision-Makers and Their Decisions in Foreign Policy

In Part 3 of this book we looked at the decision-makers in American government within the institutional frame of reference—Congress, the President, the bureaucrats, and the judges. When we focus on decision-making within particular policy areas, we discover that membership in the community of policy-makers varies considerably according to specific situations.

Decision-Making

Insofar as decision-making in the international community affects the national policies of individual countries, we must count many persons outside the United States as influential participants in the shaping of American foreign policy. Charles de Gaulle in the Fifth French Republic, Harold Wilson in Great Britain, Fidel Castro in Cuba, Abdul Nasser in Egypt, Alexsei Kosygin and Leonid Brezhnev in the Soviet Union, Chiang Kai-shek in Formosa, Mao Tse-tung and Chou En-lai in the People's Republic of China, Kurt Kiesinger in the Federal Republic of Germany, Ho Chi Minh in North Viet Nam, U Thant in the United Nations, Nguyen Van Thieu and Nguyen Cao Ky in South Viet Nam—all these and many more have played key roles in the international situation. *Their* activities on behalf of *their* respective governments—and the reactions of *our* decision-makers in defense of *our* national interests—have in large measure determined the course of American foreign policy since World War II. American foreign

---

[66]Ernest R. May, "An American Tradition in Foreign Policy: The Role of Public Opinion," in *Theory and Practice in American Politics*, edited by William H. Nelson (Chicago: The University of Chicago Press, 1964).

[67]Bernard C. Cohen, *The Press and Foreign Policy* (Princeton, N.J.: Princeton University Press, 1963).

policy has frequently been little more than *ad hoc* reactions to actions taken in the international situation. Witness the recurrent crises over Berlin, where communist maneuvers, Soviet and East German, have generally set the pattern for American policies.

Many actors on the stage of international politics, both friends and enemies, influence the course of American foreign policy. Although such powerful and high-ranking statesmen as President de Gaulle and Premier Kosygin influence American foreign policy, they do not, however, make it. A policy-maker holds a position of authority—to determine goals and to prescribe courses of action toward those goals—within a political system. American foreign policy makers derive their authority, and exercise it, within the constitutional and institutional pattern of American government. Without authority to implement policies outside the United States, they determine the goals and strategy of American foreign policy in terms of our national interests. The President of the United States, certainly one of the most powerful men in the world, is a policy-maker at home, but only an influence abroad. The same holds true for President de Gaulle, Prime Minister Wilson, and all the others who figure so prominently in international affairs. However influential they may be in international politics, they are policy-makers only within their own country, where each is accountable and responsible within the constitutional, institutional, and political framework of his own government.

From an institutional standpoint, it is relatively easy to identify the major units within the national policy machinery concerned with American foreign policy. (See Part 3.) For the most part, the principal American actors in the policy process hold official positions within these major units. Thus, for the same reason that we have excluded influential foreign statesmen from the category of policy-makers, we also exclude many influencers of domestic affairs—spokesmen for interest groups, opinion leaders, consultants of all sorts. Only those who hold official positions are the accountable and responsible decision-makers.

If we look at foreign policy, at the highest level of decision-making, we find that the top group of policy-makers represents a relatively small cluster of official positions. The President, of course, is pre-eminent; in the final analysis he is solely responsible. But the President needs, and gets, a great deal of help in making decisions. Within the Executive Office he can count on professional and political assistance from members of the White House Office staff, the National Security Council, the Bureau of the Budget, the Council of Economic Advisers, the National Aeronautics and Space Council, the Office of Science and Technology, the Office of the Special Representative for Trade Negotiations, the Office of Emergency Planning, and the Central Intelligence Agency.[68] Each of these agencies has become bureaucratized and some of them

---

[68]The current *United States Government Organization Manual* (Washington, D.C.: U.S. Government Printing Office) describes each agency and briefly outlines the assigned activities of its component units. The student should use the *Manual* as a reference for further information on each of the major units in the national policy machine.

are large. To be realistic, we should probably include only the heads or directors of these presidential agencies in the category of policy-makers who meet together with the President to consider major policy decisions.

The Central Intelligence Agency is attached, but does not seem to be specifically responsible, to the National Security Council. Ostensibly, the CIA is a service unit, an interdepartmental clearing house for all intelligence relating to national security. But the CIA is also an operating agency whose operations are not controlled by, and frequently not even known to, the regular departments. Its activities—in Latin America, Eastern Europe, and Southeast Asia—only occasionally reach the headlines, as during the Bay of Pigs invasion or the overthrow of the Diem government in Viet Nam. Thousands of high-grade specialists and professional people are employed in its huge steel and concrete establishment in Virginia, a few miles out of Washington; the nature of their employment is never discussed and the place is guarded to prevent unwanted visitors. An unknown number of CIA agents overseas are engaged in activities which are never mentioned in the public records, although it is evident, from time to time, that the agency has a decisive influence on the mainstream of American foreign policy. Enough has been said to indicate that the CIA Director is a key officer in American foreign policy.

Also within the executive branch, but outside the Executive Office of the President, we include the heads or directors of the major agencies directly involved in foreign policies and national security. The Secretary of State is officially the principal adviser to the President in the determination and execution of the foreign policy of the United States. The Secretary of Defense is the President's principal assistant in all matters relating to defense and national security. Because American foreign policy since World War II has been tied into a worldwide network of defense agreements, guaranteed by military commitments, and because continuous brushfires constantly threaten to turn the Cold War into a hot war, the Chairman of the Joint Chiefs of Staff almost always sits with the top policy-makers to represent professional military opinions which are crucial in many foreign policy decisions. Because the military assistance programs and foreign aid operations call for vast outlays of public expenditures, the Secretary of the Treasury and the Director of the Budget also belong in the top group; their advice on financial matters is at the very center of most policy decisions today. Since Hiroshima, atomic warfare has been accorded high priority in all considerations of military strategy—particularly during the Eisenhower administration, when the decision was made to rely on nuclear deterrents rather than to build up conventional armaments, and also during the Kennedy and Johnson administrations, as the presence of the Chairman of the Atomic Energy Commission at high-level policy meetings signifies.

The top group of policy-makers for the most part comprises heads of major units in the national power structure; they have direct access to the President and meet with him frequently, as a group and/or individually. Within the executive community of policy-makers, there exists a kind of pecking order; some positions (and some persons) are more equal than others. A step down from the top level policy-makers we find a second group of high-ranking policy officers who frequently meet together (but rarely with the President) for interagency planning and interagency programing. In the Eisenhower administration, the Operations Coordinating Board represented an attempt to formalize and institutionalize such interagency coordination. President Kennedy early in his administration abolished the OCB because he preferred to keep the policy process more flexible. As it turned out, however, those whom he appointed to fill the positions formerly in OCB still found it convenient and fruitful to meet informally—at the luncheon table rather than around the conference table—to coordinate and expedite interdepartmental activities. And in 1966, the arrangement was once more formalized as the Senior Interdepartmental Group (SIG), with the Under Secretary of State acting as Chairman and the members representing a half-dozen agencies with overseas responsibilities—USIA, AID, etc. Interdepartmental coordination was effected also through Interdepartmental Regional Groups (IRG); the regional assistant secretaries of state serve as chairmen of their respective groups and the operating agencies sending representatives on a regional basis.

The top policy officers, most of them heads of operating agencies, are generally backstopped by specialists and professional bureaucrats within their respective organizations. If we look at each of the agencies, we discover a hierarchy of decision-makers within each of the major units. Thus the official roster of the State Department lists some two dozen "principal officers," Under Secretaries, assistant secretaries, the counselor, the legal adviser, and others who regularly meet with the Secretary and advise him on policy matters. All the principal officers are political appointees who serve the presidential administration. But they in turn count on the thousands of permanent career people in the Department, the foreign service, and the classified civil service, to provide them with the broad range of specific intelligence which they need to properly advise the Secretary in particular situations.

In theory, the career service is politically neutral, willing and able to serve succeeding administrations without partisan prejudice or predilection. As a matter of fact, however, incoming political executives are likely to identify senior bureaucrats with the politics and policies of the outgoing administration. In 1953, senior foreign service officers, many of whom had entered the service in the era of Calvin Coolidge and Herbert Hoover, were dismayed to find themselves suspect as security risks because they had risen from the ranks in the era of Franklin D. Roosevelt and Harry S. Truman. It can be said, with some exaggeration perhaps, that conspicuous success in the outgoing administration is likely to be regarded as a handicap in the next administration, and conversely that lack of recognition and failure to get ahead in the old administration may become a professional asset with the incoming administration. Bureaucrats are persons, most of them ambitious just like other people; they want to better their positions, move into more challenging and rewarding situations and they want higher pay and more prestige. Thus during the period of presidential transition, many bright young bureaucrats may be observed pointedly detaching themselves from the outgoing administration as they jockey for position and status in the new administration.

If we look at the organizational charts, the foreign policy machine appears to be a highly rationalized hierarchy. Each office occupies a particular position in the political structure and each officer performs the duties and tasks assigned to him by statute and administrative rules. If we examine the policy process, however, we perceive a community of policy-makers rather than a schematic hierarchy. Within this community, individual policy-makers play a variety of roles, depending on the times and circumstances.

To begin with, purely personal considerations cannot be discounted in the policy process. The Secretary of the Treasury was extraordinarily influential in national security decisions during the Eisenhower administration because of President Eisenhower's implicit confidence in the opinions of George Humphrey. The Attorney General was unusually powerful in the Kennedy administration, not only because Robert Kennedy was able but because he was the President's brother. Just as personal relations between the President and his Secretary of State color their administration of foreign affairs, so also does the relationship between the Secretary of State and his principal officers shape the policy process and affect the policy output. In the Eisenhower administration, Secretary Herter played a very different role from that of Secretary Dulles, partly because Herter never enjoyed the close relationship which Dulles established with the President and partly because Herter was more inclined to seek departmental counsel than Dulles, who had remarkable confidence in his own judgment.

Although the same title remains on the door, a succession of persons in office may play very different parts in the policy process. The Special Assistant on National Security Affairs on the White House Staff has a much more influential role in the Johnson community of policy-makers than the office was accorded in the Eisenhower administration. For personal as well as circumstantial reasons, the Representative to the United Nations in the Truman administration played a much less constructive role in American foreign policy than his successors in the Eisenhower, Kennedy, and Johnson administrations. Different people holding the same office may act quite differently, partly because the passing of time inevitably changes the situation, but also because they are different persons who operate differently and work for and with different persons. Moreover, the same person in the same office may play different roles for different administrations; the obvious example is Dean Rusk, whose role as Secretary of State was quite different under President Kennedy than it became under President Johnson.

The style of an administration is determined largely by the group dynamics that exist within the President's chosen community of policy-makers. Regarding foreign policy, the relationship between the President and the Secretary of State is important, but also important are the President's relations with the Secretary of Defense, the Director of the Budget, and the Representative to the United Nations, as well as the personal relations of these men with one another and with all other members in the policy community. Hence, when an incoming President goes about selecting the principal officers of his administration, he must not only try to pick an all-star cast ("highly qualified"—"the best men available"), but he must also be sure to assemble a company of players that can perform well together.

The community of policy-makers suggests a much more personal approach to policy-making than that indicated in the *United States Government Organization Manual*. The *Manual* describes the organization and activities of each major unit in the federal government according to legal and official prescription. A casual visitor, wandering through the maze of corridors in the State Department (or the Pentagon), can observe all the *Manual* titles on the office doors. But the title on the door does not really tell who runs the office or what business is actually carried on in the office. A specific position in the departmental organization may be upgraded and given a new title to attract a particular person. One of President Eisenhower's first requests to Congress was for authorization to create a new position to signify his administration's intention of reorganizing the State Department. The high rank was crucial in recruiting a certain businessman to take on the impossible task. An especially high-sounding title may also cover up a low-grade role in foreign policy for a person representing influential interests in domestic politics—i.e., women, Negroes, or labor.

The community of policy-makers is a flexible concept. Even a conservative listing of principal officers in the major units engaged in foreign policy would include at least several hundred key positions in the executive branch. But such a large number of persons is never called together as a single group. The regular attendants at a National Security Council meeting—even during the Eisenhower administration, which was most respectful toward the official hierarchy and most sensitive to coordinated operations—might number thirty to fifty persons, with invitations issued appropriate to the agenda under consideration.

The agenda under consideration is usually the clue to the community of policy-makers. If the agenda involves global strategy, then only the top policy officers may meet with the President. If the critical issues involve military considerations, the Chairman of the Joint Chiefs of Staff may bring with him a sizeable representation from the armed services. If the problem calls for financing, the Secretary of the Treasury and the Director of the Budget may bring in a battery of fiscal experts from their respective agencies. If, on the other hand, the issue is more narrowly focused—for example, whether the United States should shift its emphasis from military support of the Shah to economic aid for the people of Iran—then the Middle East specialists and the desk officer for Iran may join in the deliberations, even though they would normally be rather far down in the hierarchy of decision-makers. In short, the community of policy-makers is a functional concept; identification of membership depends on functional roles in the policy process rather than status in the administrative hierarchy.

It is therefore not realistic to view the decision-making process in foreign policy within the strictly hierarchical pattern of the principal officers in the major executive agencies. As Dean Acheson put it (he should know because he was an Assistant Secretary of State, an Under Secretary of State, and a Secretary of State), "policy bubbles up as much as it trickles down." Ideas may move through official channels or they may be circulated through informal personal communications. In the Department of State, for example, programs are often conceived by foreign service officers in the field, or first discussed in a "country team" meeting; and high-level decisions are sometimes substantially reshaped in the programing decisions made by bureaucrats near the bottom of the totem pole.

Normally the President assumes the initiative in foreign policy, but, as we have already observed, Congress has a continuing interest in this area and actively participates at many points in the decision-making process. Congress expects to be fully informed by the administration and to be brought into the actual process of decision-making at an early stage. Hence the President and his executive agencies are in constant communication and consultation with the congressional leadership and with the committees particularly charged with national defense and foreign policy. Congress may freely debate any aspect of foreign policy; although it rarely takes an adverse stand against a declared executive policy, individual members feel free to criticize and oppose. As a way of underscoring its independent role, Congress may want to take additional action to make legitimate the official policy with which it may be in full accord. On the other hand, as a means of emphasizing national unity, the President may seek a special enabling act or congressional resolution expressing approval of a specific or general course of action, even though he may be constitutionally free to act on his own. When the President and Congress are in substantial agreement, a concurrent resolution empowering the President to act as he deems necessary to meet a crisis situation—as in the Middle East resolution of 1957 or the Cuban resolution of 1962—strengthens the position of the President in international politics. When the President asks for and fails to obtain full congressional backing, however—as happened to President Johnson on the eve of the 1967 summit meeting with the Latin American presidents at Punta del Este—or when a number of prominent senators and representatives reopen debate on the meaning of a resolution previously passed—as happened in 1967 with respect to the Gulf of Tonkin Resolution—then the position of the President becomes more difficult for him and more uncertain to the outside world than if he had acted on his own at the outset without seeming to need congressional support.

Not all members of Congress and not all members of a committee dealing with foreign affairs are equally interested or equally influential in matters of foreign policy. The President and his principal officers recognize and court those senators and representatives who have special knowledge and are actively interested, as well as those who hold positions of control in the congressional organization. As in the executive community of policy-makers, the measure of influence is not necessarily one of position or seniority. Senator Alexander Wiley, as Chairman of the Senate Committee on Foreign Relations for the first two years of the Eisenhower administration, never attained the constructive role in foreign policy achieved by his predecessor, Senator Walter George, or his successor, Senator J. W. Fulbright.

The President himself sets the style of executive-legislative relations in foreign policy. President Eisenhower's approach to Congress was respectfully institutional; he thought it more orderly to work through the congressional leadership than through individual senators and representatives. On the other hand, Presidents Kennedy and Johnson, who arrived at the White House via Capitol Hill, retained and frequently used many of their personal contacts in Congress. Whatever his personal or partisan preference, however, the President has to deal at least formally with the power structure of Congress and on a bipartisan basis.

There are different kinds of authority and influence in the congressional organization, just as there are an administrative hierarchy and a pecking order within the executive community of policy-makers. On any major policy issue, the President usually finds it politic to consult first with the top ranking *partisan leadership*—the Speaker of the House, the majority and minority floor leaders in House and Senate, and other party officers in both houses. He is also expected to consult with and fully inform the *policy leadership*—the chairmen and ranking minority members of the committees that have principal jurisdiction over foreign policy: the Senate Committee on Foreign Relations, the House Committee on Foreign Affairs, the Senate and House Committees on the Armed Services, and the Senate and House Committees on Appropriations. Other committees may share in specific foreign policy legislation—Agricultural or Banking and Currency, for example, or even the Judiciary Committees, which were very important in the long drawn-out controversy during the Eisenhower administration over the Bricker Amendment.

Congressional relations at the operational level usually involve working directly with the *policy* specialists on the subcommittees. In terms of foreign policy, the key persons on the Appropriations Committees of House and Senate are the members of the subcommittees (especially the chairmen) charged with specific consideration of appropriations for the State Department, the Defense Department, and Foreign Operations. The subcommittees of the Senate Committee on Foreign Relations and the House Committee on Foreign Affairs, which correspond to the geographical and functional bureaus in the State Department, maintain close working relations with their counterparts in the administration. Thus the subcommittee on Europe (House or Senate) works directly with the Department's Bureau on European Affairs, and the subcommittee on International Organization works with the Bureau on International Organization. Because committee assignments carry over from one session to another, some congressmen tend to make a career of policy specialization in the legislative process, and by virtue of their specialized competence enter the community of executive-legislative policy-makers whenever their particular area of specialization happens to appear on the policy agenda.

Continuity and consistency are especially important in foreign policy, for commitments and programs involve other nations. A commitment broken or a program discontinued could have serious repercussions in international relations. Hence an outgoing President is likely to move experienced career personnel into the administrative hierarchy as political executives turn in their resignations immediately prior to the transfer of power at the White House.

Every administration finds it useful to bring some seasoned foreign service officers into the community of policy-makers. For the most part, the incoming President seeks and finds his principal officers within his own party, but the bipartisan character of foreign policy makes it possible, and desirable, for him to include among his appointees qualified persons from the other party. Thus a number of distinguished names recur in the succession of administrations, John Foster Dulles, Averill Harriman, Dean Rusk, Allen Dulles, Douglas Dillon, Henry Cabot Lodge, and others.

In appraising the varying roles of individual policy-makers, we must first scrutinize interpersonal relations within the community of policy-makers. Even so, we must keep in mind that official duties and responsibilities within the institutional hierarchy may be more enduring in the overall process. On November 22, 1963, President Johnson was able to count immediately on the complete loyalty of President Kennedy's official associates. Personal considerations were irrelevant in the context of national and international crisis. It was crucial not only for the nation but also for the whole world to know that the American presidency survived intact, despite the death of its President. Word went out at once to all the embassies in Washington and to all our own diplomatic posts overseas that the succession of President Johnson would mean no change in American foreign policy. The transition from President Kennedy to President Johnson took place under tragic circumstances, but in an orderly manner within the constitutional and institutional setting.

The Decisions: Strategy and Output

The development of this chapter has been based on the assumption that foreign policy in general has a rational basis and that the community of policy-makers makes a conscious effort to act rationally. Within this context, the totality of American foreign policy can be understood and appraised in terms of (a) the national purpose and long range goals; (b) the overall guidelines for operations and programs which are intended to advance us toward our professed objectives; (c) the multiplicity of decisions for practical action in specific situations which often involve immediate goals.[69]

The broad outlines of American foreign policy have not changed since the founding of the Republic. To provide for the common defense, to promote the general welfare, and to secure the blessings of liberty — these still represent the national purpose and long-range goals of the American people. But the overall guidelines for operations and programs today must be made within the context of the modern world. Since World War II, these guidelines have remained fairly consistent, although the impact of events at home and abroad have provoked shifts in emphasis.:

(1) *We want to remain a democratic nation in a free world.* To this end we have (a) tried to strengthen the political and cultural ties between us and the countries of Western Europe; (b) set up a North Atlantic military alliance to defend our

---

[69]For two recent discussions of the grand strategy of American foreign policy, see Robert R. Bowie, *Shaping the Future* (New York: Columbia University Press, 1964) and W. W. Rostow, *View from the Seventh Floor.*

common interests against aggression; (c) tried to encourage new patterns of trade and economic association among the countries of Western Europe, between them and us, and between the entire Atlantic community and the rest of the world.

The North Atlantic Alliance today, however, stands in need of reconstruction—on both sides of the Atlantic. The United States can no longer dominate the Alliance as it did in the Alliance's early years, when the European partners were still economically devastated as a result of World War II and fearful of an imminent Soviet takeover. Today Western Europe appears politically stable, fairly prosperous, and obviously unwilling to serve as a pawn in bipolar politics between the United States and the Soviet Union. The Cold War is over in Europe and our allies in NATO cannot understand why American foreign policy moves so slowly toward *détente* between Eastern and Western Europe. The virtual secession of the French from NATO symbolizes the mounting disaffection of our European allies and the deliberate divergence of their foreign policies from ours.

On the other hand, the United States is experiencing increasing disillusionment with its European allies, who have given very little support to American foreign policy in other parts of the world, specifically in Viet Nam. We are more than irritated when our friends to whom we have given so much assistance in the past now find it politically expedient, or just good business, to maintain rapport with Hanoi, Havana, and Peking. Although the Marshall Plan has long since been terminated and the U.S. government now gives no economic aid to Western Europe, nearly a third of American private investments abroad are concentrated in Great Britain and the Common Market countries. Whatever the political or strategic bases for disruption of NATO, Europe remains a focal point of American foreign policy. Nevertheless, recent congressional proposals toward protectionism in foreign trade policies, which, if effected, would cancel out the gains made in the Kennedy Round on Tariff Negotiations and invite massive retaliation on the part of our European trade partners, are certainly not calculated to repair the growing breach in NATO.

If we really want to make NATO a bastion of freedom, we must be prepared to buckle down to the tasks imposed upon us by Article 2 of the North Atlantic Treaty: "The Parties . . . will seek to eliminate conflict in their international economic policies and will encourage economic collaboration between any or all of them." And we need also to join our allies in their efforts toward "peaceful engagement," reducing tensions between East and West wherever possible, treating different communist countries differently, and anticipating the time when it may be practical to resolve the issues between NATO and the Warsaw Pact with a treaty of mutual defense and nonaggression.

(2) *We are determined to contain communism and to resist communist aggression any place in the world.* To this end we have (a) invested in a national defense system second to none in the world, with a full spectrum of conventional weaponry for

all degrees of limited war and maximum capability to deter nuclear war; (b) entered into a series of mutual defense agreements with some forty-two different countries and have established military installations in strategic places all over the world; (c) offered both military assistance and economic support to nations everywhere in the world who need help in strengthening their own defenses and in resisting communist aggression from without or communist infiltration from within.

Starting with the premise that we could deter communist aggression with a show of military might, the grand strategy of the United States since the early 1950s has been built on an elaborate system of mutual security agreements. (See map of U.S. collective defense arrangements.) In a succession of foreign aid acts passed between 1950 and 1966, Congress has appropriated $34 billion in military assistance to some eighty countries which exhibit what the Defense Department calls a "free world orientation." Acting as "the arsenal of democracy," the United States has provided military weapons and military supports to our allies or associates in NATO, SEATO, CENTO, ANZUS; to countries that border on Communist China and the Soviet Union; to countries that have given us military base rights whether or not they show any predilection for democracy or free enterprise; to Alliance for Progress "security countries"; to developing countries in Africa and the Middle East. (We supplied military assistance both to Israel and to the Arab states both before and after the outbreak of the Middle East War in June, 1967.) A peace-loving nation, we have become the principal purveyor of the instruments of war throughout the world since World War II. We have not only furnished the newly developing nations with sophisticated weaponry; we have also helped them gear their modernization programs to increased military capability, and in so doing have frequently found it expedient to support military regimes and to supply "client states."

In this context, the war in Viet Nam, which the Johnson administration views as a "commitment" to deter communist aggression in Southeast Asia, has been bitterly debated. In the face of widely expressed disapproval of the war—manifest in public opinion polls, mass demonstrations, syndicated columns, TV programs, student resolutions, letters to newspaper editors, letters to the President and congressmen, congressional hearings, congressional debates—the administration has remained adamant in its conviction that the credibility of American foreign policy everywhere in the world depended on our stance in Viet Nam. If we welshed on our promises to South Viet Nam, it might appear to the watching world that we might in the same manner back out of other commitments when the going got rough, thus causing the whole structure of alliances to collapse for lack of faith. Moreover, if we pulled out of Viet Nam in seeming defeat, then we would have forfeited our claims to leadership in a world of power politics.

On the congressional side, however, serious doubts have been expressed both as to the morality and the feasibility of using military policy as the principal tool of foreign policy. At one point, many congressmen were in the mood to scrap the whole Foreign Assistance Act of 1967 rather than continue the military assistance programs, particularly the sale of arms to military dicta-

706

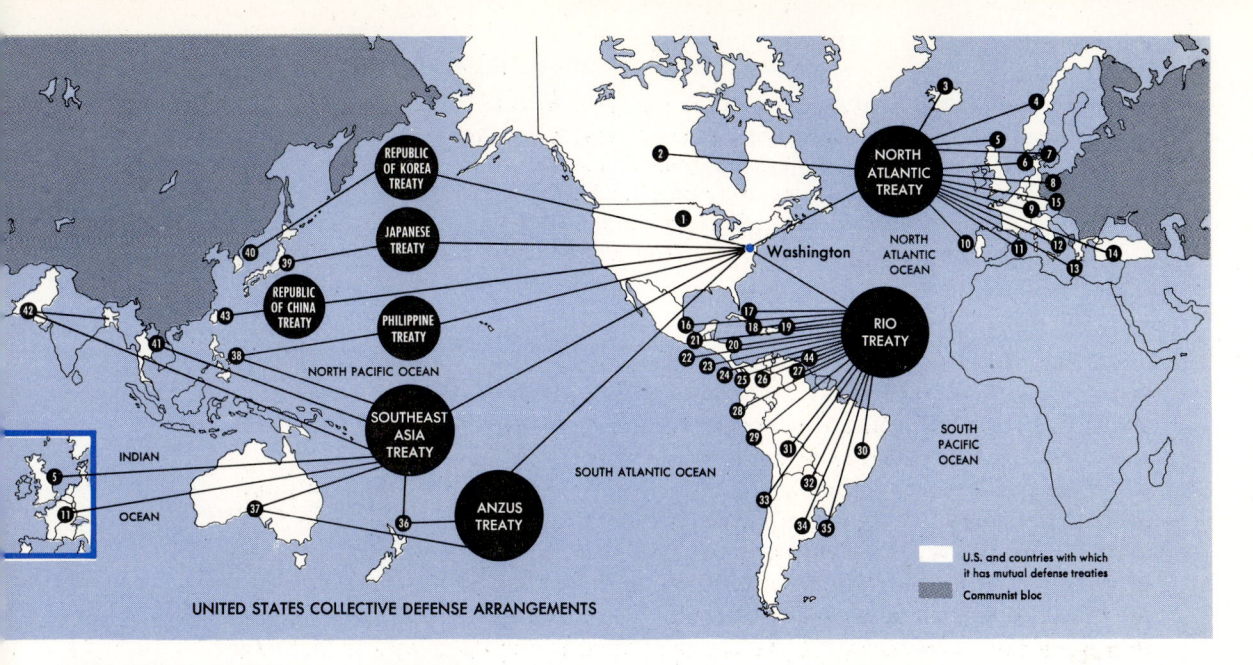

UNITED STATES COLLECTIVE DEFENSE ARRANGEMENTS

NORTH ATLANTIC TREATY
(15 Nations)

A treaty signed April 4, 1949, by which "the parties agree that an armed attack against one or more of them in Europe or North America shall be considered an attack against them all; and . . . each of them . . . will assist the . . . attacked by taking forthwith, individually and in concert with the other Parties, such action as it deems necessary including the use of armed force. . . ."

1 UNITED STATES	9 LUXEMBOURG
2 CANADA	10 PORTUGAL
3 ICELAND	11 FRANCE
4 NORWAY	12 ITALY
5 UNITED KINGDOM	13 GREECE
6 NETHERLANDS	14 TURKEY
7 DENMARK	15 FEDERAL REPUBLIC OF GERMANY
8 BELGIUM	

RIO TREATY
(22 Nations)

A treaty signed September 2, 1947, which provides that an armed attack against any American State "shall be considered as an attack against all the American States and . . . each one . . . undertakes to assist in meeting the attack. . . ."

1 UNITED STATES	22 EL SALVADOR	30 BRAZIL
16 MEXICO	23 NICARAGUA	31 BOLIVIA
17 CUBA	24 COSTA RICA	32 PARAGUAY
18 HAITI	25 PANAMA	33 CHILE
19 DOMINICAN REPUBLIC	26 COLOMBIA	34 ARGENTINA
20 HONDURAS	27 VENEZUELA	35 URUGUAY
21 GUATEMALA	28 ECUADOR	44 TRINIDAD AND TOBAGO
	29 PERU	

ANZUS (Australia—New Zealand—United States) TREATY
(3 Nations)

A treaty signed September 1, 1951, whereby each of the parties "recognizes that an armed attack in the Pacific Area on any of the Parties would be dangerous to its own peace and safety and declares that it would act to meet the common danger in accordance with its constitutional processes."

1 UNITED STATES
36 NEW ZEALAND
37 AUSTRALIA

PHILIPPINE TREATY
(Bilateral)

A treaty signed August 30, 1957, by which the parties recognize "that an armed attack in the Pacific Area on either of the Parties would be dangerous to its own peace and safety" and each party agrees that it will act "to meet the common danger in accordance with its constitutional processes."

1 UNITED STATES
38 PHILIPPINES

JAPANESE TREATY
(Bilateral)

A treaty signed January 19, 1960, whereby each party "recognizes that an armed attack against either Party in the territories under the administration of Japan would be dangerous to its own peace and safety and declares that it would act to meet the common danger in accordance with its constitutional provisions and processes." The treaty replaced the security treaty signed September 8, 1951.

1 UNITED STATES
39 JAPAN

REPUBLIC OF KOREA (South Korea) TREATY (Bilateral)

A treaty signed October 1, 1953, whereby each party "recognizes that an armed attack in the Pacific area on either of the Parties . . . would be dangerous to its own peace and safety" and that each Party "would act to meet the common danger in accordance with its constitutional processes."

1 UNITED STATES
40 REPUBLIC OF KOREA

SOUTHEAST ASIA TREATY
(8 Nations)

A treaty signed September 8, 1954, whereby each Party "recognizes that aggression by means of armed attack in the treaty area against any of the Parties . . . would endanger its own peace and safety" and each will "in that event act to meet the common danger in accordance with its constitutional processes."

1 UNITED STATES
5 UNITED KINGDOM
11 FRANCE
36 NEW ZEALAND
37 AUSTRALIA
38 PHILIPPINES
41 THAILAND
42 PAKISTAN

REPUBLIC OF CHINA (Formosa) TREATY
(Bilateral)

A treaty signed December 2, 1954 whereby each of the parties "recognizes that an armed attack in the West Pacific Area directed against the territories of either of the Parties would be dangerous to its own peace and safety," and that each "would act to meet the common danger in accordance with its constitutional processes." The territory of the Republic of China is defined as "Taiwan (Formosa) and the Pescadores."

1 UNITED STATES
43 REPUBLIC OF CHINA (FORMOSA)

Figure 16-3 Source: Department of State Bulletin (October 9, 1967).

tors in developing countries where people need elementary education and agricultural technology more than they need supersonic jet bombers.⁷⁰

The insistence of the Johnson administration that the war in Viet Nam fulfills a "commitment" has provoked many debates, in Congress and in the public forum. What is a commitment? Who has authority to make commitments that bind the United States? How and where is the United States now committed? How were the American people persuaded to move from a position of neutrality and isolation to almost singular responsibility for keeping peace in the whole world? Senator Eugene McCarthy (D.-Minn.), in Congress since 1948 and a member of the Senate Foreign Relations Committee since 1958, speaks for many thoughtful dissenters today:

"Grin and Bear It"
by George Lichty; reprinted
by permission
of Publishers-Hall Syndicate.

"...And I'll vote for a declaration of war, gentlemen, if and when the State Department can decide who is the enemy!"

> We must . . . attempt to assay our real power as compared with our assumed responsibilities. We must reassess our obligations, formal and informal, legal and extra-legal. We must establish, if we can, standards for selection of responses, both as to place and degree. We must set priorities and continue to seek, with other nations, a broader and more realistic distribution of responsibility for this world.⁷¹

(3) *We want to defend the principle of private property and the practices of private enterprise in the modern world.* To this end we have (a) offered, in varying degrees, leadership, partnership, and assistance to speed up the modernization of countries in Latin America, Africa, Asia, and the Middle East; (b) encouraged long-term programs of political socialization and economic development in the newly independent nations and offered them our immediate aid with capital investments and technological know-how; (c) tried to strengthen the Alliance for Progress between the industrial nations and the less developed nations in the western hemisphere; (d) tried to help create new patterns of partnership and assistance between the more advanced European powers and nations recently emerging from colonialism.

Congress, however, slashed its foreign assistance appropriations to a new low in 1967. The decision reflected general pique with the administration's

---

⁷⁰The Foreign Assistance Authorization Act of 1967 finally repealed the Department of Defense's authority to finance long-term credit sales of arms to poor and underdeveloped countries. Termination was set for June 30, 1968. See Senator J. William Fulbright's report to the Senate on the 1967 Act, *Congressional Record,* 90th Cong., 1st Sess., CXIII (November 8, 1967) S. 16125.

⁷¹Eugene McCarthy, *The Limits of Power* (New York: Holt, Rinehart & Winston, Inc., 1967), p. 7.

handling of foreign policy; the exigencies of Viet Nam and an overall necessity to cut expenditures; a determined resistance to tax increases and a natural inclination to cut unpopular programs; and a growing realization that twenty years of American foreign assistance programs has not made much of an impression or improvement upon the world at large.

Indeed, the gap is widening between the rich and poor nations. Each year, the rich nations, including the United States, get richer, but they give a decreasing share of their increasing GNP to the poorer nations. Current U.S. policy is to concentrate its economic assistance for "the war on hunger," helping the modernizing countries to put a lid on population explosion and to increase their capacity to produce their own food with better seed, better fertilizer, better technology, modern food processing, and more effective marketing. But this kind of policy, which is genuinely outer-directed, is not likely to have broad support at home; nor does it appeal to special interests in domestic politics. The Marshall Plan was based on a feeling of community between the American people and the people of Western Europe, as well as upon a sense of urgency to stop short the Soviet takeover of the North Atlantic community. There is no Marshall Plan projected for Asia, or for Africa, or for Latin America, however; Americans are still too isolationist to feel any close relationship to peoples who live on these other continents; and also truth to tell, the fear of communism, at least of Soviet communism, has abated with time. Hence foreign assistance programs are assigned low priority ratings on the official agenda and in performance fall far short of the basic guidelines.

(4) *We want to build a new and peaceful international order.* To this end we have (a) joined in the work of the United Nations and supported its many different activities; (b) tried to strengthen and develop regional organizations for mutual defense to supplement national devices of self-help; (c) continuously and patiently negotiated for international agreement on limitation, reduction, and control of armaments, especially the weapons of nuclear war.

As the first nuclear power in the world, and so far the only nation to have used atomic weapons in warfare, the United States has felt a strong obligation to work for peace in the world through comprehensive disarmament efforts. The limited nuclear test ban treaty of 1963, the "hotline" agreement between the United States and the Soviet Union, our approval of the UN resolution against weapons of mass destruction in space, our agreement with the Soviet Union and other nations to prevent the proliferation of nuclear weapons to nonnuclear countries, the ongoing activities of the U.S. Arms Control and Disarmament Agency, the endless disarmament negotiations in Geneva—all of these attest to our willingness to negotiate bit by bit for more effective controls of strategic armaments.

When Harlan Cleveland, then Assistant Secretary of State for International Organization Affairs, appeared before the Senate Committee on Foreign Relations in 1965, he testified that "the U.S. Government over the past twenty years has been second to none in inventing, sponsoring, supporting, and working through the international agencies which make up the existing system of world order."[72] We send official delegations every year to more than five hundred international conferences; we are dues-paying members of more than fifty international organizations; we typically provide 40 per cent of the financial resources of the international development agencies; we have supported every UN peace keeping mission. And public opinion polls indicate that the overwhelming majority of Americans support the UN.

Nevertheless, the image of America in the world today is not that of a peace-loving nation. We maintain 350,000 troops in Europe to stave off an unlikely Soviet offensive to the Atlantic; we have deployed nearly 700,000 troops in Asia from Korea to Viet Nam to deter Asian communists. We allocate more than half of our budget to national security; we are stockpiled with nuclear weapons and conventional weapons, primed for a first strike or instant retaliation way beyond the point of overkill; and we are beginning to construct antiballistic missile defenses around our principal cities and military installations. Still we spend billions of dollars every year in research and development to insure our technological superiority in all the weaponry of war. Although we subscribe to numerous pacts for mutual consultation and assistance, in the Dominican crisis of 1965 we intervened unilaterally with military force and took our case to the OAS only after the *fait accompli*. Although we are engaged in a major war in Asia which could at any time precipitate into World War III, we have not sought to resolve the issue through the UN.

Academic appraisal of American statesmanship in foreign affairs is a hazardous enterprise. Much of what goes into the formulation and execution of foreign policy depends on classified information and intelligence which are available only to official and responsible policy-makers. Assuming, however, that the theoretical construct of the politics of American democracy which we have used throughout this text has some practical validity, we venture a model of decision-making in foreign policy.

In terms of strategy, the first step in American foreign policy is to analyze our position in the external environment and to determine on a global basis as well as regionally and country by country our capacity to influence international politics. The second step is to take stock of our domestic situation, to determine where we want to go, and to set up some schedule of priorities to that end. The third step is to apprehend the plural interests within our society, and establish some criteria whereby we decide in what manner and to what extent these can and should be accommodated within the national interests. The fourth step is to fuse ideas into plans and plans into programs of action to advance our national interests in the international community. The fifth step is to organize diverse courses of action for varied situations in the external environment and at the same time to coordinate our operations abroad within guidelines that lead toward our established goals. The sixth step, and the most difficult, is to keep moving in the direction we want to go, with firmness of purpose and faith in our goals, even though sometimes immediate steps might

---

[72]*Planning for Peace*, Hearings before the Senate Committee on Foreign Relations, 89th Cong., 1st Sess., May 11, 12, 1965 (Washington, D.C.: U.S. Government Printing Office, 1965), p. 124.

temporarily move us away from them. This grand strategy calls for creative imagination as well as extraordinary political perception on the part of our top policy-makers; it requires the diplomatic skills, specialized intelligence, and worldwide experience of our foreign service together with the managerial and technical competence of the bureaucrats in many agencies. But most of all it depends on the understanding and staying power of the American people. In a democratic society, the consent of the governed controls the ultimate values in the policy process.

THE AMERICAN POLITICAL

SYSTEM IN PERSPECTIVE 17

What should this book have done for you? Our hope may be simply stated—it is that this book has given you a greater understanding of how American politics works. Remember our refusal to accept the view of theory implied in the complaint that one's college reading was "good in theory" but "inapplicable in practice." If theories fail to explain actual practices, they are simply bad theories.

If we were to list everything we hope you have learned from this book, we would have to repeat every generalization we have offered in the preceding fifteen chapters. In considering policy outputs of the American system, we have tried to re-emphasize some of the more basic conclusions and to show how they are directly related to policy. But education is not just a matter of gaining new understandings; it is also a process of "unlearning"—of ridding one's self of false conceptions. Accordingly, we shall conclude by listing a few of the misconceptions about politics that are particularly widespread and that we trust this book has helped to clear away.

"Politics Is Dirty"

This is a persistent and puzzling myth. Because the only way in which people can hope to influence public policy is through the pursuit and exercise of power—that is, through *politics*—we might assume that politics would be highly respected. Widespread suspicion of politics and politicians is even more puzzling when we remember that public officials seem, in fact, to maintain higher standards than are found in most areas of private life.

And yet the distrust persists. Apparently one reason is that politicians must make decisions of great importance to many people, and someone is always disappointed by every decision. The losers often respond to their disappointment by claiming that they got a "dirty deal." A second reason is that politics necessarily involves compromise, and it is the politicians who must make the compromises that enable people to live peaceably together—the rest of us can afford the luxury of inflexible principles and the feelings of superiority that go with them. Third, the press generally encourages an antipolitical viewpoint; the occasional crooked politician receives so much publicity that he seems typical.

Finally, Americans appear to have a double standard of morals, condemning behavior in politicians that they take for granted in their own lives. Newspaper headlines indict the public official who buys a mink coat at a wholesale price, but many of the most indignant private citizens follow the same practice. We assume that the son of a business executive, even though he may be incompetent, will be given a good job in his father's organization, but we are incensed when newspaper columnists uncover a public official's attempt to do as much for his son. In business this is regarded as "family loyalty"; in politics it is labeled "nepotism." A Sherman Adams or a Bobby Baker suffers near disgrace in public life for the very "wheeling and dealing" that we applaud on the part of the enterprising businessman. True, we have a right to expect higher standards of government officials, but we should at least be aware of the sacrifices we expect of them.

"Government Is a Great, Impersonal 'It'"

All our top policy-makers in the national government are either elected by the people or appointed by the President. Even so, many citizens regard the government almost as if decisions were made by self-appointed aliens or by a set of poorly constructed "electronic brains." To talk about the government as "we" would be somewhat unrealistic, but hardly more so than for students at the University of Michigan to say "we" are going to play the University of California in football. At least we elect our political representatives.

In their tendency to depersonalize government into "it," many Americans reflect their sense of alienation from government and politics. But to regard government as something alien is to introduce an irrational factor into our political decision-making. Like any other organization, our government is made up of human beings; it differs from other organizations in that every citizen can have a part in selecting its leaders. Nevertheless, some readers find nothing strange in a newspaper editorial that urges the government to stop some activity like hydroelectric power development and "turn it back to the people." Yet this line of argument involves illogical assumptions—namely, that government officials (who are chosen by the voters) represent interests alien to those of the people, whereas private utility executives (who are not chosen by the voters) represent interests identical with those of the people. We can work out rational arguments on both sides of questions of this sort, but not in these terms. If government is not "we," the Commonwealth and Southern Electric Company is even less so.

"The National Government Is the Worst of All"

The responsible public officials who make up this ominous "it" seem to be most foreboding at the level of the national government. A nationwide organization like the United States Steel Corporation is "the industrial family that serves America" and the AFL-CIO is made up of "the nation's workers," but our national government is "the Washington bureaucracy." Many Americans seem to have this impression: all politics is dubious, but local government is best, state government is second best, and national government is the worst of all.

In this book we have been primarily concerned with national government, but in discussing federalism we gained some insight into the comparative qualities of the national and state governments. The old Jeffersonian idea that local government was the most efficient, honest, and responsive to broad public needs seems to be an exact reversal of the facts of modern political life. The facts support a different conclusion today. Inefficiency, dishonesty, and minority domination are found most often in local governments; conditions improve in state governments; and they are at their best in the national government.

The persistence of the old attitude is not easy to explain; perhaps it is simply a case of the survival, after the facts have changed, of what may once have been good theory. Whatever the situation may have been in Jefferson's time, our problems today are national or international in scope, and the most exciting government decisions are made in Washington. As a result, politicians find a greater challenge there than in county offices, and the press and public follow decisions in the national government more closely. Moreover, the constituencies of national officials are broader and therefore serve to neutralize special interests. In short, the pressures of politics encourage a more statesmanlike performance from governors than from city councilmen, and from presidents than from governors.

Drawing by Herblock;
from *Straight Herblock*
(New York: Simon & Schuster, 1964).

"We can't burden our children with deficit spending."

"A Big Government with an Expanding Budget Is Ruinous"

Once a year, the American government engages in "the Spring rite of raising the national debt limit."[1] The annual ceremony always includes pronouncements of ultimate doom if the federal budget is not returned to the frugal practices of the pioneer American family.

This tendency to think of the national debt as similar to the indebtedness of a private family is highly misleading. To begin with, although the average family must carefully keep its expenditures below its income if it is to remain solvent, even the private citizen prospers by borrowing money and expanding his activities, not by saving string and staying out of debt.

Business enterprises and governments, however, are in a different position altogether. In order to expand their activities, they must increase their budgets and, therefore, their debts as represented by stocks and bonds. This viewpoint

[1] "T.R.B. from Washington," *The New Republic* (June 6, 1964).

is generally accepted for business corporations, but not for governments. The assumption is that corporate debts are self-liquidating, whereas government debts are simply a costly deferral of the payment of current bills. "T. R. B.," whose insights on the American scene enliven *The New Republic* every week, once engaged in a running attack on the "silly myth" that the national budget should not grow as the nation grows. "The AT&T and GM are never going to pay off their debt; not, that is, unless it wants to ruin us."[2] His argument is that government investment in good roads, better schools, and projects like the TVA is as wise as the expansion of a big corporation. Part of this investment is self-liquidating and part is not; part of it is money the government owes itself; about two-thirds of it represents actual government debt held by the public. When one stops to think in terms of the national interest, why is an expenditure of money and manpower for stronger deodorants a contribution to the national well-being and an expenditure for better schools or highways a liability?

The alleged "burden" of the national debt in recent years has decreased, not increased, if it is compared to the size of the population, the national income, or the Gross National Product. But while Americans admire growth in all other areas of activity, they seem peculiarly unable to recognize that an expanding nation requires expanding governmental activities.

"The Founding Fathers Were 'Above Politics'"

Some patriotic organizations seem to have the notion that schools can produce good Americans only if they present a "depoliticized" picture of our first great politicians. Perhaps a somewhat romanticized version must be presented at the secondary level, but to give students a false picture of democratic government is misguided patriotism. Countless Americans still have an image of George Washington, Thomas Jefferson, Alexander Hamilton, James Madison, Patrick Henry, and others marching forward in perfect unison, shoulder to shoulder, into the sunrise. Pictured as being above petty politics, these leaders are supposed to have been followed by all right-thinking men in adopting the Constitution (which Henry called "the most fatal possible plan for the enslavement of a free people"!) and to have launched the ship of state on calm waters without bickering over mere political differences.

In the real political world, on the other hand, different experiences and conflicting interests inevitably lead even the best-intentioned men to rational (and irrational) disagreements. Most of our Founding Fathers were great politicians. They were quite capable of expressing their disagreements in clear-cut terms and of throwing themselves into power struggles as lively as any that occur today. Only by understanding the special interests, the conflicting ideas, and the political strategy of the Founding Fathers can we appreciate them as real human beings—and then we can apply that understanding and appreciation to a consideration of contemporary politics.

The tragedy of the "nonpolitical" view is that it sacrifices accuracy for the sake of patriotism, and is still a poor means of molding loyal citizens. The idea that a statesman should be "above politics" is as ridiculous as the notion that

[2] *The New Republic* (June 6, 1964). Also see the issues of January 18, 1964; February 8, 1964; November 21, 1964.

the Pope or the Archbishop of Canterbury should be "above religion." But the false image of the Founding Fathers, coupled with the great respect they enjoy, leads to disillusionment when the citizen of today evaluates the performance of current office-holders and discovers that they are "mere politicians."

"The American Way Is the Only Democratic Way"

Any thinking person should be able to detect blind provincialism in political discussions, and to separate love of country from an irrational rejection of everything strange or new. Whether unfamiliar institutions deserve to be rejected or not, they should at least be evaluated on intellectually defensible grounds. Such practices as unitary government (instead of federalism), parliamentary supremacy (instead of separation of powers), multi-party politics (instead of the two-party system), and socialism (instead of capitalism), for example, may be "un-American" and even undesirable without being undemocratic.

The reverse side of this same coin, which pictures everything American as essential to democracy, is equally counterfeit. Our rulers are responsive enough to the desires of the ruled for our government to be classified as a democracy; so we can plausibly conclude that none of our key institutions is absolutely incompatible with democracy. But to conclude from this that every one of our institutions is *essential* to democracy is shabby logic. Separation of powers, and checks and balances, for example, were designed by men who were alarmed at the prospect of popular control over policy. And we have achieved a remarkable degree of democracy despite these barriers, not because of them. To claim that such institutions as these were designed in the interest of popular control is to misunderstand separation of powers and checks and balances, and to misinterpret the aims and ideas of the men who helped create them.

"The Individual Doesn't Count"

In a world of big business, big labor, and big government—where political analysis deals with groups like political parties, pressure groups, Congress, the administration, and the Supreme Court—the individual sometimes seems to have been dropped out of the picture. The individual's attitudes and interests are a product of the group affiliations and influences he has experienced since birth. Every one of these groups, however, is created out of the relations between individuls; take away the individuals and you have no groups—and no politics. Indeed, the welfare of individuals rather than of fatherland, class, or party holds the central place in democratic ideology. Human beings, not the groups into which they form, are the primary value of democratic politics.

An individual leader can, moreover, play a great role in shaping political events. If someone like Henry Luce, who headed a publishing empire including *Time, Life, Sports Illustrated,* and *Fortune,* dedicates himself to a cause, his influence may be enough to tip the scales toward success or defeat. An individual politician like the great Republican progressive, George Norris of Nebraska, may wage an unrelenting campaign for a program like the Tennessee Valley Authority and see it through to victory. People of this sort work through and upon groups, but it is their individual personalities that make the indelible impression.

What of the ordinary citizen, let's say a bricklayer? How much does he count as an individual? True, he may vote, but his vote is only one among thousands or millions; he may write a letter to his congressman or his newspaper, but again it is only one among hundreds or thousands. How can he make a greater impression on politics? If he tries to cast several ballots in a single election, he may find himself in jail; if he writes too many letters, he will be written off as a "crackpot." But he need not remain a voiceless member of the "lonely crowd." If he wants to increase his influence, he can do so by working through various groups—by joining and actively participating in a union or party organization, for example. As our study of political parties suggested, local party organizations possess considerable power, and their positions of leadership are surprisingly more open to ambitious citizens than people are aware of. Election studies have shown, in addition, that informal opinion-leaders exist at every level of society. Without commanding any official status, the politically interested and articulate citizen may not only count as an individual, but he may also assume a role of political leadership for those around him.

The bricklayer's influence may never reach a level where it can be compared with that of a Luce or a Norris, but it counts for just as much in the polling booth. And outside the polling booth, he can increase his influence through formal and informal contacts with others.

"'The Tyranny of the Majority' Is a Threat to Freedom"

This is an old notion, sufficiently respectable to be held by many college graduates. First conceived as an argument against democracy itself, the threat of majority tyranny has served as an effective weapon in opposing every extension of popular power, from universal suffrage to stronger political parties.[3] When examined in the light of actual experience in democracies, however, the threat disappears.

First, just what does the term mean? *Tyranny* is the imposition by rulers of severe deprivations upon those ruled, combined with the denial of any legal way (such as propaganda and election efforts) to eliminate those deprivations. When a citizen pays his taxes, or is required to drive within fixed speed limits, or is forbidden to engage in specified business practices, he may feel a sense of deprivation. But we do not regard him as a victim of tyranny, because he is neither treated with capricious severity nor denied an opportunity to try to change the law.

The interests and viewpoints of Americans are extremely diverse—so diverse that a majority cannot be united behind any narrowly tyrannical program. A majority coalition can be created only by a broad program representing compromises among the aims of countless minority groups. With our

[3] The alleged threat of tyranny is not, of course, the only argument against such extensions of popular power, as the discussion in Chapter 7 indicates.

overlapping group memberships and with our general commitment to popular freedom, no tyrannical policy can win majority endorsement. In the United States, truly tyrannical schemes have been heard only from the "lunatic fringe."

Perhaps a better way of dispelling fears of majority tyranny is to point out that we do not in practice find majority "rule"—i.e., majority support—even for moderate policies. Elections can hardly be regarded as endorsements of a specific policy. And even if they could, only about 65 per cent of the eligible voters turn out even when voting is heaviest; so if the winning party gets as much as 55 per cent of the votes, it has been endorsed by only about 36 per cent of the eligible voters. In the years between elections, lack of education, leisure, and political awareness reduces interest in politics to the point where a majority of citizens can hardly be called even observers, much less active supporters, of specific proposals. Robert A. Dahl, in a keen analysis of democratic theory, concludes:

> The real world issue has not turned out to be whether a majority, much less "the" majority, will act in a tyrannical way through democratic procedures to impose its will on a (or the) minority. Instead, the more relevant question is the extent to which various minorities in a society will frustrate the ambitions of one another with the passive acquiescence or indifference of a majority of adults or voters.[4]

Democracy serves to broaden participation in politics, or to increase, as Dahl says, "the number, size, and diversity of the minorities whose preferences will influence the outcome of governmental decisions."[5] Only rarely do those actively participating make up a majority. And if we do not have *majority participation*, we need not worry about *majority tyranny*.

"Free Elections Alone Will Translate Public Opinion into Policy"

This is another idea that is older than democratic government itself. But —unlike the fear of majority tyranny—this was an assumption of those who were struggling toward democracy. In America, for example, Sam Adams dissolved his political machine after the Revolution because he saw no need for such an organization once freedom had been won. Popular suffrage seemed to promise a solution for the whole problem of making government responsible to the people. Emphasis on the vote is not misplaced, for the effectiveness of all the other means of political influence stems from the basic right to vote. When the Supreme Court's repudiation of the "white primary" gave large numbers of Negro southerners the vote in 1944, for example, they soon began to use other techniques of political pressure more effectively.

For the individual citizen to cast his vote is not enough in itself, however, for individual votes are not automatically translated into public policy. If

---
[4] *A Preface to Democratic Theory* (Chicago: The University of Chicago Press, 1956), p. 133.
[5] *Ibid.*

millions of Americans were to vote as so many separate individuals, the results would be almost meaningless. Hundreds of candidates would receive votes, and pluralities as high as 10 per cent would be unusual; when the winners were announced, there would be no way of judging what policies had been endorsed. To give meaning to the vote, intermediary organizations —pressure groups and political parties—standing between the citizen and the government have proved necessary in every democracy. Political parties and pressure groups serve a "middleman" function in identifying popular interests and selecting leaders. These agencies are mentioned nowhere in the written Constitution, but they are as much a part of American politics as Congress, the President, or the Supreme Court.

"Laws Are Conceived in the Legislature"

This is a belief that is occasionally found among people unacquainted with politics, but it seldom survives even a casual study of government. In order to simplify the subject matter of politics—and to keep it noncontroversial—people sometimes fail to consider the complex problems that cannot be understood by a literal reading of the Constitution. It is not easy to explain the extra constitutional role played in legislation by pressure groups, political parties, and the President—to name but a few additional influences. No one can deny that the Constitution says that "all legislative Powers herein granted shall be vested in a Congress of the United States." So the simplest approach is to try to get across the idea that Congress legislates, the President executes, and the Supreme Court adjudicates—and let it go at that.

Even the popular press has gone beyond this simple interpretation, and any careful newspaper reader soon discovers that policy-making is shared by many who are not congressmen. Official action in Congress is the most important part of legislation, but the policy inputs of interested groups in and out of the government help shape policy before, during, and after the congressional drama.

"Policies Are Dictated by Pressure Groups"

As an extreme reaction to their discovery of the influence exerted by private groups on legislation, some people decide that policies are dictated by the ruthless application of pressure, with no regard for the public interest. And isolated incidents can be found to support this cynical view. *The Reporter* magazine revealed such an episode in connection with a tariff bill during the Eisenhower administration. The "chief of the high-tariff lobby" was reported to have furnished congressmen with copies of a bill that would have made it harder to import foreign goods. The lobbyist had left blanks in one section of the bill so that each official sponsor could fill in the names of the products made in his constituency. Sixteen representatives introduced basically similar versions of the measure. The shocking revelation was that four congressmen introduced the measure exactly as it had been given to them, without even bothering to fill in the blanks.[6]

Sorry performances of this sort by a few congressmen lead some observers to assume that the whole congressional process is an empty show, that the

[6] See "Theirs Not to Reason Why," *The Reporter* (July 6, 1954), 2.

public interest is always ignored, and that congressmen are simply puppets controlled by powerful lobbyists. A more balanced view, however, takes into account the checks on narrow minority control. First, political parties are based on a broad collection of interests, and the parties do exert considerable influence on their members in Congress. Second, every congressman knows that if he favors narrow minorities he may well be defeated in the next election. Third, the President, as a party leader with a national constitutency, also exerts pressure on congressmen, and most presidents have a broad view of the national interest. Fourth, the solidarity of any pressure group is reduced by overlapping membership in other organizations. Finally, our widespread commitment to the basic values of the "American Creed" puts a check on any pressure group that tries to ride roughshod over the interests of others. If a pressure-group spokesman violates our concept of "fair play," legislators and administrators may be alienated rather than influenced, opposing groups may gain new adherents, members of the pressure group itself may react against their spokesmen, and new opposition organizations may be created.

"Policy Reflects Consensus"

At the other extreme, some people assume that official policy always reflects consensus or general agreement. Margaret Mead, the popular anthropologist, found that this assumption was quite accurate in the rigidly traditional Balinese civilization. She says every issue there is resolved by a simple process that boils down to asking, "What is the place of this new proposal in our pattern of decreed and traditional behavior?" Americans, however, who become emotionally involved in public issues, find it difficult to imagine "a society in which issues as vital as migration or war are settled as formally, from the standpoint of public opinion, as is the date of Thanksgiving Day."[7] Certainly none of the policies we have discussed in preceding chapters reflected consensus. Policy in the United States represents the victory of one coalition of interests over another, with the losers protesting so loudly that no one can doubt their displeasure.

Balinese differ from Americans, not in having an accepted tradition, but in having a tradition that produces unquestioned answers to specific problems. Their tradition answers questions; ours provides a method for seeking answers. Any stable society requires wide acceptance of basic political procedures, and democratic government is impossible unless most of the losers as well as the winners are willing to accept policies determined by "consent of the governed." But this is quite different from *policy* by consensus. All Americans do not agree on even such underlying elements of our politics as the rules of Congress or the powers of the national government. What we *agree* on, essentially, is a method of governing in which policies reflect widespread interests without destroying the right to *disagree*. This is radically different from the idea that specific policies reflect consensus.

[7]"Public Opinion Mechanisms Among Primitive Peoples," *Public Opinion Quarterly*, I (July, 1937), 7.

People often talk about "government by consensus" as if it existed, when they really mean it is an ideal they regard as desirable. Various devices that block or delay the achievement of policies that command broad support—devices like the seniority system in Congress or the filibuster in the Senate—are thus defended on the ground that they promote the ideal of government by consensus. But this is the pursuit of a will-o'-the-wisp. A device like the filibuster gives the minority a veto over policy; it does not give us consensus. When a majority of those participating in politics are prevented from enacting a policy they want, what we actually have is minority control over policy.[8]

Minority control is certainly not consensus, although many people seem to assume that it is. If the majority is prevented from enacting a new policy, these observers point out that the existence of opposition proves the lack of consensus—and the desirability of postponing the new policy. What they fail to see is that a decision to continue an old policy is just as binding—just as much an act of government—as a decision to modify that policy. If a minority keeps an old policy in effect when a majority wants to change it, the majority is forced to accept the preference of the minority. This is no less frustrating for the majority than the requirement of observing the new policy would be for the minority. The question is not how to get consensus, but who is going to be frustrated—the majority or the minority? The seniority system and the filibuster may be justified on the grounds that they give strategic minorities a negative control over policy, and that they make more than ordinary majorities necessary to change policy; but with majorities frustrated in the first case, and with minorities frustrated in the second, this is hardly consensus.

"Ours Is a Government of Laws and Not of Men"

This idea, often heard during the American Revolution, has inspired the struggle for responsible government everywhere. It seems to be a misconception only in the literal sense. In both Europe and America, those who fought for democratic government resented the capricious and arbitrary power of rulers, from kings to local magistrates. Like any propagandists engaged in a serious political struggle, the American revolutionists exaggerated both the evils they were trying to do away with—the purely personal nature of irresponsible decisions—and the improvements they could offer—the impersonality of government under law. Without eliminating personal favoritism or malice entirely, democracy has greatly reduced the exercise of personal caprice by limiting public officials to known procedures, rules, and punishments. So in a sense we have achieved what would have been regarded in the age of monarchy as something close to "a government of laws and not of men."

To carry this concept to the extreme point of a literal belief in a government of laws and not of men, however, becomes both false and dangerous. Our government is made up of men, and our Constitution and laws are made, applied, and interpreted by men. This obvious truth is seldom overlooked so far as Congress, the President, and current laws are concerned. But some people

---

[8] As we have mentioned earlier in this chapter and elsewhere in the book, an absolute majority of the total adult population never participates actively in politics. When we talk about "majority control," then, it should be understood that we mean control by a majority of those actively participating.

tend almost to deify the Founding Fathers and, to a lesser extent, the Supreme Court. The Founding Fathers were real, live politicians rather than so many reincarnations of Moses; they met in Philadelphia rather than on Mount Sinai; and they fought out the provisions of the document among themselves rather than waiting for divine revelation. (Franklin's suggestion that they open each session with a prayer was voted down because they had no funds to pay a parson.) Similarly, the more discerning and candid Supreme Court justices themselves have reminded us that "judges do and must legislate." Constitutions and laws are not self-enforcing. The Supreme Court offers our nearest approximation to unbiased interpretation, but it speaks not with the voice of the Constitution but with the often inharmonious voices of nine justices. If the law were self-evident, if the Court's problems were simply those of nine technical experts, we would never get 5–4 decisions.

Literal belief in a government of laws and not of men is dangerous because it leads either to blindness or to disillusionment. Anyone who thinks that judicial decisions are or should be impersonal products of "the Court," for example, must either ignore split decisions or else conclude that some of the justices have lost their reasoning powers or have become scoundrels. A realistic appraisal of the Court requires an awareness that people differ on political issues and that political decisions must be made by human beings. By giving more men a voice in making laws and establishing procedures for their enforcement and interpretation, we have gone far toward insuring "a government of laws [reflecting popular preferences] and not of [a few irresponsible] men."

"Government Is Neutral"

A final misconception entertained by a great many Americans is the idea that government is neutral. Again, this is a tendency to confuse preferences with realities. It might be nice if the government really were neutral, but the notion that government is neutral simply does not fit the facts.

A useful analytical approach is to ask of any governmental arrangement or proposal: in terms of its *effect* rather than of its declared purpose, what is its function? Then ask: who is—or feels—hurt by such a function, and who is—or feels—benefited? Going further, you may use your conclusions to predict the political behavior of individuals or groups in advance. Advance knowledge about what's going to happen is as much fun in politics as in horse-racing: it is less expensive when the analysis proves faulty, and more exhilarating when the analysis proves correct. Right or wrong, the habit of prediction at least gives the observer a sense of contact with the events that are shaping the future.

Let's look at a seemingly dry and neutral feature of government—the system of apportioning representation in Congress. Using the approach we have suggested, you can easily discover from your general reading that political districting in America has long been arranged to "overrepresent" rural areas. This is certainly not a neutral arrangement. Among other things, it gives great weight in Congress to the needs of farmers. If you also know that congressmen from rural areas tend to be conservative, you can conclude that the present system of representation similarly functions to "overrepresent" the interests of larger business and allied groups.

The functions of the system of representation thus automatically benefit farmers and—in a less obvious fashion—conservative business interests. In more general terms, this feature of congressional representation is sometimes described as protecting "the minority." But "the minority" is an even more elusive term than "the majority." There are many different and conflicting minority interests, and not all of them are benefited by the system of representation. The ones that are benefited are those that dominate underpopulated political districts. Minorities within these districts, even though they are allied with majorities in "underrepresented" areas, find the districting system highly "dysfunctional." Negroes, migrant workers, tenant farmers, and sharecroppers, for example, are minorities within the overrepresented areas who are handicapped rather than helped by the system. They have more political interests in common with the factory workers, coal miners, and general wage-earners from underrepresented urban districts than with farm or mine owners in their own districts.

If you decide to try your hand at predicting future events, you will have to keep abreast of trends too recent to have been described in your college courses. Some books still say, for example, that equal representation of the states in the Senate guarantees a majority from rural areas in that body. This was actually true for so long that many political scientists still talk about the "rural" Senate and the more nearly "urban" House. In fact, however, the national census revealed as early as 1950 that only eighteen states had rural majorities, which means that almost two-thirds of the senators were elected by predominantly urban constituencies. On the other hand, the state legislatures, which are still dominated by rural areas, draw up the districts from which members of the House are chosen, and they give more House seats to rural districts. As a result, the urban-rural relationship of the two houses has actually been reversed, and the House has become the more conservative body, checking a liberal Senate! This is exactly the opposite of what the Framing Fathers apparently intended, but new realities are not—and citizens should not be—bound by the preferences of the Framers.

In view of Supreme Court decisions requiring adherence to the "one-man—one-vote" principle in both houses of state legislatures and in the national House of Representatives, we may expect the House gradually to become less conservative. This is a prediction rather than a statement of fact. The reader might keep it in mind as one test of the validity of the analysis in this book. The facts of American politics change rapidly and constantly. Unless our analysis gives the student a way of appraising future developments, it has been of little benefit. We hope it will be of some help after the contemporary facts have drastically changed.

A Bibliographical Essay

The study of American government may begin but it cannot end with a textbook. Without pretending to supply a complete bibliography, we shall suggest a number of books that the serious student can use to dig more deeply into American politics. Although this bibliography is selective—not even all the good books on any one problem can be included—many of the ones we do mention have fuller bibliographies on their specialized subjects. We list some classics that have stood the test of time but, since the text focuses on contemporary politics, most of the titles we suggest are fairly recent.

So many paperbound editions are now published that students can build a good personal library at low cost. Asterisks indicate volumes available as paperbacks.

PART ONE   The Context of American Politics

Introduction to Political Science

The systematic study of government is at least as old as Aristotle's *Politics*, but political scientists still differ among themselves as to the fields, scope, and methods of political science. *American Political Science: A Profile of a Discipline* (1964), by Albert Somit and Joseph Tanenhaus, surveys current issues and trends in the profession as viewed by members of the American Political Science Association. The authors also present an intellectual history of modern political science in *The Development of American Political Science: From Burgess to Behavioralism* (1967). In Marian D. Irish (ed.), *The Advance of the Discipline: 1948–1968*, eight essays examine new approaches to different fields of political science, including "American Government."

In *The Future of Political Science* (1963), Harold Lasswell challenges the profession to combine empirical observation with systematic analysis and offers some novel hints for significant research in political science. Carl J. Friedrich turns to the findings of psychologists, anthropologists, economists, sociologists, and historians, and tempers the traditional approach of political science with new insights and concepts in *Man and His Government: An Empirical Theory of Politics* (1963).

Theories of politics, both empirical and normative, are the concerns of Fred Frohock, *The Nature of Political Inquiry* (1967), and William T. Bluhm, *Theories of the Political*

System: Classics of Political Thought and Modern Political Analysis (1965). Arnold Brecht, in *Political Theory* (1959), states the case for empirical theory. Methodological questions are the focus of Abraham Kaplan's *The Conduct of Inquiry: Methodology for Behavioral Science** (1964).

The systems approach as developed by David Easton is presented in his *The Political System: An Inquiry into the State of Political Science* (1953), *A Framework for Political Analysis* (1965), and *A Systems Analysis of Political Life* (1965). The latter work moves toward a communications model of political life, which is also the concern of *The Nerves of Government: Models of Political Communication and Control** (1963), by Karl W. Deutsch.

Various conceptual schemes for the empirical study of politics may be found in: Arthur F. Bentley, *The Process of Government* (1908); George E. G. Catlin, *Systematic Politics: Elementa Politica and Sociologica* (1962); Robert A. Dahl, *Modern Political Analysis** (1963); Heinz Eulau, Samuel Eldersveld, and Morris Janowitz, *Political Behavior: A Reader in Theory and Research* (1956); Lewis Froman, *People and Politics** (1962); Charles Hyneman, *The Study of Politics: The Present State of Political Science* (1959); Harold D. Lasswell and Abraham Kaplan, *Power and Society: A Framework for Political Inquiry** (1950): Charles E. Merriam, *Systematic Politics** (1945); Austin Ranney (ed.), *Essays on the Behavioral Study of Politics** (1962); Herbert J. Storing (ed.) *Essays on the Scientific Study of Politics* (1962); Vernon Van Dyke, *Political Science: A Philosophical Analysis** (1960); T. D. Weldon, *The Vocabulary of Politics** (1962); and Roland Young (ed.), *Approaches to the Study of Politics** (1958).

The Cultural and Economic Context

In *The Tree of Culture** (1955), Ralph Linton offers a good introduction to the way culture shapes politics, along with other patterns of behavior. Presentations, also available in paperback editions, of the culture concept are Ruth Benedict, *Patterns of Culture** (1934), and Leslie A. White, *The Science of Culture** (1949). John Dewey's *Human Nature and Conduct* (1922) is now regarded as almost a classic analysis of the impact of culture on human nature. In a different vein, stressing intimate psychological relationships rather than culture, is Charles H. Cooley, *Human Nature and the Social Order* (1902). James C. Davis has recently returned human nature to the study of political behavior with a provocative analysis, *Human Nature in Politics: The Dynamics of Political Behavior** (1963). Political culture is the concern of the fifth volume in the Studies in Political Development series, *Political Culture and Political Development* (1965), edited by Lucien W. Pye and Sidney Verba.

Explorations in Social Change (1964), edited by George K. Zollschan and Walter Hirsch, offers a variety of essays, most of them by sociologists, presenting new forms of social theory and also discussing significant changes in the American social system which condition political behavior. Gabriel Almond, *The American People and Foreign Policy** (1950), presents a summary of many studies of the American "national character," as well as an analysis of American foreign policy in relation to that character.

General studies of the American culture by anthropologists are: Geoffrey Gorer, *The American People: A Study in National Character** (1948); Clyde Kluckhohn, *Mirror for Man: The Relation of Anthropology to Modern Life** (1949); and Margaret Mead, *And Keep Your Powder Dry: An Anthropologist Looks at America* (1942). Other social scientists have tackled the same problem: D. W. Brogan, *The American Character** (1944); and David Riesman, *The Lonely Crowd: A Study of the Changing American Character** (1953). Representatives of all the social sciences re-examine Riesman's theory in S. M. Lipset and Leo Lowenthal (eds.), *Culture and Social Character* (1961). Henry Steele Commager has collected foreign observations in *America in Perspective** (1948). William Buchanan and Hadley Cantril discuss *How Nations See Each Other* (1953), with special emphasis on American stereotypes. Twenty foreign writers develop their "images" of America, both complimentary and critical, in *As Others See Us*, edited by Franz M. Joseph (1959). Daniel J. Boorstin discusses *The Image, or What Happened to the American Dream** (1962).

The classic study of the influence of the natural environment on American politics is Frederick Jackson Turner, *The Frontier in American History* (1920). Criticisms of the

Turner thesis are presented in George Rogers Taylor (ed.), *The Turner Thesis Concerning the Role of the Frontier in American History** (1949). Lee Benson, *Turner and Beard: American Historical Writing Reconsidered* (1960), another critical reaction, suggests new hypotheses in American history. In *The Great Plains* (1931), W. P. Webb describes the way the unique environment of the Great Plains altered institutions brought from the eastern United States. Carl Becker, *Freedom and Responsibility in the American Way of Life** (1955), also considers the role of the natural environment in shaping our political heritage.

Oscar Handlin, *The Uprooted** (1951) and *Race and Nationality in American Life** (1957), are distinguished studies of the immigrant experience and the ethnic origins of the American culture. On the country's most conspicuously mistreated ethnic group, see Margaret J. Butcher, *The Negro in American Culture** (1956), and E. Franklin Frazier, *The Negro in the U.S.* (rev., 1957). *Racial Crisis in America: Leadership in Crisis** (1964), by Lewis Killian and Charles Grigg, reflects the experiences and research of two southern sociologists who discuss various aspects of current race relations; they conclude "there is no easy way out." William Brink and Louis Harris report the findings of a nationwide survey conducted by *Newsweek* in *The Negro Revolution in America** (1962). A journalistic account of the civil rights movement may be found in Charles E. Silberman, *Crisis in Black and White** (1964).

Religion and Politics* (1960), edited by Peter H. Odegard, is a collection of articles on "the religious issue," especially the Roman Catholic issue in American politics. Will Herberg, *Protestant, Catholic, and Jew** (1955), discusses the religious aspects of American society, using the sociological approach. Joseph Tussman has collected a set of significant Supreme Court decisions dealing with problems of church and state in *The Supreme Court on Church and State** (1962). Another legalistic discussion may be found in Mark de Wolfe Howe, *The Garden and the Wilderness* (1964), which deals with questions of nonbelief as belief.

Sebastian de Grazia attempts to mirror contemporary society and offers a normative, descriptive, and highly provocative picture of the world today in *Of Time, Work, and Leisure** (1962). The editors of *Fortune* point up "urban pathology" in *The Exploding Metropolis** (1958). Rayond Vernon reports for a team from the Graduate School of Public Administration at Harvard, investigating the economic base of the New York metropolitan region and making projections into the next generation in *Metropolis 1985* (1961).

Two general treatments with good bibliographies for pursuing class structure as a political force are Bernard Barber, *Social Stratification* (1957), and Kurt B. Mayer, *Class and Society** (1955). Reinhard Bendix and Seymour Martin Lipset (eds.), *Class, Status and Power: A Reader in Social Stratification* (1954), offers excellent selections. Richard Centers, *The Psychology of Social Classes* (1945), focuses more directly on the impact of class on politics. Donald R. Matthews, *The Social Background of Political Decision-Makers** (1954), includes a summary of the literature on "elite" theories as well as data on the class origins of American political leaders. C. Wright Mills has studied labor leaders, the expanding middle class, and the top decision-makers in *The New Men of Power* (1948), *White Collar** (1951), and *The Power Elite** (1956). Vance Packard offers a popular approach in *The Status Seekers** (1961).

Floyd Hunter illuminates the political importance of class structure at the local level in *Community Power Structure: A Study of Decision Makers** (1953). The same author extends his interpretation of American power structure to three levels of government—community, state, and local—in *Top Leadership, U.S.A.* (1959). Robert and Helen Lynd emphasize class differences in one of the first community studies, *Middletown: A Study in Contemporary Culture* (1929). The Lynds followed up this study with *Middletown in Transition: A Study in Cultural Conflicts* (1937). Other community studies following in this tradition are Allison Davis, Burleigh B. Gardner, and Mary R. Gardner, *Deep South: A Social Anthropological Study of Caste and Class** (1941); John Dollard, *Cast and*

Class in a Southern Town* (1949); August B. Hollingshead, *Elmtown's Youth* (1949); W. L. Warner, et al., *Democracy in Jonesville* (1949); and John R. Seeley, R. A. Sim, and E. W. Loosley, *Crestwood Heights* (1956). Maurice R. Stein, *The Eclipse of Community* (1960), surveys the literature of community studies in the United States. Robert A. Dahl investigates political power in a typical American city and offers important new insights for American government and politics in *Who Governs?** (1961). Nelson W. Polsby provides the theoretical underpinning for the same study in *Community Power and Political Theory* (1964). A book which attacks these theoretical underpinnings is Peter Bachrach, *The Theory of Democractic Elitism** (1967). Robert E. Agger, Daniel Goldrich, and Bert Swanson, in *The Rulers and the Ruled* (1964), attempt to study communities by fusing both the power elite and pluralist approaches.

L. W. Warner et al., *Social Class in America* (1949), emphasizes prestige as a means of determining social position. In a light vein, Russel Lynes' *A Surfeit of Honey* (1957) appraises the newly emerging class structure. Although social scientists have tended not to analyze themselves as a subclass, Paul V. Lazarsfeld and Wagner Thielens, Jr., have done just this in *The Academic Mind: Social Scientists in a Time of Crisis* (1958).

For the extensive literature on economics and politics, a good beginning is James Madison's *Federalist* essay No. 10. In *Capitalism, Socialism, and Democracy** (1950), Joseph Schumpeter presents a widely respected interpretation of this general problem. W. W. Rostow offers what he calls "a non-communist manifesto" in *The Stages of Economic Growth** (1960), especially illuminating on the position of the American economy in international relations. Louis M. Hacker's *American Capitalism: Its Promise and Accomplishment** (1957) traces the constructive role of American capitalism, while Adolph A. Berle and Gardner C. Means, in *The Modern Corporation and Private Property* (1932), discuss the political problems posed by a corporate economy. Edward S. Mason, *The Corporation in Modern Society* (1960), is a more recent treatment of the emergence of America's corporate economy. Eugene V. Rostow appraises the public law of American capitalism in *Planning for Freedom* (1960).

John Kenneth Galbraith discusses the paradox of private opulence and public poverty in *The Affluent Society** (1958), and he re-examines the corporate economy in *The New Industrial State* (1967). Two earlier critiques of the American economy, both including proposals for reform, are Gunnar Myrdal, *Challenge to Affluence* (1963) and Michael Reagan, *The Managed Economy* (1963). A controversial book, and one influential in official thinking about national policy, is Michael Harrington's *The Other America** (1964), which focuses on poverty in this country. Gabriel Kolko, *Wealth and Power in America* (1962), and J. Frederick Dewhurst and Associates, *America's Needs and Resources,* provide valuable data on the problems of rich and poor in the United States. Walter H. Heller, former Chairman of the President's Council of Economic Advisers, discusses the uses of the "new economics" in *New Dimensions of Political Economy* (1966).

Historical Statistics of the United States: Colonial Times to 1957 (1960) is the most informative single source on the characteristics of the American population. Here the Bureau of the Census presents historical data in tabular series on such various topics as consumer expenditures, social security, education, crime, armed forces, and veterans. The annual volumes of *Statistical Abstract of the United States* are a continuing source of current data on similar topics.

The Context of Ideas

Many books have been written about democracy and democratic government, but no official creed has ever been established. Leslie Lipson appraises the democratic record from the classical tradition to current variations in *The Democratic Civilization* (1964). Henry B. Mayo offers us *An Introduction to Democratic Theory** (1960): "The method chosen is to set up a consistent and coherent theory of democracy . . . in both operational and normative terms, to explain the system and to justify it." Neal Reimer considers *The Revival of Democratic Theory** (1962); Charles Frankel discusses *The Democratic Prospect** (1962); and Thomas L. Thorson analyzes *The Logic of Democracy** (1962). Gabriel Almond and Sidney Verba undertake a systematic investigation of *The Civic Culture: Political Attitudes and Democ-*

racy in Five Nations* (1963). Robert A. Dahl's *A Preface to Democratic Theory* (1956) is a rigorous analysis of Madisonian, populistic, and polyarchal theories of democracy.

The nature of democracy, the threats to democratic government, and defenses of democracy against alternative forms of government are found in Daniel J. Boorstin, *The Genius of American Politics* (1953); Carl J. Friedrich, *The New Image of the Common Man* (1950); Ferdinand A. Hermens, *The Representative Republic* (1958); A. D. Lindsay, *The Modern Democratic State* (1947); and J. R. Pennock, *Liberal Democracy: Its Merits and Prospects* (1950). *Political Man* (1959), by Seymour Lipset, is concerned with problems of cleavage and consensus in Western democratic society. Robert Lane's depth interviews with fifteen "common men" in "Eastport" is the basis of a penetrating analysis, *Political Ideology: Why the American Common Man Believes What He Does* (1962).

For empirical studies of totalitarian appeals in America and Europe, see Gabriel Almond, *The Appeals of Communism* (1954), and Hadley Cantril, *The Politics of Despair* (1958). Erich Fromm discusses the burdens of independence and the psychological appeal of authoritarian movements in *Escape from Freedom* (1941). On right-wing authoritarianism in America, see T. W. Adorno et al., *The Authoritarian Personality* (1950); also Daniel Bell, *The Radical Right* (1963), and Harry Overstreet and Bonaro Overstreet, *The Strange Tactics of Extremism* (1964). A reminder of the central importance of nonauthoritarian conservatism in America is found in Clinton Rossiter, *Conservatism in America* (1955).

Vernon L. Parrington's monumental work, *Main Currents in American Thought* (1930, 3 vols.), is no doubt the most widely read history of political ideas in the United States. Parrington's own convictions were so deeply held and so eloquently expressed that his work has become important as the source of his ideas no less than a history of the ideas of others. Also excellent are Merle Curti, *The Growth of American Thought* (1943); Ralph H. Gabriel, *The Course of American Democratic Thought* (1956); Louis Hartz, *The Liberal Tradition in America* (1955); and Richard Hofstadter, *The American Political Tradition* (1948). Four notable studies of American democracy by foreign commentators are Alexis de Tocqueville, *Democracy in America* (2 vols., 1954); James Bryce, *The American Commonwealth* (2 vols., 1888); Harold J. Laski, *The American Democracy* (1948); and D. W. Brogan, *Politics in America* (1954). An attempt to discuss American political thought within a context of behavioral political science is found in David Minar, *Ideas and Politics, The American Experience* (1964).

Throughout this text we have emphasized the pluralism of America. Different sections of the country react differently to current political issues. James McBride Dabbs explains Southern reactions as "the product of history" in *Who Speaks for the South?* (1964); Ralph McGill, intrepid editor of the *Atlanta Constitution*, writes from a contemporary vantage in *The South and the Southerner* (1963); Harvard professor of philosophy Perry Miller looks at New England in *Errand Into Wilderness* (1956); and Henry Nash Smith discusses *Virgin Land: The American West as Symbol and Myth* (1957). Alfred O. Hero, Jr., presents a wealth of public opinion data in *The Southerner in World Affairs* (1965).

The Constitutional Background and Federalism

No complete or accurate record of the Constitutional Convention of 1787 exists. Max Farrand has brought together the most comprehensive collection of debates in the Convention, including some timely correspondence of the Convention members, in *The Records of the Federal Convention of 1787* (1911, 1937, 4 vols.). Jonathan Elliot has collected the primary materials on the fight for ratification in *The Debates in the Several State Conventions on the Adoption of the Federal Constitution* (1835–46, 5 vols.).

The Federalist,* by Alexander Hamilton, James Madison, and John Jay, has come to be regarded as authoritative on "the intentions of the Framers," for two of the three authors were active in the Convention. A contemporary commentary, it was written as a series of partisan letters to the public in 1787 explaining and advocating the proposed Constitution. Paul Ford has gathered together considerable propaganda of the period for and against ratification in *Essays on the Constitution . . . 1787-1788* (1892).

From the legal standpoint, *The Constitution of the United States,* edited by Edward S. Corwin (1952) and revised by Norman J. Small (1964), is probably the most useful single reference volume on the "flexible Constitution." A phrase-by-phrase analysis of the Constitution, it is fully annotated with Supreme Court decisions from 1789 through 1952. The never-ending debates of Congress on the meaning of the Constitution and the nature of federalism may be traced from the first session to the present in the *Annals of Congress* (1789-1824); the *Register of Debates* (1824-27); the *Congressional Globe* (1833-1873); and the *Congressional Record* (1873 to date).

In *The American Revolution** (1957), Charles H. McIlwain offers a constitutional interpretation that is both original and provocative. A brilliant analysis of the Declaration of Independence and its philosophic import is Carl Becker, *The Declaration of Independence** (1922, 1942). Edward Dumbauld has also made a detailed interpretation of the document in *The Declaration of Independence and What It Means Today* (1950). On the Articles of Confederation, see especially Merril M. Jensen, *The Articles of Confederation* (1950); and Andrew C. McLaughlin, *The Confederation and the Constitution** (1905). Seymour Martin Lipset writes about *The First New Nation: The United States in Historical and Comparative Perspective* (1963).

There are many differing interpretations of what the Founding Fathers hoped to found. Charles A. Beard, *An Economic Interpretation of the Constitution of the United States** (1913), was highly controversial in its day and is still influential in political science. Robert E. Brown, *Charles Beard and the Constitution** (1956), and Forest McDonald, *We the People** (1958), reappraise and attempt to break down the Beard thesis, as does Lee Benson's *Turner and Beard** (1960), which uses social science techniques to deal with historical questions. Jackson Turner Main's study of *The Antifederalists: Critics of the Constitution, 1781-1788** (1961) unearths evidence that supports the Beard point of view more than that of his critics. William W. Crosskey, *Politics and the Constitution* (1953), challenges some traditional concepts of constitutional law with convincing documentation.

Andrew C. McLaughlin, *A Constitutional History of the United States* (1935), gives a general treatment of constitutional development, somewhat bent on refuting Beard. Charles Warren, *The Making of the Constitution* (1937), takes issue with the Beard interpretation in an almost day-to-day account of the Convention proceedings. Broadus Mitchell and Louise Mitchell trace the development of the Constitution, emphasizing the social background and the court decisions that have affected the meaning of the document over the years, in *A Biography of the Constitution of the United States* (1964). Arthur E. Sutherland in *Constitutionalism in America* (1965) discusses American constitutional ideas which are deep-rooted in English law from the time of the Magna Carta.

Because history is "man writ large," biographies of Founding Fathers shed light on the genesis of our constitutional government. See, for example, biographies of John Adams, Alexander Hamilton, Thomas Jefferson, James Madison, John Marshall, George Washington, James Wilson, and others. The following books also emphasize personal influence in "the critical period": Max Farrand, *The Framing of the Constitution* (1913); Hastings Lyon, *The Constitution and the Men Who Made It* (1936); Fred Rodell, *Fifty Five Men* (1936); Carl C. Van Doren, *The Great Rehearsal* (1948); and Clinton Rossiter, *1787: The Great Convention* (1966).

As to what the Constitution "really means," there is no end to controversial literature. Up to 1955, Edward S. Corwin had brought out eleven editions of *The Constitution and What It Means Today.* For varied approaches to our "flexible Constitution," see Henry S. Commager, *The American Mind** (1950); Louis Hartz, *The Liberal Tradition in America* (1955); Arthur N. Holcombe, *Our More Perfect Union* (1950); William B. Munro, *The Makers of the Unwritten Constitution* (1930); Charles E. Merriam, *The Written Constitution and the Unwritten Attitude* (1931); Howard L. McBain, *The Living Constitution* (1927, 1942); and Carl B. Swisher, *American Constitutional Development* (1954). Max Lerner's *America as a Civilization** (1957), although only partly concerned with government and constitutionalism, is packed with engrossing information, discerning observations, and exciting points of view on the American political scene. Herbert Wechsler's *Principles, Politics and Fundamental Law* (1961), propounding "neutral principles" in constitutional law, has stirred much controversy among lawyers and political scientists concerned with judicial review. Charles Black considers the Constitution as a "matter of purest politics, a structure of power" in *The Making of Constitutional Law** (1963). A content analysis of a sample of colonial newspapers attempts to discover when Americans began to think of themselves as Americans in Richard L. Merritt, *Symbols of American Community* (1966).

The role of the states in the more perfect union, and the relation of the states with one another, have always been the subject of political controversy. The Commission on Intergovernmental Relations in 1955 made *A Report to the President for Transmittal to Congress* covering many current problems of national-state relations, with emphasis on financial relations. It also published fifteen *Reports of Study Committees* (1955), which together constitute a rather complete survey of problems in "the new federalism." The Senate Sub-Committee on Intergovernmental Relations, established in 1962 under the Committee on Intergovernmental Operations, has held extensive hearings on intergovernmental issues. A similar Committee in the House has also been holding hearings. The published reports of these congressional committees cover a full spectrum of national-state relationships.

Although New Deal reforms of the 1930s evoked considerable commentary on the theory of federalism, surprisingly little research has appeared on this subject, perhaps because of the general acceptance of a prominent role for the national government. Two early studies of the "new federalism" are: Jane Perry Clark, *The Rise of a New Federalism* (1938), and V. O. Key, Jr., *The Administration of Federal Grants to States* (1937). The English scholar, Kenneth C. Wheare offers us a theoretical analysis of federalism in a comparative frame of reference, *Federal Government** (4th ed., 1964).

Other studies of American federalism include: Vincent V. Thursby, *Interstate Cooperation* (1953); Arthur W. MacMahon (ed.), *Federalism Mature and Emergent* (1955); Redding S. Sugg Jr. and George H. Jones, *The Southern Education Board: The Years of Regional Cooperation in Higher Education* (1960); and Daniel J. Elazar, *The American Partnership* (1962). *The Federal Government and Metropolitan Areas* (1960), by Robert Connery and Richard H. Leach, reads much like a staff policy paper on what "should" be the pattern of the new federalism. *Intergovernmental Relations in Review* (1960), by William Anderson, a distinguished senior political scientist synthesizes three decades of exploration and findings on this complex subject. Another seasoned scholar of state governments provides a comprehensive text in *American Intergovernmental Relations: Their Origins, Historical Development, and Current Status* (1964), by W. B. Graves. Weldon V. Barton's *Interstate Compacts in the Political Process* (1967) examines a number of compacts and discusses their utility in a federal system.

Two recent studies of federalism are *The Cities and the Federal System* (1965), by Roscoe C. Martin, and *Federalism—Origin, Operation, and Significance** (1964), by William Riker. Riker's book offers both historical and comparative perspectives. In addition, the formalism which usually marks discussions of federalism is replaced by an empirical and behavioral approach set in a deductive theoretical model.

PART TWO   Inputs of the Political System: Demands, Supports, and Apathy

Political Opinions and Political Participation

Two periodicals largely devoted to studies of political opinins and voting behavior are the *Public Opinion Quarterly* and the *International Journal of Opinion and Attitude Research*. Comprehensive annotated bibliographies (now somewhat dated) are Bruce L. Smith, Harold D. Lasswell, and

Ralph D. Casey, *Propaganda, Communication, and Public Opinion* (1946), and Bruce L. Smith and Chitra M. Smith, *International Communication and Political Opinion* (1956).

A. Lawrence Lowell, *Public Opinion and Popular Government* (1913), and Walter Lippmann, *Public Opinion** (1922), are two early studies of public opinion. More recent coverage of the field is found in William Albig, *Modern Public Opinion* (1956); Bernard Berelson and Morris Janowitz (eds.), *Reader in Public Opinion and Communication* (1950); Daniel Katz *et al.* (eds.), *Public Opinion and Propaganda: A Book of Readings* (1954). One of the Handbooks for Research in Political Behavior, *Survey Research** (1963), by Charles H. Backstrom and Gerald D. Hursh, is a do-it-yourself book covering all stages in the process of doing survey research. A technical discussion is *Survey Sampling* (1965) by Leslie Kish.

In this textbook we have found most helpful *Public Opinion and American Democracy* (1961), in which the late V. O. Key, Jr., brings together much of the new knowledge of public opinion and places it within an organized political context. Professor Key's last work (completed by Milton Cummings), *The Responsible Electorate* (1966), attempts to revise some of the conventional wisdom in the fields of public opinion and electoral behavior. Key argues that voters tend to vote according to their beliefs and suggests that earlier work had underestimated the electorate. For a brief overall consideration of the ways people arrive at political opinions and the tools that political scientists use in analyzing public opinion, we highly recommend Robert E. Lane and David O. Sears, *Public Opinion** (1964).

Various facets of psychology and politics are explored in Graham Wallas, *Human Nature in Politics* (1909); Harold D. Lasswell, *Psychopathology and Politics* (1930) and *Power and Personality* (1948); Alexander H. Leighton, *The Governing of Men* (1946); T. W. Adorno *et al.*, *The Authoritarian Personality* (1950); and H. J. Eysenck, *The Psychology of Politics* (1954). On the last two references, see the commentary in Richard Christie and Marie Jahoda, *Studies in the Scope and Method of "The Authoritarian Personality"* (1954), and the exchange of comments between Richard Christie and H. J. Eysenck in the *Psychological Bulletin* (1956). Milton Rokeach in *The Open and Closed Mind** (1960) reports on the Dogmatism scale, which measures a syndrome similar to authoritarianism but with a measure which is independent of the liberalism-conservatism dimension. Rokeach calls the two types distinguished by this scale open- and closed-minded. A similar finding of pragmatism-dogmatism is one of the ideological dimensions among Supreme Court justices in Glendon Schubert, *The Judicial Mind: Attitudes and Ideologies of Supreme Court Justices, 1946-1963* (1965).

For a thoughtful distinction between the dogmatic and single-minded individual who focuses his whole attention on a particular doctrine and the concerned citizen who has a general interest in the many facets of politics, read Eric Hoffer, *The True Believer** (1958). M. Brewster Smith, Jerome S. Bruner, and Robert W. White analyze the functions of opinions for personality in *Opinions and Personality* (1956). Herbert McClosky's articles on conservatism and personality represent a systematic examination of this problem by a contemporary political scientist. Also pertinent are Robert Lane, *Political Life: Why People Get Involved in Politics** (1959), and Heinz Eulau, *The Behavioral Persuasion in Politics** (1963).

A wide range of empirical studies represent the development of interdisciplinary research on various aspects of political socialization, especially in mass communication. Karl W. Deutsch *et. al.*, present a set of models to analyze quantitative and qualitative data on national and local patterns of political relationships in *The Integration of Political Communities** (1964). A pioneering study is Herbert Hyman's *Political Socialization* (1959). Fred Greenstein's *Children and Politics** (1965), about children's political views, suggests an interesting new approach to understanding the early stages of political socialization. Political socialization of children as it relates to systemic characteristics is the concern of David Easton in a number of recently published research reports. See also Roberta Sigel (ed.), *Political Socialization: Its Role in the Political Process** (1965).

Mass communication is a crucial tool of modern government. Two studies, one by a professional journalist, the other by a political scientist, report on the interaction of politics and the press in the communications process: Douglass Cater, *The Fourth Branch* of Government* (1959), and Dan D. Nimmo, *Newsgathering in Washington: A Study in Political Communication* (1962).

For a comprehensive summary of findings on voting behavior and for a more complete bibliography on the subject, see Seymour M. Lipset *et al.*, "The Psychology of Voting: An Analysis of Political Behavior," in Gardner Lindzey (ed.), *Handbook of Social Psychology,* II (1954). A series of election surveys begun in 1940 supplies much of our insight into voting behavior: Paul F. Lazarsfeld, Bernard Berelson, and Hazel Gaudet, *The People's Choice* (1948), and Bernard Berelson, Paul F. Lazarsfled, and William McPhee, *Voting** (1954). Eugene Burdick and Arthur J. Brodbeck have collected, in *American Voting Behavior* (1959), a series of articles re-examining the findings of the major election studies. A somewhat intemperate critique of voting studies, by Walter Berns, may be found in H. Storing (ed.), *Essays on the Scientific Study of Politics* (1962).

The Michigan Survey Research Center, which has been doing research on voting behavior since 1948, continues to furnish us with new data as well as analysis, interpretation, and projection. See Angus Campbell, Gerald Gurin, and Warren E. Miller, *The Voter Decides* (1954); Angus Campbell and Homer C. Cooper, *Group Differences in Attitudes and Votes* (1956); and Angus Campbell, P. Converse, W. Miller, and D. Stokes, *The American Voter** (1960). The recent research of the Michigan Survey Research Center concerned with electoral behavior is collected in *Elections and the Political Order* (1966), in which greater theoretical rigor and comparative perspectives augment their usual first-rate research. The mark of both recent books is a successful attempt to put politics back into the study of political behavior by considering the influence on voting of political no less than of social and economic factors.

At a more popular level, Samuel Lubell has written about *The Future of American Politics** (1952) and *Revolt of the Moderates* (1956). Louis H. Bean, *How to Predict Elections* (1948), and *Influences in the 1954 Mid-Term Elections* (pamphlet, 1954), use statistical analysis of voting "cycles" in interpreting voting behavior. In *Is There a Republican Majority?* (1954), Louis Harris appraises voting patterns in the Eisenhower era. Speical aspects of voting behavior are considered in: Harry M. Bain and Donald S. Hecock, *Ballot Position and Voter's Choice** (1957); Lawrence H. Fuchs, *The Political Behavior of American Jews* (1956); Seymour M. Lipset, *Agrarian Socialism* (1950); Henry Lee Moon, *Balance of Power: The Negro Vote* (1948); Donald S. Strong, *Urban Republicanism in the South** (1960); and Ruth G. Silva, *Rum, Religion and Votes: 1928 Re-Examined* (1962). Donald R. Matthews and James W. Prothro deal with the determinants of Negro political participation in the South in *Negroes and the New Southern Politics* (1966).

Party Politics and Political Leadership

Maurice Duverger, *Political Political Parties** (1955), is an enlightening comparative treatment; Sigmund Neumann (ed.), *Modern Political Parties* (1956), although not really a comparative analysis, offers good essays on parties in different countries. V. O. Key, Jr., *Politics, Parties, and Pressure Groups* (5th ed., 1964), and Avery Leiserson, *Parties and Politics: An Institutional and Behavioral Approach* (1958), provide excellent treatments of American political parties. Samuel J. Eldersveld, *Political Parties: A Behavioral Analysis* (1964), is both an empirical and theoretical contribution to the functions of parties. Robert Alford examines the importance of class and party in political loyalties in four countries in *Party and Society: The Anglo-American Democracies* (1963). A number of brief and refreshing accounts of American political parties have recently appeared in paperback editions: Hugh A. Bone and Austin Ranney, *Politics and Voters** (1963); Rooert A. Goldwin (ed.), *Political Parties, U.S.A.** (1964); Fred I. Greenstein, *The American Party System and the American People** (1963); Clinton Rossiter, *Parties and Politics in America** (1960); Frank Sorauf, *Political Parties in the American System** (1964); and Allen P. Sindler, *Political Parties in the United States** (1966).

Political Parties and Political Behavior* (1966), edited by William J. Crotty, Donald M.

Freeman, and Douglas S. Gatlin, presents a collection of methodological and substantive contributions. William Nisbet Chambers examines the beginnings of the party system in the United States in *Political Parties in a New Nation: The American Experience, 1776–1809** (1963), and Wilfred Binkley gives a history of shifting party doctrines and persisting bases of support in *American Political Parties* (1943).

In *The Doctrine of Responsible Party Government* (1962), Austin Ranney explores a concept that some regard as offering a model for the functioning of democratic political parties and that others regard as inappropriate or dangerous for American democracy. Pendleton Herring's *The Politics of Democracy* (1940) emphasizes the advantages of our present system of undisciplined, decentralized parties. (A somewhat revised paperback edition appeared in 1965.) E. E. Schattschneider champions disciplined, centralized parties in *Party Government** (1942), as does the Committee on Political Parties of the American Political Science Association (chaired by Professor Schattschneider) in *Toward a More Responsible Two-Party System* (1950). Frank J. Sorauf offers a stimulating and provocative discussion of interaction between party and constituency in the process of representation in *Party and Representation* (1963).

The student may compare the platforms of the parties for himself by consulting T. H. McKee (ed.), *National Conventions and Platforms of All Political Parties, 1789–1904* (1904), and K. H. Porter and D. B. Johnson, *National Party Platforms, 1840–1964* (1966). The *Congressional Quarterly*, which breaks down the votes in both houses of Congress in party terms, is a great aid in comparing the congressional record of the parties. On parties and political leaders in different sections, see: V. O. Key, Jr., *Southern Politics in State and Nation** (1949); Alexander Heard, *A Two-Party South?* (1952); Duane Lockard, *New England State Politics* (1959); and Alfred de Grazia, *The Western Republic, 1952 and Beyond* (1954). Two recent studies of third parties are: Irving Howe and Lewis Coser, *The American Communist Party: A Critical History* (1958); and Karl M. Schmidt's painstaking review of the ill-fated Progressive Party of 1948, *Henry A. Wallace: Quixotic Crusade* (1960). See also Elmo R. Richardson, *The Politics of Conservation: Crusades and Controversies* (1962).

For the study of party leadership, the works on psychology and politics cited in the previous section should prove helpful. Robert Michel's *Political Parties*,* first published in English in 1915, is a pioneering study of the psychology of power and the sociology of leadership by a distinguished French scholar. Alvin W. Gouldner's *Studies in Leadership* (1950) and Dwaine Marvick's *Political Decision Makers* (1961) are good collections of readings on the subject. Leaders at different levels are considered in Charles E. Merriam, *Four American Party Leaders* (1926); H. F. Gosnell, *Machine Politics: Chicago Model* (1937); Sonya Forthal, *Cogwheels of Democracy, A Study of the Precinct Captain* (1946); Hugh A. Bone, *Grass Roots Party Leadership* (1952); and Rexford G. Tugwell, *The Art of Politics, As Practiced by Three Great Americans* (1958). Hugh A. Bone gives us a detailed description of the eight national party committees in *Party Committees and National Politics* (1958). A more recent and somewhat more empirical study of the national party committees is found in *Politics Without Power, The National Party Committees* (1964) by Cornelius P. Cotter and Bernard C. Hennessy. The motivavations for the political activities of politicians is discussed by Joseph A. Schlesinger in *Ambition and Politics* (1966).

Pressure Groups and Public Relations

David B. Truman's *The Governmental Process* (1951) is valuable for an understanding of politics as a struggle among competing interests, and is particularly illuminating on the role of pressure groups. Other helpful general studies are: Donald C. Blaisdell, *American Democracy Under Pressure* (1957); Pendleton Herring, *Group Representation Before Congress* (1929), and *Public Administration and the Public Interest* (1936); Harold Lasswell, *Politics: Who Gets What, When, How** (1936); Charles E. Merriam, *Public and Private Government* (1944); Harmon Ziegler, *Interest Groups in American Society* (1964); Lester W. Milbrath, *The Washington Lobbyists* (1963); Raymond A. Bauer, Ithiel de Sola Pool, and Lewis Anthony Dexter, *American Business and Public Policy: The Politics of Foreign Trade* (1963), and Abraham Holtzman, *Interest Groups and Lobbying** (1966).

Many studies have been made of particular pressure groups. For the role of labor, portrayed in case studies from the 1950 elections, see Fay Caulkins, *The CIO and the Democratic Party* (1952). An insightful study of the veterans' lobby is Mary R. Dearing, *Veterans in Politics* (1952). One example of a business lobby's tactics may be found in the Federal Trade Commission's *Summary Report . . . on Efforts by Associations and Agencies of Electric and Gas Utilities to Influence Public Opinion*, Sen. Doc. No. 92, 70th Cong., 1st Sess. (1934); a highly critical study is Robert A. Brady, *Business as a System of Power* (1943). John W. Hurst, *Law and Economic Growth: The Legal History of the Lumber Industry in Wisconsin* (1964), is a thoroughgoing piece of scholarship in a much broader political context than the title suggests.

Oliver Garceau's study, *The Political Life of the American Medical Association* (1941), examines one of the most powerful pressure groups. On farm organizations and the influence of business groups on farm policy, see Wesley McCune, *The Farm Bloc* (1943), and *Who's Behind Our Farm Policy?* (1956). Peter Odegard, *Pressure Politics, The Story of the Antisaloon League* (1928), and E. E. Schattschneider, *Politics, Pressures, and the Tariff* (1935), are earlier studies of two pressure-group campaigns. Phillip O. Foss does a realistic case study of the pressure politics behind our national grazing policies in *Politics and Grass* (1960); and Robert Engler shows how "the private government that controls most of the petroleum resources of the world" affects American political life in *The Politics of Oil* (1961). Clement E. Vose examines the role of interest groups in the judicial process in *Caucasians Only: The Supreme Court, the NAACP and the Restrictive Covenant Cases* (1959). Other special studies include: Clifton Brock, *Americans for Democratic Action* (1962); Abraham Holtzman, *The Townsend Movement: A Political Study* (1963); and James H. Timberlake, *Prohibition and the Progressive Movement 1900–1920* (1963).

A broadly conceived history of advertising, written in a friendly tone, is James P. Wood, *The Story of Advertising* (1958). Otis Pease's *The Responsibility of American Advertising* (1958) is more critical. The first specific study of the application of modern public relations techniques to politics is Stanley Kelley, *Professional Public Relations and Political Power* (1956). Edward L. Bernays, a leading practitioner of the art and science of "engineering consent," has written *Propaganda* (1928), *The Engineering of Consent* (1955), and *Crystallizing Public Opinion* (1961). Vance Packard's popular-level treatment of public relations techniques, *The Hidden Persuaders** (1957), emphasizes the tremendous power of the public relations fraternity. As applied to politically oriented "institutional" advertising, however, William H. Whyte, Jr., asks *Is Anybody Listening?* (1952) and suggests that such campaigns have little influence.

Three studies from the Brookings Institution deal in part with campaign propaganda, the impact of polls and mass media, and the influence of professional public relations: Stanley Kelley, Jr., *Political Campaigning* (1960); Paul T. David, Ralph M. Goldman, and Richard C. Bain, *The Politics of National Party Conventions* (1960, revised and updated in a paperback edition, 1964); and Paul T. David (ed.), *The Presidential Election and Transition, 1960–61* (1961). Theodore H. White dramatizes the influence of the mass media, especially television, in *The Making of the President, 1960** (1961) and *The Making of the President, 1964* (1965).

Elections

For laws on voting and elections, consult the most recent edition of *The Book of the States*. See K. H. Porter, *A History of Suffrage in the United States* (1918), for the story of the extension of the franchise. Six volumes by Elizabeth C. Stanton and other suffragettes, *History of Woman Suffrage* (1881–1922), tell in detail how women won the right to vote. Richard Scammon has given us three volumes of basic reference materials and statistics on elections since 1946, *America Votes* (1956, 1958, 1960). Specialized studies of American elections are: Cortez A. M. Ewing, *Congressional Elections, 1896–1944* (1947), and *Primary Elections in* the South (1953); Paul T. David et al., *Presidential Nominating Politics in 1952* (5 vols., 1954); and Malcolm Moos, *Politics, Presidents, and Coattails* (1952). Lucius Wilmerding, Jr., provides us with an excellent historical description of *The Electoral College** (1958). Alexander Heard appraises *The Costs of Democracy** (1960) with a thorough piece of research on how nominations and elections are financed in the United States.

Paul David, Ralph M. Goldman, and Richard C. Bain have done a systematic analysis of the presidential nominating process (an outgrowth of the five-volume study of the 1952 elections sponsored by the American Political Science Association), *The Politics of National Party Conventions* (1960). New research on presidential nominations may be found in Gerald Pomper, *Nominating the President* (1963); see also Paul Tillett, *Inside Politics: The National Conventions** (1962).

An examination of the nominating process and the campaign within "the strategic environment," is *Presidential Elections: Strategies of American Electoral Politics** by Nelson W. Polsby and Aaron B. Wildavsky (1964). Anthony Downs' *An Economic Theory of Democracy** (1957) proposes a thought-provoking model for an understanding of the general function of elections in a democratic system. Lester Milbrath has attempted to collect and synthesize the propositions relating to political participation in *Political Participation: How and Why People Get Involved in Politics** (1965). The materials cited under "Political Opinions and Political Participation" are also useful in understanding the electoral system.

PART THREE   Decision-Making Agencies and Activities

Government Documents

Government documents constitute a readily available source of important primary materials on the official agencies of government. Laurence F. Schmeckebier and Roy B. Eastin furnish a valuable guide, *Government Publications and Their Use* (rev. ed., 1961).

The official text of all laws passed by Congress since the beginning is the *Statutes at Large,* now published annually. The United States *Code* contains all the general laws currently in force, consolidated and codified under fifty titles. The most recent edition was in 1958, but the *Code* is kept up to date with annual cumulative supplements. Congressional debates are reported in the *Congressional Record* (1873 to date), *Congressional Globe* (1833–73), *Register of Debates* (1824–1837), and *Annals of Congress* (1789–1824). The bound volumes of congressional debates are usually verbatim reports, although remarks made on the floor may be expunged and many speeches never given are inserted in the *Appendix* under the privilege of "leave to print." The *Hearings* of congressional committees, with transcripts of testimony, cover the whole gamut of national politics. Congressional committees also constitute a goldmine of information, especially on matters of policy, through published staff studies, reports of congressional "study missions," and committee reports to Congress. The *Congressional Directory,* published annually gives personnel data on Congress and other branches of the government. Each house also publishes its own *Manual,* containing its rules, orders, laws, and resolutions.

Presidential addresses and messages to Congress are currently printed in the *Congressional Record.* An excellent historical source is James D. Richardson's *Compilation of the Messages and Papers of the Presidents, 1789–1897.* Presidential proclamations appear in the *Statutes at Large,* and *The New York Times* regularly prints the texts of all important presidential addresses. Since 1935, all executive orders, and all administrative rules and regulations, are published daily in the *Federal Register.* The *Code of Federal Regulations* codifies the vast volume of administrative rulings; first published in 1938, it is kept up to date with cumulative supplements.

The *United States Government Organization Manual,* published annually, is the official handbook of the federal government. It contains a brief description of the principal governmental agencies, including their statutory authority, organizational outline, and functions. For more specialized departmental materials, consult the *Monthly Catalogue of*

A BIBLIOGRAPHICAL ESSAY

United States Public Documents, which lists all titles of government publications and tells where and how they may be obtained.

Since 1875, the Government Printing Office has published the decisions of the United States Supreme Court as *United States Reports,* beginning with Vol. 91. The first ninety volumes are cited by the name of the private court reporters who compiled them: Dallas, 1–4 (1790–1800); Cranch, 1–9 (1801–1815); Wheaton, 1–12 (1816–1827); Peters, 1–16 (1828–1842); Howard, 1–24 (1843–1860); Black, 1–2 (1861–1862); Wallace, 1–23 (1863–1874). *The Lawyers Edition of the U.S. Supreme Court Reports* (Rochester, N.Y.: Lawyers' Cooperative Publishing Co.) and *The Supreme Court Reporter* (St. Paul, Minn.: West Publishing Co.) are private editions, both including headnotes and annotations.

The West Publishing Company publishes the rulings of the lower federal courts. *Federal Cases,* a series of thirty volumes, contains all the lower federal court decisions from 1789 to 1880, arranged alphabetically rather than chronologically. The *Federal Reporter,* a series of 300 volumes, reports chronologically all the cases from 1880 to 1924. From 1924, the *Federal Reporter* (2nd Series) contains the decisions of the Courts of Appeals, the *Federal Supplement* the rulings of the District Courts.

Congress

Many commentators have offered useful insights into the general character, the organization, and the operation of Congress. Woodrow Wilson's *Congressional Government** (1885) remains a classic. Alfred de Grazia's *Public and Republic* (1951) examines the theory and practice of representative government, with emphasis on the historical background. Recent studies with varying points of view include Stephen K. Bailey and Howard D. Samuel, *Congress at Work* (1952); George Galloway, *The Legislative Process in Congress* (1953); Ernest S. Griffith, *Congress, Its Contemporary Role* (rev., 1956); Bertrand M. Gross, *The Legislative Struggle: A Study in Social Combat* (1953); Lewis A. Froman, *The Congressional Process** (1967).

Charles S. Clapp, on the staff at the Brookings Institution, organized a roundtable conference to give a group of congressmen a chance to discuss all facets of their work. *The Congressman: His Work As He Sees It** (1963) reports the results. John C. Wahlke and Heinz Eulau have edited a collection of essays, both behavioral and institutional analyses, in *Legislative Behavior: A Reader in Theory and Research* (1959). Roland Young examines the decision-making process of Congress and sets up a "research guide" for more exhaustive inquiries in *The American Congress* (1958). For keeping tabs on the voting record of congressmen, the *Congressional Quarterly* is almost indispensable; this privately published weekly gives the roll-call vote on all important measures, analyzes pending bills, and generally scrutinizes current congressional activities.

Stephen K. Bailey presents a case study of the Employment Act of 1946 in *Congress Makes a Law** (1950); another case study is by Daniel A. Berman, *A Bill Becomes a Law: The Civil Rights Act of 1960* (1962). A number of recent studies focus on the interaction of party and constituency in congressional politics: Julius Turner, *Party and Constituency** (1951); David B. Truman, *The Congressional Party* (1959); and Lewis A. Froman, *Congressmen and Their Constituencies** (1963). Kenneth Kofmehl examines the *Professional Staffs of Congress* (1962).

Robert L. Peabody and Nelson W. Polsby present *New Perspectives on the House of Representatives** (1964), a collection of excellent articles that demonstrate real progress in the study of legislative behavior. George B. Galloway offers us a *History of the House of Representatives* (1962). Among the many special studies of the Senate, G. H. Haynes' *The Senate of the United States* (1938) is still the standard reference, though now quite dated. Donald R. Matthews analyzes the behavior of senators as influenced by their career experiences and the environment in which they work in *U.S. Senators and Their World** (1962). J. P. Harris, *The Advice and Consent of the Senate* (1953), is a study of the

Senate role in appointments. William S. White offers an experienced Senate reporter's view of the "greatest deliberative body" in *The Citadel: The Story of the United States Senate* (1957). Senator Joseph S. Clark gives us an inside view of *The Senate Establishment** (1963).

Elections to the House are systematically investigated in Milton Cummings, *Congressmen and the Electorate: Elections for the U.S. House and the President, 1920–1964* (1967). Duncan MacRae, Jr., uses Guttman scale analysis to discover *Dimensions of Congressional Voting** (1958). MacRae systematically studies legislative behavior in France in comparison with American legislative behavior in *Parliament, Parties and Society in France, 1946–1958* (1967). At the same time, this work contains many methodological and theoretical innovations. The question of recruitment to legislative bodies is discussed by James David Barber in *The Lawmakers; Recruitment and Adaptation to Legislative Life** (1965). Although the book is substantively about freshman legislators in the Connecticut House, the theoretical insights and findings appear to have wide applicability.

For studies of the Senate and House committees, see David N. Farnsworth, *The Senate Committee on Foreign Relations* (1961); Herbert N. Caroll, *The House of Representatives and Foreign Affairs* (1958); and Robert K. Carr, *The House Un-American Activities Committee* (1952). Carl Beck has made a useful compilation of prosecutions for contempt of Congress, focusing primarily on the busy calendar of the House Committee on Un-American Activities, in *Contempt of Congress* (1959). Much has been written on congressional investigations, including Alan Barth, *Government by Investigation* (1955), and Telford Taylor, *Grand Inquest* (1955). Richard Fenno's *The Power of the Purse: Appropriations Politics in Congress* (1966) is now *the* book on congressional committees, dealing specifically with the Appropriations Committee in a systemic perspective.

The constitutional "separation of powers" complicates the overall political process. J. Leiper Freeman, *The Political Process: Executive Bureau-Legislative Committee Relations** (rev. ed., 1965), examines executive-legislative relations at the working level. *The Deadlock of Democracy: Four-Party Politics in America** (1963), by James MacGregor Burns, launches a full-scale attack on the existing political situation vis-à-vis the two congressional parties and the two presidential parties. *Continuing Crisis in American Politics** (1963), edited by Marian D. Irish, includes a number of essays on this problem. Roland Egger and Joseph Harris briefly discuss the issues between *The President and Congress** (1963), and Walter Murphy writes on *Congress and the Court: A Case Study in the American Political Process** (1962). In a more traditional vein, Edward A. Kolodziej discusses *The Uncommon Defense and Congress, 1945–1963* (1966), in which a strengthening of the role of Congress in the making of foreign policy is urged.

Because laws are made by men, biographies of congressmen often prove illuminating on personal by-play in the legislative process. Some good examples are L. S. Bushey, *Uncle Joe Cannon* (1927); George Norris, *Fighting Liberal* (1945); W. A. Robinson, *Thomas B. Reed* (1930); and H. Jerry Voorhis, *Confessions of a Congressman* (1948). *Profiles in Courage** (1958) is an entertaining, albeit hero-worshiping, study of certain United States Senators, written by President Kennedy when he was still Senator Kennedy.

The President

The literature on the presidency includes an endless succession of biographies and autobiographies. Some profess to be scholarly studies of "the life and times"; some are merely debunking, written to shock and sell; some are simply campaign materials. From the point of view of political science, we suggest Douglas Southall Freemen, *George Washington: A Biography* (6 vols., 1948–54), which was completed by J. A. Carroll and M. W. Ashworth (Vol. VII, 1957); Irving Brant, *James Madison* (1950–1960), 6 vols.; Arthur Schlesinger, Jr., *The Age of Jackson** (1945); Carl Sandburg, *Abraham Lincoln, The Prairie Years* (1926), 2 vols., and *The War Years* (1934), 4 vols.; Allan Nevins, *Grover Cleveland* (1932); Henry F. Pringle, *Theodore Roosevelt* (1931); Ray Stannard Baker, *Woodrow Wilson: Life and Letters* (1939), 8 vols.; August Hecksher (ed.), *The Politics of Woodrow Wilson* (1926); James MacGregor Burns, *Roosevelt: The Lion and the Fox* (1956); Robert E. Sherwood, *Roosevelt and Hopkins** (1948).

A BIBLIOGRAPHICAL ESSAY

To appraise first-hand accounts of recent presidencies is difficult, since the principals have still not settled their accounts with history. But we recommend as illuminating and controversial Harry S. Truman, *Memoirs* (1956) and *Truman Speaks* (1960); Dwight D. Eisenhower, *Mandate for Change 1953–56* (1963); Marquis Childs, *Eisenhower: The Captive Hero* (1958); Robert Donovan, *The Inside Story* (1956); Sherman Adams, *First Hand Account** (1961); and Emmet John Hughes, *The Ordeal of Power** (1963).

John Kennedy: A Political Profile (1960), by James MacGregor Burns, appeared as a campaign biography, but it is a more discerning study than the usual campaign material. Theodore Sorensen, who was Special Counsel to President Kennedy, gives us an inside look at *Decision-Making in the White House** (1963). Three of the recent books on the New Frontier are Arthur H. Schlesinger, Jr., *A Thousand Days: John F. Kennedy in the White House* (1965); Theodore Sorensen, *Kennedy* (1965); and Pierre Salinger, *With Kennedy* (1966).

Among general studies of the presidency, the most comprehensive is Edward S. Corwin, *The President: Office and Powers* (4th ed., 1957). More popular in treatment are Edward S. Corwin and Louis W. Koenig, *The Presidency Today* (1956); Sidney Hyman, *The American President* (1954); and Clinton Rossiter, *The American Presidency** (1956). James Hart examines the presidency in its formative years in *The American Presidency in Action, 1789* (1948). Harold Laski discusses *The American Presidency** (1940) from the British point of view. *Presidential Power** (1960), by Richard Neustadt, is concerned with "the politics of leadership," the personal power of the man in office. *The Chief Executive* (1964), by Louis W. Koenig, analyzes the power and weakness of the American presidency from George Washington to Lyndon B. Johnson. Joseph E. Kallenbach, *The American Chief Executive* (1966), considers both the presidency and its counterpart in the state governorship in an institutional and behavioral analysis of executive power in American governments.

Donald Bruce Johnson and Jack L. Walker have assembled an enterprising collection of essays by well-known authorities in *The Dynamics of the American Presidency* (1964). The institutionalization of the presidency has provoked numerous studies on the executive office. Rexford G. Tugwell provides an excellent historical survey of the American presidency since 1787, *The Enlargement of the Presidency* (1960). Richard Fenno examines *The President's Cabinet** (1959), especially its development since the Wilson administration. Corinne Silverman does a case-study on *The President's Economic Advisers** (1959). *The Presidency: Crisis and Regeneration* (1960), by Herman Finer, is a perceptive analysis of the institution, including some highly controversial recommendations.

The rise of the vice-presidency to some degree of political stature has produced a number of studies, including Edgar W. Waugh, *Second Consul* (1956); Irving G. Williams, *The American Vice-Presidency: New Look* (1954), and *The Rise of the Vice-Presidency* (1956). For different interpretations of the Cabinet at work, skim through some of the "memoirs" of Cabinet officers: James Byrnes, *Speaking Frankly* (1947), and *All In One Lifetime* (1958); *The Secret Diary of Harold Ickes: The First Thousand Days* (1953); and Frances Perkins, *The Roosevelt I Knew* (1946). *The Invisible Presidency* (1960), by Louis W. Koenig, goes beyond rumor and folklore in its account of White House favorites and personal confidantes.

Many political scientists are concerned with the theory and the practice of separation of powers. Wilfred E. Binkley takes a historical approach to the subject in *President and Congress* (1947). Pendleton Herring discusses the same problem more generally in *Presidential Leadership* (1940). On the independent regulatory commissions, which are in effect a practical denial of separation of powers, see Marver H. Bernstein, *Regulating Business by Independent Commissions* (1955). Neson W. Polsby, *Congress and the Presidency** (1964), offers a brief but insightful analysis of executive-legislative relationships.

The Bureaucrats

Leonard D. White performed a herculean task in his historical but lively consideration of our early bureaucrats, *The Federalists* (1948); *The Jeffersonians* (1951); *The Jacksonians* (1954); and *The Republican Era* (1957). White also wrote *Introduction to the Study of Public Administration*, the first textbook in public administration, in 1926; its fourth edition appeared in 1955. Recent comparative studies of the role of bureaucrats in the political system include Joseph La Palombara (ed.), *Bureaucracy and Political Development* (1963); and Ferrel Heady, *Public Adminstration: A Comparative Perspective** (1966). Anthony Downs' *Inside Bureaucracy** (1967) develops a thoughtful and provocative theory of bureaucratic decision-making.

"Older" approaches to the study of public administration were generally reform-oriented and tended to emphasize "principles" of public administration and practical problems in organization, personnel administration, and fiscal administration. Dwight Waldo, *The Administrative State* (1948) questioned the validity of principles of administration, especially those derived from scientific management in business. *Issues and Ideals in Public Administration* (1953), edited by Waldo, pursues this theme. A turning point in the study of public administration was Herbert Simon's *Administrative Behavior** (1947, rev. 1957) which focused on *behavior* in government organization, especially in decision-making. Harold Stein developed the casebook approach in *Public Administration and Policy Development* (1952).

In 1947, Talcott Parsons translated (with A. M. Henderson) and edited *The Theory of Social and Economic Organization*, a pioneer work in the systematic theory of bureaucratic organization by the German sociologist, Max Weber. This seminal study has generated various "new" approaches to the study of public administration. Recent contributions to the growing body of literature on systematic administrative theory include Peter Blau, *The Dynamics of Bureaucracy* (2nd. ed., 1963); William J. Gore, *Administrative Decision-making: A Heuristic Model* (1964); Bertram M. Gross, *The Managing of Organizations: the Administrative Struggle* (1964); Sidney Mailick and Edward H. Van Ness (eds.), *Concepts and Issues in Administrative Behavior* (1962); Robert Presthus, *The Organizational Society* (1962); Victor A. Thompson, *Modern Organization* (1961); Peter Woll, *American Bureaucracy** (1963); and Charles March, *Handbook of Organizations* (1965).

John J. Corson and Joseph P. Harris provide a brief introduction to the study of *Public Administration in Modern Society** (1963). Edwin A. Bock (ed.), James W. Fesler, Harold Stein, and Dwight Waldo discuss the tools of the trade in public administration research in *Essays on the Case Method in Public Administration* (1962). Northcote Parkinson has written an amusing but thought-provoking essay on "the rising pyramid" of governmental bureaucracy in *Parkinson's Law* (1957). For a personal approach by one who spent years in the public service, read Louis Brownlow's two volumes, *A Passion for Politics* (1955) and *A Passion for Anonymity* (1958).

Paul Van Riper gives us a *History of the United States Civil Service* (1958). A symposium by the American Assembly, edited by Wallace S. Sayre, is an historical and critical account of federal personnel management: *The Federal Government Service: Its Character, Prestige and Problems** (2nd ed., 1965). Marver H. Bernstein, *The Job of the Federal Executive* (1958), and Paul T. David and Ross Pollock, *Executives for Government* (1957), are concerned with the role of "top management," the career and political executives, in the federal service. Warner W. Lloyd, Paul Van Riper, Norman H. Martin, and Orvis F. Collins, *The American Federal Executives* (1964) present "a study of the social and personal characteristics of the civilian and military leaders of the United States government." Franklin P. Kilpatrick, Milton C. Cummings, Jr., and M. Kent Jennings report on an extensive survey by the Brookings Institution to discover what people in various categories think about the federal service, *The Image of the Federal Service* (1964); a *Source Book* presents the detailed data on which the authors base their conclusions.

Other recent empirical studies of the federal bureaucracy include Dean E. Mann with Jameson W. Poig, *The Assistant Secretaries: Problems and Processes of Appointment* (1965), and John Corson and R. Shale Paul, *Men Near the Top: Filling Key Posts in the Federal Service* (1966). Aaron Wildavsky discusses *The Politics of the Budgetary Process** (1964), in which empirical evidence and theoretical rigor combine to make very persuasive inferences about how the budget gets to be what it is. William Gore presents an overview of *Administrative Decision-Making* (1964). David T. Stanley's *The Higher Civil Service: An Evaluation of Federal Personnel Practices* (1964) is a more policy-oriented work.

Justice, Judges, and the Role of Law

The takeoff point for almost any academic discussion of justice is Plato's *Republic.** For the views of some modern scholars, see Carl J. Friedrich and John W. Chapman (eds.), *Nomos VI; Justice* (1964).

In this text, however, we have been more concerned with the role of law and the administration of justice in American government than with philosophical abstractions. For varying views of the role of lawyers and judges in the modern community, see Benjamin Cardozo, *The Nature of the Judicial Process** (1921), and *Law and Literature* (1931); Edmund Cahn, *The Sense of Injustice* (1951) and *The Moral Decision* (1955); Jerome Frank, *Law and the Modern Mind** (1930); Roscoe Pound, *Introduction to the Philosophy of Law** (rev. ed., 1954); Victor G. Rosenblum, *Law as a Political Instrument** (1955); Arthur E. Sutherland, *The Law and One Man Among Many* (1956); and Carl J. Friedrich, *The Philosophy of Law in Historical Perspective** (2nd. ed., 1963). A delightfully discursive approach to many facets of the law, justice, and life in general is provided by the letters of Mr. Justice Holmes to his contemporary, Sir Frederick Pollock, and to his long-time friend, Harold Laski: *Holmes-Pollock Letters* (1941) 2 vols., and *Holmes-Laski Letters** (1953).

On the organization and functioning of the federal judiciary, we suggest Henry M. Hart and Herbert Wechsler, *The Federal Courts and the Federal System* (1953); Lewis Mayer, *The American Legal System* (rev. ed., 1964); Jack W. Peltason, *Federal Courts in the Political Process** (1955); Walter F. Murphy and C. Herman Pritchett, *Courts, Judges, and Politics* (1961); Glendon Schubert, *Judicial Policy-Making** (1965); and Herbert Jacob, *Justice in America** (1965). For a realistic appraisal of "courthouse government," see Jerome Frank's *Courts on Trial** (1949) and *If Men Were Angels* (1942). Heinz Eulau and John D. Sprague confront some of the conventional wisdom about the role of lawyers with new empirical data in *Lawyers in Politics** (1964). Jack Peltason follows up the 1955 Supreme Court decision with a study of *Fifty-eight Lonely Men: Southern Federal Judges and School Desegregation* (1961). *The Courts, the Public and the Law Explosion** (1965), an American Assembly discussion edited by Harry W. Jones, focuses on the business and problems of the trial courts, national and state.

Selected Essays on Constitutional Law (1938), 4 vols., published under the auspices of the Association of American Law Societies, is a monumental collection of classic essays in constitutional law. Robert G. McCloskey (ed.), offers a selective and stimulating collection in *Essays in Constitutional Law** (1957). Alan Westin has drawn "a documentary portrait of one constitutional law case," *Youngstown Sheet and Tube Co.* v. *Sawyer*, covering its full course from a bargaining dispute in the steel industry to its final disposition in the Supreme Court of the United States: *The Anatomy of a Constitutional Law Case** (1958). Daniel M. Berman, *It Is So Ordered** (1966), is a detailed study of *Brown* v. *Board of Education* to show how litigation is carried all the way from the lower courts to the Supreme Court. Anthony Lewis, of *The New York Times*, discusses one case and at the same time presents a picture of the modern Supreme Court in *Gideon's Trumpet** (1964).

The Supreme Court, as a policy-making body at the highest level of American government, has been the focus of many critical studies. The standard, conservative, and generally sympathetic work is Charles Warren, *The Supreme Court in United States History* (rev., 1928). The battle between the President and the Court in the 1930s aroused public opinion to a peak of emotional intensity and provoked the legal profession and the political scientists into writing numerous argumentative monographs. Robert Jackson, in *The Struggle for Judicial Supremacy* (1941), details the "court-packing plan" of President Roosevelt and its political repercussions. Edward S. Corwin becomes over-excited in *Twilight of the Supreme Court* (1934); and Robert K. Carr is not entirely calm or dispassionate in *The Supreme Court and Judicial Review* (1942). C. Herman Pritchett's *The Roosevelt Court* (1948) attempts to analyze the political behavior of the Roosevelt Court, with emphasis on the statistical approach; he does much the same for a later Court in *Civil Liberties and the Vinson Court* (1954). The standard work on judicial review is Charles G. Haines, *The American Doctrine of Judicial Supremacy* (rev. ed., 1932). Donald G. Morgan, *Congress and the Constitution* (1966), examines a wide range of constitutional controversies in Congress in a study of constitutional law that goes well beyond court-made rules.

Because the Supreme Court in recent years has frequently been in the center of political controversy, it has evoked many new studies. Among these are: Edmond Cahn, *Supreme Court and Supreme Law* (1954); Bernard Schwartz, *The Supreme Court: Constitutional Revolution in Retrospect* (1957); Robert Jackson, *The Supreme Court in the American System of Government** (1955); and Thomas Reed Powell, *Vagaries and Varieties in Constitutional Interpretation* (1955). John P. Frank, in *Marble Palace* (1958), discusses the role of the Supreme Court today in terms of "the practicalities of power" rather than of legal theory. Alpheus T. Mason writes a shrewd and skillful analysis of the personal and political factors that have colored the judicial process in *The Supreme Court from Taft to Warren** (1958). Carl Swisher traces the more significant recent cases in constitutional law, particularly those dealing with "clear and present danger" and racial conflict, in *The Supreme Court in Modern Role* (1958). Charles Black popularizes the "legitimating" function of judicial review in *The People and the Court** (1960). Robert McCloskey puts *The American Supreme Court** (1960) in the sweep of history and finds that the Court has been most successful when it has operated nearer the margins rather than in the center of controversy.

Walter T. Murphy examines the Supreme Court as a decision-maker in the political system in the *Elements of Judicial Strategy* (1964). Whatever Charles S. Hyneman writes is bound to be scholarly, thought-provoking, and controversial; see *The Supreme Court on Trial* (1963). Henry J. Abraham offers a traditional and comparative approach to *The Judicial Process** (1962) as an introduction to a basic understanding of how the courts operate within the discipline of law. Martin Shapiro, *Law and Politics in the Supreme Court* (1964), offers some new approaches to "political jurisprudence," and treats the Supreme Court as "political scientist, labor lawmaker, tax policy maker, political theorist, and political economist."

Two recent works deal with recruitment to the judiciary. Joel Grossman takes the interest group approach in *Lawyers and Judges: The ABA and the Politics of Judicial Selection* (1965). David Danielski makes use of transactional analysis to discuss the process through which *A Supreme Court Justice is Appointed** (1964). The latter work deals with the appointment of Pierce Butler to the bench in 1922.

Students of the judicial process have recently tended to substitute quantitative methods for the traditional tools of analysis. See Glendon A. Schubert's *Constitutional Politics: The Political Behavior of Supreme Court Justices and the Constitutional Policies That They Make* (1960), *Quantitative Analysis of Judicial Behavior* (1960), and *Judicial Decision-Making* (1963). *Judicial Behavior* (1964), edited by Schubert, is a "reader in theory and research" that brings within one volume an impressive collection of essays representing an interdisciplinary and behavioral approach to the study of judicial decision-making. The culminating work in the series is his *The Judicial Mind: Attitudes and Ideologies of Supreme Court Justices, 1946–1963* (1965), in which a psychometric model of Supreme Court decision-making is tested with the empirical data of the modern Supreme Court. John Schmidhauser spotlights problems of selection and internal operation in *The Supreme Court: Its Politics, Personalities and Procedures** (1960); see also his *Constitutional Law in the Political Process* (1963). *The Supreme Court: Views from Inside** (1961), edited by Alan Westin, gives us the diverse views of nine justices on the nature of the judicial process, including a sophisticated debate on judicial activism versus judicial self-restraint. Westin has also edited another book of off-the-bench writing by Supreme Court justices, *An Autobiography of the Supreme Court* (1963).

When a judge puts on his judicial robes, he does not discard his own personality.

A BIBLIOGRAPHICAL ESSAY

Biographies of the justices are thus illuminating on the nature of the judicial process. Among many, see: Albert J. Beveridge, *Life of John Marshall* (1919), 4 vols.; Carl B. Swisher, *Roger B. Taney* (1935); Charles Fairman, *Mr. Justice Miller and the Supreme Court, 1862–1890* (1939); Willard L. King, *Melville Weston Fuller* (1950); Felix Frankfurter, *Mr. Justice Holmes and the Supreme Court** (1938); Alpheus T. Mason, *Brandeis—A Free Man's Life* (1946); Max Lerner, *The Mind and Faith of Mr. Justice Holmes* (1943); Merle J. Pusey, *Charles Evans Hughes* (1951), 2 vols.; J. Francis Paschal, *Mr. Justice Sutherland* (1951); Samuel J. Konefsky (ed.), *The Constitutional World of Mr. Justice Frankfurter* (1949); John P. Frank, *Mr. Justice Black* (1940); and Alpheus T. Mason, *Harlan Fiske Stone* (1956), and *William Howard Taft: Chief Justice* (1965). Allison Dunham and Philip B. Kurland have edited "12 short essays in legal biography" dealing with Marshall, Taney, Hughes, Stone, Bradley, Holmes, Brandeis, Sutherland, Rutledge, and others: *Mr. Justice** (1964). Wallace Mendelson's study of *Justices Black and Frankfurter* (1961) focuses on the debate between judicial activism and judicial restraint as exemplified in the work of these two great justices on the Court.

PART FOUR   Outputs of the Political Process: Rewards and Deprivations

Periodical Literature

Public policy changes so rapidly that anyone who wants to keep up will find current periodicals an essential source. In addition to a local newspaper, most people who want a full coverage of the news rely on *The New York Times;* unlike most slogans, this newspaper's claim of offering "All the News That's Fit to Print" is fairly accurate. In addition to comprehensive news reports, the *Times* prints the full text of important speeches, laws, and court decisions.

Weekly newsmagazines devote much of their space to political news and offer more interpretative treatments of important events. "The News of the Week in Review" section of the Sunday *New York Times* is probably the most impartial of these weekly surveys; its news articles follow the newspaper tradition of highly factual reporting, and its "opinion pieces" are all signed columns clearly distinguished from the news. The mass-circulation weeklies are all somewhat conservative in tone. *Time* is perhaps the most conservative of all, and its bright, authoritative tone is highly popular. *United States News and World Report* is less brash but almost equally conservative; its feature of interviews with prominent figures commands interest and sometimes "makes" news itself. *Newsweek* is perhaps the least opinionated of the three mass-circulation weeklies.

As weekly journals of opinion, *The Nation, The New Leader,* and *The New Republic* interpret events with an openly liberal bias. Although their circulation is much smaller than that of the mass-circulation weeklies, they may have a greater influence than their circulation would suggest. *The Reporter,* a biweekly, also has a liberal editorial policy; it deals less with the news of each two-week period than with interpretation and comment on more enduring problems. *The National Review* takes the conservative approach.

The *Congressional Quarterly Weekly Report* is not sold to individuals, but it is available in libraries. Since reading the daily *Congressional Record* is extremely time-consuming, the *Congressional Quarterly's* summary of debates and report of votes are an invaluable aid to the student of politics.

The "quality" monthly magazines, notably *The Atlantic* and *Harper's,* are not devoted exclusively to public affairs, but they do offer many penetrating articles on politics. These articles represent a variety of ideological positions.

Members of the American Political Science Association were recently questioned about their publication preferences in the professional journals. Those most frequently mentioned as enhancing "professional prestige" were: *American Political Science*

Review, Journal of Politics, World Politics, Political Science Quarterly, Administrative Science Quarterly, Western Political Science Quarterly, Public Administration Review, Public Opinion Quarterly, Midwest Journal of Politics, and American Behavioral Scientist. All these journals publish research findings that are concerned with basic political problems rather than with "news." The list, however, is by no means exclusive. Other prestige journals focus on special interests. For example, many law schools publish law reviews which constitute a gold mine of discussion on legal problems involved in public policies. Scholarly writing often has an incidental topical interest, and it frequently clarifies the underlying processes that produce the news. The Bulletin of the Public Affairs Information Service and the Reader's Guide to Periodical Literature are indexes for use in locating information on current affairs in a wide variety of publications.

Civil Rights and Civil Liberties

The literature on civil rights and personal liberties seems to be endless. Allen Rutland writes about The Birth of the Bill of Rights, 1776–1791 (1955). On the First Amendment, the classic discussion is Zechariah Chafee, Jr., Free Speech in the United States (1941). Glenn Abernathy emphasizes another guarantee of the First Amendment in The Right of Assembly and Association (1961). David Fellman explains what rights Americans are guaranteed when they are accused of crime in The Defendant's Rights (1958) and provides a comparative view in The Defendant's Rights Under English Law (1966). In The Rationing of Justice (1964), Arnold S. Treback gives us a pretty grim report on *how* rights are violated and *how often* in the process of criminal justice, from arrest through conviction and appeal. The Dean of the Harvard Law School, Erwin N. Griswold, treats the Fifth Amendment as a time-honored symbol of individual liberty in the Anglo-American tradition, The Fifth Amendment Today* (1955). Sidney Hook, Professor of Philosophy at New York University, takes an opposing viewpoint in Common Sense and the Fifth Amendment* (1963). Milton R. Konvitz writes about Expanding Liberties; Freedom's Gains in Postwar America (1966), a discussion of the Supreme Court's expansion of liberties.

Horace Flack examines the intent of the Framers in The Adoption of the Fourteenth Amendment (1908). The Quest for Equality (1960), by Robert J. Harris, is a witty and profound discussion of the Fourteenth Amendment as it was written and as it has been interpreted by the courts. John P. Roche, in Courts and Rights* (1961), offers us a pocket-size introduction to the American judiciary in action with emphasis on the rights of citizens in the democratic process. Henry J. Abraham, Freedom and the Court* (1967), discusses civil rights and civil liberties in the United States, with emphasis on the role of judges. Lucius J. Barker and Twiley W. Barker, Jr., discuss current civil liberties as public policy issues, emphasizing legal aspects and judicial decision-making, in Freedoms, Courts, Politics (1965).

That modern government can be a safeguard rather than a threat to liberty is evident in such official reports as To Secure These Rights (1947), by the President's Committee on Civil Rights; Whom Shall We Welcome? (1953), by the President's Commission on Immigration and Naturalization; and Equal Protection of the Laws in Public Higher Education (1960), by the United States Commission on Civil Rights. The Annual Reports of the American Civil Liberties Union are a continuing source of information on the actual as well as the legal status of civil rights in the country. The Sub-Committee on Constitutional Rights of the Senate Committee on the Judiciary is an invaluable source of primary materials—hearings, staff studies, committee reports—which illustrate how the many facets of civil rights and liberties enter into the political process and emerge as public policies.

Henry Steele Commager strongly defends the majority-rule aspect of democracy, and insists that it poses no threat to minority rights, in Majority Rule and Minority Rights (1943). In Communism, Conformity and Civil Liberties* (1955), Samuel A. Stouffer reports on American attitudes toward nonconformists during the "McCarthy era." Gunnar Myrdal's An American Dilemma: The Negro Problem and Modern Democracy* (1944, 1964) is a monumental study of American democracy, with special emphasis on the problems of Negroes. Felix E. Oppenheim analyzes behavioral concepts of freedom, unfreedom, control, and power in *Dimensions of Freedom* (1961). *The Great Rights* (1963), edited by Edmond Cahn, is a collection of essays by justices of the Supreme Court discussing various aspects of the Bill of Rights.

The rights of minority groups, as a matter of public policy, is one of the most controversial issues of our times. Henry A. Myers puts the question bluntly, *Are Men Equal?** (1945). Wallace Mendelson provides a résumé of a five-volume report of the *United States Commission on Civil Rights: Discrimination** (1962). Henry Kalven discusses *The Negro and the First Amendment* (1962). For very different viewpoints on the problem of racism in America see C. Vann Woodward, *The Strange Career of Jim Crow* (1955); Charles Morgan, *A Time to Speak* (1964); Lewis Killian and Charles Grigg, *Racial Crisis in America: Leadership in Crisis** (1964); and Benjamin Muse, *Virginia's Massive Resistance* (1961). Everett C. Ladd, Jr., presents a study of *Negro Political Leadership in the South* (1966). The *Race Relations Reporter*, published quarterly by the Vanderbilt University School of Law, is an excellent source for documentary materials on the race problem. Current development may be followed in *Southern School News*.

Recent decisions of the Supreme Court interpreting the "establishment clause" and the "free exercise" of religion have created considerable excitement. *The Wall Between Church and State** (1963), edited by Dallin H. Oaks, covers the problem from various angles. Joseph Tussman has collected the leading judicial opinions in *The Supreme Court on Church and State** (1962). Presidents from Truman to Johnson has urged change in our immigration policies. Marion T. Bennett discusses some of the issues in *American Immigration Policies* (1963). *A Nation of Immigrants*,* by President John F. Kennedy, published posthumously in 1964, was intended to back up his proposed policies to open the gates on a more rational basis than the "national origins" system.

Individual liberties versus national security is a continuing issue in American politics. For opposing views on problems of national security, see the Subcommittee on Constitutional Rights of the Senate Judiciary Committee, *Hearings, Security and Constitutional Rights* (84th Cong., 2nd Sess., 1955). For a comprehensive treatment of the legal side of the issue, see Walter Gelhorn, *Individual Freedom and Government Restraints* (1956). Within the context of Supreme Court doctrine and decision-making, Martin Shapiro presents a discussion of *Freedom of Speech: The Supreme Court and Judicial Review** (1966). Harry Howe Ransome examines the agencies and institutions created for national security since World War II, *Can American Democracy Survive Cold War?** (1963).

General Welfare and Common Defense

There is a vast amount of literature on policies to promote the general welfare and provide for the common defense. Many of the titles listed in Part One, "Cultural and Economic Context," will be useful in understanding how policy both reflects and affects the contemporary environment. Policy is goal-oriented, but the goals, like lodestars, keep moving ahead of us. President Eisenhower in 1960 appointed a Commission on National Goals; its *Report*,* with supporting essays, offered new directions for the 1960s, but already we view the future from a different perspective. In 1958, John K. Galbraith captured the mood of the time in *The Affluent Society**; Michael Harrington focuses on a different aspect in *The Other America** (1962); Hubert H. Humphrey, *War on Poverty** (1964), although a piece of campaign literature, does prefigure official policies.

For a scholarly approach to the processes and relationships by which scarce resources are translated into public policy, see Robert A. Dahl and Charles E. Lindblom, *Politics, Economics and Welfare* (1953). Also see Eugene V. Rostow, *Planning for Freedom: The Public Law of American Capitalism* (1960), and Adolf Berle, *The American Economic Republic* (1963). John R. Bunting discusses the relations of government and the economic order from the point of view of a forward-looking businessman in *The Hidden Face of Free Enterprise* (1964). Thurman Arnold in *The Folklore of Capitalism** (1938)

conveys some of the intellectually exciting ideas that fired the New Deal. Randall B. Ripley (ed.) offers a collection of brief essays that deal with the techniques of government control, *Public Policies and Their Politics* (1966).

The American economic system today is very much a part of the world economy. Raymond A. Bauer, Ithiel De Sola Pool, and Lewis Anthony Dexter have done an excellent study of foreign trade legislation in the broad context of the political process, *American Business and Public Policy: The Politics of Foreign Trade* (1963). Other books that may be helpful in understanding America's role in international economics include Gunnar Myrdal, *Beyond the Welfare State** (1960); Max F. Millikan and Donald L. M. Blackmer (eds.), *The Emerging Nations** (1961); W. W. Rostow, *The Stages of Economic Growth, A Non-Communist Manifesto** (1960); and John Kenneth Galbraith, *Economic Development* (1964).

Many people are skeptical about the economics that underlie the concept of "the Great Society." Two books that furnish considerable data on American economic resources and financial capabilities are Gabriel Kolko, *Wealth and Power in America** (1962), and James N. Morgan *et al.*, *Income and Welfare in the United States* (1962). The basic instrument for all policy-planning is the budget; see Aaron Wildavsky, *The Politics of the Budgetary Process** (1964).

Many social scientists have examined particular aspects of public policy in the general area of economics and welfare. Among these, we mention Walton H. Hamilton, *The Politics of Industry* (1957); Eveline M. Burns, *Social Security and Public Policy* (1956); Herman M. Somers and Anne R. Somers, *Doctors, Patients, and Health Insurance* (1961); Reo M. Christenson, *The Brannan Plan: Farm Politics and Policy* (1959); Robert C. Wood, *Suburbia: Its People and Their Politics** (1958); and Douglas Knight (ed.), *The Federal Government and Higher Education** (1960).

The dominating issue in American national policies of the 1960s is the common defense and national survival. But this is by no means a wholly military problem; as we have indicated in the text, the military-industrial-scientific complex pervades the American economy. *Organizing for Defense* (1961) by Paul Y. Hammond traces the development of the American military establishment in the twentieth century, concentrating more on the politics of organization than on strategic policy matters. Charles J. Hitch and Roland N. McKean stress the economic choices involved in military preparedness, *The Economics of Defense in the Nuclear Age* (1960). The American Assembly, in 1961, discussed *Arms Control: Issues for the Public.** Jack Raymond, a highly knowledgeable journalist, appraises *Power at the Pentagon* (1964).

Foreign Policy and National Security

Foreign policy is always a highly charged issue, not only in the public forum but also in the official agencies. *The Liberal Papers** (1962), with an introduction by Representative James Roosevelt, comprises a dozen essays, "reflective, critical, and constructive," by well-known social scientists, designed to publicize the foreign policy views of the "liberal group" in Congress. The *Conservative Papers** (1964), with an introduction by Representative Melvin R. Laird, brings together another group of essays, by a different but equally distinguished group of scholars, to counterpose the domestic and foreign policy views of the "conservative group" in Congress. The third volume in the series is *The Radical Papers** (1966).

Among a number of excellent overall studies of foreign policy—how it is made and how it is implemented—see Cecil V. Crabb, Jr., *American Foreign Policy in the Nuclear Age* (1965); Charles O. Lerche, *Foreign Policy of the American People* (3rd ed., 1967); James L. McCamy, *Conduct of the New Diplomacy* (1964); Paul Seabury, *Power, Freedom, and Diplomacy* (1963); and Bradford Westerfield, *The Instruments of America's Foreign Policy* (1963); and James A. Robinson, *Congress and Foreign Policy-Making: A Study in Legislative Influence and Initiative* (rev. ed., 1967). *World Pressures on American Foreign Policy** (1964), edited by Marian D. Irish, is a collection of essays by well-known political scientists who examine the pressure of external events and forces on American policy decisions. John Spanier, *American Foreign Policy Since World War II** (rev. ed., 1965), is an analytical account of American foreign policy beginning with the breakdown of our maritime alliance with the Soviet Union. Burton M. Sapin's *The Making of*

United States Foreign Policy (1966) is an institutional study of the organization of the decision-making agencies.

Many official decision-makers have published their views on foreign policy, some critical, some defensive, some after leaving office, some while still in office. Among these are Dean Acheson, *Power and Diplomacy* (1958); Thomas K. Finletter, *Foreign Policy: The Next Phase** (1960); Charles Burton Marshall, *The Limits of Foreign Policy* (1954); Robert R. Bowie, *Shaping The Future* (1964); W. W. Rostow, *View from the Seventh Floor* (1964); and Senator J. W. Fulbright, *Old Myths and New Realities** (1964), *Prospects for the West* (1963), and *The Arrogance of Power* (1966). *To Move a Nation* (1967), by Roger Hilsman, who was Assistant Secretary of State for the Far East in the Kennedy administration, discusses "the making and managing of foreign policy" from the standpoint of a professional political scientist with first-hand experience in the policy machine.

Congressional hearings, staff studies reports of study missions, and committee reports cover the whole range of American foreign policy. See especially the publications of the Senate Committee on Foreign Relations and the House Committee on Foreign Affairs. The annual congressional hearings on appropriations, requested by the various agencies concerned with foreign policy and national security, provide practical insights into the policy process as well as useful information on the programs and operations that constitute the substance of policies.

The Council of Foreign Relations' quarterly, *Foreign Affairs*, provides a forum for authoritative and scholarly articles and offers an annotated bibliography of recent books and source materials on international relations in every issue. How extensive this service is we discover in the *Foreign Affairs Bibliography 1952–62* (1964), which comprises some 8,500 listings of important books annotated by Henry L. Roberts (which explains why our selective list seems so inadequate to us!). The Council also publishes, in addition to many monographs, *Documents on American Foreign Relations* and *The United States in World Affairs*, both annual publications which are most convenient references for all students of American foreign policy. The American Assembly publishes reports of its annual meetings, many of which focus on problems of foreign policy; see, for example, *The Representation of the United States Abroad** (1956); *The Secretary of State** (1960); and *Cultural Affairs and Foreign Relations** (1963).

Perhaps the publications of the Subcommittee on National Security of the Senate Committee on Government Operations are the most illuminating source of official and unofficial views on problems relating to national security. The literature on national security is limitless, and it is difficult for the lay reader to make qualitative judgments. Henry A. Kissinger argues the feasibility of "limited nuclear war" in *Nuclear Weapons and Foreign Policy** (1957) and suggests *The Necessity for Choice** (1961). Neville Brown presents the case for *Strategic Mobility* (1964). *The Dispersion of Nuclear Weapons* (1964), edited by Richard Rosecrance, discusses the spread of nuclear weapons among the nations of the world.

On military policy, see Samuel P. Huntington, *The Soldier and the State: The Theory and Politics of Civil-Military Relations* (1957), and Edgar S. Furniss, Jr., *American Military Policy* (1957). Harry Howe Ransome throws light on an important but little understood aspect of security policy in *Central Intelligence and National Security* (1958). In *Strategic Intelligence* (1961), William M. McGovern describes the processes of gathering intelligence and then sets forth his ideas of what should be done in terms of national policy to meet "the shape of tomorrow." William W. Kaufmann explains (mostly in the words of the Secretary of Defense) *The McNamara Strategy* (1964), the development of a new method of decision-making in the Pentagon. Robert Murphy, a long-time career officer in the State Department, gives us a fascinating first-hand account of many crises in American diplomacy, especially in World War I and the years immediately following, in *Diplomat Among Warriors* (1964). Morris Janowitz is editor of a reader on *The New Military; Changing Patterns of Organization* (1964).

Don K. Price focuses on the new and expanding role of science and scientists in modern government in *The Scientific Estate* (1965); and Harold Karan Jacobson and Eric Stein, *Diplomats, Scientists, and Politicians* (1966), uses the test-ban treaty negotiations for a case study of the impact of science and technology upon foreign policy.

Floyd Matson assesses the impact of science on our twentieth century society in *Man, Science and Society* (1964). *Scientists and National Policy-Making* (1964), edited by Robert Gilpin and Christopher Wright, examines the role of the scientific establishment in national politics and public policies. Jerome B. Wiesner, former advisor to President Kennedy, is concerned with the relationships between scientists and government in *When Science and Politics Meet* (1965). J. Stefan Dupré and Sanford A. Lakoff have edited a collection of essays that deal with a wide range of issues, including the impact of science upon social thought, in *Science and the Nation** (1962).

For a comparative approach to foreign policy, see Roy Macridis, *Foreign Policy in World Politics** (3rd ed., 1967); Joseph E. Black and Kenneth W. Thompson, *Foreign Policies in a World of Change* (1963); and Kurt London, *The Making of Foreign Policy: East and West** (1965). For the role of the United States in international organizations, see John G. Stoessinger, *The United Nations and the Super Powers** (1965); and Richard N. Gardner, *In Pursuit of World Order** (1966). John D. Montgomery examines in some depth *Foreign Aid in International Politics** (1967).

Less concerned with the substance of policy, more interested in developing a systematic theory of foreign policy, a number of political scientists have recently reported on their research and findings: George Modelsky, *A Theory of Foreign Policy* (1962); Richard C. Snyder, H. S. Bruck, and Burton Sapin (eds.), *Foreign Policy Decision-Making: An Approach to the Study of International Politics* (1962); Bernard C. Cohen, *The Influence of Non-governmental Groups on Foreign Policy-Making* (1959) and *The Press and Foreign Policy** (1963); and James N. Rosenau, *Public Opinion and Foreign Policy* (1961) and (as editor) *International Politics and Foreign Policy: A Reader in Theory and Research* (1963). Thomas Schelling tackles the relationships involving *Arms and Influence* (1966).

Domestic Sources of Foreign Policy (1967), a collection of ten essays edited by James Rosenau, provides conceptual and empirical studies of the impact of domestic politics upon foreign policy.

The Declaration of Independence

(As it reads in the parchment copy)

The Unanimous Declaration of the Thirteen United States of America

When in the Course of human events, it becomes necessary for one people to dissolve the political bands, which have connected them with another, and to assume among the powers of the earth, the separate and equal station to which the Laws of Nature and of Nature's God entitle them, a decent respect to the opinions of mankind requires that they should declare the causes which impel them to the separation. — We hold these truths to be self-evident, that all men are created equal, that they are endowed by their Creator with certain unalienable Rights, that among these are Life, Liberty and the pursuit of Happiness. — That to secure these rights, Governments are instituted among Men, deriving their just powers from the consent of the governed, — That whenever any Form of Government becomes destructive of these ends, it is the Right of the People to alter or to abolish it, and to institute new Government, laying its foundation on such principles and organizing its powers in such form, as to them shall seem most likely to effect their Safety and Happiness. Prudence, indeed, will dictate that Governments long established should not be changed for light and transient causes; and accordingly all experience hath shewn, that mankind are more disposed to suffer, while evils are sufferable, than to right themselves by abolishing the forms to which they are accustomed. But when a long train of abuses and usurpations, pursuing invariably the same Object evinces a design to reduce them under absolute Despotism, it is their right, it is their duty, to throw off such Government, and to provide new Guards for their future security. — Such has been the patient sufferance of these Colonies; and such is now the necessity which constrains them to alter their former Systems of Government. The history of the present King of Great Britain is a history of repeated injuries and usurpations, all having in direct object the establishment of an absolute Tyranny over these States. To prove this, let Facts be submitted to a candid world. — He has refused his Assent to Laws, the most wholesome and necessary for the public good. — He has forbidden his Governors to pass Laws of immediate and pressing importance, unless suspended in their operation till his Assent should be obtained; and when so suspended, he has utterly neglected to attend to them. — He has refused to pass other Laws for the accommodation of large districts of people, unless those people would relinquish the right of Representation in the Legislature, a right inestimable to them and formidable to tyrants only. — He has called together legislative bodies at places unusual, uncomfortable, and distant from the depository of their public Records, for the sole purpose of fatiguing them into compliance with his measures. — He has dissolved Representative Houses repeatedly, for opposing with manly firmness his invasions on the rights of the people. — He has refused for a long time, after such dissolutions, to cause others to be elected; whereby the Legislative powers, incapable of Annihilation, have returned to the People at large for their exercise; the State remaining in the meantime exposed to all the dangers of invasion from without, and convulsions within. — He has endeavoured to prevent the population of these States; for that purpose obstructing the Laws for Naturalization of Foreigners; refusing to pass others to encourage their migrations hither, and raising the conditions of new Appropriations of Lands. — He has obstructed the Administration of Justice, by refusing his Assent to Laws for establishing Judiciary powers. — He has made Judges dependent on his Will alone, for the tenure of their offices, and the amount and payment of their salaries. — He has erected a multitude of New Offices, and sent hither swarms of Officers to harrass our people, and eat out their substance. — He has kept among us, in times of peace, Standing Armies without the Consent of our legislatures. — He has affected to render the Military independent of and superior to the Civil power. — He has combined with others to subject us to a jurisdiction foreign to our constitution, and unacknowledged by our laws; giving his Assent to their Acts of pretended Legislation. — For quartering large bodies of armed troops among us: — For protecting them, by a mock Trial, from punishment for any Murders which they should commit on the Inhabitants of these States: — For cutting off our Trade with all parts of the world: — For imposing Taxes on us without our Consent: — For depriving us in many cases, of the benefits of Trial by Jury: — For transporting us beyond Seas to be tried for pretended offenses: — For abolishing the free System of English Laws in a neighboring Province, establishing therein an Arbitrary government, and enlarging its Boundaries so as to render it at once an example and fit instrument for introducing the same absolute rule into these Colonies: — For taking away our Charters, abolishing our most valuable Laws, and altering fundamentally the Forms of our Governments: — For suspending our own Legislatures, and declaring themselves invested with power to legislate for us in all cases whatsoever. — He has abdicated Government here, by declaring us out of his Protection and waging War against us. — He has plundered our seas, ravaged our Coasts, burnt our towns, and destroyed the lives of our people. — He is at this time transporting large Armies of foreign Mercenaries to compleat the works of death, desolation and tyranny, already begun with circumstances of Cruelty & perfidy, scarcely paralleled in the most barbarous ages, and totally unworthy the Head of a civilized nation. — He has constrained our fellow Citizens taken Captive on the High Seas to bear Arms against their Country, to become the executioners of their friends and Brethren, or to fall themselves by their hands. — He has excited domestic insurrections amongst us, and has endeavoured to bring on the inhabitants of our frontiers, the merciless Indian Savages, whose known rule of warfare, is an undistinguished destruction of all ages, sexes and conditions. In every stage of these Oppressions We have Petitioned for Redress in the most humble terms: Our repeated Petitions have been answered only by repeated injury. A Prince whose character is thus marked by every act which may define a Tyrant, is unfit to be the ruler of a free people. Nor have We been wanting in attentions to our Brittish brethren. We have warned them from time to time of attempts by their legislature to extend an unwarrantable jurisdiction over us. We have reminded them of the circumstances of our emigration and settlement here. We have appealed to their native justice and magnanimity, and we have conjured them by the ties of our common kindred to disavow these usurpations, which would inevitably interrupt our connections and correspondence. They too have been deaf to the voice of justice and of consanguinity. We must, therefore, acquiesce in the necessity, which denounces our Separation, and hold them, as we hold the rest of mankind, Enemies in War, in Peace Friends. —

We, therefore, the Representatives of the united States of America, in General Congress, Assembled, appealing to the Supreme

Judge of the world for the rectitude of our intentions do, in the Name, and by the Authority of the good People of these Colonies, solemnly publish and declare, That these United Colonies are, and of Right ought to be Free and Independent States; that they are Absolved from all Allegiance to the British Crown, and that all political connection between them and the State of Great Britain, is and ought to be totally dissolved; and that as Free and Independent States, they have full Power to levy War, conclude Peace, contract Alliances, establish Commerce, and to do all other Acts and Things which Independent States may of right do. — And for the support of this Declaration, with a firm reliance on the protection of divine Providence, we mutually pledge to each other our Lives, our Fortunes and our sacred Honor.

The Constitution of the United States of America

We the People of the United States, in Order to form a more perfect Union, establish Justice, insure domestic Tranquility, provide for the common defence, promote the general Welfare, and secure the Blessings of Liberty to ourselves and our Posterity, do ordain and establish this Constitution for the United States of America.

Article I

Section 1. All legislative Powers herein granted shall be vested in a Congress of the United States, which shall consist of a Senate and House of Representatives.

Section 2. The House of Representatives shall be composed of Members chosen every second Year by the People of the several States, and the Electors in each State shall have the Qualifications requisite for Electors of the most numerous Branch of the State Legislature.

No Person shall be a Representative who shall not have attained to the age of twenty five Years, and been seven Years a Citizen of the United States, and who shall not, when elected, be an Inhabitant of that State in which he shall be chosen.

Representatives and direct Taxes shall be apportioned among the several States which may be included within this Union, according to their respective Numbers, *which shall be determined by adding to the whole Number of free Persons, including those bound to Service for a Term of Years,* and excluding Indians not taxed, *three fifths of all other persons.*[1] The actual Enumeration shall be made within three Years after the first Meeting of the Congress of the United States, and within every subsequent Term of ten Years, in such Manner as they shall by Law direct. The Number of Representatives shall not exceed one for every thirty Thousand, but each State shall have at Least one Representative; and until such enumeration shall be made, the State of New Hampshire shall be entitled to chuse three, Massachusetts eight, Rhode-Island and Providence Plantations one, Connecticut five, New-York six, New Jersey four, Pennsylvania

[1] Throughout, italics are used to indicate passages altered by subsequent amendments. In this instance, for example, see 14th Amendment.

eight, Delaware one, Maryland six, Virginia ten, North Carolina five, South Carolina five, and Georgia three.

When vacancies happen in the Representation from any State, the Executive Authority thereof shall issue Writs of Election to fill such Vacancies.

The House of Representatives shall chuse their Speaker and other Officers; and shall have the sole Power of Impeachment.

Section 3. The Senate of the United States shall be composed of two Senators from each State, *chosen by the Legislature thereof,*[2] for six Years; and each Senator shall have one Vote.

Immediately after they shall be assembled in Consequence of the first Election, they shall be divided as equally as may be into three Classes. The Seats of the Senators of the first Class shall be vacated at the Expiration of the second Year, of the second Class at the Expiration of the fourth Year, and of the third Class at the Expiration of the sixth Year, so that one third may be chosen every second Year; *and if Vacancies happen by Resignation, or otherwise, during the Recess of the Legislature of any State, the Executive thereof may make temporary Appointments until the next Meeting of the Legislature, which shall then fill such Vacancies.*[3]

No Person shall be a Senator who shall not have attained to the Age of thirty Years, and been nine Years a Citizen of the United States, and who shall not, when elected, be an Inhabitant of the State for which he shall be chosen.

The Vice President of the United States shall be President of the Senate, but shall have no Vote, unless they be equally divided.

The Senate shall chuse their other Officers, and also a President pro tempore, in the Absence of the Vice President, or when he shall exercise the Office of President of the United States.

The Senate shall have the sole Power to try all Impeachments. When sitting for that Purpose, they shall be on Oath or Affirmation. When the President of the United States is tried, the Chief Justice shall preside: And no Person shall be convicted without the Concurrence of two thirds of the Members present.

Judgment in Cases of Impeachment shall not extend further than to removal from Office, and disqualification to hold and enjoy any Office of honor, Trust or Profit under the United States: but the Party convicted shall nevertheless be liable and subject to Indictment, Trial, Judgment and Punishment, according to Law.

Section 4. The Times, Places and Manner of holding Elections for Senators and Representatives, shall be prescribed in each State by the Legislature thereof; but the Congress may at any time by Law make or alter such Regulations, except as to the Places of chusing Senators.

The Congress shall assemble at least once in every Year, and such Meeting shall be on the first Monday in December, unless they shall by Law appoint a different Day.[4]

Section 5. Each House shall be the Judge of the Elections, Returns and Qualifications of its own Members, and a Majority of each shall constitute a Quorum to do Business; but a smaller Number may adjourn from day to day, and may be authorized to compel the Attendance of absent Members, in such Manner, and under such Penalties as each House may provide.

Each House may determine the Rules of its Proceedings, punish its Members for disorderly Behaviour, and, with the Concurrence of two thirds, expel a Member.

Each House shall keep a Journal of its Proceedings, and from time to time publish the same, excepting such Parts as may in their Judgment require Secrecy; and the Yeas and Nays of the Members of either House on any question shall, at the Desire of one fifth of those Present, be entered on the Journal.

Neither House, during the Session of Congress, shall, without the Consent of the other, adjourn for more than three days, nor to any other Place than that in which the two Houses shall be sitting.

Section 6. The Senators and Representatives shall receive a Compensation for their Services, to be ascertained by Law, and paid out of the Treasury of the United States. They shall in all Cases, except Treason, Felony and Breach of the Peace, be privileged from Arrest during their Attendance at the Session of their respective Houses, and in going to and returning from the same; and for any Speech or Debate in either House, they shall not be questioned in any other Place.

No Senator or Representative shall, during the Time for which he was elected, be appointed to any civil Office under the Authority of the United States, which shall have been created, or the Emoluments whereof shall have been encreased during such time; and no Person holding any Office under the United States, shall be a Member of either House during his Continuance in Office.

[2]See 17th Amendment.
[3]See 17th Amendment.
[4]See 20th Amendment.

Section 7. All Bills for raising Revenue shall originate in the house of Representatives; but the Senate may propose or concur with Amendments as on other Bills.

Every Bill which shall have passed the House of Representatives and the Senate, shall, before it become a Law, be presented to the President of the United States; if he approve he shall sign it, but if not he shall return it, with his Objections to that House in which it shall have originated, who shall enter the Objections at large on their Journal, and proceed to reconsider it. If after such Reconsideration two thirds of that House shall agree to pass the Bill, it shall be sent, together with the Objections, to the other House, by which it shall likewise be reconsidered, and if approved by two thirds of that House, it shall become a Law. But in all such Cases the Votes of both Houses shall be determined by Yeas and Nays, and the Names of the Persons voting for and against the Bill shall be entered on the Journal of each House respectively. If any Bill shall not be returned by the President within ten Days (Sundays excepted) after it shall have been presented to him, the Same shall be a Law, in like Manner as if he had signed it, unless the Congress by their Adjournment prevent its Return, in which Case it shall not be a Law.

Every Order, Resolution, or Vote to which the Concurrence of the Senate and House of Representatives may be necessary (except on a question of Adjournment) shall be presented to the President of the United States; and before the Same shall take Effect, shall be approved by him, or being disapproved by him, shall be repassed by two thirds of the Senate and House of Representatives, according to the Rules and Limitations prescribed in the Case of a Bill.

Section 8. The Congress shall have Power To lay and collect Taxes, Duties, Imposts and Excises, to pay the Debts and provide for the common Defence and general Welfare of the United States; but all Duties, Imposts and Excises shall be uniform throughout the United States;

To borrow Money on the credit of the United States;

To regulate Commerce with foreign Nations, and among the several States, and with the Indian Tribes;

To esablish an uniform Rule of Naturalization, and uniform Laws on the subject of Bankruptcies throughout the United States;

To coin Money, regulate the Value thereof, and of foreign Coin, and fix the Standard of Weights and Measures;

To provide for the Punishment of counterfeiting the Securities and current Coin of the United States;

To establish Post Offices and post Roads;

To promote the Progress of Science and useful Arts, by securing for limited Times to Authors and Inventors the exclusive Right to their respective Writings and Discoveries;

To constitute Tribunals inferior to the Supreme Court;

To define and punish Piracies and Felonies committed on the high Seas, and Offences against the Law of Nations;

To declare War, grant Letters of Marque and Reprisal, and make Rules concerning Captures on Land and Water;

To raise and support Armies, but no Appropriation of Money to that Use shall be for a longer Term than two Years;

To provide and maintain a Navy;

To make Rules for the Government and Regulation of the land and naval Forces;

To provide for calling forth the Militia to execute the Laws of the Union, suppress Insurrections and repel Invasions;

To provide for organizing, arming, and disciplining, the Militia, and for governing such Part of them as may be employed in the Service of the United States, reserving to the States respectively, the Appointment of the Officers, and the Authority of training the Militia according to the discipline prescribed by Congress;

To exercise exclusive Legislation in all Cases whatsoever, over such District (not exceeding ten Miles square) as may, by Cession of particular States, and the Acceptance of Congress, become the Seat of the Government of the United States, and to exercise like Authority over all Places purchased by the Consent of the Legislature of the State in which the Same shall be, for the Erection of Forts, Magazines, Arsenals, dock-Yards, and other needful Buildings;—And

To make all Laws which shall be necessary and proper for carrying into Execution the foregoing Powers, and all ther Powers vested by this Constitution in the Government of the United States, or in any Department or Officer thereof.

Section 9. The Migration or Importation of such Persons as any of the States now existing shall think proper to admit, shall not be prohibited by the Congress prior to the Year one thousand eight hundred and eight, but a Tax or duty may be imposed on such Importation, not exceeding ten dollars for each Person.

The Privilege of the Writ of Habeas Corpus shall not be suspended, unless when in Cases of Rebellion or Invasion the public Safety may require it.

No Bill of Attainder or ex post facto Law shall be passed.

No Capitation, or other direct, Tax shall be laid, unless in Proportion to the Census or Enumeration herein before directed to be taken.

No Tax or Duty shall be laid on Articles exported from any State.

No Preference shall be given by any Regulation of Commerce or Revenue to the Ports of one State over those of another: nor shall Vessels bound to, or from, one State, be obliged to enter, clear, or pay Duties in another.

No Money shall be drawn from the Treasury, but in Consequence of Appropriations made by Law; and a regular Statement and Account of the Receipts and Expenditures of all public Money shall be published from time to time,

No title of Nobility shall be granted by the United States: And no Person holding any Office of Profit or Trust under them, shall, without the Consent of the Congress, accept of any present, Emolument, Office, or Title, of any kind whatever, from any King, Prince, or foreign State.

Section 10. No State shall enter into any Treaty, Alliance, or Confederation; grant Letters of Marque and Reprisal; coin Money; emit Bills of Credit; make any Thing but gold and silver Coin a Tender in Payment of Debts; pass any Bill of Attainder, ex post facto Law, or Law impairing the Obligation of Contracts, or Grant any Title of Nobility.

No State shall, without the Consent of the Congress, lay any Imposts or Duties on Imports or Exports, except what may be absolutely necessary for executing its inspection Laws: and the net Produce of all Duties and Imposts, laid by any State on Imports or Exports, shall be for the Use of the Treasury of the United States; and all such Laws shall be subject to the Revision and Controul of the Congress.

No State shall, without the Consent of Congress, lay any Duty of Tonnage, keep Troops, or Ships of War in time of Peace, enter into any Agreement or Compact with another State, or with a foreign Power, or engage in War, unless actually invaded, or in such imminent Danger as will not admit of delay.

Article II

Section 1. The executive Power shall be vested in a President of the United States of America. He shall hold his Office during the Term of four Years, and, together with the Vice President, chosen for the same Term be elected as follows:

Each State shall appoint, in such Manner as the Legislature thereof may direct, a Number of Electors, equal to the whole Number of Senators and Representatives to which the State may be entitled in the Congress but no Senator or Representative, or Person holding an Office of Trust or Profit under the United States, shall be appointed an Elector.

The Electors shall meet in their respective States, and vote by Ballot for two Persons, of whom one at least shall not be an Inhabitant of the same State with themselves. And they shall make a List of all the Persons voted for, and of the Number of Votes for each; which List they shall sign and certify, and transmit sealed to the Seat of the Government of the United States, directed to the President of the Senate. The President of the Senate shall, in the Presence of the Senate and House of Representatives, open all the Certificates, and the Votes shall then be counted. The Person having the greatest Number of Votes shall be the President, if such Number be a Majority of the whole Number of Electors appointed; and if there be more than one who have such Majority, and have an equal Number of Votes, then the House of Representatives shall immediately chuse by Ballot one of them for President; and if no Person have a Majority, then from the five highest on the List the said House shall in like Manner chuse the President. But in chusing the President, the Votes shall be taken by States, the Representation from each State having one Vote; A quorum for this purpose shall consist of a Member or Members from two thirds of the States, and a Majority of all the States shall be necessary to a Choice. In every Case, after the Choice of the President, the Person having the greatest Number of Votes of the Electors shall be the Vice President. But if there should remain two or more who have equal Votes, the Senate shall chuse from them by Ballot the Vice President.[5]

The Congress may determine the Time of chusing the Electors, and the Day on which they shall give their Votes; which Day shall be the same throughout the United States.

No Person except a natural born Citizen, or a Citizen of the United States, at the time of the Adoption of this Constitution, shall be eligible to the Office of President; neither shall any Person be eligible to that Office who shall not have attained to the Age of thirty five Years, and been fourteen Years a Resident within the United States.

In Case of the Removal of the President from Office, or of his Death, Resignation, or Inability to discharge the Powers and Duties of the said Office, the Same shall devolve on the Vice President, and the Congress may by Law provide for the Case of Removal, Death, Resignation or Inability, both of the President and Vice President, declaring what Officer shall then act as President, and such Officer shall act accordingly, until the Disability be removed, or a President shall be elected.[6]

---

[5]Superseded by the 12th Amendment.
[6]See 25th Amendment.

The President shall, at stated Times, receive for his Services, a Compensation which shall neither be encreased nor diminished during the Period for which he shall have been elected, and he shall not receive within that Period any other Emolument from the United States, or any of them.

Before he enter on the Execution of his Office, he shall take the following Oath or Affirmation: — "I do solemnly swear (or affirm) that I will faithfully execute the Office of President of the United States, and will to the best of my Ability, preserve, protect and defend the Constitution of the United States."

Section 2. The President shall be Commander in Chief of the Army and Navy of the United States, and of the Militia of the several States, when called into the actual service of the United States; he may require the Opinion, in writing, of the principal Officer in each of the executive Departments, upon any Subject relating to the Duties of their respective Offices, and he shall have Power to grant Reprieves and Pardons for Offences against the United States, except in Cases of Impeachment.

He shall have Power, by and with the Advice and Consent of the Senate, to make Treaties, provided two thirds of the Senators present concur; and he shall nominate, and by and with the Advice and Consent of the Senate, shall appoint Ambassadors, and other public Ministers and Consuls, Judges of the supreme Court, and all other Officers of the United States, whose Appointments are not herein otherwise provided for, and which shall be established by Law: but the Congress may by Law vest the Appointment of such inferior Officers, as they think proper, in the President alone, in the Courts of Law, or in the Heads of Departments.

The President shall have Power to fill up all Vacancies that may happen during the Recess of the Senate, by granting Commissions which shall expire at the End of their next Session.

Section 3. He shall from time to time give to the Congress Information of the State of the Union, and recommend to their Consideration such Measures as he shall judge necessary and expedient; he may, on extraordinary Occasions, convene both Houses, or either of them, and in Case of Disagreement between them, with Respect to the Time of Adjournment, he may adjourn them to such Time as he shall think proper; he shall receive Ambassadors and other public Ministers, he shall take Care that the Laws be faithfully executed, and shall Commission all the Officers of the United States.

Section 4. The President, Vice President, and all civil Officers of the United States, shall be removed from Office on Impeachment for, and Conviction of Treason, Bribery, or other high Crimes and Misdemeanors.

Article III

Section 1. The judicial Power of the United States, shall be vested in one supreme Court and in such inferior Courts as the Congress may from time to time ordain and establish. The Judges, both of the supreme and inferior Courts, shall hold their Offices during good Behavior, and shall, at stated Times, receive for their Services, a Compensation, which shall not be diminished during their Continuance in Office.

Section 2. The judicial Power shall extend to all Cases, in Law and Equity, arising under this Constitution, the Laws of the United States, and Treaties made, or which shall be made, under their Authority; — to all Cases affecting Ambassadors, other public Ministers and Consuls; — to all Cases of admiralty and maritime Jurisdiction; — to Controversies to which the United States shall be a Party — to Controversies between two or more States; — *between a State and Citizens of another State*[7]; — between Citizens of different States; — between Citizens of the same State claiming Lands under Grants of different States, *and between a State or the Citizens thereof, and foreign States, Citizens, or Subjects.*[8]

In all cases affecting Ambassadors, other public Ministers and Consuls, and those in which a State shall be Party, the supreme Court shall have original Jurisdiction. In all the other Cases before mentioned, the supreme Court shall have appellate Jurisdiction, both as to Law and Fact, with such Exceptions, and under such Regulations as the Congress shall make.

The Trial of all Crimes, except in Cases of Impeachment, shall be by Jury; and such Trial shall be held in the State where the said Crimes shall have been committed; but when not committed within any State, the Trial shall be at such Place or Places as the Congress may by Law have directed.

Section 3. Treason against the United States, shall consist only in levying War against them, or in adhering to their Enemies, giving them Aid and Comfort. No Person shall be convicted of Treason unless on the Testimony of two Witnesses to the same overt Act, or on Confession in open Court.

The Congress shall have Power to declare the Punishment of Treason, but no Attainder of Treason shall work Corruption of Blood, or Forfeiture except during the Life of the Person attainted.

Article IV

Section 1. Full Faith and Credit shall be given in each State to the public Acts, Records, and judicial Proceedings of every other State. And the Congress may by general Laws prescribe the Manner in which such

[7] See 11th Amendment.
[8] See 11th Amendment.

THE CONSTITUTION OF THE UNITED STATES OF AMERICA

Acts, Records, and Proceedings shall be proved, and the Effect thereof.

Section 2. The Citizens of each State shall be entitled to all Privileges and Immunities of Citizens in the several States.

A Person charged in any State with Treason, Felony, or other Crime, who shall flee from Justice, and be found in another State, shall on Demand of the executive Authority of the State from which he fled, be delivered up, to be removed to the State having Jurisdiction of the Crime.

No Person held to Service or Labour in one State, under the Laws thereof, escaping into another, shall, in Consequence of any Law or Regulation therein, be discharged from such Service or Labour, but shall be delivered up on Claim of the Party to whom such Service or Labour may be due.[9]

Section 3. New States may be admitted by the Congress into this Union; but no new State shall be formed or erected within the Jurisdiction of any other State; nor any State be formed by the Junction of two or more States, or Parts of States, without the Consent of the Legislatures of the States concerned as well as of the Congress.

The Congress shall have Power to dispose of and make all needful Rules and Regulations respecting the Territory or other Property belonging to the United States; and nothing in this Constitution shall be so construed as to Prejudice any claims of the United States, or of any particular State.

Section 4. The United States shall guarantee to every State in this Union a Republican Form of Government, and shall protect each of them against Invasion; and on Application of the Legislature, or of the Executive (when the Legislature cannot be convened) against domestic Violence.

Article V

The Congress, whenever two thirds of both Houses shall deem it necessary, shall propose Amendments to this Constitution, or, on the Application of the Legislatures of two thirds of the several States, shall call a Convention for proposing Amendments, which, in either Case, shall be valid to all Intents and Purposes, as Part of this Constitution, when ratified by the Legislatures of three fourths of the several States, or by Conventions in three fourths thereof, as the one or the other Mode of Ratification may be proposed by the Congress; Provided that no Amendment which may be made prior to the Year One thousand eight hundred and eight shall in any Manner affect the first and fourth Clauses in the Ninth Section of the first Article; and that no State, without its Consent, shall be deprived of its equal Suffrage in the Senate.

Article VI

All Debts contracted and Engagements entered into, before the Adoption of this Constitution, shall be as valid against the United States under this Constitution, as under the Confederation.

This Constitution, and the Laws of the United States which shall be made in Pursuance thereof; and all Treaties made, or which shall be made, under the Authority of the United States, shall be the supreme Law of the Land; and the Judges in every State shall be bound thereby, any Thing in the Constitution or Laws of any State to the Contrary notwithstanding.

The Senators and Representatives before mentioned, and the Members of the several State Legislatures, and all executive and judicial Officers, both of the United States and of the several States, shall be bound by Oath or Affirmation, to support this Constitution; but no religious Test shall ever be required as a Qualification to any Office or public Trust under the United States.

Article VII

The Ratification of the Conventions of nine States, shall be sufficient for the Establishment of this Constitution between the States so ratifying the Same.

Done in Convention by the Unanimous Consent of the States present the Seventeenth Day of September in the Year of our Lord one thousand seven hundred and eighty seven and of the Independence of the United States of America the twelfth. In witness whereof We have hereunto subscribed our Names.

. . .

ARTICLES IN ADDITION TO, AND AMENDMENT OF, THE CONSTITUTION OF THE UNITED STATES OF AMERICA, PROPOSED BY CONGRESS, AND RATIFIED BY THE SEVERAL STATES, PURSUANT TO THE FIFTH ARTICLE OF THE ORIGINAL CONSTITUTION.

Amendment 1

[Ratification of the first ten amendments was completed December 15, 1791]

Congress shall make no law respecting an establishment of religion, or prohibiting the free exercise thereof; or abridging the freedom of speech, or of the press; or the right of the people peaceably to assemble, and to petition the Government for a redress of grievances.

---

[9] See 13th Amendment.

Amendment II

A well regulated Militia, being necessary to the security of a free State, the right of the people to keep and bear Arms, shall not be infringed.

Amendment III

No Soldier shall, in time of peace be quartered in any house, without the consent of the Owner, nor in time of war, but in a manner to be prescribed by law.

Amendment IV

The right of the people to be secure in their persons, houses, papers, and effects, against unreasonable searches and seizures, shall not be violated, and no Warrants shall issue, but upon probable cause, supported by Oath or affirmation, and particularly describing the place to be searched, and the persons or things to be seized.

Amendment V

No person shall be held to answer for a capital, or other infamous crime, unless on a presentment or indictment of a Grand Jury, except in cases arising in the land or naval forces, or in the Militia, when in actual service in time of War or public danger; nor shall any person be subject for the same offence to be twice put in jeopardy of life or limb; nor shall be compelled in any criminal case to be a witness against himself, nor be deprived of life, liberty, or property, without due process of law; nor shall private property be taken for public use, without just compensation.

Amendment VI

In all criminal prosecutions, the accused shall enjoy the right to a speedy and public trial, by an impartial jury of the State and district wherein the crime shall have been committed, which district shall have been previously ascertained by law, and to be informed of the nature and cause of the accusation; to be confronted with the witness against him; to have compulsory process for obtaining witness in his favor, and to have the Assistance of Counsel for his defence.

Amendment VII

In Suits at common law, where the value in controversy shall exceed twenty dollars, the right of trial by jury shall be preserved, and no fact tried by a jury, shall be otherwise re-examined in any Court of the United States, than according to the rules of the common law.

Amendment VIII

Excessive bail shall not be required, nor excessive fines imposed, nor cruel and unusual punishments inflicted.

Amendment IX

The enumeration in the Constitution, of certain rights, shall not be construed to deny or disparage others retained by the people.

Amendment X

The powers not delegated to the United States by the Constitution, nor prohibited by it to the States, are reserved to the States respectively, or to the people.

Amendment XI

[January 8, 1798]

The Judicial power of the United States shall not be construed to extend to any suit in law or equity, commenced or prosecuted against one of the United States by Citizens of another State, or by Citizens or Subjects of any Foreign State.

Amendment XII

[September 25, 1804]

The Electors shall meet in their respective states and vote by ballot for President and Vice President, one of whom, at least, shall not be an inhabitant of the same state with themselves; they shall name in their ballots the person voted for as President, and in distinct ballots the person voted for as Vice President, and they shall make distinct lists of all persons voted for as President and of all persons voted for as Vice President, and of the number of votes for each, which lists they shall sign and certify, and transmit sealed to the seat of the government of the United States, directed to the President of the Senate; —The President of the Senate shall, in the presence of Senate and House of Representatives, open all the certificates and the votes shall then be counted;—The person having the greatest number of votes for President, shall be the President, if such number be a majority of the whole number of Electors appointed; and if no person have such majority, then from the persons having the highest numbers not exceeding three on the list of those voted for as President, the House of Representatives shall choose immediately, by ballot, the President. But in choosing the President, the votes shall be taken by states, the representation from each state having one vote; a quorum for this purpose shall consist of a member or members from two thirds of the states, and a majority of all the states shall be necessary to a choice. And if the House of Representatives shall not choose a President whenever the right of choice shall devolve upon them, *before the fourth day of March next following*,[10] then the Vice President shall act as President, as in the case of the death or other constitutional disability of

[10]Altered by the 20th Amendment.

THE CONSTITUTION OF THE UNITED STATES OF AMERICA

the President.—The person having the greatest number of votes as Vice President shall be the Vice President, if such number be a majority of the whole number of Electors appointed, and if no person have a majority, then from the two highest numbers on the list, the Senate shall choose the Vice President; a quorum for the purpose shall consist of two-thirds of the whole number of Senators, and a majority of the whole number shall be necessary to a choice. But no person constitutionally ineligible to the office of President shall be eligible to that of Vice President of the United States.

Amendment XIII

[December 18, 1865]

Section 1. Neither slavery nor involuntary servitude, except as a punishment for crime wherof the party shall have been duly convicted, shall exist within the United States, or any place subject to their jurisdiction.

Section 2. Congress shall have power to enforce this article by appropriate legislation.

Amendment XIV

[July 28, 1869]

Section 1. All persons born or naturalized in the United States, and subject to the jurisdiction thereof, are citizens of the United States and of the State wherein they reside. No State shall make or enforce any law which shall abridge the privileges or immunities of citizens of the United States; nor shall any State deprive any person of life, liberty, or property, without due process of law; nor deny to any person within its jurisdiction the equal protection of the laws.

Section 2. Representatives shall be apportioned among the several States according to their respective numbers, counting the whole number of persons in each State, excluding Indians not taxed. But when the right to vote at any election for the choice of electors for President and Vice President of the United States, Representatives in Congress, the Executive and Judicial officers of a State, or the members of the Legislature thereof, is denied to any of the male inhabitants of such State, being twenty-one years of age, and citizens of the United States, or in any way abridged, except for participation in rebellion, or other crime, the basis of representation therein shall be reduced in the proportion which the number of such male citizens shall bear to the whole number of male citizens twenty-one years of age in such State.

Section 3. No person shall be a Senator or Representative in Congress, or elector of President and Vice President, or hold any office, civil or military, under the United States, or under any State, who, having previously taken an oath, as a member of Congress, or as an officer of the United States, or as a member of any State legislature, or as an executive or judicial officer of any State, to support the Constitution of the United States, shall have engaged in insurrection or rebellion against the same, or given aid or comfort to the enemies thereof. But Congress may by a vote of two thirds of each House, remove such disability.

Section 4. The validity of the public debt of the United States, authorized by law, including debts incurred for payment of pensions and bounties for services in suppressing insurrection or rebellion, shall not be questioned. But neither the United States nor any State shall assume or pay any debt or obligation incurred in aid of insurrection or rebellion against the United States, or any claim for the loss or emancipation of any slave; but all such debts, obligations, and claims shall be held illegal and void.

Section 5. The Congress shall have power to enforce, by appropriate legislation, the provisions of this article.

Amendment XV

[March 30, 1870]

Section 1. The right of citizens of the United States to vote shall not be denied or abridged by the United States or by any State on account of race, color, or previous condition of servitude.

Section 2. The Congress shall have power to enforce this article by appropriate legislation

Amendment XVI

[February 25, 1913]

The Congress shall have power to lay and collect taxes on incomes, from whatever source derived, without apportionment among the several States, and without regard to any census or enumeration.

Amendment XVII

[May 31, 1913]

The Senate of the United States shall be composed of two Senators from each State, elected by the people thereof, for six years; and each Senator shall have one vote. The electors in each State shall have the qualifications requisite for electors of the most numerous branch of the State legislatures.

When vacancies happen in the representation of any State in the Senate, the executive authority of such State shall issue writs of election to fill such vacancies: *Provided,* That the legislature of any State may empower the executive thereof to make temporary appointments until the people fill the vacancies by election as the legislature may direct.

This amendment shall not be so construed as to affect the election or term of any Senator chosen before it becomes valid as part of the Constitution.

Amendment XVIII

[January 29, 1919]

Section 1. After one year from the ratification of this article the manufacture, sale, or transportation of intoxicating liquors within, the importation thereof into, or the exportation thereof from the United States and all territory subject to the jurisdiction thereof for beverage purposes is hereby prohibited.

Section 2. The Congress and the several States shall have concurrent power to enforce this article by appropriate legislation.

Section 3. This article shall be inoperative unless it shall have been ratified as an amendment to the Constitution by the legislatures of the several States, as provided in the Constitution, within seven years from the date of the submission hereof to the States by the Congress.[11]

Amendment XIX

[August 26, 1920]

The right of citizens of the United States to vote shall not be denied or abridged by the United States or by any State on account of sex.

Congress shall have power to enforce this article by appropriate legislation.

Amendment XX

[February 6, 1933]

Section 1. The terms of the President and Vice President shall end at noon on the 20th day of January, and the terms of Senators and Representatives at noon on the 3rd day of January, of the years in which such terms would have ended if this article had not been ratified; and the terms of their successors shall then begin.

Section 2. The Congress shall assemble at least once in every year, and such meeting shall begin at noon on the 3rd day of January, unless they shall by law appoint a different day.

Section 3. If, at the time fixed for the beginning of the term of the President, the President elect shall have died, the Vice President elect shall become President. If a President shall not have been chosen before the time fixed for the beginning of his term,

[11]Repealed by the 21st Amendment.

or if the President elect shall have failed to qualify, then the Vice President elect shall act as President until a President shall have qualified; and the Congress may by law provide for the case wherein neither a President elect nor a Vice President elect shall have qualified, declaring who shall then act as President, or the manner in which one who is to act shall be selected, and such person shall act accordingly until a President or Vice President shall have qualified.

Section 4. The Congress may by law provide for the case of the death of any of the persons from whom the House of Representatives may choose a President whenever the right of choice shall have devôlved upon them, and for the case of the death of any of the persons from whom the Senate may choose a Vice President whenever the right of choice shall have devôlved upon them.

Section 5. Sections 1 and 2 shall take effect on the 15th day of October following the ratification of this article.

Section 6. This article shall be inoperative unless it shall have been ratified as an amendment to the Constitution by the legislatures of three-fourths of the several States within seven years from the date of its submission.

Amendment XXI

[December 5, 1933]

Section 1. The eighteenth article of amendment to the Constitution of the United States is hereby repealed.

Section 2. The transportation or importation into any State, Territory, or possession of the United States for delivery or use therein of intoxicating liquors, in violation of the laws thereof, is hereby prohibited.

Section 3. This article shall be inoperative unless it shall have been ratified as an amendment to the Constitution by conventions in the several States, as provided in the Constitution, within seven years from the date of the submission hereof to the States by the Congress.

Amendment XXII

[February 26, 1951]

Section 1. No person shall be elected to the office of the President more than twice, and no person who has held the office of President, or acted as President, for more than two years of a term to which some other person was elected President shall be elected to the office of President more than once. But this Article shall not apply to any person holding the office of President when this Article was proposed by the Congress, and shall not prevent any person who may be holding the office of President, or acting as President, during the term within which this Article beomes operative from holding the office of President or acting as President during the remainder of such term.

Section 2. This article shall be inoperative unless it shall have been ratified as an amendment to the Constitution by the legislatures of three-fourths of the several States within seven years from the date of its submission to the States by the Congress.

Amendment XXIII

[March 29, 1961]

Section 1. The District constituting the seat of Government of the United States shall appoint in such manner as the Congress may direct:

A number of electors of President and Vice President equal to the whole number of Senators and Representatives in Congress to which the District would be entitled if it were a State, but in no event more than the least populous State; they shall be in addition to those appointed by the States, but they shall be considered, for the purposes of the election of President and Vice President, to be electors appointed by a State; and they shall meet in the District and perform such duties as provided by the twelfth article of amendment.

Section 2. The Congress shall have power to enforce this article by appropriate legislation.

Amendment XXIV

[January 23, 1964]

Section 1. The right of citizens of the United States to vote in any primary or other election for President or Vice President, for electors for President or Vice President, or for Senator or Representative in Congress, shall not be denied or abridged by the United States or any state by reason of failure to pay any poll tax or other tax.

Section 2. The Congress shall have the power to enforce this article by appropriate legislation.

Amendment XXV

[February 10, 1967]

Section 1. In case of the removal of the President from office or of his death or resignation, the Vice President shall become President.

Section 2. Whenever there is a vacancy in the office of the Vice President, the President shall nominate a Vice President who shall take office upon confirmation by a majority vote of both Houses of Congress.

Section 3. Whenever the President transmits to the President pro tempore of the Senate and the Speaker of the House of Representatives his written declaration that he is unable to discharge the powers and duties of his office, and until he transmits to them a written declaration to the contrary, such powers and duties shall be discharged by the Vice President as Acting President.

Section 4. Whenever the Vice President and a majority of either the principal officers of the executive departments or of such other body as Congress may by law provide, transmit to the President pro tempore of the Senate and the Speaker of the House of Representatives their written declaration that the President is unable to discharge the powers and duties of his office, the Vice President shall immediately assume the powers and duties of the office as Acting President.

Thereafter, when the President transmits to the President pro tempore of the Senate and the Speaker of the House of Representatives his written declaration that no inability exists, he shall resume the powers and duties of his office unless the Vice President and a majority of either the principal officers of the executive departments or of such other body as Congress may by law provide, transmit within four days to the President pro tempore of the Senate and the Speaker of the House of Representatives their written declaration that the President is unable to discharge the powers and duties of his office. Thereupon Congress shall decide the issue, assembling within forty-eight hours for that purpose if not in session. If the Congress, within twenty-one days after receipt of the latter written declaration, or, if Congress is not in session, within twenty-one days after Congress is required to assemble, determines by two-thirds vote of both Houses that the President is unable to discharge the powers and duties of his office, the Vice President shall continue to discharge the same as Acting President; otherwise, the President shall resume the powers and duties of his office.

INDEX

Aaron, Daniel, 93n
Abraham, Henry J., 570n
Academic freedom, 571-573
Academic Mind, The, 251n
Adams, James Truslow, 48n
Adams, Sherman, 423n
Adamson v. California, 580n
Adderly v. Florida, 571n
Adkins v. Children's Hospital, 607, 607n, 617n
Adler v. Board of Education, 572n
Administration of Interstate Compacts, The, 153n
Administrative law, 491
Adorno, T. W., 84n
Affluent Society, The, 58n
Afroyim v. Rusk, 560n
Agency for International Development, 477
Albertson v. Subversive Activities Control Board, 522n, 566n

Alford, Robert R., 208, 208n
Alien & Sedition Acts of 1798, 562
Aliens (see Citizenship)
Allard, Robert E., 492n
Allinsmith, Beverly, 193n
Allinsmith, Wesley, 193n
Almond, Gabriel, 5n, 7n, 15n, 17n, 18, 28n, 84n, 87n, 96n, 208, 208n, 657n, 689, 690n
Amendments to Constitution (see also Bill of Rights and individual amendments):
  procedure, 124
  restrictions, 125, 126
American Business and Public Policy, 268n, 272n, 340n, 378n, 692n
American character (see also National character):
  analysis of, 25-26
  characteristics of, 25-29

American Class Structure, The, 44n
American Commonwealth, The, 145n, 393n, 488n
American Communications Association, C.I.O. v. Douds, 564n
American Congress, The, 363n, 372n
American Constitutional Development, 530n
American Creed (see also Democracy, Democratic political theory):
  and Bill of Rights, 73
  and Constitution, 73
  and Declaration of Independence, 72
  and democratic ideology, 72, 78
  ideals of, 71-72
  and liberalism, 75
  operation of, 76

763

American Democracy: A Commentary and an Interpretation, The, 373n
American Democracy under Pressure, 277n
American Dilemma: The Negro Problem and Modern Democracy, An, 72n, 73n
American Federalism: A View from the States, 142n, 147n
American Foreign Policy in the Nuclear Age, 682n
American Foreign Policy since World War II, 653n
American judiciary (see Judges, Judiciary)
American Mind, The, 75n
American nation:
  as norm for new nations, 92
  early development, 92-135
American Partnership, The, 142n, 143, 161n
American People: A Study in National Character, The, 41n
American People and Foreign Policy, The, 28n, 87n, 657n, 689, 690n
American political system (see Political system)
American political tradition, 30-32
American politics (see also Political system, Politics):
  and American government, 5
  and public relations, 278-287
  as a system of action, 6, 19
  theory in study of, 18-21
American Presidency, The, 391n, 393n
American President, The, 390n
American Revolution, 41, 92-96, 104
American Society: A Sociological Interpretation, 24n
American State Politics, 33n, 225n, 302n
American Supreme Court, The, 539n
American Voter, The, 11n, 35n, 41n, 44n, 74n, 187, 189n, 213, 213n, 225n, 323n
American Voting Behavior, 33n, 183n, 184n
Americans for Democratic Action: Its Role in National Politics, 270n
Amicus curiae, 527
Anderson, William, 120n
And Keep Your Powder Dry: An Anthropologist Looks at America, 41n
Anti-Catholicism, 32

Apathy:
  and the American voter, 11
  function in democracy, 77
Appeals of Communism, The, 84n
Apportionment:
  and Constitution, 352
  and Fourteenth Amendment, 157
Approaches to Comparative and International Politics, 657n
Apter, David E., 76n, 96n, 212n, 326n, 545, 545n
Aptheker v. Secretary of State, 554n, 566n
Arrogance of Power, The, 682n
Articles of Confederation:
  adoption, 93
  amendments, 103-104
  and Congress, 100, 102
  and crisis of distribution, 101-102
  criticisms, 100
  difficulties with, 139
  and extradition, 151
  and full faith and credit, 151
  and interstate compacts, 152
  and national identity, 101, 139
  and participation, 102-103
  privileges and immunities, 151
  and separation of powers, 100
  and states, 100-101, 158
Asch, S. E., 201n
Atlantic Alliance: Basic Issues, The, 671n
Atlantic Alliance: Unfinished Business, The, 670n
Attitudes (see Political opinion, Public opinion)
Attorney General, responsibilities, 490, 518
Austin, John, 494
Authoritative decision-making (see Decision-makers, Outputs, Policy-making, Political system)
Authoritarian Personality, The, 84n
Azrael, Jeremy R., 332n

Bachrach, Peter, 264n
Bailey, Stephen K., 336n, 342n
Bailey v. Richardson, 464n
Bain, Richard C., 305n
Baker v. Carr, 353n, 354, 532n
Ballot:
  effects of mechanics, 321
  multiple choice, 321
  office-block, 320
  party-column, 320
  single-choice, 321
  straight ticket, 321

Bank of the United States:
  and Congress, 158-159
  and McCulloch v. Maryland, 159
Baratz, Morton S., 264n
Barker, Ernest, 382n
Barr v. Columbia, 571n
Barron v. Baltimore (1833) 127, 127n, 549, 550
Bartlett, Ruhl J., 681n
Barton, Weldon V., 153n
Basic Aims of U.S. Foreign Policy, 676n
Bauer, Raymond A., 268n, 340n, 346n, 378n, 692n
Beard, Charles, 48, 107, 107n, 230n, 341n
Becker, Carl L., 31, 31n
Becker, Theodore L., 497n
Beer, Samuel H., 333n, 334n
Bemis, Samuel Flagg, 653n
Benedict, Ruth, 24, 24n
Bentham, Jeremy, 527n
Bentley, Arthur F., 528
Berelson, Bernard R., 86n, 185n, 202n, 203n, 204n, 311n
Berle, Adolph A., 50n, 51
Berman, Daniel M., 367n
Berman v. Parker, 602n
Bern, Walter, 158n
Bernays, Edward L., 280n, 286n
Bernstein, Marver H., 470n
Betts v. Brady, 580n
Beyond the Melting Pot, 195n
Bicameralism, 359
Bill of attainder, 122
Bill of Rights (see also each amendment):
  and American Creed, 73
  and due process of law, 579
  framers of constitution, 141
  guarantees of, 186
  public awareness of, 74
  ratification of, 548
Bills (see also Congress, Decision-making, Legislation):
  and committee, 366-368
  and hearings, 366-367
  and House Rules Committee, 367
  and Presidential action, 368-369
  procedure for passage, 366-369
  and Senate committees, 367
  and Senate Policy Committee, 367
  and voting on, 368
Binkley, Wilfred, 244
Bipartisan Foreign Policy: Myth or Reality, 682n
Birth of the Bill of Rights: 1776-1791, The, 548n
Black, Charles L., 538n

764

INDEX

Black Power, 593
Blaisdell, Donald C., 277n
Blau, Peter M., 484n
Blough, William, 326n
Bobrow, Davis B., 656n
Bond v. Floyd, 578n
Bone, Hugh A., 233
Book of the States, 1966-1967, The, 298n, 301n
Boorstin, Daniel J., 89n, 662, 662n
Bowie, Robert R., 704n
Bowman, Lewis, 225n
Boynton, G. R., 225n
Bradley, Phillips, 447n
Brandeis Brief, 539
Brierly, J. L., 668n
British courts, 490-493
British Parliament, 333-334
British party system, 69
Brock, Clifton, 270n
Brodbeck, Arthur J., 33n, 183n, 184n
Brogan, D. W., 28, 28n
Bromage, Arthur W., 98n
Brown, Henry B., 49n
Brown, Robert E., 108n
Brown Shoe Co. v. U.S., 614n
Brown v. Board of Education, 150, 487, 531n, 586n, 587, 587n, 588n
 response in the South, 588-589
 results by 1966, 151
Brown v. Louisiana, 522n
Bruck, H. W., 657n
Bruner, Jerome S., 178n
Bryce, James, 145n, 393n, 418, 488, 488n, 493
Buchanan, William, 186n
Bunting, John R., 599n
Bunting v. Oregon, 607n
Burdick, Eugene, 33n, 183n, 184n
Bureaucracy (see also Civil Service, Executive agencies, Policy-making, Public administration):
 administration of law, 479-482
 American, 443-447
 committee assignment, 147
 comparative, 440-443
 and Congress, 147, 335, 371-372
 executive agencies, 454-456
 executive departments, 451-454
 functional principle, 482
 functions, 483-485
 judiciary, 481
 models, 439-440

patronage, and spoils system, 457
 and policy-making, 371-372
 political executives in policy process, 471
 and public interest, 482
 size, 444-446
 U.S. civil service, 458-564
Bureaucracy and Mobilization in Urban Politics, 208n
Bureaucracy and Political Development, 96n, 442n
Bureaucrats (see also Bureaucracy, Civil service, Executive agencies):
 in developing countries, 441-442
 the professional, and policy process, 472-473
 role in policy process, 468
Bureau of the Budget (see also Executive office of the President), 420, 424-426
Burke, Edmund, 146, 221
Burns, James MacGregor, 417n
Burstyn v. Wilson, 569n
Bush v. Orleans School Board, 151n
Business (see also Economic interests, Government):
 and big government, 58
 and the public interest, 606-607

Cabinet (see also President):
 history, 447-450
 and President, 413
 proposed changes, 450-451
 value of, 450
California politics, 221n, 302n
Campaigns (see also Elections, Political parties, Political system, Voting):
 and candidates, 203-204
 effects of, 311
 and money, 316-320
 strategies, 312-316
Campbell, Angus, 11n, 35n, 74n, 187, 189n, 194n, 203n, 205n, 213, 225n, 230n, 242n, 248n, 297n, 323n, 346n, 352n
Cannon, Clarence, 234n
Cantril, Hadley, 84n, 186
Carleton, William G., 669n
Carter v. Carter Coal Co., 619n
Cartwright, Dorwin, 201n
Caucasians Only, 528
Censorship, 568

Center, Allen H., 284n
Centers, Richard, 44n, 186
Certiorari, writ of, 521-522
Chambers, William, 224
Charles Beard and the Constitution, 108n
Chase, Harold, 505n
Chief Executive, The, 397n, 434n
Chief of state (see also President):
 comparisons, 384
 role of, 381-382
Children and Politics, 182n, 183n, 210n
Chinese Exclusion Law, 555
Chisholm v. Georgia (1793), 128-129, 129n
Church, Frank, 666n
Church and State in the United States, 574n
Citizenship:
 definition, 551-552
 and Fourteenth Amendment, 552
 and states, 554
Civic Culture, The, 208n
Civil Justice and the Jury, 517n
Civil rights (see also Bill of Rights, Citizenship, Constitution, Democracy, Individual rights and liberties):
 amendments, 549-550
 and constitutionalism, 545
 demonstrations, 590
 Negro opinion, 593
 public policy, 545
 and ratification of constitution, 548
 and riots, 594-595
 and states, 151
 and Vietnam war, 578, 595
Civil Rights Act of 1866, 549-550
Civil Rights Act of 1957, 295, 591
Civil Rights Act of 1960, 295, 591
Civil Rights Act of 1964, 295, 299, 300, 592
Civil Rights Act of 1965, 295
Civil Rights Cases (1883), 550n, 585, 585n
Civil Service (see also Bureaucracy, Executive agencies):
 employee restrictions, 461-464
 and political executives, 464-467
 and Ramspeck Act, 465
 and staff requirements, 458-460
 and tenure, 463
Civil Service Commission, 460

765

Class:
  awareness and political behavior, 44-45
  effects on attitudes, 185-186, 193
  and issues, 189
  and participation, 45, 189
  political differences, 188
  and political leadership, 46
  and politics, 43, 195
  and socialization, 185
  and tolerance, 188
  voting behavior by, 190-191
Claude, Inis L., Jr., 666n
Clausen, Aage R., 239n, 346n
Clayton Act, 616
Clayton, James E., 507n, 537n
Closed primary, 301
"Cloture" rule, 358
Cnudde, Charles F., 375n
Cochran v. Louisiana State Board of Education, 575n
Cohen, Bernard C., 696, 696n
Cohesion and group members, 268
Coker, Francis, 601n
Cole v. Young, 464, 464n
Coleman, James J., 5n, 96n
Colgrove v. Green, 353n
Colorado Politics, 221n
Coming of the New Deal, The, 627n, 633n
Commager, Henry Steele, 64n, 75n, 670n, 673n
Commercial Pictures Corp. v. Regents of New York, 569n
Commission on Organization of the Executive Branch of the Government, 481n
"Committee of the Whole," 367-368
Common Law:
  and canon law, 497-498
  and courts, 491
  customary, 497
  merchant law, 498
  nature of, 497
  origins, 497
  and right reason, 498
  Roman Codes, 498
  and rule of precedent, 492
Common Sense and World Affairs, 693n
Communications and Political Development, 96n
Communism:
  appeal, 83
  based on elite, 82
  and democracy, 81-84
  as issue in education, 572-573
  and majority rule, 81-82
  and protest vote, 83-84
  public controversy, 566-567

  in underdeveloped countries, 82-83
  variations, 82
Communism, Conformity and Civil Liberties, 32n, 38n, 75n, 567n
Communist Party, 564-565
Communist Party of U.S. v. Subversive Activities Board, 566n
Community awareness (see Nation building)
Community Power and Political Theory, 256n
Complacency, 32
Components of Defense Policy, 656n
Concepts and Issues in Administrative Behavior, 484n
Condition of American Federalism, The, 144n
Conduct of American Diplomacy, 654n
Confederation and the Constitution, The, 99n
Conference committees, 368
Conflict (see also Political system), 62-65
Conformity, 29-30
  and equality, 27
  and group judgements, 201
  and majority will, 30
  and status uncertainty, 28
Congress (see also Congressmen, House of Representatives, Interest groups, Legislation, Policy-making, Political opinions, Political system, Politics, Public opinion, Senate):
  under Articles of Confederation, 100-102
  compared with British Parliament, 333-334
  Congressional voting:
    "contingent" legislation, 419
    influence of constituency, 147-149
    and lobbying, 272
    norms and sanctions, 345-349
    party influences, 376
    and pressure groups, 265
  the Constitution:
    and admission of new states, 149
    congressional powers, 345-346
  and the Constitution, 331
  economic powers, 598
  foreign affairs, 677
  foreign aid, 687
  and general welfare, 597
  and leaders, 359

  legislative power, 418-419
  restraints, 345-346
elections:
  and campaign committees of, 234-235
  and composition, 337
  and congressional districts, 352
  local machines, 235-236
  public attention, 10
and executive agencies:
  decision-making, 369-373
  and independent regulatory commissions, 479
  influence on, 349-350
  investigation, 478-479
functions of:
  as authoritative rule-making, 335, 374-375
  communication, 143, 378
  control of immigration, 555
  decision-makers, 336
  foreign policy, 702-703
  in industrial, urban society, 335
  latent functions, 377-379
  legitimacy, 378-379
  organized minorities, 374
  passage of a bill, 366-369
  popular representation, 375-376
  regulation of commerce, 142
  role in American politics, 334-336
  rule-making activities, 335-336
  and "special" representation, 377-378
the judiciary:
  establishment of court system, 515
  federal court jurisdiction, 509
  and the judiciary, 510-511
  Supreme Court, 419, 521
norms of, 345-349
organization of:
  and access to bureaucracy, 147
  bicameral organization, 350-351
  committee system, 350-364
  leaders and bicameral system, 359
  role performance, 349
  seniority system, 364-365
  standing committees, 362-266
policy-making:
  and aliens, 557-559
  and bureaucracy, 371-372, 476-483, 478, 747
  and the citizenship, 559
  and corporate mergers, 614

766

INDEX

grants-in-aid, 168
and income taxes, 132-133
and interstate commerce, 610-611
and interstate compacts, 154-155
and judicial functions, 369-370
power of expatriation, 559-560
power of inquiry, 373
reapportionment, 352-355
political parties:
  and committee system, 363
  and leadership, 359-363
  party unity, 343-344
  selection of leaders, 359
the President:
  the administration's role, 339
  as chief legislator, 415-420
  and foreign policy, 702-703
  the Great Society, 640-641
  and policy-making, 370-371
  in war, 644
Congress and America's Future, The, 334n, 335n
Congress and Foreign Policy Making, 657n
Congress and the Constitution, 564n
Congress and the Nation, 1945-1964, 503n, 504n
Congress and the Presidency, 426
Congress: Its Contemporary Role, 252n, 364n
Congress Makes a Law, 336n
Congressional Control of Administration, 476n
Congressional Directory, 363n
Congressional districts, and state legislature, 352
Congressional Elections, 1896-1944, 303n
Congressional Government: A Study in American Policies, 364n, 378n, 416n
Congressional Process: Strategies, Rules and Procedures, The, 342n, 343n, 356n, 375n
Congressional Quarterly Weekly Report, 199n, 244n, 396n, 308n, 309n, 318n, 325n, 338n, 343n, 354n, 358n, 361n
Congressional Record, 271n, 512
Congressmen (see also Congress, Decision-makers):
  background, 337-340

and committee preference, 363-364
and constituency, influence on, 340, 342, 346
as "home town" types, 340
length of tenure, 339
and other leaders, 338-340
party membership, and identification, 342-345
Congressmen and Their Constituencies, 340n, 341n
Conscience of a Conservative, The, 324, 324n
Consensus:
  and acceptance of election results, 30
  and Democratic system, 77
  on democratic principles, 75
  V. O. Key, Jr., on, 77
  and majority rule, 76
  and minority rights, 76
Consensus and Continuity, 1776-1787, 97n, 121n
Conservatism, examined, 187
Constituency:
  of congressmen, requirements for control, 327-328
  effects of size, 341-342
  influence on Congress, 147-149
Constituents, 326-327
  relation to decision-makers, 326-327
Constitution (see also Amendments, Civil Rights, Congress, individual amendments, Individual rights and liberties, Judiciary, States, Supreme Court):
  amending:
    and change, 141
    procedure, 124-127
    restrictions, 125
  and American Creed, 73
  apportionment, 352
  Bill of Rights, 125-126, 548-550
  British, 97
  citizenship, 551
  commerce, 142
  common defense, 643
  Congress, 331
    and commerce, 142
    and common defense, 643
    and leadership, 359
    and legislation, 418
    norms and expectations, 345
    powers granted, 345-346
    qualifications, 337-338
    restraints, 345-346
    war-time interpretation, 643

constitutional law, 123
in continuance, 133-135
Convention of *1787*, 104-124
criticisms, 119
definition of, 97
due process of law, 535
economics:
  economic interpretation, 116
  economic motives, 107
  government and business, 599
elections:
  and citizenship, 559
  eligibility for national office, 289-290
and federalism, 137-138, 146-160
and foreign affairs, 676-677
and Framers, 135
and general welfare, 597
government and business, 598-599
interpretation and policy-making, 541
judiciary:
  amendments and the courts, 510
  definition of original jurisdiction, 509
  extent of "judicial power," 487, 509
  inferior courts, 488
  judges, 489, 503
  judicial behavior, 509
  judicial independence, 509
  judicial review, 524
  jurisdiction of courts, 509-510
as law and policy, 538
legislation, 418
minority rights, 65
naturalization, 557
nominating procedures, 290
personal rights v. private property, 601
political parties, 220
political philosophy, 97
popular sovereignty, 97-98
President, 387
  duties, 399-400
  economic powers, 420
  in foreign policy, 406
  qualifications, 391
  and Supreme Court, 502
ratification of, 117-120
reapportionment, 353
selection of national officials, 290
separation of powers, 99
states:
  constitutions, 97

767

governmental restrictions, 548
secession of, 150
states' rights, 146-149, 156
and status quo, 135
the Supreme Court, 509, 515, 521
taxing power, 626
treaties, 678
undemocratic aspects, 122
voting, 122
voting qualifications, 294
war powers, 117, 409, 643
Constitution of the United States of America, The, 126n
Constitutional Convention of 1787, 540
attitude toward democracy, 114-115, 120-123, 568
checks and balances, 114-115
and Congress, 111-117
and federalism, 138
and judiciary, 116
personalities, 104-107
problems, 110-111
procedures, 109-110
states' rights, 149
voting, 114, 530
Constitutional Government and Bureaucracy, 439n
Constitutional Government and Democracy, 335n
Constitutionalism, 541
Constitutional Law, 126n
Constitutional law (see also Civil rights, Constitution, individual amendments, Individual rights and liberties, Judiciary, Law, States, Supreme Court):
concept, 496-497
and Supreme Court, 144
Constitutional Politics, 497n
Constitutional rights:
of citizens overseas, 583
of defendants in federal criminal cases, 520
Conventions (see Nominations, Political parties)
Converse, Philip E., 32n, 76n, 194n, 205n, 212n, 230, 239n, 248n, 322n, 324n, 326n, 346n
Cooper, Homer C., 194n, 297n
Cooperative federalism (see also Federalism), 167
Corporations:
in modern business, 612-615
in political economy, 615
Corwin, Edward, 410n, 416n
Costs of American Governments, Facts, Trends, Myths, The, 165n, 318n
Cotter, Cornelius P., 470n

Council of Economic Advisers, 426
County party committees, 235
Courts (see also Judiciary, Law):
and adjudication, 526-532
dual system, 488
German, 493-494
Latin-American, 494
and political parties, 609
system and organization, 488
and support of values, 534
Courts on Trial, 496n, 534
Courts, The Public and the Law Explosion, The, 492n, 514n, 533n
Cox v. Louisiana, 571n
Coyle v. Smith, 149n
Crabb, Cecil V., 682n
Craig v. Harney, 515n
Crandall v. Nevada, 552, 553
Criminal law, 518
Critical Period of American History, 1783-1789, The, 99n
Crosby, John, 241, 241n
Cross-filing (see Elections, Electoral system, Nominations, Primaries), 301-302
Culture (see also American character, Environment, Political socialization, Socialization, Values):
definition, 24
opinions, 25
political behavior, 24
political system, 14
political values, 24
politics, 24-25
socialization, 24
Culture and Social Character, 26n
Cummings, Milton C., Jr., 356n, 445n, 459n
Currie, David P., 138n
Cushman, Robert E., 454n

Dahl, Robert A., 98n, 194n, 228n, 230n, 255n, 289n, 387n, 434n, 506n, 506, 620n, 658, 665, 666n
Dahlgren, Harold F., 185n
Danelski, Daniel, 508n
David, Paul T., 305n, 396n, 430n
Davies, James C., 211n
Davis, James W., 424
Davis, Kingsley, 16n
Deadlock of Democracy, The, 417n
Decision-makers (see also Bureaucracy, Decision-making, Executive agencies, Policy-making, Political system, Politics):

and ideology, 278
as independent statesmen, 326
as instructed delegates, 326
influence of pressure groups, 278
interactions, 429-432
relation to constituents, 326-327
responsible party model, 327
Decision-making (see also Decision-makers):
activities, 10
and non-decision, 264
and participation, 82
process of, 389
techniques of, 631-633
tripartite model of, 388
types of, 213
Decision-making in the White House, 400n, 423n, 436n, 654, 654n
Decision Process: Seven Categories of Functional Analysis, 388n
Declaration of Independence, 92-93
and American Creed, 72-73
and citizenship, 551
and majority rule, 65
and natural rights, 98, 546
Defendants' Rights, The, 520n
DeGrazia, Alfred, 220n
Delegates:
allotment to states, 308
selection, 306-307
"unit-rule," 310
Democracy:
acceptance of, 77
anti-democratic attacks, 81-85
and behavior, 89
capacity for conflict, 88
and change, 61, 79
commitment to, 74-76
and communism, 81-84
conditions for, 88-89
definition of, 61, 66
division of labor in, 86
dogmas, 66
equal rights, 89
freedom to criticize, 79
in Greek city-state, 66
human dignity in, 89
ideals of, 61-64
inconsistent attitudes toward, 74-75
individualism, 87
institutions of, 79-80
liberty, 80
majority rule, 64-67, 79
meaning, 61
as method of governing, 66
minority rights, 64, 67, 79
natural rights, 64
and nature of man, 62

768

one-party system, 227
and the people, 87
and political modernization, 82-83
and political participation, 87
political party system, 68
and political philosophy, 62
public opinion, 61
and social change, 64
and socialism, 80-81
and specialization, 86
stability of, 88
and technology, 88
threats to, 78-85
in underdeveloped nations, 82-83
unrealistic assumptions of, 85-88
and values, 75
Democracy and the American Party System, 252n, 253n
Democracy in America, 25n, 26n, 137n, 447n, 488n, 500n
Democracy in the United States, 85n
Democracy, Liberty and Property, 601n
Democratic creed, 66
in practice, 547
Democratic egalitarianism, 27
Democratic government, and democratic theory, 67
Democratic ideology
and American Creed, 78
as unnecessary, 77
Democratic institutions, evaluation, 68
Democratic Manual for the Democratic National Convention, 234n
Democratic political theory, (see also Democracy), 61-65
in action, 64-65
and equality, 62
and government, 67
and humanitarianism, 62-63
and individualism, 63
majority rule, 64, 67
minority rights, 65
and social progress, 63
Democratic system, and consensus, 77
Demonstration Cities and Metropolitan Act of 1966, 174
Dennis v. U.S., 68n, 565, 565n
Deportation proceedings, 561
Deputy Attorney General, 490, 518
de Roos, Robert, 372n

Desegregation (see also Individual rights and liberties, Race, Supreme Court), Brown v. Board of Education, 150
de Sola Pool, Ithiel, 268n, 340n, 346n, 378n, 692n
de Tocqueville, Alexis, 25, 27, 137, 488, 488n, 493, 500, 500n
Deutsch, Karl W., 96n, 214, 214n
Dewey, John, 24
Dexter, Lewis Anthony, 268n, 340n, 346n, 352n, 378n, 692n
Dictatorship:
degree of stability, 88
identification of, 66
Dictionary of the Social Sciences, A, 220n
Dietze, Gottfried, 528n
"Differential effects" (see also Outputs), 13
Dimensions of Freedom: An Analysis, 67n
Dimock, Marshall, 605, 605n
Diplomatic History of the United States, A, 653n
Diplomatic service (see also Civil service, Decision-makers, Foreign policy), influence in foreign policy, 664
Diplomats, Scientists, and Politicians, 665n
Direct primary (see also Elections, Electoral system, Nominations, Political parties), 301, 302
"Discharge petition," 358
District Courts of the United States, 516-517
Doctrine of Responsible Party Government, The, 252n
Domestic Sources of Foreign Policy, 657n
Doro, Marion E., 539n
Douglas, William O., 496n, 509n
Downs, Anthony, 228n, 242n
Dred Scott Case, 526, 551, 610
Dred Scott v. Sandford, 526n, 610n
Dual citizenship, 552
Due process of law (see also Individual rights and liberties), and need for counsel, 582
Dupeux, Georges, 230n
Duverger, Maurice, 230n, 231n, 232n, 237, 237n, 238n

Dynamics of th[e] [...]dency, [...]
Dynamics of B[...], 484n
Dysfunctions, 14

Eagleton, Clyde, 655n
Easton, David, 6n, 8n, 10n, 12n, 182n
Economic Concentration, 615n
Economic Interpretation of the Constitution of the United States, An, 48 48n, 107, 107n
Economic Origin of Jeffersonian Democracy, 230n
Economic Theory of Democracy, An, 228n
Economic Theory of Government, An, 242n
Economics (see also Interest groups, Pressure groups), and politics, 48-58
Edwards v. California, 554
Effects of Mass Communication, The, 199n
Eighteenth Amendment, adoption and content, 132
Eighth Amendment, adoption and content, 126
Eisenhower, Dwight D., 385n, 523n
Elazar, Daniel J., 142 142n, 143, 147n, 148n, 161n
Eldersveld, Samuel J., 222n, 223n, 315n
Electing the President, 394n
Elections (see also Campaigns, Electoral system, Nominations, Political parties, Voting):
and Congress, 240
and Constitution, 239
and electoral change, 322
and electoral continuity, 322
functional definition, 303
listing of candidates, 320
mechanics, 320-322
and nominations, 300
party change type, 322
party continuity type, 322
political purpose, 250
and President, 290
and pressure groups, 271
secret ballot, 320
types of, 322-324
Elections and the Political Order, 205n, 230n, 242n, 248n, 346n, 352n

769

Electoral College (see also Elections, Electoral system):
and conventions, 305
inequities of, 395
legal position, 292
origins, 121-122
political parties, 130
and President, 292, 394-395
and Vice-President, 292
and Twelfth Amendment, 129
Electoral Process, The, 195n, 213n
Electoral system (see also Campaigns, Elections, Political parties, Voting):
consequences of, 326
effects on party system, 230-232
identification of interests, 325
political parties, 232
Elements of Judicial Strategy, 526n
Eleventh Amendment, adoption and content, 128-129
Eligibility for office, 290
Elite theory, applicability to U.S., 264
Elliott, William J., 449n
Elman, Philip, 511n
Elmore v. Rice, 295n
Employment Act of 1946, 53
Enabling Act, 149
Enduring Federalist, The, 341n
Engel v. Vitale, 531n, 537n, 575n
Engineering of Consent, The, 280n
Enker, Arnold, 520n
Epstein, Leon J., 193n
Equal Protection Clause, 157
Equal Time: The Private Broadcasters and the Public Interest, 198n
Equality:
democratic theory, 62
majoritarianism, 64
social character, 27
and society, 27
status uncertainty, 27-29
Escape from Freedom, 84, 84n
Essays in the Public Philosophy, 64n
Essays on the American Constitution, 528n, 588n
Essays on Government, 382n
Ethnic groups, political opinions of, 193-195
Ethnocentrism, 29-32
Eulau, Heinz, 21n, 501, 501n
Evans, Rowland, 393n
Everson v. Board of Education, 575n
Ewing, Cortez A. M., 303n
Ex post facto law, 122
Extradition, 153

Factional politics, and voter turnout, 226
Facts about Government Work and Workers, 463n
Facts and Figures on Government Finance, 164n
Fainsod, Merle, 492n, 672n
Familiar Exposition of the Constitution of the United States, A, 574n
Family influence (see also Political socialization, Socialization):
and attitudes, 184
erosion of, 185
party identification, 183
political preferences, 182
socialization, 182
Farrand, Max, 108n, 230n
Farrell, R. Barry, 657n
"Favorite son" candidates, 310
Federal courts:
judges, 514
law, kinds of, 499
selection of judges, 503
Federal government, 137n
Federalism:
background, 139
concepts, 137-146
and Constitution, 137, 138, 146-160, 158
Constitutional Convention of 1787, 138, 140
cooperative federalism, 143
creative federalism, 144n, 160-174
definition, 137-138
dual federalism, 142
dysfunctional, 144
and Framing Fathers, 138
function of, 137-138
functional approach, 160
functional federalism, 144
and interstate disputes, 155
"manifest destiny," 142
models, 161
and national government, 142
national power and states' rights, 157-158
and national supremacy, 142
New Deal version, 144
operation, 137, 151
and political parties, 149
regional variations, 145
and Senate, 144
and state conflict, 156
and state sovereignty, 142
utility, 140
in various nations, 137
Federalism and the Nations of Africa, 138n
Federal law, as statutory law, 498-499
Federal Register, 479

Federal Regulation of Lobbying Act of 1946, 277
Federal-State Joint Action Committee, 162, 162n
Federal system:
"nationalization," 166
and pressure groups, 265
Feedback, in political system, 13
Fellman, David, 520n
Fenno, Richard, 20, 21, 291n, 347n, 360n, 364n, 376n, 449n, 468n
Ferguson, Harvey, 258n
Fifteenth Amendment (1870):
adoption and content, 130
white primaries, 294
Fifth Amendment:
adoption and content, 126
freedoms under, 548-549, 561-562
Filibuster, 358
First Amendment:
adoption and content, 126
and freedom of expression, 570
freedoms under, 548-549, 561-562
and religion, 575
and Sedition Act of 1798, 127
First Continental Congress, 95
First Hand Account, 423
First New Nation, The, 115n
Fiske, John, 99n
Fletcher v. Peck, 609, 609n
Foreign affairs:
and Constitution, 676
and national supremacy, 679-680
and President's role, 680-682
role in policy-making, 686
Foreign aid, and Congress, 687
Foreign Assistance Act of 1966, 691n
Foreign Assistance Act of 1967, 661n
Foreign policy:
aims, 676
analytical approach, 656
approaches to decision-making, 653-658
broad outlines of, 704
and China, 663-664
the Cold War, 656, 662, 670, 669-672
and communication, 695
conduct of, 665
Congress' role, 702-703
continuity and consistency, 703-704
decision- and opinion-makers, 691-692, 695
definition, 654
diplomat's role, 688
disarmament, 709
domestic politics, 682-687

770

INDEX

ethnocentrism, 32
external environment, 672
and federalism, 677-680
foreign aid, 687
and group dynamics, 700
hierarchy, 700-702
idealists v. realists, 655
ideology, 673-675
influences on, 686
institutional approach, 697-702
interest groups, 689-692
limits, 673
mutual security agreements, 706-707
national purpose, 675
and new nations, 662
normative approach, 655
nuclear strategy, 665
partisan politics in, 683-685
policy process, 695, 700
power relations, 662
pressure groups, 687-692
public opinion, 692-696
as rational, 604
role of personal relations, 685
structural approach, 654
traditional approach, 653-654
the United Nations, 666-669
Viet Nam, 706-708
Foreign Policy Decision Making, 657n
Foreign service, 484-485
Forrester, Ray, 126, 126n
Fosdick, Dorothy, 693, 693n
Fourteenth Amendment, 157
  adoption, 127
  "equal protection of law," 585
  reapportionment, 353
  Supreme Court, 510
Fourth Amendment:
  adoption and content, 126
  freedoms under, 548-549
Framework for Political Analysis, A, 8n
Frank, Elke, 260n, 332n, 440n
Frank, Jerome, 496, 534
Franklin, Benjamin, 92
Franklin (Albany) Plan, 92
Franklin, Julian H., 25n
Free Government in the Making: Readings in American Political Thought, 43n
Freedman v. Maryland, 570n
Freedom, rejection of, 84-85
Freedom and the Court, 570n
Freedom and Culture, 72n
Freedom and Responsibility in the American Way of Life, 31n

Freedom Ride, The, 570n
Freund, Paul, 138n, 527n
Friedrich, Carl J., 7, 8n, 86n, 89n, 335n, 439n, 442n, 532, 532n
From Construction Construed and Constitutions Vindicated, 601n
From Max Weber: Essays in Sociology, 4n, 439n
Froman, Lewis A., Jr., 340n, 341, 342n, 343, 356n, 360n, 361n, 375n
Fromm, Erich, 84
Fuchs, Lawrence E., 193n, 202n
"Full faith and credit," 152
Functions:
  basic output functions of political system:
    definition, 14
    identification of interests, 16-17
    and law, 14
    and motives, 14
    and political socialization, 15
    and purposes, 14
    selection of leaders, 16-17
  functional opinions, role of, 179
Future of American Politics, The, 240n

Galbraith, John Kenneth, 53, 612n
Galloway, George B., 358n, 377n
Garner v. Board of Public Works, 464n
Gaudet, Hazel, 311n
General Accounting Office, 477, 478
General welfare (see also Policy-making):
  Founding Fathers' concept of, 641-642
  idea, 597
  and decision-makers, 630-631
Genius of American Politics, The, 89n
Gerth, H. H., 4n, 439n
Geographic determinism, 32
Geography, and American political tradition, 30-32
Gerraty, John A., 535n
Gibbons v. Ogden, 549n, 609, 609n
Gideon's Trumpet, 580n
Gideon v. Wainwright, 534, 534n, 580-581, 580n

Girouard v. United States, 558n
Gitlin, Todd, 263n
Gitlow v. New York, 562n
Glazer, Nathan, 195n
Glenn, Norral D., 192n
Goals for Americans, 161n, 675n
Goldman, Sheldon, 504n
Goldwater, Barry M., 324n
Goldwin, Robert A., 158n
Golembouski, Robert T., 225n
Goodman, Ralph M., 305n
Gorer, Geoffrey, 41n
Gottmann, Jean, 120n
Gould, J., 220n
"Governance":
  and American government, 9
  and politics, 5
Government (see also National government, Political system, Politics):
  and big business, 50-53, 618-619
  and churches, 574
  and conflicts, 600
  definition of, 5-6, 5n
  in the economy, 53-54, 643-645
  and group interests, 5
  models, 69
  and politics, 6
  and political parties, 222
  and political system, 6
  and population shifts, 37
  responsibility, 252
  and rights, 5
  and society, 631-632
  and succession, 219-220
  types of, 66-67
  and urbanization, 39
Government and Private Enterprise, 470n
Government and the Economy, 614n
Government corporations, 455
Government expenditures:
  and business, 627-628
  and Economic Opportunity Act, 628
  growth of, 164-169
  and inflation, 164
  military, 166-167
  and national security, 627
Governmental Process, The, 219n, 221n, 255n, 256n, 259n, 276n
Graebner, Norman, 654n
Grants in aid, 637
Grass, Bertram M., 372n, 374n
Graves v. New York ex rel O'Keefe, 531n

771

"Great Society":
  factor in the war on poverty, 638
  opposition in Congress, 640-641
Greek city-state, 66
Greenstein, Fred I., 182n, 183, 183n, 210, 210n
Grigg, Charles, M., 76n, 77n, 567n
Grisham v. Hagan, 584n
Grodzins, Martin, 161
Grossman, Joel, 505n, 513n
Gross national product (GNP), 165
Group Differences in Attitudes and Votes, 194n, 297n
Group Dynamics, 201n
Groups (see Interest groups)
Grumm, John G., 231
Gulf of Tonkin Resolution, The, 681
Gunther, John, 40
Gurin, Gerald, 203n

Habeus corpus, writ of, 551
Hacker, Andrew, 338, 338n, 340n
Hamilton, Alexander, 510n
Hamilton v. Kentucky Distilleries and Wine Co., 603n
Hamilton, Walton, 600, 600n
Hammer v. Dagenhart, 617n
Hampton and Co. v. U.S., 419n
Handbook of Social Psychology, 25n
Harper, Ida Husted, 297n
Harper v. Virginia State Board of Elections, 299n, 550n, 522n
Harrington, Michael, 54, 54n, 628, 628n
Harris, Joseph P., 221n, 302n, 469n, 476n
Harris, Louis, 247n, 595
Hartz, Louis, 27n, 113, 113n
Haskins, Caryl, 662n
Heady, Terrel, 442
Health, Education and Welfare Indicators, 56n
Heart of Atlanta Motel, Inc. v. U.S., 603n
Heidenheimer, Arnold J., 490n
Heifetz, Joan, 365n
Henry, Laurin, 397n
Hepburn v. Griswold, 643n
Herring, Pendleton, 252
Hess, Robert D., 182n
Hidden Face of Free Enterprise, The, 599n
Hilsman, Roger, 468n, 469n, 473n, 663, 664n
History of Woman Suffrage, The, 297n

Hitchman Coal and Coke Co. v. Mitchell, 353n
Hoffmann, Paul J., 239n
Hofstadter, Richard, 93n
Holmes, Oliver Wendell, Justice, 496
Holtzman, Abraham, 233n
House of Representatives (see also Congress):
  committees, 367
  "discharge petition," 358
  leadership of, 359-361
  original concept of, 350-351
  "previous question," 358
  primaries, 301
  professionalization, 352
  rules of procedure, 355-358
  and states' rights, 146
  twenty-one day rule, 357
How Nations See Each Other, 186n
How Russia Is Ruled, 492n
How to Cut Paperwork, 485n
Hughes, Emmet John, 423n
Huitt, Ralph K., 260n, 332, 332n, 333, 333n, 335, 349, 350n, 361n, 362n, 369n, 375n, 377n
Humanitarianism, and democratic theory, 62-63
Human Nature in Politics: The Dynamics of Political Behavior, 211n
Humphrey's Executor v. U.S., 414n
Hunter, Floyd, 256n
Huntington, Samuel P., 334n, 335, 340n, 362n, 378n
Hyman, Herbert H., 16n, 72n, 183n, 188n, 203n
Hyman, Sidney, 313n

Ideals in democracy, 61-64
Ideas and Diplomacy, 654n
Ideas and Issues in Public Administration, 454n
Identification of interests, function, 68
Ideology:
  in America, 212-213
  and decision-makers, 278
  of public, 76-77
Ideology and Discontent, 76n, 212n, 326n
If Men Were Angels, 496n
Illinois ex rel McCollum v. Board of Education, 575n
Illinois Politics, 221n
Image of the Federal Service, The, 445, 459n
Immigrants, 555-557
  political habits of, 40-41
  status insecurity of, 42

Immigration:
  background, 555-556
  and Congress, 555-556n
  and economics and politics, 556
  "national origins" policy, 555-556
Immigration and Nationality Act (1965), 556, 557n
Impact of Negro Voting, The, 214n
In Congress Assembled, 367n
Income-tax system:
  and effects, 56, 141
  Sixteenth Amendment, 56, 141
Independent regulatory commissions, 469-471
Individual achievement, 29
Individualism:
  and democracy, 87
  and democratic theory, 63
  and majoritarianism, 64
Individual rights and liberties (see also Civil rights, Constitutional law, Judiciary):
  and general welfare, 63
  and government, 5
  and institutions, 98
Informal opinion leaders, 201
In forma pauperis, 580n
Inkeles, Alex, 17n, 25n, 177n
Inputs (see also Outputs, Political parties, Political system):
  apathy, 11-12
  and decision-making agencies, 12
  definition of, 10
  as demands, 10
  effects, 12
  and electoral system, 68
  and political parties, 68
  and political socialization, 16
  and political system 10-12
  as supports, 10-11
Inside U.S.A., 40, 40n
Institutions:
  and democracy, 79, 80
  and government, 67
  and individual liberties, 98
Integration of Political Communities, The, 96n
Interest groups (see also Decision-makers, Inputs, Political parties):
  as defined by membership, 219
  and influence on policy, 5, 87
  and political power, 255
  and rationality, 85
  and regulatory politics, 261-262
  as shapers of opinion, 219
  sources of, 258

772

INDEX

Interest Groups in American Society, 257n, 278n
Internal Security Act of 1950, 561
International Government, 655n
International Organization, 655n
International Politics and Foreign Policy, 657n
International relations (see also Foreign policy), role of competing ideologies, 674-676
Interposition, 150, 151
Interstate compacts, 153-154
Interstate Compacts in the Political Process, 153n
Interstate Co-operation: A Study of the Interstate Compact, 153n
Interstate disputes, Supreme Court rulings, problem of enforcement, 155
Introduction to the Study of Public Administration, 463n
Irish, Marian D., 423n, 448n, 648n, 672, 693n
Irony of American History, The, 31n
Is Anybody Listening?, 271n
Isolationism, 32
Issue orientation, 202-203
Issues of National Security in the 1970's, 665n
Is There a Republican Majority?, 247n

Jackson, Robert A., 511n, 531n
Jacob, Herbert, 238n
Jacob, Philip E., 96n
Jacobellis v. Ohio, 568n, 569n, 569
Jacobson, Harold Karan, 665n
Jay, John, and Constitution, 139
Jennings, M. Kent, 195n, 213n, 445n, 459n
Jensen, Merril, 99n
Jewell, Malcolm E., 354n
Johnson, Donald Bruce, 402n
Joiner, Charles W., 517n
Joint Anti-Fascist Refugee Committee v. Magrath, 495n
Jones, Charles O., 362n, 376n
Jones, George H., 154n
Jones, Harry W., 492n, 514, 514n, 515, 533n
Jordan, Amos P., Jr., 665n
Judges:
American Bar Association, 504-505
appointment of, 503
and patronage, 503-504
popular election (states), 489
qualifications and selection of, federal, 503-505
recruitment of, 489
roles of, 510-515
selection of, pressures on the, 503
and senatorial courtesy, 489, 503
Judicial activism, and the Warren court, 513
Judicial decision-making:
apathy, 528
inputs, 527
settlement of disputes, 533
Judicial norms, 488
Judicial opinions, 536
Judicial power, 509
Judicial restraint, and the Barnette Case (1943), 511-512
Judicial review, 523-525 (see also Judiciary, Law, Supreme Court):
and Congress, 510-511
and Constitution, 439, 524
definition, 524
Judiciary (see also Federal courts, Judicial review, Law, Supreme Court):
administration of justice, 533-535
and Congress, 369-371, 510-511
and constitutionality, 524
educational function, 491
function of communication, 535
function of settling disputes, 532
and group pressure, 528
independence of, 510, 537
injunction power, 617
and judicial restraint, 511-512
judicial review, 493
legislative function, 502, 538
and policy-making, 369, 370, 494, 513, 514
Justices, social and political background, 502

Kahl, Joseph A., 44n
Kaplan, Abraham, 6n
Katz, Daniel, 75n, 315n, 78n, 201n
Katzenbach v. McClung, 605n
Keech, William R., 18n, 214n

Kelly, Stanley, 279, 280, 286
Kendall, Willmoore, 252n
Kennedy, John F., 403n, 407n, 475n, 484n
Kennedy v. Mendoza, 560n
Key, V. O., Jr., 5, 28, 28n, 29n, 30, 33n, 77, 77n, 85, 85n, 131n, 191, 198n, 178n, 215n, 220n, 225n, 226, 227, 223n, 297n, 302n, 304n, 305, 322n, 326, 396n
Keyishian v. Board of Regents of New York, 572n
Kilpatrick, Franklin P., 445, 459n
Kilpatrick, James Jackson, 158n
Kinsella v. U.S. ex rel Singleton, 584n
Kissinger, Henry A., 649, 649n, 656n
Klapper, Joseph J., 199n
Kluckhohn, Clyde, 24n, 49
Koenig, Louis, 397n, 434n
Kohler, Foy D., 672n
Kolb, W. L., 220n
Kolko, Gabriel, 54n
Kort, Fred, 513n
Kraft, Joseph, 173n
Krislov, Samuel, 513n, 528

Labor movement:
history and ideology, 616-617
pressure groups and decision-makers, 619-620
role in economic policy, 615-620
Laissez faire, 50-51, 63
"Lame Duck Amendment," 131
Lane, Robert E., 45n, 181, 181n, 185n, 201n, 211n, 259n
Lang, G. E., 313n
Lang, K., 313n
LaPalombara, Joseph, 96n, 442
Laski, Harold, 373n, 393n
Lasswell, H. D., 4n, 6n, 388n
Last Hurrah, The, 240, 241n
Latent functions, 14n
Latham, Earl, 258n
Law (see also Federal courts, Judiciary, State courts, Supreme Court):
and lawyers and judges, 500
and "legal realists," 495-496
sociological school of, 495
stare decisis, 489
views of, 494-497
Law and Contemporary Problems, 572n
Law and Man, Of, 511n

773

Law and One Man among Many, The, 495n
Law and the Modern Mind, 496n
Law of Nations, The, 668n
Lawmakers in a Changing World, 260n, 332n, 333n, 396n
Lawyers, 501
Lawyers and Judges, 505n
Lawyers in Politics, 501n
Lazarsfeld, Paul F., 86n, 185n, 201n, 202n, 203n, 204n, 251n, 311n
Lazerwitz, Bernard, 247
Leach, Richard H., 153n
Leadership selection:
 and interest groups, 17
 and party systems, 68
Lectures on Jurisprudence, 495n
Legislation (see also Decision-makers, Policy-making, Politics):
 defined, 331
 initiation of, 335
 recruitment of legislators, 337-345
Legislative Procedure, 360n
Legislative Process, The, 365n, 377n
Legislative Process in Congress, The, 358n
Legislative Reorganization Act of 1946, 277n
Legislative Struggle: A study in Social Combat, The, 372n, 374n
Legislative System: Explanations in Legislative Behavior, The, 291n
Leiserson, Avery, 232n, 369n
Leppre, Mary K., 690n
Levin, Jack, 348n
Levinson, Daniel J., 25n
Lewis, Anthony, 580n
Liberal-conservative continuum, and voters, 212
Liberal Tradition in America, The, 27n, 113, 113n
Liberalism:
 examined, 187
 and voters, 212
Liberty, 80-81
Limits of Power, The, 708n
Linton, Ralph, 24n
Lippmann, Walter, 24, 24n, 64n, 95, 180
Lipset, S. M., 26n, 115, 128, 251n
Lobbying (see also Interest groups, Policy-making, Pressure groups):
 and Congress, 267, 272
 Congressional investigations, 626
 effects and importance of, 628-630
 personal backgrounds of lobbyists, 267-268
 and policy-making, 275
 role of pressure groups, 272
 and Senate, 278
Local interests:
 local machines and party power, 236-237
 and office holders, 251
Lochner v. New York, 599n, 607
Locke, John, 73, 97n, 546
"Log rolling" theory, 255
The Logic of Democracy, 61n
Lonely Crowd, The, 84n
Long, Norton, 484n
Lowell, A. Lawrence, 179n
Lowenthal, L., 26n
Lowi, Theodore J., 255n, 260, 261n, 268n
Lubell, Samuel, 212, 240n
Luce, Robert, 360n
Luther v. Borden, 156n
Lyndon B. Johnson: The Exercise of Power, 393n

Maas, Arthur A., 372n
Maccoby, Eleanor E., 184n, 191n
Machiavelli, 177
MacIver, Robert, 495
Madison, James, 123
Mailick, Sidney, 484n
Main Currents in American Thought, 73n
Majoritarianism (see also Democracy, Majority rule, Minority rights):
 and democratic theory, 64
 and equality, 64
 and individualism, 64-65
 majority control, 30, 68
 majority decisions, 65
 majority interests, 272
 minority rights, 65
Majority and minority leader, in Senate, 361-362
Majority Leader in House, 360
Majority rule, (see also Democracy, Majoritarianisn, Minority rights):
 and communism, 81-82
 and conflict, 65
 consensus, 30, 76
 and Declaration of Independence, 65
 democratic theory of, 64, 66-67, 79
 free enterprise, 80-81
 minority rights, 64, 70
Majority Rule and Minority Rights, 64n
Majority Whip of House, 360
Making of Justice, The Supreme Court in Action, The, 107, 108n, 507n, 537n
Making of United States Foreign Policy, The, 654n
Malloy v. Hogan, 581n
Man and His Government: An Empirical Theory of Politics, 7n, 442n, 532n
Man-Milieu Relationships in the Context of International Politics, 657n
Manager Economy, The, 52n
"Manifest destiny," 142
Manifest functions, 14n
Manis, Jerome G., 247n
Mapp v. Ohio, 580n
Marbury v. Madison (1803), 496, 521, 524n, 535n, 549n, 609, 609n
Martin, Curtis, 221n
Martin v. Hunter's Lessee, 678n
Martineau, Harriet, 26, 26n, 28
Marxism, 26, 27, 63, 83
Maryland Senatorial Election of 1950, 281n
Mason, Alpheus Thomas, 43n
Mass media (see also Communications):
 criticisms, 198-200
 informal leaders, 201
 and national affairs, 145
 opinion leaders, 201
 political opinions concerning, 200
 public affairs, 198
 and socialization, 196-200
Mass participation, 82
Masters, Nicholas A., 193n, 363n
Matthews, Donald R., 64, 188n, 206n, 213n, 226n, 267n, 272n, 297n, 347n, 348n, 349n, 396n, 570n, 588n, 589n
May, Ernest A., 696, 696n
Mayer, Lawrence A., 661n
Mayo, Henry B., 672n, 675
McCallum, R. B., 373n
McCarran-Walters Act, 556
McCarthy, Eugene, 708n
McClosky, H., 41n, 181, 181n, 185n, 238, 239, 567n
McClosky, Robert, 539, 539n, 540
McConnell, Grant, 255n, 341n
McCrone, Donald J., 375n
McCulloch v. Maryland (1819), 128, 128n, 158, 159-160, 549n, 552n, 609, 609n
McDonald, Forrest, 108, 108n
McElroy v. U.S. ex rel Guagliardo, 584n
McGrain v. Daughtery, 373n

INDEX

McLaughlin, A. C., 99n
McLaurin v. Oklahoma State Regents, 586n
McPee, Willam N., 86n, 185n, 202n, 203n, 204n
Mead, George Herbert, 291n
Means, Gardiner C., 50n, 51
Megaloplis, 170n
Memoirs, 396n, 401n, 405n, 418n, 449n, 645n
Mendelson, Wallace, 497n
Merton, Robert K., 14n, 20, 304n
Metropolitan America: Challenge to Federalism, 170n, 173n
Milbrath, Lester W., 206, 207n, 237n, 238n, 267n, 275, 275n
Mill, John Stuart, 562
Miller, Warren E., 203n, 205n, 215n, 239n, 327, 346n, 352n
Miller, William Lee, 93n, 315n
Miller v. United States, 578n
Mills, C. W., 4n, 256n, 439n
Milton, John, 546
Mind, Self and Society, 291n
Minority rights (see also Democracy, Majoritarianism, Majority rule):
 and consensus, 76
 and Constitution, 65
 and democratic theory, 64-67, 79
 and majority rule, 64, 65, 70
 and policy control, 13
Minow, Newton, 198n
Miranda v. Arizona, 581-582
Mirror for Man: The Relation of Anthropology to Modern Life, 24n, 27n, 49n
Missouri ex rel Gaines v. Canada, 586, 586n
Missouri v. Holland, 678
Mobility, and attitude change, 33
Mobilization of bias, 276
Modern Corporation and Private Property, The, 50n, 51
Modern Democracies, 418
Modern Political Analysis, 387n, 666n
Modern Political Parties: Approaches to Comparative Politics, 224n, 249n
Montgomery, John D., 649n
Moon, Henry Lee, 295n
Moos, Malcolm, 303n
Morgan, Donald G., 564n
Morgenthau, Hans, J., 655, 656n, 674

Morison, Samuel Eliot, 93, 93n
Morris, Arval A., 572n
Mosher, Frederick C., 165n
Moynihan, Patrick, 195n
Muller v. Oregon, 539n, 607n
Multi-party system, 230
Munger, Frank, 33n
Munn v. Illinois, 606, 607n, 610
Murphy, Walter F., 513n, 526n
Musalf, Lloyd D., 614n
Myers v. United States, 414, 414n
Myrdal, Gunnar, 71, 72

Nation-building, (see also American nation, Constitution):
 and American Federalism, 138
 and communication, 143
 crisis of common identity, 94-95
 crisis of distribution, 103
 crisis of integration, 95-102
 crisis of participation, 102-103
 crisis of penetration, 102
 and legitimacy, 96
 model of, 96
 and transportation, 143
 and U.S. Constitution, 96
Nation of States, A, 158n
National character (see also American character, Political attitudes, Public opinion):
 components, 28, 29n
 definition, 25
 social character, 30
National conventions (see also Nominations, Political parties):
 principal functions, 304
 procedures, 309-311
National defense:
 and budget, 644-645
 and Constitution, 650
 and "new industrial state," 646-650
 and research, 647
National government (see also Political system, Politics):
 expanded powers, 443
 federalism, 142
 grant-in-aid-programs, 168
 grants to states, 164
 obligations to states, 156
 regulatory activities, 630
 treaty power, 677-678
 urban demands, 162-163
National income, 55

"National interest," 63
National Labor Relations Board v. Jones and Laughlin Steel Corporation, 619n
National origins, 194
National parties (see also Political parties)
National party chairman, 233
National party committees (see also Nomination, Political parties):
 and party organization, 232-233
 weaknesses of system, 234
"National power":
 and geography, 659
 and gross national product, 660-661
 and natural resources, 660
 and population and manpower, 659
 and productive capacity, 660
National security (see also Defense policy, National defense):
 policy development, 644-645
 significant factors, 658
National Security Council, 426-427
Nationalism, 145
Nationality Act of 1960, 559
Natural rights theory, 98
Naturalization:
 and "allegiance," 558
 and formal process, 558
 and present policy, 557-560
"Nature of man," and democracy, 62
Near v. Minnesota, 569n
Nebbia v. New York, 607, 608n
Necessity for Choice, The, 649, 649n, 656n
Negro and the Ballot in the South, The, 295n
Negro Politics: The Search for Leadership, 195n
Negroes and the New Southern Politics, 188n, 206n, 226n, 297n, 570n, 589n
Nelson, William H., 696n
Neumann, Sigmund, 224n
Neustadt, Richard, 4n, 361n, 402n, 411n, 421n, 484
New American Political Economy, The, 605, 605n
Newcomb, Theodore, M., 291n
New Congress, The, 342n
New Image of the Common Man, The, 86n, 89n

775

New Industrial State, The, 53n, 612n
New Nation, The, 99n
New Perspective on the House of Representatives, 347n, 356n, 376n, 378n
New York Central Railroad Company v. White, 499n
Niebuhr, Reinhold, 31
1963-1964 American Government Annual, 448n
1967 Commission on Civil Rights Report: Voting, 295n
Nineteenth Amendment, 130, 550
Ninth Amendment, 126
Nixon, Raymond B., 199
Nolle pros, 520
Nomination (see also Conventions, Elections, Leadership selection, Voting):
  Conventions, 304, 309-311
  direct primary, 301
  effect on Presidency, 306
  "favorite son" candidates, 310
  legislative caucus, 301
  and one-party system, 303
  and President, 300
  state regulation, 300
  and Vice-Presidential candidate, 310-311
"No-party system," 226
Norms, 347-348
Norris-La Guardia Act of 1932, 353, 616
North, Barbara and Robert, 230n
Notes on the Convention, 123
Novak, Robert, 39n
Nuclear Test Ban Treaty: Demands and Supports, The, 690n
Nuclear Weapons and Foreign Policy, 656n

Object appraisal:
  definition of, 180
  and party labels, 180
Occupational status (see also Class), misidentifiers, 187
O'Connor, Edwin, 241n
Office of Economic Opportunity, 640-641
Office of Emergency Planning, 427
Office of Science and Technology, 427-428
Official agencies (see Bureaucracy, Congress, Executive agencies, Judges, Judicial system, Judiciary, Political parties, Political system, President)

Ogden, Frederic A., 131n
O'Hara, Rosemary, 239n
Oligarchy, 66
Olsen v. Nebraska, 608
On Liberty, 562
On Liberty and Considerations on Representative Government, 373n
On Understanding the Supreme Court, 527n
"One man, one vote" doctrine, 353
One-party politics:
  anti-majoritarianism, 227
  and the public, 227
  under a two-party system, 225-227
Open primary, 301
Opinion (see also Public opinion):
  basic functions of, 179-181
  culture and formation, 24-25
  and environment, 179
  input functions of, 215
  and reference groups, 180-181
Opinions and Personality, 178n, 180n
Opinion surveys, 29 (see also Opinion, Public opinion)
Oppenheim, Felix E., 67n
Ordeal of Power, The, 423n
Organization and power, 258
Organizing for National Security, 425n, 427n, 475n
Original jurisdiction, 509
Other America, The, 54, 54n, 628n
Otis, James, 48, 48n
Our Business Civilization, 48n
Our Chief Magistrate and His Powers, 400n
Outputs (see also Congress, Executive agencies, Inputs, Judiciary, Policy-making, Political system, Supreme Court):
  consequences of, 12-13
  deprivations of, 12-13
  and political socialization, 16
  and rewards, 12-13
Overlapping membership (see also Pressure groups, Interest groups):
  and cohesion, 268
  definition and consequences, 276
Oxford History of the American People, The, 93n, 120n

Packard, Vance, 25-26, 26n
Pacta sunt servanda, 687
Palko v. Connecticut, 579
Panama Refining Co. v. Ryan, 419n

Parrington, Vernon L., 73, 73n
Parties and Politics in America, 223n
Party and Policy-Making, 362n
Party Committees and National Politics, 234n
Party Government, 231n
Party Identification (see also Political parties, Political socialization):
  and congressional voting, 328, 342
  and political socialization, 204
  relation to political influence, 203-205
  and voting, 204-205
Paterson Plan, 111-112
Patterns of Culture, 24n
Peabody, R. L., 347n, 356n, 376n, 378n
Peltason, Jack W., 448n
Pendleton Act, 458
Pennock, J. Roland, 252n
People and the Court, The, 538n
People and Power: A Study of Political Behavior in America, 258n, 276n
People's Choice, The, 311n, 316n
Perception and socialization, 24
Perez v. Brownell, 559n
Personal Influence, 201n
Phillpotts, Eden, 49n
Pierce v. Society of the Sisters of Holy Names of Jesus and Mary, 575n
Plamenatz, John, 78
Planning for Peace, 710n
Plessy v. Ferguson, 150n, 595-586, 586n
Plischke, Elmer, 654n
Pluralism, 138
Pluralist Democracy in the United States, 98n, 434n, 620n
Plurality election, 231-232
Pointer v. Texas, 581n
Poland, Orville F., 165n
Policy-making (see also Bureaucracy, Congress, Decision-makers, Executive agencies, Foreign policy, Judiciary, Political parties, Supreme Court):
  and change, 605
  and Congress, 362, 366-369
  distributive arena, 260
  environment of, 390
  and group theory, 261
  judicial review, 338
  log-rolling theory, 261
  and minority groups, 496
  outputs and policies, 261
  and political executives, 472
  power-elite theory, 262
  redistributive arena, 260

776

regulatory arena, 260
and separation of powers, 431
and social security, 633-637
Political activity, 45
Political attitudes (see also
   Opinions, Political parties,
   Political socialization):
   acquisition of, 16
   and national character, 28, 29n
   status uncertainty and individual achievement, 29
Political behavior and class, 44
Political Behavior of American Jews, The, 193n, 202n
Political Behavioralism and Modern Jurisprudence, 497n
Political "bosses," 240-242
Political Community and the North Atlantic Area, 241n
Political decision-making (see Decision-makers, Policy-making, Political parties, Political system)
Political development, 94-104
Political environment (see also Culture, Political system, Socialization, Supreme Court):
   and homogeneity, 201
   operation of, 202
   and pressure groups, 264-265
   and public policies, 545
"Political gladiators," 238
Political Ideology, 241n
Political influences (see also Culture, Political environment, Political socialization, Political system):
   candidate orientation, 203-204
   issue orientation, 202-203
   party identification, 181, 203-205
Political leadership:
   and class, 44-46
   and political system, 9
   roll dispensability, 45
   and social status, 47
Political Life: How People Get Involved in Politics, 259n
Political Life: Why People Get Involved in Politics, 45n
Political Man, 251n
Political opinions (see also Congressmen, Family, Mass media, Opinions, Political parties, Political socialization, Pressure groups, Voting):
   and class, 186
   demand function of, 216

and electoral system, 214
functions of, 214-216
and national origin, 194
nature of, 177-182
permissive function of, 215
and personality, 179
and race, 194
and religion, 193-194
and residence, 192
sources of, 181-182
supportive function of, 216
Political Opposition in Western Democracies, 228n, 230n, 248n, 289n
Political participation (see also American creed, Congress, Constitution, Decision-making, Elections, Foreign policy, Majoritarianism, Political opinions, Pressure groups, Voting):
   and campaigns, 319-320
   and class, 45, 209
   definition of, 206
   and democracy, 87
   forces acting on, 207
   forms of, 206-207
   hierarchy of, 206-208
   in primaries, 302
   relation to political system, 210-212
   role definition of citizens, 208-210
   stability in, 206
   structural factors involved, 208
   and voting, 205
Political Participation, 207n, 209n
Political parties (see also Bureaucracy, Congress, Constitution, Democracy, Political system):
   attitudes, 204
   bias of system, 251
   campaigns, 235
   and choice, 222
   city committees, 235
   cohesion of, 69
   committee on resolutions, 310
   conferences, 362
   conflict in, 223, 249
   congressional campaign committees, 234, 235
   constituency, 343
   and Constitution, 220
   conventions, 304-306
   county committees, 235
   criticisms, 248-251
   decision-making, 224

and democracy, 68
development of doctrines, 242-244, 250-251
direct primary, 302
electoral bases, 246-248
electoral college, 130
electoral system, 68, 230-232
and federalism, 149
functions of, 68, 222-224, 242
input functions, 68
and governments, 222
and groups, 220
identification of basic interests, 68
labels, effect of, 204
leadership selection, 68
local machines, 236-237
majoritarianism, 224
members, 221, 237-238
methods, 221-222
national chairman, 233
national committee, 232-233
object appraisal, 223
party organization, 232-235, 238
policy orientations, 238-239
political identity, 181
political system, 222-223
and power, 221
and preference, stability of, 604-605
and President, 303-304, 416
pressure groups, 220-221, 256-257, 261-262, 275-276, 277
problem of succession, 220
and public relations, 285
purposes, 220-221
as reference groups, 181, 223
reform of, 251-253
responsibility, 250-253
senatorial campaign committees, 234-235
social bases, 244-248
state committees, 235
and Twelfth Amendment, 129-130
two-party v. one-party, 68
and voting turnout, 223, 314-315
Political Parties: A Behavioral Analysis, 222n, 223n, 231n, 237n, 238n
Political Parties in a New Nation, 224n
Political Parties in the American System, 222n, 232n
Political Parties: Their Organization and Activity in the Modern State, 230n

777

Political philosophy, 62
Political power:
   theories of, 255-256
      group or pluralistic theory, 255
      log-rolling theory, 255
Political roles:
   and political systems, 291
   and power, 4
Political science, 3, 335, 336
Political socialization, 181-206 (see also Culture, Political system):
   class status, 185
   definition of, 15, 182
   effects of, 16-17, 17n
   ethnic groups, 193
   and the family, 182
   party identification, 204
   and residence, 191
   two-party system, 232
Political system (see also Civil rights, Decision-makers, Electoral system, Government, Political opinions, Political socialization, Politics, Supreme Court, System):
   appeal of, 20
   characteristics of, 8-13
   concepts of, 4
   decision-making, 291, 336
   electoral system, 291
   function of, 13-18, 332, 487
   identification of interests, 17
   inputs of, 10-12
   internal norms of, 17
   outputs, 12-16
   party activity, 222-223
   political groups, 7
   political opinions, 212-216
   political participation, 210-212
   political roles, 7, 291
   public opinion, 177
   reapportionment, 353
   selection of leaders, 17
   separation of powers, 487-488
   socialization, 16, 196
   social structure, 95
Political System: An Inquiry into the State of Political Science, The, 6n
Political values, 23, 85
Politics (see also Political system):
   and "American character," 25-30
   and class, 43
   and culture, 23-30
   definition of, 5
   and economics, 48-51, 56-57
   and ethnic groups, 194-195
   function of, 13
   and "governance," 5

   and interest, 86
   and power, 5, 219
   and religion, 194
   and "statesmanship," 5
Politics among Nations: The Struggle for Power and Peace, 655
Politics and Social Life, 352n
Politics in England, 343n
Politics of Democracy: American Parties in Action, The, 252n
Politics of Despair, The, 84n
Politics of Industry, The, 600, 600n
Politics of Modernization, The, 96n, 545, 545n
Politics of National Party Conventions, The, 305n
Politics of Reapportionment, The, 354n
Politics of the Budgetary Process, The, 424n
Politics of the Developing Areas, The, 5n, 7n, 15n, 17n, 96n
Politics, Parties and Pressure Groups, 5n, 220n, 223n, 297n, 304n, 305n, 326n
Politics, Presidents, and Coattails, 303n
Politics, Pressures and the Tariff, 255n, 269n
Poll tax, 299
Poll Tax in the South, The, 131n
Pollock v. Farmer's Loan and Trust Co., 132n, 623n
Polsby, Nelson W., 42n, 256n, 262n, 292n, 342n, 352n, 356n, 376n, 378n, 394n, 426n
Polyansky, N. N., 492n
Pomper, Gerald, 311n
Popular participation, 68, 129-132
Popular sovereignty, 98
Population mobility and growth, effects, 33-39
Posvar, Wesley W., 649n
Potter, Pitman B., 655n
Poverty, in America, 54-55
Power, 4-5, 258
Power and International Relations, 666n
Power and Personality, 4n
Power and Society: A Framework for Political Inquiry, 6n
Power at the Pentagon, 645n, 648n
Power Elite, The, 256n
Power-elite, theory of, 255-256
Power of the Purse: Appropriations Politics in Congress, The, 20n, 21n, 291n

Preface to Democratic Theory, A, 719n
Prejudices, regional differences, 32
Presidency, The, 400n
President (see also Executive agencies, Political parties, Political system, Politics):
   and bureaucracy, 474-475, 485
   and Cabinet, 413, 447-451
   characteristics of, 391-393, 395-396
   checks and balances, 385
   and Congress, 370-371, 415-420
   and constituency, 147-148
   and Constitution, 290, 387, 391, 399-400, 406
   economic program of, 420-421
   election of, 292, 306, 394-397
   and executive agreements, 406-407
   executive offices of, 422-428
   exercise of power, 434-436
   foreign policy, 405-408, 704-703
   functions of, 432-436
   impeachment of, 403
   and independent regulatory commissions, 469-471
   independent tenure of, 417-418
   institutional approach to, 387-391
   and interest groups, 413
   and international politics, 381-387
   limitations on, 436
   nomination of, 300
   patronage, 412
   personality influence, 393, 400-404
   policy-making, 370-371
   political leadership, 432-434
   positions of:
      as Chief Executive, 383, 390, 411-415, 475
      as Chief Legislator, 415-420
      as Chief of State, 382, 404-405
      as Commander-in-Chief, 409-411
      as head of government, 382
      as party leader, 416
   powers of:
      appointment, 408, 412
      execution of laws, 532
      personal influence, 402-403
      recognition of governments, 407
      removal, 414
   and public attention, 9-10
   role of, 383-384
   Senatorial courtesy, 148, 412

INDEX

succession of, 133
and Supreme Court, 403-404
transition in, 397-399
and Twelfth Amendment, 395
and Twenty-Second Amendment, 131-132, 404
and two-party system, 229-230
veto power, 418
White House staff, 422-424
President and Congress, 249n
President: Office and Powers, The, 410n, 416n
Presidential candidates, 303-304
Presidential Election and Transition, 1960-1961, The, 396n
Presidential Elections: Strategies of American Electoral Politics, 292n, 394n
Presidential Power, 4n, 361n, 402n, 411n, 421n
Presidential primaries:
 chief functions of, 307-308
 and party nomination, 307
Presidential Transitions, 397n
Presidential veto, 369
President's Cabinet, The, 449n, 468n
Press (see Mass media)
Press and Foreign Policy, The, 696, 696n
Pressure groups (see also Interest groups):
 cohesion, 268-269
 and Congress, 265
 and decision-makers, 278
 and decision-making agencies, 256
 definition of, 256-257
 and democracy, 257, 275
 doctrines of, 269
 electioneering, 271
 "fair play," 272
 federal system, 261
 and foreign policy, 687-692
 functions of, 257
 and government organization, 265
 identification of interests, 275
 leadership, 267
 leadership selection, 275
 lobbying, 272
 Medicare, 273-275
 membership, 259
 organization of, 266-267
 overlapping membership, 268
 participation, 275
 and policy systems, 260
 and political environment, 264-265

and political influence, 259
and political parties, 220-221, 256-257, 261, 275-277
propaganda, 270
purpose of, 257
reform of, 277
regulation of, 276-278
social base of, 268-269
specialization, 259
status and access, 266
tactics of, 257, 270-275
and taxes, 623-625
Price, Don K., 472n, 649, 649n, 650
Price, H. Douglas, 351n
Price, Margaret, 295n
Prince, The, 177
Primaries (see also Nominations):
 closed primary, 301
 and cross-filing, 301-302
 function of presidential, 307
 and House of Representatives, 301
 level of participation, 302
 and nominations, 303
 and "run-off" in one-party states, 303
 and Senate, 301
Primary groups (see Family, Political socialization, Pressure groups, Socialization), 200-202
Pritchett, C. Herman, 496n, 513, 513n
Private Power and American Democracy, 255n, 341n
Private property, 601-605
Privileges and immunities (see also Citizenship), 152
Problem of the Independent Regulatory Commissions, The, 454n
Process of Government, The, 528
Professional Public Relations and Political Power, 279, 279n, 280n, 282n, 284n, 286n
Profiles in Courage, 348n
Progress and democratic theory, 63-64
Prohibition amendment, 132-133
Propaganda, 282n
"Protestant ethic," 26
Protestant Ethic and the Spirit of Capitalism, The, 27n
Prothro, James W., 18n, 26n, 77n, 188n, 206n, 213n, 226n, 297, 396n, 567n, 570n, 588n, 589n

Psychology of Social Classes, The, 44n
Public administration (see Bureaucracy, Congress, Democracy, Executive agencies)
Public Administration: A Comparative Perspective, 442
Public opinion (see also Bureaucracy, Civil service, Congress, Electoral system, Foreign policy, Interest groups, Judiciary, Mass media, Political parties, Political system, President, Pressure groups, Public policy, Supreme Court):
 analyzed, 178-179
 defined, 178, 179, 206
 and democracy, 61
 and ideology, 213
 and issues, 178
 political opinion, 179
 political role of, 213
 and political system, 177
 and power, 258
 and President, 307
 public relations, 283
 and residence, 191
 and social questions, 178
Public Opinion, 24n, 183n, 185n, 191n, 198n, 201, 215n
Public Opinion and American Democracy, 28, 28n, 29n, 77n, 178n, 215n
Public Opinion and Foreign Policy, 695n
Public Opinion and Popular Government, 179n
Public Opinion and Propaganda, 75n, 78n
Public Opinion in Soviet Russia, 17n, 177n
Public Policies and Their Politics, 632n
Public policy (see also Bureaucracy, Congress, Constitution, Judiciary, President, Pressure groups, Public opinion):
 and decision-makers, 550
 definition of, 597
 goals of, 213-214
 impermanency of, 545
 and latent public attitudes, 213
Public Policy, 649n
Public relations (see also Bureaucracy, Democracy, Electoral system, Government,

779

Mass media, Party identification, Political participation, Pressure groups, Public opinion, Voting):
  and American politics, 278-287
  basic function of, 280
  and campaigns, 281-282
  efficacy of, 281
  future of, 285
  political gains of, 285-286
  and political parties, 285
  political tactics of, 282-285
  problems, 282
  public opinion polls, 283
  threats of, 286
Public Relations Ideas in Action, 284n
Purpose of American Politics, The, 655, 656n, 675n
Pye, Lucien W., 94-95, 96n, 102, 138

Quarrels That Have Shaped the Constitution, 535n
Quartering Act, 92
Quinn v. U.S., 550n

Race (see Civil rights, Fifteenth Amendment, Immigration, Political opinion, Supreme Court, Voting):
Randolph Plan, 110-112, 115
Ranney, Austin, 221n, 252, 252n
Ransom, Harry How, 656n
"Rationality," 85-86
Raymond, Jack, 645n
Readings in Recent Political Philosophy, 495n
Readings in Social Psychology, 191n
Reagan, Michael D., 52n
Reapportionment (see also Congress, Political parties, Supreme Court, Voting):
  and Congress, 365-366
  and Constitution, 353
  effects, 354-355
  and political system, 353
  reaction, 354
  and Supreme Court, 353
Records of the Federal Convention of 1787, The, 108n, 230n
"Redistricting" (see also Reapportionment), 365-366
"Reference groups":
  definition, 180
  and political parties, 187
Regional variation, 32-33
Regulating Business by Independent Commission, 470n

Reid v. Covert, 678n
Religion (see also Public opinion, Supreme Court, Voting):
  and conscientious objectors, 577-578
  and education, 575-578
  and federal aid, 576-578
  and First Amendment, 573
  and political opinions, 193-194
Remmers, H. H., 183n
Report of the United States Commission on Civil Rights; 1959, 295n
Report on Registration and Voting Participation, 293n, 298n
Representation (see also Congress, Reapportionment):
  constitutional requirements, 146, 290
Representation in Congress, 327n
Republic, The, 16
Republican Reappraised, 243n
Residence:
  socialization, 191
  voting, 236
Responsible Electorate, The, 85n
"Responsible government," 252
Review of Bipartisan Foreign Policy Consultations since World War II, 684n
Revolt of the Moderates, 212n
Revolution in American Foreign Policy, The, 669n
Reynolds v. Sims, 157n, 353n
Rich Nations and the Poor Nations, The, 662n
Ricker, Henry W., 184n
Riesman, David, 26, 84n
Rights of the British Colonies, The, 48n
Riker, William, 85
Ripley, Randall B., 360n, 361n, 424n, 632, 632n
Rise of the Vice-Presidency, The, 429n
Robinson, James A., 657n
Robinson v. California, 580n
Roche, John P., 108n, 400n
Rochin v. California, 495n
"Roles":
  expectation, 349
  performance, 4, 349
Roosevelt, Theodore, 400n
Roots of Political Behavior, 48n
Rose, Richard, 343n
Rosenau, James N., 657n, 695, 695n
Rossiter, Clinton, 223n, 410n
Rostow, W. W., 665n, 704n
Rousseau, Jean Jacques, 64
Rowe, Leonard, 221n, 302n
Rules Committee (see also Congress), 356-357, 367

Russet, Bruce, 661, 661n
Rutland, Allen, 548n

Said, Abdul, 648n
"Sam Adam's Caucus Club," 66
Santa Clara County v. Southern P. R. Co., 585n
Sapin, Burton, 654n, 657n
Scales v. U.S., 566n
Schattschneider, E. E., 231n, 255n, 263, 263n, 269n
Schechter Poultry Corp. v. U.S., 419n, 618n
Scheiber, Harry N., 144
Schlesinger, Arthur N., Jr., 627, 627n
Schlesinger, Joseph A., 225n, 291n
Schmidhauser, John R., 502, 502n
Schneider v. Rusk, 560n
School District of Abington Township v. Schempp, 576n
Schubert, Glendon A., 497, 497n
Scientific Estate, The, 649n
Scientific Revolution and World Politics, The, 662n
Scoble, Harry M., 208, 208n
Scott v. Sandford, 551n
Sears, David O., 185n, 201n
Second Amendment, 126
Second Continental Congress, 93, 95, 99
Secretary of State, the, 453
Secretary of State, The, 472n, 649n, 650n
"Sectionalism," 192
Sedition Act of 1798, 127
Semi-Sovereign People, The, 263n
Senate (see also Congress, House of Representatives):
  "advice and consent function," 290, 678
  "cloture rule," 358
  committee action:
    bills in committees, 367
    committee leadership, 355-356
  constitutional requirements for Senators, 146, 290
  democratization, 351-352
  effect of loss, 8
  and federalism, 144
  filibuster, 358
  leadership, 361-362
  and lobbying, 278
  original form, 351
  and party organization, 234-235
  policy committees, 362, 367
  and primaries, 301
  rules of procedure, 355, 358

780

INDEX

Seventeenth Amendment, 131
  and states' rights, 146
  and Supreme Court, 512
  and treaties, 678
  and Vice-President's role, 361
Senatorial courtesy, 148, 412
Seniority system:
  in Congress, 364-365
  and southern redistricting, 365-366
Separation of powers doctrine, 99, 100, 121
Seventh Amendment, 126, 548-549
Seventeenth Amendment, 131
Shaping the Future, 704n
Shapiro, Martin, 497n
"Shared attitudes," 30
Sheatsley, Paul B., 75n, 78n, 188n, 203n
Sherman Anti-Trust Act, 611
Short Reign of Pippin IV, The, 279, 279n
Sigmund, Paul E., 25n
Simmons, J. L., 192
Single member district system, 231-232
Sixteenth Amendment, 132, 141
Sixth Amendment, 126, 548-549
Slaughter House Cases, 550n, 552n, 552-553
Slavery, 139
Small, Norman J., 126n
Smith Act of 1940, 560, 563-564
Smith, Adam, 599
Smith, Bruce L. R., 649n
Smith, M. Brewster, 178n
Smith v. Allwright, 156n, 294-295, 294n, 550n
Smithies, Arthur, 649n
Snyder, Richard C., 48n, 657n
Snyder v. Massachusetts, 495n
"Social adjustment," 180
Social Background of Political Decision-Makers, The, 46, 47n
Social change and democracy, 64
Social equality and democracy, 31
"Social mobility," 145
"Social progress and democracy," 63
Social Psychology, 291n
Social security, 635-637
Social Theory and Social Structure, 14n, 20n, 304n
Socialism and democracy, 80-81
Socialization:
  and culture, 24
  and mass media, 196, 200
  and perception, 24

and the political system, 196
  primary group influence, 200-202
Society in America, 26n
Solicitor General, 490, 518
Sorauf, Frank J., 222n, 232n
Sorensen, Theodore C., 400n, 413n, 423n, 436n, 467n, 475n, 484n, 654n
Source Book of a Study of Occupational Values and the Image of Federal Services, 459n
South Carolina v. Katzenbach, 522n, 551n
Southern Politics, 131n, 225n, 226n
Southern Regional Education Board, The, 154n
Sovereignty, in international politics, 668
Soviet government structure, 332-333
Spahr, Margaret, 495n
Spanier, John, 653n
Sparkman, John, 684n
Speaker of House, roles, 359-360
Special courts, 515n
Spencer, Herbert, 607
Sprague, John D., 501n
Sprout, Harold, 657n
Sprout, Margaret, 657n
Stamp Act, 92
Standing Committees of Congress, 358, 362-366
"Standing decisions," 263
Stare decisis, 495, 495n, 510, 534
State department, 453
State Government and Administration in the U.S., 98n
State party committees, 235
States (see also Federalism, Fourteenth Amendment):
  in Articles of Confederation, 158
  and civil rights, 151
  and Constitution, 146-149
  and federalism, 142
  and selection of delegates, 306-307
  and senatorial courtesy, 148
  and "states' rights," 127-128, 146, 150, 158
  and urban demands, 162
  and voting requirements, 294
Statesman's Yearbook, The, 381
"Statesmanship," 5
Statistical Abstract of the United States, 317n

Status of forces agreements, 583
Status Seekers, The, 26n
"Status uncertainty," 27-30, 42
Statutory law, 498-499
Steel Seizure Case (1952), 529
Steering Committee, 362
Stein, Eric, 665n
Steinbeck, John, 279
Steward Machine Co. v. Davis, 635, 635n
Stine, Leo, C., 247n
Stokes, Anson Phelps, 574n
Stokes, Donald E., 205, 215n, 242n, 324n, 327, 346n, 352n
Stone, Clarence N., 343n
Story, Joseph, 574n
Stouffer, Samuel A., 32n, 75n, 567, 567n
Stromberg, Roland N., 243n
Struggle for Judicial Supremacy, The, 511n
Study of Man, The, 24n
"Subsystem," 20
Succession, to Presidency (Twenty-fifth Amendment), 133
Sugar Act, 92
Sugg, Redding S., Jr., 153n, 154n
"Supports," (see also Inputs, Political system), 10-11
Supreme Court (see also civil rights, Federal courts, Federal law):
  and allegiance, 558
  and *amici curiae,* 527-528
  and business and public interest, 607-608
  cases, 522-523
  as censor, 568-570
  certiorari, 521-522
  and church and state, 574-575
  and Civil Rights Act of 1875, 585
  and citizenship, 560
  and Civil Rights Act of 1964, 570, 593
  and communists, 564-566
  and Congress, 536-537
  and Congress' tax power, 623
  constitutional law, 144
  and corporate mergers, 614
  criticism of, 537-538, 582
  and cruel and unusual punishment, 580
  decision process of, 529-530
  dissenting opinions, 530-532
  effect on Congress, 12
  and eminent domain, 602
  and Feinberg Law, 572

as final court of appeal, 493
and the Fourteenth Amendment, 510
and freedom of movement, 554
and *habeus corpus*, 551
interpretation, 542
and interstate commerce, 610
and interstate disputes, 155
and judicial activism, 512
jurisdiction, 521, 528
and malapportionment in states, 156-157
and National Industrial Recovery Act, 419
and "national norms," 534
and New Deal, 143-144, 618-619
and nominating process, 290
and organized labor, 617-619
and political environment, 526
and President's powers, 414
and private property, 604
and "privileges and immunities," 552
as promulgator of rules of procedure, 534
public attention, 10, 528, 536
and public policy, 538
and racial issues, 151
and reapportionment, 353
and religion in education, 575-578
as "Roosevelt court," 505-506
and selection of judges, 505, 508
and self-incrimination, 581
and "separate but equal" doctrine, 586-587
source of demands, 527
and states' rights, 609-610
and the *Steel Seizure Case*, 508
"supports," 528
and taxation, 132
and treaty power, 678
and voting, 156, 550
as "Warren court," 506-507
Supreme Court, The, 47n
Supreme Court and the Commander-in-Chief, The, 410n
Supreme Court in the American System of Government, The, 511n, 531n
Supreme Court in U.S. History, The, 513n
Supreme Court: Its Politics, Personalities, and Procedures, The, 502n
Supreme Court Justice Is Appointed, A, 508n
Survey of School Desegregation in the Southern and Border States, 1965-1966, 587n

Sutherland, Arthur E., 495, 495n
Swanson, Charles E., 196
Swearer, Howard R., 25n
Sweatt v. Painter, 586n
Swisher, Carl, 530
Swords into Ploughshares, 666n
System (see also Political system), definition, 6-7, 18-19, 20, 211, 226-227
Systems Analysis of Political Life, A, 8n

Taft-Hartley Act of 1947, 563
Taft, William Howard, 400n
Tanenhaus, Joseph, 513n
Task Force Report: The Courts, 520n
Task Force Report on Independent Regulatory Commissions, 470n
Task Force Report on Personnel and Civil Service, 466n
Taxes:
 and Congress, 621
 and Constitution, 621
 effects of, 622
 Federal income tax, 622
 influence of pressure groups, 623-625
 policy objectives, 621-622
 and political power structure, 622
 and Supreme Court, 132, 621
Taylor, John, 601n
Tenth Amendment, 126-128
Tenure of Office Act, 414
Texas v. White, 150n
Theories of Foreign Policy, 648n
Theory and Practice in American Politics, 696n
"Theory," definition and use, 18-21
Thielens, Wagner, Jr., 251n
Third Amendment, 126
Thirteenth Amendment, 127
Thorson, Thomas L., 61n
Thursby, Vincent V., 153n
Times Film Corporation v. City of Chicago, 510n
To Move a Nation, 468n, 469n, 473n, 664n
Top Leadership, U.S.A., 256n
Toscano, James V., 96n
Toth v. Quarles, 584, 584n
Toward a More Responsible Two-Party System, 250n, 253n
Transportation, and nation-building, 143
Trends in World Politics, 661n
Trevelyan, George Otto, 400n
Trial judge, 519
Trop v. Dulles, 560n

Truman, David, 219, 219n, 221, 221n, 255n, 256, 256n, 334, 334n, 335n, 351n, 360n
Truman, Harry S, 396n, 449n, 645n
Turner, Henry A., 251n
Twelfth Amendment, 129-130
Twentieth Amendment, 131
Twentieth Century Congress, A., 348
Twenty-fifth Amendment, 133
Twenty-first Amendment, 133
Twenty-fourth Amendment, 130-131, 394, 550
Twenty-second Amendment, 131-132
Twenty-third Amendment, 130
Two-Hundred Million Americans, 34n
Two-party system (see also Political parties, Voting):
 coherence and stability in government, 229
 compromise, 228-229
 evolution of, 230-232
 function, 239
 majority support, 228
 and multi-party system, 227
 and one-party system, 225-227
 plurality election, 231-232
 political socialization, 232
 and President, 229-230
 single-member district, 231-232
 unified control in government, 229

Unalienable rights:
under Declaration of Independence, 98
in democracy, 64
and general welfare, 546
Uniform Code of Military Justice, 583-584
"Unit-rule," 310
United Nations, 666-668
United Nations at Twenty-One, The, 666n
United Public Workers v. Mitchell, 462
U.S.A.: An Outline of the Country, Its People and Institutions, 28n
United States: The History of a Republic, The, 93n
U.S. Attorney, 518-519
U.S. Code, 476
U.S. Commissioner, 519
U.S. Court of Appeals, 521
U.S. economic growth, 615n
U.S. Foreign Policy, Compilation of Studies, 676n

INDEX

United States Foreign Policy, 449n
U.S. Government Organization Manual, 632-633, 697n
U.S. Marshal, 519
U.S. Senators and Their World, 267n, 272n, 278n, 347n, 348n
United States Troops in Europe, 671n
U.S. v. Adair, 617n
U.S. v. Bland, 558n
U.S. v. Brown, 566n, 619n
U.S. v. Butler, 526n, 619n
U.S. v. Caltex, Inc., 603n
U.S. v. Continental Can Co., 614n
U.S. v. Classic, 290n, 294n
U.S. v. Curtiss Wright Export Corp., 405n, 419n, 677n
U.S. v. Darby Lumber Co., 619n
U.S. v. Dennis, 68n
U.S. v. E. C. Knight Co., 611
U.S. v. E. I. DuPont de Nemours and Co., 614n
U.S. v. Harris, 277n
U.S. v. MacIntosh, 558n
U.S. v. Paramount Pictures, 569n
U.S. v. Pink, 406n, 679n
U.S. v. Schwimmer, 558, 562n
U.S. v. United States Steel Corporation, 612n
U.S. v. Wong Kim Ark, 551
"Universal suffrage," 98
University of Michigan Survey Research Center, 28, 74, 76, 185n, 247n
U.S.S.R. Courts, 490-492

Valen, Henry, 230n
Verba, Sidney, 208, 208n
Vice-President:
 constituency, 147-148
 duties of, 428-429
 election of, 292
 nomination of, 310-311, 428
 role of, 428, 361
 in the Senate, 361
View from the Seventh Floor, 665n, 704n
Views of America, 25n, 654n
Virginia Resolutions, 109-110
Vose, Clement C., 528
Voter Decides, The, 203
Voter registration, two types, 299-300
Voter turnout, 226
Voting (see also Civil rights, Class, Congress, Congressional voting, Elections, Electoral system, Liberal-conservative continuum, Party identification, Political opinions, Political parties, President, Public opinion, Public relations, Voter registration):
 behavior, 190-191
 characteristics of voters, 247
 and citizenship, 297-298
 class identification, 185
 congressional voting, 328
 "cross-pressures," 315
 Fifteenth Amendment, 130
 and ideology, 76
 "independent voters," 315-316
 information on, 74
 literacy tests, 299
 Nineteenth Amendment, 130
 poll tax, 299
 and race, 294
 rationality of voters, 85
 requirements for, 69, 292-299
  age, 298
  citizenship, 297-298
  disqualifiers, 298-299
  in general, 297
  literacy tests, 299
  poll tax, 299
  property, 294
  religion, 294
  residence, 298
 straight ticket, 321
 and Twenty-fourth Amendment, 130-131
 and women, 297
Voting: A Study of Opinion Formation in a Presidential Campaign, 86n, 185n
Voting qualifications (see Voting, requirements for)
Voting Rights Act of 1965, content and effects, 296-297, 299, 550

Wabash, St. Louis, and Pacific Ry. v. Illinois, 610n
Waging Peace, 385n, 401n, 533n
Wahlke, John C., 291n
Waldo, Dwight, 454
Walker, Jack L., 402
Walker v. Birmingham, 571n
Walrus, I. M. A., 22n, 22, 42
War on Poverty, 638-642
War on Poverty: The Economic Opportunity Act of 1964, The, 57n
Ward, Barbara, 662, 662n

Ward, Jean, 199n
Warren, Charles, 107, 108n, 513n
Washington Lobbyists, The, 267n, 275n, 278n
Watkins, Frederick M., 672n
We, the People, 108n
Wealth of Nations, The, 599
Wealth and Power in America, 54n, 56n
Web of Government, The, 495
Weber, Max, 26, 27n, 439n
Weeks, O. Douglas, 396n
Wesberry v. Sanders, 146n, 353n
West Coast Hotel Co. v. Parrish, 608, 608n
Westin, Alan F., 25n, 654n
West Virginia State Board of Education v. Barnette, 577n
Wheare, K. C., 137
White House staff, 422-424
White, Robert W., 178n, 463n
White primary, 294
Who Governs?, 194n, 255n
Why England Slept, 391n
Whyte, William H., Jr., 271n
Widery, Leonard, 400n
Wildovsky, Aaron B., 232n, 292n, 394n, 424n
Wilson, Charles, 63n
Wilson, H. Hubert, 48n
Wilson, James O., 195n
Wilson v. Bohlender, 584n
Winters, Glenn R., 492n
Winters v. New York, 568n
Williams, Irving G., 429n
Williams, Robin M., Jr., 24n
Williams v. North Carolina, 152n
Wolfinger, Raymond, 194, 365n
World Pressures on American Foreign Policy, 672n, 675n
Wright, Benjamin Fletcher, 97
Wright, Deil S., 193n
Writ of habeus corpus, 122

Yates v. United States, 565, 565n
"Yellow dog contract," 353, 617
Young, Roland, 372n
Youngstown Sheet and Tube Co. v. Sawyer, 411n, 644n

Zander, Alvin, 201n
Zeigler, Harmon, 195n, 213n, 257n
Zemel v. Rusk, 555n
Zorach v. Clauson, 575n

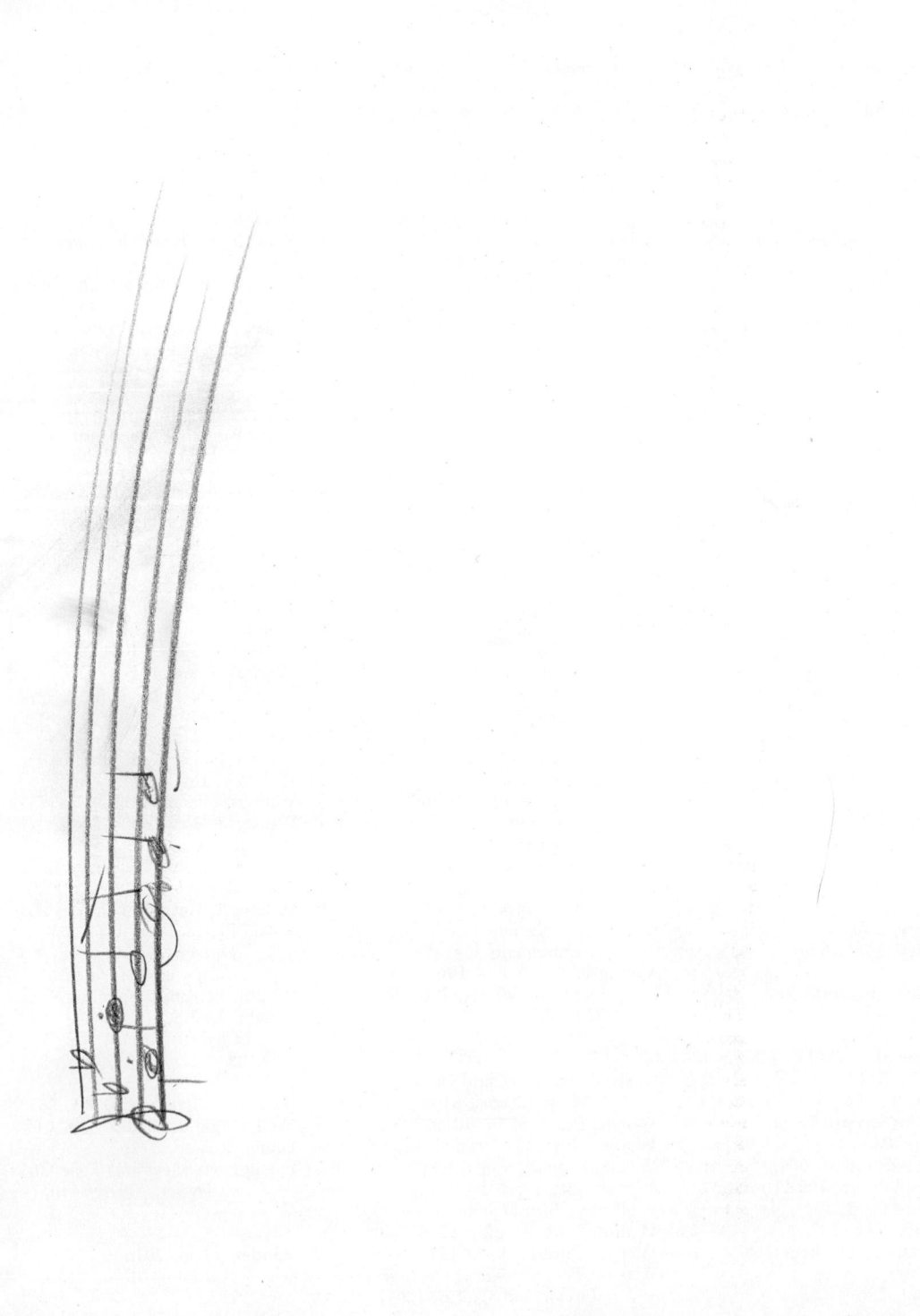